INTERNATIONAL PATENT LAW AND POLICY

■ ■ ■

By

Margo A. Bagley
University of Virginia School of Law

Ruth L. Okediji
William L. Prosser Professor of Law
University of Minnesota Law School

Jay A. Erstling
William Mitchell College of Law
Former Director, Office of the PCT, WIPO

AMERICAN CASEBOOK SERIES®
WEST₀

Mat #41441480

American Casebook Series is a trademark registered in the U.S. Patent and Trademark Office.

© 2013 LEG, Inc. d/b/a West Academic Publishing
  610 Opperman Drive
  St. Paul, MN 55123
  1–800–313–9378
West, West Academic Publishing, and West Academic are trademarks of West Publishing Corporation, used under license.

Printed in the United States of America
ISBN: 978–0–314–28787–8

DEDICATION

In loving memory of my dad: Dr. Emerson A. Cooper, 1924–2012.
To God be the glory.
—M.A.B.

For my Father in Heaven
And in loving memory of my father in Heaven:
Professor Aaron T. Gana, 1938–2007.
—R.L.O.

To Pixie.
—J.A.E.

PREFACE

The field of patent law has undergone profound changes as the combined pressures of globalization and rapid technological advances have exerted tremendous pressure on the institutions and rules that facilitate the issuance of patents and the traditional justifications for the patent system. Patents remain an important, even if at times controversial, foundation for encouraging innovation and channeling private investments into new scientific endeavors directed at enhancing human welfare. Historically, the industrial development and wealth of nations has been linked with the recognition and enforcement of patent rights, and the ability of patentees to leverage those rights in global markets. Yet, until the conclusion in 1994 of the World Trade Organization's (WTO) Agreement on Trade Related Aspects of Intellectual Property (TRIPS Agreement), scholarly commentary on international or comparative aspects of patent law was limited, and teaching materials even more so. As scholars and practitioners in the field, we recognized a need to address this gap systematically, not only for ourselves but for our students who will be practicing patent law in a vastly more complex and institutionally challenging global marketplace. The need for a text that introduces students to the core concepts, doctrines, rationales, and policy implications of global patent regulation, while also exposing them to the practice of international and comparative patent prosecution and enforcement—including multinational litigation—seemed strongly evident. And thus the idea for a casebook exclusively focused on international patent law and policy began to take shape.

This book provides a comparative overview of international patent law and policy, utilizing case law from a variety of countries; excerpts from scholarly materials representing views from vastly different jurisdictions; and international policy documents including treaties, regulations, and laws. Importantly, this book introduces students to the tensions and conflicts that characterize the international patent system, highlighting areas of controversy, presenting comparative views to facilitate analysis of how different national patent laws intersect and interact with various patent treaties, and providing a thorough examination of the practical functioning of the prosecution process in the multilateral context.

As with all book projects, our seemingly simple idea of writing a casebook on international patent law turned out to be incredibly more complex, challenging, and fulfilling than any of us imagined six years ago when our writing first began. Since then, the field of intellectual property, and patent law specifically, has experienced significant changes at national, regional, and multilateral levels. The rise of new and powerful international players in the global innovation system such as China and India, the enactment of a major patent reform bill in the United States, the intensification of efforts toward a unified European patent system complete with a regional patent court, and continued pressures from developing and emerging countries regarding the effect of the international patent system on economic development and human development needs and priorities, are all major challenges for the ongoing internationalization of patent law. Against this background of dynamic institutional, doctrinal, and cultural change in the global patent system, trade-offs between the rate of patent filings and the costs of patent administration at the national level continue to force important policy choices to the forefront of international patent governance.

We adopt an explicitly comparative approach to the study of the international patent system. We begin with the premise that the international patent framework, which formally began in 1886 with the conclusion of the Paris Convention for the Protection of Industrial Property, is now properly a "system" of international patent law. This system is not complete in all respects; it certainly is not coherent in every regard in its policy or doctrinal basis, and it remains extremely polarized in various respects, particularly in the application and enforcement of established minimum standards. Importantly, deep divisions remain between the interests of countries that represent the greatest share of the global patent landscape, so-called "emerging markets" of China, India, and Brazil, and those developing and least-developed countries whose interests in accessing patent-protected technology remain focused on ensuring that the system is appropriately balanced to facilitate the explicit public interest goals that are represented in every domestic patent regime. Throughout the book and in every chapter, we endeavor to illustrate, through case law and reference to policy materials and legal commentary, these points of tension, convergence, and compliance with global rules. Although original materials were not available for all doctrines, and not every country or region is specifically mentioned, we have made every effort to ensure that the vast trove of materials on international patent law has been represented whether in the text, in the case selection or in the Notes and Questions.

We lightly edit many of the foreign cases to give greater flexibility to teachers who may wish to emphasize different features of foreign opinions, and to provide an opportunity for students to understand the context of the case and become comfortable with different judicial styles of other legal traditions. For several Chinese and other foreign cases we utilized informal translations because we believe it is important that students preparing to practice in this brave new world must be adequately equipped to understand the way different courts and legal cultures apply the rules that have long been familiar to the traditional actors of North America and Europe.

In *Chapter 1*, we establish the legal framework for international patent law. We begin with a review of the history of the Paris Convention, identify the leading justifications for an international patent system, and then examine the developments that led up to the TRIPS Agreement in 1994, including an overview of post-TRIPS developments. Importantly, we identify and evaluate differences of opinion about the efficacy of the international patent system for economic development, and long-standing concerns of developing countries about the potential welfare costs and burdens imposed by this system.

Chapter 2 deals with procedural patent agreements, providing a comprehensive overview of the principal provisions of the Paris Convention, the Patent Cooperation Treaty (PCT), and work-sharing initiatives that have been viewed as important tools to manage the burdensome and costly process of patent prosecution faced by applicants filing in the major patent-granting offices.

In *Chapter 3*, we address substantive patent agreements, starting with the 1994 TRIPS Agreement. After providing students with a solid background of the political and negotiating context of TRIPS, we turn to the minimum mandatory provisions of the Agreement regarding patent eligibility and enforcement. Here, students will learn of the WTO's dispute settlement procedure, and study two of the seminal WTO patent cases that interpret the requirements imposed on member states. We also introduce students to the important limits of the requirements in the TRIPS Agreement, in particular those limits introduced to address the supply of patented essential medicines to qualifying countries. In this chapter, students will read an opinion from a federal court in Kenya in which the patent requirements of the TRIPS Agreement are interpreted in the context of human rights—one of the first efforts by a court in Africa to balance the role of patents with public welfare interests.

We turn in Part II of the casebook to the fundamental requirements for patentability and examine each in comparative perspective using case law from different jurisdictions. Despite significant overlap in the patent statutes of all WTO member countries, important differences remain in the requirements of patent eligibility for certain subject matter. *Chapter 4* deals with these subject matter limitations and explores in depth the primary areas of divergence among countries, namely, life forms (biotechnology), business methods and software, and pharmaceuticals and diagnostic methods.

In *Chapter 5* we cover utility, in *Chapter 6* novelty, and in *Chapter 7* inventive step/non-obviousness.

Chapter 8 covers the disclosure requirements for patents, including enablement and written description and their counterparts in other jurisdictions. We also cover the emerging disclosure of origin requirement, and the difficult question of prior-informed consent and related tensions over the protection of biological diversity, the valuable knowledge about plant and animal life held by indigenous peoples, and the demands by many developing countries for a patent system that adequately accommodates the protection of these resources. Other protection systems for plants are also discussed in this chapter as are protection regimes for designs and utility models.

In *Chapter 9*, we deal with patent prosecution in some detail, beginning with the basic patent application. We provide an overview of key aspects of internationalizing an application, features of various types of claims, the patent examination process, and patent grant and post-grant proceedings.

Finally in Part III, we cover major issues in patent litigation. First in *Chapter 10*, we address comparative approaches to infringement. Next, we deal with defenses and remedies in *Chapter 11*, and conclude with *Chapter 12* on multinational enforcement of patent rights.

In treatise, case, and article excerpts throughout the book, we have selectively omitted many citations and footnotes without using ellipses or other indicators. Within each chapter footnotes are numbered consecutively. However, within cases and other excerpted material, footnote numbers correspond to those in the original published material. In every chapter we provide notes and questions that highlight developments in international fora, as well as case updates or other relevant information from jurisdictions around the world. In addition, we help students think more deeply about the policy or doctrinal implications of the topics addressed, with questions that facilitate further study, comparison, and analysis. The result, we hope, is a rich and compelling set of materials that will equip students to understand policy arguments for the successful practice of patent law which, as they will learn from this casebook, is ineluctably now a global enterprise.

MARGO BAGLEY
RUTH OKEDIJI
JAY ERSTLING

March 2013

ACKNOWLEDGMENTS

A large number of individuals in many countries, institutions, and patent offices were critical to the completion of this casebook. We are not able to name them all individually, but we want to acknowledge how implausible this work would have been but for the strong support and enthusiasm we received as we began our research for the book.

First, our deepest gratitude to Samuel S. Bagley II, and our respective spouses: Samuel S. Bagley Sr., Dr. Tade O. Okediji, and Pixie Erstling, who bore patiently with us throughout the writing process. We also gratefully acknowledge the anonymous reviewers of early drafts of the manuscript who gave us invaluable criticism and suggestions that helped improve and strengthen various sections of the book.

In the true spirit of a casebook on an important international subject with significant comparative perspectives, various chapters were written as we traversed a number of countries—including Belgium, China, Germany, Kenya, Mexico, Nigeria, Singapore, Switzerland, Tanzania, and Uganda. We are grateful to our hosts in these various countries, and to those individuals—particularly policy officials—who provided us with information that simply could not have been otherwise known or found without their assistance and support.

Charity truly begins at home; we could not have managed, processed, and analyzed the trove of materials we gathered without the indefatigable willingness of our respective institutions to support us. We wish first to acknowledge with deep appreciation Mary Rumsey, the Foreign, Comparative & International Law Librarian at the University of Minnesota Law School, whose unrivaled commitment to tracking down the most obscure cases, directing us to unusual legal text and original foreign law sources, and helping us keep track of recent developments was surpassed only by her extraordinary efforts in providing review of our innumerable foreign and domestic citations in the final preparation of the manuscript. We are grateful to other members of the University of Minnesota Law Library, particularly David Zopfi-Jordan, Suzanne Thorpe, and Talon Powers for invaluable research and logistical support; to the wonderful law librarians of the University of Virginia School of Law, most particularly Kent Olson, Xinh Luu, Ben Doherty, and Katherine Jenkins, and to our outstanding research assistants, particularly Aditya Bharadwaj, Allyson Schmitt, Daniel Sharpe, Mingda Hang, Elizabeth Capan, Evan Carter, and Ryan Sharp. We also express our sincere gratitude to Julie Hunt, Program Manager of the Intellectual Property and Development Program, University of Minnesota, who provided overall management and supervision of the manuscript over the years, including undertaking the significant task of compiling and formatting many of the foreign materials, while also supervising several generations of research assistants; and above all to our students who, since 2007, have been the guinea pigs for early drafts of the manuscript. Thank you for your patience and your feedback over the years, which have enriched the final product immeasurably.

The following patent offices and organizations were particularly helpful to us: the World Intellectual Property Organization (WIPO); the European Patent Organization (EPO); the UK Patent Office; the United States Patent and Trademark Office (USPTO); the German Patent and Trademark Office (DPMA); and the Max Planck Institute for Intellectual Property, Competition, and Tax Law (Munich). We want to especially recognize Isabel Chng, former Register of Patents for the Intellectual Property Office of Singapore (IPOS), who generously shared her deep and broad knowledge of international patent issues, and who passed away in 2012. She will be greatly missed.

Finally, we acknowledge and thank the following authors and/or copyright owners whose works were used in this book:

Bagley, Margo A., *Patent First, Ask Questions Later: Morality and Biotechnology in Patent Law*, 45 William and Mary Law Review 469 (2003). Reprinted with permission.

Bagley, Margo A., *Patently Unconstitutional: Geographical Limitations on Prior Art in a Small World*, 87 Minnesota Law Review 679 (2003). Reprinted with permission.

Braga, Carlos Alberto Primo, *The Economics of Intellectual Property Rights and the GATT: A View from the South*, 22 Vanderbilt Journal of Transactional Law 243 (1989). Reprinted with permission.

Brewster, Rachel, *The Domestic Origins of International Agreements*, 44 Virginia Journal of International Law 501 (2004). Reprinted with permission.

Burk, Dan L. & Mark A. Lemley, *Fence Posts or Sign Posts: Rethinking Patent Claim Construction*, 157 University of Pennsylvania Law Review 1743 (2009). Reprinted with permission.

Calvert, Jane, Genomic Patenting and the Utility Requirement, 23 New Genetics & Society 301 (2004). Reprinted with permission.

de Carvalho, Nuno Pires, *Requiring Disclosure of the Origin of Genetic Resources and Prior Informed Consent in Patent Applications Without Infringing the TRIPS Agreement: The Problem and the Solution*, 2 Washington University Journal of Law & Policy 371 (2000). Reprinted courtesy of the author.

Doi, Teruo, JAPAN, in 5, International Encyclopedia of Laws: Intellectual Property 248 (Hendrik Vanhees ed., 2007).

Duncan, Jeffrey M., Michelle A. Sherwood & Yuanlin Shen, *A Comparison Between the Judicial and Administrative Routes to Enforce Intellectual Property Rights in China*, 7 John Marshall Review of Intellectual Property Law 529 (2008). Reprinted with permission.

Dutfield, Graham, *Intellectual Property & the Life Science Industries: Past, Present & Future*, 2nd edition World Scientific (2009). Reprinted courtesy of the author.

Fujino, Jinzo, *Parallel Imports of Patented Goods: The Supreme Court Talks about Its Legality* (1997).

Fukunaga, Yoshifumi, *Enforcing TRIPS: Challenges of Adjudicating Minimum Standards Agreements*, 23 Berkeley Technology Law Journal 867 (2008). Reprinted with permission.

Gadbaw, R. Michael, *Intellectual Property and International Trade: Merger or Marriage of Convenience?*, 22 Vanderbilt Journal of Transactional Law 223 (1989). Reprinted with permission.

Gana, Ruth L., *Has Creativity Died in the Third World?: Some Implications of the Internationalization of Intellectual Property*, 24 Denver Journal of International Law & Policy 109 (1995). Reprinted courtesy of the author.

GRAIN, *UPOV on the War Path*, Seedling (June 1999). Reprinted with permission.

Harhoff, Dietmar & Karin Hoisl, *Institutionalized Incentives for Ingenuity—Patent Value and the German Employees' Inventions Act*, 36 Res. Pol'y 1143 (2007). Reprinted with permission.

Helfer, Laurence R., *Toward a Human Rights Framework for Intellectual Property*, 400 University of California-Davis Law Review 971 (2007). Reprinted with permission.

Holbrook, Timothy R., *Extraterritoriality in U.S. Patent Law*, 49 William & Mary Law Review 2119 (2008). Reprinted with permission.

Janis, Mark D., *On Courts Herding Cats: Contending with the "Written Description" Requirement (and Other Unruly Patent Disclosure Doctrines)*, 2 Washington University Journal of Law & Policy 55 (2000). Reprinted courtesy of the author.

Johnson, Phillip, *Contributing to the Wrong: The Indirect Infringement of Patents*, 5 Journal of Intellectual Property Law & Practice 514 (2010). Reprinted with permission.

Joseph, Paul & Ben Mark, *Damages Inquiry: The Tail-End of a Long-Running Dispute*, 7 Journal of Intellectual Property Law & Practice (2012). Reprinted with permission.

Kastenmeier, Robert W. & David Beier, *International Trade and Intellectual Property: Promise, Risks, and Reality*, 22 Vanderbilt Journal of Transactional Law 285 (1989). Reprinted with permission.

Kieff, F. Scott, *The Case for Registering Patents and the Law and Economics of Present Patent-Obtaining Rules,* 45 Boston College Law Review 55 (2003). Reprinted courtesy of the author.

Kronstein, Heinrich & Irene Till, *A Reevaluation of the International Patent Convention*, 12 Law & Contemporary Problems, 765 (1947).

Liegsalz, Johannes & Stefan Wagner, *Patent Examination at the State Intellectual Property Office in China*, 5–8 European School of Management and Technology Working Paper No. 11–06 (2011).

Lopez, Orlando, *Should We Expand* Takeda *Beyond Chemicals: Otsuka Pharmaceuticals Co., Ltd. V. Sandoz Inc. et al. and the Problem-and-Solution Approach?* Obvipat.com (May 2012). Reprinted courtesy of the author.

Malloy, Tim & Yufeng (Ethan) Ma, *IP Enforcement in China:* Chint v. Schneider Electric, Portfolio Media, New York, IP Law 360 (October 2007).

McCarthy, J. Thomas, *Intellectual Property—America's Overlooked Export*, 20 University of Dayton Law Review 809 (1995). Reprinted with permission.

Miao, Emily, *Drafting Multilateral Pharmaceutical Applications: Guidelines for the U.S. Patent Practitioner*, AIPLA Annual Meeting (October 2007).

Mendenhall, James, *WTO Report on Consistency of Chinese Intellectual Property Standards*, ASIL Insight (Apr. 3, 2009). Reprinted with permission.

Meurer, Michael J. & Craig A. Nard, *Invention, Refinement and Patent Claim Scope: A New Perspective on the Doctrine of Equivalents*, 93 Georgetown Law Journal 1947 (2005). Reprinted with Permission.

Murray, Kali & Esther van Zimmeren, *Dynamic Patent Governance in Europe and the United States: The Myriad Example,* 19 Cardozo Journal of International Law and Comparative Law 287 (2011). Reprinted with permission.

Ng Loy, Wee Loon, *Exploring Flexibilities within Global IP Standards*, Intellectual Property Q. 162 (2009). Reprinted courtesy of the author.

Nguyen, Xuan-Thao, *Apologies as Intellectual Property Remedies: Lessons from China,* 44 Connecticut Law Review 883 (2012). Reprinted with permission.

Okediji, Ruth L., *Rules of Power in an Age of Law: Process Opportunism and TRIPS Dispute Settlement*, Handbook of International Trade, Vol. II: Economic and Legal Analyses of Trade Policy and Institutions 42–72 (E. Kwan Choi & James C. Hartigan eds., 2005). Reprinted with permission.

Orlando, Laura, *'Piracy' Provisions under the Enforcement Directive and Patent Infringement*, 2 Journal of Intellectual Property Law & Practice 642 (2007). Reprinted with permission.

Oxfam, *All Costs, No Benefits: How TRIPS-Plus Intellectual Property Rules in the U.S.-Jordan FTA Affect Access to Medicines*, Oxfam Briefing Paper (March 2007). Reprinted with permission.

Pumfrey, Nicholas et al., *The Doctrine of Equivalents in Various Regimes—Does Anybody Have It Right?*, 11 Yale Journal of Law & Technology 261 (2009). Reprinted with permission.

Reichman, J.H., *From Free Riders to Fair Followers: Global Competition Under the TRIPS Agreement*, 29 New York University Journal of International Law and Policy 11 (1996). Reprinted with permission.

Reichman, Jerome H. & Rochelle Cooper Dreyfuss, *Harmonization Without Consensus: Critical Reflections on Drafting a Substantive Patent Law Treaty*, 57 Duke Law Journal 85 (2007). Reprinted with permission.

Risch, Michael, *Reinventing Usefulness,* 2010 Brigham Young University Law Review 1195 (2010). Reprinted with permission.

Roberts, Gwilym V., Jay A. Erstling & Christian J. Girtz, *Transatlantic Patenting*, Landslide, Nov./Dec. 2009 (2009). Reprinted courtesy of Jay. A. Erstling.

Robins, Kendra, *Extraterritorial Patent Enforcement and Multinational Patent Litigation: Proposed Guidelines for U.S. Courts,* 93 Virginia Law Review 1259 (2007). Reprinted with permission.

Safrin, Sabrina, *Chain Reaction: How Property Begets Property*, 82 Notre Dame Law Review 1917 (2007). Reprinted with permission.

Sarnoff, Joshua D., *Patent-Eligible Inventions After Bilski: History and Theory*, 63 Hastings Law Journal 53 (2011). Reprinted with permission.

Stilling, William J., *Patent Term Extensions and Restoration under the Hatch-Waxman Act*, findlaw.com (2002). Reprinted courtesy of the author.

Takenaka, Toshiko, *Rethinking the United States First-to-Invent Principle From a Comparative Law Perspective*, 39 Houston Law Review 621 (2002). Reprinted courtesy of the author.

Tripp, Karen & Linda Stokley, *Changes in U.S. Patent Law Affected by the Uruguay Round Agreements Act—The GATT Implementation Leg-*

islation, 3 Texas Intellectual Property Law Journal 315 (1995). Reprinted with permission.

Vaitsos, Constantine V., *The Revision of the International Patent System: Legal Considerations for a Third World Position*, 4 World Development 85 (1976).

von Hippel, Eric, *Democratizing Innovation* 1–3, MIT Press. Reprinted with permission.

Weissbrodt, David & Kell Schoff, *Human Rights Approach to Intellectual Property Protection: The Genesis and Application of Sub-Commission Resolution 2000/7,* 5 Minnesota Intellectual Property Review 1 (2003). Reprinted with permission.

Winarski, Tyson & Adam Hess, *International Technology Trade Wars: Defending Patented Electrical Technology at the International Trade Commission*, Intellectual Property Today (Nov. 2008).

WIPO, Figure 1–Worldwide Patenting Activity: 1985–2010, World Intellectual Property Indicators (2011). Reprinted with permission.

WIPO, Figure 1–PCT Filing Activity: 1990–2010 (Figure A.1: Trend in PCT Applications), WIPO Statistics Database. Reprinted with permission.

WIPO, Figure 2–PCT Application Filings by Office (2010), Figure A.1.2: PCT Applications at Top 15 Receiving Offices (2011), WIPO Statistics Database (March 2012). Reprinted with permission.

WIPO, Figure 3–The PCT System, World Intellectual Property Organization (March 2012). Reprinted with permission.

Yuan, Arthur Tan-Chi, *Playing the Winning Cards in the Chinese Patent Invalidation Appeals*, John Marshall Law School Chinese Intellectual Property blog (March 2012). Reprinted with permission.

Yu, Peter K., *The TRIPS Enforcement Dispute*, 89 Nebraska Law Review 1046 (2011). Reprinted with permission.

SUMMARY OF CONTENTS

PREFACE V

ACKNOWLEDGMENTS IX

TABLE OF CASES XXVII

PART 1. INTRODUCTION TO THE INTERNATIONAL PATENT SYSTEM

Chapter 1. The Historical Context for Global Patent Cooperation 3
A. The Nature and Sources of International Patent Law ------------------------3
B. Justifications for a Global Patent Framework ---------------------------------- 18
C. The Quest for a Global Patent-- 40

Chapter 2. Procedural Patent Agreements 69
A. The Paris Convention -- 69
B. The Patent Cooperation Treaty (PCT) -- 93
C. Patent Worksharing Initiatives--- 117
D. Regional Patent Regimes -- 124

Chapter 3. Substantive Patent Agreements 135
A. The Agreement on Trade-Related Aspects of Intellectual Property
     Rights --- 135
B. Enforcement of Patent Rights Under the WTO Dispute Settlement
     Understanding -- 154
C. Post-TRIPS Developments --- 186

PART 2. COMPARATIVE PATENTABILITY REQUIREMENTS AND PROCUREMENT

Chapter 4. Patent Subject Matter Eligibility 225
A. Patent Eligibility of Life Forms--- 226
B. Patentability of Business Methods and Software --------------------------- 283
C. Patentability of Pharmaceuticals and Diagnostic Methods --------------- 313

Chapter 5. Utility 337
A. Practical Utility: Upstream Research-- 339
B. Industrial Application: Personal or Private Use ----------------------------- 375
C. Beneficial or Moral Utility-- 382

Chapter 6. Novelty 391
A. Defining Novelty-- 391
B. Invention Priority and Novelty-- 414
C. Territorial Limitations on Prior Art for Novelty Determinations --------- 421
D. Temporal Limitations on Prior Art: Absolute Novelty versus Grace
     Periods --- 428

Chapter 7. Inventive Step/Non-Obviousness **435**
A. The Doctrine of Inventive Step-- 435
B. The United States-- 439
C. Europe--- 466
D. Japan -- 487
E. China-- 497

**Chapter 8. Disclosure Requirements and Non-Utility Patent
 Protection** **509**
A. Patent Disclosure Requirements -- 509
B. Utility Model, Design, and Plant Protection -------------------------------- 553

Chapter 9. Patent Prosecution **589**
A. The Patent Application -- 589
B. Patent Examination --- 613
C. The Patent Grant -- 639

PART 3. MULTINATIONAL ENFORCEMENT

Chapter 10. Comparative Approaches to Patent Infringement **647**
A. Direct Infringement --- 647
B. Indirect Infringement-- 703

Chapter 11. Defenses and Remedies **723**
A. Defenses and Exceptions to Infringement -------------------------------- 723
B. Remedies-- 757

Chapter 12. Multinational Enforcement of Patent Rights **803**
A. Overview of International Obligations------------------------------------- 803
B. Regional Enforcement Initiatives --- 820
C. Administrative and Border Enforcement -------------------------------- 826
D. Multinational Patent Litigation --- 842

INDEX.. 871

TABLE OF CONTENTS

PREFACE V

ACKNOWLEDGMENTS IX

TABLE OF CASES XXVII

PART 1. INTRODUCTION TO THE INTERNATIONAL PATENT SYSTEM

Chapter 1. The Historical Context for Global Patent Cooperation 3
A. The Nature and Sources of International Patent Law --------------------------3
   1. The History of Patent Law: A Brief Overview 3
      Statute of Monopolies of 1623 4
   2. Early Harmonization Efforts: The Paris Convention for the
      Protection of Industrial Property 6
      Heinrich Kronstein & Irene Till, A Reevaluation of the
         International Patent Convention 7
      Notes and Questions 11
   3. The International Patent System in the Twenty-First Century 14
      Yoshifumi Fukunaga, Enforcing TRIPS: Challenges of
         Adjudicating Minimum Standards Agreements 14
      Note on the World Trade Organization 16
B. Justifications for a Global Patent Framework ---------------------------------- 18
   1. The International Trade Justification 19
      J. Thomas McCarthy, Intellectual Property—America's
         Overlooked Export 19
      Notes and Questions 22
   2. The Human Rights Justification 25
      David Weissbrodt & Kell Schoff, Human Rights Approach to
         Intellectual Property Protection: The Genesis and
         Application of Sub-Commission Resolution 2000/7 25
      Laurence R. Helfer, Toward a Human Rights Framework for
         Intellectual Property 31
      Notes and Questions 35
   3. The International Institutional Justification 37
      Rachel Brewster, The Domestic Origins of International
         Agreements 37
      Notes and Questions 40
C. The Quest for a Global Patent --- 40
      Jerome H. Reichman & Rochelle Cooper Dreyfuss,
         Harmonization without Consensus: Critical Reflections on
         Drafting a Substantive Patent Law Treaty 42
   1. Independence versus Territoriality.. 44
      Voda v. Cordis Corp.. 46
      Notes and Questions 50

K.K. Coral Corp. v. Marine Bio K.K. 51
Notes and Questions 54
2. The International Patent System and Developing Countries 56
Constantine V. Vaitsos, The Revision of the International
Patent System: Legal Considerations for a Third World
Position 57
Notes and Questions 60
Ruth L. Gana, Has Creativity Died in the Third World?: Some
Implications of the Internationalization of Intellectual
Property 62
Notes and Questions 66

Chapter 2. Procedural Patent Agreements **69**
A. The Paris Convention --- 69
1. National Treatment 70
2. The Right of Priority 71
Boston Scientific Scimed, Inc. v. Medtronic Vascular, Inc. 76
Edwards Lifesciences AG v. Cook Biotech Inc. 79
Notes and Questions 83
3. Independence of Patents 86
4. Inventors 86
5. Compulsory Licensing/ Working Requirements 87
6. Fees 89
7. Special Agreements 90
Notes and Questions 91
B. The Patent Cooperation Treaty (PCT) ------------------------------------- 93
1. The PCT Framework 95
a.   Receiving Offices --------------------------------------- 95
b.   International Searching Authorities --------------------- 96
c.   Designated Offices--------------------------------------- 97
d.   The International Bureau -------------------------------- 97
Notes and Questions 98
2. The PCT Procedure 100
a.   The International Stage -------------------------------- 100
(i)   Filing a PCT Application 100
(ii) International Search............................ 102
(iii) International Publication 105
(iv) International Preliminary Examination 105
b.   The National Stage------------------------------------- 106
Aristocrat Techs. Austl. Pty v. Int'l Game Tech. 107
Notes and Questions.................................. 111
3. The Impact of the PCT.................................... 113
Notes and Questions 114
Note on the Patent Law Treaty.................................. 115
C. Patent Worksharing Initiatives --- 117
1. Patent Prosecution Highways (PPHs) 117
2. Trilateral Cooperation, the IP5, the Vancouver Group, and
ASPEC.. 119
Notes and Questions 121

Note on the Substantive Patent Law Treaty (SPLT) 122
Notes and Questions 123
D. Regional Patent Regimes -- 124
   1. The European Patent Convention (EPC) 124
     Lenzing Ag's European Patent (UK) 127
     Notes and Questions 132
   2. African, Eurasian, and Gulf Cooperation Regional Patent
     Systems 132
     Notes and Questions 133

Chapter 3. Substantive Patent Agreements **135**
A. The Agreement on Trade-Related Aspects of Intellectual Property
   Rights -- 135
   1. Background and History of the TRIPS Agreement 135
     Carlos Alberto Primo Braga, The Economics of Intellectual
        Property Rights and the GATT: A View from the South 136
     Robert W. Kastenmeier & David Beier, International Trade
        and Intellectual Property: Promise, Risks, and Reality 140
     Notes and Questions 141
   2. An Overview of the TRIPS Agreement 143
     R. Michael Gadbaw, Intellectual Property and International
        Trade: Merger or Marriage of Convenience? 144
     a. Structure of the TRIPS Agreement ------------------------------- 146
     b. Basic Principles and Objectives ------------------------------- 147
     c. Standards of Protection -- 148
        Karen Tripp & Linda Stokley, Changes in U.S. Patent
          Law Effected by the Uruguay Round Agreements
          Act—The GATT Implementation Legislation 148
        Notes and Questions 150
   3. Substantive Standards in the TRIPS Agreement 151
     a. Patentable Subject Matter ------------------------------------- 151
     b. Exclusive Rights and Compulsory Licensing -------------------- 152
     c. Burden of Proof-- 154
B. Enforcement of Patent Rights Under the WTO Dispute Settlement
   Understanding -- 154
   India–Protection for Pharmaceutical and Agricultural Chemical
     Products 158
   Notes and Questions 162
   Canada—Patent Protection of Pharmaceutical Products 167
   Notes and Questions 178
   J.H. Reichman, From Free Riders to Fair Followers: Global
     Competition under the TRIPS Agreement 180
   Notes and Questions 184
C. Post-TRIPS Developments --- 186
   1. The Doha Declaration on the Trips Agreement and Public
     Health.. 186
     Declaration on the Trips Agreement and Public Health 186
     Notes and Questions 190
   2. Other Approaches to TRIPS Flexibilities 195

a. Flexibilities in TRIPS Article 31(k) ------------------------------- 196
b. Human Rights-Based Limitations on Patent Rights ----------- 198
   Asero Ochieng and Others v. Attorney-Gen. and Others....... 199
   Notes and Questions.. 214
3. Post-TRIPS Bilateralism 215
   Notes and Questions 218

PART 2. COMPARATIVE PATENTABILITY REQUIREMENTS AND PROCUREMENT

Chapter 4. Patent Subject Matter Eligibility...................................**225**
A. Patent Eligibility of Life Forms --------------------------------------- 226
   1. Lower Life Forms 226
      Diamond v. Chakrabarty 227
   2. Higher Life Forms... 232
      Harvard College v. Canada (Comm'r of Patents) 233
      Notes and Questions 240
      Monsanto Canada Inc. v. Schmeiser.............................. 240
      Notes and Questions 252
      Note on The Harvard Oncomouse and the European Patent
         Office... 255
   3. Comparative Approaches to Limits on Patenting Living Matter...... 257
      a. Europe -- 257
         Directive 98/44/EC of the European Parliament and of
            the Council on the Legal Protection of
            Biotechnological Inventions 258
         Oliver Brüstle v. Greenpeace e.V. 265
         Notes and Questions.. 276
      b. United States --- 278
         Margo A. Bagley, Patent First, Ask Questions Later:
            Morality and Biotechnology in Patent Law 278
         Notes and Questions.. 282
B. Patentability of Business Methods and Software ----------------------------- 283
   1. Europe.. 285
      Aerotel Ltd. v. Telco Holdings Ltd. and In the Matter of
         Macrossan 285
      Notes and Questions 293
   2. The Evolving State of the Law in the United States 296
      Bilski et al. v. Kappos.. 298
      Notes and Questions 309
   3. The Law in Other Countries.. 311
      Notes and Questions 312
C. Patentability of Pharmaceuticals and Diagnostic Methods ---------------- 313
   1. Pharmaceuticals.. 315
      Novartis AG v. Union of India 315
      Notes and Questions 318
   2. Diagnostic Methods... 320
      Mayo Collaborative Services v. Prometheus Laboratories, Inc..... 321
      Notes and Questions 330

Chapter 5. Utility **337**
A. Practical Utility: Upstream Research -------------------------------------- 339
   1. United States 339
      Edward J. Brenner, Commissioner of Patents v. Manson 340
      Notes and Questions 344
      In re Dane K. Fisher and Raghunath v. Lalgudi 347
      Notes and Questions 351
   2. Europe 354
      Human Genome Sciences Inc. v. Eli Lilly & Co. 356
      Notes and Questions 370
B. Industrial Application: Personal or Private Use ------------------------ 375
   Contraceptive Method/British Technology Group Decision of
      Technical Board of Appeal 3.3.1 (1994) 376
      Notes and Questions 378
C. Beneficial or Moral Utility -- 382
   Juicy Whip, Inc. v. Orange Bang, Inc. 384
   Notes and Questions 388

Chapter 6. Novelty **391**
A. Defining Novelty --- 391
   1. The "*Sine Qua Non*" of Patentability 391
      Société des Produits Nestlé S.A. 392
      Note on Comparative Approaches to Novelty 396
      Arthur Tan-Chi Yuan, Playing the Winning Cards in Chinese
        Patent Invalidation Appeals 398
      Notes and Questions 404
   2. Inherency 406
      Schering Corporation v. Geneva Pharmaceuticals, Inc. 406
      Notes and Questions 411
B. Invention Priority and Novelty --- 414
   1. First Inventor to File versus First to Invent 414
   2. Prior User Rights 418
      Notes and Questions 420
C. Territorial Limitations on Prior Art for Novelty Determinations -------- 421
   Margo A. Bagley, Patently Unconstitutional: Geographical
      Limitations on Prior Art in a Small World 423
      Notes and Questions 426
D. Temporal Limitations on Prior Art: Absolute Novelty versus Grace
   Periods -- 428
   Toshiko Takenaka, Rethinking the United States First-to-Invent
      Principle From a Comparative Law Perspective: A Proposal to
      Restructure Section 102 Novelty and Priority Provisions 430
   Notes and Questions 432

Chapter 7. Inventive Step/Non-Obviousness **435**
A. The Doctrine of Inventive Step --- 435
   1. The Origins of Inventive Step 435
   2. The Inventive Step Challenge 438
B. The United States -- 439

1. 35 U.S.C. § 103 and the *Graham v. John Deere* Inquiry 439
    Graham et al. v. John Deere Co. of Kansas City et al. 439
    Notes and Questions 442
2. The "Teaching, Suggestion, or Motivation" Approach and *KSR* 444
    KSR International Co. v. Teleflex Inc. et al. 445
    Notes and Questions 454
3. Post-*KSR* Developments 457
    Altana Pharma AG v. Teva Pharmaceuticals USA, Inc. 458
    Notes and Questions 464
C. Europe -- 466
1. The Problem-and-Solution Approach in the EPO 467
    European Patent Office Decision of the Technical Board of
        Appeal 3.5.1 of 26 September 2002 470
2. The Problem-Solution Approach in the UK................................... 475
    Actavis UK Limited v. Novartis AG.. 475
    Notes and Questions 484
D. Japan --- 487
1. Inventive Step Assessment... 487
    Intellectual Property High Court Decision, March 25, 2009 490
    Notes and Questions 491
2. Cause or Motivation.. 492
    Tokyo High Court Decision, July 23, 2002 493
    Notes and Questions 494
3. Advantageous or Unexpected Effects.. 495
4. Persons Skilled in the Art.. 495
    Notes and Questions 496
E. China--- 497
    Zhang, Xitian v. Shijiazhuang Ouyi Pharmaceutical Co., Ltd. 497
    Notes and Questions 500
    Beijing Double-crane Pharmaceutical Co., Ltd. v. Xiangbei
        Welman Pharmaceutical Co., Ltd. and Patent Re-examination
        Board of the State Intellectual Property Office............................. 502
    Notes and Questions 504
    Note on Inventive Step in the PCT 505

Chapter 8. Disclosure Requirements and Non-Utility Patent
Protection **509**
A. Patent Disclosure Requirements ------------------------------------ 509
1. Enablement... 509
    Vinylchloride Resins/Sumitomo Decision of the Technical
        Board of Appeal 3.3.1 (June 7, 1983)....................................... 510
    Notes and Questions 513
    Pharmaceutical Resources, Inc. and Par Pharmaceuticals, Inc.
        v. Roxane Laboratories, Inc. 514
    Notes and Questions 519
2. Written Description.. 521
    Ariad Pharmaceuticals, Inc. v. Eli Lilly & Co. 522
    Notes and Questions 527

Mark D. Janis, On Courts Herding Cats: Contending With the "Written Description" Requirement (and Other Unruly Patent Disclosure Doctrines) 531
    Notes and Questions 537
3. Best Mode 538
4. Disclosure of Origin... 539
    Nuno Pires de Carvalho, Requiring Disclosure of the Origin of Genetic Resources and Prior Informed Consent in Patent Applications Without Infringing the TRIPS Agreement: The Problem and the Solution 541
    Notes and Questions 544
    Sabrina Safrin, Chain Reaction: How Property Begets Property... 546
    Notes and Questions 550
B. Utility Model, Design, and Plant Protection --------------------------------- 553
    1. Utility Models... 553
    Delnorth Pty Ltd v. Dura-Post (Aust) Pty Ltd 554
    Notes and Questions 557
    2. Design Protection 559
    Samsung Electronics (UK) Limited v. Apple Inc... 560
    Notes and Questions 572
    Neoplan Bus GmbH v. Zhongwei Bus & Coach Group et al. 578
    Notes and Questions 580
    3. Plant Protection... 580
    Notes and Questions 584

Chapter 9. Patent Prosecution... 589
A. The Patent Application --------------------------------- 589
    1. Internationalizing an Application 590
    Emily Miao, Drafting Multilateral Pharmaceutical Applications: Guidelines for the U.S. Patent Practitioner..... 598
    Notes and Questions 601
    2. Claims 603
    3. Types of Applications 609
        a. Overview --------------------------------- 609
        b. Divisional Applications and Unity of Invention versus Restriction Practice --------------------------------- 611
B. Patent Examination --------------------------------- 613
    1. Substantive Examination 615
    Johannes Liegsalz & Stefan Wagner, Patent Examination at the State Intellectual Property Office in China..................... 615
    Notes and Questions 618
    2. Comparative Examination... 623
    Gwilym v. Roberts, Jay A. Erstling & Christian J. Girtz, Transatlantic Patenting... 623
    Notes and Questions 628
    3. Role of the Inventor... 630

Dietmar Harhoff & Karin Hoisl, Institutionalized Incentives
for Ingenuity—Patent Value and the German Employees'
Inventions Act 631
Notes and Questions 636
C. The Patent Grant --- 639
1. Patent Term Extension 640
2. Post-Grant Proceedings 641
   a. Nullity Proceedings --- 642
   b. Reexamination--- 642
   c. Opposition and Post-Grant Review----------------------- 643

PART 3. MULTINATIONAL ENFORCEMENT

Chapter 10. Comparative Approaches to Patent Infringement 647
A. Direct Infringement -- 647
1. Claim Construction 647
   Edward H. Phillips v. AWH Corp. 648
   Notes and Questions 654
   Monsanto Tech. LLC v. Cefetra BV 657
   Notes and Questions 664
2. Doctrine of Equivalents 665
   Festo Corp. v. Shoketsu Kinzoku Kogyo Kabushiki Co. 668
   Notes and Questions 672
   Shenzhen Triangle Science & Technology Co., Ltd. v. Compaq 674
   Notes and Questions 678
3. Purposive Construction.. 680
   Improver Corp. v. Remington Consumer Prods. Ltd..................... 681
   Notes and Questions 689
   Germany: European Patent Convention, Art.69 (1); Protocol
   on Interpretation—"Epilady Germany II" 689
   Notes and Questions 695
   Note on Post-Improver Developments in the UK...................... 696
   Notes and Questions 698
B. Indirect Infringement --- 703
1. United States... 703
   Global-Tech Appliances, Inc. v. SEB S.A. 704
   Notes and Questions 710
2. Europe and Beyond 711
   Phillip Johnson, Contributing to the Wrong: The Indirect
   Infringement of Patents 711
   Notes and Questions 718

Chapter 11. Defenses and Remedies 723
A. Defenses and Exceptions to Infringement ------------------------------- 723
1. Non-infringement and Patent Invalidity.............................. 723
   Microsoft Corp. v. i4i Limited Partnership........................... 724
   Notes and Questions 730
2. Experimental Use... 732
   Notes and Questions 737

3. Exhaustion of Patent Rights/Parallel Importation 738
    a.   United States --- 739
        Fuji Photo Film Co. v. Jazz Photo Corp. 739
        Notes and Questions.. 742
    b.   Europe --- 744
        Merck & Co. v. Primecrown Ltd. 744
        Notes and Questions.. 749
    c.   Japan -- 751
        Jinzo Fujino, Parallel Imports of Patented Goods: The
            Supreme Court Talks About Its Legality 751
        Notes & Questions.. 756
B. Remedies-- 757
  1. Injunctive Relief 758
    a.   United States --- 758
        eBay Inc. v. MercExchange, L.L.C. 759
        Notes and Questions.. 763
    b.   Europe: Cross-Border Injunctions ------------------------------- 765
        Solvay SA v. Honeywell Fluorine Products Europe B.V. 766
        Notes and Questions.. 773
  2. Damages... 775
    a.   The Patentee's Loss --- 775
        Uniloc USA, Inc. v. Microsoft Corp....................................... 776
        Notes and Questions.. 783
    b.   Defendant's Profits -- 788
        Celanese Int'l Corp. v. BP Chemicals Ltd. 788
        Notes and Questions.. 796
        Tim Malloy & Yufeng (Ethan) Ma, *IP Enforcement in*
            China: Chint v. Schneider Electric 798
        Notes and Questions.. 799
  3. Criminal Penalties 801
    Notes and Questions 802

Chapter 12. Multinational Enforcement of Patent Rights 803
A. Overview of International Obligations------------------------------------- 803
  1. The TRIPS Enforcement Standards 804
    Notes and Questions 805
  2. Implementing the Enforcement Provisions of the TRIPS
    Agreement... 807
    Sweden—Measures Affecting the Enforcement of Intellectual
        Property Rights... 808
    Notes and Questions 809
  3. Willful Infringement on a Commercial Scale: U.S. v. China and
    Implications for Patent Enforcement...................................... 811
    China—Measures Affecting the Protection and Enforcement
        of Intellectual Property Rights 812
    James Mendenhall, WTO Report on Consistency of Chinese
        Intellectual Property Standards 815
    Notes and Questions 818
B. Regional Enforcement Initiatives -- 820

1. The European Directive on the Enforcement of Intellectual
Property Rights... 820
    Laura Orlando, "Piracy" Provisions under the Enforcement
        Directive and Patent Infringement 821
    Notes and Questions 824
2. Free Trade Agreements 825
C. Administrative and Border Enforcement ------------------------------------- 826
    Jeffery M. Duncan, Michelle A. Sherwood & Yuanlin Shen, A
        Comparison Between the Judicial and Administrative Routes
        to Enforce Intellectual Property Rights in China 827
    Tyson Winarski & Adam Hess, International Technology Trade
        Wars: Defending Patented Electrical Technology at the
        International Trade Commission 831
    Notes and Questions 833
    European Union and a Member State—Seizure of Generic
        Drugs in Transit 838
D. Multinational Patent Litigation -- 842
    1. Specialized Courts.. 842
    2. Issue Preclusion... 843
        Northlake Marketing & Supply, Inc., v. Glaverbel, S.A. 844
        Notes and Questions 845
    3. Extraterritorial Approaches 847
        Transocean Offshore Deepwater Drilling, Inc. v. Maersk
            Contractors USA, Inc. 847
        Notes and Questions 852
        NTP, Inc. v. Research in Motion, Ltd............................... 853
        Notes and Questions 862
        Kendra Robins, Note, Extraterritorial Patent Enforcement and
            Multinational Patent Litigation: Proposed Guidelines for
            U.S. Courts... 863
        Notes and Questions 866

INDEX.. 871

TABLE OF CASES

The principal cases are in bold type.

Cases

Actavis UK Limited v. Novartis AG --- 475

Aerotel Ltd v. Wavecrest Group Enterprises Ltd---------------------- 486

Aerotel Ltd. v. Telco Holdings Ltd. --- **285**

AGA Medical Corporation v. Occlutech GmbH --------------------------------- 700

Air Heater Case ------------------------ 714

AlliedSignal Inc. v. DuPont Canada Inc. ------------------------------------ 785

Altana Pharma AG, v. Teva Pharmaceuticals USA, Inc. -- **458**, 464

American Fruit Growers, Inc. v. Brogdex Co. ------------------------- 228

Anchor Building Products v Redland Road Tiles ---------------------------- 715

Animal Legal Def. Fund v. Quigg-- 232

Apotex Inc. v. Nycomed Canada Inc. --- 721

Apotex, Inc. v. Wellcome Foundation Ltd. ----------------------------------- 374

Apple v. Samsung --------------------- 580

Ariad Pharmaceuticals, Inc. v. Eli Lilly & Co. ---------------------- **522**, 528

Aristocrat Techs. Austl. Pty, Ltd. v. Int'l Game Tech --------------108, 109

Aro Mfg. Co. v. Convertible Top Replacement Co. --------------------- 706

Asero Ochieng and Others v. Attorney-Gen. and Others ---- **199**

Ass'n for Molecular Pathology v. Myriad Genetics--------------------- 330

Atlas Powder Co. v. E.I. du Pont De Nemours & Co. ---------------518, 519

Automotive Tech. Int'l v. BMW of N. Am.------------------------------------ 518

Ball v. Aerosel v. Limited Brands - 458

Baxter International, Inc. v. Cobe Laboratories, Inc. -------------------- 424

Bayer AG v. Housey Pharmaceuticals -- 862

BBS Kraftfahrzeugtechnik AG v. Racimex Japan Corp. --------------- 756

Bedford v. Hunt ----------------------- 339

Beijing Double-crane Pharmaceutical Co., Ltd. v. Xiangbei Welman Pharmaceutical Co., Ltd. and Patent Re-examination Board of the State Intellectual Property Office ------------------------------- **502**

Bilski et al. v. Kappos 298, 323, 324, 325, 329

Biogen v. Medeva ---------------------- 485

BL Macchine Automatiche Spa v. Windmoller & Holscher KG ------ 774

Board of Trustees of Leland Stanford Junior University v. Roche Molecular Systems ----------------- 636

Bonito Boats, Inc. v. Thunder Craft Boats, Inc.----------------------------- 436

Boston Scientific Scimed, Inc. v. Medtronic Vascular, Inc. -------- **76**

Brenner v. Manson -------------------- 349

Brewer v. Lichtenstein--------------- 386

Brooktree Corp. v. Advanced Micro Devices -------------------------------- 386

Brown v. Duchesne-------------------- 742

Canon v. Recycle Assist-------------- 756

Case Xa ZR 130/07---------------------- 363

Caterpillar Tractor Co. v. Comm'r of Patents and Trademarks -------- 612

Catnic Components Ltd. v. Hill & Smith Ltd.[1982] R.P.C. 183, 242683

Celanese Int'l Corp. v. BP Chemicals Ltd. -------------------- **788**

Centrafarm v. Sterling Drug -------- 746

Chint Group Corp. v. Schneider Electric Low-Voltage (Tianjin) Co. --- 553

Chiron v. Murex Diagnostics, Ltd. 344

City of Elizabeth v. American Nicholson Paving Co. -------------- 423

Classen Immunotherapies, Inc. v. Biogen IDEC ------------------------- 332

Commission v. Italy ------------------- 269

Comvik v. DeTeMobil------------------ 485

Conor Medsystems Inc v. Angiotech Pharmaceuticals Inc. -------------- 701

Continental Can Co. v. Monsanto Co. --- 408

Cranway v. Playtech------------------ 714

Cross Medical Products, Inc. v. Medtronic Sofamor Danek, Inc. - 674

Cuno Engineering Corp. v. Automatic Devices Corp.------------------------ 436

Cuno Inc. v. Pall Corp. --------------- 846

Cutting Blade I Case (Schneidmesser I)-- 698

Cybor Corp. v. FAS Technologies - 655, 656

Daubert v. Merrell Dow Pharmaceuticals --------------------- 779

Decca Ltd. v. United States -------- 857

Deepsouth Packing Co. v. Laitram Corp. ----------------------------------- 856

Delnorth Pty Ltd v. Dura-Post (Aust) Pty Ltd Federal Court of Australia, Sydney ---------------- **554**

Diamond v. Chakrabarty --**227**, 235, 299, 583

Diamond v. Diehr --------------------- 300

eBay Inc. v. MercExchange **93**, 758, **759**

Ecodyne Corp. v. Croll-Reynolds Engineering -------------------------- 851

Edward H. Phillips v. AWH Corp. --- **648**

Edward J. Brenner, Commissioner of Patents v. Manson340, 349, 386

Edwards Lifesciences AG v. Cook Biotech Inc. ---------------------------- **79**

Egyptian Goddess v. Swisa ----572, 573

Eisai Co. Ltd. v. Dr. Reddy's Labs. 462, 465

Eli Lilly & Co. v. Medtronic --------- 736

European Patent Office Decision of the Technical Board of Appeal 3.5.1 of 26 September 2002 ------------------------------------- **470**

Ex Parte Jay P. Deville -------------- 455

Ex parte Jepson ----------------------- 604

Ex Parte Kurt------------------------- 455

Exela PharmaSciences, LLC v. Kappos ------------------------------------ 111

F. Hoffman-La Roche Ltd. v. Empagran S.A. ----------------------- 50

Fabio Perini SpA v. LPC Group Plc787

Fairchild Semiconductor Corp. v. Third Dimension Semiconductor-- 55

Festo Corp. v. Shoketsu Kinzoku Kogyo Kabushiki Co. ----------------- 54

Festo Corp. v. Shoketsu Kinzoku Kogyo Kabushiki Co. ------------ **668**

Flow Meter Case ----------------------- 715

Fuji Photo Film Co. v. Jazz Photo Corp. --------------------------------- **739**

Fujifilm Corp. v. Benun-------------- 743

Fujitsu Case --------------------------- 288

Fuller v. Berger ----------------------- 386

Funk Brothers Seed Co. v. Kalo Inoculant Co. --------------------229, 299

Gale Case------------------------------- 288

General Tire & Rubber Co. v. Firestone Tyre & Rubber Co. ---- 785

Generics (UK) Ltd v. H Lundbeck- 363

Georgia–Pacific Corp. v. U.S. Plywood Corp. ---------------- 777, 778, 779, 783

Gerber Garment Technology v. Lectra Systems Ltd. ------------------------ 786

Gesellschaft für Antriebstechnik mbH & Co. KG v. Lamellen und Kupplungsbau Beteiligungs KG (GAT v. LuK)----------------------- 773

Global-Tech Appliances, Inc. v. SEB S.A. ----------------------------- **704**

Gorham Co. v. White ----------------- 572

Graham et al. v. John Deere Co. of Kansas City et al. ---**439**, 445, 453, 462

Great A. & P. Tea Co. v. Supermarket Corp. ----------------------- 439, 441, 450

Greenpeace v. Plant Genetic Systems --- 256

Grimme v. Scott ----------------------- 575

Group One, Ltd. v. Hallmark Cards, Inc. ------------------------------------- 84

Grupo Promer v. OHIM-------------- 561

Haberman v. Jackel International 479

Hartranft v. Wiegmann-------------- 229

Harvard College v. Canada----- **233**, 244, 249

Hazel Grove Limited v. Euro-League Leisure ------------------------------- 715

Hilton v. Guyot ----------------------- 843

Hoechst-Roussel Pharms., Inc. v. Lehman -------------------------------- 409

Hornblower v. Boulton --------------- 236

Hotchkiss v. Greenwood 435, 440, 445, 448

Human Genome Sciences Inc. v. Eli Lilly & Co. ---------------------- **356**

Imazio Nursery, Inc. v. Dania Greenhouses--------------------581, 582

Improver Corp. v. Remington Consumer Prods. Ltd.----------- **681**

In re Abbott Respiratory ------------- 607

In re Angstadt ------------------------- 519

In re Arzberger ----------------------- 581

In re Barker --------------------------- 537

In re Bergstrom ----------------------- 410

In re Bergy----------------------------- 228

In re Bilski ----------------------------296, 297

In re Brana --------------------------346, 504

In re Comisky ------------------------- 485

In re Dane K. Fisher and Raghunath v. Lalgudi-----**347**, 466

In re Deuel----------------------------- 466

In re Fisher ---- 351, 352, 355, 371, 372, 465, 466

In re Gosteli -------------------------- 85

In re Hall ----------------------------- 424

In re Hilmer -------------------------- 84

In re Icon Health and Fitness------- 455

In re Kahn ---------------------------- 451

In re Klein --------------------------- 455

In re Klopfenstein --------------------- 426

In re Kratz ---------------------------- 410

In re Kubin --------------------------- 466

In re Lubrizol Genetics, Inc.-------- 256

In re Murphy-------------------------- 386

In re Nelson -------------------------- 386

In re Oetiker ------------------------- 442

In re President and Fellows of Harvard College--------------------- 255

In re Seaborg------------------------- 409

In re Vaeck---------------------------- 519

In re Wands --------------------514, 516

In re Watson -------------------------- 388

In the Matter of Macrossan ----- **285**

Ingersoll Milling Mach. Co. v. Granger --- 845

Innogenetics, Inc. v. Abbot Labs --- 192

Insituform Tech. Inc. v. CAT Contracting, Inc. -------------------- 674

Institute of Organic Chemistry of Chengdu Under the Chinese Academy of Sciences v. Chengdu Zhengda Electric Apparatus Factory ----------------------------------- 799

Int'l Rectifier Corp. v. Samsung Elecs. Co. ------------------------------------ 742

Island Records Limited v. Tring International Plc --------------------- 788

J.E.M. Ag Supply, Inc. v. Pioneer Hi-Bred Int'l, Inc. ------------------ 240, 583

Jazz Photo Corp. v. Int'l Trade Comm'n ------------------------------- 740

Johnson & Johnston Assoc. v. R.E. Serv. Co. ------------------------------ 673

Johnson v. Paynesville Farmers Union Cooperative Oil Co. ----------------- 253

Juicy Whip, Inc. v. Orange Bang, Inc. ----------------------------------**384**, 388

K.K. Coral Corp. v. Marine Bio K.K. ------------------------------------- **51**

Kappos v. Hyatt ----------------------- 619

Kirin-Amgen Inc. v. Hoechst Marion Roussel Ltd. -------------------------- 696

KSR International Co. v. Teleflex Inc. et al. ----**445**, 455, 462, 727, 728

Kumho Tire Co. v. Carmichael ----- 779

Lab. Corp. of Am. Holdings v. Metabolite Labs. -------------------- 296

Lenzing Ag's European Patent (UK) ---------------------------------- **127**

LG Electronics v. Hitachi ------------ 743

Litecubes, LLC v. Northern Light Products, Inc. ----------------------- 849

Losh v. Hague---------------------------- 436

Lowell v. Lewis --------------------382, 386

Lucent Technologies ------------------ 780

Madey v. Duke University ----------- 734

Marbury v. Madison ------------------- 230

Markman v. Westview Instruments, Inc. -------------------------------------- 647

Mayne Pharma Pty. Ltd. v. Pharmacia Italia -------------------------------------- 697

Mayo Collaborative Services v. Prometheus Laboratories, Inc. --- **321**

McKesson Technologies, Inc. v. Epic Systems ------------------------------ 721

Medtronic, Inc. v. Diag Corp. ------- 846

Melon Patent Case -------------------- 552

Menashe Business Mercantile v. William Hill ------------------------- 716

Merck KGaA v. Integra Lifesciences I --- 736

Merck v Stephar and Exler ---------- 745

Merrell Dow Pharmaceuticals Inc. v. H.N. Norton & Co. ------------------ 426

Merrill Lynch Case ------- 288, 289, 290

Metallizing Engineering Co. v. Kenyon Bearing & Auto Parts Co. --------- 426

Microsoft Corp. v. AT&T Corp. ---- 850, 863

Microsoft Corp. v. i4i Ltd. P'ship ------------------------------------**724**, 731

Microsoft/Data Transfer case ------- 288

Milpurrurru Case ----------------------- 63

Molnlycke AB v. Procter & Gamble Ltd ------------------------------------- 442

Monroe Auto Equipment Co. v. Heckethorn Mfg. & Supply Co. -- 453

Monsanto Canada Inc. v. Schmeiser --------------**240**, 720, 797

Monsanto Co. v. McFarling --------- 656

Monsanto Tech. LLC v. Cefetra BV --- **657**

Moulded Curbstone Case ------------ 694

Mullard v. Philco---------------------- 535

National Automatic Device Co. v. Lloyd------------------------------------- 386

Neoplan Bus GmbH v. Zhongwei Bus & Coach Group et al. ----- **578**

Netherlands v. Parliament and Council ------------------------------- 269

Nichia Corp. v. Argos Ltd. ----------- 454

Northlake Marketing & Supply, Inc., v. Glaverbel, S.A., ---------- **844**

Novartis AG v. Union of India - **315**

NTP, Inc. v. Research in Motion, Ltd. ------------------------------852, **853**

Nycomed Canada Inc. v. Teva Canada Ltd. ------------------------------------- 719

Occlutech v. AGA Medical Corp. --- 700

OddzOn v. Just Toys------------------ 456

Oliver Brüstle v. Greenpeace e.V. - 265

Organic Seed Growers and Trade Association (OSGATA) v. Monsanto --- 253

Parker v. Flook ------ 300, 325, 326, 329

Patterson v. Gaslight and Coke Co.391

PepsiCo v. Grupo Promer ----------- 561

Pfizer Inc. v. Cosmos Limited ------- 214

Pharmaceutical Resources, Inc. and Par Pharmaceuticals, Inc. v. Roxane Laboratories, Inc. ---- **514**

Pipette System Case ------------------ 715

Plastus Kreative AB v. Minnesota Mining and Manufacturing Co. --- 55

Pozzoli v. BDMO ---------------------- 476

Pregis Corporation v. Kappos ------- 111

Primos, Inc. v. Hunter's Specialties, Inc. -------------------------------------- 674

Princo Corporation, Ltd v. Koninklijke Philips Electronics ----------------- 821

Quad/Tech, Inc. v. Q.I. Press Controls B.V. ---------------------------------- 846

Qualcomm Inc v. Nokia -------------- 713

Quanta Computer, Inc. v. LG Electronics, Inc. --------------------- 742

Radio Clock II Case ------------------- 717

Radio Corp. of America v. Radio Engineering Laboratories --------- 726

Regents of the University of California v. Eli Lilly & Co. --------------522, 525

ResQNet.com, Inc. v. Lansa, Inc. -- 780

Richardson v. Stanley Works -573, 575

Rickard v. Du Bon --------------------- 386

Rite–Hite Corp. v. Kelley Co. -782, 786

Roche Nederland BV v. Primus ---- 773

Roche Products, Inc. v. Bolar Pharmaceutical Co. ---------------- 735

Sage Prods., Inc. v. Devon Indus., Inc.
-- 673
**Samsung Electronics (UK)
Limited v. Apple Inc.** ------------ **560**
Santa Clara Pueblo v. Martinez------ 50
Sara Lee/Integro Case (Coffee pods)
-- 715
Schering Corp. v. Geneva
Pharmaceuticals -------------------- 412
**Schering Corporation v. Geneva
Pharmaceuticals, Inc.**----------- **406**
Schultze v. Holtz----------------------- 386
Scott & Williams v. Aristo Hosiery Co.
--------------------------------------386, 387
Sextant Avionique, S.A. v. Analog
Devices, Inc. -------------------------- 110
Shell Development Co. v. Watson - 229
Shenzhen Taiden v. OHIM ---------- 561
Shenzhen Triangle v. Compaq 558, 642
Smith Int'l, Inc. v. Hughes Tool Co.758
Société des Produits Nestlé S.A.
-- **392**
Sodium Aluminat Case -------------- 514
**Solvay SA v. Honeywell Fluorine
Products
Europe B.V.**------------------------- **766**
Sot. Lélos kai Sia EE v.
GlaxoSmithKline ------------------- 750
South Corp. v. United States---------- 77
Spurr v. United States ---------------- 708
State Indus., Inc. v. Mor-Flo Indus,
Inc. ------------------------------------- 775
State Street Bank v. Signature
Financial Group-------------------- 283
Stein Associates, Inc. v. Heat &
Control, Inc. ---------------------------- 47
Syngenta Seeds, Inc. v. Delta Cotton
Co-Operative, Inc. ------------------ 583
Tafas v. Doll ---------------------------- 609
Tafas v. Dudas------------------------- 609
Tata Chemicals Ltd. v. Hindustan
Unilever Ltd.------------------------- 621
Texas Digital Systems, Inc. v.
Telegenix, Inc. ---------------------- 651
Therasense, Inc. v. Becton, Dickinson
& Co.----------------------------------- 620
Thomson v. American Braided Wire
-- 437
Toei Tec K.K. v. Family K.K.-------- 786
Tol-O-Matic, Inc. v. Proma Produkt-
Und Marketing Gesellschaft m.b.H
-- 386
**Transocean Offshore Deepwater
Drilling, Inc. v. Maersk
Contractors USA, Inc.**----------- **847**
Tsubakimoto Seiko v. THK K.K. --- 678
U.S. v. India --------------------------- 166
Ultramercial, LLC v. Hulu, LLC--- 332
Uniloc USA, Inc. v. Microsoft Corp.
-------------------------------------776, 783
United Horse Shoe and Nail v.
Stewart ------------------------------- 795
United States v. Dubilier Condenser
Corp. ----------------------------------- 228
United States v. Univis Lens Co. -- 743

University of Queensland v Siemens
Magnet Technology Limited------ 717
University of Western Australia v.
Gray------------------------------------- 638
University Patents, Inc. v. SmithKline
Beecham Biologicals SA ------------ 86
Vitronics Corp. v. Conceptronic,
Inc.------------------------------------- 649
Voda v. Cordis Corp. ---**46, 151, 805,
843**
Vogel v. Jones-------------------- 77, 78, 83
W.L. Gore & Assoc., Inc. v. Garlock,
Inc. ------------------------------------- 444
Warner Jenkinson Co. v. Hilton Davis
Chemical Co. --------------------667, 673
Weatherford Canada Ltd. v. Corlac
Inc. ------------------------------------- 719
Webber v. Virginia -------------------- 388
WildTangent, Inc. v. Ultramercial,
LLC -------------------------------332, 334
Wilson Sporting Goods Co. v. David
Geoffrey & Assoc. -------------------- 673
Winans v. Denmead------------------- 665
Windsurfing International Inc. v.
Tabur Marine (Great Britain) Ltd.
-- 485
Wordtech Systems, Inc. v. Integrated
Networks Solutions, Inc. ---------- 780
Yokohama Rubber Company v. Yonex
-- 680
Zenith Labs. Inc. v. Bristol-Myers
Squibb Co.----------------------------- 409
**Zhang, Xitian v. Shijiazhuang
Ouyi Pharmaceutical Co., Ltd.**
-- **497**

INTERNATIONAL PATENT
LAW AND POLICY

PART 1

INTRODUCTION TO THE INTERNATIONAL PATENT SYSTEM

∎ ∎ ∎

CHAPTER 1

THE HISTORICAL CONTEXT FOR GLOBAL PATENT COOPERATION

■ ■ ■

A. THE NATURE AND SOURCES OF INTERNATIONAL PATENT LAW

1. THE HISTORY OF PATENT LAW: A BRIEF OVERVIEW

The idea of affording special privileges to inventors to stimulate innovation and enhance public welfare dates back thousands of years. The conceptual roots of modern laws granting exclusive rights to the creators of useful inventions can be traced to ancient Greece, where rulers of certain city-states granted special protection to the producers of novel recipes. A reference to patents can also be found in Aristotle's *Politics*, written in the fourth century B.C. It mentions a proposal made by prominent Greek architect Hippodamus of Miletus calling for the establishment of an incentive system designed to reward inventors of articles beneficial to the state. However, it was not until eighteen centuries later during the Renaissance that the first patent law was enacted in Venice, Italy. The Venetian Patent Law of 1474, reproduced below, established the first modern patent system designed to regularize the previously discretionary patent grant practices of the Venetian Republic during the early fifteenth century.

VENETIAN PATENT LAW OF THE 19TH MARCH 1474

Guilio Mandich, *Venetian Patents (1450-1550)*, 30 J. PAT. OFF. SOC'Y 166, 177 (1948)

BE IT ENACTED that, by the authority of this Council, every person who shall build any new and ingenious device in this City, not previously made in our Commonwealth, shall give notice of it to the office of our General Welfare Board when it has been reduced to perfection so that it can be used and operated. It being forbidden to every other person in any of our territories and towns to make any further device conforming with and similar to said one, without the consent and license of the author, for the term of 10 years. And if anybody builds it in violation hereof, the aforesaid author and inventor shall be entitled to have him summoned before any Magistrate of this City, by which Magistrate the said infringer shall be constrained to pay him hundred ducats; and the device shall be destroyed at once.

This rudimentary legislation contained important elements of patent law that have endured until today, including requirements that the invention be new, useful, and that the inventor have an exclusive right in relation to the device for a limited duration.

The Venetian model of a formal patent system quickly spread northward, fueled by the opening of new European trade routes. Beginning in the mid-sixteenth century in Great Britain, patents quickly became an instrument of mercantilist trade policy: foreign artisans were induced to introduce new skills and technologies to Britain through the promise of special privileges. However, with the ascension of King James I to the throne in the early seventeenth century, the British patent scheme, still highly informal and discretionary, became less of an incentive system aimed at stimulating innovation and more of a tool used to bestow acts of favoritism on loyal supporters of the Crown. During the subsequent reign of Queen Elizabeth I, the considerable trade-restraining effects associated with this practice led to the enactment of the *Statute of Monopolies* of 1623 by the British Parliament. Among other privileges, the Statute declared patents illegal, except for grants to "the true and first" inventor of "new manufactures," provided the exclusive rights were not used to break the law or primarily to raise prices and obstruct trade. The provisions of the *Statute of Monopolies* quickly became a model for the North American colonies, where a similar patent statute was enacted in Massachusetts in 1641, followed by Connecticut in 1672 and South Carolina in 1691. The British statute is reproduced in part below:

STATUTE OF MONOPOLIES OF 1623
21 Jac. 1, c. 3, §6

Provided also, that any declaration before mentioned shall not extend to any letters patents and grants of privilege for the term of fourteen years or under, hereafter to be made, of the sole working or making of any manner of new manufactures within this realm to the true and first inventor and inventors of such manufactures, which others at the time of making such letters patents and grants shall not use, so as also they be not contrary to the law nor mischievous to the state by raising prices of commodities at home, or hurt of trade, or generally inconvenient: the same fourteen years to be accounted from the date of the first letters patents or grant of such privilege hereafter to be made, but that the same shall be of such force as they should be if this act had never been made, and of none other.

The next significant event in the evolution of modern patent law was the inclusion of the Intellectual Property Clause in Article I, Section 8 of the U.S. Constitution, whereby the Congress was given the power "[t]o promote the Progress of Science and useful Arts, by securing for limited

times to authors and inventors the exclusive Right to their respective
Writings and Discoveries." The Intellectual Property Clause became the
foundation for the first federal U.S. patent law—the Patent Act of 1790—
which rested on the premise that creators have rightful claim to an exclusionary property interest in their innovations. To ensure that patented
inventions were new and "useful," the Act required that two government
officials (selected from the secretary of state, the secretary of war, and the
attorney general) approve the patent and that the attorney general conduct a formal examination of the approved inventions. Like the English
Statute of Monopolies, the Act afforded creators fourteen years of protection.

In France, where, similarly to Great Britain, the patent system had
been utilized since the sixteenth century both to attract skilled artisans
and to protect established manufacturers, the opinion of the general public had traditionally gravitated toward rejection of the exclusionary effects of patent protection. Nevertheless, the turbulent events surrounding
the French Revolution and the passage of a new constitution witnessed
the enactment of the first French patent statute, the Patent Act of 1791,
and signaled a break with old customs. The Act, conceptually grounded in
the Declaration of the Rights of Man (1789), was based on the notion that
inventors possessed a natural right to the fruits of their creative endeavors. Importantly, the wide influence on the European continent of the
ideals surrounding the French Revolution, along with the significant expansion in inter-European trade, led to the proliferation of formal patent
systems across Western European nations. In the early to mid-nineteenth
century, patent statutes were adopted by Spain (1826), Portugal (1837),
Austria-Hungary (1852), and Italy (1859).

Despite strong arguments put forth about the relationship between
the protection of intellectual property, liberty and economic prosperity,
the establishment of patent protection regimes across Europe in the nineteenth century proved controversial. For example, in Holland, where a
codified patent law was enacted as early as 1817, a strong anti-patent
movement led to the complete (but ultimately temporary) abolition of patent protection in 1869. This anti-patent movement was still strong in
some European countries (e.g., Germany) even as the intensification of
cross-border trade led major industrializing nations in 1872 to begin talks
on the first multilateral intellectual property treaty—the Paris Convention for the Protection of Industrial Property (1883)—which remains the
foundation of international patent law to this day.

2. EARLY HARMONIZATION EFFORTS: THE PARIS CONVENTION FOR THE PROTECTION OF INDUSTRIAL PROPERTY

The elimination of barriers to international trade was the primary rationale for a treaty for the protection of patents. Developments in the mid-nineteenth century, most importantly the growth of cross-border commerce, soon revealed that the patchwork of early patent laws of major industrializing countries did not provide sufficient international protection for inventors. First, as we will discuss in detail in section 1.C, *infra*, intellectual property protection and the associated rights have historically been territorial in nature. Accordingly, the rights afforded under domestic patent systems were limited in scope by national boundaries. Second, still influenced by mercantilist trade policies, many early patent laws effectively excluded foreign persons from seeking patent protection in other countries. For example, under the French Patent Act of 1791 patent owners forfeited their patent if the goods were imported into, and not manufactured within, France. Because similar provisions were included in several of the earliest patent statutes, innovators needing protection in multiple jurisdictions were often forced to select specific countries in which to apply for a patent, while abandoning the possibility of protection in others. In 1872, these concerns led representatives of the major industrializing nations to gather in Vienna to discuss the possibility of an international agreement that would harmonize basic standards of patent protection and effectively eliminate existing discriminatory practices.

The catalyst for the formal commencement of negotiations for the first multilateral patent treaty was an international exhibition promoting new inventions that was sponsored by the Austro-Hungarian Empire in Vienna in 1873. At the time, applicants seeking international patent protection were hampered by the wide diversity in national laws and by the need to file multiple applications in order to avoid the possibility that the publication of an application in one country would destroy the invention's novelty in others. As a result, foreign inventors were reluctant to exhibit their inventions in Vienna for fear of inadequate legal protection. In response, the Austro-Hungarian government, urged on by the U.S., convened the Vienna Congress for Patent Reform, which emphasized the need for nations to adopt effective patent systems and urged governments "to bring about an international understanding upon patent protection as soon as possible." The French government heeded the call, and convened an International Congress on Industrial Property in Paris in 1878. That Congress determined to create "uniform legislation" in the field of industrial property. It was followed by another Congress in 1880 to debate a draft text. Finally, the Diplomatic Conference in Paris adopted the Paris Convention for the Protection of Industrial Property on March 20, 1883.

The battle to craft the Paris Convention was not easily won. Despite the enthusiasm of the United States, the Austro-Hungarian Empire, and France, a strong anti-patent mood permeated the negotiations. Germany, which at the time had recently abolished its patent law, led the anti-patent movement. Switzerland and Holland also were among the Convention's strongest opponents. Even among the pro-patent countries, a philosophical divide marked the debate, with countries such as the United States that viewed patents as a private property right on one side and countries that viewed patents as an instrument of public policy, which included most of Continental Europe, on the other.

HEINRICH KRONSTEIN & IRENE TILL, A REEVALUATION OF THE INTERNATIONAL PATENT CONVENTION
12 Law & Contemp. Probs. 765, 766–776 (1947)

The creative period of the [Paris] Union was between 1872 and 1881. During this period the negotiations on the international patent convention were the battlefield for three opposing philosophies: (1) the anti-patent movement, aimed at the destruction of the patent system; (2) the recognition of patents as private property; [and] (3) the recognition of patents as an instrument of public policy. Certainly the issue of patents *versus* no-patents had to be disposed of first. The fight on this point marked the first battle between the [pro-patent] United States and the newly organized Germany of Bismarck.

The initial invitation for an international conference on patent rights came from the Austrian Government in 1872. . . .

        . . . .

The organizers of the conference were fully aware that, in a competitive business economy, the world could not live half with patents and half without patents. The invitation to the conference sets forth the interdependence among national patent systems in the following classical statement:

> We live no longer in the day of Industrial action, which is strictly confined and is removed from foreign competition, and where slow communication prevents or delays the utilization of inventions. We live at a time of liberal Customs policy; Steam and Electricity have newly united once isolated seats of industry in a way undreamt of; and the mutual exchange of goods shows today a magnitude which a generation ago one could not have imagined. Under such altered relations the Patent granted for an invention in one country becomes in fact a restriction unprofitable and obstructive, if the same invention without limitation or increase in price, becomes in an adjoining country common property. The artisan who in the one country must work with the auxil-

iary material there patented and therefore dearer in price, will suffer an essential injury as soon as the same material is produced in the other country, not only without restriction, but with a damaging competition. Moreover a continuance of hitherto antagonistic views and measures would scarcely conduce to the preservation of general harmony; and if, for example, Patent protection were maintained in one country, so as to attract thereby skilled operatives from another, then the danger of disturbance of the International industrial balance might readily be apprehended. Such and similar inconveniences can only be met by the common action of all civilized States, disposed to the maintenance of Patent protection.

The American delegation to the Vienna conference was an able one. The Assistant Commissioner of Patents, J. M. Thacher, headed the group; his experience and knowledge of the United States patent system gave him a leading role in the negotiations. . . .

. . . .

Thacher's own report indicates the tenor of the conference. He said:

It was the general, I may say universally expressed, opinion in the congress at Vienna that in order to secure the advancement of the mechanic arts in their own countries and to prevent the emigration of their most skilled artisans, it was necessary to secure a reform in European patent legislation. . . .

. . . .

The Vienna conference made this general attitude manifest in its set of resolutions. It declared that the existence of a patent law was a requirement "of all civilized nations"; and foresaw "great injury . . . inflicted upon countries which have no rational patent laws by the native inventive talent emigrating to more congenial countries where their labor is legally protected." The conference endorsed the "English, American, and Belgian patent laws, and the draft of a patent law prepared for Germany by the society of German engineers" (Bismarck's opponents!). One small bone was thrown to the opponents of an air-tight patent system. A recommendation provided:

It is advisable to establish legal rules, according to which the patentee may be induced, in cases in which the public interest should require it, to allow the use of his invention to all suitable applicants, for an adequate compensation. . . .

. . . .

The American victory on the issue of patent *versus* no-patent, decisive as it was, merely transferred the battlefront to the next stage. This was the issue of patents as private property rights as against patents as instruments of public policy. The impending struggle was foreseen in the American-Austrian discussions of 1872. The American Government opened the dispute by complaining against the Austrian principle providing for forfeiture of patent rights if local manufacturing were not begun within one year from the grant of the patent. Here was a clear statement of the issue. John Jay, then American Ambassador in Vienna, pointed out to the Austrian Minister of Foreign Affairs on March 17, 1872:

> It has been suggested that the differences in the statutes of different countries, in regard to patents, may be generally traced to a difference in the general view taken of the character and position of the patentee; whether he is looked upon as a monopolist who owes all his rights to exceptional law, and who must be jealously watched and severely restricted; or whether he is regarded as a public benefactor, who is to be tenderly and kindly treated. The legislation of Congress has inclined more and more to the latter view; and, while adopting, as the true principle, that the inventor and public are both to be treated rationally, justly, and impartially, its tendency has been to give more and more liberally encouragement and assistance to useful inventors. . . .

This American view toward patents was novel. It stemmed from an actual faith that, in a competitive economy, patents under the control of private owners would not be subjected to abuse. The files of the United States Patent Office contain a constant reiteration of this theme; they reveal an absolute faith in the beneficent effects of an uncontrolled system. It was precisely this freedom, it was believed, which accounted for the rapid technological advance in the United States. In consequence, the Patent Office violently opposed any kind of governmental interference—whether against foreign inventors in this country or American inventors abroad. At every opportunity in the correspondence of the patent commissioners with foreign patent offices—through State Department channels or in direct negotiation—the view is developed that only international cooperation and mutual recognition of private property in patents can serve the final aim of the highest technological advance everywhere. The constant reiteration of this gospel by the most highly industrialized country in the world was bound to have an enormous effect.

But such an approach was in direct conflict with established tradition abroad. The American philosophy was genuinely new. True, the speeches of the French Revolution were aflame with this doctrine; Mirabeau exultantly speaks of inventions and patents as private property equal to any other form of private property. But, in fact, the French never drew the logical conclusion from these theories. The patent statute of France after the Revolution provided that patents should be forfeited in the event that patented goods were imported into France. Such a provision was a clear denial of the private property aspect of a patent, and made patents an instrument of public policy to bring manufacturing plants to France. This law still existed at the time of the Vienna conference.

The English patent statute of 1623 had the same purpose. Though usually called the "mother of our patent law," it differed markedly in aim, method, and field of coverage from our modern patent law. The English statute was a device for bringing new trades into England. Inventions were not new discoveries; trades and skills were "inventions" and patentable if their appearance in England was new. The English documents are replete with instances of the granting of patents for trades imported from the continent. Nor did English patents cover a strictly limited process or product. In fact, just the opposite was true. The patent was granted before the governmental authority even obtained any specifications. Not until 1780 did specification become a precondition for the grant of patents; and not until then did the concept of novelty have importance in the field of patents. Thus in the early history of Britain the issuance of a patent was essentially a political expedient; a temporary monopoly was justified if it brought new trade and skills to the island.

Obviously, the American view expressed in John Jay's letter had nothing in common with the traditional European approach. The question for the Germans—once they had abandoned their original hostility to the patent system—was which view they would adopt. Quite naturally they turned to the early English position. They were newcomers in the industrial hierarchy; they had all of the anti-monopolistic attitudes of the upstart competitor. They immediately adopted the position that patents should not be granted as a matter of right to every inventor, but should be permitted only in those fields in which the public interest justified the grant. Nor were they prepared to look upon patents as private property, to be granted to outsiders without limitation. Patents were a qualified right, subject to governmental interference in the interest of the nation. . . .

. . . .

In the meantime the American view of patents as private property came into popularity in other countries. Between 1873, the year of the Vienna conference, and 1878, the year of the Paris convention, the American view prevailed in all European countries except Germany, Switzerland, and Holland. In consequence, the following formula was submitted at the Paris meeting:

> The right of inventors and industrial creators in their own work or the right of the industrialists in their trademarks is a property right which has its basis in natural law. The law enacted by each nation does not create these rights but only regulates them.

The Swiss delegation joined issue by offering a counter motion:

> The rights of the inventor and creative worker are a creation of equitable and useful principles of the law of each nation which should reconcile this right of the inventor, based on the grant of a temporary monopoly, with the rights of society.

The Swiss motion was voted down and the "property" motion won, though the clause "which has its basis in natural law" was eliminated.

Once an international convention declared inventions and patents a type of private property, it was only logical to grant to the "owners" of such property equal protection under the law, whatever their nationality might be. In the philosophy prevailing at the end of the nineteenth century, no principle was more sacred than the mutual protection of the vested interests of private property. Once patents were recognized as a type of private property there was no possible justification for the continuance of the forfeiture penalty for importation of patented goods or for the harsh rules respecting working clauses. The French system broke down almost immediately, and the working clauses gradually fell into disuse. The priority rule made its obsequious entry as a simple convenience for the property owner.

Germany continued to remain outside of the convention during the Eighties and mid-Nineties. In that country the scope of the patent grant was limited in the interest of encouraging further invention, and patents were subjected to compulsory licensing. But in 1897, at the Brussels convention, Germany appeared and prepared the way for her retreat. One of her major concerns was the elimination of the working clause. To this end she won the ardent support of the United States.

In 1901 Germany joined the Union. In a short time she became, along with the United States, the most ardent defender of the Union. In the later conferences the two countries worked together effectively to strengthen the protections accorded the patentee. In fact, the International Patent Convention can now almost be referred to as an American-German patent alliance.

NOTES AND QUESTIONS

1. Once leading countries agreed on the importance of patent protection to reward innovation, the major task was to identify the scope of such protection on a global basis. To what extent should national justifications for the patent system influence the nature and extent of global patent protection? What principles should guide the accommodation of different national patent policies in a global patent treaty?

2. Compare the American-influenced motion with the Swiss motion submitted in preparation for the Paris Convention, *supra* p. 1012. What is the difference between the two proposals? Why do you think the reference to natural law was eliminated in the final proposal for the Paris Convention?

3. Issues of patent scope are invariably linked to the central objectives of patent protection. What *should* be the key goals of global patent protection? What features of a modern global patent system would you expect to reflect the dominance of an American property-rights approach?

4. Most of the countries that today are described as "developing" or "least-developed" were not sovereign nations at the time of the Paris Convention negotiations. Consequently, they played no role in the early philosophical debates regarding the nature and function of a global patent system. The absence of these countries from the early design and implementation of global patent norms remains a significant source of tension and disharmony in international patent relations. As with Europe, many African territories first became exposed to the various forms of intellectual property through trade relations. In describing the role of intellectual property in Africa starting in the sixteenth century, Professor Okediji argues that the patch-work system of intellectual property laws existing in Europe were used as part of a broader set of laws and institutions that governed relations between European traders in the foreign territories as colonial efforts were consolidated in the eighteenth and nineteenth centuries:

> [B]efore the conclusion of the Paris . . . Convention[,]. . . many territories in Africa, Asia and the Pacific were already affected by intellectual property regulations implemented through the various forms of formal and informal European administration in these regions . . . .

> [W]hat the Paris . . . Convention[ ] initially accomplished was the establishment of a network of relationships between the European member countries—a relationship that consolidated colonial power by expanding the geographic scope of rights acquired in the governing country to the colonies and, in some cases, the protectorates. . . . In essence, the extension of intellectual property rights was not directed at the inhabitants of the governed territories at all, but instead to facilitate commercial relations among colonial powers as trade between European powers occurred on and among the various territories on behalf of foreign sovereigns.

> Intellectual property law was not merely an incidental part of the colonial legal apparatus, but a central technique in the commercial superiority sought by European powers in their interactions *with each other* in regions beyond Europe. Granted, intellectual property systems in Europe prior to the seventeenth century were neither fully developed nor had intellectual property protection become a systematic policy designed primarily for encouraging domestic innovation. Whatever protections existed, however, would be exerted against other Europeans in colonial territories in the process of empire building. . . . Global ownership of intellectual property rights became one of a number of ways that the sovereignty of former colonies was directed away from an obligation to promote the domestic

welfare of citizens, to a duty to subordinate that welfare to the vicissitudes of the market ideology.

Ruth L. Okediji, *The International Relations of Intellectual Property: Narratives of Developing Country Participation in the Global Intellectual Property System*, 7 SING. J. INT'L & COMP. L. 315, 323–25 (2003).

Should the least-developed countries, the majority of which are in Africa, be able to rewrite some of the basic rules of the global patent system based on the argument that they were not involved in its evolution and design?

5. Do you think the economic and political history of former colonies in Africa, Asia and parts of the Americas should play a role in evaluating the relevance of the global patent system to current concerns about economic development in these regions? Did any of the motions submitted in preparation for the Paris Convention reflect similar concerns about the relationship between patents and economic growth? In what way?

6. While every country retains its own approach to patents with unique characteristics reflected in national laws, there is usually broad agreement on fundamentals among the more industrialized countries. In what ways can the developed countries address the economic development concerns of developing and least-developed countries without undermining their own interests in having a strong global patent system? There remain significant differences in views about the international patent system and its effects on economic development. We will return to these and other contentious aspects of modern international patent relations later in this Chapter and throughout this book.

Despite the difficulties encountered by negotiating parties during the talks preceding the conclusion of the Paris Convention, the final text of the Convention successfully incorporated several fundamental provisions. These provisions formed the bedrock of the modern international intellectual property system and ensured the attainment of the chief objective of the agreement: the reduction of barriers to international trade flows.

First and foremost, to eliminate the discriminatory practices of national patent systems, the Paris Convention obligated contracting states to recognize the principle of "national treatment," under which countries must afford equal treatment to both domestic and foreign inventors. Second, to ensure that applicants were not prevented from seeking protection in multiple jurisdictions, the Convention mandated member states to recognize applicants' "right of priority," whereby for twelve months after the date of their original application, applicants may apply for protection in fellow member states without fearing the loss of novelty of their inventions. These provisions will be discussed in detail in Chapter 2. Finally, to assure that the obligations of the Paris Convention were not circumvented through the conclusion of subsequent bilateral or multilateral intellectual property treaties, Article 19 permitted Paris Union members to enter into special intellectual property agreements among themselves only if those agreements did not contravene the provisions of the Convention. It was Article 19 that gained increasing importance in the evolution of the international patent system as the world entered the twentieth century.

3. THE INTERNATIONAL PATENT SYSTEM IN THE TWENTY-FIRST CENTURY

The conclusion of the Paris Convention in 1883 was undoubtedly an important first step toward the establishment of a viable international intellectual property system; nonetheless, some features of the Paris framework soon proved inadequate, given the dynamic technological and geopolitical developments after the turn of the century. As a result, between 1900 and 1979, the Paris Convention underwent six revisions designed to upgrade the system to the needs of the modern international economy. A major weakness of the Paris Convention since its inception had been the lack of an effective institutional framework charged with both administering the new regime and ensuring compliance with the regime's standards by member states. The need to improve the functioning of the international patent system, among other things, led to the formation of the World Intellectual Property Organization (WIPO) during the Stockholm Revision of the Convention in 1967. Since its establishment, WIPO—currently charged with overseeing twenty-four intellectual property treaties—has become the central hub of administration and standard-setting for the international intellectual property system. Nevertheless, discussions on the improvement of the international intellectual property scheme did not end with the creation of WIPO. By the 1980s, it became evident to policymakers in many industrialized countries that the international intellectual property system could not continue to function without an adequate enforcement framework. However, the establishment of such a framework within WIPO was not likely for a number of reasons.

YOSHIFUMI FUKUNAGA, ENFORCING TRIPS: CHALLENGES OF ADJUDICATING MINIMUM STANDARDS AGREEMENTS
23 BERKELEY TECH. L.J. 867, 871–74 (2008)

. . . .

WIPO, which was formed in 1967 as a specialized international organization, had a mandate to administer IP matters under the United Nations. The WIPO regime, however, had several defects that made it unpalatable to developed-world business interests.

The first problem was the relatively low level of minimum standards set in the conventions that the WIPO was charged with enforcing. Although these conventions did specify certain minimum standards, the contracting parties were given broad discretion as to the level of IP pro-

tections to enact. For example, a country could completely exclude pharmaceutical products from patentability or limit the duration of patent
terms to a mere seven years. In addition, the governing conventions of the
WIPO regime, particularly the Paris Convention for the Protection of Industrial Property (Paris Convention) . . . required member nations to enact only limited enforcement procedures. For example, these conventions
did not even require the exclusion or seizure of counterfeit products at
national borders. Although the drafters of the treaty may have hoped that
the fundamental principle of national treatment would ensure that member nations were incentivized to protect the IP rights of foreign nationals,
in practice national treatment failed to create the uniformly high levels of
protection desired by businesses in developed countries. National treatment requires a signatory country to provide the same IP protection to
foreigners as it does to its own nationals. However, this principle was of
little use to foreigners if a state with broad discretion did not provide adequate treatment for its own nationals.

A second shortcoming of the WIPO was that the membership of
WIPO conventions was limited and major sources of infringing goods
(particularly India, Singapore, and South Korea) were excluded. Furthermore, since not all signatories of the conventions had ratified all of
the amendments, it was "difficult to determine the exact obligations between two member states."

[In addition], the WIPO regime did not provide an effective dispute
resolution system. For example, although the Paris Convention did provide a procedure for dispute settlement, this procedure was never used in
practice. A large problem was that the jurisdiction of the International
Court of Justice (ICJ) was noncompulsory. . . . As a result, "the majority
of the member states of the convention never accepted the compulsory
jurisdiction of the ICJ . . . in IP matters." Moreover, "patent disputes were
considered to be too trivial to bring before the ICJ."

. . . .

[Finally], the developed countries were concerned about the voting
system in . . . WIPO. In . . . WIPO, as in the United Nations generally,
developed countries, developing countries, and socialist countries had
customarily voted as unified blocs, even though the individual interests of
bloc members may have diverged on particular issues. Since most IP
rights—particularly patents—were and are held by parties in developed
countries, strengthened international IP rules appeared to benefit the
developed countries while imposing costs on the other countries. Given
the WIPO membership's tendency to vote in blocs, as well as the numerical reality that the developed countries were outnumbered by the developing countries, it would have been difficult for the developed nations to
convince the other voting groups to adopt new rules within the WIPO regime. . . .

During the late 1980s, intense lobbying by a group of leading indus-trialized countries spearheaded by the U.S. led to the incorporation of the Paris Convention–centered patent system into the multilateral trade re-gime. This result was accomplished during the Uruguay Round of multi-lateral trade negotiations, which took place between 1986 and 1994 and culminated in the establishment of a new international institution, the World Trade Organization (WTO), and adoption of the most comprehen-sive multilateral intellectual property treaty to date: the Agreement on Trade-Related Aspects of Intellectual Property Rights (TRIPS Agree-ment). The TRIPS Agreement incorporated the substantive provisions of the Paris Convention (Articles 1–12 and 19) and, unlike predecessor intel-lectual property treaties, obligated its signatories to "ensure that en-forcement procedures as specified in [the Agreement] are available under their law so as to permit effective action against any act of infringement of intellectual property rights. . . ." Moreover, to assure that member states in fact comply with their obligations under the TRIPS Agreement, the negotiating parties agreed that the provisions of the Agreement should be subject to a new dispute settlement mechanism with rules codi-fied in another agreement called the Dispute Settlement Understanding (DSU), pursuant to which sanctions can be imposed on non-complying states. This strong dispute settlement mechanism provided a crucial en-forcement tool that the WIPO sorely lacked. The DSU is discussed further in Chapter 3.

NOTE ON THE WORLD TRADE ORGANIZATION

Prior to 1994, international trade relations were governed by the Gen-eral Agreement on Tariffs and Trade (GATT), completed in 1947 and amend-ed over time with approximately 200 treaty instruments, which focused prin-cipally on trade in goods. The establishment of the WTO in 1994, together with other institutional reforms including the new dispute settlement sys-tem, remains one of the most important developments in modern interna-tional economic law. In addition to the TRIPS Agreement, the Uruguay Round also produced a new GATT text (GATT 1994) and a treaty governing trade in services, the General Agreement on Trade in Services (GATS). Alt-hough GATT 1994, GATS and TRIPS are the major substantive agreements under the WTO, in reality, there are numerous agreements that form the en-tire 'Final Act' of the Uruguay Round. Further, there are a variety of Ministe-rial Decisions, Declarations, Understandings, etc., which inform the WTO governance structure and often provide a normative orientation for the obli-gations contained in the various texts. In adhering to the WTO Charter, countries are bound to all these annexed agreements and have an obligation to ensure domestic compliance with the obligations embodied in each one. Understanding the legal structure and organizational framework of the WTO is an important part of learning how this leading international organization oversees and, in some cases, directly influences the development of international patent law and policy.

The WTO's top decision-making body is the Ministerial Conference, which meets at least once every two years, and comprises the trade ministers of all WTO member states. Ministerial Conference decisions are normally made by consensus, with each country having a single vote. Importantly, since votes are not weighted, a small, least-developed WTO member has the same voting power as a large, developed country such as the United States. This approach ensures that the interests of each country are taken into account within the Organization, but, at the same time, makes collective decision making quite difficult. At present, the majority of the WTO's 159 members are developing or least-developed countries whose interests often diverge not only from those of developed countries but from each other as well.

The General Council, an organ one level below the Ministerial Conference, is made up of member country ambassadors and heads of delegations to the WTO. It convenes several times a year to review policies and issue decisions, and also meets as the Dispute Settlement Body (DSB), the authority charged with deciding trade disputes among WTO member states. As stated earlier, dispute settlement under the WTO is governed by the DSU.

The WTO Secretariat is the general administrative arm of the organization, providing professional and technical support to the member states with respect to all WTO activities and functions. The Secretariat serves an important coordination function through its professional input and assistance to the various councils and committees that carry out the work of monitoring, reporting and reviewing actions by member states regarding the implementation of the various WTO agreements. Although increasingly, many view several of the WTO's activities as affecting the direction of global intellectual property policy, responsibility for the TRIPS Agreement is vested principally in the TRIPS Council, established by Article 68. That provision states:

> The Council for TRIPS shall monitor the operation of this Agreement and, in particular, Members' compliance with their obligations hereunder, and shall afford Members the opportunity of consulting on matters relating to the trade-related aspects of intellectual property rights. It shall carry out such other responsibilities as assigned to it by the Members, and it shall, in particular, provide any assistance requested by them in the context of dispute settlement procedures. In carrying out its functions, the Council for TRIPS may consult with and seek information from any source it deems appropriate. . . .

The WTO Secretariat assists the Council with its TRIPS-specific responsibilities such as reviewing national intellectual property policies, providing technical assistance to developing and least-developed countries as issues arise within the Council, or accepting notifications under the Doha Declaration. In addition, the Council has some norm-setting responsibilities with respect to specific issues such as the protection of geographical indications, an important issue for negotiation by WTO member states. The TRIPS Council issues an annual report of its activities to the General Council.

The incorporation of intellectual property into the global trade regime, along with the ability of WTO members to enforce the multilateral standards in the TRIPS Agreement, has fundamentally transformed the international patent regime. Many of the changes and tensions brought about by the TRIPS Agreement are evident in domestic patent laws of WTO member countries and in protracted global policy debates over the effect of patents on biodiversity, protection of genetic resources, access to essential medicines for the poor, and climate change. Above all, the explicit recognition by the WTO community of the link between patent protection, trade, and economic development has raised difficult questions regarding the normative ethos underpinning the global protection of patent rights. The decision to incorporate by reference the substantive provisions of the Paris Convention has extended the geographic reach of the international system by inducing a large number of states, among them many developing and least-developed countries, to accede to the Convention. Finally, the increased credibility of the international patent system, underscored by the conclusion of the TRIPS Agreement, has intensified debates on the establishment of a "global patent" scheme, or an international patent system unconstrained by the principle of territoriality of patent rights. As you learn about the specific features of the TRIPS Agreement throughout this book, consider whether the development of international patent norms should be insulated (or isolated) from the political environment that characterizes the multilateral trade system.

———————

B. JUSTIFICATIONS FOR A GLOBAL PATENT FRAMEWORK

Since the 1870s, when discussions began on the creation of the Paris Union, national governments, along with private sector stakeholders, have sought ways to internationalize the patent system by harmonizing the acquisition of patent rights across national boundaries. More recently, significant expansion in the globalization of trade, internationalization of research, and extensive utilization of the patent system to gain competitive advantages, have intensified pressures to strengthen the global patent framework. These same developments, however, have also raised suspicions about the patent system's potential negative economic and social impacts. The intense and often highly politicized debates over the sources, nature, scope and effect of the global patent system has made it difficult to synthesize a singular theoretical framework in which all of the various facets of global patent law can be reconciled. To further complicate matters, global intellectual property agreements are "nested" within a broader set of international norms that simultaneously reinforce or stand in tension with key aspects of intellectual property protection. Below, we offer an introduction to three leading justifications for the global intellectual property system: 1) the international trade justification, which currently dominates arguments in favor of a global patent system; 2) a human rights justification, which has been used both to support and oppose global patent laws; and 3) an international institutional justification, which seeks to provide a conceptual rationale for why states enter into international agreements. As you will learn in more detail in Chapter 3, the international trade justification is the dominant justification for strong global intellectual property rights.

1. THE INTERNATIONAL TRADE JUSTIFICATION

Why is global intellectual property protection significant for U.S. interests? Consider the following excerpt by Professor McCarthy almost two decades ago at the height of the transformation of the U.S. economy:

J. THOMAS MCCARTHY, INTELLECTUAL PROPERTY— AMERICA'S OVERLOOKED EXPORT

20 U. DAYTON L. REV. 809, 809–16 (1995)

As we rush through each busy day, we often have to take no more than a hurried glance at the newspaper or at the news on television to see what's going on in the world. Sometimes we see an item that seems trivial on its face, but we subliminally recognize: "That's an amazing development! Things are changing faster than I thought."

A few years ago I saw one of those seemingly trivial facts noted in the business page and realized: "This is an important signal that the America I grew up with had irrevocably changed." What I saw in the newspaper was that the people who run the Dow Jones Index—a list of thirty industrial stocks representing a cross section of American commerce—dropped U.S. Steel from the list and replaced it with the Walt Disney Company. While the announcement may sound inconsequential, the fact that a steel giant was replaced by an entertainment empire is a symbol which keynotes the subject of this Essay.

Chicago Tribune columnist Bob Greene headlined his column on the subject: "A Mouse Replaces Men of Steel." Greene noted that the Dow Jones Index has always been the paramount financial symbol of U.S. business and industry. The Dow Jones industrial average was what American business was all about. It symbolized the source of America's strength and prosperity—or at least a dream of prosperity. A dream that has driven millions of people around the world to get to America at all costs—no matter what the odds—from countries as diverse as China, Russia, and Cuba.

Growing up in the 1940s and 1950s, I lived in what was then America's biggest factory town—Detroit, Michigan. I was taught that America was a great place to live and a robust and strong nation because it made millions of things that people all around the world wanted. Documentaries boosting American industry always seemed to include a shot of the Ford River Rouge plant (complete with smokestacks belching smoke) or a shot of white hot steel being rolled in a Pittsburgh foundry. Needless to say, U.S. Steel was a major part of that view of industrial America.

U.S. Steel stood shoulder to shoulder on the Dow Jones Index with manufacturing companies like Caterpillar, Chevron Oil, General Electric, Goodyear, and Union Carbide. What is a company whose major asset is Mickey Mouse doing with these brawny types?

The face of American business is changing, and changing fast. What America makes and what the rest of the world wants to buy is also changing. In ten years, Disney has grown "from an ailing $2 billion Hollywood also-ran into a $22 billion empire." Disney is a major entertainment company. Disney sells entertainment, leisure, and dreams to America and to the rest of the world. Disney World in Orlando, Florida is the world's most heavily visited tourist destination. Every day, dozens of jets land at Orlando's airport, bringing people from all over the world. Their destination is a place that once was covered with orange groves and swamps. Not bad for a mouse.

Disney sells entertainment through movies, videos, television programs, theme parks, books and records. But what exactly is the basis of the Disney empire? We knew that the heart of U.S. Steel was property—those huge mills spewing sparks, belching smoke and turning out rolled steel twenty-four hours a day. But what is the property that is at the heart of a company like Disney? It is a new kind of property. We call it intellectual property. Intellectual, only because it is a property right in the products of the intellect—a product of the human mind, as opposed to real estate or tangible objects.

I know that I am oversimplifying to make my point. Of course, U.S. Steel had intellectual property in know-how and engineering innovations. Disney, of course, owns a substantial amount of highly valuable real estate. But I want to focus on the heart of the fundamental differences between these two companies in order to illustrate how this simple substitution of one company for the other on the Dow Jones Index symbolizes the new era we are entering. Some call it the information age.

. . . .

Basically, the subject of all kinds of intellectual property is information. The job of intellectual property law is to create property rights in newly created information. We are continually told that we are entering. . . . [a]n age in which by far the most valuable thing to own and control is information—technological information, business information, political information and information about people. . . .

. . . .

Every newspaper in the nation regularly contains some story on a development involving intellectual property—the articles are frequently found, not on the business page, but on the front page. In the San Francisco Bay Area, many start-up companies in computer software and bio-tech are founded solely upon two or three key patent applications. Innovation has always been the engine that drives our economy, but today more people than ever before are aware of this fact and of the importance of nurturing our intellectual property system. . . .

. . . .

Our government seeks to put pressure on other governments, especially those in Asia, to raise the level of their intellectual property protection and enforcement. But why should Americans care whether the People's Republic of China winks at piracy of computer programs and compact discs?

We care because if no intellectual property protection exists regarding technical and entertainment information, then we have little to sell to the rest of the world. In the old days of selling cars, steel, and aluminum to the rest of the world, the kind of patent, trademark and copyright laws implemented by other nations did not make a lot of difference. Their intellectual property laws were their business. Now it is our business.

American businesses suffer the most when an Asian government tolerates the widespread pirating of computer programs and CDs and the Asian market becomes flooded with pirated products. This occurs because America supplies the bulk of the world's software and music, as well as video tapes. While the Asian nations produce most of the hardware used in the entertainment and computer industries, such as televisions, CD players, and PC clones, America supplies the content for that hardware—the shows, songs, and software that makes the hardware valuable. If foreign nations do not recognize or enforce intellectual property laws, then America has nothing to sell.

. . . .

If an American company sells only a few copies of a computer program or video because social customs permit widespread reproduction, then much less incentive exists to produce the product in the first place. Fewer copies will be produced and fewer Americans will be hired to produce those copies. In the information age, ineffective intellectual property protection and enforcement results in less protectable material produced. This phenomenon bodes poorly for the future of the United States, because we cannot compete in a world market for producing steel or clothes or VCRs when manufacturers in developing nations can pay what we would regard as a less than living wage. That leads to cries for protectionist legislation like trade barriers and tariffs.

. . . .

A new phenomenon in U.S. intellectual property law is that changes in our domestic law are being driven by the needs of world trade. For the first 200 years of our nation's history, we very loosely based our intellectual property laws on those of Great Britain. As the years went by, however, our laws became more and more idiosyncratic. Our intellectual property laws developed so differently from those of the rest of the world that they became a real impediment to free trade.

. . . .

Several recent changes in U.S. law were also required by the NAFTA and GATT agreements. All of these changes were driven by the need for harmonizing the United States' laws with those of our trading partners. No major trading nation in today's world can enjoy the indulgence of having intellectual property laws significantly different from those of the world community. In one sense, unusual intellectual property laws are a tariff and an unnatural barrier to world trade.

NOTES AND QUESTIONS

1. International trade is a central focus in debates over global protection of intellectual property and we discuss this further in Chapter 3. As Professor McCarthy indicates, U.S. interest in a global intellectual property system has greatly intensified in the last two decades. A 2010 press release by the Office of the United States Trade Representative (USTR) states that intellectual property theft in overseas markets "is critical to the livelihoods of the estimated 18 million Americans who work in intellectual property intensive industries." *See* Office of the U.S. Trade Representative, Special 301 Report on Intellectual Property Rights (May 4, 2010). The most recent Special 301 Report states that intellectual property infringement "undermines key U.S. comparative advantages in innovation and creativity, to the detriment of American businesses and workers." The Report continues that "[b]ecause fostering innovation and creativity is essential to our prosperity, competitiveness, and the support of an estimated 40 million U.S. jobs that directly or indirectly rely on IPR-intensive industries, USTR works to protect American inventiveness and creativity with all the tools of U.S. trade policy, including this Report." *See* RONALD KIRK, 2012 SPECIAL 301 REPORT 8 (2012), *available at* http://www.ustr.gov/sites/default/files/2012 Special 301 Report_0.pdf. What are the risks in relying on the international intellectual property system to secure or reinforce domestic economic strength? Do you think dealing with substantive patent norms in an organizational environment principally dedicated to trade liberalization is a beneficial innovation of the twenty-first century global patent system?

2. The biopharmaceutical industry, a leading patent-intensive sector, is often recognized as an important driver of the U.S. economy. According to an industry profile report, this industry alone contributed $88.5 billion to the U.S. economy in 2006, tripling the average contribution of other sectors. *See Pharmaceutical Industry Profile 2009*, PhRMA Update (Pharm. Research &

Mfr. Ass'n, Washington D.C.), Apr. 2009, at 9–12. In its 2011 industry profile, PhRMA claimed that the industry is responsible for more than 3 million jobs in the U.S. economy. *See* PHARMACEUTICAL RESEARCH AND MANUFACTURERS OF AMERICA, 2011 INDUSTRY PROFILE (2011), *available at* http://www.phrma. org/sites/default/files/159/phrma_profile_2011_final.pdf.   According   to PhRMA's President and CEO, "at a time when our innovation, entrepreneurialism and jobs dominate the national dialogue, our industry should be held up and preserved as a national treasure. It should be supported by policies that encourage growth and that reward innovation, investment and risk taking." *Id.* Are there policy tools beside patent law that could offer effective support for innovation, investment and risk taking?

3. The International Intellectual Property Alliance (IIPA) releases periodic reports on the effect of copyright protection on the U.S. economy. According to the 2011 report, U.S. gross domestic product (GDP) was $14.66 trillion in 2010. In the same year, the value added to the U.S. GDP by the "core"[1] copyright industries reached $931.8 billion, or 6.4 percent of the U.S. economy. Stephen E. Siwek, *Copyright Industries in the U.S. Economy: The 2011 Report*, I.I.P.A., at 4 (Nov. 2011), http://www.iipa.com/pdf/2011Copyright IndustriesReport.PDF. Like its predecessor, the 2011 Report noted that many patented (or patentable) technologies, such as consumer electronics, represent part of the economic value of the copyright industries because these goods facilitate the use and enjoyment of copyrighted works. *See* Stephen E. Siwek, *Copyright Industries in the U.S. Economy: The 2003–2007 Report*, I.I.P.A., at 9 (June 2009), *available at* IIPA.com. *See also* Siwek, *The 2011 Report*, *supra* at 8 (describing these as "interdependent industries" and including them as part of the "total" contribution of copyright industries to the U.S. economy. The value added to U.S. GDP by the "total" copyright industries in 2010 was $1.627 trillion, or 11.10 percent of U.S. GDP. *Id.* Do the statistics from the USTR, PhRMA, and the IIPA justify the need for stronger global patent laws? How would you respond to these figures if you represented a developing country with weak intellectual property rights?

4. According to Professor McCarthy, "unusual intellectual property laws are a tariff and an unnatural barrier to trade." Do you agree? The history of the global patent system shows that international trade flows have always played a significant role in efforts to justify the importance of an international intellectual property system. Are there any patent policy goals that may not be well served if international trade were to become the primary context for formulating domestic patent law?

5. Professor McCarthy's article focuses on the traditional intellectual property protection needs of producers of goods that might otherwise be vulnerable to free-riding. But a new paradigm of user-generated production is developing today. As explained by Professor von Hippel:

---

[1] The core industries are defined in the report as "those whose primary purpose is to create, produce, distribute or exhibit copyright materials." These industries include "newspapers and periodicals, motion pictures, recorded music, radio and television broadcasting and computer software." *Id.* at 8.

[U]sers of products and services—both firms and individual consumers—are increasingly able to innovate for themselves. User-centered innovation processes offer great advantages over the manufacturer-centric innovation development systems that have been the mainstay of commerce for hundreds of years. Users that innovate can develop exactly what they want, rather than relying on manufacturers to act as their (often very imperfect) agents. Moreover, individual users do not have to develop everything they need on their own: they can benefit from innovations developed and freely shared by others.

. . . .

The user-centered innovation process . . . is in sharp contrast to the traditional model, in which products and services are developed by manufacturers in a closed way, the manufacturers using patents, copyrights, and other protections to prevent imitators from free riding on their innovation investments. In this traditional model, a user's only role is to have needs, which manufacturers then identify and fill by designing and producing new products. The manufacturer-centric model does fit some fields and conditions. However, a growing body of empirical work shows that users are the first to develop many and perhaps most new industrial and consumer products. Further, the contribution of users is growing steadily larger as a result of continuing advances in computer and communications capabilities.

. . . .

[T]he ongoing shift of product-development activities from manufacturers to users is painful and difficult for many manufacturers. Open, distributed innovation is "attacking" a major structure of the social division of labor. Many firms and industries must make fundamental changes to long-held business models in order to adapt. Further, governmental policy and legislation sometimes preferentially supports innovation by manufacturers. Considerations of social welfare suggest that this must change. The workings of the intellectual property system are of special concern. But despite the difficulties, a democratized and user-centric system of innovation appears well worth striving for.

Eric von Hippel, Democratizing Innovation 1–3 (2005), *available at* http://web.mit.edu/evhippel/www/democ1.htm.

As you progress throughout this book, keep in mind these two very different ways of generating new products, and their contrasting implications for arguments in favor of strong intellectual property rights to incentivize innovation.

2. THE HUMAN RIGHTS JUSTIFICATION

A second justification for global intellectual property rights can be found in the international human rights regime. The principal legal source for a human rights theory for global patent law is found in Article 27(2) of the Universal Declaration of Human Rights (UDHR):

> Everyone has the right to the protection of the moral and material interests resulting from any scientific, literary or artistic production of which he [or she] is the author.

See Universal Declaration of Human Rights, G.A. Res. 217A (III), U.N. Doc. A/810, at 71 (1948).

Twenty years later, the International Covenant on Economic, Social, and Cultural Rights (ICESCR) recognized the moral and material interests of authors and inventors and the right of everyone "to enjoy the arts and to share in scientific advancement and its benefits." *See* International Covenant on Economic, Social, and Cultural Rights arts. 15(1)(b)-(c), Dec. 16, 1966, 993 U.N.T.S. 3. These provisions of the two principal human rights instruments form the legal foundation for a human rights approach to global intellectual property law. As is evident from these instruments, a human rights justification cuts simultaneously for and against strong patent rights. Intellectual property rights increasingly affect a wide range of social, political, cultural and economic interests of citizens around the world. Patents, in particular, are strongly associated with providing the incentives to induce optimal levels of private investments in life-saving and life-changing innovation. At the same time, strong global patent rights limit competition, impose burdens on downstream innovators, raise the cost of access to public goods including health and essential medicines, and constrain the scope of policy space available to governments to promote other public interest objectives. Accordingly, scholars and commentators have debated the appropriate relationship between patents and human rights.

DAVID WEISSBRODT & KELL SCHOFF, HUMAN RIGHTS APPROACH TO INTELLECTUAL PROPERTY PROTECTION: THE GENESIS AND APPLICATION OF SUB-COMMISSION RESOLUTION 2000/7

5 MINN. INTELL. PROP. REV. 1, 1–29 (2003)

I. INTRODUCTION

On August 17, 2000, the United Nations Sub-Commission on the Promotion and Protection of Human Rights (the Sub-Commission) adopted Resolution 2000/7, entitled "Intellectual Property Rights and Human Rights." This resolution signified the Sub-Commission's belief that international intellectual property regimes were not adequately accounting for human rights norms. Resolution 2000/7 called on U.N. Member States, intergovernmental bodies, and various U.N. entities to reaffirm their commitments toward the achievement of international human rights norms, adopt a human rights approach to the development of international intellectual property regimes, and further study the interaction between intellectual property protection and human rights.

. . . .

II. ELEMENTS LEADING TO THE ADOPTION OF RESOLUTION 2000/7

A. INTERNATIONAL AGREEMENTS

. . . .

1. HUMAN RIGHTS TREATIES

In Article 15 of the International Covenant on Economic, Social and Cultural Rights (ICESCR), the States Parties to the Covenant "recognize the right of everyone . . . [both] to enjoy the benefits of scientific progress and its applications", on the one hand, and to "benefit from the protection of the moral and material interests resulting from any scientific, literary or artistic production of which he is the author", on the other. Hence, international human rights law recognizes the rights of inventors and authors while simultaneously focusing on the public right to benefit from their inventions and works of art. Article 15 does not, however, indicate how a balance might be struck between the creators, the economic interests that acquire their intellectual property, and the beneficiaries of creativity.

Nevertheless, the ICESCR does contain several other provisions bearing upon access to the fruits of inventions. In Article 11, States Parties to the Covenant "recognize the right of everyone to an adequate standard of living . . . including adequate food, clothing and housing, and to the continuous improvement of living conditions." Further, States Parties recognize in Article 11 "the fundamental right of everyone to be free from hunger . . . [and accordingly agree to] improve methods of production, conservation and distribution of food by making full use of technical and scientific knowledge." In Article 12, the States Parties to the ICESCR also "recognize the right of everyone to the enjoyment of the highest attainable standard of physical and mental health" that shall be achieved by the "prevention, treatment and control . . . of diseases" as well as the "creation of conditions which would assure to all medical service and medical attention in the event of sickness."

There is another balancing process between the rights of inventors or owners of inventions under Article 15 and the rights of the hungry, ill-housed, or the sick who are protected under Articles 11 and 12. Article 2 of the ICESCR provides some guidance as to how governments should achieve these rights. Under Article 2, States Parties only agree to "take steps . . . to the maximum of available resources, with a view to achieving progressively the full realization of the rights recognized in" Articles 11, 12, and 15 of the ICESCR.

The Committee on Economic, Social and Cultural Rights, the authoritative interpreter of the ICESCR, has provided specific guidance on how to implement the general and potentially conflicting responsibilities of States Parties. The Committee has declared that States Parties have a "minimum core obligation to ensure the satisfaction of, at the very least, minimum essential levels of each of the rights." In particular, the Committee "emphasize[d] that any intellectual property regime that makes it more difficult for a State party to comply with its core obligations in relation to health, food, [or] education . . . is inconsistent with the legally binding obligations of the State party." The Committee's statement reminded States Parties of the "importance of the integration of international human rights norms into the enactment and interpretation of intellectual property law" in a balanced manner that protects "public and private interests in knowledge" without infringing on fundamental human rights.

. . . .

2. INTERNATIONAL INTELLECTUAL PROPERTY PROTECTION: THE TRIPS AGREEMENT

In adopting Resolution 2000/7, the Sub-Commission expressed a fundamental concern that the Agreement on Trade-Related Aspects of Intellectual Property does not adequately recognize human rights norms. Resolution 2000/7 reads in part:

> *Noting* . . . that actual or potential conflicts exist between the implementation of the TRIPS Agreement and the realization of economic, social and cultural rights in relation to, inter alia, impediments to the transfer of technology to developing countries, the consequences for the enjoyment of the right to food of plant variety rights and the patenting of genetically modified organisms, "bio-piracy" and the reduction of communities' (especially indigenous communities') control over their own genetic and natural resources and cultural values, and restrictions on access to patented pharmaceuticals and the implications for the enjoyment of the right to health,

> . . . .

> *Declares* . . . that since the implementation of the TRIPS Agreement does not adequately reflect the fundamental nature and indivisibility of all human rights . . . there are apparent conflicts between the intellectual property rights regime embodied in the TRIPS Agreement, on the one hand, and international human rights law, on the other.

. . . .

3. DEALING WITH DIFFERENCES AND OVERLAPS BETWEEN HUMAN RIGHTS LAW AND TRIPS

As compared with the robust sanctions-based enforcement mechanism of TRIPS within the WTO, human rights treaties have modest implementation procedures. Both the Human Rights Covenants require that States Parties report periodically on their progress in achieving the rights in the respective treaties. These reports are reviewed by 18-member treaty bodies elected by the States Parties. The treaty bodies conclude their reviews of state reports by issuing concluding comments in which issues are raised and recommendations are made. When the government needs to make a further report, usually after a couple of years, these concerns should be the subject of attention. The Human Rights Committee also has the capacity to adjudicate complaints from the individual residents of the 104 nations that have ratified the Optional Protocol to the International Covenant on Civil and Political Rights. However, Committee decisions are not considered to be binding. Indeed, human rights norms are principally implemented at the international level by persuasion and embarrassment rather than sanctions. Hence, there is an imbalance in the way international obligations are effectuated under TRIPS and human rights treaties.

A related problem posed by the creation of the WTO with its incorporation of TRIPS is its failure to address issues that arise under international law when a country has ratified treaties that may conflict with its obligations under WTO law. A nation cannot generally absolve itself of its obligations under one treaty by ratifying a second treaty later. In a situation in which there is a potential conflict, the Vienna Convention on the Law of Treaties calls for the interpretation of the two treaties so as to give effect to both. It might be argued that WTO law, including TRIPS, qualifies as *lex specialis*. However, that argument would not exempt nations from their human rights obligations and would not prevent human rights treaty bodies from assessing the human rights implications of intellectual property measures. Hence, despite the stronger implementation procedures of the WTO, governments are obligated to seek interpretations of both TRIPS and the human rights treaties that would avoid violating either treaty regime.

The WTO has given short shrift to human rights norms when deciding conflicts in the dispute resolution system. The WTO Dispute Settlement Panels and Appellate Body are primarily focused on scrutinizing the legality of national measures under GATT/WTO law. They are not required to balance various sectors of national or international law with trade law. Further, the WTO dispute resolution system has been criticized for its lack of transparency and openness to input from amici curiae and other procedures for knowledgeable input from outside the trade field. Therefore, the imbalance in the way international obligations are realized under TRIPS and the human rights treaties was a significant motivating factor in the Sub-Commission's decision to adopt Resolution 2000/7.

. . . .

C. THE NEGATIVE IMPACT OF GLOBALIZATION ON THE REALIZATION OF HUMAN RIGHTS

The Sub-Commission indicated that the negative effect of globalization on human rights was another motivating factor for the adoption of Resolution 2000/7. Specifically, the Sub-Commission relied on reports from two Special Rapporteurs, as well as from its working group on transnational corporations, to support a request for "[g]overnments and national, regional and international economic policy forums to take international human rights obligations and principles fully into account in international economic policy formulation." Because the Sub-Commission explicitly referenced these globalization reports as supporting their decision to adopt Resolution 2000/7, it is appropriate to examine those reports briefly.

1. THE SPECIAL RAPPORTEURS' PRELIMINARY REPORT

. . . The Special Rapporteurs' report began by reminding the Sub-Commission that globalization is not a purely economic phenomenon that is divorced from human values and policy decisions. Instead, the report contended that "[t]he boundaries within which the market operates are defined politically, in direct negotiations between governments in multilateral forums, such as the World Trade Organization." By asserting that political decisions shape the path of globalization, the Special Rapporteurs indicated that some human rights problems can be ameliorated at their source, by modifying the political decisions that enable globalization.

. . . .

The Special Rapporteurs' report . . . disapproved of the WTO's intellectual property protection system, positing that the TRIPS' guarantee of the patentability of plant varieties and life forms was a legal and economic usurpation. Furthermore, the Special Rapporteurs recommended that if the WTO truly desired a commitment to a balanced trade liberalization scheme, it would embrace a dialogue of inclusion for developing nation concerns.

. . . .

IV. REACTIONS TO RESOLUTION 2000/7

If the relationships between international intellectual property protection, globalization, and human rights had not been particularly visible before the summer of 2000, they certainly were subjected to more detailed scrutiny after the Sub-Commission adopted Resolution 2000/7. The Sub-Commission's resolution generated responses from U.N. bodies, intergovernmental organizations, and governments.

A. The High Commissioner's Report on TRIPS and Human Rights

Pursuant to the Sub-Commission's request, the High Commissioner for Human Rights (HCHR) submitted a report on the impact of TRIPS on human rights. The HCHR's report undertook a two-step analysis. First, the report assessed the degree to which TRIPS was compatible with a human rights approach to intellectual property protection. Second, to the extent that TRIPS did not comport with human rights standards, the report made recommendations for implementing flexibility within the TRIPS Agreement that would foster a more human rights-oriented approach to international intellectual property protection.

The HCHR determined that as currently implemented, TRIPS was not fully compatible with human rights objectives. First, the HCHR noted that "the overall thrust of the TRIPS Agreement is the promotion of innovation through the provision of commercial incentives. The various links with the subject matter of human rights . . . are generally expressed in terms of exceptions to the rule rather than the guiding principles themselves." Second, TRIPS explicitly details intellectual property rights, but refers only to general responsibilities of intellectual property holders. The HCHR indicated that, for States parties to both TRIPS and ICESCR, the balance of interests identified in TRIPS Article 7 might not be sufficient to meet its human rights obligations under ICESCR. Third, the HCHR noted that the TRIPS-imposed obligation "to provide protection for all forms of technology has an impact on States' ability to decide on development strategies." These limitations originate from similar policies in industrialized countries and do not necessarily coincide with objectives of developing nations. In addition, some developing nations lack the requisite infrastructure to implement the developed nation policies mandated by TRIPS. Further, the HCHR noted that TRIPS contained no provisions for the protection of cultural heritage and indigenous rights.

In light of these shortcomings the High Commissioner made a series of recommendations. First, States should monitor TRIPS implementation through national legislation to ensure that it meets the human rights standards detailed in the ICESCR. Second, the HCHR encouraged States to modify their intellectual property regimes to provide protection for indigenous community interests. Third, States should pass legislation that ensures access to essential drugs, so as to protect the right to the highest available standard of health. Fourth, the High Commissioner suggested that TRIPS Article 7 be amended to include an explicit reference to human rights. Finally, the High Commissioner encouraged the Sub-

Commission to continue examining the interaction of intellectual property rights and other human rights.

LAURENCE R. HELFER, TOWARD A HUMAN RIGHTS FRAMEWORK FOR INTELLECTUAL PROPERTY

40 U.C. DAVIS L. REV. 971, 975–1020 (2007)

. . . .

What little can be discerned about the intellectual property provisions of human rights law reveals a concern for balance. Both the 1948 Universal Declaration of Human Rights ("UDHR") and the 1966 International Covenant on Economic, Social, and Cultural Rights ("ICESCR" or "the Covenant") . . . offer protection to creators and innovators and the fruits of their intellectual endeavors. But they also recognize the public's right to benefit from the scientific and cultural progress that intellectual property products can engender.

Without elaboration, however, these textual provisions provide only a faint outline of how to develop human rights-compliant mechanisms to promote creativity and innovation. They also invite governments and activists on both sides of the intellectual property divide to use the rhetoric of human rights to bolster arguments for or against revising intellectual property protection standards in treaties and in national laws. Without greater normative clarity, however, such "rights talk" risks creating a legal environment in which every claim (and therefore no claim) enjoys the distinctive protections that attach to human rights.

The skeletal and under-theorized intellectual property provisions of human rights law also leave critical questions unanswered. What, for example, is the relationship between the intellectual property clauses of the UDHR and ICESCR and the remaining civil, political, social, and economic rights enshrined in human rights pantheon? And how do human rights law's intellectual property rules interface with the rules set out in multilateral agreements emanating from WIPO, the WTO, and regional and bilateral trade and investment treaties?

These uncertainties—together with the deepening crisis facing the international intellectual property system—highlight the need to develop a comprehensive and coherent "human rights framework" for intellectual property law and policy. The questions to be answered in constructing such a framework are foundational. They include issues as basic as defining the different attributes of the "rights" protected by each system; whether relevant standards of conduct are legally binding or only aspirational; whether such standards apply to governments alone or also to private parties; and adopting rules to resolve inconsistencies among overlapping international and national laws and policies. A human rights framework for intellectual property must also distinguish situations in which the two legal systems have the same or similar objectives (but may employ different rules or mechanisms to achieve those objectives), from "true conflicts" of goals or values that are far more difficult to reconcile. Finally, the framework must include an institutional dimension, one that considers the diverse international and domestic lawmaking and adjudicatory bodies in which states and non-state actors generate new rules, norms, and enforcement strategies.

. . . .

Strikingly, human rights law's inclusion of the rights of creators and inventors has not been reciprocated in the international intellectual property system. No references to "human rights" appear in multilateral treaties such as the Paris, Berne, and Rome Conventions, nor do they appear in the more recently adopted TRIPS Agreement. These treaties repeatedly describe the legal protections for authors, inventors and other intellectual property owners as "rights," "private rights," and "exclusive rights," phrases that may appear to suggest a commonality of objectives between the two legal regimes.

These linguistic and textual parallels are only superficial, however. References to rights in intellectual property treaties serve distinctive structural and institutional purposes. They help to demarcate the treaties as charters of private rather than public international law, that is, as agreements that authorize individuals and businesses to claim legal entitlements against other private parties in national courts under national laws. In addition, use of "rights" language helps to bolster claims of intellectual property owners in foreign legal systems unfamiliar with or skeptical of the entitlements the treaties create for non-nationals. The principal justifications for references to rights in intellectual property agreements are thus grounded not in deontological claims about the inherent attributes or needs of human beings, but rather arise from efforts to realize the economic and instrumental benefits of protecting intellectual property products across national borders.

. . . .

Since its inception in the late nineteenth century, the development of intellectual property protection rules occurred in a uni-modal international regime confined to intellectual property-specific diplomatic conferences and conventions. The focus of treaty-making during this formative period was the gradual expansion of protected subject matters and exclusive rights through periodic revisions to the . . . conventions. With the advent of TRIPS in 1994, the regime entered into a bimodal phrase in which rule-making competencies were shared between two intergovernmental organizations: WIPO and the WTO. By 2005, however, the international intellectual property system had morphed again, this time into a "conglomerate regime" or a "regime complex"—a multi-issue, multi-venue, mega-regime in which governments and NGOs shift norm creating initiatives from one venue to another within the conglomerate, selecting the forum in which they are most likely to achieve their objectives.

The international human rights regime has exhibited similar expansionist tendencies. . . .

Economic, social, and cultural rights are the most expansive and, for many countries, the most controversial. Whereas civil and political rights are negative liberties that require government officials to refrain from particular actions, economic, social, and cultural rights obligate governments to provide minimum levels of subsistence and well-being to individuals and groups. Achieving these goals requires affirmative measures that often have significant financial consequences and require difficult tradeoffs among competing categories of rights holders and other claimants. These affirmative obligations also create broad areas of overlap— and of potential conflict—with international intellectual property protection rules. . . .

. . . .

The creation of a human rights framework for intellectual property is still in an early stage of development. During this gestational period, government officials, international jurists, NGOs, and commentators—many of whom have divergent views concerning the appropriate relationship between human rights and intellectual property—have a window of opportunity to influence the framework's substantive content and the procedural rules that mediate relationships among its component parts. . . . I briefly sketch three hypothetical futures for the framework and explain why each of these predictions is both plausible and likely to be contested by states and non-state actors.

A. USING HUMAN RIGHTS TO EXPAND INTELLECTUAL PROPERTY

One possible future relationship between human rights and intellectual property is an expansion of intellectual property protection standards at the expense of other human rights and the interests of licensees, users, and consumers. In this vision of the future (a dystopian one, to be sure), industries and interest groups that rely upon intellectual property for their economic well-being would invoke the authors' rights and property rights provisions in human rights treaties to further augment existing standards of protection. The fear of such expansions helps to explain why some commentators are skeptical of attempts to analyze intellectual property issues in human rights terms.

Early intimations of this version of the framework's future are already apparent. . . . Constitutional courts in several European countries have recently relied on fundamental rights guarantees in their respective domestic constitutions to justify intellectual property protection. It would be but a short step for these courts to turn to international human rights law to enhance this protection still further.

. . . .

B. USING HUMAN RIGHTS TO IMPOSE EXTERNAL LIMITS ON INTELLECTUAL PROPERTY

Patent . . . owners who invoke the property rights and authors' rights provisions of human rights law to demand additional legal protections will likely face stiff resistance from user groups. These groups can draw upon other fundamental rights and freedoms to press for a competing version of the framework, one that relies on human rights law to restrict intellectual property.

. . . .

How might user groups increase the likelihood that national courts will invoke human rights law to constrain intellectual property in this way? One plausible method would be to . . . [i]ncreas[e] the number of new treaties and soft law standards that contain precise, subject-specific limits on intellectual property, improving the odds that domestic judges will refer to those limits when resolving the disputes that come before them. Such an approach also creates "strategic inconsistency" that increases pressure on government representatives in other international organizations to acknowledge these new rules and standards.

This tactic has considerable risks, however. The international legal system is disaggregated and decentralized and lacks the comprehensive normative hierarchies and enforcement mechanisms found in national laws. A surfeit of conflicting rules will further diminish the system's coherence. This could make international rules less amenable to incorporation into national law, especially for judges unsure of their authority to construe domestic statutes in harmony with those rules.

C. ACHIEVING HUMAN RIGHTS ENDS THROUGH INTELLECTUAL PROPERTY MEANS

The two future frameworks described above share a common strategy. They each take the existing baseline of intellectual property protection as a given and then invoke human rights law to bolster arguments for moving that baseline in one direction or the other.

A third human rights framework for intellectual property proceeds from a very different premise. It first specifies the minimum outcomes— in terms of health, poverty, education, and so forth—that human rights law requires of states. The framework next works backwards to identify different mechanisms available to states to achieve those outcomes. Intellectual property plays only a secondary role in this version of the framework. Where intellectual property law helps to achieve human rights outcomes, governments should embrace it. Where it hinders those outcomes, its rules should be modified (but not necessarily restricted . . .). But the focus remains on the minimum levels of human well-being that states must provide, using either appropriate intellectual property rules or other means.

A 2001 report by the U.N. High Commissioner for Human Rights analyzing the impact of TRIPS on the right to health exemplifies this outcome-focused, inductive approach. The report reviews the components of the right to health protected by article 12 of the ICESCR. According to a general comment issued by the CESCR Committee, the right to health includes an obligation for states to promote medical research and to provide access to affordable treatments, including essential drugs.

The High Commissioner's report analyzes how intellectual property affects these two obligations. It acknowledges that patents help governments promote medical research by providing an incentive to invent new medical technologies, including new drugs. But the report also asserts that pharmaceutical companies' "commercial motivation . . . means that research is directed, first and foremost, towards 'profitable' disease. Diseases that predominantly affect people in poorer countries . . . remain relatively under-researched." One way to remedy this market imperfection is to create incentives for innovation outside of the patent system.

. . . .

It is too early to predict which of these three versions of the human rights framework for intellectual property, or others yet to be identified, will emerge as dominant. What is certain is that the rules, institutions, and discourse of international human rights are now increasingly relevant to intellectual property law and policy and that the two fields, once isolated from each other, are becoming ever more intertwined.

NOTES AND QUESTIONS

1. As Professor Helfer notes, intellectual property treaties do not mention human rights. Furthermore, WIPO, the institution that historically has been charged with the harmonization of the international intellectual property system, has no expertise or resources devoted to studying the human rights framework. To what extent do you think WIPO's exclusive focus on intellectual property rights is a hindrance to its mandate to promote the global protection and harmonization of patent laws within a broader international legal system?

2. In recent years, largely in response to attacks on the patent system from non-governmental organizations and in response to the work of other inter-governmental organizations such as the World Health Organization (WHO) and the United Nations High Commission for Human Rights (UN-

HCR), WIPO has jointly sponsored activities that purport to address the intersection of intellectual property and human rights. Many observers view these efforts by WIPO as minimalist attempts to address the perceived structural problems occasioned by strong global patent laws, particularly on poor countries. However, very early in WIPO's history, a former WIPO Secretary-General advanced an intellectual property perspective to human rights:

> The protection of intellectual property concerns both the conditions governing creations of the mind and the general interests of individuals and peoples and also the economic system. Articles 22 and 27 of the Universal Declaration of Human Rights recognizes for everyone the right to "economic, social and cultural rights indispensable for the dignity and the free development of his personality" and to the "protection of the moral and material interests resulting from any scientific, literary or artistic production of which he is the author." Thus the objective sought by the authors of the International Unions for the Protection of Intellectual Property has been formally recognized by the United Nations and the competence of the Economic and Social Council is thereby established.

> It is obvious that, if the legal principles which are at the bases of the International Unions for the Protection of Intellectual Property are to triumph, the competence of these Unions should not only be recognized by the intergovernmental organizations concerned but also by the Economic and Social Council of the United Nations, because of its own competence in this field and also because one of its tasks is to coordinate international activities.

See Jacques Secretan, *Structural Evolution of the International Unions for the Protection of Industrial Property*, 1 INDUS. PROP. 170, 173 (1962). Which of Professor Helfer's three approaches to the relationship between intellectual property and human rights do you think is reflected by Mr. Secretan?

3. What do you think should be the effect of Resolution 2000/7 on the development of global patent law rules? Do you agree with the U.N. Sub-Commission that intellectual property laws are the proper concern of human rights institutions? If the "natural law" reference had remained intact in the U.S. "property" view that prevailed in the negotiations leading up to the Paris Convention, how do you think this would have affected human rights considerations of intellectual property? Are human rights a matter of "natural law?"

4. As noted by Professor Helfer, some scholars have cautioned that a human rights rationalization for the patent system may lead to arguments for a stronger global system. For example, according to Professor Raustiala:

> [T]here is no doubt that there are significant human rights implications to many IP issues—most notably, with regard to patent protection and infectious diseases, such as the HIV-Aids pandemic. But there is a downside to the embrace of IP by human rights advocates

and entities. Such attention is likely to further entrench some dangerous ideas about property: in particular, that property rights as human rights ought to be inviolable and ought to receive extremely solicitous attention from the international community. Just as the popularization of the term "intellectual property" probably helped raise the salience of the underlying rights of patent [owners] . . . — and likely enhanced political support for government intervention to protect these rights, by tapping into the strong respect for property rights present in many parts of the world—the introduction of human rights language to the policy debate over IP may have a similar strengthening influence.

Kal Raustiala, *Density and Conflict in International Intellectual Property Law*, 40 U.C. DAVIS L. REV. 1021, 1031–32 (2007).

Do you agree with Professor Raustiala?

3. THE INTERNATIONAL INSTITUTIONAL JUSTIFICATION

The history of the Paris Convention described earlier in this Chapter highlights the perspectives of the various leading economies with respect to the importance of global cooperation in patent law. The use of international agreements to foster cooperation among sovereign states on a wide range of issues is one of the salient features of modern international relations. Reflecting on the relative dominance of countries such as the U.S. and Germany at the time of the negotiations leading up to the Paris Convention, one might assume that unilateral inducements or other political threats could be used to require countries to adopt standards that comply with those of these leading countries. As you have learned, however, Germany and the United States were not exactly in agreement about the nature of the patent grant and the terms on which global patent protection should ensue. So why do states, including powerful ones like the United States, resort to international treaties? What role do domestic considerations play in the calculus leading up to a state's willingness to constrain its sovereignty in the subject-matter area of a treaty?

RACHEL BREWSTER, THE DOMESTIC ORIGINS OF INTERNATIONAL AGREEMENTS
44 VA. J. INT'L L. 501, 505–11 (2004)

II. WHY DO STATES FORM INTERNATIONAL AGREEMENTS?

States form hundreds of international agreements every year. Between 1939 and 1989, the United States alone entered into 702 Article II treaties and over 11,000 other international agreements. International legal studies scholars have long been interested in examining the content of these agreements and the resulting obligations on states but have not historically provided a strong theoretical understanding of why these agreements are formed. . . .

Institutional theory describes international agreements as [a] means of facilitating interstate cooperation. This approach has led legal scholars to conceptualize the demand for treaties as being driven by opportunities for mutual gain at the international level. As a consequence, legal scholars have tended not to examine either the domestic demand for international agreements or the domestic impact of creating international regimes. . . .

A. INSTITUTIONAL THEORY

One school of international relations thought, institutionalism, argues that treaties are mechanisms by which governments can overcome collective action problems and achieve mutual gains from cooperation. States are assumed to be unitary and rational actors interacting with one another in a state of anarchy. Anarchy implies that there is no overarching authority that can enforce agreements between states. Consequently, states face a prisoner's dilemma when considering whether to engage in international cooperation. States recognize that there are potential mutual gains from cooperation but there are also incentives to defect and no means for enforcing inter-state contracts. The prospect of greater gains from cooperation will not always be sufficient to overcome states' incentive to defect.

States can attempt to overcome the collective action problem by forming international institutions through treaty arrangements. International institutions can remedy this "political market failure" by collecting and distributing information on the prospective partners, linking issues (easing side payments in ex ante bargaining and reducing the risk of ex post defections), and decreasing the cost of additional negotiations by keeping the same institutional framework for many issues. Most importantly, institutions assure future interaction that permits states to adopt conditional strategies basing their behavior on the behavior of other actors. In sum, treaty regimes allow governments to achieve the efficiency gains of cooperation.

B. INSTITUTIONALISM IN THE STUDY OF INTERNATIONAL LAW

Institutionalism provides a basis for international legal scholars to argue that international law has independent effects on state behavior. Without treaty arrangements, states would have more difficulty maintaining cooperative relationships since the international system is riddled with informational asymmetries and high transaction costs. With international legal regimes, states will engage in more cooperative agreements leading to greater aggregate welfare gains.

This approach has had a strong and beneficial impact on the international law literature. Conceiving of treaties as mechanisms to overcome prisoner's dilemma or other mixed-motive situations has provided legal scholars with a better handle on the incentives of states to form agreements as well as potential compliance issues. The institutionalist model has been used to explain negotiations for environmental agreements and the strong record of compliance in trade issues. By describing state behavior as unitary and emphasizing the political bargaining only at the international level, however, this approach has underemphasized the diverse domestic sources of government action.

. . . .

[T]he structure of domestic law-making creates variation between liberal governments' actions in the international system. This approach emphasizes how cross-national differences in law-making processes generate different incentives for interest groups to use international law to achieve domestic policy goals.

. . . Domestic groups demand international agreements as a source of international law and domestic law. International agreements create rules for member governments in their interactions with one another internationally and for the citizens and government agencies domestically. The recognition that international agreements regulate domestic relationships, as well as international ones, changes our expectations about the demand for international agreements in several ways.

First, we should not expect treaty regimes to emerge wherever there is the possibility for overcoming collective action problems. Treaty arrangements need domestic support and not all agreements that enhance general welfare will be able to garner such support. Second, we should expect treaty negotiations to be influenced by the distributional demands of domestic groups. Even if the treaty arrangement can produce efficiency gains, we should expect those governments responsive to interest groups to be very concerned with what proportion of the gains they can acquire for such groups. Finally, we should expect that interest groups may demand international agreements for the domestic legal effects, in addition to international political effects, where treaty law has advantages over, or can supplement, statutory law.

. . . .

. . . The international effects of treaty law are clearly important to interest group and governmental decision making. Treaty arrangements allow domestic groups some measure of assurance over the actions of other states and provide the potential for international gains. The international-level effects, however, are not the only reason that domestic groups may desire treaty law. National-level effects of treaty agreements will affect the demand for international agreements as well.

NOTES AND QUESTIONS

1. What are the differences between the institutional international justi-fication and the international trade justification for global patent law? Should the United States continue to pursue international treaties whenever domestic interest groups are concerned about strengthening (or changing) the patent laws of its trading partners? What are the advantages and disad-vantages of such an approach? How should countries decide which domestic interest groups' views should prevail in the international arena?

2. Should human rights treaties prevail over international trade agree-ments in matters that affect human life, morality, or other civil liberties? Which norms should most influence the determination of which international agreements should prevail? Which institutions are best suited to make such determinations—domestic or international?

3. WIPO and the WTO are undoubtedly the most significant organiza-tions in the international intellectual property field so their interaction with human rights organizations has been the subject of sustained scrutiny by the international community. However, a number of other international organi-zations also have mandates that implicate substantive and administrative issues at the intersection of patent law and human rights. These include the Conference of the Parties to the Convention on Biological Diversity (CBD) and the United Nations Food and Agriculture Organization (FAO), among others, discussed in Chapter 8, *infra*.

C. THE QUEST FOR A GLOBAL PATENT

Today's international patent system enjoys levels of use far beyond those imagined just decades ago. The number of global patent application filings increased from 1.05 million in 1995 to 2.14 million in 2011. *See* WIPO, World Intellectual Property Indicators, 43 (2012). The biggest con-tribution to the aggregate increase in worldwide patenting activity, which grew by 7.8 percent in 2011, came from filings by China and the U.S. *See* World Intellectual Property Organization, World Intellectual Property Indicators, 6 (2012). However, the distribution of global patent filings is very uneven, with a small number of industrialized and emerging econo-mies accounting for the great majority of applications filed.

Figure 1

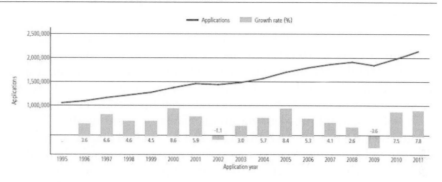

Figure A.1.1.1 Trend in patent applications worldwide

Note: World totals are WIPO estimates covering around 125 patent offices (see Data Description). These estimates include direct applications and PCT national phase entry data.

Source: WIPO Statistics Database, October 2012

SOURCE: WIPO, World Intellectual Property Indicators (2012).

This situation has raised challenges on at least two fronts. First, the increased number of patent applications and the growing complexity of the technologies they represent strain the ability of national and regional patent offices to process patent applications in a timely and effective manner. In the last two decades, patent pendency (i.e., the length of time to issue a patent) has increased markedly in major patent offices, while confidence in the quality of patent examination, and therefore in the value of granted patents, has diminished. Second, negative perceptions about the global patent system as an instrument of social policy are also on the rise. Critics have raised concerns that the global system is exacerbating the divide between rich and poor nations, hampering efforts to deal with serious public policy issues (particularly as they relate to health concerns), and privatizing and commodifying technological knowledge that should remain in the public domain.

In the context of these challenges, however, countries continue to make a case for a stronger "global patent" framework and increased patent harmonization. It is not surprising that the main protagonists are the major industrialized countries, although they are not unified on the issue. While there has been much talk of a "world patent," few, if any, of the participants in the current harmonization efforts believe that the establishment of a global patent scheme is realistic, or even desirable, in the short or medium term. Instead, the focus of debate has been on the establishment of a common operational and legal framework that would allow national and regional patent offices to improve cooperation, exchange information, share resources, and reduce duplication of work. Since a significant proportion of the recent growth in patent filings has been caused by equivalent applications (members of the same patent family) being filed in many different countries, the desirability of a global framework appears all the more compelling. *See* Gerald J. Mossinghoff & Vivian S. Kuo, *World Patent System circa 20XX, A.D.*, 38 IDEA: J.L. & TECH. 529 (1998).

If such a system could result in higher quality patent examinations, the argument goes, it would help ensure that granted patents meet established patentability criteria regardless of the country of filing. Further, reducing duplication in the work of patent offices would not only result in the faster grant of patents but also could free up resources and decrease the costs of filing and prosecuting applications internationally. Threshold access to the patent system would be eased, to the particular advantage of applicants with limited resources, and third parties would benefit from the ability to formulate reactions to granted patents earlier and more accurately. However, some suggest that a higher level of patent harmonization will present challenges for rich and poor countries alike. In the following discussion of the proposed Substantive Patent Law Treaty being negotiated at WIPO, Professors Reichman and Cooper Dreyfuss argue that deeper patent harmonization would imperil scientific progress and adversely affect the global innovation system:

JEROME H. REICHMAN & ROCHELLE COOPER DREYFUSS, HARMONIZATION WITHOUT CONSENSUS: CRITICAL REFLECTIONS ON DRAFTING A SUBSTANTIVE PATENT LAW TREATY
57 DUKE L.J. 85, 87–106 (2007)

Proposals to further harmonize domestic patent laws at the international level have understandably attracted considerable attention. As intellectual property continues to grow as a component of global trade, the costs of worldwide protection and enforcement have soared. Patent holders accordingly seek ways to acquire and maintain their exclusive rights more efficiently in an integrated world marketplace. They are also increasingly frustrated by the need to pursue multiple actions for infringement in cross-border disputes. Under the bedrock principle of territoriality, successive litigations can trigger different applications of domestic and international patent norms to the same set of facts and can lead to conflicting judgments and arguably irreconcilable outcomes.

. . . .

The effort by the World Intellectual Property Organization (WIPO) to organize a thorough exploration of the possibilities for further harmonization is . . . a welcome development to much of the patent community. Under the aegis of WIPO's Standing Committee on the Law of Patents (SCP), the Draft Substantive Patent Law Treaty (SPLT) represents an attempt "to pursue a 'deep harmonization' of both the law and practice" concerning not just the drafting, filing, and examination of patent applications, but also the cornerstone requirements of patentability. Ideally, member states would agree to adopt identical rules concerning what constitutes a novel and useful invention, when a technical advance meets the requirement for an "inventive step" (nonobviousness), and how much information must be revealed by the patent disclosure. "Deep harmonization" would also entail agreement on priority of inventorship (whether a patent is awarded to the first to invent or the first to file) and whether inventors will be accorded a grace period permitting publication for some period prior to filing. . . .

Despite the promise such an effort holds, we believe that it is unwise to move to deep substantive harmonization so quickly after the TRIPS Agreement elevated patent standards universally. These standards challenged the technological catch-up strategies of all the developing countries and saddled them with social costs they are struggling to absorb. As the endless controversies surrounding pharmaceutical patents demonstrate, higher standards of global protection—whatever their incentive effects—also generate severe and unintended distributional consequences for the developing world. A further round of harmonization will likely aggravate these and other unresolved problems without producing any offsetting user rights or concessions for these countries. On the contrary, the dynamics of TRIPS and the post-TRIPS trade agreements teach that even a development-sensitive negotiation process is likely to produce an instrument that furthers the interests of developed countries at the expense of poorer, less powerful participants.

More controversially, . . . higher levels of harmonization will harm even the developed countries, including those that are most aggressively pressing for yet another round of multilateral intellectual property negotiations. The domestic patent laws as currently practiced were largely formulated for the inventions of the Industrial Revolution, and these laws still reflect the technological premises and concepts of the creative sectors as they were then structured. Yet in this postindustrial information age, with knowledge-intensive inventions emerging from new kinds of research institutions, creative entities are organized non-hierarchically and along continuously changing lines. New players, such as universities and scientific research organizations, routinely patent their output, and whole new sectors, including biotechnology and information technology, have emerged. Until the operations of these and other new technical communities are better understood, there is a greater need for legal experimentation at the substantive level than for harmonization. In the absence of any international governance infrastructure capable of interpreting and amending the law (rather than freezing it prematurely), a compelling case can be made for delaying deep harmonization until other methods for improving the efficiency of a global patent system have been fully explored.

. . . .

It should, indeed, surprise no one that routine tinkering with a patent paradigm launched in Venice in the fifteenth century and refined by the United Kingdom in the seventeenth century cannot answer the hard questions raised by new technologies and the new modes of producing them. There are major challenges for which past experiences give only untested and untrustworthy hypotheses, with no convincing empirical studies on the horizon to resolve the doubts. . . .

1. INDEPENDENCE VERSUS TERRITORIALITY

One clear result of deep harmonization of patent law is the elimination of geopolitical boundaries as a basis for different patent law rules. The excerpt above by Professors Reichman and Cooper Dreyfuss reflects important considerations for limiting the harmonization process, despite claims of asserted gains by proponents. As noted earlier, patent law has historically been territorial in nature, with sovereign states granting patents and providing means for patentees to enforce their rights only within their borders. While national sovereignty and international comity concerns have contributed to the current system, territoriality was a natural consequence of disagreement on the scope, duration, or even desirability of patents at the time that many countries were establishing their patent systems in the late eighteenth and nineteenth centuries. Even today, there remains a lack of the necessary consensus to create a system in which the filing of a single application would result in a globally valid patent that could be asserted in a single forum regardless of where infringement occurred. If a person wants to obtain patent protection for an invention in multiple countries, she, with some exceptions, has to apply separately for a patent in each country of interest, and the exclusionary rights provided generally would not extend beyond the country's borders.

While the territoriality principle is still the foundational basis of today's patent law, there are a growing number of exceptions. For example, the current U.S. patent statute allows for extraterritorial reach in certain circumstances, such as provisions relating to products assembled abroad from components made in and shipped from the U.S. for the purpose of avoiding infringement, and products made abroad by a process patented in the U.S. *See* 35 U.S.C. § 271(f)–(g) (Supp. IV 2010). However, the primary infringement provision, 35 U.S.C. § 271(a) (2006), is explicitly territorial and defines an infringer as someone who, without authorization, "makes, uses, offers to sell, or sells any patented invention, *within the United States* or imports *into the United States* any patented invention during the term of the patent."

Even in the European Union (EU), which has eliminated territorial restrictions in numerous areas in order to create a common European market, territoriality in patent matters is still alive and well. The Brussels Convention, along with the Lugano Convention and the Brussels Regulation, provides EU-wide rules on jurisdiction and recognition of judgments and also embodies notions of patent territoriality. Article 16(4) of the Brussels Convention provides:

> The following courts shall have exclusive jurisdiction, regardless of domicile: . . .

> In proceedings concerned with the registration or validity of patents, trademarks, designs, or other similar rights required to be deposited or registered, the courts of the Contracting State in which the deposit or registration has been applied for, has taken place or is under the terms of an international convention deemed to have taken place.

See Convention on Jurisdiction and the Enforcement of Judgments in Civil and Commercial Matters art. 16(4), Mar. 1, 2002.

As will be discussed further in Chapter 10, *infra*, some patentholders have sought to use other sections of the Brussels Convention to expand the territorial limits of national courts' jurisdiction over actions alleging infringement of a foreign patent. Nevertheless, because the issue of validity is invariably intertwined with that of infringement, Article 16(4) still imposes territorial limits over such endeavors.

While hesitant to part with the degree of sovereignty over patent matters that would be necessary to establish a truly global patent system, many countries have been willing to take incremental steps in that direction under increasing pressure from multinational corporations that are frustrated by inefficient and redundant territory-based patent systems. As will be discussed in later Chapters, several multilateral treaties currently exist that allow an applicant to file one application with a central office and obtain patent protection in multiple countries. However, the patents granted from such centralized systems still must be separately enforced in each individual country in which infringement has occurred.

Not surprisingly, many patent owners would prefer not only a single global patent application process, but also a single global forum for resolving patent infringement disputes without the need for parallel or serial litigation. In the absence of a global patent court in which such actions could be brought, patentees have attempted to have domestic courts adjudicate the infringement of foreign patents along with domestic ones, with mixed results. The following case illustrates the U.S. approach to territoriality in this context.

VODA V. CORDIS CORP.

United States Court of Appeals, Federal Circuit
476 F.3d 887 (Fed. Cir. 2007)

■ GAJARSA, Circuit Judge:

I. BACKGROUND

The plaintiff-appellee Voda is a resident of Oklahoma City, Oklahoma. The defendant-appellant Cordis is a U.S.-based entity incorporated in Florida. . . . The patents at issue relate generally to guiding catheters for use in interventional cardiology. . . .Voda's [three] U.S. patents stem from a common continuation-in-part ("CIP") application filed in October 1992. . . . The foreign patents issued from a common Patent Cooperation Treaty ("PCT") application. [The PCT application, which designated the European Patent Office ("EPO") and Canada as recipients, eventually generated European, British, French, German, and Canadian patents.]

Voda sued Cordis U.S. in the United States District Court for the Western District of Oklahoma alleging infringement of his three U.S. patents. . . . Cordis U.S. answered by asserting noninfringement and invalidity of the U.S. patents.

Voda then moved to amend his complaint to add claims of infringement of the European, British, Canadian, French, and German foreign patents. Voda's amended complaint alleges that "Cordis [U.S.] has commenced and continues acts of making, selling, offering for sale and selling at least the XB guiding catheter, which is covered by [the several foreign patents] without Dr. Voda's authority. Such acts constitute infringement, under corresponding foreign law of [these several foreign patents]." Cordis U.S. has admitted that "the XB catheters have been sold domestically and internationally since 1994. . . ."

. . . .

1. AUTHORIZATION

Section 1367(a) [of Title 28 on Judiciary and Judicial Procedure] provides the statutory authority for district courts to exercise supplemental jurisdiction over certain claims outside their original jurisdiction.

> Except as provided in subsections (b) and (c) or as expressly provided otherwise by Federal statute, in any civil action of which the district courts have original jurisdiction, the district courts shall have supplemental jurisdiction over all other claims that are so related to claims in the action within such original jurisdiction that they form part of the same case or controversy under Article III of the United States Constitution. Such supplemental jurisdiction shall include claims that involve the joinder or intervention of additional parties.

. . .

In this case, it is undisputed that the district court has original federal question jurisdiction over Voda's U.S. patent infringement claims. In addition, § 1367(a) appears to authorize supplemental jurisdiction over foreign law claims in certain limited circumstances. Specifically, § 1367(a) provides the statutory authority for federal courts to exercise supplemental jurisdiction over claims that are outside the limited original jurisdiction of federal district courts, including those within the general jurisdiction of state courts. Therefore, because the "inherent powers" of state courts "permit them to entertain transitory causes of action arising under the laws of foreign sovereigns," § 1367 supplemental jurisdiction appears to include foreign law claims. Therefore, the § 1367(a) issue we discuss here is whether Voda's claims of foreign patent infringement "form part of the same case or controversy under Article III."

. . . .

a. TREATIES AS THE "SUPREME LAW OF THE LAND"

Article VI of the Constitution proclaims that "all treaties made, or which shall be made, under the authority of the United States, shall be the supreme law of the land." The Supreme Court has accordingly stated that "a treaty ratified by the United States is not only the law of this land, *see* U.S. Const., Art. II, § 2, but also an agreement among sovereign powers." . . .

The United States entered into Articles 13 through 30 of the Paris Convention for the Protection of Industrial Property ("Paris Convention") on September 5, 1970 and Articles 1 through 12 of the Paris Convention on August 25, 1973. Article 4 *bis* of the Paris Convention states that U.S. patents "shall be independent of patents obtained for the same invention in other countries" and that the "foregoing provision is to be understood in an unrestricted sense, . . . both as regards the grounds for nullity and forfeiture." In addition, Article 2(3) of the Paris Convention states that the "provisions of the laws of each of the countries of the Union relating to judicial and administrative procedure and to jurisdiction, . . . which may be required by the laws on industrial property are expressly reserved." The Paris Convention thus clearly expresses the independence of each country's sovereign patent systems and their systems for adjudicating those patents. Nothing in the Paris Convention contemplates nor allows one jurisdiction to adjudicate the patents of another, and as such, our courts should not determine the validity and infringement of foreign patents. Accordingly, while the Paris Convention contains no express jurisdictional-stripping statute, we relied on it in *Stein Associates, Inc. v. Heat & Control, Inc.*, 748 F.2d 653 (Fed. Cir. 1984)] to hold that "[o]nly a British court, applying British law, can determine validity and infringement of British patents." . . .

Subsequently, the United States adopted the Patent Cooperation Treaty ("PCT") on January 24, 1978. As with the Paris Convention, the text of the PCT maintains the independence of each country's patents. Article 27(5) states: "Nothing in this Treaty and the Regulations is intended to be construed as prescribing anything that would limit the freedom of each Contracting State to prescribe such substantive conditions of patentability as it desires."

On January 1, 1995, the United States joined the World Trade Organization, which through Article II § 2 binds all of its members to the Agreement on Trade-Related Aspects of Intellectual Property Rights ("TRIPS"). The Agreement on TRIPS contains several provisions regarding the enforcement of patents. Article 41 § 1 of the Agreement on TRIPS specifies that each country "shall ensure that enforcement procedures as specified in this Part are available under their law so as to permit effective action against any act of infringement of intellectual property rights." In addition, § 4 states that "[p]arties to a proceeding shall have an opportunity for review by a judicial authority of final administrative decisions and, subject to jurisdictional provisions in a Member's law concerning the importance of a case," and § 5 states "[i]t is understood that this Part does not . . . affect the capacity of Members to enforce their law in general." *See also id.*, art. 41–49. Like the Paris Convention, nothing in the PCT or the Agreement on TRIPS contemplates or allows one jurisdiction to adjudicate patents of another.[8] Canada, France, Germany, and the United Kingdom, which are the foreign sovereigns concerned in this case, are parties to each of these treaties. . . .

Voda asserts and one of the amicus curiae briefs suggests that these international treaties evince a trend of harmonization of patent law and thus, that allowing the exercise of supplemental jurisdiction over Voda's foreign patent infringement claims furthers the harmonization goals underlying the treaties. Regardless of the strength of the harmonization trend, however, we as the U.S. judiciary should not unilaterally decide either for our government or for other foreign sovereigns that our courts will become the adjudicating body for any foreign patent with a U.S. equivalent "so related" to form "the same case or controversy." . . . Permitting our district courts to exercise jurisdiction over infringement claims based on foreign patents in this case would require us to define the legal boundaries of a property right granted by another sovereign and then determine whether there has been a trespass to that right. . . .

---

[8] While the European Patent Convention ("EPC") states nothing of our government's intent because the United States is not a party, it may inform us on how other sovereigns treat foreign patent adjudication. Regarding claims "to the right to the grant of a European patent," the EPC has enumerated rules specifying courts of exclusive jurisdiction. European Patent Convention, Protocol on Recognition, art. 1–8, October 5, 1973. None of the treaties entered into by the United States contain such language. Moreover, while there have been working parties and draft agreements and statutes, even the members of the EPC have not yet agreed on a centralized European patent court. *See* European Patent Office, "Legislative Initiatives in European Patent Law" (July 26, 2006), *available at* http://patlaw-reform.european-patent-office.org/epla/.

b. COMITY AND RELATIONS BETWEEN SOVEREIGNS

"Comity refers to the spirit of cooperation in which a domestic tribunal approaches the resolution of cases touching the laws and interests of other sovereign states."

> Comity, in the legal sense, is neither a matter of absolute obligation, on the one hand, nor of mere courtesy and good will, upon the other. But it is the recognition which one nation allows within its territory to the legislative, executive or judicial acts of another nation, having due regard both to international duty and convenience, and to the rights of its own citizens or of other persons who are under the protection of its laws.

> . . . .

In this case, these considerations of comity do not support the district court's exercise of supplemental jurisdiction over Voda's foreign patent infringement claims. First, Voda has not identified any international duty, and we have found none, that would require our judicial system to adjudicate foreign patent infringement claims. As discussed *supra* . . . , while the United States has entered into the Paris Convention, the PCT, and the Agreement on TRIPS, nothing in those treaties contemplates or allows one jurisdiction to adjudicate the patents of another. Second, . . . Voda has not shown that it would be more convenient for our courts to assume the supplemental jurisdiction at issue. Third, with respect to the rights of our citizens, Voda has not shown that foreign courts will inadequately protect his foreign patent rights. Indeed, we see no reason why American courts should supplant British, Canadian, French, or German courts in interpreting and enforcing British, Canadian, European, French, or German patents.

Fourth, assuming jurisdiction over Voda's foreign patent infringement claims could prejudice the rights of the foreign governments. None of the parties or amicus curiae have demonstrated that the British, Canadian, French, or German governments are willing to have our courts exercise jurisdiction over infringement claims based on their patents. *Cf.* 28 U.S.C. § 1338(a) (granting federal courts exclusive jurisdiction of claims relating to U.S. patents).

. . . .

The territorial limits of the rights granted by patents are similar to those conferred by land grants. A patent right is limited by the metes and bounds of the jurisdictional territory that granted the right to exclude. . . . Therefore, a patent right to exclude only arises from the legal right granted and recognized by the sovereign within whose territory the right is located. It would be incongruent to allow the sovereign power of one to be infringed or limited by another sovereign's extension of its jurisdiction . . .

. . . .

In addition, as a rule of statutory construction, the Supreme Court "ordinarily construes ambiguous statutes to avoid unreasonable interference with the sovereign authority of other nations." *Empagran,* 542 U.S. at 164; *cf. Santa Clara Pueblo v. Martinez,* 436 U.S. 49, 60 (1978) ("[A] proper respect both for tribal sovereignty itself and for the plenary authority of Congress in [civil actions against tribal officers] cautions that we tread lightly in the absence of clear indications of legislative intent."). As discussed, there is no explicit statutory direction indicating that the district courts should or may exercise supplemental jurisdiction over claims arising under foreign patents, and the Paris Convention, PCT, and Agreement on TRIPS neither contemplate nor allow the extraterritorial jurisdiction of our courts to adjudicate patents of other sovereign nations. We have also noted the territorially limited nature of patent rights. . . . Therefore, the principle that we should "avoid unreasonable interference with the sovereign authority of other nations" applies analogously here . . . .

We would risk such interference by exercising supplemental jurisdiction over Voda's foreign patent infringement claims. Patents and the laws that govern them are often described as complex. Indeed, one of the reasons cited for why Congress established our court was because it "felt that most judges didn't understand the patent system and how it worked." . . . As such, Cordis U.S. and one of the amicus curiae assert, and Voda does not dispute, that the foreign sovereigns at issue in this case have established specific judges, resources, and procedures to "help assure the integrity and consistency of the application of their patent laws." Therefore, exercising jurisdiction over such subject matter could disrupt their foreign procedures. . . .

Accordingly, comity and the principle of avoiding unreasonable interference with the authority of other sovereigns dictate in this case that the district court decline the exercise of supplemental jurisdiction under § 1367(c).

NOTES AND QUESTIONS

1. Do you agree with the Federal Circuit's argument that global patent harmonization efforts are an insufficient basis to assert jurisdiction over foreign patents? What policy justifications can you adduce in support of the court's approach? What policy reasons can be leveled against it?

2. According to the Federal Circuit, nothing in international treaties such as the Paris Convention, the Patent Cooperation Treaty (PCT), or the TRIPS Agreement "contemplates or allows one jurisdiction to adjudicate patents of another." However, none of these agreements contain "jurisdictional

stripping" provisions either, choosing instead to leave such decisions up to individual countries.

In *Voda*, the U.S. Court of Appeals for the Federal Circuit (CAFC) rejected a district court's assertion of supplemental jurisdiction to adjudicate infringement of several foreign patents. In the following case, the Tokyo District Court takes a fundamentally different approach to the question of a foreign court's ability to adjudicate infringement of a foreign patent in the context of an unfair competition action.

K.K. CORAL CORP. V. MARINE BIO K.K.

Hesei 02 (Wa) 1943 (D. Tokyo Oct. 16, 2003)

[Summary by Dr. Shoichi Okuyama, AIPPI Journal, January 2004]

In an unfair competition case between Japanese companies concerning the dissemination of false information, a three-judge panel presided by Judge Ryoichi Mimura found no infringement on a US patent in view of the opinion expressed in the Festo US Supreme Court decision.

FACTS

A Japanese company called Coral Corporation produces and exports to the US a product containing coral fossil powder as health food. Another Japanese company called Marine Bio has US patent No. 4,540,584.[2] Marine Bio sent Coral's US dealer a warning e-mail and letter stating that the sale of the Coral product infringed on the US patent in question. Based on the Japanese Unfair Competition Prevention Law that defines announcing false information as an act of unfair competition[3] and prohibits it, Coral sued Marine Bio seeking a declaration that Defendant is not entitled to obtain an injunctive order against Plaintiff and its US customers based on the US patent with respect to the sale of the coral fossil powder product in the US. Plaintiff also sought an injunction order against Defendant to prevent Defendant from announcing and spreading notices from Japan to Plaintiff's US customers that Plaintiff's and the customers' sale in the US of the powder constitutes infringement on the US patent. Plaintiff also sought a damages award.

------

[2] The main claim of US patent No. 4,540,584 reads:

"1. A mineral supplement, comprising: coral sand as an effective component in an amount sufficient to provide calcium carbonate and other minerals as a mineral supplement for humans; wherein said coral sand is in the form of a fine powder of a particle size passing about 150 to 500 mesh."

[3] Section 2(1) provides as an act of unfair competition: an act of announcing or disseminating a false fact which harms goodwill of another person who is in a competitive relationship."

Plaintiff argued that the US patent was invalid and not infringed. In reply, Defendant argued that a Japanese court does not have international jurisdiction concerning declaratory judgment as to injunction based on a US patent, and that even if a Japanese court accepts such international jurisdiction, the enforceability of injunction orders in the US is doubtful and Plaintiff therefore lacked proper legal interest in bringing a suit before a Japanese court. Defendant also asserted that there was a literal or doctrine of equivalents infringement on its US patent.

HELD

As to the issue of international jurisdiction, the court noted that:

Concerning international jurisdiction, no general rules exist that have been internationally accepted, and international customary law has not sufficiently matured. Whether or not our country has international jurisdiction over a given case should be determined logically in the light of fairness between parties and for the idea of proper and expeditious court proceedings. For lawsuits brought before a court in our country, if any of venues provided in the Japanese Code of Civil Procedure exists in our country, unless there exist special circumstances that would make court proceedings in Japan violate fairness between parties and the idea of proper and expeditious court proceedings, our country should accept international jurisdiction over such a case.

When we look at the present case, Defendant is a Japanese corporation having its headquarters in Japan, and a normal venue exists in Japan for Defendant. Therefore, unless we have any special circumstances mentioned above, international jurisdiction should be acknowledged in Japan.

Defendant pointed out that territorialism is applicable to patents and argued that international jurisdiction should be denied in Japan for each claim mentioned above. However, the principle of territorialism for a patent means that the establishment, transfer, and effectiveness, etc. of a patent in a given country is determined by the laws of that country and the patent is effective only within the territory of the country, and relates to effects of the patent under substantive laws. It has nothing to do with international jurisdiction concerning litigation related to a patent.

A claim for injunction is based on proprietary rights of a private person, and therefore, such claim should be dealt with as an ordinary lawsuit concerning a claim under private law. The question of international jurisdiction that may exist in Japan should be decided in view of the above. If a normal venue for Defendant exists in Japan, international jurisdiction should be acknowledged in Japan. Certainly, the requirements for establishment of a patent and its effectiveness are governed by laws of each country in view of its economic policies, and to this extent, are related to policy decisions made in each country. This point should not be a reason for denying international jurisdiction in a country other than the country in which the patent is registered, while it may be considered in determining what law governs a lawsuit for injunction.

Also, in a lawsuit for denying the establishment of a patent or for invalidating a patent, sole jurisdiction is generally considered to exist in a country in which the patent is registered. In a lawsuit for injunction based on a patent, it is often possible under statutes or case law to use the invalidity of the patent as a defense against claims raised by the patentee. In such a case, even if the patentee's claim for injunction is denied because such a defense has a basis, the finding of invalidity concerning that patent, as an opinion in the decision for such lawsuit, is binding to the parties only, and the patent is never invalidated with effects on third parties in general. Thus, the allowability of invalidity defense cannot be a reason for denying international jurisdiction in countries other than the country of patent registration, and even if the other party puts up a defense of patent invalidity in a lawsuit for injunction, it does not prevent a court of a country other than the registration country from hearing such a case.

In the present case in which the existence of rights to obtain injunction based on a US patent is disputed, while it is clearly provided in US statutes that it is possible to assert a defense of patent invalidity in a lawsuit for injunctive relief (35 USC § 282(2)), the determination of invalidity of the patent in this lawsuit does not directly make the patent invalid for all third parties.

Based on the above reasoning and finding no disadvantages for Defendant in having Japanese court proceedings as compared with carrying out litigation before a US court, the court concluded that a Japanese court may have international jurisdiction in the present lawsuit. Also, the court held that even if an injunction order for a country in which the patent is registered is granted by a Japanese court, such order should be acknowledged and enforced by a court of that country, and therefore, Plaintiff has proper standing to bring the present law suit before the court.

Then, the court considered the question of infringement. The court decided that the law governing this was US law and considered literal infringement under the all element rule. Using the element-by-element analysis, the court found no literal infringement. For the doctrine of equivalents infringement, the court applied the opinion of the *Festo* US Supreme Court decision (*Festo Corp. v. Shoketsu Kinzoku Kogyo Kabushiki Co., Ltd.*, 62 U.S.P.Q. 2d 1705, 1713, 122 S. Ct. 1831 (2002)). The court noted the rebuttable presumption and the three instances in which the presumption may be overcome as provided in *Festo*. Looking at the prosecution history of the US patent, the court noted that an original main claim was narrowed by the insertion of a numerical range of about 150 to 500 mesh in order to avoid the prior art that taught a range of 20 to 60 mesh for coal sand. The lower limit of the range was clearly to avoid the prior art, but the court found that Defendant failed to show any reasons for the upper limit of 500 mesh and rebut the *Festo* presumption. Plaintiffs product contained a powder of about 5000 mesh, and no doctrine of equivalents infringement was found. The court declared that Defendant was not entitled to obtain injunction orders for the sale in the US of the coral fossil powder based on US patent No. 4,540,584.

The court then considered at length if acts committed by Defendant fell under Section 2(1)(xix) of the Japanese Unfair Competition Prevention Law. The court pointed out five points against Defendant: (1) Defendant was not a proprietor or licensee of the US patent in question when it sent the warning email and letter, (2) While Plaintiff acted immediately in response to the first warning and informed Defendant that its products fell outside the scope of the US patent, Defendant sent the second warning showing an excerpt of a Japanese court decision in an unrelated case, (3) Defendant pointed out in the second warning that Plaintiff did not have sufficient financial strength to support expensive US litigation, (4) those at the US dealer which received the warning twice were upset about the course of events and informed Plaintiff their intention to terminate business with Plaintiff, and (5) Defendant started no patent infringement litigation, and found that the acts of Defendant were acts of unfair competition under the Japanese Unfair Competition Prevention Law.

In conclusion, the court ordered Defendant not to announce or spread notices from within Japan to Plaintiff's US customers that Plaintiff's and the customers' sale in the US of the powder constitutes infringement on the US patent. The court also awarded damages of about 3 million yen (about US$ 28,000) to Plaintiff, but rejected Plaintiffs claim for a declaration that Defendant is not entitled to injunction orders against the Plaintiffs US dealer as the dealer was not a party in the present lawsuit. The court did not consider the question of validity of the US patent at issue.

NOTES AND QUESTIONS

1. Which court's approach to jurisdiction over foreign patents is more persuasive, the CAFC's in *Voda* or the Tokyo District Court in *K.K Coral*?

Does the decision of the Tokyo court suggest that it would assert jurisdiction in all cases (thus providing a convenient forum for patentees to litigate infringement of multiple foreign patents in a single action), or are there circumstances under which adjudication of a foreign patent would be considered inappropriate by the court?

2. One of the Federal Circuit's arguments in *Voda* was that global patent harmonization efforts are an insufficient basis to assert jurisdiction over foreign patents. Should this view still hold even if uniform patent rights eventually exist at the global level?

3. According to the Tokyo District Court, its adjudication of the infringement of a US patent was appropriate because even if the patent was held to be invalid by the court, such a holding would only apply to the parties to the litigation and would not affect third parties. Do you agree that such adjudication has no effect on third parties? Consider the following statement by a UK Patents Court judge, Mr. Justice Aldous, in *Plastus Kreative AB v. Minnesota Mining and Manufacturing Co.*, [1995] R.P.C. 438 (Eng.):

> For myself I would not welcome the task of having to decide whether a person had infringed a foreign patent. Although patent actions appear on their face to be disputes between two parties, in reality they also concern the public. A finding of infringement is a finding that a monopoly granted by the state is to be enforced. The result is invariably that the public have to pay higher prices than if the monopoly did not exist. If that be the proper result, then that result should, I believe, come about from a decision of a court situated in the state where the public have to pay the higher prices. One only has to imagine a decision of this court that the German public should pay to a British company substantial sums of money to realize the difficulties that might arise. I believe that, if the local courts are responsible for enforcing and deciding questions of validity and infringement, the conclusions reached are likely to command the respect of the public.

Are these concerns persuasive? Do they change your view regarding the correctness of the Tokyo District Court's decision to adjudicate infringement of a US patent? Why or why not?

4. In *Voda,* the Federal Circuit discouraged, but did not abrogate, a court's discretionary right to adjudicate issues concerning a foreign patent. In a post-*Voda* case, *Fairchild Semiconductor Corp. v. Third Dimension Semiconductor, Inc.,* 589 F. Supp. 2d 84 (D. Me. 2008), a U.S. district court in Maine chose to exercise jurisdiction in a license dispute over the scope of a Chinese patent. While noting that *Voda* "seems vehement that a United States court should almost always decline to hear a dispute about foreign patents," the court distinguished *Voda* as being based on supplemental jurisdiction, whereas the case at issue rested on diversity jurisdiction. It also concluded that any balancing of forum non conveniens factors should be "heavily

weighted in favor of the exercise of jurisdiction." Notwithstanding, U.S. court adjudication of foreign patent infringement claims is likely to be rare.

2. THE INTERNATIONAL PATENT SYSTEM AND DEVELOPING COUNTRIES

Despite its eventful history, the design of the international patent system has seldom been more economically, politically, and socially significant, as well as contentious, than it is today.

Since the end of World War II, and in the context of the post-colonial environment immediately following, the underlying economic and legal rationale of the "pro-property" view of patents which had become embedded in the international patent system has been met with deep skepticism in many developing and least-developed countries. As you learned earlier in this Chapter, antagonism toward the view of patents as property was, of course, evident in some developed countries during the early days of their own industrial and economic growth, but this was largely resolved by the conclusion of the Paris Convention. The new international "patent-divide" first emerged formally in 1961, when Brazil proposed a draft resolution before the United Nations General Assembly (U.N.G.A.) requesting a report on the role of patents in the transfer of technology to under-developed countries. The draft Brazilian Resolution among other things stated that "access to experience in the field of applied science and technology is essential to accelerate the economic development of under-developed countries and to enlarge the over-all productivity of their economies", and "in practice, access to this knowledge and experience is often limited by patents and similar arrangements designed to protect the right of ownership and exploitation of inventors of new processes, techniques and products." Finally, the draft Resolution stated that "it is in the best interest of all countries that the international patent system be applied in such a way as to reconcile the legitimate claims of patent-holders with the needs and requirements of the economic development of under-developed countries." *See* Draft Resolution, U.N.Doc A/C.2/L.565 (Nov. 8, 1961).

As finally adopted, the Resolution retained only the first and last statements. The Resolution also omitted language that had been in the draft about the failure of foreign patent owners to locally manufacture the patented product or process, restrictive provisions often contained in licensing agreements, and the effect of royalties paid for the use of foreign patents on the balance of payments of developing countries. *See* G.A. Res. 1713 (XVI), 16 U.N. GAOR, Supp. (No. 17) at 20, U.N. Doc. A/5100 (1962). The Resolution requested, among other things, a study of the effects of patents on developing countries. Many of the issues raised by the ensuing seminal report—compulsory licenses, technology transfer, and working requirements—remain controversial today. *See* United Nations, *The Role*

of Patents in the Transfer of Technology to Developing Countries, U.N.
Doc. E/3861/Rev.1. (1964).

In 2007, the WIPO General Assembly adopted the WIPO Development Agenda which consists of 45 Recommendations intended to more
coherently and systemically integrate the concerns of developing and
least-developed countries into the multilateral intellectual property system. Brazil, joined by Argentina, was again at the forefront of the initial
proposal leading up to this landmark achievement of international intellectual property policy. *See* Proposal by Argentina and Brazil for the Establishment of a Development Agenda for WIPO, WIPO Doc. No.
WO/GA/31/11 (Aug. 27 2004). The proposal was co-sponsored by Bolivia,
Cuba, the Dominican Republic, Ecuador, Egypt, Iran (Islamic Republic
of), Kenya, Peru, Sierra Leone, South Africa, Tanzania, and Venezuela.
Although not specific to patents, the Development Agenda's broad mandate that WIPO integrate economic development interests and concerns
into the international intellectual property system undoubtedly provides
an important platform for on-going calls to ensure that the patent system
is normatively balanced and serves the interests of developed and developing countries alike. For example, Cluster C, Recommendation 25, provides for "IP-related policies and initiatives necessary to promote the
transfer and dissemination of technology, to the benefit of developing
countries . . ." For the full text of the Recommendations adopted under
the Development Agenda, *see* WIPO, The 45 Adopted Recommendations
under the WIPO Development Agenda, *available at* http://www.wipo.int/
export/sites/www/ip-development/en/agenda/recommendations.pdf   (last
visited June 18, 2012).

The following excerpt from a classic text, written by Professor Vaitsos
over three decades ago, discusses issues that remain relevant to current
debates over the appropriate design of the international patent framework as well as the effects of patent protection on the development prospects of unindustrialized countries:

CONSTANTINE V. VAITSOS, THE REVISION OF THE INTERNATIONAL PATENT SYSTEM: LEGAL CONSIDERATIONS FOR A THIRD WORLD POSITION

4 WORLD DEV. 85, 85–99 (1976)

After several decades of complacent and unquestioned acceptance,
considerable attention has recently been paid by governments in developing countries as well as by international organizations to the possibility of
revising the international patent system. The renewed interest in the
subject originates from the serious inadequacies of the market for technology (within which patents have a role) and the implications of such
inadequacies for the developmental process in the Third World. The recent interest in patents has been fostered by revised or novel conceptions

regarding industrial property legislation in certain countries, while efforts at the international level have cent[e]red around the activities of
[the United Nations Conference on Trade and Development (UNCTAD)].
A report published on this subject by the UNCTAD secretariat concluded
the following:

> The available evidence suggests that the international patent
> system is not, in its present form, proving to be of benefit to the
> developing countries and that it is instead having a negative ef-
> fect on their development. [Also] . . . patent laws and practices of
> developing countries, following international standards, have le-
> galized an anomalous situation which had come to act as a re-
> verse system of preferences granted to foreign patent holders in
> the markets of developing countries.
>
>   . . . .
>
> [W]e need to acknowledge the consistency and thoroughness with
> which the patent system has been constructed. We are not dealing with a
> loose anachronism stemming from the last century (i.e., from 1883) but
> rather with a coherent 'institution' that has: (i) an ideology expressed
> through the inexact denomination of 'industrial property' that associates
> patents with forms and conceptions of property present in the world econ-
> omy; (ii) a normative base which postulates that monopoly privileges
> granted through patents promote or are necessary for inventive and in-
> vestment activities, even in developing countries, and that the benefits of
> such activities undertaken through monopoly conditions (enjoyed basical-
> ly by foreigners) exceed other costs incurred by the patent granting coun-
> try; (iii) a consistent set of legal provisions and a body of very specialized
> expertise to administer them; (iv) a relatively well-financed and well-
> managed opinion-forming and policy-influencing entity, WIPO, which
> looks after the proper administration and permanence of the patent sys-
> tem; and (v) a set of interested pressure groups whose economic prosperi-
> ty depends exclusively (such as parts of the legal profession) or greatly
> (such as the pharmaceutical transnational enterprises) on the mainte-
> nance and strength of the patent system.
>
>   . . . .
>
> Legal considerations for the revision of the international patent sys-
> tem, in order to contain and express a certain degree of relevance for de-
> veloping countries, need to explicitly recognize three fundamental factors:
>
> (1) Practically all the patents in the Third World are foreign-owned.
> As such, the monopoly privileges granted through patents have, among
> other repercussions, an international, rather than simply a domestic, in-
> come distribution effect. They also have, as a result of income flows across
> national boundaries, balance of payments implications. Furthermore, pa-
> tent protection in developing countries amounts to a policy instrument

which almost totally covers innovations realized elsewhere, namely in the industrialized countries. The [research and development (R&D)] allocations in the latter countries are hardly influenced by patent protection in the developing nations. Hence, there exists an effective divorce between patent protection in the Third World and incentives on the innovations concerned.

(2) Most of the patents granted are in the hands of a relatively small number of transnational enterprises which use patents as part of their overall business policies. This contrasts with the 'need' for protection of the individual inventors who characteristically hold most of the relatively small number of nationally-owned patents.

(3) Practically all patents granted in developing countries are never worked in their territories. As such, patent protection is not only divorced from innovative but also from investment activity, and can block the use of technology to directly work the patented processes or products. Some investment activity, though, takes place in forward-linked operations that contain imported products that are covered in one way or another by patents. What, then, are the objectives for holding unworked patents that are controlled by transnational enterprises in developing countries? There appear to be two principal reasons:

(a) They are used to preserve import markets in developing countries for the patent holders. Such import monopolies will tend to have adverse effects on the terms of trade of the importing countries. They also create monopoly conditions in forward-linked activities that use products (or processes) covered by patents. It is for this reason that any serious revision of the patent system needs to take into account the provisions on unworked patents (compulsory licences and forms of their application) and the issue of import monopolies as covered by patent privileges.

(b) Patents are used to exclude competitors, including other transnational enterprises, from investing in productive activities in developing countries and from using them as bases for exporting to the rest of the world. Such exports could take place, with varying degrees of difficulty, with or without patent protection in the rest of the world. The most convenient and effective form of erecting barriers to entry through patent protection against possible competitors appears to be at the production level rather than in the commercialization of the products involved. In this way the patent holder protects his interests at the source of production where the knowhow used can be more easily verified (in case of presumed infringement) and where the investment risks from adverse court decisions for the competitors could be the highest.

. . . .

The provisions contained in the Paris Convention . . . neglect two issues of fundamental importance for patent policy in developing countries: First, they do not distinguish between the 'need' to protect inventive activity (if such protection is needed and *if* it is socially beneficial) and the oligopoly power exercised by transnational enterprises in the world market. In the latter case certain 'rules of the game' operate. They are imposed through overall political and business considerations and/or they are translated into contractual arrangements in the sale and purchase of technology. In their strategy on patents developing countries should concentrate on considerations of the technology market rather than accept provisions that reinforce the oligopoly position of transnational enterprises. . . . Secondly, existing patent provisions do not confront adequately the fundamental link between patent protection and imports of the corresponding products in developing countries. Protection of imports should be handled through the commercial policy of a country rather than through patents.

. . . .

The efforts undertaken for a serious revision of the international patent system which will be in congruence with the development objectives of the Third World necessitate, as an integral part of the legal changes, the presence of an additional factor. The latter concerns the establishment of a body of specialized expertise, distinct to those of WIPO, who can advise developing countries on these matters and serve as a permanent observer of the evolution and performance of the patent system in the international economy.

NOTES AND QUESTIONS

1. The composition of the developing world is more complex today than it was in 1976 when Professor Vaitsos published *The Revision of the International Patent System*. Since then, the emergence of economically competitive countries such as Brazil, China, India, South Korea, and South Africa has complicated the notion of a neat division between industrialized and non-industrialized countries and changed the face of the international patent system. China and South Korea, for example, surpassed the European Patent Office in 2007, and now possess the first and fourth largest patent offices in the world in terms of the number of patent applications filed. Moreover, the number of applications filed by nationals in those countries exceeds the number of applications filed by foreigners. The 2011 WIPO Intellectual Property Report shows that while large R&D expenditures still occur mainly in high-income countries, as of 2009 China is the world's second largest R&D spender. Further, patenting by universities and public research organizations (PROs) in China, Brazil, India and South Africa has grown rapidly, with patenting by Indian PRO's at 22 percent. *See* WIPO, 2011 WORLD INTELLECTUAL PROPERTY REPORT: THE CHANGING FACE OF INNOVATION. What impact do

you think these developments may have on the formulation of international patent policy? Do these developments confirm the unwavering faith of the U.S. in the role of patents as a primary source of technological advance for all countries?

2. Recall from section 1.A, *supra*, that the requirement to work a patent locally was greatly disfavored by the U.S. and other industrialized countries during the negotiations on the first iteration of the Paris Convention. In your opinion, are the arguments advanced by Professor Vaitsos in favor of provisions on unworked patents persuasive? Given the existing socio-economic conditions in least-developed countries, should the international patent system feature an obligation to work a patent locally? What would be costs associated with such a provision? You should revisit these questions at the end of this course!

Notwithstanding the abundance of empirical research analyzing the effects of patent protection on the rate of domestic innovation and economic growth, the nature and strength of the relationship between these variables is highly contested. On one hand, "weak" patent protection arguably stimulates innovation and downstream creativity by facilitating access to knowledge goods, but may impede technology transfer from abroad as well as private investment into knowledge generation and diffusion. On the other hand, "strong" patent regimes provide an incentive structure for investment into innovative activities, but at the same time they can inhibit developing countries' access to essential medicines, compromise food security, legitimize foreign expropriation of local cultural knowledge, and restrain competition. The provision of exclusive rights to patent right-holders can have an overall negative or positive effect on a country's growth rate, depending on the particular existing macroeconomic conditions.

There are undoubtedly benefits to be derived from an appropriately balanced and implemented patent policy geared to the public interest, especially the provision of public goods such as infrastructure, public health, education, and national defense. Nonetheless, given the present socioeconomic as well as cultural conditions in many developing and least-developed countries, strong patent regimes in these countries may not lead to the realization of benefits traditionally associated with the regulation of intellectual property in industrialized countries, namely, increased domestic innovation as well as technology transfer and foreign direct investment (FDI) inflows. Consider the following excerpt discussing cultural determinants behind the differences in recognition and protection of intellectual property between indigenous societies and industrialized nations.

RUTH L. GANA, HAS CREATIVITY DIED IN THE THIRD WORLD?: SOME IMPLICATIONS OF THE INTERNATIONALIZATION OF INTELLECTUAL PROPERTY
24 DENV. J. INT'L L. & POL'Y 109, 112–42 (1995)

The central claim is that all forms of creative expression-mechanical, literary, or artistic-are value driven. The nature and variety of goods produced in any society is, initially, a function of needs as the popular adage "necessity is the mother of invention" attests. More important, however, the laws which protect these inventions—laws which define what is to be protected and how that protection is to be effected—reflect the underlying values of a society. Intellectual property law, like other law "is more than just another opinion; not because it embodies all right values, or because the values it does embody tend from time to time to reflect those of a majority or plurality, but because it is the value of values. *Law is the principle institution through which a society can assert its values.*"

. . . .

The modern debate over intellectual property protection in developing countries has failed to take account of cultural differences which affect the understanding of what constitutes property or what may rightfully be the subject of private ownership. . . . [I]t is important for the modern debate to link intellectual property laws to the social realities of societies in developing countries. Not only may this yield more effective approaches to securing enforcement of intellectual property rights in developing countries, it also presents the possibility that western based intellectual property laws may have some real impact on industrial innovative activity in these countries, thus contributing to the economic welfare of the Third World. . . . [C]ulture may influence what is created but it is those values, rooted in a conception of a good society, that determine how and what kind of intellectual property laws societies enact.

. . . .

The critical point to note about recognizing creativity in the Third World is that forms of recognition and protection are a function of, and deeply embedded in, the institutions and underlying norms of social organization. In one sense, this is no different from the forms of protection for intellectual goods in the developed world. The individualism on which property rights are based and the nature of commodification which is central to liberal market economies are reflected clearly in modern intellectual property laws.

As far back as Biblical times, these goods which are now the subject matter of intellectual property were not protected in the forms and categories of patents, copyrights, trademarks, or trade secrets. Indeed, it was not until the era of Kings in ancient Israel that material reward was given for the results of creative effort. Yet, creativity and its fruits existed, and in abundance!

. . . .

A first cause of the differences in treatment of intellectual property is that forms of property ownership in these societies are different. Many indigenous societies are not organized around individuals as such but around a clan or other extended unit. As such, "ownership" means something different from its accepted conception in Anglo-American law. Property in most western societies consists of a bundle of rights. The most important of these rights are the right to absolute possession, the right to exclude others from use, and the right to dispose of the property as one wishes. Virtually all forms of property in western societies are defined in relation to these rights; the most important right being the right to exclude. This absolutist conception of property in Anglo-American law was transferred wholesale into the domain of intellectual goods.

. . . .

A second cause of difference in intellectual property treatment in Third World countries lies in the purpose of protection. Whereas the stated underlying purpose of Anglo-American intellectual property law is to encourage creative endeavor, protection of creative endeavor in Third World societies is purposely used to achieve a myriad of social, political, and economic goals. Thus, in Imperial China, unauthorized copying was forbidden out of concern for the ways in which various commodities were identified (i.e. a form of trademark law), in an attempt to maintain the purity of classic texts as well as to fulfill the censorship function. . . . Concern for public order or morals also led to outlawing of reproduction and dissemination of "devilish books and talk," to preserve the supremacy of certain literary works and to prevent the spread of works that would denigrate imperial authority.

. . . .

A [third] cause of the differences in intellectual property treatment in indigenous societies is that the value ascribed to creative expression is jointly held by the group as a whole. This value is not material as such, thus reflecting the non-commodifiability of certain goods in these cultures. Under Aboriginal law for example, the right to create paintings and other works about creation is vested in a group of custodians who are responsible for determining "whether the stories and images may be used in a painting, who may create the painting, to whom the painting may be published, and the terms on which it may be reproduced." By maintaining such a structured form for administering the right to create, the Aboriginals are able to guard the value of the meaning of the painting to their society. The Australian Court in *Milpurrurru* recognized the personal and cultural distress that the infringing carpets had caused to the Aboriginal community, noting that the losses, "which were a reflection of the aboriginal cultural environment in which the artists reside," could be accounted for in giving award damages.

. . . .

[The final] cause of differences in recognition and protection of intellectual property between indigenous societies and industrialized nations is that the organizing principles of these societies are so different as to affect the very idea of what is considered the appropriate subject of private ownership. Most Third World societies are organized around a social unit which extends certainly beyond the individual and, in most cases, beyond the nuclear family. The forms and very definition of ownership are thus crafted in a way opposite to property conceptions of western legal and economic structures central to the development of private and public law. What is representative of intellectual property laws in these societies are thus, not surprisingly, nothing like their western counterparts.

There is one important similarity between the protection of creative endeavor under western intellectual property laws and in indigenous societies. Both aim, ultimately, to enhance public welfare by protecting the fruits of creative effort. Given the value ascribed to creativity in many indigenous societies, it seems obvious that the protection of the fruits of creative energy is essential to the well being, to the sense of identity, and to the preservation of cultural patrimony that is so vital to the viability of these groups. Similarly, the enhancement of public welfare has long been the asserted purpose of intellectual property law in Anglo-American jurisprudence. The divergent forms that these laws take . . . in indigenous societies and in the western hemisphere is the strongest testimony of the fundamentally different philosophical tenets which underlie these systems. Above all, the fact that creativity remains a vital part of life and that it holds such powerful leverage and meaning in these societies tells the rest of the world that creativity is not only alive, but that it is also central to the social, political, and economic welfare of indigenous societies.

. . . .

SOME IMPLICATIONS

It is quite clear that one of the central motivations behind the TRIPS [A]greement was to target enforceability of foreign intellectual property rights in developing countries. As such, the global model of intellectual property protection imposed by the [A]greement is not a reflection of the need to encourage creativity or to promote the public welfare. Rather, the chief aim of the [A]greement is to secure from these countries and societies the full monopoly benefits that western intellectual property laws offer. The implications of these strategic moves are many. . . .

The need to maintain incentives to encourage creative activity is limited, in many respects, to western market democracies. These democracies revolve, in large part, around individual autonomy and liberty, notwithstanding the greater social loss of nonmaterial value that individualism tends to breed. The successful commodification of intellectual goods can only be achieved in a society which embraces this sort of rugged individualism. Until indigenous societies reach this point, the international community may have to come to terms with a persistent level of piracy in international trade. Piracy, however, cannot simply be explained mechanically in economic terms based on the reasoning that poverty necessitates the availability of cheap products. For many of these societies, the difficulty in introducing western [intellectual property] principles is that these principles attempt to overturn social values which are centuries old. The laws protecting intellectual goods in these societies simply reflect fundamental notions of what the society considers to be the appropriate subject of exclusive ownership. The duplication of literary work is thus, for example, not perceived as stealing but as making a good thing accessible to the general public. Knowledge in many indigenous societies is not perceived as something that can be commodified or objectified through law. It is impossible to ignore such fundamental conceptions in these communities.

In addition to responding to a persistent level of piracy, the internationalization of intellectual property also suggests that there is some way to objectively measure protection of intellectual property. By not taking into account the possibility of alternative forms of protection, the TRIPS [A]greement, as did its predecessor treaties, presupposes that "all civilized nations" will and must recognize this global model of intellectual property protection. By mandating this model, governments in developing countries are faced with the difficult job of destroying, or at least attempting to destroy, native conceptions about life and living and about what constitutes an ordered society. The allocation of material value to goods, and the way in which this value is expressed, is grounded firmly in the history of the evolution of a people. The internationalization of intellectual property threatens to undermine, if not totally destroy, the values that indigenous systems ascribe to intellectual property and the manner in which they allocate rights to intellectual goods.

What the internationalization of intellectual property implies, ultimately, is that there is only one way to participate in the international economy and that is by playing in accordance with prescribed rules, regardless of its impact on a group of peoples. It is a message that is not unfamiliar in the history of world affairs, and yet it is a message which, so history informs us, has caused devastation of unimagined proportions to human society. The next few years will reveal just how native peoples, indigenous groups, and developing countries will fare in the preservation of their cultural patrimony and in their ability to determine the identity of their group in an increasingly hostile international economic environment.

NOTES AND QUESTIONS

1. What role should a country's stage of development play in determining what levels of patent protection it should provide? *See* Ali Imam, *How Patent Protection Helps Developing Countries*, 33 AIPLA Q.J. 377 (2005) (arguing in favor of strong patent protection in BRIC countries, but not for least developed countries).

2. Reflecting on Professor Gana's article, do you think international intellectual property policy can be reformed "to take account of cultural differences which affect the understanding of what constitutes property or what may rightfully be the subject of private ownership"? If so, what policy reforms would you propose? Given the cultural differences that exist, to what extent can inventions and other creations of the human mind be legitimately labeled "property"? Is "intellectual property" a term that has outlived its usefulness?

3. Consider the following statement from the founder of Siemens AG during the 1876 Paris Convention negotiations:

> You might consider a rule that patentees are bound to grant licenses as an interference with the right of the inventor; but such a rule is absolutely necessary. The interests of [German] industries require that licenses be made available as a matter of right. Today industry is developing rapidly; and as a result monopolization of inventions and abuse of patent rights will inevitably expose large segments of industry to serious injury. The government must protect industry against these dangers. From abroad another danger may arise. Inventive work is far more developed in England, United States and France than in Germany. Up to the present the number of patents taken out in Germany by foreigners has been small because the scope of protection given to the inventor has been insufficient. New legislation will lead to a substantial increase of foreign patentees. We shall experience a wave of foreign—particularly American—patent applications. These patents will not be taken out in order to protect industrial plants established or to be established in Germany; they will be taken out to monopolize production abroad. These articles will be imported into this country. . . . Such a danger must be met.

These words, expressing the concerns of a 19th century "developing country," mirror the concerns articulated by Professor Vaitsos in 1976. For a similar but more contemporary critique of the international patent system from one of its most trenchant critics, *see* PETER DRAHOS & JOHN BRAITHWAITE, INFORMATION FEUDALISM: WHO OWNS THE KNOWLEDGE ECONOMY? 79 -81 (2002) (arguing that the international patent system did not bring benefits to developing countries but, rather, harmed them).

4. In most developing countries there are many more patent applications filed by nonresidents than by residents. Should this fact be viewed as evidence that global patent protection offers more benefits for foreigners than for citizens? Are there benefits that can come from having high volumes of foreign patent applicants? What might those benefits be?

CHAPTER 2

PROCEDURAL PATENT AGREEMENTS

■ ■ ■

The multilateral agreements that comprise the current international system for the protection of patent rights can be divided and categorized in numerous ways. For the purposes of this book, we have chosen to divide the agreements into two basic categories: (i) procedural agreements, and (ii) substantive agreements. The primary objective of substantive patent agreements, which are discussed in Chapter 3, is either to create a framework for the grant of patent rights or to establish minimum international standards of substantive patent law, such as those relating to conditions of patentability and the scope of protection, which countries must provide to qualified rightholders. In contrast, the principal function of procedural agreements, discussed in this Chapter, is to harmonize formal processes for obtaining patent protection, and to provide a unified procedure that patent owners can utilize to obtain protection simultaneously across multiple national jurisdictions. We also include, at the end of this Chapter, regional patent-granting agreements that, while substantive in nature, still fit the theme of facilitating the obtainment of patents in multiple jurisdictions.

A. THE PARIS CONVENTION

As you learned in Chapter 1, the conclusion of the Paris Convention in 1883 was the first successful effort to create an international framework for protecting patentable inventions. The Paris Convention is an ambitious treaty that covers not only patents, but also trademarks, trade names, industrial designs, indications of source, and the repression of unfair competition. So successful was the treaty that it remains the basis for our contemporary international patent system and the starting point for all other international patent agreements.

While more than 170 countries are now party to the Paris Convention, only 11 countries signed the original text. Those countries were Belgium, Brazil, El Salvador, France, Guatemala, Italy, the Netherlands, Portugal, Serbia, Spain, and Switzerland. When the treaty entered into force on July 7, 1884, 14 countries had ratified or acceded to it. These included the 11 countries that signed the original text along with Ecuador, Tunisia, and the United Kingdom. In 1887, the United States became party to the Convention, but Germany, the last industrial power to join, did so only in 1901. Although the Convention's basic principles have remained intact, the text has not remained static. As the international industrial property system has evolved over time, provisions of the Convention have been revised and some new ones added. The current version (with the exception of a 1979 administrative amendment) dates back to 1967.

The Paris Convention is essentially a procedural treaty; it contains no provisions, for example, concerning substantive requirements for patentability or the types of inventions for which patents must be available. The Convention is nevertheless precedent-setting in several ways. Arguably the most important is that it establishes the two fundamental principles that have enabled the international patent system to grow: national treatment and the right of priority. The treaty also sets common rules that strive for balance between uniformity and national sovereignty, and it creates an administrative framework responsible for implementing and administering the Convention. Finally, the Paris Convention contains some standard-setting provisions, such as compulsory licensing stipulations, found in Article 5. The major provisions of the Convention are described below.

1. NATIONAL TREATMENT

The framers of the Paris Convention were intent on ensuring that patent applications filed by foreigners would not be subject to discriminatory treatment. The principle of national treatment, when fully applied, achieves that goal by requiring each member country—to grant the same protection to nationals of the other Paris Convention countries as it applies to its own nationals. Prior to the Paris Convention, the dominant basis for granting patent rights to foreigners was reciprocity. Under a system of reciprocity, a country would only grant to foreign applicants the rights that the applicant's own country would have provided. For example, if an applicant from country X (which only granted patents for a term of ten years) sought patent protection in country Y (which granted patents for a term of twenty years), the patent granted to the applicant by country Y would only have a term of ten years. National treatment on the other hand guarantees equal protection for foreign applicants, be they natural persons or legal entities, in dealings with other member countries.

National treatment is addressed in Articles 2 and 3 of the Paris Convention. The fundamental principle can be found in Article 2(1):

> 2(1). Nationals of any country of the Union shall, as regards the protection of industrial property, enjoy in all the other countries of the Union the advantages that their respective laws now grant, or may hereafter grant, to nationals; all without prejudice to the rights specially provided for by this Convention. Consequently, they shall have the same protection as the latter, and

the same legal remedy against any infringement of their rights, provided that the conditions and formalities imposed upon nationals are complied with.

The benefits of national treatment may apply even to nationals of non-member countries of the Paris Convention, if, in accordance with Article 3, those nationals are "domiciled" or have "real and effective industrial or commercial establishments" in a Paris member country.

The Paris Convention allows only two exceptions to the national treatment rule. The first derives from the phrase in Article 2(1), "all without prejudice to the rights specially provided for by this Convention." The purpose of this phrase is to permit member countries to conclude bilateral treaties or special agreements among themselves of which the benefits are available only to nationals of those countries. The second exception is contained in Article 2(3) of the Convention, and authorizes the imposition of special requirements on foreign applicants, provided those requirements are of a procedural or administrative nature. Virtually all countries, for example, require foreign applicants to be represented by a local patent attorney, even if national applicants are free to represent themselves. Similarly, many countries require foreign applicants or patentees to post security in the event they wish to initiate litigation, and if the foreigner is the defendant in an action, to agree to jurisdiction on the basis of the domicile or establishment of the local plaintiff.

The national treatment principle is not synonymous with a requirement to provide effective patent protection. If a Paris Convention country's patent legislation and practices are sub-standard, all that country is required to do is to provide the same sub-standard level of protection it provides to its own nationals to nationals of other Paris Convention countries. In fact, some countries did not even have a patent system when they joined the Paris Convention, including Switzerland, which was chosen to serve as the location for the Convention's administrative office. Conversely, nationals of a Convention country with sub-standard protection are entitled to all the benefits of effective protection that Convention countries with higher patent standards provide.

2. THE RIGHT OF PRIORITY

The second landmark principle of the Paris Convention is the right of priority, established in Article 4. Under this right, when patent applicants file an application in one Paris Convention member country, they, or their successors-in-title, may file applications in other member countries at any time within the following twelve months, and the later applications will be regarded as if they had been filed on the same day as the first application. Because the later applications benefit from the first application's filing date, they enjoy a priority status over any competing applications relating to the same invention filed during the twelve-month priority period. The later applications also enjoy immunity from acts accomplished after the priority filing date that would normally destroy patentability, such as publication or disclosure of the invention.

The great genius of the right of priority is that it eliminated the problem that had long plagued inventors interested in exhibiting their inventions at international fairs, namely, having to file all international patent applications simultaneously. Under the right of priority, patent applicants have twelve months (six months for design patents) to decide in which countries they need protection and to plan and organize carefully the necessary steps they must take to secure protection in the selected countries.

The major provisions of the right of priority are contained in Articles 4A(1), 4B, and 4C(1) of the Paris Convention, which provide as follows:

4A(1). Any person who has duly filed an application for a patent . . . in one of the countries of the Union, or his successor in title, shall enjoy, for the purpose of filing in the other countries, a right of priority during the periods hereinafter fixed.

4B. Consequently, any subsequent filing in any of the other countries of the Union before the expiration of the periods referred to above shall not be invalidated by reason of any acts accomplished in the interval, in particular, another filing, the publication or exploitation of the invention . . . and such acts cannot give rise to any third-party right or any right of personal possession. . . .

4C(1). The periods of priority referred to above shall be twelve months for patents.

In practical terms, the right of priority can have a determinative impact on the award of patent rights. For example, assume that Applicant A files a priority application in Country X on January 1, Applicant B files an application for the same invention in Country Y on June 1, and then Applicant A files an application in Country Y claiming priority to the Country X application on December 1. Although Applicant B's application in Country Y predates Applicant A's application by 6 months, Applicant A's application will prevail since its filing date must be considered to be January 1, the date of filing of the priority application in Country X. The right of priority can thus have a significant impact on an inventor's entitlement to a patent, particularly in highly competitive industries where parallel research is the norm and the rush to patent is a fact of life.

The right of priority is based only on the first application for the same invention filed in a Paris Convention member state. It is quite common, however, for a later application to claim "multiple priorities," that is, several applications filed within the twelve-month priority period. This may be the case particularly when an invention is still subject to ongoing refinement, improvements, or additions. In such situations, it is very useful to be able to combine the earlier applications, each of which may pertain to different features of the invention, into a single application that is filed before the end of the priority year in other Convention countries. Since research projects are often carried out multinationally, it is not uncommon for the applications that make up the multiple priorities to originate in different member countries, or for those applications to contain elements for which no priority is claimed.

Where an applicant has filed two applications pertaining to the same invention, the right of priority is based on the filing of the first, and it is generally not permissible to use only the second as the basis for priority, especially if the later application claims elements that are contained in the first application. If, however, the first application was not published and the applicant withdraws it before filing the second, the priority period can begin anew with the filing date of the second application. But in such a case, the applicant would not enjoy priority over competing applications filed, or intervening acts accomplished, between the filing dates of the first and second applications.

That being said, the withdrawal, abandonment, or rejection of the first application does not prohibit the applicant from claiming it as the basis for priority. A priority application may serve as such even if it no longer exists. The only requirement that an application must meet to constitute a priority application is that it must be, in accordance with Article 4A(2), "equivalent to a regular national filing under the domestic legislation of any country." As defined in Article 4A(3), a regular national filing is "any filing that is adequate to establish the date on which the application was filed in the country concerned. . . ." For that reason, some countries, including the United States, have taken advantage of the opportunity to permit the filing of provisional applications—i.e., applications that lack formal requirements but nevertheless are deemed sufficient to receive a filing date. Provisional applications are discussed in more detail in Chapter 9.

On September 16, 2011, President Obama signed into law the Leahy-Smith America Invents Act ("AIA"), Pub. L. No. 112–29, 125 Stat. 284. The AIA not only significantly modified the way U.S. patent law had been practiced since 1952, but as we shall discuss in subsequent Chapters, it also brought U.S. practice substantially closer to that of the rest of the world. The pre-AIA version of the U.S. Patent Act placed serious constraints on U.S. applications claiming priority to foreign applications. Because the old Act remains in force for the duration of all patents granted and all applications filed under it, it is worthwhile to consider the foreign priority challenges that the pre-AIA law posed.

Under the pre-AIA 35 U.S.C. § 102(b), an inventor could not receive a patent if "the invention was patented or described in a printed publication in this or a foreign country or in public use or on sale in this country, more than one year prior to the date of the application for patent in the United States."[1] Section 119(a) provided and continues under the AIA to provide the scope of the right of priority. Under the pre-AIA law, Section 119 read as follows (read the provisions carefully):

35 U.S.C. § 119. Benefit of earlier filing date; right of priority

(a) An application for patent for an invention filed in this country by any person who has, or whose legal representatives or assigns have, previously regularly filed an application for a patent for the same invention in a foreign country which affords similar privileges in the case of applications filed in the United States or to citizens of the United States, or in a WTO member country, shall have the same effect as the same application would have if filed in this country on the date on which the application for patent for the same invention was first filed in such foreign country, if the application in this country is filed within twelve months from the earliest date on which such foreign application was filed; **but no patent shall be granted** on any application for patent for an invention which had been patented or described in a printed publication in any country more than one year before the date of the **actual** filing of the application in this country, or which had been in public use or on sale in this country more than one year prior to such filing.

(b)(1) No application for patent shall be entitled to this right of priority unless a claim is filed in the Patent and Trademark Office, identifying the foreign application by specifying the application number on that foreign application, the intellectual property authority or country in or for which the application was filed, and the date of filing the application, at such time during the pendency of the application as required by the Director.

(2) The Director may consider the failure of the applicant to file a timely claim for priority as a waiver of any such claim. The Director may establish procedures, including the payment of a surcharge, to accept an unintentionally delayed claim under this section.

(3) The Director may require a certified copy of the original foreign application, specification, and drawings upon which it is based, a translation if not in the English language, and such other information as the Director considers necessary. Any such

---

[1] The equivalent version in the AIA (§ 102(a)(1)) provides as follows:

"A person shall be entitled to a patent unless – (1) the claimed invention was patented, described in a printed publication, or in public use, on sale, or otherwise available to the public before the effective filing date of the claimed invention...."

certification shall be made by the foreign intellectual property authority in which the foreign application was filed and show the date of the application and of the filing of the specification and other papers.

(c)In like manner and subject to the same conditions and requirements, the right provided in this section may be based upon a subsequent regularly filed application in the same foreign country instead of the first filed foreign application, provided that any foreign application filed prior to such subsequent application has been withdrawn, abandoned, or otherwise disposed of, without having been laid open to public inspection and without leaving any rights outstanding, and has not served, nor thereafter shall serve, as a basis for claiming a right of priority.

(d) Applications for inventors' certificates filed in a foreign country in which applicants have a right to apply, at their discretion, either for a patent or for an inventor's certificate shall be treated in this country in the same manner and have the same effect for purpose of the right of priority under this section as applications for patents, subject to the same conditions and requirements of this section as apply to applications for patents, provided such applicants are entitled to the benefits of the Stockholm Revision of the Paris Convention at the time of such filing.

Id. (Emphasis added). In summary, under the pre-AIA version of § 119(a), the U.S. counted backwards from the actual U.S. filing date (the actual filing date of the PCT application in PCT cases), not from the filing date of the priority application, when determining prior art under pre-AIA 35 U.S.C. § 102(b). Thus, a publication, use, or offer for sale of an invention mere days before the filing of a foreign priority application can defeat patentability of the invention in the U.S. if the PCT application, which accords the actual U.S. filing date, is filed more than one year after such publication, use, or offer for sale. This result may occur even though the PCT application was filed in time to claim priority to the foreign application. Further, the U.S. application claiming a foreign priority date must in all other respects satisfy the requirements of § 119.

This provision was particularly disadvantageous for foreign applicants and is now eliminated by the AIA, which, in section 3(g)(6), amended Section 119(a) by striking all language following the semi-colon, beginning with "but no patent shall be granted . . . ," and ending with "one year prior to such filing." The amendment entered into force on March 16, 2013.

The Paris Convention right of priority may appear straightforward, yet its implementation can be contentious, requiring a court to interpret the context surrounding the inventor's application. Consider and compare the U.S. and UK approaches in the following two cases.

BOSTON SCIENTIFIC SCIMED, INC. v. MEDTRONIC VASCULAR, INC.

United States Court of Appeals, Federal Circuit
497 F.3d 1293 (Fed. Cir. 2007)

■ MAYER, Circuit Judge:

I. BACKGROUND

This appeal stems from an interference proceeding[2] before the United States Patent and Trademark Office Board of Patent Appeals and Interferences. Scimed and Medtronic Vascular, Inc. ("Medtronic") are each assignees of different United States patent applications covering the same invention. Andrew Cragg and Michael Dake (collectively "Cragg") filed patent application 08/461,402 ("the '402 application") for the invention in question on June 5, 1995. Cragg then assigned all rights in the '402 application to Boston Scientific Technology, Inc., which later merged into Scimed, the plaintiff-appellant and current legal owner of the '402 application. Also on June 5, 1995, Thomas J. Fogarty, Timothy J. Ryan, and Kirsten Freislinger (collectively "Fogarty") filed patent application 08/463,836 ("the '836 application") for the same invention. Fogarty assigned their rights in the '836 application to a company that eventually became Medtronic, the defendant-appellee and current legal owner of the '836 application. Eric Martin, a third-party to the instant appeal, owns U.S. Patent No. 5,575,817 (the "Martin patent" or "817 Patent"), which resulted from an application filed on August 19, 1994.

On April 23, 1998, the board declared an interference between Scimed's '402 application, Medtronic's '836 application, and Martin's '817 patent. The purpose of the interference was to determine which party had priority of inventorship, thereby entitling it to the invention as set forth in the sole count of the interference. . . .

The board initially gave Cragg the benefit of the filing dates of two European patent applications filed by MinTec SARL ("MinTec"), a French company. The earlier of these dates was February 9, 1994. At the time these European applications were filed, no legal relationship existed between MinTec and Cragg, nor was MinTec acting on behalf of Cragg. Fogarty was granted the benefit of the filing date of U.S. patent application 08/255,681, which was June 8, 1994. Martin was accorded benefit of the application that led to the '817 patent, which was filed on August 19, 1994. Accordingly, the PTO initially designated Cragg as the senior party in the interference.

Fogarty responded by filing a motion attacking the priority benefit granted to Cragg. The board granted the motion, declaring Fogarty the

---

[2] [Authors' Note: The AIA makes no provision for interference proceedings since the law is based on a system of first inventor to file. Instead, it replaces interferences with derivation proceedings. See, in particular, Chapter 6, *supra*, on Novelty.]

senior party in the interference. After Cragg protested this decision, the board issued a final decision denying his request to be declared the senior party. The board ruled that Cragg was not entitled to priority benefit under 35 U.S.C. §119 because neither Cragg nor Dake had assigned their rights to MinTec until after it had filed the European applications. . . .

Scimed, the assignee of Cragg's U.S. patent application, then brought an action in the United States District Court for the District of Columbia challenging the board's final decision in the '192 interference. The district court affirmed the board's final decision, *Scimed*, 468 F. Supp.2d at 61, and Scimed filed this appeal. We have jurisdiction under 28 U.S.C. § 1295(a)(1).

II. DISCUSSION

. . . .

At issue here is whether 35 U.S.C. § 119(a) permits an applicant for a United States patent to benefit from the priority of a foreign application previously filed by an entity that was not acting on behalf of the U.S. applicant at the time of filing. We hold that it does not.

A similar issue was addressed by the Court of Customs and Patent Appeals in *Vogel v. Jones,* 486 F.2d 1068 (CCPA 1973), which, to the extent relevant here, is binding upon us, *South Corp. v. United States,* 690 F.2d 1368, 1370 (Fed.Cir.1982) (en banc). According to *Vogel*, "§ 119 gives rise to a right of priority that is personal to the United States applicant." 486 F.2d at 1072. Due to the personal nature of this right, an applicant for a U.S. patent may only benefit from the priority of a foreign application if it was filed by the U.S. applicant or "on his behalf."

Scimed argues that *Vogel* does not require the foreign applicant to have been acting on behalf of the U.S. applicant *at the time the foreign application was filed*. It points to the following passage in support:

> This practice [of allowing a U.S. applicant to claim priority from a foreign application filed by someone else] arose because it was recognized that in many foreign countries, unlike in the United States, the actual applicant for a patent can be other than the inventor, e.g., an assignee. In light of this, we regard the language in § 119 referring to legal representatives and assigns to merely represent a codification of the actual practice under [the predecessor statute to § 119]. Since under United States law an application for patent must be made by the inventor, that practice was based on the requirement that the foreign application, regardless of the identity of the applicant, must have been filed for an invention actually made by the inventive entity seeking to rely upon it for priority purposes. We think § 119 must be construed to the same end.

Id.

Scimed attempts to construe this language as permitting a U.S. applicant to benefit from a foreign application's earlier filing date whenever "the invention described in the foreign application [is the same] one actually made by the U.S. applicant,"— "regardless of the identity of the applicant' of the foreign application." According to its interpretation, "the *Vogel* court did not hold that the foreign application must have been filed by a person who was an assignee or legal representative of the U.S. inventor *at the time the foreign application was filed*, or that the foreign application must have been filed on his behalf in order for there to be priority benefit." We disagree.

Vogel clearly held that the above quoted passage "means that an applicant for a United States patent can rely for priority on the 'first filed' application by an assignee *on his behalf*." Moreover, "the existence of an application made by [the inventor's] assignee in a foreign country on behalf of one other than the United States inventor is irrelevant to his right of priority based on applications made on his behalf." In other words, while the foreign application must obviously be for the same invention and may be filed by someone other than the inventor, section 119(a) also requires that a nexus exist between the inventor and the foreign applicant at the time the foreign application was filed. Indeed, as a matter of pure logic, an entity could not have filed a foreign application "on behalf of" an inventor without the inventor's knowledge or consent; that the foreign application may have been filed in accordance with the laws of the country in which it was filed has no bearing here. Therefore, to the extent that there may have been any uncertainty or ambiguity in *Vogel*, we now explicitly hold that a foreign application may *only* form the basis for priority under section 119(a) if that application was filed by either the U.S. applicant himself, or by someone acting on his behalf *at the time the foreign application was filed*.

. . . .

III. CONCLUSION

Accordingly, the judgment of the United States District Court for the District of Columbia is affirmed.

In the United Kingdom High Court of Justice, the Honourable Mr. Justice Kitchin had to consider whether the Paris Convention requires priority claims to be filed by the same person or persons who filed the earlier application on which priority was based. *Edwards Lifesciences AG v. Cook Biotech Inc.*, [2009] EWHC 1304 (Pat), involved an action by Edwards for revocation of Cook's patent for an artificial heart valve, and a counterclaim by Cook against Edwards for infringement of the patent.

Edwards disputed Cook's claim of priority arguing that when a priority application lists multiple applicants, the application claiming priority must be made by all the same applicants (or their successors-in-title) as in the priority application. The determination of priority was pivotal in this case because a technical journal article describing the invention had been published between the date of the priority claim and the filing date of the application claiming priority. Observe in Mr. Justice Kitchin's decision the interplay between the Paris Convention, the UK Patents Act, and the Patent Cooperation Treaty (PCT) discussed later in this Chapter.

EDWARDS LIFESCIENCES AG v. COOK BIOTECH INC.

[2009] EWHC 1304 (Pat)

■ MR. JUSTICE KITCHIN:

Priority

The international application (the "PCT application") which led to the grant of the Patent has an international filing date of 31 January 2001 and it claims priority from US patent application No. 60/179,195 (the "US application") filed on 31 January 2000. The claim to priority is disputed by Edwards, a matter of some importance because, if priority is lost, Pavcnik, published later in 2000, is relevant prior art.

The priority dispute is an unusual one and depends upon the proper interpretation of Article 4 of the Paris Convention. But first I must explain the relevant factual background.

The US application was filed in the names of Joe Obermiller, Francisco Osse and Patricia Thorpe, all as joint inventors. Mr. Obermiller was an employee of Cook at the time the invention was made. Mr. Osse and Ms. Thorpe were not.

The PCT application was filed in the name of Cook but at that time the only interest it had in the invention was via Mr. Obermiller's contract of employment. It is accepted that Mr. Obermiller's interest, such as it was, belonged to Cook.

The interests of Mr. Osse and Ms. Thorpe were not assigned to Cook until September 2002, that is to say 21 months after Cook filed the PCT application but before the grant of the Patent.

In these circumstances Cook says the claim to priority is a good one because it had acquired all rights in the invention before the date of grant of the Patent and in any event always owned Mr. Obermiller's interest. Edwards says the claim is misconceived because the right of priority may only be enjoyed by the person who filed the priority application or his successor in title as at the date the right to priority is claimed, and on 31 January 2001 that was Mr. Osse, Ms. Thorpe and Cook, not Cook alone.

Entitlement to priority is addressed in section 5 of the Patents Act 1977 ("the Act") which (as it existed at the relevant time) says:

"5(1) For the purpose of this Act the priority date of an invention to which an application for a patent relates and also of any matter (whether or not the same as the invention) contained in any such application is, except as provided by the following provisions of this Act, the date of filing the application.

(2) If in or in connection with an application for a patent (the application in suit) a declaration is made, whether by the applicant or in any predecessor in title of his, complying with the relevant requirements of rules and specifying one or more earlier relevant applications for the purposes of this section made by the applicant or a predecessor in title of his and each having a date of filing during the period of twelve months immediately preceding the date of fling the application in suit, then-

(a) if an invention to which the application in suit relates is supported by matter disclosed in the earlier relevant application or applications, the priority date of that invention shall instead of being the date of filing of the application in suit be the date of filing the relevant application in which that matter was disclosed or, if it was disclosed in more than one relevant application, the earliest of them;

(b) the priority date of any matter contained in the application in suit which was also disclosed in the earlier relevant application or applications shall be the date of filing the relevant application in which that matter was disclosed or, if it was disclosed in more than one relevant application, the earliest of them."

It is also convenient to refer to section 7 of the Act which deals with the right to apply for and obtain a patent:

"7(1) Any person may make an application for a patent either alone or jointly with another.

(2) A patent for an invention may be granted-

(a) primarily to the inventor or joint inventors:

(b) in preference to the foregoing, to any person or persons who, by virtue or any enactment or rule of law, or any foreign law or treaty or international convention, or by virtue of an enforceable term of any agreement entered into with the inventor before the making of the invention, was or were at the time of the making of the invention entitled to the whole of the property in it (other than equitable interests) in the United Kingdom;

(c) in any event, to the successor or successors in title of any person or persons mentioned in paragraph (a) or (b) above or any person so mentioned and the successor or successors in title of another person so mentioned;

and to no other person.

(3) In this Act "inventor" in relation to an invention means the actual deviser of the invention and "joint inventor" shall be construed accordingly.

(4) Except so far as the contrary is established, a person who makes an application for a patent shall be taken to be the person who is entitled under subsection (2) above to be granted a patent and two or more persons who make such an application jointly shall be taken to be the persons so entitled."

Section 5, but not section 7, is one of those sections said by section 130(7) of the Act to have been framed as to have, as nearly as practicable, the same effect as the corresponding provisions of the EPC (Article 87) and the PCT (Article 8).

Of these I need only refer to the relevant parts of Article 8 of the PCT:

(1) The international application may contain a declaration, as prescribed in the Regulations, claiming the priority of one or more earlier applications filed in or for any country party to the Paris Convention for the Protection of Industrial Property.

(2) -

(a) Subject to the provisions of sub-paragraph (b), the conditions for, and the effect of, any priority claim declared under paragraph (1) shall be as provided in Article 4 of the Stockholm Act of the Paris Convention for the Protection of Industrial Property.

This takes one back to the Paris Convention (Stockholm revision), Article 4, which reads, so far as relevant:

A (1) Any person who has duly filed an application for a patent, or for the registration of a utility model, or of an industrial design, or of a trademark, in one of the countries of the Union, or his successor in title, shall enjoy, for the purpose of filing in other countries, a right of priority during the periods hereinafter fixed.

(2) Any filing that is equivalent to a regular national filing under the domestic legislation of any country of the Union or under bilateral or multilateral treaties concluded between coun-

tries of the Union shall be recognized as giving rise to the right of priority.

(3) By a regular national filing is meant any filing that is adequate to establish the date on which the application was filed in the country concerned, whatever may be the subsequent fate of the application.

. . .

D (1) Any person desiring to take advantage of the priority of a previous filing shall be required to make a declaration indicating the date of such filing and country in which it was made. Each country shall determine the latest date on which such declaration must be made.

(2) These particulars shall be mentioned in the publications issued by the competent authority, and in particular in the patents and the specifications relating thereto.

So Article 4 specifies a person is to enjoy a right of priority if he has filed a relevant application for a patent or if he is the successor in title to such a person. Successor in title here must mean successor in title to the invention, as the parties before me agreed. Further, any person wishing to take advantage of the priority of such a filing must be required to make an appropriate declaration.

Both elements of Article 4 are reflected in section 5 of the Act which requires a declaration made by the applicant which complies with the relevant rules and specifies one or more earlier relevant applications made by the applicant or a predecessor in title.

In my judgment the effect of Article 4 of the Paris Convention and section 5 of the Act is clear. A person who files a patent application for an invention is afforded the privilege of claiming priority only if he himself filed the earlier application from which priority is claimed or if he is the successor in title to the person who filed that earlier application. If he is neither the person who filed the earlier application nor his successor in title then he is denied the privilege. Moreover, his position is not improved if he subsequently acquires title to the invention. It remains the case that he was not entitled to the privilege when he filed the later application and made his claim. Any other interpretation would introduce uncertainty and the risk of unfairness to third parties. In reaching this conclusion I derive a measure of comfort from the fact that the Board of Appeal of the EPO has adopted the same approach to the interpretation of Article 87 EPC in two cases: J 0019/87 and T 0062/05.

Nevertheless, Cook contends this interpretation is inconsistent with section 7 of the Act which distinguishes between an application for a patent and its grant. Section 7(1) permits any person to make an application for a patent. Section 7(2), on the other hand, restricts the persons to whom a patent may be granted to the inventor or inventors, to any person or persons entitled to the property in the invention when it was made or to the successor or successors in title to any such person or persons. It follows, says Cook, that, as "any person", it was entitled to make the application for the Patent in January 2001 and, as the successor in title to all the inventors as a result of the assignment of September 2002, it was entitled to the grant of the Patent in April 2007. If this is the position in relation to grant then, Cook continues, it must be the same in relation to priority.

I am unable to accept this submission. The two sections are dealing with separate issues, the right to claim priority in the case of section 5, and the right to the grant of a patent in the case of section 7. Further, section 7 is not one of those sections said by section 130(7) of the Act to have a corresponding provision in the EPC, the CPC or the PCT. By contrast, section 5 has been framed so as to have the same effect as Article 8 of the PCT and so also Article 4 of the Paris Convention. I do not consider it permissible to interpret the Paris Convention in the light of section 7 of the Act. Finally, section 7 provides a complete code as to those persons entitled to the grant of a patent. In the case of a successor in title, he must have derived title by the date of grant. There is no equivalent provision in Article 4 of the Paris Convention.

I therefore conclude that the acquisition by Cook of all rights in the invention in September 2002 does not permit it to claim priority from the US application.

That leaves the alternative argument advanced by Cook, namely that it always owned Mr. Obermiller's interest in the invention and that is sufficient. I can deal with this argument quite shortly. The US application was filed in the names of Mr. Obermiller, Mr. Osse and Ms. Thorpe, all as joint inventors. It was not filed by Mr. Obermiller alone and therefore he was not "a person" who had "duly filed an application for a patent" within the meaning of Article 4A(1) of the Paris Convention. Once again, this approach is consistent with that adopted by the Board of Appeal of the EPO in case T 0788/05.

In summary, the Patent is not entitled to a priority date earlier than 31 January 2001 and so Pavcnik is relevant prior art.

NOTES AND QUESTIONS

1.   The *Scimed* court cites no statutory basis for its decision that an application filed in a foreign country will only count for priority purposes if it was filed by the U.S. applicant himself or someone acting on her behalf. Other than its reliance on *Vogel v. Jones,* 486 F.2d 1068 (C.C.P.A. 1973), why do

you think the court adopted this narrow construction of §119(a)? Can you think of any underlying policy interests that justify such an approach? What do you think are the practical effects of this rule on the timing of foreign patent filing by U.S. corporations concerned about priority?

2.   Does the *Scimed* rule essentially gut one of the main benefits of the right of priority for foreign applicants? As mentioned earlier, even with the adoption of the AIA, the provisions of the pre-AIA law, including Section 119(a), will continue in force for all granted patents and pending applications (in other words, for about the next twenty years). Thus, although the *Scimed* case will ultimately become obsolete, it will most likely continue for some time to govern the issue of whether a U.S. applicant can claim priority to a foreign application that was neither filed by the U.S. applicant nor filed on the U.S. applicant's behalf.

3. Under the pre-AIA version of Section 119, a patent could be rendered invalid by an offer for sale in the U.S. to a company, which occurred seventeen months prior to the filing of the PCT application, even though it occurred only five months prior to the filing of the U. K. priority application. *See Group One, Ltd. v. Hallmark Cards, Inc.,* 254 F.3d 1041 (Fed. Cir. 2001). In *Group One, Ltd.,* the court had to determine whether communications between the parties amounted to an offer for sale, thus triggering the on-sale bar pursuant to § 102(b). The court held that "[o]nly an offer which rises to the level of a commercial offer for sale, one which the other party could make into a binding contract by simple acceptance (assuming consideration), constitutes an offer for sale under [pre-AIA] § 102(b)." *Id.* at 1048. The court concluded that the communications by Group One did not meet this threshold. In his additional remarks, Judge Lourie agreed with the court's decision, but stated that the circumstances in *Group One Ltd.* should be construed as an offer to license. In his view, "if a license were equivalent to a sale for purposes of the on-sale bar, many patents would be invalidated long before the invention itself is put on sale because the grant of licenses often long precedes commercialization by sale of the invention. The law does not start the on-sale bar clock running when a license to an invention is executed." *Id.* at 1053. Other than the words used in a transaction, how would you distinguish between an offer for sale and an offer to license? Read § 102(b) and § 119(a) carefully. Does the statutory language provide a basis to exclude licenses from triggering the on-sale bar?

4. To the extent the right of priority is meant principally to assist foreign inventors secure patent rights in countries that are party to the Paris Convention, the on-sale bar does not facially appear to conflict with this key provision of international patent law. Do you think U.S. implementation of the right of priority, as expressed in the pre-AIA version of § 119(a), treats foreign and domestic applicants the same?

5. U.S. implementation of the right of priority had long been the subject of controversy, due largely to the decision in *In re Hilmer,* 359 F.2d 859 (C.C.P.A 1966), a case that has received great criticism for discriminating against foreign inventors. The decision in *Hilmer* provides that while a U.S.

application may benefit from a claim of foreign priority for the purpose of obtaining an earlier U.S. filing date, it cannot rely on the priority date for the purpose of serving as patent-defeating prior art. As a result, the only effective filing date on which a published U.S. application or granted U.S. patent can be used to defeat a competing application, outside the context of an interference proceeding, is its U.S. filing date, not its earlier foreign priority date. This distinction between the effective date for filing and the effective date for prior art is unique to U.S. law. For an article critical of biases against foreign applicants under the PCT system in post-TRIPS U.S. law, and its relationship to the *Hilmer* doctrine, *see* Sean A. Passino, Stephen B. Maebius & Harold C. Wegner, *Foreign-Filed PCT Applications: An Aysmmetrical Patent-Defeating Effect*, 85 J. P. & TRADEMARK OFF. SOC'Y 874 (2003). The AIA eliminates this discrepancy in new Section 102(d) by giving U.S. applications patent defeating effect as of their foreign priority date for whatever is disclosed on that date.

6. To test your understanding of the right of priority, consider the following: On June 15, 2005, Sangeeta, an Indian engineer working in Mumbai, filed a patent application with the Indian Patent Office for a particular species of chemical compounds having novel antibacterial properties. On September 1, 2005, Sharon, a U.S. engineer working in Minneapolis, filed an application for the same species of compounds with the USPTO. On February 10 and March 15, 2006, Sangeeta published two articles disclosing the compound in American technical journals, and on June 10, 2006, she filed an application for her invention in the USPTO, claiming priority to the Indian application.

a. Given that both India and the U.S. are parties to the Paris Convention, who should be considered to have the earliest filing date?

b. What if Sangeeta were deemed to have abandoned her Indian application for failure to pay the requisite fees or if the Indian Patent Office determined that the compound was not patentable?

c. Assume now that the USPTO issues Sangeeta a patent for her invention on July 1, 2008. When should the twenty-year patent term expire? *See* Article 4*bis*(5) of the Paris Convention, which provides that "[p]atents obtained with the benefit of priority shall, in the various countries of the Union, have a duration equal to that which they would have, had they been applied for or granted without the benefit of priority."

d. What if Sangeeta's U.S. application included broader claims than her Indian application? For example, if Sangeeta's U.S. application also claimed a genus of compounds that included not only the species claimed in the Indian application, but other species as well, would Sangeeta be entitled to claim the benefit of her earlier filing date for the genus claims? Section 119(a) provides that the U.S. application must be for the same invention as that disclosed in the priority application. Is Sangeeta's U.S. application for the "same invention"? *See In re Gosteli,* 872 F.2d 1008 (Fed. Cir. 1989) (holding that the applicants were not entitled to benefit from the foreign priority date, without which the application was deemed invalid for lack of novelty).

7. For a European Patent Office (EPO) example of the complexities that sometimes arise in implementing the Paris Convention right of priority, *see* the well-known *University Patents* case, Case G03/98, University Patents, Inc. v. SmithKline Beecham Biologicals SA, 2000 E.P.O.R. 33 (EPO Enlarged Bd. App. 2000) (deciding that, for purposes of benefiting from a six-month grace period under the European Patent Convention, the relevant date for calculating the period is the date of the actual filing of the European patent application, not the date of priority). The EPO and the European Patent Convention (EPC) will be discussed further at the end of this Chapter.

3. INDEPENDENCE OF PATENTS

The principle of independence of patents, provided for in Article 4*bis* of the Convention, provides that a patent, or patent application, cannot be refused or invalidated in one member country on the grounds that a patent or an application has been refused, invalidated, or is no longer maintained in another. The principle also makes clear that a member country cannot be obliged to grant a patent just because a patent for the same invention was previously granted in another country. Article 4*bis* states, in part, as follows:

> 4*bis*(1). Patents applied for in the various countries of the Union by nationals of countries of the Union shall be independent of patents obtained for the same invention in other countries, whether members of the Union or not.

> (2). The foregoing provision is to be understood in an unrestricted sense, in particular, in the sense that patents applied for during the period of priority are independent, both as regards the grounds for nullity and forfeiture, and as regards their normal duration.

Article 4*bis* was not part of the original text of the Paris Convention, but was added during the treaty's first revision in 1900 to reinforce the principle that the fate of a patent or patent application in one member country should not be determinative of the fate of its counterparts in others. The provision has particular practical relevance when a patent applicant files applications for an invention, the subject matter of which may prove not to be patentable in some countries but patentable in others (for example, a business method), or when a patent owner chooses to abandon a patent in some countries but to maintain it elsewhere.

4. INVENTORS

Until the AIA, U.S. patent law required that a patent application had to be filed in the name of the inventor as applicant. In all other countries, however, an application could be filed in the name of the inventor's employer or an assignee. To prevent the inventor from remaining unknown, Article 4*ter* of the Paris Convention provides that the inventor "has the right to be mentioned as such in the patent." Ensuring the *right of the inventor to be mentioned* not only protects the right of inventors to recognition, it also serves to safeguard their material interests. This is particularly the case in countries such as Germany or Japan where employee-inventors are entitled to special remuneration based on the commercial value of their inventions. Where inventors are omitted or incorrectly mentioned, most Paris Convention countries provide for administrative remedies to rectify the error.

The AIA changed longstanding U.S. law by permitting patent applications to be filed in the name of the assignee. Section 4(b) of the Act amends § 118 of the Patent Act and states, "[a] person to whom the inventor has assigned or is under an obligation to assign the invention may make an application for patent." Similarly, Article 4*quater* of the Convention ensures the right of patent applicants and patent owners to apply for and maintain their patents even if the sale of the patented product, or the product obtained from a patented process, is "subject to restrictions or limitations" imposed by domestic law. This change is discussed in more detail in Chapter 9, *infra*.

5. COMPULSORY LICENSING/ WORKING REQUIREMENTS

Some of the most vexing international patent law questions have been concerned about how countries may respond to the *importation* of articles covered by patents, what the consequences should be of *failure to work* a patented invention, and to what extent countries should permit *compulsory licensing*. While these questions have been addressed more recently in the WTO TRIPS Agreement, Article 5A of the Paris Convention was an early attempt to resolve them.

Article 5A, which was added in 1958 at a Paris Convention revision conference in Lisbon, deals with whether and, if so, to what extent obligations may be put on patent owners to exploit ("work") an invention in the country in which the patent has been granted. The issue of importation of patented articles focuses on whether a patent owner should be required to manufacture a patented invention in the patenting country. If the patent owner chooses not to manufacture the product in the country where the patent has been granted, but rather only to import it, can the country take action on the grounds that it has been unduly deprived of the full economic benefits of the patented technology? Article 5A(1) answers that question largely in the negative, by providing as follows:

5A(1). Importation by the patentee into the country where the patent has been granted of articles manufactured in any of the countries of the Union shall not entail forfeiture of the patent.

In other words, the rights of patent owners who merely import a patented product into the patenting country may not be invalidated, revoked, repealed, or otherwise terminated, provided the product was manufactured in another Paris Convention country.

Nevertheless, the Paris Convention expressly allows member countries to take action against patent owners in the event they abuse their patent rights, in particular by failing to work, or only insufficiently working, a patented invention. The principal remedy provided by the Convention, found in Article 5A(2) is "legislative measures providing for the grant of compulsory licenses." Where compulsory licenses prove insufficient, however, Article 5A(3) permits "forfeiture or revocation of a patent" in certain circumstances.

There is no obligation to work a patented invention in the United States, thus it sometimes is difficult to understand the justification for such a requirement, even though it exists to varying degrees in most national patent laws. The requirement of working is based on the public policy consideration that to promote technological advancement, a fundamental rationale for the establishment of a patent system, the grant of patent rights should serve to introduce new inventions into the country and not to block or unduly monopolize their use. Countries should be entitled to ensure that they are able to reap the benefits of new technologies, and if a patent is being used to prevent them from doing so, they should be free to put limitations on the patent grant. In fact, the laws of only fifteen countries do not include penalties for non-working. *See* 2–8 WORLD PATENT LAW & PRACTICE § 8.01 (John P. Sinnott ed., 2012). Moreover, in most countries with working requirements, importation does not suffice to meet the requirement. *See id.* at § 8.05.

Another significant rationale for a working requirement is protection of domestic jobs and government revenue. To illustrate, when a foreign inventor from Country X obtains a patent in Country Y and supplies Y's domestic market with products imported from Country X, the result is likely to be an outflow of funds from Country Y to Country X. However, if Country Y requires patentees to "work" patented inventions in Country Y or allows for compulsory licenses in the case of non-working, more financial benefits should accrue to Country Y since the patented products will be produced domestically, not imported.

Despite these concerns, countries recognize that the requirement to work a patent cannot be without qualification. The introduction of a new invention into a country takes time and it is not feasible to introduce the invention in all countries at once. Therefore, the provisions on the grant of compulsory licenses and forfeiture in Article 5A of the Paris Convention seek to strike a balance between the interests of member countries in preventing abuses and the practical realities that patent owners must face in commercializing their inventions. Article 5A imposes a balance by introducing time limits and other constraints on the grant of a compulsory license. In accordance with Article 5A(4), a third party may not request a compulsory license for failure to work before at least four years from the date on which the patent application was filed or three years from the date on which the patent was granted, whichever date occurs later. In addition, a compulsory licensing request must be refused by the relevant Paris Convention member, at least for a period of time, if the owner of a patent that is the subject of a compulsory licensing request can justify its failure to work the invention "by legitimate reasons." Even if a license is granted, certain limitations apply. Among them are that compulsory licenses must be non-exclusive, meaning that patent owners reserve the right to grant licenses to other third parties as well as to work their inventions themselves, and the recipients of compulsory licenses may not transfer them to other third parties. In accordance with Article 5A(3), even where the grant of a compulsory license appears insufficient to resolve patent abuse, "no proceedings for the forfeiture or revocation of a patent may be instituted before the expiration of two years from the grant of the first compulsory license."

It is important to note that the limitations of Article 5A apply only to compulsory licenses for non-working or insufficient working. National legislation may, under the Paris Convention, provide for the grant of compulsory licenses on other grounds, in particular on the grounds of public health, national security, excessive pricing, or the imposition of unreasonable terms or restrictive measures, without the time limits or other constraints imposed by the Convention. The controversial role of compulsory licensing in facilitating access to public goods, including essential medicines and transfer of climate-friendly technologies, will be discussed more fully in Chapter 3.

6. FEES

Once a patent is granted, its continued maintenance is generally dependent not only on compliance with requirements to work the invention, but also on the payment of fees. Failure to pay maintenance fees, which in most countries must be paid annually, can result in the revocation of the patent. In recognition of the difficulty that international fee payments may entail, Article 5*bis* of the Convention requires member countries to allow a grace period of at least six months beyond the due date for receipt of maintenance fees, and it permits the restoration of patents that have lapsed because of non-payment. To discourage habitual late payments, however, it also permits member countries to require the payment of a surcharge in the event of late payment.

7. SPECIAL AGREEMENTS

Had the Paris Convention merely established a set of rights and obligations in the field of industrial property, it would have been a remarkable accomplishment. But the Paris Convention did more. In Article 1(1), it also established a "Union for the Protection of Industrial Property"—a single administrative entity linking all countries party to the Convention. The entity comprises three organs: (i) an Assembly (Article 13), which consists of all member countries and is responsible for policy making; (ii) an Executive Committee (Article 14), which consists of one-fourth of the member countries and is responsible for oversight and ensuring implementation of the Assembly's policies; and (iii) the International Bureau (Article 15), which is the secretariat of the Union responsible for carrying out all administrative tasks. The International Bureau was the predecessor to the World Intellectual Property Organization (WIPO).

The goal of WIPO, as expressed in the preamble to the WIPO Convention, is to "encourage creative activity, [and] promote the protection of intellectual property throughout the world." Under Article 4 of the Convention, the chief functions of WIPO include: (i) "[d]evelopment of measures designed to facilitate the efficient protection of intellectual property throughout the world and to harmonize national legislation in this field", (ii) "cooperat[ion with] States requesting legal-technical assistance in the field of intellectual property", and (iii) "conclusion of international agreements designed to promote the global protection of intellectual property." In 1974, through the initiative of the Organization's Coordination Committee, WIPO was transformed into a specialized agency of the United Nations with a mandate to administer intellectual property matters recognized by UN member states, including ongoing administration of the Paris Convention.

As the importance of intellectual property has grown, so has WIPO. It now administers a total of twenty-five treaties and has a broad program of work that seeks to:

- harmonize national intellectual property legislation and procedures;
- provide services for international applications for industrial property rights;
- exchange information about intellectual property;
- provide legal and technical assistance to developing and other countries;
- facilitate the resolution of private intellectual property disputes; and
- marshal information technology as a tool for storing, accessing, and using valuable intellectual property information.

Arguably, the WIPO Convention anticipated the growth in importance of intellectual property and provided for it, all the while preserving its own preeminent status and that of the Paris Convention, as well as other treaties administered under its auspices.

One of the most important administrative provisions of the Paris Convention is Article 19, which gives member countries the right to enter into *special agreements*, either bilaterally or multilaterally, for the protection of industrial property. Article 19 makes clear that the framers of the Paris Convention intended to give member countries freedom in legislating on patent matters not covered by the treaty itself; however, article 19 also imposes the condition that the special agreements "do not contravene the provisions of this Convention." The Patent Cooperation Treaty, discussed in the next section, is the first and one of the most important special agreements concluded in accordance with Article 19 of the Paris Convention.

NOTES AND QUESTIONS

1. Since its establishment in 1967, the institutional preeminence of WIPO in intellectual property standard-setting and administration has been the subject of significant attention from scholars, policy makers, and nongovernmental organizations. While the value of a single, expert institution has been recognized as an important aspect in the stability and consistency of the international patent system, some scholars have argued that having other international organizations more actively involved in norm-setting will enhance the quality of multilateral intellectual property governance particularly with respect to interests of concern to developing countries. According to Professor Okediji, WIPO's preeminence in intellectual property was the result of a deliberate strategy to limit the role of other international organizations whose view of intellectual property was more accountable to social and public welfare concerns. She argues that multi-institutional norm-setting is vital to effectively address issues affecting the global innovation system:

> [Today], the question of institutional choice for global IP norm development is no longer merely . . . about the role of IP in economic growth. . . . [T]he emergence of a range of new issues . . . compel a new institutional recipe for meeting the demands of a global environment . . . suffused with new forms of digitally inspired creative endeavours, cross-cultural innovation, scientific databases and the emergence of highly sophisticated research tools, all affected to some degree by the elaboration of global IP rules. Added to this rich and promising global innovation frontier are the pressing issues of public health, the risks and promise of agricultural biotechnology and the challenge of climate change. Undoubtedly, institutional coordination and collaboration will play an important role in efforts to address these critical global issues and to more precisely manage

increasingly scarce political and economic resources. Nowhere has this been more apparent than in the critical work of the World Health Organization (WHO) with respect to mobilizing efforts between WIPO, the WTO and other agencies, directed at normatively sensitive and practically oriented solutions to address global public health needs with full awareness of the IP constraints in place.

. . . WIPO's global IP norms became increasingly entrenched in an economic theory devoid of such concerns at precisely the same period in which international institutions were being consciously designed to respond to the demands and interests of developing countries and even as a robust doctrine of state accountability for the welfare of its citizens was codified through the development of international human rights law. Throughout these fundamental shifts in the international legal system, IP norms and the treaties negotiated in WIPO remained largely insulated from demands for a socially and culturally relevant normative IP framework.

Ruth L. Okediji, *WIPO-WTO Relations and the Future of Global Intellectual Property Norms*, 39 NETHERLANDS Y.B. INT'L LAW 69, 84-85 (2008).

What are the advantages of having a single international organization responsible for the international patent system? What are the disadvantages?

2. Of what practical significance is naming the inventor on a patent application as provided under Article 4*ter* of the Paris Convention? Recall from Chapter 1 the different views of the need for a global patent system and the divergent views of the U.S. and Switzerland. Which philosophical perspective is most consistent with Article 4*ter*?

3. Compulsory licenses have long been a feature of the global intellectual property system. Although they are often viewed as a controversial device to help address the interests of developing countries in having access to patented technologies, in fact, many highly industrialized countries, including Belgium, Canada, France, Japan, and Israel, have some form of compulsory license provisions in their domestic patent legislation. What justifies the use of compulsory licenses in industrialized countries? Can you think of other ways to accomplish the objectives that might cause a government to issue a compulsory license?

4. Debate over the appropriateness of compulsory licenses or patent working requirements goes to the heart of the question whether patents should be viewed as personal property rights or as instruments of public policy. In light of the prevailing view of patents as property at the conclusion of the Paris Convention, why do you think these issues remain part of the global patent system? How well do you think the Paris Convention addresses the tension between the interest in protecting an inventor's rights and safeguarding concerns of access to new technologies in developing countries? Read Article 5A carefully. What other criteria would you suggest should be added to the considerations for granting a compulsory license?

5. Assume that countries have decided to revise Article 5A with the possibility of completely eliminating compulsory licenses and proscribing national legislation that penalizes inventors for failure to work a patent. If you were a delegate to these negotiations, what arguments would you make in support of retaining a compulsory license provision in the Paris Convention?

6. In *eBay Inc. v. MercExchange, L.L.C.,* 547 U.S. 388 (2006), the US. Supreme Court ruled that patentees are not automatically entitled to injunctive relief, but instead courts must apply a multifactored test similar to other areas of law in which injunctions are an available remedy. *Id.* at 391–92. Some commentators suggest that this decision effectively establishes a de facto compulsory license in U.S. patent law. *See e.g.,* Charlene A. Stern-Dombal, *Tripping Over Trips: Is Compulsory Licensing Under eBay at Odds with US Statutory Law Requirements and TRIPS,* 41 SUFFOLK U. L. REV. 249, 261 (2007). Do you agree? If so, do you think the U.S. is in compliance with the compulsory license requirements of Article 5A? Of Article 31(b) of the TRIPS Agreement? You should revisit this question after you have covered Chapter 3.

7. Despite the successes of the Paris Convention, critics have also identified many flaws in the agreement, including: its failure to address the scope of patentable subject matter; provide a minimum patent term; place sufficient restrictions on the grant of compulsory licenses and working requirements; or provide meaningful dispute resolution. This dissatisfaction led, over time, to negotiations on other treaties, in particular the WTO TRIPS Agreement, discussed in Chapter 1, *supra,* and Chapter 3, *infra,* providing stronger, more substantive protections and enforcement provisions.

B. THE PATENT COOPERATION TREATY (PCT)

One WIPO achievement about which there is little debate is the Patent Cooperation Treaty (PCT). The PCT, a treaty concluded at the Washington Diplomatic Conference in 1970, revolutionized the international patent system by creating a unified procedure to facilitate the filing of patent applications worldwide. Under the PCT framework, an applicant can apply for patent rights in any number of PCT member countries by filing a single "international" application instead of having to file separate applications in every country in which she desires protection. Moreover, filing an international application entitles the applicant to receive a non-binding search of the prior art and a preliminary opinion on the invention's patentability, both prepared by a major patent office, as well as to have the application published by the International Bureau of WIPO. If the applicant chooses, she may also amend the application's claims and/or description before entering the national stage, which entails turning the international application into a national application in each of the countries in which the applicant wishes to pursue patent protection. At a time when the growing complexities of international trade were beginning to make a simple twelve-month Paris Convention priority right appear insufficient, the PCT provided a streamlined international system that smoothed the way for growth in global patenting activity.

The origins of the PCT date back to the mid-1960s when national patent offices first began to worry about growing numbers of patent applications and the increasing backlogs they created. At that time, patent applications both in the U.S. and abroad remained unpublished prior to grant, and very long pendencies meant that applications were kept secret for unduly long periods. When the patents did finally issue, the applicants' economic interest in their inventions had often already declined. At the same time, growth in international trade meant that applicants were seeking protection in more and more countries, and many complained that the need to file multiple applications was unnecessarily burdensome, in particular when the applications resulted in redundant patent examinations.

The drafters of the PCT set out to craft a system that would, as far as possible, resolve the growing issues of inefficiency and redundancy. Although those issues still plague the patent system today, the PCT has proven to be a great success. With a membership of 146 countries as of June 2012, it can be argued that the PCT is well established as one of the major accomplishments of the international patent system.

Success did not come immediately, however. The PCT system became operative in 1978, and that year applicants filed only about 650 international applications worldwide. Nonetheless, rapid technological innovation, increase in international trade flows, and the increasing attention to intellectual property enforcement that began in the mid-1980s and intensified in the 1990s, gave the PCT the takeoff it needed. Between 1995 and 2001, the filing of PCT applications grew by about 18 percent annually. The year 2001 marked the first one in which more than 100,000 PCT applications were filed. By the end of 2011, that number had grown to 182,354, representing an 11 percent increase over 2010. *See* WIPO, World Intellectual Property Indicators, 62 (2012).

FIGURE 1

PCT FILING ACTIVITY: 1990–2011

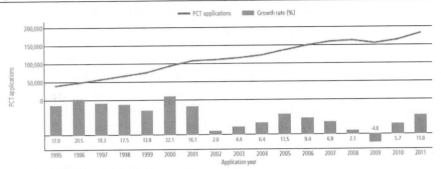

Figure A.5.1.1 Trend in PCT applications

Note: Data refer to the international phase of the PCT system. Counts are based on the international application date.

Source: WIPO Statistics Database, October 2012

1. THE PCT FRAMEWORK

Despite its stated objective to "simplify and render more economical the obtaining of protection for inventions where protection is sought in several countries," the PCT system in fact features a dense and complicated regulatory framework that is anything but simple. The system comprises not only the PCT itself, but also a complex and often amended set of Regulations that add specificity to the Treaty's provisions, and Administrative Instructions that direct the technical interactions among national patent offices and WIPO. In addition, a set of bilateral agreements regulates relations between WIPO and the national and regional offices that serve as the PCT International Searching and Preliminary Examining Authorities, and International Search and Preliminary Examination Guidelines govern the manner in which those offices are to perform their functions. Finally, PCT Receiving Office Guidelines define the functions and responsibilities of national patent offices to receive, validate, and accord a filing date to PCT applications.

The complexity of the PCT framework is driven, at least in part, by one of the system's most noteworthy features—the sharing of responsibilities between national patent offices and WIPO. Under the PCT, a national office may carry out three separate functions, each of which is central to the system, while WIPO serves as the system's hub.

a. Receiving Offices

Article 10 of the PCT provides: "The international application shall be filed with the prescribed receiving Office, which will check and process it as provided in this Treaty and the Regulations." Almost all national patent/industrial property offices act as "PCT Receiving Offices," which are an applicant's primary line of contact with the PCT system. The role of receiving offices is to serve as the locus for the filing of PCT applications and to ensure that the applications comply with the Treaty's procedural requirements. Receiving offices verify that applications have been validly filed and contain the necessary supporting data, ensure that applications comprise at least a claim and a description (the minimum requirements for meeting the definition of an application under Article 11 of the PCT), and accept the payment of fees. If applications meet the Treaty's formal requirements, receiving offices grant them an international filing date and communicate the application documents to international authorities (discussed below) and to WIPO. If applications fail to meet the minimum requirements, receiving offices notify applicants and invite them to make the necessary corrections.

Almost all international applications claim priority under the Paris Convention to an earlier-filed national application. A recent amendment to Rule 26*bis* of the PCT Regulations has added a new responsibility to the role of receiving offices in cases in which applicants fail to file international applications within the twelve-month priority period. Under new Rule 26*bis*.3, receiving offices now have the authority to restore the right of priority. Two conditions govern this new rule: the request to restore priority must be filed within two months of the end of the priority period; and, depending upon each receiving office's procedures, the request must assert that the failure to file on time either was unintentional or took place despite the exercise of all due care. As the *Scimed* and *Edwards Lifesciences* cases above point out, however, the question of whether a PCT application has successfully claimed priority is ultimately a decision for the national courts of the country in which the ensuing patent is being litigated.

b. International Searching Authorities

In addition to serving as receiving offices, several experienced patent offices serve as "International Searching Authorities" pursuant to Article 16 of the PCT. Article 15 of the Treaty provides that "each international application shall be the subject of international search," and it is the responsibility of the international authorities to carry out patent searches to discover the relevant prior art, to establish an International Search Report for each application, to examine applications and any subsequent amendments that applicants may make, and to prepare an opinion and preliminary report on patentability for each application. There are currently seventeen international authorities: the national patent offices of Australia, Austria, Brazil, Canada, China, Egypt, Finland, India, Israel, Japan, the Republic of Korea, the Russian Federation, Spain, Sweden, and the United States; the European Patent Office (EPO); and the Nordic Patent Authority, which is a consortium of the patent offices of Denmark, Iceland, and Norway.

Brazil, Egypt, India, and Israel are the newest members of this exclusive club. In accordance with Article 16(3) of the PCT, and as was the case with all the authorities, the countries' proposals to be appointed as international authorities were discussed and adopted by the PCT member countries at the annual meeting of the PCT Assembly, the PCT's governing body. Article 16(3) also provides that to be approved as an international authority, a national office or intergovernmental organization is required to satisfy the minimum requirements laid down in the PCT Regulations. Under Rule 36.1 of the Regulations, an international authority must:

(i)   Employ at least one-hundred full-time staff with sufficient technical qualifications;

(ii)   Possess or have access to the prescribed minimum documentation required to carry out proper international searches;

(iii)   Have a staff capable of searching the required technical fields and with language capacity to understand at least those languages in which the prescribed minimum documentation is written or translated; and

(iv)   Have in place a quality management system and appropriate internal review arrangements.

c. Designated Offices

The third function of patent offices within the PCT system is to serve as "Designated Offices." The role of a designated office is, with only few exceptions, identical to the traditional role of a national patent office. A designated office's responsibilities begin when the PCT system's international phase ends. When an international application enters the national phase—or national stage—before a particular patent office, it is treated as a national application. The role of a designated office is to process the application in accordance with local patent procedure and, on the basis of national law, either reject the application or grant a patent.

d. The International Bureau

The role of the International Bureau of WIPO is to serve as the administrator and secretariat of the PCT system. WIPO is the guardian and publisher of all PCT applications filed worldwide, and it serves as the coordinator of the PCT system among offices and authorities. It convenes and organizes meetings at which PCT issues are discussed and amendments to the PCT Regulations adopted, offers assistance to current and potential PCT member countries, publishes information about the system, and provides advice and training to PCT applicants.

WIPO also has an important translation function. Under Rule 48.3 of the PCT Regulations, applications may be filed for publication in any of the PCT system's ten official languages: Arabic, Chinese, English, French, German, Japanese, Korean, Portuguese, Russian, and Spanish. For the purpose of uniformity, however, English and French serve as the system's anchor languages. WIPO therefore maintains a large team of translators who produce English and/or French translations of all abstracts, titles of inventions, and text matter in drawings of applications filed in PCT languages other than English or French, and English translations of all international search reports and preliminary reports on patentability not established in English.

In addition, WIPO maintains its own receiving office—currently the sixth largest worldwide—where applicants from any PCT country can file applications in any language. When applicants file in non-official languages, PCT Rule 12.3 gives them a one-month period to translate their application into a language acceptable for international search and publication.

———————

NOTES AND QUESTIONS

1. Can you think of any benefits a country might gain when its national office serves as an ISA under the PCT system? Consider the following observation of the aspirations of a new ISA, the Brazilian Patent Office (NIIP):

> NIIP is working hard to make itself the trusted office in South America. . . . In NIIP's eyes the only way to create a stable patent regime in South America is to build a regional network and then link that regional network to the international network of ISAs that will administer the system globally. NIIP's organizational goal is to become the trusted regional node and interface between the global and regional systems. Few other offices in South America are in a position to take on this role because, amongst other things, it requires a government to invest in building up a patent office to the level of an ISA.

PETER DRAHOS, THE GLOBAL GOVERNANCE OF KNOWLEDGE: PATENT OFFICES AND THEIR CLIENTS 254 (2010).

Joining the PCT system may have negative repercussions for a developing country? Professor Drahos contrasts Vietnam, which joined the PCT in 1993 and saw a sharp increase in patent applications, particularly pharmaceutical patent applications, with Cambodia, a country that has not yet joined the PCT:

> Both Cambodia and Vietnam have become integrated into the international patent treaty framework with one critical difference. Cambodia is not yet a member of the PCT. It does have a patent office that accepts applications, but the number of applications is very low [13 in 2007, compared to over 12,000 in Vietnam in 2004]. The

lesson is fairly clear. Developing countries that want to avoid truck-loads of patents showing up on the doorstep of their patent office, because, for instance, they fear the effects of pharmaceutical patent-ing, should not join the PCT or delay for as long as possible.

Id. at 270.

2. Are the national policy benefits associated with the PCT system suffi-cient reason to encourage developing and least-developed countries to estab-lish national patent offices with functioning receiving offices and a corps of patent examiners? Why or why not? What if a country had little or no patent activity and few, if any, trained patent agents? For an argument that estab-lishing patent offices can induce innovation in developing countries, *see* Tade O. Okediji & Ruth L. Okediji, *Patents and Innovation in Colonial India: Evi-dence from 1763–1893* (manuscript 000124, University of Minnesota mimeo Series, 2009–2010).

3. What drawbacks might there be in having the global patent admin-istration system so heavily dependent on local office patent practices? How might any such weaknesses be corrected in the PCT? Examine carefully Ta-ble 1 below, which shows the top fifteen countries where applicants filed the most PCT applications in 2010. Why do you think the PCT has been so suc-cessful in industrialized countries? Note that since 2010, Asia is the biggest PCT filing region with 38.8 percent of total applications in 2011. Most of the Asian filings originated from East Asia (Japan, China and South Korea). Within Asia, the strongest growth came from China (+35.3 percent), which is now the fourth biggest PCT filing country worldwide. South Korea and Japan also experienced substantial growth, while PCT filings in European countries largely declined and the U.S., whose filers remained the biggest users of the PCT system, saw an increase in filings of 9.2 percent. *See* WIPO, PCT YEARLY REVIEW: THE INTERNATIONAL PATENT SYSTEM (2012), *available at* http://www. wipo.int/export/sites/www/freepublications/en/patents/901/wipo_pub_901_ 2012.pdf. Do you think there is a link between the number of filings and the economic growth countries are experiencing?

4. In 2009, the PCT experienced its first annual decrease in filings since the system's creation. According to WIPO, international patent filings fell by 4.5 percent. This decrease was not as low as had been earlier predicted, and the rate of international filings actually increased in several East Asian countries but declined sharply in leading industrialized countries including the U.S. (11.4 percent) and Germany (11.2 percent). *See* WIPO, Press Re-lease, International Patent Filings Dip in 2009 amid Global Economic Down-turn, WIPO Doc. PR/2010/632 (Feb.8,2010), *available at* http://www.wipo.int/ pressroom/en/articles/2010/article_0003.html. By 2011, however, the number of PCT filings had rebounded to a new high of 182,354, an 11 percent increase over 2010 filings. Are there any conclusions that should be drawn between global patent filings and economic activity?

TABLE 1

PCT APPLICATION FILINGS BY OFFICE 2011

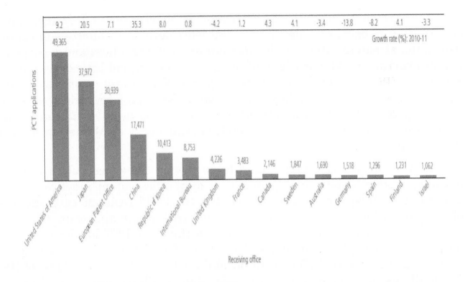

Figure A.1.2: PCT applications at top 15 receiving offices, 2011

Note: The figures given for PCT applications filed in 2011 are WIPO estimates.

Source: WIPO Statistics Database, March 2012

2. THE PCT PROCEDURE

The PCT procedure consists of two "stages" (as they are referred to in the U.S.) or two "phases" (as they are referred to in the rest of the world): international, and national. Each comprises several steps, which are discussed below.

a. The International Stage

The international stage, which constitutes the heart of the PCT scheme, is a centralized procedure consisting of four main steps: (i) the filing of an international application and its initial processing; (ii) the preparation of an international search report and written opinion on patentability; (iii) the publication of the application; and (iv) an international preliminary examination of the application.

(i) Filing a PCT Application

In accordance with PCT Article 11, the filing of an international application has the effect of a "regular national filing" in each of the PCT member countries. In other words, a PCT application must be regarded, at least initially, as if it were a national application filed in every PCT member country. To meet the requirements of Article 11, only two basic conditions must be met. The first is that an applicant (only one if several applicants file jointly) must be a national or resident of a PCT member country. The second is that the application must contain four essential elements: A part that appears to be a description of the invention; a part that appears to be a claim; the applicant's name and nationality or residence; and an indication that the application is being filed under the PCT.

Applicants generally file international applications with their own national receiving offices. They may also file (as mentioned above) directly with WIPO's own receiving office; however, in the case of U.S. applicants and those from a few other countries with security regulations in place, the ability to file directly with WIPO is conditioned upon first obtaining a foreign filing license from the national patent office.

PCT Article 8 and Rule 4.10 of the PCT Regulations expressly provide that PCT applications may claim the priority of one or more Paris Convention priority applications. In practice, almost all PCT applications are subsequent filings that benefit from the filing date of the earliest-filed priority application. It is for that reason that the PCT timeline (see Figure 2 below) begins with the filing of a priority application, and dates and deadlines throughout the PCT procedure are generally calculated from the priority filing date.

FIGURE 2

The PCT System

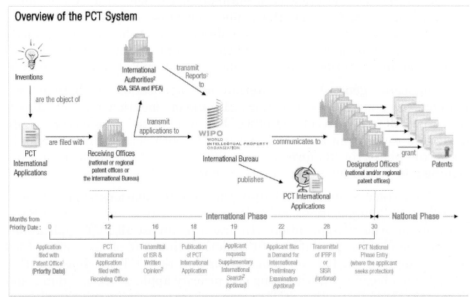

(ii) International Search

Article 15 of the PCT mandates that every international application shall be the subject of an international search, carried out by an International Authority chosen by the applicant from among the authorities designated by the receiving office. Currently, U.S. applicants can choose the United States Patent and Trademark Office (USPTO), the Australian Patent Office (IP Australia), the European Patent Office, the Korean Intellectual Property Office, or the Russian Patent Office (Rospatent) as a searching authority. In making the choice, applicants often consider factors such as thoroughness of search (e.g., the European Patent Office has the reputation of being especially thorough), cost (e.g., the Korean Office is the least expensive without seeming to sacrifice quality), subject matter of the invention (e.g., Australia limits the technical scope of searches it performs; only the USPTO searches inventions concerning surgical methods), or geographical region where the invention is going to be most heavily exploited.

The objective of the international search is to discover "relevant prior art," which Rule 33.1(a) defines as:

[E]verything which has been made available to the public anywhere in the world by means of written disclosure (including
drawing and other illustrations) and which is capable of being of
assistance in determining that the claimed invention is or is not
new and that it does or does not involve an inventive step (i.e.,
that it is or is not obvious), provided that the making available to
the public occurred prior to the international filing date.

Given the enormous amount of prior art in the world, it is not surprising that the PCT limited itself to written disclosures and excluded
oral ones. However, many countries, including most of Europe, Japan,
Argentina, Brazil, Canada, India, Republic of Korea, and Russia, provide
that oral disclosures, even those made outside the country, also constitute
prior art. It is clear, therefore, that the international search may leave
relevant disclosures uncovered. Another limitation concerns the scope of
the search. Although the PCT defines prior art as extending to "anywhere
in the world," practical realities dictate that international authorities restrict their searches geographically. Accordingly, Rule 34 of the PCT Regulations permits authorities to focus their searches on the PCT "minimum
documentation," which includes patent documents and technical literature from major industrialized countries.

The international search is carried out by a patent examiner in accordance with detailed International Search and Preliminary Examination Guidelines. The Guidelines resemble national practice manuals and
were agreed upon, after lengthy discussion, by all the international authorities. The international search is a unilateral process with no additional input from the applicant or opportunity to intervene. The search
results in the issuance, by the examiner, of an international search report
and a written opinion on the patentability of the invention claimed in the
international application.

a. International Search Report

An international search report consists mainly of a listing of references to published patents and technical journal articles that might have
a bearing on the invention's novelty or inventive step (non-obviousness).
For each reference cited, the report contains an indication of the extent to
which the document is merely relevant to patentability, or whether it in
fact discloses the invention in whole or in part. The report may also contain observations concerning the requirement of unity of invention. Rule
13.1 of the PCT Regulations requires that an application relate "to one
invention only or to a group of inventions so linked as to form a single
general inventive concept." If in the opinion of the patent examiner an
application relates to more than one invention or inventive concept, the
examiner will search only the first claimed invention unless the applicant
pays additional fees.

The written opinion on patentability, which issues together with the search report, is the examiner's non-binding view on whether the invention appears to be patentable in light of the results of the international search. The written opinion is intended to be helpful not only to applicants, but also to designated offices, particularly in those countries that make patenting decisions largely on the basis of the search report.

The principal value of the international search process is to help applicants evaluate their chances of obtaining patents in PCT member countries, and to provide an opportunity to remedy flawed applications. A favorable international search report and written opinion, in which the documents cited do not raise issues of patent-destroying prior art, tends to indicate a strong patent application with a good chance of speedy grant in the national stage. If, on the other hand, the search report and written opinion are unfavorable, PCT Article 19 permits applicants to amend their claims in order to distinguish their inventions from the prior art cited in the search report. Because Article 19 prohibits the amended claims from going beyond the disclosure of the invention as contained in the originally filed application, amendments filed under Article 19 tend to narrow or limit the scope of the claimed invention. In cases where the search report and written opinion reveal that the invention is simply not patentable, regardless of any amendments that the applicant may file, applicants may choose to abandon the application and thereby save the time, effort, and money that entering national stage would require, or they may opt to ensure the invention's continued confidentiality by withdrawing the application prior to publication.

b. Supplementary Search

Among the latest additions to the PCT is the establishment of a system of supplementary international search. Supplementary search is based on the notion that in today's globalized, highly technological world, a single international search of the prior art may not always be sufficient. For example, an applicant hoping to market her invention in several regions of the world may wish a more complete overview of the prior art than one international searching authority can provide. This may especially be the case if the applicant believes that prior art documents in a language that the designated authority lacks capacity to search thoroughly (for example, the USPTO searching Russian-language patent documents) may have special relevance to her patent application.

The supplementary international search system, which is embodied in new Rule 45*bis* of the PCT Regulations, gives applicants the option to request one or more additional searches, in addition to the main international search, to be carried out by international searching authorities other than the authority carrying out the main search. Depending upon how it wishes to carry out its obligations, the supplementary searching authority is free to undertake a new, complete search or to limit itself to a top-up search, filling in the gaps left by the main international authority. As of June 2011, Austria, the European Patent Office, Finland, the Nordic Patent Institute, Russia, and Sweden had signed on as supplementary authorities, while the other international searching authorities indicated a lack of current interest in assuming the additional responsibilities. Whether PCT applicants will embrace supplementary international search as a useful and effective tool will remain an open question for some time to come.

(iii) International Publication

WIPO publishes all international applications and international search reports shortly after the expiration of eighteen months from the priority date. The publication takes two forms: the full text of the application and search report; and an abbreviated format that includes basic bibliographic data about the applicant and inventor, the title of the invention, an abstract providing a brief overview of the invention, and a representative drawing of the invention. The priority application on which the international application is based, the written opinion on patentability, a limited list of the countries in which the applicant has entered the national stage, and any additional documentation and correspondence are also subsequently made available on the publication website.

The date of publication constitutes the date on which PCT applications become part of the prior art for purposes of an international search. International publication may also have the effect of national publication, particularly with respect to providing provisional protection for inventions, although such national effect is frequently accorded only in the case of applications published in the country's official language. Published international applications (indeed, all published patent applications) contain a wealth of scientific and technical information. An application's bibliographic data, description, and claims provide unparalleled insight into the research activities and the state of the art of competitors. They serve as catalysts for technology transfer and as the starting point for the development of new technologies. They may often also provide a sound basis for making investment decisions.

(iv) International Preliminary Examination

The fourth and final step in the international stage is an optional one, currently used by only a small minority of applicants. International preliminary examination is a second evaluation of the potential patentability of an invention. It is based largely on the international search report, and the examiner applies the same standards as those on which the written opinion on patentability was established. The purpose of international preliminary examination is to give applicants a second chance. If applicants wish not only to amend their claims, but also to amend the description and/or application drawings in order to overcome defects cited in the international search report or written opinion, or if they wish to take issue with the opinion's conclusions, international preliminary examination provides the means to do so. The opportunity to amend the claims, description, and/or drawings during the international preliminary examination procedure is provided for in Article 34 of the PCT. It entitles applicants to participate actively in the examination process by submitting arguments in response to the international search and by having an interview or dialogue with the examiner. At the end of the process, the examiner issues an international preliminary examination report, titled International Preliminary Report on Patentability, which may contain the examiner's views on whether the amendments overcome the cited defects in the application, or whether the applicant's arguments rebut the issues raised in the written opinion, and therefore on whether, in the examiner's nonbinding opinion, the claimed invention is patentable.

Prior to April 2002, requests for preliminary examination were routinely filed by applicants, not so much because of interest in the examination results, but rather as a way to extend the time within which an applicant had to enter the national phase from twenty to thirty months. Amendments to the PCT now allow an applicant to obtain the full thirty months without requesting an IPRP, thereby avoiding unnecessary work on the part of the examining authority.

International preliminary examination provides the only opportunity that applicants have in the international stage to influence an examiner's findings. Those findings are final, however, as an international preliminary report on patentability is not subject to appeal. For that reason, as well as for the fact that the same amendments and arguments can usually be made before each national office in the national stage, roughly only about 10 percent of PCT applicants avail themselves of the international preliminary examination procedure.

b.   The National Stage

Applicants enter the national stage by pursuing their applications in the national patent offices of the PCT countries in which they desire protection. As illustrated in the *Scimed* case, Chapter 2 A. *supra*, once an application enters the national stage, national law governs the substantive conditions of patentability, and the decision to grant or refuse a patent remains solely within the jurisdiction of each office. The national stage thus reflects the fact that the PCT is an application filing system, not a patent issuing one. The most compelling advantage for using the PCT is that applicants need not enter the national stage until the end of the thirtieth month from the priority filing date (with some countries permitting entry at the end of the thirty-first month), or at least eighteen months later than the twelve-month priority period provided by the Paris Convention. Moreover, the entry requirements are minimal; they usually consist of hiring a local patent attorney, paying fees, and in some cases filing a translation of the application in the national language or submitting powers of attorney. WIPO supplies the application file, including the published version of the application, the international search report, any amendments that have been filed, the written opinion or international preliminary report on patentability, and a copy of the priority patent application.

The additional 18 months afforded to enter the national phase allow applicants to defer national patent filing costs, and give them more time to evaluate their inventions and carefully select the countries in which to seek protection. That selection is one of the most crucial decisions applicants have to make. Factors that applicants tend to consider include identifying where the invention is likely to be manufactured, sold or licensed, where competitors are likely to operate, where related research and development efforts are centered, where future investments are likely to be found, and where patent enforcement is likely to be effective. Since the life of a patent is twenty years from the date of filing, applicants cannot afford to adopt short-term views in making national stage entry decisions. In particular, failure to carefully observe the procedural requirements of national laws could have important ramifications.

Like *Scimed,* the following case illustrates that, interpretation of the enabling provisions for PCT obligations in U.S. law is squarely within the province of the courts.

ARISTOCRAT TECHS. AUSTL. PTY V. INT'L GAME TECH.

United States Court of Appeals, Federal Circuit

543 F.3d 657 (Fed. Cir. 2008)

■ LINN, Circuit Judge:

I. BACKGROUND

Aristocrat Technologies Australia Pty, Ltd. and Aristocrat Technologies, Inc. (collectively, "Aristocrat") compete with International Game Technology and IGT (collectively, "IGT") in the market for electronic gaming machines. Aristocrat is the assignee of U.S. Patent Nos. 7,056,215 ("the '215 patent") and 7,108,603 ("the '603 patent"), both of which relate to a "slot machine game and system with improved jack-pot feature." Prosecution of these patents began in Australia, when, starting on July 8, 1997, Aristocrat filed two provisional patent applications directed to the inventions embodied in the patents-in-suit. One year later, Aristocrat filed a Patent Cooperation Treaty application ("the PCT application") in Australia, claiming priority to the previously filed provisional applications. The PCT application was subsequently published. Pursuant to 35 U.S.C. § 371 and 37 C.F.R. § 1.495, Aristocrat was required to pay the fee for the U.S. national stage of the PCT application by January 10, 2000—

thirty months after the filing date of the first Australian provisional application.

The U.S. Patent and Trademark Office ("PTO") did not receive Aristocrat's national filing fee until January 11, 2000—one day late. The PTO consequently mailed a notice of abandonment to Aristocrat, which stated, among other things, that Aristocrat "may wish to consider filing a petition to the Commissioner under 37 CFR 1.137(a) or (b) requesting that the application be revived." J.A. at 642. In lieu of filing a petition to revive the abandoned application, Aristocrat responded by filing a Petition to Correct the Date-In-that is, to correct the date on which the PTO received its national filing fee. The PTO denied the petition without prejudice, after Aristocrat failed to provide sufficient evidence to corroborate the date the filing fee was mailed. It is unclear when Aristocrat received the PTO's denial, but it later filed a petition to revive the '215 patent application under 37 C.F.R. § 1.137(b), claiming that the delay in paying the national stage filing fee was "unintentional." *Id.* at 660–61. The PTO granted the petition to revive on September 3, 2002. . . . Following the PTO's revival, Aristocrat resumed prosecution of the '215 patent application, and later filed the '603 patent application as a continuation of the '215 patent application. The '215 patent issued on June 6, 2006, and the '603 patent issued on September 19, 2006.

In June 2006, Aristocrat filed suit against IGT for infringement of the '215 patent in the United States District Court for the Northern District of California. Aristocrat amended its complaint to assert infringement of the '603 patent when that patent issued. IGT answered and subsequently moved for summary judgment of invalidity. It argued that the '215 patent was invalid because, after it was abandoned, Aristocrat was required to show that its delay was "unavoidable" in order to revive the application, not merely that its delay was "unintentional." Thus, according to IGT, the PTO "improperly revived" the '215 patent application by requiring Aristocrat only to show "unintentional delay." IGT also argued that the '603 patent was invalid, contending that since the '215 patent application was not lawfully revived, it constituted prior art to, and thus anticipated, the '603 patent under 35 U.S.C. § 102(b).

The district court granted IGT's motion. It first concluded that the Patent Act permitted revival of an abandoned patent application only upon a showing of "unavoidable delay." *Aristocrat Techs. Austl. Pty, Ltd. v. Int'l Game Tech.*, 491 F. Supp.2d 916, 924–29 (N.D. Cal. 2007). Next, the district court found that IGT was permitted, pursuant to 35 U.S.C. § 282, to raise the PTO's alleged improper revival as a defense to infringement. The district court also concluded, alternatively, that it possessed authority to review the PTO's revival of the '215 patent application under the Administrative Procedure Act, 5 U.S.C. § 701 *et seq.* ("APA"). After concluding that Aristocrat abandoned the '215 patent application and failed to meet the more exacting "unavoidable delay" standard when attempting to revive it, the district court deemed the '215 patent invalid. Finally, the district court also deemed the '603 patent invalid, under the rationale that if the '215 patent application was not properly revived, then it constituted invalidating prior art under 35 U.S.C. § 102(b). Following its grant of summary judgment, the district court entered final judgment in favor of IGT. . . .

Aristocrat timely appealed. . . .

II. DISCUSSION

. . . .

B. Analysis

1. *The '215 Patent*

The threshold issue in this appeal is whether "improper revival" may be raised as an invalidity defense in an action involving the infringement or validity of a patent. The district court, relying on 35 U.S.C. §§ 282(2) and (4), decided that question affirmatively. The district court also found that the APA provided a separate basis upon which to review the PTO's revival of the '215 patent. We conclude that "improper revival" may not be raised as a defense in an action involving the validity or infringement of a patent.

Section 282 of title 35 provides a catalog of defenses available in an action involving the validity or infringement of a patent:

(1) Noninfringement, absence of liability for infringement or unenforceability,

(2) Invalidity of the patent or any claim in suit on any ground specified in part II of this title as a condition for patentability,

(3) Invalidity of the patent or any claim in suit for failure to comply with any requirement of sections 112 or 251 of this title,

(4) Any other fact or act made a defense by this title.

The first and third enumerated categories are not asserted by IGT as bases for its invalidity defense. At issue are the second and fourth. We discuss each in turn.

Section 282(2) authorizes an invalidity defense based "on any ground specified in part II of this title as a condition for patentability." A defense falling under this section thus has two prerequisites: it must fall within part II of title 35 and it must be a "condition for patentability." The district court determined that "[b]ecause Section 133's six-month deadline for prosecuting an application is specified within part II of Title 35, it necessarily provides an available defense where a patentee has abandoned, and failed to lawfully revive, a patent application." *Aristocrat*, 491 F. Supp.2d at 930. What the district court failed to address, however, is whether the proper revival of an abandoned application is a "condition for patentability."

. . . .

While there are most certainly other factors that bear on the validity or the enforceability of a patent, utility and eligibility, novelty, and non-obviousness are the only so-called conditions for patentability. For example, section 112 unquestionably provides certain additional requirements for a patent to be valid, one of which, for instance, is that the patented invention be enabled by the specification. 35 U.S.C. § 112, 1. But the requirements in section 112 are not conditions for patentability; they are merely requirements for obtaining a valid patent. Indeed, section 282 itself draws a distinction between invalidity based "on any ground specified in part II of this title as a condition for patentability," 35 U.S.C. § 282(2), and invalidity "for failure to comply with any requirement of sections 112 or 251," 35 U.S.C. § 282(3). *See Sextant Avionique, S.A. v. Analog Devices, Inc.,* 172 F.3d 817, 829 (Fed. Cir. 1999). Section 282(3), relating to invalidity under section 112, would be redundant if the requirements in section 112 were conditions for patentability because, if so, that defense would fall within the boundaries of section 282(2). Section 282(2), by virtue of its applicability to "condition[s] for patentability," relates only to defenses of invalidity for lack of utility and eligibility, novelty, and non-obviousness, and does not encompass a defense based upon the alleged improper revival of a patent application.

. . . .

The salient question, . . . is whether improper revival is "made a defense" by title 35. We think that it is not. Congress made it clear in various provisions of the statute when it intended to create a defense of invalidity or noninfringement, but indicated no such intention in the statutes pertaining to revival of abandoned applications. . . . What is important . . . is simply that sections 133 and 371, relied upon by IGT, provide none of the signals that Congress has given in other circumstances to indicate that these sections provide a defense to an accused infringer. Rather, these provisions merely spell out under what circumstances a patent application is deemed abandoned during prosecution and under what circumstances it may be revived. . . . Because the proper revival of an abandoned application is neither a fact or act made a defense by title 35 nor a ground specified in part II of title 35 as a condition for patentability, we hold that improper revival may not be asserted as a defense in an action involving the validity or infringement of a patent.

. . . .

. . . There is good reason not to permit procedural irregularities during prosecution, such as the one at issue here, to provide a basis for invalidity. Once a patent has issued, the procedural minutiae of prosecution have little relevance to the metes and bounds of the patentee's right to exclude. If any prosecution irregularity or procedural lapse, however minor, became grist for a later assertion of invalidity, accused infringers would inundate the courts with arguments relating to every minor transgression they could comb from the file wrapper. This deluge would only detract focus from the important legal issues to be resolved-primarily, infringement and invalidity. . . .

. . . .

III. CONCLUSION

For the reasons discussed above, we reverse the district court's grant of summary judgment and remand for proceedings consistent with this opinion.

―――――――

NOTES AND QUESTIONS

1. Do you agree that "procedural irregularities" should not provide a basis to defend a patent against claims of infringement? If such irregularities have the effect of being more burdensome on foreign patent applicants, would this constitute a violation of the national treatment rule?

2. In *Exela PharmaSciences, LLC v. Kappos,* 2012 WL 3638552 (2012), the district court approved a different strategy for patent infringement defendants to challenge the improper revival of a patent later asserted against them. The court denied a motion by the USPTO to dismiss a declaratory judgment action against the USPTO for issuing the patent. Thus, improper revival may not be raised as a defense to infringement, but may be the basis of a separate action against the USPTO. However, on December 6, 2012, the Federal Circuit held in a different case, *Pregis Corporation v. Kappos,* 2012 WL 6051956, that a competitor who has been sued as an infringer cannot lodge an Administrative Procedure Act (APA) challenge against the USPTO's issuance of a patent. Consequently, this issue is likely to be the subject of a petition for certiorari to the U.S. Supreme Court in the future.

3. Should it be the sole province of a patent examiner to decide whether a specific deviation from an established process incorporating international obligations into national law is sufficient to cause a foreign applicant to lose rights to her patent under domestic law? In what ways can the international patent system be used to constrain the potential discriminatory exercise of discretion by patent offices? In an important article analyzing 150 years of the practices of patent offices, Professor Lerner concludes that the flexibility accorded to patent offices in wealthier countries is often restricted. Further, in common law countries, responsibility for deciding issues of patentability is evenly divided between patent offices and the court. Civil law countries, on the other hand, rely primarily on the courts to determine issues of validity

and the discretion of the patent office is significantly limited. *See* Josh Lerner, *150 Years of Patent Office Practice*, 7 AM. L. & ECON. REV. 112 (2005).

4. The *Aristocrat* court states that "the requirements in section 112 are not conditions for patentability; they are merely requirements for obtaining a valid patent." Do you agree? What is the basis for this distinction? Is such a distinction cognizable under the TRIPS Agreement?

5. ABC Corp., a mid-sized manufacturing company located in Portland, Oregon, has acquired several U.S. patents but has never sought foreign patent protection. It has just created a new, innovative product line that it believes has international market potential. As a result, it has begun thinking about acquiring foreign patents and developing an international patent filing strategy. What strategic considerations should the company keep in mind?

6. A simple and effective way for a company to start thinking about international patenting is to ask key questions about the relevant technology, business, and potential countries of foreign filing. The goal of any international filing strategy is to gain the greatest competitive impact from the fewest patents, since filing in either too many or too few countries can prove costly. What are some of the specific questions that a company should ask?

7. As companies consider issues such as what is the technology's potential return on investment, where might licensing be desired, or where the business' distribution networks are best located, it needs to focus on more than just its present situation. Given the limited term of a patent, these considerations should also reflect the company's long-term plans and objectives as well as the foreign filing countries' future market and intellectual property prospects. Whenever the answers indicate that it would be beneficial for the company to maintain patent prosecution flexibility, keep its filing options open, or defer large-scale costs in exchange for paying a relatively small up-front fee (which is practically always the case), the company should consider using the PCT.

8. A sound patent filing strategy also strives to minimize costs while maximizing impact during the life of a patent. One of the most effective tactics a company can adopt is to abandon any patent that is no longer viable. In most countries, the amount of periodic maintenance fees that a company must pay to keep a patent in force increases as the patent ages. It is typical, in fact, for 75 percent of the total fee to fall due in the patent's final ten years of life. Abandoning a patent that no longer adds value to a company's business not only saves money, it also provides a valuable revenue source for filing new applications. The same can be said for PCT applications. Where an international search report and written opinion predict little likelihood that an invention can be patented, abandoning the application simply by never entering the national stage can save a company a great deal of time, effort, and money. Since the invention was disclosed when the application was published, which makes the invention part of the prior art, the company can also be assured that no one else can patent it.

9. The cost of filing a PCT application is considerable. Applicants must pay a transmittal fee to the receiving office, an international filing fee to the International Bureau of WIPO, and an international search fee to the international searching authority. Depending primarily on the choice of searching authority, and because each authority gets to set its own fee, the application filing fee can range from as little as $2,008 to more than $4,203, based on June 2011 fee rates.

3. THE IMPACT OF THE PCT

The PCT system has had an impact not only on international patent filing, but also on the development of patent practice and procedure worldwide. A growing number of countries, including Singapore and Israel, make patent grant decisions at least in part on the basis of positive international search reports and written opinions. Similarly, Egypt, along with a number of other emerging economies, has looked to the PCT International Search and Examination Guidelines as the model for their own national search procedures. Furthermore, the aspirations of some countries, such as India and Brazil, to serve as PCT international authorities have led those countries to focus enhanced attention toward improving the quality and efficiency of their national offices and examining corps.

The PCT has also played a role in the harmonization of patent practice. For example, the PCT criteria for unity of invention as relating to "one invention only or a group of inventions so linked as to form a single general inventive concept" has been adopted by many national offices in their national practice. Even the USPTO applies the unity of invention concept when it acts in a PCT capacity, including as a designated office during the national stage, despite its adherence to the alternative notion of "restriction practice" for U.S. national applications. Under restriction practice, "[i]f two or more independent and distinct inventions are claimed in one application," the applicant may be required to restrict the application to one invention only. *See* 35 U.S.C. § 121 (2006). Unity of invention and restriction practice are discussed in more detail in Chapter 9.

Perhaps the PCT's greatest impact stems from the fact that a system composed of more than 140 countries and more than one-hundred patent offices that are all required to perform PCT functions can operate smoothly and continue to gain momentum. It is difficult to determine whether the PCT is flourishing despite great diversity in legal, linguistic, and national practice cultures, or because of it. The PCT's strength may well lie in the balance it has struck between achieving harmonized procedures and accommodating peculiarities in national law and practice. How that balance evolves over time could determine the PCT's future.

NOTES AND QUESTIONS

1. Starting around the year 2000, WIPO spearheaded a process to reform the PCT Regulations. Among the last reforms adopted were a series of provisions to provide safeguards for applicants in the event they made errors in the PCT filing process. Since most errors concern either missed deadlines or clerical mistakes in applications, the safeguard reform efforts focused on those two areas. Among the deadlines that applicants tend to miss, the two most crucial are the twelve-month priority filing date and the national phase entry date. The PCT now permits a two month grace period for both, although many limitations and restrictions apply. In order to benefit from the grace period, applicants need to establish—depending upon the country concerned—that their failure to meet the deadline was either unintentional or that it happened despite their exercise of all due care. Unfortunately for applicants, not all countries have adopted these safeguards.

With respect to the provisions concerning reinstatement of a missed priority date, *see* PCT Rules 26*bis*.3 and 49*ter*. With respect to the provisions concerning reinstating of rights following a missed national phase entry date, *see* PCT Rule 49.6.

2. The new PCT Regulations often contradict provisions of national law; countries have therefore been free to opt out of the new rules, at least until such time as they can amend their national legislation to conform to the new requirements. Why should countries not be automatically bound by PCT Regulations just as citizens are by agency regulations?

3. A second recently adopted safeguard effort attempts to reconcile the fact that applicants frequently file patent applications at the last moment and under great pressure. As a result, they sometimes submit applications with sentences, paragraphs, or whole portions missing, or with clerical errors that a trained eye would recognize as an obvious mistake. To deal with the problem of applications filed with missing parts, the PCT adopted a rather clever solution. All priority applications are now deemed to be incorporated by reference into their corresponding international applications. If the priority applications contain the part that is missing from their international counterparts, applicants can simply request that the priority applications be used to fill the international applications' gap. *See* PCT Regulations, Rules 4.18 and 20.6. Here too, however, a significant number of countries have chosen not to recognize this safeguard for the time being.

4. With respect to obvious sorts of clerical errors, for example, typing the abbreviation for meter (m) instead of for millimeter (mm), the PCT Regulations have also attempted to provide a solution. International authorities can now correct the mistake if they conclude that it was obvious both that "something else was intended," and that "nothing else could have been intended other than the proposed rectification." Unlike the other safeguard provisions, PCT member countries cannot opt out of this reform. Consequently, they must recognize and accept all obvious mistakes corrected by international authorities. *See* PCT Regulations, Rules 43.6*bis* and 91.1. What do you think

accounts for the way the PCT treats the applicability of this rule versus the other reforms?

5. Not all reform efforts proved successful. One proposal that failed to gain acceptance concerned an initiative by the Swiss Government, supported by many developing countries, to recognize traditional knowledge and genetic resources within the PCT system. Switzerland proposed to amend the PCT Regulations explicitly to enable PCT member countries to require patent applicants, upon or after entry of their international applications into the national phase of PCT procedure, to declare the source of genetic resources and/or traditional knowledge, if their inventions were directly based on such resources or knowledge. To satisfy the requirement, Switzerland further proposed that applicants should have the possibility to declare the source at the time of filing their PCT applications or later during the international phase. In case a PCT application did not contain the required declaration, national law could provide that the application would not be processed until the patent applicant furnished the declaration. The primary policy objective of the disclosure requirement was to make access to genetic resources and traditional knowledge more transparent within the context of patent protection and to promote the sharing of benefits arising out of their use. The Swiss proposal met with stiff resistance from the United States, Canada, Australia, Japan, and other industrialized countries, and although Switzerland has never formally withdrawn it, the proposal is rarely discussed and no longer realistically figures on the PCT reform agenda. It, however, remains an important issue in other international fora including the Convention on Biological Diversity (CBD). We discuss the CBD and protection of traditional knowledge and genetic resources in Chapter 8.

NOTE ON THE PATENT LAW TREATY

The Patent Law Treaty (PLT), a treaty also administered by WIPO, was concluded in June 2000 and entered into force in April 2005. Currently, the PLT's membership consists of only thirty-two countries, a number that belies the influence the treaty has had on the evolution of international and national patent law. The United States Senate ratified the PLT in 2007, but it was not implemented until President Obama signed the Patent Law Treaties Implementation Act of 2012 (Pub. Law 112–211) on December 18, 2012. The provisions of the Act will come into effect on December 18, 2013. Because the PLT's provisions have been incorporated into the PCT regulations, the European Patent Convention and national legislation, the treaty's impact on patent procedure and practice has already proven to be considerable. The PLT is unusual in that membership is open not only to countries, but also to regional patent offices. *See* Article 20. To date, however, the European Patent Office is the only regional office that has signed the treaty and it is still contemplating ratifying it.

It is important to note that the PLT deals with procedural requirements only. Article 2(2) of the PLT expressly states that the treaty has no applicability to substantive patent law. The principal objective of the PLT is to make patent filing and prosecution more user-friendly by creating common procedural rules and requirements that patent offices of all member countries must respect. The treaty applies both to national and regional patent applications, as well as to international applications filed under the PCT. The PLT attempts to achieve its objective by stipulating maximum formalities that offices may apply and prohibiting offices from creating additional requirements in respect of matters covered by the treaty. Under Article 2, however, countries are free to establish procedural requirements that are more favorable to patent applicants and owners than those provided in the treaty.

One of the most important provisions of the PLT is contained in Article 5, which requires a patent office to accept and accord a filing date to an application if the application complies with three simple formalities: (i) it contains an indication that what has been filed is intended as an application, (ii) the applicant is identified, and (iii) the application contains what appears to be a description of the invention. Even if those requirements are not fully met, however, an office may accord a filing date to an application provided that evidence of the applicant's identity accompanies the application, and it may accept a drawing in place of a written description. In light of the importance of an application's filing date in identifying relevant prior art and in settling competing patent claims between competitors, the relaxed procedures required by the PLT may have a significant impact on patenting outcomes.

Under Article 6, the treaty also sets a common standard for the form and content of national or regional patent applications, which effectively mimics the form and content of PCT applications, and provides for the adoption of standardized international forms essential to the patent prosecution process. To that end, WIPO has published model forms relating to the act of filing an application, granting power of attorney, and requesting a change of name or address, the correction of mistakes, and the recording of a license or security interest.

The PLT permits member countries to require that an applicant or patent owner be represented by an attorney or agent in procedures before the patent office; however, as provided by Article 7, individual applicants or owners must be permitted to represent themselves for the purposes of filing an application, paying a fee, or filing a copy of a previously submitted application. In a similar effort to reduce burdens on applicants, the PLT restricts the ability of patent offices to require the submission of additional evidence or documentation in support of patent applications, or unnecessarily to demand copies of priority applications or their translations. In accordance with Article 6(6), a patent office may only require the submission of evidence to support the formal contents of an application, declarations of priority, or the authenticity of translations where that office has a reasonable doubt as to the veracity of the matter submitted. Moreover, an office may not require applicants to submit copies of their priority applications if they were previously filed with the same office or are available electronically, nor may it demand the translation of foreign priority applications into the office's national language unless the office believes that the validity of the priority claim is relevant to the determination of whether the invention claimed is patentable. *See* WIPO, Regulations under the Patent Law Treaty, Rule 4(3) and (4).

While the above provisions do simplify and streamline patent procedure, arguably the PLT's most important contributions to patent prosecution are the provisions of Articles 11 to 13, which introduce important safeguards to prevent the loss of substantive rights if certain time limits or formal requirements are not met. It is those provisions that served as the basis for the reform of the PCT discussed earlier in this Chapter. It is interesting to note that while the PLT still has few members, it has won consensus and approval among both industrialized and developing countries. With time, its membership is most likely to increase and its provisions firmly integrated in national patent law and practice.

C. PATENT WORKSHARING INITIATIVES

The three treaties discussed thus far in this Chapter are designed to help applicants obtain patents in multiple locations. However, none of the treaties results in a patent. Applicants still must enter the national phase, usually requiring substantive examination, in each country or region in which they desire patent protection. This redundancy of examination, which is built into the global patent system by territoriality constraints, is widely seen as inefficient, time-consuming, and expensive, as it requires the same subject matter to be examined multiple times by different offices to achieve patent protection in multiple countries. The patent offices of several countries are exploring a variety of ways—short of a global patent—to alleviate some of these issues, including Patent Prosecution Highways and a variety of other cooperative ventures.

1. PATENT PROSECUTION HIGHWAYS (PPHs)

PPHs, originally an initiative of the Japan Patent Office, are bilateral agreements between the patent offices of two countries or regions that allow for expedited application prosecution in certain circumstances. To use the PPH, an applicant must have received a ruling from either office that at least one claim in an application is patentable. The applicant may then request that the other office fast-track the examination of corresponding claims in corresponding applications. According to the USPTO, which as of June 2012 had PPHs or pilot PPHs in place with the patent offices of Australia, Austria, Canada, China, Denmark, the European Patent Office, Finland, Germany, Hungary, Iceland, Israel, Japan, Korea, Mexico, Norway, Russia, Singapore, Spain, Sweden, Taiwan, and the UK, the PPH is designed to "leverage fast-track patent examination procedures already available in both offices to allow applicants to obtain corresponding patents faster and more efficiently."

Beginning in January 2010, the USPTO expanded the PPH system to include PCT applications, and it began signing PCT-PPH agreements with other international searching authorities. Under PCT-PPH agreements currently in force with Australia, Austria, the European Patent Office, Finland, Japan, Korea, Russia, and Spain, a PCT applicant who receives a written opinion or international preliminary examination report from one of those international searching authorities, or from the USPTO acting as international searching authority, may request the other office to fast track the examination of corresponding claims during the national phase.

The latest addition to the PPH arsenal is an enhanced framework pilot program known as PPH Mottainai. "Mottainai" is a Japanese term meaning "a sense of regret concerning waste when the intrinsic value of an object or resource is not properly utilized" (*see* Patent Prosecution Highway Portal Site, http://www.jpo.go.jp/cgi/linke.cgi?url=/ppph-portal/index.htm, last visited June 18, 2012). In order to minimize the regret, PPH Mottainai permits applicants to request participation in the program on the basis of results available on any patent family member from any office participating in the pilot. Prior to Mottainai, eligibility was limited to reuse of search and examination results from a partner office on the priority (first-filed) application in a patent family. In addition to the USPTO, the offices participating in the pilot include the Canadian Intellectual Property Office, Japan Patent Office, IP Australia, National Board of Patents and Registration of Finland, Rospatent (Russia), Spanish Patent and Trademark Office, and United Kingdom Intellectual Property Office.

Other patent offices are pursuing PPH agreements with the same vigor as the USPTO, with the result that offices are creating an intricate and overlapping PPH web. The Japan Patent Office, for example, has PPHs with the patent offices of the U.S., Austria, Canada, Denmark, the European Patent Office, Finland, Germany, Korea, Mexico, Russia, Singapore, Spain, Sweden, and the UK, as well as a "pre-pilot" program with China. Japan also has PCT-PPH agreements with the U.S., the European Patent Office, Finland, Spain, Sweden, and Mexico.

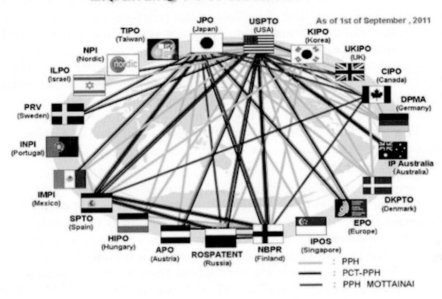

Source: Japan Patent Office

The following diagram illustrates the basic PPH process.

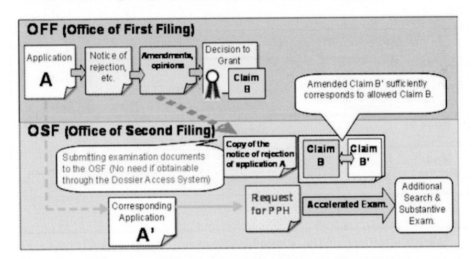

Source: Japan Patent Office

2. TRILATERAL COOPERATION, THE IP5, THE VANCOUVER GROUP, AND ASPEC

Since 1983, the European Patent Office (EPO), Japan Patent Office (JPO), and USPTO, which together process a majority of patent applications filed worldwide, have been involved in a trilateral cooperation initi-

ative involving sharing information on search and examination procedures and other efforts to reduce inefficiencies and redundancies in the
patent grant procedure. The objectives of the trilateral initiative include
improving the quality of examination processes at the three offices, developing common search tools, harmonizing office practices, and exploiting
the results of search and examination through work sharing. The offices
undertake the preparation of comparative studies on laws, regulations,
and practices governing search and examination and have initiated projects that deal with subjects as diverse as the development of machine
translation tools for searching patent documents and the harmonization
of biotechnology examination processes for single nucleotide polymor-
phisms and haplotypes.

A recent trilateral office worksharing initiative, referred to as "Triway," is a pilot program to leverage the searching expertise of each office.
The purpose of Triway is to permit the trilateral offices to conduct prior
art searches on corresponding applications in a more timely and efficient
manner. Under Triway, each Office would conduct a search of the application, and the results of those searches would then be shared among the
offices in order to reduce overall search and examination workloads. The
following diagram illustrates the workings of the Triway initiative. The
pilot program was launched in July 2008 and was scheduled to last one
year. It was limited to one-hundred applications from all areas of technology.

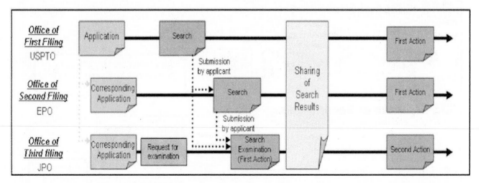

Source: Trilateral.net

With the offices of the Republic of Korea (KIPO) and China (SIPO)
consistently recording the highest growth in application filings over the
last several years, the trilateral cooperation has recently taken steps to
expand the cooperation to include these offices. This expanded cooperation initiative is dubbed the IP5 (KIPO, SIPO, EPO, JPO, and USPTO),
and in 2008, the IP5 agreed to work toward eliminating unnecessary duplication of work among all the offices, enhancing patent examination efficiency and quality, and guaranteeing stability of patent rights. Together, the five offices receive 90 percent of all patent applications filed in the

world each year. The heads of the five offices meet annually to discuss progress on a variety of worksharing projects led by the member offices.

The Vancouver Group, established in 2008, is a work-sharing consortium that consists of the patent offices of Australia, Canada, and the United Kingdom. The objectives of the Vancouver Group are twofold: to share information and experiences on common issues and areas relevant to managing a *mid-sized* national patent office; and to contribute to a more effective multilateral approach to worksharing. In March 2011, the Vancouver Group launched a pilot system to facilitate access to search and examination results among the Group's offices. Called CASE (Centralized Access to Search and Examination), the system consists of a common digital library of the search and examination results of the participating offices. The Vancouver Group has estimated that the worldwide patent backlog to which the duplication of work has contributed has cost the global economy £7.6 billion for every year of extra delay, and if CASE proves successful in decreasing the delay, it is likely to lead to closer collaboration among larger groups of patent offices.

The ASEAN Patent Examination Cooperation (ASPEC) is a regional cooperation program between the patent offices of Brunei Darussalam, Cambodia, Indonesia, Lao PDR, Malaysia, the Philippines, Singapore, Thailand, and Vietnam. Active since 2009, ASPEC has as its purpose the sharing of search and examination results between the participating offices to allow patent applicants to obtain corresponding applications faster, more efficiently, and with a higher quality end product. In April 2012, ASPEC moved to operating in the English language in all offices.

NOTES AND QUESTIONS

1. A somewhat more controversial work sharing proposal is the New Route, which was initiated by the JPO and supported by the USPTO, but so far resisted by the EPO. The New Route effectively would create a thirty-month priority period outside the scope of the PCT. To date, the New Route has seen few takers and is likely to fade into oblivion. What value do you think the New Route would add to the international administration of patent law? Why do you think the USPTO supported it?

2. Patent Prosecution Highways, the Triway, the New Route, CASE, and ASPEC are all designed to increase speed, efficiency and quality in the patent examination process. Which approach seems most likely to be beneficial to applicants? Why? Can you suggest a better system for addressing the redundancy in examination issues? What public welfare gains might result from a more efficient global patent prosecution system? Do you see any disadvantages? To whom?

3. Consider the following worksharing characterization:

One can think of three kinds of worksharing based on the kinds of information that is shared between [offices]. First, Patent Offices can share and mutually exploit the information of searching prior arts. This process is called *"Search sharing."* . . . Second, it is possible for offices to share . . . information . . . in the process of examination. This is called *Action sharing."* . . . Finally, it is possible for an office to cooperate with other offices by sharing its final decision. This is called *"decision sharing."* . . . .

. . . .

[D]ecision sharing is useful when *substantive patent law* is harmonized. . . . If two countries share a similar rule of patentability, the second office could dramatically reduce the need for further examination. . . . One case example shows that an applicant in Japan obtained a patent decision from Korea [the two countries have almost identical substantive law] in only 28 days by using PPH.

Dongwook Chun, *Patent Law Harmonization in the Age of Globalization: The Necessity and Strategy for a Pragmatic Outcome*, 93 J. PAT. & TRADEMARK OFF. SOC'Y 127, 148–54 (2011). What do these types of sharing say about the level of trust and harmonization that will be necessary for effective worksharing in the future?

4. If the New Route were to take hold, it is likely that membership would be restricted to industrialized countries with sophisticated patent offices. What impact might such an occurrence have on developing countries and their ability to benefit from the patent system?

NOTE ON THE SUBSTANTIVE PATENT LAW TREATY (SPLT)

Much of the material discussed in this Chapter has centered around agreements on procedural requirements, and shows the success the international community has achieved in procedural harmonization. Attempts at substantive agreements, however, have proven less fruitful. Following the conclusion of the PLT, WIPO sought to continue its patent harmonization effort by standardizing substantive aspects of patent law. Although a draft of the SPLT exists, no consensus for its conclusion has been reached, nor is it likely that such an agreement can be achieved in the short term. Of particular note is the rift in agreement between industrialized and developing countries, as noted in the excerpt by Professors Reichman and Cooper Dreyfuss in Chapter 1, *supra*, p. 42.

At its most basic level, the SPLT seeks to set universal standards for assessing patentability and validity by establishing rules governing the sufficiency of disclosure, claim drafting, and claim interpretation, as well as defining pertinent terms such as prior art, novelty, inventive step/nonobviousness, and industrial applicability/utility. Regulating those issues, however, requires resolution of numerous others, such as claim breadth, the grace period, applicability of oral disclosure and non-public use, sharing and recognition of search and examination results, and definition of a "person of ordinary skill in the art." These and other related issues form the subject matter of subsequent Chapters of this text.

After years of discussion and revisions, member delegations could not reach a consensus on the pertinent issues, nor could they fully agree on how future work on substantive harmonization should proceed. Although the outlook for the SPLT does not appear promising, WIPO member countries all seem to agree that the goals of reducing the overall costs of obtaining international patent protection and increasing efficiency and predictability in the administration of the international patent process are laudable ones.

While the SPLT has not garnered worldwide support, other international and regional agreements have been adopted that have succeeded in regulating substantive aspects of patent law. Those agreements are the subject of the next Chapter.

NOTES AND QUESTIONS

1. What should the scope of a substantive patent law treaty comprise? Should it attempt to exert jurisdiction beyond the scope of the PCT? Should it seek to change established national systems indirectly (consider, for instance, the pressure that had been placed on the United States to replace its long-established first-to-invent tradition with a first-inventor-to-file system)? What about assisting developing countries with the development of their national patent systems? How much influence should substantive harmonization have on these developing systems?

2. Is the goal of substantive harmonization to replace individualized national systems altogether? Does the development of substantive harmonization preclude existence of national systems even if a global system has not been officially declared? Would substantive harmonization be more acceptable, or advance more quickly, if it were first made applicable only to PCT international applications entering the national stage? Is it possible to restrict substantive harmonization only to international applications entering the national stage?

3. Does the objective of harmonization conflict with the principle of independence of patents and even with national sovereignty? Recall from Chapter 1, *supra*, the concerns articulated by Professors Reichman and Cooper Dreyfuss about substantive patent law harmonization. As they observe, even among the most industrialized countries, there remain significant policy and administrative differences in their patent systems. Given what you have now learned about the global procedural framework for patents, especially efforts for further cooperation among the major patent offices, do you think these concerns are justified?

4. It sometimes appears that countries are eager to promote harmonization as long as their national systems and laws remain relatively unchanged. To what extent should countries be required to relinquish national practices in the interests of harmonization? What external pressures might motivate them to do so? What sorts of pressures might motivate them to resist?

D. REGIONAL PATENT REGIMES

While the TRIPS and TRIPS-plus agreements discussed in Chapter 3, *infra*, mandate minimum standards of patent protection, other treaties streamline the process of obtaining and enforcing patents simultaneously in multiple countries within a geographic region. The most successful example of this type of treaty is the European Patent Convention, but international agreements also exist among two regional groups of African countries, a group of Arab states, and between Russia and a group of its former dependent territories. Because these treaties facilitate the grant of patents with regional scope, they constitute exceptions to the strictly national territorial model of patent rights and, in the longer term, they may serve to promote greater patent system harmonization worldwide.

1. THE EUROPEAN PATENT CONVENTION (EPC)

The most significant regional patent treaty is the Convention on the Grant of European Patents ("EPC"), signed in 1973 by a group of countries seeking to create a uniform European patent system. The EPC entered into force on October 7, 1977, and as of June 2012 had grown to a membership of thirty-eight contracting member countries and two extension states. The principal accomplishment of the treaty is that it established the European Patent Office (EPO) and endowed the EPO with a system of substantive and procedural rules that permit it to grant European patents, valid in all member countries with only a single application. Membership in the EPO is not limited to European Union (EU) countries, although all EU countries are members. "Extension states" are expected to become full-fledged EPC members in due course, but during the interim phase they are included within the scope of a European patent application and European patent applicants may obtain patent protection in them.

Under the EPC, an applicant is entitled to file and prosecute a single, unitary application that covers all member and extension countries. When the EPO grants a European patent, it is comparable to the grant of a bundle of national patents that become valid in each particular country once the patent owner completes some registration formalities. From that point on, each country must treat the European patent as equivalent to a national patent and must grant the patent owner the same rights as would be conferred by a national patent. An applicant may still apply for patent protection in each individual EPC member country exclusively or concurrently, but all EPC countries are required to modify their national laws to comply with the EPC.

The entry into force of two agreements marked a new chapter in the life of the European patent system. On December 13, 2007, EPC 2000, which is a revised version of the EPC, came into effect. While EPC 2000 kept intact the substance of European patent law, it refined European patent procedure, incorporated some of the features of the PLT, and generally made it easier to file European patent applications. For example, EPC 2000 relaxes the requirements for obtaining a filing date, allows applications to be filed in any language, and eliminates the need for applicants to select and designate upfront those EPC countries in which they desire to pursue patent protection.

May 1, 2008, saw the entry into force of the London Agreement, a text that was adopted by EPC member countries on October 17, 2000. The London Agreement eases some of the costly and time-consuming translation requirements that burdened the national registration of European patents. Prior to the London Agreement, the entire patent specification (the text of the patent) had to be translated into the national language of every EPC member country in which the patentee chose to register the European patent. Now, however, countries party to the agreement have waived the translation requirement either entirely or in part. As a result, for applications the description of which is filed in English, either no additional translation is required (the case, for example, in France, Germany, and Switzerland), or only the claims need to be translated into the national language (the case, for example, in Denmark, the Netherlands, and Sweden). *See Agreement on the Application of Article 65 EPC – London Agreement*, O.J. EPO 2001, 550.

Translation issues have long plagued the development of the European patent system. The EPC was negotiated alongside another European agreement, the Community Patent Convention (CPC), a treaty designed to create a centralized system for the issuance and enforcement of a single unitary patent within the EU. However, when talks stalled on the CPC, in large part due to concerns about making patent translations available in all EU languages (twenty-three at present) and the costs involved, the parties decided to move forward with the EPC and continue to work on the CPC separately. The success of the EPC, along with the fact that the CPC has not yet been concluded, suggests the decision was a wise one. For many years, there seemed little likelihood that agreement on the CPC could be achieved; however, the emergence of machine translation and other electronic translation tools and the high costs of obtaining patent protection in Europe have given new life to the effort to achieve a unitary patent. As further noted in Chapter 10, the European Commission, in conjunction with twenty-five EU member states, is moving forward with an enhanced cooperation initiative to create two EU regulations, one for a unitary EU patent that would be granted by the EPO, the other for the supporting translation regime. *See* EUROPEAN COMMISSION, PROPOSAL FOR A REGULATION OF THE EUROPEAN PARLIAMENT AND OF THE COUNCIL IMPLEMENTING ENHANCED COOPERATION IN THE AREA OF CREATION OF UNITARY PATENT PROTECTION (2011), *available at* http://ec.europa.eu/internal_market/indprop/docs/patent/com2011-215-final_en.pdf. Applicants could choose to pursue either the unitary EU patent instead of or in addition to the traditional European patent bundle granted by the EPO. Moreover, applicants could still choose to obtain individual patents from national offices. At the same time, an agreement to create a European patent court is also being pursued, but as of this writing, there are still several obstacles to implementation of both sets of initiatives.

Regardless of the fate of the unitary patent regime, the EPC system is a proven success. Over 244,000 European applications were filed in 2011, 74 percent of which were international applications filed under the PCT and converted to European applications when they entered the regional phase. About 28 percent of all applications came from U.S. applicants while an increasing percentage (32 percent in 2011) came from Japan, South Korea and China. *See* http://www.epo.org/about-us/office/annual-report/2011/statistics-trends.html. A more detailed analysis of some of the substantive requirements of the EPC is included throughout this book.

Similar to most national legislation worldwide, including the new U.S. America Invents Act, the EPC provides for post-grant opposition. Within nine months following the grant of a European patent, any interested party may file an opposition on the basis that the invention is not patentable, that the patent does not disclose the invention in a sufficiently clear and complete manner, or that subject matter of the patent extends beyond the content of the application. If the EPO grants the opposition, the patent is revoked with retroactive effect in all designated countries. As with examination decisions, opposition decisions can be appealed to one of the EPO Boards of Appeal, of which there are twenty-seven Technical Boards and one Legal Board. Questions from a Board of Appeal or the President of the EPO can be referred to the EPO Enlarged Board of Appeal, which is the EPO's highest adjudicating body.

Post-grant opposition can be particularly useful for third parties interested in challenging a national patent obtained through the EPO. As the following case illustrates, applicants choosing the EPO over national patent offices are, in one sense, putting all of their eggs in one basket, which can be risky indeed.

LENZING AG'S EUROPEAN PATENT (UK)

In the High Court of Justice – Queen's Bench Division and In the Patents Court
[1997] R.P.C. 245

Before: Mr. Justice JACOB

. . . .

It is first necessary to explain the legal framework of the problem. Until 1978, a patent for an invention in the United Kingdom could only be obtained by application to the United Kingdom Patent Office. The procedures for this were laid down in the Patents Act 1949 and the Rules made pursuant to the rule- making power conferred by the Act. Ultimately any decision adverse to an applicant could be the subject of appeal to the Patents Court. Patents in other countries had to be obtained by applications to the national patent office of each country concerned. This was widely regarded as wasteful. It meant, for instance, that if you wanted a patent in "n" European countries, you had to apply in different national patent offices. Each of these would (or might since some did not) search the prior art to see whether the invention was new. Further each country had its own, distinct, substantive laws of validity and infringement.

Accordingly in 1973 a number of European countries entered into the European Patent Convention ("EPC"). This set up the European Patent Office ("EPO") in Munich. The 1977 Patents Act was passed, as its recital says, "to give effect to certain international conventions" of which the EPC was one. I described the broad effect of the position prevailing after the 1977 Act came into force (mid-1978) in Aumac Limited's Patent as follows:

"One can obtain a patent in this country by one of two routes. One can simply apply to the British Patent Office who will process the application and if all goes well grant the patent. One can also or alternatively apply to the EPO. This operates as a central processing patent office for the states parties to the EPC. In making one's application there, one must "designate" the states in which one wants a patent. Once the EPO grants a patent it takes effect in each designated state in the same way as a patent from the national office of that state. A patent granted by the EPO which takes effect here is called a "European patent (UK)". There is provision that one cannot at the same time have a patent granted by a national office and the EPO for the same invention. The EPO patent prevails and the corresponding national patent must be revoked. But this happens only when the EPO grants the patent. Until then one can process an application through the two systems simultaneously. Once the EPO has granted a patent, there is a system of "opposition" (really revocation) which is operated by the EPO whereby it is possible to apply within 9 months of grant to have the EPO patent revoked. If it is, the revocation works for all designated states—a central "knock-out" system."

Lenzing's patent has been knocked out centrally. Can they challenge that knock-out at least so far as the United Kingdom patent is concerned? That is what I have to decide.

The patent concerned is (or was) No. 0,356,419. Lenzing applied for it in the EPO on 7 August 1989. It is for a process for making cotton-like fabric from wood. Following examination the patent was granted on 16 December 1992. Opposition was entered in the EPO by Courtaulds plc and Akzo Fazer AG within the 9 month period from grant provided for by Article 89(1) of the EPC. On 6 May 1994 the Opposition Division orally announced its decision, refusing the opposition. It gave its reasons on 4 July 1994. The opponents appealed to the BoA, to which appeals lie pursuant to the provisions of Articles 106–111. Another Courtaulds company (Courtaulds Fibres (Holdings) Ltd.) was permitted to join in the appeal. The BoA received written submissions. It held an oral hearing on 3 May 1996. In accordance with its usual practice (a practice often criticised), following an adjournment of an hour or so, it announced its decision. The patent was revoked. Written reasons followed on 12 July 1996. The fact of revocation was recorded on the register of European Patents kept by the EPO. I do not know the precise date of such recordal but it must have been shortly after the decision was given. There is no attempt to attack that entry in these proceedings. The decision was duly communicated to the Comptroller-General of Patents who caused an entry to be made in the United Kingdom register of patents to the effect that the patent was revoked. The communication took the form of the supply of the information on a tape or disc which the Comptroller simply ran to alter the electronically kept Register. He did not purport to exercise his discretion.

Meanwhile proceedings had started in the [UK] Patents Court. Courtaulds, believing that the patent represented a major threat to their investment in a new plant in the United Kingdom, on 29 September 1994 petitioned to revoke the European patent (UK). This was just after the Opposition Division had upheld the patent. In November Lenzing attacked, serving a writ for infringement. It was duly agreed that both proceedings should run together. Discovery took place and the trial date was set for December 1996. The revocation of the Patent intervened. Courtaulds now apply for the action to be dismissed and for their costs of the action and petition.

Lenzing say that the written reasons for the decision show that there was a serious procedural injustice. In particular they say that the reasons were never put to them, either at the hearing or before, and were not argued by the opponents. They say that there was thereby:

(1) a breach of "natural justice";

(2) a breach of Article 113 of the EPC (that "decisions of the EPO may only be based on grounds or evidence on which the parties

concerned have had an opportunity to present their comments"); and

(3) a breach of Article 11 of the Rules of Procedure of the BoA, which empowers the Board "to send with the summons to oral hearing a communication drawing attention to matters which seem to be of especial significance."

Lenzing further say that the decision was irrational or perverse, misunderstanding and misconstruing both the cited prior art and their patent. And they say that the BoA made up its mind in advance of the hearing and that such was admitted by the Chairman of the Board in a conversation with their patent agent. This makes the procedural misfeasance allegations all the more serious: the claim is that the Board knew in advance of the grounds of their proposed decision, yet deliberately kept it back. Lenzing say that if they had known of the point, they could have answered it or offered suitable amendments to their patent to deal with it.

Lenzing say the result of the events which they allege is that the decision of the BoA should be regarded as a nullity. They accept that judicial review will not lie against the impugned decision itself (because of the immunity of the EPO from process) but, they say, that does not prevent a collateral attack. They make that attack in three ways:

(1) In resisting Courtaulds' applications for the infringement claim to be struck out and for their costs of their petition for revocation;

(2) In seeking judicial review of the Comptroller's action in recording on the Register of patents an entry to the effect that the patent has been revoked;

(3) In applying by motion to the Patents Court pursuant to section 34 of the Patents Act 1977 directly for an order that the Register be rectified so as to remove that entry.

Admittedly the procedures in which the question arises are different, but, say Lenzing, given the fact that the decision should be regarded as a nullity, all three procedures (or at least one or other of them) are appropriate. . . .

Courtaulds wish to dispute all of the allegations of fact. The EPO is not in a position even to go into them—its position is that its Boards of Appeal are an international tribunal over which national courts have no supervisory power. So it is not necessary or legitimate to go into the facts. The EPO does not appear before me. It has never been (and could not be) served in accordance with any Rule of Court, though it has been given notice of these proceedings. It has immunity from any relevant process for reasons I will examine later.

. . . .

Lenzing now accepts that domestic judicial review proceedings will not lie against the EPO. Originally . . . they sought an order that the decision of the BoA insofar as it purported to revoke their European patent (UK) be revoked. An awful muddle therefore follows if they are right in saying that the decision can be treated as a nullity. The register of European patents under Article 127 will continue to record the revocation of the European patent by the BoA whatever is done to the United Kingdom Register. And Courtaulds and Akzo, who perfectly properly were parties to the appeal before the EPO will, so far as this country is concerned, in effect be deprived of that appeal. By our law the appeal has not happened, but it has as far as the EPO is concerned. I mention Akzo particularly because they are not parties to the present proceedings and it is doubtful whether they could be made such. More generally anyone who consulted the EPO register and said "The patent is gone for all Europe: I need not bother to look at national registers" would be misled. And even more seriously, anyone who in reliance on the revocation as being final has made an investment accordingly (either by way of direct investment in plant or R&D or on the stock market) would be adversely affected.

Lenzing accept that all that follows from their argument. Nonetheless they boldly submit that Parliament did intend that there could be inquiry by way of collateral attack here into the acts of a Board of Appeal of the EPO and that was intended by Parliament. Further, they say, it would require very strong language indeed for Parliament to exclude an inquiry into the lawfulness of what was done to deprive a party of a United Kingdom property right. They say no such language is used here. Thus, it would follow, that the decision of the BoA should be treated in just the same way as that of a domestic tribunal with this limited, but irrelevant limitation, that the decision itself cannot be directly quashed or attacked.

Courtaulds and the Comptroller say that the whole Lenzing approach is misconceived. They begin by pointing out that the EPC as such is an international treaty, taking effect in public international law. It establishes by Article 1 "A system of law common to the Contracting States for the grant of patents." That follows the recital specifying the States' desire that there be a "single procedure for the grant of patents."

It is, I think clear, (and Mr. Prescott Q.C. for Lenzing did not really contest otherwise) that the "opposition" procedure was and is really regarded so far as the Convention is concerned as part of the grant process. It is somewhat Pickwickian to describe a post-grant attack on a patent as "opposition" but the word does convey the notion that one is concerned with the early life of the patent. Hence the fact that the attack must be within 9 months of grant. The founding fathers of the Convention had to choose between an opposition proper — which would or could have the result that the applicant could be kept out of his monopoly for many years—and this form of "belated opposition." They chose the latter. We had a similar system under the 1949 Act in addition to true opposition. It is still a patent office jurisdiction, and although, so far as I know there is no explicit decision to that effect, I imagine that the standard applied (other than on questions of law) is to give any benefit of the doubt to the patentee, there being an opportunity later in national courts for a further and better attack on the patent. Be that as it may, I think it is indisputable that under the Convention the contracting States intended that the opposition procedure and result should apply to the European patent as a whole. That is so as a matter of public international law. And that is what the United Kingdom signed up to in joining the EPC.

Next, say Courtaulds, the activities of the EPO are not governed by English law and are not justiciable in English courts. It is not open to the English courts to consider whether or not the decision was "in excess" of the powers of the BoA. They say that is so even if the BoA had taken a bribe to reach its decision. That may well be a matter which would allow another Board to set the earlier decision aside (as fraud in our courts enables an earlier decision to be set aside) but that is a matter for the new system of law created by the EPC on the international plane.

Thus, say Courtaulds and the Comptroller, all that Parliament has required in the 1977 Act, sections 77(2) and 77(4A) is proof that the EPO has, acting in purported exercise of its powers under the EPC (of which it, and not national courts are the judge), revoked a European patent. Once that is shown, then our law automatically treats the European patent (and with it the European patent (UK)) as revoked. The Comptroller in making the entry in the register is acting in a purely administrative capacity, just recording what has been done. I have no doubt that Courtaulds and the Comptroller are right. . . . This country has agreed with the other States members of the EPC that the final arbiter of revocation under the new legal system is to be the Board of Appeal of the EPO. Other States would be justly entitled to complain if we in this country were to ignore such a final decision . . . .

Mr. Prescott devised a more limited class of attack, public policy . . . . This is the principle that the English court will not recognise and enforce a judgment of a foreign court where the proceedings in that court were in breach of the principles of "natural justice" (the English law term for the right to fair hearing—"due process" as the Americans call it). This, I felt, was Mr. Prescott's most attractive argument. Why should the English court (or for that matter any other national court) have to accept a decision of a BoA reached by unfair means? The answer, which I think is clear, is that it would be contrary to the international treaty even to inquire into the question. Mr. Prescott's appeal to public policy is met by a conflicting policy. The United Kingdom and the other Member States have agreed at an international level via the EPC that the BoA is the final arbiter of oppositions. It is the agreed EPO equivalent of the House of Lords, Cour de Cassation, or Bundesgerichthof. It is not for national courts to query its doings, whether in a direct or collateral attack.

Mr. Prescott's final main submission was this: that the EPO was different from other international organisations. Unlike, say, the Tin Council, it is a body whose decisions take effect in national law. He said (correctly) that those decisions only take effect by virtue of an Act of Parliament. So the EPO should be regarded as a public body constituted by Act of Parliament, rather like any other United Kingdom decision making tribunal. This is fallacious. The EPO is clearly recognised on the plane of international law. The Patents Act causes its decisions to be recognised here as a matter of national law. But its decisions remain decisions at the international level so it is no business of our courts to go into them.

NOTES AND QUESTIONS

1. In the UK *Lenzing AG* case, the court concluded that it had no power to remedy the EPO BoA opposition decision even if gross malfeasance had occurred because the EPO is not subject to any national law. Should the EPO be subject to the jurisdiction of any court? An international tribunal, such as a WTO dispute panel?

2. A revision to the EPC that took effect in 2007 pursuant to EPC 2000 provides a direct response to the fairness concern posed in *Lenzing*. Article 112(a) provides any party to an EPO Board of Appeal decision the right to appeal to the EPO Enlarged Board of Appeal where there has been a fundamental procedural defect, such as a violation of a party's right to be heard on an issue.

------

2. AFRICAN, EURASIAN, AND GULF COOPERATION REGIONAL PATENT SYSTEMS

There are two regional patent systems in Africa, the African Regional Industrial Property Organization (ARIPO) and the Organisation Africaine de la Propriété Intellectuelle (OAPI). ARIPO grants patents for a group of English-speaking countries while OAPI grants patents for French-speaking countries.

Like the EPO, ARIPO provides a streamlined application and examination system for applicants seeking patents in multiple ARIPO countries. After grant, the ARIPO patent is subject to the national laws of each designated state and has the same effect as a patent granted by the national office. As of this writing, eighteen states are members of ARIPO.

OAPI was formed in 1977 by a group of African countries that gained their independence from France between 1958 and 1960. Unlike ARIPO or the EPC, the sixteen member countries of OAPI do not have national patent granting systems; OAPI grants a single patent that is valid in all member countries. While the substantive law is the same across all member countries, interpretations can differ and a patent may be invalidated in one country yet remain enforceable in the other member countries.

The Eurasian Patent Organization (EAPO) issues patents for Russia and eight of its former dependent territories. The dissolution of the USSR in 1991 created considerable uncertainty regarding intellectual property protection in the region prompting many newly formed states to set up their own patent offices. However, there was also a strong desire for a regional system of harmonized laws that would facilitate multi-country patent procurement. The result was the Eurasian Patent Convention which took effect in 1995. While similar to the EPC in many ways, an EA PO patent offers a significant advantage: a single language, Russian, resulting in lower costs by eliminating the need for translations.

The Gulf Cooperation Council (GCC) patent office has, since 1992, granted patents in a single language, Arabic, for the countries of Bahrain, Kuwait, Oman, Qatar, UAE, and Saudi Arabia. As with other regional patents, GCC patents must be enforced in each jurisdiction. Applicants can still choose the alternative of filing in national offices.

NOTES AND QUESTIONS

1. What advantages do regional patent systems offer to patentees? Do you think regional systems would do a better job of reflecting public policy concerns of their member states?

2. What should be the relationship between the "global" patent system and the regional systems? Should the regional systems be encouraged to follow the practices and procedures adopted by major patent offices such as the USPTO or the EPO?

CHAPTER 3

SUBSTANTIVE PATENT AGREEMENTS

■ ■ ■

A. THE AGREEMENT ON TRADE-RELATED ASPECTS OF INTELLECTUAL PROPERTY RIGHTS

The multilateral agreements (PC, PCT, and PLT) discussed in the previous Chapter can be considered "procedural" because they relate principally to processes for obtaining patent protection. For example, Article 27 of the PCT states that "[n]othing in this Treaty and the [PCT] Regulations is intended to be construed as prescribing anything that would limit the freedom of each Contracting State to prescribe such *substantive* conditions of patentability as it desires." (Emphasis added). The international accords discussed in this Chapter set minimum standards of protection that countries must provide to all qualifying subject matter and encompass rules concerning patent eligibility, patentability requirements, and standards of protection.

1. BACKGROUND AND HISTORY OF THE TRIPS AGREEMENT

As you learned in Chapter 1, the TRIPS Agreement is the principal international agreement in the global patent system. To fully appreciate the unprecedented nature and scope of the treaty, the ongoing tensions it has elicited within the current system of international intellectual property regulation, and the continuing pressure it exerts on all countries regardless of level of development, it is important to understand the political and economic context in which the contentious beginnings of the TRIPS Agreement are grounded.

The formal commencement of the Uruguay Round of multilateral trade negotiations was launched by the Punta del Este Declaration of September 20, 1986. The Declaration, which set forth the basis on which the whole round would proceed, addressed negotiations on intellectual property as part of the section on trade in goods. The relevant portion of the Declaration states as follows:

MINISTERIAL DECLARATION ON THE URUGUAY ROUND

Part I. Negotiations on Trade in Goods

. . . .

135

Trade-related aspects of intellectual property rights, including trade in counterfeit goods

In order to reduce the distortions and impediments to international trade, and taking into account the need to promote effective and adequate protection of intellectual property rights and to ensure that measures and procedures to enforce intellectual property rights do not themselves become barriers to legitimate trade, the negotiations shall aim to clarify GATT provisions and elaborate as appropriate new rules and disciplines. Negotiations shall aim to develop a multilateral framework of principles, rules and disciplines dealing with international trade in counterfeit goods, taking into account work already undertaken in the GATT.

These negotiations shall be without prejudice to other complementary initiatives that may be taken in the World Intellectual Property Organization and elsewhere to deal with these matters.

The fact that intellectual property was explicitly identified in the Punta del Este Declaration was itself a major victory for the United States and its allies. This was not the first time that intellectual property rights had been addressed within the GATT system and an agreement between disparately situated countries was not easily obtained. While the successful conclusion of the TRIPS Agreement represented a fundamental acknowledgment of the increasing importance of invention and knowledge-based trade in the international economy, the decision to formally incorporate an intellectual property agreement into the international trade system proved controversial. Recall from Chapter 1 that the move was initiated largely by industrialized countries impatient with the pace of progress on new intellectual property standards and, as the following excerpts emphasize, the absence of an enforcement mechanism within WIPO.

CARLOS ALBERTO PRIMO BRAGA, THE ECONOMICS OF INTELLECTUAL PROPERTY RIGHTS AND THE GATT: A VIEW FROM THE SOUTH

22 VAND. J. TRANSNAT'L L. 243, 245–51 (1989)

By the end of the Tokyo Round (1979), both developed and developing contracting parties of the GATT shared a sense of frustration. . . . [T]here was a widespread feeling that the multilateral trade system was not working well. For the LDCs, the shortcomings of the "special and differential treatment approach" (S&D) coupled with GATT's deficient coverage of their main trade interests were the basic reasons for frustration. For the industrialized countries, frustration reflected the concern with *free-*

rider behavior by LDCs and the recognition of the growing importance of trade issues that was not dealt with properly in the GATT—such as services, intellectual property rights, trade-related investment measures, and high-technology trade. The economic crisis of the early 1980s put additional pressure on the system because it accelerated the adoption of protectionist measures throughout the world. Against this background, the United States called a GATT Ministerial Meeting in 1982 to serve as a *launch pad* for a new round of multilateral trade negotiations (MTN).

The agenda suggested by the United States included the so-called *new themes*, a more stringent discipline for agricultural export subsidies and the creation of a safeguards code. To a certain extent, the American proposal tried to pave the way for a GATT *reform* (that is, the inclusion of the new themes). By putting together the new themes with issues of interest to numerous countries (agriculture and safeguards), the American negotiators expected to find enough support for the launching of a new round. This agenda, however, was not well received in Geneva. The European Community, particularly France, was skeptical about the prospects of trade liberalization efforts amid world recession. The LDCs stressed that the main problems with the multilateral trade system, from their point of view, were related to the lack of compliance by industrialized countries with GATT disciplines in traditional trade areas (such as agriculture, textiles, and clothing). Accordingly, the task of recovering the GATT's credibility would be best served not by extending its disciplines to new areas, but by addressing the *old* problems of the system.

. . . .

It is worth mentioning at this point that intellectual property considerations were present in the GATT since its origin. Article IX, for instance, establishes that marks of origin (trade names, geographical indications, etc.) should not be used in such a way as to hamper international trade. This article also seeks to prevent misleading indications of the "true origin of a product, to the detriment of such distinctive regional or geographical names of products as are protected by legislation." Article XX(d), in turn, places the adoption or enforcement of measures necessary to secure "the protection of patents, trademarks and copyrights, and the prevention of deceptive practices" among the so called general exceptions in the GATT. These measures, as long as they are non-discriminatory and necessary to assure compliance with GATT-compatible laws and regulations, are not bound by GATT disciplines. In addition, there are references in articles XII:3(c) and XVIII:10 to the fact that trade restrictions allowed under balance-of-payments crises should not be inconsistent with intellectual property rights laws.

It is also true that many instruments negotiated under GATT auspices, using GATT procedures and practices, took into account intellectual property rights—such as the 1958 recommendation on marks of origin, the Customs Valuation Code, and the Standards Code negotiated during the Tokyo Round. The 1982 Ministerial Declaration nevertheless constituted a major development in the history of intellectual property rights in the GATT system. It is important to remember that since 1978 the United States had attempted to garner support for an Anti-Counterfeiting Code. This effort, which gradually gained support from the European Community, Japan, and Canada, did not reach the *consensus* level needed for incorporation in the results of the Tokyo Round. With the Ministerial Declaration, however, the debate on intellectual property rights gained new momentum. In 1984, the GATT established a Group of Experts to study trade aspects of commercial counterfeiting. Although this Group could not reach a final decision, the growing concern for intellectual property-related issues paved the way for the inclusion of TRIPs in the Uruguay Round.

The road to the Uruguay Round, however, was not an easy one. The idea of a new round of MTN was raised again by Japan in 1983. By 1985, the common perception that the multilateral trading system was in jeopardy fostered the search for compromises to bridge the gap between developed and developing countries. The introduction of the *dual track* approach, concerning negotiations on services, is a good example in this context. After tense negotiations, the eighth round of MTN was finally launched in September of 1986.

The fact that TRIPs became a subject for negotiation in the Round did not mean that an international consensus on the issue had been reached. Actually, it only meant a change in the focus of the debate which became centered on the issue of the coverage of the negotiations. The Ministerial Declaration of Punta del Este represents a masterpiece of diplomatic compromise and, consequently, allows many interpretations. . . .

. . . .

It is quite clear in this Declaration that a major objective of the negotiations should be the drafting of an Anti-Counterfeiting Code (*a multilateral framework*). In this context, one could say that the American position had finally been vindicated. Ironically, this objective was now further down on the American intellectual property rights agenda. By 1986, pushed by the interests of knowledge-intensive industries, the United States saw as its main objective the development of a set of standards for intellectual property rights protection in order to curb "piracy." These standards, "presumably . . . modelled after United States legislation," and the GATT's dispute-settlement mechanism, would provide the means for enhancing intellectual property rights protection on a world-wide basis. The adoption of such standards in the GATT system would mean a radical departure from the original GATT approach to intellectual property. As described above, the only GATT provision which requires the protection of intellectual property rights by contracting parties is article IX (6).

One could argue, however, that the Declaration provides for such a broad negotiating objective to the extent that "effective and adequate protection of intellectual property rights" is accepted as a necessary condition to reduce the distortions and impediments to international trade.

From the point of view of the LDCs, such an objective was well beyond the legal mandate for negotiations on TRIPs at the Uruguay Round. The LDCs accepted the existence of a clear mandate to negotiate trade in counterfeit goods, but these negotiations should be restricted to the examination of the trade effects of counterfeiting without entering the discussion of "what constitutes counterfeiting." Another facet of the LDCs' position was the resistance to any attempt to transform the negotiations into "an exercise to set standards of protection of intellectual property rights or to attempt to raise the levels of such protection under existing multilateral agreements through the strengthening of enforcement procedures. . ." LDCs also emphasized their strong support for the existing international agreements administered by the World Intellectual Property Organization (WIPO)—that is, the Paris Convention (patents, utility models, designs and trademarks, trade names, and appellation of origin), the Berne Convention (copyrights), the Madrid and Lisbon Agreements (repression of false or deceptive indications of source on goods, and the protection and registration of appellations of origin)—and by the United Nations Educational, Scientific and Cultural Organization (UNESCO)— namely, the Universal Copyright Convention. By disputing the adequacy of GATT as a forum for a broad debate on intellectual property rights, the LDCs raised jurisdictional arguments against the American agenda.

The other major players from the First World, the European Community, and Japan, adopted a less radical approach in the negotiations compared to the United States. Both Japan and the European Community supported the goal of better intellectual property rights protection around the world. Yet, they did not share the United States' enthusiasm concerning the use of GATT to set international standards for intellectual property systems. Among their major concerns was the use of national intellectual property laws as "barriers to legitimate trade," as in the case of section 337 [of U.S. Trade law]. There were also significant differences in terms of negotiating tactics. The European Community, for instance, suggested that negotiations should first address the issue of repression of counterfeiting and piracy. . . .

ROBERT W. KASTENMEIER & DAVID BEIER, INTERNATIONAL TRADE AND INTELLECTUAL PROPERTY: PROMISE, RISKS, AND REALITY

22 VAND. J. TRANSNAT'L L. 285, 286–92 (1989)

Intellectual property protection for goods and services has become increasingly important to United States business in recent years. In the postwar era, the relative percentage of United States exports with a high intellectual property content (for example, chemicals, books, movies, records, electrical equipment, and computers) has more than doubled to more than twenty-five percent of all United States exports. Royalties received by United States industries from the licensing of intellectual property exceeds $8 billion per year, which is more than six times the amount paid to foreign firms. Equally significant are the losses that occur when such goods and services are pirated. According to some estimates, the value of lost sales due to unauthorized copying of United States products throughout the world exceeds $40 billion per year. The increasing importance attached to trade-oriented intellectual property, growing levels of piracy facilitated by emerging technologies, and expanding research and development costs has motivated businesses to seek governmental intervention to protect their intellectual property rights. The most comprehensive initiatives yet undertaken have been certain congressional efforts to improve United States intellectual property law. Parallel to these initiatives has been the effort to include intellectual property standards, norms, and enforcement minimums as a code beneath the GATT umbrella.

. . . .

International recognition of the connection between intellectual property and the world of international trade is a relatively new phenomenon. This linkage began in a publicly evident manner during the 98th Congress with the enactment of a series of measures requiring the Reagan Administration to examine the "adequacy and effectiveness" of the intellectual property laws of our trading partners, as a part of the trade assessment process. This largely bilateral approach assumed that the United States could obtain significant changes in the intellectual property laws of other countries through the threat/negotiation process. For some American business interests, the results of this initiative were necessarily under-inclusive. Moreover, because the potential impact of such a technique on some of the United States trading partners was limited, American businesses began to advocate the use of the GATT forum for enhanced intellectual property protection. Some advocates of the GATT process also saw it as complementary to the bilateral process. They argued that GATT standards could be applied to bilateral negotiations. Alternatively, some advocates of the GATT initiative viewed it as a useful device for energizing the other United Nations organizations responsible for intellectual property matters.

Genuinely disenchanted with the existing multilateral intellectual property fora (the World Intellectual Property Organization (WIPO) and UNESCO), and the absence of enforceable minimum standards within existing multilateral intellectual property treaties, the United States private sector considered using the GATT as a vehicle for improving the level of international multilateral standards. Members of the United States business community whose products rely on intellectual property protection—and their Congressional allies—urged the United States Government to attempt to include intellectual property protection in the then-forthcoming round of GATT talks.

The United States promoted its position to the other GATT contracting parties. This effort succeeded in producing the Punta del Este Declaration. . . .

. . . .

A December 1988 meeting in Montreal, Canada reviewed the progress made thus far in the Uruguay Round with respect to intellectual property. Four distinct positions emerged, without any signs of reconciliation between them. The United States, the European Community, and Japan were united in their willingness to negotiate substantive standards. The countries comprising the Association of Southeast Asian Nations (ASEAN) were willing to continue the discussions, but argued that the end product should reflect the developmental differences of the Third World. Canada, and Switzerland, whose intellectual property laws are generally adequate, but who wish to see the standard-setting exercise include as many GATT signatory or contracting parties as possible, appeared more willing to enter into negotiations even if they produced lower intellectual property standards. The fourth approach, articulated by the Indian and Brazilian delegations, was shared by several developing countries, including some Latin American nations. This group questioned the nature and scope of the Punta del Este Mandate and sought to have intellectual property standards set by WIPO, if at all. These nations apparently have concluded that WIPO would be a more sympathetic forum for the preservation of their existing intellectual property laws. Therefore, they insisted on studying topics that would lead to the diminution of intellectual property protection, such as compulsory licensing. In sum, the developing nations' view was largely antithetical to the view articulated by the negotiators from the United States, the European Community, and Japan.

NOTES AND QUESTIONS

1. As the excerpts above indicate, there was no consensus among the developed countries for inclusion of substantive intellectual property standards

in the Uruguay Round negotiations. There were even deeper divisions between the developed and developing countries. What do you make of the fact that the developing countries most vocal in their opposition to the integration of intellectual property rights in the Uruguay Round, such as India and Brazil have since the conclusion of the Round, emerged as important sources of cutting-edge innovation in areas from software to biotechnology? What about the fact that some countries reputed to be havens for intellectual property infringement, notably China, were not involved in the Uruguay Round process yet are now significant players in the international patent system? China became a WTO member, and thus subject to the TRIPS Agreement, in 2001.

2. The concerted efforts of private industry groups in the United States, European Union, and Japan are largely to be credited with the successful inclusion of intellectual property in the Uruguay Round. In the United States, an ad hoc group comprised of chief executive officers of major companies representing the software, pharmaceutical and entertainment industries formed the Intellectual Property Committee (IPC). This committee, wielding tremendous economic and political clout, initiated and led U.S. government efforts at the multilateral level to develop the TRIPS Agreement. A number of TRIPS scholars have been highly critical of this use of private power to, in effect, shape laws both within and outside of the U.S., particularly given the significant public policy interests implicated by intellectual property regulation. For an important work exploring the strategic involvement of private industry groups in the evolution of the TRIPS Agreement, *see* SUSAN K. SELL, PRIVATE POWER, PUBLIC LAW: THE GLOBALIZATION OF INTELLECTUAL PROPERTY RIGHTS (2003).

3. Since the conclusion of the TRIPS Agreement, the role of private interests in shaping intellectual property laws has been the subject of heightened scrutiny, most of it critical. Why do you think this is the case? Can you think of any reasons why intellectual property rights should be insulated from the reach of private interest groups? Do you think civil society organizations and non-profit organizations, who have also become significant actors on the global scene, should also be criticized for their role in influencing national or international intellectual property norms?

4. As we point out throughout this book, significant normative differences exist between the opinions of developed and developing countries, including the least-developed countries, regarding the benefits of strong intellectual property rights and their effect on economic development. Private industry groups are usually associated with arguments that support strong intellectual property rights as a source of economic growth while civil society organizations generally are associated with arguments that advocate for strong limitations on such rights. These ideological positions tend to be approximated with the tension between the "incentive" and "public interest" sides of the patent bargain. Recall from Chapter 1 the various arguments between countries such as the United States and Switzerland with respect to the justifications for a global patent system and whether patent rights should

be treated as property or as a public trust. In light of the history of the TRIPS negotiations, how far along have we come in the debate? Based on the excerpts above, how different are the issues and justifications that were raised in the mid-nineteenth century when the Paris Convention was being negotiated and the early twenty-first century as the TRIPS Agreement was concluded?

5. The conceptual link between trade and intellectual property is best framed in terms of the principle of comparative advantage. According to Professor Reichman, the logic of the TRIPS Agreement is aptly summed up by this classic rationale for liberal trade policy:

> Among the many causes of the drive to overcome preexisting territorial limitations on intellectual property rights, two merit attention here. First, the growing capacity of manufacturers in developing countries to penetrate distant markets for traditional industrial products has forced the developed countries to rely more heavily on their comparative advantages in the production of intellectual goods than in the past. Second, the rise of knowledge-based industries radically altered the nature of competition and disrupted the equilibrium that had resulted from more traditional comparative advantages. Not only is the cost of research and development often disproportionately higher than in the past, but the resulting innovation embodied in today's high-tech products has increasingly become more vulnerable to free-riding appropriators.

J.H. Reichman, *Universal Minimum Standards of Intellectual Property Protection Under the TRIPS Component of the WTO Agreement*, 29 INT'L LAW. 345, 346 (1995).

Do you agree that shifting comparative advantage in significant sectors of one country justifies a global legal response in the form of a treaty to ensure protection for those sectors? What other ways exist to deal with technological shifts that occasion significant investments of private capital? Do you think any of those alternatives would be more efficient than multilateral global negotiations? Would they be as effective?

2. AN OVERVIEW OF THE TRIPS AGREEMENT

The successful conclusion of the TRIPS Agreement during the Uruguay Round of multilateral trade negotiations manifested the importance of intellectual property protection in global economic relations, and reflected the desire "to reduce distortions and impediments to international trade" that may result from differences in levels of protection and enforcement of intellectual property rights. The Agreement established mandatory minimum standards of protection that every WTO member must provide for patents as well as other types of intellectual property in order to narrow variations across national intellectual property systems, and provide greater uniformity, stability, and predictability of protection worldwide. These new minimum standards were, in many cases, significantly higher than the standards of protection previously afforded to rights holders by many WTO member countries. Importantly, unlike previous multilateral intellectual property accords, the dispute resolution framework designed to settle disputes arising among member states over the protection of intellectual property rights meant that there existed potential for the development of a set of truly global intellectual property norms.

Recall from Chapter 2 that the Paris Convention and the PCT, two leading WIPO-administered patent treaties, evolved incrementally on the basis of consensus of all the member countries. Due to the nature of standard-setting activities in WIPO bodies, discussions within the Organization were largely informed by national experiences, and progress in negotiations over issues could be blocked even if only a single member country objected. The Uruguay Round provided a forum where, unlike WIPO, the developed countries could maximize their influence and impose obligations on all WTO member countries even before a consensus had emerged. Because there was never a complete "buy-in" from all WTO member countries, however, the TRIPS Agreement carries with it a certain level of mistrust, and developing countries in particular have been the source of strong opposition to the further strengthening of minimum global levels of intellectual property protection. The political and economic environment in which the TRIPS Agreement was negotiated raised important questions about the conditions under which developed countries, led by the United States, and developing countries might benefit under a new intellectual property order based on minimum, mandatory substantive intellectual property rights. In addition, however, was a realization that there would be possible costs to the United States of merging intellectual property rights with the liberal trading system. Consider the following excerpt:

R. MICHAEL GADBAW, INTELLECTUAL PROPERTY AND INTERNATIONAL TRADE: MERGER OR MARRIAGE OF CONVENIENCE?

22 VAND. J. TRANSNAT'L L. 223, 226–30 (1989)

Until relatively recently, intellectual property and international trade policies were relegated to distinct and separate spheres. Each was based upon its own set of domestic laws and international agreements, although common principles such as national treatment were central features of the international agreements in both domains. Entirely distinct bureaucracies administered these laws and agreements both at the national and international levels, and their efforts were rarely viewed as requiring coordination, except perhaps in light of foreign political—as distinct from economic-policy considerations.

More than any other factor, the concerns of the private sector seem to have been instrumental in changing this perspective. . . .

. . . .

. . . [T]he United States Government began to reevaluate its policy of benign neglect toward United States investment abroad, and attention turned to the United States Trade Representative (USTR) as the agency most receptive to industry concerns and in the best position to coordinate efforts by the United States Government to develop responses. By 1979, USTR had authority to address investment issues both through the negotiation of agreements and the use of trade measures . . . .

. . . [T]he private sector began to look to trade policy as a tool to deal with a range of issues beyond the traditional scope of trade negotiations-issues that relate to the entire environment that United States companies confront in other countries. The private sector was attracted to the network of procedures, advisory mechanisms, and political relationships which gave industry a greater feeling that its concerns were understood and that the strategy it worked out with the United States Government would be implemented in a forthright, assertive manner, with greater insulation from foreign policy-inspired interference than had characterized the resolution of such issues in the past.

Companies ultimately saw the possibility that the United States Government would be willing to use the leverage inherent in access to the United States market as a means of stimulating countries to upgrade their level of protection. Not coincidentally, some of the countries that posed the most serious problems were heavily dependent upon trade with the United States.

. . . .

[T]rade leverage has proved most effective in stimulating reforms in countries that are especially dependent upon trade with the United States. When such countries' access to the markets of Europe and Japan is included, the case for accommodating concerns about intellectual property rights is two to four times as compelling. A trade-leveraged strategy is likely to be less effective in countries that are less dependent on exports to the Western industrialized nations, or in which other considerations outweigh the trade implications of failure to address United States concerns.

The United States strategy of conditioning trade concessions on provision of intellectual property protection inevitably had to confront the issue of its compatibility with the framework of rules and negotiating procedures in GATT. The effectiveness of trade leverage is in fact quite limited if its use cannot somehow be justified under the GATT rules. The use of measures whose GATT-consistency is questioned provokes accusations of unilateralism and raises the threat that other countries will feel justified in responding in kind. . . .

This . . . argues strongly for a new agreement that binds GATT members to a higher standard of obligation with respect to intellectual property rights than is presently mandated in any international agreement. This approach is problematic, however, because it puts the issue entirely into a negotiating context; that is, to obtain concessions on standards from other GATT members, the United States and others would be expected to offer something in return. Like-minded countries will likely be willing to accept the minimum standards that the United States seeks in return for a commitment that the United States will forego recourse to unilateral responsive measures (other than those contemplated by the agreement). But for countries unwilling to embrace the standards, there are only two alternatives in this paradigm: (1) persuade the United States and other countries to agree to compromise on the standard of protection; or (2) provide concessions in other areas. The first of these alternatives is unacceptable to the United States business community and the second is highly problematic.

———————

As concluded, the Uruguay Round negotiations were successful because at some level they were a "win-win" for all countries. In exchange for stronger standards of intellectual property protection through the TRIPS Agreement, developing countries gained concessions and market access in areas such as textiles and agriculture where they have traditionally held a comparative advantage over the developed countries. However, it has proved difficult for the United States and the European Union to honor their obligations given the politically sensitive nature of these industries in domestic markets. Accordingly, the perceived legitimacy of the "TRIPS bargain" has been far less robust than ideally should be the case. Further, as you will learn later in this Chapter, several U.S. trading partners (some of them allies during the Uruguay Round negotiations) have observed that the United States has not been in full compliance with the TRIPS Agreement.

a. Structure of the TRIPS Agreement

The TRIPS Agreement is divided into five substantive and two administrative parts. The substantive portion of the Agreement is divided as follows:

- Part I (Arts. 1–8) consists of general provisions and basic principles applicable to all areas of intellectual property;
- Part II (Arts. 9–40) is devoted to setting standards concerning the availability, scope and use of intellectual property

rights in each of the subject areas covered by the Agreement (patents, trademarks, copyrights, etc.);

- Part III (Arts. 41–61) deals with the enforcement of IP rights;
- Part IV (Art. 62) provides for procedures concerning the acquisition and maintenance of IP rights; and
- Part V (Arts. 63–64) establishes the TRIPS dispute resolution procedure.

b. Basic Principles and Objectives

Among the noteworthy provisions of Part I of the Agreement is Article 2, which incorporates the substantive provisions of the Paris Convention (Articles 1–12, and 19), and expressly obliges WTO member countries to comply with them. The implications of requiring WTO member countries to obey the terms of the Paris Convention are significant. Since several WTO members are not party to the Paris Convention (e.g., Kuwait, Myanmar, and Taiwan), the TRIPS Agreement extends the reach of the Convention to them. It also effectively attaches a dispute resolution mechanism, not previously a feature of the Paris Convention, which can be invoked when one WTO member country accuses another of a Convention violation. Moreover, requiring compliance signals that the Paris Convention is not only the basis for the TRIPS Agreement, but it is also the starting point upon which the Agreement adds specificity and detail as well as new standards not found in the earlier text. In this latter respect, the TRIPS Agreement can be viewed as "Paris-plus."

Article 3 of the TRIPS Agreement reiterates the obligation of national treatment as provided in the Paris Convention, according to which "[e]ach Member shall accord to the nationals of other Members treatment no less favorable than that it accords to its own nationals." Article 4, however, adds a new feature to the multilateral intellectual property framework—the concept of most-favored-nation (MFN) treatment. As provided in the Agreement, "any advantage, favor, privilege or immunity" regarding intellectual property protection that a WTO member country grants to the nationals of another country must be granted "immediately and unconditionally" to the nationals of all other member countries. The requirement of most-favored-nation treatment applies even if the advantage is more favorable than that which the WTO member affords to its own nationals. However, derogations from MFN are allowed in certain circumstances. For example, countries may join a free trade agreement that discriminates against goods from outside the area.

Part I also lays out the underlying objectives of the Agreement. Foremost among them is the notion that intellectual property protection should contribute to the promotion of innovation and technology transfer. To achieve this goal, Article 7 of the Agreement stipulates that intellectual property rights and obligations should be balanced, to the mutual advantage of both producers and users of intellectual property, and that protection should be carried out in a manner "conducive to enhancing social and economic welfare." Recognizing that the absence of balance can lead to abuses by rights holders, TRIPS Article 8 permits WTO member countries to adopt measures in their national laws or regulations "to protect public health and nutrition," "to promote the public interest in sectors of vital importance to their socio-economic and technological development," and "to prevent the resort to practices which unreasonably restrain trade or adversely affect the international transfer of technology." The Doha Declaration on the TRIPS Agreement and Public Health, which will be discussed later in this Chapter, was adopted at a WTO Ministerial meeting in 2001 in an effort to reinforce flexibilities countries have under the TRIPS Agreement to act in the interest of national public health priorities.

c. Standards of Protection

While Part I sets forth the fundamental objectives and basic principles of the TRIPS Agreement, Part II attempts to infuse them with meaning and specificity by establishing substantive standards of protection with respect to each of the subject areas covered by the Agreement. In some cases, the standards merely codify prevailing practice, but in others, they set requirements higher than those existing in many member countries. The adoption of the TRIPS Agreement has therefore required most countries, including the United States, to amend at least some provisions of their national patent laws.

KAREN TRIPP & LINDA STOKLEY, CHANGES IN U.S. PATENT LAW EFFECTED BY THE URUGUAY ROUND AGREEMENTS ACT—THE GATT IMPLEMENTATION LEGISLATION

3 TEX. INTELL. PROP. L.J. 315, 315–21 (1995)

The Uruguay Round of the General Agreement on Trade and Tariffs Negotiations (GATT) came to a close on December 15, 1993. . . . On December 8, 1994, almost one year after the close of the GATT negotiations, President Clinton signed the Uruguay Round Agreements Act into law in the United States. This act is the legislation implementing the World Trade Organization (WTO)/GATT and its accompanying Trade Related Aspects of Intellectual Property Rights (TRIPs) provisions in the United States. The TRIPs provisions of the WTO/GATT implementation legislation make sweeping and significant changes to current intellectual property law, particularly for patents. . . .

. . . .

I. PATENT TERM CHANGED TO TWENTY YEARS FROM DATE OF FILING

The most significant change brought about by the Uruguay Round Agreements Act is that the term of a United States patent will be twenty years, measured from the date of filing of the patent application, rather than seventeen years, measured from the date of issue of the patent. This means that the patent term will begin on the date that the patent issues and will end twenty years from the date on which the application for the patent was filed in the United States. A continuation or a continuation-in-part patent application may still be filed with the benefit of the filing date of the parent, for purposes of priority. However, the term of the continuation or continuation-in-part patent will be measured from the date of filing of the parent application, rather than from the date of issue of the continuation or continuation-in-part patent. Similarly, the term of a divisional patent application will be measured from the date the parent application is filed. Where there is more than one parent application, the patent term of all the descendants shall be measured from the date the earliest parent application is filed. . . .

. . . .

II. PROVISIONAL APPLICATIONS ESTABLISHED IN CREATING A "DOMESTIC PRIORITY SYSTEM"

Provisional applications may be filed beginning June 8, 1995. The purpose of a provisional application is to provide a priority date that will not be counted in the patent term. The provisions of the Paris Convention for Protection of Industrial Property do not allow inclusion of the Paris Convention priority period in the patent term. Provisional applications are intended to place U.S. applicants on equal footing with foreign applicants with respect to the patent term.

. . . .

III. Foreign Activity May Be Used to Show Date of Invention

For proving a date of invention, parties will be able to rely on inventive activity occurring outside the United States in a World Trade Organization (WTO) member country. Inventive activity for proving a date of invention will no longer be restricted to activity occurring within the United States or in NAFTA countries Canada and Mexico. Foreign companies and multinationals will no longer be limited to the filing dates of their foreign priority applications to establish a date of invention made abroad. This change will apply to applications filed on or after January 1, 1996. . . .

IV. SCOPE OF INFRINGEMENT BROADENED

Effective January 1, 1996, offers to sell a patented invention—a patented product or a patented process—or a product made from a patented process, will infringe the patent if the sale will occur before the expiration of the patent term. Similarly, offers to sell a component known to be especially made or adapted for a patented invention will be sufficient to establish contributory infringement if the sale will occur before the expiration of the patent term. The existing exceptions to infringement of section 271(e) of the Patent Act will continue to apply.

Also, effective January 1, 1996, importing a patented invention—a patented product or patented process—as well as importing a product made by a process patented in the United States, will infringe the patent. Similarly, importing a component known to be especially made for the invention will be sufficient to establish contributory infringement.

NOTES AND QUESTIONS

1. Although the push for TRIPS originated from the United States, it is not entirely clear that the industry groups or Congress fully appreciated the fact that U.S. law would also be more than minimally affected by the substantive requirements of the Agreement. Unlike other areas of intellectual property law, however, especially copyright law, Congress has been more willing to make adjustments to patent laws to comply with TRIPS standards. Despite these efforts, however, there remained important areas where U.S. law was not fully consistent with the demands of the international patent system. *See, e.g.,* 2 Moy's Walker on Patents § 8:98 (4th ed.) (2003 & 2009 Supp.) (noting that despite NAFTA and TRIPS, "foreign activities can be relied upon to prove a date of invention only if the foreign inventor has himself attempted to cover that subject matter in a claim of a United States patent or patent application.") *See also* Sean A. Passino, Stephen B. Maebius & Harold C. Wegner, *Foreign-Filed PCT Applications: An Asymmetrical Patent-Defeating Effect*, 85 J. PAT. & TRADEMARK OFF. SOC'Y 874, 874 (2003) (remarking that PCT related changes introduced by the 1999 American Inventors Protection Act were "a major sore point in the international patent community"). The 2011 America Invents Act (AIA) amendments further reduced but did not completely eliminate such inconsistencies. Throughout this book, we note areas of continued divergence between the patent law of the United States and several other countries, as well as areas that, while not facially inconsistent with treaty provisions, nonetheless may have a prejudicial effect on innovation occurring outside the United States.

2. To what extent do you think the international patent system is effective if countries are still free to enact domestic laws that have the effect of favoring their citizens? Is it just a matter of time before full harmonization of intellectual property standards is achieved, or should there always be a basis for countries to consider domestic interests in enacting new legislation? Before you answer this question, consider TRIPS Article 8.1 which states:

Members may, in formulating or amending their laws and regulations, adopt measures necessary to protect public health and nutrition, and to promote the public interest in sectors of vital importance to their socio-economic and technological development, provided that such measures are consistent with the provisions of this Agreement.

3. Recall the Federal Circuit's decision in *Voda v. Cordis Corp.,* 476 F.3d 887 (Fed Cir. 2007) that you read in Chapter 1, *supra* p. 45. If international harmonization is not regarded by the court as a sufficient basis to assert jurisdiction over foreign patents, should it be enough to restrain Congress from engaging in protectionist patent legislation? Should these two institutions— courts and Congress—be equally responsible and accountable to the obligations contained in international treaties that the U.S. has signed?

4. The Preamble to the TRIPS Agreement states that the signatory countries recognize "the underlying public policy objectives of national systems for the protection of intellectual property, including developmental and technological objectives." This provision has been widely cited by developing and least-developed countries as a basis for limitations to strong patent rights in their domestic legislation. Can this language also be construed to provide a basis for U.S. laws, agency regulations, or practices that favor U.S. patent applicants? Can it be the basis for U.S. efforts through bilateral treaties to further strengthen global patent rights beyond what is in the TRIPS Agreement? We will return to the topic of bilateral trade agreements and intellectual property rights later in this Chapter.

3. SUBSTANTIVE STANDARDS IN THE TRIPS AGREEMENT

a. Patentable Subject Matter

The patent-related provisions (Articles 27–34) of the Agreement are relatively few in number, but they are quite extensive in scope. TRIPS Article 33 fills a gap in the Paris Convention by providing that patent protection must be available for a minimum of twenty years, a standard that most WTO countries other than the United States, Japan, and a few others had already adopted prior to TRIPS. Article 27.1 tackles the more controversial issue of patentable subject matter by requiring that patent protection must be available for both products and processes in all areas of technology, provided that the inventions to be protected are new, involve an inventive step, and are capable of industrial application. Article 27.1 was—and remains—controversial because it goes well beyond the bounds of the Paris Convention. As was mentioned in Chapter 2, the Paris Convention is silent on the issue of scope of patent protection, and that silence permitted many countries to exclude certain essential products, such as pharmaceuticals and agrochemicals, from the scope of patentable subject matter. As a result, in the pre-TRIPS era, countries that did not protect pharmaceutical or agrochemical products (e.g., India) were able to produce lawful generic versions of those products by inventing around the patented process. As discussed further below, apart from a few narrow exceptions, such wholesale exclusion of a particular group of products from the coverage of the patent system is no longer possible under the TRIPS framework.

Product patenting was among the most contentious and heatedly fought issues that marked the TRIPS negotiations. Although the question was ultimately resolved in favor of requiring protection, a compromise was struck with respect to the provision's effective date. Article 65.4 provides that if a developing country did not provide product patent protection in a particular area of technology when the TRIPS Agreement entered into force on January 1, 1995, it had up to January 1, 2005, to amend its national legislation in order to provide for protection. During the transition period, applications for pharmaceutical or agrochemical patents could be filed with the patent offices of the countries concerned, but those offices had no obligation to examine the applications until the expiration of the period. Least-developed countries (LDCs) have been given until 2013 to comply with TRIPS generally and until 2016 to provide pharmaceutical product patent protection (with the right to request additional extensions), and they do not have to comply with TRIPS Art. 70.8 and 70.9. In November 2011, Bangladesh, an LDC, requested an extension of the 2013 deadline. At the time of this writing, the request is pending before the TRIPS Council.

While the United States has adopted the principle that "anything under the sun that is made by man" should be eligible for patent protection, most countries have traditionally declared certain categories of inventions to be outside the scope of patentable subject matter. In conformity with that prevailing practice, Articles 27.2 and 27.3 give member countries freedom, if they so choose, to exclude certain types of inventions from patentability. For example, countries may refuse to patent an invention if its commercial exploitation would be contrary to public order or morality, or would endanger health or the environment. They can also refuse to patent diagnostic, therapeutic, and surgical methods for the treatment of humans or animals, as well as "plants and animals other than micro-organisms, and essentially biological processes for the production of plants or animals other than non-biological and microbiological processes." Under TRIPS Article 27.3(b), however, new plant varieties may not be excluded from the scope of patent protection unless a *sui generis* system, such as one for breeders' rights, is in place to protect them. We discuss the issue of new plant varieties in Chapter 8.

b. Exclusive Rights and Compulsory Licensing

Unlike the Paris Convention, which is silent on the matter, the TRIPS Agreement enumerates the exclusive rights that a member country must ensure are conferred on patent owners. Article 28.1 distinguishes between product and process patents and mandates the following rights for each:

(a) where the subject matter of a patent is a product, to prevent third parties not having the owner's consent from the acts of: making, using, offering for sale, selling, or importing for these purposes that product;

(b) where the subject matter of a patent is a process, to prevent third parties not having the owner's consent from the act of using the process, and from the acts of: using, offering for sale, selling, or importing for these purposes at least the product obtained directly from the process.

Recognizing that patent owners may abuse rights afforded to them, the Agreement also permits limited exceptions to the rights conferred, as well as the grant of compulsory licenses. Article 31 of the TRIPS Agreement, which refers to a compulsory license as "use without authorization of the right holder," provides rather exacting conditions that member countries must put into place in order to safeguard the interests of patent owners. Those conditions, while subject to exceptions, include ensuring that:

- the proposed user has made efforts to obtain authorization from the right holder on reasonable commercial terms and conditions and that such efforts have not been successful with a reasonable period of time;

- the scope and duration of such use [is] limited to the purpose for which it was authorized;

- the use is non-exclusive, non-assignable, and "authorized predominantly for the supply of the domestic market";

- the use can be terminated "if and when the circumstances which led to it cease to exist or are unlikely to recur";

- the patent owner is paid adequate remuneration and any decision relating to remuneration is subject to judicial review;

- the legal validity of any decision relating to the authorization of such use shall be subject to judicial review or other independent review by a distinct higher authority; and

- judicial review is available in the case of decisions to revoke or forfeit a patent.

To facilitate conformity with the particularly detailed nature of the TRIPS compulsory licensing requirements, a few of the countries that joined the WTO following adoption of the TRIPS Agreement chose to rely on the language of the TRIPS provisions, and echoed it in their national patent legislation.

c. Burden of Proof

The final patent-specific provision of the TRIPS Agreement is Article 34, which concerns the burden of proof in civil proceedings for process patent infringement. As noted above, Article 28(b) of the Agreement provides that patents granted for a process of manufacture must give rise to exclusive rights not only in the process but also in the product obtained directly from the process. This provision was the subject of heated discussion during the Uruguay Round negotiations, but Article 34 proved even more contentious. Article 34 provides that in cases of alleged process patent infringement where the product is identical to the product obtained by the patented process, courts may place the burden of proof on the defendant to prove that "the process to obtain an identical product is different from the patented process." The provision therefore shifts the traditional allocation of the burden of proof away from the right holder, and requires alleged infringers to show that they have not used a patented process. In the absence of such proof, in particular where the product obtained by the patented process is new, or where the patent owner was unable to determine the actual process used by the defendant, the courts must find that the defendant is liable for infringing the patented process.

B. ENFORCEMENT OF PATENT RIGHTS UNDER THE WTO DISPUTE SETTLEMENT UNDERSTANDING

Article 41 of the TRIPS Agreement obligates all WTO member countries to ensure that enforcement procedures are available under domestic law "to permit effective action against any act of infringement of intellectual property rights covered by this Agreement, including expeditious remedies to prevent infringements and remedies which constitute a deterrent to further infringements." The Agreement does not mandate the establishment of a specialized intellectual property judicial system, but it does require that the system of enforcement be fair, equitable, reasonably prompt, uncomplicated, and subject to judicial review. In particular, judicial authorities must, under the Agreement, have the authority to order the production of evidence, issue injunctions, require the infringer to pay damages and expenses, order the destruction of infringing goods, and take prompt and effective *ex parte* measures to prevent imminent infringement or preserve evidence. The Agreement thus echoes the policy of the United States and other developed countries that having intellectual property laws is not enough; the judicial system must be prepared to enforce them.

The TRIPS Agreement is the first (and only) multilateral intellectual property accord featuring a formal framework for the resolution of disputes among members concerning the fulfillment of obligations under the treaty. Article 64 of the Agreement not only makes disputes subject to the WTO dispute settlement procedure, it also requires member countries to refer disputes to the procedure rather than taking matters into their own hands. The WTO Understanding on the Rules and Procedures Governing the Settlement of Disputes, adopted simultaneously with the TRIPS Agreement, controls the dispute settlement procedure and provides that consultations should play a central role. A member country initiates the procedure by requesting consultations with an alleged offending country, and the alleged offender is obligated to commence consultations within the following thirty days. If there is no settlement of the dispute within sixty days of the request for consultations, or if the request for consultations is rejected, the complainant country may request the establishment of a dispute resolution panel, which normally consists of three experts from countries not party to the dispute.

After receiving evidence, a WTO panel will normally complete its work within six months and submit its reports to the Dispute Settlement Body (DSB), which is made up of all WTO member countries. Unless the DSB decides by consensus not to adopt the panel report, or one of the parties to the dispute notifies the Council of its intent to appeal the report's findings, the report is adopted within sixty days of its issuance. If an appeal is lodged, an appellate panel, also consisting of three members, will be convened to review the issues of law covered in the panel report, and to examine the legal interpretations developed by the panel. The appellate panel will normally issue its report within sixty days of the decision to appeal, and that report must be accepted by the parties, unless the DSB decides by consensus to reject it.

If the final report finds in favor of the complainant, the offending country will have to notify the WTO whether it intends to implement the adopted recommendations, in which case the DSB will review implementation until it determines that the country is in compliance with its TRIPS obligations. In the event the offending country declines or fails to implement the recommendations, however, the complainant country may seek compensation, or, more typically, request the DSB to suspend trade concessions or other obligations to the offending country. The following flowchart illustrates the WTO dispute settlement process.

WTO Dispute Settlement Process

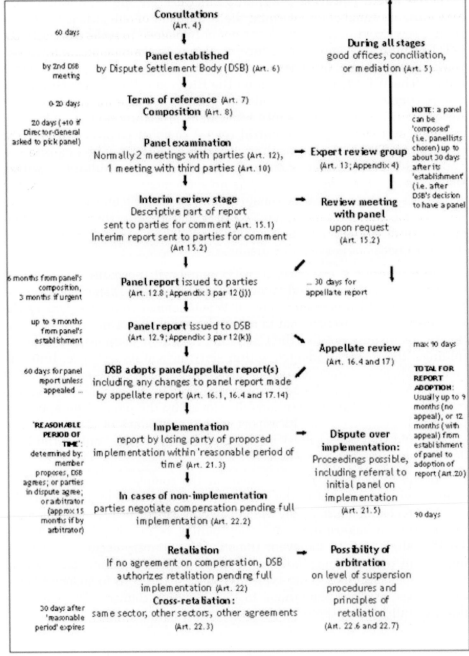

Source: WTO

The WTO dispute settlement process is largely seen as a success compared to the predecessor GATT regime; in fact, 332 WTO cases were filed between 1995 and 2005 versus 300 total cases brought under GATT between 1947 and 1994. Moreover, in its relatively short history, the WTO has already resolved several patent cases. As noted earlier, TRIPS Article 27 requires member countries to provide patent protection in all areas of technology, a requirement largely designed to ensure product patent protection for pharmaceuticals and agricultural chemicals by developing countries and LDCs. In exchange, countries not previously providing such protection received a transition period in which to bring their laws into compliance with Article 27. But in exchange for the transition period, such countries, other than LDCs, had to provide a way (called a "mailbox system") for eligible inventions applied for after the entry into force of the TRIPS agreement to be examined for patentability once the transition periods expired. Moreover, owners of patents obtained in other countries on such inventions could apply, in transitioning countries, for up to five years of exclusive marketing rights (EMRs). Under the 2001 Doha Declaration, discussed below, LDCs do not have to comply with Article 27 before January 1, 2016. Mailbox systems and EMRs are provided for in TRIPS Article 70.8 and 70.9:

? reconcile

mailbox apps to preserve novelty + priority in agro + pharma

70.8 Where a Member does not make available as of the date of entry into force of the WTO Agreement patent protection for pharmaceutical and agricultural chemical products commensurate with its obligations under Article 27, that Member shall:

> (a) notwithstanding the provisions of Part VI, provide as from the date of entry into force of the WTO Agreement a means by which applications for patents for such inventions can be filed;

> (b) apply to these applications, as of the date of application of this Agreement, the criteria for patentability as laid down in this Agreement as if those criteria were being applied on the date of filing in that Member or, where priority is available and claimed, the priority date of the application; and

> (c) provide patent protection in accordance with this Agreement as from the grant of the patent and for the remainder of the patent term, counted from the filing date in accordance with Article 33 of this Agreement, for those of these applications that meet the criteria for protection referred to in subparagraph (b).

70.9 Where a product is the subject of a patent application in a Member in accordance with paragraph 8(a), exclusive marketing rights shall be granted, notwithstanding the provisions of Part VI, for a period of five years after obtaining marketing approval in that Member or until a product patent is granted or rejected in that Member, whichever period is shorter, provided that, subsequent to the entry into force of the WTO Agreement, a patent application has been filed and a patent granted for that product in another Member and marketing approval obtained in such other Member.

Compliance with TRIPS Article 70.8 was the subject of the first TRIPS dispute brought before the WTO. The Appellate Body decision illustrates some of the flexibility inherent in the TRIPS Agreement—members are allowed to determine how best to meet their obligations, but only up to a point.

INDIA–PROTECTION FOR PHARMACEUTICAL AND AGRICULTURAL CHEMICAL PRODUCTS

Report of the Appellate Body
WT/DS50/AB/R
19 December 1997

[India appealed from the conclusions made by a WTO dispute resolution panel in the Panel Report, *India-Patent Protection for Pharmaceutical and Agricultural Chemical Products* (the "Panel Report"), which considered a complaint by the United States against India concerning, among other things, the absence in India of a means for the filing of patent applications for pharmaceutical and agricultural chemical products pursuant to Article 70.8 of the TRIPS Agreement. The Panel concluded that India had not complied with its obligations under Article 70.8(a) because it had "failed to establish a mechanism that adequately preserves novelty and priority in respect of applications for product patents in respect of pharmaceutical and agricultural chemical inventions during the transitional period to which it is entitled under Article 65 of the Agreement." Arguing that the Panel erred in its findings, India contended that "it has established, through 'administrative instructions,' 'a means' by which applications for patents for pharmaceutical and agricultural chemical products (often referred to as 'mailbox applications') can be filed" and that this mechanism satisfied TRIPS Article 70.8.]

45. . . . The Panel misunderstands the concept of legitimate expectations in the context of the customary rules of interpretation of public international law. The legitimate expectations of the parties to a treaty are reflected in the language of the treaty itself. The duty of a treaty interpreter is to examine the words of the treaty to determine the intentions of the parties. This should be done in accordance with the principles of treaty interpretation set out in Article 31 of the *Vienna Convention*. But these principles of interpretation neither require nor condone the imputation into a treaty of words that are not there or the importation into a treaty of concepts that were not intended.

46. In *United States – Standards for Reformulated and Conventional Gasoline*, we set out the proper approach to be applied in interpreting the *WTO Agreement* in accordance with the rules in Article 31 of the *Vienna Convention*. These rules must be respected and applied in interpreting

the *TRIPS Agreement* or any other covered agreement. The Panel in this case has created its own interpretative principle, which is consistent with neither the customary rules of interpretation of public international law nor established GATT/WTO practice. Both panels and the Appellate Body must be guided by the rules of treaty interpretation set out in the *Vienna Convention*, and must not add to or diminish rights and obligations provided in the *WTO Agreement*.

. . . .

48. For these reasons, we do not agree with the Panel that the legitimate expectations of Members *and* private rights holders concerning conditions of competition must always be taken into account in interpreting the *TRIPS Agreement*.

. . . .

57. . . . The Agreement takes into account, *inter alia*, "the need to promote effective and adequate protection of intellectual property rights." We believe the Panel was correct in finding that the "means" that the Member concerned is obliged to provide under Article 70.8(a) must allow for "the entitlement to file mailbox applications and the allocation of filing and priority dates to them." Furthermore, the Panel was correct in finding that the "means" established under Article 70.8(a) must also provide "a sound legal basis to preserve novelty and priority as of those dates." These findings flow inescapably from the necessary operation of paragraphs (b) and (c) of Article 70.8.

58. However, we do *not* agree with the Panel that Article 70.8(a) requires a Member to establish a means "so as to eliminate any reasonable doubts regarding whether mailbox applications and eventual patents based on them could be rejected or invalidated because, at the filing or priority date, the matter for which protection was sought was unpatentable in the country in question." India is *entitled*, by the "transitional arrangements" in paragraphs 1, 2 and 4 of Article 65, to delay application of Article 27 for patents for pharmaceutical and agricultural chemical products until 1 January 2005. In our view, India is obliged, by Article 70.8(a), to provide a legal mechanism for the filing of mailbox applications that provides a sound legal basis to preserve both the novelty of the inventions and the priority of the applications as of the relevant filing and priority dates. No more.

. . . .

60. India insists that it has done that. India contends that it has established, through "administrative instructions," a "means" consistent with Article 70.8(a) of the *TRIPS Agreement*. According to India, these "administrative instructions" establish a mechanism that provides a sound legal basis to preserve the novelty of the inventions and the priority of the applications as of the relevant filing and priority dates consistent with Arti-

cle 70.8(a) of the *TRIPS Agreement*. According to India, pursuant to these "administrative instructions," the Patent Office has been directed to store applications for patents for pharmaceutical and agricultural chemical products separately for future action pursuant to Article 70.8, and the Controller General of Patents Designs and Trademarks ("the Controller") has been instructed not to refer them to an examiner until 1 January 2005. According to India, these "administrative instructions" are legally valid in Indian law, as they are reflected in the Minister's Statement to Parliament of 2 August 1996. And, according to India:

> There is . . . *absolute certainty* that India can, when patents are due in accordance with subparagraphs (b) and (c) of Article 70.8, decide to grant such patents on the basis of the applications currently submitted and determine the novelty and priority of the inventions in accordance with the date of these applications.

61. India has not provided any text of these "administrative instructions" either to the Panel or to us.

62. Whatever their substance or their import, these "administrative instructions" were not the initial "means" chosen by the Government of India to meet India's obligations under Article 70.8(a) of the *TRIPS Agreement*. The Government of India's initial preference for establishing a "means" for filing mailbox applications under Article 70.8(a) was the Patents (Amendment) Ordinance (the "Ordinance"), promulgated by the President of India on 31 December 1994 pursuant to Article 123 of India's Constitution. Article 123 enables the President to promulgate an ordinance when Parliament is not in session, and when the President is satisfied "that circumstances exist which render it necessary for him to take immediate action." India notified the Ordinance to the Council for TRIPS, pursuant to Article 63.2 of the *TRIPS Agreement*, on 6 March 1995. In accordance with the terms of Article 123 of India's Constitution, the Ordinance expired on 26 March 1995, six weeks after the reassembly of Parliament. This was followed by an unsuccessful effort to enact the Patents (Amendment) Bill [of] 1995 to implement the contents of the Ordinance on a permanent basis. This Bill was introduced in the Lok Sabha (Lower House) in March 1995. After being passed by the Lok Sabha, it was referred to a Select Committee of the Rajya Sabha (Upper House) for examination and report. However, the Bill was subsequently not enacted due to the dissolution of Parliament on 10 May 1996. From these actions, it is apparent that the Government of India initially considered the enactment of amending legislation to be necessary in order to implement its obligations under Article 70.8(a). However, India maintains that the "administrative instructions" issued in April 1995 effectively continued the mailbox system established by the Ordinance, thus obviating the need for a formal amendment to the Patents Act or for a new notification to the Council for TRIPS.

63. With respect to India's "administrative instructions," the Panel found that "the current administrative practice creates a certain degree of legal insecurity in that it requires Indian officials to ignore certain mandatory provisions of the Patents Act" and that "even if Patent Office officials do not examine and reject mailbox applications, a competitor might seek a judicial order to do so in order to obtain rejection of a patent claim."

64. India asserts that the Panel erred in its treatment of India's municipal law because municipal law is a fact that must be established before an international tribunal by the party relying on it. In India's view, the Panel did not assess the Indian law as a fact to be established by the United States, but rather as a law to be interpreted by the Panel. India argues that the Panel should have given India the benefit of the doubt as to the status of its mailbox system under Indian domestic law. India claims, furthermore, that the Panel should have sought guidance from India on matters relating to the interpretation of Indian law.

. . . .

66. In this case, the Panel was simply performing its task in determining whether India's "administrative instructions" for receiving mailbox applications were in conformity with India's obligations under Article 70.8(a) of the *TRIPS Agreement*. It is clear that an examination of the relevant aspects of Indian municipal law and, in particular, the relevant provisions of the Patents Act as they relate to the "administrative instructions," is essential to determining whether India has complied with its obligations under Article 70.8(a). There was simply no way for the Panel to make this determination without engaging in an examination of Indian law. But, as in the case cited above before the Permanent Court of International Justice, in this case, the Panel was not interpreting Indian law "as such;" rather, the Panel was examining Indian law solely for the purpose of determining whether India had met its obligations under the *TRIPS Agreement*. To say that the Panel should have done otherwise would be to say that only India can assess whether Indian law is consistent with India's obligations under the *WTO Agreement*. This, clearly, cannot be so.

. . . .

68. And, just as it was necessary for the Panel in this case to seek a detailed understanding of the operation of the Patents Act as it relates to the "administrative instructions" in order to assess whether India had complied with Article 70.8(a), so, too, is it necessary for us in this appeal to review the Panel's examination of the same Indian domestic law.

69. To do so, we must look at the specific provisions of the Patents Act. Section 5(a) of the Patents Act provides that substances 'intended for use, or capable of being used, as food or as medicine or drug" are not patentable. "When the complete specification has been led in respect of an appli-

cation for a patent," section 12(1) *requires* the Controller to refer that application and that specification to an examiner. Moreover, section 15(2) of the Patents Act states that the Controller "shall refuse" an application in respect of a substance that is not patentable. We agree with the Panel that these provisions of the Patents Act are mandatory.

And, like the Panel, we are not persuaded that India's "administrative instructions" would prevail over the contradictory mandatory provisions of the Patents Act. We note also that, in issuing these "administrative instructions," the Government of India did not avail itself of the provisions of section 159 of the Patents Act, which allows the Central Government "to make rules for carrying out the provisions of [the] Act" or section 160 of the Patents Act, which requires that such rules be laid before each House of the Indian Parliament. We are told by India that such rulemaking was not required for the "administrative instructions" at issue here. But this, too, seems to be inconsistent with the mandatory provisions of the Patents Act.

70. We are not persuaded by India's explanation of these seeming contradictions. Accordingly, we are not persuaded that India's "administrative instructions" would survive a legal challenge under the Patents Act. And, consequently, we are not persuaded that India's "administrative instructions" provide a sound legal basis to preserve novelty of inventions and priority of applications as of the relevant filing and priority dates.

71. For these reasons, we agree with the Panel's conclusion that India's "administrative instructions" for receiving mailbox applications are inconsistent with Article 70.8(a) of the *TRIPS Agreement*.

NOTES AND QUESTIONS

1. Although developing countries were obliged to start examining pharmaceutical product patent applications as of January 2005, the mailboxes in some patent offices still contain unexamined applications. If you were a patent counsel for a pharmaceutical company with pending applications in several mailboxes, would you view this situation as a cause for alarm?

2. How would you describe the construction of the TRIPS Agreement adopted by the Appellate Body in *India–Protection for Pharmaceutical and Agricultural Chemical Products*? Shortly after the conclusion of the Uruguay Round, a debate between Professor Jackson and Ms. Bello raised an important question about the nature of the various agreements that comprise the Uruguay Round: Are the agreements rule-based such that countries cannot legitimately deviate from them or are they more like contract rights in which one party may engage in an efficient breach and pay for any noncompliance? According to Ms. Bello, "the WTO rules are simply not "binding" in the traditional sense. . . . To put it simply, a government could renege on

its negotiated commitment not to exceed a specified tariff on an item, provided it restored the overall balance of GATT concessions through compensatory reductions in tariffs on other items." *See* Judith Hippler Bello, *The WTO Dispute Settlement Understanding: Less Is More,* 90 AM. J. INT'L L. 416, 416–417 (1996). For example, in a copyright case brought by the EU, the U.S. Copyright Act's "small business exception" in § 110(5) was found to be in violation of TRIPS Article 13. The United States has paid the EU millions of dollars in temporary settlements but still has not brought the law into compliance. In response to Ms. Bello, Professor Jackson reviewed the provisions of the DSU and argued that "the DSU clearly establishes a preference for an *obligation to perform* the recommendation; notes that the matter shall be kept under surveillance until performance has occurred; indicates that compensation shall be resorted to only if the *immediate* withdrawal of the measure is impracticable; and provides that in *nonviolation* cases, there is *no* obligation to withdraw an offending measure, which strongly implies that in *violation* cases there *is* an obligation to perform." *See* John H. Jackson, *The WTO Dispute Settlement Understanding – Misunderstandings on the Nature of Legal Obligation,* 91 AM. J. INT'L L. 60, 63 (1997). He concluded that the DSU rules are "binding in the traditional *international law* sense" and that they should have an important effect in domestic U.S. jurisprudence, as in the jurisprudence of many other nation-states. *Id.* at 63–64. What view of the TRIPS Agreement did the Appellate Body adopt? Which do you find most persuasive? What are the most serious implications of the view proposed by Ms. Bello? By Professor Jackson?

3. India amended its patent law, with effect from January 1, 2005, to comply with its TRIPS obligations, ending a deliberate national strategy, in effect since 1970, of denying patent protection to pharmaceutical products in order to create a domestic pharmaceutical industry with low drug prices for Indian consumers. Prior to 1970, almost 90 percent of patents in India were held by foreigners and were not worked in India. Foreign multinational corporations controlled 80 percent of the drug market in India and, according to the Kefauver U.S. Senate report, drugs in India were among the highest priced in the world. For example, an anti-anxiety drug, Meprobamate, cost 147 percent more in India than in the U.S. at the time of the report. The 1959 Ayyangar Committee Report on the Indian patent system recommended the abolition of patents on pharmaceutical, chemical and food products (though processes were still patentable) to allow the creation and growth of an indigenous pharmaceutical industry. The strategy, implemented in the Indian Patent Act of 1970, was clearly a success. India is among the top five bulk drug manufacturers in the world and has the largest number of FDA-approved manufacturing facilities outside of the U.S. It is also the fourteenth largest exporter of drugs and exported $3.2 billion in drugs to more than sixty-five countries in 2003. *See* Shamnad Basheer, *India's Tryst with TRIPS: The Patents (Amendment) Act, 2005,* 1 INDIAN J. L. & TECH. (2005), *available at* http://www.ijlt.in/. *See also* Janice M. Mueller, *The Tiger Awakens: The Tumultuous Transformation of India's Patent System and the Rise of Indian Pharmaceutical Innovation,* 68 U. PITT. L. REV. 491 (2007).

4. What are some of the implications for national sovereignty of the decision in *India—Protection for Pharmaceutical and Agricultural Chemical Products?* Did the Appellate Body report unduly intrude on India's right to interpret its national law and to set its own priorities concerning conditions of competition? India's method of complying with TRIPS suggests that there may still be meaningful flexibilities that countries can use to exercise sovereign rights regarding patent protection and public policy. One of the amendments to the Indian Patent Act is Section 3(d), which excludes patent protection for "the mere discovery of a new form of a known substance which does not result in the enhancement of the known efficacy of that substance or the mere discovery of any new property or new use for a known substance." This provision has been employed to reject mailbox pharmaceutical patent applications, such as one by Novartis for a different crystal form of its cancer drug, Gleevec. In 2006, Novartis challenged the amendment in the Indian High Court as not compliant with TRIPS and lost. The court concluded that it did not have jurisdiction to adjudicate validity of a TRIPS violation. The decision, which will be discussed further in Chapter 4, is now on appeal to the Indian Supreme Court.

As discussed in the Tripp & Stokley excerpt, *supra*, compliance with TRIPS required several changes to U.S. law. However, contrary to most developing countries and LDCs, the United States did not have to make the biggest TRIPS-related legal change of providing product patent protection for pharmaceuticals and agricultural chemicals. While U.S. law has allowed for product patent protection for pharmaceuticals since the enactment of the Patent Act of 1790, a surprising number of highly developed countries with well-established patent systems only introduced such protection relatively recently. For example, Germany introduced product patents for pharmaceuticals in 1968, Japan in 1976, Switzerland in 1977, Italy in 1978, and Canada in 1987. Arguably, providing protection only for processes used in the development of medicines allowed domestic industries in these countries to develop expertise in pharmaceutical production gradually, and supply national markets with competitively priced products, aiding public health policy objectives. By contrast, the TRIPS Agreement required developing countries to provide such protection a mere ten years after the effective date of the Agreement (twenty-one years for LDCs). Moreover, countries seeking to take advantage of TRIPS flexibilities to effectuate public health policies, such as Thailand (discussed *infra*), often face threats of trade sanctions by the United States, and heavy criticism by industry and other stakeholders. Is this simply the price of globalization or might adjustments be needed in the TRIPS framework to better balance intellectual property protection with the responsibilities of sovereign nations to meet the public health needs of their citizens? In a recent report, The United Nations Conference on Trade and Development argued that the use of IP flexibilities is important for sustainable growth in Africa. *See* UNCTAD, *Ecomonic Development in Africa Report*, 91 (2012). According to the agency, "[i]t is important in particular that IPR [intellectual property rights] facilitate technological development and do not act as a barrier preventing African countries from accessing and using the tech-

4 suggested reforms in Africa!

nologies necessary for leapfrogging." The Agency suggests four reforms to the global IPR regime could be supportive of development in Africa: "(a) broader room for compulsory licensing. . . ; (b) strengthening patenting standards, particularly standards of breadth and novelty; (c) limiting the length of patent protection; and (d) allowing innovators to use existing patented knowledge to generate new innovations." Do you agree?

5. In 2003 the World Health Organization (WHO) created the Commission on Intellectual Property Rights, Innovation, and Public Health to study how intellectual property rights affect access to public health, particularly with respect to diseases that disproportionately impact developing countries. In 2006, the Commission issued its report, entitled "Public Health, Innovation, and Intellectual Property Rights." The preface to the report contains the following statement:

> Intellectual property rights are important, but as a means not an end. How relevant they are in the promotion of the needed innovation depends on context and circumstance. We know they are considered a necessary incentive in developed countries where there is both a good technological and scientific infrastructure and a supporting market for new health-care products. But they can do little to stimulate innovation in the absence of a profitable market for the products of innovation, a situation which can clearly apply in the case of products principally for use in developing country markets. The effects of intellectual property rights on innovation may also differ at successive phases of the innovation cycle—from basic research to a new pharmaceutical or vaccine. . .

> Whereas there is an innovation cycle in developed countries which broadly works to provide the health care required by their inhabitants, this is far from being the case in developing countries to meet the needs of their people, in particular poor people.

COMMISSION ON INTELLECTUAL PROPERTY RIGHTS, INNOVATION, AND PUBLIC HEALTH, PUBLIC HEALTH, INNOVATION, AND INTELLECTUAL PROPERTY RIGHTS: REPORT OF THE COMMISSION ON INTELLECTUAL PROPERTY RIGHTS, INNOVATION AND PUBLIC HEALTH X (2006) *available at* http://www.who.int/intellectual property/report/en/index.html.

To what extent should organizations such as the WHO play a role in informing the debate over the appropriate balance of patent law and policy? How much deference should be paid to their public health expertise in determining future international patent policy?

6. Public health is not the only issue demanding the attention of the international patent community. In 2008, the European Patent Office held its first conference on Patenting and Climate Change, bringing together participants from forty-five countries to discuss how patents can support, or inhibit, innovations that benefit the environment. As nations seek solutions to global warming and climate change, would the advancement of technology be better

served if national laws were free to exclude crucial environmental inventions from the scope of patentability?

7. WTO disputes normally involve an allegation that a member has violated or failed to comply with some aspect of the treaty, such as in the *U.S. v. India* case. But in some situations a dispute can be launched even though no agreement has been violated. For example, if a country agrees to reduce its tariff on a product but later subsidizes domestic production so that the effect on competition is the same as if the tariff had been retained, there would be no violation of the agreement, but the member would effectively have circumvented its WTO obligation. Such "non-violation" complaints are allowed for goods and services, but members agreed not to use them under TRIPS for the first five years of the Agreement, a moratorium that has been extended since then. The issue of whether non-violation complaints should be allowed under TRIPS remains contentious, with some countries arguing for their use and others seeking to have the moratorium continued or made permanent. Should non-violation complaints ever be allowed under TRIPS?

8. The WTO remedy of suspension of trade concessions in the event an offending country fails to implement a final dispute settlement report is generally most effective when the offending country is dependent on the complainant country for trade. The remedy is likely to have little or no impact when the offending country does not need to rely on the complainant country. This disparity in dependency is often the case in trade between developing and industrialized countries, where, for example, developing Country A may carry out 50 percent of its trade with industrialized Country B, but Country B, which has many more significant trading partners, may carry out only 0.5 percent of its trade with Country A. In such situations, not only could country B withstand the imposition of trade sanctions with no deleterious effect on its economy, it could also continue to cause injury to country A with virtual impunity. Are there ways to redress the potential imbalance in the dispute settlement framework? For example, would it be an appropriate remedy to permit developing and least-developed countries to suspend their TRIPS obligations with respect to an offending industrialized country? When the U.S. was deemed in violation of its WTO obligations in relation to cotton subsidies and failed to comply in 2009, Brazil was allowed to cross-retaliate in the area of intellectual property. The decision could have resulted in, among other things, the suspension of royalty payments on patented and copyrighted goods but the two countries agreed to a settlement before such actions were implemented. *See* Pedro Paranaguá, *The US-Cotton Case: The Truth Behind Brazil's Cross-Retaliation Against US Intellectual Property*, Intell. Prop. Watch (Mar. 18, 2010), http://www.ip-watch.org/weblog/2010/03/18/the-us-cotton-case-the-truth-behind-brazil%e2%80%99s-cross-retaliation-against-us-intellectual-property/. Similarly, on January 28, 2013, the WTO Dispute Settlement Body gave Antigua and Barbuda the right to cross-retaliate against the United States, in an amount not exceeding $21 million annually, by suspending intellectual property protection as a sanction for the U.S.'s failure to comply with its commitments under GATS. *See* William New, *WTO: Antigua to Retaliate Against U.S. by Suspending IP Rights Protection*, IP-Watch, Jan-

uary 28, 2013. For a broader discussion of this option see Frederick M. Abbott, *Cross-Retaliation in TRIPS: Options for Developing Countries*, International Centre for Trade and Sustainable Development, Issue Paper No. 8, (Apr. 2009). What other remedies would you propose?

As noted earlier, the importance of striking an appropriate balance between the public interest and concerns of intellectual property rights holders is most notably expressed in Article 7 of the TRIPS Agreement. With specific reference to patents, however, Article 30 acknowledges the right of member states to enact some limitations to patent rights. It states:

Exceptions to Rights Conferred

Members may provide limited exceptions to the exclusive rights conferred by a patent, provided that such exceptions do not unreasonably conflict with a normal exploitation of the patent and do not unreasonably prejudice the legitimate interests of the patent owner, taking account of the legitimate interests of third parties.

The following TRIPS dispute decision provides an important analysis of how "limited" a member's domestic exceptions must be to comply with the Agreement.

CANADA—PATENT PROTECTION OF PHARMACEUTICAL PRODUCTS

Report of the Panel
WT/DS114/R
17 March 2000

[On 11 November 1998, the European Communities (EC) and their member states requested that the WTO Dispute Settlement Body (DSB) establish a panel to examine the consistency of §§ 55.2(1)-(2) of the Canadian Patent Act and implementing regulations with the requirements of the TRIPS Agreement. The provisions at issue authorized the manufacture and stockpiling of patented pharmaceutical products intended for sale without the consent of the patent owner during the period of six months before the expiry of the 20-year patent term. The provisions also authorized the manufacture, use, or sale of a patented product for regulatory review purposes. Section 55.2(1), the "regulatory review exception," provides:

It is not an infringement of a patent for any person to make, construct, use or sell the patented invention solely for uses reasonably related to the development and submission of information required under any law of Canada, a province or a country other than Canada that regulates the manufacture, construction, use or sale of any product.

Section 55.2(2) of the Patent Act, "the stockpiling exception," provides:

> It is not an infringement of a patent for any person who makes, constructs, uses or sells a patented invention in accordance with subsection (1) to make, construct or use the invention, during the applicable period provided for by the regulations, for the manufacture and storage of articles intended for sale after the date on which the term of the patent expires.

The EC argued that as a result of the disputed provisions, Canada only provided for 19 years and six months of the minimum patent protection as mandated by Articles 28.1 and 33 of the TRIPS Agreement. In response, Canada requested the Panel to dismiss the EC complaint, submitting that its exceptions to the exclusive rights conferred by a patent: (i) were "limited exceptions" within the meaning of TRIPS Article 30; and (ii) "did not reduce the term of protection accorded to a patent, because they did nothing to impair a patentee's right to exploit its patent for the full term of protection by working the patent for its private commercial advantage."]

II. FACTUAL ASPECTS

. . . .

2.5 The regulatory review procedure is time consuming. It may take from one to two-and-a-half years to complete. However, prior to this period, a generic manufacturer will have spent from two to four years in the development of its regulatory submission. Thus, the overall time required for a generic manufacturer to develop its submission and to complete the regulatory review process ranges from three to six-and-a-half years. After the development of its regulatory submission, the generic manufacturer will file an Abbreviated New Drug Submission ("ANDS") with Health Canada. The generic manufacturer files an ANDS because, typically, it is relying on comparative studies to a drug product that has proven to be safe and effective. An innovator, on the other hand, would file a New Drug Submission, since it must provide full pre-clinical and clinical data to establish the safety and efficacy of the drug in question. For an innovator, it takes approximately eight to 12 years to develop a drug and receive regulatory approval, which takes place during the 20-year patent term. The resulting period of market exclusivity under the current Canadian Patent Act varies from drug to drug. Estimated averages, at the time that the Act came into force, range from eight to ten years, according to the Pharmaceutical Manufacturers Association of Canada (PMAC), or 12 to 14 years, according to the Canadian Drug Manufacturers Association (CDMA).

. . . .

VII. FINDINGS

A. MEASURES AT ISSUE

7.1 At issue in this dispute is the conformity of two provisions of Canada's *Patent Act* with Canada's obligations under the *Agreement on Trade-Related Aspects of Intellectual Property Rights* ("the TRIPS Agreement"). The two provisions in dispute, Sections 55.2(1) and 55.2(2) of the Patent Act, create exceptions to the exclusive rights of patent owners. Under Article 28.1 of the TRIPS Agreement, patent owners shall have the right to exclude others from making, using, selling, offering for sale or importing the patented product during the term of the patent. According to Article 33 of the TRIPS Agreement, the term of protection available shall not end before the expiration of a period of 20 years counted from the filing date of the application against which the patent was granted. Sections 55.2(1) and 55.2(2) allow third parties to make, use or sell the patented product during the term of the patent without the consent of the patent owner in certain defined circumstances.

. . . .

C. PRINCIPLES OF INTERPRETATION

7.13 The legal issues in this dispute primarily involve differences over interpretation of the key TRIPS provisions invoked by the parties, chiefly Articles 27.1, 30 and 33. The rules that govern the interpretation of WTO agreements are the rules of treaty interpretation stated in Articles 31 and 32 of the Vienna Convention. The starting point is the rule of Article 31(1) which states:

> "A treaty is to be interpreted in good faith in accordance with the ordinary meaning to be given to the terms of the treaty in their context and in the light of its object and purpose."

The parties have submitted arguments on each of these elements, as well as further arguments based on subsequent practice by certain WTO Members, thus relying on Article 31(3)(b), which reads in relevant part as follows:

> "There shall be taken into account, together with the context: (a) [. . .]; (b) any subsequent practice in the application of the

treaty which establishes the agreement of the parties regarding its interpretation."

The parties have also advanced arguments based on the negotiating history of the TRIPS provisions in dispute. Negotiating history falls within the category of "Supplementary Means of Interpretation" and is governed by the rule of Article 32 of the Vienna Convention, which provides as follows:

"Recourse may be had to supplementary means of interpretation, including the preparatory work of the treaty and the circumstances of its conclusion, in order to confirm the meaning resulting from the application of Article 31, or to determine the meaning when the interpretation according to Article 31:

(a) leaves the meaning ambiguous or obscure; or

(b) leads to a result which is manifestly absurd or unreasonable."

. . . .

7.15 As a consequence of the extended context that has to be taken into account when interpreting provisions of the TRIPS Agreement, the Panel, in considering the negotiating history of the TRIPS Agreement, concluded that interpretation may go beyond the negotiating history of the TRIPS Agreement proper and also inquire into that of the incorporated international instruments on intellectual property.

. . . .

E. SECTION 55.2(2) (THE STOCKPILING EXCEPTION)

. . . .

7.17 The Panel began by considering the claims of violation concerning Section 55.2(2), the so-called stockpiling provision. It began by considering the EC claim that this measure was in violation of Article 28.1 of the TRIPS Agreement, and Canada's defence that the measure was an exception authorized by Article 30 of the Agreement.

7.18 . . . . There was no dispute as to the meaning of Article 28.1 exclusive rights as they pertain to Section 55.2(2) of Canada's Patent Act. Canada acknowledged that the provisions of Section 55.2(2) permitting third parties to "make", "construct" or "use" the patented product during the term of the patent, without the patent owner's permission, would be a violation of Article 28.1 if not excused under Article 30 of the Agreement. The dispute on the claim of violation of Article 28.1 involved whether Section

55.2(2) of the Patent Act complies with the conditions of Article 30.

7.19 The TRIPS Agreement contains two provisions authorizing exceptions to the exclusionary patent rights laid down in Article 28—Articles 30 and 31. Of these two, Article 30—the so-called limited exceptions provision—has been invoked by Canada in the present case. It reads as follows:

"Exceptions to Rights Conferred

Members may provide limited exceptions to the exclusive rights conferred by a patent, provided that such exceptions do not unreasonably conflict with the normal exploitation of the patent and do not unreasonably prejudice the legitimate interests of the patent owner, taking account of the legitimate interests of third parties."

7.20 Both parties agreed upon the basic structure of Article 30. Article 30 establishes three criteria that must be met in order to qualify for an exception: (1) the exception must be "limited"; (2) the exception must not "unreasonably conflict with normal exploitation of the patent"; (3) the exception must not "unreasonably prejudice the legitimate interests of the patent owner, taking account of the legitimate interests of third parties." The three conditions are cumulative, each being a separate and independent requirement that must be satisfied. Failure to comply with any one of the three conditions results in the Article 30 exception being disallowed.

7.21 The three conditions must, of course, be interpreted in relation to each other. Each of the three must be presumed to mean something different from the other two, or else there would be redundancy. Normally, the order of listing can be read to suggest that an exception that complies with the first condition can nevertheless violate the second or third, and that one which complies with the first and second can still violate the third. The syntax of Article 30 supports the conclusion that an exception may be "limited" and yet fail to satisfy one or both of the other two conditions. The ordering further suggests that an exception that does not "unreasonably conflict with normal exploitation" could nonetheless "unreasonably prejudice the legitimate interests of the patent owner."

7.22 Canada argued that Section 55.2(2) complies with each of the three conditions of Article 30. The European Communities argued that Section 55.2(2) fails to comply with any of the three conditions.

. . .

. . . .

7.26 In the Panel's view, Article 30's very existence amounts to a recognition that the definition of patent rights contained in Article 28 would need certain adjustments. On the other hand, the three limiting conditions attached to Article 30 testify strongly that the negotiators of the Agreement did not intend Article 30 to bring about what would be equivalent to a renegotiation of the basic balance of the Agreement. Obviously, the exact scope of Article 30's authority will depend on the specific meaning given to its limiting conditions. The words of those conditions must be examined with particular care on this point. Both the goals and the limitations stated in Articles 7 and 8.1 must obviously be borne in mind when doing so as well as those of other provisions of the TRIPS Agreement which indicate its object and purposes.

. . . .

7.31 The Panel agreed with the EC interpretation that "limited" is to be measured by the extent to which the exclusive rights of the patent owner have been curtailed. The full text of Article 30 refers to "limited exceptions to the exclusive rights conferred by a patent." In the absence of other indications, the Panel concluded that it would be justified in reading the text literally, focusing on the extent to which legal rights have been curtailed, rather than the size or extent of the economic impact. In support of this conclusion, the Panel noted that the following two conditions of Article 30 ask more particularly about the economic impact of the exception, and provide two sets of standards by which such impact may be judged. The term "limited exceptions" is the only one of the three conditions in Article 30 under which the extent of the curtailment of rights as such is dealt with.

. . . .

7.33 The Panel could not accept Canada's argument that the curtailment of the patent owner's legal rights is "limited" just so long as the exception preserves the exclusive right to sell to the ultimate consumer during the patent term. Implicit in the Canadian argument is a notion that the right to exclude sales to consumers during the patent term is the essential right conveyed by a patent, and that the rights to exclude "making" and "using" the patented product during the term of the patent are in some way secondary. The Panel does not find any support for creating such a hierarchy of patent rights within the TRIPS Agreement. If the right to exclude sales were all that really mattered, there would be no reason to add other rights to exclude "making" and "using". The fact that such rights were included in the TRIPS Agreement, as they are in most national patent laws, is strong evidence that they are considered a meaningful and independent part of the patent owner's rights.

7.34 In the Panel's view, the question of whether the stockpiling exception is a "limited" exception turns on the extent to which the patent owner's rights to exclude "making" and "using" the patented product have been curtailed. The right to exclude "making" and "using" provides protection, additional to that provided by the right to exclude sale, during the entire term of the patent by cutting off the supply of competing goods at the source and by preventing use of such products however obtained. With no limitations at all upon the quantity of production, the stockpiling exception removes that protection entirely during the last six months of the patent term, without regard to what other, subsequent, consequences it might have. By this effect alone, the stockpiling exception can be said to abrogate such rights entirely during the time it is in effect.

7.35 In view of Canada's emphasis on preserving commercial benefits *before* the expiration of the patent, the Panel also considered whether the market advantage gained by the patent owner in the months after expiration of the patent could also be considered a purpose of the patent owner's rights to exclude "making" and "using" during the term of the patent. In both theory and practice, the Panel concluded that such additional market benefits were within the purpose of these rights. In theory, the rights of the patent owner are generally viewed as a right to prevent competitive commercial activity by others, and manufacturing for commercial sale is a quintessential competitive commercial activity, whose character is not altered by a mere delay in the commercial reward. In practical terms, it must be recognized that enforcement of the right to exclude "making" and "using" during the patent term will necessarily give all patent owners, for all products, a short period of extended market exclusivity after the patent expires. The repeated enactment of such exclusionary rights with knowledge of their universal market effects can only be understood as an affirmation of the purpose to produce those market effects.

7.36 For both these reasons, the Panel concluded that the stockpiling exception of Section 55.2(2) constitutes a substantial curtailment of the exclusionary rights required to be granted to patent owners under Article 28.1 of the TRIPS Agreement. . . . [I]t was clear to the Panel that an exception which results in a substantial curtailment of this dimension cannot be considered a "limited exception" within the meaning of Article 30 of the Agreement.

. . . .

F. SECTION 55.2(1) (THE REGULATORY REVIEW EXCEPTION)

. . . .

7.45 In the Panel's view, however, Canada's regulatory review exception is a "limited exception" within the meaning of TRIPS Article 30. It is "limited" because of the narrow scope of its curtailment of Article 28.1 rights. As long as the exception is confined to conduct needed to comply with the requirements of the regulatory approval process, the extent of the acts unauthorized by the right holder that are permitted by it will be small and narrowly bounded. Even though regulatory approval processes may require substantial amounts of test production to demonstrate reliable manufacturing, the patent owner's rights themselves are not impaired any further by the size of such production runs, as long as they are solely for regulatory purposes and no commercial use is made of resulting final products.

. . . .

7.51 The second condition of Article 30 prohibits exceptions that "unreasonably conflict with a normal exploitation of the patent". Canada took the position that "exploitation" of the patent involves the extraction of commercial value from the patent by "working" the patent, either by selling the product in a market from which competitors are excluded, or by licensing others to do so, or by selling the patent rights outright. The European Communities also defined "exploitation" by referring to the same three ways of "working" a patent. The parties differed primarily on their interpretation of the term "normal".

7.52 . . . Canada considered that the regulatory review exception of Section 55.2(1) does not conflict with "normal exploitation" because it does not conflict at all with the patent owner's exclusive marketing rights throughout the term of the patent. To be sure, the value derived from the exercise of exclusive marketing rights during the term of the patent is the key ingredient in the exploitation of a patent. The issue in dispute, however, was whether the concept of "normal exploitation" *also* includes the additional period of market exclusivity that would be obtained, *after* the term of the patent, if patent rights could be used to prevent competitors from obtaining, or taking steps to obtain, marketing authorization during the term of the patent. By inference, Canada's assertion that "normal exploitation" is sufficiently safeguarded by protecting market exclusivity during the term of the patent amounted to an assertion that these post-expiration forms of market exclusivity should not be considered as normal exploitation.

. . .

. . . .

7.55 The normal practice of exploitation by patent owners, as with owners of any other intellectual property right, is to exclude all forms of competition that could detract significantly from the economic returns anticipated from a patent's grant of market exclusivity. . . Protection of all normal exploitation practices is a key element of the policy reflected in all patent laws. Patent laws establish a carefully defined period of market exclusivity as an inducement to innovation, and the policy of those laws cannot be achieved unless patent owners are permitted to take effective advantage of that inducement once it has been defined. . .

7.57 The Panel considered that Canada was on firmer ground, however, in arguing that the additional period of de facto market exclusivity created by using patent rights to preclude submissions for regulatory authorization should not be considered "normal". The additional period of market exclusivity in this situation is not a natural or normal consequence of enforcing patent rights. It is an unintended consequence of the conjunction of the patent laws with product regulatory laws, where the combination of patent rights with the time demands of the regulatory process gives a greater than normal period of market exclusivity to the enforcement of certain patent rights. It is likewise a form of exploitation that most patent owners do not in fact employ. For the vast majority of patented products, there is no marketing regulation of the kind covered by Section 55.2(1), and thus there is no possibility to extend patent exclusivity by delaying the marketing approval process for competitors.

. . . .

7.60 The third condition of Article 30 is the requirement that the proposed exception must not "unreasonably prejudice the legitimate interests of the patent owner, taking into account the legitimate interests of third parties". . . .

. . . .

7.69 To make sense of the term "legitimate interests" in this context, that term must be defined in the way that it is often used in legal discourse—as a normative claim calling for protection of interests that are "justifiable" in the sense that they are supported by relevant public policies or other social norms. . . We may take as an illustration one of the most widely adopted Article 30-type exceptions in national patent laws—the exception under which use of the patented product for scientific experimentation, during the term of the patent and without consent, is not an infringement. It is often argued that this exception is based on the notion that a key public policy purpose underlying patent laws is to facilitate the dissemination and advancement of technical knowledge and that allowing the patent owner to prevent experimental use during the term of the patent would frustrate part of the purpose of the requirement that the nature of the invention be disclosed to the public. To the contrary, the argument concludes, under the policy of the patent laws, both society and the scientist have a "legitimate interest" in using the patent disclosure to support the advance of science and technology. While the Panel draws no conclusion about the correctness of any such national exceptions in terms of Article 30 of the TRIPS Agreement, it does adopt the general meaning of the term "legitimate interests" contained in legal analysis of this type. . .

7.74 This second line of argument called attention to the fact that patent owners whose innovative products are subject to marketing approval requirements suffer a loss of economic benefits to the extent that delays in obtaining government approval prevent them from marketing their product during a substantial part of the patent term. According to information supplied by Canada, regulatory approval of new pharmaceuticals usually does not occur until approximately eight to 12 years after the patent application has been filed, due to the time needed to complete development of the product and the time needed to comply with the regulatory procedure itself. The result in the case of pharmaceuticals, therefore, is that the innovative producer is in fact able to market its patented product in only the remaining eight to 12 years of the 20-year patent term, thus receiving an effective period of market exclusivity that is only 40–60 per cent of the period of exclusivity normally envisaged in a 20-year patent term. The EC argued that patent owners who suffer a reduction of effective market exclusivity from such delays should be entitled to impose the same type of delay in connection with corresponding regulatory requirements upon the market entry of competing products. . . .

. . . .

Applied to the regulatory review exception, this argument called for the removal of such exceptions so that patent owners may use their exclusionary patent rights to prevent competitors from engaging in product development and initiating the regulatory review process until the patent has expired. The result of removing the exception would be to allow patent owners to create a period of further, de facto market exclusivity after the expiration of the patent, for the length of time it would take competing producers to complete product development and obtain marketing approval.

. . . .

7.78 The type of normative claim put forward by the EC has been affirmed by a number of governments that have enacted *de jure* extensions of the patent term, primarily in the case of pharmaceutical products, to compensate for the de facto diminution of the normal period of market exclusivity due to delays in obtaining marketing approval. According to the information submitted to the Panel, such extensions have been enacted by the European Communities, Switzerland, the United States, Japan, Australia and Israel. The EC and Switzerland have done so while at the same time allowing patent owners to continue to use their exclusionary rights to gain an additional, de facto extension of market exclusivity by preventing competitors from applying for regulatory approval during the term of the patent. The other countries that have enacted *de jure* patent term extensions have also, either by legislation or by judicial decision, created a regulatory review exception similar to Section 55.2(1), thereby eliminating the possibility of an additional de facto extension of market exclusivity.

7.79 This positive response to the claim for compensatory adjustment has not been universal, however. In addition to Canada, several countries have adopted, or are in the process of adopting, regulatory review exceptions similar to Section 55.2(1) of the Canadian Patent Act, thereby removing the de facto extension of market exclusivity, but these countries have not enacted, and are not planning to enact, any *de jure* extensions of the patent term for producers adversely affected by delayed marketing approval. When regulatory review exceptions are enacted in this manner, they represent a decision not to restore any of the period of market exclusivity due to lost delays in obtaining marketing approval. Taken as a whole, these government decisions may represent either disagreement with the normative claim made by the EC in this proceeding, or they may simply represent a conclusion that such claims are outweighed by other equally legitimate interests.

. . . .

7.82 On balance, the Panel concluded that the interest claimed on behalf of patent owners whose effective period of market exclusivity had been reduced by delays in marketing approval was neither so compelling nor so widely recognized that it could be regarded as a "legitimate interest" within the meaning of Article 30 of the TRIPS Agreement. Notwithstanding the number of governments that had responded positively to that claimed interest by granting compensatory patent term extensions, the issue itself was of relatively recent standing, and the community of governments was obviously still divided over the merits of such claims. Moreover, the Panel believed that it was significant that concerns about regulatory review exceptions in general, although well known at the time of the TRIPS negotiations, were apparently not clear enough, or compelling enough, to make their way explicitly into the recorded agenda of the TRIPS negotiations. The Panel believed that Article 30's "legitimate interests" concept should not be used to decide, through adjudication, a normative policy issue that is still obviously a matter of unresolved political debate.

. . . .

7.84 Having reviewed the conformity of Section 55.2(1) with each of the three conditions for an exception under Article 30 of the TRIPS Agreement, the Panel concluded that Section 55.2(1) does satisfy all three conditions of Article 30, and thus is not inconsistent with Canada's obligations under Article 28.1 of the TRIPS Agreement.

NOTES AND QUESTIONS

1. Do you agree with the conclusion of the *Canada* panel that a provision permitting the stockpiling of patented pharmaceutical products during the final six months of the patent term constitutes a substantial curtailment of exclusive rights? Can a contrary argument be made that prohibiting testing or stockpiling results in an undue extension of the twenty-year patent term?

2. The *Canada* panel essentially provides both sides with a victory by striking the stockpiling provision while upholding the regulatory review provision. Central to its conclusion regarding the regulatory review provision was the notion that the issue was still in considerable flux at the country level and thus that "Article 30's "legitimate interests" concept should not be used to decide, through adjudication, a normative policy issue that is still obviously "a matter of unresolved political debate." Ironically, Directive 2004/27/EC of the European Parliament and of the Council of 31 March 2004, contains the same type of regulatory review exemption that the EC had complained of in the *Canada* case. What does this *volte-face* say about the wisdom of the *Canada* panel's decision on the regulatory review exemption issue?

3. Article 30 was derived from the famous (or infamous) three-step test in copyright law. Originally codified in Article 9(2) of the Berne Convention for the Protection of Literary and Artistic works, the three-step test governed the scope of exceptions or limitations member countries could impose on copyrighted works. As integrated into the TRIPS Agreement, however, the three-step test was expanded to govern exceptions and limitations to all copyright interests, not just the reproduction right. Article 13 provides: "Members shall confine limitations or exceptions to exclusive rights to certain special cases which do not conflict with a normal exploitation of the work and do not unreasonably prejudice the legitimate interests of the right holder." This wording differs only slightly from Article 30.

In 2008, The Max Planck Institute for Intellectual Property, Competition and Tax Law issued a declaration that calls for a balanced interpretation of the "three-step test" of Article 13. Among other principles, the Declaration states:

> Limitations and exceptions do not conflict with a normal exploitation of protected subject matter, if they:
>
> - are based on important competing considerations; or
>
> - have the effect of countering unreasonable restraints on competition, notably on secondary markets, particularly where adequate compensation is ensured. . . .

> The Three-Step Test should be interpreted in a manner that respects the legitimate interests of third parties, including:
>
> - interests deriving from human rights and fundamental freedoms;
>
> d. interests in competition, notably on secondary markets; and
>
> e. other public interests, notably in scientific progress and cultural, social, or economic development.

See MAX PLANCK INSTITUTE FOR INTELLECTUAL PROPERTY, DECLARATION: A BALANCED INTERPRETATION OF THE "THREE-STEP TEST" IN COPYRIGHT LAW, *available at* http://www.ip.mpg.de/files/pdf2/declaration_three_step_test_final_english1.pdf.

Do you think this proposed approach should be adopted by TRIPS panels in construing Article 30? If the panel in the *Canada—Patent Protection of Pharmaceutical Products* had adopted this approach, do you think it would have made a difference in its interpretation of Article 30?

————————————

Given the significant need in most developing and least-developed countries, for relatively easy and cheap access to new technologies, the TRIPS Agreement clearly imposes significant innovation costs on such countries. As earlier observed, most of the major developing countries, India and Brazil most notably, strongly resisted the incorporation of intellectual property in the multilateral trade regime. Upon conclusion of the Uruguay Round, there emerged a rich body of literature analyzing the logic and rationale behind the ultimate acquiescence of the developing countries, who far outnumber developed countries, to the TRIPS Agreement. Consider the following excerpt discussing the future prospects these countries could have under the new WTO-administered system:

J.H. REICHMAN, *FROM FREE RIDERS TO FAIR FOLLOWERS: GLOBAL COMPETITION UNDER THE TRIPS AGREEMENT*
29 N.Y.U. J. INT'L L. & POL. 11, 14–93 (1996)

In principle, the TRIPS Agreement should replace a patchwork system of territorial regulation (that allowed free-riders in some countries readily to appropriate the fruits of foreign investment in technical innovation) with a global competitive framework built around the international minimum standards of protection adopted for specified intellectual creations. . . . In practice, however, any given state's approach to compliance with this Agreement will vary with its own national innovation strategy and with the formal and informal industrial policies chosen to effectuate it. In this context, the developed and developing countries appear to be heading in opposite directions, and the tensions engendered by their conflicting interests complicate the process of consolidating the TRIPS Agreement for the immediate future.

. . . .

II. COMPETITIVE ROLE OF THE DEVELOPING COUNTRIES IN AN INTEGRATED WORLD MARKET

In the developed countries, adoption of the TRIPS Agreement seems to have further whetted the protectionist appetites of those powerful industrial combinations that have successfully captured the legislative and administrative exponents of trade and intellectual property policies in recent years. The traditional internal dialogues within these countries have consequently assumed a high-protectionist bias favoring creators and investors, with a concomitant stifling of pro-consumer and pro-competitive voices.

. . . .

[I]n both the European Union and the United States, established intellectual property rights are being expanded, new sui generis laws are proliferating, and antitrust or competition laws are being relaxed with a view to facilitating joint research by natural competitors... Given the cumulative effect of these and other laws, the competitive ethos characteristic of the nineteenth and early twentieth centuries may give way to a system in which virtually all products sold on the general products market come freighted with some form of exclusive property right . . . .

Behind these high-protectionist trends there usually lies a defensive mentality that tends to view national innovation policy in terms of preserving the dominant position of existing technology-exporting firms. Such policies are rooted in fears that leakage and spillovers will facilitate valuable applications of research results outside the originating countries and, ever more frequently, in newly industrialized or developing countries. By combining the market power of natural competitors with strengthened international intellectual property protection, oligopolists in developed countries seek to make it harder for firms in developing countries to gain access to the most valuable technologies or otherwise to catch up with the leaders in the global market for higher-tech products.

. . . .

It follows that the developing countries should seek to maintain the maximum amount of competition in their domestic markets that is consistent with a good faith implementation of the international minimum standards of intellectual property protection. In carrying out this task, they will find much room to maneuver from within the international conventions themselves, which leave wide and crucial issues, especially scope of protection issues, to the vagaries of the WTO Member States' domestic laws. In other words, the wholesale elevation of minimum standards under the TRIPS Agreement cannot obscure the extent to which the "grey" or ill-defined areas of national intellectual property laws persist in an unharmonized state under the existing international conventions. How single states mesh these "grey areas" with the express norms embodied in the TRIPS Agreement will initially determine the level of competition in single markets and will eventually determine the regulatory balance for the global market as a whole.

III. A PRO-COMPETITIVE STRATEGY FOR IMPLEMENTING THE TRIPS AGREEMENT

A pro-competitive strategy for implementing the TRIPS Agreement in developing countries (as distinct from LDCs, which are relegated to a slower track), consists of at least five component factors. First, the developing countries may tilt their domestic patent, copyright and related intellectual property laws to favor second-comers, especially local competitors, rather than distant proprietary rights holders, to the full extent that good faith compliance with both national treatment and the relevant TRIPS standards still permits. Second, and closely related, the developing countries should distance themselves from protectionist measures being adopted in the developed countries, and they may use tailor-made applications of competition law to curb the adverse effects of these measures on their domestic economies and to limit the abusive exercise of market power in general. Third, developing countries may institute incentive structures likely to stimulate subpatentable innovation at the local level with fewer anticompetitive effects than the hybrid regimes of exclusive property rights proliferating in the developed countries. Fourth, the developing countries may resist any further elevation of international intellectual property standards beyond the levels set in the TRIPS Agreement unless they are offered countervailing trade concessions or until their own technological prowess justifies the social costs of such regimes. Fifth, the developing countries may exploit new means of acquiring and disseminating scientific and technical knowledge by resorting to the global information infrastructure, and they should potentiate both their physical capacity to access such knowledge and the intellectual skills to process the information conveyed. . . .

IV. PRESENT TENSIONS AND THE PROSPECTS FOR A FUTURE EQUILIBRIUM

. . . .

Progress in the developing countries . . . depends on the maintenance of a suitable balance between incentives to create and the resulting opportunities for free competition, and they stand to benefit most from a balance that errs on the side of competition. In rationalizing their national systems of innovation, the developing countries will accordingly want to gear their intellectual property policies (and related competition law policies) to the pace of their own technological development and to their efforts to accelerate the acquisition of technical knowledge generally. . .

. . . .

The guiding principle is to meet over-protection abroad with corresponding degrees of lesser protection at home in order to stimulate competitive advantages in exploiting spillovers, leakage, and the products of reverse engineering. However, the needs of local innovators will change over time, and newly industrialized countries may reach a stage where they require stronger intellectual property protection than is good for less developed countries. . . .

. . . .

If the institutions responsible for securing compliance with the TRIPS Agreement can successfully manage the clash of interests between developed and developing countries in the short and medium terms, it should allow the positive economic effects of the Uruguay Round to make themselves felt across national boundaries over time. The stronger competitive tides rising in the global marketplace could then gradually influence the business strategies of single firms as much as or more than the economic policies of single nation states. As entrepreneurs in developing countries think more like those who manage small and medium-sized firms in the developed countries, the affinities between them may soon outweigh their perceived differences. This sharing of interests should, in turn, weaken the North-South divisions that characterized multilateral negotiations in the past, and could lead to healthy transnational alliances and networks between small and medium-sized firms everywhere.

. . . .

Governments may reinforce [such] informal networks by encouraging working relationships between local entities and foreign universities, research institutes, and trade associations. When necessary, local investors (and governments) may resort to the worldwide labor market for the skills and expertise in question. To the extent that underemployment in developed countries continues to generate more trained personnel than some of these countries can currently absorb, it creates opportunities for a reverse brain drain that could help to implant strategically important skills in developing countries. The ability to use cheap unskilled labor in other facets of production may offset some of the costs of this strategy.

. . . .

Even the most pro-competitive approach to implementing international intellectual property rights may prove unavailing, however, if developing countries do not further rationalize and invigorate their antitrust or competition laws. While preserving the bases for healthy competition under local conditions, these reforms may reduce the trade-distorting effects of undue concentration in the developed countries, which higher levels of international intellectual property protection tend to magnify. . . .

. . . .

To the extent that developed countries opt to shelter manufacturers of high-tech products behind artificial barriers to entry, the allegiance of developing countries to a more pro-competitive strategy will in and of itself shorten their catch-up period, promote leapfrogging, and gradually augment their share of the world market for these goods. The more that the developed countries retreat from their historical commitment to free competition as the basic instrument of economic policy, moreover, the more the developing countries will promote the interests of consumers and second-comers everywhere if they maintain a healthy balance between incentives to create and the public interest in free competition in their domestic jurisdictions.

The developing countries may thus inherit the historical role of defending the competitive ethos against overly protectionist demands in all the relevant international forums. If, as one hopes, the developed countries regain their confidence and eventually retreat from current protectionist strategies, then the restoration of more competitive conditions in both developed and developing countries could usher in an unprecedented epoch of investment and technological innovation from which all humanity stands to gain.

NOTES AND QUESTIONS

1. Professor Reichman bases his analysis on the notion that industrialized country efforts to expand and strengthen intellectual property rights are inherently protectionist and anti-competitive and that developing country resistance is pro-competitive. On what grounds does he base this assertion? Do you agree?

2. If one adopts the arguments by Professor Reichman, the recipe for developing country success under the TRIPS regime is for developing countries to safeguard and exploit the flexibilities inherent in the Agreement. As noted earlier, India has followed that strategy by, among other things, limiting pharmaceutical patentability through Section 3(d). In an article describing the Appellate Body's approach to TRIPS interpretation as a "cautious, strict constructionist," Professor Reichman presciently outlined the justifications for flexibility within the TRIPS Agreement:

> Deference to local law and strict construction of treaties have ... become the pedestal on which the Appellate Body's TRIPS jurisprudence rests. As a result, the seminal decision in *US v. India* seems certain to reinforce the residual power of states to forge their own intellectual property laws and policies, within the reserved powers of GATT 1994, Article XX(d), except insofar as the black letter rules of the TRIPS Agreement otherwise clearly overrule or circumscribe such exercise of residual power. By the same token, one can no longer argue that activist panels may fill the gaps in international intellectual property law by reference to the "legitimate expectations of members and private rights holders concerning conditions of competition" . . . .

> The Appellate Body's decision in *US v. India* should logically strengthen the ability of developing countries to resist the bullying tactics of the developed countries that were previously described. The latter have continued to press the developing countries (and their advisors) to adopt versions or interpretations of the international intellectual property standards that conform to the developed countries' own laws and practices or to positions they staked out during the multilateral negotiations. Yet, as the Appellate Body makes clear, position papers deposited in the course of the negotiations do not constitute controlling sources of law because only the black letter rules apply; and the means of implementing them are expressly reserved to local law in Article 1 of the TRIPS Agreement.

> The developing countries remain free, therefore, to adopt a more pro-competitive approach to implementing the TRIPS Agreement ... provided that such implementation remains consistent with a good faith application of the relevant international standards of intellectual property protection.

Jerome H. Reichman, *Securing Compliance with the TRIPS Agreement after US v. India*, 1 J. INT'L ECON. L. 585, 596–97 (1998).

3. Brazil, another developing country, took a different approach to limit pharmaceutical patents through perceived TRIPS flexibilities. The country implemented a law specifying that after a pharmaceutical patent application is examined, it would not be allowed to issue until after a separate body, the National Sanitary Supervision Agency (analogous to the FDA in the U.S.), reviewed the application and concluded issuance of a patent would not be unduly detrimental to the public interest. Can you make an argument that this strategy is not TRIPS compliant? The Attorney General effectively nullified the regulation in 2011, possibly based on pressure from the patent office, which considered the "prior approval" process an interference in its area of competence. *See AGU's Opinion Confirms the Powers of the ANVISA and INPI Patent Medicines* (Jan. 25, 2011), *translated at* http://translate. google.com/translate?sl=auto&tl=en&u=http://www.agu.gov.br/sistemas/site/ TemplateImagemTextoThumb.aspx?idConteudo%3D153676%26id_site%3D3. In addition, Brazilian law allows for compulsory licenses to be granted on patented products where the patent owner fails to work the patent in Brazil within three years of the patent grant. The United States brought a WTO complaint against Brazil for its compulsory licensing provision in 2001 but the case settled after Brazil countered with its own request for a WTO panel charging that the U.S. violates TRIPS because, under the Bayh-Dole Act (35 U.S.C. § 204 (2006)) government-funded inventions are to be manufactured "substantially in the United States." What does this dispute say about the necessity for full TRIPS compliance?

4. The post-TRIPS era has been marked by a tug-of-war between the U.S. and other industrialized countries, which have sought to raise the standards required by TRIPS, and many developing countries, which have sought to maintain or lower them. As noted in the discussion on Post-TRIPS Bilateralism, *infra*, while neither side has prevailed multilaterally, TRIPS-plus requirements have been included in some bilateral and regional trade agreements with developing countries. For example, while not mandated by TRIPS, bilateral agreements require developing countries to provide patent term extensions, restrict third-party use of test data, or limit compulsory licensing. What impact may such agreements have on the development of future international patent policy as well as on the ability of developing countries to reap the benefits of a patent system? Professors Dinwoodie and Dreyfuss provide a comprehensive analysis of TRIPS disputes, flexibilities, and overall impact in *Graeme B. Dinwoodie & Rochelle C. Dreyfuss, A Neofederalist Vision of TRIPS: Building Resilient International intellectual Property System* (Oxford University Press, 2012).

5. Developing countries generally have fought against enlarging the scope of patent rights. They have also argued strongly in both the WTO and WIPO in favor of intellectual property protection for traditional knowledge and genetic resources. The United States and several other industrialized countries have resisted with just as much fervor. What accounts for this "flip-

flopping" of positions, with developing countries advocating to limit competition and industrialized countries seeking to maintain it? What does this say about the nature of patent policy making? For an interesting explanatory theory of this phenomenon, *see* Sabrina Safrin, *Chain Reaction: How Property Begets Property,* 82 NOTRE DAME L. REV. 1917 (2007).

C. POST-TRIPS DEVELOPMENTS

1. THE DOHA DECLARATION ON THE TRIPS AGREEMENT AND PUBLIC HEALTH

Striking an appropriate balance between the protection of intellectual property rights and public health considerations, particularly access to medicines, was perhaps the greatest challenge the negotiators of the TRIPS Agreement had to face. Although the Agreement contains flexibilities, largely in the form of compulsory licensing provisions, which allow the incorporation of exceptions and limitations to intellectual property rights into domestic legislation, the issue as to how far member countries should be allowed to go in using these flexibilities to meet their public health needs proved contentious. For example, some countries wondered whether the need to provide access to essential medicines was the sort of "national emergency" or a case of "extreme urgency" that Article 31 of the TRIPS Agreement contemplated in permitting a compulsory license without trying to obtain the authorization of the patentee. That question, along with others, was largely answered at a WTO Ministerial meeting on November 14, 2001, with the adoption of the Doha Declaration on the TRIPS Agreement and Public Health.

DECLARATION ON THE TRIPS AGREEMENT AND PUBLIC HEALTH
WT/MIN(01)/DEC/2
Adopted on 14 November 2001

1. We recognize the gravity of the public health problems afflicting many developing and least-developed countries, especially those resulting from HIV/AIDS, tuberculosis, malaria and other epidemics.

2. We stress the need for the WTO Agreement on Trade-Related Aspects of Intellectual Property Rights (TRIPS Agreement) to be part of the wider national and international action to address these problems.

3. We recognize that intellectual property protection is important for the development of new medicines. We also recognize the concerns about its effects on prices.

4. We agree that the TRIPS Agreement does not and should not prevent Members from taking measures to protect public health. Accordingly, while reiterating our commitment to the TRIPS Agreement, we affirm

that the Agreement can and should be interpreted and implemented in a manner supportive of WTO Members' right to protect public health and, in particular, to promote access to medicines for all.

In this connection, we reaffirm the right of WTO Members to use, to the full, the provisions in the TRIPS Agreement, which provide flexibility for this purpose.

5. Accordingly and in the light of paragraph 4 above, while maintaining our commitments in the TRIPS Agreement, we recognize that these flexibilities include:

(a) In applying the customary rules of interpretation of public international law, each provision of the TRIPS Agreement shall be read in the light of the object and purpose of the Agreement as expressed, in particular, in its objectives and principles.

(b) Each Member has the right to grant compulsory licences and the freedom to determine the grounds upon which such licences are granted.

(c) Each Member has the right to determine what constitutes a national emergency or other circumstances of extreme urgency, it being understood that public health crises, including those relating to HIV/AIDS, tuberculosis, malaria and other epidemics, can represent a national emergency or other circumstances of extreme urgency.

(d) The effect of the provisions in the TRIPS Agreement that are relevant to the exhaustion of intellectual property rights is to leave each Member free to establish its own regime for such exhaustion without challenge, subject to the MFN and national treatment provisions of Articles 3 and 4.

6. We recognize that WTO Members with insufficient or no manufacturing capacities in the pharmaceutical sector could face difficulties in making effective use of compulsory licensing under the TRIPS Agreement. We instruct the Council for TRIPS to find an expeditious solution to this problem and to report to the General Council before the end of 2002.

7. We reaffirm the commitment of developed-country Members to provide incentives to their enterprises and institutions to promote and encourage technology transfer to least-developed country Members pursuant to Article 66.2. We also agree that the least-developed country Members will not be obliged, with respect to pharmaceutical products, to implement or apply Sections 5 and 7 of Part II of the TRIPS Agreement or to enforce rights provided for under these Sections until 1 January 2016, without prejudice to the right of least-developed country Members to seek

66.2 encourages technology transfer

- They keep delaying implementation in LDCs b/c of issues w/ access to medicine it will cause.

other extensions of the transition periods as provided for in Article 66.1 of the TRIPS Agreement. We instruct the Council for TRIPS to take the necessary action to give effect to this pursuant to Article 66.1 of the TRIPS Agreement.

———————

The Doha Declaration therefore makes clear that the TRIPS Agreement should be interpreted in a manner supportive of public health and nothing in the Agreement should be seen as preventing countries from taking measures to protect it.

However, one question remained outstanding. Article 31(f) of the TRIPS Agreement provides that production under compulsory licensing must be "predominantly for the supply of the domestic market." That provision has been viewed by some countries as limiting the amount of pharmaceuticals a country could export when a product was made under a compulsory licensing scheme, with the result that countries that lacked the capacity to produce pharmaceuticals could be denied access to an inexpensive source of essential medicines. On August 30, 2003, the WTO General Council adopted a decision that waived member countries' obligations under Article 31(f) and allowed any member to export pharmaceutical products made under compulsory licenses, provided that the country complied with a lengthy list of conditions arguably designed to deter any non-essential use of the provision, as illustrated in the following flowchart.

31(f) waived

→ However, waiver process too complicated to be effective.

DOHA DECLARATION PARAGRAPH 6 IMPLEMENTATION FLOWCHART

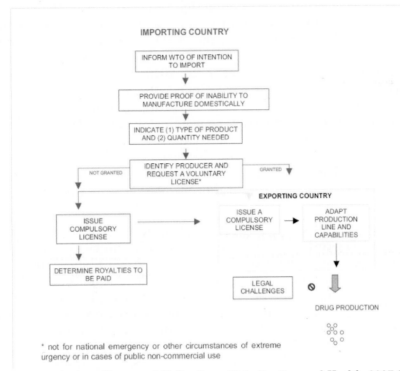

Source: Vanessa Kerry and Kelley Lee, *Globalization and Health,* 2007 3:3

For the text of the decision, *see* WTO, Implementation of Paragraph 6 of the Doha Declaration on the TRIPS Agreement and Public Health, General Council Decision of 30 August 2003, WT/L/540 (2003).

When the draft decision was presented to the WTO General Council, the U.S. and some other industrialized country members expressed concern that it would be used to undermine patent protection. To calm those fears, the Council chairperson added a statement "represent[ing] several key shared understandings of Members." Among those understandings was that the system established by the decision "should be used in good faith to protect public health and . . . not be an instrument to pursue industrial or commercial policy objectives," and "that the purpose of the Decision would be defeated if products supplied under [it] are diverted from the markets for which they are intended." While lacking legal force, the statement has been considered an integral part of the decision.

The most recent chapter in the development of the Doha Declaration came on December 6, 2005, when the WTO General Council adopted a decision transforming the waiver contained in the decision of August 30, 2003, into a permanent amendment of the TRIPS Agreement and adding additional details for ensuring proper use of the system. The amendment, which would create a new Article 31*bis* and a new Annex to the TRIPS Agreement, requires ratification by two-thirds of the WTO member countries to become binding. The deadline for ratification was December 1, 2007; however, only fourteen countries (including the United States) had acted by the deadline. In response, the WTO General Council extended the deadline for ratification until December 31, 2009, then to December 31, 2011, and currently to December 31, 2013. Despite the extensions, only forty-four WTO members had accepted the amendment as of June 15, 2012. The WTO keeps a tally of ratifying countries at http://www.wto.org/english/tratop_e/trips_e/amendment_e.htm. Once the number of acceptances reaches two-thirds of the WTO membership, the amendment will take effect in those members and will replace the 2003 waiver for them. For each of the remaining WTO member countries, the waiver will continue to apply until that member accepts the amendment and it takes effect.

Thus far, the waiver has been a failure in terms of increasing the availability of low-cost drugs to countries lacking sufficient manufacturing capacity. Although the provision has been in place since 2003, only one country, Rwanda, has made use of it to obtain a drug from Canada, a process that took approximately two years to complete. The complexity of the waiver provisions, combined with the heavy pressure faced by other countries taking advantage of TRIPS flexibilities, likely are the primary reasons for the provision's disuse.

NOTES AND QUESTIONS

1. Consider the following statement by one of the leading experts on TRIPS and public health, Professor Abbott:

> There may be a better international approach than the present one to the development and distribution of new medicines. The current system involves constant tension between patent holder and consumer, mediated through a complex body of rules. . . . The [WTO Decision on Implementation of Para. 6 of the Doha Declaration on TRIPS and Public Health, dealing with TRIPS Art. 31(f)] may not be the first-best instrument from anybody's perspective, but it does give countries lacking adequate manufacturing capacity some flexibility to make use of compulsory licensing . . . The adoption of the Decision shows that the WTO can address important issues of social concern. But adoption standing alone does not show that the WTO can do so effectively. Effective implementation of the Decision is threatened by newly negotiated bilateral and regional agreements.

See Frederick Abbott, *The WTO Medicines Decision: World Pharmaceutical Trade and the Protection of Public Health*, 99 AM. J. INT'L L. 317, 358 (2006).

TRIPS-plus bilateral and regional agreements are discussed in Part C.3 *infra*. What recourse do developing and least-developed countries have? For a detailed analysis of the WTO decision and the flexibilities available under TRIPS in relation to medicines, see CYNTHIA M. HO, ACCESS TO MEDICINE IN THE GLOBAL ECONOMY: INTERNATIONAL AGREEMENTS ON PATENT AND RELATED RIGHTS (2011).

2. On November 29, 2006, the Director General of the Department of Disease Control, Ministry of Public Health of Thailand, announced the issuance of a compulsory license for the patented drug Efavirenz (sold in Thailand under the trademark Stocrin® by Merck), a highly effective HIV antiretroviral. The compulsory license was permitted to remain in effect until December 31, 2011. It was limited to doses for 200,000 persons entitled to treatment under the Thai national health system, and it required a royalty payment of 0.5 percent of the total sales value of the drug. It was no surprise that the reaction of the U.S. pharmaceutical industry was highly critical.

In addition to the compulsory license for Stocrin, Thailand also issued compulsory licenses for a second HIV/AIDS drug Kaletra® (Abbott) and a heart disease drug Plavix® (Bristol Myers Squibb). In retaliation, Abbott announced that it would introduce no new drugs in Thailand. Compulsory licenses for infectious diseases are not surprising, but what is the justification for a compulsory license on a drug to treat a chronic or non-communicable disease (NCD) like heart disease? Consider the following statement from the World Health Organization:

> [C]hronic diseases and poverty are tied into a vicious cycle, and their impact shackles the macroeconomic development of many countries. Heart disease, stroke and diabetes alone are estimated to reduce the gross domestic product by between 1% and 5% per year in low-and middle-income countries experiencing rapid economic growth. In China, the Russian Federation and India, estimated losses in national income over the next 10 years due to these diseases are (in international dollars) $558,000 million, $303,000 million and $237,000 million, respectively.

World Health Organization, *Report by the Secretariat, Prevention and Control of Noncommunicable Diseases: Implementation of the Global Strategy*, WHO Doc. A60/15, at 3 (Apr. 5, 2007).

On September 19, 2011, world leaders gathered in New York to address the rapidly growing problem of the rise of NCDs as causes of death. The meeting marked only the second time in history that the United Nations held a summit to address a world health issue. A 2011 World Health Organization report pegs NCDs as accounting for 36 million of the 57 million global deaths in 2008. Many newer drugs used to treat these conditions are extremely expensive, and also lucrative, for drug companies because they involve complex molecules called biologics and are meant to be taken for the remainder of a patient's life. In fact, Roche derives half of its $24 billion annual sales from just three biologics: Rituxan, Avastin, and Herceptin. However, recent reports indicate that generic manufacturing companies in India and China are investing in facilities and otherwise gearing up to produce and distribute generic copies (call "biosimilars") of many of these drugs, with the issuance of compulsory licenses from each government. Does TRIPS Art. 31 permit compulsory licenses for NCDs? Should it?

3. Do you think compulsory licenses are a legitimate means to address national income loss due to prevalent disease? Why should patent owners, in effect, subsidize the health care costs of foreign citizens? There is a growing awareness that many developing countries are facing a "double burden" of infectious and chronic disease that they are ill-equipped to handle. For example, in 2006, Thailand had an average per capita income of $8.19 per day, $5.22/day for the bottom 80 percent of the population. Yet the pre-compulsory license price of Plavix was $2/day, close to 40 percent of the average income of the bottom 80 percent of the population. What are the implications of this trend and these statistics for global drug development and protection? For a bit of irony, *see Innogenetics, Inc v. Abbott Labs, No. 05-C-0575-C,* 2007 WL 5431017 (W.D. Wis. Jan. 12, 2007), in which Abbott, in effect, requested it be granted a "compulsory license" to continue producing a drug after it had been found liable for patent infringement.

4. On March 9, 2012, the Indian Patent Office Controller General authorized India's first post-TRIPS compulsory license to Natco Pharma for Sorafenib, a generic version of Nexavar, a liver and kidney cancer drug patented and sold by Bayer Healthcare AG. Natco will have to pay Bayer a royalty of 6 percent of net sales of the drug. The decision was based on the drug's high price, that it was only available to 2 percent of the relevant population, as well as the fact that Bayer did not locally produce the drug but imported it. Bayer has decided to appeal the decision stating that "the order of the Patent Controller of India damages the international patent system and endangers pharmaceutical research." Interestingly, the compulsory license has already had an impact, as other pharmaceutical companies have begun to reduce prices on their anti-cancer drugs in response. If brought before the WTO DSB, should the reasons for granting the compulsory license cited by the controller be considered TRIPS compliant? Why or why not?

5. The issue of TRIPS and public health is a thorny one with no easy solutions. While compulsory licenses have their place, they will never be a complete solution to the problem, as explained by Professor Kapczynski:

> Often the poor (and especially the very poor) are so poor that they make up very little of an expected market for an innovation. Giving them access to goods by exempting them from exclusion rights can thus yield more in access than it would compromise in terms of innovation. Even from an efficiency perspective, and certainly from a distributive perspective, such users should ride for free if the scheme can be administered with reasonable accuracy and without excessive expense.

But the free-riding strategy has clear limitations. It may be difficult or costly to identify the poor. And, at some point, access for the poor will undercut incentives substantially enough to undermine incentives to generate information. . . It is no accident that the global access to medicines campaign and its focus on addressing patent barriers to medicines arose out of the HIV/AIDS movement. A large enough community of people living with HIV in wealthy countries existed to attract investment into new medicines to treat HIV. No similar interest exists in developing treatments for conditions such as extensively drug-resistant tuberculosis (TB)—the largest impact of which is felt in South Africa. No patent exception can give patients with this form of TB better access to simple and fast-acting medicines, because such medicines do not exist. . .

In other words, using IP to generate innovation will undersupply not just access for the poor but also production for the poor. . . The problem will appear to be the most acute when the rich and the poor have different information needs, because here the information goods that the poor need will not be developed at all. This is an evident problem in health, in which the global poor disproportionately suffer from communicable diseases that have little or no impact in the global North.

Amy Kapczynski, *The Cost of Price: Why and How to Get Beyond Intellectual Property Internalism*, 59 UCLA L. REV. 970, 998–1000 (2012).

Some commentators, such as consumer advocate Jamie Love, suggest that solutions outside of the patent system must be sought to allow countries to provide affordable drugs to their citizens while ensuring pharmaceutical companies can reap the profits necessary to incentivize continued new drug development. In recent years, a range of policy instruments to induce pharmaceutical innovation have been proposed as alternatives or supplements to the patent system, including a global fund to incentivize drug development, buy-outs of patents (e.g., reimbursement of R&D costs) on drugs for global diseases, direct grants to compensate for R&D expenditures, patent term extensions for technologies that have significant application to global health pandemics, so called "wild-card" patents (allowing a company to choose a patent from its portfolio that would benefit from term extension in exchange for commercializing a technology for which there is a limited market or other disincentives to exploitation), the Medicines Patent Pool, and much more. *See, e.g.*, Thomas Pogge, *The Health Impact Fund: Boosting Pharmaceutical Innovation without Obstructing Free Access*, 18 CAMBRIDGE Q. HEALTHCARE ETHICS 78 (2009) (global fund); William W. Fisher & Talha Syed, *Global Justice in Healthcare: Developing Drugs for the Developing World*, 40 U.C. DAVIS L. REV 581 (2007); B. Spellberg *et al.*, *Societal Costs Versus Savings from Wild-Card Patent Extension Legislation to Spur Critically Needed Antibiotic Development*, 35 INFECTION 167 (2007); Kevin Outterson, *Patent Buy-Outs for Global Disease Innovations for Low- and Middle-Income Countries*, 32 AM. J. L. & MED. 159 (2006) (buyouts); James Love & Tim Hubbard, *Prizes for Inno-*

vation of New Medicines and Vaccines, 18 ANNALS HEALTH L. 155, 155–57 (2009) (prizes). The recently launched WIPO RE:SEARCH initiative aims to provide a searchable, public database of intellectual property assets and resources (including know-how) available for research and development for drugs to treat neglected tropical diseases, tuberculosis, and malaria http://www.wipo.int/research/en/. Of the above proposals and initiatives, prize systems have received some of the most significant attention as a way to reward innovation. Do you think incentivizing pharmaceutical research through prizes could be as successful as the patent system has been in inducing the development and adequate supply of new drugs? To what extent does your answer depend on how the prize system is designed? For a review of the various prize design options, *see* Michael Abramowicz, *Perfecting Patent Prizes,* 56 VAND. L. REV. 115 (2003).

6. While the *Canada—Patent Protection* panel report serves to reinforce the rights of the patentee, it also recognizes that those rights have limits. Compulsory licensing is one of the most effective remedies a government can employ to limit the scope of exclusive rights accorded by a patent. As noted in Chapter 2, Article 5A of the Paris Convention expressly permits the grant of compulsory licenses to prevent the abuses that may result from the failure to exploit a patented invention. The Convention provides little detail, however, other than to stipulate minimum time limits before a member country may act, guarantee that patent owners must have an opportunity to justify their inaction, and require that any compulsory license must be non-exclusive and non-transferable. Recall from p. 153, *supra*, that Article 31 of the TRIPS Agreement refers to a compulsory license as "use without authorization of the right holder," and provides rather exacting conditions that member countries must put into place in order to safeguard the interests of patent owners.

7. In order to ensure conformity with the particularly detailed nature of the compulsory licensing requirements in the TRIPS Agreement, a few of the countries that joined the WTO following adoption of the TRIPS Agreement (e.g., Jordan), chose to rely on the language of the TRIPS provisions, and echoed it in their national patent legislation. *See* Articles 22–26 of the Patents of Invention Law, Law No. 32 of 1999, as amended by Temporary Law No. 71 of 2001 of the Kingdom of Jordan, WIPO Doc. JO024EN. Even some highly developed countries, such as Belgium and Switzerland, have chosen to create new compulsory licensing provisions for public health purposes. *See* Esther Van Zimmeren & Geertrui Van Overwalle, *A Paper Tiger: Compulsory License Regimes for Public Health,* 42 INT'L REV. INTELL. PROP. & COMP. L. 4 (2011). As of May 2012, at least fourteen developing countries had issued compulsory licenses which were predominately for public health-related government use. These countries included Brazil, Ecuador, Ghana, Guinea, India, Indonesia, Malaysia, Mozambique, Rwanda, Swaziland, Taiwan, Thailand, Zambia and Zimbabwe. *See* CAROLYN DEERE, THE IMPLEMENTATION GAME: THE TRIPS AGREEMENT AND THE GLOBAL POLITICS OF INTELLECTUAL PROPERTY REFORM IN DEVELOPING COUNTRIES 83 (2009).

2. OTHER APPROACHES TO TRIPS FLEXIBILITIES

Designing appropriate limitations to the exclusive rights associated with a patent grant is an exercise fraught with tension, uncertainty and, in many respects, political compromise. This is certainly true at the domestic level in the U.S., where the task of maintaining the appropriate balance between the incentive to innovate and access to new technologies and information is divided between Congress and the courts. The "patent balance," like its counterpart in the copyright arena, is typically used as a proxy for measuring the extent to which public interest concerns are properly accommodated in the intellectual property system. Over the years, the leading patent systems of the world have developed a rich and culturally relevant jurisprudence regarding limitations to patent rights. These limitations are found in the legislative texts of domestic patent laws, but also often originate as judicially created exceptions or limitations as courts interpret statutes in light of national constitutional and public policy objectives. See, e.g., the Supreme Court of Canada's *Harvard College* decision excerpted in Chapter 4. In this way, public interest norms are embedded in the architecture of the various institutions and regulatory agencies that together effectuate the means by which "progress" and "public welfare" interests are served by the patent system.

Limitations and exceptions to patent rights are the least harmonized area of global patent law. For developing countries in particular, the freedom to enact limitations and exceptions within their domestic patent laws is of particular importance with respect to facilitating access to essential medicines and other public goods, as well as for promoting local indigenous innovation which would ordinarily involve some level of imitation and reverse engineering. Given the many serious issues affecting these countries, important attention has focused on how specific provisions of the TRIPS Agreement affect delineations of a country's discretion to enact exceptions to patent rights. As evidenced by the decision in *Canada—Patent Protection of Pharmaceutical Products*, the starting point for considering so-called "TRIPS Flexibilities" is Article 30. Additionally, scholars have pointed to the Preamble and Objectives of the TRIPS Agreement as sources of authority for countries to enact TRIPS flexibilities consistent with their domestic national priorities and economic development concerns. *See* Keith E. Maskus, *Using the International Trading System to Foster Technology Transfer for Economic Development*, 2005 MICH. ST. L. REV. 219, 223–24, and Peter K. Yu, *The Objectives and Principles of the TRIPS Agreement*, 46 HOUS. L. REV. 979, 1014 (2009). Below we discuss two other potential sources of limitations on TRIPS-mandated patent rights, one within the Agreement (Art. 31(k)) and one outside of TRIPS (human rights).

a. Flexibilities in TRIPS Article 31(k)

Recently, Professor Ng-Loy has argued that other provisions of the TRIPS Agreement, specifically Article 31, offer additional opportunities for developing countries to supply pharmaceutical products for public health considerations. In analyzing TRIPS flexibilities in the laws of India and Singapore, Professor Ng-Loy focuses on a particularly difficult question surrounding the Paragraph 6 solution, namely, whether pharmaceutical products produced in one country may be exported to another country that lacks domestic capacity to manufacture such products:

> [In] the second sentence in para. 9 of the 2003 WTO decision, there is a clear acknowledgement that pharmaceutical products produced under a compulsory licence *can* be exported in circumstances falling outside of the waiver system. This possibility lies in art. 31(k) which gives WTO countries the discretion not to comply with the export restriction in art. 31(f) when issuing a compulsory licence to "remedy a practice determined after judicial or administrative process to be anticompetitive". This flexibility in art. 31(k) is particularly attractive for a country with very strong generic drug manufacturing capacities and which is looking to help its generic drug sector grow by manufacturing patented drugs for export. India is one such country.

> India is probably the best-known example of how a country very successfully built up a strong generic-based pharmaceutical sector, by making use of the flexibilities in the transitional provision of the TRIPs Agreement which allowed developing countries to delay granting product patent protection in certain areas of technology till 2005. When this grace period came to an end on January 1, 2005, India's patent law had to be amended to provide patent protection for pharmaceutical products developed by the research-based drug companies. But at the same time, other amendments were made to help its generic drug companies cope with this new situation. In particular, s.92A was introduced to allow a generic drug company to apply for a compulsory licence to manufacture the patented pharmaceutical products for export. . . . which . . . implements the waiver system of the 2003 WTO decision. More interesting is s.92A(3) which alludes to the presence of other provisions in India's Patents Act allowing a compulsory licensee to export the pharmaceutical products manufactured under the compulsory licence, and preserving the applicability of these provisions. . . .

> Section 90(1)(vii) allows the export of patented products manufactured under the compulsory licence where the grant of the licence is needed to supply or develop a market for the export of the patented product made in India. In the context of patented

drugs, the patentee's refusal to grant a licence on reasonable terms to allow the Indian generic drug companies to supply an external demand could be raising barriers to market entry in a way that hinders the development or growth of the generic drug sector in India. Analysed in this way, the patentee may be engaging in anti-competitive practices. Arguably, s.90(1)(vii) of India's patent law falls within the flexibilities permitted by art. 31(k) of the TRIPs Agreement.

It is even clearer that s.90(1)(ix) of India's patent law *is* put in place to take advantage of the flexibilities in art. 31(k). This section allows for the export of patented products made under a compulsory licence where the compulsory licence is granted "to remedy a practice determined after judicial or administrative process to be anti-competitive". This is the exact phrase used in art. 31(k) [of the TRIPS Agreement]. Section 90(1)(ix) has to be read with the substantive provision in India's patent law which sets out the grounds on which a compulsory licence may be granted. There are three grounds: (a) where the reasonable requirements of the public with respect to the patented invention have not been satisfied; (b) where the patented invention is not available to the public at a reasonable or affordable price; and (c) that the patented invention is not worked in the territory of India.

If the patentee refuses to supply patented drugs at an affordable price to the public in another country (one which may have the drug manufacturing capacity and therefore does not qualify for the waiver system in the 2003 WTO decision) and this refusal is determined by the other country's judicial or administrative body to be anti-competitive, a generic drug company in India could potentially apply for the grant of a compulsory licence to manufacture the drugs and, under the authority of s.90(1)(ix), the compulsory licence could permit export of these drugs to this other country.

Singapore, too, has a provision in its patent law which, in theory at least, is wide enough to allow a compulsory licence to be issued to manufacture patented drugs for export purposes. To appreciate the breadth of this provision, it is necessary to have some background to this provision. Prior to July 1, 2004, s.55 of the Singapore Patents Act provided that a compulsory licence could be granted, upon the expiry of three years from the grant of a patent, on the ground that a market for the patented invention was not being supplied, or was not being supplied on reasonable terms, in Singapore. If a compulsory licence was granted on this basis, it was specifically provided in s.55(4) (c) that the licence was to be "limited to the supply of the patented invention predominantly in Singapore". This state of the affairs had to change, upon the conclusion of the US–Singapore FTA in 2003, because of the obligation therein to allow the grant of compulsory licences to a third party (other than the Government) in only one situation, namely, to remedy anti-competitive practices. To implement this obligation, s.55 was amended. The current position allows a compulsory licence to be issued where the grant of the licence "is necessary to remedy an anti-competitive practice". More significantly, the export-restriction in s.55(4)(c) was deleted. The implication arising from this deletion must be that it is now possible, when a compulsory licence is issued in Singapore to remedy an anti-competitive practice, for the licence to permit exportation of the products made under the compulsory licence.

The Singapore law on compulsory licensing of patents is consistent with . . . art. 31(k).

Ng-Loy Wee Loon, *Exploring Flexibilities within the Global IP Standards*, 2 INTELL. PROP. Q. 162, 181–84 (2009).

Read TRIPS Article 31(k) closely. Do you agree with Professor Ng-Loy's analysis? Are India and Singapore in compliance with the TRIPS Agreement?

b. Human Rights-Based Limitations on Patent Rights

As noted in the Weissbrodt and Schoff excerpt in Chapter 1, in August of 2000, the United Nations Subcommission for the Protection and Promotion of Human Rights issued a unanimous resolution with the following conclusion:

> Since the implementation of the TRIPS Agreement does not adequately reflect the fundamental nature and indivisibility of all human rights, including the right to health, the right to food, and the right to self-determination, there are apparent conflicts between the intellectual property rights regime embodied in the TRIPS Agreement . . . and international human rights law.

Recall from Chapter 1 that human rights theories have informed justifications for international intellectual property rights. In light of the significant effect of pharmaceutical products on human health and well-being, what exactly can a human rights approach to global patent rights contribute to the debate about patents and access to medicines? The following High Court of Kenya case illustrates how constitutionally based human rights justifications can be balanced against patent rights in the access to medicines context.

ASERO OCHIENG AND OTHERS V. ATTORNEY-GEN. AND OTHERS

High Court of Kenya

Petition No. 409 of 2009 (H.C.K.) (Kenya, 2010)

JUDGMENT

INTRODUCTION

1. This petition raises critical issues pertaining to the constitutional right of citizens to the highest attainable standard of health. The petitioners are all citizens of Kenya who describe themselves as living positively with HIV/AIDS. They are apprehensive that their rights under the Constitution are threatened by the enactment of the Anti-Counterfeit Act, 2008, specifically sections 2, 32 and 34 thereof. They see these provisions as affecting or likely to affect their access to affordable and essential drugs and medicines including generic drugs and medicines thereby infringing their fundamental right to life, human dignity and health as protected by Articles 26(1), 28 and 43 of the Constitution of Kenya.

2. By their Amended Petition dated 3rd November 2010, the petitioners seek the following prayers:

    (a) A declaration that the fundamental right to life, human dignity and health as protected and envisaged by Articles 26(1), 28 and 43 of the Constitution encompasses access to affordable and essential drugs and medicines including generic drugs and medicines.

    (b) A declaration that in so far as the Anti Counterfeit Act, 2008 severely limits access to affordable and essential drugs and medicines including generic medicines for HIV and AIDS, it infringes on petitioners right to life, human dignity and health guaranteed under Articles 26(1), 28 and 43 of the Constitution.

    (c) A declaration that enforcement of the Anti Counterfeit Act, 2008 in so far as it affects access to affordable and essential drugs and medication particularly generic drugs is a breach of the petitioner's right to life, human dignity and health guaranteed under the Constitution.

. . . .

6. On the 17th of January, 2011, Mr. Anand Grover, the United Nations Special Rapporteur for Health, pursuant to orders made by Musinga, J, was joined as an Interested Party. . . .

THE PETITIONERS' CASE

9. The petitioners are adults who have been living with HIV for periods ranging between 8 and 19 years. They have been taking HIV drugs for

the last ten years or so since generic anti-retroviral (ARV) HIV drugs became widely available following the enactment of the Industrial Property Act, 2001. They take 1st line ARVs consisting mainly of 3TC, AZT and NVP, two tablets per day as prescribed.

10. The 1st petitioner depones that she gets her medication free of charge from *Medicins Sans Frontieres* (MSF) which runs a programme in conjunction with the government of Kenya to provide cheap and free access to medicines. The 2nd petitioner, who is also infected with HIV but is not currently on HIV drugs, has a 5 year old son infected since birth and who is on the 1st line anti-retroviral medication 3TC, AZT and NVD. He, too, receives his medication free of charge through a project funded by the government of Kenya and MSF. Like the other petitioners, she is unemployed and would not be in a position to afford any of the HIV/AIDS medication if she was required to purchase the drugs for her son. The 3rd petitioner, who has been living with HIV/Aids for 8 years, is also unemployed and receives his medication free of charge through a government programme. He started receiving a regular supply after the passage of the Industrial Property Act in 2001 which allowed the entry into the country of generic drugs.

. . . .

12. In his submissions on behalf of the petitioners, Mr. Luseno stated that the petitioners are users of generic drugs which are taken daily, and this daily usage guarantees them the right to life without which no one can enjoy any other right in the constitution. In recognition of the special status of persons affected and living with HIV and AIDS, the government enacted the HIV and AIDS Prevention and Control Act, 2006 whose object was to extend to persons affected by HIV full protection of their human rights and civil liberties. This required that the government ensures availability of resources to ensure access to HIV drugs.

. . . .

15. The petitioners submit that if the [Anti-Counterfeit] Act is applied and enforced, their right to life, human dignity and health as guaranteed under Articles 26(1), 28 and 43 of the Constitution is likely to be infringed. The availability and access to generic drugs will be severely restricted; such generic drugs and medication will be deemed counterfeit goods within the meaning of the Act and therefore liable to seizure at any time; and the cost of treatment for the petitioners will be likely to increase as they will be forced to rely on more expensive branded drugs. This, in turn, will result in fewer people having access to the essentials drugs for treatment of HIV and AIDS.

16. The petitioners submit further that the application and enforcement of the Act is in breach of the State's undertaking under the HIV and AIDS Prevention and Control Act, 2006 . . . [and] is likely to intentionally de-

prive the petitioners of their right to life, human dignity and health in contravention of Articles 26(1), 28 and 43 of the Constitution.

. . . .

18. The petitioners also argue that Section 2 of the Act subjects Kenyans to laws of other countries, as it accords owners of intellectual property rights in other countries the right to enforce those rights in Kenya without regard or compliance with Kenyan laws. The section, and indeed the entire Act, is in breach of international law to which Kenya was a party. Mr. Luseno submitted that Article 51 of the Agreement on Trade Related Aspects of Intellectual Property Rights (TRIPS) of the World Trade Organisation (WTO) limits the use of the term "counterfeiting" to counterfeit trademark goods; that the TRIPS Agreement forms part of Kenyan law in line with the provisions of Article 2 of the Constitution of Kenya; that the term 'counterfeit' as used in the Act goes beyond its internationally accepted legal meaning.

19. Mr. Luseno submitted with regard to Section 34 of the Act that it imports remedies which are exercisable by the police on suspicion by an owner of intellectual property rights that there are counterfeit which have been imported. According to the petitioners, all the medicines they rely on are imported. Mr. Luseno submitted that 90% of persons with HIV use generic drugs imported by the government and donors. Should the police, on suspicion, detain the drugs at the port, the impact before a court is moved for an order to allow release of the goods to the market would be devastating. For petitioners who use the drugs daily, there may be loss of life by the time the suspicions are investigated. Section 2 seems to impose a burden on the user to satisfy the Commissioner that the drugs are not counterfeit and thus limits access to essential drugs and medication.

. . . .

22. The petitioners' position is that they are not opposed to the fight against counterfeiting, but they are a special class that was asking that legislation passed should not be contradictory of the state's positive obligations towards them. They referred to the incidents in other jurisdictions in which the application of provisions similar to section 2, 32 and 34 of the Act had led to seizure of generic drugs to the detriment of persons living with HIV. The incidents in question were the seizure by customs authorities in the Netherlands of generic drugs for HIV destined for Brazil in December 2008 and the seizure in Germany of generic drugs manufactured in India which were bound for Vanuatu.

23. Mr. Luseno asked the court to take cognizance of the decision of Wendoh J who in granting conservatory orders in the matter had noted that ambiguity in the legislation is against the right to life; that suspicion in Section 34 will be used against access to the drugs, and that there has

to be a better way of controlling counterfeit drugs. He argued that since the issuance of the conservatory orders, the government has been able to control counterfeiting without putting the petitioners at risk. He stated that the petitioners were asking government to consider the Act again and re-draft it as the lack of access to HIV drugs constitutes a real threat to life. . . .

25. On the respondent's submissions, Mr. Luseno pointed out that the state itself could not distinguish between counterfeit and generics and the respondent's counsel had used the word counterfeit in referring to generics consistently. He contended that if the government itself could not come out clearly as to what is counterfeit or generic, the risk that the Commissioner of Police would not be able to make the distinction was clear.

THE INTERESTED PARTY'S CASE

. . . .

27. The position of the Interested Party, like that of the petitioners, is that the Act threatens the right to life, dignity and health of the petitioners and other persons infected with HIV. . . .

28. With regard to the right to life, the Interested Party submitted that HIV is a life-threatening virus and that anti retroviral therapy is the most effective intervention for the survival of persons infected with the virus. When taken regularly as prescribed, such therapy is associated with a 90% reduction in deaths caused by AIDS.

. . . .

31. The Interested Party argued also that the Act poses a threat to the rights of children. Article 53(2) of the Constitution guarantees to every child the right to basic health care services. Further, the state and everyone else is enjoined to have the best interests of the child as the primary consideration in all matters involving children.

32. Like the petitioners, the Interested Party impugns Section 2 of the Act where it refers to protection of patents in Kenya or elsewhere. Mr. Ombati submitted that the nature of patent law is that it does not have international application, but the Act opens the door for anyone with a patent to come and have it protected in Kenya.

SUBMISSIONS BY THE AMICUS

33. The Special Rapporteur, Mr. Anand Grover, states that he filed his submissions in this matter in fulfilment of his mandate as outlined in Human Rights Council Resolution 6/29. He states that the resolution obliges the Special Rapporteur to make recommendations on issues surrounding the Right to Health, particularly in relation to laws, policies and practices that may represent obstacles to the right being realised. . . .

34. According to the Special Rapporteur, while the objective of the Act is to prohibit trade in counterfeit goods, it is likely, as currently written, to endanger the constitutional right to health guaranteed under Article 43 and in turn the right to life under Article 26 of the Constitution. This is so because the definition of counterfeit drugs in section 2 of the Act includes the "manufacture, production. . .or making, whether in Kenya or elsewhere, of any goods whereby those protected goods are imitated in such manner and to such a degree that those other goods are identical or substantially similar copies of the protected goods." In his view, this definition would certainly encompass generic medicines produced in Kenya and elsewhere and thus is likely to adversely affect the manufacture, sale, and distribution of generic equivalents of patented drugs. It does not include an exception for medications, and does not 'avert' to the existence of generic drugs.

35. The Special Rapporteur submits that the definition of 'counterfeiting' within the Act effectively conflates generic medicines with medicines which are produced in violations of private intellectual property rights, and this conflation of legitimately produced generic medicines with those that possibly violate intellectual property rights is likely to have a serious adverse impact on the availability, affordability and accessibility of low-cost, high-quality medicines.

36. This would lead to a situation in which medicines that are approved by regulatory authorities as being safe and effective are seized on the grounds that they are "counterfeit"; generic medicines destined for importation to Kenya being seized due to the uncertainty surrounding possible infringement of the Act upon delivery; significant delays of shipments of imported generic drugs at ports of entry to Kenya for inspection or legal clarification purposes; seizure of medicines at Kenyan ports by customs officials and police officers who are not specially trained to recognise the difference between counterfeit and generic products and an increase in the price of ARVs within Kenya which would make them expensive and financially inaccessible to those who need them.

37. The resulting limited access by patients to generic, medication will be a violation of their right to health as guaranteed by the Constitution and international treaties. . . .

THE RESPONDENT'S CASE

38. Ms. Kimaiyo for the respondents, in opposing the petition submitted that the government cares for people with HIV/AIDS and has put in place mechanisms for their care and passed the HIV and AIDS Prevention and Control Act 2006. She relied on the submissions dated 9th January 2012 and the affidavit of Allan George Njogu Kamau, the Chairman of the Board of the Anti-Counterfeit Agency and argued that the term 'generic drugs' is not synonymous with "counterfeit drugs".

39. According to the respondents, the duties of the state under Article 43 are to ensure that its people attain the highest standard of healthcare. It is also the duty of the state to ensure that they enjoy the right to life. This is why the state enacted the Anti-Counterfeit Act as allowing counterfeit drugs will lead to death, and the Act was intended to protect citizens. The Act does not intend to bar generic drugs but seeks to prohibit trade in counterfeits in Kenya. She submits that the term "counterfeit medicines" is given the same definition in the Act as it is given by the World Health Organisation. . . .

. . . .

41. To the petitioners' submission that the Act should expressly provide for exemption of generic drugs from the definition of counterfeits, the respondents argue that this is to demand too much as the Industrial Property Act did not provide just for importation of generic drugs but for other essential goods. It would not therefore make sense to name each and every limitation when such limitation could be captured in a proviso. The respondents referred to the proviso to section 2 which states that nothing in the provision shall derogate from the existing provisions under the Industrial Property Act and submitted that in the event of a conflict in interpretation, the provisions of the Industrial Property Act shall prevail.

. . . .

43. With regard to the issue of whether or not the provisions in question are in breach of the constitutional rights of the petitioners, the respondents submitted that interpretation of the provisions of the Anti-Counterfeit Act does not and will not lead to violation of rights. The intention of the Act was to protect the lives of Kenyans from those few individuals who would deal with counterfeit goods, including drugs, for profit. For the court to grant the declarations sought would lead to breach, not protection, of the petitioners' fundamental rights. The Anti-Counterfeit Act provides sufficient safeguards for users of anti-retroviral drugs against those who market counterfeit goods but also ensures that they access anti-retroviral drugs. The petition is therefore an abuse of the court process which ought to be dismissed.

THE SOCIO-ECONOMIC CONTEXT

44. In considering the issues that arise in this petition, it is important to bear in mind the socio-economic context in which they arise.

45. There can be no dispute that HIV AIDS constitutes a serious threat to the health and life of the petitioners in particular but to others within the general public who may be infected by the virus. This is particularly so with regard to children and women. The Interested Party has pointed out at Paragraph 27 of its Answer in Support of the Petition that

[a]pproximately 110,000 children are born with HIV as a result of mother to child transmission of HIV. Scientists have accumulated significant research-generated evidence to show that with appropriate and affordable treatment this could be cut by between 30 and 50%.

46. The state also recognises the challenges that HIV poses. In the Kenya National Aids Strategic Plan 2004–2009 that was made within the same period that the Anti-Counterfeit Act was enacted and commenced operation, the state notes that HIV/AIDS continues to be a major challenge to the country's socio-economic development. It notes that since the first case was discovered in the country in 1984, over 1.5 million people have died due to AIDS-related illnesses. This has resulted in 1.8 million children left as orphans. The state notes, however, that a combination of factors, including antiretroviral therapy, have led to a decrease in the incidence and the numbers of those dying from HIV/AIDS.

47. In the 2010 Country Report to the United Nations General Assembly Special Session on HIV and AIDS, the National Aids Control Council, citing the Kenya AIDS Indicators Survey (2007) states that the average HIV prevalence among the general population aged 15–49 stands at 7.4%. Women have a higher prevalence compared to men, with women standing at 8.4% against 5.4% percent for men. It estimates the number of people living with HIV at between 1.3 to 1.6 million.

48. The Kenya National HIV and AIDS Estimates (2010) puts the cumulative number of children infected by HIV at 184,052 by 2009. It notes that the state has therefore put in place mechanisms to prevent mother to child transmission, with the Country Report indicating that in 2009, about 58,591 HIV positive pregnant women received antiretroviral prophylaxis to reduce the risk of mother-to-child transmission of HIV.

49. The Country Report estimates that more than 2.4 million children are orphans, half of them due to HIV and AIDS. Many of these orphans are in households that are targeted to receive government support in order to have improved access to nutrition, education and health. This underlines more than anything else the low economic circumstances in which many of those infected with HIV live.

50. In light of the above statistics, it is not hard to see the socio-economic implications of HIV/AIDS. It is now commonly acknowledged that without medical intervention and treatment, a person infected with HIV ultimately succumbs to the opportunistic infections that occur as a result of the compromised immune system. Many of those who are infected with the virus are, like the petitioners, unemployed and therefore financially incapable of procuring for themselves the anti-retroviral branded medication that they need to remain healthy. They are therefore dependent on generic anti-retroviral medication which is much cheaper and therefore more accessible to them.

51. From the pleadings and submissions before me, it is common ground that until the passage of the Industrial Property Act in 2001 (Act No. 3 of 2001), it was not possible for poor people infected with HIV/AIDS to access anti-retroviral medication as the only ones available were expensive branded medicine. Generic anti-retroviral drugs were not available in Kenya as the existing legislation did not allow parallel importation of generic drugs and medicines. Section 58 (2) of the Industrial Property Act, 2001 as read with Rule 37 of the Industrial Property Regulations, 2002, allowed the parallel importation of generic drugs. It is on the basis of this legislation that availability and access to anti-retroviral drugs has increased and greatly enhanced the life and health of persons such as the petitioners who have been living with HIV/AIDS.

52. It is against this context that any legislative measure that would affect accessibility and availability of anti-retroviral medicines must be viewed. If such measure would have the effect of limiting access, then such measure would ipso facto threaten the lives and health of the petitioners and others infected with HIV and Aids, and would be in violation of their rights under the Constitution.

53. I take this view because, from the pleadings and submissions before me, while the petitioners, Interested Party and the Amicus on one hand and the respondents on the other have taken diametrically opposed positions on this petition, they are in agreement that the petitioners have certain rights which are guaranteed under the Constitution and by international law. The petitioners, as citizens of Kenya, have the right to life guaranteed under Article 26(1); they have the right to human dignity provided for under Article 28; they also have the right to the highest attainable standard of health guaranteed under Article 43(1) of the Constitution.

. . . .

55. The rights which the petitioners see as likely to be violated by the implementation of the Act are guaranteed under the Constitution of Kenya and under international law. . . . . Article 2 of the Constitution now makes it clear that all international treaties to which Kenya is a party are now part of the laws of Kenya. I am therefore bound by the Constitution to have regard to these treaties.

56. In my view, the right to health, life and human dignity are inextricably bound. There can be no argument that without health, the right to life is in jeopardy, and where one has an illness that is as debilitating as HIV/AIDS is now generally recognised as being, one's inherent dignity as a human being with the sense of self worth and ability to take care of oneself is compromised. What may not be agreed upon by the parties is the meaning and implication of the right to health, and the nature and implication of the positive obligation that recognition of this right in the Constitution and international treaties places on the state.

MEANING AND IMPLICATION OF THE RIGHT TO HEALTH

57. Article 43(1) of the Constitution of Kenya provides that

> Every person has the right—

> (a) to the highest attainable standard of health, which includes the right to health care services, including reproductive health care;

58. Article 12(1) of the International Covenant on Economic, Social and Cultural Rights provides as follows: 'The States Parties to the present Covenant recognize the right of everyone to the enjoyment of the highest attainable standard of physical and mental health.'

59. The Convention then sets out at Article 12(2) the steps that each state party should take to achieve the full realization of this right. Such steps include the

> 'prevention, treatment and control (of) epidemic, endemic, occupational and other diseases'

> and

> 'The creation of conditions which would assure to all medical service and medical attention in the event of sickness.'

. . . .

61. In General Comment No. 14 on the Right to Health, the Committee on Economic, Social and Cultural Rights notes that

> [h]ealth is a fundamental human right indispensable for the exercise of other human rights. Every human being is entitled to the enjoyment of the highest attainable standard of health conducive to living a life in dignity.

62. The Committee notes further that:

> The reference in article 12, paragraph 1, of the Covenant to "the highest attainable standard of physical and mental health" is not confined to the right to health care. On the contrary, the drafting history and the express wording of article 12, paragraph 2, acknowledge that the right to health embraces a wide range of socio-economic factors that promote conditions in which people can lead a healthy life, and extends to the underlying determinants of health, such as food and nutrition, housing, access to safe and potable water and adequate sanitation, safe and healthy working conditions, and a healthy environment.

63. The "socio-economic factors that promote conditions in which people can lead a healthy life" imply, in my view, a situation in which people have access to the medication they require to remain healthy. If the state

fails to put in place such conditions, then it has violated or is likely to violate the right to health of its citizens.

64. The Committee on Economic, Social and Cultural Rights notes further in General Comment No. 17 on the right of Everyone to benefit from the protection of the moral and material interests resulting from any scientific, literary or artistic production of which he or she is the author, UN doc. E/C.12/GC/17, 12 January, 2006, para. 35 that:

> 'States parties thus have a duty to prevent unreasonably high costs for access to essential medicines.'

65. The right to access medicine has also been recognised as an essential component of the right to health in other jurisdictions. In South Africa, the Constitutional Court, in the case of Minister of Health and Others -v- Treatment Action Campaign and Others (*supra*) held that the failure of the state to ensure access to the drug Nevirapine to pregnant women to prevent mother to child transmission of HIV was a violation of the constitutional right to the highest attainable standard of health.

66. The state's obligation with regard to the right to health therefore encompasses not only the positive duty to ensure that its citizens have access to health care services and medication but must also encompass the negative duty not to do anything that would in any way affect access to such health care services and essential medicines. Any legislation that would render the cost of essential drugs unaffordable to citizens would thus be in violation of the state's obligations under the Constitution.

. . . .

THE ANTI-COUNTERFEIT ACT, ACT NO. 13 OF 2008

68. The Act was passed in 2008 and received Presidential assent on 24th of December 2008. The Act commenced on the 7th of July 2009 in terms of Legal Notice No. 115. The Preamble to the Act states that it is an Act of Parliament intended to 'prohibit trade in counterfeit goods, to establish the Anti-Counterfeit Agency, and for connected purposes.'

69. The respondents have argued that the intention behind the Act was to prohibit trade in counterfeit goods, including counterfeit medicines, which pose a danger to the life and health of Kenyans. The petitioners, while acknowledging the need to control trade in counterfeit goods, see the implementation of the Act in its present form as likely to lead to violation of their right to life, human dignity and health.

70. That there has been a problem with counterfeit goods entering the country and there is therefore a need to prohibit such trade is not in dispute. The right of holders of intellectual property rights to benefit from their innovations is also recognised, and the enactment of the Act may have been intended to be in fulfilment of Kenya's obligations under TRIPS to protect the rights of patent holders. The Amicus argues, howev-

er, that Kenya has fulfilled its obligations under TRIPS by enacting the Industrial Property Act 2001. . . . The Anti-Counterfeit Act appears to have been intended to bolster the protection of intellectual property rights by providing criminal sanctions for infringement.

. . . .

SECTION 2 OF THE ACT

72. The petitioners impugn section 2 of the Act as likely to lead to an interpretation that includes generic drugs among counterfeit medicine and therefore lead to their criminalisation and seizure under Section 32 and 34 respectively. The Amicus argues that the Act conflates generic medicine with counterfeit medicine and is thus in agreement with the petitioners that the Act may lead to the seizure and thereby shortage of the generic drugs which are essential for the survival of the petitioners.

73. Section 2 provides as follows:

> "[c]ounterfeiting" means taking the following actions without the authority of the owner of intellectual property right subsisting in Kenya or elsewhere in respect of protected goods-
>
> (a) the manufacture, production, packaging, re-packaging, labeling or making, whether in Kenya or elsewhere, of any goods whereby those protected goods are imitated in such manner and to such a degree that those other goods are identical or substantially similar copies of the protected goods;
>
> (b) the manufacture, production or making, whether in Kenya or elsewhere, the subject matter of that intellectual property, or a colourable imitation thereof so that the other goods are calculated to be confused with or to be taken as being the protected goods of the said owner or any goods manufactured, produced or made under his licence;
>
> (c) the manufacturing, producing or making of copies, in Kenya or elsewhere, in violation of an author's rights or related rights;
>
> (d) in relation to medicine, the deliberate and fraudulent mislabeling of medicine with respect to identity or source, whether or not such products have correct ingredients, wrong ingredients, have sufficient active ingredients or have fake packaging;

74. According to the respondents, this definition is the same as that used by the World Health Organisation (WHO). However, the WHO defines counterfeits in its Factsheet as 'Spurious/falsely-labelled/falsified/counterfeit medicines are medicines that are deliberately and fraudulently mislabelled with respect to identity and/or source' and notes that such counterfeit drugs may be 'compounded 'using the wrong ingredients, insufficient active ingredients, without active ingredients, or with fake packaging.'

75. The danger that the petitioners see in the possibility of the terms 'generic' and counterfeit' being used interchangeably is borne out by the fact that there have been instances, admittedly in other jurisdictions, in which generic medication has been seized while in transit on the basis that it is counterfeit. Such seizures have affected users of generic drugs in developing countries which, like Kenya, have large populations dependent on generic HIV medication for survival. The nature of international trade being the way it is, the risk of seizure of generic drugs bound for Kenya, whether at Kenyan ports or outside this country, cannot be ruled out.

76. Section 2 of the Act uses the words 'whether or not such products have correct ingredients, wrong ingredients, have sufficient active ingredients or have fake packaging.' As the Amicus points out, generic drugs 'have the same composition and contain the same substances as patented formulations of the same drug, and are essentially identical copies, therefore can be used for the same purposes as their non-generic counterparts.'

77. The World Health Organisation defines generic medicine as "a pharmaceutical product, usually intended to be interchangeable with an innovator product, that is manufactured without a licence from the innovator company and marketed after the expiry date of the patent or other exclusive rights". Generic drugs thus '. . .have correct ingredients. . . ' and 'sufficient active ingredients' within the meaning of section 2 of the Anti-Counterfeit Act. In a legal regime that is focused on protection of intellectual property rights, the danger that such generic drugs can be seized under section 32 and 34 of the Act is therefore manifest.

78. In my view, the definition of 'counterfeit' in section 2 of the Act is likely to be read as including generic medication. I would therefore agree with the Amicus that the definition 'would encompass generic medicines produced in Kenya and elsewhere and thus is likely to adversely affect the manufacture, sale, and distribution of generic equivalents of patented drugs. This would affect the availability of the generic drugs and thus pose a real threat to the petitioners' right to life, dignity and health under the Constitution.

79. The respondents argue that the intention of the Act is to safeguard the petitioners and others against the use of counterfeit medicines. A reading of the Act, however, shows a different intention. Section 32 provides as follows:

It shall be an offence for any person to–

(a) have in his possession or control in the course of trade, any counterfeit goods;

(b) manufacture, produce or make in the course of trade, any counterfeit goods;

(c) sell, hire out, barter or exchange, or offer or expose for sale, hiring out, barter or exchange any counterfeit goods;

(d) expose or exhibit for the purposes of trade any counterfeit goods;

(e) distribute counterfeit goods for purposes of trade or any other purpose;

(f) import into, transit through, tranship within or export from Kenya, except for private and domestic use of the importer or exporter as the case may be, any counterfeit goods;

(g) in any other manner, dispose of any counterfeit goods in the course of trade.

80. Section 33(1) of the Act provides that

Any holder of an intellectual property right, his successor in title, licensee or agent may, in respect of any protected goods, where he has reasonable cause to suspect that an offence under section 32 has been or is being committed, or is likely to be committed, by any person, lay a complaint with the Executive Director.

81. At section 34(1) the Act provides that

34. (1) The owner of an intellectual property right, who has valid grounds for suspecting that the importation of counterfeit goods may take place, may apply to the Commissioner in the prescribed manner to seize and detain all suspected counterfeit goods which are–

(a) goods featuring, bearing, embodying or incorporating the subject matter of that intellectual property right or to which the subject matter of that right has been applied; and

(b) imported into or enter Kenya during the period specified in the application:

82. Clearly, as the above provisions show, the tenor and object of the Act is to protect the intellectual property rights of individuals. This explains the rights granted to the intellectual property holder to complain about suspected violation of Intellectual property rights through trade in counterfeit goods, and the powers granted to the Commissioner appointed under Section 13(1) of the Kenya Revenue Authority Act to seize suspected goods upon the complaint of a patent holder. Had the primary intention been to safeguard consumers from counterfeit medicine, then the Act should have laid greater emphasis on standards and quality.

83. The Anti-Counterfeit Act has, in my view, prioritised enforcement of intellectual property rights in dealing with the problem of counterfeit medicine. It has not taken an approach focused on quality and standards

which would achieve what the respondents have submitted is the purpose behind the Act: the protection of the petitioners in particular and the general public from substandard medicine. Protection of consumers may have been a collateral issue in the minds of the drafters of the Act. This is why for instance, the rights of consumers of generic medicine are alluded to in the proviso to Section 2 of the Act.

84. However, the right to life, dignity and health of people like the petitioners who are infected with the HIV virus cannot be secured by a vague proviso in a situation where those charged with the responsibility of enforcement of the law may not have a clear understanding of the difference between generic and counterfeit medicine. The primary concern of the respondent should be the interests of the petitioners and others infected with HIV/AIDS to whom it owes the duty to ensure access to appropriate health care and essential medicines. It would be in violation of the state's obligations to the petitioners with respect to their right to life and health to have included in legislation ambiguous provisions subject to the interpretation of intellectual property holders and customs officials when such provisions relate to access to medicines essential for the petitioners' survival. There can be no room for ambiguity where the right to health and life of the petitioners and the many other Kenyans who are affected by HIV/AIDS are at stake.

85. Further, contrary to the respondents' counsel's assertion, the Anti-Counterfeit Act, being later in time, would prevail over the Industrial Property Act in the event of a conflict, and the proviso to Section 2 may not be of much help to the petitioners. Should the Act be implemented as it is, the danger that it poses to the right of the petitioners to access essential medicine which they require on a daily basis in order to sustain life is far greater and more critical than the protection of the intellectual property rights that the Act seeks to protect. The right to life, dignity and health of the petitioners must take precedence over the intellectual property rights of patent holders.

86. While such intellectual property rights should be protected, where there is the likelihood, as in this case, that their protection will put in jeopardy fundamental rights such as the right to life of others, I take the view that they must give way to the fundamental rights of citizens in the position of the petitioners. As the Committee on Economic Social and Cultural rights notes at paragraph 35 of General Comment No. 17:

> Ultimately, intellectual property is a social product and has a social function. States parties thus have a duty to prevent unreasonably high costs for access to essential medicines, plant seeds or other means of food production, or for schoolbooks and learning materials, from undermining the rights of large segments of the population to health, food and education. Moreover, States parties should prevent the use of scientific and technical pro-

gress for purposes contrary to human rights and dignity, including the rights to life, health and privacy, e.g. by excluding inventions from patentability whenever their commercialization would jeopardize the full realization of these rights. . . . States parties should also consider undertaking human rights impact assessments prior to the adoption and after a period of implementation of legislation for the protection of the moral and material interests resulting from one's scientific, literary or artistic productions.

87. In view of the matters set out above, I find that Sections 2, 32 and 34 of the Anti Counterfeit Act threaten to violate the right to life of the petitioners as protected by Article 26 (1), the right to human dignity guaranteed under Article 28 and the right to the highest attainable standard of health guaranteed under Article 43 (1) and grant the declarations sought as follows:

> (a) The fundamental right to life, human dignity and health as protected and envisaged by Articles 26(1), 28 and 43(1) of the Constitution encompasses access to affordable and essential drugs and medicines including generic drugs and medicines.
>
> (b) In so far as the Anti-Counterfeit Act, 2008 severely limits or threatens to limit access to affordable and essential drugs and medicines including generic medicines for HIV and AIDS, it infringes on the petitioners' right to life, human dignity and health guaranteed under Articles 26(1), 28 and 43(1) of the Constitution.
>
> (c) Enforcement of the Anti Counterfeit Act, 2008 in so far as it affects access to affordable and essential drugs and medication particularly generic drugs is a breach of the petitioners' right to life, human dignity and health guaranteed under the Constitution.

88. It is incumbent on the state to reconsider the provisions of section 2 of the Anti-Counterfeit Act alongside its constitutional obligation to ensure that its citizens have access to the highest attainable standard of health and make appropriate amendments to ensure that the rights of petitioners and others dependent on generic medicines are not put in jeopardy.

89. I am grateful to the parties for their well-researched submissions and authorities.

90. This petition revolved around critical issues of great public interest and I therefore make no order as to costs.

MUMBI NGUGI, Judge

NOTES AND QUESTIONS

1. On April 20, 2012, Kenya's High Court ordered the revision of the Anti-Counterfeit Act of 2008 on the grounds that in its current form the Act threatens access to affordable generic medicine. ANGOP, Kenya Ruling Upholds Access to Generic Drugs (Apr. 21, 2012) http://www.portalangop.co.ao/motix/en_us/noticias/africa/2012/3/16/Kenyan-court-ruling-upholds-access-generic-drugs,40b30da6-1904-456b-8b90-a34f0955f684.html. The ruling follows the April 2010 order in *Ochieng and Others v. Attorney-General and Others*, *supra*, that temporarily suspended the implementation of the Act, which had come into effect in July 2009, with respect to generic medicine. THE PHARMALETTER, *Kenya Court Set to Deliver Ruling on Anti-Counterfeit Law* (Jan. 27, 2012), http://www.thepharmaletter.com/file/110588/kenya-court-set-to-deliver-ruling-on-anti-counterfeit-law.html.

2. The Anti-Counterfeiting Act at issue in *Ochieng* seems to have been particularly egregious in that it prevented the importation into Kenya of drugs that were protected by patent in countries outside of Kenya, even if there was no Kenyan patent. This law was itself apparently the result of outside influences lobbying the government of Kenya for stronger protection for pharmaceutical products. *See* Suleiman Mbatiah, *Kenya: Pharmaceutical Companies Pushing Anti-Counterfeit Law*, INTERPRESSSERVICE NEWS AGENCY (Jun. 14, 2010), http://www.ipsnews.net/2010/06/kenya-pharmaceutical-companies-pushing-anti-counterfeit-law/. Both the petitioners and the Court referred to events and decisions taking place outside of Kenya, such as the seizure of generic drugs in the EU. How important do you think these outside influences were on the Court's ultimate decision? What impact might the foreign interests behind the law have had on the Court's view that the law was "to protect the intellectual property rights of individuals," not to safeguard public health?

3. In *Pfizer Inc. v. Cosmos Limited*, Case No. 49 (2006) (Industrial Property Tribunal) (Kenya), the court found a generic manufacturer liable for infringing a patent on the HIV/AIDS drug azithromycin dehydrate. Cosmos argued that it was entitled to make and import the drug because it was used for the treatment of opportunistic infections in HIV/AIDS patients. The court disagreed, noting that Cosmos had not followed the requirements for obtaining a compulsory license from the government to exploit the patented product without authorization from the patent-holder. Is the Kenya High Court's decision in *Ochieng* consistent with the Kenya Industrial Property Tribunal's decision in *Pfizer*?

4. Despite the prospects for flexibilities to pursue public interest goals through the patent system, many developing and least-developed countries have not integrated exceptions and limitations to patent rights in their national laws. Instead, some countries adopted provisions that exceeded the substantive requirements of the TRIPS Agreement. Regional intellectual property offices such as OAPI played a key role in influencing member governments to adopt these TRIPS-plus provisions. *See* Carolyn Deere, THE IMPLEMENTATION GAME: THE TRIPS AGREEMENT AND THE GLOBAL POLITICS OF

INTELLECTUAL PROPERTY REFORM IN DEVELOPING COUNTRIES 255–58 (2009). Indeed, under the revised Bangui Agreement, which governs the intellectual property framework for OAPI members, a judicial procedure in national civil courts is required before any of the flexibilities in the Doha Declaration can be used. *See id.* at 257. Why do you think regional offices would encourage such strong patent standards? Why do you think the countries agreed to them?

3. POST-TRIPS BILATERALISM

Post-TRIPS WTO Ministerial meetings have been noteworthy for the lack of progress in both trade and intellectual property negotiations. The most recent Doha Round (named for the city in which the Round began), also called the "Development Round," was intended to provide an opportunity for issues of particular relevance to developing and least-developed countries, such as disclosure of origin and prior informed consent in relation to genetic resources, to take center stage at the WTO and in any newly adopted TRIPS amendments. Not surprisingly, while developing countries have aspired to roll back some of the requirements of the TRIPS Agreement during the Doha negotiations, many developed countries have pushed strongly for the adoption of even higher levels of global IP protection. To date, neither group has succeeded to any meaningful extent. As a result, the Doha Round has been widely perceived by scholars and policy makers as a failure, with the only significant progress in the patent arena being the adoption of the Doha Declaration on the TRIPS Agreement and Public Health, and the controversial amendment of TRIPS permitting the supply of drugs produced under compulsory licensing to other countries in need of such drugs but lacking the manufacturing capacity to produce them.

While negotiations in the multilateral WTO arena stagnated in recent years, several developed countries, in particular the U.S. along with EU and European Free Trade Area countries (Norway, Iceland, Switzerland, and Lichtenstein), quietly revived the use of regional and bilateral agreements to achieve concessions and increase minimum levels of patent protection in exchange for preferential trade benefits. Between 2002 and 2007 alone, the United States concluded negotiations on eleven bilateral and regional free trade agreements.[1] Congress made possible this flurry of treaty activity when it passed the Bipartisan Trade Promotion Authority Act of 2002, which provided the executive branch with "fast-track" authority to conclude agreements with U.S. trading partners. *See* Bipartisan Trade Promotion Authority Act, Pub. L. No. 107–210 (2002).

Under the fast-track system, Congress, when presented with a proposed treaty, was required to vote on an agreement as a whole, within a

---

[1] U.S.—Singapore, Chile, Australia, Morocco, Bahrain, Oman, Panama, South Korea, Peru, Columbia and CAFTA. *See* http://www.ustr.gov for more information and agreement texts.

limited period of time of sixty legislative days, and without adding amendments to it. Additionally, the introduction to the Act explicitly outlined "TRIPS-plus" bilateral agreement objectives in the IP arena, and commanded that "the provisions of any multilateral or bilateral trade agreement governing intellectual property rights that is entered into by the United States reflect a standard of protection similar to that found in United States law." *Id.*

Individual agreements differ in specific terms, but the following "TRIPS-plus" provisions appear in at least one bilateral or regional FTA:

- Mandatory treaty accessions;[2]
- Patent term extensions—for delays in patent examination/regulatory approval;
- Third-party use for marketing approval;
- Patent-holder consent to third party marketing approval;
- Restrictions on third-party use of test data (typically five-year exclusions from use for marketing approval for pharmaceuticals, ten years for agricultural chemicals);
- No third-party reliance on patent-holder marketing approval;
- Patent protection for new uses of known products;
- Limits on excluding life forms from patentability;
- Parallel importation restrictions; and
- Compulsory licensing restrictions.

While all of the studied agreements require accession to other international IP agreements, such as the PCT or the Budapest Treaty, discussed in Chapter 8, and U.S. and EFTA agreements contain patent term extension and test data protection provisions, the remaining provisions are found only in select U.S. agreements. Nonetheless, European countries still benefit from these U.S. efforts. As cogently explained by Professors Vaver and Basheer:

> Europe does not presently compel other states to increase the level of patent rights beyond TRIPs, in the way the US is acting. Rather, its policy seems to be to ensure that the domestic law of its trading partners is framed to comply with most recent international norms: TRIPs of course, but also the Paris Convention and the Patent Cooperation Treaty. For countries wanting to join the EU, the early adoption of laws that mirror the EU's serve as a pre-entrance test.
>
> There is a subtlety to this stand-back policy. The US is left to do the running on raising the patent hurdles in free trade agreements as part of its overall strategy to raise global intellectual

---

[2] Requiring that parties accede to one or more of: UPOV, PCT, PC, PLT, the Budapest Convention, or TRIPS.

property levels of protection. One purpose is to stack the deck even higher in favour of big pharma in its never-ending war against generic imitators, wherever they are and wherever they market or export their products.

The US may negotiate the national and regional free trade agreements bilaterally, but the agreements also benefit Europe, including foreign companies with European bases.

Consider the issue of what categories of inventions are patentable. Once a new standard of patentability becomes part of domestic law and is extended to that country's nationals because of a bilateral trade agreement, that country must, under the national treatment requirements of the WTO agreement or Paris convention, also extend that standard to the nationals of all other WTO and Paris Convention states—including European states. At some point, the standard may become so prevalent as to become a new norm of international law. The stage is then set for the inclusion of such a term in the next round of TRI Ps negotiations, causing non-observance to become subject to sanction under TRIPs disputes resolution procedures.

David Vaver & Shamnad Basheer, *Popping Patented Pills: Europe and a Decade's Dose of TRIPs*, E.I.P.R. 282 [2006].

Nevertheless, recently, the European Union has been pushing for higher levels of IP protection in the FTAs it is negotiating, such as the EU-India FTA, and allegedly has sought in some agreements not only TRIPS-plus provisions, but EU-Plus and EU-Extra provisions.

U.S. bilateral activity slowed considerably around 2008 out of concern that the bilateral initiatives were not achieving U.S. interests; however, agreements recently were finalized with South Korea, Colombia, and Panama. Moreover, the United States has also pushed negotiation of two highly controversial IP enforcement treaties; the Anti-Counterfeiting Trade Agreement (ACTA) and the Transpacific Partnership Agreement (TPP). Part of the controversy surrounding each of these two treaties is the highly secretive nature of the negotiations taking place, with little opportunity for outsiders to provide input until the text is revealed as a fait accompli. While both agreements are largely focused on copyright and trademark enforcement, they both contain provisions that many NGOs and patient advocacy groups find troubling as they may severely limit access to medicines around the world. The current TPP negotiating parties are: Australia, Brunei Darussalam, Chile, Malaysia, New Zealand, Peru, Singapore, Vietnam, and the United States. ACTA has been signed, but not ratified, by Australia, Canada, the European Union, Japan, Morocco, New Zealand, Singapore, South Korea, and the United States. *See* Joint Statement of Health Action International (HAI) Europe, Oxfam, Médecins Sans Frontières (MSF) and the Trans Atlantic Consumer Dia-

logue (TACD) call on EU parliamentarians to condemn ACTA independently of the ECJ referral (March 29, 2012), https://www.
laquadrature.net/files/26%20Mar%202012%20Joint%20Statement%20
Call%20on%20MEPs%20to%20condemn%20ACTA%20independently%20
of%20the%20ECJ%20referral.pdf, and Susan K. Sell, *TRIPS Was Never
Enough: Vertical Forum Shifting, FTAs, ACTA, and TPP*, 18 J. INTELL.
PROP. L. 447 (2011).

One of the most controversial FTAs negotiated after the conclusion of
the TRIPS Agreement was the "CAFTA-DR," the Central America-
Dominican Republic Free Trade Agreement. Originally negotiated between the United States and Costa Rica, Nicaragua, Honduras, El Salvador, and Guatemala, and denominated CAFTA, the "DR" was added when
the Dominican Republic—with whom the U.S. had been separately negotiating—was added to the treaty in 2004. As the United States' third
largest export market in Latin America (behind Mexico and Brazil), Central America and the Dominican Republic were logical targets for U.S.
trade agreement attention. However, U.S. inclusion in CAFTA-DR of several "TRIPS-plus" provisions drew significant criticism, even from members of the U.S. Congress. Nevertheless, all signatories to the agreement
have ratified the treaty and it is in force for all seven countries.

NOTES AND QUESTIONS

1. In some respects, U.S. intellectual property policy abroad seems inconsistent with the domestic state of affairs. As one commentator notes regarding CAFTA:

> . . . Several civil society groups have noted the irony of USTR's push
> for "TRIPSplus" standards at the same time as Congress is debating
> options for improving the affordability of medicines within US bor-
> ders. While several US states are approving legislation to enable US
> citizens to buy medicines more cheaply from Canada, USTR is push-
> ing for agreements that prevent citizens in developing countries
> from doing the same.

Isabelle Scherer, *The Domino Effect of US FTAs: Public Health Groups,
Members of Congress Claim CAFTA Will Choke Access to Medicines*, Intell.
Prop. Watch (Nov. 4, 2004).

What possible negative consequences do U.S. citizens face as a result of
IP standards becoming more stringent through "TRIPS-plus" provisions in
bilateral and regional trade agreements?

2. Data exclusivity provisions in FTAs are interesting and controversial
because of their potential to create patent-like protection in the absence of
actual patent protection. Article 39 of TRIPS provides in part:

> Members, when requiring, as a condition of approving the market-
> ing of pharmaceutical or of agricultural chemical products which
> utilize new chemical entities, the submission of undisclosed test or

other data, the origination of which involves a considerable effort, **shall protect such data against unfair commercial use**. In addition, Members shall protect such data against disclosure, **except where necessary to protect the public**, or unless steps are taken to ensure that the data are protected against unfair commercial use. (emphasis added).

No time period is specified in Article 39, but several FTAs require countries to provide five to ten years of protection for data submitted to regulatory authorities to gain marketing approval for new drugs. Thus, even if a drug is denied patent protection, or the patent covering it has expired, competing manufacturers would be unable to market a generic version as reproducing the clinical data would be infeasible and unethical. Such provisions are considered by some to be "TRIPS-plus" as they require countries to provide more protection than does TRIPS. In particular, Article 39.3 requires protection of data against unfair commercial use, but such wording does not mandate exclusivity; protection could be provided by compensation for data use. Moreover, abbreviated drug marketing approval processes may not qualify as unfair commercial use if they are expressly provided for by law. *See* Tahir Amin et al., THE IMPACT OF ARTICLE 39.3 IN INDIA: A PRACTICAL PERSPECTIVE 11 (2006), http://iilj.org/research/documents/TheImpactofArticle39.3inIndiaA PracticalPerspective.pdf; and Carlos M. Correa, *Data Exclusivity for Pharmaceuticals: TRIPS Standards and FTAs*, *in* RESEARCH HANDBOOK ON THE PROTECTION OF IP UNDER WTO RULES 717 (Carlos M. Correa ed., 2010).

3. Not surprisingly, the U.S. government touts the benefits of FTAs for developing countries. Consider the following comments regarding the U.S.-Jordan FTA:

> The Jordan–US FTA is today flaunted by US officials and the US Trade Representative (USTR) as a success, an example of a country where "globalization has benefited" its economy, including "increased economic growth generally, and in particular, benefits for Jordan's pharmaceutical and bio-medical technology industries". These benefits, the argument continues, are reflected in a growing presence of multinational pharmaceutical enterprises in Jordan, enhanced accessibility and availability of drugs to all Jordanians at lower prices. Claims have also been made that the Jordan–US FTA has improved the ability of local firms to produce generic drugs and engage in new, innovative research and development in collaboration with major international pharmaceutical firms. As the Congressman James Moran recently wrote to the American Congress: "Since enactment of the FTA, the Jordanian drug industry has begun to develop its own innovative medicines" and has improved "access to new medicines" at affordable prices.

Hamed El-Said & Mohammed El-Said, *TRIPS-Plus Implications for Access to Medicines in Developing Countries: Lessons from Jordan–United States Free Trade Agreement*, 10 J. WORLD INTELL. PROP. 438, 439 (2007) (citations omitted).

However, there is another view. Jordan was the first Arab country to sign an FTA with the United States, and that agreement was the first to contain TRIPS-plus provisions. According to the OXFAM, the agreement has not benefited the Jordanian people or drug industry:

> Since the US-Jordan FTA was formally enacted . . ., TRIPS-plus rules have given multinational pharmaceutical companies more tools to prevent generic competition with their products. In fact, most pharmaceutical companies have not bothered to apply for patent protection for medicines launched onto the Jordanian market. Instead, multinational drug companies rely on TRIPS-plus . . . data exclusivity, to prevent generic competition for many medicines. . . . most multinational companies decided not to file patent applications after the US-Jordan FTA was signed because: (1) Jordan is not a member of the Patent Co-operation Treaty (PCT), thereby making patent filings expensive, complicated, and time-consuming for new medicines;25 (2) many medicines without a generic equivalent would have qualified for little or no patent protection in Jordan due to the original patent filing date; and (3) pharmaceutical companies concluded that data exclusivity effectively prevents generic competitors from entering the market for five years following registration of the originator medicine. In fact, of the 21 multinational drug companies, only three bothered to patent medicines that they launched onto the Jordanian market by mid-2006. . . . Recently, multinational drug companies have started to file patent applications for drug precursors that will eventually be launched on the Jordanian market. . . . Data exclusivity will ensure that even if a patent application is rejected, the pharmaceutical company can secure at least five years of monopoly protection. . . .

> [N]ew medicines to treat diabetes and heart disease cost anywhere from two to six times more in Jordan than in Egypt, where there are no TRIPS-plus barriers. . . . In 2002, medicines with no generic equivalent comprised only three per cent of the Jordanian market by value. Since then, medicines with no generic equivalent have progressively captured a larger share of the domestic market and, by the second quarter of 2006, these medicines comprised 9.4 per cent.
> . . . Furthermore, local generics companies complain that multinational pharmaceutical companies neither signed more licensing agreements nor transferred technology to local manufacturers. Thus, most new medicines are imported rather than produced locally. According to the Jordanian Association of Pharmaceutical Manufacturers (JAPM), most licensing agreements that are in effect today were signed before 1999.

All Costs, No Benefits: How TRIPS-Plus Intellectual Property Rules in the US-Jordan FTA Affect Access to Medicines, Oxfam Briefing Paper (March

2007), http://www.oxfam.org/sites/www.oxfam.org/files/all%20costs,%20no% 20benefits.pdf.

What advice would you give to countries considering adopting TRIPS-plus provisions in an FTA? Should other international law regimes, specifically human rights, always trump intellectual property provisions in regional trade agreements? Should arguments based in human rights doctrine be available for citizens, whose lives arguably are adversely impacted by TRIPS-plus provisions, even when their national laws make no provision for a constitutional right to health or access to medicines? Is a constitutional right to health legally distinct from a constitutional right to access to medicines?

PART 2

COMPARATIVE PATENTABILITY REQUIREMENTS AND PROCUREMENT

■ ■ ■

CHAPTER 4

PATENT SUBJECT MATTER ELIGIBILITY

■ ■ ■

The question of what types of inventions should be eligible for patent protection is important, controversial, and continues to elude harmonization efforts. As discussed in Chapter 3, TRIPS Article 27.1 requires member countries to provide patent protection to inventions "whether products or processes, in all fields of technology" and to make patent rights enjoyable "without discrimination as to the place of invention, the field of technology and whether products are imported or locally produced." However, Articles 27.2 and 27.3 provide a laundry list of inventions members can exclude from patentability. Those provisions state as follows:

(2) Members may exclude from patentability inventions, the prevention within their territory of the commercial exploitation of which is necessary to protect *ordre public* or morality, including to protect human, animal or plant life or health or to avoid serious prejudice to the environment, provided that such exclusion is not made merely because the exploitation is prohibited by their law.

(3) Members may also exclude from patentability:

(a) diagnostic, therapeutic and surgical methods for the treatment of humans or animals;

(b) plants and animals other than micro-organisms, and essentially biological processes for the production of plants or animals other than non-biological and microbiological processes. . . .

Many countries and regions also have statutory provisions explicitly excluding certain types of subject matter from patent protection. For example, EPC Articles 52(2) and (4) state:

(2) The following in particular shall not be regarded as inventions . . .

(a) discoveries, scientific theories and mathematical methods;

(b) aesthetic creations;

(c) schemes, rules and methods for performing mental acts, playing games or doing business, and programs for computers;

(d) presentations of information. . . .

(4) Methods for treatment of the human or animal body by surgery or therapy and diagnostic methods practised on the human or animal body shall not be regarded as inventions. . .

In patent systems around the world, there is little disagreement on the patent eligibility of most traditional types of inventions, such as machines or industrial chemicals. The chief areas of divergence are in the fields of biotechnology, business and diagnostic methods, computer software, and, as noted in Chapter 3, the scope and availability of protection for pharmaceuticals. Patent eligibility is a threshold determination regarding the *kinds* of inventions that may be patented. Even after clearing the eligibility hurdle, inventions still must be deemed patentable under the remaining patentability criteria, including novelty, industrial applicability, and inventive step. This Chapter examines significant differences in national patent subject matter standards and highlights the key rationales behind the disparate treatment of inventions in these often contested areas.

A. PATENT ELIGIBILITY OF LIFE FORMS

Accompanying recent momentous breakthroughs in biotechnology (biotech) research, the patent eligibility of "human-made" life forms is a topic that has, in the last several decades, received significant attention by both scholars and policy makers worldwide. Governmental and nongovernmental organizations in several countries have commissioned studies and drafted reports on the ethical and moral issues associated with patenting certain biotech inventions. The diversity of approaches to patent subject matter eligibility used by countries to address these issues derives largely from cultural norms and public policy considerations. Some countries have also made distinctions between the eligibility of higher and lower life forms.

1. LOWER LIFE FORMS

Overall, the United States traditionally has taken a much broader view of patent subject matter eligibility than most other countries and does not have explicit statutory bars to any of the categories of inventions identified in TRIPS Articles 27.2 or 27.3. In fact, until the 2011 AIA codification of the Weldon Amendment (regarding human organisms and discussed *infra* at p. 283), the only subject matter explicitly barred from patentability by statute related to atomic weapons:

No patent shall hereafter be granted for any invention or discovery which is useful solely in the utilization of special nuclear material or atomic energy in an atomic weapon. Any patent granted for any such invention or discovery is revoked, and just compensation shall be made therefor.

42 U.S.C. § 2181 (2006).

The Supreme Court decision below, the first dealing with patenting life forms, explains the basis and contours of the U.S. viewpoint.

DIAMOND V. CHAKRABARTY

Supreme Court of the United States
447 U.S. 303 (1980)

■ BURGER, C.J.:

We granted certiorari to determine whether a live, human-made micro-organism is patentable subject matter under 35 U.S.C. § 101.

I.

In 1972, respondent Chakrabarty, a microbiologist, filed a patent application, assigned to the General Electric Co. The application asserted 36 claims related to Chakrabarty's invention of "a bacterium from the genus *Pseudomonas* containing therein at least two stable energy-generating plasmids, each of said plasmids providing a separate hydrocarbon degradative pathway."[1] This human-made, genetically engineered bacterium is capable of breaking down multiple components of crude oil. Because of this property, which is possessed by no naturally occurring bacteria, Chakrabarty's invention is believed to have significant value for the treatment of oil spills.[2]

Chakrabarty's patent claims were of three types: first, process claims for the method of producing the bacteria; second, claims for an inoculum comprised of a carrier material floating on water, such as straw, and the new bacteria; and third, claims to the bacteria themselves. The patent examiner allowed the claims falling into the first two categories, but rejected claims for the bacteria. His decision rested on two grounds: (1) that micro-organisms are "products of nature," and (2) that as living things they are not patentable subject matter under 35 U.S.C. § 101.

Chakrabarty appealed the rejection of these claims to the Patent Office Board of Appeals, and the Board affirmed the Examiner on the se-

---

[1] Plasmids are hereditary units physically separate from the chromosomes of the cell. In prior research, Chakrabarty and an associate discovered that plasmids control the oil degradation abilities of certain bacteria. In particular, the two researchers discovered plasmids capable of degrading camphor and octane, two components of crude oil. In the work represented by the patent application at issue here, Chakrabarty discovered a process by which four different plasmids, capable of degrading four different oil components, could be transferred to and maintained stably in a single *Pseudomonas* bacterium, which itself has no capacity for degrading oil.

[2] At present, biological control of oil spills requires the use of a mixture of naturally occurring bacteria, each capable of degrading one component of the oil complex. In this way, oil is decomposed into simpler substances which can serve as food for aquatic life. However, for various reasons, only a portion of any such mixed culture survives to attack the oil spill. By breaking down multiple components of oil, Chakrabarty's micro-organism promises more efficient and rapid oil-spill control.

cond ground.[3] Relying on the legislative history of the 1930 Plant Patent Act, in which Congress extended patent protection to certain asexually reproduced plants, the Board concluded that § 101 was not intended to cover living things such as these laboratory created micro-organisms.

The Court of Customs and Patent Appeals, by a divided vote, reversed on the authority of its prior decision in *In re Bergy*, 563 F.2d 1031, 1038 (1977), which held that "the fact that microorganisms . . . are alive . . . [is] without legal significance" for purposes of the patent law.[4] . . . The Commissioner of Patents and Trademarks . . . sought certiorari. . . .

II.

. . . .

The question before us in this case is a narrow one of statutory interpretation requiring us to construe 35 U.S.C. § 101 which provides:

> Whoever invents or discovers any new and useful process, machine, manufacture, or composition of matter, or any new and useful improvement thereof, may obtain a patent therefor, subject to the conditions and requirements of this title.

Specifically, we must determine whether respondent's microorganism constitutes a "manufacture" or "composition of matter" within the meaning of the statute.[5]

III.

In cases of statutory construction we begin, of course, with the language of the statute. . . . And "unless otherwise defined, words will be interpreted as taking their ordinary, contemporary common meaning." . . . . We have also cautioned that courts "should not read into the patent laws limitations and conditions which the legislature has not expressed." *United States v. Dubilier Condenser Corp.*, 289 U.S. 178, 199 (1933).

Guided by these canons of construction, this Court has read the term "manufacture" in § 101 in accordance with its dictionary definition to mean "the production of articles for use from raw or prepared materials by giving to these materials new forms, qualities, properties, or combinations, whether by hand-labor or by machinery." *American Fruit Growers, Inc. v. Brogdex Co.*, 283 U.S. 1, 11 (1931). Similarly, "composition of matter" has been construed consistent with its common usage to include "all compositions of two or more substances and . . . all composite articles, whether they be the results of chemical union, or of mechanical mixture,

---

[3] The Board concluded that the new bacteria were not "products of nature," because *Pseudomonas* bacteria containing two or more different energy-generating plasmids are not naturally occurring.

[4] *Bergy* involved a patent application for a pure culture of the micro-organism *Streptomyces vellosus* found to be useful in the production of lincomycin, an antibiotic.

[5] This case does not involve the other "conditions and requirements" of the patent laws, such as novelty and nonobviousness. 35 U.S.C. §§ 102, 103.

or whether they be gases, fluids, powders or solids." *Shell Development Co. v. Watson,* 149 F. Supp. 279, 280 (D.C.1957) (citing 1 A. DELLER, WALKER ON PATENTS § 14, p. 55 (1st ed. 1937)). In choosing such expansive terms as "manufacture" and "composition of matter," modified by the comprehensive "any," Congress plainly contemplated that the patent laws would be given wide scope.

The relevant legislative history also supports a broad construction. The Patent Act of 1793, authored by Thomas Jefferson, defined statutory subject matter as "any new and useful art, machine, manufacture, or composition of matter, or any new or useful improvement [thereof]." Act of Feb. 21, 1793, § 1, 1 Stat. 319. The Act embodied Jefferson's philosophy that "ingenuity should receive a liberal encouragement." 5 WRITINGS OF THOMAS JEFFERSON 75–76 (Washington ed. 1871). Subsequent patent statutes in 1836, 1870, and 1874 employed this same broad language. In 1952, when the patent laws were recodified, Congress replaced the word "art" with "process," but otherwise left Jefferson's language intact. The Committee Reports accompanying the 1952 Act inform us that Congress intended statutory subject matter to "include anything under the sun that is made by man." S. REP. NO. 1979, 82d Cong., 2d Sess., 5 (1952); H.R. REP. NO. 1923, 82d Cong., 2d Sess., 6 (1952).[6]

This is not to suggest that § 101 has no limits or that it embraces every discovery. The laws of nature, physical phenomena, and abstract ideas have been held not patentable. . . . Thus, a new mineral discovered in the earth or a new plant found in the wild is not patentable subject matter. Likewise, Einstein could not patent his celebrated law that $E=mc^2$; nor could Newton have patented the law of gravity. Such discoveries are "manifestations of . . . nature, free to all men and reserved exclusively to none." *Funk Brothers Seed Co. v. Kalo Inoculant Co.,* 333 U.S. 127, 130 (1948). . . .

Judged in this light, respondent's micro-organism plainly qualifies as patentable subject matter. His claim is not to a hitherto unknown natural phenomenon, but to a nonnaturally occurring manufacture or composition of matter—a product of human ingenuity "having a distinctive name, character [and] use." *Hartranft v. Wiegmann,* 121 U.S. 609, 615 (1887). . . .

[T]he patentee has produced a new bacterium with markedly different characteristics from any found in nature and one having the potential for significant utility. His discovery is not nature's handiwork, but his own; accordingly it is patentable subject matter under § 101.

---

[6] This same language was employed by P. J. Federico, a principal draftsman of the 1952 re-codification, in his testimony regarding that legislation: "[U]nder section 101 a person may have invented a machine or a manufacture, which may include anything under the sun that is made by man. . . . " Hearings on H.R. 3760 before Subcommittee No. 3 of the House Committee on the Judiciary, 82d Cong., 1st Sess., 37 (1951).

. . . .

Congress [has] recognized that the relevant distinction [is] not between living and inanimate things, but between products of nature, whether living or not, and human-made inventions. Here, respondent's micro-organism is the result of human ingenuity and research. . . .

. . . .

It is, of course, correct that Congress, not the courts, must define the limits of patentability; but it is equally true that once Congress has spoken it is "the province and duty of the judicial department to say what the law is." *Marbury v. Madison,* 1 Cranch 137, 177 (1803). Congress has performed its constitutional role in defining patentable subject matter in § 101; we perform ours in construing the language Congress has employed. . . .

. . . .

To buttress his argument, the petitioner, with the support of amicus, points to grave risks that may be generated by research endeavors such as respondent's. The briefs present a gruesome parade of horribles. Scientists, among them Nobel laureates, are quoted suggesting that genetic research may pose a serious threat to the human race, or, at the very least, that the dangers are far too substantial to permit such research to proceed apace at this time. We are told that genetic research and related technological developments may spread pollution and disease, that it may result in a loss of genetic diversity, and that its practice may tend to depreciate the value of human life. These arguments are forcefully, even passionately, presented; they remind us that, at times, human ingenuity seems unable to control fully the forces it creates—that, with Hamlet, it is sometimes better "to bear those ills we have than fly to others that we know not of."

It is argued that this Court should weigh these potential hazards in considering whether respondent's invention is patentable subject matter under § 101. We disagree. The grant or denial of patents on microorganisms is not likely to put an end to genetic research or to its attendant risks. The large amount of research that has already occurred when no researcher had sure knowledge that patent protection would be available suggests that legislative or judicial fiat as to patentability will not deter the scientific mind from probing into the unknown any more than Canute could command the tides. Whether respondent's claims are patentable may determine whether research efforts are accelerated by the hope of reward or slowed by want of incentives, but that is all.

What is more important is that we are without competence to entertain these arguments—either to brush them aside as fantasies generated by fear of the unknown, or to act on them. The choice we are urged to make is a matter of high policy for resolution within the legislative process after the kind of investigation, examination, and study that legislative bodies can provide and courts cannot. That process involves the balancing of competing values and interests, which in our democratic system is the business of elected representatives. Whatever their validity, the contentions now pressed on us should be addressed to the political branches of the Government, the Congress and the Executive, and not to the courts.

. . . Our task, rather, is the narrow one of determining what Congress meant by the words it used in the statute; once that is done our powers are exhausted. Congress is free to amend § 101 so as to exclude from patent protection organisms produced by genetic engineering. . . . Or it may choose to craft a statute specifically designed for such living things. But, until Congress takes such action, this Court must construe the language of § 101 as it is. The language of that section fairly embraces respondent's invention.

Accordingly, the judgment of the Court of Customs and Patent Appeals is

Affirmed.

Mr. Justice BRENNAN, with whom Mr. Justice WHITE, Mr. Justice MARSHALL, and Mr. Justice POWELL join, dissenting.

I agree with the Court that the question before us is a narrow one. Neither the future of scientific research, nor even, the ability of respondent Chakrabarty to reap some monopoly profits from his pioneering work, is at stake. Patents on the processes by which he has produced and employed the new living organism are not contested. The only question we need decide is whether Congress, exercising its authority under Art. I, § 8, of the Constitution, intended that he be able to secure a monopoly on the living organism itself, no matter how produced or how used. Because I believe the Court has misread the applicable legislation, I dissent.

The patent laws attempt to reconcile this Nation's deep seated antipathy to monopolies with the need to encourage progress. Given the complexity and legislative nature of this delicate task, we must be careful to extend patent protection no further than Congress has provided. In particular, were there an absence of legislative direction, the courts should leave to Congress the decisions whether and how far to extend the patent privilege into areas where the common understanding has been that patents are not available.

In this case, however, we do not confront a complete legislative vacuum. [Justice Brennan then discusses the Plant Patent Act of 1930 and the Plant Variety Protection Act as two more specific statutes indicating Congressional intent to exclude living inventions from the utility patent statute. Eds]

[T]he Court's decision does not follow the unavoidable implications of the statute. Rather, it extends the patent system to cover living material even though Congress plainly has legislated in the belief that § 101 does not encompass living organisms. It is the role of Congress, not this Court, to broaden or narrow the reach of the patent laws. This is especially true where, as here, the composition sought to be patented uniquely implicates matters of public concern.

2. HIGHER LIFE FORMS

In *Diamond v. Chakrabarty*, the court gave a green light to biotech researchers and investors by confirming that "life" can constitute patent-eligible subject matter, despite the concerns expressed by the dissenters. Patent offices in other countries, both developed and developing, also began to recognize the patentability of microorganisms such as bacteria. Then, on April 7, 1987, the USPTO announced that it considered "non-naturally occurring, non-human multicellular living organisms, including animals, to be patentable subject matter" based on the *Chakrabarty* decision. News of the Office's plans to patent animals created significant public controversy and generated calls for bans on both the underlying research and patents on genetically modified animals. Opponents of patents for animals also sought relief in court. Nine plaintiffs, including the Animal Legal Defense Fund, the American Society for the Prevention of Cruelty to Animals, and the Humane Farming Association, filed suit alleging that the USPTO Commissioner had violated the Administrative Procedures Act in filing the Notice without complying with the required public notice and comment period. *See Animal Legal Def. Fund v. Quigg,* 932 F.2d 920, 924 (Fed. Cir. 1991). In affirming dismissal of the suit for lack of standing, the Court of Appeals for the Federal Circuit noted:

> Essentially, appellants assert a right, as members of the public particularly interested in animals, to sue for what they perceive to be an unwarranted interference with the discretionary judgment of an examiner. However, it must be noted that whether patents are allowable for animal life forms is not a matter of discretion but of law. . . . Thus, if we assume examiners must follow the Notice—which the Commissioner denies—such action has no effect on the ultimate validity of any patent. *Either the subject matter falls within section 101 or it does not, and that question does not turn on any discretion residing in examiners.*

Id. at 929–930 (emphasis added). The Court's words made clear the absence of any authority on the part of the USPTO to deny patents on otherwise patentable subject matter.

On April 12, 1988, almost a year to the day after its earlier announcement, the USPTO heralded the issuance of the world's first patent on a higher life form, in this case a mouse, as "a singularly historic event." *See* Keith Schneider, *Harvard Gets Mouse Patent, a World First*, N.Y. TIMES, Apr. 13, 1988, at A22. The mouse, developed by Harvard researchers Philip Leder and Timothy Stewart, was genetically modified to increase its chances of developing cancer, making it a more useful research subject. While no court challenges were made to the issuance of the Harvard mouse patent in the United States, the application received a far different reception in some other countries, as illustrated in the following decision from Canada.

HARVARD COLLEGE V. CANADA (COMM'R OF PATENTS)

Supreme Court of Canada
[2002] 4 S.C.R. 45

■ BASTARACHE J.:

I. INTRODUCTION

This appeal raises the issue of the patentability of higher life forms within the context of the [*Canadian*] *Patent Act*, R.S.C. 1985, C. P-4. The respondent, the President and Fellows of Harvard College [Harvard], seeks to patent a mouse that has been genetically altered to increase its susceptibility to cancer, which makes it useful for cancer research. The patent claims also extend to all non-human mammals which have been similarly altered.

II. FACTUAL BACKGROUND

On June 21, 1985, [Harvard] applied for a patent on an invention entitled "transgenic animals." The invention aims to produce animals with a susceptibility to cancer for purposes of animal carcinogenic studies. The animals can be used to test a material suspected of being a carcinogen by exposing them to the material and seeing if tumours develop. Because the animals are already susceptible to tumour development, the amount of material used can be smaller, thereby more closely approximating the amounts to which humans are actually exposed. In addition, the animals will be expected to develop tumours in a shorter time period. The animals can also be used to test materials thought to confer protection against the development of cancer.

The technology by which a cancer-prone mouse ("oncomouse") is produced is described in the patent application disclosure. The oncogene (the cancer-promoting gene) is obtained from the genetic code of a non-mammal source, such as a virus. A vehicle for transporting the oncogene into the mouse's chromosomes is constructed using a small piece of bacterial DNA referred to as a plasmid. The plasmid, into which the oncogene has been "spliced," is injected into fertilized mouse eggs, preferably while they are at the one-cell stage. The eggs are then implanted into a female host mouse, or "foster mother," and permitted to develop to term. After the offspring of the foster mother are delivered, they are tested for the presence of the oncogene; those that contain the oncogene are called "founder" mice. Founder mice are mated with mice that have not been genetically altered. In accordance with Mendelian inheritance principles, 50 percent of the offspring will have all of their cells affected by the oncogene, making them suitable for the uses described above.

In its patent application, the respondent seeks to protect both the process by which the oncomice are produced and the end product of the process, i.e. the founder mice and the offspring whose cells are affected by the oncogene. The process and product claims also extend to all non-human mammals. In March 1993, by Final Action, a Patent Examiner rejected the product claims (claims 1 to 12) as being outside the scope of the definition of "invention" in s. 2 of the *Patent Act*, but allowed the process claims (claims 13 to 26). In August 1995, after a review by the Commissioner of Patents and a hearing before the Patent Appeal Board, the Commissioner confirmed the refusal to grant a patent for claims 1 to 12. The Federal Court Trial Division dismissed the respondent's appeal from the decision of the Commissioner. The respondent's further appeal to the Federal Court of Appeal was allowed by a majority of the court. . . . The Commissioner of Patents appeals from that decision.

III. RELEVANT STATUTORY PROVISIONS

Patent Act, R.S.C. 1985, c. P-4:

2. In this Act, except as otherwise provided,

"invention" means any new and useful art, process, machine, manufacture or composition of matter, or any new and useful improvement in any art, process, machine, manufacture or composition of matter. . . .

. . . .

V. ANALYSIS

. . . .

The definition of invention in s. 2 of the *Patent Act* lists five categories of invention: art (*réalisation*), process (*procédé*), machine (*machine*), manufacture (*fabrication*) or composition of matter (*composition de matières*). The first three, "art," "process" and "machine," are clearly inapplicable when considering claims directed toward a genetically engineered non-human mammal. If a higher life form is to fit within the definition of invention, it must therefore be considered to be either a "manufacture" or a "composition of matter."

[The Federal Court of Appeal] concluded that the oncomouse was a "composition of matter," and therefore did not find it necessary to consider whether it was also a "manufacture." In coming to this conclusion, [the court relied] on the following definition of "composition of matter" adopted by the majority of the U.S. Supreme Court in [*Diamond v. Chakrabarty*, 447 U.S. 303, 308 (1980)]:

> . . . all compositions of two or more substances and . . . all composite articles, whether they be the results of chemical union, or of mechanical mixture, or whether they be gases, fluids, powders or solids.

In Chakrabarty, the majority attributed the widest meaning possible to the phrases "composition of matter" and "manufacture" for the reason that inventions are, necessarily, unanticipated and unforeseeable. . . .

I agree that the definition of invention in the *Patent Act* is broad. Because the Act was designed in part to promote innovation, it is only reasonable to expect the definition of invention to be broad enough to encompass unforeseen and unanticipated technology. I cannot however agree with the suggestion that the definition is unlimited in the sense that it includes "anything under the sun that is made by man." In drafting the *Patent Act*, Parliament chose to adopt an exhaustive definition that limits invention to any "art, process, machine, manufacture or composition of matter." Parliament did not define "invention" as "anything new and useful made by man." By choosing to define invention in this way, Parliament signalled a clear intention to include certain subject matter as patentable and to exclude other subject matter as being outside the confines of the Act. This should be kept in mind when determining whether the words "manufacture" and "composition of matter" include higher life forms.

With respect to the meaning of the word "manufacture" (*fabrication*), although it may be attributed a very broad meaning, I am of the opinion that the word would commonly be understood to denote a non-living mechanistic product or process. For example, the *Oxford English Dictionary* (2nd ed. 1989), vol. IX, at p. 341, defines the noun "manufacture" as the following:

> [T]he action or process of making by hand. . . . The action or process of making articles or material (in modern use, on a large scale) by the application of physical labour or mechanical power.

The *Grand Robert de la langue française* (2nd ed. 2001), vol. 3, at p. 517, defines thus the word "*fabrication*":

[TRANSLATION]

> Art or action or manufacturing. . . The manufacture of a technical object (by someone). Manufacturing by artisans, by hand, by machine, industrially, by mass production. . .

. . . .

. . . In my view, while a mouse may be analogized to a "manufacture" when it is produced in an industrial setting, the word in its vernacular sense does not include a higher life form. The definition in *Hornblower v. Boulton* (1799), 8 T.R. 95, 101 E.R. 1285 (Eng. K.B.), cited by the respondent, is equally problematic when applied to higher life forms. In that case, the English courts defined "manufacture" as "something made by the hands of man" (at p. 1288). In my opinion, a complex life form such as a mouse or a chimpanzee cannot easily be characterized as "something made by the hands of man."

As regards the meaning of the words "composition of matter," I believe that they must be defined more narrowly than was the case in *Chakrabarty, supra,* at p. 308 namely "all compositions of two or more substances and . . . all composite articles." If the words "composition of matter" are understood this broadly, then the other listed categories of invention, including "machine" and "manufacture," become redundant. This implies that "composition of matter" must be limited in some way. Although I do not express an opinion as to where the line should be drawn, I conclude that "composition of matter" does not include a higher life form such as the oncomouse. . . .

[T]here are a number of factors that make it difficult to regard higher life forms as "composition[s] of matter." First, the *Oxford English Dictionary, supra*, vol. III, at p. 625, defines the word "composition" as "[a] substance or preparation formed by combination or mixture of various ingredients" . . . . Within the context of the definition of "invention," it does not seem unreasonable to assume that it must be the inventor who has combined or mixed the various ingredients. Owing to the fact that the technology by which a mouse predisposed to cancer is produced involves injecting the oncogene into a fertilized egg, the genetically altered egg would appear to be cognizable as "[a] substance or preparation formed by combination or mixture of various ingredients" or as [translation] "[a]ction or manner of forming a whole . . . by assembling several parts." However, it does not thereby follow that the oncomouse itself can be understood in such terms. Injecting the oncogene into a fertilized egg is the but-for cause of a mouse predisposed to cancer, but the process by which a fertilized egg becomes an adult mouse is a complex process, elements of which require no human intervention. The body of a mouse is composed of various ingredients or substances, but it does not consist of ingredients or substances that have been combined or mixed together by a person. Thus, I am not satisfied that the phrase "composition of matter" includes a higher life form whose genetic code has been altered in this manner.

It also is significant that the word "matter" captures but one aspect of a higher life form. As defined by the *Oxford English Dictionary, supra*, vol. IX, at p. 480, "matter" is a "[p]hysical or corporeal substance in general . . . , contradistinguished from immaterial or incorporeal substance (spirit, soul, mind), and from qualities, actions, or conditions." . . . . Although some in society may hold the view that higher life forms are mere "composition[s] of matter," the phrase does not fit well with common understandings of human and animal life. Higher life forms are generally regarded as possessing qualities and characteristics that transcend the particular genetic material of which they are composed. A person whose genetic make-up is modified by radiation does not cease to be him or her-self. Likewise, the same mouse would exist absent the injection of the on-cogene into the fertilized egg cell; it simply would not be predisposed to cancer. The fact that it has this predisposition to cancer that makes it valuable to humans does not mean that the mouse, along with other ani-mal life forms, can be defined solely with reference to the genetic matter of which it is composed. The fact that animal life forms have numerous unique qualities that transcend the particular matter of which they are composed makes it difficult to conceptualize higher life forms as mere "composition[s] of matter." It is a phrase that seems inadequate as a de-scription of a higher life form.

. . . .

Patenting higher life forms would involve a radical departure from the traditional patent regime. Moreover, the patentability of such life forms is a highly contentious matter that raises a number of extremely complex issues. If higher life forms are to be patentable, it must be under the clear and unequivocal direction of Parliament. For the reasons dis-cussed above, I conclude that the current Act does not clearly indicate that higher life forms are patentable. Far from it. Rather, I believe that the best reading of the words of the Act supports the opposite conclu-sion—that higher life forms such as the oncomouse are not currently pa-tentable in Canada.

. . . .

[S]everal of the issues raised by the interveners and in the literature are . . . directly related to patentability and to the scheme of the *Patent Act* itself. These issues, which pertain to the scope and content of the mo-nopoly right accorded to the inventor by a patent, have been explored in depth by the Canadian Biotechnology Advisory Committee (CBAC) . . . . In June 2002, the CBAC released its final report [titled] *The Patenting of Higher Life Forms and Related Issues*. The report recommends that high-er life forms should be patentable. Nonetheless, it concludes . . . that giv-en the importance of issues raised by the patenting of higher life forms and the significant "values" content of the issues raised, Parliament and not the courts should determine whether and to what degree patent rights ought to extend to plants and animals.

Two of the issues addressed by the CBAC (farmers' privilege and in-nocent bystanders) arise out of the unique ability of higher life forms to self-replicate. Because higher life forms reproduce by themselves, the grant of a patent covers not only the particular plant, seed or animal sold, but also all of its progeny containing the patented invention. In the CBAC's view, this represents a significant increase in the scope of rights offered to patent holders that is not in line with the scope of patent rights provided in other fields.

One significant concern arising out of the increased scope of patent protection is the impact that it will have on Canada's agricultural industry. The CBAC recommends that a farmers' privilege provision be included in the Act. The privilege would permit farmers to collect and reuse seeds harvested from patented plants and to breed patented animals for their own use, so long as these were not sold for commercial breeding purposes. Although the CBAC puts forward suggestions pertaining to the general nature of such a provision, it nonetheless recognizes that more work would need to be done to identify the extent of the privilege in relation to plants and animals.

Another concern identified by the CBAC in respect to self-replication pertains to infringement. The CBAC observes that since plants and animals are often capable of reproducing on their own, it must be recognized that they will not always do so under the control or with the knowledge of those who grow the plants or raise the animals. Patent law does not currently require a patent holder to prove that an alleged infringer knew or ought to have known about the reproduction of a patented invention. An "innocent bystander" may therefore be faced with high costs to defend a patent infringement suit and an award of damages for infringement without a countervailing remedy against the patent holder. The CBAC correspondingly recommends that the *Patent Act* contain a provision that would allow the so-called "innocent bystander" to rebut the usual presumption concerning knowledge of infringement in respect of inventions capable of reproducing, such as plants, seeds and animals.

. . . .

There is no doubt that two of the central objects of the Act are "to advance research and development and to encourage broader economic activity." As noted earlier, this does not, however, imply that "anything under the sun that is made by man" is patentable. Parliament did not leave the definition of invention open, but rather chose to define it exhaustively. Regardless of the desirability of a certain activity, or the necessity of creating incentives to engage in that activity, a product of human ingenuity must fall within the terms of the Act in order for it to be patentable. . . .

. . . .

Based on the language and the scheme of the Act, both of which are not well accommodated to higher life forms, it is reasonable to assume that Parliament did not intend the monopoly right inherent in the grant of a patent to extend to inventions of this nature. It simply does not follow from the objective of promoting ingenuity that all inventions must be patentable, regardless of the fact that other indicators of legislative intention point to the contrary conclusion.

. . . .

The respondent notes that the Commissioner of Patents has since 1982 accepted that lower life forms come within the definitions of "composition of matter" and "manufacture" and has granted patents on such life forms accordingly. It adds that the *Patent Act* does not distinguish, in its definition of invention, between subject matter that is less complex (lower life forms) and subject matter that is more complex (higher life forms). It submits that there is therefore no evidentiary or legal basis for the distinction the Patent Office has made between lower life forms such as bacteria, yeast and moulds, and higher life forms such as plants and animals.

. . . .

Though this Court is not faced with the issue of the patentability of lower life forms, it must nonetheless address the respondent's argument that the line between higher and lower life forms is indefensible. As discussed above, I am of the opinion that the unique concerns and issues raised by the patentability of plants and animals necessitate a parliamentary response. Only Parliament has the institutional competence to extend patent rights or another form of intellectual property protection to plants and animals and to attach appropriate conditions to the right that is granted. In the interim, I see no reason to alter the line drawn by the Patent Office. The distinction between lower and higher life forms, though not explicit in the Act, is nonetheless defensible on the basis of common sense differences between the two. Perhaps more importantly, there appears to be a consensus that human life is not patentable; yet this distinction is also not explicit in the Act. If the line between lower and higher life forms is indefensible and arbitrary, so too is the line between human beings and other higher life forms.

. . . .

Finally, the respondent refers to the World Trade Organization's *Agreement on Trade Related Aspects of Intellectual Property Rights* (TRIPS), and the *North American Free Trade Agreement* (NAFTA), which both contain an article whereby members may "exclude from patentability" certain subject matter, including plants and animals other than micro-organisms. The respondent argues that it is apparent from this provision that plants and animals are considered patentable, unless specifically excluded from patentability. I see little merit to this argument since the *status quo* position in Canada is that higher life forms are not a patentable subject matter, regardless of the fact that there is no explicit exclusion in the *Patent Act*. In my view, the fact that there is a specific exception in TRIPS and NAFTA for plants and animals does however demonstrate that the distinction between higher and lower life forms is widely accepted as valid.

. . . .

VI. CONCLUSION

For the reasons given above, the appeal is allowed. . . .

––––––––––––

NOTES AND QUESTIONS

1. What factors do you think are responsible for the different treatment of the patentability of life forms between Canada and the United States reflected in *Harvard College* despite the nearly identical patent statutory provisions on which it and *Diamond v. Chakrabarty* are based? Before the *Harvard College* case, the U.S. Supreme Court in *J.E.M. Ag Supply, Inc. v. Pioneer Hi-Bred Int'l, Inc.,* 534 U.S. 124 (2001), used virtually identical reasoning (and similar language) to that in *Diamond v. Chakrabarty* to uphold the patent eligibility of plants—higher life forms—under 35 U.S.C. § 101. This suggests that the distinction is really not that of higher versus lower life forms. Which Court's exercise in statutory interpretation do you find more persuasive and why?

2. The prevailing Justices in the *Diamond v. Chakrabarty* decision placed heavy emphasis on the importance of a patent incentive to encourage genetic research, which at the time was a fledgling field. How should this rationale be viewed in light of the public policy concerns raised by the Canadian Supreme Court in *Harvard College*?

3. If a WTO member country filed a complaint against Canada, how do you think a WTO dispute panel would rule on the TRIPS-compatibility of the *Harvard College* decision? Does a WTO panel have jurisdiction to rule on this question? Read Article 64(2) of the TRIPS Agreement before attempting this question!

––––––––––––

What the Canadian Supreme Court "took away" from patent eligibility in *Harvard College*, it "returned" in a sense two years later in the following case.

MONSANTO CANADA INC. v. SCHMEISER

Supreme Court of Canada
[2004] 1 S.C.R. 902

PANEL: McLachlin C.J. and Iacobucci, Major, Bastarache, Binnie, Arbour, LeBel, Deschamps and Fish JJ.

The judgment of McLachlin C.J. and Major, Binnie, Deschamps and Fish JJ. was delivered by

■ McLACHLIN C.J. and FISH J.: —

I. INTRODUCTION

This case concerns a large scale, commercial farming operation that grew canola containing a patented cell and gene without obtaining licence or permission. The main issue is whether it thereby breached the Patent Act, R.S.C. 1985, c. P-4. We believe that it did.

In reaching this conclusion, we emphasize from the outset that we are not concerned here with the innocent discovery by farmers of "blow-by" patented plants on their land or in their cultivated fields. Nor are we concerned with the scope of the respondents' patent or the wisdom and social utility of the genetic modification of genes and cells—a practice authorized by Parliament under the Patent Act and its regulations.

. . . .

II. THE SALIENT FACTS

Percy Schmeiser has farmed in Saskatchewan for more than 50 years. In 1996 he assigned his farming business to a corporation in which he and his wife are the sole shareholders and directors. He and his corporation grow wheat, peas, and a large amount of canola.

. . . .

Schmeiser never purchased Roundup Ready Canola nor did he obtain a licence to plant it. Yet, in 1998, tests revealed that 95 to 98 percent of his 1,000 acres of canola crop was made up of Roundup Ready plants. The origin of the plants is unclear. They may have been derived from Roundup Ready seed that blew onto or near Schmeiser's land, and was then collected from plants that survived after Schmeiser sprayed Roundup herbicide around the power poles and in the ditches along the roadway bordering four of his fields. The fact that these plants survived the spraying indicated that they contained the patented gene and cell. The trial judge found that "none of the suggested sources [proposed by Schmeiser] could reasonably explain the concentration or extent of Roundup Ready canola of a commercial quality" ultimately present in Schmeiser's crop. . . .

The issues on this appeal are whether Schmeiser infringed Monsanto's patent, and if so, what remedies Monsanto may claim.

III. ANALYSIS

A. THE PATENT: ITS SCOPE AND VALIDITY

Canola is a valuable crop grown in Canada and used to make edible oil and animal feed. The respondents are the licensee and owner, respectively, of Canadian Patent No. 1,313,830. This patent, titled "Glyphosate-

Resistant Plants," was issued on February 23, 1993, and expires on February 23, 2010. It discloses the invention of genetically engineered genes and cells containing those genes which, when inserted into plants (in this case canola), dramatically increase their tolerance to herbicides containing glyphosate. Ordinarily, glyphosate inhibits an enzyme essential for plant survival. Most plants sprayed with a glyphosate herbicide do not survive, but a canola plant grown from seed containing the modified gene will survive.

Since 1996, canola seed containing the patented gene and cell has been produced in Canada under licence from the respondents; this seed has been marketed to farmers under the trade name "Roundup Ready Canola," reflecting its resistance to the glyphosate herbicide "Roundup" manufactured by the respondents. Roundup can be sprayed after the canola plants have emerged, killing all plants except the canola. This eliminates the need for tillage and other herbicides. It also avoids delaying seeding to accommodate early weed spraying.

In 1996, approximately 600 Canadian farmers planted this Roundup Ready Canola on 50,000 acres. By 2000, approximately 20,000 farmers planted 4.5 to 5 million acres—nearly 40 percent of all canola grown in Canada.

Monsanto requires a farmer who wishes to grow Roundup Ready Canola to enter into a licensing arrangement called a Technology Use Agreement ("TUA"). The licensed farmers must attend a Grower Enrollment Meeting at which Monsanto describes the technology and its licensing terms. By signing the TUA, the farmer becomes entitled to purchase Roundup Ready Canola from an authorized seed agent. They must, however, undertake to use the seed for planting a single crop and to sell that crop for consumption to a commercial purchaser authorized by Monsanto. The licensed farmers may not sell or give the seed to any third party, or save seed for replanting or inventory.

The TUA gives Monsanto the right to inspect the fields of the contracting farmer and to take samples to verify compliance with the TUA. The farmer must also pay a licensing fee for each acre planted with Roundup Ready Canola. In 1998, the licensing fee was $ 15 per acre.

A Roundup Ready Canola plant cannot be distinguished from other canola plants except by a chemical test that detects the presence of the Monsanto gene, or by spraying the plant with roundup. A canola plant that survives being sprayed with Roundup is Roundup Ready Canola.

The trial judge found the patent to be valid. He found that it did not offend the Plant Breeders' Rights Act, S.C. 1990, c. 20, and held that the difficulty of distinguishing canola plants containing the patented gene and cell from those without it did not preclude patenting the gene. The trial judge also rejected the argument that the gene and cell are unpatentable because they can be replicated without human intervention or control.

. . . .

Everyone agrees that Monsanto did not claim protection for the genetically modified plant itself, but rather for the genes and the modified cells that make up the plant. Unlike our colleague, Arbour J., we do not believe this fact requires reading a proviso into the claims that would provide patent protection to the genes and cells only when in an isolated laboratory form.

Purposive construction of patent claims requires that they be interpreted in light of the whole of the disclosure, including the specifications. . . . In this case, the disclosure includes the following:

. . . .

BACKGROUND OF THE INVENTION

The object of this invention is to provide a method of genetically transforming plant cells which causes the cells and plants regenerated therefrom to become resistant to glyphosate and the herbicidal salts thereof.

. . . .

A purposive construction therefore recognizes that the invention will be practised in plants regenerated from the patented cells, whether the plants are located inside or outside a laboratory. It is difficult to imagine a more likely or more evident purpose for patenting "a method of genetically transforming plant cells which causes the cells and plants regenerated therefrom to become resistant to glyphosate".

More particularly, the patented claims are for:

1. A *chimeric gene*: this is a gene that does not exist in nature and is constructed from different species.

2. An *expression vector*: this is a DNA molecule into which another DNA segment has been integrated so as to be useful as a research tool.

3. A *plant transformation vector*: used to permanently insert a chimeric gene into a plant's own DNA.

4. Various species of *plant cells* into which the chimeric gene has been inserted.

5. A *method of regenerating a glyphosate-resistant plant*. Once the cell is stimulated to grow into a plant, all of the differentiated cells in the plant will contain the chimeric gene, which will be passed on to offspring of the plant.

The appellant Schmeiser argues that the subject matter claimed in the patent is unpatentable. While acknowledging that Monsanto claims protection only over a gene and a cell, Schmeiser contends that the result of extending such protection is to restrict use of a plant and a seed. This result, the argument goes, ought to render the subject matter unpatentable, following the reasoning of the majority of this Court in Harvard College v. Canada (Commissioner of Patents), [2002] 4 S.C.R. 45, 2002 SCC 76 ("Harvard Mouse"). In that case, plants and seeds were found to be unpatentable "higher life forms".

This case is different from *Harvard Mouse*, where the patent refused was for a mammal. The Patent Commissioner, moreover, had allowed other claims, which were not at issue before the Court in that case, notably a plasmid and a somatic cell culture. The claims at issue in this case, for a gene and a cell, are somewhat analogous, suggesting that to find a gene and a cell to be patentable is in fact consistent with both the majority and the minority holdings in *Harvard Mouse*.

. . . .

Whether or not patent protection for the gene and the cell extends to activities involving the plant is not relevant to the patent's validity. It relates only to the factual circumstances in which infringement will be found to have taken place, as we shall explain below. Monsanto's patent has already been issued, and the onus is thus on Schmeiser to show that the Commissioner erred in allowing the patent. . . . He has failed to discharge that onus. We therefore conclude that the patent is valid.

[The Court concluded that Mr. Schmeiser did not "make" the patented gene. —EDS.]

2. APPLICATION OF THE LAW

The trial judge's findings of fact are based, essentially, on the following uncontested history.

Mr. Schmeiser is a conventional, non-organic farmer. For years, he had a practice of saving and developing his own seed. The seed which is the subject of Monsanto's complaint can be traced to a 370-acre field, called field number 1, on which Mr. Schmeiser grew canola in 1996. In 1996 five other canola growers in Mr. Schmeiser's area planted Roundup Ready Canola.

In the spring of 1997, Mr. Schmeiser planted the seeds saved on field number 1. The crop grew. He sprayed a three-acre patch near the road with Roundup and found that approximately 60 percent of the plants survived. This indicates that the plants contained Monsanto's patented gene and cell.

In the fall of 1997, Mr. Schmeiser harvested the Roundup Ready Canola from the three-acre patch he had sprayed with Roundup. He did not sell it. He instead kept it separate, and stored it over the winter in the back of a pick-up truck covered with a tarp.

A Monsanto investigator took samples of canola from the public road allowances bordering on two of Mr. Schmeiser's fields in 1997, all of which were confirmed to contain Roundup Ready Canola. In March 1998, Monsanto visited Mr. Schmeiser and put him on notice of its belief that he had grown Roundup Ready Canola without a licence. Mr. Schmeiser nevertheless took the harvest he had saved in the pick-up truck to a seed treatment plant and had it treated for use as seed. Once treated, it could be put to no other use. Mr. Schmeiser planted the treated seed in nine fields, covering approximately 1,000 acres in all.

Numerous samples were taken, some under court order and some not, from the canola plants grown from this seed. Moreover, the seed treatment plant, unbeknownst to Mr. Schmeiser, kept some of the seed he had brought there for treatment in the spring of 1998, and turned it over to Monsanto. A series of independent tests by different experts confirmed that the canola Mr. Schmeiser planted and grew in 1998 was 95 to 98 percent Roundup resistant. . . .

Dr. Downey testified that the high rate of post-Roundup spraying survival in the 1997 samples was "consistent only with the presence in field number 2 of canola grown from commercial Roundup tolerant seed." According to Dr. Dixon, responsible for the testing by Monsanto US at St. Louis, the "defendants' samples contain[ed] the DNA sequences claimed in claims 1, 2, 5, and 6 of the patent and the plant cell claimed in claims 22, 23, 27, 28 and 45 of the patent" . . . . As the trial judge noted, this opinion was uncontested.

The remaining question was how such a pure concentration of Roundup Ready Canola came to grow on the appellants' land in 1998. The trial judge rejected the suggestion that it was the product of seed blown or inadvertently carried onto the appellants' land:

> It may be that some Roundup Ready seed was carried to Mr. Schmeiser's field without his knowledge. Some such seed might have survived the winter to germinate in the spring of 1998. However, I am persuaded by evidence of Dr. Keith Downey . . . that none of the suggested sources could reasonably explain the concentration or extent of Roundup Ready canola of a commercial quality evident from the results of tests on Schmeiser's crop.

He concluded, at para. 120:

> I find that in 1998 Mr. Schmeiser planted canola seed saved from his 1997 crop in his field number 2 which he knew or ought to have known was Roundup tolerant, and that seed was the primary source for seeding and for the defendants' crops in all nine fields of canola in 1998.

In summary, it is clear on the findings of the trial judge that the appellants saved, planted, harvested and sold the crop from plants containing the gene and plant cell patented by Monsanto. The issue is whether this conduct amounted to "use" of Monsanto's invention—the glyphosate-resistant gene and cell.

. . . .

In this regard, the first and fundamental question is whether Monsanto was deprived in whole or in part, directly or indirectly, of the full enjoyment of the monopoly that the patent confers. And the answer is "yes".

Monsanto's patent gives it a monopoly over the patented gene and cell. The patent's object is production of a plant which is resistant to Roundup herbicide. Monsanto's monopoly enabled it to charge a licensing fee of $ 15 per acre to farmers wishing to grow canola plants with the patented genes and cells. The appellants cultivated 1030 acres of plants with these patented properties without paying Monsanto for the right to do so. By cultivating a plant containing the patented gene and composed of the patented cells without licence, the appellants thus deprived Monsanto of the full enjoyment of its monopoly.

. . . .

. . . [I]t is suggested that because Monsanto's claims are for genes and cells rather than for plants, it follows that infringement by use will only occur where a defendant uses the genes or cells in their isolated, laboratory form. This argument appears not to have been advanced in any detail at trial or on appeal, but is the position taken by our colleague, Arbour J.

It is uncontested that Monsanto's patented claim is only for the gene and cell that it developed. This, however, is the beginning and not the end of the inquiry. The more difficult question—and the nub of this case—is whether, by cultivating plants *containing the cell and gene*, the appellants used the patented components of those plants. The position taken by Arbour J. assumes that this inquiry is redundant and that the only way a patent may be infringed is to use the patented invention in isolation.

This position flies in the face of century-old patent law, which holds that where a defendant's commercial or business activity involves a thing of which a patented part is a significant or important component, infringement is established. It is no defence to say that the thing actually used was not patented, but only one of its components.

. . . .

Provided the patented invention is a significant aspect of the defendant's activity, the defendant will be held to have "used" the invention and violated the patent. If Mr. Schmeiser's activities with Roundup Ready Canola plants amounted to use interfering with Monsanto's full enjoyment of their monopoly on the gene and cell, those activities infringed the patent. Infringement does not require use of the gene or cell in isolation.

. . . Mr. Schmeiser argued at trial that he should not be held to have "used" Monsanto's invention because he never took commercial advantage of the special utility that invention offered—resistance to Roundup herbicide. He testified that he never used Roundup herbicide as an aid to cultivation. (That he used it in 1996 in his initial gathering of the Roundup Ready seed is clear.)

. . . .

Perhaps the appellants' failure to spray with Roundup herbicide is a way of attempting to rebut the presumption of use that flows from possession. However, the appellants have failed to rebut the presumption.

Their argument fails to account for the stand-by or insurance utility of the properties of the patented genes and cells. Whether or not a farmer sprays with Roundup herbicide, cultivating canola containing the patented genes and cells provides stand-by utility. The farmer benefits from that advantage from the outset: if there is reason to spray in the future, the farmer may proceed to do so.

. . . .

Further, the appellants did not provide sufficient evidence to rebut the presumption of use. It may well be that defendant farmers could rebut the presumption by showing that they never intended to cultivate plants containing the patented genes and cells. They might perhaps prove that the continued presence of the patented gene on their land was accidental and unwelcome, for example, by showing that they acted quickly to arrange for its removal, and that its concentration was consistent with that to be expected from unsolicited "blow-by" canola. Knowledge of infringement is never a necessary component of infringement. However, a defendant's conduct on becoming aware of the presence of the patented invention may assist in rebutting the presumption of use arising from possession.

However, the appellants in this case actively cultivated canola containing the patented invention as part of their business operations. Mr. Schmeiser complained that the original plants came onto his land without his intervention. However, he did not at all explain why he sprayed Roundup to isolate the Roundup Ready plants he found on his land; why he then harvested the plants and segregated the seeds, saved them, and kept them for seed; why he next planted them; and why, through this husbandry, he ended up with 1030 acres of Roundup Ready Canola which would otherwise have cost him $15,000. In these circumstances, the presumption of use flowing from possession stands unrebutted.

. . . [Appellants also] contend that the patent should be given a narrow scope for infringement purposes, since the plants reproduce through the laws of nature rather than through human intervention. Thus, they argue, propagation of Roundup Ready Canola without a licence cannot be a "use" by them because plants are living things that grow by themselves.

. . . .

The appellants' argument . . . ignores the role human beings play in agricultural propagation. Farming is a commercial enterprise in which farmers sow and cultivate the plants which prove most efficient and profitable. Plant science has been with us since long before Mendel. Human beings since time immemorial have striven to produce more efficient plants. Huge investments of energy and money have been poured into the quest for better seeds and better plants. One way in which that investment is protected is through the Patent Act giving investors a monopoly when they create a novel and useful invention in the realm of plant science, such as genetically modified genes and cells.

Finally, many inventions make use of natural processes in order to work. For example, many valid patents have referred to various yeasts, which would have no practical utility at all without "natural forces.". . .

The issue is not the perhaps adventitious arrival of Roundup Ready on Mr. Schmeiser's land in 1998. What is at stake in this case is sowing and cultivation, which necessarily involves deliberate and careful activity on the part of the farmer. The appellants suggest that when a farmer such as Mr. Schmeiser actively cultivates a crop with particular properties through activities such as testing, isolating, treating, and planting the desired seed and tending the crops until harvest, the result is a crop which has merely "grown itself." Such a suggestion denies the realities of modern agriculture.

Inventions in the field of agriculture may give rise to concerns not raised in other fields—moral concerns about whether it is right to manipulate genes in order to obtain better weed control or higher yields. It is open to Parliament to consider these concerns and amend the Patent Act should it find them persuasive.

Our task, however, is to interpret and apply the Patent Act as it stands, in accordance with settled principles. Under the present Act, an invention in the domain of agriculture is as deserving of protection as an invention in the domain of mechanical science. Where Parliament has not seen fit to distinguish between inventions concerning plants and other inventions, neither should the courts.

Invoking the concepts of implied licence and waiver, the appellants argue that this Court should grant an exemption from infringement to "innocent bystanders". The simple answer to this contention is that on the facts found by the trial judge, Mr. Schmeiser was not an innocent bystander; rather, he actively cultivated Roundup Ready Canola. Had he been a mere "innocent bystander", he could have refuted the presumption of use arising from his possession of the patented gene and cell. . . .

The appellants argue, finally, that Monsanto's activities tread on the ancient common law property rights of farmers to keep that which comes onto their land. Just as a farmer owns the progeny of a "stray bull" which wanders onto his land, so Mr. Schmeiser argues he owns the progeny of the Roundup Ready Canola that came onto his field. However, the issue is not property rights, but patent protection. Ownership is no defence to a breach of the *Patent Act*.

We conclude that the trial judge and Court of Appeal were correct in concluding that the appellants "used" Monsanto's patented gene and cell and hence infringed the *Patent Act*.

. . . .

The reasons of Iacobucci, Bastarache, Arbour and LeBel JJ. were delivered by

ARBOUR J. (dissenting in part):

. . . .

This case was decided in the courts below without the benefit of this Court's decision in *Harvard College v. Canada* (Commissioner of Patents). . . . The heart of the issue is whether the Federal Court of Appeal's decision can stand in light of our decision in that case.

More specifically, the trial judge interpreted the scope of the Monsanto patent without the benefit of the holding in *Harvard College* that higher life forms, including plants, are not patentable. Both lower court decisions "allo[w] Monsanto to do indirectly what Canadian patent law has not allowed them to do directly: namely, to acquire patent protection over whole plants" . . . .

Such a result is hard to reconcile with the majority decision in *Harvard College*. . . . It would also invalidate the Patent Office's longstanding policy of not granting exclusive rights, expressed in a patent grant, over higher life forms, that was upheld in *Harvard College*. . . .

The two central issues here, the scope of Monsanto's patent and whether agricultural production of Roundup Ready Canola constitutes an infringing use, are determined by a purposive construction of the patent claims and the proper application of the majority decision in *Harvard College*. . . . Monsanto is on the horns of a dilemma; a narrow construction of its claims renders the claims valid but not infringed, the broader construction renders the claims invalid. . . .

In light of *Harvard College*, I conclude that the patent claims here cannot be interpreted to extend patent protection over whole plants and that there was no infringing use. I need not review, and take no issue with the factual overview of the case provided in my colleagues' reasons.

. . . .

The issue in *Harvard College, supra,* was whether a mouse that was genetically modified to make it susceptible to cancer was the valid subject matter for a patent claim. The majority found that higher life forms were not "compositions of matter".". Plants were clearly included in the category of higher life forms. . . . Accordingly, plants do not fit within the definition of an "invention": Patent Act, R.S.C. 1985, c. P-4, s. 2.

The majority approved the line drawn by the Patent Office between unpatentable higher life forms, patentable lower life forms, and patentable processes for engineering transgenic higher life forms in the laboratory: *Harvard College.* . . .

. . . .

Thus, in *Harvard College,* claims for a genetically modified plasmid and the process claims to genetically modify a mouse so that it became susceptible to cancer were found to be valid. Claims for the mouse itself were found to be invalid by the Patent Commissioner and that finding was upheld by this Court. No other claims were at issue in *Harvard College;* transgenic mammalian eggs (single cells) were not claimed, although the majority suggested in obiter that such a claim may be the valid subject matter of a patent claim. . . .

. . . .

The classic rule is "what is not claimed is considered disclaimed." The inventor may not get exclusive rights to an invention that was not part of the public disclosure of the invention. The public must be able to predict the activities that will infringe on the exclusive rights granted to the patentee. . . .

So long as the claims are interpreted fairly and knowledgeably, if the patentee has limited the claims, then the public is entitled to rely on that limitation. . . . An inventor cannot enlarge the scope of the grant of exclusive rights beyond that which has been specified. . . . However, the full specification may be looked at to discern the scope of the claims. . . . The claims are invalid if they are broader than the disclosures. . . .

. . . .

It is clear from the specification that Monsanto's patent claims do not extend to plants, seeds, and crops. It is also clear that the gene claim does not extend patent protection to the plant. The plant cell claim ends at the point where the isolated plant cell containing the chimeric gene is placed into the growth medium for regeneration. Once the cell begins to multiply and differentiate into plant tissues, resulting in the growth of a plant, a claim should be made for the whole plant. However, the whole plant cannot be patented. Similarly, the method claim ends at the point of the regeneration of the transgenic founder plant but does not extend to methods for propagating that plant. It certainly does not extend to the offspring of the regenerated plant.

In effect, the patent claims grant Monsanto a monopoly over the chimeric gene and the cell into which it is inserted and the method for doing so. Therefore, no other biotechnology company can use the chimeric gene to create a glyphosate-resistant plant cell that can then be regenerated into a glyphosate-resistant plant.

. . . .

I will assume . . . that the appellants planted seeds containing Monsanto's patented gene and cell. I agree with my colleagues that the appellants did not make or construct the gene or cell contained in the canola crop and did not use Monsanto's patented process.

. . . .

In the result, the lower courts erred not only in construing the claims to extend to plants and seed, but in construing "use" to include the use of subject matter disclaimed by the patentee, namely the plant. The appellants as users were entitled to rely on the reasonable expectation that plants, as unpatentable subject matter, fall outside the scope of patent protection. Accordingly, the cultivation of plants containing the patented gene and cell does not constitute an infringement. The plants containing the patented gene can have no stand-by value or utility as my colleagues allege. To conclude otherwise would, in effect, confer patent protection on the plant.

. . . .

There is no claim for a "glyphosate-resistant" plant and all its offspring. Therefore saving, planting, or selling seed from glyphosate-resistant plants does not constitute an infringing use.

. . . .

The Canadian Biotechnology Advisory Committee, in Patenting of Higher Life Forms and Related Issues (June 2002), suggests that the . . . use of biologically replicating organisms as a "vehicle" for genetic patents may overcompensate the patentee both in relation to what was invented, and to other areas of invention. The [Canadian Biotechnology Advisory Committee] explains the point as follows:

> Because higher life forms can reproduce by themselves, the grant of a patent over a plant, seed or non-human animal covers not only the particular plant, seed or animal sold, but also all its progeny containing the patented invention for all generations until the expiry of the patent term. . . . In addition, much of the value of the higher life form, particularly with respect to animals, derives from the natural characteristics of the original organism and has nothing to do with the invention. In light of

these unique characteristics of biological inventions, granting the patent holder exclusive rights that extend not only to the particular organism embodying the invention but also to all subsequent progeny of that organism represents a significant increase in the scope of rights offered to patent holders. It also represents a greater transfer of economic interests from the agricultural community to the biotechnology industry than exists in other fields of science.

. . . .

III. DISPOSITION:

I would allow the appeal with costs to the appellants throughout.

NOTES AND QUESTIONS

1. In *Monsanto Canada Inc. v. Schmeiser,* [2004] 1 S.C.R. 902, the majority held that claims to genetically modified seeds (lower life forms) extend protection over plants grown from those seeds (higher life forms), turning the patent eligibility question into a claim drafting issue. Following the logic in *Schmeiser,* claims to a genetically modified egg would grant patent protection over the higher life form animal resulting from that egg, seemingly in direct contravention of *Harvard College.* Do you agree with the *Schmeiser* majority that its decision is consistent with both the majority and dissenting opinions in *Harvard College*?

2. The fact that Mr. Schmeiser deliberately harvested, saved and replanted Roundup Ready (RR) seed appears to be viewed quite negatively by the Court. Do you consider Mr. Schmeiser's actions wrongful? Should he be able to do what he wants with items that come, unsolicited, onto his property? What about the fact that the RR plants take up space on his property that he could otherwise have used to plant other crops of his choosing? Monsanto's Technology Use Agreement (TUA) mentioned in the case allows the company to capture virtually all of the positive externalities generated by their genetically modified inventions, while court decisions such as the one in *Schmeiser* allow the company to avoid many of the negative externalities. As one commentator notes:

> Under current law in most states, the non-GM farmer shoulders the responsibility for protecting his crop from GM contamination. Conversely, the patent owner seemingly bears no responsibility to prevent the contamination, but retains ownership in the patented traits even when the traits contaminate a neighboring field. . . . [This situation] fosters a bizarre legal scenario in which the owner of a patented trait responsible for crop contamination could sue the owner of the contaminated crop for patent infringement.

Amanda L. Kool, *Halting Pig in the Parlor Patents: Nuisance Law as a Tool to Redress Crop Contamination*, 50 JURIMETRICS J. 453, 454 (2010).

In fact, the notion that "ownership is no defence to a breach of the Patent Act" (*Monsanto v. Schmeiser*, para. 96) arguably gives Monsanto an incentive to develop GMO crops that spread to other fields farther and faster. However, this result is being challenged, at least in the United States. In *Johnson v. Paynesville Farmers Union Cooperative Oil Co.,* 802 N.W.2d 383 (Minn. Ct. App. 2011), the Minnesota Court of Appeals approved an organic farmer's trespass suit against neighboring farmers over pesticide drift contamination, a decision that could be the basis of similar suits for GMO contamination. Also, in *Organic Seed Growers and Trade Association (OSGATA) v. Monsanto, No. 11–2163,* 2012 WL 607560 (S.D.N.Y. 2012), eighty-plus organic farmers, seed businesses, and organic agricultural organizations represented by the Public Patent Foundation sought a declaratory judgment of non-infringement if their fields are contaminated by Monsanto's transgenic crops, noting that Monsanto has already sued more than one-hundred farmers for patent infringement and settled with hundreds more. The district court granted Monsanto's motion to dismiss for lack of standing but at the time of this writing, the case is on appeal to the Court of Appeals for the Federal Circuit.

3. Although *Monsanto* won the case and received injunctive relief, Mr. Schmeiser did not have to pay the company a single penny in damages. In a portion of the decision not reproduced above, the Court explained why:

> The Patent Act permits two alternative types of remedy: damages and an accounting of profits. Damages represent the inventor's loss, which may include the patent holder's lost profits from sales or lost royalty payments. An accounting of profits, by contrast, is measured by the profits made by the infringer, rather than the amount lost by the inventor. Here, damages are not available, in view of Monsanto's election to seek an accounting of profits.
>
> It is settled law that the inventor is only entitled to that portion of the infringer's profit which is causally attributable to the invention . . . . "[I]t is essential that the losses made good are only those which, on a common sense view of causation, were caused by the breach" . . . .
>
> . . . On the facts found, the appellants made no profits *as a result of the invention.*
>
> Their profits were precisely what they would have been had they planted and harvested ordinary canola. They sold the Roundup Ready Canola they grew in 1998 for feed, and thus obtained no premium for the fact that it was Roundup Ready Canola. Nor did they gain any agricultural advantage from the herbicide resistant nature of the canola, since no finding was made that they sprayed with Roundup herbicide to reduce weeds. The appellants' profits

arose solely from qualities of their crop that cannot be attributed to the invention.

On this evidence, the appellants earned no profit from the invention and Monsanto is entitled to nothing on their claim of account.

Monsanto Canada Inc. v. Schmeiser, para. 100–105.

Do you think the remedy would have been different if Monsanto had elected damages? Why or why not? We will study damages for patent infringement in Chapter 11.

————————

Despite decisions like *Monsanto v. Schmeiser* that appear to align closely with the U.S. position on patentability of life forms, there remain important concerns and policy differences between countries on this issue. Even in cases where the question of patentability is positively decided, the reasoning provided reflects the strong sentiments on both sides of the debate. In the European Patent Office, concerns about the patentability of life forms are addressed via EPC Article 53:

> European patents shall not be granted in respect of: (a) Inventions the commercial exploitation of which would be contrary to *ordre public* or morality . . . ."

In *Plant Genetic Systems v. Greenpeace, Ltd.*, T 0356/93, 1995 Official J. Eur. Pat. Off. 545 (1995), an EPO Technical Board of Appeal expounded on the meaning and application of the morality and *ordre public* provisions:

> Article 53(a) EPC excludes from patentability "inventions the publication or exploitation of which would be contrary to "ordre public" or morality, provided that the exploitation shall not be deemed to be so contrary merely because it is prohibited by law or regulation in some or all of the Contracting States".

> As is apparent from the historical documentation, the EPC Working Party recognised that "there was no European definition of morality". Its members were, therefore, unanimously of the opinion that the "interpretation of the concept of morality should be a matter for European institutions" . . . . The same applies to the concept of "ordre public" . . . . Thus, prior to any assessment of the patentability of the claimed subject-matter under Article 53(a) EPC, the meaning of these concepts must be defined by way of interpretation.

> It is generally accepted that the concept of "ordre public" covers the protection of public security and the physical integrity of individuals as part of society. This concept encompasses also the protection of the environment. Accordingly, under Article 53(a) EPC, inventions the exploitation of which is likely to breach public peace or social order (for example, through acts of terrorism) or to seriously preju-

dice the environment are to be excluded from patentability as being contrary to "ordre public".

The concept of morality is related to the belief that some behaviour is right and acceptable whereas other behaviour is wrong, this belief being founded on the totality of the accepted norms which are deeply rooted in a particular culture. For the purposes of the EPC, the culture in question is the culture inherent in European society and civilisation. Accordingly, under Article 53(a) EPC, inventions the exploitation of which is not in conformity with the conventionally-accepted standards of conduct pertaining to this culture are to be excluded from patentability as being contrary to morality.

The second half-sentence of Article 53(a) EPC contains the qualification "that the exploitation shall not be deemed to be so contrary merely because it is prohibited by law or regulation in some or all of the Contracting States". This qualification makes clear that the assessment of whether or not a particular subject-matter is to be considered contrary to either "ordre public" or morality is not dependent upon any national laws or regulations. Conversely and by the same token, the Board is of the opinion that a particular subject-matter shall not automatically be regarded as complying with the requirements of Article 53(a) EPC merely because its exploitation is permitted in some or all of the Contracting States. Thus, approval or disapproval of the exploitation by national law(s) or regulation(s) does not constitute per se a sufficient criterion for the purposes of examination under Article 53(a) EPC.

Id. at para. 3–7.

Despite this careful exposition of Article 53(a), the EPO generally approaches the interpretation of Article 53(a) on a case-by-case basis and, in so doing, is able to adopt a narrow or liberal lens in viewing the question of patentability as each situation demands.

NOTE ON THE HARVARD ONCOMOUSE AND THE EUROPEAN PATENT OFFICE

The Harvard oncomouse patent application in Europe initially received a reception no warmer across the Atlantic in the EPO than in Canada. In applying Article 53(a) to the Harvard oncomouse, the EPO Examining Division chose a very narrow focus for its inquiry, ignoring any objections to patents on animals in principle. *See In re President and Fellows of Harvard College,* Examining Division of the European Patent Office, [1991] E.P.O.R. 525, 527. Instead, the Examining Division employed a balancing test, noting that "[f]or each individual invention [involving higher life forms] the question of morality has to be examined and possible detrimental effects and risks have to be weighed and balanced against the merits and advantages aimed at." *Id.* at 527. The Examining Division then set about balancing three stated interests:

(1) the interest in remedying human diseases, (2) the interest in protecting the environment from the uncontrolled spread of unwanted genes, and (3) the interest in avoiding cruelty to animals.

On the first interest, remedying human diseases, the Examining Division came down on the side of patentability, noting that the invention could be of great benefit to mankind if it could help in the search for a cure for cancer, one of the most frequent causes of human death. For the second interest, protection of the environment, the Examining Division admitted that the introduction of such genetically modified animals into the environment could cause unforeseen environmental problems. However, the Examining Division did not consider this concern to be a significant bar to a patent since the animals would be used solely in laboratory settings and would not be released into the general environment. Finally, the third interest, preventing cruelty to animals, did not militate against patentability because, while more of the animals with the oncogene would develop painful cancers, the invention allowed the use of fewer animals in total so the invention would, in effect, reduce the overall extent of animal suffering. In allowing a patent on the invention to issue, the Examining Division also noted the absence of suitable alternatives as animal models are currently considered "indispensable" in testing.

The decision of the EPO did not diminish the controversy regarding the mouse patent. Even though the patent issued, it quickly became the target of more than a dozen petitions to the EPO opposing its grant and was finally maintained in amended form in 2004. Nevertheless, unlike the U.S., the test applied by the EPO provides a mechanism for evaluating the patent eligibility of morally controversial biotech inventions *before* granting a patent. For example, a different transgenic mouse, one genetically modified to lose its hair so that it would be useful in human baldness studies, apparently failed the balancing test according to a notice from the EPO to the Upjohn Corporation, the owner of the mouse application. Although the degree of animal suffering would ostensibly be similar, the interest in curing baldness was not as compelling as the interest in curing cancer. *See* Steve Conner, *Patent Ban on Baldness 'Cure' Mouse*, Independent (London), Feb. 2, 1992 at 5.

Balancing competing interests is not the only approach the EPO has taken when evaluating the applicability of the Article 53(a) exception. In two other cases, different bodies within the EPO articulated two additional morality tests: (1) The unacceptability test, which asks whether commercial exploitation of the invention would be considered to be wrong in light of conventionally accepted standards of conduct of European culture; and (2) the public abhorrence test, which asks whether the commercial exploitation of the invention would be abhorrent to the European public. *See Greenpeace v. Plant Genetic Systems*, [1995] E.P.O.R. 357, 366, *In re Lubrizol Genetics, Inc.*, (Lubrizol II), EP-B1–122 791, 1990 O.J. E.P.O. 71 (Opp. Div.), reprinted in 21 Int'l Rev. Indus. Prop. & Copyright L. 487 (1990); and *Hormone Relaxin, [1995] E.P.O.R. 541.*

3. COMPARATIVE APPROACHES TO LIMITS ON PATENTING LIVING MATTER

As noted above, unlike the statutory patent eligibility provisions in the United States and Canada, the European Patent Convention's Article 53(a) allows for an explicit consideration of the moral implications of patenting a particular invention. Consistent with TRIPS Article 27(2), many other countries consider such implications in patent eligibility as well. For example, under Section 32 of the Japan Patent Act (1959, as amended): "inventions liable to contravene public order, morality or public health shall not be patented." *See* Japan Patent Act, Law No. 121 of 1959, amended by Law No. 220 of 1999, art. 32, *translated in* http://www.wipo.int/clea/docs_new/pdf/en/jp/jp036en.pdf. Article 32 of the Korean Patent Act (2009) states: "[A]ny invention that is liable to contravene public order or morality or to injure public health shall not be patented." *See* Republic of Korea, Patent Act (Act No. 950, promulgated on December 31, 1961, as last amended on January 30, 2009 by Act No. 9381), *available at* http://www.wipo.int/wipolex/en/text.jsp?file_id=214464#LinkTarget_1346. And Article 5 of the China Patent Law Third Revision (2008) provides that "[p]atent rights shall not be granted for invention-creations that violate the law or social ethics, or harm public interests . . . ." *See* Patent Law of the People's Republic of China (2009),) Art. 5, *available at* http://www.chinaipr.gov.cn/lawsarticle/laws/lawsar/patent/201101/1186462_1.html. These are just a few of the many national provisions prohibiting patents on the basis of moral or ethical considerations.

As is now evident, biotechnological inventions tend to be more likely to raise these issues than traditional patent subject matter. In light of this concern, a group of European countries took the affirmative step of going beyond their national laws to clarify the limits of biotech patentability in the region.

a. Europe

A key consequence of the decision of the U.S. Supreme Court in *Diamond v. Chakrabarty* was a significant increase in private investment in biotechnology research. The substantial expansion of biotech-related industries was, however, limited primarily to the U.S. market. In the EU, the uncertainty caused by diverging national approaches toward the protection of biotechnological inventions along with the fact that unlike the U.S. Patent Act, the EPC (Article 53(a)) explicitly brings moral considerations into the patentability equation, led to the relocation of some European biotech firms to the United States In 1996, a study published by the EU Economic and Social Committee found that the USPTO issued 65 percent of the world's patents for biotechnological innovation and the U.S. biotech industry comprised 1,300 firms, while the EU's share of worldwide patenting activity was 15 percent and its industry composed of only

485 firms. *See* Opinion of the Economic and Social Committee on the "Proposal for a European Parliament and Council Directive on the Legal Protection of Biotechnological Inventions," 1996 O.J. (C 295) 11 (EC) at §§ 1.2.2–1.3.2. This state of affairs led to calls for reform of European patent law, which culminated in the enactment in 1998 of the EU Directive 98/44/EC on the legal protection of biotechnological inventions. The chief aim of the Directive, key provisions of which are excerpted below, is to encourage investment in the field of biotechnology within the EU by harmonizing national protection of biotechnological inventions.

DIRECTIVE 98/44/EC OF THE EUROPEAN PARLIAMENT AND OF THE COUNCIL ON THE LEGAL PROTECTION OF BIOTECHNOLOGICAL INVENTIONS
O.J. (L 213), 13–21 (EC)

PREAMBLE

. . . .

(3) Whereas effective and harmonized protection throughout the Member States is essential in order to maintain and encourage investment in the field of biotechnology;

. . . .

(5) Whereas differences exist in the legal protection of biotechnological inventions offered by the laws and practices of the different Member States; whereas such differences could create barriers to trade and hence impede the proper functioning of the internal market;

(6) Whereas such differences could well become greater as Member States adopt new and different legislation and administrative practices, or whereas national case-law interpreting such legislation develops differently;

(7) Whereas uncoordinated development of national laws on the legal protection of biotechnological inventions in the Community could lead to further disincentives to trade, to the detriment of the industrial development of such inventions and of the smooth operation of the internal market;

. . . .

(14) Whereas a patent for invention does not authorise the holder to implement that invention, but merely entitles him to prohibit third parties from exploiting it for industrial and commercial purposes; whereas, consequently, substantive patent law cannot serve to replace or render superfluous national, European or international law which may impose restrictions or prohibitions or which concerns the monitoring of research and of the use or commercialisation of its results, notably from the point of view of the requirements of public health, safety, environmental protec-

tion, animal welfare, the preservation of genetic diversity and compliance with certain ethical standards;

. . . .

(16) Whereas patent law must be applied so as to respect the fundamental principles safeguarding the dignity and integrity of the person; whereas it is important to assert the principle that the human body, at any stage in its formation or development, including germ cells, and the simple discovery of one of its elements or one of its products, including the sequence or partial sequence of a human gene, cannot be patented; whereas these principles are in line with the criteria of patentability proper to patent law, whereby a mere discovery cannot be patented;

. . . .

(37) Whereas the principle whereby inventions must be excluded from patentability where their commercial exploitation offends against *ordre public* or morality must also be stressed in this Directive;

(38) Whereas the operative part of this Directive should also include an illustrative list of inventions excluded from patentability so as to provide referring courts and patent offices with a general guide to interpreting the reference to *ordre public* and morality; whereas this list obviously cannot presume to be exhaustive; whereas processes, the use of which offend against human dignity, such as processes to produce chimeras from germ cells or totipotent cells of humans and animals, are obviously also excluded from patentability;

(39) Whereas *ordre public* and morality correspond in particular to ethical or moral principles recognised in a Member State, respect for which is particularly important in the field of biotechnology in view of the potential scope of inventions in this field and their inherent relationship to living matter; whereas such ethical or moral principles supplement the standard legal examinations under patent law regardless of the technical field of the invention;

. . . .

(42) Whereas, moreover, uses of human embryos for industrial or commercial purposes must also be excluded from patentability; whereas in any case such exclusion does not affect inventions for therapeutic or diagnostic purposes which are applied to the human embryo and are useful to it;

(43) Whereas pursuant to Article F(2) of the Treaty on European Union, the Union is to respect fundamental rights, as guaranteed by the European Convention for the Protection of Human Rights and Fundamental Freedoms signed in Rome on 4 November 1950 and as they result from the constitutional traditions common to the Member States, as general principles of Community law;

. . . .

CHAPTER 1: PATENTABILITY

Article 1

1. Member States shall protect biotechnological inventions under national patent law. They shall, if necessary, adjust their national patent law to take account of the provisions of this Directive.

2. This Directive shall be without prejudice to the obligations of the Member States pursuant to international agreements, and in particular the TRIPs Agreement and the Convention on Biological Diversity.

Article 2

1. For the purposes of this Directive,

(a) 'biological material' means any material containing genetic information and capable of reproducing itself or being reproduced in a biological system;

(b) 'microbiological process' means any process involving or performed upon or resulting in microbiological material.

2. A process for the production of plants or animals is essentially biological if it consists entirely of natural phenomena such as crossing or selection.

Article 3

1. For the purposes of this Directive, inventions which are new, which involve an inventive step and which are susceptible of industrial application shall be patentable even if they concern a product consisting of or containing biological material or a process by means of which biological material is produced, processed or used.

2. Biological material which is isolated from its natural environment or produced by means of a technical process may be the subject of an invention even if it previously occurred in nature.

Article 4

1. The following shall not be patentable:

(a) plant and animal varieties;

(b) essentially biological processes for the production of plants or animals.

2. Inventions which concern plants or animals shall be patentable if the technical feasibility of the invention is not confined to a particular plant or animal variety.

3. Paragraph 1(b) shall be without prejudice to the patentability of inventions which concern a microbiological or other technical process or a product obtained by means of such a process.

Article 5

1. The human body, at the various stages of its formation and development, and the simple discovery of one of its elements, including the sequence or partial sequence of a gene, cannot constitute patentable inventions.

2. An element isolated from the human body or otherwise produced by means of a technical process, including the sequence or partial sequence of a gene, may constitute a patentable invention, even if the structure of that element is identical to that of a natural element.

3. The industrial application of a sequence or a partial sequence of a gene must be disclosed in the patent application.

Article 6

1. Inventions shall be considered unpatentable where their commercial exploitation would be contrary to ordre public or morality; however, exploitation shall not be deemed to be so contrary merely because it is prohibited by law or regulation.

2. On the basis of paragraph 1, the following, in particular, shall be considered unpatentable:

(a) processes for cloning human beings;

(b) processes for modifying the germ line genetic identity of human beings;

(c) uses of human embryos for industrial or commercial purposes;

(d) processes for modifying the genetic identity of animals which are likely to cause them suffering without any substantial medical benefit to man or animal, and also animals resulting from such processes.

Article 7

The Commission's European Group on Ethics in Science and New Technologies evaluates all ethical aspects of biotechnology.

CHAPTER 2: SCOPE OF PROTECTION

Article 8

1. The protection conferred by a patent on a biological material possessing specific characteristics as a result of the invention shall extend to any biological material derived from that biological material through propagation or multiplication in an identical or divergent form and possessing those same characteristics.

2. The protection conferred by a patent on a process that enables a biological material to be produced possessing specific characteristics as a result of the invention shall extend to biological material directly obtained through that process and to any other biological material derived from

the directly obtained biological material through propagation or multiplication in an identical or divergent form and possessing those same characteristics.

Article 9

The protection conferred by a patent on a product containing or consisting of genetic information shall extend to all material, save as provided in Article 5(1), in which the product is incorporated and in which the genetic information is contained and performs its function.

The implementation of Directive 98/44/EC by EU member states proved difficult and, to date, the Directive's goal of harmonizing national patent practices for the biotechnology sector within the EU has not been achieved in full. Several EU member states defied EU law by failing to create national laws to implement the Directive by the July 30, 2000 deadline, exposing those states to legal action and sanctions by other members. Opposition to the Directive was so fierce, however, that four of the fifteen EU member states were still out of compliance in 2005 and the last state to complete implementation, Bulgaria, did not do so until late 2006. While all member countries have now implemented the Directive, the form of the implementation has generated controversy in some instances. For example, implementing legislation in both France and Germany narrowly limits gene patent protection to the specific use detailed in the patent. Consequently, broad gene claims in patents issued by the European Patent Office may not be valid in those countries.

Article 6, paragraph 1 of the European Union Biotechnology Directive essentially restates the EPC Article 53(a) position that "[I]nventions shall be considered unpatentable where their commercial exploitation would be contrary to ordre public or morality." Paragraph 2 of Article 6 then takes the further step of providing an explicit, non-exclusive list of subject matter that would be considered contrary to *ordre public* or morality if commercially exploited. The European Patent Organization, although not an arm of the EU, voluntarily complied with the Biotech Directive by amending the EPC implementing regulations to incorporate certain of its provisions in relation to Article 53(a). *See* European Patent Office, *Revision of the European Patent Convention (EPC 2000) Synoptic Presentation EPC 1973/2000—Part II: The Implementing Regulations*, O.J.E.P.O. 43 (Spec. Ed. 5/2007). In particular, Rule 23(d)[1] (now Rule 28(c) as a result of renumbering to implement EPC 2000) entitled "Exceptions to Patentability" provides:

---

[1] Rule 23(d) is now Rule 28(c) as a result of renumbering to implement EPC 2000.

Under Article 53(a), European patents shall not be granted in respect of biotechnological inventions which, in particular, concern the following:

    (a) processes for cloning human beings;

    (b) processes for modifying the germ line genetic identity of human beings;

    (c) uses of human embryos for industrial or commercial purposes;

    (d) processes for modifying the genetic identity of animals which are likely to cause them suffering without any substantial medical benefit to man or animal, and also animals resulting from such processes.

The EPO has cited Rule 23 in rejections of patent applications claiming products created through the destruction of human embryos to obtain embryonic stem cells. In April 2006, questions regarding the rejection of the Wisconsin Alumni Research Foundation's (WARF) patent application relating to such stem cell products were referred to the EPO Enlarged Board of Appeals to provide clarification on the parameters of the Rule 23(d) exceptions.

In the WARF case, the EPO Examining Division rejected certain claims in WARF's European application under Rule 23(d) EPC in conjunction with Article 53(a) EPC. The rejected claims, which were directed to, among other things, cell cultures comprising primate embryonic stem cells and methods of maintaining such cell cultures, were deemed to violate the prohibitions because they required the use and destruction of human embryos as starting material.

The examiners considered it irrelevant that the claimed subject matter related to cell cultures and not to a method of producing the cell cultures because the only way to obtain the cell cultures was through destruction of a human embryo. WARF appealed the decision to the EPO Board of Appeals which, because of the importance of the issue, referred four questions to the Enlarged Board of Appeals (EBOA) for decision. The EBOA heard oral arguments in June 2008 on the following questions:

1. Does Rule 23d(c) [now 28(c)] EPC apply to an application filed before the entry into force of the rule?

2. If the answer to question 1 is yes, does Rule 23d(c) [now 28(c)] EPC forbid the patenting of claims directed to products . . . which . . . at the filing date could be prepared exclusively by a method which necessarily involved the destruction of the human embryos from which the said products are derived, if the said method is not part of the claims?

3. If the answer to question 1 or 2 is no, does Article 53(a) EPC forbid patenting such claims?

4. In the context of questions 2 and 3, is it of relevance that after the filing date the same products could be obtained without . . . the destruction of human embryos?

In a November 2008 decision,[2] the EBOA answered "yes" to questions 1 and 2 (negating the need to answer question 3), and "no" to question 4, thus agreeing with the rejection of WARF's human embryonic stem cell culture claims. The EBOA began by interpreting the Rule 23d(c) prohibition in the context of Article 53(a) EPC and Article 27(2) of TRIPS, which contain similar wording, and noted that "[t]he forbidden exploitation must be something contravening the underlying legal principles of all contracting states." In considering the various arguments for and against allowing patenting of the claim, the EBOA broadly construed both the implementing rule and the concept of "invention," noting that "[a] claimed new and inventive product must first be made before it can be used. Such making is the ordinary way commercially to exploit the claimed invention and falls within the monopoly granted . . . ." The EBOA ultimately concluded, considering the intentions of the legislators, that "it is not the fact of the patenting itself that is considered to be against ordre public or morality, but it is the performing of the invention, which includes a step (involving the destruction of a human embryo) that has to be considered to contravene those concepts." *Id.* at paragraphs 25 and 29. However, stem cell cultures obtainable from existing stem cell lines arguably still could be patented under the decision.

As noted above, the Patent Act of Japan contains a provision similar to Article 53(a) of the EPC. Although WARF did not seek a patent on the cell cultures in Japan, the Japanese Patent Office (JPO) apparently also has denied patents on claims involving human embryonic stem cell-derived inventions in other cases. *See* Yoichi Yoshizawa, *Comparative Analysis on Patentability of Human Embryonic Stem Cells* 49–54 (Sept. 11, 2006) (unpublished LL.M. IP thesis, Munich Intellectual Property Law Center) (on file with authors). However, a more recent commentary suggests this view may be changing and that the JPO is open to patenting human embryonic stem cell inventions. Koichi Sumikura, *The Issues Surrounding Patent Protection for Human-Embryonic Stem Cells and Therapeutic Cloning in Japan*, 13 MPI STUD. INTELL. PROP. COMPETITION & TAX L. 111, 115–116 (2009). Finally in China, the SIPO Examination Guidelines for Article 5 of the 3rd Revision of the Chinese Patent Act, which provides that inventions incompatible with law, social morality, or public interest shall not be patented, list as unpatentable human embryonic stem cells and processes to prepare them, as well as the human body at all stages of development.

---

[2] Case G2/06, WARF/stem cells, [2009] E.P.O.R. 15, at para. 1 (Enlarged B. App. 2008).

Patent offices are not alone in invoking this morality-based patentability limitation. In December 2006, the German Federal Patent Court (GFPC) partially revoked claims in a German patent to Dr. Oliver Brüstle on similar grounds to those articulated by the EPO Enlarged Board of Appeals in the WARF decision. The GFPC ruled that claims to stem cells and methods for producing them that could involve the destruction of human embryos violated the *ordre public* and morality provision of the German Patent Act. The decision was appealed to the Bundesgerichtshof, the German Supreme Court, which decided to refer several questions to the Court of Justice of the European Union on the proper interpretation of the Biotech Directive. The Court of Justice answered in the following decision.

OLIVER BRÜSTLE V. GREENPEACE E.V.
Court of Justice of the European Union
Case C-34/10 (Grand Chamber), 18 October 2011

REFERENCE for a preliminary ruling under Article 267 TFEU from the Bundesgerichtshof (Germany), made by decision of 17 December 2009, received at the Court on 21 January 2010.

JUDGMENT

1 This reference for a preliminary ruling concerns the interpretation of Article 6(2)(c) of Directive 98/44/EC of the European Parliament and of the Council of 6 July 1998 on the legal protection of biotechnological inventions (OJ 1998 L 213, p. 13; 'the Directive').

2 The reference has been made in proceedings brought by Greenpeace e.V. ('Greenpeace') seeking annulment of the German patent held by Mr. Brüstle, which relates to neural precursor cells and the processes for their production from embryonic stem cells and their use for therapeutic purposes.

LEGAL CONTEXT

AGREEMENTS BINDING THE EUROPEAN UNION AND/OR THE MEMBER STATES

. . . .

4 Article 52(1) of the Convention on the Grant of European Patents, signed at Munich on 5 October 1973 ('the CGEP'), to which the European Union is not party, but of which the Member States are signatories, reads as follows:

'European patents shall be granted for any inventions, in all fields of technology, provided that they are new, involve an inventive step and are susceptible of industrial application.'

5. Article 53 of the CGEP states:

'European patents shall not be granted in respect of:

> (a) inventions the commercial exploitation of which would be contrary to "ordre public" or morality; such exploitation shall not be deemed to be so contrary merely because it is prohibited by law or regulation in some or all of the Contracting States.'

EUROPEAN UNION LEGISLATION

6. [The Court reproduced the preamble to the Directive—Eds.]

. . .

7. The Directive provides:

'Article 1

1. Member States shall protect biotechnological inventions under national patent law. They shall, if necessary, adjust their national patent law to take account of the provisions of this Directive.

. . . .

Article 5

1. The human body, at the various stages of its formation and development, and the simple discovery of one of its elements, including the sequence or partial sequence of a gene, cannot constitute patentable inventions.

2. An element isolated from the human body or otherwise produced by means of a technical process, including the sequence or partial sequence of a gene, may constitute a patentable invention, even if the structure of that element is identical to that of a natural element. . .

Article 6

1. Inventions shall be considered unpatentable where their commercial exploitation would be contrary to *ordre public* or morality; however, exploitation shall not be deemed to be so contrary merely because it is prohibited by law or regulation.

2. On the basis of paragraph 1, the following, in particular, shall be considered unpatentable:

. . .

> (c) uses of human embryos for industrial or commercial purposes;

. . .'

NATIONAL LAW

8. Paragraph 2 of the Patentgesetz (Law on patents), as amended for the purposes of transposition of Article 6 of the Directive (BGBl. 2005 I, p. 2521; 'the PatG'), is worded as follows:

'1. Patents may not be granted for inventions whose commercial exploitation would be contrary to *ordre public* or morality; however, exploitation shall not be deemed to be so contrary merely because it is prohibited by law or regulation.

2. In particular, patents shall not be awarded for:

. . .

(3) uses of human embryos for industrial or commercial purposes;

. . .

The application of points (1) to (3) shall be governed by the appropriate provisions of the Embryonenschutzgesetz [(Law on the protection of embryos; "the EschG")].'

9. Paragraph 21 of the PatG provides:

'1. A patent shall be revoked (Paragraph 61) if it appears that:

the object of the patent is not patentable pursuant to Paragraphs 1 to 5.'

10. Under Paragraph 22(1) of the PatG:

'A patent shall be declared void on application (Paragraph 81) if it appears that one of the grounds set out in Paragraph 21(1) applies, or that the scope of the protection conferred by the patent has been extended.'

11. Paragraphs 1(1), point 2, and 2(1) and (2) of the EschG of 13 December 1990 define as a criminal offence the artificial fertilisation of ova for a purpose other than inducing pregnancy in the woman from whom they originate, the sale of human embryos conceived *in vitro* or removed from a woman before the end of the nidation process in the uterus, or their transfer, acquisition or use for a purpose other than their preservation, and the *in vitro* development of human embryos for a purpose other than inducing pregnancy.

12. Under Paragraph 8(1) of the EschG, an embryo is a fertilised human ovum capable of development, from the time of karyogamy, and any cell removed from an embryo which is 'totipotent', that is to say, able to divide and develop into an individual provided that the other conditions necessary are satisfied. A distinction must be made between those cells and pluripotent cells, which are stem cells which, although capable of developing into any type of cell, cannot develop into a complete individual.

13. Under Paragraph 4 of the Gesetz zur Sicherstellung des Embryonenschutzes im Zusammenhang mit Einfuhr und Verwendung menschlicher embryonaler Stammzellen (Law to ensure the protection of

embryos in connection with the importation and use of human embryonic stem cells) (BGBl. 2002 I, p. 2277) of 28 May 2002:

'(1) The importation and use of embryonic stem cells are prohibited.

(2) By derogation from subparagraph 1 above, the importation and use of embryonic stem cells shall be authorised for purposes of research on the conditions set out in Paragraph (6) if:

1. the authorising authority is satisfied that

(a) the embryonic stem cells were obtained before 1 May 2007 in accordance with the legislation in force in the State of origin and have been preserved in culture or stored thereafter in cryopreserved form (lineage of embryonic stem cells);

(b) the embryos from which they originate were produced by *in vitro* fertilisation with a view to inducing pregnancy and became definitively superfluous to that purpose and there is no evidence that this was for reasons connected with the embryos themselves;

(c) no remuneration or other valuable benefit has been granted or promised in consideration of the donation of the embryos for the purpose of obtaining stem cells, and,

2. the importation and use of the embryonic stem cells does not infringe any other provisions of law, in particular those of the EschG.

3. Authorisation shall be refused if the embryonic stem cells were manifestly obtained in contravention of the founding principles of the German legal order. It shall not be refused on the ground that the stem cells were obtained from human embryos.'

14. Under Paragraph 5(1) of that Law:

'Research work on embryonic stem cells may be carried out only if it is scientifically established that

1.   that work pursues high-level research aims for the increase of scientific knowledge in the area of basic research or serves to extend medical knowledge in connection with the development of diagnostic, preventive or therapeutic procedures for human use. . .'

The dispute in the main proceedings and the questions referred for a preliminary ruling.

15. Mr. Brüstle is the holder of a German patent, filed on 19 December 1997, which concerns isolated and purified neural precursor cells,

processes for their production from embryonic stem cells and the use of neural precursor cells for the treatment of neural defects.

16. It is claimed in the patent specification filed by Mr. Brüstle that the transplantation of brain cells into the nervous system is a promising method of treatment of numerous neurological diseases. The first clinical applications have already been developed, in particular for patients suffering from Parkinson's disease.

17. In order to remedy such neural defects, it is necessary to transplant immature precursor cells, still capable of developing. In essence, that type of cell exists only during the brain's development phase. The use of cerebral tissue from human embryos raises significant ethical questions and means that it is not possible to meet the need for the precursor cells which are required to provide publicly available cell treatment.

18. However, according to the specification, embryonic stem cells offer new prospects for the production of cells for transplantation. Being pluripotent, they can develop into all types of cells and tissues and can be conserved during many passages in the state of pluripotentiality and can multiply. The patent at issue seeks, in those circumstances, to make it possible to resolve the technical problem of producing an almost unlimited quantity of isolated and purified precursor cells having neural or glial properties, obtained from embryonic stem cells.

19. On application by Greenpeace, the Bundespatentgericht (Federal Patent Court) ruled, on the basis of Paragraph 22(1) of the PatG, that the patent at issue was invalid in so far as it covers precursor cells obtained from human embryonic stem cells and processes for the production of those precursor cells. The defendant appealed against that judgment to the Bundesgerichtshof (Federal Court of Justice).

20. In the view of the referring court, the outcome of the application for annulment depends on whether the technical teaching of the patent at issue, in so far as it concerns precursor cells obtained from human embryonic stem cells, is excluded from patentability under Paragraph 2(2), first sentence, point 3, of the PatG. The answer to that question depends in turn on the interpretation which should be given in particular to Article 6(2)(c) of the Directive.

21. According to the referring court, having regard to the fact that Article 6(2) of the Directive does not allow the Member States any discretion as regards the fact that the processes and uses listed therein are not patentable (*see* Case C-377/98 *Netherlands* v. *Parliament and Council* [2001] ECR I-7079, paragraph 39, and Case C-456/03 *Commission* v. *Italy* [2005] ECR I-5335, paragraph 78 et seq.), the reference made in the second sentence of Paragraph 2(2) of the PatG to the EschG, particularly to the definition of an embryo which Paragraph 8(1) of that Law gives, cannot be regarded as the fruit of the task left to Member States to put Arti-

cle 6(2)(c) of the Directive into concrete terms in that regard, even though
the Directive did not expressly define the concept of embryo. The only
possible interpretation of that concept is European and unified. In other
words, the second sentence of Paragraph 2(2) of the PatG and, in particular, the concept of embryo which it uses cannot be interpreted differently
from that of the corresponding concept in Article 6(2)(c) of the Directive.

22. With that in mind, the referring court seeks, inter alia, to ascertain whether the human embryonic stem cells which serve as base material for the patented processes constitute 'embryos' within the meaning of
Article 6(2)(c) of the Directive and whether the organisms from which
those human embryonic stem cells can be obtained constitute 'human
embryos' within the meaning of that article. In that regard, it notes that
the human embryonic stem cells which serve as base material for the patented processes are not all totipotent cells, some being only pluripotent
cells obtained from embryos at the blastocyst stage. It is also uncertain as
to the classification, in the light of the concept of embryo, of blastocysts
from which human embryonic stem cells can also be obtained.

23. In those circumstances, the Bundesgerichtshof decided to stay the
proceedings and refer the following questions to the Court for a preliminary ruling:

'1. What is meant by the term "human embryos" in Article 6(2)(c)
of [the Directive]?

(a) Does it include all stages of the development of human life,
beginning with the fertilization of the ovum, or must further
requirements, such as the attainment of a certain stage of development, be satisfied?

(b) Are the following organisms also included:

– fertilized human ova into which a cell nucleus from a
mature human cell has been transplanted;

– fertilized human ova whose division and further development have been stimulated by parthenogenesis?

(c) Are stem cells obtained from human embryos at the blastocyst stage also included?

2. What is meant by the expression "uses of human embryos for
industrial or commercial purposes"? Does it include any commercial exploitation within the meaning of Article 6(1) of [the
Directive], especially use for the purposes of scientific research?

3. Is technical teaching to be considered unpatentable pursuant
to Article 6(2)(c) of the Directive even if the use of human embryos does not form part of the technical teaching claimed with
the patent, but is a necessary precondition for the application of
that teaching:

– because the patent concerns a product whose production necessitates the prior destruction of human embryos,

– or because the patent concerns a process for which such a product is needed as base material?'

CONSIDERATION OF THE QUESTIONS REFERRED

THE FIRST QUESTION

24. By its first question, the referring court asks the Court to interpret the concept of 'human embryo' within the meaning of and for the purposes of the application of Article 6(2)(c) of the Directive, that is to say, for the sole purpose of ascertaining the scope of the prohibition on patentability laid down in that provision.

25. It must be borne in mind that, according to settled case-law, the need for a uniform application of European Union law and the principle of equality require that the terms of a provision of European Union law which makes no express reference to the law of the Member States for the purpose of determining its meaning and scope must normally be given an independent and uniform interpretation throughout the European Union. . . .

26. Although the text of the Directive does not define human embryo, nor does it contain any reference to national laws as regards the meaning to be applied to those terms. It therefore follows that it must be regarded, for the purposes of application of the Directive, as designating an autonomous concept of European Union law which must be interpreted in a uniform manner throughout the territory of the Union.

27. That conclusion is supported by the object and the aim of the Directive. It follows from recitals 3 and 5 to 7 in the preamble to the Directive that it seeks, by a harmonisation of the rules for the legal protection of biotechnological inventions, to remove obstacles to trade and to the smooth functioning of the internal market that are brought about by differences in national legislation and case-law between the Member States, and thus, to encourage industrial research and development in the field of genetic engineering (see, to that effect, *Netherlands* v *Parliament and Council*, paragraphs 16 and 27).

28. The lack of a uniform definition of the concept of human embryo would create a risk of the authors of certain biotechnological inventions being tempted to seek their patentability in the Member States which have the narrowest concept of human embryo and are accordingly the most liberal as regards possible patentability, because those inventions would not be patentable in the other Member States. Such a situation would adversely affect the smooth functioning of the internal market which is the aim of the Directive.

29. That conclusion is also supported by the scope of the listing, in Article 6(2) of the Directive, of the processes and uses excluded from patentability. It is apparent from the case-law of the Court that, unlike Article 6(1) of the Directive, which allows the administrative authorities and courts of the Member States a wide discretion in applying the exclusion from patentability of inventions whose commercial exploitation would be contrary to *ordre public* and morality, Article 6(2) allows the Member States no discretion with regard to the unpatentability of the processes and uses which it sets out, since the very purpose of this provision is to delimit the exclusion laid down in Article 6(1). It follows that, by expressly excluding from patentability the processes and uses to which it refers, Article 6(2) of the Directive seeks to grant specific rights in this regard (see *Commission* v *Italy*, paragraphs 78 and 79).

30. As regards the meaning to be given to the concept of 'human embryo' set out in Article 6(2)(c) of the Directive, it should be pointed out that, although, the definition of human embryo is a very sensitive social issue in many Member States, marked by their multiple traditions and value systems, the Court is not called upon, by the present order for reference, to broach questions of a medical or ethical nature, but must restrict itself to a legal interpretation of the relevant provisions of the Directive (*see*, to that effect, Case C-506/06 *Mayr* [2008] ECR I-1017, paragraph 38).

31. It must be borne in mind, further, that the meaning and scope of terms for which European Union law provides no definition must be determined by considering, inter alia, the context in which they occur and the purposes of the rules of which they form part. . . .

32. In that regard, the preamble to the Directive states that although it seeks to promote investment in the field of biotechnology, use of biological material originating from humans must be consistent with regard for fundamental rights and, in particular, the dignity of the person. Recital 16 in the preamble to the Directive, in particular, emphasises that 'patent law must be applied so as to respect the fundamental principles safeguarding the dignity and integrity of the person.'

33. To that effect, as the Court has already held, Article 5(1) of the Directive provides that the human body at the various stages of its formation and development cannot constitute a patentable invention. Additional security is offered by Article 6 of the Directive, which lists as contrary to *ordre public* or morality, and therefore excluded from patentability, processes for cloning human beings, processes for modifying the germ line genetic identity of human beings and uses of human embryos for industrial or commercial purposes. Recital 38 in the preamble to the Directive states that this list is not exhaustive and that all processes the use of which offends against human dignity are also excluded from pa-

tentability (*see Netherlands* v *Parliament and Council*, paragraphs 71 and 76).

34. The context and aim of the Directive thus show that the European Union legislature intended to exclude any possibility of patentability where respect for human dignity could thereby be affected. It follows that the concept of 'human embryo' within the meaning of Article 6(2)(c) of the Directive must be understood in a wide sense.

35. Accordingly, any human ovum must, as soon as fertilised, be regarded as a 'human embryo' within the meaning and for the purposes of the application of Article 6(2)(c) of the Directive, since that fertilisation is such as to commence the process of development of a human being.

36. That classification must also apply to a non-fertilised human ovum into which the cell nucleus from a mature human cell has been transplanted and a non-fertilised human ovum whose division and further development have been stimulated by parthenogenesis. Although those organisms have not, strictly speaking, been the object of fertilisation, due to the effect of the technique used to obtain them they are, as is apparent from the written observations presented to the Court, capable of commencing the process of development of a human being just as an embryo created by fertilisation of an ovum can do so.

37. As regards stem cells obtained from a human embryo at the blastocyst stage, it is for the referring court to ascertain, in the light of scientific developments, whether they are capable of commencing the process of development of a human being and, therefore, are included within the concept of 'human embryo' within the meaning and for the purposes of the application of Article 6(2)(c) of the Directive.

38. In the light of the foregoing considerations, the answer to the first question is that:

– any human ovum after fertilisation, any non-fertilised human ovum into which the cell nucleus from a mature human cell has been transplanted and any non-fertilised human ovum whose division and further development have been stimulated by parthenogenesis constitute a 'human embryo' within the meaning of Article 6(2)(c) of the Directive;

– it is for the referring court to ascertain, in the light of scientific developments, whether a stem cell obtained from a human embryo at the blastocyst stage constitutes a 'human embryo' within the meaning of Article 6(2)(c) of the Directive.

THE SECOND QUESTION

39. By its second question, the referring court asks whether the concept of 'uses of human embryos for industrial or commercial purposes' within the meaning of Article 6(2)(c) of the Directive also covers the use of human embryos for purposes of scientific research.

40. In that regard, it must be pointed out that the purpose of the Directive is not to regulate the use of human embryos in the context of scientific research. It is limited to the patentability of biotechnological inventions.

41. With regard, therefore, solely to the determination of whether the exclusion from patentability concerning the use of human embryos for industrial or commercial purposes also covers the use of human embryos for purposes of scientific research or whether scientific research entailing the use of human embryos can access the protection of patent law, clearly the grant of a patent implies, in principle, its industrial or commercial application.

42. That interpretation is supported by recital 14 in the preamble to the Directive. By stating that a patent for invention 'entitles [its holder] to prohibit third parties from exploiting it for industrial and commercial purposes', it indicates that the rights attaching to a patent are, in principle, connected with acts of an industrial or commercial nature.

43. Although the aim of scientific research must be distinguished from industrial or commercial purposes, the use of human embryos for the purposes of research which constitutes the subject-matter of a patent application cannot be separated from the patent itself and the rights attaching to it.

44. The clarification in recital 42 in the preamble to the Directive, that the exclusion from patentability set out in Article 6(2)(c) of the Directive 'does not affect inventions for therapeutic or diagnostic purposes which are applied to the human embryo and are useful to it' also confirms that the use of human embryos for purposes of scientific research which is the subject-matter of a patent application cannot be distinguished from industrial and commercial use and, thus, avoid exclusion from patentability.

45. That interpretation is, in any event, identical to that adopted by the Enlarged Board of Appeal of the European Patent Office regarding Rule 28(c) of the Implementing Regulations to the CGEP, which uses precisely the same wording as Article 6(2)(c) of the Directive (see decision of 25 November 2008, G 2/06, *Official Journal EPO*, May 2009, p. 306, paragraphs 25 to 27).

46. The answer to the second question is therefore that the exclusion from patentability concerning the use of human embryos for industrial or commercial purposes in Article 6(2)(c) of the Directive also covers use for purposes of scientific research, only use for therapeutic or diagnostic purposes which is applied to the human embryo and is useful to it being patentable.

THE THIRD QUESTION

47. By its third question, the referring court asks the Court, in essence, whether an invention is unpatentable even though its purpose is not the use of human embryos, where it concerns a product whose production necessitates the prior destruction of human embryos or a process for which requires a base material obtained by destruction of human embryos.

48. It is raised in a case concerning the patentability of an invention involving the production of neural precursor cells, which presupposes the use of stem cells obtained from a human embryo at the blastocyst stage. It is apparent from the observations presented to the Court that the removal of a stem cell from a human embryo at the blastocyst stage entails the destruction of that embryo.

49. Accordingly, on the same grounds as those set out in paragraphs 32 to 35 above, an invention must be regarded as unpatentable, even if the claims of the patent do not concern the use of human embryos, where the implementation of the invention requires the destruction of human embryos. In that case too, the view must be taken that there is use of human embryos within the meaning of Article 6(2)(c) of the Directive. The fact that destruction may occur at a stage long before the implementation of the invention, as in the case of the production of embryonic stem cells from a lineage of stem cells the mere production of which implied the destruction of human embryos is, in that regard, irrelevant.

50. Not to include in the scope of the exclusion from patentability set out in Article 6(2)(c) of the Directive technical teaching claimed, on the ground that it does not refer to the use, implying their prior destruction, of human embryos would make the provision concerned redundant by allowing a patent applicant to avoid its application by skillful drafting of the claim.

51. Again, the Enlarged Board of Appeal of the European Patent Office reached the same conclusion when asked about the interpretation of Rule 28(c) of the Implementing Regulations to the CGEP, the wording of which is identical to that of Article 6(2)(c) of the Directive (*see* decision of 25 November 2008, paragraph 22, referred to in paragraph 45 above).

The answer to the third question is therefore that Article 6(2)(c) of the Directive excludes an invention from patentability where the technical teaching which is the subject-matter of the patent application requires the prior destruction of human embryos or their use as base material, whatever the stage at which that takes place and even if the description of the technical teaching claimed does not refer to the use of human embryos.

NOTES AND QUESTIONS

1. In *Brüstle v. Greenpeace*, the CJEU notes in paragraph 45 that the EPO Enlarged Board of Appeal (EBOA) in its WARF decision also concluded that the use of human embryos for scientific research included in a patent application is considered industrial or commercial use. However, the Court went beyond the EBOA in concluding that inventions that involved the destruction of a human embryo at any time in their past were unpatentable under the Directive. Thus EPO-issued patents claiming inventions derived from pre-existing cell lines would appear to be invalid after *Brüstle*. Do you agree with either of these approaches to the patenting of human-embryo-derived inventions?

2. Interestingly, the research that yielded the claimed inventions was legal in Germany and was in fact funded in part by the German government. But what is legal in a country may not be objectively moral. Consider one commentator's view of the decision:

> More mischievous patent attorneys will be starting to consider what patents in other areas of technology might be vulnerable as a result of this decision. Does the use of slave labour to mine metals such as tin, tantalum, tungsten and gold for the mobile phone industry mean that mobile phone patents are immoral?

Philip Webber, *Brüstle: What Will Happen Next?*, IPKAT BLOG, (Oct. 29, 2011, 9:57 P.M.), http://ipkitten.blogspot.com/2011/10/brustle-what-will-happen-next.html.

Should moral, legal, or ethical violations involved in making an invention affect an inventor's ability to obtain or enforce a patent on the invention? For a further analysis of these issues, *see Margo A. Bagley, The New Invention Creation Boundary in Patent Law,* 51 WM. & MARY L. REV. 577 (2009). Similarly, the Chinese SIPO Examination Guidelines interpret Article 5 of the Patent Act as banning patents on human embryonic stem cells and processes to obtain them, as noted earlier. Yet, the *National Eleventh Five-year Development Plan of Sciences and Technology* (2006) listed as one of the main goals in the area of developmental and reproductive research "establish[ing] primate embryonic stem cell banks that are based mainly on human beings." Available (in Chinese) at http://www.most.gov.cn/kjgh/kjfzgh/200610/t 20061031_55485_6.htm. However, the *National Twelfth Five-year Development Plan of Sciences and Technology* (2011) does not explicitly mention human embryonic stem cell research. Instead, this more recent plan emphasizes other specific areas such as research on stem cell re-programing, self-renewal, and pluripotency; recognition of new stem cell markers; translational research of stem cells, etc. The omission of human embryonic stem cell research does not necessarily indicate a policy change but it remains to be seen whether such research is promoted in China in the future. Available (in Chinese) at http://www.most.gov.cn/mostinfo/xinxifenlei/gjkjgh/201107/t201107 13_88230_6.htm.

3. Does the *Brüstle* decision violate the TRIPS Agreement? Article 27(2) provides:

> Members may exclude from patentability inventions, the prevention within their territory of the commercial exploitation of which is necessary to protect ordre public or morality, including to protect human, animal or plant life or health or to avoid serious prejudice to the environment, provided that such exclusion is not made merely because the exploitation is prohibited by their law.

However, if the research is legal, then how can preventing the commercial exploitation of the invention be contrary to morality? Without patent protection, arguably more research involving human embryos can take place (although there may be a reduced financial incentive to do so). Consider this argument:

> How can a state realistically claim that the prevention of the commercial exploitation of the invention is necessary if it simultaneously allows said commercial exploitation? . . . [I]n order to comply with this TRIPS provision [27(2)], a country should guarantee that there is a symmetrical correspondence between ethical norms built inside patent law and moral provisions applied outside patent law.

Enrico Bonadio, *Stem Cells Industry and Beyond: What is the Aftermath of Brüstle?*, 95 EUR. J. RISK REG. 93 (2012). Do you agree? If not, why not?

4. Although the EPO has exhibited a willingness to evaluate questions of morality and public order posed, in particular, by biotech inventions, the Office in most cases has come down on the side of permitting the grant of patents, often with some modification to the claims. The EPO Guidelines for Substantive Examination provide instruction to examiners on the standard to apply in evaluating morality and public order. Part C, Chapter IV, § 4.1 of the Guidelines states:

> Any invention the commercial exploitation of which would be contrary to "ordre public" or morality is specifically excluded from patentability. The purpose of this is to deny protection to inventions likely to induce riot or public disorder, or to lead to criminal or other generally offensive behaviour. Anti-personnel mines are an obvious example. This provision is likely to be invoked only in rare and extreme cases. A fair test to apply is to consider whether it is probable that the public in general would regard the invention as so abhorrent that the grant of patent rights would be inconceivable. If it is clear that this is the case, objection should be raised under Art. 53(a); otherwise not.

The standard in the EPO Examination Guidelines for applying Article 53(a) is whether it is probable that the public in general would regard the invention as so abhorrent that the grant of patent rights would be inconceivable. Is it sufficiently clear, appropriate and workable? Can you articulate a more helpful standard? Are patent examiners likely to be qualified to address moral issues? If not, can moral issues still play a role in patentability determinations? If so, how? If not, should morality determinations be left to some other entity or simply ignored?

5. Like many other countries, the morality exception to patentability in India has seen little use historically. However, Professor Basheer has uncovered a rather interesting application of the provision:

> Right[] from its inception in 1911, the Indian Patent regime has always had a 'morality' exception. Section 3 (b) of the Patents Act articulates this exception as any invention, 'the primary or intended use of which would be contrary to law or morality or injurious to public health.'

> . . . [T]here appears to be only one unreported instance of the use of this exception by the Indian Patent Office. The invention in this case related to medicinal powder prepared from skeletal remains of dead bodies dug up within a week of burial. Digging up graves for profit- oriented purposes was seen as highly objectionable by the patent office.

> In light of the above, one may be tempted to relegate the morality exception to something of a non-starter. However, it is important to remember that this exception was dormant in most other regimes and triggered off mainly when confronted with biotechnology applications. In the Indian context, the patent office screened out problematic biotechnology applications using a constricted definition of manufacture, internal guidelines, delayed examination tactics etc. With most of these grounds no longer available, it is quite possible that the patent office may now turn to the morality exception.

Posting of Shamnad Basheer to Spicy IP, *Grave Diggers, "Immoral" Patents and the NBRA,* http://spicyipindia.blogspot.com/2008/07/grave-diggers-immoral-patents-and-nbra.html (July 30, 2008).

b. United States

While the U.S. Patent Act contains no patent subject matter constraints on grounds stated in TRIPS Article 27, nor a provision similar to EPC Article 53 (a), the issuance of patents on morally controversial biotech inventions has led to calls for Congress to explicitly limit patent protection based on moral considerations. Consider the following excerpt from an article by Professor Bagley in which she questions the wisdom of the U.S. approach to the patenting of morally controversial biotech inventions.

MARGO A. BAGLEY, PATENT FIRST, ASK QUESTIONS LATER: MORALITY AND BIOTECHNOLOGY IN PATENT LAW
45 WM. & MARY L. REV. 469 (2003)

In [the article] "Cloning Trevor," journalist Kyla Dunn chronicles the unsuccessful efforts of a group of scientists at Advanced Cellular Technologies (ACT) to create an embryonic clone of a two-year-old boy afflicted with a rare genetic disorder. Theoretically, the development of such an embryo, made with one of the boy's skin cells and a donated human egg, could yield embryonic stem cells which, when injected back into the boy, might halt and reverse the disorder. This effort is an example of therapeutic cloning—the creation of genetically modified embryos that ultimately will be destroyed in order to produce cures for various human ailments. By contrast, reproductive cloning has as its aim the development, also from a genetically modified embryo, of a fully formed child. Therapeutic cloning is less abhorrent to many than reproductive cloning, but both are morally controversial, and neither type of research is eligible for federal funding. Instead, private sector entities, like the ACT researchers that attempted to clone Trevor, are funding work in these areas.

While federal funding may not be available for cloning research, federal patent protection, which provides an incentive for private funding, is available. For example, a cloning patent was issued to the University of Missouri in April 2001, claiming inventions directed to, among other things, methods for "producing a cloned mammal" and for "producing a cloned mammalian embryo." Moreover, the patent disclosure states that "the present invention encompasses the living, cloned *products* produced by each of the methods described herein." The patent and news reports of other human cloning activity drew critical reaction, commentary, and calls for legislative action from a variety of sources. However, none of the proposed amendments, either to ban patents on cloning or to ban cloning research, have been enacted to date.

Why is the federal government granting exclusive property rights, which in effect act as indirect research funding, in inventions for which it will not, for public policy reasons, provide direct research funding? Patents can be seen as a type of indirect funding because they provide incentives for parties to undertake expensive and risky research. Patents induce upfront funding of projects with the expectation that monopoly profits can be generated over the long term. This situation, which appears inconsistent, does not necessarily involve active and deliberate congressional authorization of patents on such morally controversial inventions. Rather, Congress simply may not appreciate the ramifications of its inaction in sustaining the current "patent first, ask questions later" U.S. patent regime.

Under a "patent first, ask questions later" approach, a patent issues, and to the extent its claimed subject matter conflicts with norms or values held by a meaningful portion of society, the patent generates, among other things, public expressions of outrage, questions of how it issued in the first place, and often calls for Congress to address the perceived problem legislatively. . . .

. . . .

The U.S. patent system has not always had this "patent first" approach to moral issues. For many years a judicially created "moral utility" doctrine served as a type of gatekeeper of patent-eligible subject matter. The doctrine allowed both the USPTO and courts to deny patents on morally controversial subject matter under the fiction that such inventions were not "useful." The gate, however, is currently untended, as a result of judicial decisions that interpreted the scope of the statutory utility and subject matter standards under the Patent Act of 1952 in a way that left no room for a moral utility doctrine. Beginning in 1980 with *Diamond v. Chakrabarty* and continuing to the present, the Supreme Court has expansively and consistently held that Congress intended the definition of subject matter eligible for protection under the 1952 Patent Act to include any type of living or nonliving matter, as long as it is "made by man." Combining these decisions with the Court's generous deference to Congress in Intellectual Property Clause matters means that no explicit basis exists for denying patent protection to otherwise patentable, morally controversial subject matter. . . .

Members of Congress may not appreciate fully this change of events because of statements by the USPTO declaring that it would deny patents on certain morally controversial inventions for public policy or, in the case of inventions comprising humans, Thirteenth Amendment reasons. Members of Congress have cited such statements in arguments against specific legislation directed at banning human-cloning patents. The USPTO, however, is claiming power that it does not have. The Supreme Court has already interpreted the patent statute without reference to any limits based on moral considerations and the idea that the Thirteenth Amendment could support the denial of patents, on genetically modified previable fetuses for example, is doctrinally unsound. The USPTO . . . lacks the authority to deny patents on morally controversial inventions, even ones that comprise human genetic subject matter, and has in fact issued patents encompassing human genetic subject matter, despite earlier pronouncements.

Further complicating congressional action to address the patent eligibility of morally controversial biotech subject matter may be misunderstandings of the basic nature of the U.S. patent-grant system. The Patent Act of 1952 entitles a person to a patent on her invention if it meets the statutory requirements for patentability, which include novelty, utility, and non-obviousness. As most of the morally controversial biotech inventions are new and targeted at curing human disease, if only tangentially, such express statutory requirements have not and likely will not prove too difficult to surmount. In the absence of statutory limits, researchers and their patent attorneys are making patent policy and determining the limits of patent eligibility by the subject matter described in their patent applications. Congress may not be aware that inaction on its part has placed patent applicants in the position of de facto arbiters of patent eligibility, thereby providing private entities with incentives, via granted patents, to develop and exploit morally controversial inventions without engaging in any analysis of the policy implications of such decisions. . . .

Facially, the U.S. "patent first" approach appears to reflect a normative congressional choice of a system that defaults in favor of patent eligibility while leaving specific subject matter exclusions for subsequent reactive legislation. However, appearances can be deceiving. Congress could certainly have chosen to create a "patent first" system in which advancing technology was the only concern. Alternatively, Congress could acquiesce in the operation of such a system by declining to enact legislation to correct it. A variety of evidence suggests, however, that Congress has not intentionally created such a system, nor intentionally acquiesced in such a system. . . .

Without statutory bars to the issuance of morally controversial patents, the public and Congress are continually in a reactive instead of proactive mode in assessing the potential impact of patenting such subject matter. Issues surrounding takings and government interference with property rights and contractual relations complicate and confound Congress' ability to adequately define patent eligible subject matter after the fact. In addition, a lack of public understanding regarding how the patent system operates likely traps some people in the "is-ought fallacy;" the erroneous assumption that because the law allows some governmental action, such as the issuance of a morally controversial patent, that action must be proper. Finally, as with therapeutic cloning, the ends to be achieved by exploitation of these patents, such as curing serious human ailments, are seductively desirable and politically explosive. These factors combine to make the necessary, but ex post, inquiry into whether the morally controversial "means" to achieve these desirable ends are appropriate subjects for patent protection, exceedingly difficult to undertake.

. . . .

Admittedly, while a "patent first" approach is problematic, good reasons clearly exist for leaving questions of morality out of patent law. Some commentators point to the patent system being ill-equipped to engage in such inquiries that are better left to regulatory agencies. Others correctly note that denying patents on morally controversial inventions will not stop the underlying research that is the source of public concern. Still others posit that failing to grant patents on promising technology, perhaps because of public misunderstandings of science, may hinder important discoveries and deny life-saving cures to millions. In essence they argue that the system is not broken, and to the extent it is, it would be better not to fix it because the solution-any type of morality-based limitation-could be far worse than the current problem.

. . . .

. . . [L]egislation excluding morally controversial subject matter from patent protection would not stop research into such subject matter from taking place. Rather, it would reduce the incentives for conducting the research and keep certain fruits of such research in the public domain precisely because either the underlying activity is either (1) so controversial that the government should not place its imprimatur on it via a patent grant, or (2) so socially beneficial that government should not grant anyone exclusive rights in it. . . .

Undoubtedly, such legislation could have the effect of reducing discoveries and innovations in certain biotech areas of inquiry, a consequence which cannot be dismissed lightly. Because patents require disclosure, such legislation could also have the negative effect of keeping such research hidden from public view and potential regulations. However, there are already areas of scientific research society does not promote or condone for moral reasons, such as various types of experiments on human subjects, despite the fact that useful, even life-saving information might be generated thereby. The blurring of the line between human and nonhuman animals occasioned by biotechnological advances and the lack of consensus on when life begins for human embryos and fetuses used for research purposes, among other things, supports the desirability of having at least an initial decision regarding the patent eligibility of morally controversial biotech subject matter be made by an informed Congress. . . .

NOTES AND QUESTIONS

1. The U.S. "patent first, ask questions later" approach to morally controversial biotech subject matter stands in contrast to the "ask questions first, then patent" approach of countries having statutory morality inquiries, such as EPC member states. Which approach to patentability seems preferable and why? For a cogent argument that moral considerations should be left out of patent law *see Donna M. Gitter, Led Astray by the Moral Compass: Incorporating Morality into European Union Biotechnology Patent Law,* 19 BERKELEY J. INT'L L. 1 (2001). The U.S. "moral utility" doctrine is discussed further in Chapter 5.

2. In a part of the article not reproduced above, Professor Bagley argues that patents create incentives to engage in morally controversial research activity and observes that Congress has not shied away from regulating other morally controversial subjects such as guns, abortion, and pornography. Is regulating the patenting of morally controversial subject matter qualitatively different from these other targets of congressional action? What other mechanisms would you suggest as alternatives for (or in addition to) explicit morality-based limits on patent subject matter?

3. The various policy rationales for specific aspects of national patent laws illustrate a key challenge in efforts to harmonize global standards for patentable subject matter; namely, the cultural, ethical and political factors that shape domestic values. In interpreting and applying national laws, courts increasingly are called upon to evaluate international treaty provisions. What factors should weigh most heavily when a national court evaluates domestic considerations regarding patentability against TRIPS Article 27(1)?

4. Article 27 of the TRIPS Agreement allows countries to exclude inventions from patentability based on morality considerations. To what extent does the Agreement's deference to national prerogatives in this area suggest limitations on global patent policy and harmonization initiatives? How, if at all, should moral considerations affect global patent standards? What about when national standards conflict? What institution is best suited to determine if a country's refusal to patent an invention is merely trade protectionism disguised as an ethical/moral argument? Should such policy decisions be subject to global review at all?

5. Congress arguably targeted the morality-based aspects of patent regulation in 2004 with the Weldon Amendment to the Omnibus Appropriations Bill (Pub. L. No. 108–199, 118 Stat. 3). The Amendment, deemed a "clarification" of the USPTO's 1987 policy against patenting humans (1077 O.G. 24 (April 21, 1987)), stated that "[n]one of the funds appropriated or otherwise made available under this Act may be used to issue patents on claims directed to or encompassing a human organism." However, the provision failed to define the term "human" and did not amend the patent statute to provide a basis for the rejection of a claim. Moreover, as part of a spending bill, the Amendment was a temporary measure that expired at the end of each year. Nonetheless, the provision was included in spending bills each year between 2004 and 2010, and finally was incorporated into the U.S. Patent Act in Section 33(a) of the 2011 America Invents Act, which states: "Notwithstanding any other provision of law, no patent may issue on a claim directed to or encompassing a human organism." Do you see any potential problems with the wording of this provision? How might you improve it?

B. PATENTABILITY OF BUSINESS METHODS AND SOFTWARE

Another key contested area characterized by considerable divergence across national approaches is the patent eligibility of business methods and computer software. Similarly to biotechnological inventions, the United States has been at the forefront of full recognition of both business methods and software as patentable subject matter and innovators in both fields have been able to obtain patent protection since the 1990s. In particular, in 1998, the Court of Appeals for the Federal Circuit noted (in dicta) in *State Street Bank v. Signature Financial Group,* 149 F.3d 1368

(Fed. Cir. 1998), that business methods as such were patent-eligible inventions:

> Today, we hold that the transformation of data, representing discrete dollar amounts, by a machine through a series of mathematical calculations into a final share price, constitutes a practical application of a mathematical algorithm, formula, or calculation, because it produces "a useful, concrete and tangible result"—a final share price momentarily fixed for recording and reporting purposes and even accepted and relied upon by regulatory authorities and in subsequent trades.

Id. at 1373.

The decision almost immediately resulted in a veritable flood of business method patent applications, many of them Internet-related, to the USPTO where previously there had been just a trickle. As business method patents were granted by the USPTO, infringement suits asserting these patents sprouted like weeds, generating concerns regarding the appropriateness of such subject matter for patent protection and the ability of the USPTO to grant high quality patents in this area.

In Europe, on the other hand, the patentability of business methods and computer software has been complicated by Article 52(2) of the EPC, which explicitly excludes stand-alone (i.e., non-technical/non-computer implemented) "schemes, rules and methods for . . . doing business, and programs for computers" from patent-eligible subject matter. Similarly, in Japan, where patent-eligibility standards resemble those of the EPO, examination guidelines of the JPO prevent the patenting of "methods for doing business as such" "because they do not utilize a law of nature." *See* JAPAN PATENT OFFICE, EXAMINATION GUIDELINES FOR PATENT AND UTILITY MODEL IN JAPAN, REQUIREMENTS FOR PATENTABILITY: INDUSTRIALLY APPLICABLE INVENTIONS, § 1.1(4) (2012). The following UK decision discusses not only the differences in approach to this subject matter in the U.S. and Europe, but also the differences within Europe which, following defeat of an EU Software Directive in 2005 (which would have aided harmonization across Europe similarly to the Biotech Directive), continues to exhibit marked variations in approaches to the patent eligibility of business methods and software.

1. EUROPE

AEROTEL LTD. V. TELCO HOLDINGS LTD. AND IN THE MATTER OF MACROSSAN

UK Supreme Court of Judicature, Court of Appeal (Civil Division)
[2006] EWCA (Civ) 1371 (Eng.); 1 All E.R. 225

■ Lord Justice JACOB:

These two appeals are about some of the categories declared by Art. 52(2) and (3) of the European Patent Convention ("EPC") not to be "inventions" and so unpatentable. The "Aerotel appeal" is in what was a patent action between Aerotel and Telco. Sued for infringement, Telco counter-claimed for revocation of Aerotel's Patent No. 2,171,877. . . .

. . . .

The other appeal (the "Macrossan appeal") arrives here by a different route. Mr. Macrossan is the applicant for a UK patent, No GB0314464.9. The Office took the view that the subject-matter was unpatentable. . . .

. . . .

THE APPROACH TO THE LEGISLATION

As we have said these appeals turn on the application of Art.52(2) and 52(3) of the EPC. The provision was implemented in UK law by s.1(2) of the Patents Act 1977. Although s.1(2) pointlessly uses somewhat different wording from that of the EPC no-one suggests that it has any different meaning. So we, like the parties before us, work directly from the source. . . .

. . . .

ARTICLE 52: GENERAL CONSIDERATIONS

Article 52 reads:

"(1) European patents shall be granted for any inventions which are susceptible of industrial application, which are new and which involve an inventive step.
(2) The following in particular shall not be regarded as inventions within the meaning of paragraph 1:
　(a) discoveries, scientific theories and mathematical methods;
　(b) aesthetic creations;
　(c) schemes, rules and methods for performing mental acts, playing games or doing business, and programs for computers;
　(d) presentations of information.
(3) The provisions of paragraph 2 shall exclude patentability of the subject-matter or activities referred to in that provision

only to the extent to which a European patent application or European patent relates to such subject-matter or activities as such."

The provisions about what are not to be "regarded as inventions" are not easy. Over the years there has been and continues to be much debate about them and about decisions on them given by national courts and the Boards of Appeal of the EPO. . . . There has also been much political debate too: some urging removal or reduction of the categories, others their retention or enlargement. With the political debate we have no concern— it is our job to interpret them as they stand.

. . . .

THE POSITION OUTSIDE EUROPE

The position is different in Europe from that in the USA. Not only is there no equivalent of Art.52(2) in the U.S. statute but the courts have positively held that the types of patentable invention should be given "wide scope". The general approach is that found in the Supreme Court case of *Diamond v Chakrabarty*. . . . The actual decision in *Chakrabarty*, that new and non-obvious microorganisms could be patented, is not that remarkable to European eyes for microorganisms are patentable as such under the EPC (only plants and animals are excepted by Art. 53(b)). But the expansive approach of the majority opinion (given by Burger CJ) in the Supreme Court goes wider. . . .

. . . .

The endorsement of the "anything under the sun that is made by man" approach led to further expansion of what is patentable in the US. [the court went on to discuss State Street Bank and other cases expanding patent eligible subject matter in the United States.]

. . . .

OTHER CONSIDERATIONS

Before moving on we would add three things. First there has been some political pressure on Europe to remove or reduce the categories of non-inventions. Part of that has come, Mr. Birss [counsel for the UK patent office] told us, from the fact that TRIPS . . . does not have the same explicit categories of non-invention as the EPC. . . .

. . . .

Secondly there is pressure from would-be patentees on patent offices. People are applying for what are, or arguably are, business method and computer program patents in significant numbers. This is evidenced, for example, by the fact that whereas a few years ago the Comptroller only had one or two hearings a year concerned with these topics, he now has about four a week—a number are waiting on the outcome of these appeals.

This pressure in part stems from the fact that . . . people have been getting patents for these subject-matters in the USA. Since they can get them there, they must as a commercial necessity apply for them everywhere. If your competitors are getting or trying to get the weapons of business method or computer program patents you must too. An arms race in which the weapons are patents has set in. . . .

Thirdly it by no means follows that because of pressure from applicants, the grant of patents for excluded categories should be allowed or that the excluded categories (particularly business methods and computer programs) should be construed narrowly. Just as with arms, merely because people want them is not sufficient reason for giving them.

Fourthly despite the fact that such patents have been granted for some time in the U.S., it is far from certain that they have been what Sellars and Yeatman would have called a "Good Thing." The patent system is there to provide a research and investment incentive but it has a price. That price (what economists call "transaction costs") is paid in a host of ways: the costs of patenting, the impediment to competition, the compliance cost of ensuring non-infringement, the cost of uncertainty, litigation costs and so on. There is, so far as we know, no really hard empirical data showing that the liberalisation of what is patentable in the USA has resulted in a <u>greater</u> rate of innovation or investment in the excluded categories. Innovation in computer programs, for instance, proceeded at an immense speed for years before anyone thought of granting patents for them as such. There is evidence, in the shape of the mass of U.S. litigation about the excluded categories, that they have produced much uncertainty. If the encouragement of patenting and of patent litigation as industries in themselves were a purpose of the patent system, then the case for construing the categories narrowly (and indeed for removing them) is made out. But not otherwise.

In our opinion, therefore, the court must approach the categories without bias in favour of or against exclusion. . . .

. . . .

THE CASE LAW

. . . .

It is clear that a whole range of approaches have been adopted over the years both by the EPO and national courts. . . .

The decisions of the EPO Boards of Appeal are mutually contradictory. To say that is not to criticise anyone. On the contrary the Boards of Appeal have each done what they think is right in law—as befits tribunals exercising a judicial function. But surely the time has come for matters to be clarified by an [EPO] Enlarged Board of Appeal. . . .

Our summary of the various approaches which have been adopted is as follows:

THE CONTRIBUTION APPROACH

Ask whether the inventive step resides only in the contribution of excluded matter—if yes, Art.52(2) applies. This approach was supported by Falconer J in *Merrill Lynch* but expressly rejected by this Court.

THE TECHNICAL EFFECT APPROACH

Ask whether the invention as defined in the claim makes a technical contribution to the known art—if no, Art.52(2) applies. A possible clarification (at least by way of exclusion) of this approach is to add the rider that novel or inventive purely excluded matter does not count as a "technical contribution". This is the approach (with the rider) adopted by this Court in *Merrill Lynch*. It has been followed in the subsequent decisions of this Court, *Gale* and *Fujitsu*. The approach (without the rider as an express caution) was that first adopted by the EPO Boards of Appeal, *see Vicom, IBM/Text processing* and *IBM/Data processor network*.

THE "ANY HARDWARE" APPROACH

Ask whether the claim involves the use of or is to a piece of physical hardware, however mundane (whether a computer or a pencil and paper). If yes, Art.52(2) does not apply. This approach was adopted in three cases, *Pension Benefits, Hitachi* and *Microsoft/Data transfer* (the "trio"). It was specifically rejected by this Court in *Gale*.

However there are variants of the "any hardware" approach: [the court discussed the three conflicting variants used in the Pension Benefits, Hitachi, and Microsoft/Data Transfer cases].

DISCUSSION

We begin with the last approach, that a claim to hardware is enough, an approach shared by the trio. Some examples outside the context of computer programs and methods of doing business show why it must be wrong. Consider for instance the following:

> a claim to a book, e.g. to a book containing a new story the key elements of which are set out in the claim;

> a claim to a standard CD player or iPod loaded with a new piece of music.

Everyone would agree that the claims must be bad—yet in each case as a whole they are novel, non-obvious and enabling. To deem the new music or story part of the prior art (the device of *Pension Benefits* and *Hitachi*) is simply not intellectually honest. And, so far as we see, the *Mi-*

crosoft approach, which discards that device, would actually lead to patentability.

There is moreover a clear conflict between the variants. Mr. Birss described the first two as "The Lord Giveth, the Lord Taketh away." The giving is the passing of Art.52(2), the taking away being the device of treating the excluded matter as known. Mr. Macrossan rightly pointed out that this was not so with the third variant—as he put it "the Lord Giveth but the Lord Doth not Always Taketh away."

. . . .

The fact is that this court is bound by its own precedent: that decided in *Merrill Lynch, Gale* and *Fujitsu*—the technical effect approach with the rider. We think we must apply it as we understand it, namely as set out above. That we will proceed to do.

However before doing so we must consider the approach which the Comptroller, through Mr. Birss, urges upon us. We must in particular consider whether it is consistent with that which has already been decided.

The approach is in 4 steps:

(1) properly construe the claim
(2) identify the actual contribution;
(3) ask whether it falls solely within the excluded subject matter;
(4) check whether the actual or alleged contribution is actually technical in nature.

The Comptroller submits that this approach is structured and thus helpful to the public and examiner alike and is consistent with the principles enunciated in *Merrill Lynch*. . . .

No-one could quarrel with the first step—construction. You first have to decide what the monopoly is before going on the question of whether it is excluded. Any test must involve this first step.

The second step—identify the contribution—is said to be more problematical. . . . [I]t is an exercise in judgment probably involving the problem said to be solved, how the invention works, what its advantages are. What has the inventor really added to human knowledge perhaps best sums up the exercise. The formulation involves looking at substance not form—which is surely what the legislator intended.

. . . .

The third step—is the contribution solely of excluded matter?—is merely an expression of the "as such" qualification of Art.52(3). . . Ask whether the contribution thus identified consists of excluded subject matter as such? . . .

The fourth step—check whether the contribution is "technical"—may not be necessary because the third step should have covered that. It is a necessary check however if one is to follow *Merrill Lynch* as we must.

As we have said this test is a re-formulation of the approach adopted by this court in *Fujitsu:* it asks the same questions but in a different order.

. . . .

Accordingly we propose to apply the Comptroller's structured approach to both cases under appeal. To these we now turn.

THE AEROTEL APPEAL

1. The patent has two sets of claims, method claims (1–8) and system claims (9–23). It is only necessary to set out claims 1 and 9:

> 1. A method of making a telephone call from any available telephone, comprising: obtaining a special code by making a prepayment; inserting the prepayment in a memory in a special exchange and being allocated to the special code in the memory for use in verifying a calling party call; dialling the special exchange when a telephone call connection is desired; inputting the special code for verification; inputting the number of called party; verifying at the special exchange by checking the special code and comparing the prepayment less any deductions for previous calls in the memory with the minimum cost of a call to the called party station; connecting the called and calling parties' stations in response to said verification; monitoring the remaining prepayment less deductions for the running cost of the call; and disconnecting the call when the remaining prepayment has been spent by the running cost of the call.

> 9. A telephone system for facilitating a telephone call from any available telephone station, comprising:

>> means for coupling a calling party station to a special exchange;

>> memory means in the special exchange for storing customer special codes and prepayment information individual to each customer;

>> means for verifying the calling party responsive to a code transmitted from the calling party station to the special exchange so as to verify that the code matches the special customer code in the memory means and the calling party has unused credit;

>> means for connecting said calling party station to a called station responsive to the verification.

We concentrate on the system claim first. Although called a "system" it is actually a claim to a physical device consisting of various components. Mr. Thorley helpfully provided a simplified diagram of it:

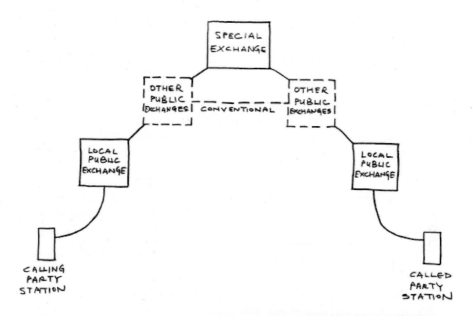

A conventional method of making a phone call involves the caller dialling the callee's number. The call goes through a number of public exchanges with an ultimate connection to the callee. The conventional route is shown in dotted lines. A system of measuring call duration applied to appropriate rates computes the cost. If the caller has no account running from his station (*e.g.* is in a call box) he will have to pre-pay. The patentee's idea is to have an extra piece of equipment which he calls a "special exchange." The caller has an account with the owner of that and deposits a credit with him. The caller has a code. To make a call he calls the number of the special exchange and inputs his code and then the callee's number. If the code is verified and there is enough credit he is put through: the call will be terminated if his credit runs out.

The important point to note is that the system as a whole is new. And it is new in itself, not merely because it is to be used for the business of selling phone calls. So, moving on to step two, the contribution is a new system. It is true that it could be implemented using conventional computers, but the key to it is a new physical combination of hardware. It seems to us clear that there is here more than just a method of doing business as such. That answers the third step. Finally the system is clearly technical in nature. We see no Art.52(2) objection to the claim.

Turning to the method claims, they are essentially to the use of the new system. Given that that is free of a s.52(2) objection, then the narrower claim to its use must be too. Again the contribution is not just a method of doing business but the use of a new apparatus for such a method. So there is more than just a business method. And the method involves the use of apparatus and so is technical.

. . . .

We therefore allow the appeal. . . .

THE MACROSSAN APPEAL

We borrow the description of Mr. Macrossan's application from Mann J and the hearing officer: "The application claims a patent for an automated method of acquiring the documents necessary to incorporate a company. It involves a user sitting at a computer and communicating with a remote server, answering questions. . . ."

. . . .

The method is clearly intended in practice to be one carried out by a user accessing an internet site, though, as Mr. Macrossan points out, that is not necessarily so. . . .

The principal points before Mann J. were concerned with excluded matters. Mann J. held that the application was;

    a)   for a method of performing a mental act as such;

    b)   not for a method of doing business;

    c)   for a computer program as such.

    . . . .

We turn to a method of doing business as such. Step 1 of the structured approach (construe the claim) causes no difficulty. Step 2 calls for an assessment of the inventor's contribution. That again poses little difficulty. Mr. Macrossan does not suggest he has invented any new kind of hardware. What he has thought of is an interactive system which will do the job which otherwise would have been done by a solicitor or company formation agent. Questions are asked, the answers incorporated in the draft, and depending on some particular answers, further questions are asked and the answers incorporated. That is his contribution.

Step 3—is that contribution solely excluded matter? That depends on the meaning of "a scheme rule or method of doing business as such". The hearing officer held that the claim was indeed just for that . . .

. . . [and] thus concluded that the claim was indeed to a method of doing business as such.

. . . .

. . . Mr. Macrossan's method is for the very business itself, the business of advising upon and creating appropriate company formation documents. The final step is to ask whether there is anything technical about the contribution—there obviously is none beyond the mere fact of the running of a computer program.

We turn to the "computer program as such" objection. Here Mann J. and the hearing officer were unanimous in saying the exclusion applied and we agree. Applying the structured test, again there is no difficulty over step 1. Step 2—what is the contribution?—is again straightforward. It is to provide a computer program (in practice probably an interactive website) which can be used to carry out the method. The hardware used is standard and is not part of the contribution. Step 3—is the contribution solely of excluded matter?—is again easy. The contribution is just the devised program up and running. Step 4—is that contribution technical?—is again easy. No. So the exclusion applies.

Accordingly we hold that Mr. Macrossan's idea is excluded from patentability. . . .

NOTES AND QUESTIONS

1. At the conclusion of the *Aerotel/Macrossan* decision, Lord Justice Jacob made an open plea to the EPO to bring clarity to the interpretation of the Article 52 EPC exclusions. He wrote:

> It is formally no business of ours to define questions to be asked of an Enlarged Board of Appeal. What we say now is only put forward in case the President of the EPO finds it helpful. If he thinks it pointless or arrogant of us to go this far, he is of course entirely free to ignore all we say. Nonetheless in the hope that there is a spirit of co-operation between national courts and the EPO we ventured to ask the parties what questions might be posed by the President of an Enlarged Board pursuant to Art.112. As we have said the British Comptroller of Patents has encouraged us in this course. . . . Having considered the drafts, the questions which we think might be put are as follows:
>
> > What is the correct approach to adopt in determining whether an invention relates to subject matter that is excluded under Article 52? How should those elements of a claim that relate to excluded subject matter be treated when assessing whether an invention is novel and inventive under Articles 54 and 56? And specifically: Is an operative computer program loaded onto a medium such as a chip or hard drive of a computer excluded by Art.52(2) unless it produces a technical effect, if so what is meant by 'technical effect'? What are the key characteristics of the method of doing business exclusion?
>
> How would you answer these questions?

2. Recall from Chapter 2 that the Enlarged Board of Appeals (EBOA) is the highest appellate body in the European Patent Office and questions can be referred to it from an EPO Board of Appeal or from the President of the EPO. While then-EPO President Alain Pompidou declined to refer Lord Justice Jacob's questions to the EBOA, in October of 2008, Pompidou's successor to the EPO Presidency, Alison Brimelow, did refer four questions regarding computer-implemented inventions to the EPO Enlarged Board of Appeal:

> Can a computer program only be excluded as a computer program as such if it is explicitly claimed as a computer program?

> 2.(a) Can a claim in the area of computer programs avoid exclusion under Art. 52(2)(c) and (3) merely by explicitly mentioning the use of a computer or a computer-readable data storage medium?

> 2.(b) If question 2(a) is answered in the negative, is a further technical effect necessary to avoid exclusion, said effect going beyond those effects inherent in the use of a computer or data storage medium to respectively execute or store a computer program?

> 3.(a) Must a claimed feature cause a technical effect on a physical entity in the real world in order to contribute to the technical character of the claim?

> 3.(b) If question 3(a) is answered in the positive, is it sufficient that the physical entity be an unspecified computer?

> 3.(c) If question 3(a) is answered in the negative, can features contribute to the technical character of the claim if the only effects to which they contribute are independent of any particular hardware that may be used?

> 4.(a) Does the activity of programming a computer necessarily involve technical considerations?

> 4.(b) If question 4(a) is answered in the positive, do all features resulting from programming thus contribute to the technical character of a claim?

> 4.(c) If question 4(a) is answered in the negative, can features resulting from programming contribute to the technical character of a claim only when they contribute to a further technical effect when the program is executed?

Why do you think President Brimelow made this referral? Is it relevant that she was formerly the head of the UK Patent Office? Are there are other questions that should have been referred?

3. On May 12, 2010, the EPO Enlarged Board of Appeals (EBOA) handed down its opinion "In Relation to a Point of Law Referred by the President of the European Patent Office pursuant to Article 112(1)(b) EPC." In case number G 3/08, the EBOA *dismissed* President Brimelow's referral siding with several of the approximately one-hundred *amicus curiae* briefs filed in response to the referral who questioned its admissibility. In a fifty-six-page

opinion, the EBOA analyzed the relevant case law and concluded there was a "divergence" between two decisions of the EPO Technical Boards of Appeal that did not rise to the level of an actual conflict between Board decisions as summarized in the EBOA's headnotes:

> Different decisions by a single Technical Board of Appeal in differing compositions may be the basis of an admissible referral by the President of the EPO of a point of law to the Enlarged Board of Appeal pursuant to Article 112 (1) (b) EPC. . . . As the wording of Article 112 (1) (b) EPC is not clear with respect to the meaning of "different/abweichende/divergent" decisions the provision has to be interpreted in the light of its object and purpose according to Article 31 of the Vienna Convention on the Law of Treaties (VCLT). The purpose of the referral right under 112 (1) (b) EPC is to establish uniformity of law within the European patent system. Having regard to this purpose of the presidential right to refer legal questions to the Enlarged Board of Appeal the notion "different decisions" has to be understood restrictively in the sense of "conflicting decisions" . . . . T 0424/03, *Microsoft* does deviate from a view expressed in T 1173/97, *IBM*, concerning whether a claim to a program on a computer-readable medium necessarily avoids exclusion from patentability under Article 52(2) EPC. However this is a legitimate development of the case law and there is no divergence which would make the referral of this point to the Enlarged Board of Appeal by the President admissible.

See Patentability of Programs for Computers, G 3/08 at 2–3 (2010) (Enlarged Bd. App.). The Board further noted that "case law in new legal and/or technical fields does not always develop in linear fashion" and that "earlier approaches may be abandoned or modified" all within the legitimate development of the law. Thus, in the absence of conflicting Board of Appeal decisions, the EBOA concluded that the legal requirements for a referral were not met. Nevertheless, the EBOA did admit that:

> While the referral has not actually identified a divergence in the case law, there is at least the potential for confusion, arising from the assumption that any technical considerations are sufficient to confer technical character on claimed subject-matter, a position which was apparently adopted in some cases (e.g. T 769/92, *Sohei*, Headnote 1). However T 1173/97, *IBM* sets the barrier higher in the case of computer programs. It argues that all computer programs have technical effects, since for example when different programs are executed they cause different electrical currents to circulate in the computer they run on. However such technical effects are not sufficient to confer "technical character" on the programs; they must cause further technical effects. In the same way, it seems to this Board, although it may be said that all computer programming involves technical considerations since it is concerned with defining a method which can be carried out by a machine, that in itself is not

enough to demonstrate that the program which results from the programming has technical character; the programmer must have had technical considerations beyond "merely" finding a computer algorithm to carry out some procedure.

Id. at para. 13.5.

Does this statement by the EBOA eliminate the confusion in assessing an invention's technical character? What is the state of patentability of computer-implemented inventions in Europe following this opinion?

---

2. THE EVOLVING STATE OF THE LAW IN THE UNITED STATES

The issuance of patents on e-commerce models, financial and accounting methods, and more in the wake of the State Street Bank decision generated consternation and criticism in many quarters, including from parties pursuing such patents for defensive and other reasons. Consider the sentiments of IBM, the company with the largest portfolio of business method patents, in an amicus brief filed in *In re Bilski,* 545 F.3d 943 (Fed. Cir. 2008):

> The lack of a plausible justification for patents on abstract business methods, coupled with the anticompetitive consequences of issuing these patents, counsels that this Court clarify that patentable subject matter is limited to inventions involving technological contributions. Modern society's dizzying pace of technological change, with its accompanying changes to marketplace conditions and commercial practices, should by no means lead to an alteration of these established principles.

Brief of Amicus Curiae IBM in Support of Neither Party, *In re Bilski (2008)* (No. 2007–1130), 31–32, *available at* http://www.patentlyo.com/patent/bilski.ibm.pdf.

In *Lab. Corp. of Am. Holdings v. Metabolite Labs., Inc.,* 548 U.S. 124, 125 (2006), the patentee was charged with seeking to 'claim a monopoly over a basic scientific relationship,'. . . namely, the relationship between homocysteine and vitamin deficiency." The Court dismissed the grant of certiorari in the case as improvidently granted because the patent subject matter question had not been properly raised in the lower court. In dissent, Justice Breyer, joined by Justices Stevens and Souter, took the opportunity to send a warning signal regarding the breadth of the State Street decision:

> Neither does the Federal Circuit's decision in *State Street Bank* help respondents. That case does say that a process is patentable if it produces a "useful, concrete, and tangible result." But this

Court has never made such a statement and, if taken literally, the statement would cover instances where this Court has held the contrary. The Court, for example, has invalidated a claim to the use of electromagnetic current for transmitting messages over long distances even though it produces a result that seems "useful, concrete, and tangible." *Morse.* Similarly the Court has invalidated a patent setting forth a system for triggering alarm limits in connection with catalytic conversion despite a similar utility, concreteness, and tangibility. *Flook.* And the Court has invalidated a patent setting forth a process that transforms, for computer-programming purposes, decimal figures into binary figures—even though the result would seem useful, concrete, and at least arguably (within the computer's wiring system) tangible. *Gottschalk.*

Id. at 136–137.

Apparently heeding the warning, the Court of Appeals for the Federal Circuit (CAFC) retreated from its broad view of business method patent eligibility *en banc* in *In re Bilski,* 545 F.3d 943 (Fed. Cir. 2008), a case involving a claim to a method of hedging risks in commodities trading. In an exhaustive decision that generated several dissenting opinions, the court articulated the "machine or transformation" test for determining the patent eligibility of a process. This test, claimed by the CAFC to have been gleaned from several Supreme Court decisions, states that a process must either be implemented on a machine or it must transform an article to a different state or thing to be eligible for patent protection.

The Supreme Court granted certiorari in *Bilski* and, in a 5–4 decision, declined to ratify the Federal Circuit's categorical imposition of the machine or transformation test. Instead, the Court called for a flexible approach to patent eligibility; it upheld the rejection of Bilski's application but on the ground that Bilski's business method was an unpatentable abstract idea. Four justices, however, would have rejected Bilski's patent application on the ground that business methods do not, as a matter of law, constitute patent-eligible subject matter.

The Supreme Court's decision is lengthy and somewhat confusing as all portions did not garner a majority. Justice Kennedy delivered the opinion of the Court. Chief Justice Roberts, and Justices Thomas and Alito joined the entire opinion; Justice Scalia joined the opinion except for Parts II-B-2 and II-C-2. Justice Stevens filed a concurring opinion (the final opinion of his Supreme Court career), in which Justices Ginsburg, Breyer, and Sotomayor joined. Justice Breyer also filed a concurrence, in which Justice Scalia joined in part. The following excerpts are from Justice Kennedy's and Justice Steven's opinions:

BILSKI ET AL. V. KAPPOS

United States Supreme Court
130 S. Ct. 3218 (2010)

■ Justice KENNEDY delivered the opinion of the Court, except as to Parts II-B-2 and II-C-2.

The question in this case turns on whether a patent can be issued for a claimed invention designed for the business world. The patent application claims a procedure for instructing buyers and sellers how to protect against the risk of price fluctuations in a discrete section of the economy. Three arguments are advanced for the proposition that the claimed invention is outside the scope of patent law: (1) it is not tied to a machine and does not transform an article; (2) it involves a method of conducting business; and (3) it is merely an abstract idea. The Court of Appeals ruled that the first mentioned of these, the so-called machine-or-transformation test, was the sole test to be used for determining the patentability of a "process" under the Patent Act, 35 U.S.C. § 101.

I

Petitioners' application seeks patent protection for a claimed invention that explains how buyers and sellers of commodities in the energy market can protect, or hedge, against the risk of price changes. The key claims are claims 1 and 4. Claim 1 describes a series of steps instructing how to hedge risk. Claim 4 puts the concept articulated in claim 1 into a simple mathematical formula. Claim 1 consists of the following steps:

> "(a) initiating a series of transactions between said commodity provider and consumers of said commodity wherein said consumers purchase said commodity at a fixed rate based upon historical averages, said fixed rate corresponding to a risk position of said consumers;

> "(b) identifying market participants for said commodity having a counter-risk position to said consumers; and

> "(c) initiating a series of transactions between said commodity provider and said market participants at a second fixed rate such that said series of market participant transactions balances the risk position of said series of consumer transactions." . . .

The remaining claims explain how claims 1 and 4 can be applied to allow energy suppliers and consumers to minimize the risks resulting from fluctuations in market demand for energy. For example, claim 2 claims "[t]he method of claim 1 wherein said commodity is energy and said market participants are transmission distributors." . . . Some of these claims also suggest familiar statistical approaches to determine the inputs to use in claim 4's equation. For example, claim 7 advises using well-known random analysis techniques to determine how much a seller will gain "from each transaction under each historical weather pattern." . . .

The patent examiner rejected petitioners' application, explaining that it "'is not implemented on a specific apparatus and merely manipulates [an] abstract idea and solves a purely mathematical problem without any limitation to a practical application, therefore, the invention is not directed to the technological arts.'" . . . The Board of Patent Appeals and Interferences affirmed, concluding that the application involved only mental steps that do not transform physical matter and was directed to an abstract idea. . . . .

The United States Court of Appeals for the Federal Circuit heard the case en banc and affirmed. . . .

. . . The court held that "[a] claimed process is surely patent-eligible under § 101 if: (1) it is tied to a particular machine or apparatus, or (2) it transforms a particular article into a different state or thing." . . . The court concluded this "machine-or-transformation test" is "the sole test governing § 101 analyses," . . . and thus the "test for determining patent eligibility of a process under § 101." . . . Applying the machine-or-transformation test, the court held that petitioners' application was not patent eligible. . . .

. . . .

II

A

Section 101 . . . specifies four independent categories of inventions or discoveries that are eligible for protection: processes, machines, manufactures, and compositions of matter. "In choosing such expansive terms . . . modified by the comprehensive 'any,' Congress plainly contemplated that the patent laws would be given wide scope." *Diamond v. Chakrabarty,* 447 U.S. 303, 308, (1980). Congress took this permissive approach to patent eligibility to ensure that "'ingenuity should receive a liberal encouragement.'" . . .

The Court's precedents provide three specific exceptions to § 101's broad patent-eligibility principles: "laws of nature, physical phenomena, and abstract ideas." *Chakrabarty, supra,* at 309, 100 S. Ct. 2204. While these exceptions are not required by the statutory text, they are consistent with the notion that a patentable process must be "new and useful." And, in any case, these exceptions have defined the reach of the statute as a matter of statutory *stare decisis* going back 150 years. . . . The concepts covered by these exceptions are "part of the storehouse of knowledge of all men . . . free to all men and reserved exclusively to none." *Funk Brothers Seed Co. v. Kalo Inoculant Co.,* 333 U.S. 127, 130, (1948).

The § 101 patent-eligibility inquiry is only a threshold test. Even if an invention qualifies as a process, machine, manufacture, or composition of matter, in order to receive the Patent Act's protection the claimed invention must also satisfy "the conditions and requirements of this title." Those requirements include that the invention be novel, . . .nonobvious, . . . and fully and particularly described . . . .

The present case involves an invention that is claimed to be a "process" under § 101. . . .

. . . .

The Court first considers two proposed categorical limitations on "process" patents under § 101 that would, if adopted, bar petitioners' application in the present case: the machine-or-transformation test and the categorical exclusion of business method patents.

B

1

Under the Court of Appeals' formulation, an invention is a "process" only if: "(1) it is tied to a particular machine or apparatus, or (2) it transforms a particular article into a different state or thing." This Court has "more than once cautioned that courts 'should not read into the patent laws limitations and conditions which the legislature has not expressed.'" *Diamond v. Diehr*, 450 U.S. 175, 182, 101 S.Ct. 1048, 67 L.Ed.2d 155 (1981). In patent law, as in all statutory construction, "[u]nless otherwise defined, 'words will be interpreted as taking their ordinary, contemporary, common meaning.' " *Diehr, supra,* at 182, 101 S. Ct. 1048. . . . The Court has read the § 101 term "manufacture" in accordance with dictionary definitions, . . . and approved a construction of the term "composition of matter" consistent with common usage, ...

Any suggestion in this Court's case law that the Patent Act's terms deviate from their ordinary meaning has only been an explanation for the exceptions for laws of nature, physical phenomena, and abstract ideas. *See Parker v. Flook,* 437 U.S. 584, 588–589 (1978). This Court has not indicated that the existence of these well-established exceptions gives the Judiciary *carte blanche* to impose other limitations that are inconsistent with the text and the statute's purpose and design. Concerns about attempts to call any form of human activity a "process" can be met by making sure the claim meets the requirements of § 101.

Adopting the machine-or-transformation test as the sole test for what constitutes a "process" (as opposed to just an important and useful clue) violates these statutory interpretation principles. Section 100(b) provides that "[t]he term 'process' means process, art or method, and includes a new use of a known process, machine, manufacture, composition of matter, or material." The Court is unaware of any "'ordinary, contemporary, common meaning,'" *Diehr, supra,* at 182, 101 S. Ct. 1048, of the definitional terms "process, art or method" that would require these terms to be tied to a machine or to transform an article. . . .

. . . .

The Court of Appeals incorrectly concluded that this Court has endorsed the machine-or-transformation test as the exclusive test. It is true that *Cochrane v. Deener,* 94 U.S. 780, 788, 24 L.Ed. 139 (1877), explained that a "process" is "an act, or a series of acts, performed upon the subject-matter to be transformed and reduced to a different state or thing." More recent cases, however, have rejected the broad implications of this dictum; and, in all events, later authority shows that it was not intended to be an exhaustive or exclusive test. *Gottschalk v. Benson,* 409 U.S. 63, 70, 93 S.Ct. 253, 34 L.Ed.2d 273 (1972), noted that "[t]ransformation and reduction of an article 'to a different state or thing' is the clue to the patentability of a process claim that does not include particular machines." At the same time, it explicitly declined to "hold that no process patent could ever qualify if it did not meet [machine or transformation] requirements." *Id.,* at 71, 93 S.Ct. 253. *Flook* took a similar approach, "assum[ing] that a valid process patent may issue even if it does not meet [the machine-or-transformation test]." 437 U.S., at 588, n. 9, 98 S.Ct. 2522.

This Court's precedents establish that the machine-or-transformation test is a useful and important clue, an investigative tool, for determining whether some claimed inventions are processes under § 101. The machine-or-transformation test is not the sole test for deciding whether an invention is a patent-eligible "process."

2

It is true that patents for inventions that did not satisfy the machine-or-transformation test were rarely granted in earlier eras, especially in the Industrial Age . . . . But times change. Technology and other innovations progress in unexpected ways. . . .

The machine-or-transformation test may well provide a sufficient basis for evaluating processes similar to those in the Industrial Age-for example, inventions grounded in a physical or other tangible form. But there are reasons to doubt whether the test should be the sole criterion for determining the patentability of inventions in the Information Age. As numerous *amicus* briefs argue, the machine-or-transformation test would create uncertainty as to the patentability of software, advanced diagnostic medicine techniques, and inventions based on linear programming, data compression, and the manipulation of digital signals. . . .

In the course of applying the machine-or-transformation test to emerging technologies, courts may pose questions of such intricacy and refinement that they risk obscuring the larger object of securing patents for valuable inventions without transgressing the public domain. . . . As a result, in deciding whether previously unforeseen inventions qualify as patentable "process[es]," it may not make sense to require courts to confine themselves to asking the questions posed by the machine-or-transformation test. Section 101's terms suggest that new technologies may call for new inquiries. . . .

. . . .

C

1

Section 101 similarly precludes the broad contention that the term "process" categorically excludes business methods. The term "method," which is within § 100(b)'s definition of "process," at least as a textual matter and before consulting other limitations in the Patent Act and this Court's precedents, may include at least some methods of doing business. *See, e.g.,* Webster's New International Dictionary 1548 (2d ed.1954) (defining "method" as "[a]n orderly procedure or process . . . regular way or manner of doing anything; hence, a set form of procedure adopted in investigation or instruction"). The Court is unaware of any argument that the "'ordinary, contemporary, common meaning,'" *Diehr, supra,* at 182, 101 S. Ct. 1048, of "method" excludes business methods. Nor is it clear how far a prohibition on business method patents would reach, and whether it would exclude technologies for conducting a business more efficiently. . . .

The argument that business methods are categorically outside of § 101's scope is further undermined by the fact that federal law explicitly contemplates the existence of at least some business method patents. Under 35 U.S.C. § 273(b)(1), if a patent-holder claims infringement based on "a method in [a] patent," the alleged infringer can assert a defense of prior use. For purposes of this defense alone, "method" is defined as "a method of doing or conducting business." § 273(a)(3). In other words, by allowing this defense the statute itself acknowledges that there may be business method patents. Section 273's definition of "method," to be sure, cannot change the meaning of a prior-enacted statute. But what § 273 does is clarify the understanding that a business method is simply one kind of "method" that is, at least in some circumstances, eligible for patenting under § 101.

A conclusion that business methods are not patentable in any circumstances would render § 273 meaningless. This would violate the canon against interpreting any statutory provision in a manner that would render another provision superfluous. . . . This principle, of course, applies to interpreting any two provisions in the U.S. Code, even when Congress enacted the provisions at different times. . . . This established rule of statutory interpretation cannot be overcome by judicial speculation as to the subjective intent of various legislators in enacting the subsequent provision. Finally, while § 273 appears to leave open the possibility of some business method patents, it does not suggest broad patentability of such claimed inventions.

2

Interpreting § 101 to exclude all business methods simply because business method patents were rarely issued until modern times revives many of the previously discussed difficulties. At the same time, some business method patents raise special problems in terms of vagueness and suspect validity. . . . The Information Age empowers people with new capacities to perform statistical analyses and mathematical calculations with a speed and sophistication that enable the design of protocols for more efficient performance of a vast number of business tasks. If a high enough bar is not set when considering patent applications of this sort, patent examiners and courts could be flooded with claims that would put a chill on creative endeavor and dynamic change.

In searching for a limiting principle, this Court's precedents on the unpatentability of abstract ideas provide useful tools. . . .

. . . .

III

Even though petitioners' application is not categorically outside of § 101 under the two broad and atextual approaches the Court rejects today, that does not mean it is a "process" under § 101. Petitioners seek to patent both the concept of hedging risk and the application of that concept to energy markets. Rather than adopting categorical rules that might have wide-ranging and unforeseen impacts, the Court resolves this case narrowly on the basis of this Court's decisions in *Benson, Flook,* and *Diehr,* which show that petitioners' claims are not patentable processes because they are attempts to patent abstract ideas. Indeed, all members of the Court agree that the patent application at issue here falls outside of § 101 because it claims an abstract idea.

In *Benson,* the Court considered whether a patent application for an algorithm to convert binary-coded decimal numerals into pure binary code was a "process" under § 101. . . . The Court first explained that "'[a] principle, in the abstract, is a fundamental truth; an original cause; a motive; these cannot be patented, as no one can claim in either of them an exclusive right.'" . . . The Court then held the application at issue was not a "process," but an unpatentable abstract idea. . . A contrary holding "would wholly pre-empt the mathematical formula and in practical effect would be a patent on the algorithm itself." . . .

In *Flook,* the Court considered the next logical step after *Benson.* The applicant there attempted to patent a procedure for monitoring the conditions during the catalytic conversion process in the petrochemical and oil-refining industries. The application's only innovation was reliance on a mathematical algorithm. . . . *Flook* held the invention was not a patentable "process." The Court conceded the invention at issue, unlike the algorithm in *Benson,* had been limited so that it could still be freely used outside the petrochemical and oil-refining industries. . . . Nevertheless, *Flook* rejected "[t]he notion that post-solution activity, no matter how conventional or obvious in itself, can transform an unpatentable principle into a patentable process." . . . The Court concluded that the process at issue there was "unpatentable under § 101, not because it contain[ed] a mathematical algorithm as one component, but because once that algorithm [wa]s assumed to be within the prior art, the application, considered as a whole, contain[ed] no patentable invention." . . . As the Court later explained, *Flook* stands for the proposition that the prohibition against patenting abstract ideas "cannot be circumvented by attempting to limit the use of the formula to a particular technological environment" or adding "insignificant postsolution activity." . . .

Finally, in *Diehr,* the Court established a limitation on the principles articulated in *Benson* and *Flook.* The application in *Diehr* claimed a previously unknown method for "molding raw, uncured synthetic rubber into cured precision products," using a mathematical formula to complete some of its several steps by way of a computer. . . . *Diehr* explained that while an abstract idea, law of nature, or mathematical formula could not be patented, "an *application* of a law of nature or mathematical formula to a known structure or process may well be deserving of patent protection." . . . *Diehr* emphasized the need to consider the invention as a whole, rather than "dissect[ing] the claims into old and new elements and then . . . ignor[ing] the presence of the old elements in the analysis." Finally, the Court concluded that because the claim was not "an attempt to patent a mathematical formula, but rather [was] an industrial process for the molding of rubber products," it fell within § 101's patentable subject matter. . . .

In light of these precedents, it is clear that petitioners' application is not a patentable "process." Claims 1 and 4 in petitioners' application explain the basic concept of hedging, or protecting against risk: "Hedging is a fundamental economic practice long prevalent in our system of commerce and taught in any introductory finance class." . . . The concept of hedging, described in claim 1 and reduced to a mathematical formula in claim 4, is an unpatentable abstract idea, just like the algorithms at issue in *Benson* and *Flook.* Allowing petitioners to patent risk hedging would pre-empt use of this approach in all fields, and would effectively grant a monopoly over an abstract idea.

Petitioners' remaining claims are broad examples of how hedging can be used in commodities and energy markets. *Flook* established that limiting an abstract idea to one field of use or adding token postsolution components did not make the concept patentable. That is exactly what the remaining claims in petitioners' application do. . . . Indeed, these claims add even less to the underlying abstract principle than the invention in *Flook* did, for the *Flook* invention was at least directed to the narrower domain of signaling dangers in operating a catalytic converter.

* * *

Today, the Court once again declines to impose limitations on the Patent Act that are inconsistent with the Act's text. The patent application here can be rejected under our precedents on the unpatentability of abstract ideas. The Court, therefore, need not define further what constitutes a patentable "process," beyond pointing to the definition of that term provided in § 100(b) and looking to the guideposts in *Benson, Flook,* and *Diehr*.

And nothing in today's opinion should be read as endorsing interpretations of § 101 that the Court of Appeals for the Federal Circuit has used in the past. . . . It may be that the Court of Appeals thought it needed to make the machine-or-transformation test exclusive precisely because its case law had not adequately identified less extreme means of restricting business method patents, including (but not limited to) application of our opinions in *Benson, Flook,* and *Diehr*. In disapproving an exclusive machine-or-transformation test, we by no means foreclose the Federal Circuit's development of other limiting criteria that further the purposes of the Patent Act and are not inconsistent with its text.

. . . .

Justice STEVENS, concurring in the judgment.

In the area of patents, it is especially important that the law remain stable and clear. The only question presented in this case is whether the so-called machine-or-transformation test is the exclusive test for what constitutes a patentable "process" under 35 U.S.C. § 101. It would be possible to answer that question simply by holding, as the entire Court agrees, that although the machine-or-transformation test is reliable in most cases, it is not the *exclusive* test.

I agree with the Court that, in light of the uncertainty that currently pervades this field, it is prudent to provide further guidance. But I would take a different approach. Rather than making any broad statements about how to define the term "process" in § 101 or tinkering with the bounds of the category of unpatentable, abstract ideas, I would restore patent law to its historical and constitutional moorings.

For centuries, it was considered well established that a series of steps for conducting business was not, in itself, patentable. In the late 1990's, the Federal Circuit and others called this proposition into question. Congress quickly responded to a Federal Circuit decision with a stopgap measure designed to limit a potentially significant new problem for the business community. It passed the First Inventors Defense Act of 1999 (1999 Act), 113 Stat. 1501A-555 (codified at 35 U.S.C. § 273), which provides a limited defense to claims of patent infringement for "method[s] of doing or conducting business." Following several more years of confusion, the Federal Circuit changed course, overruling recent decisions and holding that a series of steps may constitute a patentable process only if it is tied to a machine or transforms an article into a different state or thing. This "machine-or-transformation test" excluded general methods of doing business as well as, potentially, a variety of other subjects that could be called processes.

The Court correctly holds that the machine-or-transformation test is not the sole test for what constitutes a patentable process; rather, it is a critical clue. But the Court is quite wrong, in my view, to suggest that any series of steps that is not itself an abstract idea or law of nature may constitute a "process" within the meaning of § 101. The language in the Court's opinion to this effect can only cause mischief. The wiser course would have been to hold that petitioners' method is not a "process" because it describes only a general method of engaging in business transactions-and business methods are not patentable. More precisely, although a process is not patent-ineligible simply because it is useful for conducting business, a claim that merely describes a method of doing business does not qualify as a "process" under § 101.

. . . .

Because the text of § 101 does not on its face convey the scope of patentable processes, it is necessary, in my view, to review the history of our patent law in some detail. This approach yields a much more straightforward answer to this case than the Court's. As I read the history, it strongly supports the conclusion that a method of doing business is not a "process" under § 101. . . .

[*Justice Stevens then engaged in a detailed history of U.S. patent law culminating in an analysis of the oft-quoted phrase, "anything under the sun," to make the case that business methods are not patentable subject matter within the meaning of the U.S. Patent Act.*—Eds.]

Since at least the days of Assyrian merchants, people have devised better and better ways to conduct business. Yet it appears that neither the Patent Clause, nor early patent law, nor the current § 101 contemplated or was publicly understood to mean that such innovations are patentable. . . .

. . . .

On one side of the balance is whether a patent monopoly is necessary to "motivate the innovation." . . . Although there is certainly disagreement about the need for patents, scholars generally agree that when innovation is expensive, risky, and easily copied, inventors are less likely to undertake the guaranteed costs of innovation in order to obtain the mere possibility of an invention that others can copy. Both common sense and recent economic scholarship suggest that these dynamics of cost, risk, and reward vary by the type of thing being patented. And the functional case that patents promote progress generally is stronger for subject matter that has "historically been eligible to receive the protection of our patent laws" than for methods of doing business.

Many have expressed serious doubts about whether patents are necessary to encourage business innovation. Despite the fact that we have long assumed business methods could not be patented, it has been remarked that "the chief business of the American people, is business." Federal Express developed an overnight delivery service and a variety of specific methods (including shipping through a central hub and online package tracking) without a patent. Although counterfactuals are a dubious form of analysis, I find it hard to believe that many of our entrepreneurs forwent business innovation because they could not claim a patent on their new methods.

"[C]ompanies have ample incentives to develop business methods even without patent protection, because the competitive marketplace rewards companies that use more efficient business methods." Innovators often capture advantages from new business methods notwithstanding the risk of others copying their innovation. Some business methods occur in secret and therefore can be protected with trade secrecy. And for those methods that occur in public, firms that innovate often capture long-term benefits from doing so, thanks to various first mover advantages, including lockins, branding, and networking effects. Business innovation, moreover, generally does not entail the same kinds of risk as does more traditional, technological innovation. It generally does not require the same "enormous costs in terms of time, research, and development," and thus does not require the same kind of "compensation to [innovators] for their labor, toil, and expense." . . .

Nor, in many cases, would patents on business methods promote progress by encouraging "public disclosure." . . . Many business methods are practiced in public, and therefore a patent does not necessarily encourage the dissemination of anything not already known. And for the methods practiced in private, the benefits of disclosure may be small: Many such methods are distributive, not productive-that is, they do not generate any efficiency but only provide a means for competitors to one-up each other in a battle for pieces of the pie. And as the Court has explained, "it is hard to see how the public would be benefited by disclosure" of certain business tools, since the nondisclosure of these tools "encourages businesses to initiate new and individualized plans of operation," which "in turn, leads to a greater variety of business methods." . . .

In any event, even if patents on business methods were useful for encouraging innovation and disclosure, it would still be questionable whether they would, on balance, facilitate or impede the progress of American business. For even when patents encourage innovation and disclosure, "*too much* patent protection can impede rather than 'promote the Progress of . . . useful Arts.' " . . .

The primary concern is that patents on business methods may prohibit a wide swath of legitimate competition and innovation. As one scholar explains, "it is useful to conceptualize knowledge as a pyramid: the big ideas are on top; specific applications are at the bottom." The higher up a patent is on the pyramid, the greater the social cost and the greater the hindrance to further innovation. Thus, this Court stated in *Benson* that "[p]henomena of nature . . . , mental processes, and abstract intellectual concepts are not patentable, as they are the basic tools of scientific and technological work." . . . Business methods are similarly often closer to "big ideas," as they are the basic tools of *commercial* work. They are also, in many cases, the basic tools of further business innovation: Innovation in business methods is often a sequential and complementary process in which imitation may be a "*spur* to innovation" and patents may "become an *impediment*." "Think how the airline industry might now be structured if the first company to offer frequent flyer miles had enjoyed the sole right to award them." "[I]mitation and refinement through imitation are both necessary to invention itself and the very lifeblood of a competitive economy." . . .

    . . . .

These effects are magnified by the "potential vagueness" of business method patents. . . . When it comes to patents, "clarity is essential to promote progress." . . . Yet patents on methods of conducting business generally are composed largely or entirely of intangible steps. Compared to "the kinds of goods . . . around which patent rules historically developed," it thus tends to be more costly and time consuming to search through, and to negotiate licenses for, patents on business methods. . . .

The breadth of business methods, their omnipresence in our society, and their potential vagueness also invite a particularly pernicious use of patents that we have long criticized. As early as the 19th century, we explained that the patent laws are not intended to "creat[e] a class of speculative schemers who make it their business to watch the advancing wave of improvement, and gather its foam in the form of patented monopolies, which enable them to lay a heavy tax upon the industry of the country, without contributing anything to the real advancement of the arts." . . . Yet business method patents may have begun to do exactly that. . . .

These many costs of business method patents not only may stifle innovation, but they are also likely to "stifle competition." . . . Even if a business method patent is ultimately held invalid, patent holders may be able to use it to threaten litigation and to bully competitors, especially those that cannot bear the costs of a drawn out, fact-intensive patent litigation. That can take a particular toll on small and upstart businesses. Of course, patents always serve as a barrier to competition for the type of subject matter that is patented. But patents on business methods are patents on business itself. Therefore, unlike virtually every other category of patents, they are by their very nature likely to depress the dynamism of the marketplace.

. . . .

The Constitution grants to Congress an important power to promote innovation. In its exercise of that power, Congress has established an intricate system of intellectual property. The scope of patentable subject matter under that system is broad. But it is not endless. In the absence of any clear guidance from Congress, we have only limited textual, historical, and functional clues on which to rely. Those clues all point toward the same conclusion: that petitioners' claim is not a "process" within the meaning of § 101 because methods of doing business are not, in themselves, covered by the statute. In my view, acknowledging as much would be a far more sensible and restrained way to resolve this case. Accordingly, while I concur in the judgment, I strongly disagree with the Court's disposition of this case.

NOTES AND QUESTIONS

1. If you were a tenth justice on the Court, whose opinion would you have joined—Justice Kennedy's or Justice Stevens's? Why? Of what consequence would it have been had the dissenting opinion been the majority?

2. What is your view of Justice Stevens's warning that business method patents might hinder rather than foster innovation? Are the U.S. (*Bilski*) and UK (*Aerotel*) cases reconcilable?

3. The majority opinion in *Bilski* has come under criticism for failing to provide guidance as to what constitutes an abstract idea. As a result, critics predict an onslaught of new litigation as applicants, the USPTO, and the courts struggle to figure out what sorts of business methods are too abstract to be patentable. Not surprisingly, the USPTO and courts have continued to rely largely on the machine-or-transformation (MOT) test post-*Bilski* for lack of a better compass. In particular, the USPTO responded to *Bilski* by issuing an Interim Guidance for Determining Subject Matter Eligibility for Process Claims in View of *Bilski v. Kappos* (*Interim Bilski Guidance* (2010); *see* http://www.uspto.gov/patents/law/exam/bilski_guidance_27jul2010.pdf). The USPTO's cover memorandum provides in part as follows:

> Under the *Interim* Bilski *Guidance*, factors that weigh in favor of patent-eligibility satisfy the criteria of the machine-or-

transformation test or provide evidence that the abstract idea has been practically applied, and factors that weigh against patent-eligibility neither satisfy the criteria of the machine-or-transformation test nor provide evidence that the abstract idea has been practically applied. A summary sheet of these factors is also attached to this memorandum. The machine-or-transformation test remains an investigative tool and is a useful starting point for determining whether a claimed invention is a patent-eligible process under 35 U.S.C. § 101. The *Interim* Bilski *Guidance* provides additional factors to aid in the determination of whether a claimed method that fails the machine-or-transformation test is nonetheless patent-eligible (i.e., is not an abstract idea), and also whether a claimed method that meets the machine-or-transformation test is nonetheless patent-ineligible (i.e., is an abstract idea). Since claims directed to abstract ideas were not patent-eligible prior to *Bilski*, subject matter eligibility outcomes based on the *Interim* Bilski *Guidance* are not likely to change in most cases. The difference is that in some rare cases, factors beyond those relevant to machine-or-transformation may weigh for or against a finding that a claim is directed to an abstract idea.

Id.

The summary sheet lists the first factor weighing toward eligibility as "recitation of a machine or transformation (either express or inherent)" and the first factor weighing against eligibility as "no recitation of a machine or transformation." Is this in conformity with the decision? Why or why not? A 2011 article by a respected group of academics outlined the problems with this default reliance on the MOT test and argued instead that, post-*Bilski*, the focus of Section 101 method claim analyses should be on the scope or breadth of the claim, not its abstractness:

> The abstract ideas limitation on patentable subject matter has long been a puzzle, one *Bilski* did little to resolve. We think the dominant conception of § 101 as a gatekeeper, excluding certain inventions from the patent system altogether, is wrong. We don't exclude inventions from patentability because the invention is too abstract. We refuse to patent certain claims when those claims reach too broadly and thereby threaten downstream innovation. Reconceiving abstract ideas as a scope limitation not only helps to explain the case law, but it avoids the disastrous consequences associated with the machine-or-transformation test.

Mark A. Lemley, Michael Risch, Ted Sichelman & R. Polk Wagner, *Life after Bilski*, 63 STAN. L. REV. 1313, 1346 (2011). Do you agree that a gatekeeper role should not be the dominant function for Section 101? Revisit this question after reading the *Mayo v. Prometheus* decision in the next section, where the U.S. Supreme Court cites this article approvingly for some of its points.

4. The full inclusion of business methods as patent-eligible subject matter in the United States has led to patents in a particularly controversial area: tax reduction strategy. As of January 2010, about ninety patents had been issued and over 136 such applications published for tax-related advice, including patents on a purchase of an annuity contract to fund a charitable remainder trust (No. 7,149,712) and on a tax-deferred real estate transaction (No. 6,292,788). *See* Ollie Tinsley, *Section of Taxation: Tax Strategy Patenting Task Force*, ABA (Feb. 16, 2010). Such patents raise a variety of concerns, including lack of prior art and infringement liability for tax advisors and a concomitant increase in the cost of tax law compliance. Outcry over such patents led to the introduction of a bill in Congress to ban such patents as well as an Internal Revenue Service proposal to require a special disclosure if a taxpayer uses a patented tax planning method to achieve a tax benefit. Should such methods be patentable like any other method or excluded from patentability? What might be particularly troubling about the issuance of such patents? The America Invents Act specifically targeted tax strategy patents in Section 14 of the Act, which deems such strategies part of the prior art and thus incapable of distinguishing a claimed invention from the prior art. The section has exclusions for tax preparation and financial management methods.

3. THE LAW IN OTHER COUNTRIES

While differences clearly exist between the protections offered by different countries for business method and computer-implemented inventions, there are many similarities. According to patent practitioners from several countries:

> It will be a while before some clarity and consistency are achieved among jurisdictions. What is clear is that filing of applications for business methods is increasingly common around the world. However, the patent offices of the various jurisdictions are still reluctant to grant patents for pure business methods.

> In Australia, to be patentable, the claimed method must involve a "physical effect" in order to constitute an "artificially created state of affairs." Similarly, in Canada, business methods are not excluded from patentability and some cases may even suggest a trend towards their greater acceptance. However, it appears that for now, the Office will be applying the same patentability standard to business methods that they apply to other inventions. The trend in China is to allow business methods that are software-related. Similarly, in Japan, business method inventions are regarded as part of software-related inventions and, thus, are assessed according to the similar standards. Business methods are per se excluded from patentability in both India and the UK However, it has generally been interpreted that business

methods that are tied to computer means or hardware are not excluded from patentability in these countries.

See Eugene F. Derényi et al., *Protection of Business Method Patents Outside the United States*, LANDSLIDE (June 2009), at 18, 23.

Recently, New Zealand decided to repeal and replace its patent law (Patents Act 1953) with a new law that makes most software unpatentable. The only exception is for inventions that contain embedded software. In its commentary on the proposed Patents Bill, the Commerce Committee of the New Zealand Parliament stated the following:

> We recommend amending clause 15 to include computer programs among inventions that may not be patented. We received many submissions concerning the patentability of computer programs. Under the Patents Act 1953 computer programs can be patented in New Zealand provided they produce a commercially useful effect. Open source, or free, software has grown in popularity since the 1980s. Protecting software by patenting is inconsistent with the open source model, and its proponents oppose it. A number of submitters argued that is no "inventive step" in software development, as "new" software invariably builds on existing software. They felt that computer software should be excluded from patent protection as software patents can stifle innovation and competition, and can be granted for trivial or existing techniques. In general we accept this position.

New Zealand Parliament, Commerce Committee, *Patents Bill: Commentary* (2010) at http://legislation.govt.nz/bill/government/2008/0235 /latest/ whole.html.

In the debates that led to the new legislation, the New Zealand Computer Society supported the prohibition on software patenting, arguing that copyright protection for computer software was sufficient and that patent protection had the chilling effect of attracting "patent trolls." The New Zealand Information and Communications Technology Group, an IT industry association, opposed the prohibition, however, warning that it could hamper innovation and that software patents are essential for global competition. *See* Emma Woollacott, *New Zealand Bans Software Patents*, TG DAILY (July 15, 2010) , 6:31 A.M.), http://www.tgdaily.com/ business-and-law-features/50667-new-zealand-bans-software-patents.

NOTES AND QUESTIONS

1. What do you think are the strongest policy reasons for restricting patents on computer software and methods of doing business? What are the strong policy reasons for permitting them? Does the TRIPS Agreement per-

mit New Zealand and other countries to exclude patents for business methods in their domestic patent laws? Does it make a difference if the determination to exclude business methods patent eligibility comes from the courts? Should it make a difference?

2. Assume you are consulted by a developing country seeking to develop a software and IT industry. What advice regarding patentability would you give them? What factors do you think you would need to weigh?

3. Should national differences in the level of patent protection provided to computer software and business methods be tolerated? Are there advantages to permitting variations in treatment? Or would the world be a better place if a single standard were adopted? If so, what should that standard be?

4. As noted by Lord Justice Jacob in *Aerotel*, the broad approach to patent eligibility evidenced by *State Street* in the United States put pressure on other countries to do likewise. Consider the advice for China offered by two commentators:

> As a nation relatively lagging behind others in the IPR field, China should intensify its research on business method patent theory and legislation, and study of cases in the area, draw on the experience of the developed countries, such as the U.S., Japan, and European countries, [and] learn from their lessons. . .

Steve Song & Guowei Liu, *Patent Eligibility of Business Methods in China from US Perspective*, CHINA PATENTS & TRADEMARKS 54, 59 (2011).

What lessons should China and other emerging economies take away from the experience of the United States and Europe regarding business method patents?

C. PATENTABILITY OF PHARMACEUTICALS AND DIAGNOSTIC METHODS

As noted in Chapter 3, while many countries have historically allowed patents on *processes* to make drugs, the patenting of pharmaceutical *products* has been controversial in many countries for a very long time. Drugs can mean the difference between life and death, giving governments and the public strong interest in their development and protection. But drugs can also be extremely profitable, and patent protection can play a significant role in that profitability. Consider the following discussion of the development of pharmaceutical patenting across borders by Professor Dutfield:

> Historically, it was common to exclude medicines from patentability ostensibly because it was deemed immoral, though this was often really to protect domestic infant industries. Sometimes it was considered to be rather shocking for health researchers to even consider applying for a patent. Such policies and views may

and do shift in light of experience, as happened in Britain after penicillin. But moral considerations may continue to create legal uncertainties in patent law and affect attempts at substantive legal harmonization across jurisdictions and in international law.

. . . .

[T]he modern pharmaceutical industry can be said, in part, to be an offshoot of the dyestuff industry. . . .

With the patenting of fine chemicals and processes to make them, new science-based industries appeared almost from nothing and these generated huge revenues. The patent stakes for such firms, whether they were innovators or imitators, were immense. Consequently, success depended often on clever use of the patent systems of their own countries *and* of their overseas markets. Their ability to be strategic about patenting . . . depended on what patent laws allowed them to protect, or to get away with. Consequently, the chemical industries became active lobbyists influencing as far as they could the drafting of patent laws. Where they found underprotection (as they saw it), companies would join with rivals to persuade the government to strengthen protection. Where they found overprotection, they would lobby either for less protection, or alternatively collaborate with other firms to mitigate market distortions arising from either too many patents or from the monopolies created by small numbers of overly broad patents. They would do this, for example, by pooling their patents or shifting their operations to neighboring countries. When patents were insufficient to keep prices high for lengthy periods, companies sometimes formed price-fixing cartels. When one looks at the business practices of today's pharmaceutical and biotechnology companies, it becomes obvious that these lessons were learned from the dyemakers 130 years earlier when they were starting also to make drugs. Furthermore, governments became aware of the economic stakes involved and consequently became very interested not only in their own patent laws but in those of their perceived economic competitors. Again, this is very much the case today.

GRAHAM DUTFIELD, INTELLECTUAL PROPERTY RIGHTS & THE LIFE SCIENCE INDUSTRIES: PAST, PRESENT & FUTURE 7, 12-13 (2nd ed. World Scientific 2009).

The patent eligibility of pharmaceuticals had been clearly established in all developed countries by the late 1980s and has been further reaffirmed by Article 27 of the TRIPS Agreement. With respect to developing countries, the majority of which did not afford patent protection to pharmaceuticals prior to the conclusion of the Uruguay Round, the TRIPS

Agreement mandated the recognition of patent eligibility of pharmaceutical innovation within ten years after the effective date of the Agreement (i.e. by 1 January, 2005). However, even after the expiration of the ten-year transitional period, some developing countries, seeking to advance their domestic public health concerns, have attempted to finesse their TRIPS obligations with respect to the protection of pharmaceuticals, a move that has drawn heavy criticism from the pharmaceutical industry as well as threats of trade sanctions by certain developed countries.

1. PHARMACEUTICALS

Consider the following challenge to a patentability limitation in the amended Indian Patent Act of 2005:

NOVARTIS AG V. UNION OF INDIA

In the High Court of Judicature at Madras
W.P. Nos.24759 and 24760 of 2006
(Madras H.C., Aug. 6, 2007)

COMMON ORDER

[Novartis brought this action challenging a decision of the Indian Patent Office, which rejected claims to a different form of the company's anti-leukemia drug Gleevec based on Section 3(d) of the amended Indian Patent Act.]

2. In this judgment, for convenience sake, we will hereinafter refer [to] the [Indian] Patents Act as the "Principal Act"; Ordinance 7/2004 introducing an amendment to section 3(d) of the Act as the "Ordinance"; Amending Act of 2005 amending section 3(d) of the Act as the "Amending Act"; section 3(d) as the amended section and the Act after the amendment as the "Amended Act". The challenge to the amended section is mainly on two grounds namely,

(a) it is not compatible to the Agreement on Trade Related Aspects of Intellectual Property Rights, hereinafter referred to as "TRIPS" for convenience sake; and

(b) it is arbitrary, illogical, vague and offends Article 14 of the Constitution of India.

For a better understanding of the attack to the amended section, we feel that it is desirable to extract hereunder section 3(d) of the Principal Act; the nature of amendment to that section sought to be brought in by the Ordinance and the amended section itself:

"Unamended section 3(d):

[The following are not inventions within the meaning of this Act-...] [t]he mere discovery of any new property or new use of a known substance or of the mere use of a known process, machine or apparatus unless such known process results in a new product or employs at least one new reactant.

. . . .

Section 3(d) as amended by the Patents (Amendment) Act, 2005 with effect from 01.01.2005:

> [The following are not inventions within the meaning of this Act-...] [t]he mere discovery of a new form of a known substance which does not result in the enhancement of the known efficacy of that substance or the mere discovery of any new property or new use for a known substance or of the mere use of a known process, machine or apparatus unless such known process results in a new product or employs at least one new reactant.

Explanation [provided in the Amended Act to section 3(d) as amended by the Patents (Amendment) Act]:

> For the purposes of this clause, salts, esters, ethers, polymorphs, metabolites, pure form, particle size isomers, mixtures of isomers, complexes, combinations and other derivatives of known substance shall be considered to be the same substance, unless they differ significantly in properties with regard to efficacy."

. . . .

5. On the submissions made by the learned senior counsels on either side, we are of the considered opinion that the following issues arise for consideration in [this case]:

> (a) Assuming that the amended section is in clear breach of Article 27 of "TRIPS" and thereby suffers the wise of irrationality and arbitrariness violating Article 14 of the Constitution of India, could the courts in India have jurisdiction to test the validity of the amended section in the back drop of such alleged violation of "TRIPS"? OR
>
> Even if the amended section cannot be struck down by this court for the reasons stated above, cannot this court grant a declaratory relief that the amended section is not in compliance of Article 27 of "TRIPS"?
>
> (b) If it is held that courts in India have jurisdiction to go into the above referred to issue, then, is the amended section compatible or non-compatible to Article 27 of "TRIPS"?
>
> (c) Dehors issues (a) and (b) referred to above, could the amended section be held to be violative of Article 14 of the Constitution of India on the ground of vagueness, arbitrariness and conferring un-canalised powers on the Statutory Authority?

6. Let us take the first issue.

. . . .

8. . . . [W]e are of the considered view that in whichever manner one may name it namely, International Covenant, International Treaty, International Agreement and so on and so forth, yet, such documents are essentially in the nature of a contract. . . .

Therefore there cannot be any difficulty at all in examining such treaties on principles applied in examining contracts. Under these circumstances, when a dispute is brought before a court arising out of an International Treaty, courts would not be committing any error in deciding the said dispute on principles applicable to contracts. In other words, the court has to analyse the terms of such International Treaty; the enforceability of the same; by whom and against whom; and if there is violation, is there a mechanism for solving that dispute under the treaty itself? Based on such construction of the International Treaty namely, "TRIPS", it is argued very strenuously by the learned counsels appearing for the contesting parties that there is a settlement mechanism under the Treaty itself and therefore even assuming without conceding that the petitioner has the right to enforce the terms of the said Treaty, yet, he must go only before the Dispute Settlement Body provided under the "TRIPS" itself. Article 64 of "TRIPS" is pressed into service to sustain this point. It is contended by [the counsel for the respondents] that the settlement mechanism provided under Article 64 of "TRIPS" is governed by the procedure as understood by the World Trade Organisation. [Respondents' counsel] took us through the said Dispute Settlement Understanding . . . and we find that it contains comprehensive provisions for resolving the disputes arising out of any [WTO agreement, including TRIPS] . . . . Therefore we have no difficulty at all that Article 64 of "TRIPS" read with World Trade Organisation's understanding on Rules and Procedures governing the settlement of disputes provides a comprehensive settlement mechanism of any dispute arising under the [TRIPS] [A]greement. Article 3 of the Rules declares that the dispute settlement system of the World Trade Organisation is to provide security and predictability to the multilateral trading system. When such a comprehensive dispute settlement mechanism is provided as indicated above and when it cannot be disputed that it is binding on the member States, we see no reason at all as to why the petitioner, which itself is a part of that member State, should not be directed to have the dispute resolved under the dispute settlement mechanism referred to above. Several nations in the world are parties to "TRIPS" as well as the [Agreement Establishing the WTO]. The agreements are discussed, finalised and entered into at the higher level of the nations participating in such meeting. Therefore it is binding on them. When such participating nations, having regard to the terms of the agreement and the complex problems that may arise out of the agreement between nation[s] . . . , decide that every participating nation shall have a Common Dispute Settlement Mechanism, we see no reason at all as to why we must disregard it. As we began saying that any International Agreement possesses the basic nature of an ordinary contract and when courts respect the choice of jurisdiction fixed under such ordinary contract, we see no compelling reasons to deviate from such judicial approach when we consider the choice of forum arrived at in International Treaties. Since we have held that this court has no jurisdiction to decide the validity of the amended section, being in violation of Article 27 of "TRIPS", we are not going into the question whether any individual is conferred with an enforceable right under "TRIPS" or not. For the same reason, we also hold that we are not deciding issue No.(b) namely, whether the amended section is compatible to Article 27 of "TRIPS" or not.

. . . .

10. Let us now take the last issue for consideration. . . .

. . . .

16. . . . [Relying on precedent], it is clear that Article 14 [of the Indian Constitution] can be invoked only when it is shown that in the exercise of a discretionary power there is a possibility of a real and substantial discrimination and such exercise interferes with the fundamental right guaranteed by the Constitution. . . . It is not shown by the learned senior counsels appearing for the petitioners before us that in the exercise of the discretionary power by the Patent controller, any of the petitioner's fundamental rights are violated namely, to carry on the trade or the petitioner stand singularly discriminated. We find that the amended section by itself does not discriminate nor does it prohibit the trade being carried on.

. . . .

18. . . . [T]he amended section has in-built measures to guide the Statutory Authority in exercising its power under the Act. We have also found that the amended section does not suffer from the vice of vagueness, ambiguity and arbitrariness. The Statutory Authority would be definitely guided in deciding whether a discovery is an invention or not by the materials to be placed before him by the Patent applicant. If that is so, . . . we have to necessarily state that the amended section cannot be invalidated solely on the ground that there is a possibility of misusing the power.

19. . . . [F]or all the reasons stated above, on issue (c) we hold that the amended section is not in violation of Article 14 of the Constitution of India. . . .

NOTES AND QUESTIONS

1. Review Article 3(d) of the Indian Patent Act excerpted in the *Novartis* case. As a matter of statutory construction, should it be read as a limitation

on patentable subject matter or as an interpretation of patentability criteria such as non-obviousness? How did the *Novartis* court construe Article 3(d)? You should return to this question after you have read Chapter 7.

2. Should the interpretation of Article 3(d) of the Indian Patent Act be subject to scrutiny by an international body? How would you make the case that Article 3(d) of the Indian Patent Act is consistent with Article 27 of the TRIPS Agreement? How would you make the case that it is inconsistent? Which argument do you think is most compelling? What do you think is the intended purpose of Article 3(d)? For a recent article discussing the normative and strategic importance of India's creative implementation of TRIPS obligations, including Article 3(d), and highlighting its importance for other developing countries and the international intellectual property system generally, *see* Amy Kapczynski, *Harmonization and Its Discontents: A Case Study of TRIPS Implementation in India's Pharmaceutical Sector*, 97 CAL. L. REV. 1571 (2009).

3. One of the subject matter topics on which countries diverge is the treatment of claims to "new uses" of known substances, in particular claims to a second medical use or indication or new forms of a known compound. Such claims are of special interest in the pharmaceutical arena as a way to extend the market exclusivity of a drug in a strategy called "life cycle management" or, more perjoratively, "evergreening." As explained by the European Generic Medicines Association:

> Evergreening, in one common form, occurs when the brand-name manufacturer literally "stockpiles" patent protection by obtaining separate 20-year patents on multiple attributes of a single product. These patents can cover everything from aspects of the manufacturing process to tablet colour, or even a chemical produced by the body when the drug is ingested and metabolised by the patient.

> In the 1980s the list of a drug's properties eligible for patenting was relatively limited. They included: primary uses, processes and intermediates, bulk forms, simple formulations, [and] composition of matter.

> During the 1990s the catalogue grew to 18, nearly four times the amount of a decade earlier, to include patents on such additional aspects as: expansive numbers of uses, methods of treatment, mechanism of action, packaging, delivery profiles, dosing regimen, dosing range, dosing route, combinations, screening methods, chemistry methods, biological target[s], and field of use. . . .

Eur. Generic Med. Assoc., *Evergreening: Evergreening of Pharmaceutical Market Protection*, available at http://198.170.119.137/gen-evergrn.html (last visited July 2, 2012).

Many countries allow such patent claims, including the United States, Canada and member countries of the EPO; however, some do not, such as India, as discussed in the Novartis case. To what extent is the issue of the patentability of a new form of a compound, such as a salt, a question of patent subject matter as opposed to novelty or inventive step?

4. In addition to Article 3(d), several other controversial amendments to the Indian Patent Act relate to the protection of pharmaceuticals. Professor Basheer provides a useful overview of the provisions and associated issues in *India's Tryst with TRIPS*, 1 INDIAN J.L. & TECH. 15 (2005). For a concise overview of India's TRIPS compliance issues and the *Novartis* case, *see* Janice Mueller, *Taking TRIPS to India: Novartis, Patent Law and Access to Medicines*, 356 NEW ENG. J. MED. 541 (2007).

5. Novartis appealed its loss in the *Novartis v. Union of India* case to the Indian Supreme Court. Novartis challenged the legality of Section 3(d) of the Patent Act as well as how Section 3(d) is being applied by the Patent Office. Novartis claims that the fact that its new form of Gleevec (alternate spelling) has reduced side effects should suffice for a showing of enhanced efficacy, while the Patent Office position is that a drug must show enhanced therapeutic efficacy. Patient advocate groups have picketed Novartis headquarters demanding that the company drop the case and stating that "the case that Novartis is pursuing in India is really aimed at closing down any space left for generic companies to operate [sic] [a]nd to really push TRIPS-plus and IP-plus measures on India in a way that will really constrain not only the medicine in question, but any future medicines." Rachel Marusak Hermann, *Novartis Before India's Supreme Court: What's Really at Stake?*, INTELL. PROP. WATCH (Mar. 2, 2012). Novartis disputes that contention and argues that India is denying it the intellectual property protection it counts on to fuel future R&D research. Which argument do you find more compelling? On April 1, 2013, the Indian Supreme Court affirmed the decision of the Patent Office rejecting the patentability of Gleevec under §3(d) of the Indian Patent Act. See *Norvatis AG v. Union of India and Others*, Civil Appeal Nos. 2717-2727 of 2013 (Supreme Court of India).

---

2. DIAGNOSTIC METHODS

Traditional pharmaceutical development has focused on disease targets and developing drugs that are used on a wide variety of patients. But differences in a patient's genetic or metabolic profile, for example, can cause a drug not to be effective in treating a particular condition. Developments in personalized medicine seek to change that, by allowing drug treatments to be tailored to individuals based on the analysis of a variety of information about them in conjunction with known information about a particular drug.

Some patents relating to personalized drug treatment raise profound concerns as they seem to cover fundamental truths about correlations in the known world. That issue came before the U.S. Supreme Court in *Labcorp. v. Metabolite* in 2006, but the Court dismissed certiorari as improvidently granted as the subject matter eligibility issue had not been properly raised in the lower court. Justice Breyer's dissent from the Court's decision not to decide the case is quoted in the *State Street Bank* discussion in Section 3 above regarding business method patents. The two Justices who joined Breyer in the *Labcorp* dissent, Stephens and Souter, are no longer on the Court; nevertheless, in a unanimous decision that carried clear echoes of his *Labcorp* dissent, Justice Breyer further explored the patent subject matter limits in 35 U.S.C. § 101 as they relate to diagnostic methods.

MAYO COLLABORATIVE SERVICES V. PROMETHEUS LABORATORIES, INC.

United States Supreme Court
132 S. Ct. 1289 (2012)

■ BREYER, J., delivered the opinion for a unanimous Court.

. . . .

I

A

The patents before us concern the use of thiopurine drugs in the treatment of autoimmune diseases, such as Crohn's disease and ulcerative colitis. When a patient ingests a thiopurine compound, his body metabolizes the drug, causing metabolites to form in his bloodstream. Because the way in which people metabolize thiopurine compounds varies, the same dose of a thiopurine drug affects different people differently, and it has been difficult for doctors to determine whether for a particular patient a given dose is too high, risking harmful side effects, or too low, and so likely ineffective.

At the time the discoveries embodied in the patents were made, scientists already understood that the levels in a patient's blood of certain metabolites, including, in particular, 6–thioguanine and its nucleotides (6–TG) and 6–methyl–mercaptopurine (6–MMP), were correlated with the likelihood that a particular dosage of a thiopurine drug could cause harm or prove ineffective. *See* U.S. Patent No. 6,355,623, col.8, ll.37–40, 2 App. 10. ("Previous studies suggested that measurement of 6–MP metabolite levels can be used to predict clinical efficacy and tolerance to azathioprine or 6–MP" (citing Cuffari, Théorêt, Latour, & Seidman, 6–Mercaptopurine Metabolism in Crohn's Disease: Correlation with Efficacy and Toxicity, 39 Gut 401 (1996))). But those in the field did not know the precise correlations between metabolite levels and likely harm or ineffectiveness. The patent claims at issue here set forth processes embodying researchers' findings that identified these correlations with some precision.

More specifically, the patents—U.S. Patent No. 6,355,623 ('623 patent) and U.S. Patent No. 6,680,302 ('302 patent)—embody findings that concentrations in a patient's blood of 6–TG or of 6–MMP metabolite beyond a certain level (400 and 7000 picomoles per 8x10 ^{8} red blood cells, respectively) indicate that the dosage is likely too high for the patient, while concentrations in the blood of 6–TG metabolite lower than a certain level (about 230 picomoles per 8x10 ^{8} red blood cells) indicate that the dosage is likely too low to be effective.

The patent claims seek to embody this research in a set of processes. Like the Federal Circuit we take as typical claim 1 of the 623 Patent, which describes one of the claimed processes as follows:

> "A method of optimizing therapeutic efficacy for treatment of an immune-mediated gastrointestinal disorder, comprising:

> "(a) administering a drug providing 6–thioguanine to a subject having said immune-mediated gastrointestinal disorder; and

> "(b) determining the level of 6–thioguanine in said subject having said immune-mediated gastrointestinal disorder,

> "wherein the level of 6–thioguanine less than about 230 pmol per 8x10 ^{8} red blood cells indicates a need to increase the amount of said drug subsequently administered to said subject and

> "wherein the level of 6–thioguanine greater than about 400 pmol per 8x10 ^{8} red blood cells indicates a need to decrease the amount of said drug subsequently administered to said subject." '623 patent, col.20, ll.10–20, 2 App. 16.

For present purposes we may assume that the other claims in the patents do not differ significantly from claim 1.

B

Respondent, Prometheus Laboratories, Inc. (Prometheus), is the sole and exclusive licensee of the '623 and '302 patents. It sells diagnostic tests that embody the processes the patents describe. For some time petitioners, Mayo Clinic Rochester and Mayo Collaborative Services (collectively Mayo), bought and used those tests. But in 2004 Mayo announced that it intended to begin using and selling its own test—a test using somewhat higher metabolite levels to determine toxicity (450 pmol per $8x10^8$ for 6–TG and 5700 pmol per $8x10^8$ for 6–MMP). Prometheus then brought this action claiming patent infringement.

The District Court found that Mayo's test infringed claim 7 of the '623 patent. In interpreting the claim, the court accepted Prometheus' view that the toxicity-risk level numbers in Mayo's test and the claim were too similar to render the tests significantly different. The number Mayo used (450) was too close to the number the claim used (400) to matter given appropriate margins of error. The District Court also accepted Prometheus' view that a doctor using Mayo's test could violate the patent even if he did not actually alter his treatment decision in the light of the test. In doing so, the court construed the claim's language, "indicates a need to decrease" (or "to increase"), as not limited to instances in which the doctor actually decreases (or increases) the dosage level where the test results suggest that such an adjustment is advisable. [S]ee also Brief for Respondent (describing claimed processes as methods "for improving . . . treatment . . . by using individualized metabolite measurements *to inform* the calibration of . . . dosages of . . . thiopurines" (emphasis added)).

Nonetheless the District Court ultimately granted summary judgment in Mayo's favor. The court reasoned that the patents effectively claim natural laws or natural phenomena—namely the correlations between thiopurine metabolite levels and the toxicity and efficacy of thiopurine drug dosages—and so are not patentable.

On appeal, the Federal Circuit reversed. It pointed out that in addition to these natural correlations, the claimed processes specify the steps of (1) "administering a [thiopurine] drug" to a patient and (2) "determining the [resulting metabolite] level." These steps, it explained, involve the transformation of the human body or of blood taken from the body. Thus, the patents satisfied the Circuit's "machine or transformation test," which the court thought sufficient to "confine the patent monopoly within rather definite bounds," thereby bringing the claims into compliance with § 101. . . .

Mayo filed a petition for certiorari. We granted the petition, vacated the judgment, and remanded the case for reconsideration in light of *Bilski,* 130 S. Ct. 3218, which clarified that the "machine or transformation test" is not a definitive test of patent eligibility, but only an important and useful clue. *Id.,* at 130 S. Ct., at 3234–3235. On remand the Federal Circuit reaffirmed its earlier conclusion. It thought that the "machine-or-transformation test," understood merely as an important and useful clue, nonetheless led to the "clear and compelling conclusion . . . that the . . . claims . . . do not encompass laws of nature or preempt natural correlations." 628 F.3d 1347, 1355 (2010). Mayo again filed a petition for certiorari, which we granted.

II

Prometheus' patents set forth laws of nature—namely, relationships between concentrations of certain metabolites in the blood and the likelihood that a dosage of a thiopurine drug will prove ineffective or cause harm. Claim 1, for example, states that *if* the levels of 6–TG in the blood (of patient who has taken a dose of a thiopurine drug) exceed about 400 pmol per 8x10⁸ red blood cells, *then* the administered dose is likely to produce toxic side effects. While it takes a human action (the administration of a thiopurine drug) to trigger a manifestation of this relation in a particular person, the relation itself exists in principle apart from any human action. The relation is a consequence of the ways in which thiopurine compounds are metabolized by the body—entirely natural processes. And so a patent that simply describes that relation sets forth a natural law.

The question before us is whether the claims do significantly more than simply describe these natural relations. To put the matter more precisely, do the patent claims add *enough* to their statements of the correlations to allow the processes they describe to qualify as patent-eligible processes that *apply* natural laws? We believe that the answer to this question is no.

A

If a law of nature is not patentable, then neither is a process reciting a law of nature, unless that process has additional features that provide practical assurance that the process is more than a drafting effort designed to monopolize the law of nature itself. A patent, for example, could not simply recite a law of nature and then add the instruction "apply the law." Einstein, we assume, could not have patented his famous law by claiming a process consisting of simply telling linear accelerator operators to refer to the law to determine how much energy an amount of mass has produced (or vice versa). Nor could Archimedes have secured a patent for his famous principle of flotation by claiming a process consisting of simply telling boat builders to refer to that principle in order to determine whether an object will float.

What else is there in the claims before us? The process that each claim recites tells doctors interested in the subject about the correlations that the researchers discovered. In doing so, it recites an "administering" step, a "determining" step, and a "wherein" step. These additional steps are not themselves natural laws but neither are they sufficient to transform the nature of the claim.

First, the "administering" step simply refers to the relevant audience, namely doctors who treat patients with certain diseases with thiopurine drugs. That audience is a pre-existing audience; doctors used thiopurine drugs to treat patients suffering from autoimmune disorders long before anyone asserted these claims. In any event, the "prohibition against patenting abstract ideas 'cannot be circumvented by attempting to limit the use of the formula to a particular technological environment.'" *Bilski, supra,* 130 S. Ct., at 3230 (quoting *Diehr,* 450 U.S., at 191–192).

Second, the "wherein" clauses simply tell a doctor about the relevant natural laws, at most adding a suggestion that he should take those laws into account when treating his patient. That is to say, these clauses tell the relevant audience about the laws while trusting them to use those laws appropriately where they are relevant to their decisionmaking (rather like Einstein telling linear accelerator operators about his basic law and then trusting them to use it where relevant).

Third, the "determining" step tells the doctor to determine the level of the relevant metabolites in the blood, through whatever process the doctor or the laboratory wishes to use. As the patents state, methods for determining metabolite levels were well known in the art. '623 patent, col.9, ll.12–65, 2 App. 11. Indeed, scientists routinely measured metabolites as part of their investigations into the relationships between metabolite levels and efficacy and toxicity of thiopurine compounds. '623 patent, col.8, ll.37–40, *id.,* at 10. Thus, this step tells doctors to engage in well-understood, routine, conventional activity previously engaged in by scientists who work in the field. Purely "conventional or obvious""[pre]-solution activity" is normally not sufficient to transform an unpatentable law of nature into a patent-eligible application of such a law. *Flook,* 437 U.S. at 590; *see also Bilski,* 130 S. Ct., at 3230 ("[T]he prohibition against patenting abstract ideas 'cannot be circumvented by' . . . adding 'insignificant post-solution activity'" (quoting *Diehr, supra,* at 191–192)).

Fourth, to consider the three steps as an ordered combination adds nothing to the laws of nature that is not already present when the steps are considered separately. *See Diehr, supra,* at 188, ("[A] new combination of steps in a process may be patentable even though all the constituents of the combination were well known and in common use before the combination was made"). Anyone who wants to make use of these laws must first administer a thiopurine drug and measure the resulting metabolite concentrations, and so the combination amounts to nothing significantly more than an instruction to doctors to apply the applicable laws when treating their patients.

The upshot is that the three steps simply tell doctors to gather data from which they may draw an inference in light of the correlations. To put the matter more succinctly, the claims inform a relevant audience about certain laws of nature; any additional steps consist of well-understood, routine, conventional activity already engaged in by the scientific community; and those steps, when viewed as a whole, add nothing significant beyond the sum of their parts taken separately. For these reasons we believe that the steps are not sufficient to transform unpatentable natural correlations into patentable applications of those regularities.

B

1

A more detailed consideration of the controlling precedents reinforces our conclusion. The cases most directly on point are *Diehr* and *Flook,* two cases in which the Court reached opposite conclusions about the patent eligibility of processes that embodied the equivalent of natural laws. The *Diehr* process (held patent eligible) set forth a method for molding raw, uncured rubber into various cured, molded products. The process used . . . the Arrhenius equation, to determine when . . . to open the press. It consisted in effect of the steps of: (1) continuously monitoring the temperature on the inside of the mold, (2) feeding the resulting numbers into a computer, which would use the Arrhenius equation to continuously recalculate the mold-opening time, and (3) configuring the computer so that at the appropriate moment it would signal "a device" to open the press. *Diehr,* 450 U.S., at 177–179.

The Court pointed out that the basic mathematical equation, like a law of nature, was not patentable. But it found the overall process patent eligible because of the way the additional steps of the process integrated the equation into the process as a whole. . . . It nowhere suggested that all these steps, or at least the combination of those steps, were in context obvious, already in use, or purely conventional. And so the patentees did not "seek to pre-empt the use of [the] equation," but sought "only to foreclose from others the use of that equation in conjunction with all of the other steps in their claimed process." *Ibid.* These other steps apparently added to the formula something that in terms of patent law's objectives had significance—they transformed the process into an inventive application of the formula.

The process in *Flook* (held not patentable) provided a method for adjusting "alarm limits" in the catalytic conversion of hydrocarbons. . . . The claimed process amounted to an improved system for updating . . . alarm limits through the steps of: (1) measuring the current level of the variable, *e.g.,* the temperature; (2) using an apparently novel mathematical algorithm to calculate the current alarm limits; and (3) adjusting the system to reflect the new alarm-limit values. . . .

The Court, as in *Diehr,* pointed out that the basic mathematical equation, like a law of nature, was not patentable. But it characterized the claimed process as doing nothing other than "provid[ing] a[n unpatentable] formula for computing an updated alarm limit. . . . [T]he other steps in the process did not limit the claim to a particular application. Moreover, "[t]he chemical processes involved in catalytic conversion of hydrocarbons[,] . . . the practice of monitoring the chemical process variables, the use of alarm limits to trigger alarms, the notion that alarm limit values must be recomputed and readjusted, and the use of computers for 'automatic monitoring-alarming'" were all "well known," to the point where, putting the formula to the side, there was no "inventive concept" in the claimed application of the formula. *Id.,* at 594."[P]ost-solution activity" that is purely "conventional or obvious," the Court wrote, "can[not] transform an unpatentable principle into a patentable process."*Id.,* at 589, 590.

The claim before us presents a case for patentability that is weaker than the (patent-eligible) claim in *Diehr* and no stronger than the (unpatentable) claim in *Flook.* Beyond picking out the relevant audience, namely those who administer doses of thiopurine drugs, the claim simply tells doctors to: (1) measure (somehow) the current level of the relevant metabolite, (2) use particular (unpatentable) laws of nature (which the claim sets forth) to calculate the current toxicity/inefficacy limits, and (3) reconsider the drug dosage in light of the law. These instructions add nothing specific to the laws of nature other than what is well-understood, routine, conventional activity, previously engaged in by those in the field. And since they are steps that must be taken in order to apply the laws in question, the effect is simply to tell doctors to apply the law somehow when treating their patients. The process in *Diehr* was not so characterized; that in *Flook* was characterized in roughly this way.

2

Other cases offer further support for the view that simply appending conventional steps, specified at a high level of generality, to laws of nature, natural phenomena, and abstract ideas cannot make those laws, phenomena, and ideas patentable. . . .

. . . .

In *Bilski* the Court considered claims covering a process for hedging risks of price changes by, for example, contracting to purchase commodities from sellers at a fixed price, reflecting the desire of sellers to hedge against a drop in prices, while selling commodities to consumers at a fixed price, reflecting the desire of consumers to hedge against a price increase. One claim described the process; another reduced the process to a mathematical formula. . . . The Court held that the described "concept of hedging" was "an unpatentable abstract idea." . . . The fact that some of the claims limited hedging to use in commodities and energy markets and specified that "well-known random analysis techniques [could be used] to help establish some of the inputs into the equation" did not undermine this conclusion, for "*Flook* established that limiting an abstract idea to one field of use or adding token postsolution components did not make the concept patentable." . . .

. . . .

3

. . . .

[E]ven though rewarding with patents those who discover new laws of nature and the like might well encourage their discovery, those laws and principles, considered generally, are "the basic tools of scientific and technological work." . . . And so there is a danger that the grant of patents that tie up their use will inhibit future innovation premised upon them, a danger that becomes acute when a patented process amounts to no more than an instruction to "apply the natural law," or otherwise forecloses more future invention than the underlying discovery could reasonably justify. *See* generally Lemley, Risch, Sichelman, & Wagner, *Life After* Bilski, 63 STAN. L. REV. 1315 (2011) (hereinafter Lemley, et al.,) (arguing that § 101 reflects this kind of concern); *see also* C. Bohannan & H. Hovenkamp, *Creation without Restraint: Promoting Liberty and Rivalry in Innovation* 112 (2012) ("One problem with [process] patents is that the more abstractly their claims are stated, the more difficult it is to determine precisely what they cover. They risk being applied to a wide range of situations that were not anticipated by the patentee"); W. Landes & R. Posner, *The Economic Structure of Intellectual Property Law* 305–306 (2003) (The exclusion from patent law of basic truths reflects "both . . . the enormous potential for rent seeking that would be created if property rights could be obtained in them and . . . the enormous transaction costs that would be imposed on would-be users [of those truths]").

The laws of nature at issue here are narrow laws that may have limited applications, but the patent claims that embody them nonetheless implicate this concern. They tell a treating doctor to measure metabolite levels and to consider the resulting measurements in light of the statistical relationships they describe. In doing so, they tie up the doctor's subsequent treatment decision whether that treatment does, or does not, change in light of the inference he has drawn using the correlations. And they threaten to inhibit the development of more refined treatment recommendations (like that embodied in Mayo's test), that combine Prometheus' correlations with later discovered features of metabolites, human physiology or individual patient characteristics. The "determining" step too is set forth in highly general language covering all processes that make use of the correlations after measuring metabolites, including later discovered processes that measure metabolite levels in new ways.

. . . .

III

We have considered several further arguments in support of Prometheus' position. But they do not lead us to adopt a different conclusion. First, the Federal Circuit, in upholding the patent eligibility of the claims before us, relied on this Court's determination that "[t]ransformation and reduction of an article 'to a different state or thing' is *the clue* to the patentability of a process claim that does not include particular machines." . . . It reasoned that the claimed processes are therefore patent eligible, since they involve transforming the human body by administering a thiopurine drug and transforming the blood by analyzing it to determine metabolite levels. 628 F.3d, at 1356–1357.

The first of these transformations, however, is irrelevant. As we have pointed out, the "administering" step simply helps to pick out the group of individuals who are likely interested in applying the law of nature. *See supra*, at 1297. And the second step could be satisfied without transforming the blood, should science develop a totally different system for determining metabolite levels that did not involve such a transformation. *See supra*, at 1302. Regardless, in stating that the "machine-or-transformation" test is an *"important and useful clue "* to patentability, we have neither said nor implied that the test trumps the "law of nature" exclusion. *Bilski, supra,* 130 S. Ct., at 3225–3227 (emphasis added). That being so, the test fails here.

Second, Prometheus argues that, because the particular laws of nature that its patent claims embody are narrow and specific, the patents should be upheld. Thus, it encourages us to draw distinctions among laws of nature based on whether or not they will interfere significantly with innovation in other fields now or in the future. Brief for Respondent 42–46; *see also* Lemley 1342–1344 (making similar argument).

But the underlying functional concern here is a *relative* one: how much future innovation is foreclosed relative to the contribution of the inventor. A patent upon a narrow law of nature may not inhibit future research as seriously as would a patent upon Einstein's law of relativity, but the creative value of the discovery is also considerably smaller. And, as we have previously pointed out, even a narrow law of nature (such as the one before us) can inhibit future research. . . .

In any event, our cases have not distinguished among different laws of nature according to whether or not the principles they embody are sufficiently narrow. *See, e.g., Flook,* 437 U.S. 584 (holding narrow mathematical formula unpatentable). And this is understandable. Courts and judges are not institutionally well suited to making the kinds of judgments needed to distinguish among different laws of nature. And so the cases have endorsed a bright-line prohibition against patenting laws of nature, mathematical formulas and the like, which serves as a somewhat more easily administered proxy for the underlying "building-block" concern.

. . . .

Fourth, Prometheus, supported by several *amici,* argues that a principle of law denying patent coverage here will interfere significantly with the ability of medical researchers to make valuable discoveries, particularly in the area of diagnostic research. That research, which includes research leading to the discovery of laws of nature, is expensive; it "ha[s] made the United States the world leader in this field"; and it requires protection. Brief for Respondent 52.

Other medical experts, however, argue strongly against a legal rule that would make the present claims patent eligible, invoking policy considerations that point in the opposite direction. The American Medical Association, the American College of Medical Genetics, the American Hospital Association, the American Society of Human Genetics, the Association of American Medical Colleges, the Association for Molecular Pathology, and other medical organizations tell us that if "claims to exclusive rights over the body's natural responses to illness and medical treatment are permitted to stand, the result will be a vast thicket of exclusive rights over the use of critical scientific data that must remain widely available if physicians are to provide sound medical care." Brief for American College of Medical Genetics et al. as *Amici Curiae* 7; *see also* App. to Brief for Association Internationale pour la Protection de la Propriete Intellectuelle et al. as *Amici Curiae* A6, A16 (methods of medical treatment are not patentable in most of Western Europe).

We do not find this kind of difference of opinion surprising. Patent protection is, after all, a two-edged sword. On the one hand, the promise of exclusive rights provides monetary incentives that lead to creation, invention, and discovery. On the other hand, that very exclusivity can impede the flow of information that might permit, indeed spur, invention, by, for example, raising the price of using the patented ideas once created, requiring potential users to conduct costly and time-consuming searches of existing patents and pending patent applications, and requiring the negotiation of complex licensing arrangements. At the same time, patent law's general rules must govern inventive activity in many different fields of human endeavor, with the result that the practical effects of rules that reflect a general effort to balance these considerations may differ from one field to another. *See* Bohannan & Hovenkamp, Creation without Restraint, at 98–100.

In consequence, we must hesitate before departing from established general legal rules lest a new protective rule that seems to suit the needs of one field produce unforeseen results in another. And we must recognize the role of Congress in crafting more finely tailored rules where necessary. Cf. 35 U.S.C. §§ 161–164 (special rules for plant patents). We need not determine here whether, from a policy perspective, increased protection for discoveries of diagnostic laws of nature is desirable.

* * *

For these reasons, we conclude that the patent claims at issue here effectively claim the underlying laws of nature themselves. The claims are consequently invalid. And the Federal Circuit's judgment is reversed.

NOTES AND QUESTIONS

1. In *Mayo*, the Court further clarified the limits of the machine or transformation (MOT) test, setting a higher bar for transformation than had the Federal Circuit. As in *Bilski*, the Court eschewed the use of bright line rules or shortcuts in analyzing subject matter eligibility.

In one sense, *Mayo* unites two strands of controversial patent subject matter: biotechnology (implicating products of nature) and business methods/computer-implemented inventions (implicating abstract ideas), a joining that clearly can be seen in *Ass'n for Molecular Pathology v. Myriad Genetics,*

Inc., 132 S. Ct. 1794 (2012), opinion below, 653 F.3d 1329 (Fed. Cir. 2011). Shortly after deciding *Mayo*, the Supreme Court granted cert. in *Myriad* and vacated and remanded the case for consideration in light of *Mayo.* In *Myriad*, a large group of plaintiffs (patients, researchers, organizations and others all represented by the American Civil Liberties Union and The Public Patent Foundation) challenged the validity of selected claims in several of Myriad's patents on the Breast Cancer Susceptibility Genes (BRCA 1 and BRCA2) and related methods, as ineligible under § 101. Judge Robert Sweet of the District Court for the Southern District of New York invalidated all of the claims, finding claims to isolated DNA and cDNA to be unpatentable as lacking characteristics "markedly different" from sequences found in nature. He also invalidated claims to various methods, such as "detecting a germline alteration in a BRCA1 gene" by analyzing a sequence from a human sample as abstract idea comparisons that failed the MOT test.

The Federal Circuit reversed as to all except the method of comparison claims, concluding that the isolated DNA and cDNA claims constituted patent-eligible subject matter because, among other things, covalent bonds were broken in the isolation process. Also, the court upheld the following method claim as patent eligible:

> 20. A method for screening potential cancer therapeutics which comprises: growing a transformed eukaryotic host cell containing an altered BRCA1 gene causing cancer in the presence of a compound suspected of being a cancer therapeutic, growing said transformed eukaryotic host cell in the absence of said compound, determining the rate of growth of said host cell in the presence of said compound and the rate of growth of said host cell in the absence of said compound and comparing the growth rate of said host cells, wherein a slower rate of growth of said host cell in the presence of said compound is indicative of a cancer therapeutic.

653 F.3d at 1335.

Do you think this claim is patent eligible in light of *Mayo v. Prometheus*? For a classic study on the issues associated with patenting DNA, *see* Nuffield Council on Bioethics, *The Ethics of Patenting DNA: A Discussion Paper* (2002). On November 30, 2012, the U.S. Supreme Court again granted certiorari in the *Myriad* case to decide the single question "Are human genes patentable?"

Interestingly, in Australia, Myriad's BRCA patent claims were also upheld by a lower court as a "manner of manufacture," the statutory patent eligibility requirement in the Australian Patent Act. While disagreeing with the U.S. Federal Circuit's reasoning, the judge *in Cancer Voices Australia v Myriad Genetics Inc.* [2013] FCA 65, concluded that the composition of matter claims covered a manner of manufacture. After concluding the that gene patent claims were patent eligible because "a product that consists of an artificially created state of affairs which has economic significance will constitute a 'manner of manufacture,'" the judge referred to the U.S. case:

. . . it seems to me that the[U.S.] *Myriad* decision does not provide any direct assistance to either side in the present case. I say this for two reasons. First, the law in Australia is different. . . It must also be recognised, especially as the *Myriad* case heads to the US Supreme Court, that the constitutional setting in which patent legislation operates in the US is quite different to that in which patent legislation operates in this country. Secondly, the evidence in the *Myriad* case was not the same as the evidence in the present cast. And at least in relation to the matter of covalent bonds, I have taken a different view of the facts to that taken by Judge Lourie.

Id. at para. 135. An appeal in this case is expected.

2. Two months after deciding *Mayo*, the U.S. Supreme Court was again faced with a petition for certiorari involving an alleged abstract idea. In *WildTangent, Inc. v. Ultramercial, LLC,* 132 S. Ct. 2431 (2012), opinion *infra*, *Ultramercial, LLC v. Hulu, LLC,* 657 F.3d 1323 (Fed. Cir. 2011) the question presented was "[w]hether, or in what circumstances, a patent's general and indeterminate references to 'over the Internet' or at 'an Internet website' are sufficient to transform an unpatentable abstract idea into a patentable process for purposes of 35 U.S.C. § 101"?" Petition for a Writ of Certiorari at i, WildTangent, Inc. v. Ultramercial, LLC, 132 S. Ct. 2431 (2012). In the court below, Judge Rader, writing for the panel, had downplayed the significance of the § 101 inquiry:

> The '545 patent claims a method for distributing copyrighted products (e.g., songs, movies, books) over the Internet where the consumer receives a copyrighted product for free in exchange for viewing an advertisement, and the advertiser pays for the copyrighted content. . . .
>
> . . . .
>
> [A]s § 101 itself expresses, subject matter eligibility is merely a threshold check; claim patentability ultimately depends on "the conditions and requirements of this title," such as novelty, nonobviousness, and adequate disclosure. By directing attention to these substantive criteria for patentability, the language of § 101 makes clear that the categories of patent-eligible subject matter are no more than a "coarse eligibility filter." In other words, the expansive categories—process, machine, article of manufacture, and composition of matter—are certainly not substitutes for the substantive patentability requirements set forth in § 102, § 103, and § 112 and invoked expressly by § 101 itself.

Id. at 1324–1326.

Judge Rader appeared to suggest that less focus be put on the Section 101 inquiry and more on Sections 102, 103 and 112, an argument he made explicitly in additional views in *Classen Immunotherapies, Inc. v. Biogen IDEC*, 659 F.3d 1057 (Fed. Cir. 2011):

This court should decline to accept invitations to restrict subject matter eligibility. . . .

The patent eligibility doctrine has always had significant unintended implications. . . . For instance, eligibility restrictions usually engender a healthy dose of claim-drafting ingenuity. In almost every instance, patent claim drafters devise new claim forms and language that evade the subject matter exclusions. These evasions, however, add to the cost and complexity of the patent system. . . .

By creating obstacles to patent protection, the real-world impact is to frustrate innovation and drive research funding to more hospitable locations. To be direct, if one nation makes patent protection difficult, it will drive research to another, more accommodating, nation.

Id. at 1074–1075.

Interestingly, this argument also was advanced by the government in *Mayo v. Prometheus.* But in a portion of the decision not reproduced above, the Court in *Mayo* declined to pursue such a course noting:

[T]he Government argues that virtually any step beyond a statement of a law of nature itself should transform an unpatentable law of nature into a potentially patentable application sufficient to satisfy § 101's demands. Brief for United States as *Amicus Curiae.* The Government does not necessarily believe that claims that (like the claims before us) extend just minimally beyond a law of nature should receive patents. But in its view, other statutory provisions—those that insist that a claimed process be novel, 35 U.S.C. § 102, that it not be "obvious in light of prior art," § 103, and that it be "full[y], clear[ly], concise[ly], and exact[ly]" described, § 112—can perform this screening function. In particular, it argues that these claims likely fail for lack of novelty under § 102.

This approach, however, would make the "law of nature" exception to § 101 patentability a dead letter. The approach is therefore not consistent with prior law. The relevant cases rest their holdings upon section 101, not later sections. . . .

We recognize that, in evaluating the significance of additional steps, the § 101 patent-eligibility inquiry and, say, the § 102 novelty inquiry might sometimes overlap. But that need not always be so. And to shift the patent-eligibility inquiry entirely to these later sections risks creating significantly greater legal uncertainty, while assuming that those sections can do work that they are not equipped to do.

What role would laws of nature, including newly discovered (and "novel") laws of nature, play in the Government's suggested "novelty" inquiry? Intuitively, one would suppose that a newly discovered law of nature is novel. The Government, however, suggests in effect that the novelty of a component law of nature may be disregarded when evaluating the novelty of the whole. But §§ 102 and 103 say nothing about treating laws of nature as if they were part of the prior art when applying those sections. Cf. *Diehr,* 450 U.S., at 188, 101 S. Ct. 1048 (patent claims "must be considered as a whole"). And studiously ignoring *all* laws of nature when evaluating a patent application under §§ 102 and 103 would "make all inventions unpatentable because all inventions can be reduced to underlying principles of nature which, once known, make their implementation obvious." *Id.,* at 189, n. 12. *See also* Eisenberg, Wisdom of the Ages or Dead–Hand Control? Patentable Subject Matter for Diagnostic Methods After *In re Bilski,* 3 Case W. Res. J.L. Tech. & Internet 1 (2012); 2 D. Chisum, Patents § 5.03[3] (2005). . . .

. . . .

These considerations lead us to decline the Government's invitation to substitute §§ 102, 103, and 112 inquiries for the better established inquiry under § 101.

Who do you think has the better argument, Judge Rader or Justice Breyer, and why? For a scholarly article also making this proposal *see* Dennis D. Crouch & Robert P. Merges, *Operating Efficiently Post-*Bilski *by Ordering Patent Doctrine Decision-Making,* 25 BERKELEY TECH. L.J.1673 (2010). On May 20, 2012, the U.S. Supreme Court granted cert. in *WildTangent* and vacated and remanded the decision for the Federal Circuit to reconsider in light of *Mayo v. Prometheus. WildTangent, Inc. v. Ultramercial, LLC,* 132 S. Ct. 2431 (2012).

3. While the Court articulates and relies on the non-statutory exclusions from patent-eligible subject matter—laws of nature, physical phenomena and abstract ideas—it says very little about their origins. According to Professor Sarnoff, the exclusions have deep roots in a rather surprising place:

By the late eighteenth century, notwithstanding changing theological conceptions and the growth of atheism, nature was understood as "one grand, interrelated design, comprehensible by rational investigation," the understanding of which would benefit all humans. During this period, invention was still understood in the classical sense of uncovering something in nature that had been present all along, through the mechanism of divine providence in permitting human access to such knowledge. The divine creations of science, nature, and broad abstract ideas that were revealed to humanity through the efforts of scientists and philosophers, "those favoured mortals . . . who share that ray of divinity which we call genius," were thus intended to be freely available. And "[i]f the inventor was no more than God's instrument in bringing His gifts to the community, then he could at most claim user's rights over them."

Moreover, the divine origins of discoveries of nature, and their initial status as commons property, imposed moral duties to freely share knowledge of science, nature, and ideas. . . . As Edward Walterscheid noted, the medieval belief that "genius was a gift of God . . . largely precluded an earlier development of the concept of intellectual property. For how could one properly seek to obtain commercial value from that which was perceived to have been granted by the grace of God?" Although times were changing, they had not done so for patents on science, nature, and ideas—and still have not done so.

. . . .

Further, it was commonly recognized at that time that property rights in functional ideas (inventions) . . . did not arise under natural law. Such invention rights could exist only by the positive act of a government—through the grant of patents—and were not otherwise recognized at common law. Utilitarian philosophers in the late eighteenth century therefore felt the need to articulate a call for government intervention to create rights to inventions as incentives for their production and distribution. But these positive law rights did not and, given contemporaneous deontological moral beliefs, could not attach to the science, nature, and ideas themselves, only to the creative human applications that the inventor had actually discovered. And, as aptly put by the late nineteenth century patent law scholar William Robinson, the religious prohibition on creating such property and the obligation to share new discoveries corresponded with the utilitarian goal of promoting progress, whether understood as creative development or as dissemination: "To benefit by the discoveries of his fellow-men is thus not only a natural right, it is also the natural duty which every man owes to himself and to society; and the mutual, universal progress thence resulting is the fulfillment of the earthly destiny of the human race." As described above, these commitments have been preserved throughout the more than two hundred years of American patent law doctrine; we continue to recognize the exclusions for science, nature, and ideas as a matter of stare decisis.

Joshua D. Sarnoff, *Patent-Eligible Inventions After Bilski: History and Theory*, 63 HASTINGS L.J. 53, 89–90 (2011). Should the religious origins and purposes of the exclusions be relevant to their interpretation and application today?

CHAPTER 5

UTILITY

■ ■ ■

Utility, referred to most often as industrial applicability or usefulness, is a further requirement of patentability. Utility is one of the oldest consistently applied patentability requirements in the world. Recall from Chapter 1 the Venetian Patent Act of 1474, which required the invention to have been "reduced to perfection so that it can be *used* and operated." Article 27.1 of the TRIPS Agreement requires patents to be available for inventions in all areas of technology so long as the inventions "are new, involve an inventive step and are capable of industrial application" and notes that "capable of industrial application" may be deemed synonymous with "useful." However, the standard for satisfying the utility requirement is relatively modest throughout the world, and patent challenges on grounds of lack of utility are infrequent, especially for electrical or mechanical inventions. The utility requirement does not mandate that an invention be a commercial success or that it represent an improvement over the prior art. In the United States, for example, the utility requirement simply derives from the pronouncement in 35 U.S.C. § 101 that "whoever invents . . . any new and *useful* process . . . may obtain a patent therefor . . . ." Thus, utility may be found even though an invention is unimportant, inconsequential, or just plain silly. Consider U.S. Patent No. 4,608,967 (the '967 patent), issued in 1986, which discloses a "Pat on the Back Apparatus," which is defined as "[a] self-congratulatory apparatus having a simulated human hand [that is] manually swingable into and out of contact with the user's back."

The drawing below from the patent illustrates the apparatus and how it works. The patent specification states that the invention "is useful for providing a self-administered pat-on-the-back or a congratulatory gesture" and that it "may be used for amusement or for a needed psychological lift." Such statements, which are rarely questioned by patent examiners even if the invention's proposed benefit seems slight or ridiculous, are generally more than sufficient to meet the utility threshold.

PAT ON THE BACK APPARATUS – US PATENT NO. 4,608,967

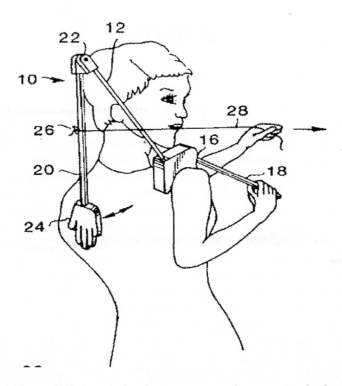

Nonetheless, differences in the way countries approach the utility requirement suggest that this invention might fail the standard in some jurisdictions. It is not at all certain that the "Pat on the Back" apparatus would meet an industrial applicability standard in countries that require an invention to be capable of exploitation in an industry. These differences in approach to the utility requirement should not be surprising in light of our discussion in Chapter 1 of the varying national views of the patent system, including the manufacturing and policy-oriented perspectives that were evident in local working requirements codified in the patent laws of many countries. Recall that such working requirements were also present in the Statute of Monopolies as well as in the Venetian Patent Act.

As we shall see in this Chapter, employing a more or less restrictive utility requirement can allow a country to further important policy objectives. For example, requiring a practical, presently available, specific and substantial utility can limit the patenting of upstream research; imposing a requirement of usefulness in an industry can immunize personal activity from infringement liability; and invoking a requirement of social utility can deny a government imprimatur to morally controversial inventions. In the next section, we explore the most basic expression of the utility requirement—"practical" or "specific utility"—as applied to the patenting of early stage inventions in the United States and the UK.

A. PRACTICAL UTILITY: UPSTREAM RESEARCH

1. UNITED STATES

In the United States, the utility requirement has both a constitutional and a statutory dimension. Article 1, sec. 8, cl. 8 of the Constitution authorizes Congress to grant exclusive rights to promote the progress of "useful" arts, which at the time meant helpful or valuable trades. The low threshold for utility evident in most technological areas in the United States is generally traced to the case of *Bedford v. Hunt*, 3 F. Cas. 37 (C.C.D. Mass. 1817). In that decision, Justice Story defined the meaning of the term "useful":

> By useful invention, in the statute, is meant such a one as may be applied to some beneficial use in society, in contradistinction to an invention, which is injurious to the morals, the health, or the good order of society. It is not necessary to establish, that the invention is of such general utility, as to supersede all other inventions now in practice to accomplish the same purpose. It is sufficient, that it has no obnoxious or mischievous tendency, that it may be applied to practical uses, and that so far as it is applied, it is salutary. If its practical utility be very limited, it will follow, that it will be of little or no profit to the inventor; and if it be trifling, it will sink into utter neglect. The law, however, does not look to the degree of utility; it simply requires, that it shall be capable of use, and that the use is such as sound morals and policy do not discountenance or prohibit.

Id. at 37.

Thus, at a minimum, to be useful, an invention must work (operable utility), and it must be applicable to practical uses (practical utility). Under such a standard, meeting the utility requirement would not be an issue for the vast majority of inventions (except in the area of morally controversial inventions, discussed in more detail in section C, *infra*). However, advances in the chemical and biotechnology fields have led to an increase in so-called "speculative" inventions: inventions with the potential for significant benefit to society, but whose use is not yet known. These sorts of inventions, which may involve gene sequences, genetic fragments, nucleotide sequences, proteins, molecules, or other complex compounds, pose to patent examiners and courts around the world the issue of how to distinguish between speculation and utility. At what point does the former become the latter? The U.S. Supreme Court first addressed this issue in the following case.

EDWARD J. BRENNER, COMMISSIONER OF PATENTS V. MANSON

Supreme Court of the United States
383 U.S. 519 (1966)

■ Mr. Justice FORTAS delivered the opinion of the Court.

. . . .

In December 1957, Howard Ringold and George Rosenkranz applied for a patent on an allegedly novel process for making certain known steroids. . . . United States Patent No. 2,908,693 issued late in 1959.

In January 1960, respondent Manson . . . filed an application to patent precisely the same process described by Ringold and Rosenkranz. He asserted that it was he who had discovered the process, and that he had done so before December 17, 1956. Accordingly, he requested that an 'interference' be declared in order to try out the issue of priority between his claim and that of Ringold and Rosenkranz.

A Patent Office examiner denied Manson's application, and the denial was affirmed by the Board of Appeals within the Patent Office. The ground for rejection was the failure 'to disclose any utility for' the chemical compound produced by the process. . . . This omission was not cured, in the opinion of the Patent Office, by Manson's [later] reference to an article in the November 1956 issue of the Journal of Organic Chemistry . . . which revealed that steroids of a class which included the compound in question were undergoing screening for possible tumor inhibiting effects in mice, and that a homologue [a chemically related compound] adjacent to Manson's steroid had proven effective in that role. . . .

The Court of Customs and Patent Appeals (hereinafter CCPA) reversed . . . . Certiorari was granted . . . to resolve this running dispute over what constitutes 'utility' in chemical process claims. . . .

. . . .

II.

Our starting point is the proposition, neither disputed nor disputable, that one may patent only that which is "useful." . . . Suffice it to say that the concept of utility has maintained a central place in all of our patent legislation, beginning with the first patent law in 1790 and culminating in the present law's provision that 'Whoever invents or discovers any new and useful process, machine, manufacture, or composition of matter, or any new and useful improvement thereof, may obtain a patent therefor, subject to the conditions and requirements of this title.'

As is so often the case, however, a simple, everyday word can be pregnant with ambiguity when applied to the facts of life. That this is so is demonstrated by the present conflict between the Patent Office and the CCPA over how the test is to be applied to a chemical process which yields an already known product whose utility-other than as a possible object of scientific inquiry-has not yet been evidenced. . . .

. . . .

The second and third points of respondent's argument present issues of much importance. Is a chemical process 'useful' within the meaning of § 101 either (1) because it works—i.e., produces the intended product? or (2) because the compound yielded belongs to a class of compounds now the subject of serious scientific investigation? These contentions present the basic problem for our adjudication. Since we find no specific assistance in the legislative materials underlying § 101, we are remitted to an analysis of the problem in light of the general intent of Congress, the purposes of the patent system, and the implications of a decision one way or the other.

In support of his plea that we attenuate the requirement of 'utility,' respondent relies upon Justice Story's well-known statement that a 'useful' invention is one 'which may be applied to a beneficial use in society, in contradistinction to an invention injurious to the morals, health, or good order of society, or frivolous and insignificant' [*Lowell v. Lewis*]—and upon the assertion that to do so would encourage inventors of new processes to publicize the event for the benefit of the entire scientific community, thus widening the search for uses and increasing the fund of scientific knowledge. Justice Story's language sheds little light on our subject. Narrowly read, it does no more than compel us to decide whether the invention in question is 'frivolous and insignificant'—a query no easier of application than the one built into the statute. Read more broadly, so as to allow the patenting of any invention not positively harmful to society, it places such a special meaning on the word 'useful' that we cannot accept it in the absence of evidence that Congress so intended. There are, after all, many things in this world which may not be considered 'useful' but which, nevertheless are totally without a capacity for harm.

It is true, of course, that one of the purposes of the patent system is to encourage dissemination of information concerning discoveries and inventions. And it may be that inability to patent a process to some extent discourages disclosure and leads to greater secrecy than would otherwise be the case. The inventor of the process, or the corporate organization by which he is employed, has some incentive to keep the invention secret while uses for the product are searched out. However, in light of the highly developed art of drafting patent claims so that they disclose as little useful information as possible-while broadening the scope of the claim as widely as possible-the argument based upon the virtue of disclosure must be warily evaluated. Moreover, the pressure for secrecy is easily exaggerated, for if the inventor of a process cannot himself ascertain a 'use' for that which his process yields, he has every incentive to make his invention known to those able to do so. Finally, how likely is disclosure of a patented process to spur research by others into the uses to which the product may be put? To the extent that the patentee has power to enforce his patent, there is little incentive for others to undertake a search for uses.

Whatever weight is attached to the value of encouraging disclosure and of inhibiting secrecy, we believe a more compelling consideration is that a process patent in the chemical field, which has not been developed and pointed to the degree of specific utility, creates a monopoly of knowledge which should be granted only if clearly commanded by the statute. Until the process claim has been reduced to production of a product shown to be useful, the metes and bounds of that monopoly are not capable of precise delineation. It may engross a vast, unknown, and perhaps unknowable area. Such a patent may confer power to block off whole areas of scientific development, without compensating benefit to the public. The basic quid pro quo contemplated by the Constitution and the Congress for granting a patent monopoly is the benefit derived by the public from an invention with substantial utility. Unless and until a process is refined and developed to this point—where specific benefit exists in currently available form—there is insufficient justification for permitting an applicant to engross what may prove to be a broad field.

. . . .

This is not to say that we mean to disparage the importance of contributions to the fund of scientific information short of the invention of something 'useful,' or that we are blind to the prospect that what now seems without 'use' may tomorrow command the grateful attention of the public. But a patent is not a hunting license. It is not a reward for the search, but compensation for its successful conclusion. . . .

The judgment of the CCPA is reversed.

Mr. Justice HARLAN, concurring in part and dissenting in part.

. . . .

Respondent has contended that a workable chemical process, which is both new and sufficiently nonobvious to satisfy the patent statute, is by its existence alone a contribution to chemistry and 'useful' as the statute employs that term. Certainly this reading of 'useful' in the statute is within the scope of the constitutional grant, which states only that '(t)o promote the Progress of Science and useful Arts,' the exclusive right to 'Writings and Discoveries' may be secured for limited times to those who produce them. Art. I, s 8. Yet the patent statute is somewhat differently worded and is on its face open both to respondent's construction and to the contrary reading given it by the Court. In the absence of legislative history on this issue, we are thrown back on policy and practice. Because I believe that the Court's policy arguments are not convincing and that past practice favors the respondent, I would reject the narrow definition of 'useful' and uphold the judgment of the Court of Customs and Patent Appeals (hereafter CCPA).

The Court's opinion sets out about half a dozen reasons in support of its interpretation. Several of these arguments seem to me to have almost no force. For instance, it is suggested that '(u)ntil the process claim has been reduced to production of a product shown to be useful, the metes and bounds of that monopoly are not capable of precise delineation' . . . and '(i)t may engross a vast, unknown, and perhaps unknowable area.' . . . . I fail to see the relevance of these assertions; process claims are not disallowed because the products they produce may be of 'vast' importance nor, in any event, does advance knowledge of a specific product use provide much safeguard on this score or fix 'metes and bounds' precisely since a hundred more uses may be found after a patent is granted and greatly enhance its value.

The further argument that an established product use is part of '(t)he basic quid pro quo' . . . for the patent or is the requisite 'successful conclusion' . . . of the inventor's search appears to beg the very question whether the process is 'useful' simply because it facilitates further research into possible product uses. The same infirmity seems to inhere in the Court's argument that chemical products lacking immediate utility cannot be distinguished for present purposes from the processes which create them, that respondent appears to concede and the CCPA holds that the products are nonpatentable, and that therefore the processes are nonpatentable. Assuming that the two classes cannot be distinguished, a point not adequately considered in the briefs, and assuming further that the CCPA has firmly held such products nonpatentable, this permits us to conclude only that the CCPA is wrong either as to the products or as to the processes and affords no basis for deciding whether both or neither should be patentable absent a specific product use.

More to the point, I think, are the Court's remaining, prudential arguments against patentability: namely, that disclosure induced by allowing a patent is partly undercut by patent-application drafting techniques, that disclosure may occur without granting a patent, and that a patent will discourage others from inventing uses for the product. How far opaque drafting may lessen the public benefits resulting from the issuance of a patent is not shown by any evidence in this case but, more important, the argument operates against all patents and gives no reason for singling out the class involved here. The thought that these inventions may be more likely than most to be disclosed even if patents are not allowed may have more force; but while empirical study of the industry might reveal that chemical researchers would behave in this fashion, the abstractly logical choice for them seems to me to maintain secrecy until a product use can be discovered. As to discouraging the search by others for product uses, there is no doubt this risk exists but the price paid for any patent is that research on other uses or improvements may be hampered because the original patentee will reap much of the reward. From the standpoint of the public interest the Constitution seems to have resolved that choice in favor of patentability.

What I find most troubling about the result reached by the Court is the impact it may have on chemical research. Chemistry is a highly interrelated field and a tangible benefit for society may be the outcome of a number of different discoveries, one discovery building upon the next. To encourage one chemist or research facility to invent and disseminate new processes and products may be vital to progress, although the product or process be without 'utility' as the Court defines the term, because that discovery permits someone else to take a further but perhaps less difficult step leading to a commercially useful item. In my view, our awareness in this age of the importance of achieving and publicizing basic research should lead this Court to resolve uncertainties in its favor and uphold the respondent's position in this case.

. . . .

Fully recognizing that there is ample room for disagreement on this problem when, as here, it is reviewed in the abstract, I believe the decision below should be affirmed.

NOTES AND QUESTIONS

1. The Court's interpretation of the utility requirement in *Brenner v. Manson* reflects a policy choice regarding the point at which patent protection should be given to an invention. In one sense, the quid pro quo of the patent grant (disclosure in exchange for exclusivity) is not satisfied by being able to successfully make a compound that has no known use. Deferring the patent grant until the use of the compound is both known and disclosed in the patent application ensures a threshold level of informational benefit to the public and maintains incentives for other researchers to continue to explore beneficial uses for the technology. According to the Court, in the absence of a known utility for an invention, granting a patent may amount to "permitting an applicant to engross what may prove to be a broad field." Do you agree or do you side with the dissent? What policy objective do you think the Court was trying to advance? Is a robust utility requirement the most effective doctrinal tool to accomplish the task? What about the costs, some of which were mentioned by the dissent, of reserving patent protection only for inventions with known utility?

2. The UK Patent Office *Examination Guidelines for Patent Applications Relating to Biotechnological Inventions* (2009) echo a concern similar to the Court's in *Brenner v. Manson*. Citing the 1996 UK Court of Appeal decision in *Chiron v. Murex Diagnostics, Ltd.*, [1996] F.S.R. 153 (Eng. C.A.), the Guidelines state:

In *Chiron Corp*, the Court of Appeal observed that section 4(1) is not satisfied if the product made is useless. . . . It is therefore necessary to consider whether the invention claimed has a useful purpose, and whether the specification identifies any practical way of exploiting it. It is not the purpose of a patent to reserve an unexplored field of research for an applicant.

Id. at paragraph 51.

Likewise, in its submission to WIPO's Standing Committee on Patents (SCP), the Brazilian Association of Intellectual Property (ABPI) asserted that Article 15 of the Brazilian Industrial Property Law has a similar requirement for known utility. Article 15 of the Brazilian Patent Law provides that "inventions . . . are considered to be susceptible of industrial application when they can be made or used in any kind of industry." According to ABPI, this implies that an invention "must: (i) be feasible, i.e., it can be reduced to practice; (ii) *have a known utility*, otherwise it would not have a practical application; and (iii) be of a technical or technological nature, otherwise it would not relate to industry." *See* WIPO, *"Industrial Applicability" and "Utility" Requirements: Commonalities and Differences,* WIPO Doc. SCP/9/5 at 4 (2003).

3. As mentioned previously, the TRIPS Agreement makes utility a condition of international patent law by incorporating it into the Agreement's provisions on patentable subject matter. TRIPS Article 27.1 requires that patents be made available for inventions that are "capable of industrial application" or, in the terminology preferred by the U.S., Australia and Canada, for inventions which are "useful." For definitional purposes however, footnote 5 of Article 27 states that the phrase "'capable of industrial application' may be deemed by a Member to be synonymous with the [term] . . . 'useful'. . . ." In sum, the TRIPS Agreement accommodates the jurisprudence associated with the two concepts. Despite the difference in terminology, the two concepts overlap significantly. Nevertheless, there can be distinctions in the emphasis placed on certain requirements depending on what standard is adopted by a given country, and a difference in which inventions qualify for patent protection. A country may adopt either terminology (with its associated nuances or distinctive areas of emphasis) and be fully in compliance with its TRIPS obligations.

4. In the United States, inventions in many industries encounter no problems with practical utility, resulting in a differential application of the utility requirement for inventions in the chemical and biotechnology arena which tend to be more susceptible, as a class, to having this deficiency. As explained by Professors Burk and Lemley:

Beginning with *Brenner v. Manson*, the courts have required proof that a new chemical molecule or chemical process display some concrete and terminal application before it can be patented. In the case of pharmaceuticals, the PTO subsequently elevated this holding to require proof of therapeutic efficacy before a patent could issue. The Federal Circuit has weakened this rule somewhat, holding that indicators of therapeutic efficacy, such as animal modeling or in vitro data, can satisfy the utility requirement. . . .

Under these cases, the standard for utility in the life sciences is different—and substantially higher—than the standard in any other industry. This higher standard is similarly apparent in a related life sciences manifestation of the *Brenner* legacy regarding patents on DNA molecules, especially short or partial gene sequences such as ESTs. The PTO's Utility Guidelines for such patents require a showing of "specific," "substantial," and "credible" applications not found in examination of other technologies. . . .

Thus, the utility doctrine constitutes an example of a macro policy lever: It creates a blanket rule for one set of cases that differs from the rule in others. . . .

Dan L. Burk & Mark A. Lemley, *Policy Levers in Patent Law*, 89 VA. L. REV. 1575, 1644–1646 (2003).

Does the TRIPS Agreement require consistent application of the utility standard across domestic sectors? Read Articles 7 and 8 of the TRIPS Agreement. In what ways might the requirement of known utility as articulated by the Court in *Brenner* contribute to the ideals expressed in these provisions?

———————

The *Brenner* decision was criticized by many as having the potential to inhibit research in the chemical area and as deviating from established law. As a result, it was construed narrowly and limited to its particular facts. The applicant supplied no utility for the steroids produced by the claimed process at the time of filing. In fact, in *In re Brana*, 51 F.3d 1560 (Fed. Cir. 1995), the U.S. Court of Appeals for the Federal Circuit relaxed the utility requirement post-*Brenner* in the area of pharmaceuticals in a case that also dealt with anti-tumor steroidal compounds. There, the court did not even mention *Brenner v. Manson* despite the similarities in subject matter and issue. However, beginning in the late 1980s, the USPTO began to receive increasing numbers of applications on gene-related patent inventions, many of which raised the same kinds of early-stage patenting policy concerns as did the invention in *Brenner v. Manson*. In 2001, the USPTO published Utility Guidelines to aid examiners (and applicants) dealing with such applications. While the Guidelines applied to all applications, they were deemed to be "particularly relevant in areas of emerging technologies, such as gene-related technologies, where uses for new materials that have not been fully characterized are not readily apparent." *See* Final Guidelines for Determining Utility of Gene-Related Inventions, *available at* www.uspto.gov/news/pr/2001/01-01.jsp. The Guidelines deemed rejections inappropriate for inventions with a "well-established utility," and explained that:

> An invention has a well-established utility (1) if a person of ordinary skill in the art would immediately appreciate why the invention is useful based on the characteristics of the invention (e.g., properties

or applications of a product or process), and (2) the utility is specific, substantial, and credible.

Examiners were further instructed that:

> If the applicant has asserted that the claimed invention is useful for any particular practical purpose (i.e., it has a "specific and substantial utility") and the assertion would be considered credible by a person of ordinary skill in the art, do not impose a rejection based on lack of utility.

66 Fed. Reg. 1092 (2001).

USPTO ignores Brenner ruling.

The following case concerning the patenting of Expressed Sequence Tags, or ESTs, gene fragments that can be used as research tools, provided a vehicle for the Federal Circuit to revisit the reasoning of *Brenner v.* Manson, and to consider the viability of the USPTO's Utility Examination Guidelines.

IN RE DANE K. FISHER AND RAGHUNATH V. LALGUDI

United States Court of Appeals, Federal Circuit
421 F.3d 1365 (Fed. Cir. 2005)

■ MICHEL, Chief Judge.

Dane K. Fisher and Raghunath Lalgudi (collectively "Fisher") appeal from the decision of the U.S. Patent and Trademark Office ("PTO") Board of Patent Appeals and Interferences ("Board") affirming the examiner's final rejection of the only pending claim of application Serial No. 09/619,643 (the "'643 application"), entitled "Nucleic Acid Molecules and Other Molecules Associated with Plants," as unpatentable for lack of utility under 35 U.S.C. § 101 . . . .

. . . .

The claimed invention relates to five purified nucleic acid sequences that encode proteins and protein fragments in maize plants. The claimed sequences are commonly referred to as "expressed sequence tags" or "ESTs." Before delving into the specifics of this case, it is important to understand more about the basic principles of molecular genetics and the role of ESTs.

Genes are located on chromosomes in the nucleus of a cell and are made of deoxyribonucleic acid ("DNA"). DNA is composed of two strands of nucleotides in double helix formation. The nucleotides contain one of four bases, adenine ("A"), guanine ("G"), cytosine ("C"), and thymine ("T"), that are linked by hydrogen bonds to form complementary base pairs (i.e., A-T and G-C).

When a gene is expressed in a cell, the relevant double-stranded DNA sequence is transcribed into a single strand of messenger ribonucleic acid ("mRNA"). Messenger RNA contains three of the same bases as DNA (A, G, and C), but contains uracil ("U") instead of thymine. mRNA is released from the nucleus of a cell and used by ribosomes found in the cytoplasm to produce proteins.

Complementary DNA ("cDNA") is produced synthetically by reverse transcribing mRNA. cDNA, like naturally occurring DNA, is composed of nucleotides containing the four nitrogenous bases, A, T, G, and C. Scientists routinely compile cDNA into libraries to study the kinds of genes expressed in a certain tissue at a particular point in time. One of the goals of this research is to learn what genes and downstream proteins are expressed in a cell so as to regulate gene expression and control protein synthesis.

An EST is a short nucleotide sequence that represents a fragment of a cDNA clone. It is typically generated by isolating a cDNA clone and sequencing a small number of nucleotides located at the end of one of the two cDNA strands. When an EST is introduced into a sample containing a mixture of DNA, the EST may hybridize with a portion of DNA. Such binding shows that the gene corresponding to the EST was being expressed at the time of mRNA extraction.

Claim 1 of the '643 application recites:

A substantially purified nucleic acid molecule that encodes a maize protein or fragment thereof comprising a nucleic acid sequence selected from the group consisting of SEQ ID NO: 1 through SEQ ID NO: 5.

The ESTs set forth in SEQ ID NO: 1 through SEQ ID NO: 5 are obtained from cDNA library LIB3115, which was generated from pooled leaf tissue harvested from maize plants . . . grown in the fields at Asgrow research stations. SEQ ID NO:1 through SEQ ID NO:5 consist of 429, 423, 365, 411, and 331 nucleotides, respectively. When Fisher filed the '643 application, he claimed ESTs corresponding to genes expressed from the maize pooled leaf tissue at the time of anthesis. Nevertheless, Fisher did not know the precise structure or function of either the genes or the proteins encoded for by those genes.

The '643 application generally discloses that the five claimed ESTs may be used in a variety of ways, including: (1) serving as a molecular marker for mapping the entire maize genome, which consists of ten chromosomes that collectively encompass roughly 50,000 genes; (2) measuring the level of mRNA in a tissue sample via microarray technology to provide information about gene expression; (3) providing a source for primers for use in the polymerase chain reaction ("PCR") process to enable rapid and inexpensive duplication of specific genes; (4) identifying the presence or absence of a polymorphism; (5) isolating promoters via chromosome walking; (6) controlling protein expression; and (7) locating genetic molecules of other plants and organisms. . . .

In a final rejection, dated September 6, 2001, the examiner rejected claim 1 for lack of utility under § 101. The examiner found that the claimed ESTs were not supported by a specific and substantial utility. She concluded that the disclosed uses were not specific to the claimed ESTs, but instead were generally applicable to any EST. For example, the examiner noted that any EST may serve as a molecular tag to isolate genetic regions. She also concluded that the claimed ESTs lacked a substantial utility because there was no known use for the proteins produced as final products resulting from processes involving the claimed ESTs. The examiner stated: "Utilities that require or constitute carrying out further research to identify or reasonably confirm a 'real world' context of use are not substantial utilities."

. . . .

The Board considered each of Fisher's seven potential uses . . . [and] concluded that Fisher's asserted uses for the claimed ESTs tended to the "insubstantial use" end of the spectrum between a substantial and an insubstantial utility.

The Board also concluded that using the claimed ESTs to isolate nucleic acid molecules of other plants and organisms, which themselves had no known utility, is not a substantial utility. . . .

Additionally, the Board addressed the remaining asserted utilities, highlighting in particular the use of the claimed ESTs to monitor gene expression by measuring the level of mRNA through microarray technology and to serve as molecular markers. The Board found that using the claimed ESTs in screens does not provide a specific benefit because the application fails to provide any teaching regarding how to use the data relating to gene expression. . . . The Board analogized the facts to those in *Brenner v. Manson,* 383 U.S. 519 (1966), in which an applicant claimed a process of making a compound having no known use. In that case, the Supreme Court affirmed the rejection of the application on § 101 grounds. Here, the Board reasoned: "Just as the process in *Brenner* lacked utility because the specification did not disclose how to use the end-product, the products claimed here lack utility, because even if used in gene expression assays, the specification does not disclose how to use SEQ ID NO: 1–5 specific gene expression data." . . . The Board offered a similar rationale for the use of the claimed ESTs as molecular markers. . . . Accordingly, the Board affirmed the examiner's rejection of the '643 application for lack of utility under § 101. . . .

. . . .

Fisher asserts that the Board unilaterally applied a heightened standard for utility in the case of ESTs, conditioning patentability upon "some undefined 'spectrum' of knowledge concerning the corresponding gene function." Fisher contends that the standard is not so high and that

Congress intended the language of § 101 to be given broad construction. In particular, Fisher contends that § 101 requires only that the claimed invention "not be frivolous, or injurious to the well-being, good policy, or good morals of society," essentially adopting Justice Story's view of a useful invention from *Lowell v. Lewis* . . . . Under the correct application of the law, Fisher argues, the record shows that the claimed ESTs provide seven specific and substantial uses, regardless whether the functions of the genes corresponding to the claimed ESTs are known. . . .

. . . .

We agree . . . that none of Fisher's seven asserted uses meets the utility requirement of § 101. Section 101 provides: "Whoever invents . . . any new and *useful* . . . composition of matter . . . may obtain a patent therefor . . . ." *(*Emphasis added*)*. In *Brenner,* the Supreme Court explained what is required to establish the usefulness of a new invention . . . . Contrary to Fisher's argument that § 101 only requires an invention that is not "frivolous, injurious to the well-being, good policy, or good morals of society," the Supreme Court appeared to reject Justice Story's de minimis view of utility. . . . In its place, the Supreme Court announced a more rigorous test, stating:

> The basic *quid pro quo* contemplated by the Constitution and the Congress for granting a patent monopoly is the benefit derived by the public from an invention with *substantial utility*. Unless and until a process is refined and developed to this point—where *specific benefit exists in currently available form*—there is insufficient justification for permitting an applicant to engross what may prove to be a broad field. (emphases added).

Following *Brenner,* our predecessor court, the Court of Customs and Patent Appeals, and this court have required a claimed invention to have a specific and substantial utility to satisfy § 101. . . .

. . . .

Courts have used the labels "practical utility" and "real world" utility interchangeably in determining whether an invention offers a "substantial" utility. Indeed, the Court of Customs and Patent Appeals stated that "'[p]ractical utility' is a shorthand way of attributing 'real-world' value to claimed subject matter. In other words, one skilled in the art can use a claimed discovery in a manner which provides some *immediate benefit to the public*." . . . It thus is clear that an application must show that an invention is useful to the public as disclosed in its current form, not that it may prove useful at some future date after further research. Simply put, to satisfy the "substantial" utility requirement, an asserted use must show that that claimed invention has a significant and presently available benefit to the public. . . .

. . . .

Turning to the "specific" utility requirement, an application must disclose a use which is not so vague as to be meaningless. . . . Thus, in addition to providing a "substantial" utility, an asserted use must also show that that claimed invention can be used to provide a well-defined and particular benefit to the public. . . .

We agree with the Board that the facts here are similar to those in *Brenner*. There, as noted above, the applicant claimed a process for preparing compounds of unknown use. Similarly, Fisher filed an application claiming five particular ESTs which are capable of hybridizing with underlying genes of unknown function found in the maize genome. The *Brenner* court held that the claimed process lacked a utility because it could be used only to produce a compound of unknown use. . . . Applying that same logic here, we conclude that the claimed ESTs, which do not correlate to an underlying gene of known function, fail to meet the standard for utility intended by Congress.

NOTES AND QUESTIONS

1. In determining whether utility exists for purposes of § 101 of the U.S. patent statute, why should the uses enumerated by Fisher not be sufficient? Reconsider the U.S. Supreme Court's opinion in *Brenner v. Manson*. Did the Court require that patent applicants *know* the utility of their invention or that there be some utility for the invention? Given the constitutional goal to "promote the Progress of Science" why should a de minimis test for utility (i.e., one that recognizes the benefits of the dissemination) be insufficient for patentability?

2. Would you recommend a de minimis test of utility for a country with low levels of scientific research capacity? Why or why not? One of the objectives of the TRIPS Agreement is to promote the transfer and dissemination of technology. *See* TRIPS Agreement, Article 7. What standard of utility do you think would best facilitate achievement of this goal?

3. In a cogent dissent, Judge Rader took issue with the majority's minimization of the usefulness of ESTs in *In re Fisher*:

Fisher's claimed EST's *are* beneficial to society. As an example, these research tools "may help scientists to isolate the particular underlying protein-encoding genes. . . [with the] overall goal of such experimentation . . . presumably [being] to understand the maize genome[.]" *Majority Opinion*, at 1373. . . .

These research tools are similar to a microscope; both take a researcher one step closer to identifying and understanding a previously unknown and invisible structure. Both supply information about a molecular structure. Both advance research and bring scientists closer to unlocking the secrets of the corn genome to provide

better food production for the hungry world. If a microscope has
§ 101 utility, so too do these ESTs.

The Board and this court acknowledge that the ESTs perform a
function, that they have a utility, but proceed quickly to a value
judgment that the utility would not produce enough valuable information. The Board instead complains that the information these
ESTs supply is too "insubstantial" to merit protection. Yet this conclusion denies the very nature of scientific advance. Science always
advances in small incremental steps. While acknowledging the patentability of research tools generally (and microscopes as one example thereof), this court concludes with little scientific foundation
that these ESTs do not qualify as research tools because they do not
"offer an immediate, real world benefit" because further research is
required to understand the underlying gene. This court further
faults the EST research for lacking any "assurance that anything
useful will be discovered in the end." These criticisms would foreclose much scientific research and many vital research tools. Often
scientists embark on research with no assurance of success and
knowing that even success will demand "significant additional research."

In re Fisher, 421 F.3d at 1380.

Recall the discussion above regarding the policy functions for which the
utility standard was designed. Whose opinion do you find more consistent
with the underlying policy rationale for the utility standard, Judge Rader's or
that of the majority?

4. What are the practical or conceptual difficulties presented in comparing ESTs (from the broad field of biogenetics) to microscopes (from the broad
field of engineering)? What aspect of this comparison do you think was most
useful to the putative patentee? What was most detrimental? Can you think
of a more persuasive analogy? *See In re Fisher*, 421 F.3d at 1373 (describing
the comparison of ESTs to microscopes as "flawed.")

5. The USPTO's Manual of Patent Examining Procedure (MPEP) defines
the Utility Examination Guideline requirement of a specific and substantial
utility as follows:

A "specific utility" is *specific* to the subject matter claimed and can
"provide a well-defined and particular benefit to the public." . . .
This contrasts with a *general* utility that would be applicable to the
broad class of the invention. . . . For example, indicating that a compound may be useful in treating unspecified disorders, or that the
compound has "useful biological" properties, would not be sufficient
to define a specific utility for the compound.

[T]o satisfy the "substantial" utility requirement, an asserted use
must show that the claimed invention has a significant and presently available benefit to the public. . . . the following are examples of
situations that require or constitute carrying out further research to

identify or reasonably confirm a "real world" context of use and, therefore, do not define "substantial utilities":

(A) Basic research such as studying the properties of the claimed product itself or the mechanisms in which the material is involved;

(B) A method of treating an *unspecified* disease or condition;

(C) A method of assaying for or identifying a material that itself has no specific and/or substantial utility;

(D) A method of making a material that itself has no specific, substantial, and credible utility; and

(E) A claim to an intermediate product for use in making a final product that has no specific, substantial and credible utility.

Id. at § 2107.01.

The Office also rejects "throw away" utilities, a famous example being using transgenic mice as snake food. Such a use is neither specific (all mice could serve as snake food) nor substantial (considering the cost to develop the mouse it also seems incredible that it would be used as snake food). The Office assesses "credibility" from the perspective of one of ordinary skill in the art in view of the totality of information available. For example, an invention that defies the second law of thermodynamics would be deemed an incredible invention. It is important to keep in mind that all three requirements must be met. For example, the claimed uses for the ESTs in *Fisher* were credible (use as markers, probes, etc.), but were neither specific nor substantial.

6. As noted earlier in this Chapter, the U.S. utility standard (outside of the biotechnology and chemical arts) generally is perceived as less rigorous than its European or Japanese counterparts. Recent scholarship has explored ways to strengthen the standard to facilitate greater consistency with the expected quid pro quo to which the Court in *Brenner* referred. For example, in addition to operable utility and practical utility, Professor Risch would add another utility-based hurdle to U.S. patent law; namely, a test for commercial utility:

The proposed test would find commercial utility present with sufficient evidence to convince a person with skill in the art that a) there is a market for the invention, and that b) the invention can be manufactured at a cost sufficient to fulfill market demand. Given that more than 50% of patents wind up being worthless, an initial review to determine which patents are most likely to be worthless should be practically achievable.

The test would be applied in a manner similar to that of operable and practical utility, such that *expectations* justify utility even if the expectations prove incorrect in hindsight. Furthermore, no invention is complete without commercial utility. Thus, if a person with skill in the art would not expect the invention to be manufacturable in commercial quantities as of the filing date, then the patent would not issue even if the patentee proves skeptics wrong. However, because it is based on expectations, the test does not require actual commercial production, which might conflict with rules that penalize sales of patented inventions before filing. Likewise, a patent expected to succeed would not be void simply because a product incorporating the patent flops in the market.

The first factor seems straightforward; in order to be commercially useful, some group of people must want to purchase it. The primary doctrinal oddity is that a person having skill in the art of the invention will usually not be an economist or other person with sufficient information to assess market demand. As a result, the test would likely be applied as a determination a skilled artisan would make with the benefit of information from those who know about market demand. . . .

The second factor constrains the result somewhat, by only allowing a finding of commercial utility where there is evidence that near-term market demand can be satisfied. The factor bars inventions that will remain so expensive to reproduce for such a long period of time that many who might want to purchase the invention are unable to obtain it.

Michael Risch, *Reinventing Usefulness,* 2010 BYU L. REV. 1195, 1240–42.

Do you think the U.S. needs such a test? *See also* Ted Sichelman, *Commercializing Patents*, 62 STAN. L. REV. 341, 365 (2010) (advocating higher utility threshold) and Christopher A. Cotropia, *The Folly of Early Filing in Patent Law*, 61 HASTINGS L.J. 65, 120–122 (2009) (proposing actual reduction to practice requirement for patent applications).

7. Recall from Chapter 1 our discussion of the concerns of developing and least-developed countries about the global patent system. If you were assisting the patent office of one of these countries in drafting regulations to interpret the utility standard, which of the three tests above (operable utility, practical utility, or commercial utility), alone or in combination, would you recommend for adoption and why?

2. EUROPE

Article 57 of the European Patent Convention (to which all EU member states are party), requires a patentable invention to be susceptible or capable of industrial applicability, meaning that it "can be made or used in any kind of industry, including agriculture," with "industry" being interpreted in the broadest possible sense. Submissions from the EPO to WIPO identified three specific types of inventions for which industrial applicability could play a decisive role in a patentability determination:

(1) those which appear to be impossible to carry out because they contravene the laws of physics (for example, a perpetual motion

machine); (2) those concerning methods which could be considered to fall entirely within the private or personal sphere; and (3) those involving gene sequences, for which the industrial application must be disclosed.

WIPO, *"Industrial Applicability" and "Utility" Requirements: Commonalities and Differences,* WIPO Doc. SCP/9/5, at 2 (2003).

Regarding the third category, as discussed in Chapter 4, EU member countries must also comply with the EU Biotechnology Directive which explicitly controls the patenting of genomic material.

Article 5 of the Directive provides:

1. The human body, at the various stages of its formation and development, and the simple discovery of one of its elements, including the sequence or partial sequence of a gene, cannot constitute patentable inventions.

. . . .

3. The industrial application of a sequence or partial sequence of a gene must be disclosed in the patent application.

Recitals 22 to 24 to Article 5 further clarify industrial application requirements for genomic materials under the Directive:

22. . . . . Whereas the industrial application of a sequence or partial sequence [of a gene] must be disclosed in the patent application as filed;

23. Whereas a mere DNA sequence without indication of a function does not contain any technical information and is therefore not a patentable invention;

24. Whereas, in order to comply with the industrial application criterion it is necessary in cases where a sequence or partial sequence of a gene is used to produce a protein or part of a protein, to specify which protein or part of a protein is produced or what function it performs . . . .

The requirements of EPC Article 57 and Article 5 of the EU Biotech Directive apply not only to inventions such as the ESTs at issue in *In re Fisher,* but also the full-length genes addressed in the following case.

HUMAN GENOME SCIENCES INC. V. ELI LILLY & CO.

United Kingdom Supreme Court
[2011] UKSC 51

■ LORD NEUBERGER.

INTRODUCTION

1. This appeal is concerned with the validity of a patent which claims the nucleotide sequence of the gene which encodes for a novel protein (and which has further associated claims). . . . [T]he primary issue on this appeal raises a difficult question, namely the way in which the requirement of industrial applicability in Articles 52 and 57 of the European Patent Convention ("the EPC") extends to a patent for biological material.

. . . .

THE PATENT IN SUIT

3. The patent in suit ("the Patent") is European Patent (UK) 0,939,804. It describes the encoding nucleotide, the amino acid sequence, and certain antibodies, of a novel human protein, which it calls Neutrokine-α, and includes contentions as to its biological properties and therapeutic activities, as well as those of its antibodies. These contentions are predictions, which are substantially based on the proposition that Neutrokine-α is a member of the TNF ligand superfamily.

4. The application for the Patent was filed by Human Genome Sciences Ltd ("HGS") on 25 October 1996, and it was granted by the Examining Division of the European Patent Office ("the EPO") to HGS on 17 August 2005. Accordingly, the Patent's validity is to be judged as at October 1996.

. . . .

10. In very summary terms, the disclosure of the Patent . . . includes the following features: (i) the existence and amino acid sequence of Neutrokine-a, (ii) the nucleotide sequence of the gene encoding for Neutrokine-a, (iii) the tissue distribution of Neutrokine-a, (iv) the expression of Neutrokine-a by its mRNA (the encoding gene) in T-cell and B-cell lymphomas, and (v) the information that Neutrokine-a is a member of the TNF ligand superfamily.

. . . .

22. A family or superfamily of proteins is a group of proteins, all of which enjoy a significant degree of homology, i.e. they all have certain specified structural characteristics. Although the distinction is not always observed, members of a particular family will normally have close structural similarity and similar functions, whereas members of a particular superfamily, while retaining related structural characteris-

tics, will often be more distantly related and will include members which have similar functions but also may include members with different functions. However, even that is an over-simplification, as, in some cases, proteins will have pleiotropic functions, "that is to say a multitude of different effects on different cell types, driving multiple biological processes"—per Kitchin J at [2008] RPC 29, para 71. Accordingly, there will be cases where members of a family or superfamily have some functions which are common to all (or a majority) of the members, and other characteristics which are unique to one member (or a few members).

23. The TNF superfamily is sufficiently described for present purposes as consisting of certain cytokines with common structural molecular characteristics. . . . As the Patent records, the founding member of the superfamily was TNF-α, which, by 1996, had long been known as a cytokine with a significant role in regulating immune cells; at least eight other members of the family had been found, including one called TNF-B.

. . . .

THE PROCEEDINGS IN THE EPO AND IN THE ENGLISH COURTS

27. The central issue both in the High Court proceedings before Kitchin J and in the opposition proceedings before the EPO was whether, in the light of the common general knowledge at October 1996, by disclosing . . . [namely the existence and structure of Neutrokine-α, the sequence of its encoding DNA, its tissue distribution, its expression, and its membership of the TNF ligand superfamily], the Patent satisfied Articles 52 and 57 of the EPC so as to enable HGS to claim the encoding gene for Neutrokine-α.

28. Article 52 of the EPC provides that an invention cannot be patented unless it is "susceptible of industrial application". Article 57 of the EPC ("Article 57") goes on to state that an invention is susceptible of industrial application "if it can be made or used in any kind of industry, including agriculture." In its various decisions discussed below, the Board always refers to Article 57 alone, and I will adopt the same approach.

29. After the grant of the Patent to HGS, it was the subject of opposition proceedings brought in the EPO by Eli Lilly and Company ("Eli Lilly"). Following an oral hearing before the Opposition Division of the EPO ("the OD") in June 2008, the Patent was revoked on the basis that the claimed invention constituted, as the Judge put it, a claim to an arbitrary member of the TNF ligand superfamily without a known function.

30. HGS appealed against the OD's decision to the Board, which, after a hearing lasting around a day and a half, in a decision given on 21 October 2009, allowed the appeal. The Board's decision was, in very

summary terms, based on the ground that the notional addressee of the Patent would have appreciated that, "in the light of the common general knowledge of the TNF ligand superfamily and its properties", Neutrokine-α would, as the Patent states, be "active in directing the proliferation, differentiation, and migration of [T-cells]", and that was a sufficient function to vindicate the Patent under Article 57—*see* T 0018/09, paras 23–24. Accordingly, the Board referred the case back to the OD with a direction that the Patent be maintained.

31. Meanwhile, Eli Lilly brought parallel proceedings in the High Court for revocation of the Patent in this jurisdiction. The proceedings came before Kitchin J, who, after a hearing held over some thirteen days, decided to revoke the Patent. His decision was, again in very summary terms, based on the conclusion that, in the light of the common general knowledge, the notional addressee of the Patent would have concluded that the "functions" of Neutrokine-α "were, at best, a matter of expectation and then at far too high a level of generality to constitute a sound or concrete basis for anything except a research project"—*see* [2008] RPC 29, para 234.

32. Kitchin J's decision was given on 31 July 2008, after the decision of the OD, but before HGS had appealed to the Board. HGS appealed against Kitchin J's decision to the Court of Appeal, who, on 9 February 2010, dismissed the appeal—[2010] EWCA Civ 33, [2010] RPC 14. The Court of Appeal's reasoning effectively followed and approved that of Kitchin J, although it was given after the ruling of the Board. In his judgment, with which Hallett LJ and Lewison J agreed, Jacob LJ discussed the reasoning of the Board in T0018/09. It is, of course, against the decision of the Court of Appeal which HGS now appeal.

33. HGS's case on this appeal is that, notwithstanding Kitchin J's impressively full and careful analysis of the law, the relevant technology, the Patent and the expert evidence, and its affirmation by the Court of Appeal, his decision that the Patent failed to satisfy Article 57 was wrong. . . . In summary, HGS contends that the reasoning of the Board was correct, and that it shows that Kitchin J and the Court of Appeal set too high a standard for industrial applicability in the context of a patent for biological material.

. . . .

THE REASONING AND CONCLUSIONS OF KITCHIN J AND OF THE BOARD

. . . .

70. As to the overall effect of the teaching of the Patent, it is convenient to refer to what Kitchin J said at [2008] RPC 29, paras 231–233, as the view which he expressed was very similar to that of the Board,

and was not challenged in this court by HGS. In those paragraphs, he summarised his view as to what the Patent disclosed thus:

"231. In this case I am quite satisfied that the skilled person would consider the Patent does not of itself identify any industrial application other than by way of speculation. . . [I]t contains an astonishing range of diseases and conditions which Neutrokine-α and antibodies to Neutrokine-α may be used to diagnose and treat and there is no data of any kind to support the claims made. The skilled person would consider it totally farfetched that Neutrokine-α could be used in relation to them all and . . . would be driven to the conclusion that the authors had no clear idea what the activities of the protein were and so included every possibility. To have included such a range of applications was no better than to have included none at all.

232. But that is not the end of the matter because the disclosure must be considered in the light of the common general knowledge . . . . The skilled person would have known that TNF was involved as a primary mediator in immune regulation and the inflammatory response and had an involvement in a wide range of diseases as septic shock, rheumatoid arthritis, inflammatory bowel disease, tissue rejection, HIV infection, and some adverse drug reactions. He would have known that all the members of the TNF ligand superfamily identified hitherto were expressed by T-cells and played a role in the regulation of T-cell proliferation and T-cell mediated responses. Further, . . . the skilled person would anticipate that the activities of Neutrokine-a might relate to T-cells and, in particular, be expressed on T-cells and be a co-stimulant of B-cell production; that it might play a role in the immune response and in the control of tumours and malignant disease; that it might have an effect on B-cell proliferation . . ."

. . . .

74. The Judge also considered in some detail the work carried out since October 1996, and concluded at [2008] RPC 29, para 176, that this work established Neutrokine-α's functions more clearly, and in particular that it "plays a significant and particular role in the proliferation and differentiation of B-cells . . . [and] in the regulation of T-cell proliferation and activation". He went on:

"Neutrokine-α has now been shown to have an important role in the development of autoimmune disease and B-cell cancers; but, at the same time, much of its biology remains unclear and is the subject of continuing study by many different research centres. In my judgment the nature and extent of all this research work, the limited conclusions ultimately drawn and the amount of work that remains to be done point strongly to the conclusion that the therapeutic and diagnostic applications suggested in the Patent were indeed speculative."

75. Turning then to the passage in which he expressed his conclusions, [2008] RPC 29, paras 230 and 234–5, Kitchin J said this:

"230. I accept that the contribution made by HGS was to find Neutrokine-α and to identify it as a member of the TNF ligand superfamily. However it is clear from the cases to which I have referred that simply identifying a protein is not necessarily sufficient to confer industrial utility upon it. . . . It may be sufficient if the identification of the protein will immediately suggest a practical application, such as was the case with insulin, human growth hormone and erythropoietin. But if the function of the protein is not known or is incompletely understood and if no disease has been attributed to a deficiency or excess of it, then the position may well be different. In these cases the industrial utility must be identified in some other way.

. . .

234. Does [the] common general knowledge, taken as a whole, disclose a practical way of exploiting Neutrokine-α? Or does it provide a sound and concrete basis for recognising that Neutrokine-α could lead to practical application in industry? In my judgment it does not. The fact that Neutrokine-α might be expected to play a role in regulating the activities of B-cells and T-cells and play an unspecified role in regulating the immune and inflammatory response did not reveal how it could be used to solve any particular problem. Neither the Patent nor the common general knowledge identified any disease or condition which Neutrokine-α could be used to diagnose or treat. Its functions were, at best, a matter of expectation and then at far too high a level of generality to constitute a sound or concrete basis for anything except a research project.

235. I believe this conclusion is confirmed by the activities of those in the pharmaceutical industry in the years following the filing of the application. HGS, Lilly and Biogen (and possibly others too) carried out research programmes to try and find out where Neutrokine-α was expressed, where its receptors were expressed and what its activities appeared to be. They carried out *in vitro* assays and animal studies and determined that it appeared to have an activity in relation to B lymphocytes with a particular biological profile. On the basis of this work they recognised that it was an important therapeutic target—some two to three years after the application for the Patent had been filed. It is significant

that in so doing they considered that its utility might lie in the treatment of B-cell disorders of particular kinds."

76. The passage I have just quoted from Kitchin J's judgment encapsulates Eli Lilly's case, and HGS's case is well summarised in the Board's reasoning at T0018/09, paras 22–26. The first of those paragraphs sets the scene in terms of the general approach:

"22. As pointed out in T 870/04, [paras 5 and 6], in many cases the allocation of a newly found protein to a known protein family with known activities suffices to assign a specific function to the protein because normally the members of the family share a specific function. This may be a well-characterized and perfectly understood function which provides in a straightforward manner enough support for industrial applicability. In such cases, the *'immediate concrete benefit'* is manifest. In other cases, where the members of a protein family have different, pleiotropic effects which may even be opposite and neither completely characterized nor understood, no effect can be assigned to a new member without relying on some experimental data. Between these two extreme situations, a variety of other situations may arise for which a detailed examination of all the facts may be required. Indeed, this is the case for the TNF ligand superfamily."

77. In the next two paragraphs, the Board sought to follow that approach in relation to the instant Patent:

"23. As known in the art and acknowledged in the [Patent], all members of the TNF ligand superfamily are known to participate in the regulation of (immune) cell proliferation, activation, and differentiation, and are involved in various medical conditions. They are pleiotropic cytokines which display a wide range of activities and have distinctive, but also overlapping biological functions. . . . As acknowledged in the art, a feature common to all members (without exception) of the TNF ligand superfamily is the expression on activated T-cells and the ability to co-stimulate T-cell proliferation. . . In view of the assignment of Neutrokine-a to the family, the skilled person expects it to display this common feature, the relevant question here being whether anything in the Patent specification contradicts this expectation.

24. The Patent specification, besides providing the undisputed structural identification of Neutrokine-a as a member of the TNF ligand superfamily, also provides some further relevant technical data which are fully in line with the expected properties of a member of that superfamily. In particular, it discloses the tissue distribution of Neutrokine-a mRNA expression using

the nucleic acid sequence encoding the Neutrokine-a protein, as a cDNA probe and, as expected, reports—although without concrete experimental data—the expression of Neutrokine-a in activated T-cells. . . . It further states that '(l)ike other members of TNF family, Neutrokine-a exhibits activity on leukocytes including for example monocytes, lymphocytes and neutrophils. For this reason Neutrokine-a is active in directing the proliferation, differentiation and migration of these cell types'. . . . This broad statement, far from contradicting the ability of Neutrokine-a to co-stimulate T-cell proliferation, actually supports it. In the light of the common general knowledge of the TNF ligand superfamily and its properties, no serious doubts can be cast on this explicit additional information. Nor can this information be taken as a mere theoretical or purely hypothetical assumption. First of all, it is plausible and, secondly, there is ample post-published evidence on file confirming both the presence of Neutrokine-a on activated T-cells and its ability to co-stimulate T-cell proliferation."

78. The Board then turned to Eli Lilly's contention that "in view of the numerous contradictory statements and of the broad range of conditions and diseases referred to in the patent-in-suit, the skilled person would have disregarded such information as constituting only hypothetical assumptions or speculations", and said this at T 0018/09, para 26:

"When reading the patent specification, a skilled person would distinguish the positive technical information such as that mentioned above from other allegedly contradictory and broad statements found in the patent-in-suit, such as . . . the wide range of activities and conditions for which Neutrokine-α could be useful. This is because the skilled person realises that the description of the structure of Neutrokine-α, its structural assignment to the family of TNF ligands, and the reports about its tissue distribution and activity on leucocytes, are the first essential steps at the onset of research work on the newly found TNF ligand superfamily member. In view of the known broad range of possible activities of such a molecule, the skilled person is aware of the fact that the full elucidation of all properties requires further investigations which will gradually reveal them. In this context, the skilled person regards the long listing of possible actions of Neutrokine-α and of medical conditions in which it might take part as the enumeration or generalisation of the properties of the TNF ligand superfamily. This is seen as the frame in which the newly found molecule has to be placed as one could prima facie have a reasonable expectation that most of them could in fact be present."

79. The Board accordingly concluded at T 0018/09, para 27 that "the description of the patent delivers sufficient technical information, namely the effect of Neutrokine-α on T-cells and the tissue distribution of Neutrokine-α mRNA, to satisfy the requirement of disclosing the nature and purpose of the invention and how it can be used in industrial practice."

. . . .

FOLLOWING THE BOARD'S JURISPRUDENCE

83. Where the EPO decides that a patent, or a claim in a patent, is invalid, then that is the end of the issue (subject, of course, to the patentee or applicant appealing to the Board) in relation to all countries which are signatories to the EPC. Where, however, the EPO decides that a patent, or a particular claim, is valid, then, as this case shows, it is still open to a national court to decide that the patent, or claim, is invalid within its territorial jurisdiction. In all cases, however, the EPO and each national court are, of course, applying the principles contained in the EPC. It is plainly appropriate in principle, and highly desirable in practice, that all these tribunals interpret the provisions of the EPC in the same way.

84. In a number of recent decisions of the House of Lords, attention has been drawn to "the importance of UK patent law aligning itself, so far as possible, with the jurisprudence of the EPO (and especially decisions of its Enlarged Boards of Appeal)", to quote Lord Walker in *Generics (UK) Ltd v. H Lundbeck A/S* [2009] UKHL 12; [2009] RPC 13, para 35. It is encouraging that the same approach is being adopted in Germany by the Bundesgerictshof—see *Case Xa ZR* 130/07 (10 September 2009), para 33.

85. However, as Lord Walker went on to explain in *Generics* [2009] RPC 13, para 35, "National courts may reach different conclusions as to the evaluation of the evidence in the light of the relevant principles" even though "the principles themselves should be the same, stemming as they do from the EPC". Thus, the EPO (or another national court) and a national court may come to different conclusions because they have different evidence or arguments, or because they assess the same competing arguments and factual or expert evidence differently, or, particularly in a borderline case, because they form different judgments on the same view of the expert and factual evidence.

. . . .

87. Further, while national courts should normally follow the established jurisprudence of the EPO, that does not mean that we should regard the reasoning in each decision of the Board as effectively binding on us. There will no doubt sometimes be a Board decision which a national court considers may take the law in an inappropriate direction,

misapplies previous EPO jurisprudence, or fails to take a relevant argument into account. In such cases, the national court may well think it right not to apply the reasoning in the particular decision. While consistency of approach is important, there has to be room for dialogue between a national court and the EPO (as well as between national courts themselves). Nonetheless, where the Board has adopted a consistent approach to an issue in a number of decisions, it would require very unusual facts to justify a national court not following that approach.

      . . . .

DID THE COURTS BELOW FOLLOW THE BOARD'S JURISPRUDENCE?

103. As already mentioned, despite its very wide-ranging and generalised suggestions as to the uses to which Neutrokine-α and its antibodies might be put, over and above revealing the existence and structure of the new protein and its encoding gene, the only relevant teaching of the Patent ultimately arises from its teaching as to the tissue distribution of Neutrokine-α, its expression in T-cell and B-cell lymphomas, and the fact that it is a member of the TNF ligand superfamily. Accordingly, the question is whether the Judge was right, or at least entitled, to conclude that the inferences which would have been drawn from this in 1996 would not have been enough to satisfy Article 57.

104. The determination of that issue, as I see it, ultimately involves focussing on the Judge's conclusion. . . . [H]e concluded that the fact that the description in the Patent, even taken together with knowledge which should be attributed to its addressee, neither "reveal[ed] how [Neutrokine-α] could be used to solve any particular problem" nor "identified any disease or condition which [it] could be used to diagnose or treat" was fatal to the patent's validity. He considered that the functions of Neutrokine-α "were, at best, a matter of expectation and then at far too high a level of generality to constitute a sound or concrete basis for anything except a research project".

105. My initial reaction, like that of the Court of Appeal, was that this was a conclusion to which Kitchin J, as the trial judge, who had heard a great deal of evidence, which he had impressively and cogently analysed, was entitled to come, and with which it would be inappropriate to interfere. Standing back, it also seemed to be a conclusion which could be said to accord with good sense. As he held in the next paragraph of his judgment (also quoted in para 75 above), it required what may fairly be characterised as a research project to enable the therapeutic qualities of Neutrokine-α to be identified, or, as HGS would put it, to be confirmed.

106. However, on further reflection . . . I have come to the conclusion that the basis upon which the Judge decided the issue was

not consistent with the approach adopted by the Board in the decisions which are discussed above.

107. The essence of the Board's approach in relation to the requirements of Article 57 in relation to biological material may, I think, be summarised in the following points:

The general principles are:

(i) The patent must disclose "a practical application" and "some profitable use" for the claimed substance, so that the ensuing monopoly "can be expected [to lead to] some . . . commercial benefit" (T 0870/04, para 4, T 0898/05, paras 2 and 4);

(ii) A "concrete benefit", namely the invention's "use . . . in industrial practice" must be "derivable directly from the description", coupled with common general knowledge (T 0898/05, para 6, T 0604/04, para 15);

(iii) A merely "speculative" use will not suffice, so "a vague and speculative indication of possible objectives that might or might not be achievable" will not do (T 0870/04, para 21 and T 0898/05, paras 6 and 21);

(iv) The patent and common general knowledge must enable the skilled person "to reproduce" or "exploit" the claimed invention without "undue burden", or having to carry out "a research programme" (T 0604/04, para 22, T 0898/05, para 6);

Where a patent discloses a new protein and its encoding gene:

(v) The patent, when taken with common general knowledge, must demonstrate "a real as opposed to a purely theoretical possibility of exploitation" (T 0604/04, para 15, T 0898/05, paras 6, 22 and 31);

(vi) Merely identifying the structure of a protein, without attributing to it a "clear role", or "suggest[ing]" any "practical use" for it, or suggesting "a vague and speculative indication of possible objectives that might be achieved", is not enough (T 0870/04, paras 6–7, 11, and 21; T 0898/05, paras 7, 10 and 31);

(vii) The absence of any experimental or wet lab evidence of activity of the claimed protein is not fatal (T 0898/05, paras 21 and 31, T 1452/06, para 5);

(viii) A "plausible" or "reasonably credible" claimed use, or an "educated guess", can suffice (T 1329/04, paras 6 and 11, T 0640/04, para 6, T 0898/05, paras 8, 21, 27 and 31, T 1452/06, para 6, T 1165/06 para 25);

(ix) Such plausibility can be assisted by being confirmed by "later evidence", although later evidence on its own will not do (T 1329/04, para 12, T 0898/05, para 24, T 1452/06, para 6, T 1165/06, para 25);

(x) The requirements of a plausible and specific possibility of exploitation can be at the biochemical, the cellular or the biological level (T 0898/05, paras 29–30);

Where the protein is said to be a family or superfamily member:

(xi) If all known members have a "role in the proliferation, differentiation and/or activation of immune cells" or "function in controlling physiology, development and differentiation of mammalian cells", assigning a similar role to the protein may suffice (T 1329/04, para 13, T 0898/05, para 21, T 1165/06, paras 14 and 16, and T 0870/04, para 12);

(xii) So "the problem to be solved" in such a case can be "isolating a further member of the [family]" (T 1329/04, para 4, T 0604/04, para 22, T 1165/06, paras 14 and 16);

(xiii) If the disclosure is "important to the pharmaceutical industry", the disclosure of the sequences of the protein and its gene may suffice, even though its role has not "been clearly defined" (T 0604/04, para 18);

(xiv) The position may be different if there is evidence, either in the patent or elsewhere, which calls the claimed role or membership of the family into question (T 0898/05 para 24, T 1452/06, para 5);

(xv) The position may also be different if the known members have different activities, although they need not always be "precisely interchangeable in terms of their biological action", and it may be acceptable if "most" of them have a common role (T 0870/04, para 12, T 0604/04, para 16, T 0898/05, para 27).

. . . .

109. [I]t seems to me that, subject to dealing with a number of specific arguments to the contrary, the disclosure of the existence and structure of Neutrokine-α and its gene sequence, and its membership of the TNF ligand superfamily should have been sufficient, taking into account the common general knowledge, to satisfy the requirements of Article 57, in the light of the principles which I have attempted to summarise in para 107 above. Points (viii), (ix) and (x) appear to apply so far as the plausibility of at least some of the claims are concerned, and points (xi), (xii) and (xiii) all appear to be satisfied, given the evidence in relation to the TNF ligand superfamily (and point (xiv) cannot be invoked by Eli Lilly).

. . . .

111. [T]he Board's conclusion was effectively this, that the disclosure of what was accepted to be a new member of the TNF ligand superfamily (coupled with details of its tissue distribution) satisfied Article 57, because all known members were expressed on T-cells and were able to co-stimulate T-cell proliferation, and therefore Neutrokine-α would be expected to have a similar function. This conclusion was supported, or reinforced, by the statement that Neutrokine-α was expressed in B-cell and T-cell lymphomas (referred to in T 0018/09, para 30), and indeed by the interest and effort in the pharmaceutical industry in finding a new member of the superfamily (as explained by Kitchin J at [2008] RPC 29, paras 72–74).

THE ARGUMENTS IN SUPPORT OF THE CONCLUSION REACHED BELOW

112. The first argument to the contrary is based on the fact that the members of the TNF ligand superfamily were known to have pleiotropic effects. On behalf of Eli Lilly, Mr. Waugh QC therefore relies on point (xv) i.e. that the claim to a new member of a superfamily is not good enough because the known members of the family have different activities. In my opinion, that point does not apply in a case where all known members of the superfamily also manifest to a significant degree common activities which are, of themselves, enough to bring the patent within the ambit of points (xi), (xii) and (xiii).

113. Given that the fact that all known family members have sufficient common features to satisfy those points can justify a patent for a new member, it would seem somewhat bizarre if the fact that they had additional, but differing, qualities, should preclude the grant of such a patent. The disclosure of a new member would not only be of greater potential value than if the additional qualities did not exist, but the reason for the grant of the patent is the perceived value of a new member because of the common features of all known members, a feature which is unaffected by the additional qualities.

. . . .

116. A second argument raised against validity is the unsatisfactory drafting of the Patent (mentioned by the Court of Appeal at [2010] RPC 14, para 148). If the Judge had found that the drafting of the specification of the Patent was so confusing and potentially misleading that the skilled reader would have been put off the scent in relation to what would otherwise have been appreciated from common general knowledge and reading the literature as to the potential and plausible uses to which the disclosure could be put, that may well have been a problem for HGS's case. However, although the Judge was (in my view, rightly) critical about the drafting of the specification, he did not any-

where in his full and careful judgment say, or even suggest, that its wide-ranging prolix contents would have actually diverted the notional addressees, the appropriately skilled persons, from what they would otherwise have understood the Patent to be revealing, in the light of what was appreciated about the properties of the known members of the TNF ligand superfamily. Indeed, Mr. Thorley QC, for HGS, identified passages in the evidence of Professor Saklatvala, which would have made such a finding difficult to justify.

. . . .

119. A third argument is based on the Judge's remarks at [2008] RPC 29, paras 176 and 234, that the disclosure in the Patent as to the uses of Neutrokine-α, even when taken together with common general knowledge, was no more than "speculative" and did not give rise to an "immediate concrete benefit"– i.e. invoking on points (ii) and (iii). This argument (which was also relied on by the Court of Appeal—*see* at [2010] RPC 14, para 132) proceeds on the implicit assumption that the disclosure of the Patent as summarised in para 108 above is not sufficient in itself to satisfy the requirements of Article 57.

. . . .

121. The Court of Appeal made much of the Board's statement that a patent should yield an "immediate concrete benefit" *(see* at [2010] RPC 14, paras 146, 149, 155 and 156). I certainly accept that, in some cases, different tribunals can and will legitimately come to different views as to whether a particular claimed invention can satisfy the requirement of providing an "immediate concrete benefit". However, I am not persuaded that such an argument is open to Eli Lilly in this case. In my view, the Court of Appeal's approach, like that of the Judge, was implicitly predicated on the mistaken basis that it was not enough for the Patent to satisfy the requirements of points (xi) to (xiii).

122. Further, at least in the context of the present case, I do not consider that the Courts below gave proper weight to points (viii), (ix) and (x). In particular, in my judgment, the Court of Appeal did not approach the concept of plausibility consistently with the jurisprudence of the Board. That is well demonstrated by Jacob LJ's observation at [2010] RPC 14, para 112, that "[i]t is not good enough to say this protein or any antibody to it probably has a pharmaceutical use. Such a statement is indeed plausible, but is of no real practical use. You are left to find out what that use is." If the statement "is indeed plausible", then, in the absence of any reason to the contrary, it at least *prima facie* satisfies the requirements of Article 57 according to the Board.

. . . .

127. A further argument, which is really another formulation of the same point, is that, as was emphasised by the Court of Appeal at [2010]

RPC 14, para 152, one important reason why Kitchin J reached a different conclusion from the Board was because he concluded that the necessary assays to determine the precise role and potential of the patent's disclosure would be a "complex task", whereas the Board thought it would simply involve "standard assays"—compare [2008] RPC 29, para 77, and T 0018/09, para 29 respectively.

128. As the Court of Appeal rightly observed, such a conflict is entirely legitimate and understandable, in view of the different evidence, the benefit of cross-examination, and/or the room for difference of opinion between two tribunals. In another case, such a difference in assessment of the evidence could well justify a difference in outcome. But not in this case. Once one concludes that the effect of the Board's jurisprudence is that, in the light of the common general knowledge, the disclosure of Neutrokine-α as a member of the TNF ligand superfamily (coupled with its amino acid and encoding gene sequences and the tissues in which it is expressed), the claims in relation to the invention's potential satisfy Article 57. As a result, the relevance of the degree of effort needed in relation to any subsequent work falls away. (The same point undermines Eli Lilly's reliance on a number of other small differences between the findings of the Judge and the Board on the expert evidence).

CONCLUSION ON THE MAIN ISSUE, ARTICLE 57

129. Accordingly, I would allow HGS's appeal on the issue as to whether the Patent satisfied the requirements of Article 57, and hold that it does. As explained, I have reached this conclusion by applying my understanding of the jurisprudence of the Board to the facts found by Kitchin J. However, particularly as I have stated . . . above that there is good sense in the contrary conclusion reached by the Judge and the Court of Appeal, it is right to emphasise that there is also good sense in the result which, at least in my view, is mandated by the Board's approach to the law in this field.

130. Just as it would be undesirable to let someone have a monopoly over a particular biological molecule too early, because it risks closing down competition, so it would be wrong to set the hurdle for patentability too high. . . . Quite where the line should be drawn in the light of commercial reality and the public interest can no doubt be a matter of different opinions and debate. However, in this case, apart from the fairly general submissions of the parties and of the BIA, we have not had any submissions on such wider policy considerations.

. . . .

CONCLUSION

140. It follows from this that, at least in my opinion, HGS's appeal on the Article 57 issue should be allowed . . . and the case should be remitted to the Court of Appeal to deal with the outstanding issues.

NOTES AND QUESTIONS

1. In a portion of the *HGS v. Eli Lilly* decision not reproduced above, Lord Neuberger opined on the different approach to the utility requirement for biological material taken by U.S. courts:

> 38. As for the US courts, their approach to the question of what constitutes "any new and useful . . . composition of matter" under section 101 of 35 USC was considered by the US Supreme Court in *Brenner v Manson*, and by the US Court of Appeals for the Federal Circuit in *Fisher v Lalgudi* (and both decisions are discussed and quoted from by the Judge at [2008] RPC 29, paras 218–224).

> 39. The analyses in the US cases deserve great respect, and it is interesting to note that, in *Fisher*, the US Court of Appeals referred to a requirement that "an invention is useful to the public as disclosed in its current form" as opposed to "prov[ing] useful at some future date after further research", and that the invention "can be used to provide a well-defined and particular benefit to the public."

> 40. However, there are obvious risks in relying on US jurisprudence when considering the precise nature of the requirements of Article 57 in relation to a claim for a patent for biological material under the EPC. There have been moves over the past fifty years (and more) to harmonise patent law across jurisdictions (the EPC and TRIPS—the Trade-Related Aspects of Intellectual Property Protection—being two important examples), and it is a laudable aim to seek to ensure that all aspects of the law of patents are identical throughout the world. However, the achievement of such an aim is plainly not currently practicable, and, although they have a great deal in common, there are significant and fairly fundamental differences (over and above the different words used in Articles 52 and 57 of the EPC and section 101 of 35 USC) between US patent law and the EPC (two notorious examples being the first to file rule in Europe, and file wrapper estoppel in the US).

> 41. Accordingly, particularly when it comes to a nice question such as the precise delineation of boundaries between patentability and unpatentability on the ground of industrial application, it would be unsurprising if the law was not identical under the two jurisdictions.

Id. at para. 38–41.

Do you agree with the Court's refusal to align its decision with that of courts in the United States? In your view, which decision takes the correct approach to the utility of biological material, *In re Fisher* (U.S.) or *HGS v. Eli Lilly* (UK)?

2. In another portion of the *HGS v. Eli Lilly* decision not reproduced above, the Court noted the intervention of the BioIndustry Association (BIA) in the proceedings:

> 96. The BioIndustry Association ("the BIA"), which has intervened in these proceedings, describes itself as "a trade association for innovative enterprises in the UK's bioscience sector" and its membership extends to hundreds of companies with an aggregate turnover in 2010 of about £5.5bn, and around 36,000 employees.

> 97. The requirements of clarity and certainty in this area of law are emphasised by the BIA. As its submissions also explain, after the discovery of a naturally occurring molecule, particularly a protein and its encoding gene, a large amount of research and development is required before there can be any therapeutic benefit. It is therefore important for bioscience companies to be able to decide at what stage to file for patent protection. Thus,

>> "If the application is filed early . . . [t]he company will be left with no patent protection, but would have disclosed its invention in the published patent application to competitors. If the application is filed late, there is a risk in such a competitive environment where several companies may be working on the same type of research projects, that a third party will already have filed a patent application covering the same or a similar invention, in which case the company may not be able to gain any patent protection for its work and by continuing their programme they may risk infringing that third party's patents. In both cases, the company will have lost much of the benefit of its costly research and development."

> 98. Similarly, funding for research and development on the potential therapeutic value of a newly discovered and characterised protein or its antibodies is dependent on the funders being reasonably confident that the patent (or patent application) concerned will be reasonably safe from attack (or likely to be granted). It is also relevant that bioscience companies attract investment by reference to their patent portfolios, which gives rise to the same need for certainty.

> 99. As the BIA suggests, it is worth remembering the purpose of the patent system, namely to provide a temporary monopoly as an incentive to innovation, while at the same time facilitating the early dissemination of any such innovation through an early application for a patent, and its subsequent publication. Although this is

true in any sector, it has particular force in the pharmaceutical field, where even many of those who are sceptical about the value of intellectual property rights accept that there is a public interest in, and a commercial need for, patent protection.

100. For obvious reasons, the BIA has not set out to support either of the two parties to this appeal in its trenchant written submissions in these proceedings. However, it does suggest that if we agree with the reasoning of the Court of Appeal there is at least a risk that it will "make it appreciably harder for patentees to satisfy the requirement of industrial applicability in future cases." If that were so, it is suggested that this "would cause UK bioscience companies great difficulty in attracting investment at an early stage in the research and development process".

Id. at para. 96–100.

Do you think the BIA's intervention influenced the outcome in this case? Should it have? In other words, should courts consider the types of policy issues raised by the BIA (and voiced by the dissent in *Brenner v. Manson*) when interpreting statutory provisions?

3. What factors do you think should guide courts in determining whether a particular biogenomic or invention is "useful"? Should different standards apply? The Federal Circuit in *In re Fisher* stressed a robust usefulness standard for ESTs. In *Eli Lilly*, the UK court focused on the EPO Boards of Appeal requirement of a "sufficient function" for the biological material. Is having a function synonymous with being useful? According to one commentator:

> [I]n gene patenting there is the assumption that if the *function* of a gene is known then its utility is known. The EU Directive (1998) says that 'a mere DNA sequence without indication of a function does not contain any technical information and is therefore not a patentable invention' (paragraph 23). So if we do know the function of a gene, we potentially have a patentable invention. At first glance it seems strange that knowing the function of a gene is sufficient to show that the gene is a useful invention, since function is normally thought of as something a gene does which contributes to the maintenance, operation or persistence of the organism. Physiological function does not intuitively seem to demonstrate the broader social utility that we might think would be necessary for a patent . . . .

Jane Calvert, *Genomic Patenting and the Utility Requirement*, 23 NEW GENETICS & SOC'Y 301, 303–304 (2004).

Do you agree?

4. In her article, Dr. Calvert identifies at least three possible types of utility for gene patents:

The first type of utility I call 'anthropocentric' utility. This is utility that does not rely on what a gene does in the organism; it is something we impose on the gene from our human perspective. One example would be the utility of non-coding DNA in disease diagnosis; another would be genetic fingerprinting. In the case of genetic fingerprinting, the function of DNA is not to make it easier to identify criminals at a crime scene, but we can use the DNA for this purpose from our anthropocentric perspective. With anthropocentric utility it is not necessary to know anything about the physiological function of the DNA that is being used.

The second type of utility can be called 'physiological function" An example of this type of utility is a gene that produces a protein that interacts with the HIV virus. This is something the gene does anyway, whether we pay any attention or not, it is not something we impose on it from our human perspective (although we do, of course, have a particularly human interest in the HIV virus).

A third type of utility falls between these two. It can be called 'manipulated physiological function.' This is where we (anthropocentrically) manipulate the natural function of the gene to fulfill a certain objective. Examples here would be GM crops and gene therapy. The natural functions of these genes have been anthropocentrically altered to be useful for our purposes.

Id. at 307.

Are these categories helpful? Read TRIPS Article 27. Is there any basis for suggesting that these types of utility do not satisfy the standard set forth in that provision?

5. The utility/industrial applicability doctrine provides courts with a policy lever to control the timing of patenting in order to facilitate downstream developments. Are there any downsides to this approach? Consider the significant research and development resources most developed countries invest in basic science. Should the discovery of new information upon which further research is built, and patents eventually issue, be a sufficient benefit to society to merit some reward even if not a patent? Would you support legislative efforts to give "research patents" to scientists whose research activities produce valuable information but for which there is no known utility? Should such scientists be rewarded with a percentage of royalty streams for patents that incorporate that knowledge?

6. To establish a global requirement that inventions be useful is one thing, but applying this standard to new scientific fields shows the limits of broad harmonization of legal standards. For example, if an invention is deemed "useful" by scientists in Country A, but not by those in Country B because of the latter's level of scientific knowledge, should Country B nevertheless recognize the validity of such a patent issued by Country A? Does TRIPS Article 27 *require* that Country B protect such an invention? What can Country B do to defend against arguments that the invention satisfies TRIPS

standards because of its utility to scientists in another WTO member country?

7. No multilateral agreement, including the TRIPS Agreement, defines utility. Indeed, the patent laws of most countries also do not have a definition of utility. Patent offices, however, most notably the USPTO and EPO, issue guidelines that more specifically identify criteria for the patentability requirements. Guidelines issued by one of the major patent offices (USPTO, EPO, JPO) often will influence the others regarding the specific subject matter. For example, the 2001 USPTO Utility Examination Guidelines influenced the UK Patent Office and the EPO, which both adopted similar standards. At least one commentator has argued that the U.S. had first mover advantage in setting the global standard for the utility requirement. *See* Sivaramjani Thambisetty, *Legal Transplants in Patent Law: Why "Utility" Is the New "Industrial Applicability,"* 49 JURIMETRICS J. 155 (2009) (noting that "the USPTO's efforts in drafting detailed guidelines, based on an informed debate, quickly became a focal point for patent offices in other jurisdictions"). Are there any dangers in such legal transplantation between patent offices?

8. In *Apotex, Inc. v. Wellcome Foundation Ltd.*, 2002 SCC 77 [2002] 4 S.C.R. 153 (Can.), the Supreme Court of Canada was called upon to judge the patentability of AZT as a treatment for HIV and AIDS. Apotex, a generic drug manufacturer, contended that the usefulness of AZT was merely speculative at the time the Wellcome Foundation Ltd. filed its patent application. In holding that the Wellcome Foundation had fulfilled the utility requirement, the Court considered the question at what point in time does speculation become utility. According to the Court, the answer lies in the doctrine of "sound prediction":

> 66. The doctrine of "sound prediction" balances the public interest in early disclosure of new and useful inventions, even before their utility has been verified by tests (which in the case of pharmaceutical products may take years) and the public interest in avoiding cluttering the public domain with useless patents, and granting monopoly rights in exchange for misinformation.

> . . . .

> 70. The doctrine of sound prediction has three components. Firstly, as here, there must be a factual basis for the prediction. . . . Secondly, the inventor must have at the date of the patent application an articulable and "sound" line of reasoning from which the desired result can be inferred from the factual basis. . . . Thirdly, there must be proper disclosure. Normally, it is sufficient if the specification provides a full, clear and exact description of the nature of the invention and the manner in which it can be practiced . . . . It is generally not necessary for an inventor to provide a theory of *why* the invention works. Practical readers merely want to know that it does work and how to work it. In this sort of case, however, the sound

prediction is to some extent the *quid pro quo* the applicant offers in exchange for the patent monopoly. . . .

71. It bears repetition that the soundness (or otherwise) of the prediction is a question of fact. Evidence must be led about what was known or not known at the priority date. . . . Each case will turn on the particularities of the discipline to which it relates. In this case, the findings of fact necessary for the application of "sound prediction" were made and the appellants have not, in my view, demonstrated any overriding or palpable error.

Id.

Does the Canadian doctrine of sound prediction resolve the problem of speculative utility? How is it different from speculative utility? Is sound prediction compatible with U.S. and EPO standards?

B. INDUSTRIAL APPLICATION: PERSONAL OR PRIVATE USE

Countries that adopt the "capable of industrial application" standard generally require inventions to exhibit some form of industrial or physical activity of a technical character; nevertheless, they tend to define the term "industrial" in a broad sense. Article 57 of the European Patent Convention, for example, provides that "[a]n invention shall be considered as susceptible of industrial application if it can be made or used in any kind of industry, including agriculture." Likewise, the JPO Examination Guidelines provide in Part II, Ch. 1, § 2 that "'industry' is interpreted in a broad sense, including mining, agriculture, fishery, transportation, telecommunications, etc., as well as manufacturing."[1] However, Japan, the countries of the European Patent Organisation (which administers the European Patent Convention), and many others distinguish between industrial and personal applicability, and will not permit patents for methods that are applied only for purely personal or private use. One example of such an invention, which the JPO Guidelines describe as "commercially inapplicable and hence industrially inapplicable" is a method of smoking. *See* Examination Guidelines for Patent and Utility Model in Japan, pt. II, ch. 1, § 2.1.2(i) (June 2009). Another example can be found in the following decision of the Technical Board of Appeal of the EPO, which deals with whether an application for a method of contraception that is applied in the private and personal sphere of a human being is susceptible of industrial application.

---

[1] In no case, however, does the term include methods of human or animal medical treatment, since they are expressly excluded from the scope of patentable subject matter.

CONTRACEPTIVE METHOD/BRITISH TECHNOLOGY GROUP
DECISION OF TECHNICAL BOARD OF APPEAL 3.3.1 (1994)

T 0074/93, 1995 Official J. Eur. Pat. Off. 712

SUMMARY OF FACTS AND SUBMISSIONS

I. European patent application No. 88 904 588.6 relating to alicyclic compounds and their contraceptive use was filed as an international application on 27 May 1988, claiming priority from an earlier application in the United Kingdom of 2 June 1987. The Examining Division refused the application on 2 September 1992 in a decision based on Claims 1 to 10 as filed by letter of 3 August 1992.

II. The application was refused because Claim 5, which relates to the use of a compound for applying to the cervix of a female capable of conception, was not susceptible of industrial application as required by Article 57 EPC insofar as the compound was to be applied to the cervix of a *human* female. Such use was regarded as a purely personal use carried out in private by women themselves. There was no industry which offered women the service of applying the compounds for them.

. . . .

REASONS FOR THE DECISION

. . . .

2. *Main request*

. . . .

2.2. The primary issue to be dealt with is whether the subject-matter of Claim 5 is susceptible of industrial application according to Article 57 EPC.

The objection raised by the Examining Division that the application of a contraceptive to the cervix of a human female is a purely personal use which does not meet the requirement of Article 57 EPC has not been dispelled by the Appellant.

2.2.1. The Board agrees with the appellant's submission that the principle can be derived from the EPC that appropriate protection should be given to technical inventions. The latter must however fulfil the general criteria in Article 52(1) EPC. . . This means that the general principle of patentability can apply only if the alleged invention is susceptible of industrial application.

. . . .

2.2.3. The Board also agrees with the appellant that a method of contraception is not excluded *per se* from patentability under the aspects of industrial application as stipulated in Articles 57 and 52(4), first sentence, EPC. Pregnancy is not an illness and therefore its prevention is not in general therapy according to Article 52(4). . . . It seems to have been widely accepted in the Contracting States that such methods may be susceptible of industrial application . . . . It is, however, not sufficient for such methods to be susceptible of industrial application in general. Rather, the invention as claimed in the specific case must fulfil the requirement of Article 57 EPC.

2.2.4. The method as claimed in Claim 5 is intended for application by the woman herself. Even the appellant has not contested the fact that such application is not normally part of an industry as required in Article 57 EPC. Nevertheless they are of the opinion that industrial applicability has been established by the two examples given by them [(1) application by a prostitute charging her client a price which included a contraceptive; (2) application by a nurse to a disabled woman unable to apply it to herself], in which the method is alleged to be part of an industry.

2.2.5. These examples are not convincing.

2.2.5.1. In the case of the prostitute, the appellant referred to the "oldest industry in the world". Since "industry" in the field of industrial property is widely understood in its broadest sense (Article 2(3) of the Paris Convention), such a liberal interpretation may also apply to Article 57 EPC. But the decisive question is not whether a prostitute's profession is an industry, but whether the application by a prostitute of a contraceptive composition to the cervix is part of an industry. This is not the case. The application of a contraceptive composition to the cervix as claimed is not part of the business relationship between a prostitute and her client, and the contract between them does not cover the question of which means of contraception she may apply to herself. She has the freedom and responsibility to decide which one to choose, taking into consideration factors such as tolerance or reliability. This holds true at least as long as the client is not affected; if the prostitute applied contraceptive means to her client, their use might become part of the business relationship. As long as she applies them to herself and protects herself outside her contact with the client, the client is in no way involved and the application remains in the private and personal sphere of the prostitute.

A prostitute may have a professional interest in not becoming pregnant, in order to remain able to pursue her profession. This is, however, neither her only nor her predominant interest in using a contraceptive. The prostitute has a serious interest in not becoming pregnant from a client for purely private and personal reasons, because this could affect her future life to a much higher degree than the temporary inability to practice. Also, a pregnancy arising from a nonprofessional relationship could damage her professional perspectives. Nevertheless, the use of a contraceptive in a private relationship could hardly be regarded as being of an industrial character. This shows that the mere motive for using a contraceptive is of minor importance for the question of industrial application.

2.2.5.2. The example of the contraceptive cream being applied to a disabled person by a nurse is different insofar as another person is involved in the application. The fact that this person acts professionally is not sufficient to make the application of the contraceptive an industrial activity. The nurse does not offer contraception to the disabled person as an industry but to help her satisfy her strictly personal needs. It follows from this that the nature of the activity is not changed by the fact that it is not exercised by the disabled woman herself but by her assistant acting according to her instructions. That is the difference between the present case and cases of cosmetic treatment, in which the Board has regarded the requirements of Article 57 EPC as satisfied because there are enterprises whose object is to beautify the human body. . . .

2.2.6. In determining the borderline between industrial activities, in which the effects of patents have to be respected, and private and personal activities, which should not be adversely affected by the exercise of these rights, the Board has taken into consideration the fact that Article 57 EPC may be regarded as an expression of the general idea that any natural person has the right to have his or her privacy respected. The core of this right must not be taken away from anybody. Therefore the fact that for some women contraception is connected with professional activities does not give an act, which is in essence private and personal, an industrial character. It has to be stressed that this does not apply to contraception in general, but to the specific type of application of a composition as claimed in Claim 5.

. . . .

The question as to whether it would be sufficient for an industrial application to be expected in future may be left unanswered. Even if the Board were to accept the appellant's position in this respect, it would not be sufficient simply to make an unsubstantiated allegation to this effect. Without any specific indication the Board is not in a position to accept that the requirement of Article 57 EPC is fulfilled.

A patent cannot therefore be granted on the basis of the main request.

NOTES AND QUESTIONS

1. Why should it matter that a particular invention is applied in the personal space of an individual? What policy concerns can you discern in the EPO's holding in *British Technology Group/Contraceptive Method*?

2. In *Feminine Hygiene Device/Ultrafem, Inc.*, EPO Technical Board of Appeal Decision No. T 1165/97 of February 15, 2000, the Board of Appeal set aside a decision of the Examining Division refusing to grant a patent for a method of feminine hygiene that the Division concluded was not susceptible

of industrial application. The Examining Division had relied primarily on the *British Technology Group* case in concluding that the invention, a method of collecting and disposing of vaginal discharge, was not patentable. The Board of Appeal distinguished the two cases as follows:

> 3.1 It is the view of the Board that the method as claimed by the above mentioned independent claims ... complies with the requirements of Article 57 EPC, which consider an invention as susceptible of industrial application if it can be made or used in any kind of industry.
>
> Such a method can be performed by an enterprise of which the object is to assist women in collecting a sample of their vaginal discharge, e.g., for subsequent visual, chemical or bacterial inspection or for extraction of one or more of its components for use in industrial preparation of pharmaceutical compositions. Whether such enterprises actually exist is not relevant for the purposes of Article 57 EPC, what counts is the possibility that such a service may be offered by an enterprise. . . .
>
> At present there exist (hospital) laboratories offering the service of taking samples of body fluids (e.g., blood, sputum, mucus) for further analysis. Such services are performed for a fee and are run on a commercial basis. They perform their functions "continually, independently and for financial gain. . . ." It is not inconceivable that such services are extended to the provision and placement of a vaginal discharge collector, collection of vaginal discharge therein and the retrieval and subsequent disposal of the collector as presently claimed in the method claims of the third and fourth auxiliary request.
>
> 3.2 In decision T 74/93 relied upon by the Examining Division the Board considered that a method of contraception which was to be applied in the private and personal sphere of the woman in question was not susceptible of industrial application. . . .
>
> In one example it was discussed whether the fact that a nurse could be applying the method to a disabled person was sufficient to fulfill the requirement of industrial applicability. The Board deciding case T 74/93 considered that the fact that such a nurse acts professionally did not suffice to make the application of the method an industrial activity. The service of applying the contraceptive method was not offered as an industry but to satisfy the strictly personal needs of the disabled person. It followed therefrom that the nature of the activity was not changed by the fact that it was not exercised by the disabled person in question, but by her assistant following her instructions.
>
> In the present case, it can be foreseen that application and retrieval of the discharge collector is performed by a professional in the service of an enterprise. However, in contrast to the case of decision T

74/93, this service is not one satisfying only the strictly personal needs of the woman in question. Collecting a sample may be caused by external reasons, e.g. the advice of a medical practitioner to have such a sample taken for further diagnosis. Moreover, in the situation described above, the person taking the sample will generally not be acting on the instructions of the woman in question, but rather on the basis of the instructions supplied with the collector itself, if necessary supplemented by instructions issued by his/her superior.

Id. at para. 3.1–3.2.

Are you persuaded by the distinction the EPO draws between the two cases?What value is served by requiring that a patent applicant link her invention to an industry? How might the EPO's reasoning in the *British Technology Group* case affect the prospect that some inventions can trigger the establishment of new industries?

3. Do you think it makes sense to differentiate between personal and industrial applicability? Is there an argument that the market will serve as a sufficient disincentive to seeking patents for inventions that are applicable only in the personal or private sphere or is there a completely different policy concern at issue? Which do you think is the better approach: the U.S. "utility" requirement under which the *British Technology Group* invention would have been patentable, or the EPO "industrial applicability" requirement? Why?

4. Review the excerpt by Professor Risch in Note 6, *supra* at p. 353. Is commercial utility another way of requiring industrial applicability, or is it something different?

5. Efforts to develop global harmonized minimum substantive norms for patent law have been resisted by many developing countries who have long been concerned about the effect of harmonized patent rules on their ability to access technology and to develop national polices conducive to their economic priorities. The proposed WIPO Substantive Patent Law Treaty (SPLT) would harmonize differences in the "industrial applicability" and "utility" standards. A draft Article 12(4) provided three alternatives to reconcile the practical differences between the two standards:

A. A claimed invention shall be industrially applicable (useful). It shall be considered industrially applicable (useful) if it can be made or used for exploitation in any field of [commercial][economic] activity.

B. A claimed invention shall be industrially applicable (useful). It shall be considered industrially applicable (useful) if it can be made or used for exploitation in any kind of industry. "Industry" shall be understood in its broadest sense, as in the Paris Convention.

C. A claimed invention shall be industrially applicable (useful). It shall be considered industrially applicable (useful) if it has a specific, substantial and credible utility.

See WIPO Standing Committee on the Law of Patents, *"Industrial Applicability" and "Utility" Requirements: Commonalities and Differences,* WIPO Doc. SCP/9/5 (2003).

Do you think any of these alternatives will establish a truly global, uniform approach to utility? Should such uniformity be an objective of the global patent system?

6. Utility/industrial applicability inquiries often intertwine with other patentability requirements. As noted in Chapter 3, TRIPS Article 27.3 allows countries to exclude from patentability diagnostic, surgical and therapeutic methods for treating humans or animals. In discussing exclusions from patent-eligible subject matter, the WIPO Standing Committee on the Law of Patents recognized that "in some countries, inventions concerning diagnostic, surgical or therapeutic methods for the treatment of humans or animals are not patentable because they are not regarded as inventions that meet the requirement of industrial applicability." *See* WIPO, *Exclusions from Patentable Subject Matter and Exceptions to the Rights,* WIPO Doc. SCP/13/3 at 13 (2009). However, it should be noted that lack of industrial applicability is not the basis for such exceptions in the EPC. According to the EPO Enlarged Board of Appeal in G 1/04, *Diagnostic Methods* (2006), OFF. J. EUR. PAT. OFF. 334, "The motive for the change [in EPC 2000] was the realisation that these methods were excluded from patentability for reasons of public health and that, consequently, one should not base the argument on lack of industrial applicability anymore."

7. In a 2001 informal paper, WIPO, The Practical Application of Industrial Applicability/Utility Requirements Under National and Regional Laws (2001), WIPO acknowledged the blending of substantive patentability requirements and concluded:

> It is apparent that the notions of "industrial applicability" and "utility" are broad and, at least in part, overlap. Further, they relate to other substantive requirements of patentability. Therefore, for the purposes of full harmonization of substantive patent law, the industrial applicability/utility requirement cannot be considered separately from other requirements. In this regard, the SCP may wish to consider the possibility of examining substantive patentability requirements *as a whole,* without giving too much focus on the terminology "industrial applicability" or "utility."

Id. at 6.

Do you agree that utility/industrial applicability should be subsumed in a consideration of substantive patentability requirements (e.g., novelty, subject matter eligibility) "as a whole"?

C. BENEFICIAL OR MORAL UTILITY

Article 27(2) of the TRIPS Agreement provides that member countries have a right to exclude inventions from patentability in order to protect morality and public order:

> Members may exclude from patentability inventions, the prevention within their territory of the commercial exploitation of which is necessary to protect *ordre public* or morality, including to protect human, animal or plant life or health or to avoid serious prejudice to the environment, provided that such exclusion is not made merely because the exploitation is prohibited by their law.

This standard is reflected in patent laws worldwide. For example, Article 32 of the Patent Act of Japan provides ". . . any invention that is liable to injure public order, morality, or public health shall not be patented." Article 5 of the Patent Law of the People's Republic of China provides in part "patent rights shall not be granted for invention-creations that violate the law or social ethics, or harm public interests." And Article 25(4) of the South African Patent Act provides in part "[a] patent shall not be granted (a) for an invention the publication or exploitation of which would be generally expected to encourage offensive or immoral behaviour."

However, as noted in Chapter 4, no such statutory provision is present in U.S. law. Instead, fairly early in the development of U.S. patent law, courts considered the morality of an invention under the rubric of the utility requirement. Justice Story is credited with providing the first articulation of the doctrine in his jury instruction in *Lowell v. Lewis*, 15 F. Cas. 1018 (C.C.D. Mass. 1817). He explained that:

> The patent act uses the phrase 'useful invention' mere[ly] incidentally; it occurs only in the first section, and there it seems merely descriptive of the subject matter of the application. . . All that the law requires is, that the invention should not be frivolous or injurious to the well-being, good policy, or sound morals of society. The word 'useful,' therefore, is incorporated into the act in contradistinction to mischievous or immoral. For instance, a new invention to poison people, or to promote debauchery, or to facilitate private assassination, is not a patentable invention. But if the invention steers wide of these objections, whether it be more or less useful is a circumstance very material to the interests of the patentee, but of no importance to the public.

Id. at 1019 (citations omitted).

Justice Story's language provided the foundation for what came to be known as the "moral utility" doctrine—the idea that to be "useful" within the meaning of the patent statute, and thus eligible for patent protection, an invention had to meet certain judicially identified standards of morality. For more than 150 years, courts cited this requirement as the basis for rejecting a variety of morally controversial inventions, including gambling machines and fraudulent articles such as incredible medical devices, a process for spotting tobacco leaves to make them appear to be of higher quality, and stockings that appeared to have a seam (suggesting higher quality) but which were actually seamless.

The USPTO continued to reject applications, and U.S. courts continued to invalidate "obnoxious or mischievous" patents, in particular those that were deemed to be deceptive or immoral, until 1977 when the USPTO signaled a change of policy in *Ex parte Murphy,* 200 U.S.P.Q. (BNA) 801, 803 (B.P.A.I. 1977). In that case, the Board of Patent Appeals and Interferences concluded that "this Office should not be the agency which seeks to enforce a standard of morality with respect to gambling, by refusing, on the ground of lack of patentable utility, to grant a patent on a game of chance if the requirements of the Patent Act otherwise have been met." Today, as noted in the Manual of Patent Examining Procedure ("MPEP") Section 706.03(a), which provides instructions for patent examiners: "A rejection under 35 U.S.C. § 101 for lack of utility should *not* be based on grounds that the invention is frivolous, fraudulent or against public policy." (Emphasis in original, citations omitted).

As a result, instead of an invention being ineligible for patent protection if it could be used unlawfully, an invention could meet the moral utility requirement if it had at least one moral, legal purpose. As noted by the USPTO Board of Patent Appeals and Interferences in *Ex parte Murphy*: "[E]verything [is] useful within the meaning of the law, if it is used (or designed and adapted to be used) to accomplish a good result, though in fact it is oftener used (or is as well or even better adapted to be used) to accomplish a bad one[.]" 200 U.S.P.Q. (BNA) 801, 802 (BPAI 1977). Eventually, however, courts began refusing to impose any morality requirement at all. The courts acknowledged that it was an area in which Congress could legislate, but that such determinations were not the proper purview of the judiciary or the USPTO.

In 1998, the moral utility doctrine seemed on the verge of revival when the USPTO threatened to invoke the requirement in response to a controversial patent application. The application, filed by activist Jeremy Rifkin and biologist Stuart Newman, claimed the invention of human-animal chimera, creatures made, in theory, by blending human cells with those of various animals such as mice, chimpanzees, pigs, or baboons. The applicants actually had not made such creatures, nor did they want anyone else to make them. Rather, their purpose in filing the application was to provoke a debate and force Congress, the courts, or the USPTO to draw the line on patent-eligible subject matter.

Shortly after receiving the chimera application, the USPTO issued a media advisory in which it cited Justice Story's quote in *Lowell v. Lewis* and posited that "inventions directed to human/non-human chimera could, under certain circumstances, not be patentable because, among other things, they would fail to meet the public policy and morality aspects of the utility requirement." *See* U.S. Pat. Off., Media Advisory 98–6, *Facts on Patenting Life Forms Having a Relationship to Humans* (April 1, 1998). Nevertheless, by its own admission in a more recent statement, the USPTO acknowledged that it is without authority to deny a patent based on morality or public policy concerns. In addressing a public comment that the USPTO should deny patents on DNA for the public good, the Office stated:

> The scope of subject matter that is eligible for a patent, the requirements that must be met in order to be granted a patent, and the legal rights that are conveyed by an issued patent, are all controlled by statutes which the USPTO must administer. . . . Congress creates the law and the Federal judiciary interprets the law. The USPTO must administer the laws as Congress has enacted them and as the Federal courts have interpreted them. Current law provides that when the statutory patentability requirements are met, there is no basis to deny patent applications. . . .

Utility Examination Guidelines, 66 FED. REG. 1092, 1095 (Jan. 5, 2001).

Not long after the USPTO issued its Media Advisory, the Court of Appeals for the Federal Circuit handed down the following decision, addressing the moral utility requirement.

JUICY WHIP, INC. V. ORANGE BANG, INC.

United States Court of Appeals, Federal Circuit
185 F.3d 1364 (Fed. Cir.1999)

■ BRYSON, Circuit Judge.

The district court in this case held a patent invalid for lack of utility on the ground that the patented invention was designed to deceive customers by imitating another product and thereby increasing sales of a particular good. We reverse and remand.

I

Juicy Whip, Inc., is the assignee of United States Patent No. 5,575,405, which is entitled "Post-Mix Beverage Dispenser With an Associated Simulated Display of Beverage." A "post-mix" beverage dispenser stores beverage syrup concentrate and water in separate locations until the beverage is ready to be dispensed. The syrup and water are mixed together immediately before the beverage is dispensed, which is usually after the consumer requests the beverage. In contrast, in a "pre-mix" beverage dispenser, the syrup concentrate and water are pre-mixed and the beverage is stored in a display reservoir bowl until it is ready to be dispensed. The display bowl is said to stimulate impulse buying by providing the consumer with a visual beverage display. A pre-mix display bowl, however, has a limited capacity and is subject to contamination by bacteria. It therefore must be refilled and cleaned frequently.

The invention claimed in the '405 patent is a post-mix beverage dispenser that is designed to look like a pre-mix beverage dispenser. The claims require the post-mix dispenser to have a transparent bowl that is filled with a fluid that simulates the appearance of the dispensed beverage and is resistant to bacterial growth. The claims also require that the dispenser create the visual impression that the bowl is the principal source of the dispensed beverage, although in fact the beverage is mixed immediately before it is dispensed, as in conventional post-mix dispensers.

Claim 1 is representative of the claims at issue. It reads as follows:

In a post-mix beverage dispenser of the type having an outlet for discharging beverage components in predetermined proportions to provide a serving of dispensed beverage, the improvement which comprises:

a transparent bowl having no fluid connection with the outlet and visibly containing a quantity of fluid;

said fluid being resistant to organic growth and simulating the appearance of the dispensed beverage;

said bowl being positioned relative to the outlet to create the visual impression that said bowl is the reservoir and principal source of the dispensed beverage from the outlet; and

said bowl and said quantity of fluid visible within said bowl cooperating to create the visual impression that multiple servings of the dispensed beverage are stored within said bowl.

Juicy Whip sued defendants Orange Bang, Inc., and Unique Beverage Dispensers, Inc., (collectively, "Orange Bang") in the United States District Court for the Central District of California, alleging that they were infringing the claims of the '405 patent. Orange Bang moved for summary judgment of invalidity, and the district court granted Orange Bang's motion on the ground that the invention lacked utility and thus was unpatentable under 35 U.S.C. § 101.

The court concluded that the invention lacked utility because its purpose was to increase sales by deception, i.e., through imitation of another product. The court explained that the purpose of the invention "is to create an illusion, whereby customers believe that the fluid contained in the bowl is the actual beverage that they are receiving, when of course it is not." Although the court acknowledged Juicy Whip's argument that the invention provides an accurate representation of the dispensed beverage for the consumer's benefit while eliminating the need for retailers to clean their display bowls, the court concluded that those claimed reasons for the patent's utility "are not independent of its deceptive purpose, and are thus insufficient to raise a disputed factual issue to present to a jury." The court further held that the invention lacked utility because it "improves the prior art only to the extent that it increases the salability of beverages dispensed from post-mix dispensers"; an invention lacks utility, the court stated, if it confers no benefit to the public other than the opportunity for making a product more salable. Finally, the court ruled that the invention lacked utility because it "is merely an imitation of the premix dispenser," and thus does not constitute a new and useful machine.

II

Section 101 of the Patent Act of 1952, 35 U.S.C. § 101, provides that "[w]hoever invents or discovers any new and useful process, machine, manufacture, or composition of matter, or any new and useful improvement thereof," may obtain a patent on the invention or discovery. The threshold of utility is not high: An invention is "useful" under section 101 if it is capable of providing some identifiable benefit. *See Brenner v. Manson,* 383 U.S. 519, 534 (1966); *Brooktree Corp. v. Advanced Micro Devices, Inc.,* 977 F.2d 1555, 1571 (Fed.Cir.1992) ("To violate § 101 the claimed device must be totally incapable of achieving a useful result"); *Fuller v. Berger,* 120 F. 274, 275 (7th Cir.1903) (test for utility is whether invention "is incapable of serving any beneficial end").

To be sure, since Justice Story's opinion in *Lowell v. Lewis,* 15 F. Cas. 1018 (C.C.D.Mass.1817), it has been stated that inventions that are "injurious to the well-being, good policy, or sound morals of society" are unpatentable. As examples of such inventions, Justice Story listed "a new invention to poison people, or to promote debauchery, or to facilitate private assassination." *Id.* at 1019. Courts have continued to recite Justice Story's formulation, *see Tol-O-Matic, Inc. v. Proma Produkt-Und Marketing Gesellschaft m.b.H.,* 945 F.2d 1546, 1552–53 (Fed.Cir.1991); *In re Nelson,* 280 F.2d 172, 178–79 (CCPA 1960), but the principle that inventions are invalid if they are principally designed to serve immoral or illegal purposes has not been applied broadly in recent years. For example, years ago courts invalidated patents on gambling devices on the ground that they were immoral, *see e.g., Brewer v. Lichtenstein,* 278 F. 512 (7th Cir.1922); *Schultze v. Holtz,* 82 F. 448 (N.D.Cal.1897); *National Automatic Device Co. v. Lloyd,* 40 F. 89 (N.D.Ill.1889), but that is no longer the law, *see In re Murphy,* 200 USPQ 801 (PTO Bd. App.1977).

In holding the patent in this case invalid for lack of utility, the district court relied on two Second Circuit cases dating from the early years of this century, *Rickard v. Du Bon,* 103 F. 868 (2d Cir.1900), and *Scott &*

Williams v. Aristo Hosiery Co., 7 F.2d 1003 (2d Cir.1925). In the *Rickard* case, the court held invalid a patent on a process for treating tobacco plants to make their leaves appear spotted. At the time of the invention, according to the court, cigar smokers considered cigars with spotted wrappers to be of superior quality, and the invention was designed to make unspotted tobacco leaves appear to be of the spotted-and thus more desirable-type. The court noted that the invention did not promote the burning quality of the leaf or improve its quality in any way; "the only effect, if not the only object, of such treatment, is to spot the tobacco, and counterfeit the leaf spotted by natural causes." *Id.* at 869.

The *Aristo Hosiery* case concerned a patent claiming a seamless stocking with a structure on the back of the stocking that imitated a seamed stocking. The imitation was commercially useful because at the time of the invention many consumers regarded seams in stockings as an indication of higher quality. The court noted that the imitation seam did not "change or improve the structure or the utility of the article," and that the record in the case justified the conclusion that true seamed stockings were superior to the seamless stockings that were the subject of the patent. *See Aristo Hosiery,* 7 F.2d at 1004. "At best," the court stated, "the seamless stocking has imitation marks for the purposes of deception, and the idea prevails that with such imitation the article is more salable." *Id.* That was not enough, the court concluded, to render the invention patentable.

We decline to follow *Rickard* and *Aristo Hosiery,* as we do not regard them as representing the correct view of the doctrine of utility under the Patent Act of 1952. The fact that one product can be altered to make it look like another is in itself a specific benefit sufficient to satisfy the statutory requirement of utility.

It is not at all unusual for a product to be designed to appear to viewers to be something it is not. For example, cubic zirconium is designed to simulate a diamond, imitation gold leaf is designed to imitate real gold leaf, synthetic fabrics are designed to simulate expensive natural fabrics, and imitation leather is designed to look like real leather. In each case, the invention of the product or process that makes such imitation possible has "utility" within the meaning of the patent statute, and indeed there are numerous patents directed toward making one product imitate another. *See, e.g.,* U.S. Pat. No. 5,762,968 (method for producing imitation grill marks on food without using heat); U.S. Pat. No. 5,899,038 (laminated flooring imitating wood); U.S. Pat. No. 5,571,545 (imitation hamburger). Much of the value of such products resides in the fact that they appear to be something they are not. Thus, in this case the claimed post-mix dispenser meets the statutory requirement of utility by embodying the features of a post-mix dispenser while imitating the visual appearance of a pre-mix dispenser.

The fact that customers may believe they are receiving fluid directly from the display tank does not deprive the invention of utility. Orange Bang has not argued that it is unlawful to display a representation of the beverage in the manner that fluid is displayed in the reservoir of the invention, even though the fluid is not what the customer will actually receive. Moreover, even if the use of a reservoir containing fluid that is not dispensed is considered deceptive, that is not by itself sufficient to render the invention unpatentable. The requirement of "utility" in patent law is not a directive to the Patent and Trademark Office or the courts to serve as arbiters of deceptive trade practices. Other agencies, such as the Federal Trade Commission and the Food and Drug Administration, are assigned the task of protecting consumers from fraud and deception in the sale of food products. *Cf. In re Watson,* 517 F.2d 465, 474–76 (CCPA 1975) (stating that it is not the province of the Patent Office to determine, under section 101, whether drugs are safe). As the Supreme Court put the point more generally, "Congress never intended that the patent laws should displace the police powers of the States, meaning by that term those powers by which the health, good order, peace and general welfare of the community are promoted." *Webber v. Virginia,* 103 U.S. (13 Otto) 344, 347–48 (1880).

Of course, Congress is free to declare particular types of inventions unpatentable for a variety of reasons, including deceptiveness. *Cf.* 42 U.S.C. § 2181(a) (exempting from patent protection inventions useful solely in connection with special nuclear material or atomic weapons). Until such time as Congress does so, however, we find no basis in section 101 to hold that inventions can be ruled unpatentable for lack of utility simply because they have the capacity to fool some members of the public. The district court therefore erred in holding that the invention of the '405 patent lacks utility because it deceives the public through imitation in a manner that is designed to increase product sales.

REVERSED and REMANDED.

NOTES AND QUESTIONS

1. The decision in *Juicy Whip, Inc. v. Orange Bang, Inc.,* 185 F.3d 1364 (Fed. Cir. 1999), read in conjunction with the U.S. Supreme Court's pronouncement in *Diamond v. Chakrabarty, supra* Chapter 4, that it had "no competence" to address the "high policy" questions surrounding the moral and ethical issues generated by the patenting of genetic material, indicates that, for good or ill, morality-based inquiries are outside the scope of patent law in the U.S. On what does the Federal Circuit base its repudiation of the moral utility requirement?

2. Not surprisingly, *Juicy Whip* has not stopped parties from continuing to raise moral utility arguments in litigation. In early 2011, eighty-three or-

ganic and conventional farmers and other concerned organizations, along with the Public Patent Foundation, sued the Monsanto Company for a declaratory judgment of non-infringement of Monsanto's patents on RoundUp Ready® herbicide-resistant transgenic seeds. *OSGATA et. al. v. Monsanto Co.*, First Amended Complaint, No. 11-cv-2163-NRB (S.D.N.Y. Jun. 1, 2011). The plaintiffs do not wish to use transgenic seed but are afraid of their crops being contaminated by Monsanto's seed, losing their organic certification, and potentially being subject to patent infringement liability. Monsanto is known for vigorously enforcing its patents against farmers, having brought over a hundred lawsuits and settled hundreds of other such disputes. According to the plaintiffs:

> [P]atents on transgenic seed fail to satisfy the requirement of both the Constitution and the Patent Act that only technology with a beneficial societal use may be patented. . . . Because transgenic seed, and in particular Monsanto's transgenic seed, is "injurious to the wellbeing, good policy, or sound morals of society" and threatens to "poison people," Monsanto's transgenic seed patents are all invalid. . . .

> Monsanto's most predominant transgenic trait is glyphosate tolerance. This trait makes crops tolerant of Monsanto's nonselective, glyphosate-based herbicide, called Roundup. Roundup causes severe injury or destruction when applied to crops that are not glyphosate tolerant. . . . [A]s Monsanto's transgenic seed becomes more widely used, then so too will glyphosate. As such, the existence of Monsanto's transgenic seed is directly responsible for the increased use of glyphosate, . . . which studies have shown is harmful to human health. . . . Studies suggest an association between glyphosate use and the risk of non-Hodgkin lymphoma. . . . Another study that included more than fifty thousand pesticide applicators suggested a link between glyphosate use and multiple myeoloma. . . . There are also serious questions about whether transgenic seed itself has an effect on human health [citing research] . . . . Others have suggested an association between Monsanto's transgenic seed, its inherent increase in glyphosate use and animal miscarriages. . . .

> While transgenic seed poses many dangers for society, its purported benefits have not been achieved. While Monsanto makes many bold promises for its transgenic seed, those promises have universally been proven false. . . . [T]he Attorney General of West Virginia filed suit against Monsanto just last fall after his office determined that several published tests contradicted the yield results claimed by Monsanto in its advertising. . . .

> [E]vidence shows that the increased use of glyphosate caused by Monsanto's transgenic seed has in turn caused weeds to become resistant to the herbicide. . . . Thus, despite all of the hype, using transgenic seed actually increases costs, reduces production, and exacerbates environmental harms. . . .

> [A]s Justice Story explained in *Lowell v. Lewis*, inventions that are "injurious to the wellbeing, good policy, or sound morals of society" are unpatentable. . . . For at least the reasons discussed above regarding the perils of transgenic seed, Monsanto's transgenic seed is not "useful," and, therefore, Monsanto's transgenic seed patents are all invalid.

First Amended Complaint at para. 4, 105–120, 144.

In a separate brief, the plaintiffs note that "Monsanto spends much of its brief trying to defend the social utility of transgenic seed. As described in the Amended Complaint, Monsanto's transgenic seed is no more useful for society than some of its past products, like Agent Orange, DDT, PCB's and other toxins, all of which Monsanto said were safe at the time, but were later proven not to be." *OSGATA et al. v. Monsanto* Co., Brief by Plaintiffs Defending Standing, No. 1:11-cv-02163-NRB at 8 (S.D.N.Y. August 11, 2011). Should such concerns be considered in the patentability or patent validity analysis? For additional views on this topic see, e.g., Elizabeth A. Rowe, *Patents, Genetically Modified Food, and IP Overreaching,* 64 SMU L. REV. 859 (2011) and Zachary Lerner, Comment, *Rethinking What Agriculture Could Use: A Proposed Heightened Utility Standard for Genetically Modified Food Patents,* 55 U. KAN. L. REV. 991, 1014–20 (2007).

3. Of course, moral considerations are not completely absent from U.S. patent law, as several provisions do discourage some dishonest activity. For example, inventors who intentionally mislead the patent office during the patent-obtaining process (inequitable conduct, 37 C.F.R. § 1.56) are sanctioned, and patents where the inventive concept itself was stolen from another (pre-AIA 35 U.S.C. § 102(f)) are disallowed. Beyond these, questions of the behavior of a patent applicant, questions regarding the morality of an invention largely lie outside the scope of the U.S. patent inquiry. Is this a prudent policy? Should the U.S. consider questions of morality in the patentability analysis? *See* Margo A. Bagley, *Patent First, Ask Questions Later: Morality and Biotechnology in Patent Law*, 45 WILLIAM & MARY L. REV. 469 (2003).

CHAPTER 6

NOVELTY

■ ■ ■

A. DEFINING NOVELTY

1. THE "*SINE QUA NON*" OF PATENTABILITY

Novelty, the requirement that an invention be in some way "new," has always been a feature of patent systems around the globe. Recall that the Venetian Patent Act of 1474 discussed in Chapter 1, only allowed for patent protection for a "*new* and ingenious device."

Early conceptions of novelty, including under the English Statute of Monopolies, differed from the modern view by allowing knowledge new to the realm but known elsewhere to be patentable. Prior public local knowledge or use of the invention, however, would void patentability. As explained by the English Court of Appeals in the case of *Patterson v. Gaslight and Coke Co.*, [1877] 3 App. Cas. 239 (H.L.) 244 (appeal taken from Eng.) (quoting W. M. Hindmarch, A TREATISE ON THE LAW RELATING TO PATENT PRIVILEGES FOR THE SOLE USE OF INVENTIONS 33 (1846)):

> If the public once becomes possessed of an invention by any means whatever, no subsequent patent for it can be granted either to the true or first inventor himself, or any other person, for the public cannot be deprived of the right to use the invention, and a patentee of the invention could not give any consideration to the public for the grant, the public already possessing everything that he could give.

Just how "new" an invention has to be for patentability has been a question of degree that can vary considerably from country to country based on differing definitions of prior art and public policy goals. The term "prior art" used generically refers to the body of information against which a claimed invention is compared in determining whether the invention is novel. In its broadest form, prior art includes all publicly accessible information available prior to a certain date, generally the filing date of the application for patent. An applicant need not actually be aware of prior art cited against her application for the information to be considered prior art. Knowledge of all of the relevant art is presumed on the part of the hypothetical person having ordinary skill in the art (PHOSITA).

Today, novelty is the *sine qua non* of patentability, the essential element every invention must have to be worthy of patent protection. Without the novelty requirement, the grant of a patent would not provide the public with the disclosure of new information. Rather, it would allow patentees to exclude the public from the use of information already in its purview. As noted above, national and regional provisions regarding novelty may differ on how broadly or narrowly prior art is defined. An example of a broad definition of "prior art" appears in EPC Article 54 which provides, in part:

(1) An invention shall be considered to be new if it does not form part of the state of the art.

(2) The state of the art shall be held to comprise everything made available to the public by means of a written or oral description, by use, *or in any other way*, before the date of filing of the European patent application.

(3) Additionally, the content of European patent applications as filed, the dates of filing of which are prior to the date referred to in paragraph 2 and which were published on or after that date, shall be considered as comprised in the state of the art.

Convention on the Grant of European Patents, Art. 54, Oct. 5, 1973, 1065 U.N.T.S. 199 (emphasis added).

The following case illustrates the application of Article 54 in the European Patent Office (EPO).

SOCIÉTÉ DES PRODUITS NESTLÉ S.A.
Opposition by Chris Hansen A/S and Mars UK Limited
EPO Board of Appeals – T_0690/04–3.3.09
March 1, 2007

[Food product companies **Chris Hansen** and **Mars UK** (Respondents I and II respectively) are opposing the grant of a European patent to Nestlé, parent company of Nestlé Purina Pet Care Company. The main ground for the opposition is that the claimed invention lacks novelty in view of the prior art; namely, sales of pet food products in Denmark and the U.S. before the patent application priority date. EDS.]

3. Novelty (Article 54 EPC)

3.1 Claim 2 of the patent . . . is directed to a cereal product having the following features:

  a) a dried

  b) ready-to-eat cereal product comprising

  c) a gelatinised

  d) starch matrix which includes

  e) a coating containing

f) a probiotic micro-organism, wherein

g) the coating comprises a carrier substrate which contains the micro-organism. . . .

3.2 Respondent II denied the novelty of the subject-matter of Claim 2 . . . over the prior public uses of the Eagle Pack Products and the Wysong Products.

3.3 According to EPO practice concerning the determination of whether an invention has been made available to the public by prior use it is necessary to clarify when the act of prior use occurred, what was made available to the public through that use and the circumstances of the act of use, i.e. where, how and by whom the subject-matter was made public through that use. . . .

3.4 The Wysong International Vitality Feline product.

3.4.1 The "when" issue

This prior use objection is based essentially on the affidavit of Dr. Randy L. Wysong, founder and director of the Wysong Corporation, Midland, Michigan, United States of America, and the clarifications filed with letter dated 29 January 2007.

Dr. Wysong stated that Wysong Corporation had been selling dry pet food containing probiotics since the 1980s. These products included the "Vitality Feline" product (also called "Vitality Dry Kattefoder" when sold in Denmark) which is considered to anticipate the subject-matter of Claim 2 of the main request. Respondent II filed photographs of a package of a "Vitality Feline" product and several invoices showing that the product was available to the public before the priority date of the patent in suit, i.e. before 9 January 1997.

[These photographs] include[] pictures of the front and back of the packaging for the "Vitality Feline" product. The package was sold in Denmark and is referred to as "Vitality Feline" on the back side and had been relabelled as "Vitality Dry Kattefoder" on the front side. Dr. Wysong explained in point 17 of his affidavit that the reference "951106" on the reverse side of the package referred to the date 6 November 1995 and the Board has no reason to doubt the accuracy of this statement as this manner of codifying a date on a printed publication is conventional. Respondent II further filed two invoices showing that "Vitality Dry Kattefoder" had been sold in Denmark on 7 November 1996 and 26 March 1996 and submitted two declarations by Ms. M. L. Møller . . . and Ms. B. Hermansen . . . which state that they recognised with complete certainty the packages of "Vitality Dry Kattefoder" as those which they had purchased in various pet shops in Ballerup and Roedrove in 1995 or 1996. The Appellant questioned whether the [Vitality] product could have been sold in Denmark because the batch code and the expiration date of the product were not given on the package. Without this information the product could not have been sold legally in any EU country.

The Board notes that the evidence provided by Respondent II undoubtedly shows that the product was marketed before the priority date of the patent. The absence of an adequate selling authorisation by the competent administrative EU bodies cannot impair the accuracy of the available evidence. In fact, Respondent II actually confirmed during the oral proceedings that the product had later to be withdrawn from the market due to the absence of such authorisation.

Respondent II provided further evidence that certain Wysong products, including the Vitality Feline product now under consideration, were available also in the United States. . . .

In summary, the evidence filed by Respondent II establishes that the product "Vitality Feline" was produced and sold by Wysong Corporation before the priority date of the patent.

3.4.2 The "what" issue

It remains to decide if this product anticipates the subject-matter of Claim 2.

The Vitality Feline product is a dried (moisture max. 12%) ready-to-eat (see feeding guide) cereal product containing several starch sources (wheat, rice, corn and extruded soybeans) and a source of live (viable) naturally occurring micro-organisms (Streptococcus faecium, Lactobacillus acidophilus, Lactobacillus casei, Lactobacillus lactis and Saccharomyces cerevisiae) having a probiotic activity which has not been quantified. Thus, the Vitality Feline product shows features a), b), d) and f) of Claim 2 of the patent in suit.

It remains to be established whether this product also anticipates the remaining features of Claim 2, namely that the starch is gelatinised (feature c)) and that it includes a coating (feature e)) which contains the probiotic micro-organism (feature g)).

To prove that the Vitality Feline product also anticipates features c), e), and g), Respondent II relied essentially on the declarations by Dr. R. L. Wysong, explaining the process of preparation of the Wysong products and on an information video produced in 1991 and its transcript published in 1993, also explaining how the Wysong products were prepared. This video film is mentioned on the [Vitality] package together with the information that it could be purchased from Wysong Corporation.

Respondent II filed a copy of the final frame of this video showing that it was made in 1991 and a transcript excerpt of the video including the preparation process of the Wysong products. . . .

The process as described in [the video transcript] indicates . . . that the Wysong products were prepared by extrusion cooking to produce gelatinized starches (feature c)). The extruded product was dried and could have various liquids and powder applied to it before it was finally put into its final package . . . . [I]t is explained that fragile ingredients such as essential fatty acids and probiotic and enzymes could be incorporated after processing to prevent their destruction. The addition of a fatty acid and a probiotic after the extrusion step results in a coating containing the probiotic micro-organism (features e) and g)).

The disclosure of [the video transcript] is confirmed by page 2 of the affidavit of Dr. Wysong explaining that the Wysong process involves the extrusion cooking of, amongst other ingredients, cereal grains resulting in a kibble product having a gelatinised starch matrix. The extruded kibbles are then dried and coated with the heat-sensitive products. . . .

The Appellant pointed out that the sale of a product constituted prior art only if the skilled person could analyse the product and reproduce it without undue burden. It doubted that an analysis of the product would reveal to a skilled person all the features of a product falling within the scope of the patent, in particular because in its opinion the identity of the micro-organism, the amount of viable micro-organism present and the presence of a carrier substrate could not be determined without ambiguity.

The Board cannot accept this argument of the Appellant. As explained above, the subject-matter of Claim 2 lacks novelty because the product Vitality Feline and a process for its production were available to the public before the priority date of the patent. Under these circumstances, it is not necessary that the skilled person could analyse the product, because he would know its constitution from the ingredients listed in [the Vitality product] and the method of preparation described in the prepublished transcript.

Notwithstanding the above and for the sake of completeness, the Board notes that it considers that the skilled person could analyze the "Vitality Feline" in order to confirm its constitution. It is within the knowledge of the skilled person how to determine the degree of gelatinization of a given starch by using physical, chemical and biochemical methods such as loss of birefrigerance, increase in viscosity, differential scanning calorimetry, etc. It is also within the skilled person's capacity to find out if the product includes a coating containing the probiotic micro-organism.

This analysis was in fact made on the [Vitality] product by Ms. Jensen, the Laboratory Manager in [Chris] Hansen during 1996 and 1997, who, notwithstanding her cautious language, confirmed in her affidavit . . . that the "Vitality Dry Kattefoder" is coated and contained a large quantity of lipid and that the bacteria were ("suspected to be") incorporated into the fatty substance . . . . (The use of the word "suspected" in this statement cannot detract from the fact that verifying this "suspicion", if wished, would not go beyond routine analysis techniques).

3.5 Thus, the product Vitality Feline shows all the features of Claim 2 of the patent in suit . . . . The subject-matter of this Claim 2 lacks therefore novelty (Article 54 EPC).

NOTE ON COMPARATIVE APPROACHES TO NOVELTY

The term "anticipation" used by the Board in the *Nestlé* case, is simply the opposite of novelty. If an invention is anticipated by the prior art, it is not new. Although definitions of prior art differ on territorial and temporal bases, as will be discussed later in this Chapter, the general approach to novelty is quite similar in Europe, the U.S., Japan, and most other countries. In the U.S., a claimed invention is anticipated if each of its elements is present in a single prior art reference that would enable a PHOSITA to make the invention.

There are exceptions to this "single reference" rule: A reference can be anticipating if the PHOSITA could take its disclosure in combination with her own ordinary skill and be in possession of the invention. Also, extrinsic evidence generally can be used to educate a judge about what a reference would disclose to the PHOSITA. Finally, additional documents can add elements to the reference but only if they were appropriately mentioned in the reference so as to be considered "incorporated by reference." The EPO Examination Guidelines describe a very similar approach:

> It should be noted that in considering novelty (as distinct from inventive step . . .), it is not permissible to combine separate items of prior art together. . . . However, if a document (the "primary" document) refers explicitly to another document as providing more detailed information on certain features, the teaching of the latter is to be regarded as incorporated into the document containing the reference, if the document referred to was available to the public on the publication date of the document containing the reference. . . . It is further permissible to use a dictionary or similar document of reference in order to interpret a special term used in a document. . . . A document takes away the novelty of any claimed subject-matter derivable directly and unambiguously from that document including any features implicit to a person skilled in the art in what is expressly mentioned in the document. . . . In determining novelty, a prior document should be read as it would have been read by a person skilled in the art on the relevant date of the document.

EPO, Guidelines for Examination in the European Patent Office, Pt. C, Ch. IV-27, Secs. 9.1–9.3 (April 2010).

The approach to novelty in Japan appears consistent with the U.S. and EPO approaches. The Japanese Patent Examination Guidelines on Novelty state:

1.2.4 Inventions Described in Distributed Publications . . .(3) Inventions that have been described in publications

The expression "inventions described in publications" means inventions recognized from the descriptions in the publications or equivalents to such descriptions in the publications.

The expression "equivalents to such descriptions" means those that persons can derive from the descriptions based on their common general knowledge (Note) as of the filing.

Note: The term "common general knowledge" means obvious knowledge derived from the general knowledge or experience of a person skilled in the art, including well-known arts or commonly used arts.

Also, the term "well-known arts" means the arts generally known in the technical field, such as those published in a significant number of documents and known in the field widely enough that it is not necessary to submit any examples of the arts. The term "commonly used arts" means the arts well-known and commonly used.

1.5.4 Comparing the Claimed Inventions and Cited Inventions

(1) The claimed inventions and cited inventions are compared by identifying corresponding and differing points between matters used to specify the claimed invention and matters required to express the cited inventions by words (hereinafter called "matters used to specify the cited inventions") . . . .

(4) Combinations of two or more independent cited inventions should not be compared to the claimed inventions.

1.5.5 Determining the Novelty of the Claimed Inventions

(1) When the difference between the matters used to specify the invention in the claimed inventions themselves and those used to specify the cited inventions is not found after the comparison, the claimed inventions are not novel. Any difference between these two matters involves the novelty of the claimed inventions.

Examination Guidelines for Patent and Utility Model in Japan: Novelty and Inventive Step, Ch. 2, pp. 3, 14 (2005).

In each of these jurisdictions, the novelty of an invention is compared to a single prior art reference (invention, publication, item in public use), with consideration being given to information that would be known to a PHOSITA from the reference. Such an inquiry is designed to prevent the patenting of information already available to the public, a goal sought by patent regimes worldwide. For a helpful overview of distinctions and similarities between approaches to novelty and priority in the USPTO, JPO, and EPO, *see* Toshiko

Takenaka, *Rethinking the United States First-to-Invent Principle from a Comparative Law Perspective: A Proposal to Restructure § 102 Novelty and Priority Provisions,* 39 HOUS. L. REV. 621 (2002).

The following summary and translation from the John Marshall Law School Chinese Intellectual Property blog site http://chineseip.jmls.edu/sites/en/playing-winning-cards-chinese-patent-invalidation-appeals, shows a similarly broad approach to novelty and prior art in China as we see elsewhere. The rights at issue are design patents, not utility patents, and thus cover only the appearance of an article of manufacture. Nevertheless, applications for design patents are subject to the same requirements of novelty and nonobviousness as inventions protected by utility patents. Design patents are discussed in more detail in Chapter 8.

ARTHUR TAN-CHI YUAN, PLAYING THE WINNING CARDS IN CHINESE PATENT INVALIDATION APPEALS
03/21/2012

In a series of 7 cases[1] before the Beijing First Intermediate People's Court, the Cincinnati-based company, The United States Playing Card Company ("USPC"), was dragged into a patent invalidation slugfest with a Chinese patentee over playing cards and [playing card casings]. The USPC has been a winner in all these cases due to their timely filing of invalidation proceedings before the Patent Reexamination Board of the State Intellectual Property Office ("PRB"), as well as timely registration of their trademarks and clever litigation strategy.

One Patent, Please

The case started when USPC decided to invalidate a total of 7 patents filed and owned by plaintiff of the lawsuit, Mr. Zeng Qingsong. The invalidation proceedings were before the PRB. In all 7 cases, the PRB invalidated the patents. The plaintiff thereafter sought judicial review of the PRB's administrative decisions.

Zeng filed 7 design patents in a span of about 3 months on playing card designs and designs on boxes housing the playing cards. These design patents are:

---

[1] Case numbers 39, 43, 46, 1201, 1202, 1203, and 1204.

Table 1

Design patent #	Filing date	Design
2007303 16154.2	10/29/ 2007	组件1后视图 · 组件1主视图 · 组件2主视图 · 组件3主视图 · 组件55后视图 · 组件55主视图

Design patent #	Filing date	Design
2007303 16153.8	10/29/ 2007	组件1~组件54后视图 · 组件1主视图 · 组件2主视图 · 组件3主视图 · 组件55后视图 · 组件55主视图

Design patent #	Filing date	Design
2007300 60301.4	7/24/ 2007	

Design patent #	Filing date	Design
2007303 16152.3	10/29/ 2007	

Design patent #	Filing date	Design
2007303 16150.4	10/29/ 2007	展开图　　　　　　　　　主视图

Design patent #	Filing date	Design
2007303 16151.9	10/29/ 2007	展开图　　　　　　　　　主视图

Design patent #	Filing date	Design
2007300 60715.7	7/27/ 2007	主视图

From Table 1 above, Zeng received 3 design patents on the playing cards with July 24, 2007 as the earliest filing date among the three (*see* 200730060301.4 patent). In addition, he also received 3 design patents on the box of the playing cards with all three patent applications filed on October 29, 2007.

There is a problem, however, with this approach. According to Article 13 of the Implementing Regulations of the Patent Law of China[2] ("Regulations") 2001:

> **For any identical invention-creation, only one patent right shall be granted.**
>
> Two or more applicants who respectively file, on the same day, applications for patent for the identical invention-creation, as provided for in Article 9 of the Patent Law, shall, after receipt of a notification from the Patent Administration Department under the State Council, hold consultations among themselves to decide the person or persons who shall be entitled to file the application (emphasis added).

Therefore, USPC argued before the PRB that Zeng's duplicated patents was a violation of Article 13 of the Regulations. So, if anything, Zeng should have only received 1 design patent on the playing cards: 200730060301.4 ("card patent"), and another design patent on the box of the playing cards: 200730316150.4 ("box patent").

Zeng disagreed and argued that the 2001 Regulations are not applicable because USPC challenged his patents in the PRB on February 1, 2010. Instead, the new Regulations issued on January 9, 2010 and the new Patent Law of 2008 should be the governing law and regulations.

The Beijing First Intermediate People's Court ("Court") readily rejected Zeng's argument because the new patent law of 2008 and the new Regulations of 2010 expressly stated that they apply to patent applications filed on or after the effective date of the law and the Regulation, which was October 1, 2009 and February 1, 2010, respectively. The patents in question were filed in 2007, which means the patent law of 2001 and the Regulations of 2001 were [in] application. [T]he PRB correctly applied the right Regulations. As such, the invalidity decisions of the 4 patents were upheld.

Likelihood of Confusion

Secondly, the USPC also argued that the three remaining patents were also invalid due to lack of novelty and inventiveness before the PRB. In support of its arguments, the USPC used its own registered Chinese trademarks as evidence. The USPC has registered two trademarks:

---

[2] http://www.chinadaily.com.cn/bizchina/2006-04/17/content_569565_2.htm.

Table 2

TM Registration #	Filing date	Mark design
1222497	8/8/ 1997	
3214771	6/18/ 2002	

The USPC thus argued that its registered trademarks were filed and published before the filing date of Zeng's two patents. In addition, although the joker figure and the bee in the card patent are facing in a different direction from that in the USPC's 3214771 trademark design, they are substantially similar and would cause a likelihood of confusion to the public as to the source of the product. Similarly, Zeng's box patent used texts "3cc," but they are written in a similar style that is close to the USPC's 1222497 trademark of "Bee."

Zeng argued . . . that there was no likelihood of confusion about the use of the joker figure on a bee and the word "Bee." In addition, [he argued that] patent rights and trademark rights are separate rights.

The PRB agreed with the USPC's arguments and invalided the patents. The Court affirmed the PRB's decision. In its affirmance, the Court found that Article 23[3] of the Patent Law of 2001 was dispositive:

> Any design for which patent right may be granted must not be identical with or similar to any design which, before the date of

---

[3] http://www.chinaiprlaw.com/english/laws/laws4.htm.

filing, has been publicly disclosed in publications in the country or abroad or has been publicly used in the country, and must not collide with any legal prior rights obtained by any other person.

The Court found that, although there are differences in the design of Zeng's design patents, Zeng's design patents are similar to the USPC's registered marks, which [were] publicly disclosed in publications in China. And, Zeng's design patent rights are in conflict with the USPC's trademark rights, which were obtained legally prior to Zeng's.

Therefore, the USPC was successful in defeating the remaining 3 design patents by Zeng.

Thoughts

1. One would ask: "Why [were] Zeng's duplicated patents [] granted and issued in the first place?" The answers lie in that design patents in China have a lower standard of novelty and inventiveness.

2. Also, a Chinese design patent has a term of 10 years from the date of filing (Article 42 of the Chinese Patent Law 2008), whereas a US design patent has a term of 14 years from issuance, not filing.

3. [The] Patent Reexamination Board is an administrative agency that handles all patent invalidation proceedings. If a party is dissatisfied with its ruling, the Beijing First Intermediate Court has the sole jurisdiction to hear the administrative appeal, or known as the "administrative litigation" in China.

4. This case clarifies the retroactive application of the third amendments to the Chinese patent law (2008) and the implementing regulations of the patent law of 2010.

NOTES AND QUESTIONS

1. In the Chinese design patent cases, the prior art references were registered trademarks, a completely different type of intellectual property. Why was that difference not relevant to the decision on novelty?

2. In *Société des Produits Nestlé*, the EPO Board of Appeal (BOA) held that claim 2 of the patent application was anticipated/lacking in novelty, based on evidence in the form of product samples, photograph, invoices, and affidavits. Why does the use of these diverse references not violate the single reference rule? What functions do the additional items serve? Note that the location of sales of the product was irrelevant to the question of novelty—sales, public use, publication, or even oral disclosure anywhere in the world destroy novelty for a claimed invention under the EPC.

3. A common adjunct to the requirement that a reference identically disclose a claimed invention to be anticipating is the requirement that the reference be enabling. In other words, the reference must enable a PHOSITA to make the invention. In the United States, this is a different enablement requirement than the one found in statutory provisions, such as 35 U.S.C. § 112, that requires an inventor to enable a PHOSITA to make and use the invention. As explained by Professor Seymore:

> Although similar to its statutory cousin, anticipatory enablement is a narrower doctrine. A prior art reference need not demonstrate utility in order to anticipate. And an anticipatory reference need only enable what falls precisely within the scope of the claim-at-issue and nothing more. By comparison, an enabling description for patent-supporting purposes must enable the full scope of the claimed subject matter. These differing standards reveal a curious asymmetry: a description that is sufficient to anticipate a claim for patent-defeating purposes might be insufficient to enable a claim for patent-supporting purposes.

Sean B. Seymore, *Rethinking Novelty in Patent Law*, 60 DUKE L.J. 919, 933 (2011).

For more on the patent-supporting enablement requirement, see the discussion on written description and enablement in Chapter 8. Can you think of any practical or policy reasons that justify this "curious asymmetry"?

4. One novelty topic on which countries clearly differ in approach is the prior art effect of applications filed before, but published after, an application under examination for novelty. Such earlier filed applications are not available to the public at their filing date but may still be used as novelty-defeating prior art references as of that date to avoid double patenting: the obtaining of two patents on the same invention. The EPO takes a "photographic novelty" approach to such applications. Under EPC Article 54(3), the earlier-filed application is only prior art as to the subject matter explicitly disclosed therein. In other words, only if the subject matter of the later application is "photographically identical" to the earlier application will it be rejected as lacking novelty. Such applications are often referred to as "secret prior art."

5. Secret prior art applications in the EPO are only considered prior art for purposes of determining the novelty of an invention, not for inventive step. By contrast, in the United States under pre-AIA 35 U.S.C. § 102(e), and AIA § 102(a)(2), filed-but-unpublished patent applications can be used in both novelty and non-obviousness determinations. Some other countries, such as Japan, take a middle approach and include implicitly disclosed information as well as equivalents thereto, but only for novelty not inventive step. What might be some benefits or drawbacks of each approach? What underlying policy norms do you think influence the approach adopted by different countries? How would these differences affect your counsel to a client inquiring about strategies for patent prosecution in different jurisdictions? For a concise discussion of the need for harmonization in this area *see* Heinz Bardehle, *Patent*

Harmonization: Quo Vadis?, 88 J. PAT. & TRADEMARK OFF. SOC'Y 644 (2006). *See also* Kate H. Murashige, *The Hilmer Doctrine, Self-Collision, Novelty and the Definition of Prior Art*, 26 J. MARSHALL L. REV. 549 (1993) (offering a cogent analysis of the problems that can arise in the consideration of secret prior art).

6. Consider Article 13 of the Implementing Regulations of the Patent Law of China ("Regulations") 2001 reproduced in the Chinese design patent cases excerpted above. While not exactly secret prior art, the provision still is directed at avoiding double patenting. What reasons underlie prohibitions against double patenting? Note that in the context of a single applicant, as in the Chinese design patent cases, Article 13 works to prevent double patenting. Where, however, two inventors file applications on the same day claiming the same invention, this provision requires the inventors to resolve priority disputes among themselves. We will return to this topic later in section B, *infra*.

2. INHERENCY

Requiring patentable inventions to be novel in view of the prior art seems a fair requirement in light of the goals and purposes of patent law and the powerful right to exclude that a patent affords. It seems only logical that an inventor should be precluded from asserting rights over information already available to the public. However, it is not always clear that the information has been made available to the public; the information may be inherently present but not expressly disclosed. Determining when a claimed invention is inherently present in the prior art, and therefore anticipated, can be a complex and murky undertaking, as illustrated by the following case.

SCHERING CORPORATION V. GENEVA PHARMACEUTICALS, INC.

United States Court of Appeals, Federal Circuit
339 F.3d 1373 (Fed. Cir. 2003)

■ RADER, C.J.:

    . . .

Schering Corporation (Schering) owns the '233 and '716 patents on antihistamines. Antihistamines inhibit the histamines that cause allergic symptoms.

The prior art '233 patent covers the antihistamine loratadine, the active component of a pharmaceutical that Schering markets as CLARITIN™. Unlike conventional antihistamines when CLARITIN™ was launched, loratadine does not cause drowsiness.

The more recent '716 patent at issue in this case covers a metabolite of loratadine called descarboethoxyloratadine (DCL). A metabolite is the compound formed in the patient's body upon ingestion of a pharmaceutical. The ingested pharmaceutical undergoes a chemical conversion in the digestion process to form a new metabolite compound. The metabolite DCL is also a non-drowsy antihistamine. The '716 patent issued in April 1987 and will expire in April 2004 (the '233 patent issued in 1981 and has since expired) . . . .

Structurally, loratadine and its metabolite DCL differ only in that loratadine has a carboethoxy group (i.e., -COOEt) on a ring nitrogen, while DCL has a hydrogen atom on that ring nitrogen:

Loratadine ('233 patent)   **DCL ('716 patent)**

Claim 1 of the '716 patent covers DCL (for X = Cl), its fluorine analog, and their salts; claim 3 covers only DCL and its salts:

1. A compound of the formula . . . wherein X represents Cl or F:

3. A compound having the structural formula . . . .

The '233 patent issued on August 4, 1981, over one year before the earliest priority date of the '716 patent, February 15, 1984. The '233 patent is thus prior art to the '716 patent. *See* 35 U.S.C. § 102(b) (2000) ("A person shall be entitled to a patent unless . . . the invention was patented . . . in this or a foreign country . . . more than one year prior to the date of the application for patent in the United States."). The '233 patent discloses a class of compounds including loratadine. . . . The '233 patent claims loratadine in claim 7. . . . The '233 patent claims four other compounds in claims 8–11. . . . The '233 patent does not expressly disclose DCL and does not refer to metabolites of loratadine.

The numerous defendants-appellees sought to market generic versions of loratadine once the '233 patent expired [leading Schering to file suit for infringement] . . . . The district court concluded that the '233 patent anticipated claims 1 and 3 of the '716 patent under 35 U.S.C. § 102(b). The district court therefore granted the appellees' motions for summary judgment of invalidity. Schering timely appealed to this court. . . .

II.

. . . .

A.

A patent is invalid for anticipation if a single prior art reference discloses each and every limitation of the claimed invention. . . . Moreover, a prior art reference may anticipate without disclosing a feature of the claimed invention if that missing characteristic is necessarily present, or inherent, in the single anticipating reference. *Continental Can Co. v. Monsanto Co.,* 948 F.2d 1264, 1268 (Fed. Cir. 1991). . . .

The record shows that DCL necessarily and inevitably forms from loratadine under normal conditions. DCL is a necessary consequence of administering loratadine to patients. The record also shows that DCL provides a useful result, because it serves as an active non-drowsy antihistamine. In sum, this court's precedent does not require a skilled artisan to recognize the inherent characteristic in the prior art that anticipates the claimed invention.

B.

This court recognizes that this may be a case of first impression, because the prior art supplies no express description of any part of the claimed subject matter. The prior art '233 patent does not disclose any compound that is identifiable as DCL. In this court's prior inherency cases, a single prior art reference generally contained an incomplete description of the anticipatory subject matter, i.e., a partial description missing certain aspects. Inherency supplied the missing aspect of the description. Upon proof that the missing description is inherent in the prior art, that single prior art reference placed the claimed subject matter in the public domain. This case does not present the issue of a missing feature of the claimed invention. Rather, the new structure in this case, DCL, is not described by the prior '233 patent.

Patent law nonetheless establishes that a prior art reference which expressly or inherently contains each and every limitation of the claimed subject matter anticipates and invalidates. . . . In . . . prior cases, however, inherency was only necessary to supply a single missing limitation that was not expressly disclosed in the prior art. This case, as explained before, asks this court to find anticipation when the entire structure of the claimed subject matter is inherent in the prior art.

Because inherency places subject matter in the public domain as well as an express disclosure, the inherent disclosure of the entire claimed subject matter anticipates as well as the inherent disclosure of a single feature of the claimed subject matter. The extent of the inherent disclosure does not limit its anticipatory effect. In general, a limitation or the entire invention is inherent and in the public domain if it is the "natural result flowing from" the explicit disclosure of the prior art. . . .

In reaching this conclusion, this court is aware of *In re Seaborg,* 328 F.2d 996 (CCPA 1964). In that case, this court's predecessor considered claims drawn to an isotope of americium made by nuclear reaction in light of a prior art patent disclosing a similar nuclear reaction process but with no disclosure of the claimed isotope. The court reversed a United States Patent and Trademark Office rejection of the claims for lack of novelty. This court's predecessor found that the prior art process did not anticipate the claims because the process would have produced at most one billionth of a gram of the isotope in forty tons of radioactive material, i.e., the isotope would have been undetectable. *Id.* at 998–99. In this case, DCL forms in readily detectable amounts as shown by the extensive record evidence of testing done on humans to verify the formation of DCL upon ingestion of loratadine. . . .

Turning to this case, the use of loratadine would infringe claims 1 and 3 of the '716 patent covering the metabolite DCL. This court has recognized that a person may infringe a claim to a metabolite if the person ingests a compound that metabolizes to form the metabolite. *See Hoechst-Roussel Pharms., Inc. v. Lehman,* 109 F.3d 756, 759 (Fed. Cir. 1997) ("[T]he right to exclude may arise from the fact that when administered, [the accused product] metabolizes into another product . . . which Hoechst has claimed."); *see also Zenith Labs., Inc. v. Bristol-Myers Squibb Co.,* 19 F.3d 1418, 1421–22 (Fed. Cir. 1994) (stating that a compound claim could cover a compound formed upon ingestion). An identical metabolite must then anticipate if it is earlier in time than the claimed compound.

The record shows that the metabolite of the prior art loratadine is the same compound as the claimed invention. Claims 1 and 3 are compound claims in which individual compounds are claimed in the alternative in Markush format. DCL is within the scope of claims 1 and 3. Because the prior art metabolite inherently disclosed DCL, claims 1 and 3 are anticipated and invalid. In other words, the record shows that a patient ingesting loratadine would necessarily metabolize that compound to DCL. That later act would thus infringe claims 1 and 3. Thus, a prior art reference showing administration of loratadine to a patient anticipates claims 1 and 3.

C.

. . . .

Anticipation does not require the actual creation or reduction to practice of the prior art subject matter; anticipation requires only an enabling disclosure. . . . Thus, actual administration of loratadine to patients before the critical date of the '716 patent is irrelevant. The '233 patent suffices as an anticipatory prior art reference if it discloses in an enabling manner the administration of loratadine to patients. . . .

An anticipatory reference need only enable subject matter that falls within the scope of the claims at issue, nothing more. To qualify as an enabled reference, the '233 patent need not describe how to make DCL in its isolated form. The '233 patent need only describe how to make DCL in any form encompassed by a compound claim covering DCL, *e.g.*, DCL as a metabolite in a patient's body. The '233 patent discloses administering loratadine to a patient. A person of ordinary skill in the art could practice the '233 patent without undue experimentation. The inherent result of administering loratadine to a patient is the formation of DCL. The '233 patent thus provides an enabling disclosure for making DCL.

D.

Finally, this court's conclusion on inherent anticipation in this case does not preclude patent protection for metabolites of known drugs. With proper claiming, patent protection is available for metabolites of known drugs. *Cf. In re Kratz*, 592 F.2d 1169, 1174 (CCPA 1979) (stating that a naturally occurring strawberry constituent compound does not anticipate claims to the substantially pure compound); *In re Bergstrom*, 427 F.2d 1394, 1401–02 (CCPA 1970) (stating that a material occurring in nature in less pure form does not anticipate claims to the pure material).

But those metabolites may not receive protection via compound claims. In this case, for instance, claims 1 and 3 broadly encompass compounds defined by structure only. Such bare compound claims include within their scope the recited compounds as chemical species in any surroundings, including within the human body as metabolites of a drug. As this case holds, these broad compound claims are inherently anticipated by a prior art disclosure of a drug that metabolizes into the claimed compound.

A skilled patent drafter, however, might fashion a claim to cover the metabolite in a way that avoids anticipation. For example, the metabolite may be claimed in its pure and isolated form, as in *Kratz* and *Bergstrom,* or as a pharmaceutical composition (e.g., with a pharmaceutically acceptable carrier). The patent drafter could also claim a method of administering the metabolite or the corresponding pharmaceutical composition. The '233 patent would not provide an enabling disclosure to anticipate such claims because, for instance, the '233 patent does not disclose isolation of DCL.

The '716 patent contains claims 5–13 covering pharmaceutical compositions and claims 14–16 covering methods of treating allergic reactions by administering compounds that include DCL. These claims were not found anticipated by the '233 patent. . . .

CONCLUSION

The district court did not err in finding that the '233 patent discloses administering loratadine to a patient, and that DCL forms as a natural result of that administration. The district court correctly concluded that DCL is inherent in the prior art. The district court correctly granted summary judgment that claims 1 and 3 are invalid as anticipated by the '233 patent.

NOTES AND QUESTIONS

1. As the majority notes, the question of whether a claimed invention can be invalidated for lack of novelty where the prior art supplies no express description of *any part* of the claimed subject matter appears to be a matter of first impression for the court and its decision was not without controversy. The denial of a request for rehearing of the *Schering Corp. v. Geneva* case *en banc* resulted in two dissenting opinions. In one, Judge Newman argued that:

> The law is that a product is "anticipated" if it is not new. Conversely, it is not anticipated if it is new. . . . No precedent supports the position that a product whose existence was not previously known and is not in the prior art is always unpatentable on the ground that it existed undiscovered. If the law is to be changed in this direction it must be done *en banc.*

> . . . .

> The panel appears to have reached the correct result of no liability for infringement, but for the wrong reason. According to the briefs, the defendants are doing only what was claimed in the expired loratidine patent, not in suit. However, instead of simply ruling that Schering cannot prevent the practice of the expired patent in accordance with its teachings, the panel strains to hold that this new-

ly discovered, previously unknown product cannot be validly patented. That is not the law.

Schering Corp. v. Geneva Pharmaceuticals, Inc., 348 F.3d 992, 993–94 (Fed. Cir. 2003).

Is Judge Newman's critique circular? If practicing art taught in an expired patent results in the creation of a new, previously unknown product, why shouldn't someone be able to claim the new product as "novel"?

2. What policy concerns may be animating the majority's decision? If the point of the inherency doctrine is to prevent claims for things that are not new, does it make sense that a pure and isolated form of a metabolite, which already exists in nature, can survive a novelty inquiry as the court suggests?

3. As you read in Chapter 4, p. 319 *supra,* the term "evergreening" refers to attempts by owners of patents on lucrative pharmaceutical products, to effectively extend the term of exclusivity for those products by obtaining additional patents on product features, variations etc. Reread that note now. Would you consider the *Schering* case to be an example of evergreening? Is the court expanding the doctrine of inherency to address this type of strategic patenting? What do you think are the principal arguments against evergreening of pharmaceutical patents? How would you defend the practice of evergreening on efficiency grounds? Public policy grounds?

4. The United States is not alone in taking a broad view of inherency in the pharmaceutical context. In *Merrell Dow Pharmaceuticals Inc. v. H.N. Norton & Co.,* [1996] R.P.C. 76 (H.L.), the UK House of Lords struck down a patent on the acid metabolite of the previously patented antihistamine terfenadine, which is produced in the liver after a person swallows terfenadine. While disclaiming application of the doctrine of inherency, the court's reasoning is instructive and largely parallel to the Federal Circuit's:

> An anticipation is the traditional English term for that part of the state of the art which is inconsistent with the invention being new. . . . In this case, [it is argued] that the invention had been anticipated in two ways. First . . . it had been *used* before the priority date [because] "Terfenadine was made available to and used by volunteers in clinical trials in 1977/1978". They had made the acid metabolite in their livers and experienced its anti-histamine effects. Secondly, . . . before the priority date the invention had been *disclosed* in the specification of the terfenadine patent. That was a publicly available document which told one how to make terfenadine and that it should be taken for its anti-histamine effect. The inevitable result of following those instructions was to make the acid metabolite. I shall call these two arguments anticipation by use and anticipation by disclosure. . . . It may be helpful at this point to highlight the similarities and the distinctions between the case for anticipation by use, which I have rejected, and the case for anticipation by disclosure, which I have accepted. In both cases no one was aware that the acid metabolite was being made. In the case of antic-

ipation by use, however, the acts relied upon conveyed no information which would have enabled anyone to work the invention, i.e. to make the acid metabolite. The anticipation in this form relies solely upon the fact that the acid metabolite was made, . . . It disavows any reliance upon extraneous information, such as the formula for making terfenadine and the instructions to take it for its antihistamine effect. Anticipation by disclosure, on the other hand, relies upon the communication to the public of information which enables it to do an act having the inevitable consequence of making the acid metabolite. The terfenadine specification teaches that the ingestion of terfenadine will produce a chemical reaction in the body and for the purposes of working the invention in this form, this is a sufficient description of the making of the acid metabolite. Under the description the acid metabolite was part of the state of the art.

. . .

. . . .

But the argument in this appeal for anticipation by disclosure involves no "doctrine of inherency". It does not claim that the acid metabolite must be deemed to have been made available by the teachings of the terfenadine patent even though all information about it remained hidden. It claims instead that the acid metabolite was sufficiently disclosed under the description "an anti-histamine chemical reaction in the human body which occurs after taking terfenadine". The respondents say that for the purposes of the particular invention in issue, the specification contained sufficient information about the acid metabolite to make it part of the state of the art. For the reasons I have given, I think it did. I would therefore dismiss the appeal.

Id. at 84, 90, and 93.

Is there a meaningful difference between the reasoning used by the *Schering* and *Merrell Dow* courts? Did the Federal Circuit uphold anticipation based on use or disclosure?

5. Article 27.1 of the TRIPS Agreement provides that "[s]ubject to the provisions of paragraphs 2 and 3, patents shall be available for any inventions, whether products or processes, in all fields of technology, provided that they are *new*, involve an inventive step and are capable of industrial application." Does the inherency doctrine as articulated by the Federal Circuit in the *Schering* decision violate this provision? To what extent and on what grounds should countries be free to determine the exact contours of the global legal requirement that patents must cover inventions that are "novel"?

6. As discussed in the previous section, to destroy the novelty of a claimed invention, a prior art reference must enable a PHOSITA to make the invention. In one sense, the inherency doctrine turns this enablement requirement on its head. As explained by Professors Mueller and Chisum:

> We acknowledge the irony that prior art that explicitly describes a claimed invention but does not enable at least its making (if not its use) is not enough to anticipate (i.e. destroy novelty), yet prior art that is silent as to an element of a claimed invention but which if practiced would inevitably result in the creation of that limitation does anticipate under the theory of inherency. . . .

> In cases such as *Schering*, the Federal Circuit has wielded the doctrine of anticipation by inherency as a rather blunt instrument to combat perceived patent evergreening. We support cabining the doctrine in favor of more robust tools for policing patent validity. . . Patent claims . . . should be held anticipated under principles of inherency only when the inherency is truly inevitable. . . . To establish that one practicing the prior art would inevitably have produced a claimed invention, that prior art must satisfy a heightened level of enablement . . . . whatever teaching was explicitly provided by the prior art, . . . must be so clear that when replicated, no more than de minimis experimentation would be required to obtain the claimed invention.

Janice M. Mueller & Donald S. Chisum, *Enabling Patent Law's Inherent Anticipation Doctrine,* 45 HOUS. L. REV. 1101, 1104, 1163–1164 (2008). *See also* Dan L. Burk & Mark A. Lemley, *Inherency,* 47 WM. & MARY L. REV. 371, 374 (2005) (articulating a "public benefit" test for anticipation by inherency).

Do you agree that such limitations on the doctrine of inherency are needed? Is the inherency doctrine an appropriate tool for addressing the practice of evergreening? What other doctrines in patent law do you think might be better suited for this purpose?

B. INVENTION PRIORITY AND NOVELTY

1. FIRST INVENTOR TO FILE VERSUS FIRST TO INVENT

Generally speaking, a patent gives its owner the right to exclude others from making, using, selling, offering to sell, or importing the invention during the term of the patent. If, however, two or more inventors come up with the same invention and file for a patent, the system needs a way to determine who gets the patent, since only one patent will issue per invention. For decades, the United States stood alone in awarding the patent to the inventor who could establish the earliest invention date (first to invent or "FTI"). The earlier invention date was deemed novelty-destroying prior art against the second inventor negating her right to obtain a patent on the earlier invented subject matter. 35 U.S.C. §§ 102(g) and 135 (2006).

That all is changed, however, for applications effectively filed on or after March 16, 2013, the effective date of the Leahy-Smith America Invents Act (AIA) prior art provisions. Then the United States joins all other countries in awarding, with some caveats that will be explained later, the patent to the inventor who wins the race to the patent office and files an application covering the invention first (first inventor to file or FITF).

Even before the AIA, however, the United States did not have a pure FTI system. Statutory bars tied to the filing date of a patent application prevented an applicant from obtaining a patent if, for example, she failed to file an application for the invention within one year of exposing the invention to the public (recall 35 U.S.C. § 102(b), cited by the Federal Circuit in *Schering* as providing the basis for the '233 patent to anticipate claims in the '716 patent). Consequently, when an invention had been publicly disclosed, there was already a need for speedy filing within the U.S. patent system.

Nevertheless, aside from the statutory bars, for the millions of pre-AIA patents and patent applications in force and pending, patentability before the United States Patent and Trademark Office (USPTO or "the Office") is tied to an applicant's invention date, relative to the prior art. If two inventors file applications in the USPTO claiming the same invention, the Office generally will initiate an interference proceeding to determine which applicant is the first inventor and thus entitled to a patent on the claimed invention. Interference proceedings are priority contests: If a claimant can prove that she is the first inventor of the disputed subject matter and has not abandoned, suppressed or concealed the invention, then she is entitled to a patent. Alternatively, interference proceedings can be used to show that, for some reason other than priority of invention, such as fraud in procuring the patent or derivation of the invention from someone else, another party is not entitled to a patent.

A stated goal of the AIA is international harmonization. According to the Act's preamble:

> It is the sense of the Congress that converting the United States patent system from 'first-to-invent' to a system of 'first inventor to file' will improve the United States' patent system and promote harmonization of the United States' patent system with the patent systems commonly used in nearly all other countries throughout the world with whom the United States conducts trade and thereby promote greater international uniformity and certainty in the procedures used for securing the exclusive rights of inventors to their discoveries.

Leahy-Smith America Invents Act, Pub. L. No. 112–29, 126 Stat. 284 (2011).

But if harmonization is the goal, the AIA does not achieve it, as it creates a priority regime unlike any other in the world. In fact, it creates not a FITF system, but a First Inventor to File or Disclose then File (FITFODTF) system.

The key provisions of the new 35 U.S.C. § 102 that create this unique regime provide:

(a) Novelty; Prior Art.—A person shall be entitled to a patent unless —

(1) the claimed invention was patented, described in a printed publication, or in public use, on sale, or otherwise available to the public before the effective filing date of the claimed invention; or

(2) the claimed invention was described in a patent issued under section 151, or in an application for patent published or deemed published under section 122(b), in which the patent or application, as the case may be, names another inventor and was effectively filed before the effective filing date of the claimed invention.

Thus § 102(a) now defines prior art as basically any kind of public disclosure in paragraph (1), and patent filing disclosures (published U.S. and PCT applications that are effectively filed before the effective filing date of the application at issue) in paragraph (2).

The exceptions to § 102(a)'s new broad definition of prior art are located in new § 102(b):

(b) Exceptions.—

(1) Disclosures made 1 year or less before the effective filing date of the claimed invention.—A disclosure made 1 year or less before the effective filing date of a claimed invention shall not be prior art to the claimed invention under subsection (a)(1) if—

(A) the disclosure was made by the inventor or joint inventor or by another who obtained the subject matter disclosed directly or indirectly from the inventor or a joint inventor; or

(B) the subject matter disclosed had, before such disclosure, been publicly disclosed by the inventor or a joint inventor or another who obtained the subject matter disclosed directly or indirectly from the inventor or a joint inventor.

(2) DISCLOSURES APPEARING IN APPLICATIONS AND PATENTS.—A disclosure shall not be prior art to a claimed invention under subsection (a) (2) if—

(A) the subject matter disclosed was obtained directly or indirectly from the inventor or a joint inventor;

(B) the subject matter disclosed had, before such subject matter was effectively filed under subsection (a)(2), been publicly disclosed by the inventor or a joint inventor or another who obtained the subject matter disclosed directly or indirectly from the inventor or a joint inventor . . .;

Thus, under § 102(b)(1), the disclosure of an inventor's work by her or someone who got it from her will not bar her from obtaining a patent if made one year or less before her effective filing date. A third-party disclosure also will not bar her if it is made one year or less before her filing date and she had previously publicly disclosed it. Under § 102(b)(2), a published U.S. or PCT patent application disclosing the applicant's claimed invention will not be prior art if it is her own work or if she publicly disclosed the subject matter prior to the published application being effectively filed.

These provisions are complicated, non-intuitive, and sure to spawn a wealth of litigation in the coming years. But to illustrate the uniqueness of the new U.S. system, consider the following hypothetical scenario:

Tom invents a new compound X in the United States in April 2013. Heng Hui independently invents compound X in Singapore in May 2013 and publicly discloses it at a trade show there in August 2013. Tom files a patent application in the USPTO claiming X in September 2013. Heng Hui, after receiving permission from the Singapore Intellectual Property Office (IPOS) to file abroad, files a patent application in the USPTO claiming X in November 2013. Tom's application is published by the USPTO in March 2015. Who has priority, Tom or Heng Hui?

Heng Hui has priority, even though Tom was the first inventor to file an application claiming X in the USPTO. This is because Heng Hui avoids public use through the § 102(b)(1)(A) grace period by filing within one year of her public disclosure. Also, her public use avoids Tom's application publication through § 102(b)(2)(B). Finally, Heng Hui's public use in Singapore is § 102(a)(1) prior art to Tom, defeating his ability to obtain a patent on X. Thus, the first inventor to file loses because the second inventor to file disclosed first.

Congress's goal of harmonizing U.S. patent priority rules with those of the rest of the world may have been laudable, but it was doomed to failure even without the AIA's FITFODTF idiosyncrasies. This is because although prior to the AIA all countries except the United States operated under FITF patent regimes, many differences existed, and still exist, in how priority is determined from country to country. FITF countries even differ on how to handle two applications claiming the same invention that are filed on the same day. In Japan, for example, the Office requires competing applicants to consult among themselves and decide who gets the patent; if they cannot decide, no one gets the patent:

Article 39: Prior Application

(1) Where two or more patent applications claiming identical inventions have been filed on different dates, only the applicant who filed the patent application on the earliest date shall be entitled to obtain a patent for the invention claimed.

(2) Where two or more patent applications claiming identical inventions have been filed on the same date, only one applicant, who was selected by consultations between the applicants who filed the said applications, shall be entitled to obtain a patent for the invention claimed. Where no agreement is reached by consultations or consultations are unable to be held, none of the applicants shall be entitled to obtain a patent for the invention claimed.

[Patent Law of Japan], Law No. 121 of 1959, *amended by* Law No. 220 of 1999, art. 39.

As noted in the Playing card cases *supra*, China has a similar approach to determining priority between competing inventors. Article 13 of the Implementing Regulations of the Patent Law of China ("Regulations") 2001 requires applicants for patents for identical invention to "hold consultations among themselves" to decide who shall be entitled to file the application.

In contrast, the European Patent Office might in theory issue two patents on the same invention because under Article 54, neither is before (and thus not prior art to) the other. As explained in the Guidelines for Examination in the European Patent Office: "Should two applications of the same effective date be received from two different applicants, each must be allowed to proceed as though the other did not exist." Pt. C, Ch. IV-24, Sec. 7.4 (June 2012). Apparently, if this rare circumstance occurs, examiners encourage applicants to differentiate their claims sufficiently that any patents that issue do not overlap. The U.S. AIA does not specify how such a tie is to be resolved.

2. PRIOR USER RIGHTS

Secret use of an invention by a third-party does not destroy novelty as to another inventor who independently created and seeks to patent an invention, as it does not make the invention publicly available. Prior user rights allow such third party secret use of an invention to continue after a patent issues, on a royalty-free basis, as long as the third party was using the invention, secretly for some specified period of time before the patent application was filed. Most major countries that have a FITF system also provide prior user rights, the exceptions being Canada, with no prior user rights, and India, where such rights are limited to pharmaceutical products.

Prior user rights are personal and generally transferable only with the sale of the business in which they were used. These rights dilute the exclusivity and thus the value that a patent normally provides by allowing someone other than the patent owner to practice the invention. Prior user rights also risk reducing the incentive to obtain a patent because an inventor can keep her invention secret and continue to practice it after another entity obtains a patent. An illustrative provision is Article 79 of the Patent Act of Japan, which provides for prior user rights as follows:

Article 79: Non-exclusive license by virtue of prior use

Where, at the time of filing of a patent application, a person who has made an invention by himself without knowledge of the contents of an invention claimed in the patent application or has learned the invention from a person just referred to, has been commercially working the invention in Japan or has been making preparations therefore, such person shall have a non-exclusive license on the patent right under the patent application. Such license shall be limited to the invention which is being worked or for which preparations for working are being made and to the purpose of such working or the preparations therefore.

[Patent Law of Japan], Law No. 121 of 1959, amended by Law No. 220 of 1999, art. 79, *translated in* http://www.wipo.int/clea/docs_new/pdf/en/jp/jp036en.pdf.

The form and scope of the prior user right can vary considerably by jurisdiction. However, courts generally require proof of knowledge of the invention and commercial exploitation (or significant preparation) prior to the application filing date. In some cases, actual prior use may not be required. France, for example, has a "prior personal possession" defense that can shield a party (e.g., an academic) from infringement liability based solely on their prior knowledge of the invention.

Under the U.S. FTI system, there had been a default preference for inventors to seek patents and disclose inventions rather than to keep inventions as trade secrets. The only prior user rights under the FTI system in U.S. patent law were for business method patents under 35 U.S.C. § 273(c) which was introduced in the American Inventor's Protection Act of 1999, Public Law 106–113, § 1000(a)(9), 113 Stat. 1501A-552, due to concerns about this new area of patent-eligible subject matter. Today, the AIA's move to a FITFODTF system also includes an expansion of the coverage of § 273(c) to all technological areas, and provides an infringement defense to third parties who can demonstrate commercial use of a claimed invention for at least a year before the patent application filing date.

There are limitations and exceptions to the defense, such as a geographical limitation to sites where the invention had been in use prior to the critical date, and an exception for university-owned patents that may be in violation of TRIPS since it voids the defense in infringement suits by U.S., but not foreign, universities. *See* Dennis Crouch, *"How the AIA Violates TRIPS,"* PATENTLY-O (Aug. 28, 2012, 5:57 A.M.), http://www.patent lyo.com/patent/2012/08/how-the-aia-violates-trips.html.

The AIA also required the USPTO to report to Congress on the use of prior user rights in other industrialized countries, with a special focus on issues such as the effect of such rights on innovation rates, start-up access to venture capital, and universities. The USPTO issued its Report in January 2012. The Report concluded, among other things, that the AIA prior user rights provision "strikes the right balance" with its limitations, that there is no substantial evidence of a negative impact of such right on innovation rates, access to venture capital, etc., and that it is "pro-manufacturing and pro-jobs." *See* U.S. Pat. and Trademark Off., *Report on the Prior User Rights Defense, Report to Congress* 2 (2012), *available at* http://www.uspto.gov/aia_implementation/20120113-pur_report.pdf. For an analysis of the advantages and drawbacks of prior user rights *see* Carl Shapiro, *Prior User Rights*, 96 AM. ECON. REV. 92 (2006). *See also* Samson Vermont, *Independent Invention as a Defense to Patent Infringement,* 105 MICH. L. REV. 475 (2006); and Mark A. Lemley, *Should Patent Infringement Require Proof of Copying?*, 105 MICH. L. REV. 1525 (2007).

NOTES AND QUESTIONS

1. How would you reconcile the policy concerns underlying the novelty inquiry with a system of prior user rights? Given the widespread use of prior user rights in numerous countries, should there be efforts to harmonize this area of patent law? Many least-developed countries are still in the process of updating their patent laws to comply with the TRIPS Agreement. Would you recommend that they adopt a regime of prior user rights?

2. Interestingly, university researchers in Europe had lauded the pre-AIA U.S. FTI regime as beneficial to their U.S. counterparts. According to ProTon Europe, the pan-European network of knowledge transfer offices and companies affiliated with universities and other public research organizations:

> European universities and other public research organizations still file on average 5 times *less* patent applications than their U.S. counterparts, although the total research budgets are comparable. The lower propensity to patent is attributable to 2 main factors: . . . . [2] The fact that the U.S. patent system is much more favourable to universities than the European system. In addition to lower cost and single language, the U.S. universities are taking advantage of the protection of inventors by the *first-to-invent principle*, a grace period of one year, the continuation-in-part system, provisional ap-

plications, 50% reduction in filing and maintenance fees, no maintenance fees before grant, wider patentable inventions, etc. *There is no question that the U.S. universities could not have achieved the reported benefits for the U.S. economy in terms of new products, new companies, and new jobs with the patent system available in Europe.*

PROTON EUROPE, PROTON EUROPE RECOMMENDS IMPROVEMENTS TO THE PATENT SYSTEM IN EUROPE IN ORDER TO FACILITATE KNOWLEDGE TRANSFER FROM PUBLIC RESEARCH 2–3 (2007), *cited in* Margo A. Bagley, *The Need for Speed (and Grace): Issues in a First-Inventor-to-File World*, 23 BERKELEY TECH. L.J. 1035, 1047 (2008) (emphasis added).

In the statement above, ProTon Europe cites the FTI principle as one of several U.S. patent system features beneficial to university researchers. Another cited benefit, a one-year grace period, is discussed later in this Chapter. For differing views on the potential harms for university and other small entity inventors under a first-inventor-to-file regime, *see* David S. Abrams and R. Polk Wagner, *Poisoning the Next Apple? How the America Invents Act Harms Inventors* 65 STANFORD L. REV. (forthcoming 2013); and Dennis D. Crouch, *Is Novelty Obsolete? Chronicling the Irrelevance of the Invention Date in U.S. Patent Law*, 16 MICH. TELECOMM. & TECH. L. REV. 53 (2009). *See also* Margo A. Bagley, *The Need for Speed (and Grace): Issues in a First-Inventor-To-File World*, 23 BERKELEY TECH. L.J. 1035, 1047 (2008).

C. TERRITORIAL LIMITATIONS ON PRIOR ART FOR NOVELTY DETERMINATIONS

Countries define novelty either globally, allowing for all publicly accessible information available anywhere in the world to be considered in the analysis, or territorially, limiting the analysis by geographical boundaries. As will be discussed below, such territorial limitations may have the effect of placing information publicly available in one part of the world under patent protection in another.

Throughout history, patents often have been used to facilitate public policy objectives. For example, recall that the English Statute of Monopolies of 1623 allowed patents to be granted for "new manufactures within this realm," thus allowing for patents to be granted to importers of technology that was new to England but known in another part of the world. Such patents provided incentives to bring new industry, products, and knowledge to England that would enhance the quality of life of its citizenry and the economic development of the country.

A policy of ignoring non-documentary prior art existing outside a country's borders was a common feature of world patent statutes for decades but in recent times, many countries, such as Japan, Canada, China, and the member countries of the European Patent Convention, have eliminated such distinctions. While several smaller countries have retained geographical limitations on prior art, among major patent-granting countries, only the laws of the United States and the Republic of Korea still contain such provisions. However, the AIA eliminates the geographical limitation for patents issuing on applications filed on or after March 16, 2013 and defines prior art broadly in new § 102(a)(1) to cover the claimed invention being "patented, described in a printed publication, or in public use, on sale, *or otherwise available to the public before the effective filing date of the claimed invention.*"

In the United States, § 102 of the Patent Act identifies the knowledge against which patentability is assessed and details the grounds upon which an applicant can be denied a patent, based on either lack of novelty of the invention or loss of right to the invention. Just like EPC Article 54, § 102's novelty, or anticipation, requirement is only met if each and every element of the claimed invention is disclosed in a single prior art reference. Additionally, the reference must enable a person of ordinary skill in the field of the invention to make the invention. If these requirements are met, then a claimed invention is not "new" because it is fully disclosed in a reference that is accessible to the interested public.

Because the AIA is prospective in its application, for the next twenty years and more patents issued under the pre-AIA § 102 will be subject to a definition of prior art limited, in some respects, by geography. Three of the five pre-AIA § 102 subsections, (a), (b), and (g)(2), contain a geographical limitation to "this country," the United States, for non-patent, non-printed publication prior art. Sections 102(d) and (e) of the pre-AIA law also contain geographical limitations on prior art, the first focused on foreign applications, the second on U.S. patents and applications. The (a)(e), and (g)(2) provisions read:

A person shall be entitled to a patent unless—

(a) the invention was known or used by others *in this country*, or patented or described in a printed publication in this or a foreign country, before the invention thereof by the applicant for patent, or

(b) the invention was patented or described in a printed publication in this or a foreign country or in public use or on sale *in this country*, more than one year prior to the date of the application for patent in the United States, or . . .

(g)(2) before such person's invention thereof, the invention was made *in this country* by another inventor who had not abandoned, suppressed, or concealed it. In determining priority of invention under this subsection, there shall be considered not only the respective dates of conception and reduction to practice of the invention, but also the reasonable diligence of one who was first to conceive and last to reduce to practice, from a time prior to conception by the other. (emphasis added)

There are two key differences between the prior art provisions in 35 U.S.C. § 102(a) and (g)(2) on the one hand and § 102(b) on the other:

(1) *Triggering Event*: Prior art under § 102(a) and (g) is determined as of the date the applicant invented the claimed subject matter, whereas prior art under § 102(b) is determined as of the date that is one year before the U.S. patent application filing date.

(2) *Who Can Trigger It*: Only a third party can create prior art under § 102(a) and (g) (since, by definition, the inventor cannot publicly know or use the invention before she has invented it), whereas the inventor *or* a third party can create prior art under § 102(b) because the critical date is tied to the filing of the patent application. However, public activities of an inventor that are directed to reducing the invention to practice—experiments to determine that it works for its intended purpose—are not public uses of the invention but rather, are experimental uses and do not trigger the § 102(b) one-year clock. *See City of Elizabeth v. American Nicholson Paving Co.*, 97 U.S. 126 (1877).

The earliest U.S. patent statutes took a global view of prior art, free from geographical limitations. Such limits were introduced, however, in the Patent Act of 1836. The distinction between documentary evidence and other types of use apparently arose, at least in part, from a perception that foreign knowledge and/or use was not sufficiently accessible to the interested public in the U.S. for it to be deemed to be in the global public domain. On the other hand, the description of an invention in a patent or printed publication, existing anywhere in the world was deemed to destroy novelty as long as the reference was *accessible* to the interested public. While this dichotomy may have made sense in 1836, in the twenty-first century, judicial interpretations of "public accessibility" combined with changes in the accessibility of foreign public knowledge and/or use rendered geographical limitations problematic at best, resulting in the AIA changes.

However, aside from the pre-AIA geographical limitations, U.S. law pre- *and* post-AIA, reflects a fairly broad view of the scope of prior art, as described in the following excerpt by Professor Bagley.

MARGO A. BAGLEY, PATENTLY UNCONSTITUTIONAL: GEOGRAPHICAL LIMITATIONS ON PRIOR ART IN A SMALL WORLD
87 MINN. L. REV. 679, 708 (2003)

Section 102(b) [of the U.S. Patent Act] places no geographical limitation on prior art if it is in the form of a patent or a printed publication. In terms of what constitutes a "printed publication," the phrase "has been interpreted to give effect to ongoing advances in the technologies of data storage, retrieval, and dissemination." Consequently, information on microfilm, videotape, or even the Internet can be a "printed publication" within the meaning of Section 102(b) if it meets the key requirement: Public accessibility. Printed publications are prior art if they are publicly accessible. As noted by the Court of Appeals for the Federal Circuit (CAFC): "[b]ecause there are many ways in which a reference may be disseminated to the interested public, 'public accessibility' has been called the touchstone in determining whether a reference constitutes a printed publication bar under 35 U.S.C. Section 102(b)."

But just what level of public accessibility is required for a printed publication? Apparently, the bar is quite low. In *In re Hall*, the CAFC held that a copy of a doctoral thesis, in German, indexed and listed in a card catalogue in a German library on the edge of the black forest, and only available there, is prior art here in the US, despite the difficulty of access or of one's even knowing such a document existed. The court made its position quite clear: "[W]e reject appellant's legal argument that a single cataloged thesis in one university library does not constitute sufficient accessibility to those interested in the art exercising reasonable diligence."

The rule regarding the meaning of "patented" in section 102(b) is similar. Information is "patented" within the meaning of section 102(b) if it is "available to the public" and the rights granted are both "substantial and exclusive." Thus, a German design patent called a "Geschmacksmuster," available for viewing only by traveling to the particular city courthouse in Germany where the registered design is deposited, is prior art under section 102. The reasoning employed by the CAFC in reaching this conclusion is telling:

> We recognize that Geschmackmuster on display for public view in remote cities in a far-away land may create a burden of discovery for one without the time, desire, or resources to journey there in person or by agent to observe that which was registered and protected under German law. Such a burden, however, is by law imposed upon the hypothetical person of ordinary skill in the art who is charged with knowledge of all the contents of the relevant prior art.

Thus, for both patents and printed publications, the section 102 requirements of public accessibility and public availability have been broadly construed in the context of foreign art despite the burden such a requirement may impose on patent applicants.

Furthermore, even the section 102(b) concept of "public use" in this country has been interpreted expansively. In *Baxter International, Inc. v. Cobe Laboratories, Inc.,* use of a novel centrifuge in a private laboratory in a National Institutes of Health ("NIH") building was deemed a prior art "public use" under section 102(b). The court reasoned from the policies underlying the public use bar that because there was no control over the invention by the inventor, and because the laboratory was in a public building, anyone "who saw the centrifuge in operation would have reasonably believed [it] was publicly available." Judge Newman, in dissent, commented on the breadth of this ruling, noting that "this new category of internal laboratory use is immune to the most painstaking documentary search."

The public accessibility standard enunciated in these decisions seems to be one of "constructive" accessibility, and it is determined on a case-by-case basis. Under this standard, the only types of information that should not qualify as prior art would be secret information or information unavailable because of a political or other extraordinary barrier. For example, if a country did not allow U.S. citizens to freely enter its borders, public knowledge and/or use there might be considered, on those facts, not publicly accessible.

The reasoning behind these expansive judicial constructions is simple: The Constitution prohibits Congress from granting exclusive patent rights over subject matter in the public domain:

> Congress in the exercise of the patent power may not overreach the restraints imposed by the stated constitutional purpose. . . . Moreover, Congress may not authorize the issuance of patents whose effects are to remove existent knowledge from the public domain, or to restrict free access to materials already available.

The prohibition is particularly applicable to section 102(b) because:

> The novelty and non-obviousness requirements express a congressional determination that the purposes behind the [Intellectual Property] Clause are best served by free competition and exploitation of either that which is already available to the public or that which may be readily discerned from publicly available material.

Congress' wisdom in making foreign patents and printed publications prior art from the earliest patent act, when they were surely difficult for inventors and other interested persons to obtain, is clearly evident today. Inventors (and the general public) now have fingertip access to millions of foreign patents and printed publications via the Internet and commercial databases, as well as easy access by mail, library and even cheap international travel opportunities.

———————

NOTES AND QUESTIONS

1. In its 2004 *In re Klopfenstein* decision (380 F.3d 1345), the U.S. Court of Appeals for the Federal Circuit expanded the scope of patent-invalidating prior art by broadly interpreting the phrase "printed publication" to include fairly ephemeral scientific poster presentations. The court held that university researchers who presented study results at a scientific conference more than two years before filing a patent application claiming the invention were barred from patenting the disclosed invention even though no copies of any enabling document were distributed. The holding was based on the fact that slides disclosing the later-claimed invention were displayed on posters at the conference for two-and-a-half days without any notice that note taking was prohibited. The decision is significant because previous decisions in the U.S. had required distribution of at least some copies or the indexing and cataloging of at least one physical copy of a reference before considering such information to be patent-defeating prior art. Based on the court's reasoning in *In re Klopfenstein*, should sand paintings drawn by elders during Native American ritualistic ceremonies depicting a novel invention constitute a "printed publication"? Should it matter than non-tribal members are strictly forbidden from attending such ceremonies?

2. Because the phrase "printed publication" is retained in the AIA version of § 102, the wealth of interpretative case law on the meaning of the phrase will still apply. What is unclear, however, is the meaning of the new phrase "or otherwise available to the public" and whether it eliminates some types of non-public information that was judicially deemed prior art under pre-AIA § 102. *See Metallizing Engineering Co. v. Kenyon Bearing & Auto Parts Co.*, 153 F.2d 516 (2d Cir. 1946).

3. The delineation of prior art is an important aspect of maintaining the patent balance between promoting innovation and preserving for free public use those things that do not represent new contributions to the field. Sometimes, however, the justification for such line drawing can be difficult to discern, particularly in cases in which an inventor has introduced an economically viable innovation that may have existed in a different state of nature but only through the inventor's efforts did the product become available in a functional way to the general public. Consider the example given by the UK House of Lords in *Merrell Dow Pharmaceuticals Inc. v. H.N. Norton & Co.*, [1996] R.P.C. 76 (H.L.):

> 36. . . . The Amazonian Indians have known for centuries that cinchona bark can be used to treat malarial and other fevers. They used it in the form of powdered bark. In 1820, French scientists discovered that the active ingredient, an alkaloid called quinine, could be extracted and used more effectively in the form of sulphate of quinine. In 1944, the structure of the alkaloid molecule ($C_{20}H_{24}N_2O_2$) was discovered. This meant that the substance could be synthesised.

37. Imagine a scientist telling an Amazonian Indian about the discoveries of 1820 and 1944. He says: "We have found that the reason why the bark is goo*d for fevers is that it contains an alkaloid with a rather* complicated chemical structure which reacts with the red corpuscles in the bloodstream. It is called quinine." The Indian replies: "That is very interesting. In my tribe, we call it the magic spirit of the bark." Does the Indian know about quinine? My Lords, under the description of a quality of the bark which makes it useful for treating fevers, he obviously does. I do not think it matters that he chooses to label it in animistic rather than chemical terms. He knows that the bark has a quality which makes it good for fever and that is one description of quinine.

38. On the other hand, in a different context, the Amazonian Indian would not know about quinine. If shown pills of quinine sulphate, he would not associate them with the cinchona bark. He does not know quinine under the description of a substance in the form of pills, and he certainly would not know about the artificially synthesised alkaloid.

Id. at 88.

Why should patent law not reward such welfare enhancing contributions to society? Note that in such cases, the inventor's efforts may, in fact, be deemed "novel" for purposes of U.S. patent law, but may be questioned on other fronts such as "non-obviousness." In this regard, novelty and non-obviousness police, in different ways, the patent policy that rewards significant ingenuity that adds to the state of art in a given field.

4. The patent statutes of countries that have eliminated (or never included) geographical limitations on prior art take a global view of the public domain available to the hypothetical person of ordinary skill in the art. For example, China recently eliminated its geographical limitations on prior art in 2008 (effective in 2009) and Japan eliminated geographical limitations on prior art from its law in 1999 (effective in 2001). Thus, under Article 29 of the Patent Act of Japan, applicants cannot patent:

> [I]nventions which were publicly known in *Japan or elsewhere* . . . inventions which were publicly worked in *Japan or elsewhere*; . . . inventions which were described in a distributed publication or made available to the public through electric telecommunication lines in *Japan or elsewhere* prior to the filing of the patent application.

Consider the following statement from the *Report of the Planning Subcommittee of the Industrial Property Council: To the Better Understanding of Pro-Patent Policy*, which led to the removal of territorial limitations on prior art in Japan:

> [I]f patents are granted . . . in Japan for inventions known or worked overseas . . . technology able to be freely used overseas cannot be used in Japan, thereby causing a delay in the development of

technology. In addition, this may also give the impression of encouraging the imitation of technology . . . resulting in a system that
. . . run[s] contrary to the direction in which Japan is heading of
shifting from catch-up-type to frontier-type research and development. In addition, since it has become relatively easy to conduct
surveys about facts relating to known or worked inventions overseas
. . . due to the progress of transportation means in recent years, the
formation of a border-less economy and the progress of means of
providing information . . . there is no longer any reason to establish
regional standards for known or worked inventions in Japan.

Japanese Patent Office, *available at* http://www.jpo.go.jp/shiryou_e/
toushin_e/shingikai_e/report.pdf (Nov. 1998).

Do you find this reasoning persuasive? Unlike the United States and Japan, the EPC never contained a geographical limitation on prior art. Would
you expect EPC Article 54's broad view of prior art as comprising "everything
made available to the public by means of a written or oral description, by use,
or in any other way, before the date of filing of the European patent application" to help or hinder innovative research in Europe? What about the new
U.S. definition in the AIA?

D. TEMPORAL LIMITATIONS ON PRIOR ART: ABSOLUTE NOVELTY VERSUS GRACE PERIODS

In addition to variations in the territorial scope of prior art for novelty determinations, modern patent regimes also differ on temporal scope,
operating absolute novelty or relative novelty regimes. In absolute novelty regimes, the general rule is that any disclosure of an invention to the
public prior to the application filing date voids novelty and bars patent
protection for the invention. Relative novelty regimes employ grace periods that insulate some amount of pre-filing public disclosure from the
novelty analysis.

A "grace period" is a length of time in which a patent application can
be filed after public exposure of an invention without impairing its novelty for patentability purposes. Pre-AIA law required inventors to file patent applications in the USPTO within one year of disclosing the invention to the public; otherwise they would forfeit the right to patent the invention and a similar result occurs under the AIA. Grace periods can provide inventors with valuable time to, among other things, gather information on the commercial viability of an invention, publish information
about the invention for academic advancement purposes, and obtain funding to prepare and prosecute a patent application. Conversely, a grace
period may create uncertainty for third parties who see an invention or
publication describing an invention in public but will not know whether
the inventor is seeking patent protection generally until after the grace
period plus the eighteen month pre-publication period has expired.

The pre-AIA U.S. grace period provided in 35 U.S.C. § 102(b), insulated an inventor against personal or third-party disclosures of the claimed invention in patents, printed publications, or geographically specific public uses or sales of the invention of the claimed invention that took place up to one year before she filed her patent application. In combination with the FTI system, this meant, for example, that a U.S. inventor could safely sell products she had invented or publish a paper on the invention up to a year before filing an application without losing the right to a patent. If, for example, a competitor saw the inventor's disclosure during this period and developed an obvious variation of it (or came up with it independently) and filed a patent application before the first inventor, the first inventor would still be able to obtain her patent through an interference proceeding and prevent a patent from issuing to the first filer. This has all changed under the AIA. The grace period is significantly restricted and now may be interpreted to only protect against identical disclosures to what the inventor previously disclosed, making an inventor vulnerable to disclosure of obvious variants of earlier disclosures. *See* § 102(b).

Ironically, at around the same time the United States was restricting the grace period in the AIA, Japan was expanding the scope of its six-month grace period from a list of designated activities (e.g., Internet and designated academic society disclosures covered, but television and non-designated academic societies not covered) to a more comprehensive focus on any activity of the inventor that results in an invention becoming public (other than disclosure through a patent, design, trademark, or utility model application). *See* Japan Patent Act, Article 30. As a result of the change, which went into effect in April of 2012, the Japan Patent Office has seen a 70 precent increase in requests for application of the grace period (unlike in the U.S., JPO applicants must request application of the grace period at the patent application filing date), with most of the increase coming from university and small and medium-sized enterprise (SME) inventors. *See* Japan Patent Office, *Study on the Grace Period: Revision of Patent Law in Japan, available at* http://www.trilateral.net/events/meetings/nov2012/jpo-gp.pdf.

While a few other countries like Canada and Thailand have a one-year grace period, most countries limit such a period to six months and generally constrain the circumstances under which a grace period can be invoked. The following excerpt provides a brief perspective on the interplay between novelty, priority, and the grace period in Japan and the EPO.

TOSHIKO TAKENAKA, RETHINKING THE UNITED STATES
FIRST-TO-INVENT PRINCIPLE FROM A COMPARATIVE LAW
PERSPECTIVE: A PROPOSAL TO RESTRUCTURE SECTION
102 NOVELTY AND PRIORITY PROVISIONS

39 HOUS. L. REV. 621, 624–630 (2002)

1. Novelty. Novelty provisions of major first-to-file countries, namely those of the European Patent Convention (EPC) and Japanese Patent Law (JPL), have simple and short definitions of prior art; any form of disclosure gives rise to the prior art, regardless of the actor of such disclosure. For example, the EPC provides the following definition of novelty:

> (1) An invention shall be considered to be new if it does not form part of the state of the art.

> (2) The state of the art shall be held to comprise everything made available to the public by means of a written or oral description, by use, or in any other way, before the date of filing of the European patent application . . .

Unlike the U.S. provision, neither the European nor Japanese provisions distinguish the definition of prior art by actors and thus do not have separate provisions for the inventor's and others' actions. . . . The simple, key concept to make information give rise to prior art is public accessibility. Under the European and Japanese novelty approaches, any information made publicly available in any form of publication anywhere in the world, as of the date of application, constitutes prior art. . . .

Although technically not available as of the application date of the subject matter under examination, first-to-file countries also view subject matter described in an application pending in their own patent office as prior art, provided that the application is later published through an eighteen-month publication, thereby becoming publicly available. . . . Both the EPC and JPL adopted the "whole contents" approach, making the whole contents of European and Japanese applications the prior art as of the filing date. With respect to applications claiming priority right under the Paris Convention, the whole contents of applications become the prior art as of the priority date.

As an exception to this simple novelty principle, most first-to-file countries provide a grace period provision. One commentator from a first-to-file country defines grace period as a specific period of time prior to the filing of a patent application by the inventor or his or her successor in title, during which time disclosures of an invention do not forfeit a right to patent the invention. Under the first-to-file system, grace period provisions are provided as an exception to the principle that novelty is determined as of the application date. Because grace periods are an exception and not a rule, conditions that allow one to take advantage of the grace period are very restrictive. . . . To limit the scope of subject matter that can take advantage of the exception, the vast majority of countries have adopted a disclosure-specific grace period, in which only certain categories of disclosure are qualified to take advantage of a grace period. The most common disclosure-qualified categories include: experimental use, disclosure by an applicant, disclosure by a third party, abuse of right, display at an international exhibition, and presentation at a scientific meeting. Further, applicants cannot take advantage of the system unless they invoke the grace period at the date of application and submit evidence of the claimed subject matter.

One extreme example of the first-to-file grace period is the system under the EPC. The scope of disclosure that can take advantage of the EPC grace period is very limited, and applicants must meet procedural requirements to invoke the system. In contrast, the Japanese grace period is more general than that of the European system and includes a broad range of inventors' activities to take advantage of the system. Under the Japanese system, an applicant can take advantage of the grace period not only with subject matter that is identical to the subject matter disclosed prior to the date of application, but also obvious subject matter. . . .

2. Priority. The priority provisions of major first-to-file countries are predicated on a simple rule: a patent should be granted to the first applicant. For example, EPC Article 60, Paragraph 2 provides:

> If two or more persons have made an invention independently of each other, the right to the European patent shall belong to the person whose European patent application has the earliest date of filing; however, this provision shall apply only if this first application has been published under Article 93 and shall only have effect in respect of the Contracting States designated in that application as published.

Because priority is granted based on the date an applicant files an application to be examined by the European Patent Office (EPO), a procedure to decide the priority among more than one application is unnecessary as long as the dates are clear. When more than two applicants file applications for the same invention on the same date, the EPO gives patents to both applicants.

The Japanese rule is very similar to the European rule, except in the manner that the Japanese rule handles more than one application with the same application date. The JPL requires applicants who filed for the same invention on the same date to negotiate for an agreement to identify one applicant who will obtain the patent. If applicants cannot reach an agreement, the Japan Patent Office (JPO) refuses to give a patent to either party. This practice avoids an expensive proceeding to award the priority among applicants who filed their applications on the same day.

These rules also apply to the determination of priority during the grace period. Under the grace period provisions of first-to-file countries, if a third party files prior to the date of application by the inventor who disclosed the same invention during the grace period, the inventor's application is rejected for being the second to file. If the third party's date of application is after the inventor's date of disclosure, the disclosure destroys the novelty of the third-party application, and thus a patent is granted to neither party.

NOTES AND QUESTIONS

1. As Professor Takenaka notes, the limited grace period provided in many FITF regimes only provides protection against disclosures made by or derived from the applicant and does not impact priority. So what happens if an inventor publishes an article disclosing her invention during the grace period, and a second independent inventor files an application first on the same invention? It depends. As shown in the Tom/Heng Hui example on pp. 427–428, under the AIA the first inventor/second filer is entitled to the patent. But in South Korea, for example, the first inventor would not be entitled to a patent because she was not the first inventor to file. But the second inventor also would not be entitled to the patent because the first inventor's publication would be novelty-precluding prior art to her since the grace period does not protect against third-party disclosures. *See* Man-Gi Paik & Jae-Choon You, *Korea: What Korea's Patent Reforms Mean for You*, MANAG. INTELL. PROP. (Oct. 1, 2006). A general grace period in conjunction with a FTI system, such as existed in the U.S. pre-AIA law, avoided these issues as the first inventor/second filer could establish her right to a patent in an interference proceeding.

2. Several European countries had grace period provisions before joining the EPC, and several countries still retain varying types of grace periods in national law. Grace periods in Spain and Portugal, for example, are a derogation from the EPC and thus do not apply to European patents issued for those countries; only inventors seeking national patents may benefit from them. For a thorough treatment of the benefits and drawbacks of introducing a grace period in Europe, *see* Joseph Straus, *Grace Period and the European and International Patent Law—Analysis of Key Legal and Socio-Economic Aspects*, 20 IIC STUDIES 1 (2001).

3. Neither the TRIPS Agreement nor the Paris Convention explicitly address prior art grace periods, leaving such determinations up to individual member countries. The European Patent Convention (EPC) operates on an absolute novelty basis, with limited exceptions for certain types of disclosures (evident abuse or display at an international exhibition) occurring within six months of the application filing date. Moreover, the grace period dates from the filing of the actual European patent application, not a priority application, effectively eliminating the benefit of the grace period for foreign applicants who choose to take advantage of the Paris Convention right of priority after filing a first application in their home country. *See* Case G03/98, *Uni-*

versity Patents, Inc. v. SmithKline Beecham Biologicals SA, 2000 E.P.O.R. 33 (EPO Enlarged Bd. App. 2000).

4. A persuasive argument in favor of harmonizing the grace period is related to the growing global emphasis on the knowledge dissemination function of patents. In the U.S., academic inventions are disclosed in scientific journals earlier than European academic inventions. This has been attributed by some to the strong pre-AIA grace period provision in U.S. patent law. When U.S. inventors desire international protection, the lag period for disclosure in journals is longer, but disclosure by U.S. inventors is still more likely to occur earlier than their European counterparts. *See* Chiara Franzoni & Giuseppe Scellato, *The Grace Period in International Patent Law and Its Effect on the Timing of Disclosure*, 39 RESEARCH POL'CY 200 (2010) (concluding based on empirical data that USPTO international filings on average are published 9.9 months after filing compared with 16.2 months after EPO filings. Purely domestic patents are published in scientific journals an average of 2.8 months after filing.) *Id.* at 209. Do you think a harmonized grace period is an effective mechanism to encourage early disclosure by inventors? Do you think the opportunity costs for academic inventors who may risk losing patent protection in some countries justifies a harmonized grace period? Does your answer depend on the number of inventions that originate from public universities and research institutes? What impact, if any, might the narrower grace period in the U.S. AIA have on the above trends? For more on the importance of the grace period to university inventors, *see* Margo A. Bagley, *Academic Discourse and Proprietary Rights: Putting Patents in Their Proper Place*, 47 B.C.L. REV. 217 (2006).

CHAPTER 7

INVENTIVE STEP/NON-OBVIOUSNESS

■ ■ ■

This Chapter will examine the patentability requirement of inventive step (as it is generally known), or non-obviousness (as it is known in the U.S.).[1] While most national laws have adopted a uniform definition of inventive step, patent offices vary in the analytical methods they use to assess whether inventions meet the requirement. In order to get a sense of some of the dominant methods, this Chapter will focus on the criteria for evaluating inventive step adopted by the U.S. Patent and Trademark Office (USPTO), the European Patent Office (EPO), the State Intellectual Property Office of China (SIPO), and the Japan Patent Office (JPO), which together examine a major proportion of the world's patent filings.

A. THE DOCTRINE OF INVENTIVE STEP

1. THE ORIGINS OF INVENTIVE STEP

As early as 1850, the U.S. Supreme Court recognized that something more than novelty was required for an invention to be patentable. In *Hotchkiss v. Greenwood*, 52 U.S. 248 (1850), the Court held that the mere substitution of one material for another in the manufacture of a product (in this case, the substitution of clay or porcelain for wood in the manufacture of doorknobs) did not result in a patentable invention even if the substitution was novel and represented an advance over the prior art. The Court reasoned as follows:

> The improvement consists in the superiority of the material, which is not new, over that previously employed in making the knob. . . . But this, of itself, can never be the subject of a patent. No one will pretend that a machine, made, in whole or in part, of materials better adapted to the purpose for which it is used than the materials of which the old one is constructed, and for that reason better and cheaper, can be distinguished from the old one; or, in the sense of the patent law, can entitle the manufacturer to a patent. . . . The difference is formal, and destitute of ingenu-

---

[1] The prevailing international term for the requirement is "inventive step" and, accordingly, that term will also be used in this Chapter, but it should be understood that the term is used synonymously with the term "non-obvious" or "non-obviousness." *See* TRIPS Agreement, Art. 27, fn. 5 ("For the purposes of this Article, the terms 'inventive step' and 'capable of industrial application' may be deemed by a Member to be synonymous with the terms 'non-obvious' and 'useful' respectively").

ity or invention. It may afford evidence of judgment and skill in
the selection and adaptation of the materials in the manufacture
of the instrument for the purposes intended, but nothing more.

Id. at 266.

Hotchkiss illustrates that the aim of patent law is to reward only
those inventions that objectively advance the state of the art and contribute to technological development. Even if it is novel, an invention that is
simply a minor improvement or an obvious combination of known elements is generally not deemed worthy of a patent. As the U.S. Supreme
Court more recently restated, "concepts within the public grasp, or those
so obvious that they readily could be, are the tools of creation available to
all." *See Bonito Boats, Inc. v. Thunder Craft Boats, Inc.,* 489 U.S. 141,156
(1989).

Although the U.S. courts had long held that an invention needed
something in addition to novelty to merit a patent, it was not until the
enactment of the 1952 Patent Act that the additional requirement—non-
obviousness—was codified. Section 103 of the Patent Act requires that an
invention as a whole must not have been obvious at the time the invention was made to a person having ordinary skill in the art. It also specifies that "patentability shall not be negatived by the manner in which the
invention was made." This language nullified the "flash of creative genius" requirement previously imposed by the Supreme Court in *Cuno Engineering Corp. v. Automatic Devices Corp.,* 314 U.S. 84 (1941). There, the
court had stated "[a] new device, however useful it may be, must reveal
the flash of creative genius not merely the skill of the calling. If it fails, it
has not established its right to a private grant on the public domain." *Id.*
at 91. With the new § 103, however, inventions created through deliberate, incremental effort, and serendipitous discoveries are equally eligible
for patent protection. Professor Duffy provides an enlightening history of
the development of the non-obviousness requirement, including the flash
of genius test, in John F. Duffy, *Inventing Invention: A Case Study of Legal Innovation,* 86 Tex. L. Rev. 1 (2007).

While U.S. pronouncements on the requirement of non-obviousness
were groundbreaking, the development of English law predated that of
the United States. The 1838 case of *Losh v. Hague,* 1 Webster's Pat. Cas.
202 (1838), to which the U.S. Supreme Court referred in *Hotchkiss,* dealt
with the patentability of improvements to carriage wheels for railroad
use. In instructing the jury on the law, Lord Abinger, C.B., noted:

> [B]ut it would be a very extraordinary thing to say, that because
> all mankind have been accustomed to soup with a spoon, that a
> man could take out a patent because he says you might eat peas
> with a spoon. The law on the subject is this; that you cannot
> have a patent for applying a well-known thing which might be
> applied to 50,000 different purposes, for applying it to an opera-

tion which is exactly analogous to what was done before. Suppose a man invents a pair of scissors to cut cloth with; if the scissors were never invented before, he could take out a patent for it. If another man found he could cut silk with them, why should he take out a patent for that?

Id. at 208.

The specific use of the term "obvious" as a disqualifier for patent protection also comes from English law. Its origin is the 1889 case of *Thomson v. American Braided Wire,* (1889) 6 R.P.C. 518, 528 (H.L.) (UK), which involved a patent for a particular use of wire to make bustles for women's dresses. In that case, the House of Lords said that "the mode in which the tube of braided wire is made available as a bustle by the use of clamps applied and fixed in the manner described, appears . . . to be simple and efficient, and *not so obvious as to occur to everyone* contemplating the use of braided wire for the purpose of a bustle" (emphasis added). The UK codified the requirement of non-obviousness in 1932, but it used an additional term—inventive step—to describe it. Section 3(f) of the 1932 UK Patents and Design Act provided that a patent may be revoked on grounds that "the invention is obvious and does not have an inventive step having regard to what was known or used prior to the date of the patent."

Many civil law countries also required some form of non-obviousness as a condition of patentability, but like their common law counterparts, codification of the requirement came later. France, for example, did not formally add an obviousness requirement until 1968, but French courts routinely held that inventions that were trivial modifications of the prior art could not be deemed novel. German courts required that inventions produce a technical advance in the art and also possess a sufficient level of "inventivity" well before the notion of inventive step was codified in the German Patent Law. And Japanese law, which is modeled after the German, added an obviousness requirement in 1959, but had traditionally required patentable inventions to demonstrate an advantage over the prior art.

Patent systems worldwide now routinely apply the requirement that an invention must not be obvious to a person of ordinary skill in the art if it is to be deserving of a patent. This requirement has become an internationally accepted norm. It is embedded not only in the patent laws of all countries with modern patent legislation, but also in the PCT (Article 33(1) and (3)) and Article 27 of the TRIPS Agreement which provides that "[p]atents *shall* be available for any inventions, whether products or processes, in all fields of technology, provided that they are new, involve an inventive step, and are capable of industrial application." Accordingly, the domestic patent legislation of Member States of the WTO must incorporate the non-obviousness standard.

2. THE INVENTIVE STEP CHALLENGE

Despite the universal recognition of the requirement, standards vary from country to country for assessing whether an invention possesses inventive step. It is widely conceded that the determination of inventive step is a challenging exercise. In essence, it requires an examiner objectively to decide whether an invention would have been obvious to a hypothetical person who possesses ordinary, reasonable skill in the technology of the invention based on the prior art available at the time the invention was made. Recall from Chapter 6 that such a hypothetical person is often referred to as a PHOSITA (person having ordinary skill in the art). The hypothetical person is deemed to be ordinary to ensure that extraordinary levels of skill are not attributed to him or her, which would result in virtually all inventions being declared obvious. In setting the level of "ordinary-ness," examiners or courts are supposed to look at factors such as the typical educational level of people in the technical field, the complexity of the field and of the particular technology, and the degree to and speed at which the technology and the field are changing. The construct of the ordinary person is not without contradiction, however, for whereas the hypothetical person is just ordinary, she or he is presumed to have complete and perfect knowledge of all the relevant prior art.

As you learned in Chapter 6, an invention will be considered to lack novelty only if all its features can be found in a single prior art reference. However, a patent examiner may look at several relevant prior art references at once to determine whether or not an invention possesses inventive step. If the examiner concludes that it would have been obvious for a PHOSITA to have arrived at the claimed invention by combining features found in one reference with features found in others, the examiner will reject the patent application on grounds that the invention does not sufficiently advance the state of the art to merit the grant of exclusive rights. Conversely, if the examiner concludes that a person of ordinary skill would not have been expected to combine the references in question, the invention will be considered to possess inventive step.

Among the challenges that examiners face in assessing inventive step, therefore, is the need to distinguish among combinations of prior art references that bear no obvious relation to each other from those that do. This is an especially difficult burden because inventive step must not be assessed on the basis of hindsight. In other words, examiners must avoid examining the invention on the basis of knowledge we have today; instead, they must step back in time and carry out the examination in relation to the state of the art either when the invention was made or when the patent application claiming the invention was filed. In light of this challenge, it is no surprise that national and regional patent offices adopt different analytical methods to discern the presence of an inventive step.

B. THE UNITED STATES

1. 35 U.S.C. § 103 AND THE *GRAHAM V. JOHN DEERE* INQUIRY

In the United States, the requirement of inventive step is contained in § 103 of the Patent Act of 1952, which provides that a patent application should be rejected "[i]f the differences between the subject matter sought to be patented and the prior art are such that the subject matter as a whole would have been obvious at the time the invention was made to a person having ordinary skill in the art to which such subject matter pertains."[2] Non-obviousness is the most commonly litigated patent validity issue and, according to Professors Allison and Lemley, it is the requirement that usually leads to patent invalidation. *See* John R. Allison & Mark A. Lemley, *Empirical Evidence on the Validity of Litigated Patents*, 26 AIPLA Q.J. 185, 208–209 (1998). The seminal decision interpreting § 103 is *Graham v. John Deere Co.*, decided by the U.S. Supreme Court in 1966 and providing the Court's first interpretation of this provision.

GRAHAM ET AL. V. JOHN DEERE CO. OF KANSAS CITY ET AL.

Supreme Court of the United States
383 U.S. 1 (1966)

■ Mr. Justice CLARK delivered the opinion of the Court.

After a lapse of 15 years, the Court again focuses its attention on the patentability of inventions under the standard of Art. I, § 8, cl. 8, of the Constitution and under the conditions prescribed by the laws of the United States. Since our last expression on patent validity, *A. & P. Tea Co. v. Supermarket Corp.*, 340 U.S. 147 (1950), the Congress has for the first time expressly added a third statutory dimension to the two requirements of novelty and utility that had been the sole statutory test since the Patent Act of 1793. This is the test of obviousness, i.e., whether "the subject matter sought to be patented and the prior art are such that the subject matter as a whole would have been obvious at the time the invention was made to a person having ordinary skill in the art to which said subject matter pertains. Patentability shall not be negatived by the manner in which the invention was made." § 103 of the Patent Act of 1952, 35 U.S.C. § 103 (1964 ed.).

---

[2] Pursuant to the 2011 America Invents Act, effective March 16, 2013, the quoted language from § 103 will be replaced with the following: "[i]f the differences between the claimed invention and the prior art are such that the claimed invention as a whole would have been obvious before the effective filing date of the claimed invention to a person having ordinary skill in the art to which such subject matter pertains." This new language reflects the new focus on the filing date instead of the invention date.

The questions, involved in each of the companion cases before us, are what effect the 1952 Act had upon traditional statutory and judicial tests of patentability and what definitive tests are now required. We have concluded that the 1952 Act was intended to codify judicial precedents embracing the principle long ago announced by this Court in *Hotchkiss v. Greenwood,* 11 How. 248 (1851), and that, while the clear language of § 103 places emphasis on an inquiry into obviousness, the general level of innovation necessary to sustain patentability remains the same.

. . . .

IV.

. . . .

The first sentence of [§ 103] is strongly reminiscent of the language in *Hotchkiss*. Both formulations place emphasis on the pertinent art existing at the time the invention was made and both are implicitly tied to advances in that art. The major distinction is that Congress has emphasized "nonobviousness" as the operative test of the section, rather than the less definite "invention" language of *Hotchkiss* that Congress thought had led to "a large variety" of expressions in decisions and writings. In the title itself the Congress used the phrase "Conditions for patentability; *nonobvious subject matter*" (italics added), thus focusing upon "nonobviousness" rather than "invention." The Senate and House Reports, S. Rep. No 1979, 82d Cong., 2d Sess. (1952); H.R. Rep No 1923, 82d Cong., 2d Sess. (1952), reflect this emphasis in these terms:

> Section 103, for the first time in our statute, provides a condition which exists in the law and has existed for more than 100 years, but only by reason of decisions of the courts. An invention which has been made, and which is new in the sense that the same thing has not been made before, may still not be patentable if the difference between the new thing and what was known before is not considered sufficiently great to warrant a patent. That has been expressed in a large variety of ways in decisions of the courts and in writings. Section 103 states this requirement in the title. It refers to the difference between the subject matter sought to be patented and the prior art, meaning what was known before as described in section 102. If this difference is such that the subject matter as a whole would have been obvious at the time to a person skilled in the art, then the subject matter cannot be patented.

> That provision paraphrases language which has often been used in decisions of the courts, and the section is added to the statute for uniformity and definiteness. This section should have a stabilizing effect and minimize great departures which have appeared in some cases." H.R., *supra*, at 7; S. Ref., *supra*, at 6.

It is undisputed that this section was, for the first time, a statutory expression of an additional requirement for patentability, originally expressed in *Hotchkiss*. . . .

V.

. . . .

While the ultimate question of patent validity is one of law, *A. & P. Tea Co. v. Supermarket Corp., supra* at 155, the § 103 condition, which is but one of three conditions, each of which must be satisfied, lends itself to several basic factual inquiries. Under § 103, the scope and content of the prior art are to be determined; differences between the prior art and the claims at issue are to be ascertained; and the level of ordinary skill in the pertinent art resolved. Against this background, the obviousness or non-obviousness of the subject matter is determined. Such secondary considerations as commercial success, long felt but unsolved needs, failure of others, etc., might be utilized to give light to the circumstances surrounding the origin of the subject matter sought to be patented. As indicia of obviousness or nonobviousness, these inquiries may have relevancy. *See* Note, *Subtests of "nonobviousness": A Nontechnical Approach to Patent Validity*, 112 U. Pa. L. Rev. 1169 (1964).

This is not to say, however, that there will not be difficulties in applying the nonobviousness test. What is obvious is not a question upon which there is likely to be uniformity of thought in every given factual context. The difficulties, however, are comparable to those encountered daily by the courts in such frames of reference as negligence and scienter, and should be amenable to a case-by-case development. We believe that strict observance of the requirements laid down here will result in that uniformity and definiteness which Congress called for in the 1952 Act.

While we have focused attention on the appropriate standard to be applied by the courts, it must be remembered that the primary responsibility for sifting out unpatentable material lies in the Patent Office. To await litigation is—for all practical purposes—to debilitate the patent system. . . . The [non-obviousness] standard has remained invariable in this Court. Technology, however, has advanced—and with remarkable rapidity in the last 50 years. Moreover, the ambit of applicable art in given fields of science has widened by disciplines unheard of a half century ago. It is but an evenhanded application to require that those persons granted the benefit of a patent monopoly be charged with an awareness of these changed conditions. The same is true of the less technical, but still useful arts. He who seeks to build a better mousetrap today has a long path to tread before reaching the Patent Office.

NOTES AND QUESTIONS

1. Recall that courts in many jurisdictions had applied the inventive step standard before it was included in national patent legislation. It should not be surprising, then, that judicial articulations included elements not strictly embedded in the rule. As the Supreme Court noted in *Graham v. John Deere,* secondary considerations such as "commercial success, long felt but unsolved needs, failure of others, etc.," can be employed in the non-obviousness determination. Today, evidence of such "objective indicia of non-obviousness" is often used by applicants to attempt to rebut an examiner's *prima facie* obviousness rejection:

> The *prima facie* case is a procedural tool of patent examination, allocating the burdens of going forward as between examiner and applicant. . . . [T]he examiner bears the initial burden, on review of the prior art or on any other ground, of presenting a *prima facie* case of unpatentability. If that burden is met, the burden of coming forward with evidence or argument shifts to the applicant. After evidence or argument is submitted by the applicant in response, patentability is determined on the totality of the record, by a preponderance of the evidence with due consideration to persuasiveness of argument.

> If examination at the initial stage does not produce a *prima facie* case of unpatentability, then without more the applicant is entitled to grant of the patent.

In re Oetiker, 977 F.2d 1443, 1445 (Fed. Cir. 1992) (citations omitted).

In order to succeed, however, the applicant must demonstrate to the examiner's satisfaction that there is a nexus between the proffered evidence and the claimed invention. Without such a nexus, the examiner will treat the evidence as having no weight.

Read Article 27 of the TRIPS Agreement again. Is it TRIPS compliant for a country to utilize secondary considerations in lieu of, or as a proxy for, a pure inventive step requirement and analysis?

2. In *Aerotel Ltd. v. Wavecrest Group Enterprises Ltd.,* [2008] EWHC 1180 (Pat) (14 May 2008) the UK High Court cautioned against relying too heavily on secondary considerations in determining obviousness:

> 143. It should also be remembered that when present, commercial success is at best a secondary measure or aid by which to assess obviousness. It is I think, well to keep in mind the observations of Sir Donald Nicholls V-C on this point in *Molnlycke AB v. Procter & Gamble Ltd* [1994] RPC 49 at 112–113. When the issue is one of obviousness, the court's task is to determine as a fact what is included in the state of the art and then again to find as a fact, whether in the light of the state of the art the relevant inventive step is obvious. . . . Secondary evidence such as evidence of contemporaneous events had its place, he said, and the importance of it varied from

case to case. Nevertheless it "had to be kept firmly in its place". By itself, commercial success is "of very little importance".

144. Successful licencing may of course have been the result of a number of variables which have nothing to do with the Patent (or its US equivalent): commercial considerations, the notorious cost of IP litigation, the parties' respective negotiating skills and so on.

Id. at para. 143- 144.

Do you agree with the UK court that successful patent licensing is not a good proxy for assessing inventive step? Why? What policy arguments could be made in favor of generous resort to secondary considerations to determine inventive step? What policy arguments could be made against it?

3. On appeal, the UK Court of Appeal affirmed the finding that the invention, a method of making telephone calls and a telephone system, was obvious and that Aerotel had failed to show that its commercial success as evidenced by its licensing agreements was a result of the invention. *Aerotel Ltd v. Wavecrest Group Enterprises Ltd & Ors* [2009] EWCA Civ 408 [30], (Eng.) According to the Court, "[a] grateful market did not immediately fall upon this invention, saying 'this is the answer to our problems.' When the invention was made known absolutely nothing happened. The world beat a path to the door of Ralph Waldo Emerson's inventor of a better mousetrap, but the path to Aerotel's door remained untrodden." *Id.* at para. 30. . . . Do the Court of Appeal's comments support or weaken the case for a significant role for commercial success in determining inventive step? For a thoughtful critique of commercial success as a secondary consideration, *see* Robert P. Merges, *Commercial Success and Patent Standards: Economic Perspectives on Innovation*, 76 CAL. L. REV. 805 (1988).

4. The Paris Convention did not codify a requirement for inventive step, and, as mentioned earlier, the first international treaty to incorporate the standard was the PCT in 1970. However, the Strasbourg Convention on the Unification of Certain Points of Substantive Law on Patents is a multilateral treaty completed by the Council of Europe in 1963 which included the "inventive step" requirement. Though the treaty did not enter into force until 1980, it influenced the drafting of the PCT. Article 1 of the Strasbourg Convention states:

In the Contracting States, patents shall be granted for any inventions which are susceptible of industrial application, which are new and which involve an inventive step. An invention which does not comply with these conditions shall not be the subject of a valid patent. A patent declared invalid because the invention does not comply with these conditions shall be considered invalid ab initio.

Convention on the Unification of Certain Points of Substantive Law, Nov. 27, 1963, 1249 U.N.T.S. 369 [Strasbourg Convention].

5. What justifies a *global* requirement for inventive step/non-obviousness in national patent laws? Would you support an international rule that har-

monizes approaches to the use of secondary considerations in assessing inventive step? Recall from Chapter 2, *supra*, that most developing and least-developed countries do not have substantive patent examination capability. Accordingly, for these countries, the question of how to evaluate inventive step/non-obviousness, and the related role of secondary considerations, is largely irrelevant, or is it? Is there any benefit (or harm) to the U.S. public if a patent issues in Botswana for an invention that is obvious or lacks inventive step under Botswana law? What about harm to the public in Botswana?

6. What factors are appropriate in the evaluation of secondary considerations? Consider that inventors in developing and least-developed countries operate under severe socio-economic constraints including lack of adequate physical infrastructure, and access to water, electricity, and transportation. Low levels of formal education and low life-expectancy rates are also typical characteristics of developing societies. Should these factors play any role in evaluating obviousness/inventive step with regard to inventions from developing or least-developed countries? Is it desireable for the obviousness/inventive step evaluation to be country or culture specific?

7. Ascertaining the level of ordinary skill in the pertinent art, which is one of the inquiries that the Court directed in *Graham v. John Deere*, is not an easy task. The PHOSITA is always a hypothetical construct; she or he is never the inventor, the examiner, the judge, or any particular expert. Moreover, even if the subject matter of the patent application is the result of joint inventorship, U.S. practice dictates that the person of ordinary skill should always be a single person, not a hypothetical group even though data indicates that most significant inventions are the products of teams working at around the same time on the same idea. *See* Mark A. Lemley, *The Myth of the Sole Inventor,* 110 MICH. L. REV. 709 (2012).

2. THE "TEACHING, SUGGESTION, OR MOTIVATION" APPROACH AND *KSR*

Since the task of the examiner is to compare the disclosures in the relevant prior art to the disclosures in the claims that are the subject of the patent application, the examiner must first determine what prior art to compare. In many countries, all prior art that is considered relevant for the determination of novelty is also considered relevant for the determination of inventive step (subject to the analogous art limitation, discussed *infra* pp. 454–455, including unpublished pending patent applications (i.e., "secret" prior art)), and the PHOSITA is presumed to have constructive knowledge of all of it. Although combining prior art references is inherent in the concept of inventive step, the Court of Appeals for the Federal Circuit was loath to permit combination on the basis of hindsight analysis. The court feared that an examiner might "fall victim to the insidious effect of a hindsight syndrome wherein that which only the inventor taught is used against its teacher." *W.L. Gore & Assoc., Inc. v. Gar-*

lock, Inc., 721 F.2d 1540, 1553 (Fed. Cir. 1983*)*. In order to prevent the inventor's patent application from becoming the blueprint a patent examiner would use to find obviousness, the court imposed a requirement, not found in *Graham v. John Deere*, that prior art references should be combined only where there was a particular reason for doing so. That reason would exist, according to the court, when there was a specific teaching, suggestion or motivation ("TSM") that would cause a PHOSITA to combine the prior art references, and which, once combined, would result in a reasonable expectation of success that the invention could be made. This test required an examiner to look for clear, specific evidence showing a teaching, suggestion, or motivation to combine prior art references that flowed primarily from the references themselves or the knowledge of those skilled in the art. In other words, the examiner had to identify some objective teaching that would lead her or him to conclude that a PHOSITA would combine references. Short of that objective showing, the examiner was bound to conclude that the invention possessed inventive step. Criticisms of the shortcomings of the TSM test came to a head in the following case.

KSR International Co. v. Teleflex Inc. et al.
550 U.S. 398 (2007)

■ Justice KENNEDY delivered the opinion of the Court.

    . . .

In *Graham v. John Deere Co. of Kansas City*, 383 U.S. 1 (1966), the Court set out a framework for applying the statutory language of § 103, language itself based on the logic of the earlier decision in *Hotchkiss v. Greenwood*, 52 U.S. 248 (1851), and its progeny. The analysis is objective:

> Under § 103, the scope and content of the prior art are to be determined; differences between the prior art and the claims at issue are to be ascertained; and the level of ordinary skill in the pertinent art resolved. Against this background the obviousness or nonobviousness of the subject matter is determined. Such secondary considerations as commercial success, long felt but unsolved needs, failure of others, etc., might be utilized to give light to the circumstances surrounding the origin of the subject matter sought to be patented.

Id., at 17–18.

While the sequence of these questions might be reordered in any particular case, the factors continue to define the inquiry that controls. If a court, or patent examiner, conducts this analysis and concludes the claimed subject matter was obvious, the claim is invalid under § 103.

. . . Because the Court of Appeals addressed the question of obviousness in a manner contrary to § 103 and our precedents, we granted certiorari. We now reverse.

I

A

In car engines without computer-controlled throttles, the accelerator
pedal interacts with the throttle via cable or other mechanical link. The
pedal arm acts as a lever rotating around a pivot point. In a cable-
actuated throttle control the rotation caused by pushing down the pedal
pulls a cable, which in turn pulls open valves in the carburetor or fuel injection unit. The wider the valves open, the more fuel and air are released, causing combustion to increase and the car to accelerate. When
the driver takes his foot off the pedal, the opposite occurs as the cable is
released and the valves slide closed.

In the 1990's it became more common to install computers in cars to
control engine operation. Computer-controlled throttles open and close
valves in response to electronic signals, not through force transferred
from the pedal by a mechanical link. Constant, delicate adjustments of air
and fuel mixture are possible. The computer's rapid processing of factors
beyond the pedal's position improves fuel efficiency and engine performance.

For a computer-controlled throttle to respond to a driver's operation
of the car, the computer must know what is happening with the pedal. A
cable or mechanical link does not suffice for this purpose; at some point,
an electronic sensor is necessary to translate the mechanical operation
into digital data the computer can understand.

Before discussing sensors further we turn to the mechanical design of
the pedal itself. In the traditional design a pedal can be pushed down or
released but cannot have its position in the footwell adjusted by sliding
the pedal forward or back. As a result, a driver who wishes to be closer or
farther from the pedal must either reposition himself in the driver's seat
or move the seat in some way. In cars with deep footwells these are imperfect solutions for drivers of smaller stature. To solve the problem, inventors, beginning in the 1970's, designed pedals that could be adjusted
to change their location in the footwell. Important for this case are two
adjustable pedals disclosed in U.S. Patent Nos. 5,010,782 (filed July 28,
1989) (Asano) and 5,460,061 (filed Sept. 17, 1993) (Redding). The Asano
patent reveals a support structure that houses the pedal so that even
when the pedal location is adjusted relative to the driver, one of the
pedal's pivot points stays fixed. The pedal is also designed so that the
force necessary to push the pedal down is the same regardless of adjustments to its location. The Redding patent reveals a different, sliding
mechanism where both the pedal and the pivot point are adjusted.

We return to sensors. Well before Engelgau applied for his challenged patent, some inventors had obtained patents involving electronic pedal sensors for computer-controlled throttles. These inventions, such as the device disclosed in U.S. Patent No. 5,241,936 (filed Sept. 9, 1991) ('936), taught that it was preferable to detect the pedal's position in the pedal assembly, not in the engine. The '936 patent disclosed a pedal with an electronic sensor on a pivot point in the pedal assembly. U.S. Patent No. 5,063,811 (filed July 9, 1990) (Smith) taught that to prevent the wires connecting the sensor to the computer from chafing and wearing out, and to avoid grime and damage from the driver's foot, the sensor should be put on a fixed part of the pedal assembly rather than in or on the pedal's footpad.

In addition to patents for pedals with integrated sensors inventors obtained patents for self-contained modular sensors. A modular sensor is designed independently of a given pedal so that it can be taken off the shelf and attached to mechanical pedals of various sorts, enabling the pedals to be used in automobiles with computer-controlled throttles. One such sensor was disclosed in U.S. Patent No. 5,385,068 (filed Dec. 18, 1992) ('068). . . .

. . . .

This short account of pedal and sensor technology leads to the instant case.

B

KSR, a Canadian company, manufactures and supplies auto parts, including pedal systems. Ford Motor Company hired KSR in 1998 to supply an adjustable pedal system for various lines of automobiles with cable-actuated throttle controls. KSR developed an adjustable mechanical pedal for Ford and obtained U.S. Patent No. 6,151,976 (filed July 16, 1999) ('976) for the design. In 2000, KSR was chosen by General Motors Corporation (GMC or GM) to supply adjustable pedal systems for Chevrolet and GMC light trucks that used engines with computer-controlled throttles. To make the '976 pedal compatible with the trucks, KSR merely took that design and added a modular sensor.

Teleflex is a rival to KSR in the design and manufacture of adjustable pedals. . . . [I]t is the exclusive licensee of the Engelgau patent. Engelgau filed the patent application on August 22, 2000 as a continuation of a previous application for U.S. Patent No. 6,109,241, which was filed on January 26, 1999. He has sworn he invented the patent's subject matter on February 14, 1998. The Engelgau patent discloses an adjustable electronic pedal described in the specification as a "simplified vehicle control pedal assembly that is less expensive, and which uses fewer parts and is easier to package within the vehicle." Engelgau, col. 2, lines 2–5, Supplemental App. 6. Claim 4 of the patent, at issue here, describes:

"A vehicle control pedal apparatus comprising:

- a support adapted to be mounted to a vehicle structure;

- an adjustable pedal assembly having a pedal arm moveable in for[e] and aft directions with respect to said support;

- a pivot for pivotally supporting said adjustable pedal assembly with respect to said support and defining a pivot axis; and

- an electronic control attached to said support for controlling a vehicle system;

- said apparatus characterized by said electronic control being responsive to said pivot for providing a signal that corresponds to pedal arm position as said pedal arm pivots about said pivot axis between rest and applied positions wherein the position of said pivot remains constant while said pedal arm moves in fore and aft directions with respect to said pivot."

Id., col. 6, lines 17–36, Supplemental App. 8 (diagram numbers omitted).

We agree with the District Court that the claim discloses "a position-adjustable pedal assembly with an electronic pedal position sensor attached to the support member of the pedal assembly. Attaching the sensor to the support member allows the sensor to remain in a fixed position while the driver adjusts the pedal." . . .

. . . .

Upon learning of KSR's design for GM, Teleflex sent a warning letter informing KSR that its proposal would violate the Engelgau patent. "'Teleflex believes that any supplier of a product that combines an adjustable pedal with an electronic throttle control necessarily employs technology covered by one or more'" of Teleflex's patents. KSR refused to enter a royalty arrangement with Teleflex; so Teleflex sued for infringement, asserting KSR's pedal infringed the Engelgau patent and two other patents. Teleflex later abandoned its claims regarding the other patents and dedicated the patents to the public. The remaining contention was that KSR's pedal system for GM infringed claim 4 of the Engelgau patent. Teleflex has not argued that the other three claims of the patent are infringed by KSR's pedal, nor has Teleflex argued that the mechanical adjustable pedal designed by KSR for Ford infringed any of its patents.

C

The District Court granted summary judgment in KSR's favor. After reviewing the pertinent history of pedal design, the scope of the Engelgau patent, and the relevant prior art, the court considered the validity of the contested claim. By direction of 35 U.S.C. § 282, an issued patent is presumed valid. The District Court applied *Graham*'s framework to determine whether under summary-judgment standards KSR had overcome the presumption and demonstrated that claim 4 was obvious in light of the prior art in existence when the claimed subject matter was invented. *See* § 102(a).

The District Court determined, in light of the expert testimony and the parties' stipulations, that the level of ordinary skill in pedal design was "'an undergraduate degree in mechanical engineering (or an equivalent amount of industry experience) [and] familiarity with pedal control systems for vehicles.'" The court then set forth the relevant prior art, including the patents and pedal designs described above.

Following *Graham*'s direction, the court compared the teachings of the prior art to the claims of Engelgau. It found "little difference." Asano taught everything contained in claim 4 except the use of a sensor to detect the pedal's position and transmit it to the computer controlling the throttle. That additional aspect was revealed in sources such as the '068 patent and the sensors used by Chevrolet.

Under the controlling cases from the Court of Appeals for the Federal Circuit, however, the District Court was not permitted to stop there. The court was required also to apply the TSM test. The District Court held KSR had satisfied the test. It reasoned (1) the state of the industry would lead inevitably to combinations of electronic sensors and adjustable pedals, (2) Rixon provided the basis for these developments, and (3) Smith taught a solution to the wire chafing problems in Rixon, namely locating the sensor on the fixed structure of the pedal. This could lead to the combination of Asano, or a pedal like it, with a pedal position sensor.

    . . . .

With principal reliance on the TSM test, the Court of Appeals reversed. It ruled the District Court had not been strict enough in applying the test, having failed to make "finding[s] as to the specific understanding or principle within the knowledge of a skilled artisan that would have motivated one with no knowledge of [the] invention' . . . to attach an electronic control to the support bracket of the Asano assembly." The Court of Appeals held that the District Court was incorrect that the nature of the problem to be solved satisfied this requirement because unless the "prior art references address[ed] the precise problem that the patentee was trying to solve," the problem would not motivate an inventor to look at those references.

    . . . .

That it might have been obvious to try the combination of Asano and a sensor was likewise irrelevant, in the court's view, because " '[o]bvious to try' has long been held not to constitute obviousness." . . .

. . . .

II

A

We begin by rejecting the rigid approach of the Court of Appeals. Throughout this Court's engagement with the question of obviousness, our cases have set forth an expansive and flexible approach inconsistent with the way the Court of Appeals applied its TSM test here. To be sure, *Graham* recognized the need for "uniformity and definiteness." Yet the principles laid down in *Graham* reaffirmed the "functional approach" of *Hotchkiss*. To this end, *Graham* set forth a broad inquiry and invited courts, where appropriate, to look at any secondary considerations that would prove instructive.

Neither the enactment of § 103 nor the analysis in *Graham* disturbed this Court's earlier instructions concerning the need for caution in granting a patent based on the combination of elements found in the prior art. For over a half century, the Court has held that a "patent for a combination which only unites old elements with no change in their respective functions . . . obviously withdraws what is already known into the field of its monopoly and diminishes the resources available to skillful men." *Great Atlantic & Pacific Tea Co. v. Supermarket Equipment Corp.*, 340 U.S. 147, 152 (1950). This is a principal reason for declining to allow patents for what is obvious. The combination of familiar elements according to known methods is likely to be obvious when it does no more than yield predictable results. . . .

. . . .

. . . When a work is available in one field of endeavor, design incentives and other market forces can prompt variations of it, either in the same field or a different one. If a person of ordinary skill can implement a predictable variation, § 103 likely bars its patentability. For the same reason, if a technique has been used to improve one device, and a person of ordinary skill in the art would recognize that it would improve similar devices in the same way, using the technique is obvious unless its actual application is beyond his or her skill. . . . [A] court must ask whether the improvement is more than the predictable use of prior art elements according to their established functions.

Following these principles may be more difficult in other cases than it is here because the claimed subject matter may involve more than the simple substitution of one known element for another or the mere application of a known technique to a piece of prior art ready for the improvement. Often, it will be necessary for a court to look to interrelated teachings of multiple patents; the effects of demands known to the design community or present in the marketplace; and the background knowledge possessed by a person having ordinary skill in the art, all in order to determine whether there was an apparent reason to combine the known elements in the fashion claimed by the patent at issue. To facilitate review, this analysis should be made explicit. *See In re Kahn,* 441 F.3d 977, 988 (CA Fed. 2006). [R]ejections on obviousness grounds cannot be sustained by mere conclusory statements; instead, there must be some articulated reasoning with some rational underpinning to support the legal conclusion of obviousness"). As our precedents make clear, however, the analysis need not seek out precise teachings directed to the specific subject matter of the challenged claim, for a court can take account of the inferences and creative steps that a person of ordinary skill in the art would employ.

B

When it first established the requirement of demonstrating a teaching, suggestion, or motivation to combine known elements in order to show that the combination is obvious, the Court of Customs and Patent Appeals captured a helpful insight. . . . [A] patent composed of several elements is not proved obvious merely by demonstrating that each of its elements was, independently, known in the prior art. Although common sense directs one to look with care at a patent application that claims as innovation the combination of two known devices according to their established functions, it can be important to identify a reason that would have prompted a person of ordinary skill in the relevant field to combine the elements in the way the claimed new invention does. This is so because inventions in most, if not all, instances rely upon building blocks long since uncovered, and claimed discoveries almost of necessity will be combinations of what, in some sense, is already known.

Helpful insights, however, need not become rigid and mandatory formulas; and when it is so applied, the TSM test is incompatible with our precedents. The obviousness analysis cannot be confined by a formalistic conception of the words teaching, suggestion, and motivation, or by over-emphasis on the importance of published articles and the explicit content of issued patents. The diversity of inventive pursuits and of modern technology counsels against limiting the analysis in this way. In many fields it may be that there is little discussion of obvious techniques or combinations, and it often may be the case that market demand, rather than scientific literature, will drive design trends. Granting patent protection to advances that would occur in the ordinary course without real innovation retards progress and may, in the case of patents combining previously known elements, deprive prior inventions of their value or utility.

In the years since the Court of Customs and Patent Appeals set forth the essence of the TSM test, the Court of Appeals no doubt has applied the test in accord with these principles in many cases. There is no necessary inconsistency between the idea underlying the TSM test and the *Graham* analysis. But when a court transforms the general principle into a rigid rule that limits the obviousness inquiry, as the Court of Appeals did here, it errs.

C

The flaws in the analysis of the Court of Appeals relate for the most part to the court's narrow conception of the obviousness inquiry reflected in its application of the TSM test. In determining whether the subject matter of a patent claim is obvious, neither the particular motivation nor the avowed purpose of the patentee controls. What matters is the objective reach of the claim. If the claim extends to what is obvious, it is invalid under § 103. One of the ways in which a patent's subject matter can be proved obvious is by noting that there existed at the time of invention a known problem for which there was an obvious solution encompassed by the patent's claims.

The first error of the Court of Appeals in this case was to foreclose this reasoning by holding that courts and patent examiners should look only to the problem the patentee was trying to solve. The Court of Appeals failed to recognize that the problem motivating the patentee may be only one of many addressed by the patent's subject matter. The question is not whether the combination was obvious to the patentee but whether the combination was obvious to a person with ordinary skill in the art. Under the correct analysis, any need or problem known in the field of endeavor at the time of invention and addressed by the patent can provide a reason for combining the elements in the manner claimed.

The second error of the Court of Appeals lay in its assumption that a person of ordinary skill attempting to solve a problem will be led only to those elements of prior art designed to solve the same problem. The primary purpose of Asano was solving the constant ratio problem; so, the court concluded, an inventor considering how to put a sensor on an adjustable pedal would have no reason to consider putting it on the Asano pedal. Common sense teaches, however, that familiar items may have obvious uses beyond their primary purposes, and in many cases a person of ordinary skill will be able to fit the teachings of multiple patents together like pieces of a puzzle. Regardless of Asano's primary purpose, the design provided an obvious example of an adjustable pedal with a fixed pivot point; and the prior art was replete with patents indicating that a fixed pivot point was an ideal mount for a sensor. The idea that a designer hoping to make an adjustable electronic pedal would ignore Asano because Asano was designed to solve the constant ratio problem makes little sense. A person of ordinary skill is also a person of ordinary creativity, not an automaton.

The same constricted analysis led the Court of Appeals to conclude, in error, that a patent claim cannot be proved obvious merely by showing that the combination of elements was "obvious to try." When there is a design need or market pressure to solve a problem and there are a finite number of identified, predictable solutions, a person of ordinary skill has good reason to pursue the known options within his or her technical grasp. If this leads to the anticipated success, it is likely the product not of innovation but of ordinary skill and common sense. In that instance the fact that a combination was obvious to try might show that it was obvious under § 103.

The Court of Appeals, finally, drew the wrong conclusion from the risk of courts and patent examiners falling prey to hindsight bias. A factfinder should be aware, of course, of the distortion caused by hindsight bias and must be cautious of arguments reliant upon *ex post* reasoning. *See Graham*, 383 U.S., at 36 (warning against a "temptation to read into the prior art the teachings of the invention in issue" and instructing courts to "guard against slipping into the use of hindsight"' (quoting *Monroe Auto Equipment Co. v. Heckethorn Mfg. & Supply Co.*, 332 F.2d 406, 412 (6th Cir. 1964)). Rigid preventative rules that deny factfinders recourse to common sense, however, are neither necessary under our case law nor consistent with it. . . .

. . . .

III

When we apply the standards we have explained to the instant facts, claim 4 must be found obvious. We agree with and adopt the District Court's recitation of the relevant prior art and its determination of the level of ordinary skill in the field. As did the District Court, we see little difference between the teachings of Asano and Smith and the adjustable electronic pedal disclosed in claim 4 of the Engelgau patent. A person having ordinary skill in the art could have combined Asano with a pedal position sensor in a fashion encompassed by claim 4, and would have seen the benefits of doing so.

. . . .

B

The District Court was correct to conclude that, as of the time Engelgau designed the subject matter in claim 4, it was obvious to a person of ordinary skill to combine Asano with a pivot-mounted pedal position sensor. There then existed a marketplace that created a strong incentive to convert mechanical pedals to electronic pedals, and the prior art taught a number of methods for achieving this advance. The Court of Appeals considered the issue too narrowly by, in effect, asking whether a pedal designer writing on a blank slate would have chosen both Asano and a modular sensor similar to the ones used in the Chevrolet truckline and disclosed in the '068 patent. The District Court employed this narrow inquiry as well, though it reached the correct result nevertheless. The proper question to have asked was whether a pedal designer of ordinary skill, facing the wide range of needs created by developments in the field of endeavor, would have seen a benefit to upgrading Asano with a sensor. . . .

. . . Technological developments made it clear that engines using computer-controlled throttles would become standard. As a result, designers might have decided to design new pedals from scratch; but they also would have had reason to make pre-existing pedals work with the new engines. Indeed, upgrading its own pre-existing model led KSR to design the pedal now accused of infringing the Engelgau patent.

For a designer starting with Asano, the question was where to attach the sensor. The consequent legal question, then, is whether a pedal designer of ordinary skill starting with Asano would have found it obvious to put the sensor on a fixed pivot point. The prior art discussed above leads us to the conclusion that attaching the sensor where both KSR and Engelgau put it would have been obvious to a person of ordinary skill. . . .

NOTES AND QUESTIONS

1. Did *KSR* change the inventive step standard as set forth in *Graham v. John Deere* or just provide better tools to make the determination? Given the centrality of the PHOSITA construct in assessing inventive step, should there be guiding international principles to aid courts and patent offices? If so, what factors should be relevant in a global context? The EU has traditionally opposed the inclusion of methods of evaluating patentability standards, including inventive step, in patent treaties. Accordingly, few commentators expect *KSR* to have any significant effect on patent practice in Europe. *See, e.g.,* Dugie Standeford, *KSR Decision May Impact EU Patent Process But Not Harmonisation,* INTELL. PROP. WATCH (June 1, 2007), http://www.ip-watch.org/weblog/index.php?p=636. Nonetheless, a few courts in other jurisdictions have cited the *KSR* decision with approval. For example, a decision by the British Court of Appeal underscoring the importance of an objective approach to obviousness cited the KSR decision in its analysis. *See Nichia Corp. v. Argos Ltd.,* [2007] EWCA Civ 741, 23 (Ct. of Appeal 2007) (Pill, Rix, Jacob, JJ.) (cautioning against rigid application of the UK's "problem-solution" approach to obviousness). The problem-solution approach is discussed in section C *infra.* Although an objective approach is desirable, hindsight bias may be unavoidable, or at least, according to one commentator, remains a serious problem post-*KSR. See* Gregory N. Mandel, *Another Missed Opportunity: The Supreme Court's Failure to Define Nonobviousness or Combat Hindsight Bias in KSR v. Teleflex,* 12 LEWIS & CLARK L. REV. 323 (2008).

2. The doctrine of analogous art limits the prior art that can be used in an obviousness rejection to that which is either (1) within the field of the inventor's endeavor, or (2) if not within the same field, reasonably pertinent to the particular problem the inventor was trying to solve. The doctrine thus

cabins the scope of the inventive step inquiry by recognizing limits on the combinations of prior art of which a PHOSITA can be expected to be aware.

In *KSR*, the Supreme Court cast doubt on the continued vitality of the doctrine of analogous art when it noted that "[w]hen a work is available in one field of endeavor . . . [this] can prompt variations of it, either in the same field or a different one." *KSR Int'l Co. v. Teleflex Inc.* et al., 550 U.S. 398, 417 (2007). In response to this statement, the USPTO issued guidelines which, while reaffirming the two-pronged approach, added the following caveat: "[P]rior art that is in a field other than that of the applicant, or solves a problem which is different from that which the applicant was trying to solve, may also be considered for the purposes of 35 USC 103." *See* MPEP § 2141. Despite this seeming weakening of the doctrine of analogous art, the USPTO Board of Patent Appeals and Interferences has at least twice since *KSR*, disqualified a reference from being used in a § 103 rejection on the basis that it was not from an analogous art. *See Ex Parte Kurt* (BPAI 11/30/07) and *Ex Parte Jay P. Deville*, 2011 WL 4007710, (Bd. Pat. App. & Inter.), Sept. 6, 2011. Moreover, the Court of Appeals for the Federal Circuit recently reaffirmed the viability of the doctrine by concluding that five references did not qualify as analogous art:

> A reference qualifies as prior art for an obviousness determination under § 103 only when it is analogous to the claimed invention. . . .We agree with Mr. Klein that the Board's conclusory finding that Roberts, O'Connor, and Kirkman are analogous is not supported by substantial evidence. . . . [Also,] Greenspan and De Santo are not analogous, Mr. Klein argues, because they do not address multiple ratios or have a "movable divider." We agree. . . . [S]ince we have determined that the Board's finding that the five references at issue are analogous art is not supported by substantial evidence, the references do not qualify as prior art under 35 U.S.C. § 103.

In re Klein, 647 F.3d 1343, 1347–1352 (Fed. Cir. 2011).

3. The XYZ Health and Fitness Co. is the manufacturer of treadmills and other fitness devices. It is seeking reexamination of a patent it obtained on a treadmill with a folding base that allows the base to swivel to an upright position for storage. The patent claims a gas spring as a means for stably retaining the treadmill base in its upright position. The prior art at issue consists of an advertisement by a competitor for a folding treadmill that demonstrates all of XYZ's claims other than the gas spring, and a patent for a folding bed that discloses dual action gas springs that support the weight of the bed in both its open and closed positions. There is no specific reference that teaches or suggests combining the two. XYZ contends that the patent for the folding bed should not be considered part of the relevant prior art because it falls outside the scope of treadmill art and addresses a different problem than that addressed in the XYZ patent. In a post-*KSR* world, would you conclude that a PHOSITA would have nevertheless found it obvious to combine the two teachings? *See In re Icon Health and Fitness, Inc.*, 496 F.3d 1374 (Fed. Cir. 2007).

4. In 2004, Congress passed the Collaborative Research and Technology Enhancement Act, 118 Stat. 3596, codified at 35 U.S.C. § 103(c)(2) (2006), (the CREATE Act), a provision narrowly tailored to remove a specific impediment to the patenting of collaborative research results, which often involve university researchers and industry scientists. Prior to the passage of the CREATE Act, the joint collaboration of coworkers for the *same* employer could not be used as prior art for obviousness against later work pursuant to § 103(c), but that protection did not extend to the collaborations of coworkers from *different* organizations (such as those in university-industry joint research agreements). The CREATE Act eliminated the "same/different" organization distinction by disqualifying from the state of the art for determining obviousness "secret" prior art which is the work of researchers from different research organizations *if* there was a pre-existing agreement for research collaboration. The Act overruled the CAFC's 1995 decision in *OddzOn v. Just Toys,* 122 F.3d 1396 (Fed. Cir. 1997), and extended the non-obviousness safe harbor of 35 U.S.C. § 103(c) to include prior inventions of researchers from *different* organizations operating pursuant to a joint research agreement. As amended by the CREATE Act, 35 U.S.C. § 103(c) currently provides:

(1) Subject matter developed by another person, which qualifies as prior art only under one or more of subsections (e), (f), and (g) of section 102 of this title [35 USCS § 102], shall not preclude patentability under this section where the subject matter and the claimed invention were, at the time the claimed invention was made, owned by the same person or subject to an obligation of assignment to the same person.

(2) For purposes of this subsection, subject matter developed by another person and a claimed invention shall be deemed to have been owned by the same person or subject to an obligation of assignment to the same person if—

(A) the claimed invention was made by or on behalf of parties to a joint research agreement that was in effect on or before the date the claimed invention was made;

(B) the claimed invention was made as a result of activities undertaken within the scope of the joint research agreement; and

(C) the application for patent for the claimed invention discloses or is amended to disclose the names of the parties to the joint research agreement.

(3) For purposes of paragraph (2), the term "joint research agreement" means a written contract, grant, or cooperative agreement entered into by two or more persons or entities for the performance of experimental, developmental, or research work in the field of the claimed invention.

However, effective March 16, 2013, as codified by the America Invents Act (AIA) of 2011, the CREATE Act provisions will be incorporated into the new 35 U.S.C. § 102 and will apply to both novelty and non-obviousness determinations. Another AIA change to the provisions that should benefit inventors is that the joint research agreement will only need to be in effect before the filing date, not the invention date, of the claimed invention.

5. The CREATE Act, like the Bayh-Dole Act discussed in Chapter 9, *infra*, is an example of Congress choosing to facilitate university-industry technology transfer policy through patent law. Is it appropriate for a country's patent laws to promote policy objectives not justified in the utilitarian incentive system underlying patent rights?

3. POST-*KSR* DEVELOPMENTS

The USPTO responded to the *KSR* opinion by issuing revised examination guidelines. *See* Department of Commerce, Patent and Trademark Office, Examination Guidelines for Determining Obviousness Under 35 U.S.C. 103 in View of the Supreme Court Decision in KSR International Co. v. Teleflex Inc., 72 Fed. Reg. 57526 (October 10, 2007). The guidelines emphasize the centrality of the *Graham v. John Deere Co.* factual inquiries and attempt to accommodate the Supreme Court's call for a flexible and functional approach to assessing inventive step in at least two ways. First, they reduce dependence on documentary prior art as the source of knowledge and ability that examiners may presume a PHOSITA would possess at the time of invention. The guidelines state:

> [T]he focus when making a determination of obviousness should be on what a person of ordinary skill in the pertinent art would have known at the time of the invention, and on what such a person would have reasonably expected to have been able to do in view of that knowledge. This is so regardless of whether the source of that knowledge and ability was documentary prior art, general knowledge in the art, or common sense.

72 Fed. Reg. 57526 at 57527.

The second way in which the guidelines establish a more flexible approach is by reducing reliance on the TSM test. Responding to the Supreme Court's call to abandon rigid, formalistic rules, the guidelines cite seven rationales that examiners may adopt to support rejections on the basis of obviousness; teaching, suggestion, or motivation come in only in seventh position. *See* 72 Fed. Reg. 57526 (Oct. 9, 2007).

The guidelines direct examiners to articulate clearly the reasons underpinning their conclusions on obviousness, and identified those grounds as follows:

(A) Combining prior art elements according to known methods to yield predictable results;

(B) Simple substitution of one known element for another to obtain predictable results;

(C) Use of known technique to improve similar devices (methods, or products) in the same way;

(D) Applying a known technique to a known device (method, or product) ready for improvement to yield predictable results;

(E) 'Obvious to try'—choosing from a finite number of identified, predictable solutions, with a reasonable expectation of success;

(F) Known work in one field of endeavor may prompt variations of it for use in either the same field or a different one based on design incentives or other market forces if the variations would have been predictable to one of ordinary skill in the art;

(G) Some teaching, suggestion, or motivation in the prior art that would have led one of ordinary skill to modify the prior art reference or to combine prior art reference teachings to arrive at the claimed invention.

72 Fed. Reg. 57259, (Oct. 9, 2007). The 2007 KSR Guidelines also were incorporated into the MPEP. *See* MPEP § 2141 (8th ed. 2001) (Rev. 6, Sept. 2007).

On September 1, 2010, an update to the USPTO Guidelines on obviousness went into effect. *See 2010 KSR Guidelines Update, 75 Fed. Reg.* 53643 (Sept. 1, 2010). The Update was issued to "provide additional guidance in view of decisions by the United States Court of Appeals for the Federal Circuit since KSR." *Id.* citing *Ball v. Aerosel v. Limited Brands,* 555 F.3d 984 (Fed. Cir. 2009), the 2010 Update requires patent examiners, like the courts, to provide explicit analysis for rejections on obviousness grounds. *Id.* at 53645. The 2010 Update also makes clear that examiners "should not withdraw any rejection solely on the basis that the invention lies in a technological area ordinarily considered to be unpredictable." *Id.* Using post-*KSR* case law from the Federal Circuit, the 2010 Update is a helpful guide through the current landscape of the inventive step doctrine in the U.S. Together with the 2007 KSR Guidelines, the 2010 Update "provide a more complete view of the state of the law of obviousness." *Id.* at 53646. The following case is mentioned in the 2010 Update and illustrates the effect of *KSR* in the chemical arts.

ALTANA PHARMA AG v. TEVA PHARMACEUTICALS USA, INC.

United States Court of Appeals, Federal Circuit
566 F.3d 999 (Fed. Cir. 2009)

■ WARD, District Judge [sitting by designation].

. . . .

I. BACKGROUND

Appellants, Altana Pharma AG and Wyeth, accuse appellees, Teva Pharmaceuticals USA, Inc. ("Teva"), Sun Pharmaceutical Industries, Ltd. ("Sun"), et al. (collectively, "Defendants") of infringing U.S. Patent No. 4,758,579 ("the '579 patent"). Wyeth is the exclusive licensee of the '579 patent in the United States. . . .

The '579 patent is directed to the compound pantoprazole, the active ingredient in Altana's antiulcer drug Protonix®. The compound pantoprazole belongs to a class of compounds known as proton pump inhibitors ("PPIs") that are used to treat gastric acid disorders in the stomach. PPIs inhibit gastric acid secretion through their action on the gastric acid pump. When triggered by the body, the gastric acid pump is established in the secretory canaliculus of the stomach's parietal cells via the enzyme H^+, K^+–ATPase. Once triggered, the pump transports protons, H^+, from the inside of the parietal cell into the cell's secretory canaliculus in exchange for potassium ions, K^+, which the pump transports from the canaliculus to the inner portion of the cell. The availability of potassium ions within the canaliculus is attributable to the migration of potassium chloride, KCI, into the canaliculus, also from the inside of the parietal cell. As the pump reabsorbs the K^+ in exchange for H^+ extrusion, the Cl^- remains in the canaliculus, resulting in the formation of hydrochloric acid, HCI, within the canaliculus, which is then secreted into the stomach.

Although the operation of the gastric acid pump was known at the time of the invention at issue, the mechanism by which PPIs inhibit the gastric acid pump was not understood in the art until after the effective filing date of the '579 patent. Part of the uncertainty surrounding the method of action for PPIs is attributable to the fact that PPIs are prodrugs, which are drugs that convert to their active form after they are delivered within a patient's body, which typically exhibits a pH of about 5 to about 7. In this regard, PPIs are acid-activated prodrugs that are converted into their active form in the highly acidic environment, having a pH of about 1, within the secretory canaliculus of parietal cells. Once converted to its active form, the PPI thereafter binds to one or more cysteine amino acids in the acid pump. This binding inhibits the operation of the gastric acid pump.

The first commercialized PPI compound was omeprazole, which was approved for use by the U.S. Food and Drug Administration ("FDA") in 1989 under the trade name Prilosec ®. Omeprazole was first synthesized by AB Hassle (now known as AstraZeneca) in 1979 and is the subject of U.S. Patent No. 4,255,431 ("the '431 patent"). Omeprazole or Prilosec ® is well known today as a blockbuster drug for the treatment of patients that suffer from heartburn, as well as other symptoms that stem from gastroesophageal reflux disease ("GERD"). After the successful commercialization of Prilosec ®, many drug companies, including Byk Gulden (Altana's predecessor), began to develop new PPIs to compete with omeprazole.

Altana's research efforts resulted in the issuance of U.S. Patent No. 4,555,518 ("the '518 patent") and the '579 patent. The application for the '518 patent was filed before the '579 patent, and contained a pharmacology section that compared the effectiveness of 18 claimed compounds against four prior art compounds. The '518 patent refers to one of the 18 compounds chosen for testing as compound 12. The '579 patent, which is not related to the '518 patent, claims PPI compounds that are structurally similar to the compounds claimed in the '518 patent. Pantoprazole, the compound at issue in this litigation, exhibits a structure that is very similar to compound 12 from the '518 patent.

There are three main structural elements to the PPI molecular backbone: the benzimidazole ring, the methylsulfinyl bridge, and the pyridine ring. The general formula of the PPI disclosed in the '579 patent is reproduced below:

'579 patent at 2:5–15. The issues in this case primarily relate to the pyridine ring (the right-most structure on the above compound), specifically, the radicals located on the pyridine ring (indicated by R2, R3, and R4). The '579 patent teaches that "R3 represents a 1–3C–alkoxy radical, one of the radicals R2 and R4 represents a 1–3C–alkoxy radical and the other represents a hydrogen atom (—H) or a 1–3C–alkyl radical." *Id.* at 2:28–31.

. . . The only structural difference between compound 12 and pantoprazole is the substituent (or radical) at the 3–position of the pyridine ring. In compound 12, it is a methyl group (—CH_3), whereas in pantoprazole, it is a methoxy group (—OCH_3).

On or about April 6, 2004, Teva filed an Abbreviated New Drug Application ("ANDA") pursuant to the Hatch–Waxman Act, requesting FDA approval to sell a generic version of Protonix ® prior to the expiration of the '579 patent. Sun filed similarly directed ANDA applications on or about March 1, 2005, and June 25, 2005. Both Teva and Sun filed paragraph IV certifications in conjunction with their respective ANDA applications. Following the submission of these ANDA applications, Altana filed suit against Teva and, subsequently, against Sun. The district court consolidated these cases.

Altana filed a motion for preliminary injunction on June 22, 2007. In opposition to this motion, both Teva and Sun conceded infringement; however, they maintained that the '579 patent is invalid. Specifically, the defendants argued that the '579 patent was obvious in light of the teachings in the following prior art references: (1) Altana's '518 patent, (2) the Sachs article, (3) the Bryson article, and (4) the '431 patent (covering omeprazole).

In the district court, the defendants' obviousness analysis focused on the selection of compound 12 from the '518 patent as a lead compound for modification. The defendants argued that the Sachs article provided motivation for one of skill in the art to lower the pKa of a PPI to a value of 4 in order to provide better stability of the compound in the patient's body. The pKa value of a compound is measured on a logarithmic scale, and indicates the degree of the willingness of the compound to accept or donate a proton. The lower the numerical pKa of a compound, the more acidic and less basic it is. Thus, at pH 5, a compound with a pKa of 4 would be more stable than the compound with a pKa of 5. The defendants' position was that Sachs taught that a pKa value of 4 was a desirable characteristic in a PPI because it would improve the stability of a PPI in the body prior to its introduction to the parietal cells of the stomach. The defendants further argued that the Bryson article taught how to lower the pKa value. In particular, they argued that Bryson taught that a methoxy group at the 3–position of a pyridine ring provides a lower pKa than a methyl group in that same position. Finally, the defendants argued that the '431 patent demonstrated the feasibility of substituting a methoxy group for a methyl group at the 3–position of the pyridine ring in a PPI.

. . . .

II. DISCUSSION

. . . .

2. DISTRICT COURT'S OBVIOUSNESS ANALYSIS

Altana challenges the district court's obviousness analysis on the merits. Altana argues that the district court clearly erred when it determined that the defendants' obviousness defense had substantial merit. In particular, Altana argues that the district court allowed the defendants to select compound 12 of the '518 patent as a lead compound when the prior art suggested the availability of numerous other compounds that were at least as promising to modify as compound 12. In addition, Altana contends that the district court's findings with respect to the teaching of Bryson are clearly erroneous. We examine each argument.

Obviousness is ultimately a question of law, based on underlying factual determinations. The factual determinations that form the basis of the legal conclusion of obviousness include (1) the scope and content of the prior art; (2) the level of ordinary skill in the art; (3) the differences between the claimed invention and the prior art; and (4) evidence of secondary factors, known as objective indicia of non-obviousness. *Graham v. John Deere Co.,* 383 U.S. 1, 17–18 (1966). This court recently explained that "[w]here, as here, the patent at issue claims a chemical compound, the analysis of the third Graham factor (the differences between the claimed invention and the prior art) often turns on the structural similarities and differences between the claimed compound and the prior art." *Eisai Co. Ltd. v. Dr. Reddy's Labs., Ltd.,* 533 F.3d 1353, 1356–57 (Fed.Cir. 2008). Thus, to establish a prima facie case of obviousness in cases involving new chemical compounds, the accused infringer must identify some reason that would have led a chemist to modify a known compound in a particular manner. This standard is consistent with the legal principles announced in the Supreme Court's decision in *KSR Int'l Co. v. Teleflex Inc.,* 550 U.S. 398 (2007).

Obviousness based on structural similarity may be proven by the identification of some motivation that would have led one of ordinary skill in the art to select and modify a known compound in a particular way to achieve the claimed compound. The requisite motivation can come from any number of sources and need not necessarily be explicit in the art. Instead, "it is sufficient to show that the claimed and prior art compounds possess a 'sufficiently close relationship . . . to create an expectation,' in light of the totality of the prior art, that the new compound will have 'similar properties' to the old." . . .

Our review of the district court's decision is limited, and it is important to place the district court's findings in perspective. Applications for preliminary injunctions are typically presented on an abbreviated record without the benefit of a full trial. In this case, the district court carefully explained that its obviousness findings were preliminary. In the district court, the defendants attempted to prove that the claims were vulnerable because one of skill in the art would have selected a number of compounds disclosed in the '518 patent, including compound 12, as a starting point for further development. Based on the record before it, the district court found that "Defendants have raised a substantial argument that compound 12 was a natural choice for further development in this regard."

Ample evidence supported this finding. First, the '518 patent claimed that its compounds, including compound 12, were improvements over the prior art, specifically omeprazole (the first successful PPI). In addition, compound 12 was disclosed as one of the more potent of the eighteen compounds of the '518 patent for which data was provided during prosecution. Moreover, the patent examiner relied on the compounds of the '518 patent during the prosecution of the '579 patent. . . .

Beyond this evidence, the district court considered the opinions of qualified experts. The defendants supported their obviousness argument with the Declaration of Prof. Lester A. Mitscher, Ph.D. Dr. Mitscher was amply qualified to express opinions on the subject matter involved in this case. Dr. Mitscher expressed his opinion that Altana's '518 patent (which disclosed compound 12) was "on the cutting edge of PPI development in June 1984." Dr. Mitscher provided the district court with an overview of the history of PPIs and the state of the art as of June 1984. In particular, Dr. Mitscher stated that one of skill in the art would have selected the 18 exemplary compounds (including compound 12) of the '518 patent over omeprazole from which to pursue further development efforts designed to improve the quality and effectiveness of PPIs. Although Altana's expert suggested that one of skill in the art would have selected omeprazole over the compounds of the '518 patent, in part because of toxicity concerns, the district court apparently accepted Dr. Mitscher's contrary opinion. The district court's reliance on Dr. Mitscher's opinion was not clearly erroneous.

Beyond the finding that those of skill in the art would have pursued the 18 exemplary compounds in the '518 patent, the district court also found that one of skill in the art would have found compound 12, in particular, a natural choice for further development efforts. This finding is supported by evidence that compound 12 was one of the more potent PPI compounds disclosed in the '518 patent. Although potency is not dispositive, the district court believed—not unreasonably—that the potency of the compound was a factor that would have led one of skill in the art to select compound 12 from the group for further study. It bears mention that Altana itself had selected compound 12 for further development efforts, although the inventor stated that he ultimately developed pantoprazole by using an unwanted by-product from his scale up work as a starting point, rather than compound 12.

Altana suggests that the prior art would not have directed one of skill in the art to select compound 12 over the approximately 90 compounds claimed to be improvements in the '518 and other prior art patents, or, for that matter, over the thousands of other compounds included in the prior art disclosures. In light of Dr. Mitscher's declaration, however, the district court had a sufficient evidentiary basis for rejecting that position. Moreover, to the extent Altana suggests that the prior art must point to only a single lead compound for further development efforts, that restrictive view of the lead compound test would present a rigid test similar to the teaching-suggestion-motivation test that the Supreme Court explicitly rejected in *KSR*. . . . The district court in this case employed a flexible approach—one that was admittedly preliminary—and found that the defendants had raised a substantial question that one of skill in the art would have used the more potent compounds of the '518 patent, including compound 12, as a starting point from which to pursue further development efforts. That finding was not clearly erroneous.

The district court determined that the Sachs article taught those of skill in the art that an effective PPI should have a pKa of 4 because a pKa of 4 would lead to better stability of the compound within the body. Thus, according to the district court, one of skill in the art would have been motivated to modify the prior art compounds to reduce their pKa to 4. It is not disputed that the author of the Sachs article, Dr. George Sachs, is one of the leading researchers in the PPI development field. As such, the district court was entirely justified in selecting the Sachs article as relevant prior art. Moreover, although Altana disputed the teachings of Sachs before the district court, Altana does not challenge on appeal the district court's findings with respect to the Sachs teachings. Instead, Altana contends that the district court made a factual error in interpreting the Bryson article which requires reversal. We now turn to that issue.

The Bryson article teaches the pKa values of various chemical groups, including methoxy groups, at the 3–position of a simple pyridine ring. The defendants argued that Bryson taught that a methoxy group at the 3–position of the pyridine ring would have a lower pKa value than if it had a methyl group at that position. The district court accepted this argument, but stated "[a]ccording to Bryson, the pKa value of a methoxy group at such a position is 4; however, the pKa of a methyl group at this position is 5." The district court also stated: "Bryson undisputably taught that a compound with a methoxy group at the 3 position of the pyridine ring would have a lower pKa value (namely a pKa of 4) that [sic] a compound with a methyl group at that position." The district court concluded that "[w]hen Bryson's teachings are combined with the structure of compound 12 and combined with Dr. Sachs's teachings, Defendants have raised a substantial question that this combination was at the very least obvious to try and that such would lead to a predictable variation of compound 12, i.e., a compound with better pH5 stability."

. . . .

III. CONCLUSION

For the aforementioned reasons, we affirm.

NOTES AND QUESTIONS

1. As noted earlier, *Altana v. Teva*, 566 F.3d 999 (Fed. Cir. 2009), is one of the cases described by the USPTO as instructive on the non-obviousness analysis post-*KSR*. As the Guidelines explain:

> Obviousness of a chemical compound in view of its structural similarity to a prior art compound may be shown by identifying some line of reasoning that would have led one of ordinary skill in the art to select and modify the prior art compound in a particular way to produce the claimed compound. The necessary line of reasoning can

be drawn from any number of sources and need not necessarily be explicitly found in the prior art of record. . . . In response to Altana's argument that the prior art must point to only a single lead compound for further development, the Federal Circuit stated that a 'restrictive view of the lead compound test would present a rigid test similar to the teaching-suggestion-motivation test that the Supreme Court explicitly rejected in *KSR* * * *. The district court in this case employed a flexible approach . . . and found that the defendants had raised a substantial question that one of skill in the art would have used the more potent compounds of [Altana's prior art] patent, including compound 12, as a starting point from which to pursue further development efforts. That finding was not clearly erroneous.'

75 Fed. Reg. 53643 (2010), http://edocket.access.gpo.gov/2010/pdf/2010-21646.pdf.

In view of the court's reasoning in *Altana*, would you expect it to be easier or more difficult to obtain and retain a patent on a chemical invention post-*KSR*? Why? For an insightful analysis of non-obviousness in the pharmaceutical context post-*KSR*, *see* Rebecca S. Eisenberg, *Pharma's Nonobvious Problem*, 12 LEWIS & CLARK L. REV. 375 (2008).

2. Imagine you are a judge adjudicating a pharmaceutical patent infringement case similar to *Altana*. The defendant proffers a prior art lead compound that is structurally similar to the claimed compound, is useful for the same indications, and only differs in the substituent at the 4-position of the pyridine ring. In the lead compound the 4-position contains a trifluoro group that confers lipophilicity (a beneficial feature making the compound more soluble in oil) on the lead compound. The substituent in the 4-position of the claimed compound is known to reduce lipophilicity. Should the claimed compound be deemed obvious in view of the lead compound? *See Eisai Co. Ltd. v. Dr. Reddy's Labs., Ltd.,* 533 F.3d 1353 (Fed. Cir. 2008*).*

3. In Chapter 5, we discussed the requirement that an invention must be useful to be patentable. Recall that in *In re Fisher*, Chief Judge Rader of the Court of Appeals for the Federal Circuit dissented from what he perceived to be a "misuse" of the utility doctrine instead of the non-obviousness requirement. He explained:

In truth, I have some sympathy with the Patent Office's dilemma. The Office needs some tool to reject inventions that may advance the "useful arts" but not sufficiently to warrant the valuable exclusive right of a patent. The Patent Office has seized upon this utility requirement to reject these research tools as contributing "insubstantially" to the advance of the useful arts. The utility requirement is ill suited to that task, however, because it lacks any standard for assessing the state of the prior art and the contributions of the claimed advance. The proper tool for assessing sufficient contribution to the useful arts is the obviousness requirement of 35 USC

103. Unfortunately this court has deprived the Patent Office of the obviousness requirement for genomic inventions. *See In re Deuel* (CAFC 1995). . . . Nonetheless, rather than distort the utility test, the Patent Office should seek ways to apply the correct test, the test used worldwide for such assessments (other than in the United States), namely inventive step or obviousness.

In re Fisher, 421 F.3d 1365, 1381–82 (Fed. Cir. 2005).

In *In re Deuel,* 51 F.3d 1552 (Fed. Cir. 1995), the Court of Appeals for the Federal Circuit held that a prior art reference teaching a method of gene cloning, together with a reference disclosing a partial amino acid sequence of a protein, did not render DNA molecules encoding the protein obvious. "Knowledge of a protein does not give one a conception of a particular DNA encoding it." The case also held that "obvious to try" is an inappropriate test for obviousness.

Armed with *KSR*'s embrace of the "obvious to try "rationale, Judge Rader, in *In re Kubin,* 561 F.3d 1351 (Fed. Cir. 2009), effectively reversed *Deuel,* holding that a claimed polynucleotide would have been obvious over the known protein that it encodes where the PHOSITA would have had a reasonable expectation of success in deriving the claimed polynucleotide using standard biochemical techniques, and a PHOSITA would have had a reason to try to isolate the claimed polynucleotide. Noting that the *In re Deuel* "obvious to try" holding had been "unambiguously discredited" in *KSR*, the court in *Kubin* has, in a sense, returned the obviousness inquiry to biotech inventions.

C. EUROPE

The European Patent Office (EPO) traditionally has been perceived to require a higher level of inventive step than the USPTO. This difference may be attributable, at least in part, to the EPO's practice of examining inventive step on the basis of a "problem-and-solution" approach. The EPO's inventive step analysis is governed by Article 56 of the European Patent Convention (EPC), which provides that "[a]n invention shall be considered as involving an inventive step if, having regard to the state of the art, it is not obvious to a person skilled in the art." Unlike U.S. practice, Article 56 also provides that the state of the art for purposes of assessing inventive step excludes "secret prior art," that is, applications filed prior to the filing date of the European patent application at issue, but published only after the filing date. With the exception of unpublished prior art, all references and teachings available to a person skilled in the art can be considered for evaluating inventive step.

1. THE PROBLEM-AND-SOLUTION APPROACH
IN THE EPO

The problem-and-solution approach that guides the EPO analysis is grounded in Rule 42(1)(c) of the Implementing Regulations under the European Patent Convention. The rule states that "[t]he description [of the invention] shall disclose the invention, as claimed, in such terms that the technical problem, even if not expressly stated as such, and its solution can be understood, and state any advantageous effects of the invention with reference to the prior art." Guidance in making sense of the problem-and-solution approach can be found in numerous decisions of the Boards of Appeal of the EPO as well as in the Guidelines for Examination in the European Patent Office, Part C, Ch. IV, § 11 of which is devoted to examining for inventive step. The EPO Guidelines are the equivalent of the USPTO's Manual of Patent Examining Procedure. Section 11.7 of the Guidelines specifically addresses the problem-and-solution approach.

The problem-and-solution approach basically consists of three stages: (i) identifying the "closest prior art" to the claimed invention, (ii) determining the "objective technical problem" that the invention claims to solve, and (iii) in light of the prior art as a whole, assessing whether or not a skilled person could have, in an obvious manner, derived the solution to the technical problem from the closest prior art.

In practice, the problem-and-solution approach is substantially more mechanical than the USPTO's *Graham v. John Deere* formulation. Selecting the closest prior art requires the examiner to identify a single prior art reference that is directed to a similar purpose, effect, or use as the claimed invention and that would constitute the best hypothetical starting point for creating the invention. Once selected, the examiner needs to determine the extent to which the invention's technical features can be distinguished, either in terms of structure or function, from the technical features of the closest prior art. The objective technical problem consists in determining the modifications or adaptations necessary to provide the closest prior art with the distinguishing technical features embodied in the invention—in other words, filling the gap. It is important to note that the problem derived by the examiner need not be the same as the problem provided by the applicant in the patent application, especially if the prior art cited by the examiner differs from the prior art with which the applicant was familiar. In addition, because an invention must possess a technical character in order to be granted a European patent, any non-technical features that an invention may comprise are discounted in the examination for inventive step, regardless of how novel or innovative those features may be.

In the final stage of assessing inventive step, once the examiner has arrived at the technical problem by comparing the invention and the closest prior art, the examiner needs to answer the question "whether there is any teaching in the prior art as a whole that *would* . . . have prompted the skilled person, faced with the objective technical problem, to modify or adapt the closest prior art while taking account of that teaching, thereby arriving at something falling within the terms of the claims, and thus achieving what the invention achieves." EPO Examination Guidelines, § 11.7.3 [emphasis added]. When the answer to the question is negative, the invention is deemed to possess inventive step.

Noteworthy in the above question is that it employs the word "would" and not the word "could." In what is referred to as the "could-would approach," examiners are instructed not to ask whether a skilled person *could* have arrived at the invention by modifying or adapting the closest prior art, but rather whether that person *would* have done so. An invention possesses inventive step in accordance with the problem-and-solution approach, therefore, if the skilled person *would not* have sought to arrive at the invention by adapting or modifying the closest prior art, even though such a person might theoretically have been incited by the prior art to do so.

The problem-solution approach can be helpfully illustrated as a five-step process:

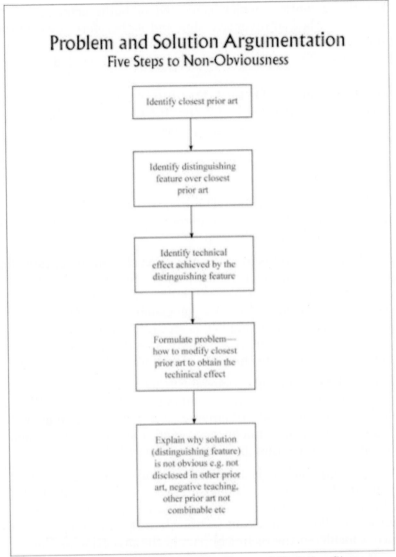

Source: Gwilym Roberts, Jay Erstling, and Christian Girtz,
"Transatlantic Patenting," 2 LANDSLIDE 30, 32 (2009).

The following decisions of the Technical Board of Appeal of the EPO
and the UK High Court illustrate application of the problem-solution approach in different jurisdictions. The UK case presents an appeal from a
lower court decision invalidating patent claims to a sustained release
pharmaceutical composition. The EPO case concerns an appeal from oppositions filed against the grant of a patent for GSM (Global System for
Mobile Communications) mobile telephone technology. The patent covered a method for digital mobile telephone systems in which a subscriber
identity module (SIM) was allocated at least two identities that were selectively activated by the user. The relevant EPO opposition division

found that the invention, which consisted of both technical and non-technical features, lacked inventive step and it therefore revoked the patent, despite the fact that the invention's non-technical features were sufficiently inventive. The patentee, Comvik GSM AB, appealed.

EUROPEAN PATENT OFFICE DECISION OF THE TECHNICAL BOARD OF APPEAL 3.5.1 OF 26 SEPTEMBER 2002

Case Number: T 0641/00–3.5.1

. . . .

REASONS FOR THE DECISION

1. The appeal is admissible. The appeal is not allowable, however, since the invention as claimed is not patentable in terms of Articles 52(1)[1] and 56 EPC for lack of inventive step.

2. Article 56 EPC states in its English text that an invention shall be considered to involve an inventive step, if having regard to the state of the art, it is not obvious to a person skilled in the art. The equally authentic French and German texts are somewhat more informative in that they can best be rendered in English as stating that an invention shall be considered as based on inventive activity if a skilled person cannot derive it in an obvious manner from the state of technology.

3. The legal definition of Article 56 EPC is to be put into context with the remaining patentability requirements of Articles 52 to 57 EPC, these articles implying the general principles that patents shall be available for inventions in all fields of technology . . . , and that technical character is a sine qua non for an invention in the sense of the EPC. . . .

4. On this approach it is legitimate to have a mix of technical and "non-technical" features . . . appearing in a claim, even if the non-technical features should form a dominating part. . . . It follows that the board, although allowing a mix of technical and non-technical features to be claimed, considered the technical part of the invention as the basis for assessing inventive step.

5. Furthermore, based on the ordinary meaning to be given the terms of Article 56 EPC in their context in the EPC, and consistent in particular with Rule 27 EPC[3], as a test for whether an invention meets the requirements of Article 56 EPC, the boards of appeal have developed and applied a method known as the "problem-and-solution approach", according to which an invention is to be understood as a solution to a technical problem. This approach requires identification of the technical field of the in-

---

[1] Article 52(1) EPC provides as follows: "European patents shall be granted for any inventions, in all fields of technology, provided that they are new, involve an inventive step and are susceptible of industrial application."

[3] In the revised Implementing Guidelines adopted on December 7, 2006, Rule 27 is now Rule 42.

vention (which will also be the field of expertise of the person skilled in the art to be considered for the purpose of assessing inventive step), the identification of the closest prior art in this field, the identification of the technical problem which can be regarded as solved in relation to this closest prior art, and then an assessment of whether or not the technical feature(s) which alone or together form the solution claimed, could be derived as a whole by the skilled person in that field in an obvious manner from the state of the art. For the purpose of the problem-and-solution approach, the problem must be a technical problem, it must actually be solved by the solution claimed, all the features in the claim should contribute to the solution, and the problem must be one that the skilled person in the particular technical field might be asked to solve at the priority date. In this context "problem" is used merely to indicate that the skilled person is to be considered as faced with some task . . . , not that its solution need necessarily involve any great difficulty. If the above conditions are not met by a problem as formulated, then it is usually necessary to reformulate the problem. There may also be cases where the features claimed fall into two or more groups, each group serving to solve a particular technical problem quite unrelated to the technical problem solved by the other groups. In such a case the obviousness of each group as a solution to its problem needs to be considered in isolation . . . . If no technical problem can be derived from the application, then an invention within the meaning of Article 52 EPC does not exist. . . .

6. Further, where a feature cannot be considered as contributing to the solution of any technical problem by providing a technical effect it has no significance for the purpose of assessing inventive step.

. . . .

In the present Board's view, this finding is entirely consistent with the general requirement for an invention to have technical character, leading to the conclusion that an invention in the sense of Article 52 EPC can only be made up of those features which contribute to said technical character.

7. The technical problem should not be formulated to refer to matters of which the skilled person would only have become aware by knowledge of the solution now claimed. Such formulation of the problem involving inadmissible hindsight of the solution must be avoided by reformulation of the technical problem to be solved. Thus a problem should not contain pointers to the solution or partially anticipate it. However, in the Board's view this principle applies to those aspects of the subject matter claimed which contribute to the technical character of the invention and hence are part of the technical solution. Merely because some feature appears in the claim does not automatically exclude it from appearing in the formulation of the problem. In particular where the claim refers to an aim to be achieved in a nontechnical field, this aim may legitimately appear in the

formulation of the problem as part of the framework of the technical problem that is to be solved, in particular as a constraint that has to be met. Thus in T 1053/98 . . . the Board (in a different composition) considered it necessary to formulate the technical problem in such a way that there was no possibility of an inventive step being involved by purely non-technical features. Such a formulation of the problem could refer to the nontechnical aspect of the invention as a given framework within which the technical problem was posed. The approach adopted in this decision thus accepts it as correct to formulate the technical problem to include non-technical aspects whether novel or not: these nontechnical aspects are thus not to be regarded as contributing to the solution.

. . . .

8. Finally, the identification of the skilled person may also need careful consideration. The skilled person will be an expert in a technical field. If the technical problem is concerned with a computer implementation of a business, actuarial or accountancy system, the skilled person will be someone skilled in data processing, and not merely a business man, actuary or accountant.

9. [The] starting point for examining inventive step is, in the present case, prior art document D8. It describes features of the GSM network standards at the stage of implementation reached in 1990 and the so-called Subscriber Identity Module (SIM) in particular, which is part of the mobile station and stores all the subscriber related information elements contained in the individual mobile stations, allowing the system to identify, authenticate and locate the subscriber in the network . . . . The remaining part of the mobile station is "a universal equipment operable by different subscribers in turn, each using his own SIM" . . . .

The GSM standards address not only technical issues but also administrative and commercial aspects of the network management. In particular the separation of subscriber related and universal functions provide, from the network operator's point of view, "a great flexibility in the subscription management." Although not explicitly dealt with in document D8, the commercial aspects of a subscription management imply that the network operator has at its disposal the technical and administrative means for charging the calling costs to the individual subscriber. The SIM, in the "GSM network operation phase" . . . is personalized (allocated to a given subscriber) and, from a process point of view, a GSM application enabling the subscriber technically to access the system. The GSM application may be one of several applications, for example when the SIM is part of an ISO standardized multi-application IC card supporting in addition to the GSM application a number of other applications. On such an active multi-application card the GSM application can be selected by appropriate commands . . . .

10. Claim 1 defines that "the subscriber identity module (SIM) is allocated at least two identities". Figure 6 of the present patent specification, however, shows an "active card modified for use as a subscriber identity module" including two standard modules . . . , each module providing a fully functional GSM application. The term "subscriber identity module" as used in the patent, therefore, has to be construed to include the multi-application card disclosed in document D8, except for the claim feature that "at least two identities" are allocated, which means in the terminology of document D8 that not only one but at least two of the applications supported by the active multi-application card are GSM applications.

11. According to document D8, each single subscriber identity module is allocated an identity which is the basis for different identity data (among others, the personal identity number IMSI to which a MSISDN number is allocated). The network location registers including the Home Location Register HLR . . . maintain the correspondence between all these numbers. Since the GSM standards require that the subscriber identity data are stored in the network home database, a user selecting a GSM application automatically and selectively activates the desired identity in the home database of the network operator from the subscriber unit. Only one GSM application can be allocated to an IMSI identity at a time. By means of the MSISDN number allocated to the subscriber identity incoming calls are automatically set up against the activated identity according to the information stored in the home database.

12. With reference to appellant's main request it follows that document D8 anticipates all features of claim 1 but the following:

(i) the subscriber identity module is allocated at least two identities,

(ii) said at least two identities being selectively usable, and

(iii) the selective activation being used for distributing the costs for service and private calls or among different users.

13. Distributing costs according to specific schemes (features (ii) and (iii)), however, is not disclosed as a technical function of the system: it is left to the user to decide and to select the desired identity and to the network operator to use the additional identity data in one or other way. The inconveniences to be eliminated are actually not located in any technical aspects of the network system, distributing costs according to the claimed kind of cost attributing scheme is rather a financial and administrative concept which as such does not require the exercise of any technical skills and competence and does not, on the administrative level, involve any solutions to a technical problem. Technical aspects first come into play with the implementation of such a scheme on the GSM system. In other words, the claimed concept of selectively distributing the costs for service

and private calls or among different users does as such not make a contribution to the technical character of the invention.

14. According to the patent specification, eliminating inconveniences caused by distributing costs for service and private calls or among different users is an object of the invention. This is not yet formulated as a technical problem. To arrive at the technical problem this object needs to be reformulated as being to implement the GSM system in such a way as to allow user-selectable discrimination between calls for different purposes or by different users. In fact, the technical professional would, in a realistic situation, receive knowledge of the cost distribution concept as part of the task information given to him to indicate the services to be provided to the customer.

15. From document D8, the skilled person, an expert in GSM systems, knows that before access to a GSM network can be granted, the mobile station has to be personalized by means of a subscriber identity module, providing the IMSI number which identifies the account to which the calling costs are to be charged. Discriminating between calls originating from one and the same mobile station, therefore, requires the allocation of different IMSI numbers, or in other terms, the implementation of a corresponding number of GSM applications (feature (i)). Faced with this technical requirement, the skilled person finds a solution in document D8 . . . : the use of an active multi-application card providing the necessary commands for selecting the desired application (feature (ii)), and thus the desired identity which a GSM system can use for charge collection.

Finally, any technical considerations which might be involved in implementing the specific use according to feature (iii) on the GSM system derive from the prior art in a straightforward way. In the GSM system costs are charged to the identity used for making a call and this remains the same according to the invention. The patent in suit does not disclose or claim any new way of charging costs, but only correlates more than one identity with one and the same subscription under the discrimination aspect, thus requiring—if at all—only minor modifications of the network's home database. In the Board's view, such considerations do not involve any technical ingenuity and hence cannot contribute positively to inventive step.

In consequence, the claimed invention, insofar as it has technical character, is obvious in the light of document D8 so that the method of claim 1 does not meet the patentability requirement of inventive step (Articles 52(1) and 56 EPC).

---

2. THE PROBLEM-SOLUTION APPROACH IN THE UK

ACTAVIS UK LIMITED V. NOVARTIS AG

United Kingdom High Court of Justice, Court of Appeal (Civil Division)
[2010] EWCA Civ 82, February 17, 2010

■ Lord Justice JACOB:

1. Novartis appeals Warren J's decision . . . [2009] EWHC 41 (Ch), that its [European Patent] (UK) 0948320 is invalid for obviousness.

. . . .

THE PATENT AND ITS BACKGROUND

3. The Patent, whose priority date is October 1996, is for a sustained release formulation of fluvastatin. In 1996 fluvastatin was a well-known statin available in an immediate release formulation consisting of capsules containing 20 or 40 mg of the sodium salt. By that date there was a strong and well-known school of thought in favour of a dosage regime consisting of a 40 mg capsule to be taken twice a day.

4. Also at the priority date there was extensive knowledge of sustained release formulations generally. The Patent puts it this way under the heading "background art":

[0002] In recent years there has been a large increase in the development and use of sustained-release tablets which are designed to release the drug slowly after ingestion. With these types of dosage forms, the clinical utility of drugs can be improved by means of improved therapeutic effects, reduced incidence of adverse effects and simplified dosing regimens.

Mr Meade [appearing for Norvatis] suggested that this paragraph should be read as specific to the invention and was saying that the invention would lead to improved therapeutic effects, reduced adverse effects and simplified dosing regimens. But it is clear that it is no more than a general background statement about the increasing use of sustained release drugs and the reasons therefor. It is saying you may or may not get improved therapy (for one or other or both reasons) and you will (obviously) get a simplified dosing regime. That was common general knowledge.

. . . .

8. The Patent then goes on to discuss statins generally and then fluvastatin, which it acknowledges is known. It then suggests that its solubility is so great that one would expect problems in creating a sustained release formulation. . . .

9. The Patent then says what problem the invention is aimed at:

[0015] ... [T]here is a need for pharmaceutical formulations of HMG-CoA reductase inhibitors which avoid the above mentioned drawbacks and are possible to prepare, e.g., without including large amounts of slow release excipients or the use of highly advanced techniques. Preferably, the production costs of the formulations should be low.

Clearly in context the "need" referred to is a need for slow-release formulations, not merely any kind of formulation. That is the problem the invention of the Patent seeks to overcome.

10. The clear message of all this is simple: there is a need for a sustained release formulation of fluvastatin but its solubility is so high that there is at least a perception that any of the conventional methods would not work.

. . . .

16. . . . Although there were lurking in the background some arguments about other claims, the only claim which really matters is claim 1, as permitted to be amended by Warren J:

> A sustained release pharmaceutical composition comprising a water soluble salt of fluvastatin as active ingredient and being selected from the group consisting of matrix formulations, diffusion-controlled membrane coated formulations and combinations thereof, wherein the sustained release formulation releases the active ingredient over more than 3 hours.

OBVIOUSNESS: THE LAW

17. The statutory question is beguilingly simple and is set out in the European Patent Convention, enacted by the Patents Act 1977. The Convention says;

. . . .

Art 56 Inventive Step

> An invention shall be considered as involving an inventive step if, having regard to the state of the art, it is not obvious to a person skilled in the art.

So at bottom the question is simply whether the invention is obvious.

. . .

18. In our courts we have found a structure helpful to approach—not answer—the question. In its latest refinement (see *Pozzoli v. BDMO* [2007] FSR 37) it runs as follows:

(1)(a) Identify the notional "person skilled in the art"

(b) Identify the relevant common general knowledge of that person;

(2) Identify the inventive concept of the claim in question or if that cannot readily be done, construe it;

(3) Identify what, if any, differences exist between the matter cited as forming part of the "state of the art" and the inventive concept of the claim or the claim as construed;

(4) Viewed without any knowledge of the alleged invention as claimed, do those differences constitute steps which would have been obvious to the person skilled in the art or do they require any degree of invention?

Obvious for the purposes of step 4 means technically rather than commercially obvious.

. . . .

21. . . . . Step 4 is the key, statutory step.

22. I am conscious that some appear to think that this structured process is something peculiarly British. I do not think it is. It merely makes explicit that which is implicit in all other approaches.

. . . .

25. [An] approach, often used in the EPO both for examination and opposition is the "problem and solution approach" ("PSA") . . . . [It has] three main stages:

(i)   determining the "closest prior art,"

(ii) establishing the "objective technical problem" to be solved, and

(iii) considering whether or not the claimed invention, starting from the closest prior art and the objective technical problem, would have been obvious to the skilled person.

26. I have a few comments about the PSA. First, and most important, is to emphasise that no-one suggests or has ever suggested that it is the only way to go about considering obviousness. The Guidelines say no more than that the examiner should "normally" apply it. That makes sense for an examining office which needs a common structured approach. When it comes to a national court making a full multifactorial assessment of all relevant factors (which may include so-called "secondary indicia" such as commercial success, especially if there has been a long-felt want) it may perhaps be used less often—particularly where there is significant room for argument about what the "objective technical problem" is. In this case, however, as will be seen, I think the approach is indeed useful.

27. My second comment is about stage 1—identify the closest piece of prior art. It is not related to the remaining steps. It is about where they start from. Generally it is an immensely practical way of dealing with the

fact that practitioners before the Office seem to think they can improve opposition attacks by the citation of a very large number of pieces of prior art. Currently there is nothing in the procedural rules (for instance a fee or costs sanction) to prevent this. Nor, in many cases, have practitioners themselves developed a culture of identifying their best piece or pieces (perhaps 2 or 3 maximum) of prior art. What is the Office to do when faced with a profligate number of citations? Laboriously consider the question of obviousness over each, one by one? Even though there may be fifty or more? That would be intolerable besides leading to even worse delays than there are now. So step 1 is essentially Office protective. It is an attempt to identify the best obviousness attack. The logic is simple: if that succeeds it does not matter if there are other attacks which might also succeed. And if it fails, other, weaker attacks would also do so.

. . . .

29. It will be noticed that there is nothing like PSA step 1 in the *Pozzoli/Windsurfing* approach. The reason is essentially this: that practitioners before the English Patents Court have learned to confine themselves to their best cases, especially by the time of trial. English patent judges are simply not faced with profligate citations. And indeed if a party attempted to indulge in profligate citation it would be likely to find that when the case-management stage of the case was reached, it would be made to identify its best case, or few best cases. Moreover wasteful conduct, which would generally include profligate citation of prior art, is likely be met with adverse costs orders.

30. I turn to the next step—establishing the "objective technical problem." The Guidelines say this:

> In the context of the problem-and-solution approach, the technical problem means the aim and task of modifying or adapting the closest prior art to provide the technical effects that the invention provides over the closest prior art. The technical problem thus defined is often referred to as the **"objective technical problem"**.
>
> The objective technical problem derived in this way may not be what the applicant presented as "the problem" in his application. The later may require reformulation, since the objective technical problem is based on objectively established facts, in particular appearing in the prior art revealed in the course of the proceedings, which may be different from the prior art of which the applicant was actually aware at the time the application was filed. In particular, the prior art cited in the search report may put the invention in an entirely different perspective from that apparent from reading the application only.

31. There is recognition here of that fact that in many cases the patentee did not start from the closest piece of prior art identified by step 1. He may have thought he was solving some larger or different problem. He may not have known of this piece of prior art.

32. The "reformulation" referred to thus involves the court or tribunal artificially creating a problem supposed to be solved by the invention. It is perhaps here that there can be real difficulties: for so much may depend on that reformulation however objectively one attempts the reformulation.

. . . .

34. For myself, I think the re-formulation—which really means retrospective construction—of a problem is perhaps the weakest part of the PSA. It will be noted that with the *Pozzoli/Windsurfing* approach, once one has finished the orienting step 3, the question is simply left open: is the invention obvious? There is no attempt to force the question into a problem/solution.

35. Moreover the PSA does not really cope well with cases where the invention involves perceiving that there is a problem, or in appreciating that a known problem, perhaps "put up with" for years, can be solved. Take for instance the "Anywayup Cup" case, *Haberman v. Jackel International* [1999] FSR 683. The invention was a baby's drinker cup fitted with a known kind of valve to prevent it leaking. Babies drinker cups had been known for years. Parents all over the world had put up with the fact that if they were dropped they leaked. No-one had thought to solve the problem. So when the patentee had the technically trivial idea of putting in a valve, there was an immediate success. The invention was held non-obvious, a conclusion with which most parents would agree. Yet fitting reasoning to uphold the patent into a PSA approach would not really work. For by identifying the problem as leakage and suggesting it can be solved, one is halfway to the answer—put in a valve.

36. Another aspect of obviousness which is not readily answered by the PSA is illustrated by the 5¼ inch plate paradox. This runs like this. Suppose the patent claim is for a plate of diameter 5¼ inches. And suppose no-one can find a plate of that particular diameter in the prior art. Then (a) it is novel and (b) it is non-obvious for there is no particular reason to choose that diameter. The conclusion, that the plate is patentable, is so absurd that it cannot be so.

37. What then is the answer to the paradox? It is this: the 5¼ inch limitation is purely arbitrary and non-technical. It solves no problem and advances the art not at all. It is not inventive. And although "inventive step" is defined as being one which is not obvious, one must always remember the purpose of that definition—to define what is inventive. That which is not inventive by any criteria is not made so by the definition.

Trivial limitations, such as specifying the plate diameter, or painting a known machine blue for no technical reason are treated as obvious because they are not inventive.

38. The PSA does not assist in providing an answer to the paradox. This is for the simple reason that there is no problem and so no solution to it.

39. Having said that the PSA has its limitations I hasten to add this: the PSA is apt to work very well when there is no need to reformulate the problem. This, as will be seen, is such a case. And it also generally works where, although there needs to be a reformulation, the reformulation is not controversial.

40. The last step of the PSA, asking whether the invention is obvious starting from the closest prior art and the objective technical problem corresponds to *Pozzoli/Windsurfing* step 4, though the latter is not limited to any "objective technical problem". As I have said it leaves the question unconstrained by any necessary requirement to identify a problem.

41. That is because in the end obviousness is a multifactorial question. Kitchin J put thus in a manner approved by Lord Hoffmann at [42] in *Conor*:

> The question of obviousness must be considered on the facts of each case. The court must consider the weight to be attached to any particular factor in the light of all the relevant circumstances. These may include such matters as the motive to find a solution to the problem the patent addresses, the number and extent of the possible avenues of research, the effort involved in pursuing them and the expectation of success. (*Generics v. Lundbeck* [2007] RPC 32 at [72]).

42. Finally I should say a word about what is sometimes called the could/would point. For it was part of Mr. Meade's submissions that even though it was conceded that the idea of a slow-release formulation of fluvastatin would occur to the skilled person, that was not enough to make a claim to it obvious. It was necessary to show that skilled person *would* implement it.

. . . .

47. [However], a requirement that an idea can only be held obvious upon proof that it would actually be implemented would make many self-evident ideas non-obvious. For many obvious ideas may not be worth implementing commercially.

. . . .

THE JUDGMENT UNDER APPEAL

51. The Judge analysed the evidence in detail, for which I am very grateful. Because of that it is unnecessary to go over it all again. Before going to the Judge's conclusions, it is worth noting that Actavis put its case higher than it needed to. It advanced a case that a sustained release form of fluvastatin would be expected not only to be a more convenient formulation for patient compliance but would be likely to have significant medical advantages, namely improved therapeutic effect and fewer side effects. Hence, the argument ran, there was a strong motive to create a sustained release form and a strong expectation that all three types of benefit would be obtained, the two medical and the convenience.

52. On the facts the Judge rejected the "medical advantage" motivation as having a significant enough expectation of success. But he did accept the "more convenient" advantage point. His detailed summary of the position, which is unchallenged, reads as follows:

> [312] In the light of the totality of the evidence, the essentials of which I have discussed above, I reach the following conclusions:
>
> . . .
>
> d. The skilled team would seek to identify the benefits (or incentives) and problems (or disincentives) of a sustained release formulation.
>
> e. The team would regard improved patient compliance as a benefit which would certainly be obtained if a satisfactory formulation of an 80 mg dose could be successfully achieved.
>
> f. The team would be concerned about clinical efficacy. It would be uncertain about whether improvement could be achieved. It could not be ruled out. But it certainly could not be said with any confidence that any improvement would be achieved, nor that there was a strong expectation that it would be achieved.
>
> g. The team would also be concerned with side-effects. Again, it would be unable to predict with anything approaching certainty that any reduction in the risk of side-effects would be achieved, but there would be some hope of reduced risks of hepatotoxicity (on a population basis as explained above) and a reasonable expectation of improvements in myopathy. However, neither of these was seen as serious problems with fluvastatin at the priority date.
>
> h. The team would have, as a result of common general knowledge and secondary common general knowledge, an expectation of being able to develop an 80 mg sustained release formu-

lation which released over at least 3 hours *in vivo* and would be
confident that it would have some clinical efficacy. But it would
have no confidence that it would achieve better, or even the
same, efficacy as the existing maximum dosage of 2 x 40 mg daily immediate release. It would expect, but could not be certain,
that this would not produce a greater risk of side-effects than the
existing maximum dosage.

    i. It would have been rational, from a technical perspective,
for the team to have produced a sustained release formulation
for 80 mg once daily dosage with a view to improved patient
compliance, anticipated reduction in side-effects and possible
improved efficacy. But in the light of the uncertainties, such a
course might well be seen as commercially unjustifiable; but that
would be a matter for the decision of commercial people not of
the skilled team.

    j. The team, if it were asked to do so, would be confident of
producing a sustained release formulation of fluvastatin at various doses which had the release characteristics *in vitro* described
in the Patent. It would be confident that such a formulation
could be taken by humans and would have some therapeutic effect albeit perhaps of lesser efficacy than the equivalent dosage
taken in immediate release form as a single dose (up to 40 mg
daily) or two doses (up to 80 mg daily). There would, however, be
no reason for producing such a formulation for its own sake if it
were thought impossible or highly unlikely that such a formulation would have, or would lead to a product which would have,
improved efficacy and/or reduced side-effects.

53. I should also set out a further finding:

    [320] The Patent claims that, surprisingly, fluvastatin sodi-
um exhibits particularly favourable release characteristics. The
evidence, however, shows that the high absolute solubility of a
drug is a problem only at very high and very low levels. The evidence also shows that the high (but not very high) solubility of
fluvastatin would not have been seen as a serious problem at
least *in vitro*; it would only have been seen as limiting the available technology for producing a sustained release formulation re-
leasing *in vitro* over a period of 3 hours or more.

54. So the whole basis for the invention as set out in the Patent was
destroyed. The Patent says the skilled man would think the solubility of
fluvastatin was so high that the skilled man would think a sustained release form could not be made. But that was not so. The skilled man would
not think that, based on his common general knowledge alone. The problem presented in the Patent was illusory (Lloyd LJ's happy choice of
word)—it was in reality a non-problem because fluvastatin is not so high-

ly soluble that the skilled person would expect it to be impossible or difficult to make a sustained release form.

. . . .

56. Mr Meade had to accept that the basis of the invention as presented by the patentee would not in reality have been seen as a problem
by the skilled person. So he pointed to the PSA, submitting that this
clearly allowed for a reformulation of the problem. It would be good
enough to support the Patent if there was another problem in the way.
That problem, he suggested was this: that the skilled person would not
have a sufficient expectation of success to make it worthwhile trying to
make a sustained release formulation. This case should be considered on
an "obvious to try" basis. And because of an insufficient expectation of
success Actavis should fail.

57. The Judge went along with this approach, but only up to a point.
For after his summary of the facts he went on to conclude that the invention was not obvious on the basis of a notional project to develop a sustained release formulation which had a fair expectation of success. By
"success" he meant a formulation which had improved therapeutic effects
or fewer side effects as compared with immediate release formulations.

58. Having got this far the judge went on to consider the case on the
basis of the 5¼ inch plate paradox. At this point he held that there was no
motivation to produce a sustained release form and said this:

> [323] In my judgment, this absence of motivation does not
> prevent claim 1 from being technically obvious. The skilled team
> would, for reasons already given, not reject a sustained release
> formulation out of hand. Even though its focus will be on the end
> result of an 80 mg once daily formulation having improved effi-
> cacy and less serious side effects, coupled with better patient
> compliance, the concept of sustained release will be present. It
> does not need a commercial boss to ask the question "Can you
> make a formulation [within claim 1]" for the skilled formulator
> to appreciate its technical obviousness any more than it needs a
> commercial boss to ask a similar question of the plate designer
> for that designer to appreciate the technical obviousness of the
> odd-sized plate. I conclude that claim 1 is obvious over the com-
> mon general knowledge.

. . . .

60. Because of the way the Judge dealt with the matter, Mr Meade
appealed in respect of the "technically obvious" finding and Mr Wyand
challenged the decision that apart from that point the invention was not
obvious. I have to say I do not think that the two-bite approach is actually
a convenient way to deal with obviousness. It is, after all, a multifactorial assessment. The thing to do is to identify all the relevant factors,

orientate oneself à la *Pozzoli* and then decide whether the invention is obvious.

61. I start with Mr Wyand's challenge. He submitted that the Judge had made an error in assessing what was meant by "success" in terms of the Patent. It was not improved clinical efficacy or the same efficacy with fewer side effects. It was simply a sustained release formulation which one would expect to work. Moreover if one wanted a motive, there was one—improved patient compliance. Whether it was worth actually developing such a formulation (there would be costs of testing and compliance with regulatory requirements) was irrelevant. As the Patent said at [15] there was a need for a slow release formulation which it was possible to prepare.

62. I accept that submission. Once the obstacle put forward in the Patent against being able to make a sustained formulation was shown to be illusory, then a sustained release formulation is obvious. You might get better efficacy or fewer side effects, but you would certainly get better compliance. In *Pozzoli* terms the only difference between the prior art and the claim is the idea of making a sustained release formulation. For that there was a technical motivation and no difficulty, real or apparent.

63. The PSA gives the same answer. What is the objective problem? Why that which the patentee himself stated—to produce a sustained release form of fluvastatin. Was the solution obvious? Yes, any of the standard methods for such formulations would clearly work: there is no reason why they would not.

64. There is no need and it would be wrong to re-formulate the problem as suggested by Mr Meade. This is not a case where some prior art unknown to the patentee has turned up. Nor is it right to reformulate the problem as one of looking for better medical effects when that was not the problem as seen by the patentee or to reformulate the solution as having found such effects when the patentee has not promised any.

. . . .

66. The upshot is that I would uphold the decision of the Judge. Unlike him, however, I do not think the case was finely balanced. Once the basis of the Patent was proved illusory there was nothing left to save it. . . .

NOTES AND QUESTIONS

1. Does the court in *Actavis* apply the problem-and-solution approach in the same way as the EPO in *Comvik*? What interpretive tools dominate the analysis of inventive step in *Actavis*? In *Comvik*? Which decision is more persuasive?

2. Is the argument in *Actavis* that there is no inventive step or that there is no technical problem to be solved? According to the Board of Appeals in

Comvik, "for the purpose of the problem-and-solution approach, the problem must be a technical problem, it must actually be solved by the solution claimed, all the features in the claim should contribute to the solution, and the problem must be one that the skilled person in the particular technical field might be asked to solve at the priority date." *Comvik v. DeTeMobil, supra,* at para. 5. As thus formulated, in what way is the approach to inventive step in Europe different from that in the United States? How should the policy goals underlying patent law affect which approach to obviousness is most appropriate?

3. The decision in *Comvik* characterizes the invention as lacking inventive step. However, a significant part of the reason it lacks inventive step is because some features of the invention fall within patent subject matter eligibility exclusions (lack of technical character). A similar confluence of subject matter eligibility and inventive step in a business method/computer implemented invention can be seen in the U.S. Federal Circuit decision of *In re Comisky,* 499 F.3d 1365 (Fed. Cir. 2007). There, after concluding that certain claims which involved use of a general purpose computer comprised patent-eligible subject matter, the court noted that "[t]he routine addition of modern electronics to an otherwise unpatentable invention typically creates a prima facie case of obviousness." What might account for this interplay between subject matter eligibility and inventive step?

4. Despite the fact that countries that are part of the EPO have harmonized their national legislation with the European Patent Convention, national courts sometimes take somewhat different approaches from that of the EPO in ruling on inventive step. As seen in the *Actavis* decision, in the UK for example, instead of focusing just on the closest piece of prior art, courts will also look to the common general knowledge in the art and impute that knowledge to the PHOSITA. As a result, if the common general knowledge fills the gap between the closest prior art and what is being claimed, the invention will be held to lack inventive step. *See Windsurfing International Inc. v. Tabur Marine (Great Britain) Ltd.,* [1985] R.P.C. 59 (C.A. (Civ.) 1984). And in Germany, based on the old principle that inventions should substantially advance the art, German courts tend to give evidence of unexpected results or superior advantage greater weight than does the EPO in finding inventive step. Do such approaches make more sense than the highly mechanized one of the EPO? Why or why not?

5. Decisions about obviousness are inherently subjective, and the various tests used to determine whether an invention satisfies the inventive step/non-obviousness standard are in part designed to help curb the potential for arbitrariness. Lord Justice Jacob of the UK Court of Appeal (Civil Division) in *Aerotel v. Wavecrest Group Enterprises, Ltd.* [2009] EWCA Civ 408 quoted approvingly from an earlier UK decision *Biogen v. Medeva* [1997] RPC 1:

> The need for appellate caution in reversing the judge's evaluation of the facts is based upon much more solid grounds than professional courtesy. It is because specific findings of fact, even by the most me-

ticulous judge, are inherently an incomplete statement of the impression which was made upon him by the primary evidence. His expressed findings are always surrounded by a penumbra of imprecision as to emphasis, relative weight, minor qualification and nuance (as Renan said, *la vérité est dans la nuance*), of which time and language do not permit exact expression, but which may play an important part in the judge's overall evaluation. . . . When the application of a legal standard such as negligence or obviousness involves no question of principle but is simply a matter of degree, an appellate court should be very cautious in differing from the judge's evaluation."

Aerotel Ltd v. Wavecrest Group Enterprises Ltd, [2009] EWCA Civ 408 [25], (Eng.).

Do you agree?

6. Given the weaknesses of the problem-and-solution approach discussed by the court in *Actavis,* would you recommend this approach to patent offices or courts in developing countries?

7. In the chemical arts, Europe and the United States may not be far apart at all in their approaches to determining the presence of an inventive step. This is because the "lead compound" approach exemplified in the *Altana Pharma v. Teva Pharmaceuticals* case in section B.3, *supra,* is very similar to the problem-solution approach. As one commentator explains:

> [T]he obviousness analysis for a claim for a chemical composition starts with the identification of a lead compound that would be the most promising to modify and, after identifying the lead compound, determines whether the prior art would have provided a reason or motivation to modify the lead compound in a manner that shows obviousness of the claimed chemical composition. . . . [This] approach has a strong similarity to the European problem-and-solution approach. In the European problem-and-solution approach to the examination of inventive step (a.k.a. obviousness), the first step is the determination of the "closest prior art." In determining the closest prior art, the first consideration is a similar purpose or effect. In order to determine non-obviousness, the problem being solved by the claimed invention is identified and a determination is made as to whether it was obvious to provide the differences between the claimed invention and the closest prior art in order to solve the problem.

> Comparing the two approaches, . . . the lead compound is similar to the closest prior art. In the problem-and-solution approach, the determination of whether it would have been obvious to provide the differences between the claimed invention and the closest prior art relies on the "could/would analysis"—whether the prior art would ("not simply could, but would") have led one skilled in the art trying to solve the problem to provide the differences between the claimed

invention and the closest prior art. The "could/would analysis" is very similar to . . . the determination of whether the prior art would have provided a reason or motivation to modify the lead compound.

Although we are not clamoring for a return to the TSM approach that led to the *KSR* decision, the problem- and-solution approach, within the expanded framework for motivation given in *KSR*, would provide a rational approach to obviousness determination which will make the life of the patent practitioners more bearable.

Orlando Lopez, *Should We Expand* Takeda *Beyond Chemicals: Otsuka Pharmaceuticals Co., Ltd. v. Sandoz Inc.* et al. *and the Problem-and-Solution Approach?* OBVIPAT (May 15, 2012), http://www.obvipat.com/2012/05/should-we-expand-takeda-beyond-chemicals-otsuka-pharmaceuticals-co-ltd-v-sandoz-inc-et-al-and-the-problem-and-solution-approach/.

Do you agree that applying the problem-solution approach to all technologies in the U.S. would be preferable to the *KSR* framework? If not, why not?

D. JAPAN

The requirement of inventive step was added to Japanese law in 1959. Section 29(2) of the Japan Patent Act (Law No. 121 of April 13, 1959, as amended)[3] provides that "[w]here, prior to the filing of the patent application, a person ordinarily skilled in the art of the invention would have been able to easily make the invention . . . a patent shall not be granted. . . ." The Japanese Examination Guidelines for Patent and Utility Model offer detailed assistance (in Part II, Ch. 2, § 2) on how the provision should be applied. They underscore that the purpose of the provision, just as in the U.S. and Europe, is to prevent the grant of patents that do not contribute to, and may even hamper, technological progress. The basic procedure for determining inventive step in Japan is similar to that in the U.S., but the process also contains elements akin to the European approach.

1. INVENTIVE STEP ASSESSMENT

The determination of inventive step in the JPO, like that in the EPO, is basically a three-step process. In the first step, the examiner selects and assesses the body of prior art relevant to the claimed invention. From that body of art, the examiner selects the one reference that most closely resembles the invention at issue, which is known as the prime cited art. Like the USPTO, the second step consists of comparing the prime cited art with the invention to determine the structural similarities and differences. The comparison of claimed inventions and cited inventions is plagued by the same concerns faced in other countries about examiner hindsight bias or, as described by a recent Japanese case study on in-

---

[3] Unofficial English translation furnished by the Japan Patent Office.

ventive step, concern that the "finding of the cited invention was forcedly approximated to the claimed invention in finding the cited invention from the cited document." *See* JAPANESE PATENT OFFICE, INTELLECTUAL PROPERTY POLICY COMMITTEE, CASE STUDY ON INVENTIVE STEP 2 (2010). In the third step before the JPO, the examiner attempts to determine whether the prime cited art or other cited prior art, as well as well-known and commonly used art, would have caused a person skilled in the art to have arrived at the claimed invention. Unlike the U.S., but similar to Europe and China, "secret prior art" cannot be considered in evaluating inventive step. The chart below illustrates the approach to inventive step in Japan.

The excerpted cases below, culled from the JPO study cited earlier, illustrate various aspects of the Japanese approach that recently have been clarified.

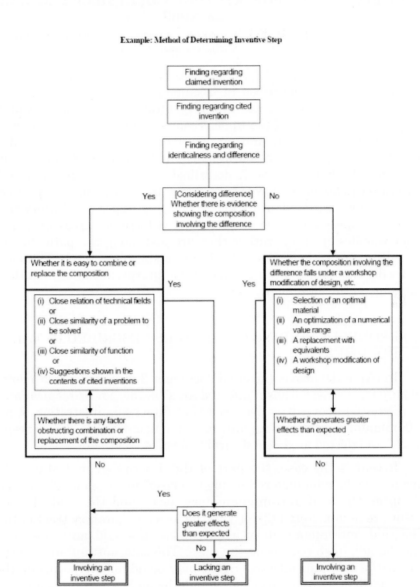

Source: Modified flowchart from JPO Examination Department's "FY2006 Report on Inventive Step Review"

INTELLECTUAL PROPERTY HIGH COURT DECISION, MARCH 25, 2009

(2008 Gyo-ke) 10261, "Xylitol concoction for treatment of condition of upper respiratory tract")[4]

[In this case, the defendant asserted that the description of his treatment method, described in Document 2 [(A) to (G)] as a treatment method for a disease of the lower respiratory tract, also included the treatment of diseases of the upper respiratory tract because it can be administered intra-nasally and an average person would understand that from the description in the document. The Court determined that just because nasal administration is described as a path to directly administer aerosol particles to the lower respiratory tract, it cannot be inferred that nasal administration is a method of treating upper respiratory tract diseases. The nose and upper respiratory tract are not areas that the treatment was designed for; rather they are just along the path that reaches the ultimate destination of the lower respiratory tract. Therefore, the Court declined to extend the defendant's interpretation beyond the literal language in the document.–EDS.]

. . .

B. ERRONEOUS FINDING OF MATTERS DESCRIBED IN THE CITED DOCUMENT 2

In (A) to (D) above, the cited document 2 discloses a treatment method only for diseases whose "infected area" is the "lower respiratory tract." In (E) to (G) above, it is disclosed that direct administration of an anti-inflammatory agent and an anti-infective agent to the "lower respiratory tract," an infected area, is a desirable form of treatment.

If that is the case, the part of the description that states that the "agent may be administered inside the nose" in the said (G), "In a desirable form, the said anti-inflammatory agent and the said anti-infective agent are administered directly to the lower respiratory tract of the host. The said anti-inflammatory agent and/or the said anti-infective agent may be administered inside the nose. The said anti-inflammatory agent and/or the said anti-infective agent may be administered inside the nose in the form of aerosol particles," should be understood to mean that aerosol particles are administered to "inside the nose" from the nostril which is the entrance route to directly administer the said anti-inflammatory agent and the said anti-infective agent to the "lower respiratory tract," which is the affected area. It cannot be understood that the said anti-inflammatory agent and the said anti-infective agent are administered to the nose for the purpose of treating the nose on the assumption that the nose itself is an infected area.

---

[4] Excerpted from Japanese Patent Office, Intellectual Property Policy Committee, Case Study on Inventive Step (2010, p. 3) *available at* http://www.jpo.go.jp/kijun/kijun2/pdf/tukujitu_casesstudy/progre_en.pdf

Therefore, the finding of the trial decision that "the cited document 2 describes that the anti-infective agent can be administered to the nose, an infected area (summary of matters (G))" is incorrect.

C. JUDGMENT ON THE ASSERTION OF THE DEFENDANT IN CONNECTION WITH THE ERRONEOUS FINDING OF MATTERS DESCRIBED IN THE CITED DOCUMENT 2

In response, the defendant asserts that a person skilled in the art can understand the description that "[t]he said anti-infective agent can be administered locally, orally, in the vein or in the abdominal cavity. Local administration is desirable. The first advantage of local administration of a treatment agent is that a higher concentration of agent can be delivered to an infected tissue with a lower total dose to patients than what is required for systemic administration, enabling the avoidance of known side effects of a high dose agent, for example, systemic administration of corticosteroid" mentions an infectious respiratory disease not only of the "lower respiratory tract" but also of the "upper respiratory tract." This is because the fact that nasal administration as well as oral administration can be chosen as an administration route with regard to "the anti-infective agent" for various infectious respiratory diseases was well known before the priority date of this application.

However, the said assertion of the defendant cannot be adopted.

It is natural to interpret the said description of the defendant's citation as about a disease whose infected area is the "lower respiratory tract" based on the description which repeatedly mentions that the cited document 2 is for providing a treatment method for a disease whose infected area is the "lower respiratory tract.". At the same time, even if it is publicly known that "intranasal administration" as well as "oral administration" can be chosen as an administration route of an "anti infectious agent" for a respiratory disease, this cannot constitute a ground to interpret the description of the cited document 2 as one that includes the "upper respiratory tract" contrary to the clear description stated in the cited document 2 that it is for providing a treatment method for a disease of the "lower respiratory tract." Therefore, the said assertion of the defendant cannot be adopted.

NOTES AND QUESTIONS

1. In the *Xylitol* case, the Japanese Intellectual Property High Court dismissed the description of public knowledge of intranasal administration of a drug as a basis for expanding the literal wording of the cited document. What policy justifications might exist for limiting the use of arguments about the state of the public's knowledge? How should the content and state of prior

art in a given field be determined, and by whom using what kinds of evidence?

2. The defendant in this case argued that the established prior art made clear that the affected area in the cited document was the "upper respiratory tract" despite the document's explicit reference to providing a method of treatment for diseases of the "lower respiratory tract." What factors do you think should prevail in comparing or interpreting the scope and content of a cited document with a claimed invention? Is it appropriate to limit the evaluation of prior art strictly to the language used in the document?

2. CAUSE OR MOTIVATION

Similar to the USPTO, a JPO examiner must consider every feature of the claimed invention, not simply the purely technical ones that contribute to the invention's solution. The examiner is also directed to look for a cause or motivation in the cited prior art, or in well-known, commonly used art, that would cause a person skilled in the art to arrive at the claimed invention from the prime cited art. Unless a cause or motivation can be identified, the invention is deemed to possess inventive step.

There are generally four types of cause or motivation that will create a presumption of lack of inventive step in Japan:

- where the technical field of the claimed invention and that of the cited prior art are closely related;
- where the prior art reveals a close similarity to the problem the claimed invention is attempting to solve, or where the claimed invention represents merely a juxtaposition of technical features over the prior art, the optimization of a known numerical value range, or the replacement of one known element with an equivalent;
- where the function, mechanisms, or operation of the claimed invention and the cited prior art are closely similar; or
- where there are suggestions to the claimed invention in the prior art.

The presumption in the above cases may be overcome, however, if the claimed invention possesses advantageous or unexpected effects, or other secondary indicia of inventive step, over the cited prior art. This is particularly so with respect to genus-species inventions, which the Guidelines refer to as "selection inventions," or inventions with numerical ranges.

The case excerpt below, *Engine ignition device,* illustrates application of the inventive step requirement where the technical fields are closely related. In this case, the Tokyo High Court agreed with the trial decision that there was a motivation stemming from the prior art.

TOKYO HIGH COURT DECISION, JULY 23, 2002
(2000 (Gyo-ke) 388, "Engine ignition device")[5]

[In this case, the invention described in document 1 is an ignition device for an internal combustion engine for motor vehicles powered by a battery. The invention described in document 2 is an ignition device for an internal-combustion engine with its battery charged with the output from an AC generator being used as a DC power source. These inventions are extremely similar because document 2 does not explicitly state that it cannot be applied to motor vehicles. Both of the documents can be applied to a universal problem: starting engines using output from an AC generator in a case where battery voltage drops. The key issue addressed by the court is whether there is cause or motivation to apply the constituent in document 2 to the invention in document 1. –EDS.]

. . .

(2) According to the contents of descriptions in document 1 and document 2, the invention described in document 1 relates to an ignition device of internal-combustion engine for motor vehicles powered by a battery. The ignition device described in document 2 is identified as an ignition device for internal-combustion engines equipped with its battery charged with output from an AC generator as a DC power source. Moreover, it is clear that the content of description in document 2 does not exclude its application to motor vehicles so that the invention described in document 1 and the ignition device described in document 2 are similar in the technical field of "an ignition device for on-vehicle internal-combustion engine powered by a battery."

The decision focused on close similarity of the technical fields of document 1 and document 2, and a person skilled in the art could have easily arrived at the constituent (constituent in connection with the difference 1) to charge the battery in document 1 with output from the AC generator by applying the constituent described in document 2 to the invention in document 1. Therefore, there is no error in the judgment.

Then, close similarity of the technical fields mentioned above could also serve as a cause or motivation to combine document 1 and document 2.

(3) The plaintiff asserts that there is not a problem of corrected invention in document 1 and document 2 so that there is no cause or motivation to combine matters described in both documents, and that therefore, a person skilled in the art could not easily arrive at the application of the constituent of document 2 to the invention described in document 1.

---

[5] Excerpted from Japanese Patent Office, Intellectual Property Policy Committee, Case Study on Inventive Step (2010, p. 11) available at http://www.jpo.go.jp/shiryou/kijun/kijun2/pdf/tukujitu_casestudy/progre_en.pdf.

However, Reference Otsu No.1 and Reference Otsu No.2 describe that an engine is started by output from an AC generator in a case where the battery voltage drops. . . . Also they describe the fact that, in that case, the engine cannot be ignited because of low output of the AC generator, and as a means to solve such a problem, the constituent in which output from a rectifier connected to the AC generator is directly connected to the second side of the ignition coil (Reference Otsu No.1) or the constituent which inserts an adjusting resistance (Reference Otsu No.2) are shown. Both of them suggest a means to enable start-up of engines using output from the AC generator in a case where battery voltage drops. These examples indicate that the problem of corrected invention that "enabling start-up of engines even in a case where battery voltage drops" asserted by plaintiff is recognized as universal in the field of ignition device of internal-combustion engine including motor vehicle and is a well-known problem to a person skilled in the art.

In such situation where a universal or a well-known problem exists, it can be said that there exists a cause or motivation to apply the constituent of document 2 to the invention of document 1 regardless of whether a problem of corrected invention is presented in document 1 and document 2. Moreover, there is no obstructive factor in reaching the constituent that the battery of document 1 is charged with output from the AC generator by applying the constituent described in document 2 to the invention described in document 1. Therefore, the assertion by the plaintiff with regard to this point cannot be adopted.

NOTES AND QUESTIONS

1. The *Engine ignition device* case involved close similarity of technical fields while other cases have dealt with the similarity of problems to be solved between the claimed inventions and the cited inventions. *See, e.g.,* Intellectual Property High Court Decision, July 19, 2007 (2006 (Gyo-ke) 10488 "Drive circuit"). Should there be a difference in how courts assess cause or motivation in these two contexts? What policy justifications support the view that it is appropriate to consider the technical difficulty involved in assessing whether there is a general cause or motivation to combine what is cited in an applicant's document and the well-known art?

2. The plaintiff in the *Engine ignition device* case argued that a person skilled in the art could not easily arrive at the application of the cited document to the claimed invention. The Tokyo High Court disagreed, noting that several references already noted the problem that the plaintiff's invention sought to address. According to the court, since the problem was so well-known, there existed a cause or motivation sufficient to deny the presence of inventive step. Is the extent to which a problem is known an appropriate proxy for determining cause or motivation?

3. ADVANTAGEOUS OR UNEXPECTED EFFECTS

Although both Japanese and U.S. practice permit the consideration of secondary considerations or objective indicia of non-obviousness, the procedure for asserting them differs. In the USPTO, an examiner generally will not consider the existence of secondary indicia at the initial examination stage, leaving it to the patent applicant to assert it as a rebuttal argument if the examiner makes a prima facie case of obviousness. In the JPO, however, the examiner considers secondary indicia, including factors such as commercial success or long-felt need, as part of the original assessment of inventive step. Patent applicants therefore need to disclose their inventions' advantageous or unexpected effects or other secondary indicia *in the patent application*, at least to a degree for the examiner to infer them, if the examiner is to take them into consideration. It is also essential that the effects bear a causative link to the technical features of the invention, not to features such as successful sales promotion or marketing. In Japanese parlance, advantageous or unexpected results are referred to as "koka," and the *koka* must be causatively linked to the "yoshi," or gist (technical features) of the invention; as in the United States, there must be a "nexus" between the secondary considerations and the claimed invention. While secondary indicia may thus play a role in the initial assessment of inventive step, it is interesting to note that they are rarely invoked in practice in Japan once an examiner has made a finding of lack of inventive step. For more on this requirement, *see Japanese Examination Guidelines*, Part II, Chapter 2, 2.5 (3) (citing Decision by the Tokyo High Court, October 27, 1998 [Heisei 9 (Gyo Ke) 198]) and David Abraham, *Shino–Sei:Japanese Inventive Step Meets U.S. Non-Obviousness*, 77 J. PAT. & TRADEMARK OFF. SOC'Y 528, 531 (1995).

4. PERSONS SKILLED IN THE ART

Japanese inventors often work in teams, and it is common practice for all members of the team to be mentioned as inventors in patent applications. It is not surprising, therefore, that a Japanese examiner may define a PHOSITA as a group of persons, particularly in respect of applications for highly advanced and complex technology. If the examiner further defines the group of persons as spanning various technical fields and imputes to the group ordinary skill for each one of them, the PHOSITA will likely be deemed to have a broader scope of knowledge than the PHOSITA's U.S. hypothetical counterpart. *See* Amy Nelson, *Obviousness or Inventive Step as Applied to Nucleic Acid Molecules: A Global Perspective*, 6 N. CAROLINA J. L. & TECH. 1, 25 (2004).

NOTES AND QUESTIONS

1. What are the practical consequences of the differences between the U.S., Japanese and European approaches to inventive step? Would you describe these differences as substantive or merely stylistic? A recent comparative study commissioned by the EPO/USPTO/JPO Trilateral Cooperation Initiative compares the handling of the inventive step/non-obviousness inquiry in each office. *See* "Catalogue of Differing Practices/Remaining Differences" (2012) *available at* http://www.trilateral.net/catalogue/catalogue2012.pdf. Another useful comparison of the approaches of these three systems, particularly after the KSR decision, is provided in Tomotaka Homma, *Comparing Japanese and U.S. Standards of Obviousness: Providing Meaningful Guidance After KSR*, 48 IDEA 3449 (2008) and for a seminal historical overview, *see* Tetsu Tanabe & Harold C. Wegner, *Japanese Patent Law*, AIPPI JAPAN (1979).

2. Article 27 of the TRIPS Agreement provides that member countries must grant patents to inventions that, *inter alia*, possess inventive step, but the Agreement neither defines the term nor instructs member countries as to how it should be applied. As countries devise and refine standards and tests for inventive step, what factors should they take into consideration? What policy interests might come into play in setting an appropriate standard? Is it possible for a country to violate Article 27 by establishing too low a standard? If so, how?

3. One of the inventive step-related topics on which countries diverge is the treatment of claims to "new uses" of known substances, in particular, claims to a second medical use or indication. Such claims are of special interest in the pharmaceutical arena as a way to extend the life cycle of a drug through a process called "evergreening" which we discussed earlier in Chapter 4.

Many countries allow such claims, including the United States, Canada, and member countries of the EPO; however, some do not. For example, the India Patents Act, as amended in 2005 to comply with the TRIPS Agreement, contains a new Section 3(d) which provides that "the mere discovery of a new form of a known substance which does not result in the enhancement of the known efficacy of that substance" is not patentable. It then provides that salts, esters, ethers, polymorphs, metabolites, and the like, shall be considered as the same substance unless they "differ significantly in properties with regard to efficacy." One particularly interesting aspect of Section 3(d) is the fact that, like the approach used in the *Comisky* and *Comvik* cases excerpted earlier in this Chapter, its application involves both questions of patent subject matter eligibility and inventive step. In 2007, the Madras Chennai High Court upheld a Section 3(d) rejection of a Novartis patent application for the anti-cancer drug Gleevec, where the drug involved was deemed to be simply a different form of an existing compound without the requisite enhanced efficacy. *See Novartis AG v. Union of India*, 2007 A.I.R. 24759 (Madras H.C.), *supra*, Chapter 4.

E. CHINA

China has only had a patent law since 1984, but the country has experienced a meteoric rise in the use of its patent system both by Chinese nationals and foreign inventors. In 2010, China ranked third in the world in the number of utility patent applications, and by 2012, China's State Intellectual Property Office had become number one in the world in patent applications received. *See* WIPO, 2012 WIPO World Intellectual Property Indicators, *available at* http://www.wipo.int/ipstats/en/wipi/index.html. The Third Revision of the Patent Law of the People's Republic of China, which became effective in October 2009, continues to include the inventive step requirement in Article 22:

> Article 22. Any invention or utility model for which patent right may be granted must possess novelty, inventiveness and practical app1icability.. . .
>
> Inventiveness means that, as compared with the technology existing before the date of filing, the invention has prominent substantive features and represents a notable progress and that the utility model has substantive features and represents progress.

http://www.sipo.gov.cn/sipo_English/laws/lawsregulations/200804/t20080 416_380327.html.

While the language of the provision reads somewhat differently from that in the U.S., EPO, and Japan, the analysis, as illustrated in the following decisions, appears quite familiar.

ZHANG, XITIAN V. SHIJIAZHUANG OUYI PHARMACEUTICAL CO., LTD.

Beijing Higher People's Ct. 2007 (China)[6]

FACTS AND PROCEDURAL HISTORY

The patent at issue is for an invention entitled "Separation of Amlodipine Enantiomers." The holder of the patent is Xitian Zhang, the plaintiff. The date of the application is February 21, 2000. SIPO granted the patent right on January, 29, 2003.

In the patent application, there are three separate patent claims:

- The first invention claim is a method for separating the (R)(+) and (S)(-) isomers of amlodipine from a mixture. The main feature of this method is the following chemical reaction: using chiral auxiliary deuterated dimethyl sulfoxide (DMSO-d6) or organic solvents containing DMSO-d6, the

---

[6] Summaries of the two Chinese cases in this section were translated by Dr. Mingda Hang. Original decision (in Chinese) is available at http://www.law-lib.com/cpws/cpws_view.asp?id= 200401023403.

mixture of isomers will react with D- or L-tartaric acid (separation chiral reagent), resulting in separated precipitations of (S)(-) amlodipine tartrate and (R)(+) amlodipine tartrate. In this reaction, the molar ratio of amlodipine to tartaric acid is about 0.25.

- The second claim is a dependent claim based on the first claim. It includes two additional technical features. The first one is to limit the molar ratio of DMSO-d6 to amlodipine to equal or exceed 1. The second feature is to limit the organic solvents containing DMSO-d6 which can be separated by precipitation to water, sulfoxides, ketones, amides, esters, chlorinated hydrocarbons, and hydrocarbons.

- The third claim is a dependent claim based on the first and second claims. The complexes that precipitated separately are (R)(+) amlodipine-half-D-tartaric acid-single-DMSO-d6 and (S)(-) amlodipine-half-D-tartaric acid-single-DMSO-d6.

The invalidity request against this patent is raised by the Shijiazhuang Ouyi Pharmaceutical Co., Ltd. ("Ouyi") and the Shijiazhuang Zhongqi Pharmaceutical Technology Co., Ltd. ("Zhongqi"). They argue that this patent violates the requirements set forth in Article 22 Section 3 [inventiveness] of the Chinese Patent Law.

On April 1st, 2006, the Patent Reexamination Committee issued No.7955 decision on the invalidity request: 1) the first claim and the part of the third claim dependent on the first claim are invalid; 2) the second claim and the part of the third claim dependent on the second claim are upheld as valid.

Xitian Zhang (the holder of the disputed patent) appealed the No.7955 decision to the Beijing No.1 People's Intermediate Court. After losing that appeal, Zhang appealed to the Beijing People's High Court and also lost that appeal.

THE COURT'S REASONING ON THE INVALIDITY OF THE FIRST CLAIM:

The court noted that the central issue of this case is whether the first claim of the disputed patent meets the requirement of inventiveness. The court cited to the Chinese Patent law, which prescribes that inventiveness means that compared with existing technologies [the prior art], the invention possesses prominent substantive features and represents a remarkable advancement.

The court further noted that in the field involving chemical reactions or pharmaceutical inventions, a person who is familiar with the art could think to use a structurally, physically, or chemically identical or similar compound to replace the corresponding compound using existing techniques without any creative effort. In the inventiveness inquiry, if a chemically, physically identical/similar compound is used for the same application, to meet the inventiveness requirement there must be an unexpected outcome. The unexpected outcome can either be a substantive improvement or an outcome that cannot be deduced from public knowledge.

First inquiry: whether the invention is nonobvious in light of current techniques [prior art] (the three-step/tripartite analysis):

1. Determination of the most closely-related current technique [prior art]: Ouyi and Zhongqi presented the evidence of Pfizer's No. 95192238.6 patent. Pfizer's patent was publicly disclosed on March 5th, 1997.

2. Determine the differentiating feature between this invention and the prior art. The court also needs to determine the practical technical problem that the invention has solved. The difference between the disputed patent in this case and Pfizer's patent is they used different chiral auxiliaries: DMSO-d6 is used in the disputed patent and DMSO is used in Pfizer's patent. Pfizer's patent also disclosed the cosolvents, which include water, ketones, alcohols, ethers, amides, esters, chlorinated hydrocarbons, nitrile or hydrocarbon. The practical problem solved by the invention described in the disputed patent is to obtain the dextrarotary isomer of amlodipine.

3. Finally, determine whether the invention is obvious to a person who is familiar with the art.

Based on the description in the disputed patent, the technical problem claimed to be solved is that it can achieve a higher optical purity and yield in separating the mixture of amlodipine enantiomers. The solution of this technical problem is based on the replacement of DMSO with DMSO-d6 as the chiral auxiliary.

It is very easy for persons who are familiar with the art to reach the conclusion that DMSO-d6, which has a similar chemical nature to DMSO, could also be used as the chiral auxiliary to separate the amlodipine enantiomers.

The court noted that DMSO-d6 is mainly used for NMR [spectroscopy] and is much more expensive than DMSO. In addition, before the disclosure of the patent at issue, the replacement of DMSO with DMSO-d6 had never been publicly disclosed. But there is no technical barrier to such a replacement.

Second Inquiry: When the invention does not meet the non-obviousness requirement, the second inquiry is to determine whether the invention can achieve an unexpected technical outcome. If it does achieve such an unexpected technique outcome, then the invention possesses inventiveness, but if it does not, the inventiveness inquiry ends and the invention at issue fails the validity test.

Unexpected technical outcomes are usually proved through experimental data. The burden of providing such data is on the holder of the disputed patent. If no sufficiently reliable experimental data is provided to prove unexpected outcome, the inventiveness of the invention cannot be determined.

In this case, the technical effects of separating the mixture of amlodipine enantiomers are mainly the optical purity and the yield. The disputed patent disclosed 5 application examples and Pfizer's patent disclosed 11 application examples. The comparison must be done among examples obtained under similar experimental conditions. Among the disclosed examples in the two patent descriptions, examples 1 and 4 of the disputed patent have the same experimental conditions as examples 9 and 10 in Pfizer's patent. Therefore, the comparison should be done between these two sets of examples.

The optical purities in examples 9 and 10 are both 99.5% and the yield in example 9 is 67%. The optical purity in example 1 of the disputed patent is 99.9% and 99.2%, for example 4, the yield of example 1 is 68%. Therefore, there is no substantial improvement in the purity or the yield.

The data provided by the holder of the disputed patent did not prove there is an unexpected improvement or outcome.

In summary, claim 1 of the patent is not nonobvious compared to the reference documents, and there was no unexpected technical outcome. A person familiar with the art can obtain the technique described in claim 1 from the comparative document without creative input. Therefore, claim 1 fails the inventiveness requirement of Chinese Patent Law Article 22 Section 3.

NOTES AND QUESTIONS

1. As described by the Beijing Higher People's Court above, how similar is the Chinese approach to evaluating inventive step to that in the United States? How about as compared to the Japanese approach? Is the tripartite/three-step analysis functionally equivalent to the EPO's problem-solution approach? Can you discern any ways in which it is different?

2. The Beijing Higher People's Court divides its analysis into two stages: a first inquiry that looks at the claimed invention in light of the prior art, and a second inquiry that evaluates whether the invention can achieve unexpected technical outcomes despite an initial determination that the invention does not satisfy the requirement of non-obviousness/inventive step. Why not

analyze the prospect of an "unexpected technical outcome" as part of the inquiry under the first step of the non-obviousness/inventive step analysis? What are the advantages or disadvantages of this two-stage approach? Is it the same as the U.S. approach in which the examiner establishes a prima facie case of obviousness (*see* p. 442, Note 1, *supra*) that the applicant then must attempt to rebut with secondary considerations?

3. In its assessment of whether the invention at issue has an unexpected technical outcome, the Beijing Higher People's Court held that the technical effect of the substituted chemical compound is supposed to be better optical purity and yield, but that the patentee did not establish that the substitution of DMSO with DMSO-d6 actually provides any improvement in those parameters. The court also notes that substituting DMSO with DMSO-d6 had not been previously disclosed but minimized the importance of that finding by noting there was no technical barrier to the substitution and intimating that the higher cost of DMSO-d6 was the reason for the lack of substitution. Consider the USPTO's second rationale for establishing a prima facie case of obviousness in the 2007 post-*KSR* Guidelines which appears similar:

B. Simple Substitution of One Known Element for Another to Obtain Predictable Results

To reject a claim based on this rationale, Office personnel must resolve the *Graham* factual inquiries. Office personnel must then articulate the following:

(1) a finding that the prior art contained a device (method, product, etc.) which differed from the claimed device by the substitution of some components (step, element, etc.) with other components;

(2) a finding that the substituted components and their functions were known in the art;

(3) a finding that one of ordinary skill in the art could have substituted one known element for another, and the results of the substitution would have been predictable; and

(4) whatever additional findings based on the *Graham* factual inquiries may be necessary, in view of the facts of the case under consideration, to explain a conclusion of obviousness.

The rationale to support a conclusion that the claim would have been obvious is that the substitution of one known element for another would have yielded predictable results to one of ordinary skill in the art at the time of the invention.

72 Fed. Reg. 57530.

However, as discussed in the Notes following the next case (*Beijing Double-crane*), in China, evidence submitted to show unexpected results needs to be present in the application as filed.

BEIJING DOUBLE-CRANE PHARMACEUTICAL CO., LTD. V. XIANGBEI WELMAN PHARMACEUTICAL CO., LTD. AND PATENT RE-EXAMINATION BOARD OF THE STATE INTELLECTUAL PROPERTY OFFICE

The Supreme People's Court (China, 2011)

CASE SUMMARY

PROCEDURAL HISTORY

Guangzhou Welman Pharmaceutical Co., Ltd. (hereinafter referred to as "Guangzhou Welman") is the patentee of the "Anti beta-lactamase antibiotic compound" patent (the disputed patent at issue in this case). Beijing Double-crane Pharmaceutical Co., Ltd. (hereinafter referred to as "Double-crane") filed a request to invalidate the disputed patent with the Patent Re-examination Board. According to the request, the [State Intellectual Property Office (SIPO)] Patent Re-examination Board issued No. 8113 Decision of Invalidation Request, and invalidated the disputed patent for lack of inventiveness.

Guangzhou Welman challenged the decision by filing an administrative lawsuit with the Beijing First Intermediate People's Court which upheld the No. 8113 Decision.

Guangzhou Welman then appealed to the Beijing Higher People's Court (during the appeal, the patentee of the disputed patent, Guangzhou Welman changed the name of the company to Xiangbei Welman). In the appeal, the Beijing Higher People's Court decided that the disclosed technology on the combinations of drugs in the reference document and the disputed compound are essentially different, and it is not obvious to one skilled in the art. The court accordingly overruled the first trial decision and the No. 8113 decision, and ordered the Patent Re-examination Board to issue a new decision on the invalidation request.

Double-crane then appealed to the Supreme People's Court [Supreme Court]. The Supreme Court granted review on March 1, 2011.

During the Supreme Court review, Xiangbei Welman presented a compilation of new evidence, which included studies on Cefotaxime Sodium and Sulbactam, and studies on Piperacillin and Sulbactam,etc. Based on this evidence, Xiangbei Welman argued that to understand and solve the issues regarding safety, efficacy and stability of the compound in order to obtain the patent, it had engaged in a series of pharmacological/toxicological experiments to test the chronic toxicity, acute toxicity, and in vitro antibacterial effects of the drug.

Xiangbei Welman further argued that not all relevant experiments and studies need to be recorded in the patent description. Because the art at issue is pharmaceutical, it must meet the drug registration requirements on safety, efficacy, and stability. No matter how the patent description is written, the improving work done by Xiangbei Welman on the compound's safety, efficacy, and stability cannot be denied.

On December 17, 2011, the Supreme Court revoked the decision by the Beijing Higher People's court and reinstated the No. 8113 decision of the SIPO Patent Re-examination Board and first trial decision.

COURT'S REASONING

The Supreme Court first noted that although clinical drug combination and compound preparation are two different technological fields, they are very closely-related. The Supreme Court additionally noted that when given sufficiently disclosed technological information on the clinical drug combination, one who is skilled in the art should be able to obtain the technology revealed in the patent. If sufficient technological information has been disclosed in the [prior art] reference documents, one skilled in the art could understand the technology and be motivated to obtain the technology of the disputed patent.

Second, the Supreme Court noted that patent law is substantively different from other laws or regulations relating to drug invention and manufacturing in their legislative aims, subject matter, and specific standards. Therefore, the patent could be granted as long as it conforms to Chinese patent law and there is no need to further consider other legislation or regulations relating to research and production of drugs [such as regulatory approval requirements].

Third, the Supreme Court noted that the disclosed technical details in the patent description are the basis for patent examination. They also serve the purposes of educating and informing the public so the technology can be spread and applied. Therefore, the technology solutions not disclosed in a patent description usually cannot be considered as the basis for evaluating whether the patent application has met the legal requirements for granting the patent right. Otherwise, it would be against the "first to file" principle set forth in the patent law and the underlying nature of "disclosure in exchange for protection" in patent law. The Supreme Court further noted that the patent applicant has the right to determine the scope of the disclosure in the patent description and can reasonably reserve some of the technical details, but the patent applicant should shoulder the burden for unfavorable consequences resulting from such nondisclosure.

In conclusion, although Xiangbei Welman claimed that they have conducted research and experiments to solve the safety, efficacy, and stability problems of the disputed drug, such technology is not included in the patent description. Therefore, such evidence cannot be used to determine the disputed novelty/inventiveness of the patent or the innovative development over the prior art on safety, effectiveness and stability.

NOTES AND QUESTIONS

1. Do you agree with the Supreme People's Court that evidence generated to support drug regulatory marketing approval (like FDA approval in the U.S.) is not necessarily relevant to the determination of an invention's patentability? In *In re Brana,* 51 F.3d 1560 (Fed. Cir. 1995), the Federal Circuit similarly discounted the relevance of such evidence to patentability determinations, but for an apparently different reason:

> The Commissioner, as did the Board, confuses the requirements under the law for obtaining a patent with the requirements for obtaining government approval to market a particular drug for human consumption. . . . FDA approval, however, is not a prerequisite for finding a compound useful within the meaning of the patent laws. Usefulness in patent law, and in particular in the context of pharmaceutical inventions, necessarily includes the expectation of further research and development. The stage at which an invention in this field becomes useful is well before it is ready to be administered to humans. Were we to require Phase II testing in order to prove utility, the associated costs would prevent many companies from obtaining patent protection on promising new inventions, thereby eliminating an incentive to pursue, through research and development, potential cures in many crucial areas such as the treatment of cancer.

Id. at 1567–68.

In *Brana,* the court seems to be making it easier for applicants to obtain patents by noting that the rigorous and expensive testing necessary for FDA approval is not required for patentability. But the Supreme Court seems to be discounting the relevance of such data for inventive step determinations, arguably making it more difficult for applicant's to obtain patents. What different policy goals in the U.S. and China may be guiding these approaches?

2. In China, secondary considerations are relevant to the inventiveness determination. However, as noted by the Supreme People's Court in *Beijing Double-crane,* if the evidence supporting inventiveness is not present in the patent application as filed, it cannot be considered, as that would violate the "first to file" rule and negate the disclosure quid pro quo of the patent grant. As noted in Section D *supra,* the approach in Japan is similar. Interestingly, as one commentator notes, in China, evidence of commercial success is not subject to this limitation:

> Different from other evidentiary materials showing the inventive step, materials used to demonstrate "commercial success of inventions" are not required to be disclosed prior to the date of application of the patent, even [if] the majority of them occurred after the date of application of the patent, thus proving that the technical solution protected by the patent has directly caused the commercial success.

Zhang Peng, *Impact of "Commercial Success of Inventions" upon Judgment of Inventive Step*, CHINA INTELLECTUAL PROPERTY, (June 1, 2012), http://ipr.chinadaily.com.cn/2012-01/06/content_14395653.htm.

3. Should there be any limit on the scope of what an applicant can introduce as evidence of inventive step after the filing date? Do you agree with the Chinese court that such limits are more consistent with the "first to file" principle? Would the absence of a limitation be inconsistent with the social bargain that gives a patentee protection in exchange for disclosure? In fact, most countries require that the invention be adequately disclosed in the patent application as filed such that a person of ordinary skill in the art could practice the invention after the patent expires. *See, e.g.*, U.S. Patent Act 35 U.S.C. § 112, paragraph 1.

4. The limitation on submitting evidence of novelty or non-obviousness generated after the filing date and not disclosed in the patent application as filed is not present in U.S. patent law. As the USPTO Manual of Patent Examining Procedure (MPEP) explains:

> If a prima facie case of obviousness is established, the burden shifts to the applicant to come forward with arguments and/or evidence to rebut the prima facie case. Rebuttal evidence and arguments can be presented in the specification, by counsel, or by way of an affidavit or declaration under 37 CFR 1.132 . . . . Rebuttal evidence may include evidence of "secondary considerations," such as "commercial success, long felt but unsolved needs, [and] failure of others." Rebuttal evidence may also include evidence that the claimed invention yields unexpectedly improved properties or properties not present in the prior art. Rebuttal evidence may consist of a showing that the claimed compound possesses unexpected properties. A showing of unexpected results must be based on evidence, not argument or speculation. . . . However, to be entitled to substantial weight, the applicant should establish a nexus between the rebuttal evidence and the claimed invention, i.e., objective evidence of nonobviousness must be attributable to the claimed invention.

MPEP 2145 (citations omitted).

NOTE ON INVENTIVE STEP IN THE PCT

Under current PCT procedures, the assessment of inventive step is part of the preparation of the written opinion (a document similar to a first office action in the USPTO), which occurs as part of the international search process. In addition to Article 33(3) of the Treaty, Rule 65 of the PCT Regulations, and Chapter 13 of the PCT International Search and Preliminary Examination Guidelines, adopted in 2004, provide guidance on the determination of inventive step.

The PCT's approach to inventive step is basically an amalgamation of the procedures of the three offices discussed in this Chapter. The PCT is particularly instructive in providing definitions for a few of the key elements that govern the inventive step process. Some of the features that characterize the PCT's approach are as follows:

a. An invention will lack inventive step if the invention as a whole, compared to the prior art as a whole, would have been obvious to a person skilled in the art. In making this determination, examiners may combine multiple items of prior art and are instructed to "take into consideration the claim's relation not only to individual documents or parts thereof taken separately but also to combinations of such documents or parts of documents, where such combinations are obvious to a person skilled in the art" (¶ 13.01 of the Guidelines).

b. The PCT Regulations, in Rule 64.1(a), define prior art as "everything made available to the public anywhere in the world by means of written disclosure . . . provided that such making available occurs prior to the relevant date." The relevant date is either the international filing date of the international application or, where the international application claims the priority of an earlier application, the filing date of the priority application.

c. The term "obvious" is defined as "that which does not go beyond the normal progress of technology but merely follows plainly or logically from the prior art, that is, something which does not involve the exercise of any skill or ability beyond that to be expected of the person skilled in the art" (¶ 13.03).

d. A person skilled in the art should be presumed:

- to be a hypothetical person having ordinary skill in the art and aware of what was common general knowledge in the art;

- to have had access to everything in the prior art, in particular the references cited in the international search report; and

- to have had at his/her discretion the normal means and capacity for routine experimentation.

In addition, if the problem on which the invention is based and which arises from the closest prior art prompts the person skilled in the art to seek its solution in another technical field, the person skilled in the art is also the person skilled in that field. Moreover, the person skilled in the art need not be an individual. Where the invention concerns a highly advanced technology or involved a specialized process, the PCT Guidelines provide that it may be more suitable to think of the person skilled in the art as a research or production team.

e. The PCT Guidelines endorse the problem-solution approach as a suitable way to carry out the inventive step analysis. In general, however, examiners are instructed to act as follows in accordance with ¶ 13.10:

The examiner should identify the closest prior art as the basis for the assessment of inventive step. This is considered to be that combination of features derivable from one single reference that provides the best basis for considering the question of obviousness. In determining the scope of the disclosure of the items of prior art, in addition to the explicit disclosure, an implicit disclosure, that is, a teaching which a person skilled in the art could reasonably draw from the explicit disclosure, should also be taken into account. The critical time for the determination of such disclosure is the claim date of the application concerned. The general knowledge of the person skilled in the art on the relevant date of the claim should also be taken into account.

f. Finally, the PCT Guidelines provide that it is appropriate to combine prior art references where it would be obvious to the person skilled in the art to make such a combination. Factors that would make a combination obvious are where the nature and content of the references are such as to prompt combination or association with one another, where the references come from similar or neighboring technical fields, and where the references are reasonably pertinent to the particular problem which the invention solves.

CHAPTER 8

DISCLOSURE REQUIREMENTS AND NON-UTILITY PATENT PROTECTION

■ ■ ■

A. PATENT DISCLOSURE REQUIREMENTS

In Chapters 4–7, we considered the primary patentability requirements of subject matter, novelty, non-obviousness/inventive step, and utility/industrial applicability. Two more substantive patentability requirements bear special mention: enablement and written description. They are being covered separately in this Chapter because, unlike novelty and inventive step, for example, where a patent examiner looks to the prior art to see if the patentability requirement is met for each claim, the patent specification itself must provide the necessary fulfillment of these requirements. The specification must enable a person having ordinary skill in the art (PHOSITA) to practice the invention without undue experimentation, and it must provide an adequate written description of the invention that will convey to a PHOSITA that the inventor was in possession of the claimed invention at the filing date. Both of these requirements are discussed in more detail below.

1. ENABLEMENT

While the patent statutes of countries may differ in the precise wording used, a universal requirement is that an application must "disclose the invention in a manner sufficiently clear and complete for it to be carried out by a person skilled in the art." *See* EPC Article 83. Known simply as the "enablement" requirement, this aspect of the application process is designed to further the goal of enhancing the public store of knowledge particularly to the benefit of follow-on inventors/innovators, and to ensure that the invention can be practiced by persons of skill in the art when the patent term expires.

While seemingly straightforward, the enablement requirement has given rise to considerable litigation. Questions have arisen, for example, about how complete the disclosure must be in order to be deemed sufficient and whether the issue of sufficiency must be decided solely on the basis of the content of the claims. An early European Patent Office Board of Appeal decision addressed both those questions in the Sumitomo case (T 14/83) below.

VINYLCHLORIDE RESINS/SUMITOMO DECISION OF THE TECHNICAL BOARD OF APPEAL 3.3.1 (JUNE 7, 1983)

T 14/83, 3 Official J. Eur. Pat. Off. 105 (1984), [1979-85] E.P.O.R. C726

SUMMARY OF FACTS AND SUBMISSIONS

I. European patent application No. 79 300 604.0, filed on 11 April 1979 and published on 17 October 1979 under publication No. 0 004 795, claiming the priority of the Japanese prior application of 12 April 1978, was refused by decision of the Examining Division of the European Patent Office dated 18 August 1982 on the basis of the amended claim 1 filed with the letter dated 8 June 1982. This claim reads as follows:

> A method for producing a vinyl chloride resin which comprises polymerizingither
>
> (a) vinyl chloride or
>
> (b) a mixture of a major amount of vinyl chloride and a minor amount of at least one monomer copolymerisable therewith in the presence of 0.01 to 10% by weight, based on the weight of the vinyl chloride monomer, of at least one polyfunctional monomer having two or more ethylenic double bonds in the molecule, characterised in that polymerization is carried out until at least 60 weight % of the total monomer in the polymerization system is polymerized, and at a temperature of 0° to 50°C, the amount and identity of the polyfunctional monomer, the percentage conversion of the total monomer and the polymerization temperature and, in the case of (b), the amount and identity of copolymerizable monomer being so selected that a vinyl chloride resin consisting of (i) 10 to 80% by weight of tetrahydrofuran-insoluble vinyl chloride resin gel fraction and (ii) 90 to 20% by weight of tetrahydrofuran-soluble fraction having an average polymerization degree of 1,000 or more is produced.

II. The stated ground for the refusal was insufficient disclosure according to Article 83 EPC ["The European patent application must disclose the invention in a manner sufficiently clear and complete for it to be carried out by a person skilled in the art."]. Neither claim 1 nor the matter of the application as a whole would enable the expert readily to select the parameters required for a consistently successful preparation of the resin. It could not be accepted that it would be a routine matter for the skilled man to select from 4 to 6 different parameters by experimentation to obtain the correct method of polymerization and then to test the product for gel content and molecular weight to establish that the desired end result had been achieved. The question of admissibility and clarity of claim 1 was not considered and the substantive examination of the application in suit was deferred.

III. The appellants lodged an appeal against the decision on 28 October 1982, and submitted a Statement of Grounds on 22 December 1982, enclosing two amended claims in which the above two alternatives a) and b) indicating how to carry out the invention were split into separate claims. The appellants submit that claim 1 now specifies that the expert must select three parameters, i.e. the amount and identity of the polyfunctional monomer and the polymerization temperature such that the required product is produced. To select the polyfunctional monomer the skilled man would merely have recourse to his experience in the art and then alter the other two parameters by using a particular amount of polyfunctional monomer and a particular temperature roughly lying in the middle of the allowed ranges or in the preferred ranges. He would then check to see whether the product produced had the required composition which involves measurements of the gel content of the tetrahydrofuran-insoluble fraction (hereinafter referred to "gel fraction',) and average polymerization degree of the tetrahydrofuran-soluble fraction (hereinafter simply referred to "polymerization degree" of the "solublefraction"). In most cases, even if the expert did not choose these values for temperature and amount of polyfunctional monomer, the product obtained would indeed have the required composition. In the event of failing to achieve the desired composition, the expert could clearly see from tables 1 to 3 of the specification how to achieve the goal envisaged. Claim 2 now specifies, according to the submission of the appellants, that there are additionally two parameters which affect the composition of the product, but these are conventional in the art. As could be seen in Appendix III of the Statement of Grounds of Appeal the balance between the gel content and polymerization degree is not very greatly affected by the presence of a monofunctional comonomer.

IV. On the Board's advice the appellants finally submitted on 11 April 1983 7 redrafted claims, the first of which, recombining the two alternatives of the invention, has the following wording:

> A method for producing a vinyl chloride resin consisting of (i) 10 to 80% by weight of tetrahydrofuran-insoluble vinyl chloride resin gel fraction and (ii) 90 to 20% by weight of tetrahydrofuran-soluble fraction having an average polymerization degree of 1,000 or more characterised by polymerizing
>
> either
>
> (a) vinyl chloride or
>
> (b) a mixture of a major amount of vinyl chloride and a minor amount of at least one monofunctional monomer copolymerizable therewith in the presence of 0.01 to 10% by weight, based on the weight of the vinyl chloride monomer, of at least one copolymerizable polyfunctional monomer having two or more ethylenic double bonds in the molecule, at a temperature in the range of

from 0° to 50°C and until at least 60 weight % of the total monomer in the polymerization system is polymerized.

The appellants request that the decision refusing the application be set aside and that a patent be granted on this basis.

REASONS FOR THE DECISION

. . .

3. Pursuant to Article 83 EPC the invention is sufficiently clearly and completely disclosed if it can be carried out by a person skilled in the art. The source of the disclosure of the invention within the European patent application is of no importance. The question of whether or not an invention is disclosed must not be judged solely on the basis of the claims, as the Examining Division did. It is true that the Examining Division made the routine statement that neither the matter of claim 1 nor the matter of the specification as a whole could be successfully repeated. Nevertheless it neglected the relevance of the tabular results of experiments in the description of the invention.

4. The present invention is concerned with a process for the production of vinyl chloride resins consisting of 10 to 80% by weight of a "gel fraction" and the balance of a "soluble fraction" with an average polymerization degree of 1000 or more. This task is said to be achieved in the simpler of its alternative solutions (method (a) of claim 1) by combination of the following simplified features (a) copolymerization of vinyl chloride with a polyfunctional monomer (b) the latter being added in an amount of 0.01 to 10% by weight based on the weight of vinyl chloride (c) using a polymerization temperature between 0 and 50°C (d) until at least 60% by weight of the monomers is polymerized. Accordingly, the features (b), (c) and (d) are quantitatively fixed ranges of values, whilst feature (a), i.e. the nature of the polyfunctional monomer, is defined in the main claim by the number of ethylenic double bonds and comprehensively illustrated in the description. There can be no doubt that a process including these features can be carried out by an expert, which was not contested by the Examining Division.

5. However, the Division took the position that the specification as filed did not tell the expert how to select the parameters required for a consistently successful preparation of the resin. The Division relies here particularly on the comparative results forming part of the original description, which results demonstrate the occasional lack of success of the claimed process to achieve its objective, notwithstanding strict adherence to the features as claimed. . . .

6. However, occasional lack of success of a claimed process does not impair its feasibility in the sense of Article 83 EPC if, e.g., some experimentation is still to be done to transform the failure into success, provided that such experimentation is not undue and does not require inventive

activity. In the present case experimentation was altogether unnecessary, since tables [included in the description] give sufficient instruction to the skilled reader on how to operate the process in the event of failure. . . . [E]mpirical rules [disclosed in the description] about the influence of alteration of the polymerization temperature and the amount of polyfunctional comonomer on the resulting resin enable the skilled person, notwithstanding occasional lack of success when applying the individual process variables, to realise the desired result. . . .

7. [I]n conclusion, it is clear that the expert who carried out the claimed processes strictly in accordance with the instructions and occasionally missed the desired target at the first attempt would be able to bring about the desired composition of the resin quickly and reliably by having recourse to the said empirical rules disclosed in the description of the present specification. . . .

9. Accordingly, the invention defined by the present claims is considered to have been sufficiently clearly and completely disclosed within the meaning of Article 83 EPC. Mention should also be made that in the event that such a teaching cannot be defined in a claim precisely enough to rule out occasional lack of success, such a claim is not to be objected to provided it is possible to deduce from the description the action to be taken—which also cannot be precisely defined—by way of fine tuning of the variables.

10. From the foregoing, it follows that the decision under appeal is not supported by the grounds for refusal. However, the patent sought cannot be granted at present, since substantive examination has not yet been completed.

For these reasons, It is decided that:

1. The decision of the Examining Division of the European Patent Office dated 18 August 1982 is set aside.

2. The case is remitted to the first instance for substantive examination on the basis of the 7 claims dated 11 March 1983, received on 11 April 1983.

Notes and Questions

1. Do you agree with the EPO Board of Appeal that a patent applicant should not have to set forth in precise terms the exact steps necessary for someone skilled in the art to successfully carry out the claimed process? Does enablement serve any distinct policy goals which could *not* be better served by other patentability requirements such as utility? Should experts be used to determine if a specification is sufficiently enabled or should the judgment of an examiner be sufficient?

2. In *Vinylchloride Resins,* the Board of Appeal noted that an occasional lack of success does not violate EPC Article 83 so long as a person skilled in the art does not have to engage in "undue experimentation." Does the Board of Appeal's reasoning represent a trade-off between the construction of the PHOSITA and the sufficiency of the enablement?

3. Japanese law is much in alignment with that of the EPO as articulated in the *Vinylchloride Resins* decision. Section 36(4) of the Japanese Patent Act (Act No. 121 of 1959 as amended) provides that, "[t]he statement of the detailed explanation of the invention ... shall be clear and sufficient as to enable any person ordinarily skilled in the art to which the invention pertains to work the invention." The Tokyo High Court, in Case No. 199/1975, known as the *Sodium Aluminate* case, held that the provision does not require that the description disclose every element of the invention. If an undisclosed element is readily understandable to a person skilled in the art, "without explicit explanation," the enablement requirement will be deemed to have been met.

In the United States, the enablement requirement is contained in 35 U.S.C. § 112, which provides, in part, that "[t]he specification shall contain a written description of the invention, and of the manner and process of making and using it, in such full, clear, concise, and exact terms as to enable any person skilled in the art to which it pertains, or with which it is most nearly connected, to make and use the same ..."

In *In re Wands*, 858 F.2d 731 (Fed. Cir. 1988), the U.S. Court of Appeals for the Federal Circuit established eight factors relevant to determining whether the enablement requirement has been met: (1) the quantity of experimentation necessary; (2) the amount of direction or guidance presented; (3) the presence or absence of working examples; (4) the nature of the invention; (5) the state of the prior art; (6) the relative skill of those in the art; (7) the unpredictability of the art; and (8) the breadth of the claims. As the following case illustrates, to meet the enablement requirement, the disclosure in an application containing broad claims for an invention in a highly unpredictable field of art where the relative skill of those in the art is untested requires far greater clarity, exactitude, and detail than for an application narrowing claiming an invention in a highly predictable field of art.

PHARMACEUTICAL RESOURCES, INC. AND PAR PHARMACEUTICALS, INC. V. ROXANE LABORATORIES, INC.

United States Court of Appeals, Federal Circuit
253 Fed.App'x. 26 (Fed. Cir. 2007).

■ MOORE, Circuit Judge.

Pharmaceutical Resources, Inc. and Par Pharmaceuticals, Inc. (Par, collectively) appeal the district court's grant of summary judgment of invalidity of the asserted claims in U.S. Patent Nos. 6,593,318 (the '318 patent) and 6,593,320 (the '320 patent) in favor of defendant Roxane Laboratories, Inc. (Roxane). Because the district court properly determined that the asserted claims of the '318 and '320 patents are invalid as a matter of law under 35 U.S.C. § 112, first paragraph, for lack of enablement, we *affirm* the judgment.

BACKGROUND

The '320 patent is a divisional of the '318 patent. Both patents share a common specification, which was first filed as Serial No. 09/063,241 ("the '241 application," now U.S. Patent No. 6,028,065). The '318 and '320 patents relate to stable flocculated suspensions of megestrol acetate and methods for making such suspensions.

Bristol-Myers Squibb (BMS) was the first company to develop and patent a liquid pharmaceutical composition of megestrol acetate. BMS' U.S. Patent No. 5,338,732 (the Atzinger patent) teaches that stable suspensions of megestrol acetate can be created but that the type and concentration of the surfactant in solution is critical to creating a stable flocculated suspension. The Atzinger patent discloses only one stable flocculated suspension composition, combining megestrol acetate with polyethylene glycol as a wetting agent and polysorbate 80 as a surfactant.

When Par formulated a generic version of BMS's patented product, it sought to design around the Atzinger patent claims by utilizing other surfactants and wetting agents. In developing its own product, Par discovered that flocculated suspensions of megestrol acetate could be formed using a much wider range of ingredients and concentrations than taught in the Atzinger patent, including other surfactants and wetting agents. Through those efforts, Par received a series of patents on its flocculated suspensions, including the '318 and '320 patents.

Par brought the present suit in 2003, asserting that Roxane infringes certain claims in the '318 and '320 patents. Roxane denies infringement and asserts that the claims of the '318 and '320 patents are invalid and unenforceable. After the district court issued a *Markman* order, Roxane moved for summary judgment of invalidity, arguing, *inter alia*, that the asserted claims in the '318 and '320 patents are invalid for lack of enablement. At issue are independent claims 19 and 41 of the '318 patent (and claims 20, 25–27, 32, 34, 42, 47, and 53 dependent thereon) and independent claim 1 from the '320 patent (and claims 2 and 6 dependent thereon). Claim 19 of '318 patent recites:

> Claim 19. An oral pharmaceutical composition in the form of a stable flocculated suspension in water comprising: (a) megestrol acetate; (b) at least two compounds selected from the group consisting of polyethylene glycol, propylene glycol, glycerol, and sorbitol; and (c) a surfactant.

The district court granted Roxane's motion for summary judgment, concluding that "as a matter of law Par is not entitled to the broad claims it asserts in this action."

Par appeals the district court's grant of summary judgment of invalidity. We have jurisdiction pursuant to 28 U.S.C. § 1295(a)(1).

ANALYSIS

We review a district court's grant of summary judgment de novo, reapplying the standard applicable at the district court. . . . Although a patent claim is presumed enabled unless proven otherwise by clear and convincing evidence . . . to defeat Roxane's motion for summary judgment Par must put forth evidence that does "more than simply raise some doubt regarding enablement: 'If the evidence is merely colorable, or is not significantly probative, summary judgment may be granted.' "

Whether the subject matter of a patent claim satisfies the enablement requirement under 35 U.S.C. § 112, first paragraph, is a question of law, reviewed de novo, based on underlying facts, reviewed for clear error. . . . In *In re Wands,* 858 F.2d 731, 737 (Fed.Cir.1988), this court set forth eight factors relevant to the enablement analysis:

> (1) the quantity of experimentation necessary, (2) the amount of direction or guidance presented, (3) the presence or absence of working examples, (4) the nature of the invention, (5) the state of the prior art, (6) the relative skill of those in the art, (7) the predictability or unpredictability of the art, and (8) the breadth of the claims.

In this case, Par sought extremely broad claims in a field of art that it acknowledged was highly unpredictable, therefore, Par has set a high burden that its patent disclosure must meet to satisfy the requisite *quid pro quo* of patent enablement. . . . The scintilla of evidence put forward by Par to suggest that the claims are enabled, most of which actually conflicts with the intrinsic evidence in this case, does not raise a genuine issue of material fact. . . .

A. Unpredictability of the Art

In this case, *all* of the record evidence establishes that the art of making stable flocculated suspensions of megestrol acetate is highly unpredictable. The common disclosure of the '318 and '320 patents discusses this unpredictability:

> The surfactants in a stable flocculated suspension need to be selected carefully and be used within a critical concentration range because even minor changes can have an effect on the properties of such a stable formulation. This is particularly true for megestrol acetate because predictability based on prior art teachings does not apply in this case, as noted hereinabove.

'318 Patent col.3 1.66-col.4 1.5. Par also stressed the unpredictability of this particular pharmaceutical formulation field during prosecution of the '241 application:

> [B]ased on the uncertainty of results once any modification in types of ingredients or amounts is made, as discussed in the prior art including Atzinger at al. [sic] . . ., a person skilled in the art would not have any reasonable expectation of success in maintaining a stable flocculated suspension of megestrol acetate once a change in the type or amount of surfactant or wetting agent is made.

The extrinsic evidence also supports the conclusion that the relevant field is unpredictable. During its previous litigation with BMS, for instance, Par relied in part on the unpredictability of this art field. Par's technical expert opined on the nature of the art, stating:

> Formulating a flocculated suspension is, in my view, one of the most delicate formulation efforts in terms of balancing the excipients, and it is also very difficult to predict in terms of what its properties will be or what the effect of different excipients will be. There is no known method in the art to predict whether a change in inactive ingredients will produce a stable suspension.

In the current litigation, Par's technical expert, Dr. Klibanov, explained that "megestrol acetate is sufficiently unique as a compound [such] that prior art references teaching how to wet other insoluble compounds provide absolutely no guidance with regard to wetting megestrol acetate." Similarly, Dr. Chao, a named inventor of the '318 and '320 patents, testified that predictions could not be made regarding whether or not particular combinations of ingredients including megestrol acetate would form a stable flocculated compound, but rather, this required actual experimentation.

A. Breadth of the Claims

In addition, the district court concluded that claims 19 and 41 of the '318 patent and claim 1 of the '320 patent "have an extraordinarily broad scope."

Par argued that the claims at issue are not as broad as suggested by the district court because the hypothetical pharmaceutical formulator would start experimenting with the twenty-two surfactants that the United States Pharmacopoeia and National Formulary (USP-NF) has recognized and approved for use in oral pharmaceuticals in order to practice the invention. In addition, Par argues that the district court erred in assuming that the claims covered use of a surfactant in *any* concentration.

The claims allow the choice of *any* surfactant in *any* concentration (with the exception that claim 1 of the '320 patent does not permit polysorbate as the surfactant if polyethylene glycol is the chosen wetting agent). The language of the claims and the specification both suggest that the claims encompass hundreds of possible surfactants. Par admitted as much in oral argument. Further, the disclosure of the '318 and '320 patents list dozens of "suitable" surfactant genera beyond those listed by the USP-NF.

Moreover, nothing in the language of the claims limits the concentration of surfactant. The specification gives a preferred concentration range for only one surfactant, docusate sodium. To the extent that Par now suggests that an ordinarily skilled artisan would know that surfactant concentrations over 0.030% weight-per-volume would not work, it follows that a large part of the asserted claims' scope is directed toward inoperative embodiments. The number of inoperative combinations is significant when assessing the experimentation that an ordinarily skilled artisan would need to practice the claimed invention. *Atlas Powder Co. v. E.I. du Pont de Nemours & Co.*, 750 F.2d 1569, 1576 (Fed.Cir.1984).

We thus conclude that the district court properly determined that the claims at issue "have an extraordinarily broad scope." The district court also correctly noted in its analysis that our case law requires that the full scope of the claims be enabled.

B. Enablement of the Asserted Claims

Taking into account the broad scope of the claims and the highly unpredictable nature of the art, Par's evidence regarding enablement fails to establish a genuine issue of material fact as to whether or not the claims are enabled and therefore fails to defeat summary judgment.

Par's specification discloses only three working examples, utilizing only one new surfactant. Given the highly unpredictable nature of the invention and the extremely broad scope of the claims, these three working examples do not provide an enabling disclosure commensurate with the entire scope of the claims.

Additionally, the two declarations from Par's expert witnesses on the issue of enablement are conclusory and lack evidentiary support or specifics as to the experimentation that would be needed to practice the entire scope of the claims. Accordingly, these declarations are legally insufficient to raise a genuine issue of material fact as to whether the claims are enabled. *See, e.g., Automotive Tech. Int'l v. BMW of N. Am., Inc.*, 501 F.3d 1274, 1284–85 (Fed.Cir.2007) ("[H]aving failed to provide any detail regarding why no experimentation was necessary, the declaration does not create a genuine issue of material fact as to enablement.").

Finally, Par argues that its own experiments with megestrol acetate solutions, to which the inventor, Dr. Femia, testified, are sufficient to create a genuine issue of material fact regarding enablement of the asserted claims. The district court determined that this evidence supports a conclusion of lack of enablement because it evidences numerous unsuccessful attempts by Par to practice subject matter within the scope of the claims.

Interpreting Dr. Femia's testimony in the light most favorable to Par, that Dr. Femia was successful in formulating the claimed composition with seven surfactants, gives rise to "merely colorable" evidence, and fails to create a genuine issue of material fact as to enablement of the full scope of the claims. It is highly relevant that the intrinsic evidence stresses the criticality of the choice of surfactant and concentration. Given this fact, the extraordinarily broad scope of the claims, which encompasses hundreds of surfactants, the high degree of unpredictability of the art, and the minimal guidance provided by the three working examples in the specification, the mere fact that Par's inventors were able to create successfully a stable flocculated megestrol acetate suspension with seven surfactants does not create a genuine issue of material fact regarding enablement.

Based on the foregoing, we conclude as a matter of law that each of the asserted claims of the '318 and '320 patents is invalid under 35 U.S.C. § 112, first paragraph, for lack of enablement. Accordingly, we affirm.

NOTES AND QUESTIONS

1. Why should the three working examples listed in the specification be insufficient to enable the entire set of claims? Is the court in *Roxane Laboratories, Inc.* simply using enablement as a doctrinal tool to constrain the scope of claims in the specification? A number of important cases in the U.S. have established the requirement that the enabling disclosure should be reasonably related to the scope of the claims. *See, e.g., In re Angstadt*, 537 F.2d 498, 502 (CCPA 1976). However, the Federal Circuit also has stated that "patent applicants are not required to disclose every species encompassed by their claims, even in an unpredictable art. . . . [T]here must be sufficient disclosure, either through illustrative examples or terminology, to teach those of ordinary skill how to make and use the invention as broadly as it is claimed." *See In re Vaeck*, 947 F.2d 488, 496 (Fed. Cir. 1991). In light of these cases, are you persuaded that the court's decision in *Roxane Laboratories* struck the right balance?

2. In contrast to *Roxane Laboratories*, the Federal Circuit decision in *Atlas Powder Co. v. E.I. du Pont de Nemours & Co.*, 750 F.2d 1569 (Fed. Cir. 1984) involving a "predictable art," was much less stringent on the perquisites for meeting the enablement requirement. There, Du Pont defended an action for infringement brought by Atlas Powder, the owner of a patent relating to blasting agents, by alleging that the Atlas patent failed to meet the 35 U.S.C. § 112 enablement requirement. In rejecting Du Pont's allegation of lack of enablement, the court noted not only that the presence of some inoperative combinations in the claims did not negate enablement, but also that

the use of prophetic examples (examples of experiments that had not actually been performed but were hypothetical) could establish enablement:

> To be enabling under § 112, a patent must contain a description that enables one skilled in the art to make and use the claimed invention. . . . That some experimentation is necessary does not preclude enablement; the amount of experimentation, however, must not be unduly extensive. . . .

> We agree with the district court's conclusion on enablement. Even if some of the [combinations claimed in the patent] were inoperative, the claims are not necessarily invalid. 'It is not a function of the claims to specifically exclude . . . possible inoperative substances. . . .' Of course, if the number of inoperative combinations becomes significant, and in effect forces one of ordinary skill in the art to experiment unduly in order to practice the claimed invention, the claims might indeed be invalid. That, however, has not been shown to be the case here.

> Du Pont [further] contends that, because the [patent's] examples are 'merely prophetic,' they do not aid one skilled in the art in making the invention. Because they are prophetic, argues Du Pont, there can be no guarantee that the examples would actually work.

> Use of prophetic examples, however, does not automatically make a patent non-enabling. The burden is on one challenging validity to show by clear and convincing evidence that the prophetic examples together with other parts of the specification are not enabling. Du Pont did not meet that burden here. To the contrary, the district court found that the 'prophetic' examples of the specification were based on actual experiments that were slightly modified in the patent to reflect what the inventor believed to be optimum, and hence, they would be helpful in enabling someone to make the invention.

Id. at 1576–1577. What policy considerations justify a different enablement standard for unpredictable arts? Could those concerns be more effectively addressed through a more robust construction of the PHOSITA in the relevant field?

3. Review the EPO decision in *Vinylchloride Resins, supra.* Does the reasoning of the Board of Appeal suggest a similar link in the EPO between enablement and the scope of the claims? The EPO Guidelines for Examination state:

> [W]here the claims cover a broad field, the application should not usually be regarded as satisfying the requirements of Art. 83 unless the description gives a number of examples or describes alternative embodiments or variations extending over the area protected by the claims. However, regard must be had to the facts and evidence of the particular case. There are some instances where even a very broad field is sufficiently exemplified by a limited number of examples or even one example.

EPO Guidelines for Examination pt. F, ch. 3, sec. 1.

4. In determining the right "scope" of patent claims, courts must balance the interests of follow-on inventors and innovators who could be unjustly blocked by overly broad claims. Conversely, simply awarding protection only for the embodiments disclosed, may result in the issued patent having little economic value. *See* Robert P. Merges & Richard R. Nelson, *On the Complex Economics of Patent Scope,* 90 COLUM. L. REV. 839, 845 (1990). How well do you think the enablement requirement addresses this concern?

2. WRITTEN DESCRIPTION

In addition to meeting the enablement requirement, the patent application must also provide a written description that supports the application's claims, in effect showing that the inventor had possession of the subject matter at the time of filing and is not over-claiming. The Korean Patent Act is typical in this regard and provides in Article 42(4)(ii) that "the claim(s) shall be supported by a detailed description of the invention." Likewise, EPC Article 84 provides that "[t]he claims shall define the matter for which protection is sought. They shall be clear and concise and be supported by the description."

Although a disclosure may enable a person of ordinary skill in the art to make and use an invention broader than that originally claimed in the application, amended claims will fail if the written description in the application as originally filed lacks evidence that the inventor was in possession of the invention as encompassed by those broader claims. Professor Janice Mueller offers an excellent example of the distinction between the enablement and written description requirements as applied to amended or later-filed claims:

> Assume that a patent application as filed discloses and claims a red widget. No other color of widget is mentioned, nor is any suggestion made in the application that the claimed widget could be any color other than red. Although a person of ordinary skill in the art might arguably be *enabled* by this disclosure to make widgets of other colors (such as blue widgets or yellow widgets), a generic claim later presented during the course of the patent application's prosecution that recited 'a widget of a primary color' would not be valid under the written description of the invention requirement. This is because the as-filed patent application did not provide a written description of 'the invention,' as later claimed generically; the application showed only that the inventor was in possession of red widgets when she filed. Thus, the later-filed generic claim would not be entitled to the earlier filing date of the application as the *prima facie* date of invention of the claimed genus of primary color widgets.

Janice M. Mueller, PATENT LAW (3d ed. 2009) at 127.

The written description has traditionally served as a method of policing priority to ensure that claims are adequately supported and therefore entitled to the prior-art-limiting filing date attributed to them. Such priority-related issues tend to arise when claims are added or amended in a pending application, when an application claims domestic or foreign priority to an earlier-filed application, or when an applicant under U.S. law asserts claims in an interference proceeding. EPC Article 123(2) is a case in point. The provision states that "[a] European patent application or a European patent may not be amended in such a way that it contains subject-matter which extends beyond the content of the application as filed." Similarly, Article 19(2) of the Patent Cooperation Treaty provides that "amendments shall not go beyond the disclosure in the international application as filed." The written description requirement ensures compliance with such provisions.

In 1997, the U.S. Court of Appeals for the Federal Circuit expanded the focus of the written description requirement by holding that an *originally* filed claim could lack an adequate written description in *Regents of the University of California v. Eli Lilly & Co.,* 119 F.3d 1559 (Fed. Cir. 1997). This expanded written description doctrine is unique to U.S. patent law. Although it has yet to be adopted by courts outside of the United States, the expansion was recently reaffirmed in *Ariad Pharmaceuticals, Inc. v. Eli Lilly & Co.,* in an *en banc* decision of the U.S. Court of Appeals for the Federal Circuit.

ARIAD PHARMACEUTICALS, INC. V. ELI LILLY & CO.

United States Court of Appeals, Federal Circuit
598 F.3d 1336 (Fed. Cir. 2010)

■ LOURIE, Circuit Judge:

Ariad Pharmaceuticals, Inc., Massachusetts Institute of Technology, the Whitehead Institute for Biomedical Research, and the President and Fellows of Harvard College (collectively, "Ariad") brought suit against Eli Lilly & Company ("Lilly") in the United States District Court for the District of Massachusetts, alleging infringement of U.S. Patent 6,410,516 ("the '516 patent"). After trial, at which a jury found infringement, but found none of the asserted claims invalid, a panel of this court reversed the district court's denial of Lilly's motion for judgment as a matter of law ("JMOL") and held the asserted claims invalid for lack of written description.

Ariad petitioned for rehearing *en banc,* challenging this court's interpretation of 35 U.S.C. § 112, first paragraph, as containing a separate written description requirement. Because of the importance of the issue, we granted Ariad's petition and directed the parties to address whether § 112, first paragraph, contains a written description requirement separate from the enablement requirement and, if so, the scope and purpose of that requirement. We now reaffirm that § 112, first paragraph, contains a written description requirement separate from enablement, and we again reverse the district court's denial of JMOL and hold the asserted claims of the '516 patent invalid for failure to meet the statutory written description requirement.

The '516 patent relates to the regulation of gene expression by the transcription factor NF-êB. The inventors of the '516 patent were the first to identify NF-êB and to uncover the mechanism by which NF-êB activates gene expression underlying the body's immune responses to infection. . . . [T]he inventors recognized that artificially interfering with NF-êB activity could reduce the harmful symptoms of certain diseases, and they filed a patent application on April 21, 1989, disclosing their discoveries and claiming methods for regulating cellular responses to external stimuli by reducing NF-êB activity in a cell.

Ariad brought suit against Lilly on June 25, 2002, the day the '516 patent issued. Ariad alleged infringement of claims 80, 95, 144, and 145 by Lilly's Evista® and Xigris® pharmaceutical products.

> . . .

The [asserted] claims are . . . genus claims, encompassing the use of all substances that achieve the desired result of reducing the binding of NF-êB to NF-êB recognition sites. Furthermore, the claims, although amended during prosecution, use language that corresponds to language present in the priority application [for example:]

> 80. [A method for modifying effects of external influences on a eukaryotic cell, which external influences induce NF-êB-mediated intracellular signaling, the method comprising altering NF-êB activity in the cells such that NF-êB-mediated effects of external influences are modified, wherein NF-êB activity in the cell is reduced] wherein reducing NF-êB activity comprises reducing binding of NF-êB to NF-êB recognition sites on genes which are transcriptionally regulated by NF-êB.

> . . . .

[A]lthough the parties take diametrically opposed positions on the existence of a written description requirement separate from enablement, both agree that the specification must contain a written description of the invention to establish what the invention is. The dispute, therefore, centers on the standard to be applied and whether it applies to original claim language.

As in any case involving statutory interpretation, we begin with the language of the statute itself.... Section 112, first paragraph, reads as follows:

The specification shall contain a written description of the invention, and of the manner and process of making and using it, in such full, clear, concise, and exact terms as to enable any person skilled in the art to which it pertains, or with which it is most nearly connected, to make and use the same, and shall set forth the best mode contemplated by the inventor of carrying out his invention.

According to Ariad, a plain reading of the statute reveals two components: a written description (i) of the invention, and (ii) of the manner and process of making and using it. Yet those two components, goes Ariad's argument, must be judged by the final prepositional phrase; both written descriptions must be "in such full, clear, concise, and exact terms as to enable any person skilled in the art . . . to make and use the same." Specifically, Ariad parses the statute as follows:

The specification shall contain

[A] a written description

[i] of the invention, and

[ii] of the manner and process of making and using it,

[B] in such full, clear, concise, and exact terms as to enable any person skilled in the art to which it pertains, or with which it is most nearly connected, to make and use the same . . .

Ariad argues that its interpretation best follows the rule of English grammar that prepositional phrases (here, "of the invention," "of the manner and process of making and using it," and "in such full, clear, concise, and exact terms") modify another word in the sentence (here, "written description"), and that it does not inexplicably ignore the comma after "making and using it" or sever the "description of the invention" from the requirement that it be in "full, clear, concise, and exact terms," leaving the description without a legal standard.

Ariad also argues that earlier versions of the Patent Act support its interpretation. Specifically, Ariad contends that the first Patent Act, adopted in 1790, and its immediate successor, adopted in 1793, required a written description of the invention that accomplished two purposes: (i) to distinguish the invention from the prior art, and (ii) to enable a person skilled in the art to make and use the invention. Ariad then asserts that when Congress assigned the function of defining the invention to the claims in 1836, Congress amended the written description requirement so that it served a single purpose: enablement.

Lilly disagrees, arguing that § 112, first paragraph, contains three separate requirements. Specifically, Lilly parses the statute as follows:

(1) "The specification shall contain a written description of the invention, *and* "

(2) "The specification shall contain a written description . . . of the manner and process of making and using it, in such full, clear, concise, and exact terms as to enable any person skilled in the art to which it pertains, or with which it is most nearly connected, to make and use the same, *and* "

(3) "The specification . . . shall set forth the best mode contemplated by the inventor of carrying out the invention."

Lilly argues that Ariad's construction ignores a long line of judicial precedent interpreting the statute's predecessors to contain a separate written description requirement, an interpretation Congress adopted by reenacting the current language of § 112, first paragraph, without significant amendment.

We agree with Lilly and read the statute to give effect to its language that the specification "shall contain a written description of the invention" and hold that § 112, first paragraph, contains two separate description requirements: a "written description [i] of the invention, *and* [ii] of the manner and process of making and using [the invention]". 35 U.S.C. § 112, ¶ 1 (emphasis added). On this point, we do not read Ariad's position to be in disagreement as Ariad concedes the existence of a written description requirement. Instead Ariad contends that the written description requirement exists, not for its own sake as an independent statutory requirement, but only to identify the invention that must comply with the enablement requirement.

But, unlike Ariad, we see nothing in the statute's language or grammar that unambiguously dictates that the adequacy of the "written description of the invention" must be determined solely by whether that description identifies the invention so as to enable one of skill in the art to make and use it. The prepositional phrase "in such full, clear, concise, and exact terms as to enable any person skilled in the art . . . to make and use the same" modifies only "the written description . . . of the manner and process of making and using [the invention]," as Lilly argues, without violating the rules of grammar. That the adequacy of the description of the manner and process of *making* and *using* the invention is judged by whether that description enables one skilled in the art to *make* and *use* the same follows from the parallelism of the language.

. . .

In contrast to amended claims, the parties have more divergent views on the application of a written description requirement to original claims. Ariad argues that *Regents of the University of California v. Eli Lilly & Co.,* 119 F.3d 1559 (Fed. Cir.1997), extended the requirement beyond its proper role of policing priority as part of enablement and transformed it into a heightened and unpredictable general disclosure requirement in place of enablement. Rather, Ariad argues, the requirement to describe what the invention is does not apply to original claims because original claims, as part of the original disclosure, constitute their own written description of the invention. Thus, according to Ariad, as long as the claim language appears *in ipsis verbis* in the specification as filed, the applicant has satisfied the requirement to provide a written description of the invention.

Lilly responds that the written description requirement applies to all claims and requires that the specification objectively demonstrate that the applicant actually invented—was in possession of—the claimed subject matter. Lilly argues that § 112 contains no basis for applying a different standard to amended versus original claims and that applying a separate written description requirement to original claims keeps inventors from claiming beyond their inventions and thus encourages innovation in new technological areas by preserving patent protection for actual inventions.

Again we agree with Lilly. If it is correct to read § 112, first paragraph, as containing a requirement to provide a separate written description of the invention, as we hold here, Ariad provides no principled basis for restricting that requirement to establishing priority. Certainly nothing in the language of § 112 supports such a restriction; the statute does not say "[t]he specification shall contain a written description of the invention *for purposes of determining priority*." And although the issue arises primarily in cases involving priority, Congress has not so limited the statute, and neither will we.

Furthermore, while it is true that original claims are part of the original specification, that truism fails to address the question whether original claim language necessarily discloses the subject matter that it claims. Ariad believes so, arguing that original claims identify whatever they state, *e.g.*, a perpetual motion machine, leaving only the question whether the applicant has enabled anyone to make and use such an invention. We disagree that this is always the case. Although many original claims will satisfy the written description requirement, certain claims may not. For example, a generic claim may define the boundaries of a vast genus of chemical compounds, and yet the question may still remain whether the specification, including original claim language, demonstrates that the applicant has invented species sufficient to support a claim to a genus. The problem is especially acute with genus claims that use functional language to define the boundaries of a claimed genus. In such a case, the functional claim may simply claim a desired result, and may do so without describing species that achieve that result. But the specification must demonstrate that the applicant has made a generic invention that achieves the claimed result and do so by showing that the applicant has invented species sufficient to support a claim to the functionally-defined genus.

Recognizing this, we held in *Eli Lilly* that an adequate written description of a claimed genus requires more than a generic statement of an invention's boundaries . . . . [W]e held that a sufficient description of a genus instead requires the disclosure of either a representative number of species falling within the scope of the genus or structural features common to the members of the genus so that one of skill in the art can "visualize or recognize" the members of the genus. We explained that an adequate written description requires a precise definition, such as by structure, formula, chemical name, physical properties, or other properties, of species falling within the genus sufficient to distinguish the genus from other materials. We have also held that functional claim language can meet the written description requirement when the art has established a correlation between structure and function. But merely drawing a fence around the outer limits of a purported genus is not an adequate substitute for describing a variety of materials constituting the genus and showing that one has invented a genus and not just a species.

In fact, this case similarly illustrates the problem of generic claims. The claims here recite methods encompassing a genus of materials achieving a stated useful result, i.e., reducing NF-êB binding to NF-êB recognition sites in response to external influences. But the specification does not disclose a variety of species that accomplish the result. Thus . . . that specification fails to meet the written description requirement by describing only a generic invention that it purports to claim.

. . .

Ariad argues that *Eli Lilly* constituted a change in the law, imposing new requirements on biotechnology inventions. We disagree. Applying the written description requirement outside of the priority context in our 1997 *Eli Lilly* decision merely faithfully applied the statute, consistent with Supreme Court precedent and our case law. . . . Neither the statute nor legal precedent limits the written description requirement to cases of priority or distinguishes between original and amended claims . . . . The application of the written description requirement to original language was raised in [previous cases] and is raised again by the parties here. Once again we reject Ariad's argument and hold that generic language in the application as filed does not automatically satisfy the written description requirement.

NOTES AND QUESTIONS

1. Does the plain language of §112 dictate a particular interpretation of the written description requirement or are the arguments put forth by Ariad and Eli Lilly based principally on policy? How would you defend the court's

rationale for agreeing with Eli Lilly's interpretation? What are the benefits of the view adopted by the court? The limits?

2. The Federal Circuit's evolution of the written description requirement which culminated in *Ariad* has been controversial. *See, e.g.,* Janice M. Mueller, T*he Evolving Application of the Written Description Requirement to Biotechnological Inventions*, 13 BERKELEY TECH. L.J. 615 (1998). The *Ariad* decision makes clear that there is a written description requirement separate from the enablement requirement. Less clear, however, is what applicants will have to establish to meet the requirement in a given case. As Judge Rader noted in his dissent from the *Ariad* decision:

> Under this new doctrine, patent applicants will face a difficult burden in discerning proper claiming procedure under this court's unpredictable written description of the invention requirement. The court talks out of both sides of its mouth as it lays out the test. On the one hand, the test seems to require the fact finder to make a subjective inquiry about what the inventor possessed. . . . On the other, the court states that the test requires an objective inquiry into the four corners of the specification from the perspective of a person of ordinary skill in the art. But a test becomes no less subjective merely because it asks a fact finder to answer the subjective question objectively. This court still asks the fact finder to imagine what a person of skill in the art would have understood the inventor to have subjectively possessed based on the description in the specification (which of course by definition describes the exact same invention according to this court's claim construction rules) . . . .

> In sum, the statute supplies a test for description that has operated marvelously for decades, if not centuries. If this court perceives a need for renewed attention to description requirements, it should strengthen its enablement jurisprudence instead of making new rules. Invention of new technologies strengthens and advances the "useful arts," but invention of new doctrines frustrates and confuses the law.

598 F.3d at 1366–67.

Do you agree that the majority invented a new doctrine? Or did it simply apply an old doctrine to a new factual scenario?

3. Some of the concerns animating the court's decision in *Ariad* may seem familiar to you. In a sense, they echo the upstream patenting concerns discussed in Chapter 5, *supra*, in relation to the utility/industrial applicability requirement. In *Ariad*, the inventors recognized that it would be useful to reduce NF-êB binding activity but did not take the next step of identifying compounds having that effect. Rather, they claimed methods of achieving the desired result that would be infringed by others who actually took the time and effort to develop the requisite species. Arguably, allowing such claims would disincentivize the later development of such compounds and stifle advances in the art in a manner similar to the way allowing patents on com-

pounds with no known use (e.g., *Brenner v. Manson*) could disincentivize efforts to find uses for them. Is this a valid concern in the *Ariad* context? Why should these inventors not be able to reap rewards for their important observations regarding NF-êB?

4. EPC Article 84 provides that claims must be supported by the description. As interpreted by the EPO Boards of Appeal, this provision requires that the subject matter of the claim be taken from the description and does not permit the claiming of something that is not described. In Amendments/Xerox, Technical Board of Appeal 3.2.1 decision T 133/85, 1988 Official J. Eur. Pat. Off. 441, the Board ruled that a claim that did not include a feature described in the application as an essential feature of the invention, and which was therefore inconsistent with the description, was not supported by the description within the meaning of Article 84. The Board also took the opportunity to distinguish between the objective of Article 84 and that of Article 123(2), which requires support for amended claims proposed during the course of prosecution or opposition:

> The requirement of Article 84 EPC in respect of the claims of an application should be clearly distinguished from the provision in Article 123(2) EPC.

> Article 123(2) EPC, in contrast to Article 84 EPC, is of course only concerned with determining the allowability of an amendment proposed during the course of prosecution of an application (or proposed during an opposition), and is not applicable if no amendment has been proposed.

> However, it follows from the above that if an amendment to an application (either the description or the claims) is proposed, the application must be examined to ensure that the requirements of both Article 123(2) EPC and Article 84 EPC are met.

> The requirement of Article 123(2) EPC is clearly different from the requirement of Article 84 EPC, both as a matter of wording and as a matter of substance.

> As background to Article 84 EPC, it is noted that the description and the claims of a patent application have different functions. The primary function of the description is to enable a person skilled in the art thereafter to be able to carry out the invention. The primary function of the claims is to define the matter for which protection is sought in terms of the technical features of the invention (*see* Rule 29 EPC); thereafter the actual protection (i.e. the monopoly) given by a granted patent in each designated State is determined in accordance with Article 69 EPC by reference to the claims, ultimately by the courts of such States.

> Thus, the requirement in Article 84 EPC that the claims shall be supported by the description is of importance in ensuring that the monopoly given by a granted patent generally corresponds to the invention which has been described in the application, and that the

claims are not drafted so broadly that they dominate activities which are not dependent upon the invention which has been described in the application. On the other hand, Article 84 EPC clearly envisages (by the use of the word "supported") that the "matter for which protection is sought" can be defined in a generalised form, compared to the specific description of the invention. The permissible extent of generalisation from the description to the claims, having regard to the requirement of Article 84 EPC, is a question of degree and has to be determined, having particular regard to the nature of the invention which has been described, in each individual case.

In contrast, Article 123(2) EPC only requires to be considered when an amendment is proposed, either to the claims or to the description. For an amendment to be allowable, the application after amendment must not "contain subject-matter which extends beyond the content of the application as filed". Clearly the function of this provision is to prevent the addition of subject-matter to a patent application after the date of filing.

Id. at 11–12.

To what extent do you think the EPO's approach is akin to or different from the approach taken by the Federal Circuit in the *Ariad* case? Does the approach adopted by the EPC, which provides separately that the description must support the claims and that it must also support any amendments, make sense? Does it help in understanding the written description requirement? For a comparison of the European and U.S. approaches to enablement for biotech inventions, *see* Sven J.R. Bostyn, ENABLING BIOTECHNOLOGICAL INVENTIONS IN EUROPE AND THE UNITED STATES: A STUDY OF THE PATENTABILITY OF PROTEINS AND DNA SEQUENCES WITH SPECIAL EMPHASIS ON THE DISCLOSURE REQUIREMENT (EPO 2001).

5. For non-biological inventions, providing a written description that enables a skilled person to practice the invention normally can be achieved using words and drawings alone. However, for inventions that involve the use of biological material, words and drawings may be insufficient for enablement. In such cases, an applicant can meet the requirement by depositing a sample of the inventive biological material with an international depository authority under the auspices of the Budapest Treaty on the International Recognition of the Deposit of Microorganisms for the Purpose of Patent Procedure Apr. 28, 1977, 32 U.S.T. 1241, 1861 U.N.T.S. 361.

Administered by WIPO, the Budapest Treaty provides a certification process for depositories that maintain microorganism samples such that a deposit in a single International Depository Authority (IDA) will fulfill the deposit requirement for the patent office of any of the seventy-eight countries signatory to the Treaty. *See* Article 3. The Regulations under the Budapest Treaty require that a deposit be made for a minimum term of thirty years, and at least five years after the most recent request for a sample received by the IDA. *See* Rule 9.1. As of October 2012, forty-one IDAs accept deposits under the Treaty: seven in the United Kingdom; three each in the Russian Federation and the Republic of Korea; two each in Australia, China, India, Italy, Japan, Poland, Spain, and the United States; and one each in Belgium, Bulgaria, Canada, Chile, the Czech Republic, Finland, France, Germany, Hungary, Latvia, the Netherlands, and Slovakia.

In 2010, the USPTO conducted a survey of 6,865 final patent application rejections issued over a four-and-a-half year period between 2005 and 2010. The survey found that a written description rejection was made in about 9.7 percent of all applications during that time period. The rejections were directed particularly at claims that employed unsupported functional language, or that merely set forth a desired result without any indication of what achieved that result. *See* "Director's Forum" blog (May 5, 2010), at http://www.uspto.gov/blog/director/entry/written_description_little_used_perhaps.

Analogs to the written description requirement appear in the laws of other jurisdictions as well, as does the tension with the enablement requirement. The following excerpt describes the written description/enablement interplay in the EPO and UK.

MARK D. JANIS, ON COURTS HERDING CATS: CONTENDING WITH THE "WRITTEN DESCRIPTION" REQUIREMENT (AND OTHER UNRULY PATENT DISCLOSURE DOCTRINES)
2 WASH. U. J.L. & POL'Y 55, 88–107 (2000)

The "written description" jurisprudence demonstrates that modern U.S. courts periodically perceive a need to reach beyond the enablement criterion to redress an alleged disclosure deficiency. . . . [B]oth European and British law also appear burdened with doctrines that are analogous to the U.S. written description requirement.

A. "Sufficiency" and "Support" in European Patent Law

Although the rhetorical labels certainly differ, a similar pattern of disclosure doctrines, evident in the bifurcation of enablement and written description in U.S. law, is also present in European patent law. Not surprisingly, one also finds the attending expressions of confusion. Disclosure requirements under the European Patent Convention ("EPC") rest upon a core requirement of enablement, embodied in EPC article 83. However, the EPC also includes, in article 84, the requirement that the claims be "clear and concise and be supported by the description."

This distinction matters. Compliance with article 83's enablement requirement is an issue both for original examination and for post-grant opposition. In contrast, compliance with article 84 is strictly a matter for original examination, a matter that excited considerable commentary in Europe, especially in the context of allegedly overbroad biotechnology claims. As a conceptual matter and as a matter of practical consequences, it is necessary to attempt to distinguish between article 83 "sufficiency" and article 84 "support," just as it is necessary under current U.S. patent law to distinguish between enablement and written description. It is perhaps telling, then, that the attempt to articulate a standard for article 84 "support" that is truly distinct from article 83 "sufficiency" has not revealed any profound insight. Instead, the project has generated rhetoric and reasoning quite comparable to U.S. written description jurisprudence. . . .

1. Artificial Distinctions Between "Sufficiency" and "Support"

EPO jurisprudence on article 84 does embrace the notion, familiar to U.S. adequacy of disclosure law, that requiring a strict correlation between the scope of the express disclosure and the scope of the claim is counterproductive. For example, in T 133/85, the Board of Appeal acknowledged that a principal purpose of the support requirement in article 84 is to modulate the "width" of the claims, yet the Board made clear it considered that the term "support" allows for some "generalization" of the claim vis a vis the description:

> [T]he requirement in Article 84 EPC that the claims shall be supported by the description is of importance in ensuring that the monopoly given by a granted patent generally corresponds to the invention which has been described in the application, and that the claims are not drafted so broadly that they dominate activities which are not dependent upon the invention which has been described in the application. On the other hand, Article 84 EPC clearly envisages (by use of the word 'supported') that the 'matter for which protection is sought' can be defined in a generalised form, compared to the specific description of the invention.

> This issue raises the difficult question of how much claim "generalization" the patentee may undertake before crossing over into the prohibited practice of claiming "covetously." The European Patent Office (EPO) Guidelines for Examination attempt to flesh out this concept, but make little headway. The Guidelines take refuge in the proposition that the extent of allowable disconnect or generalization between the claims and the disclosure is a matter for case-by-case resolution. Beyond this broad pronouncement, the Guidelines do little more than restate the article 83 enablement standard. . . .

EPO case law under the article 84 support requirement reflects this same overlap with article 83. For example, in T 409/91, the claim at issue was directed to a fuel oil containing wax particles of a specified size. The disclosure described fuel oil compositions including not only wax particles within the claimed size range, but also specified additives as to which the claims were silent. The Board found numerous problems with this disconnect between the scope of the disclosure and the scope of the claims. First, according to the Board, the article 84 support requirement reflected the general principle that "the definitions in the claims should essentially correspond to the scope of the invention as disclosed in the description." However, as the Board articulated the rationale of article 84, it lapsed into enablement language: "[T]he claims should not extend to subject matter which, after reading the description, would still not be at the disposal of the person skilled in the art."

Indeed, if the evidence had in fact shown, as the Board suggested it did, that a skilled artisan could not have prepared the claimed composition without using the additive one might suppose there would be no need to resort to article 84, because there would surely be an enablement problem. The Board, in fact, proceeded to find an article 83 enablement violation. In so doing, the Board again confronted the problem of relating article 83 to the article 84 support requirement:

> Although the requirements of [a]rticle 83 and [a]rticle 84 are directed to different parts of the patent application, since [a]rticle 83 relates to the disclosure of the invention, whilst [a]rticle 84 deals with the definition of the invention by the claims, the underlying purpose of the requirement of support by the description ... and of the requirement of sufficient disclosure is the same, namely to ensure that the patent monopoly should be justified by the actual technical contribution to the art. Thus, a claim may well be supported by the description in the sense that it corresponds to it, but still encompass subject matter which is not sufficiently disclosed within the meaning of [a]rticle 83 EPC as it cannot be performed without undue burden, or vice versa.

This broad pronouncement carries the tone of rationality, but sheds little light on any distinction between the two requirements ... the distinction seems more hypothetical than real ....

In the United States, the deployment of an illusory written description requirement has had adverse consequences for coherence. Interestingly, some of the same consequences are seen in EPO case law. For example, the EPO may be willing to allow article 84 support considerations to influence claim construction. Similarly, and perhaps more significantly, the EPO has held that a lack of clarity objection could be reformulated as an insufficiency objection and thus be raised post-grant, even though an article 84 objection would not be available post-grant.

. . .

B. The "Fair Basis" Requirement in British Jurisprudence

British patent law provides an interesting illustration of transition and fluidity in the application of adequacy of disclosure requirements. The "fair basis" requirement is of particular interest as a rough analog to the EPC article 84 "support" requirement and to the U.S. "written description" requirement. The rise, fall, and arguable recent resuscitation of the "fair basis" requirement in British patent law provides yet another illustration of the phenomenon whereby courts turn to ancillary disclosure doctrines to buttress the enablement requirement.

1. "Fair Basis" Before the 1977 Act

Even before British patent law required formal claims, patentees began to include language in their applications directed at identifying invention scope. Thus, courts became sensitive to the potential for "disconformity" between the disclosure and these proto-claims. When the British statute began to mandate claims, the disconformity defense persisted. Similarly, disconformity had a role in assuring congruence between the disclosure in a provisional specification and the complete specification.

Unfortunately, the notion of disconformity was never articulated with any great precision. Instead, in *Mullard Radio*, the leading pre-1949 enunciation, the court gave the test in terms that did little beyond restating the question: "[A] claim may be for an article which is new, which is useful and which has subject-matter, yet it may be too wide a claim because it extends beyond the subject-matter of the invention." . . .

The 1949 Act turned away from the generic disconformity concept, omitting the provision allowing patent revocation "on any ground on which a patent might have been repealed by scire facias," and instead included a revocation provision that specified a multiplicity of possible grounds of revocation. Regarding adequacy of disclosure, section 32 contained two subsections that bear a fairly close resemblance to current U.S. law under 35 U.S.C. § 112, first paragraph. Section 32(1)(h) included enablement and best mode requirements:

> [A] patent may . . . be revoked by the court on any of the following grounds . . .: that the complete specification does not sufficiently and fairly describe the invention and the method by which it is to be performed, or does not disclose the best method of performing it which was known to the applicant for the patent and for which he was entitled to claim protection.

Separately, section 32(1)(i) encompassed claim ambiguity, but also injected a "fair basis" requirement, whereby "a patent may . . . be revoked by the court [[if] any claim of the complete specification is not fairly based on the matter disclosed in the specification. While some authorities have cautioned against reliance on pre-1949 "disconformity" precedent to explain the statutory fair basis requirement, the precedent undoubtedly formed an important part of the backdrop for understanding the fair basis requirement. As the court put it in *Olin Matheison*:

> [The fair basis provision] was introduced into the 1949 Act at the same time as the removal of the provision, contained in the pre-

vious Act, for revocation "on any ground on which a patent might have been repealed by scire facias . . . In other words, section 32(1) covers the objection discussed at length in the case of . . . [*Mullard v. Philco*] that a claim which is a "covetous" claim, or one in which the claim does not "equiparate" with the consideration given by the disclosure, is a bad claim. This requirement [[]] has always been fundamental in our patent law, and section 32(1) certainly includes it, but it is not, of course, limited to it.

. . .

2. "Fair Basis" in Modern British Patent Law

The role of the fair basis requirement in modern British patent law remains a matter of considerable complexity. The 1977 Act significantly reformulated the grounds for revoking a patent for inadequate disclosure. Eliminating the multiplicity of grounds set forth in sections 32(1)(h) and (i) of the 1949 Act, the 1977 Act instead articulated a generic insufficiency requirement: "[a patent may be revoked if] the specification of the patent does not disclose the invention clearly enough and completely enough for it to be performed by a person skilled in the art." [section 72(1)(c)]. It seems clear that this language carries forward the insufficiency (enablement) standard from the 1949 Act and eliminates the "best method" requirement.

The fate of the fair basis requirement, however, seems less clear from the language of section 72(1)(c). Some courts and commentators, noting the excision of the specific "fairly based" language from the new provision, understandably assumed that the fair basis requirement had disappeared as a ground of revocation. This assumption drew additional force from the language of section 14 of the 1977 Act. Section 14, which sets forth the adequacy of disclosure requirements for pending applications, includes language nearly identical to the section 72(1)(c) insufficiency requirement. However, section 14 also includes a separate requirement that the claims be "supported" by the description. Therefore, the fair basis requirement, to the extent that it survived the 1977 Act, served only as a ground for rejecting a pending application under a "lack of support" rubric of section 14(5)(c). Consequently, litigants could not raise a fair basis challenge to a granted patent. This, of course, conforms with the current European practice. Nevertheless, some judges and commentators have expressed frustration with the discontinuity between pre-grant and post-grant adequacy of disclosure requirements.

Against this backdrop, in a remarkable feat of statutory construction, the House of Lords resuscitated the fair basis requirement in *Biogen, Inc. v. Medeva, Inc.*, a landmark decision on biotechnology patenting. Although Lord Hoffman's opinion in *Biogen* addresses inventive step and enablement, its treatment of fair basis is most pertinent in the fair basis context. Lord Hoffman acknowledged that the fair basis requirement had disappeared from the face of the statute, but nevertheless insisted that the fair basis "principle" remained:

> [T]he disappearance of 'lack of fair basis' as an express ground for revocation does not in my view mean that general principle which it expressed has been abandoned. The jurisprudence of the EPO shows that it is still in full vigor and embodied in articles 83 and 84 of the EPC, of which equivalents in the 1977 Act are section 14(3) and (5) and section 72(1)(c).

In Lord Hoffman's view, the general principle is that the claim must remain confined to the extent of the technical contribution as described in the patent.

Although the statutory construction that carries the fair basis "principle" forward into section 72(1)(c) may not provide illumination for those in the United States, other aspects of the opinion bear consideration. First, the fact that Lord Hoffman felt compelled to reach beyond enablement to a "support" rationale is significant; his opinion contains parallels to the written description requirement in the United States. Second, notwithstanding Lord Hoffman's careful elucidation of the relationship between the relevant provisions on sufficiency and support (both in the priority context and as grounds for revocation), the *Biogen* standard for "support" does not meaningfully confine judges' discretion to strike down claims for inadequate disclosure. Criticizing the lower courts and the EPO for inquiring whether the disclosure could "deliver the goods across the full width of the patent or priority document," Lord Hoffman set out a vivid governing rubric that has the fluidity of the "possession" standard. Lord Hoffman stated, "it is not whether the claimed invention could deliver the goods, but whether the claims cover other ways in which they might be delivered: ways which owe nothing to the teaching of the patent or any principle which it disclosed." Lord Hoffman proceeded to outline two ways in which the breadth of a claimed invention might exceed the technical contribution in the disclosure; yet he framed both possibilities in the rhetoric of enablement.

Thus, even this relatively brief excursion through *Biogen* seems to confirm observations from U.S. written description law as to both the nature and likely costs of disclosure doctrines that supplement enablement, be they called "support," "fair basis," or something else. Certainly, the support/fair basis notion, as articulated in *Biogen*, appears to leave judges with wide discretion to strike down claims for insufficient supporting disclosure. Presumably, this remains true even if contestants have not proven a violation. Although this discretion may often be deployed wisely by experienced jurists, like Lord Hoffman, the *Biogen* standard indeed confers vast discretion.

IV.

Only a few years after the arrival of the written description requirement in U.S. law, Judge Markey recognized its character:

> How incongruous. How exaltive of form over substance. How illustrative of stare decisis rampant. The board is saying that it doesn't *matter* that one discloses an invention in such "clear, concise and exact terms" (enablement) as to enable its practice, the very purpose and quid pro quo of the patent system from its inception. [*In re Barker,* 559 F.2d 588, 594 (C.C.P.A. 1977) (Markey, J. dissenting)].

Judge Markey had it right. The written description requirement is at worst indecipherable, and at best unruly, even when considered in isolation. Viewed together with other disclosure doctrines under U.S. law (e.g., enablement, best mode, utility), the entire exercise of making patent disclosure law very much resembles the proverbial herding of cats, both in its level of cacophony and its likely futility. Comparative analysis reinforces this proposition: written description analogs such as "support" in European patent law and "fair basis" in British patent law seem as indeterminate as the written description requirement. This result occurs despite the best efforts of leading jurists.

Today, however, after repeated (and more aggressive) Federal Circuit invocations of the written description requirement, the weight of stare decisis hangs even heavier. Moreover, comparative study suggests that the written description requirement or analogous doctrines simply may be part of the *realpolitik* of patent disclosure law. Accordingly, it may be overly optimistic to propose that the Federal Circuit dispose of the written description requirement altogether with one bold stroke, or alternatively that Congress address the matter. This does not mean, however, that we ought to resign ourselves to the status quo regarding the written description requirement. Reconsideration of the doctrine with adjustments is possible.

NOTES AND QUESTIONS

1. Do you agree with Professor Janis that the written description requirement should be eliminated, or at least adjusted? If so, what type of adjustment should be made and with what goal?

2. As described by Professor Janis, are the written description, sufficiency, and fair basis requirements equivalent doctrines? Other than the shared characteristic of indeterminacy which is highlighted by Professor Janis, what other similarities in structure or content do you glean from this analysis of the comparative disclosure approaches of the U.S., EU, and the UK? Are there any notable dissimilarities?

3. Is the judicial discretion to strike down claims afforded by the written description/sufficiency/fair basis requirements truly desirable? In arguing for retention of the written description requirement in light of inadequacies in enablement law, Professor Lefstin notes:

> The enablement inquiry tends to be fact-intensive, requiring evidence of what one of ordinary skill in the art could or could not accomplish with certain efforts given the state of the art. The inquiry may require extensive expert testimony and may not be amenable to early judicial intervention. In contrast, written description is a question of what the patent specification discloses: does the text of the patent disclose the invention defined by the claims? No less than most other inquiries in patent law, this question is resolved from the perspective of one of ordinary skill in the art. Nevertheless, the underlying question in written description, what information is conveyed by the patent specification, may be more capable of judicial resolution than questions about the behavior or thought processes of technological artisans. To the extent that we desire more judicial control over patent scope and desire such control not be confined by the particular testimony adduced in a given case, written description may be a more appealing doctrine than enablement.

Jeffrey A. Lefstin, *The Formal Structure of Patent Law and the Limits of Enablement*, 23 BERKELEY TECH L. J. 1141, 1215–1216 (2008). Do you think we need both requirements to adequately cabin claim scope?

3. BEST MODE

In the U.S., a patent specification is required to include "the best mode contemplated by the inventor of carrying out his invention" at the time of filing the patent application. *See* 35 U.S.C. §112. A number of countries, such as China, India, and Japan, have a best mode/best method/ preferred method-type requirement, if not in their statutory provisions, then in examination guidelines, although there may be no penalty for non-compliance. *See, e.g.,* Bingbin Lu, *Best Mode Disclosure for Patent Applications: An International and Comparative Perspective*, 16 J. INTELL. PROP. RTS. 409, 413 (2011). For example, the Japanese Patent and Utility Model Examination Guidelines state:

> 3.2.1 Practices in Enablement Requirement
>
> (1)Mode for carrying out the invention
>
>> It is necessary to state in the detailed explanation of the invention at least one mode that an applicant considers to be the best (see, Note) among the "modes for carrying out the invention" showing how to carry out the claimed invention in compliance with the requirement in Article 36(4)(i).

(Note) . . . It would be noted that regarding a point to state what the applicant considers to be the best, it is not required as a requirement based on Article 36(4)(i). Therefore it does not constitute reasons for refusal even if it is clear that what an applicant considers to be the best has not been stated.

http://www.jpo.go.jp/tetuzuki_e/t_tokkyo_e/Guidelines/1_1.pdf. The idea behind the requirement is the sensible one that an inventor (or other applicant) should not be able to simply disclose enough information that someone could practice the invention, but keep the best conditions to herself as a trade secret. Because the requirement varies so significantly from country to country, the stringency of the requirement in the U.S. has been unpopular with foreign applicants, who saw it as a trap for the unwary and a tool to increase patent litigation costs and complexity. Moreover, because the requirement relates to the applicant's *subjective* best mode, and applicants are under no duty to update the best mode with new information that they learn while prosecuting the application, its value has been questioned. The America Invents Act of 2011 (AIA) retained the statutory best mode requirement but, curiously, removed best mode violations from being a basis for patent invalidity or unenforceability proceedings commenced on or after September 16, 2011. In other words, as in Japan, there appears to be no clear penalty for violating the best mode requirement. While an examiner could refuse to grant a patent if the best mode were not disclosed, examiners normally are not in a position to make such a determination. However, a patent attorney's failure to comply with the requirement could, in theory, result in sanctions of some sort. The uncertainty created by the AIA on this issue likely will remain until Congress takes action to further amend the statute.

4. DISCLOSURE OF ORIGIN

The requirement that an inventor adequately disclose her invention to the public in the patent document so that the interested public can be in possession of the invention when the patent expires is part of the quid pro quo of the patent grant. It provides the basis for the enablement and written description requirements, and their global counterparts, described above, and has long been a feature of the patent laws. In recent years, however, a new disclosure requirement has emerged for biotechnological inventions: the requirement that an inventor disclose not just the invention, but the origin of the materials and knowledge used to create the invention.

This Disclosure of Origin (DOO) requirement is controversial, in part because it is designed to combat "biopiracy": the patenting of genetic resources and associated traditional knowledge from a foreign country without compensating the keepers of the resources and the holders of the knowledge. "Traditional Knowledge" is a catch-all term that includes tradition-based inventions, creations, and scientific discoveries resulting from intellectual activity in the industrial or scientific fields. Patent-related genetic resource/traditional knowledge disputes regarding Indian neem and turmeric, Mexican yellow ("enola") beans, Ecuadorean Ayahuasca, and the Nigerian serendipity berry, to name a few, have all been categorized as biopiracy. For examples and discussions of perceived instances of biopiracy, *see* Lorna Dwyer, *Biopiracy, Trade, and Sustainable Development*, 19 COLO. J. INT'L ENVTL. L. & POL'Y 219, 227–231 (2008); and Cynthia M. Ho, *Biopiracy and Beyond: A Consideration of Socio-Cultural Conflicts with Global Patent Policies*, 39 U. MICH. J.L. REFORM 433, 473 (2006). *See also* David Llewelyn, INVISIBLE GOLD IN ASIA: CREATING WEALTH THROUGH INTELLECTUAL PROPERTY, pp. 210–212 (Marshall Cavendish 2010) for a fascinating example of perceived biopiracy in the development of the chronic pain drug Ziconotide (Prialt).

However, the United States and some other developed countries are fundamentally opposed to the grafting of a DOO requirement into patent law. As stated in a U.S. Group response to a 2010 AIPPI questionnaire on the "*Requirement of Indicating the Source and/or Country of Origin of Genetic Resources and Traditional Knowledge in Patent Applications*":

> While the United States has been monitoring the proposals that have been made in a variety of fora to allow or mandate that national patent legislation require the declaration of the source of genetic resources and traditional knowledge in patent applications as well as demands for sharing of benefits from the commercialization of products utilizing them, the US government, with the strong support of US companies, has taken the position that these initiatives are unwise and unnecessary. There are no pending bills or discussions that would suggest that legislation will be introduced on these issues within the United States. It should also be noted that the United States is not a party to the Convention on Biological Diversity [CBD], and no pending legislation exists that would alter that status.

International Association for the Protection of Intellectual Property (AIPPI), *Questionnaire February 2010: Special Committees Q 94— WTO/TRIPS and Q166—Intellectual Property and Genetic Resources, Traditional Knowledge and Folklore on the Requirement of Indicating the Source and/or Country of Origin of Genetic Resources and Traditional Knowledge in Patent Applications: Communication from the US Group* (Apr. 7, 2010). Indeed, although then-President Bill Clinton signed the CBD in 1993, the treaty was never ratified by the U.S. Senate.

The Convention on Biological Diversity, which went into effect in 1993, contains several key principles, including the following:

-States have sovereign control over biological resources within their borders and shall ensure conservation of same;

-States shall endeavor to create conditions to facilitate access on mutually agreed terms and subject to prior informed consent;

-There should be fair and equitable sharing of benefits of use of genetic resources with providing party; and

-Wider application of Traditional Knowledge (TK) shall be with the approval and involvement of TK holders.

Convention on Biological Diversity, June 5, 1992, 1760 U.N.T.S. 79, 143, 152.

The following excerpt explains both the link between the DOO requirement and the CBD, and the tension between the DOO requirement and TRIPS.

NUNO PIRES DE CARVALHO, REQUIRING DISCLOSURE OF THE ORIGIN OF GENETIC RESOURCES AND PRIOR INFORMED CONSENT IN PATENT APPLICATIONS WITHOUT INFRINGING THE TRIPS AGREEMENT: THE PROBLEM AND THE SOLUTION
2 WASH. U. J.L. & POL'Y 371 (2000)

The requirement that applicants for patents in the field of biotechnology disclose the source of the genetic resources eventually used as raw materials or tools in the inventive activity and, in addition, provide information (and evidence, if any, by means of contracts or licenses) on prior informed consent is not a new concept. It is a consequence of article 15 of the Convention on Biological Diversity (CBD), which deals with access to genetic resources. Paragraph four states that access, where granted by the country of origin, "shall be on mutually agreed terms and subject to provisions of this Article." Paragraph five adds that access "shall be subject to prior informed consent of the Contracting Party providing such resources, unless otherwise determined by that Party." In addition, paragraph seven establishes that the contracting parties shall take legislative action in order to ensure "sharing . . . the benefits arising from the commercial and other utilization of genetic resources with the Contracting Party providing such resources." Article 8(j) of the CBD establishes that national legislation should "encourage the equitable sharing of the benefits arising from the utilization of knowledge, innovations, and practices of indigenous and local communities . . . relevant for the conservation and sustainable use of biological diversity."

The argument for the Requirement is that researchers and companies from developed countries are using genetic resources extracted from biodiversity-rich countries without appropriate authorization in order to obtain new technologies, inventions, techniques, and products. Further-more, in many instances members of local, traditional communities, who cooperate with researchers to provide the lead for the identification and discovery of those genetic resources and their active principles, seldom receive payment. The press has described this frequently as "biopiracy" and this characterization has generated strong public indignation in de-veloping countries.

In order to maintain a record of inventions that were developed with the use of genetic resources conserved in situ and/or traditional or indige-nous knowledge, it has been proposed that patent applications disclose this information. In the absence of proper authorization, the countries of origin could then make the patent holders accountable for any infringe-ment of the national laws implementing the mentioned CBD provisions. In other words, a specific provision of patent law would serve the imple-mentation of an environmentally related treaty.

So far, the Requirement has been incorporated into two statutes: An-dean Decision No. 391 of August 16, 1996, which establishes a Common Regime on Access to Genetic Resources; and the Biodiversity Law (No. 7788) of Costa Rica enacted May 27, 1998. Under both statutes patent applicants are obliged to provide patent offices with information concern-ing the origin of the genetic resource in question and some proof of prior informed consent from government authorities as well as traditional knowledge holders, whenever the resource will be obtained through their technical knowledge. As an intellectual property-related proposal, it could be expected that it would find its way to the two intergovernmental or-ganizations that cover patent matters: the WTO and the WIPO. . . .

Strictly speaking, the Requirement, to the extent it concerns infor-mation that does not relate directly to the activity of inventing, does not characterize the invention itself. In this sense, it is not a "substantive" requirement. Unlike novelty, non-obviousness, utility, and unity—the four patentability requirements that concern the substance, i.e., the very essence of the inventive activity—the Requirement is an accessory, which relates to the invention collaterally. . . .

The issue is whether the Requirement described above complies with the standards concerning the availability of patent rights established by the TRIPS Agreement. . . . Article 27.1 lists the substantive conditions of patentability: "[P]atents shall be available for any inventions . . . provided they are new, involve an inventive step and are capable of industrial ap-plication." . . .

The Requirement quite obviously is not compatible with article 27.1. The manner of obtaining genetic resources used in the development of inventions is an external condition. The outcome of the inventive activity is indeed independent of the ways and means employed to reach it. The situation that arises from an invention derived from the use of genetic resources that have been illegally extracted from their in situ environment is similar to the situation of an invention that has been developed with the assistance of a stolen microscope. This event would infringe the common law but not patent law under article 27.1 of the TRIPS Agreement. In both situations inventors would still be entitled to the patent, provided the conditions of patentability were met. Nonetheless they would be subject to criminal and civil liability for stealing (both the genetic resources, depending on the existence of appropriate legislation, and the microscope) in the country from which the resources had been taken.

. . .

To make the granting and validity of those patents dependent on the meeting of the Requirement conflicts with the obligations imposed on WTO members by the TRIPS Agreement. Nevertheless, courts should be able to sanction the lack of candor of patent applicants who knowingly failed to disclose the source in a manner that would facilitate benefit sharing, as established by article 15 of the CBD. Actually, the determination that the concealment of information might lead to the implementation of public policies concerning benefit sharing is fraudulent is a matter of law. Consequently, any attempt to enforce patent rights thus obtained would be an abuse of rights. In compliance with paragraph 2 of article 8 of the TRIPS Agreement and given that infringement both direct and contributory is a tort, it can be imposed that one must have clean hands to obtain relief from an equity court. Only after a patentee abandons its unlawful practice and the effects of the misuse are completely dissipated may it sue infringers. In the case of the Requirement, this implies that patent owners would have to disclose the origin and obtain the appropriate authorizations from the appropriate stakeholders (governments, local authorities, and traditional knowledge holders) before the patent rights could be enforced against infringers.

In sum, the national or regional laws of WTO members that restrict access to the genetic resources found in their territory may require that patent applicants indicate, if known, the source of genetic resources directly or indirectly used in obtaining the invention. The lack of that indication by a patent applicant who knew or had reason to know constitutes fraud. Therefore, the enforcement of the resulting patent therefore, may be deemed an abuse of rights.

In the same vein, if one obtains the genetic resource directly or indirectly used in making a patented invention in a country that has adopted legislation requiring prior informed consent, the failure to obtain that consent constitutes fraud and, therefore, an attempt to enforce that patent may be deemed an abuse of rights. In both cases the patentee's cleaning his hands by providing the missing information and/or obtaining the required prior consent, would purge the abuse of rights.

NOTES AND QUESTIONS

1. Since the writing of Dr. Pires de Carvalho's article, many countries have added DOO requirements to their patent laws or enacted special biodiversity protection legislation containing similar provisions. Consider, for example, two provisions in the Third Revision of the Chinese Patent Law:

> Article 5. Patent rights shall not be granted for invention-creations that violate the law or social ethics, or harm public interests. Patent rights shall not be granted for inventions that are accomplished by relying on genetic resources which are obtained or used in violation of the provisions of laws and administrative regulations. . . .

> Article 26. [W]ith regard to an invention-creation accomplished by relying on genetic resources, the applicant shall, in the patent application documents, indicate the direct and original source of the genetic resources. If the applicant cannot indicate the original source, he shall state the reasons.

Patent Law of the People's Republic of China, Third Revision (2008). Article 5 thus makes violation of genetic resource acquisition laws in creating an invention a basis for denying patentability or invalidating a patent, and Article 26 requires applicants to disclose the country of origin of relevant genetic resources in addition to the direct supplier. Failure to supply the required information is a basis for rejecting claims in an application, but apparently not for invalidating an already issued patent. Does Article 5 violate TRIPS Article 27.1?

2. The laws of some other countries reflect a different approach. For example, a Brazilian law regulating access to components of Brazilian genetic heritage contains a variety of penalties for violation of genetic resource laws in creating patentable inventions. Such penalties include payment to the Federal Government of at least 20 percent of the gross income or royalties from commercializing or licensing the resulting product (benefit sharing) and suspension or cancellation of the resulting patent. Also, the origin of genetic material used in creating an invention must be disclosed in the patent application. Brazilian Provisional Act, No. 2,186–16, Title VII, Art. 26, Title VIII, Art. 30, Title IX, Art. 31 (August 23, 2001).

India's Biodiversity Act has even stiffer penalties: imprisonment, while also allowing for retroactive permission and the imposition of benefit-sharing conditions. The law provides in part:

> 6. (1) No person shall apply for any intellectual property right, by whatever name called, in or outside India for any invention based on any research or information on a biological resource obtained from India without obtaining the previous approval of the National Biodiversity Authority before making such application:

> Provided that if a person applies for a patent, permission of the National Biodiversity Authority may be obtained after the acceptance

of the patent but before the sealing of the patent by the patent authority concerned.

(2) The National Biodiversity Authority may, while granting the approval under this section, impose benefit sharing fee or royalty or both or impose conditions including the sharing of financial benefits arising out of the commercial utilisation of such rights. . . .

Penalties.

55. (1) Whoever contravenes or attempts to contravene or abets the contravention of the provisions of section 3, section 4, or section 6 shall be punishable with imprisonment for a term which may extend to five years, or with fine which may extend to ten lakh rupees and where the damage caused exceeds ten lakhs such fine may be commensurate with the damage caused, or with both. . . .

57. (1) Where an offence or contravention under this Act has been committed by a company, every person who at the time the offence or contravention was committed was in charge of, and was responsible to the company for the conduct of the business of the company, as well as the company, shall be deemed to be guilty of the offence or contravention and shall be liable to be proceeded against and punished accordingly:

Provided that nothing contained in this sub-section shall render any such person liable to any punishment provided in this Act, if he proves that the offence or contravention was committed without his knowledge or that he had exercised all due diligence to prevent the commission of such offence or contravention.

India Biodiversity Act (2002), *available at* http://www.wipo.int/wipolex/ en/details.jsp?id=6058. Should simply filing a patent application be grounds for the imposition of criminal penalties? Why or why not? For a discussion of the potential impact of illegal, immoral, or unethical activity in creating inventions on later-obtained patent rights, *see* Margo A. Bagley, *The New Invention Creation Activity Boundary in Patent Law,* 51 WILLIAM & MARY L. REV. 577 (2009).

3. A study for the EU Commission generated by the Queen Mary Institute categorizes DOO regimes as: (1) strong—mandatory disclosure accompanied by access and benefit sharing provisions, including proof of legal acquisition; (2) medium—mandatory disclosure only; and (3) weak—disclosure is simply "encouraged or even expected but not required." Queen Mary Intellectual Property Institute, REPORT ON DISCLOSURE OF ORIGIN IN PATENT APPLICATIONS, 5 (Oct. 2004). Belgium, India, Peru, the Andean Communities and Brazil all fit in the "strong" category; Denmark, Switzerland, Norway, and New Zealand are examples of "medium" regimes; and Egypt, the EU, Germany, Romania, Spain, and Sweden are given as examples of "weak" DOO regimes.

The following excerpt posits an intriguing theory regarding the origins and concerns behind the DOO requirement and the CBD itself. We suggest revisiting the *Diamond v. Chakrabarty* decision in Chapter 4 before reading the excerpt.

SABRINA SAFRIN, CHAIN REACTION: HOW PROPERTY BEGETS PROPERTY

82 NOTRE DAME L. REV. 1917 (2007)

Before *Chakrabarty*, with the notable exception of certain man-made plants that received a limited form of intellectual property protection in a few countries, types of living organisms, whether naturally occurring or man-made through traditional breeding, could not be exclusively owned. For example, while a person might own a particular dog, no one could own a breed of dog. Moreover, nations treated genetic material as an open access resource. As with the living resources of the high seas, states did not assert sovereignty over genetic material nor did they seek to appropriate it. No single individual, corporation or nation held an exclusive right to prevent others from using the resource generally.

The *Chakrabarty* case generated numerous amicus briefs. All knew that if the Supreme Court allowed Dr. Chakrabarty to patent his genetically engineered oil-eating microbe, others would seek to patent and hence enjoy property rights over their man-made living creations. Indeed, in the ten years following Chakrabarty's victory, patents were extended in rapid order to isolated and purified genetic sequences, to man-made plants, and to animals. Unanticipated, however, was how the propertization of living organisms and their genetic material would set off a chain reaction of collateral propertization of unmodified genetic and other naturally-occurring biological material. First, the governments of developing countries began to assert sovereign ownership rights over raw genetic material in their countries and to restrict access to such material. Second, patients began to assert property or other legal rights in biological specimens, such as blood or tissue samples, that they had contributed in the course of receiving medical treatment. By the turn of the millennium, raw biological material increasingly moved from an open access or global commons good to a private or government-owned good. . . .

Developing countries harbor the greatest amount of the world's naturally occurring genetic material because they comprise most of the countries which hug the equatorial line where the greatest numbers of life forms concentrate. Why, these countries asked, should individuals and companies from gene-poor developed countries obtain genetic material free of charge from gene-rich developing countries when they then patent these genes and at times sell them back to the country where the genetic material originated? Moreover, developing countries faced increasing pressure to extend patent protection to man-made living organisms and their genetic material. In the late 1980s, the United States began to require, as a condition of free trade relations, that other countries extend intellectual property protection to bioengineered and other goods. This link between trade and intellectual property rights blossomed in full with the 1994 adoption of the Agreement on Trade-Related Aspects of Intellectual Property Rights ("TRIPS Agreement") as part of the world trading system. The TRIPS Agreement required countries to extend intellectual property protection to most bioengineered goods or face trade sanctions.

In response to the propertization of improved genetic material, developing countries pressed for the international recognition of sovereign rights over raw genetic material in the 1992 Convention on Biological Diversity (CBD). The CBD no longer considered genetic resources to form part of "the common heritage of mankind," as had traditionally been the case, but rather to fall within the province of sovereigns who would control access to such material. Since 1993, over forty nations have passed or are in the process of passing laws which greatly restrict access to raw genetic material in their countries. Under these laws, the national government either owns all raw genetic material in the country or greatly restricts access to it through a multilayered consent process. . . .

The key operating dynamic is that of a tit-for-tat. Namely, if developed countries assert and demand that developing countries recognize intellectual property rights over man-made living organisms and isolated and purified genetic sequences, then developing countries believe that they should also assert property interests over the raw genetic material that may contribute to the patented goods. Raw genetic material has contributed to pharmaceutical innovations and improved crops from time immemorial. Yet sovereigns only asserted ownership rights over this material after the patent system recognized private ownership rights over the material and internationalized these property rights through pre-TRIPS agreements and eventually through the TRIPS Agreement itself. Public statements of developing country leaders also evidence this responsive dynamic. . . .

Most knowledge that we use is both traditional and free. It consists of human innovation and insight developed over millennia and passed down from generation to generation. A child born today will benefit from language that she made no contribution to creating. She will use numbers and a system of mathematics for free. She will enjoy food, songs and dances developed by generations long gone. She will inherit a range of methodologies from the tying of shoelaces to the manipulation of a range of tools and objects. We take the free availability of most information as a given. No one thinks to thank the Chinese, let alone pay a royalty to China, whenever eating pasta. Mexico holds no intellectual property right in the widespread use of aloe vera in soaps and moisturizers. Our use of Arabic numerals generates no royalties for Arab nations nor do parents pay a royalty to Israel whenever they name a child Jacob or Hannah.

Yet, today many nations demand the development of intellectual property regimes to cover "traditional knowledge." A flurry of international activity has materialized on this issue. . . . In 1999, the Parties to the CBD established a working group to address traditional knowledge issues, and the 1992 CBD itself exhorts nations to respect and protect traditional knowledge. The CBD working group has met four times, and numerous regional and experts meetings have convened on the topic as well. Even the World Trade Organization has taken up the issue, calling upon the TRIPS Council "to examine . . . the protection of traditional knowledge and folklore." A study by WIPO indicated that the majority of countries surveyed believe in the need for an international agreement for the protection of expressions of folklore. Several nations, such as Brazil and Panama, have already enacted measures purporting to protect traditional knowledge.

What has occurred to cause nations to demand the extension of intellectual property rights to tradition? Anthropologist Michael Brown observes that "[i]n the late 1980s, ownership of knowledge and artistic creations traceable to the world's indigenous societies emerged, seemingly out of nowhere, as a major social issue." However, something did happen in the late 1980s that likely engendered such demands: the internationalization of intellectual property. In the late 1980s, the United States began to impose trade sanctions against countries that accorded little or no protection to U.S. intellectual property goods, pursuant to a new U.S. law called "Special Clause 301." As mentioned earlier, the United States also made trade with it conditioned upon the granting of intellectual property rights in a number of bilateral agreements. Moreover, in 1986 and 1987, the United States and the European Union linked intellectual property and trade in the negotiating mandate for the Uruguay Round of the General Agreement on Tariffs and Trade. The 1994 adoption of the TRIPS Agreement, which emerged from the Uruguay Round, required countries to put in place, as a condition of participating in the world trading system, copyright, patent, trademark and trade secret laws. Beginning in the late 1980s, developing countries were forced to extend a host of intellectual property protection to a vast range of knowledge that had hitherto remained free in their countries. They responded to these first generation intellectual property rights by demanding in numerous international fora the development of second generation intellectual property rights which would propertize traditional knowledge generated in their countries that had previously remained open.

One can see this nexus between the internationalization of Western intellectual property protection and the movement to propertize traditional knowledge in multiple contexts. For example, developing countries strongly object to the requirement that they extend patent protection to pharmaceutical goods. This requirement appeared in several pre-TRIPS bilateral agreements, and the TRIPS Agreement mandates such protection. In turn, developing country demands for the extension of intellectual property protection to traditional knowledge often concern the protection of folk remedies . . . .

Even the language used by those demanding the creation of intellectual property rights over traditional knowledge indicates the relationship between the internationalization of intellectual property and the demand to fashion new intellectual property rights to cover traditional knowledge. Developed countries and their companies repeatedly decried the widespread copying of Western drugs, movies, songs and software as "piracy." Mimicking such characterization, those advocating the creation of property rights over traditional knowledge reciprocally characterize the uncompensated use of traditional knowledge as "piracy."

While the national governments of developing countries respond to the internationalization of intellectual property by demanding new forms of intellectual property, the demands by indigenous groups for the protection of their traditional knowledge, while sometimes reactive to Western intellectual property, can stem from other concerns. For example, indigenous groups sometimes seek to protect and control knowledge that they consider sacred or private. They may also seek to prevent persons from fraudulently depicting an item as an authentic native craft. Addressing these concerns, however, does not require the creation of new property rights but can be met with legislation that prohibits certain bad acts. . . .

Underlying the creation of property rights over raw genetic and biological material is a desire by those demanding such rights that others not exploit them. When individuals and corporations began to patent isolated and purified genetic sequences, cell lines and living organisms, those from whom the raw biological material came felt exploited. Nations with a history of colonial exploitation had a heightened sensitivity to such exploitation. They no longer viewed the sharing of raw biological material as international collaboration but rather as "biocolonialism." As the President of Tanzania said, "[M]ost of us in developing countries find it difficult to accept the notion that biodiversity should [flow freely to industrial countries] while the flow of biological products from the industrial countries is patented, expensive and considered the private property of the firms that produce them. This asymmetry . . . is unjust." Developing countries created property rights over material that they had previously shared to prevent others from taking advantage of them.

A similar sentiment animates patient property claims to biological specimens. Patients willingly donated biological specimens when they believed they were contributing to a greater social good. The obtainment of patent rights by researchers and institutions over cell lines and genetic sequences breached this cooperative spirit. Contributors, like those who joined the effort to find the gene responsible for Canavan disease . . . felt taken advantage of. Their fury and sense of violation do not stem from concern over lost potential economic opportunities, but rather from being played the patsy.

In the case of traditional knowledge, when developed countries began to insist that developing countries cease copying intellectual property goods developed in the West, developing countries expressed resentment over the knowledge that they had shared with the West. It was one thing for societies effectively to share knowledge with each other. It was quite another for technologically-advanced societies to wrap their knowledge in a web of intellectual property protections, while freely using the traditional knowledge of their less developed counterparts.. . .

The chain reaction theory . . . has cautionary implications. It predicts that the more property rights a society recognizes the more property rights it will have in the future. Consequently, policy makers must exercise extreme caution before bowing to the demands of those who initially seek new or expanded property rights. Granting these rights will likely unleash a chain reaction of demands for, and result in the creation of, additional, unanticipated and potentially undesirable property regimes.

NOTES AND QUESTIONS

1. Do you agree that *Chakrabarty* and its progeny are appropriately correlated to claims by developing and least-developed countries for recognition of ownership over raw genetic material? Is Professor Safrin simply cautioning against the expansive reach of modern patent (and indeed all intellectual property) laws in the developed countries or is she pointing to the moral force of the demands by the developing and least-developed countries as the quid pro quo for the TRIPS-era? Is the chain reaction advanced by Professor Safrin the inevitable trade-off (no pun intended!) of global patent law harmonization efforts?

2. Should intangible property rights in inventions be treated similarly to rights in biological or genetic material? As noted by Professor Safrin, property begets property; yet not all property interests are equal. Do you think the demands of the developing and least-developed countries could be met in ways other than through a regime of exclusive rights?

3. In July 2008, a group of World Trade Organization (WTO) member countries introduced a proposed amendment to the Agreement on Trade-Related Aspects of Intellectual Property (TRIPS) which would address these issues as follows:

Members agree to amend the TRIPS Agreement to include a mandatory requirement for the disclosure of the country providing/source of genetic resources, and/or associated traditional knowledge for which a definition will be agreed, in patent applications. Patent applications will not be processed without completion of the disclosure requirement.

Members agree to define the nature and extent of a reference to Prior Informed Consent [PIC] and Access and Benefit Sharing [ABS].

Text based negotiations shall be undertaken . . . to implement the above. Additional elements . . ., such as PIC and ABS as an integral part of the disclosure requirement and post-grant sanctions [such as invalidity or unenforceability], may also be raised and shall be considered in these negotiations.

Draft Modalities for TRIPS Related Issues, TN/C/W/52 (July 19, 2008). The sponsors were Albania, Brazil, China, Colombia, Ecuador, the European Communities, India, Indonesia, the Kyrgyz Republic, Liechtenstein, the Former Yugoslav Republic of Macedonia, Pakistan, Peru, Sri Lanka, Switzerland, Thailand, Turkey, the ACP Group, and the African Group. These same countries were also pushing for an amendment addressing protection of geographical indications of origin in tandem with this proposal. *See* TRIPS: Geographical Indications, Background and the current situation, available at http://www.wto.org/english/tratop_e/trips_e/gi_background_e.htm.   The amendment did not pass, but its introduction may have provided an impetus for the Nagoya Protocol, discussed *infra*.

4. On October 29, 2010, CBD members adopted the Nagoya Protocol on Access to Genetic Resources and the Fair and Equitable Sharing of Benefits Arising from their Utilization. The Nagoya Protocol is a supplementary agreement to the CBD that creates an international framework for access to genetic resources and traditional knowledge with prior informed consent and mutually agreed terms, including terms on fair and equitable benefit sharing from use of genetic resources and associated traditional knowledge. As of March 2013, ninety-two countries had signed the agreement but only fifteen had ratified it. It will not come into force until ninety days after deposit of the fiftieth instrument of ratification. *See* http://www.cbd.int/abs/about. The Nagoya Protocol may be a step forward, but some contend it did not go far enough in addressing human genetic resources and traditional knowledge in particular. *See, e.g.,* M. Nöthling Slabbert, *The Legal Regulation of Access and Benefit-Sharing with Regard to Human Genetic Resources in South Africa,* 74 J. CONTEMP. ROMAN-DUTCH L. 605 (2011); and Reji K. Joseph, *International Regime on Access and Benefit Sharing: Where Are We Now?,* 12 ASIAN BIOTECH & DEV. REV. 77–94 (2010). On January 15, 2013, the European Parliament published a resolution calling for, among other things, swift ratification of the Nagoya Protocol, and the imposition of a requirement that patent applicants disclose the origin of genetic resources used in creating their inventions. *See* EUROPEAN PARLIAMENT RESOLUTION OF 15 JANUARY 2013 ON DEVELOPMENT ASPECTS OF INTELLECTUAL PROPERTY RIGHTS ON GENETIC RESOURCES: THE IMPACT ON POVERTY REDUCTION IN DEVELOPING COUNTRIES

(2012/2135(INI)) available *at* http://www.europarl.europa.eu/sides/getDoc.do?type=TA&language=EN&reference=P7-TA-2013-7.

5. On May 4, 2011, the EPO issued European patent number EP 1962578 to Monsanto Invest B.V. on closterovirus-resistant melon plants. According to the EPO:

> The plants are made resistant by the introduction of a gene from another melon plant by way of a conventional breeding method involving the use of a genetic marker ("marker-assisted breeding"). The gene which is responsible for the resistance was first found in a melon plant in India and catalogued in 1961. It has been publicly available since 1966.

> http://www.epo.org/news-issues/issues/melon.html.

Two oppositions to the melon patent were filed before the opposition period ended in February 2012: one based on lack of novelty and inventive step filed by Nunhems, the vegetable seed-producing subsidiary of Bayer Crop-Science, the other from a coalition of NGOs acting under the heading "No patents on seeds." *See* EPO, The Melon Patent Case-FAQ, http://www.epo.org/news-issues/issues/melon.html. The coalition has asserted technical arguments against the patent and the opposition papers also charge that the melon claimed "is not patentable under Article 53(a) as it is against order public for violating provisions of the Indian Biological Diversity Act, 2002." If Monsanto did not comply with the biodiversity law in India in obtaining genetic material for its invention, should that be grounds for invalidating the patent under Article 53(a)?

The coalition apparently is supported by a diverse group of organizations, including the Berne Declaration (Switzerland), GeneWatch (UK), Greenpeace (Germany), Misereor (Germany), Development Fund (Norway), No Patents on Life (Germany), Reseau Semences Paysannes (France) and Swissaid (Switzerland). These organizations are seeking a revision of EPC to exclude breeding material, plants and animals and food from patentability. More than 250 organizations and over 50,000 individuals have signed a petition to this effect. *See* Vandana Shiva, *Opposition to Monsanto's Patent on Indian Melon*, NAVDANYA (Feb. 3, 2012), http://www.navdanya.org/news/223-opposition-to-monsantoas-patent-on-indian-melon.

6. During its General Assemblies in October 2012, WIPO Member States agreed to a year-long work plan during which developing and least-developed countries hope sufficient progress will be made toward a treaty on the protection of genetic resources, traditional knowledge and folklore. Work on this issue is the focus of the WIPO Intergovernmental Committee on Intellectual Property and Genetic Resources, Traditional Knowledge and Folklore (IGC) which was established in October 2000. The most current IGC texts which are the basis for the ongoing negotiations are available at http://www.wipo.int/tk/en/igc/index.html.

B. UTILITY MODEL, DESIGN, AND PLANT PROTECTION

While this casebook, and most of patent law in general, concerns itself primarily with standard invention patents, other types exist, and the initial decision of which type of patent to apply for can play an important part in patent prosecution. Other types include utility models, design patents, innovation patents, and plant patents, although in some countries, the particular instrument of protection is not denoted a "patent" at all, such as the Community design right in the EU.

1. UTILITY MODELS

Utility models originated in 1891 in Germany, where—known as a *Gebrauchsmuster*—they still constitute an important form of national protection for certain inventions. The requirements for a utility model are generally less stringent than those for a patent, and applicants most often seek utility model protection for products or innovations of an incremental nature that may not necessarily meet the patentability criteria (although applicants also use utility models as a method of getting protection quickly). Utility models require novelty, but the standard of obviousness or inventive step is generally much lower than that for a patent and, in some cases, it is absent altogether. The application process is usually simple and straightforward because most countries do not subject utility model applications to substantive examination, and the time from application to registration is consequently quite short, often less than six months. The term of protection for utility models, however, is also relatively short, ranging from about seven to ten years.

Almost ninety countries provide utility model protection; *see* WIPO, *Where Can Utility Models Be Acquired?* http://www.wipo.int/sme/en/ip_business/utility_models/where.htm, for a list. China currently registers more utility models than any other country. In 2009, applicants filed more than 310,700 utility model applications with China's State Intellectual Property Office, as compared with more than 314,500 invention patent applications. Of the utility model applicants, 99.4 percent were Chinese nationals, making utility model registration an overwhelmingly preferred domestic form of protection in China. By contrast, foreign applicants accounted for over 27 percent of the Chinese invention patent applications in 2009. It is interesting to note that the largest infringement damage award ever granted in China involved a utility model. In 2007, in the case of *Chint Group Corp. v. Schneider Electric Low-Voltage (Tianjin) Co.*, the Wenzhou Intermediate People's Court ordered Schneider to pay $48.5 million in damages. The case settled in 2009 for $23 million.

In Australia, utility models are referred to as innovation patents. They were introduced into Australian law in 2001 as a replacement for the former system of petty patents in order to provide more effective and accessible protection for incremental inventions. What distinguishes innovation patents from standard patents is the requirement that an invention must possess "innovative step"—as opposed to the inventive step required for patents discussed in Chapter 7. The following 2008 Federal Court of Australia decision (affirmed by the Full Court in 2009) addressed the meaning of innovative step for the first time.

DELNORTH PTY LTD V. DURA-POST (AUST) PTY LTD

Federal Court of Australia, Sydney
[2008] FCA 1225

■ GYLES, J.

This case concerns alleged infringement of, and alleged invalidity of, three innovation patents, a new breed of patent that was introduced into the Patents Act 1990 (the Act) effective from 24 May 2001 by the Patents Amendment (Innovation Patents) Act 2000. It followed the Report of the Advisory Council on Intellectual Property (ACIP). The Explanatory Memorandum stated the objectives of the amendment as follows:

The purpose of the proposed innovation patent system is to stimulate innovation in Australian [Small to Medium Enterprises]. It would do this by providing Australian businesses with industrial property rights for their lower level inventions. Industrial property rights are not available for these inventions at present, which means competitors may be able to copy them. For this reason, a firm making lower level inventions cannot be certain of capturing the benefits that come from their commercial exploitation. This lowers the incentive to innovate.

The term of an innovation patent is eight years rather than 20 years as is the case with a standard patent (s 68). Claims are limited to five (s 40(2)(c)).

If a complete application for an innovation patent is made, and if it passes what is described as a formalities check, the Commissioner must accept the patent request and complete specification (s 52). There is a special regime for examination, re-examination and opposition to innovation patents set out in Ch 9A of the Act.... "Patentable invention" is differently defined for the purposes of a standard patent and for the purposes of an innovation patent in s 18 of the Act—the principal difference lies in the fact that, for the former, an inventive step is required and, for the latter, an innovative step. There is apparently no overseas equivalent of innovation patents and the researches of counsel have not turned up any relevant decisions dealing with revocation of innovation patents.

. . .

On 25 November 2005, Application for Innovation Patent No 2005100978 (Patent No 1) was filed and was certified on 2 February 2006. On 24 February 2006, this proceeding was commenced by Delnorth against the respondent Dura-Post (Australia) Pty Ltd (Dura-Post) for infringement of Patent No 1 based upon the manufacture and sale of roadside posts under the name Flexi-Steel post.

On 18 April 2006, Application for Innovation Patent No 2006100297 (Patent No 2) was filed and it was certified on 6 July 2006. The cross-claim and particulars of invalidity were filed by Dura-Post on 5 May 2006.

On 15 August 2006, Application for Innovation Patent No 2006100696 (Patent No 3) was filed and certified on 5 October 2006. By 15 August 2006 Delnorth had manufactured and sold what was known as an "Ezy-Drive Steel Flex" post. The pleadings were amended to allege infringement of Patent No 2 and Patent No 3. Dura-Post denies infringement and claims that Patents No 1, 2 and 3 are each invalid....

Innovative step

Issue 13: What is the proper construction of s 7(4) of the Act? Section 7(4), (5) and (6) are as follows:

"Innovative step

(4) For the purposes of this Act, an invention is to be taken to involve an innovative step when compared with the prior art base unless the invention would, to a person skilled in the relevant art, in the light of the common general knowledge as it existed in the patent area before the priority date of the relevant claim, only vary from the kinds of information set out in subsection (5) in ways that make no substantial contribution to the working of the invention.

(5) For the purposes of subsection (4), the information is of the following kinds:

(a) prior art information made publicly available in a single document or through doing a single act;

(b) prior art information made publicly available in 2 or more related documents, or through doing 2 or more related acts, if the relationship between the documents or acts is such that a person skilled in the relevant art would treat them as a single source of that information.

(6) For the purposes of subsection (4), each kind of information set out in subsection (5) must be considered separately."

"Prior art base" is defined in Sch 1 to mean (so far as is relevant):

"(a) in relation to deciding whether an invention does or does not involve an inventive step or an innovative step:

(i) information in a document that is publicly available, whether in or out of the patent area; and

(ii) information made publicly available through doing an act, whether in or out of the patent area."

"Prior art information" is defined in Sch 1 to mean (so far as is relevant):

"(c) for the purposes of subsection 7(5)-information that is part of the prior art base in relation to deciding whether an invention does or does not involve an innovative step."

This issue lies at the heart of the difference between an innovation patent and a standard patent. So far as the latter is concerned, s 7(2) and s 7(3) are as follows:

"Inventive step

(2) For the purposes of this Act, an invention is to be taken to involve an inventive step when compared with the prior art base unless the invention would have been obvious to a person skilled in the relevant art in the light of the common general knowledge as it existed in the patent area before the priority date of the relevant claim, whether that knowledge is considered separately or together with the information mentioned in subsection (3).

(3) The information for the purposes of subsection (2) is:

(a) any single piece of prior art information; or

(b) a combination of any 2 or more pieces of prior art information;

being information that the skilled person mentioned in subsection (2) could, before the priority date of the relevant claim, be reasonably expected to have ascertained, understood, regarded as relevant and, in the case of information mentioned in paragraph (b), combined as mentioned in that paragraph."

Section 18(1A) commences with the words:

". . . an invention is a patentable invention for the purposes of an innovation patent if the invention, so far as claimed in any claim:

. . .

(b) when compared with the prior art base as it existed before the priority date of that claim:

. . .

(ii) involves an innovative step;"

That is the same in structure as s 18(1) dealing with standard patents and an inventive step.

It is submitted for Dura-Post that there is a difference between the invention, on the one hand, and the innovative step, on the other, based upon the language of s 18(1A) and s 7(4) as the invention has to "involve" an innovative step.

. . .

There is no need to search for some particular advance in the art to be described as an innovative step which governs the consideration of each claim. The first step is to compare the invention as claimed in each claim with the prior art base and determine the difference or differences. The next step is to look at those differences through the eyes of a person skilled in the relevant art in the light of common general knowledge as it existed in Australia before the priority date of the relevant claim and ask whether the invention as claimed only varies from the kinds of information set out in s 7(5) in ways that make no substantial contribution to the working of the invention. It may be that there is a feature of each claim which differs from the prior art base and that could be described as the main difference in each case but that need not be so. Section 7(4), in effect, deems a difference between the invention as claimed and the prior art base as an innovative step unless the conclusion which is set out can be reached. If there is no difference between the claimed invention and the prior art base then, of course, the claimed invention is not novel.

The phrase "no substantial contribution to the working of the invention" involves quite a different kind of judgment from that involved in determining whether there is an inventive step. Obviousness does not come into the issue. The idea behind it seems to be that a claim which avoids a finding of no novelty because of an integer which makes no substantial contribution to the working of the claimed invention should not receive protection but that, where the point of differentiation does contribute to the working of the invention, then it is entitled to protection, whether or not (even if), it is obvious. Indeed, the proper consideration of s 7(4) is liable to be impeded by traditional thinking about obviousness.

NOTES AND QUESTIONS

1. In *Delnorth Pty Ltd v. Dura-Post (Aust) Pty Ltd*, the court held that an innovation patent may be awarded even when the invention claimed is obvious, provided that it makes a contribution that is "real" or "of substance" to the working of the invention. Thus innovation patents can provide important protection for incremental inventions that would not meet the non-obviousness requirements for a utility patent but still represent an advance. Is there any downside to the issuance of such innovation patents?

2. As noted above, utility models may be granted with no substantive examination at all, as is the case in China. For countries that allow such rights to be granted without substantive examination, an opportunity for the patent office to consider the validity of a utility model asserted in infringement litigation can be critically important. Thus defendants charged with infringing utility models generally will seek reexamination or institute a nullity action to challenge the validity of the grant. We study an example of the importance of such a reexamination proceeding to infringement litigation in the *Shenzhen Triangle v. Compaq* case, involving a Chinese utility model, in Chapter 10, *infra*.

3. A significant amount of patent litigation in Germany, the country with the most patent suits in Europe, involves utility models. *See* Michael C. Elmer & Stacy D. Lewis, *Where to Win: Patent-Friendly Courts Revealed*, MANAGING INTELL. PROP. 4 (2010). It appears utility models are used strategically in Germany because they generally are granted more quickly by the patent office (due to the lower requirements for novelty and non-obviousness), and thus can be asserted against an alleged infringer while a utility patent application covering aspects of the same invention is still undergoing examination. Then, if and when the utility patent issues, it can be added to the utility model lawsuit so that any resulting injunction will last for the duration of the utility patent, not just the shorter term of the utility model. With the increasing numbers of utility models being filed in China and the potential for significant damages awards available, it is likely that litigation involving such utility models will increase there as well; possibly to the detriment of foreign companies who, so far, are not meaningfully availing themselves of this useful tool. For differing views on the benefits of utility models in China in particular, *see* Patricia E. Campbell & Michael Pecht, *The Emperor's New Clothes: Intellectual Property Protections in China*, 7 J. BUS. & TECH. L. 69, 90, 91 (2012), and Mark S. Zhai, *The Chinese Utility Model Patent Is Destroying Innovation in China*, 39 AIPLA Q.J. 413, 423–424 (2011).

4. Recall that the principal distinction between a utility model and a patent is the degree of inventive step required. What policy objectives justify utility models as a form of protection? Is the degree of innovation required sufficient to justify the award of exclusive rights? Why or why not? Should more nations, particularly those at less sophisticated levels of industrial development, be encouraged to adopt systems of utility model protection?

5. In 1995 the European Commission initiated work on a proposal to establish a Community-wide directive on the protection of inventions by utility model. The initiative was suspended in 2000 because of lack of support from member nations. Similarly, there have been unheeded calls for the United States to adopt a system of utility model protection. *See, e.g.,* Mark D. Janis, *Second Tier Patent Protection,* 40 HARV. INT'L L.J. 151 (1999). Why do you think the idea of harmonized utility model protection has not caught on across Europe and in the U.S.?

2. DESIGN PROTECTION

A *design patent* is a patent granted on the ornamental design of a functional item. While a standard invention patent protects the way an article is used or works, a design patent protects the way it looks. As an example, the following is the U.S. design patent, granted in 1915, for the original Coca Cola® bottle:

A design patent is a type of design right. Article 25 of the TRIPS Agreement requires that "[m]embers shall provide for the protection of independently created industrial designs that are new or original"; however, the Agreement does not stipulate the means of protection that countries must adopt. While the U.S. and China protect designs through the grant of patents, most countries, including the members of the EU, Brazil, Canada, South Africa, Japan, and Korea, protect designs as a distinct intellectual property right separate from patents. For example, the Office for Harmonization in the Internal Market (OHIM), the EU agency responsible for Community design protection, grants a Registered Community Design (RCD). An RCD, which protects "the appearance of the whole or a part of a product resulting from the features of, in particular, the lines, contours, colours, shape, texture and/or materials of the product itself and/or its ornamentation," has an initial five-year duration, which can be renewed for successive periods of five years up to a maximum of twenty-five years. *See* Articles 3(a), 12, Council Regulation (EC) No 6/2002 of 12 December 2001 on Community Designs, 2002 O.J. (L 3) 1. While the design covered by the RCD is required to be novel, the OHIM does not engage in a novelty examination during the registration process. Thus design protection can be obtained often more quickly and less expensively than utility patent protection, yet, can be just as valuable if infringement is found and an EU-wide injunction is granted. The following decision from the UK concerning the famous Apple tablet computer, the iPad, illustrates the infringement analysis for an RCD.

SAMSUNG ELECTRONICS (UK) LIMITED V. APPLE INC.
UK Court of Appeal [2012] EWCA Civ. 1339

SIR ROBIN JACOB . . . GIVING THE FIRST JUDGMENT AT THE INVITATION OF LONGMORE LJ:

1. HHJ Birss QC sitting as a Deputy Judge of the Patents Court, gave two judgments in favour of Samsung (I shall use "Samsung" variously to mean Samsung Electronics (UK) Ltd., the UK subsidiary of the Korean company Samsung Electronics Co. Ltd, "SEC", or the entire Samsung Group. The context will make it clear which). The judgments are under appeal by Apple. By the first, of 9th July 2012, Judge Birss held that three Samsung Galaxy tablet computers, the 10.1, the 8.9 and the 7.7 did not infringe Apple's registered Community Design No. 000181607–0001. By the second, of 18th July 2012, he held that Apple should be compelled to publicise the fact that it had lost in manners specified in the consequential order. . . .

. . .

3. Because this case (and parallel cases in other countries) has generated much publicity, it will avoid confusion to say what this case is about and not about. It is not about whether Samsung copied Apple's iPad. Infringement of a registered design does not involve any question of whether there was copying: the issue is simply whether the accused design is too close to the registered design according to the tests laid down in the law. . . Likewise there is no issue about infringement of any patent for an invention.

4. So this case is all about, and only about, Apple's registered design and the Samsung products. The registered design is not the same as the design of the iPad. It is quite a lot different. For instance the iPad is a lot thinner, and has noticeably different curves on its sides. . . . Whether the iPad would fall within the scope of protection of the registered design is completely irrelevant. We are not deciding that one way or the other. This case must be decided as if the iPad never existed.

5. Other disputes between the parties in other countries have concerned other intellectual property rights. We are not concerned with any of them. So far as this registered design and the three Samsung tablets is concerned I simply . . . record the position. . . . [The judge then proceeded to note the pending status of Apple/Samsung Community Design cases in the Netherlands, Spain, and Germany, noting the EU-wide injunction issued in Germany that this UK decision effectively overruled, while simultaneously nullifying the other proceedings. He also mentioned the litigation in the U.S. regarding the Apple design patent which corresponds to the Community Design Registration and which also had been resolved in Samsung's favor, noting that U.S. design patent infringement is "somewhat different" than that for an RCD. -EDS.]

6. The upshot of all this is that there is now no injunction anywhere based on the registered design or its equivalent.

The non-infringement appeal

7. The Community Design involved was registered on 24th May 2004—an aeon ago in terms of computers. It consists of seven views. The product in which the design is intended for incorporation is a "handheld computer".
. . .

9. The legal test for infringement—the scope of protection—is set out in Art. 10 of the Community Design Regulation EC 6/2002:

> Article 10 Scope of protection
>
> 1. The scope of the protection conferred by a Community design shall include any design which does not produce on the informed user a different overall impression.
>
> 2. In assessing the scope of protection, the degree of freedom of the designer in developing his design shall be taken into consideration.

10. The notional character whose attributes the court has to adopt is the "informed user." The Judge dealt with these attributes:

> [33] The designs are assessed from the perspective of the informed user. The identity and attributes of the informed user have been discussed by the Court of Justice of the European Union in *PepsiCo v. Grupo Promer* (C-281/10P) [2012] FSR 5 at paragraphs 53 to 59 and also in *Grupo Promer v. OHIM* [2010] ECDR 7, (in the General Court from which *PepsiCo* was an appeal) and in *Shenzhen Taiden v. OHIM*, case T-153/08, 22 June 2010, BAILII: [2010] EUECJ T-153/08.
>
> [34] Samsung submitted that the following summary [culled from the CJEU decisions] characterises the informed user. . . .:

He (or she) is a user of the product in which the design is intended to be incorporated, not a designer, technical expert, manufacturer or seller.

However, unlike the average consumer of trade mark law, he is particularly observant;

He has knowledge of the design corpus and of the design features normally included in the designs existing in the sector concerned;

He is interested in the products concerned and shows a relatively high degree of attention when he uses them;

He conducts a direct comparison of the designs in issue unless there are specific circumstances or the devices have certain characteristics which make it impractical or uncommon to do so.

[35] I would add that the informed user neither (a) merely perceives the designs as a whole and does not analyse details, nor (b) observes in detail minimal differences which may exist.

11. Subject to two minor criticisms to which I will come, Mr Silverleaf on behalf of Apple accepted this summary of the law. Note that it includes reference to the *Grupo Promer/Pepsico* case, both before the General Court of the CJEU and before the CJEU itself (the case name is different but it is the same case). And note further that the CJEU expressly approved what the General Court had said about the informed user:

[53] It should be noted, first, that Regulation No 6/2002 does not define the concept of the 'informed user'. However, as the Advocate General correctly observed in points 43 and 44 of his Opinion, that concept must be understood as lying somewhere between that of the average consumer, applicable in trade mark matters, who need not have any specific knowledge and who, as a rule, makes no direct comparison between the trade marks in conflict, and the sectoral expert, who is an expert with detailed technical expertise. Thus, the concept of the informed user may be understood as referring, not to a user of average attention, but to a particularly observant one, either because of his personal experience or his extensive knowledge of the sector in question. . .

. . . .

13. Apple's first criticism of the Judge's approach in law was this: it submitted that the informed user, noting that the design was from 2004, would know and expect that advances in technology would make thinner tablets possible. Hence, it suggested, the informed user would give little significance to the thickness of the design as registered.

14. I do not agree for two reasons. First is that the scope of protection is for the design as registered, not some future, even if foreseeable, variant. Second is that Apple's point cuts both ways: if the informed user could foresee thinner tablets ere long so could Apple whom the informed user would take to have the same prevision. Thus the informed user would take the thickness to be a deliberate design choice by Apple.

15. The second criticism was based on the fact that the Judge took account of the fact that the Samsung products had the trade mark Samsung on both their fronts and backs. It was submitted that the informed user would disregard the trade mark altogether as being a mere conventional addition to the design of the accused product.

16. Actually what the Judge said about the trade mark being on the front of the Samsung tablets was said in the context that Apple was contending that a feature of the registered design was "A flat transparent surface without any ornamentation covering the front face of the device up to the rim." He said:

> [113] All three tablets are the same as far as feature (ii) is concerned. The front of each Samsung tablet has a tiny speaker grille and a tiny camera hole near the top edge and the name Samsung along the bottom edge.

> [114] The very low degree of ornamentation is notable. However a difference is the clearly visible camera hole, speaker grille and the name Samsung on the front face. Apple submitted that the presence of branding was irrelevant .... However in the case before me, the unornamented nature of the front face is a significant aspect of the Apple design. The Samsung design is not unornamented. It is like the LG Flatron. I find that the presence of writing on the front of the tablet is a feature which the informed user will notice (as well as the grille and camera hole). The fact that the writing happens to be a trade mark is irrelevant. It is ornamentation of some sort. The extent to which the writing gives the tablet an orientation is addressed below.

> [115] The Samsung tablets look very close to the Apple design as far as this feature is concerned but they are not absolutely identical as a result of a small degree of ornamentation.

17. So what the Judge was considering was the fact that unlike the design, the front face had some sort of ornamentation which happened to be a trade mark (plus speaker grill and camera hole). Little turned on it in his view, he called it "a small degree of ornamentation." But it was a difference.

18. I think the Judge was correct here. If an important feature of a design is no ornamentation, as Apple contended and was undisputed, the Judge was right to say that a departure from no ornamentation would be taken

into account by the informed user. Where you put a trade mark can influence the aesthetics of a design, particularly one whose virtue in part rests on simplicity and lack of ornamentation. The Judge was right to say that an informed user would give it appropriate weight—which in the overall assessment was slight. If the only difference between the registered design and the Samsung products was the presence of the trade mark, then things would have been different.

19. Much the same goes for the Samsung trade mark on the back of the products. Apple had contended that a key feature was "a design of extreme simplicity without features which specify orientation." Given that contention the Judge can hardly have held that an informed user would completely disregard the trade marks both front and back which reduce simplicity a bit and do indicate orientation.

20. There was no error of law here—and in any event the point was not one on which the case turned as the Judge made clear. . . .

25. Having got these minor skirmishes out of the way, I turn to the main question, was the Judge wrong in his assessment of a different overall impression to the informed user?

. . . .

27. [M]r Silverleaf submitted he [was]: that he approached the design corpus wrongly and failed properly to consider the designs as a whole. The heart of the latter submission was that the Judge went about the comparison exercise piecemeal, feature by feature, and failed to have regard to the overall impression of the registered design as compared with any of the items of prior art contained within the design corpus. . . .

28. I accept that submission as a matter of law. But I do not think the Judge remotely did that. The Judge was entirely aware of the need to consider the overall impression of the design as it would strike the informed user bearing in mind both the design corpus and the extent of design freedom. He said so both at the outset and at his conclusion:

> [31] I start by reminding myself that what really matters is what the court can see with its own eyes. . . . The most important things are the registered design, the accused object and the prior art and the most important thing about each of these is what they look like.

> [32] I also remind myself that while the exercise is a visual one, judgments have to be written and reasons necessarily expressed in words. However I must bear in mind that it is the overall impression which counts and not a verbalised list of features, . . .

And, when he came to consider the overall impression of the Apple design having considered the various features of the design:

[178] Having gone through the various features individually it is necessary to pull it all together and consider the overall impression of the Apple design on an informed user.

29. It is of course the case that, of necessity, the Judge had to go through a "verbalised list of features." Apple can hardly complain about that since the Judge used the very list of seven features it had identified and invited him to use.

30. I do not think it worthwhile or correct to consider each feature in all the meticulous detail which the Judge, of necessity, had to undertake. I shall concentrate on the most important.

31. However before I do so it should be noted that Samsung did not contend that any of these features were "dictated solely by function." Such a feature is excluded from consideration by virtue of Art. 81. It means a feature which is purely functional, not to some degree chosen for the purpose of enhancing the product's visual appearance . . . .

32. However Samsung did submit, and the Judge accepted, that in some respects there is only a limited degree of freedom for any designer of a tablet computer, particularly in relation to the appearance of the front and rather more for the back.

33. I turn to the front first. For it is obviously the most important feature of all, that which strikes the eye and would strike the eye of the informed user as most important. Its features are verbalised by the first four features identified by Apple:

> (i) A rectangular, biaxially symmetrical slab with four evenly, slightly rounded corners;

> (ii) A flat transparent surface without any ornamentation covering the entire front face of the device up to the rim;

> (iii) A very thin rim of constant width, surrounding and flush with the front transparent surface;

> (iv) A rectangular display screen surrounded by a plain border of generally constant width centred beneath the transparent surface.

I would add one other feature, that the edges of the front as shown on the representations are sharp. The sides are at 90° to the plane of the front face. So the thin rim has only its side visible on a front view.

34. I propose to consider design restraint first. The Judge held that:

> [104] The rectangular display screen is totally banal and determined solely by function. Apart from that there are some other design constraints applicable to this feature but they do not account for the identity between the Samsung tablets and the Apple design. These devices do not need to have biaxial symmetry

nor be strictly rectangular. Nevertheless the significance of this identity is reduced by the fact that there are other designs in the design corpus which are very similar too.

35. So you could have a front face of somewhat different shape, but the general shape (rectangular with rounded edges) is not that significant. I do not see how that assessment can be criticised.

36. As to item (ii) (transparent and flat over the entire face with no ornamentation), the Judge found that flatness was common and transparency essential. He held that there was a certain amount of design freedom (you could have a bezel or raised frame). Touch screen technology meant you did not need a raised frame to protect the screen. The degree of ornamentation of the front was a matter of designer choice.

37. As to the thin rim:

> [119] As before, this aspect of the design is the product of trade offs by the designer which include functional considerations but also include aesthetics. The designer can choose to have a flush rim or a bezel, can choose the rim thickness and whether it is constant around the device. Within a general overall constraint, the designer has significant aesthetic design freedom.

38. And as to the border within the frame:

> [126] I find that there is a degree of design constraint applicable here. The devices need some kind of border. The border need not be as described in feature (iv) but there are limits on design freedom.

The Judge added this:

> [127] Irrespective of the matter of design freedom, to my eye, feature (iv) would strike the informed user as a rather common feature.

39. All of this appears to be a proper assessment of the degree of design freedom. In overall terms for a hand-held tablet (1) you need a flat transparent screen, (2) rounded corners are unremarkable (and have some obvious functional value in a hand-held device), and (3) you need a border of some sort for functional reasons. There is some design freedom as regards ornamentation, the rim, the overall shape (rectangular or with some curved sides) but not a lot. And the main thing, the screen itself was something with which the informed user would be familiar . . . .

40. The Judge also cannot be faulted in his assessment of the design corpus in relation to the front of hand-held computers. Of particular relevance are the following:

The Flatron

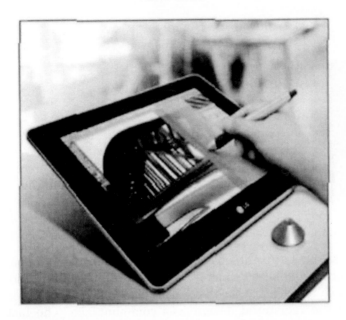

We were shown a physical example of this. The front is very close to that of the registered design, save that it departs from lack of orientation by a little LG logo. The back is rather different, as I shall come to.

Ozolins, US Patent Appn. 2004/0041504 A1

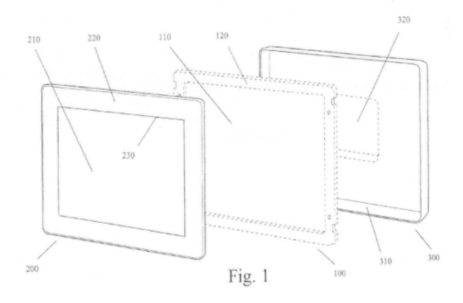

Fig. 1

Bloomberg (A Community RD of 2003)

41. There was a debate, entirely sterile as far as I can see, about whether other Bloomberg publications showed the same thing or something similar. I do not go into it, for there was no suggestion that the appearance of the front of the registered design was commonplace. The fact remains that other items of the design corpus show fronts very close to the Apple design.

42. Mr Silverleaf complained that the judge referred to a "family" of designs having similar fronts. But I see no significance in that. He clearly recognised that fronts of this sort were not commonplace, and so, whether one called the above three designs a "family" is immaterial.

43. As to the sides, it is rather apparent that the Apple design has the 90° sharp edge to which I have referred. It matters because the informed user (indeed any user) would notice it. It gives the Apple design a sharp outline. The Judge called it a "crisp edge." The Samsung products are very different in relation to this and the sides generally. Before us Apple put in an exhibit (without complaint from Mr Carr) which illustrates this vividly because it has been enlarged and shows the side views of the registered design and the three accused products on the same scale:

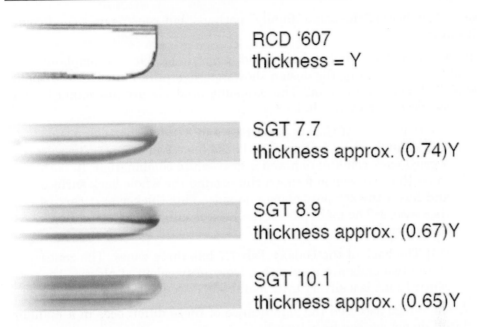

RCD '607
thickness = Y

SGT 7.7
thickness approx. (0.74)Y

SGT 8.9
thickness approx. (0.67)Y

SGT 10.1
thickness approx. (0.65)Y

By contrast with the crisp edge of the design, all three of the Samsung products have a side which curves a little outwards (so a bit bezel-like) before curving back in and under. And none of them have a vertical portion.

44. Apple's features (v) and (vi) related to the back and sides of the design:

v) A substantially flat rear surface which curves upwards at the sides and comes to meet the front surface at a crisp outer edge;

vi) A thin profile, the impression of which is emphasised by (v) above.

45. The Judge said of feature (v):

[150] There is one serious design constraint applicable to this feature. The back needs to be generally flat. Apart from that there is considerable design freedom. The sides are very similar but these kinds of sides for products are not unusual. The informed user would recognise the Apple design in this respect as belonging to a familiar class of products with somewhat curved sides and a fairly crisp edge. The Samsung tablets are members of the same familiar class.

I cannot see how there could be any complaint about this. Actually to my eye what he said was if anything too favourable to Apple. For there is surely a real design difference between Apple's sharp edge, vertical side followed by a nearly circular arc of rounding and each of Samsung's products. Members of the same "family" perhaps, but cousins or second cousins at most.

46. As to the back, as the Judge said it had to be flat. No complaint was made about that. But the design shows more: a pure flat surface without embellishment of any kind. The Samsung products are altogether busier in ways described by the Judge . . .

> [13] The backs of Galaxy Tabs 10.1 and 8.9 have what Samsung call a clutch purse feature. The backs have two colours. There is a gray/black combination and a gray/white combination. In both cases the gray region forms a rim around the whole back surface and has a thicker part along one side. This thicker part carries the camera. The main part of the back is either black or white as the case may be.

> [14] The back of the Galaxy Tab 7.7 has three zones. The zones at the two ends are a smooth silvery gray coloured plastic. The central zone is a silvery gray metal with a rougher texture.

47. The Judge assessed the significance of these differences in a manner which I do not see can be bettered . . . .

48. As to Apple's final feature, "Overall, a design of extreme simplicity without features which specify orientation", the Judge accepted that accurately applied to the registered design. As I have said he noted that the Samsung products did have features which specified orientation (notably the trade mark but also the camera and speaker) and the other matters which made them more complicated design-wise.

49. Mr Silverleaf had another complaint. He submitted that insofar as there were items of the design corpus which had fronts very similar to that of the registered design, those items had very different backs—nothing like the flat back and the sides of the registered design. So if you looked at the designs as whole—in the round—the design corpus products produced a very different impression whereas the impressions produced by the Samsung products and the registered design produced were much the same.

50. Thus, for instance, although the Flatron had a large front face looking very close to the design (and Samsung) the back was different. It looked like this:

The stand . . . could be optionally fitted to the silvered computer which could be hand-held. So it is irrelevant. But the lump on the back of the screen was integral with it. No doubt it contained functional electronics and the like. We were shown a physical example of the Flatron—it is much bigger than any of the Samsung products (or an iPad for that matter). Just about hand-holdable.

51. I do not accept Mr Silverleaf's criticism for three reasons. First, whilst of course the statutory question requires the court to consider the reaction of the informed user to the "overall impression," any sort of user, informed or not, would be apt notionally to consider the front and back rather separately. Secondly at least to my mind the Flatron in particular, looks very much like a two-part construction—like a large tablet with something stuck on to its back. And thirdly even if Mr Silverleaf were right, the implication is that the back matters rather a lot. Assuming that to be so it would lead the notional informed user to notice how different the backs of the Samsung products are as compared with the registered design (much thicker, even in the case of the 7.7, quite different curvatures, no sharp edge, and busier flat portion) . . . .

52. There is also this—a point I have touched on before and which the Judge rightly thought important. The Samsung products are all significantly and immediately noticeably thinner than the registered design. Even the 7.7 which, being the smallest is relatively thicker than the other two, is visually significantly thinner. Doubtless that is why it was contended, wrongly as I have said, that the informed user would pay little attention to thinness. I think the Judge would have been wrong if he had not held that the informed user would consider the relative thinness of the product as forming a significant part of the overall impression.

53. Overall I cannot begin to see any material error by the Judge. He may have been wrong about how many Bloombergs there were or how another piece of the design corpus, Stevenson was to be understood, but that in no

way impairs his overall conclusion, arrived at by using his own eyes and taking into account both the design corpus and the extent to which there was design freedom:

> [190] The informed user's overall impression of each of the Samsung Galaxy Tablets is the following. From the front they belong to the family which includes the Apple design; but the Samsung products are very thin, almost insubstantial members of that family with unusual details on the back. They do not have the same understated and extreme simplicity which is possessed by the Apple design. They are not as cool. The overall impression produced is different.

54. I would add that even if I were forming my own view of the matter, I would have come to the same conclusion and for the same reasons. If the registered design has a scope as wide as Apple contends it would foreclose much of the market for tablet computers. Alterations in thickness, curvature of the sides, embellishment and so on would not escape its grasp. Legitimate competition by different designs would be stifled. [The judge went on to uphold the order that Apple publicize the non-infringement decision]

. . .

88. In the result I would dismiss both appeals . . . .

NOTES AND QUESTIONS

1. As the court noted in the *Samsung v. Apple* case (so styled because Samsung sued for a declaration of non-infringement and Apple countered with an infringement claim), the court noted that Apple had obtained a design patent in the U.S. on the same design as was protected by the RCD, and in U.S. litigation, Samsung's tablet also escaped design infringement liability. Recall from Chapter 2 that the Paris Convention right of priority applies to designs, but with only a six-month priority period. Thus the RCD must have been filed within six months of the filing date of the U.S. design patent application from which it claimed priority.

2. As Sir Robin Jacob noted in *Samsung v. Apple*, design patent infringement in the U.S. is "somewhat different" to infringement of an RCD. *Id.* at para. 5. An *en banc* Court of Appeals for the Federal Circuit reaffirmed the "ordinary observer" test in *Egyptian Goddess v. Swisa*, 543 F.3d 665 (Fed. Cir. 2008), as the sole test for determining design patent infringement. The test, articulated in *Gorham Co. v. White*, 81 U.S. 511, 528 (1871), is "[I]f, in the eye of an ordinary observer, giving such attention as a purchaser usually gives, two designs are substantially the same, if the resemblance is such as to deceive such an observer, inducing him to purchase one supposing it to be the other, the first one patented is infringed by the other." In *Egyptian Goddess,*

the Federal Circuit rejected its "point of novelty" test, previously used in conjunction with the "ordinary observer" test:

> [T]his court has held that proof of similarity under the ordinary observer test is not enough to establish design patent infringement. Rather, the court has stated that the accused design must also appropriate the novelty of the claimed design in order to be deemed infringing [the "point of novelty" test] . . . . [W]e conclude that the point of novelty test, as a second and free-standing requirement for proof of design patent infringement, is inconsistent with the ordinary observer test . . . Applying the ordinary observer test with reference to prior art designs [avoids] problems created by the separate point of novelty test. One such problem is that the point of novelty test has proved difficult to apply in cases in which there are several different features that can be argued to be points of novelty in the claimed design. In such cases, the outcome of the case can turn on which of the several candidate points of novelty the court or factfinder focuses on. The attention of the court may therefore be focused on whether the accused design has appropriated a single specified feature of the claimed design, rather than on the proper inquiry, i.e., whether the accused design has appropriated the claimed design as a whole. . . . Our rejection of the point of novelty test does not mean, of course, that the differences between the claimed design and prior art designs are irrelevant. To the contrary, examining the novel features of the claimed design can be an important component of the comparison of the claimed design with the accused design and the prior art. But the comparison of the designs, including the examination of any novel features, must be conducted as part of the ordinary observer test, not as part of a separate test focusing on particular points of novelty that are designated only in the course of litigation.

Id. at 670–678.

How might eliminating the point of novelty test affect the infringement determination? Would you expect infringement to be easier or more difficult to establish? The *Egyptian Goddess* case and the point of novelty test are analyzed in historical perspective in James Juo, Egyptian Goddess: *Rebooting Design Patents and Resurrecting* Whitman Saddle, 18 FED. CIR. BAR J. 429 (2009).

3. The Federal Circuit recently added a further refinement to the ordinary observer test by noting that purely functional design features can be abstracted (i.e. not considered) when comparing a patented design to an allegedly infringing design. *See Richardson v. Stanley Works, Inc.*, 597 F.3d 1288 (Fed. Cir. 2010). Is this approach simply a variation of the point of novelty test in reverse, or an important and prudent development? If a function can be performed many ways, how can one determine if a particular feature is purely functional? For a critical analysis of the functionality doctrine in

design protection law, see Jason J. DuMont and Mark D. Janis, *Functionality in Design Protection Systems*, 19 J. INTELL. PROP. L. 261 (2012).

4. On 24th July 2012 the German Court of Appeal, the Oberland-esgericht, granted Apple's request for an EU-wide injunction against the Samsung 7.7 tablet. The injunction was granted after Judge Birss's UK decision finding no infringement by the Samsung 7.7 of Apple's RCD. In a portion of the *Samsung v. Apple* decision not reproduced above, Sir Jacob took issue with the action of the German Court:

> I cannot understand on what basis the Court thought it had jurisdiction to grant interim relief. I do not think it did for several reasons.

> Firstly it is common ground that no German court was "first seized" of the claim for a declaration of non-infringement. Indeed given that Apple withdrew its claim for infringement in Germany, no German court appears even now to be seized of a claim for infringement. It is true that Samsung applied for declarations of non-infringement on the same day, 8th September 2011 in Spain, the Netherlands and England and Wales and there could be (but I think rather overtaken by events given that the trial and appeal are over here) a dispute about which case started first in point of time. After all there is now a Community-wide decision on the point, now affirmed on appeal. One would think that ought to put an end to all other litigation about it.

> Secondly I cannot see any basis for an interim injunction. The UK court had already granted a final declaration. Moreover it was sitting not just as a UK court but as a Community Court. Interim injunctions are what you grant in urgent cases where there is not enough time to have a full trial on the merits. That was not this case. Lord Grabiner told us that the Oberlandesgericht had jurisdiction pursuant to Art. 31 of the Brussels Regulation EC/44/2001. But that relates to "provisional, including protective measures." There was no room for "provisional" measures once Judge Birss, sitting as a Community Court had granted a final declaration of non-infringement.

> Further Judge Birss was not sitting as a purely national court. He was sitting as a Community design court, see Arts. 80 and 81 of the Designs Regulation 44/2001. So his declaration of non-infringement was binding throughout the Community. It was not for a national court—particularly one not first seized—to interfere with this Community wide jurisdiction and declaration.

> The Oberlandesgericht apparently also thought it had jurisdiction because the party before it was SEC whereas the party before the English court was SEC's UK subsidiary. With great respect that is quite unrealistic commercially—especially as I shall recount below, Apple at least took the view that SEC would be liable for the subsid-

iary's actions. They were all one "undertaking". I use the word of EU law for this sort of situation.

What the Oberlandesgericht did not do was to consider Judge Birss's decision in detail. It gave only meagre reasons for saying "The Court cannot concur with the interpretation of the High Court". I regret that. In *Grimme v. Scott* [2010] EWCA Civ 1110, this Court said:

> [63] Broadly we think the principle in our courts—and indeed that in the courts of other member states—should be to try to follow the reasoning of an important decision in another country. Only if the court of one state is convinced that the reasoning of a court in another member state is erroneous should it depart from a point that has been authoritatively decided there. Increasingly that has become the practice in a number of countries, particularly in the important patent countries of France, Germany, Holland and England and Wales. Nowadays we refer to each other's decisions with a frequency which would have been hardly imaginable even twenty years ago. And we do try to be consistent where possible.

> [64] The Judges of the patent courts of the various countries of Europe have thereby been able to create some degree of uniformity even though the European Commission and the politicians continue to struggle on the long, long road which one day will give Europe a common patent court.

That principle was not followed by the Oberlandesgericht. If courts around Europe simply say they do not agree with each other and give inconsistent decisions, Europe will be the poorer.

Id. at para. 56–63. What does this kerfluffle between the UK and German courts say about the real level of harmonization of an ostensibly harmonized (RCD) right? For more on cross-border injunctions, *see* Marketa Trimble, *Cross-Border Injunctions in U.S. Patent Cases and Their Enforcement Abroad*, 13 MARQ. INTELL. PROP. L. REV. 331 (2009).

5. While the RCD system is registration only, U.S. law requires design patent applications to be substantively examined for novelty and non-obviousness. However, according to Professor Crouch the U.S. actually has a *de facto* registration system that is pretty close to the RCD now:

> [T]he USPTO's examination of design patent novelty can best be described as a farce. In a 2010 study, I found that the vast majority of design patent applications do not receive even a single rejection during the examination process and only 1.2% are the subject of an obviousness or novelty rejection.

Dennis Crouch, *UK Appellate Court Confirms Pan-European Win for Samsung on iPad Community Design Charges*, PATENLYO (Oct. 18, 2010). What are the benefits and disadvantages of granting protection (and the right to sue for infringement) to designs that have not first been evaluated for novelty?

6. In another portion of the *Samsung v. Apple* decision not reproduced above, the court discussed the legal effect of dotted lines in the Apple RCD drawing:

> There is one other point about how the informed user would assess the registered design, a point decided by the Judge adversely to Samsung. Views 0001.1 and 0001.3 show the front of the tablet. There is a rectangular dotted line shown. Apple submitted, and the Judge accepted, that the dotted line indicated a frame below a glass face—of the kind now familiar on all sorts of touch-screen devices. Samsung ran a complicated point based on the guidelines for examination. It submitted these would lead the informed user to conclude that the dotted lines were there to indicate that a feature was not protected: thus the fact that the Samsung device does have a "frame" is to be disregarded.

> This is faintly absurd: a bit like the notice-board reading "Ignore this notice." For if there were no dotted rectangular line, the front face of the design as registered would be entirely plain. So it would then be for the informed user to form a judgment as to whether a tablet with a frame created a different overall impression. In short, on Samsung's contention if there were no dotted lines the position would the same as if they were there.

> The Judge rejected the contention. He was right to do so. The simplest explanation ... is this: the drawings have hatching which clearly indicates a flat, shiny, surface. This goes over the dotted line. So the latter is there to show a border below the shiny transparent surface.

> Mr Silverleaf submitted further that the informed user would know about flat screens with "frames" under the glass. They were known and the frames had a known, technical purpose of providing space for the necessary electronics. This, the informed user would readily see, is what is being shown here, that with which he is familiar. I agree. The point has repercussions, however, on the scope of protection.

[2012] EWCA Civ 1339, para. 21–24. This interpretation is contrary to how the U.S. treats such dotted lines in design patents. Consider, for example, U.S. design patent Des. 391,999 for an "Activity Block." Figure 1 shows a toy block and a dotted line drawing of an elephant, to indicate that *something*, not necessarily that elephant, can be inserted inside the block:

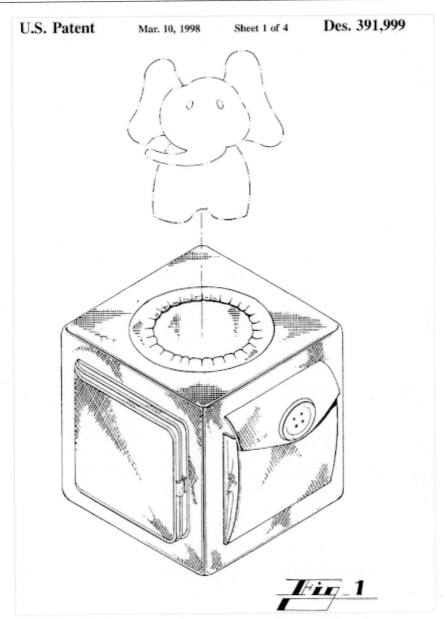

U.S. Patent   Mar. 10, 1998   Sheet 1 of 4   Des. 391,999

Fig. 1

The patent states "[t]he broken line showing of the insertable toy is for illustrative purposes only and forms no part of the claimed design."

In commenting on the *Samsung v. Apple* court's dotted line discussion, Professor Crouch notes:

Although minor in the context of this appeal, Lord Justice Jacob has an interesting comment on the dotted "ghost" lines that have become common in US design patent drafting. According to the MPEP, those lines are allowed as "Environmental structure" so long as "clearly designated as environment in the specification." MPEP § 1503. The Apple registration included a dotted line frame showing the boundary of the operational portion of its screen. Samsung unsuccessfully argued that dotted line should not be given any patentable weight based upon what Jacob, LJ calls "a complicated point based on the guidelines for examination." . . . . This development if applied broadly could actually become a major source of contention and difficulty in implementing the global design rights system suggested by the Hague Agreement.

Dennis Crouch, *UK Appellate Court Confirms Pan-European Win for Samsung on iPad Community Design Charges, supra.*

In 2009, China received over 351,300 design patent applications, making China the world's leader in design protection; it received 521,468 such applications in 2011. Almost 97 percent of the applications come from Chinese applicants. Article 2 of the Chinese Patent Law defines a patentable design as "a new design of a product's shape, pattern or the combination thereof, or the combination of its color and shape and/or pattern, that is aesthetically pleasing and industrially applicable." Recent amendments to the Chinese law, which came into effect on October 1, 2009, established a worldwide absolute novelty test for protection. Also, in Article 23, the new law requires that a design "must be substantially different from prior designs or a combination of features of prior designs." Previously, the Act required only that the design not be similar to prior designs. In addition, in an attempt to prevent copied trademarks from being patented as designs, Article 25(5) of the Act excludes graphic designs from protection if their main function is identification.

The leading design patent case in China concerns a design patent for a bus. The owner of the design patent, a German bus manufacturer, sued two Chinese companies for infringement. As the following summary explains, the case illustrates the value of design patent protection in creating infringement liability for competitors.

NEOPLAN BUS GMBH V. ZHONGWEI BUS & COACH GROUP ET AL.

File No. N090103

Two Chinese Companies Lose Bus Design Patent Infringement Case to German Bus Maker[1]

www.chinacourt.org, Jan. 21, 2009

At the conclusion of trial proceedings that lasted two years, the Beijing First Intermediate People's Court handed down its decision in a well-publicized bus patent infringement case. The case was among those that have attracted the most attention since China's entry into the WTO. The court held that the "A9" design buses made and sold by Yancheng Zhong-

---

[1] Text edited by the authors for grammar and style.

wei Bus and Coach Group (Zhongwei Group) and Zonda Industrial Group infringed the design patent right of the German bus maker Neoplan Bus GmbH, owner of the patent to the design of the "Starliner" bus. The two Chinese companies were ordered to pay damages in the amount of RMB 21.16 million (about US $3.11 million).

On September 23, 2004, Neoplan Bus of Germany applied for a design patent for its Starliner buses and started manufacturing and selling the buses in China. In the spring of 2006, Neoplan Bus determined that Yancheng Zhongwei Bus and Coach Group and Zonda Industrial Group were making and selling buses that infringed the Starliner design patent. Beijing Zhongtong Xinghua Auto Sales Co., Ltd. was also found selling the allegedly infringing buses in Beijing. Neoplan sued, requesting an injunction and damages in the amount of RMB 40 million. In order to establish infringement, Neoplan Bus furnished RMB 934,000 for the notarized purchase of a bus manufactured by the defendants.

As this was the first case in which a foreign company sued Chinese companies for patent infringement in the bus manufacturing industry, the case was considered one of the ten most influential law suits in 2006 as well as one of the ten top news stories in the bus manufacturing industry. Recognizing the importance of the case, the Beijing First Intermediate People's Court appointed a judge with a background in the automobile industry and a people's assessor with a Ph.D. in Automobile Studies.

The Zhongwei Group, which had earlier been granted a design patent for its A9 bus, argued that it had independently developed the bus design and had used it prior to the use of the Starliner design. The court held that the Zhongwei Group did not have sufficient evidence to establish that it had independently developed the bus design or that it had the priority of use. The court also held that the Zhongwei Group's design patent, although granted by the State Intellectual Property Office, was invalid since it was anticipated by the Neoplan Bus design patent. The court judged that the differences the A9 bus exhibited from the Starliner patented design were minor and did not alter the overall visual impression of the buses. The court therefore ruled that the A9 bus incorporated the plaintiff's patented "Starliner" design and infringed the plaintiff's patent right. The court ordered Beijing Zhongtong Xinghua Auto Sales Co., Ltd. immediately to stop selling the infringing A9 buses. The court ordered Zhongwei Group and Zonda Group immediately to stop making and selling the infringing A9 buses, to pay damages for economic loss in the amount of RMB 20 million, and to compensate Neoplan Bus in the amount of RMB 1.16 million for expenses it paid to stop the infringing act.

NOTES AND QUESTIONS

1. The design patent at issue in the *Neoplan Bus* case was eventually invalidated by the SIPO Patent Re-examination Board on February 25, 2010. The infringement case was reversed by the Beijing High Court on August 10, 2012. For a summary, see http://www.iprights.com/content.output/1164/1164/ Resources/China%20IP%20Express/China%20IP%20Express%20351%20 (September%202012).mspx. Nevertheless, as *Neoplan Bus* and the worldwide *Apple v. Samsung* litigation indicate, design protection can be very beneficial. The advantages of design protection include speedy examination, the establishment of an alternative basis for alleging infringement, and the possible remedies of an injunction and damages.However, historically, relatively few American businesses took advantage of design protection, and even fewer today tend to take advantage of it in countries like China. Why do you think this is so? What advice would you give to an American company that might have protectable designs?

2. On December 18, 2012, President Obama signed into law the Patent Law Treaties Implementation Act of 2012, Pub. Law 112–211, implementing the Patent Law Treaty (discussed in Chapter 2, *supra*) and the Hague Agreement Concerning the International Deposit of Industrial Designs (Hague Agreement). The Act will go into effect on December 18, 2013. The Hague Agreement first entered into force in 1925 and is part of a Hague system of several treaties. Countries can choose which of the treaties to join and still be part of the Hague system. The U.S. is joining the most recent Hague treaty, the 1999 Geneva Act, which will allow applicants to file international design applications at the USPTO for transmittal to the WIPO International Bureau (IB) for registration in designated contracting states. It also will allow foreign applicants to obtain a U.S. design patent based on filing an international design application that designates the U.S., though the international application still will be subject to examination in the USPTO. In addition, the term for a U.S. design patent will increase from fourteen years to fifteen years from grant. The Paris Convention right of priority still applies under the Hague system.

Under the Hague system, applications may be filed in English, French, or Spanish, and once received by the International Bureau, undergo a formalities examination and then are recorded and published in the WIPO International Designs Bulletin. If any contracting state concludes a registered design does not meet its registration criteria (e.g., novelty), it must notify the IB within up to twelve months that it is refusing registration. If it does not make such a notification, the design is deemed registered in that state.

3. PLANT PROTECTION

TRIPS Article 27.3(b) allows countries to exclude plants from patent protection as long as an effective *sui generis* system of protection is provided for plant varieties. Many countries, including most developed countries, allow at least some plants to be protected by utility patents. Cases such as *Monsanto v. Schmeiser* in Chapter 4, *supra*, and *Monsanto v. Cefetra*, in Chapter 10, *infra*, involve utility patent protection for sexually reproducible plants—plants that reproduce via seeds.

While the phrase "plant patent" may be used generically to denote utility patents covering plants, the term has a specific meaning in the United States. A plant patent is a particularly U.S. form of protection. The Plant Patent Act (PPA), 35 U.S.C. §§161–164, enacted in 1930, allows the grant of a patent to anyone who has invented or discovered and asexually reproduced any distinct and new variety of plant, including cultivated sports, mutants, hybrids, and newly found seedlings, other than a tuber-propagated plant or a plant found in an uncultivated state. An asexually reproduced plant is one that is propagated by means other than from seeds, such as by the rooting of cuttings (by layering, budding, or grafting). The term of a plant patent is the same as for a utility patent—twenty years from the date on which the application was filed—and other conditions of patentability apply equally to plant patents.

However, these conditions do not apply seamlessly with respect to plant innovations nor do they embody the same jurisprudence. For example, with respect to subject matter eligibility, although § 161 extends protection to anyone who "invents or discovers and asexually reproduces any distinct and new variety of plant," the predecessor provision to §161 historically has been interpreted to exclude bacteria on grounds that the legislative history of plant patent protection is limited to plants in the standard meaning of the term. *See In re Arzberger*, 112 F.2d 834 (CCPA 1940). This explains, in part, why the utility patent regime has since become the primary home for bacteria-related inventions. Similarly, the Federal Circuit has ruled that the term "variety" in §161 "cannot be read as affording plant patent protection to a range of plants" as is the case under the U.S. Plant Variety Protection Act. *See Imazio Nursery, Inc. v. Dania Greenhouses*, 69 F.3d 1560, 1567 (Fed. Cir. 1995). According to the court, asexual reproduction is a requirement that controls the scope of plant patent protection and thus it limits eligibility to a single plant and its asexually reproduced progeny. *Id.*

Other differences between plant and utility patent protection include the notion of "distinctness" rather than "utility" in §161, and challenges in applying novelty and statutory bars, non-obviousness and disclosure standards to plant patents as these standards are commonly understood in utility patents. *See* Mark D. Janis, et. al., INTELLECTUAL PROPERTY RIGHTS IN PLANTS, Chapter 9, (forthcoming OUP 2013).

Plant patents also are available in South Korea, through legislation originally modeled after the U.S. PPA. There are some key differences however, as tuber-propagated plants are no longer excluded from protection in South Korea. Also, a 2006 amendment to the South Korean Patent Act appears to allow sexually reproducible plants to be protected under the act as well. *See* K.S. Yoon, *Plant Variety Protection in the Republic of Korea, in* AGRICULTURAL BIOTECHNOLOGY AND INTELLECTUAL PROPERTY PROTECTION: SEEDS OF CHANGE 273–280 (Jay P. Kesan ed., 2007).

While most countries grant exclusive rights for new varieties of plants, they tend to do so in the context of *sui generis* protection systems outside the confines of patent law. The German Plant Variety Protection Law, as amended, is typical. It grants protection to a plant variety if it is "1. distinct, 2. homogeneous, 3. stable, 4. new, and 5. designated by means of a registrable variety denomination" Art. 1. The recipient of plant variety protection is entitled to the following rights:

> 1. (a) to produce, to condition for the purpose of propagation, to place on the market, to import or export propagating material of the protected variety or (b) to stock such material for any of the purposes mentioned in item (a),
>
> 2. To carry out any acts mentioned in item 1 with respect to other plants or parts of plants or directly obtained products thereof if propagating material was used in their production without the consent of the owner.
>
> *Id.* at Art. 10.

The protection lasts for twenty-five years (except for certain varieties and tree species that last for thirty), but it is subject to certain limitations. For example, it does not extend to acts carried out "privately and for non-commercial purposes" or "for experimental purposes in relation to the protected variety" Article 10a.

As with designs, an EU-wide Community Plant Variety Right (CPVR) is available as an alternative to national protection. The CPVR is granted by the Community Plant Variety Office, based in Angers, France, and is valid for a maximum of twenty-five years, or thirty years for vines, trees, and potatoes (if the annual maintenance fee is paid). The United States also has a specific Plant Variety Protection Act (PVPA), 7 U.S.C. §§ 2321–2582. Enacted in 1970, it gives breeders exclusive rights in new, distinct, uniform, and stable sexually reproduced or tuber-propagated plant varieties for up to twenty-five years. The PVPA differs from the PPA in that the latter is limited to asexually reproduced plants. The PVPA also differs from utility patent protection for plants in important ways. Under the PVPA, protected varieties can be used and reproduced for plant breeding or other research (i.e. to come up with a new variety) and farmers can save protected seed for replanting (not sale). In addition, infringement of a PVPA certificate (which is issued by the USDA, not the USPTO), is harder to establish, in that the plaintiff must show that the defendant dispensed the variety in a propagatable form without notice of it being a protected variety and also that the defendant did not have notice that it had received such a protected variety. *See Syngenta Seeds, Inc. v. Delta Cotton Co-Operative, Inc.*, 457 F.3d 1269 (Fed. Cir. 2006).

In *J.E.M. Ag Supply, Inc. v. Pioneer Hi-Bred International, Inc.*, 534 U.S. 124 (2001), the United States Supreme Court confirmed that plants were eligible for utility patent protection under 35 U.S.C. 101, upholding the USPTO's sixteen-year practice of granting such patents. In the decision, the Court reiterated its reasoning from *Diamond v. Chakrabarty*, 447 U.S. 303 (1980), that Congress intended a broad scope for patent-eligible subject matter, and that living things were eligible for protection. The Court also dismissed the argument that Congress's passage of the more specific Plant Patent Act of 1930 and Plant Variety Protection Act of 1970 statutes meant plants were excluded from utility patent protection, noting the differing requirements for, and coverage of, the three statutes.

At the international level, Article 27.3(b) of the TRIPS Agreement requires member states to adopt an effective *sui generis* system for plant varieties or provide patent protection for such subject matter. One prominent example of a *sui generis* system for plant varieties is the International Union for the Protection of New Varieties of Plants (UPOV). Established in 1961, UPOV comprises two different protocols—a 1978 Convention and 1991 Convention each with its own distinct standards. Applications for protection must be filed pursuant to national law. However, applications filed in one country may be used as a basis to claim priority for an application filed in another UPOV member country. After registration of a plant variety, the breeder has the exclusive right to exclude others from (1) producing the multiplying material of the variety; (2) selling, offering, or exposing that material to sale; (3) importing or exporting the material; (4) repeating the use of the new variety for the commercial production of other varieties; and (5) using ornamental plants or parts thereof that normally are not commercialized for propagation with the purpose of producing ornamental plants or cut flowers. Such rights cover all botanic genres and species (although some countries such as Canada exclude algae, bacteria, and fungi).

Protection for a plant variety under UPOV 1978 and UPOV 1991 is based on four requirements: the variety must be novel, distinctive, uniform and stable. However, important differences exist between the two protocols. In general, UPOV 1991 is considered a stronger regime of protection for plant varieties. It was established specifically to strengthen breeders' rights and does not exempt farmers from prohibitions on seed saving, a fact that has led many commentators and non-governmental organizations to deem UPOV 1991 as "TRIPS-plus" and fundamentally incompatible with the interests and priorities of developing countries. This is particularly unfortunate because TRIPS requires developing countries to provide a system of plant protection and UPOV 1978 is closed to new members, leaving such countries with the option of joining UPOV

1991 or having to create their own system—a daunting proposition. To date the EU and 68 other countries are members of UPOV.

NOTES AND QUESTIONS

1. Why should agricultural innovation be protected under a different regime than innovation in other areas? What are the advantages of a *sui generis* system over patents for agricultural inventions? *See* Mark D. Janis & Stephen Smith, *Technological Change and the Design of Plant Variety Protection Regimes*, 82 CHI.-KENT L. REV. 1557 (2007) (arguing that in the plant variety context, general unfair competition principles can be adapted to technological change more easily than can exclusive rights and exemptions).

2. One *sui generis* plant variety protection regime that explicitly seeks to balance the rights of breeders and farmers is India's Protection of Plant Varieties and Farmer's Rights Act (PPVFRA). Enacted in 2001, PPVFRA contains elements of UPOV 1978, 1991, and other *sui generis* provisions favorable to farmers. In particular, the Act contains:

> Breeders rights: exclusive right to "produce, sell, market, distribute, import or export" their variety (imprisonment penalties for violation);

> Explicit farmer's rights: the right to "save, use, sow, resow, exchange, share or sell [their] farm produce including seed of a variety protected under this Act . . . provided that the farmer[s] shall not be entitled to sell branded seed of a variety protected under this Act;"

> Protection against Terminator seeds: breeders are forbidden from marketing a variety that prevents a plant from germinating a second time;

> Benefit sharing: when a breeder use a farmers' variety to breed a new variety, the breeder must pay a royalty into the National Gene Fund, which gives benefits to farmers;

> System of dual rights: breeders are rewarded for their innovation by being able to control the commercial marketplace; farmers can engage in their livelihood.

See PPVFRA, http://agricoop.nic.in/PPV&FR%20Act,%202001.pdf. *See also* Christoph Antons, *The International Debate about Traditional Knowledge and Approaches in the Asia-Pacific Region, in* TRADITIONAL KNOWLEDGE, TRADITIONAL CULTURAL EXPRESSIONS AND INTELLECTUAL PROPERTY LAW IN THE ASIA-PACIFIC REGION 63–64 (Christoph Antons ed., 2009).

3. Important and controversial concerns regarding the relationship between food security and protection for agricultural innovation have become entrenched in the mélange of post-TRIPS concerns about heightened global intellectual property standards. Consider the following:

> The UPOV Convention sets out rules for granting monopoly rights over the results of plant breeding. . . . The 1978 Act gives breeders

exclusive ownership over the commercial use of varieties for the purpose of production and sale. The 1978 Act offers two explicit limitations on the monopoly right of the breeder. The first is that other breeders may freely use UPOV-protected varieties for further research. The second is farmers are free to reuse the seed for next year's sowing under certain conditions. When UPOV revised its convention in 1991, it narrowed down the exemption for competing breeders and it deleted the so-called farmers' privilege. Furthermore, the 1991 Act extends the breeders' monopoly right to the products of the farmer's harvest. Any country wishing to join UPOV today must sign the 1991 treaty. The implications of doing so are truly profound:

Impact on producers:

UPOV as such introduces legal and economic restrictions on farmers' livelihood practices. Farmers' rights become nothing but a "privilege" under the 1978 treaty and under the 1991 treaty it is up to individual governments to offer farmers some legal space to reuse proprietary seeds. As a general principle, access to genetic resources is restricted under UPOV whether for production or breeding purposes. Although farmers are responsible for 80–90% of the seed supply in the South, this will massively shift to private control under plant variety rights regimes imposed by the World Trade Organisation. Contrary to what many people assume, private breeders do take farmers to court for alleged piracy of proprietary seed and they are actively pursuing more powerful means to prevent the reuse of seed on the farm (such as contract law governing purchase agreements, "terminator" type technologies and hybridisation).

Genetic erosion:

UPOV is biased towards the specific needs of industrial agriculture, especially through its Distinction-Uniformity-Stability criteria; the uniformity criterion alone has been singled out as promoting the loss of genetic diversity in agriculture. By allowing companies to collect royalties on seed sales, UPOV stimulates the corporate takeover of plant breeding which means fewer actors supplying the market, also leading to erosion. Corporations are not in the business of genetic conservation (they rely on genebanks for that) and tend to work with highly stabilised elite material with wide adaptation. Through intensive promotional or marketing efforts, these varieties tend to replace more diverse traditional materials, and consequently the diversity being used by farmers declines. These are the trends: the reports on varietal replacement and the narrowing genetic base of modern cultivars are readily available.

Adverse impacts on R&D:

Impact studies conducted in one UPOV member state, the USA, report a decline in the flow of germplasm among breeders, a decline in the sharing of scientific information and a decline in the rate of progress in plant breeding. Scant other studies have been done in countries with UPOV experience, despite nearly 40 years of practice. It is noteworthy, however, that UPOV was obliged to revise its treaty in 1991 in order to address an important dysfunction in its own system: instead of providing an incentive for innovation (the breeding of truly novel varieties), UPOV was providing an incentive for plagiarism (breeders could make minor changes to existing varieties and still call them "new" for the purpose of legal protection).

See GRAIN, *UPOV on the War Path*, SEEDLING (June 1999).

4. By contrast, a 2005 UPOV Impact Study of five member countries (Argentina, China, Kenya, Poland, and the Republic of Korea), found economic, health, and social benefits associated with implementation of the UPOV system of protection. *See* Int'l Union for the Protection of New Varieties of Plants, UPOV REPORT ON THE IMPACT OF PLANT VARIETY PROTECTION (2005). These countries also reported an increase in the overall numbers of plant varieties developed after the introduction of the UPOV system. What do you make of the two divergent views of the UPOV and plant variety protection in general? According to a 2010 WIPO publication:

> [F]indings show that introducing the UPOV system contributes to more diverse types of breeders and encourages breeding activity. The public sector is often an important PVP user, and PVP also encourages investment in plant breeding. The graph above [not shown- EDS.] reflects, for example, the growth in government investment in plant breeding in the Republic of Korea (UPOV member since 2002) under the Research and Development Fund for Plant Breeding. Under this scheme, the government matches private investment with public funds, the graph thus reflecting an equivalent, significant increase in private investment.

http://www.wipo.int/wipo_magazine/en/2010/03/article_0007.html.

5. In addition to statutory and treaty-based protection regimes for plants, breeders also have technological protection mechanisms that enable them to maintain varying levels of exclusivity and control over cultivated and modified plants. A traditional mechanism is the production of hybrid seeds that do not "breed true" after one or more generations, necessitating the purchase of new seeds by farmers (as opposed to relying on saved seed) in order to achieve the cultivated benefits. More controversial technological control mechanisms include "terminator" and "traitor" genetic use restriction technologies (GURTs). "Terminator" seeds are genetically modified to become sterile after a single planting season, while "Traitor" seeds require some type of treatment of the seed to activate the gene each planting season. Such technologies may allow seed developers to avoid expensive patent infringement suits against farmers who save seeds, but what might be some of the downsides of such technology and for whom? *See, e.g.,* Dan L. Burk, *Legal Con-*

straint of Genetic Use Restriction Technologies, 6 MINN. J.L. SCI. & TECH. 335 (2004).

6. There appears to be an increasing tension between patent rights and plant breeders' rights. A 2009 report from the Netherlands Centre for Genetic Research identified several challenges for plant breeders created by developments in the patenting of plants:

> Plant breeder's rights and patent rights may be conflicting in plant breeding. Specific liberties of breeders and farmers [e.g., saving seed, experimentation] are lost with the patentability of plant-related inventions... Patent rights hold possibilities for strategic use, which may lead to lack of clarity in the market and to monopolistic behavior... Plant breeder's rights have no such effects.... Patent rights, together with the way these are granted and exerted, contributes to a decreasing diversity in breeding companies and threatens innovation in plant breeding...[T]he patent system needs to be amended... Amendments of regulations is necessary to increase the room for innovation in plant breeding. This can be reached by restricting the scope of patents in plant breeding and more specifically by reinstating the exemption of patents on plant(varieties) or by introducing full breeder's exemption in patent rights. Both options should preferably be implemented at the European level, possible via a revision of the Biotechnology Directive, and preferably in consultation with other countries with a significant breeding sector (such as the USA, Japan, and China).

Niels Louwaars et al., *Breeding Business: The Future of Plant Breeding in the Light of Developments in Patent Rights and Plant Breeder's Rights* 2–3 (2009). Considering our discussion in Chapter 4 of the difficulties surrounding enactment of the EU Biotech Directive, amending it may prove quite a feat. Can you think of other policy options that might alleviate some of the problems identified by the report?

CHAPTER 9

PATENT PROSECUTION

■ ■ ■

In patent parlance, the process through which an inventor obtains a patent is called "prosecution" and includes the drafting of an application describing, defining, and claiming the invention, as well as the administrative colloquy between the applicant or her representative and the patent office regarding the prepared application. There are numerous similarities in prosecution practice present in virtually all patent systems. For example, all systems require compliance with certain formalities in filing an application (e.g., payment of a designated fee, and identification of the applicant). However, differences between national systems can be significant and make transnational patent prosecution challenging. While almost all major patent-granting offices will engage in substantive examination of a patent application to ensure that it complies with specific patentability requirements (e.g., novelty, inventive step, and industrial applicability), several smaller offices including Belgium and the patent offices of most African countries do not. These offices issue patents either with no substantive examination at all or with the substantive examination having been performed by a foreign patent office. Moreover, some countries require applicants to obtain government permission before filing a patent application in a foreign country while others do not.

With such a wealth of prosecution differences existing globally, the goal of this Chapter is not to canvas all or even most of these distinctions. Rather, the focus will be on key prosecution-related topics such as the form and content of the patent application and the patentability requirements to which it must conform, post-grant procedures such as patent correction mechanisms, and issues relating to the role of the inventor in prosecution and beyond.

A. THE PATENT APPLICATION

To obtain a patent on an invention, an inventor must prepare and file an application disclosing and claiming the invention. The disclosure is contained in a section of the patent application called the specification, which includes claims. The patent application includes drawings as well as other information such as an abstract of the invention, title of the invention, and geographic location information for the inventor(s)/assignee(s). In most jurisdictions, the specification generally comprises the following sections: (i) background; (ii) summary of the invention; (iii) drawings, if any; and (iv) detailed description of the invention, which may include examples. Examples may be working examples, which have actually been performed (and are described using the past tense), or they may be paper (also known as "prophetic") examples that the inventor believes will work (and thus are described in the present tense) despite not having actually performed them. The specification concludes with one or more claims covering the specific subject matter of the inventive concept (although in many countries a filing date may be obtained even if no claims are originally filed). Even though these basic features can be found in patent applications the world over, preparing an application for filing in multiple jurisdictions can be quite expensive and can create unique challenges for applicants.

1. INTERNATIONALIZING AN APPLICATION

As discussed in Chapter 3, all member states of the WTO are required to provide patent protection to inventors (subject to LDC transition periods). However, the vast majority of inventors will only seek patents in a small number of countries. The "IP5" comprises the five largest patent offices in the world in terms of the number of applications received: the State Intellectual Property Office of China (SIPO), the United States Patent & Trademark Office (USPTO), the Japan Patent Office (JPO), the Korean Intellectual Property Office (KIPO), and the European Patent Office (EPO). Combined, these offices receive 90 percent of all patent applications filed worldwide. *See* http://www.fiveipoffices.org/about-us.html. Until relatively recently, the Trilateral Cooperation Offices—EPO, JPO and USPTO—stood apart as the largest offices and accounted for approximately 80 percent of patent applications. These three offices have been working somewhat cooperatively since 1983. *See* http://www.tri lateral.net. So-called "triadic patents" comprise patents obtained in the Trilateral offices on the same invention by the same applicant/inventor. The number of triadic patents obtained by applicants can be a useful metric for a country's innovative activity. According to the EU Commission, "triadic patents are the most valuable ones and are considered the best patent indicator for innovation." *See Communication from the Commission to the European Parliament and the Council—Enhancing the Patent System in Europe, at 5,* COM (2007) 165 final (Mar. 4, 2007).

Figure 1 shows samples of a triadic patent family for a "Ratchet Wrench," including the full U.S. patent (minus two drawings pages), the front page of the Japanese patent, and portions of the European Patent.

FIGURE 1

US006435060B1

(12) **United States Patent**   (10) **Patent No.:**   **US 6,435,060 B1**

Izumisawa   (45) **Date of Patent:**   **Aug. 20, 2002**

(54) **RATCHET WRENCH**

(75) Inventor: **Nobuyuki Izumisawa**, Tokyo (JP)

(73) Assignee: **Kabushiki Kaisha Shinano Seisakusho**, Tokyo (JP)

(*) Notice: Subject to any disclaimer, the term of this patent is extended or adjusted under 35 U.S.C. 154(b) by 98 days.

(21) Appl. No.: **09/691,559**

(22) Filed: **Oct. 18, 2000**

(51) Int. Cl.[7] B25B 13/46

(52) U.S. Cl. 81/57.39; 81/57.26

(58) Field of Search 81/57.11, 57.26, 81/57.39, 60

(56)   **References Cited**

U.S. PATENT DOCUMENTS

4,748,872 A	*	6/1988	Brown	....	81/57.26
5,022,289 A	*	6/1991	Butzen	....	81/57.39
5,142,952 A	*	9/1992	Putney et al.	....	81/57.39
5,784,934 A	*	7/1998	Izumisawa	....	81/57.26
6,298,753 B1	*	10/2001	Izumisawa	....	81/57.39

* cited by examiner

Primary Examiner—Joseph J. Hail, III
Assistant Examiner—Joni B. Danganan

(74) *Attorney, Agent, or Firm*—Jordan and Hamburg LLP

(57)   **ABSTRACT**

A ratchet wrench includes a handle and a head. The handle has a motor accommodated within. The head is provided with a ratchet mechanism having a rotary tightening member which is to be rotated by drive power from the motor. A pin extends in a transverse direction with respect to the axis of the handle so as to connect the head with the handle. A crankshaft is connected to an output shaft of the motor. A crankpin of the crankshaft is rotatably fitted into a first drive bush. The first drive bush is fitted into a first drive member such that the first drive bush is slidable in the transverse direction. The first drive member is connected to the pin in such a manner that the first drive member is rotatable about the pin and slidable along the pin. A second drive member is connected to the pin in such a manner that the second drive member is rotatable about the pin and slidable together with the first drive member along the pin. The second drive member is fitted into a second drive bush so as to be slidable in a direction parallel to the axis of the head. A yoke is connected to the second drive bush in such a manner that the yoke is swingable relative to the second drive bush and is connected to the rotary tightening member via the ratchet mechanism.

4 Claims, 3 Drawing Sheets

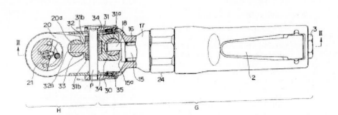

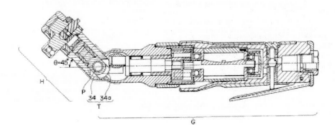

US 6,435,060 B1

1

RATCHET WRENCH

BACKGROUND OF THE INVENTION

1. Field of the Invention

The present invention relates to a ratchet wrench, and particularly to a head-tiltable-type ratchet wrench whose head can be tilted relative to a handle.

2. Background of the Invention

Japanese Patent Application Laid-Open (kokai) No. 10-217140 discloses a conventional ratchet wrench having a rotatable head.

In the disclosed ratchet wrench, upon operation of a lever, pressurized air is fed to a motor, so that the motor operates. The motor rotates a drive member, which in turn rotates a first bevel gear. The first bevel gear rotates a third bevel gear via a second bevel gear. The third bevel gear rotates a drive shaft to which a socket is fixed, so that the socket rotates to tighten or loosen a threaded fastening element. Upon release of the lever, the feed of the air to the motor is stopped and the drive shaft stops its rotation. When the position of the head is changed relative to the handle, a pin is moved to a release position, and the head is pivoted to a selected position. As described above, the conventional ratchet wrench includes a plurality of bevel gears provided between the head and the handle so as to enable pivoting of the head in a plane containing the axis of the handle.

Need for a ratchet wrench which can tighten or loosen a threaded fastening element at a difficult-to-access location has become stronger, as has need for a ratchet wrench which permits an operator to insert the ratchet wrench into a narrower space than in the case of the conventional ratchet wrench currently in use.

In order to insert a ratchet wrench into a narrower space, the head, which is a rotatable or tiltable portion, of a ratchet wrench is desired to be as short as possible. Since the conventional ratchet wrench disclosed in the above-described patent publication has the bevel gears between the head and the handle, the head cannot be shortened.

SUMMARY OF THE INVENTION

In consideration of the above-described problem of the conventional ratchet wrench, an object of the present invention is to provide a ratchet wrench whose head can be made shorter in order to enable insertion into narrower spaces.

The present invention provides a ratchet wrench comprising: a handle within which a motor Is accommodated; a head provided with a ratchet mechanism having a rotary tightening member which is to be rotated by drive power from the motor; a pin extending in a transverse direction with respect to the axis of the handle so as to connect the head with the handle; a crankshaft connected to an output shaft of the motor; a first drive bush into which a crankpin of the crankshaft is rotatably fitted; a first drive member into which the first drive bush is fitted to be slidable in a direction substantially perpendicular to the axis of the pin, the first drive member being connected to the pin in such a manner that the first drive member is rotatable about the pin and slidable along the pin; a second drive member connected to the pin in such a manner that the second drive member is rotatable about the pin and slidable together with the first drive member along the pin; a second drive bush into which the second drive member is fitted so as to be slidable in a direction parallel to the axis of the head; and a yoke which is connected to the second drive bush in such a manner that the yoke is swingable relative to the second drive bush, the

2

yoke being connected to the rotary tightening member via the ratchet mechanism.

The ratchet wrench of the present invention enables a worker to tighten or loosen a bolt, nut, or other fastening element in a state in which the head is directed to a desired angular direction.

Preferably, the ratchet wrench of the present invention further includes a tilt mechanism which locks the head at an angle selected from a plurality of angles relative to the axis of the handle. The head is securely locked to the handle, so that a bolt or nut within a small space is tightened or loosened securely and easily.

Preferably, the tilt mechanism includes an engagement member having a toothed portion, the engagement member being fixed to the head and rotatably connected to the pin; and a lock pin which is disposed in a front portion of the handle and is engaged with the engage member so as to lock the head. This structure enables a worker to direct the head to a desired angular direction through a simple operation of holding the handle in one hand and the head in the other hand and bending the ratchet wrench about the axis of the pin.

Preferably, the crankshaft is connected to the motor via a reduction gear mechanism.

BRIEF DESCRIPTION OF THE DRAWINGS

FIG. 1 is a front view of the ratchet wrench according to an embodiment of the present invention;

FIG. 2 is a sectional view of the ratchet wrench taken along line II—II in FIG. 1; and

FIG. 3 is a sectional view of the ratchet wrench with the head being tilted at an angle θ=45°.

DESCRIPTION OF THE PREFERRED EMBODIMENT

An embodiment of the present invention will be described in detail with reference to the drawings.

FIG. 1 is a front view of a ratchet wrench according to an embodiment of the present invention, a portion of which is sectioned in order to show the internal structure thereof. FIG. 2 is a sectional view of the ratchet wrench taken along line II—II in FIG. 1. FIG. 3 is a sectional view of the ratchet wrench whose head is tilted at 45° with respect to the axis of a handle.

As shown in the drawings, the ratchet wrench includes a handle G, a head H, and a pin P. The handle G has a motor 1 accommodated therein. The head H is provided with a ratchet mechanism 21 including a rotary tightening member 22 which is operated by drive power from the motor 1. The pin P extends in a transverse direction of the handle G and connects the handle G with the head H. In the present embodiment, the motor 1 is an air motor. However, the present invention can be applied to an electrically-driven ratchet wrench.

Upon operation of an open-close lever 2, the air motor 1 is operated by pressurized air fed from an air induction port 3 via an open-close valve 4, so that a shaft 9 of the air motor 1 rotates. A motor housing 5 is covered with a body cover 23, which serves as a grip of the ratchet wrench. The body cover 23 is preferably formed of resin.

In the air motor 1, a rotor 6 is rotatably supported by bearings 7 and 8 fixed to the motor housing 5. The shaft 9 is rotatably supported by the bearing 8. The tip end of the shaft 9 is in engagement with a reduction gear mechanism 10.

US 6,435,060 B1

3

The reduction gear mechanism 10 includes three idle gears 12, an internal gear 13, and a cage 14. The idle gears 12 are in meshing-engagement with the shaft 9. The internal gear 13 is in meshing-engagement with the idle gears 12 and is fixed into a driver housing 17, which is coupled with the motor housing 5 by way of a lock ring 24. The cage 14 is coupled to each of the idle gears 12 via a respective idle pin 25 and is in engagement with a crankshaft 15.

In the present embodiment, the three idle gears 12 are disposed around the shaft 9. Each of the idle gears 12 is rotatably fixed onto the corresponding idle pin 25. The cage 14 is fixed to the idle pins 25 (three idle pins in the present embodiment), so that when the idle gears 12 revolve around the shaft 9, the cage 14 rotates about its axis and the crankshaft 15 rotates.

In the driver housing 17, one end of the crankshaft 15 located on the side of the reduction gear mechanism 10 is rotatably supported by a bush 26, and the other end located on the side of a ratchet mechanism 21 (described later) is rotatably supported by a needle bearing 16.

The crankshaft 15 has a crank pin 18 projecting from a tip end surface 15a at an eccentric position. The crank pin 18 is rotatably fitted into a first drive bush 30. The first drive bush 30 is fitted in a groove 31a of a first drive member 31 such that the first drive bush 30 is slidable along the groove 31a (in the direction perpendicular to the sheet in FIG. 1). The first drive member 31 is connected to the pin P such that the first drive member 31 is slidable along the pin P and is rotatable about the pin P.

The first drive member 31 includes forked connecting portions 31b which are connected to the pin P. The second drive member 32 is disposed between the connecting portions 31b and is rotatably connected to the pin P in such a manner that the second drive member 32 is slidable together with the drive member 31.

A drive pin 32a of the second drive member 32 is fitted into a second drive bush 33 such that the drive pin 32a is slidable in a direction parallel to the axis of the head. The second drive bush 33 is fitted into a recess 20a of a yoke 20, so that the drive pin 32a is swingable relative to the yoke 20. The yoke 20 is connected to a rotary tightening member 22 via the ratchet mechanism 21.

The ratchet wrench is provided with a tilt mechanism T which locks the head H at an angle selected from a plurality of angles to which the head H can be tilted relative to the handle G through pivoting motion about the pin P.

The tilt mechanism T includes a pair of tilt covers 34 and a pair of lock pins 35. The tilt covers 34 are fixed to upper and lower side surfaces of the head H (in FIG. 1) and are supported by the pin P at the opposite ends thereof. Each of the tilt covers 34 has a toothed portion 34a formed on the rear portion thereof. The lock pins 35 are embedded in the front end portion at positions corresponding to those of the tilt covers 34. Each lock pin 35 is pressed against the toothed portion 34a of the corresponding tilt cover 34.

In the present embodiment, the toothed portion 34a includes nine grooves formed at intervals of 11.25° about the axis of the pin P. Therefore, the head can be tilted relative to the handle G at an angle selected from nine angles; i.e., 0° (horizontal position), −11.25°, −22.5°, −33.75°, −45°, +11.25°, +22.5°, +33.75°, and +45° ("−" indicates the downward direction and "+" indicates the upward direction in FIG. 3).

4

FIG. 3 shows a state in which the head H has been tilted upward to the angle θ=+45°.

When an object, such as a bolt or nut, is tightened by use of the ratchet wrench having the above-described structure, the head H is directed to a desired angle direction relative to the handle G, the rotary tightening member 22 is engaged with the object, and the open-close lever 2 is operated. As a result, the air motor 1 operates, and the shaft 9 rotates together with the rotor 6.

The rotation speed of the shaft 9 is reduced through the reduction gear mechanism 10. The rotational motion of the shaft 9 is transmitted to the first drive member 31 and the second drive member 32 via the crankshaft 15 and is converted to a reciprocating motion along the pin P. The reciprocating motion of the second drive member 32 is transmitted to the yoke 20, so that the yoke 20 swings repeatedly. The swinging motion of the yoke 20 is converted to rotational motion of the rotary tightening member 22, whereby the bolt or nut is tightened.

What is claimed is:

1. A ratchet wrench comprising:

a handle within which a motor is accommodated;

a head provided with a ratchet mechanism having a rotary tightening member which is to be rotated by drive power from the motor;

a pin extending in a transverse direction with respect to the axis of the handle so as to connect the head with the handle;

a crankshaft connected to an output shaft of the motor;

a first drive bush into which a crankpin of the crankshaft is rotatably fitted;

a first drive member into which the first drive bush is fitted to be slidable in a direction substantially perpendicular to the axis of the pin, the first drive member being connected to the pin in such a manner that the first drive member is rotatable about the pin and slidable along the pin;

a second drive member connected to the pin in such a manner that the second drive member is rotatable about the pin and slidable together with the first drive member along the pin;

a second drive bush into which the second drive member is fitted so as to be slidable in a direction parallel to the axis of the head; and

a yoke which is connected to the second drive bush in such a manner that the yoke is swingable relative to the second drive bush, the yoke being connected to the rotary tightening member via the ratchet mechanism.

2. A ratchet wrench according to claim 1, including a tilt mechanism which locks the head at an angle selected from a plurality of angles relative to the axis of the handle.

3. A ratchet wrench according to claim 2, wherein the tilt mechanism includes an engagement member having a toothed portion, the engagement member being fixed to the head and rotatably connected to the pin; and a lock pin which is disposed in a front portion of the handle and is engaged with the engage member so as to lock the head.

4. A ratchet wrench according to claim 1, wherein the crankshaft is connected to the motor via a reduction gear mechanism.

* * * * *

(19)日本国特許庁（ＪＰ）　　(12)公開特許公報（Ａ）　　(11)特許出願公開番号

特開2002-79473

（P2002-79473A）

(43)公開日　平成14年3月19日（2002.3.19）

(51)Int.Cl.^{7}	識別記号	FI		テーマコード(参考)
Ｂ２５Ｂ　21/00		Ｂ２５Ｂ　21/00		Ｃ
				Ｍ

審査請求　未請求　請求項の数4　ＯＬ　（全5頁）　最終頁に続く

(21)出願番号	特願2000-271053（P2000-271053）	(71)出願人	391051452
(22)出願日	平成12年9月7日（2000.9.7）		株式会社信濃製作所
			東京都板橋区徳丸1丁目20番17号
		(72)発明者	泉輝　信行
			東京都板橋区徳丸1丁目20番17号　株式会社信濃製作所内
		(74)代理人	100072936
			弁理士　大橋　勇　（外1名）

(54)【発明の名称】　ラチェットレンチ

(57)【要約】

【課題】　より狭い場所へのアクセスが可能となるようにヘッドの長さを短くすることができるラチェットレンチを提供する。

【解決手段】　内部にモーターが内蔵されたハンドルＧと、前記モーターに連結されたクランクシャフトからの動力により作動する回動締付部を有するラチェット機構21を備えるヘッドＨと、前記ハンドルＧと前記ヘッドＨ連結すると共に横断方向に伸びるピンＰを有するラチェットレンチであって、前記クランクシャフト15のクランクピン18を回転可能に嵌挿する第1ドライバブシュ30と、前記第1ドライバブシュ30を上下に摺動可能に嵌挿すると共に前記ピンＰに回転可能かつ横方向に摺動可能に連結された第1ドライバ31と、前記ピンＰに回動可能かつ前記第1ドライバ31と共に横方向に摺動可能に連結された第2ドライバ32と、前記第2ドライバ32を前後に摺動可能に嵌挿する第2ドライバブシュ33と、前記第2ドライバブシュ33に摺動可能に連結されるとともに、前記ラチェット機構21を介して前記回動締付部に接続されるヨーク20とを備えた。

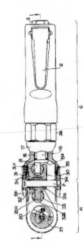

(19) Europäisches Patentamt
European Patent Office
Office européen des brevets

(11) EP 1 186 381 A1

(12) **EUROPEAN PATENT APPLICATION**

(43) Date of publication:
13.03.2002 Bulletin 2002/11

(51) Int Cl.⁷: **B25B 21/00**, B25B 23/00

(21) Application number: 00122901.2

(22) Date of filing: 20.10.2000

(84) Designated Contracting States:
AT BE CH CY DE DK ES FI FR GB GR IE IT LI LU
MC NL PT SE
Designated Extension States:
AL LT LV MK RO SI

(30) Priority: 07.09.2000 JP 2000271053

(71) Applicant: KABUSHIKI KAISHA SHINANO
SEISAKUSHO
Tokyo (JP)

(72) Inventor: Izumisawa, Nobuyuki,
c/o K. K. Shinano Seisakusho
Tokyo (JP)

(74) Representative: Prüfer, Lutz H., Dipl.-Phys. et al
PRÜFER & PARTNER GbR,
Patentanwälte,
Harthauser Strasse 25d
81545 München (DE)

(54) **Ratchet wrench**

(57) A ratchet wrench includes a handle(G) and a head(H). The handle(H) has a motor(1) accommodated within. The head(H) is provided with a ratchet mechanism(21) having a rotary tightening member(22) which is to be rotated by drive power from the motor(1). A pin (P) extends in a transverse direction with respect to the axis of the handle(G) so as to connect the head(H) with the handle(G). A crankshaft(15) is connected to an output shaft(9) of the motor(1). A crankpin(18) of the crankshaft(15) is rotatably fitted into a first drive bush(30). The first drive bush(30) is fitted into a first drive member(31) such that the first drive bush(30) is slidable in the transverse direction. The first drive member(31) is connected to the pin(P) in such a manner that the first drive member (31) is rotatable about the pin(P) and slidable along the pin(P). A second drive member(32) is connected to the pin(P) in such a manner that the second drive member (32) is rotatable about the pin(P) and slidable together with the first drive member(31) along the pin(P). The second drive member(32) is fitted into a second drive bush(33) so as to be slidable in a direction parallel to the axis of the head(H). A yoke(20) is connected to the second drive bush(33) in such a manner that the yoke (20) is swingable relative to the second drive bush(33) and is connected to the rotary tightening member(22) via the ratchet mechanism (21).

FIG.1

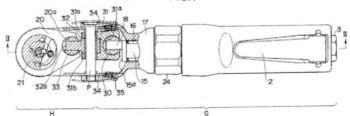

EP 1 186 381 A1

EP 1 186 381 A1

Description

BACKGROUND OF THE INVENTION

Field of the Invention:

[0001] The present invention relates to a ratchet wrench, and particularly to a head-tiltable-type ratchet wrench whose head can be tilted relative to a handle.

Background of the Invention:

[0002] Japanese Patent Application Laid-Open (kokai) No. 10-217140 discloses a conventional ratchet wrench having a rotatable head.
[0003] In the disclosed ratchet wrench, upon operation of a lever, pressurized air is fed to a motor, so that the motor operates. The motor rotates a drive member, which in turn rotates a first bevel gear. The first bevel gear rotates a third bevel gear via a second bevel gear. The third bevel gear rotates a drive shaft to which a socket is fixed, so that the socket rotates to tighten or loosen a threaded fastening element. Upon release of the lever, the feed of the air to the motor is stopped and the drive shaft stops its rotation. When the position of the head is changed relative to the handle, a pin is moved to a release position, and the head is pivoted to a selected position. As described above, the conventional ratchet wrench includes a plurality of bevel gears provided between the head and the handle so as to enable pivoting of the head in a plane containing the axis of the handle.
[0004] Need for a ratchet wrench which can tighten or loosen a threaded fastening element at a difficult-to-access location has become stronger, as has need for a ratchet wrench which permits an operator to insert the ratchet wrench into a narrower space than in the case of the conventional ratchet wrench currently in use.
[0005] In order to insert a ratchet wrench into a narrower space, the head, which is a rotatable or tiltable portion, of a ratchet wrench is desired to be as short as possible. Since the conventional ratchet wrench disclosed in the above-described patent publication has the bevel gears between the head and the handle, the head cannot be shortened.

SUMMARY OF THE INVENTION

[0006] In consideration of the above-described problem of the conventional ratchet wrench, an object of the present invention is to provide a ratchet wrench whose head can be made shorter in order to enable insertion into narrower spaces.
[0007] The present invention provides a ratchet wrench comprising: a handle within which a motor is accommodated; a head provided with a ratchet mechanism having a rotary tightening member which is to be rotated by drive power from the motor; a pin extending in a transverse direction with respect to the axis of the handle so as to connect the head with the handle; a crankshaft connected to an output shaft of the motor; a first drive bush into which a crankpin of the crankshaft is rotatably fitted; a first drive member into which the first drive bush is fitted to be slidable in a direction substantially perpendicular to the axis of the pin, the first drive member being connected to the pin in such a manner that the first drive member is rotatable about the pin and slidable along the pin; a second drive member connected to the pin in such a manner that the second drive member is rotatable about the pin and slidable together with the first drive member along the pin; a second drive bush into which the second drive member is fitted so as to be slidable in a direction parallel to the axis of the head; and a yoke which is connected to the second drive bush in such a manner that the yoke is swingable relative to the second drive bush, the yoke being connected to the rotary tightening member via the ratchet mechanism.
[0008] The ratchet wrench of the present invention enables a worker to tighten or loosen a bolt, nut, or other fastening element in a state in which the head is directed to a desired angular direction.
[0009] Preferably, the ratchet wrench of the present invention further includes a tilt mechanism which locks the head at an angle selected from a plurality of angles relative to the axis of the handle. The head is securely locked to the handle, so that a bolt or nut within a small space is tightened or loosened securely and easily.
[0010] Preferably, the tilt mechanism includes an engagement member having a toothed portion, the engagement member being fixed to the head and rotatably connected to the pin; and a lock pin which is disposed in a front portion of the handle and is engaged with the engage member so as to lock the head. This structure enables a worker to direct the head to a desired angular direction through a simple operation of holding the handle in one hand and the head in the other hand and bending the ratchet wrench about the axis of the pin.
[0011] Preferably, the crankshaft is connected to the motor via a reduction gear mechanism.

BRIEF DESCRIPTION OF THE DRAWINGS

[0012]

FIG. 1 is a front view of the ratchet wrench according to an embodiment of the present invention;
FIG. 2 is a sectional view of the ratchet wrench taken along line II-II in FIG. 1; and
FIG. 3 is a sectional view of the ratchet wrench with the head being tilted at an angle θ=45°.

DESCRIPTION OF THE PREFERRED EMBODIMENT

[0013] An embodiment of the present invention will be described in detail with reference to the drawings.

2

5   EP 1 186 381 A1   6

the yoke 20 is converted to rotational motion of the rotary tightening member 22, whereby the bolt or nut is tightened.

Claims

1. A ratchet wrench comprising:

    a handle within which a motor is accommodated;

    a head provided with a ratchet mechanism having a rotary tightening member which is to be rotated by drive power from the motor;

    a pin extending in a transverse direction with respect to the axis of the handle so as to connect the head with the handle;

    a crankshaft connected to an output shaft of the motor;

    a first drive bush into which a crankpin of the crankshaft is rotatably fitted;

    a first drive member into which the first drive bush is fitted to be slidable in a direction substantially perpendicular to the axis of the pin, the first drive member being connected to the pin in such a manner that the first drive member is rotatable about the pin and slidable along the pin;

    a second drive member connected to the pin in such a manner that the second drive member is rotatable about the pin and slidable together with the first drive member along the pin;

    a second drive bush into which the second drive member is fitted so as to be slidable in a direction parallel to the axis of the head; and

    a yoke which is connected to the second drive bush in such a manner that the yoke is swingable relative to the second drive bush, the yoke being connected to the rotary tightening member via the ratchet mechanism.

2. A ratchet wrench according to claim 1, including a tilt mechanism which locks the head at an angle selected from a plurality of angles relative to the axis of the handle.

3. A ratchet wrench according to claim 2, wherein the tilt mechanism includes an engagement member having a toothed portion, the engagement member being fixed to the head and rotatably connected to the pin; and a lock pin which is disposed in a front portion of the handle and is engaged with the engage member so as to lock the head.

4. A ratchet wrench according to claim 1, wherein the crankshaft is connected to the motor via a reduction gear mechanism.

4

The samples in Figure 1 illustrate the parts of a patent application described earlier. Study these samples carefully. You will notice that the specifications of the U.S. and European patents are virtually identical, suggesting the application was "internationalized" to make it suitable for filing globally. Applicants seeking patent protection in multiple jurisdictions face the dilemma of drafting their applications to comply with diverse requirements and rules. They also face the high costs of translating their applications into the languages required by various offices. The following excerpt suggests ways to internationalize a patent application to address the requirements of multiple offices and reduce prosecution costs at the same time. Although focusing on pharmaceutical inventions and U.S. drafters, this counsel is useful for inventions and practitioners in other technical and geographic areas as well.

EMILY MIAO, DRAFTING MULTILATERAL PHARMACEUTICAL APPLICATIONS: GUIDELINES FOR THE U.S. PATENT PRACTITIONER

(Oct. 19, 2007) (Paper Presented at AIPLA Annual Meeting)

A. Introduction

Foreign patent protection has become increasingly important in the global marketplace, yet U.S. patent practitioners often prepare patent applications without paying attention to patent requirements abroad. Usually, U.S. patent practitioners will file their patent applications through the PCT system and will think of foreign requirements at the point when the application is about to enter the national phase. As will be discussed, early consideration of application drafting issues can help save time and money and ultimately enhance the likelihood of obtaining broad, valid claims that can be enforced abroad.

[M]uch of the requirements for preparing foreign patent applications for pharmaceutical subject matter are generally the same as those for other subject matter . . . .

B. Application drafting strategy

As a threshold matter, preparing multilateral or global applications based on the PCT format rather than U.S. application format is recommended because even if the client decides not to pursue foreign protection, a properly drafted multilateral application will satisfy U.S. requirements. Furthermore, a multilateral application can be filed in various foreign jurisdictions with minor modifications and at a significant cost saving for the client.

Foreign filing costs are directly related to the number of application pages and claims and therefore can be readily controlled by the patent drafter, particularly if the so-called "problem/solution" philosophy is adhered to during drafting of the application. In many foreign patent systems, notably Europe and Japan, the so-called "problem/solution" philosophy has been adopted with respect to the description of patent applications. In addition to focusing the application, the application of this philosophy in drafting multilateral applications may be useful in overcoming "lack of inventive step" rejections which are commonly applied to applications originating from the U.S. . . . .

1. The Background section

Long-winded background sections in U.S. patent applications do little to advance the claimed invention and add to translation fees. Rather than provide an exhaustive tutorial of well-known aspects of the invention and description of the prior art, the Background section in multilateral applications should be limited to describing the problem(s) to which the invention is directed.

Any prior art discussion in the Background section may not ultimately be directed to the most relevant prior art. At least in the pharmaceutical field, experience has shown that the more relevant prior art is often uncovered in Europe and Japan rather than in the U.S. Furthermore, discussions concerning the differences between the prior art and invention in the Background section may give rise to prosecution history estoppel, at least in the U.S. While most foreign countries do not have a duty of candor, significant prior art [references] should be brought to the attention of foreign counsel so that they can be addressed during prosecution, generally in the form of claim amendments and/or brought to the attention of foreign patent offices.

The description of principles or elements of the invention as well as the description of the inventive solution to the problem should be reserved for the Detailed Description as inclusion of such descriptions may imply that at least part, if not all, of the invention is known in the art.

2. The Summary of the Invention section

An exhaustive "Summary of the Invention" section of a U.S. patent application not only adds to translation costs but can have a negative consequence in introducing unintended limiting characterizations of the invention. The Summary section should be as broad as the broadest independent claim and include the claims in paraphrased form. Instead of defining what the invention is in characterizing terms (e.g., the present invention comprises . . .), phrases such as "an embodiment of the invention" or "an aspect of the invention" should be used to avert limiting characterizations.

The Summary section should not include actual or implied assertions regarding essential or critical elements of the invention as it may be difficult to remove such an element from the claim later on if it turns out the element identified as being essential is not. Similarly, a description of "objects" of the invention should not be included in the Summary section since some foreign countries may require proof of the achievement of those objects in order to demonstrate patent infringement.

3. The Detailed Description section

The Detailed Description section should contain a full and clear description of the novel features of the invention as well as the description of the inventive solution to the problem raised in the Background section. The description should explain how one carries out the invention in as much detail as possible. Any unexpected results are highly desirable and should be discussed in this section as well. . .

Terminology used in this section should have established meaning in the art and those meanings should be acceptable in foreign countries. If multiple meanings of a term exist, then the meaning of the term should be explained.

The wording of claims should closely correspond to the wording in the Detailed Description. Furthermore, claim elements should be investigated to identify possible patentable subject matter for inclusion into the application since it is often necessary to add limitations to a claim to overcome prior art and the degree of disclosure required to support a claimed element in foreign countries may be greater than it is in the U.S. In Europe, for instance, only explicitly disclosed language in the specification can be used in the claims.

Cross-references to other U.S. applications often appear in U.S. applications such as "see co-pending U.S. application XYZ, which is incorporated by reference herein in its entirety." When seeking to rely upon disclosures contained in other documents, care must be taken to ensure that these referenced documents have already been published and that they are properly incorporated by reference, otherwise an insufficient disclosure objection may arise and the applicant may be unable to rely on such materials unless the applicant demonstrate that the information is in the common general knowledge. In China, an insufficient disclosure rejection of an application that relies on an unpublished U.S. application incorporated by reference cannot be overcome by submitting the cited U.S. application during prosecution. If a particular disclosure such as a chemical reaction or assay conditions is important in producing a claimed invention, make sure that the referenced application has already been published by the filing date of the foreign application.

For a pharmaceutical application directed to a new chemical compound, a number of foreign countries, especially China, require that the application disclose the specific medical use, pharmacological efficacy, effective amount and method of administration. Furthermore, if the skilled artisan cannot reasonably predict that the invention would provide the asserted use and efficacy on the basis of the prior art theories, the description should also disclose experimental evidence (including animal data) or clinical results sufficient to prove the technical solution of the invention solves the technical problem or achieves the asserted technical effect.

The claimed invention should be supported by many possible examples to permit broad interpretations. While many foreign countries do not require an actual demonstration of utility with respect to pharmaceutical inventions, failure to include examples that support the stated pharmaceutical effect can be fatal to patentability in some countries. In China, an insufficient disclosure rejection under Article 26(3) for lack of pharmaceutical data cannot be overcome by submitting data during prosecution. Even if the description generally describes unexpected pharmaceutical activity and effect, experimental data demonstrating the stated activity and effect is required.

4. The Claims section

Large numbers of claims is a significant cost factor for foreign applications, especially for pharmaceutical applications involving DNA and protein sequences. Many foreign countries and regions include a cost penalty for [excessive] claims . . . including Europe and Japan. Furthermore, large numbers of claims require more translation and work for foreign counsel. While reducing the number of claims to the absolute minimum for costs reason alone is not advisable, particularly where valuable claims are involved, obtaining good patent coverage at a reasonable cost can be readily achieved by careful selection of what is claimed and how it is claimed. Having a reasonable number and variety of claims in the multilateral application is desirable for a number of reasons, including avoiding the need to add claims later on during prosecution and risking new matter objections.

To contain costs in foreign applications, the claims, both dependent and independent, should be primarily directed to subject matter that supports patentability, not subject matter that adds little in terms of patentability. Multiple dependent claims should be considered as another method for limiting the number of claims.

NOTES AND QUESTIONS

1. Attempts to "internationalize" a patent application as advised above can create certain risks for an applicant. Efforts to be concise to save translation costs may create other costs related to the scope of protection of the issued patent or validity issues related to adequate enablement or written description. Some experts suggest drafting two or more different applications, or at least claim sets, designed to comply with, and take advantage of, unique features and requirements of the U.S., Japanese, and European patent systems. Recall our discussion of the PCT system in Chapter 2, *supra*. What factors should influence a client's decision to file in foreign jurisdictions?

2. The harmonization of patent prosecution may serve the interests of applicants and patent offices from the major industrialized countries by, among other things, reducing costs and eliminating redundancies. Can the same be said for patent offices and applicants in developing countries? What are the advantages and disadvantages, if any, to developing country patent

offices of adopting the prosecution practices of their industrialized counterparts? How easy do you think it would be for developing country patent offices to resist such practices? Interestingly, the TRIPS Agreement does not address application prosecution practices. Instead, such issues are the focus of other agreements, namely, the Paris Convention (PC), the Patent Cooperation Treaty (PCT), the Patent Law Treaty (PLT), and various bilateral and trilateral initiatives such as the patent prosecution highways discussed in Chapter 2. Why do you think this is so?

3. As you learned in Chapter 2, the PC, PCT, and PLT facilitate the filing of applications in multiple jurisdictions by extending the time to file, reducing filing requirements, and more. However, applicants still may face significant hurdles to filing applications in multiple countries. One such hurdle is the requirement that an applicant obtain a foreign filing license. Many jurisdictions, including the UK, China, the United States, and India, require applicants to file domestically, and/or otherwise obtain permission, before filing an application in a foreign country covering an invention made in the home country. This requirement is normally animated by national security concerns and allows a government to determine if an invention should be maintained in secrecy and not disclosed (for some period of time) to foreign patent offices. Penalties for failing to obtain permission may include fines, imprisonment, and the inability to obtain a patent on the invention in the home country. For example, Article 20 of the People's Republic of China Patent Act (2008) provides in part:

> Any unit or individual that intends to apply for patent in a foreign country for an invention or utility model accomplished in China shall submit the matter to the patent administration department under the State Council for confidentiality examination.
>
> . . .
>
> With regard to an invention or utility model for which an application is filed for a patent in a foreign country in violation of the provisions of the first paragraph of this Article, if an application is also filed for the patent in China, patent right shall not be granted.

Patent Law (adopted by Standing Comm. Nat'l People's Cong., Mar. 12, 1984, last amended Dec. 27, 2008) art. 20 (2008) (China).

4. In some cases, concerns of a more economic nature may influence foreign filing requirements. As discussed in Chapter 8, *supra*, in a provision clearly designed to facilitate the sharing of benefits from inventions made with genetic resources from India, the Indian Biological Diversity Act (2002) penalizes applicants who file for patent protection covering inventions made with biological resources from India without first obtaining permission from the relevant authority.

5. In the United States, an applicant is deemed to have such permission (called a foreign filing license) six months after filing an application in the USPTO, though one can petition to be granted such a license earlier. Also, applicants may file PCT applications on inventions made in the United

States with the USPTO as the Receiving Office without obtaining a foreign filing license. However, if the application is placed under a secrecy order in the United States, it will not be forwarded to the International Bureau for publication or further processing while the secrecy order is in place.

2. CLAIMS

In any country, the claims are the single most important part of a patent application. No matter how extensive or grandiose the written description portion of the document, what the inventor ultimately may exclude others from practicing is the subject matter defined by the claims. Claim drafting is considered more of an art than a science and can consume years of practice before real proficiency is attained.

Claims can be independent or dependent. Independent claims stand alone whereas a dependent claim "depends from" and explicitly refers to another claim and incorporates the subject matter of that claim, further defining or adding elements to the invention. Study the patents in Figure 1, *supra*, again. For convenience, the claims of the U.S. ratchet wrench patent (the '060 patent) are reproduced below:

1. A ratchet wrench comprising: a handle within which a motor is accommodated; a head provided with a ratchet mechanism having a rotary tightening member which is to be rotated by drive power from the motor; a pin extending in a transverse direction with respect to the axis of the handle so as to connect the head with the handle; a crankshaft connected to an output shaft of the motor; a first drive bush into which a crankpin of the crankshaft is rotatably fitted; a first drive member into which the first drive bush is fitted to be slidable in a direction substantially perpendicular to the axis of the pin, the first drive member being connected to the pin in such a manner that the first drive member is rotatable about the pin and slidable along the pin; a second drive member connected to the pin in such a manner that the second drive member is rotatable about the pin and slidable together with the first drive member along the pin; a second drive bush into which the second drive member is fitted so as to be slidable in a direction parallel to the axis of the head; and a yoke which is connected to the second drive bush in such a manner that the yoke is swingable relative to the second drive bush, the yoke being connected to the rotary tightening member via the ratchet mechanism.

2. A ratchet wrench according to claim 1, including a tilt mechanism which locks the head at an angle selected from a plurality of angles relative to the axis of the handle.

3. A ratchet wrench according to claim 2, wherein the tilt mechanism includes an engagement member having a toothed por-

tion, the engagement member being fixed to the head and rotatably connected to the pin; and a lock pin which is disposed in a front portion of the handle and is engaged with the engage member so as to lock the head.

4. A ratchet wrench according to claim 1, wherein the crankshaft is connected to the motor via a reduction gear mechanism.

U.S. Patent No. 6,435,060 B1, col. 4.

Claim 1 of the '060 patent is an independent claim and claims 2–4 are dependent claims. Multiple dependent claims depend from and refer to more than one previous claim and incorporate the subject matter of the referenced claims in the alternative. Claim 4 of the '060 patent could be rewritten as a multiple dependent claim in the following form: "A ratchet wrench according to claims 1, 2, or 3, wherein the crankshaft is connected to the motor via a reduction gear mechanism."

A claim typically appears as a single sentence comprising a preamble (e.g., "a ratchet wrench"), which names the invention; a transition phrase (e.g., "comprising"), which has a special meaning in the law and generally indicates whether the claim is open to additional elements; and a body, listing elements of the invention and how they are connected (e.g., "the crankshaft is connected to the motor via a reduction gear mechanism"). Some offices, such as the EPO (Examination Guidelines Rule 29), USPTO (37 C.F.R. § 1.75(e)), and SIPO (Implementing Regulations Rule 22), prefer, but do not require, claims to instead be in a "Jepson" format, named after the inventor who first used such a claim format successfully. *Ex parte Jepson*, 1917 Dec. Comm'r Pat. 62. In Jepson claims, the preamble is a phrase that is admitted to be prior art, the transition is of the form "wherein the improvement comprises" or "characterized in that . . ." or similar language, and the remainder is the technical improvement over the prior art. Claims tend to follow established formats and appear quite similar from country to country, which is not surprising, considering the widespread use of the Paris Convention priority and the PCT system to file applications covering the same invention in multiple countries. However, a variety of other special claim formats exist, such as Markush, product-by-process, and Beauregard claims. Some represent quirks of particular jurisdictions while others, such as functional claims, are used more globally. Three claim formats are discussed below: (i) omnibus claims,(ii) functional claims, and (iii) Swiss-type claims.

An omnibus claim refers to the remainder of the specification and drawings to define the invention. For example, a claim to "a hamburger, as shown and described" is an omnibus claim. Such claims are allowed in countries that retain "central claiming" aspects such as Germany and most other European countries, although their use is discouraged; see, for example, EPO Examination Guidelines Rule 29(6). In these countries, the claim identifies the center or core of the invention. Omnibus claims are not allowed for utility patents in the United States, given its peripheral claiming system. Under the peripheral claiming system, claims are required to "particularly point out and distinctly claim" the invention by defining its periphery—i.e., its metes and bounds. The purpose of the requirement is to give third parties requisite notice of the proprietary scope of the patent so they can govern their behavior to avoid infringement. However, omnibus claims are required in U.S. design and plant patents, which are limited to a single claim. For example, the claim of a design patent on a table (which would only protect the table's appearance, not its function), could read "the ornamental design for a table, as shown and described."

In theory, a peripheral claiming system provides superior notice to other inventors compared to a central claiming system but this does not appear to be the reality. As explained by Professors Burk and Lemley:

> Patents are, in theory, a legal right to exclude competitors from using the patentee's invention. Exactly what the patentee gets to prevent others from using depends, however, on how the law defines the scope of the patent right. In modern American patent doctrine, we define what the patentee owns not by what she actually built or disclosed, but by what she claimed. Courts and commentators regularly analogize patent claims as akin to the "metes and bounds" of a real property deed, defining the outer boundaries of a "property" right conferred on the patentee. According to this view, known as the peripheral claiming approach, words of a claim form a sort of conceptual "fence" that marks the edge of the patentee's rights. . .

> [This peripheral claiming approach] isn't working . . . parties and courts seem unable to agree on what particular patent claims mean. Patent law has provided none of the certainty associated with the definition of boundaries in real property law. Literally every case involves a fight over the meaning of multiple terms, and not just the complex technical ones. Recent Federal Circuit cases have had to decide plausible disagreements over the meanings of the words "a," "or," "to," "including," and "through," to name but a few. Claim construction is sufficiently uncertain that many parties don't settle a case until after the court has construed the claims, because there is no baseline for agreement on what the patent might possibly cover. . . .

> The problem is not just lack of understanding. Rather, claim construction may be inherently indeterminate: it may simply be impossible to cleanly map words to things. Patent attorneys seize on such indeterminacy to excuse infringement or to expand their client's exclusive rights. . . . The key feature of peripheral claiming, setting out clear boundaries to warn the public of what

is and is not claimed—the "notice function" of patents that has received so much attention in recent years—increasingly seems to be an illusion. And it is a dangerous illusion, because it means that courts define the scope of legal rights not by reference to the invention but by reference to semantic debates over the meaning of words chosen by lawyers. . . .

There is an alternative. Before 1870, the scope of U.S. patents was determined using a system of "central claiming." Under a central-claiming approach, the patentee does not delineate the outer reach of what it claims. Rather, the patentee discloses the central features of the invention—what distinguishes it from the prior art—and the courts determine how much protection the patent is entitled to by looking at the prior art that cabins the invention, how important the patentee's invention was, and how different the accused device is. In some countries elements of that system remain to this day, and indeed there are vestiges of central claiming in the U.S. patent system. . . .

If the goal of peripheral claiming was to establish fence posts marking the boundary of the patent, we can think of central claiming as replacing fence posts with sign posts identifying new inventions. Whereas peripheral claiming purports to mark the outermost boundary of the patentee's claims, central claiming describes the core or gist of the patentee's contribution to technology. . . [T]he way for the patent system to move ahead may be by looking behind. Rather than relying on the illusion of peripheral fence posts, patent law may do better to once again look to central sign posts.

Dan L. Burk & Mark A. Lemley, *Fence Posts or Sign Posts: Rethinking Patent Claim Construction*, 157 U. PA. L. REV. 1743, 1744–1747 (2009) (citations omitted).

The "vestiges" of central claiming in the U.S. system include the use of omnibus claims in design and plant patents, discussed in Chapter 8, *supra*, and means plus function claims, which are provided for in 35 U.S.C. §112 and discussed briefly below. For an analysis of central vs. peripheral claiming in patents and beyond, *see* Jeanne C. Fromer, *Claiming Intellectual Property*, 76 U. CHI. L. REV. 719 (2009).

Functional claims allow elements of an invention to be described by their function (e.g., "means for fastening") as opposed to their structure (e.g., "a button"). The structure for performing the stated function is disclosed in the remainder of the specification and is considered, along with its equivalents, to be part of the claim. Functional claims can be helpful in defining combination inventions wherein a particular function can be performed by a variety of elements. Such claims are provided for by statute in the United States at 35 U.S.C. § 112, ¶ 6. Most other countries do not have statutory provisions specifying how such claims are to be interpreted. Thus, while other offices generally will accept such claims, their scope and interpretation can vary widely.

There are also types of claims that are useful for particular categories of inventions. One such example is a "Swiss-type claim," a claim given its name because it was first allowed by the Swiss Patent Office. A Swiss-type claim is a claim that covers a second or subsequent new medical use of a known substance or composition. Assume, for example, that a researcher discovers that acetylsalicylic acid (the active chemical in aspirin) not only cures headaches, but also cures athlete's foot. If the researcher wishes to claim protection for this new medical use with a Swiss-type claim, she will formulate her claim as follows: "the use of composition A [in this case, acetylsalicylic acid] in the manufacture of a medicament for the treatment of disorder B" [in this case, athlete's foot]. The purpose of a Swiss-type claim is to permit protection for an invention that would otherwise not be patentable. In the above example, the researcher would not be able to obtain protection for acetylsalicylic acid, since it is known and lacks novelty. The only novel aspect of the invention is the use of the acid as a method of treatment for athlete's foot. However, under Article 53(c) of the EPC, as well as under the laws of a majority of countries, methods of treatment of the human body are not regarded as patentable inventions. A Swiss-type claim circumvents that limitation because it does not claim the treatment itself, but rather only the manufacture of the medicament that permits the treatment to take place.

Swiss-type claims are unnecessary in countries that permit the patenting of methods of medical treatment, such as the United States. Further, following the EPO Enlarged Board of Appeals decision in *In re Abbott Respiratory*, G 0002/08 (2010), *available at* http://www.epo.org/law-practice/case-law-appeals/recent/g080002ex1.html, Swiss-style claims are no longer allowed at the EPO for applications having a filing date on or after January 11, 2011. EPC Article 54((5) EPC 2000 explicitly allows for a known substance to be patented for a specific therapeutic use, such as a different dosage regime, as long as the method is not in the prior art. According to the Enlarged Board: "Where the subject matter of a claim is rendered novel only by a new therapeutic use of a medicament, such claim may no longer have the format of a so called Swiss-type claim as instituted by decision G 5/83." *Id.* at para. 7.1.3. Instead, second medical use claims can be written as "Substance X for the treatment of disease Y."

As the brief description of the omnibus, functional and Swiss-type claims above illustrate, claim formats can be powerful tools for patentees to control and expand the subject matter others will be excluded from practicing. As Professor Drahos's extensive study based on interviews with 45 patent offices concludes:

The monopoly heart of the patent system lies in the claims that are applied for and granted. . . . [T]he patent system is a system of private taxation. Through claims the drafter determines the products and activities that are to be the subject of this power of taxation.

It is in the drafting of patent claims that so much of the relentless gaming of the patent system is to be found. . . . So, for example, the patenting of naturally occurring biological materials can be achieved of a claim format that distinguishes the natural from the isolated or purified material is accepted by an office. 'An isolated Y comprising sequence X' is one example of this kind of patent drafting magic. . . . [B]y accepting different types of claims, patent offices expand the operation of the patent system and in some cases circumvent restrictions on patentability. During the course of the fieldwork more than one attorney suggested that through the art of claiming much could be done to avoid restrictions on patentability and improve protection for clients. This is almost certainly no idle boast. Much of the practical impact of any national patent system lies not in what the patent statute says is or is not patentable, but rather in what types of claims the patent office recognizes.

PETER DRAHOS, THE GLOBAL GOVERNANCE OF KNOWLEDGE: PATENT OFFICES AND THEIR CLIENTS 79–81 (2010).

The terms "patented invention" and "claimed invention," though commonly used, are somewhat misleading in that they suggest that each patent contains only one invention. A patent may disclose one broad inventive concept, but it can include as many inventions as it has claims because each claim covers an invention and the patentability requirements must be met for each claim. While words in a patent application generally are given their ordinary meaning, in some countries, a patentee is allowed to be her own lexicographer and can give a special meaning to a word as long as that special meaning is explicitly stated in the patent.

As the Maio excerpt indicates, p. 601, *supra,* patent applications may contain an extremely large number of claims, which can make a patent examiner's job difficult and burdensome. Some patent offices have therefore taken measures to attempt to reduce the number of claims that applicants file. Rule 43(5) of the EPC Implementing Regulations states that "[t]he number of claims shall be reasonable with regard to the nature of the invention claimed." This provision arguably provides a basis for an EPO examiner to object to an application containing an excessive number of claims. Another way in which the EPO limits claims is by charging excess claim fees. There are no charges for the first fifteen claims, then 500 euros for each additional claim above sixteen.

In 2007, the USPTO sought to implement rules limiting an applicant to five independent/twenty-five total claims (unless the applicant could support why additional claims are needed), a move that, along with proposed changes limiting the use of continuing applications (discussed later in this Chapter) raised the ire of patent practitioners and many corporate patent assignees. Implementation of the rules was initially blocked by a court order in *Tafas v. Dudas*, 541 F. Supp. 2d 805 (E.D. Va. 2008). However, on appeal, the U.S. Court of Appeals for the Federal Circuit in *Tafas v. Doll,* 559 F.3d 1345 (Fed. Cir. 2009) held that almost all the proposed rules were procedural in nature and therefore constituted valid acts within the USPTO's rule-making power. Nonetheless, the Undersecretary of Commerce for Intellectual Property and Director of the USPTO, David Kappos, withdrew the contested rules. 74 Fed. Reg. 52,686 (Oct. 14, 2009).

Claims are, however, limited under the new accelerated examination track offered since September 26, 2011 by the USPTO. Called "Track 1" prioritized examination, this expedited option (examination is to be completed within twelve months of filing) is available to applicants for utility or plant patents who pay a special fee of $4000 (as of March 16, 2013), or $2000 for small entities, whose applications include no more than four independent and thirty total claims and no multiple dependent claims, and who file electronically. Exceeding claim restrictions or petitioning for an extension of time during Track 1 terminates the prioritized exam, moving the application to a slower track.

3. TYPES OF APPLICATIONS

a. Overview

During the course of prosecuting a patent, an applicant may use several different types of applications to achieve protection for her invention. Provisional applications are available in many countries, including Australia, Singapore, Japan, the UK, the United States, China, and New Zealand, as a less expensive way to secure a filing date for priority purposes. Provisional applications offer applicants a lower filing fee and an additional twelve months in which to determine whether to file a regular non-provisional application for a patent. Provisional applications also protect an applicant's right to file in other countries as long as the provisional application is filed before the invention is disclosed to the public. The provisional application is not examined, and will simply lapse after twelve months and have no further effect unless a regular non-provisional application is filed by that time. Importantly, filing a provisional application does not start the twenty-year patent term clock ticking. Term is counted from the filing of the first non-provisional application.

In the United States, non-provisional applications include regular, continuing (continuation, continuation-in-part, divisional), and reissue applications. A continuing application follows an original non-provisional application while a reissue application can be filed by a patentee who wishes to correct an error in an issued patent.

Continuation applications are primarily used by applicants who want to pursue additional claims to an invention disclosed in an earlier application (called a "parent" or "original" application). The continuation uses the same specification as the parent application, can claim priority from the filing date of the parent, must name at least one of the same inventors as in the parent, and must be filed during the pendency of the parent at the USPTO. While filing a continuation used to be a key way to move past an examiner's final rejection of claims, many applicants now simply file a Request for Continued Examination (RCE) and pay a fee, which effectively removes the final rejection and allows them to continue prosecution in the same application. Patent examiners routinely reject the claims initially filed in an application based on combinations of prior art references, usually patents or other published documents that, in the examiner's view, disclose the claimed invention. In the United States, the availability of continuing applications and RCEs means that the cycle of examiner rejections and applicant responses to rejections can go on for years and can easily consume tens of thousands of dollars before an examiner concludes a patent should issue on a claimed invention, or the applicant either appeals or gives up and abandons the application.

Continuation-in-part (CIP) applications have the features of continuations except that they also contain some new matter not present in the parent application. Thus, the common matter is entitled to the filing date of the parent but the new matter, and any new claims relying on it, is only entitled to the filing date of the CIP. Nevertheless, the term of a patent issuing from a CIP is still measured from the earliest effective non-provisional filing date.

Continuation practice has been seen as somewhat controversial and out of harmony with patent practice worldwide. Although countries permit the filing of divisional applications (discussed below) in accordance with Article 4G of the Paris Convention, the filing of continuation and CIP applications is unique to the United States. As a result, some critics view the U.S. system, which gives patent applicants "several cracks at the bat," as adding significant delay and uncertainty to patent prosecution. They also argue that the ability to use continuing applications to track competitors' products and align patent claims with them gives applicants undue power and permits them to gain unfair and unnecessary advantage over competitors. *See, e.g.,* Mark A. Lemley & Kimberly A. Moore, *Ending Abuse of Patent Continuations,* 84 B.U. L. REV. 65 (2004).

b. Divisional Applications and Unity of Invention versus Restriction Practice

As noted earlier, each patent application can contain more than one invention as evidenced by the claims, but an application should not contain more than one inventive concept (or group of related inventions). When an application contains more than one inventive concept, an examiner may require the application to be divided, with one application covering only a single inventive concept. In the United States, concern over multiple inventions in an application is addressed in § 121 of the Patent Act, which governs so-called "restriction practice." Pursuant to §121, an examiner generally will require "restriction" if the claims are directed to "independent and distinct" inventions. In such a case, the examiner will refuse to examine all the claims in the application, and instead will require the applicant to elect one invention (covered by one or more claims) for examination. The applicant may then pursue any other inventions disclosed in that parent application in one or more divisional applications. In Europe, Japan, and elsewhere, combining independent inventions into a single application violates the requirement of "unity of invention." Unity of invention is directed to ensuring that patent relate to only one invention or one group of related inventions. When an examiner is of the opinion that this requirement has been violated, the result is similar to that under restriction practice; namely, that one invention will be examined in the parent application and claims to other inventions can be sought in divisional applications.

Unity of invention differs in a subtle way from restriction practice, however. Under unity of invention, an application may include a group of inventions, provided those inventions are linked so as to form a single general inventive concept. For this requirement to be met, all the independent claims in the application must share the same novel and nonobvious feature. An application claiming an apparatus (for example, a chair), a method of manufacture of the apparatus, and a new use for the apparatus may therefore be deemed to possess unity of invention, and the examiner will examine all the claims without requiring the election of a single invention and the filing of divisional applications claiming the others.

Unity of invention and restriction practice are largely administrative conveniences providing greater revenue to patent offices from the additional filing fees of the divisional applications, and easier searching and classification for the examiners. At times, however, the distinction between unity of invention and restriction practice can make a significant difference in prosecution.

Consider the following: Application A is a patent application filed directly with the USPTO. Application B is an identical application to Application A, but it is filed as a PCT application. Rule 13.1 of the Regulations under the PCT adopts the unity of invention standard. The rule provides that "[t]he international application shall relate to one invention only or to a group of inventions so linked as to form a single general inventive concept ('requirement of unity of invention')." The PCT also places limitations on the actions national patent offices may take when an international application enters the national stage in any country. For example, Article 27(1) provides: "No national law shall require compliance with requirements relating to the form or contents of the international application different from or additional to those which are provided for in this Treaty and the Regulations." Application A receives a restriction requirement from the USPTO. The PCT International Searching Authority does not raise a unity of invention objection against Application B during the international stage. Application B enters the national stage in the United States. Given the interplay between PCT Rule 13.1 and Article 27(1), may the USPTO restrict Application B just as it did Application A? The answer, according to *Caterpillar Tractor Co. v. Comm'r of Patents and Trademarks*, 650 F. Supp. 218 (E.D. Va. 1986), is "no." Although the *Caterpillar* case dealt with earlier versions of the PCT Regulations and the U.S. Code of Federal Regulations, the court held that to permit the issuance of a restriction requirement would "be contrary to the PCT and thus contrary to law." The PCT in this scenario not only trumps national law, it provides patent prosecution options not available to direct national applicants.

While applicants most often file divisional applications in response to restriction or unity of invention objections, divisional applications, like U.S. continuation applications, also serve as convenient prosecution tools. Because divisional applications carve out distinct and independent inventions from the parent application, they are helpful, for example, when a patent office allows some claims in an application but refuses others. In such cases, filing a divisional application may allow an applicant to resubmit the non-allowed claims while obtaining a patent covering the allowed ones. This type of voluntary divisional application will be treated as a new application separate and independent from the parent application, but it will retain the parent's filing date and the right to claim the same priority.

Not surprisingly, applicants frequently file divisional applications toward the end of the prosecution process, causing complaints from patent offices that they contribute to patent examination backlogs. In response, the EPO amended its regulations to limit the opportunities for divisional filing. The new regulations, which went into effect on April 1, 2010, provide that divisional applications must be filed no later than two years from the first examination report on any patent application in a family of parents and divisionals, or within two years of a specific non-unity of invention objection, whichever is latest. Divisional applications must therefore be filed at earlier stages of the prosecution process rather than at the end, which may considerably hamper their value as a prosecution strategy.

B. PATENT EXAMINATION

As noted earlier, virtually all major patent systems require substantive examination of patent applications to ensure compliance with novelty, inventive step, and other conditions of patentability while certain smaller/lower volume offices do not. A country might choose to forego substantive examination for a variety of reasons, including limited resources and/or a low number of patent applications received. Training and maintaining a cadre of professional patent examiners is expensive, and a government faced with limited resources may choose to direct its funds to higher-priority needs. Alternatively, as only a small percentage of patents are ever litigated, a government may choose to simply register patents and allow litigation of the important ones to uncover any issues of patent validity. The drawback, of course, is that competitors may be negatively impacted by the issuance of patents that do not meet the patentability requirements for that country and that would not have been granted if domestic substantive examination had taken place.

Some commentators suggest that a patent registration system need not be limited to small countries/low volume offices, but could be a desirable policy choice for the United States to adopt. *See, e.g.,* F. Scott Kieff, *The Case for Registering Patents and the Law and Economics of Present Patent-Obtaining Rules*, 45 B.C. L. REV. 55 (2003). According to Professor Kieff:

> The hypothetical model patent system differs from our present one in that patent applications would be merely registered in the Patent Office rather than examined. Under the present system, patent applications are filed in the Patent Office and examined for compliance with the legal rules for patentability by technically and legally trained staff of that administrative agency. Under the examination process, also called patent prosecution, the ex parte exchange between the applicant and the Patent Office examiner typically lasts about three years before an application that has not been either finally rejected or abandoned issues as a patent. Having been examined, issued patents enjoy a procedural and substantive presumption of validity, and a party challenging a patent must prove invalidity under the heightened standard for civil litigation of "clear and convincing evidence."

> In the proposed registration model, patent applications would be filed with the Patent Office but not examined. The Patent Office would maintain original files and make authentic copies available publicly . . . . In addition, the presumption of validity would be eliminated, or at least relaxed, thereby allowing invalidity to

be judged under the standard ordinarily used in civil litigation of "a preponderance of the evidence."

Recent work by Mark Lemley sheds some light on the strengths of soft-look systems—such as the present system and the proposed registration model—as compared with hard-look systems in which patents are examined with stricter scrutiny. Lemley shows that "[b]ecause so few patents are ever asserted against a competitor, it is much cheaper for society to make detailed validity determinations in those few cases than to invest additional resources examining patents that will never be heard from again."

Lemley explores one important reason why the making of detailed validity determinations in litigation instead of in the Patent Office leads to lower net costs across all patents when he offers the core insight that litigation and its threat operate to provide important information about society's level of interest in a given patent—only those patents that matter receive a hard look. But this information could be provided through other means, perhaps even directly to the Patent Office, which leaves open the issue of which method of providing this information is cheapest.

A more complete exploration of this open issue is therefore required to understand the many reasons why the costs of providing such information through litigation are less. One advantage of litigation is that, because it comes later, it allows more information about society's interest in the patent to accrue, thereby decreasing the likelihood of error associated with *ex ante* efforts to predict which patents should receive close attention. Another advantage is that ex post selection of those patents that turn out to matter raises fewer administrative and public choice problems than would ex ante efforts because the attention of both proponents and opponents of a given patent are more likely to be at a peak in later litigation. Decision making through litigation mitigates many of the well-known problems associated with making award-type decisions.

Id. at 70–73 (citations omitted).

While the United States had a registration system from 1793 to 1836, and its current system is costly to maintain and often criticized, despite the above-noted advantages of a registration system there are no indications that it, or any other major patent granting country or regional office, intends to move to a registration system for patents. There are, of course, other policy implications for registration versus examination systems. For example, an examination system may improve the quality of patents, facilitate a more robust public domain in terms of weeding out non-patentable things; and enhance competition. Registration systems may be more efficient administratively but may fail to enhance the over-all amount or quality of technical skill or information in circulation in the local market. The patent offices of Belgium, South Africa, Uganda, Nigeria, and the OAPI are among the few purely registration systems where patents can issue without any local substantive examination. Such offices originally adopted a patent registration approach to avoid the significant costs associated with employing and training examiners to conduct substantive examination. For example, when the Intellectual Property Office of Singapore (IPOS) first began granting patents under the Patent Law of 1995, only a handful of employees were on staff to handle patent matters. IPOS currently does not engage in substantive examination of patent applications (although recent amendments to the patent law will be changing that and the office is expected to begin hiring examiners soon); however, to obtain a patent in Singapore, an applicant must have obtained substantive examination from one of a list of designated foreign patent offices or the PCT International Bureau. Thus, as substantive examination is the dominant regime in the major patent issuing countries, we will focus on a comparative overview of this approach for the remainder of this Chapter.

1. SUBSTANTIVE EXAMINATION

Recently, countries such as China, India and Brazil have emerged as leading contenders in patent examination and issuance. Together with Russia, the so called BRIC countries received 25 percent of patent applications filed worldwide in 2010, all but India experiencing growth in applications received. *See* WIPO, 2012 WIPO IP FACTS AND FIGURES, 17 (2012), *available at* http://www.wipo.int/export/sites/www/free publications/en/statistics/943/wipo_pub_943_2012.pdf.

Recall from Chapter 1 that in 2011, China's patent office took the number one spot from the USPTO in terms of the number of utility patent applications it receives each year. *See* WIPO, WORLD INTELLECTUAL PROPERTY INDICATORS 48 (2012). As noted in Chapter 8, China is also number one in terms of design and utility model applications received. The following excerpt discusses the patent examination process in China.

JOHANNES LIEGSALZ & STEFAN WAGNER, PATENT EXAMINATION AT THE STATE INTELLECTUAL PROPERTY OFFICE IN CHINA

Eur. Sch. of Mgmt. and Tech. Working Paper No. 11–06, 5–8 2011)

. . . .

The PRC joined the World Intellectual Property Organization (WIPO) in 1980 and consequently paved the way for an IPR system that complies with international standards. Five years later, in 1985, the PRC also signed the Paris Convention for the Protection of Industrial Property and in 1993 the Patent Cooperation Treaty. In becoming a member of the WTO in 2001, China reached another important milestone and adheres to the TRIPS agreement. Today, the PRC has implemented laws for all relevant IPRs such as patents, trademarks and copyrights. All IPRs are filed at branches such as the Patent Office of the SIPO. These offices are responsible for the acceptance, examination and publication of all IPR related documents. Concerning IPR-related disputes, the PRC has established a system of people's courts that enforce IPR laws. This tiered system is divided into the Supreme, Higher, Intermediate and Basic People's Courts. At the Intermediate People's Court level and above, there are specialized divisions for IPR disputes.

[The] Chinese patent law was enacted by the Standing Committee of the sixth National Congress in 1984 and is the governing legislation for the protection of technological inventions in China. It went into force in 1985 and was amended three times, in 1992, 2000 and 2008. In Art. 2 of the Implementing Regulations of the Patent Law of the People's Republic of China, an invention is defined as "any new technical solution relating to a product, a process, or improvement thereof." According to the patent law, patents can be granted to inventions that fulfill the basic requirements of Art. 22: novelty, inventiveness and practical applicability. With the exception of some minor differences, these standards are largely comparable to the regulations of the USPTO and the EPO.

Before the date of filing of a patent application no identical invention or utility model can have been publicly disclosed in the PRC or in any other country in order to meet the novelty criterion. During the examination of the novelty of an application, examiners have to follow the principle of individual comparison. This means each document of prior reference is compared with the technical solution of the invention under review. In the case of two or more applications on the same subject matter by different applicants, the patent should be granted to the first applicant; this is commonly known as the first-to-file principle. The requirement of inventiveness applies to an invention if it has prominent substantive features and represents a notable progress, compared with the technology existing before the date of filing (state of the art). In order to prove this criterion all relevant prior art is compared to the technical solution of the current application. The third criterion—practical applicability—requires that inventions can be made or used and can produce effective results. "Made or used" refers to the commercial production or utilization of an invention. An invention is not seen as practically applicable if it is non-reproducible or if unique natural conditions are necessary.

According to Art. 3 of the Chinese patent law, the patent administration department under the State Council is responsible for the patent examination throughout the country. It receives and examines patent applications and grants patent rights for inventions. There are three major routes to file a patent at the SIPO. The direct way is to file the patent as a Chinese priority filing. Note that a Chinese priority filing is mandatory for inventions made in the PRC by Chinese individuals and entities. Because China adheres to the Paris Convention for the Protection of Intellectual Property, a second filing option is to extend a foreign application by a subsequent SIPO application within the priority year. There also exists a third option, based on the PCT treaty. An applicant may file an international PCT application at any of the defined receiving offices. This allows the applicant to delay the decision as to which jurisdiction he is seeking patent protection for up to 30 months.

A patent application has to contain a description of the underlying invention, an abstract and the claims supplemented by technical drawings if necessary. The basic application fee of Renminbi Yuan (RMB) 950 is comparable to the online filing fee of EUR 100 at the EPO. After an application has been filed at the SIPO, the examination procedure follows. . . . During the examination, an applicant may amend an application as long as the amendments are within the scope of the initially submitted documents. The applicant may *withdraw* the application at any time during examination. If the invention fulfills the basic formality requirements, it will be classified according to the International Patent Classification IPC by the patent examiner. Eighteen months after the application was filed the document will be published; however, the publication may take place earlier at the applicant's request.

Within three years after the filing date the applicant may request a substantive examination of the filed patent invention. If the applicant fails to do so, the application is deemed to have been withdrawn by the applicant. The fee for requesting substantive examination is RMB 2,500. If the examination finds that the invention is not in line with Chinese patent law, the SIPO has to notify the applicant. The applicant will then

cant pays the renewal fees. These annual renewal fees increase over time, from RMB 900 in the first 3 years to RMB 8,000 during the 16th year. In the case of a refused application, the applicant may request a re-examination by the SIPO Patent Re-Examination Board or directly file a judicial appeal within a certain time limit. Furthermore, the first administrative or judicial decision can be appealed as the Chinese court system always permits at least two instances of appeal. Once a patent is granted, Chinese patent law allows any party to ask the SIPO Patent Re-Examination Board to invalidate the patent. The Re-Examination Board has the option to maintain the patent as granted, revoke the patent or maintain the patent in an amended form. If the person who requested the invalidation or the patent holder is not satisfied with the decision of the Re-Examination Board to maintain or invalidate the patent in dispute, another judicial proceeding can be initiated.

NOTES AND QUESTIONS

1. Patent law is relatively new to China; the country has only had a patent act since 1984. However, patents have been increasing in importance in China due to the size of the market, their perceived link with innovation and national competitiveness, the significant domestic capacity to copy innovative products, and also as a result of pressure from other countries to strengthen overall levels of intellectual property protection.

2. In a portion of the study not reproduced above, the authors report a troubling finding:

> Most interestingly, we find that Chinese applicants achieve faster patent grants when compared to applicants from other countries, in particular to non-Asian applicants. While this effect might be due to a language advantage of domestic applicants, it might also be a sign of positive discrimination of Chinese applicants. Finding that the speed advantage of domestic applicants is more pronounced in areas that are of high importance to the Chinese economy does not alleviate this concern. While we are unable to ultimately answer the question whether discrimination of applicants is taking place, further research is warranted. . . . Also, applications filed by applicants with a clear focus on the Chinese market as well as by applicants that have filed a high number of applications at the SIPO are characterized by shorter duration of patent examination. Taken together, these findings imply that having experience in dealing with the SIPO can significantly reduce the grant lags to be expected. For firms having no or little experience in dealing with Chinese patent authorities it might therefore pay-off to contract an external law firm that is experienced in dealing with the SIPO.

Id. at 27–28.

The authors also point to a study suggesting other patent offices including the EPO (Germany) and JPO may also effectively discriminate against foreign applicants by granting patents to domestic applicants more quickly. However, there are a variety of other possible reasons for the disparities, including foreign applicant language difficulties and lack of familiarity with the office and its procedures. *See* Paul H. Jensen, *Alfons Palangkaraya & Elizabeth Webster, Disharmony in International Patent Office Decisions,* 15 FED. CIR. B.J. 679, 695–699 (2006). Of course, U.S. patent law has long had statutory provisions that were facially neutral but had a discriminatory impact on foreign applicants, such as 35 U.S.C. §104, which, prior to amendments resulting from NAFTA and TRIPS, and which was eliminated by the America Invents Act (AIA), prevented applicants from relying on inventive activity outside of the United States to establish entitlement to a patent. Is there any recourse for applicants who feel they are being discriminated against during prosecution at a foreign office? *See* TRIPS Art. 3 and 4.

In the United States, substantive examination automatically follows the examination for compliance with formalities such as proper documentation, payment of fees, and the required oath. The U.S. Patent Act provides that an applicant is entitled to a patent unless the USPTO, through its examiners, can establish otherwise. Consequently, the burden is on the examiner, in the first instance, to show that a claimed invention fails to meet one or more statutory requirements. Once compliance with all requirements is established, a patent will issue from the USPTO. If compliance is not established, the applicant will have the opportunity to abandon the application or appeal the examiner's rejection(s) to the Patent Trial and Appeal Board, and from there to the Court of Appeals for the Federal Circuit, and ultimately to the United States Supreme Court. An alternative route of appeal from a USPTO Board decision is to the District Court for the Eastern District of Virginia under 35 U.S.C. §145, and then to the Federal Circuit and the Supreme Court. Bringing a civil action in district court allows an applicant to introduce evidence that was not presented to the USPTO. *See Kappos v. Hyatt*, 132 S.Ct. 1690 (2012).

In other countries, substantive examination is not automatic and must be requested within a specified period of time (e.g., three years in the EPO, SIPO, and JPO; seven years in the German patent office) or the application will be deemed abandoned. Regardless of whether substantive examination is requested, applications normally will be published eighteen months after their filing date. However, in the U.S., applicants can avoid having their applications published if they notify the USPTO that they will not file for patent protection on the same invention in a foreign country. The independent inventor lobby in the United States was able to obtain this concession in the American Inventor's Protection Act of 1999. It allows an applicant interested solely in the U.S. market to keep his or her invention a trade secret if the patent application ultimately is rejected. However, under the pseudo first-inventor-to-file regime created by the AIA, recall that applicants have an incentive to publicly disclose their inventions at the time they file their applications in order to maintain priority over third-party inventors as discussed in Chapter 6, *supra*.

At least two other examination-related features are relatively unique to U.S. patent law. One is the duty of candor. USPTO rules require that patent applicants and their attorneys abide by a duty to disclose to the patent office all known information material to an invention's patentability, in particular, all known relevant prior art. Because patents are "affected with a public interest," and prosecution is an *ex parte* proceeding with virtually no third-party involvement, imposing on a patent applicant a duty to be candid with the USPTO seems reasonable. In the United States, parties accused of patent infringement routinely respond at least in part by charging the patentee with having engaged in inequitable conduct during patent prosecution. A charge of inequitable conduct requires a finding of materiality and intent to deceive. 37 C.F.R. § 1.56. Notably, if inequitable conduct is established, it does not simply result in the invalidation of claims tainted by the bad activity; rather, the entire patent is deemed unenforceable.

The inequitable conduct defense has been invoked with such frequency it has been called a "plague" on patent litigation. In an *en banc* 2011 decision, *Therasense, Inc. v. Becton, Dickinson & Co.*, 649 F.3d 1276, the Court of Appeals for the Federal Circuit raised the materiality and intent to deceive standards required for a finding of inequitable conduct. To find the requisite intention to deceive the Office, the applicant (or anyone associated with prosecuting the application) must have engaged in a knowing and deliberate deception, such deception being the single most reasonable inference able to be drawn from the evidence presented. In addition, to find the requisite materiality, the deception must be the "but-for" cause of the Office allowing the patent. In other words, but for the deception (withholding material information or presenting false or misleading information) the patent would not have issued. Alternatively, the materiality prong can be met by the applicant engaging in affirmative acts of egregious misconduct, such as filing a false affidavit. For a forward-looking essay on the problems engendered by the defense and its prospects after *Therasense*, *see* John M. Golden, *Patent Law's Falstaff: Inequitable Conduct, the Federal Circuit, and Therasense*, 7 WASH. J.L. TECH. & ARTS 353 (2012).

Following passage of the America Invents Act (AIA), the bases on which a challenger can assert inequitable conduct have been reduced in a variety of ways. First, the AIA creates a new supplemental examination proceeding which appears to allow an applicant to purge earlier inequitable conduct during application prosecution (35 U.S.C. §257(c)). Second, it removes the requirement that certain acts be done "without deceptive intent" from several provisions in the U.S. Patent Act, including filing a reissue application (§251), correcting inventorship (§§116(c), 256(a)), foreign filing violations (§§184, 185), instituting a suit on a patent containing an invalid claim (§288), and disclaiming a claim (§253). Finally, as noted earlier, the AIA has eliminated "best mode" violation-based challenges.

With a substantial reduction in the range of offenses that could trigger an inequitable conduct claim, the question arises why other countries never enacted such a requirement. At least one legal scholar has argued that other means exist in most countries to challenge the validity of improperly granted patents thus obviating adoption of a strict obligation of candor on the part of applicants and attorneys participating in the examination process. *See* Paul M. Janicke, *Do We Really Need So Many Mental and Emotional States in United States Patent Law?*, 8 TEX. INTELL. PROP. L.J. 279, 292 (2000). Others point to the "English rule" adopted by many countries by which courts routinely award attorney fees to the winning party (so patentees may be less likely to sue on flawed patents), as well as the absence of U.S.-style broad discovery, without which inequitable conduct is less likely to be uncovered. *See* Martin J. Adelman, Randall R. Rader & John R. Thomas, CASES AND MATERIALS ON PATENT LAW 586 (3d ed. 2009). Nevertheless, there still are countries with disclosure provisions which, if violated, can have a similar effect to inequitable conduct in the United States. For example, Section 8 of the Indian Patent Act provides:

> Information and undertaking regarding foreign applications
>
> (1) Where an applicant for a patent under this Act is prosecuting either alone or jointly with any other person an application for a patent in any country outside India in respect of the same or substantially the same invention, or where to his knowledge such an application is being prosecuted by some person through whom he claims or by some person deriving title from him, he shall file along with his application or subsequently within the prescribed period as the Controller may allow
>
> (a) a statement setting out detailed particulars or such application; and
>
> (b) an undertaking that, [up to the date of grant of patent in India,] he would keep the Controller informed in writing, from time to time, of [detailed particulars as required under] clause (a) in respect of every other application relating to the same or substantially the same invention, if any, filed in any country outside India subsequently to the filing of the statement referred to in the aforesaid clause, within the prescribed time.
>
> (2) At any time after an application for patent is filed in India and till the grant of a patent or refusal to grant of a patent made thereon, the Controller may also require the applicant to furnish details, as may be prescribed, relating to the processing of the application in a country outside India, and in that event the applicant shall furnish to the Controller information available to him within such period as may be prescribed.

The Patent Act, No. 39 of 1970, INDIA CODE (1970).

In *Tata Chemicals Ltd. v. Hindustan Unilever Ltd.*, M.P. Nos.73 of 2011, and M.P. Nos.7, 16, and 22 of 2012, ORA/18/2010/PT/MUM (IPAB June 12, 2012), the Intellectual Property Appellate Board (IPAB), broadly interpreted the term "country" in Section 8 to include an international filing under the PCT. Thus a negative PCT International Preliminary Examination Report

(IPER) on the issues of novelty, inventive step and industrial applicability should have been submitted to the Indian Patent Office by the applicant, even though the key prior art document cited by the IPER had been cited by the Indian examiner and the rejection overcome by the Applicant. According to the Board:

> It is not enough that the Examiner knew that this prior art was there, the respondent ought to have disclosed the results of the IP-ER. The IPER rejected the claims 1 to 3 on both the grounds of novelty and inventive step. It is not for us to conjecture what effect this might have had on the examiner here if he had the benefit of the IPER. This is the object and purpose of enacting Section 8. . . . [T]his information would be of great use for a proper examination of the application. It is no answer to say anyway the office looked at EP'578 [the document cited in the IPER]. The Patent Office did not *see* the IPER. The learned counsel for the respondent submitted that this lapse is of a de-minimis nature; we do not think that honestly furnishing the information or particulars allows a de-minimis qualification.

> The Act requires compliance with Section 8(1) and 8(2) and the patent applicant must comply with the same. Otherwise the patent is liable to be revoked.

Id. at para. 106–107.

Thus, prudent applicants in countries with provisions regarding candor should disclose both foreign and PCT prosecution results to the patent office.

The other feature relatively unique to U.S. patent law is the ability of applicants to file "continuing applications," mentioned previously, and thus extend the period of prosecution throughout the term of the patent, if so desired. A continuing application (or a continuation) is, at its most basic, an application that has been re-filed with the USPTO, most frequently following the rejection of some or all of the original (or parent) application's claims. Applicants file continuations in order to continue negotiating with the USPTO examiner, to submit new claims, or to amend existing ones. If the USPTO allows the continuation, it will issue a patent that expires twenty years from the filing date of the parent application.

While most applicants file continuations following final rejections, applicants may choose to file a continuing application even after the parent application has been allowed in order, for example, to broaden claims or align them more closely with their competitors' products to maximize the chance of success in a potential infringement suit.

Although continuations are unique to the United States, many countries do have divisional applications, which are a type of continuing application except that the ability to prolong prosecution is constrained. Also, several countries, including India, Australia, and New Zealand, also have so-called "patents of addition." A patent of addition can have a somewhat similar effect as a continuation-in-part application (CIP) as it allows a patent to be granted for a modification to or improvement of an invention on which a main patent previously has been granted. Like a patent from a continuation application, the patent of addition runs for the same term of protection as the main patent, subject to possible term extensions.

2. COMPARATIVE EXAMINATION

The process of patent examination tends to follow a similar pattern among countries that engage in substantive examination. Nevertheless, differences in examination guidelines and practices lead to a variety of ways in which applicants are required to draft and prosecute applications. The following article, which takes the form of a dialogue between a London-based European patent attorney and a Minneapolis-based U.S. academic and former Director of the PCT, discusses European and U.S. prosecution practices and policies that are slowly converging, but it also points to some persistent significant differences.

GWILYM V. ROBERTS, JAY A. ERSTLING & CHRISTIAN J. GIRTZ, TRANSATLANTIC PATENTING

LANDSLIDE, Nov./Dec. 2009, at 30

Gwilym: Everyone is fascinated by our transatlantic relationship. I recently had the pleasure of reading *The American* by Henry James about a young U.S. businessman who has made his fortune in railroads and is doing the grand European tour in the mid 19th century. His attempts to win a Parisian wife from a noble family are captivating and have surprising results, but the main theme of the story is about the meeting of the two civilizations, New World and Old World. I would argue that the New World is somewhere else again now and it is interesting to assess how close U.S. and EP practice have come in this Brave Old World. . .

Jay: Not to belabor the literary references, but I think Dickens' "[i]t was the best of times, it was the worst of times" also has something to say about the current state of transatlantic patenting. The difficulties that patent offices—especially the USPTO—are facing, combined with the [current] economy, are pushing offices to take work sharing and harmonization seriously and to consider initiatives that they might have dismissed not too long ago. It will be interesting to see just how close U.S. and EP practice moves, particularly in light of the influence that new "New World" offices like China and India might exert, but it is just as interesting to take a look at the differences that are likely to persist. Hopefully our discussion will shed some light on both of these. Why don't you start at the beginning, with an invention?

Gwilym: It doesn't matter where you are; the reassuring news is that the patent system still requires an invention. The exact levels of inventiveness vary, but my experience has been that this affects the way you pre-

sent the arguments rather than the strength of the arguments themselves . . . .

So let's assume we have an invention—now we need to write the application. I would liken filing a patent application in Europe to heading off into
the empty desert on your camel—you need to take all your provisions
with you as you set off because you won't be able to add anything later on.
This is because the EPO approach to "added matter" is enormously strict
to the extent that usually explicit textual basis for any wording changes is
required.

So everything has to go in. The drawings need to be described well
enough that they can be reproduced from words alone. If you would like a
feature to be importable from the description into the claims, you need to
be able to show that it does not need to be accompanied by the other features in conjunction with which it is described. You also will need to be
able to show that it would be combinable with the existing claims features. The best way to ensure this has always been to use dependent
claims wisely and while multiple dependencies do help to keep the numbers down, the limit of 15 claims before fairly hefty claims fees become
due is a major constraint. In my experience it differs from the U.S. approach, where there is a little more flexibility. Continuing the desert
analogy, you guys seem to have a few fast-food marts, petrol stations, and
convenience stores along the roadside.

Jay: I agree. It seems that the U.S. system does have more flexibility in
prosecuting patents than the EPO approach, and I wonder whether this
difference reflects historical policy considerations favored by the respective systems. An underlying goal in the United States, as you know, was
to encourage as much innovation as possible, particularly by the little
guy. We have always romanticized the notion of the lone inventor, and we
have been reluctant to adopt policies that discourage that notion. So to
encourage invention, we needed a system that was supple and somewhat
forgiving, and that also provided broad exclusive rights and strong remedies . . . .

From the eyes of a U.S. practitioner, it seems that the European system
and the national systems on which it was based were predicated more on
the need to reward innovation among existing players—the big guys, if
you will—rather than trying to bring the little guy into the fold. So the
system needed to encourage early disclosure (hence, first-to-file) and to
reward existing players that already had the structure to file quickly. It
makes sense, then, that Europe placed emphasis on the details of the
claims as filed, ensuring that all of the provisions were initially included.
The natural result was a system with less flexibility, but also one that
tended to be less litigious. But that was then. I think general consensus
now is that however real those philosophical policy differences might have
been, they are much less relevant to today's world . . . . But given that EP

practice is still somewhat less flexible despite movement to the contrary, what additional things should U.S. practitioners consider when converting a U.S. application into a European one?

Gwilym: When we start off on our journey, we bring our tools along as well—we'll need something to back up our arguments of nonobviousness. The European Patent Office is very unlikely to be persuaded by inventive step (nonobviousness) arguments that can't be derived from information found in the application as filed. This does not need to be an explicit reference to nonobviousness, but the advantages attached to a feature need to be derivable.

Jay: And that creates a potential issue. Some tension exists in U.S. practice when using terms like "advantageous" or "preferable" when reciting features. The use of those terms is not in favor because they may read whatever is advantageous or preferable into the claim and make it a required part (excluding everything else).

The problem with reading the recited "advantageous" or "preferable" features into the claim is not in getting the patent to issue, but in litigation. By showing a preference for one embodiment, you may be ruling something else out. Essentially, the limitation is in seeking coverage of non-stated alternatives using the Doctrine of Equivalents. Your "advantageous" or "preferable" embodiment may be used as evidence against you in claim construction, thus limiting your possible patent coverage in later infringement or interference actions. It is a much better idea to use generic language like "first embodiment" or "an embodiment" when reciting features. Can't that work?

Gwilym: We don't need to use words like "advantageous" or "preferable." For example, "cause and effect" language is acceptable. Having recited a feature, you might add that certain effects are achieved as a result of inclusion of that feature. It is best to cite as many effects as you can for each feature, to give best basis for an inventive step argument later. . .

Jay: [W]hat are some [other] issues that the European practitioner needs to consider?

Gwilym: We have oases of common sense! There are tricks and tweaks we can apply at filing to help with the budget but possibly of more interest is substantive examination—that is, Extended European Search Reports (EESR) examination reports where the examiner raises his substantive objections. There is no question that these are still of a very high quality, despite ever increasing productivity targets. A good invention has strong prospects of going to grant; a poor one may face problems. But prosecution practice can still influence the outcome.

It is probably worth mentioning that we are happy to start in Europe with broadly worded claims as long they are clear, include the point of novelty, and have enough additional features for the supporting inventive argument to have context—in other words, the EPO will accept claims directed to the invention rather than the product. The examiner concentrates on the independent claims and issues of patentability, clarity, and sufficiency (enablement) in particular. Most European practitioners are strong on the "first hit" approach—that is, if you fire off your best efforts on the first substantive response, you can maximize your prospects of pushing the application through to grant. The examiners seem to dig their heels in with repeated arguments on the same unamended claim and we are being called to a hearing (Oral Proceedings) after fewer and fewer actions now.

We can strengthen our position by using "Auxiliary Requests," which are effectively cascades of claim sets from strongest to weakest that we can file at the same time and the EPO is very good at looking at all of them and identifying whether there is patentable subject matter in any of them. It does not succumb to the temptation of looking for the "easiest option" but will consider each request in turn so this can be a very good approach effectively giving multiple bites at the cherry. I would say that it is a little harder than it used to be to get a patent granted at the EPO, but usually we feel that we have a good and fair hearing. . . .

Jay: . . . Let's switch gears here. There has been some discussion about reforming divisional practice in Europe. We know divisional applications have been useful. How has it worked and why is there talk of reform?

Gwilym: The EPO has made it very clear they don't like it, but the practice of divisional patent applications provide[d] a strong backup route in Europe. . .

There ha[d] been some concern at the EPO about the "abuse" of divisional patent applications. The Enlarged Board of Appeal found, however, that there was no abuse as practitioners are working within the scope of the EPC. Even so, the EPO will, from . . . April [2010], restrict the opportunity for filing divisionals. From then divisionals must effectively be filed within 24 months of the first examination report on the earliest parent or a later "unity of invention" objection. It may be that a strategy will develop whereby a full review of the parent application will be carried out prior to the 24-month cutoff and all required divisionals will be filed at that stage, as a matter of good practice . . .

Jay: [Consider] the concept of unity of invention. A rough equivalent in the United States is a restriction on claims. The U.S. practitioner has several ways of responding to such a restriction, and also has several other tools at his disposal when considering claiming priority to an earlier-filed application or when hoping to continue an application. Requests for continued examination (RCEs), continuations, continuations-in-part (CIPs), and divisional applications all provide flexibility in this field and have become essential elements of U.S. prosecution. . .Needless to say, any limitation on continuations would drastically alter U.S. practice.

But we can't lose sight of the end goal of having a patent granted. Because the grant of a European patent isn't the end of the road—the patent must be validated in each country—and in light of the need to manage costs, what should the European practitioner know about proceeding after the EPO grants a patent?

Gwilym: As most people know, the European patent application is a "bundle" of national patent applications and after grant it splinters into national patents in each country, where relevant steps are taken. This has become a lot cheaper since the London Agreement dispensed with translations for a number of countries, and efforts continue to unify the system further and in particular allow for centralized infringement proceedings rather than country by country. But we do not have a United States of Europe yet. Of course, we do have the opposition proceedings at the EPO. As long as an opposition is launched within nine months of grant of a patent, it is possible to knock it out across Europe through proceedings based at the EPO.

An upshot of the current fragmented system is that claims can be read differently in different jurisdictions and the test for determining the true scale of the patent claim differs subtly but enough that decisions vary from country to country. There is guidance within the EPC that all countries are supposed to follow, but it does not seem to have pinned anyone down except that the concept of file wrapper estoppel has been expressly rejected.

Jay: So to sum up, it seems that, from a big-picture perspective, we are moving closer together, but from a micro perspective, there are still significant differences. It will be interesting to see if [future case law, potential new EPO and USPTO rules] and changes in European practice, such as the restrictions on divisionals, continue the momentum of bridging gaps or create new ones. My bet is that the forward momentum will continue, which will benefit applicants on both sides of the "pond." If we can focus on making prosecution more cost-effective, reliable, efficient, and sound, we may indeed be moving towards the "best of times."

Any final comments, Gwilym?

Gwilym: Globalization is not a word that is well received these days, but my own view is that we are close to a globally harmonized patent system, if not a unitary global patent system.

Best practice for the United States and Europe means much the same thing. We can be a little more relaxed in Europe about what is said during prosecution and a little less relaxed about the latitude for amendment of a patent application during its life. Just as in Henry James' day, the American in Europe needs to exercise a little caution, but I am glad to say that these days the outcome is likely to be more cheerful than it was for his protagonist!

NOTES AND QUESTIONS

1. Recall from Chapter 3, and as noted in the excerpt above, as a result of the London Agreement, fewer translations may be required to enter the national stage in EPO contracting states. As of March 2011, France, Germany, Luxembourg, Monaco, Switzerland/Liechtenstein, and the UK do not require translation of the specification of the European patent. Latvia, Lithuania, Slovenia, Croatia, Denmark, Hungary, Iceland, the Netherlands, and Sweden all require that a translation of the claims into one of their official languages be supplied; however, the last six countries dispense with further translation requirements if the European patent has been granted in (or translated into) English or supplied in the respective official language.

On March 10, 2011, the EU Council authorized the use of an enhanced cooperation procedure to create a single EU patent valid in twenty-five of the twenty-seven member states. The two dissenting states, Italy and Spain, primarily object to the fact that the language regime of the unitary patent will be that of the EPC: English, German, and French. Creation of the unitary EU patent is expected to eliminate the current process of national validation of EPO-granted European patents for participating countries, which should provide even more benefits than the London Agreement for patentees desiring protection in multiple European jurisdictions. The future unitary patent would be valid immediately throughout the territory of the EU member states participating in the enhanced cooperation in the (EPO) grant language. While progress is being made on this initiative, as we will discuss in Chapter 10, the exact form of the patent and litigation scheme ultimately will determine its usefulness.

2. It appears that applicants and patent offices are often at loggerheads, with applicants seeking ways to make prosecution more cost-effective and flexible and patent offices striving to make patent examination more efficient and structured. Are these interests really at odds? What common goals should applicants and examiners share regardless of the jurisdiction in which the patent is being prosecuted? Consider the following national patent office initiatives:

a. KIPO has instituted a "customer-tailored three-track examination system" in an effort to manage application backlogs and work flow. Under the system, applicants choose one of the following examination tracks: accelerated, regular, or customer-deferred. The accelerated track is for applicants who wish to acquire patent rights as rapidly as possible in order, for example, to secure a market position or institute an infringement action. Examination under the accelerated track results in a first office action within two to three months of the request. Customer-deferred examination is intended for applicants who need time to commercialize their inventions. Under customer-deferred examination, applicants determine when they want their applications examined, and examination begins within three months of the applicants' requests. Under the regular track, which is the default route, a first office action will generally be produced within sixteen months from the request for examination.

b. The Danish Patent Office has instituted a commercial search service. It will carry out pre-application prior-art searches, clearance searches, and free-to-operate searches for applicants of any country.

c. The UK Patent Office provides a non-binding validity opinion (novelty and inventive step assessment only) to help parties settle or avoid litigation.

d. In the Japan Patent Office, a patentee can file a "Hantei" request for an opinion on whether a device infringes (or is an equivalent of) the claims of a patent, and a competitor can also file a "Hantei" request to determine whether their activity (or proposed activity) comes within the claims of a patent. Upon receiving a request for a "Hantei," the JPO will set up a three-examiner panel to provide an objective, neutral, advisory opinion. The opinion can be used by a requesting party in patent infringement litigation, but it is not binding on any court.

e. The EPO, JPO, and USPTO are working on the establishment of a common application format that would standardize the formal aspects of patent applications across the three countries and allow applicants to file the application documents (description, claims, abstract, and drawings) in a uniform manner in all three offices.

f. The USPTO has introduced several initiatives to expedite and improve patent examination and reduce backlogs. In one, called Project Exchange, applicants with multiple pending applications can receive expedited review of one application in exchange for withdrawing an unexamined application. The other, entitled the Green Technology Pilot Program, permits patent applications pertaining to environmental quality, energy conservation, development of renewable energy resources, and greenhouse gas emission reduction to be advanced out of turn for examination and accorded special status for review. Importantly, the first USPTO satellite office, the Elijah J. McCoy United States Patent and Trademark Office, recently opened in Detroit, MI, and three other offices in Dallas, TX, Denver, CO, and Silicon Valley, CA will open within a few years. The new locations are expected to boost USPTO examiner hiring efforts and provide additional convenience for applicants.

g. On June 19, 2012, SIPO issued "Administrative Measures on Prioritized Examination of Patent Applications," which became effective August 1, 2012. The measures allow for a speedier examination of certain types of invention patent applications (completion within one year instead of the current three to five year average examination period). Prioritized examination is available for applications in a variety of areas, including green technology fields, such as energy conservation, environmental protection, new materials or new energy vehicles, and inventions of national or public importance.

Which of these initiatives do you think is the most valuable for applicants? Which would you identify as most likely to improve the efficiency and quality of the patent examination process?

3. ROLE OF THE INVENTOR

The level of involvement of an inventor in patent prosecution can vary significantly across jurisdictions. While an inventor generally can choose to prepare, file and prosecute the application *pro se*, most inventors choose to hire a patent attorney or patent agent to handle the process.

Under Article 4*ter* of the Paris Convention, described in detail in Chapter 2, an inventor has the right to be "mentioned as such in the patent," although the application may be filed by someone else, often the assignee. For corporate researchers, inventors generally will have assigned the ownership rights to their inventions to their employer as a condition of employment, and the employer will prosecute the application and enforce any resulting patent. Under current U.S. law, the application must nevertheless be filed in the name of the inventor, while in most other countries the employer can file the application in its own name.

As also noted in Chapter 2, the Patent Law Treaty (PLT) has played a role in facilitating multinational patent application filing. A key objective of the PLT is to make it easier for applicants to obtain a filing date in multiple countries by eliminating certain formal requirements. As such, under the PLT, all that a member country can require in order for an applicant to obtain a filing date are: (1) an indication that what has been filed is intended as an application; (2) identification of the applicant (who may not be the inventor); and (3) that the application contains what appears to be a description of the invention.

The United States finally ratified the PLT with the Patent Law Treaties Implementaiton Act of 2012, eliminating the requirement of a claim in a non-provisional application and increasing filing flexibility in other ways. The AIA has brought the United States into somewhat closer alignment with other countries by allowing patent applications to be filed by the assignee. However, the patent ultimately granted must still be to the inventor (the real party in interest) and the inventor must still make an oath that she believes herself to be the original (or an original if a joint inventor) inventor of the claimed invention.

In many companies throughout the world, researchers are hired to invent, and must agree, either as a condition of their employment or as a matter of law, to transfer the rights to inventions they develop to their employers. In some countries, including Germany, Japan, Austria, South Korea, China, Sweden, Mexico, France, Italy, Greece, and Israel, such employee inventors may be entitled to compensation based on the value of patents the company obtains on such inventions. For example, in Germany, there is a fairly detailed statutory inventor compensation scheme with guidelines to aid in the determination of the appropriate level of compensation. *See* German Employees' Inventions Act (1957), Arbeitnehmererfindungesetz, ArbNErfG (Employees' Inventions Act), *available at* http://www.gesetze-im-internet.de/arbnerfg/ (in German; English translation *available at* http://www.wipo.int/wipolex/en/text.jsp?file_id=126211). U.S. patent law leaves the matter of employee compensation for inventive activity to private contracting with one notable exception: the Bayh-Dole Act of 1980. *See* 35 U.S.C. §§ 200–211. Under Bayh-Dole, universities and government contractors may take title to inventions developed with federal funds and grant exclusive licenses to entities willing to commercialize those inventions. In exchange, the university agrees to pursue patents on the inventions, seek licensees, and comply with a variety of other requirements, including sharing any profits resulting from licensed patents with the inventors.

The following article provides an overview of the German system for employee inventor compensation and highlights the employee inventor systems in several countries.

DIETMAR HARHOFF & KARIN HOISL, INSTITUTIONALIZED INCENTIVES FOR INGENUITY—PATENT VALUE AND THE GERMAN EMPLOYEES' INVENTIONS ACT
36 RES. POL'Y 1143 (2007)

INSTITUTIONALIZED COMPENSATION SCHEMES IN VARIOUS COUNTRIES

In Germany, the rights and liabilities within an employer–employee-inventor relationship are governed by a specific legal institution. Comparable legal regulations only exist in Denmark, Finland, Norway and Sweden. We briefly consider a few features of these systems before turning to the German institutions.

The Swedish Employees' Invention Act is of dispositive nature, i.e., the legal provisions may be amended by the employer or the employee as long as the employee's basic right to compensation is not affected. Basically, the Swedish Employees' Invention Act distinguishes between two types of employee inventions: the work-related invention and the invention arising outside the context of employment. The rights on work-related inventions are fully transferred to the employer. For the second type, the rights to the invention remain with the employee. The employee may apply for a patent before reporting the invention to the employer, however, she must offer the employer the right to use the invention.

The Danish Employees' Invention Act is similar to the Swedish law. The right to the invention remains with the employee-inventor. The inventor is obliged to report all inventions to the employer. For inventions which were made in the course of the employee's normal work the employer can claim the right to the invention. The claiming of the right has to be declared no later than four months from receipt of the invention report. Disagreements are brought before a board of arbitration. The inventor's claim to a reasonable compensation is deemed to be satisfied with his regular salary.

In the United Kingdom, France, Italy, Austria, the Netherlands and Japan, regulations concerning employee-invention are part of the respective national patent laws. According to Section 39 (1) of the English Patents Act inventions "made in the course of the normal duties of the employee" or made in the course of "duties falling outside his normal duties, but specifically assigned to him" belong to the employer. The remaining inventions belong to the inventor himself. Compensation is to be paid only if the invention is of outstanding benefit to the employer (Section 40 (1) English Patents Act). Disputes concerning the compensation are submitted to court or are decided by the comptroller within the firm (Section 41 English Patents Act).

The French Patent Law also assigns inventions which are made in fulfillment of an employment contract to the employer. The employee-inventor may come into possession of additional compensation (compensation beyond normal salary) if a claim to compensation is regulated by plant agreement (*i.e.*, between employer and works council) or by contractual agreements between employer and inventor. Disputes concerning compensation have to be resolved by an arbitration commission or in court.

The Italian legal regulations differ from the French ones with respect to inventor compensation. If no special arrangements have been made, the inventor is entitled to a reasonable compensation, depending on the economic value of the invention. The amount payable to the inventor decreases with the degree of involvement of the employer in the creation of the invention . . . .

The Japanese Patent Act basically assigns the right to the invention to the employee (§ 35 Japanese Patent Act). The employer receives the right to a non-exclusive license and is not obligated to pay compensation. Assignment of an employee-invention to the employer may be regulated in advance by contract or employment negotiations. In this case, the right to the invention is passed to the employer or the employer receives an exclusive license. The employee is then entitled to receive a reasonable remuneration on the part of the employer.

In Switzerland and Liechtenstein employee-inventions are subject to civil law. According to Art 332 Obligation Law (Obligationenrecht), patentable and not patentable inventions made during the employee's normal work duties are to be reported to the employer. Rights to the invention are assigned to the employer. Payment of compensation is compulsory. The amount of payment depends on the economic value of the service invention, the duties and position of the employee in the firm, the contribution made by the employer and by third parties, and finally on the extent internal equipment has been used for making the invention. Disputes have to be solved by [a] labor court.

In the United States and in Canada, there exist no special legal provisions pertaining to inventor compensation. Basically, the inventor principle is applied which means that the invention belongs to the inventor. Therefore, patents are always applied for in the inventor's name, and are then assigned to the employer. Conditions concerning an assignment of the invention to the employer are to be regulated by contractual agreements. Typical employment contracts in the US therefore specify the following obligations for employee-inventors: first, the employee-inventor has to notify the employer of each invention made. Second, the employee-inventor has to keep secret any invention or company related information, and finally, the inventor has to confer all rights to the invention to the employer during the employer-employee relationship. The employee-inventor in return has no legal claim to compensation. Compensation may also be determined in the employment contract. In cases where no contractual agreements exist between the employer and the employee-inventors and where the employer was instrumental in making the invention (*e.g.*, by providing the inventor with the necessary tools, materials, or financial resources), the employer receives a "shop right." Due to this shop right, the employer obtains a non-exclusive license. In exchange, the employer pays a license-fee of 1 US$ representing a symbolic inventor compensation . . . .

REGULATIONS OF THE GERMAN EMPLOYEES' INVENTIONS ACT AS OF 1957

In its current form, the German Employees' Inventions Act applies to all patentable inventions (patented or not) or inventions which are eligible for a utility model as well as to any other technical improvement proposals made by employees (§§2, 3 ArbNErfG). The Act applies to inventions made by inventors in organizations which are governed under German law or in German subsidiaries of international organizations. It provides a set of rules concerning rights and liabilities of both the employer and the employee.

The Act distinguishes between service inventions and free inventions. Service inventions are inventions which either result from the obligatory activity of the employee in the company or ". . . are substantially based on experience or activities of the company" (§4 ArbNErfG). Other inventions, for instance, inventions made by employees during their leisure time or by self-employed inventors, are free inventions. According to §5 ArbNErfG the employee is obligated to report a service invention to the employer immediately. Within the period of four months from the receipt of the report of the invention, the employer can claim the invention on a restricted or unrestricted basis (§6 ArbNErfG). If the employer does not claim the invention the legal title to the invention is released to the inventor. In case of an unrestricted claim to the invention, all rights to the invention are transferred to the employer, and the employer is obliged to file a national patent application for the invention. A restricted claim provides the employer with a non-exclusive right to use the invention, which implies that the employer is not allowed to grant licenses on the patented invention. Restricted claims turn out to be quite infrequent — in our data, only 2.6 percent of all patents are claimed by the employer on a restricted basis. In the case of a restricted claim, the employer has no obligation to file a German patent application. An inventor, who wants his invention to be protected by a patent, has to file the application in his own name.

Once the invention is claimed, either in restricted or unrestricted form, the employer has the obligation to reasonably compensate the inventor. The inventor's right to remuneration arises as soon as the employer has claimed the right to the service invention (unrestricted claiming of right) or as soon as the employer has claimed the right to the invention and uses it (restricted claiming of right). Guidelines for the Remuneration of Employees' Inventions in Private Employment were first issued by the Federal Minister for Labor and Social Affairs (Bundesminister für Arbeit und Sozialordnung) in 1959. These guidelines are based upon the Remuneration Guidelines for Subordinates' Inventions from March 20, 1943. They regulate in some detail how the compensation is determined. The compensation is supposed to be proportional to the value of the invention. According to Section 1 of the guidelines, three different methods exist for calculating the value of the invention:

- by using a licensing analogy, i.e., by determining the license fee that would have to be paid for the use of a comparable invention owned by a third party,

- by calculating the benefits from the invention accruing to the employer, i.e., the difference between costs and revenues resulting from the use of the invention, or

- by estimation of the value of the invention, i.e., by determining the price which would have had to be paid by the company to buy the invention from a free inventor.

The estimation of the value of the invention provides the basis for the calculation of the compensation payable to the inventor. In a second step, the share of value accruing to the inventor(s) is determined. According to §9 (2) ArbNErfG, the proportion attributable to the inventor(s) depends:

- on the economic exploitability of the service invention, *i.e.*, the value of the invention, which is determined according to the three above described methods,

- on the duties and position of the employee in the company, *i.e.*, the share of the inventor in the creation of the service invention decreases the more it is expected of him by reason of his position and by the amount of salary paid to him at the time of the report of the invention, and also

- on the degree of involvement of the company in the creation of the service invention, i.e., the share of the inventor in the creation of the service invention increases the greater his own initiative in recognizing the problem, and the smaller the company's support with technical assistance.

If more than one employee-inventor is responsible for a service invention, the relative contributions of the inventors have to be specified. §12 (2) ArbNErfG constitutes that the compensation must be determined for each inventor separately. Each inventor has to be informed about the total amount of remuneration and the share received by the other coinventors.

Disputes arising between employees and employer regarding the inventors' compensation can be brought before the Board of Arbitration at the German Patent and Trademark Office in Munich or Berlin (§§28–36 ArbNErfG). The Arbitration Board issues a proposal for a settlement. This proposal is binding for both parties unless a written opposition is filed within one month. Should an appeal be filed against the proposal, the proceedings before the Arbitration Board are deemed to have been unsuccessful and the filing of an action with the court having jurisdiction (the respective district court) is possible. On average, fewer than 100 disputes per year are negotiated before the Arbitration Board (GPTO 2003). Compared to the annual number of patent applications to which the German Employees' Inventions Act applies, this number is quite small.

NOTES AND QUESTIONS

1. Which type of system would you expect be more conducive to motivating inventive activity: a detailed employee inventor compensation scheme, such as exists in Germany, or a less regulated system perhaps governed by contract or industry practice similar to the United States? What advantages or disadvantages might each type of system provide?

2. In 2005, Japan revised its employee inventor compensation law, which applies if there is no contract or if a court determines that the contract terms are unreasonable. Pursuant to Article 35 of the Japanese Patent Act, employees should be compensated using the employer's profits and contributions in respect of the invention as a reference point. This revision has generated considerable concern in Japan and elsewhere, as its parameters are unclear and the potential for employer liability is substantial. Under the previous version of the law, Dr. Shuji Nakimura, inventor of the blue LED, sued his former employer (who had given him a bonus of only $150 for developing the invention) for $190 million as reasonable compensation. He ultimately settled for $8 million. What are the possible benefits to a country in enacting a pro-employee inventor compensation law? What are the risks of such a law?

3. As a result of the Bayh-Dole Act, some U.S. university researchers have become millionaires through statutorily mandated royalty sharing. For example, under Emory University's Intellectual Property Policy, inventors receive 100 percent of net royalties up to $25,000, 33 percent of net revenue up to $4 million, and 25 percent of net revenue over $4 million. *See* Emory University, Intellectual Property Policy 7.6.05, *available at* http://policies. emory.edu/7.6. Consequently, Emory's 2005 sale of the royalty stream for the patented HIV drug Emtriva® for $540 million turned three faculty inventors of the drug into millionaires. Other U.S. universities and their faculty inventors have also reaped significant financial rewards from the licensing of (mostly patented) university inventions. For example, in 2009, the University of Minnesota, New York University, and Northwestern University generated over $95 million, $113 million, and $161 million, respectively, in technology licensing revenue. *See Licensing Revenue and Patent Activity, 2009 Fiscal Year*, CHRON. HIGHER EDUC. (Dec. 17, 2010). Should the United States adopt a uniform law requiring employers to compensate employees for inventions? Should developing countries adopt the Bayh-Dole approach to incentivizing the patenting of university-generated inventions? For a cogent argument against such a move, *see* Anthony D. So et al., *Is Bayh-Dole Good for Developing Countries? Lessons from the US Experience*, 6 PUB. LIBR. SCI. BIOLOGY 2078 (2008).

4. Sometimes a slight difference in the wording of an assignment agreement or an employment contract can result in an employer's loss of rights in a researcher's invention. Two cases, one from the United States and one from Australia, point out the importance of carefully drafting such agreements:

In *Board of Trustees of Leland Stanford Junior University v. Roche Molecular Systems, Inc.*, 583 F.3d 832 (Fed. Cir. 2009), *aff'd*, 131 S. Ct. 2188

(2011), the Federal Circuit held that the term "agree to assign" as used in a patent assignment clause did not constitute an immediate transfer of rights from the inventor-assignor to the employer-assignee. Rather, the language conveyed only an intent to assign patent rights at a later, unspecified time.

The *Stanford* case involved three patents that claimed methods for quantifying HIV in human blood samples and correlating those measurements to the therapeutic effectiveness of antiretroviral drugs using the polymerase chain reaction (PCR) technique. To develop the technology in question, Stanford hired a research fellow in 1988 and had him sign a "Copyright and Patent Agreement" that obligated him to assign his inventions to the University. The agreement provided: "I agree to assign or confirm in writing to Stanford and/or Sponsors that right, title and interest in . . . such inventions as required by Contracts or Grants."

A short while thereafter, but while still employed by Stanford, the researcher sought the assistance of Cetus, a private company that developed PCR techniques. At Cetus' request, the researcher signed the company's "Visitor's Confidentiality Agreement," which provided that the researcher "will assign and do[es] hereby assign to Cetus, my right, title, and interest in each of the ideas, inventions, and improvements" that the researcher may devise "as a consequence of" his work at the company. In 1991, Roche purchased Cetus' PCR business and began manufacturing HIV detection kits.

In 1992 Stanford filed the parent patent application that resulted from the researcher's work. The researcher did not execute a written assignment to Stanford of the researcher's rights to the invention until 1995. Ten years later, in 2005, Stanford sued Roche alleging that Roche's HIV detection kits infringed Stanford's patents.

The Court of Appeals for the Federal Circuit held in favor of Roche on the basis that researcher did not obtain an actual assignment from Stanford until 1995. The court determined that the "agree to assign" language of the Stanford agreement reflected "a mere promise to assign rights in the future," with the consequence that the researcher "agreed only to assign his invention rights to Stanford at an undetermined time."

In contrast, in light of the Cetus agreement's unequivocal "will assign and do hereby assign" language, execution of that agreement effected a present assignment to Cetus of the researcher's future inventions and provided Cetus with immediate equitable title to any inventions that the researcher might create. Because the court determined that Cetus' equitable title was converted to legal title in 1992 when the parent application was filed, Cetus' legal title to the invention vested first, rendering the researcher's 1995 assignment to Stanford invalid. Stanford's failure to draft an agreement that transferred rights automatically upon creation of an invention consequently cost Stanford its right to the very valuable patents in this case. The United States Supreme Court granted certiorari and affirmed, making clear that the Bayh-Dole Act did not change the default rule in patent law that rights to an invention initially vest in the inventor, not the inventor's employer. For a criticism of the U.S. law in this area as compared to the German system, *see* Toshiko Takenaka, *Serious Flaw of Employee Invention Ownership Under the Bayh-Dole Act in Stanford v. Roche: Finding the Missing Piece of the Puzzle in the German Employee Act*, 20 TEX. INTELL. PROP. L.J. 281 (2012).

The Australian case, *University of Western Australia v. Gray,* [2009] FCAFC 116, concerned a professor of surgery who signed a standard university employment contract. The contract provided that Professor Gray's duties included teaching, conducting examinations, directing and supervising work in his field, undertaking research, and organizing and stimulating research among his staff and students. During his tenure at the university, Professor Gray undertook research into metastatic liver and bowel cancers, and he developed technologies for the production and use of microspheres for the targeted treatment of tumors. He filed several patent applications in his and others' names. Professor Gray left the university in 1997 and assigned his rights to the patents to Sirtex Medical, a company created for the purpose of commercializing Professor Gray's technologies. Professor Gray was a director of the company and had a significant ownership interest in it.

The university filed suit against Professor Gray for breach of his employment contract. Although the university's standard contract contained no express terms concerning inventive activity, the university maintained that the contract included implied terms that created an "implied duty to invent," which in turn required Professor Gray to notify the university about his inventions, prohibited him from patenting them himself, and required him to assign his patent rights to the university.

The full Federal Court of Australia held in favor of Professor Gray, ruling that a duty to research does not carry with it a duty to invent. The Court determined that there was nothing in Professor's Gray's contract that permitted it to imply a duty to provide the university with the benefit of the professor's inventions, even though Professor Gray's research was of the sort likely to produce inventive results. The Court based its decision on detailed findings about the nature of Professor Gray's work as an academic researcher, which it concluded was substantially different from the nature of the work of a commercial researcher: Professor Gray was free to choose the subject matter and direction of his research; he was not under an obligation of secrecy and was free to publish his work; he could collaborate with researchers at other institutions; and he secured a significant portion of the funding for his research on his own. The Court therefore sent a clear message that if a university wants to ensure that it retains rights to its researchers' inventions, it should include an express "duty to invent" provision and clear assignment language in its employment contracts.

5. Provisions relating to employee inventions are found not only in the legislation of industrialized countries, but also in the laws of some developing countries. The following is a description of the law on employee inventions in Nigeria:

Employee inventions are addressed in the Patents and Designs Act of 1970, which essentially restates the common law. This law declares that inventions "made by an employee in the course of the employee's employment or in the execution of a contract for the performance of a specific work" belong to the employer or the party that commissioned the work. If the invention was made in the course of the employee's employment, then the employee is not entitled to any additional remuneration. However, if the employment does not require the usage of any form of "inventive activity," then the employee is entitled to some form of award, taking into account the employee's salary and the importance of the invention. In general, the laws addressing employee inventions are seen as being "in a less than satisfactory state" because the laws are "heavily weighted against the employee."

Donald J. Ying, Comment, *A Comparative Study of the Treatment of Employee Inventions, Pre-Invention Assignment Agreements, and Software Rights*, 10 U. PA. J. BUS. & EMP. L. 763, 775–776 (2008) (quoting Chioma Kanu Agomo, *in* 10 INTERNATIONAL ENCYCLOPAEDIA FOR LABOUR LAW AND INDUSTRIAL RELATIONS, Nigeria-1, Nigeria-81 (Roger Blanpain ed.1992).

What approach toward the regulation of employee inventors would you expect to be most beneficial for promoting inventive activity and technological advancement in research institutions in developing countries? What factors should the governments of such countries consider in determining how to allocate rights to employee inventions?

C. THE PATENT GRANT

The grant of a patent after substantive or, in the case of a registration system, formal examination, marks the beginning of the enforceable life of the patent. Although a patent's term is measured from the filing date of the first non-provisional domestic application, it actually begins on the date the patent issues. *See, e.g.,* 35 U.S.C. § 154; EPC, Art. 64, Japanese Patent Act Art. 66. This is also the date on which the patentee can employ the rights provided under the relevant patent law, such as excluding others from making, using, selling, offering to sell, and importing the patented invention. *See* 35 U.S.C. § 271; TRIPS Art. 28. After a patent issues in the United States, and even before one issues in many other regions such as the EPO, a patentee/applicant must pay escalating maintenance fees to keep the patent in force. Such fees are required annually in the EPO and in many patent offices worldwide. In the United States, such fees are required at four, seven, and eleven year intervals. Patents can expire prematurely if a patentee fails to pay maintenance fees on the patent when due. *See* TRIPS Art. 62. Also, in the United States, patentees sometimes disclaim the terminal portion of the term of a patent in order to overcome an obviousness-type double patenting rejection. *See* 35 U.S.C. § 253.

1. PATENT TERM EXTENSION

Article 33 of TRIPS states that the term of patent protection "shall not end before the expiration of a period of twenty years counted from the filing date." This sets a minimum term for patents; however, members are free to provide for longer protection. The following provides a succinct summary of patent term extension possibilities in the United States:

> Present patent laws consist of four forms of patent extension. The first and least common form of extension arises when Congress enacts private legislation. The second form commonly called an adjustment is governed by 35 U.S.C. § 154. Section 154 may be evoked to extend a patent term for delays within the U.S. Patent and Trademark Office (USPTO) during patent prosecution. A third form of patent term extension comes from the Uruguay Rounds Agreements Act enacted in 1994. This Act amended 35 U.S.C. § 154 so that patents filed on or after June 8, 1995 have a patent term of twenty years from the date they are filed. Previously, patents had a seventeen-year term from the date they issued. However, design patents still only have a fourteen-year term from the date of patent grant. According to Section 154(c), all patents (other than design patents) that were in force on June 8, 1995, or that issued on an application that was filed before June 8, 1995, have a term that is the greater of the twenty years from filing or seventeen years from issue. The fourth form of patent extension commonly called a patent term restoration was created in 1984 when Congress passed the Drug Price Competition and Patent Restoration Act also known as the Hatch-Waxman Act. The Act added Section 156 to the Patent Act permitting patent term extension for patents on products (or processes for making or using the same) that are human drug products, medical devices, food additives, and color additives subject to regulation under the Federal Food, Drug and Cosmetic Act. The Act restores a portion of the patent term during which the patentee is unable to sell or market a product while awaiting government approval, such as the Food and Drug Administration's (FDA) review of a prescription drug. In 1988, the Generic Animal Drug and Patent Term Restoration Act in 1988 added animal drug and veterinary biological products to the list of products eligible for a term extension.

William J. Stilling, *Patent Term Extensions and Restoration under the Hatch-Waxman Act*, FINDLAW (Nov. 20, 2002), *available at* http://library.findlaw.com/2002/Nov/20/132408.html. When the United States joined the Hague design treaty via the Patent Law Treaties Implementation Act of 2012, it increased the term of design patents to fifteen years from grant.

Many countries provide Hatch-Waxman-like term extensions/term restorations for pharmaceuticals. For example, after a patent on a plant or medicinal product expires in an EU member country, the patentee can seek a supplementary protection certificate (SPC), which may provide up to five additional years of marketing exclusivity for the product if it meets certain requirements. *See* Council Regulation (EEC) No 1768/92 of 18 June 1992 concerning the creation of a supplementary protection certificate for medicinal products, 1992 O.J. (L 182) 1; Regulation (EC) No 1610/96 of the European Parliament and of the Council of 23 July 1996 Concerning the Creation of a Supplementary Protection Certificate for Plant Protection Products, 1996 O.J. (L 198) 30. The SPC was designed to compensate for the extensive regulatory approval process for such products. SPC's are granted on a country-by-country basis and thus are not EU-wide. An SPC technically is not a patent term extension, as it only arises after the patent expires, but it has a similar effect.

In addition to explicit term extension provisions for drugs that many countries provide, sometimes as a result of accession to a free trade agreement, many countries also provide a type of patent term extension for pharmaceuticals via data and/or marketing exclusivity protection for new clinical studies and/or new chemical entities. With data exclusivity, a regulatory agency, such as the U.S. Food and Drug Administration (FDA), will not accept an application that relies on an originator company's clinical test data for drug approval during the period of exclusivity. With marketing exclusivity, a regulatory agency will not approve another company's marketing application for a drug during the term of exclusivity. By denying competitors access to clinical data submitted to a regulatory agency for marketing approval, for a term of years, the patentee can extend the period of exclusivity, since generic products cannot be marketed without such approval. As discussed in Chapter 3, data exclusivity provisions also appear in several bilateral/regional free trade agreements as TRIPS-plus provisions. *See, e.g.,* U.S.-Singapore Free Trade Agreement, May 6, 2003, 42 I.L.M. 1026, U.S.-Jordan Free Trade Agreement, Oct. 24, 2000, 41 I.L.M. 63, and the Dominican Republic-Central America Free Trade Agreement, Aug. 5, 2004, 43 I.L.M. 514. In addition, many countries such as the U.S. and EU member countries offer pediatric and orphan drug exclusivity. Pediatric exclusivity provides a six-month extension of exclusivity added to the end of a patent and is available to companies in exchange for testing a drug in children. Orphan drug exclusivity provides marketing exclusivity (seven years in the United States) for the creation of drugs for rare diseases and other financially unattractive medical conditions, even for unpatented drugs.

2. POST-GRANT PROCEEDINGS

After a patent issues, it may be subject to challenge in the patent office and/or in court through nullity actions or in patent infringement or declaratory judgment litigation where patent validity is contested. "Reexamination," "post-grant opposition," and "post-grant review" are all different names for patent office proceedings in which third parties can challenge granted patents. These proceedings can differ in form and substance by jurisdiction but tend to have commonalities between them, as discussed below. Patent owners also may correct errors in patents using various measures; for example, reissue proceedings, certificates of correction, and disclaimers in the USPTO. In other countries, patent correction is also available through proceedings in the patent office, such as the Japanese request for correction, or in a court, such as the amendment procedures available in a German Federal Patent Court nullity action. Three of the most important of these proceedings—nullity actions, reexaminations, and oppositions—are discussed in more detail below.

a. Nullity Proceedings

In many countries, the determination of the infringement and validity of a patent is handled in separate actions in separate tribunals. *See, e.g.*, the Chinese *Shenzhen Triangle v. Compaq* case excerpted in Chapter 10, *infra*, where a court action was stayed pending a SIPO reexamination proceeding to assess validity. In such jurisdictions, issued patents can be invalidated only in nullity or opposition proceedings brought during the enforceable life of the patent. Nullity actions generally can be brought by any person, can be based on any patentability ground, and, depending on the particular jurisdiction, can be brought in a specialized patent court, a general court, or in the patent office. A nullity decision may partially or completely invalidate a patent and in some cases, such as in the German Federal Patent Court, the patentee may have the opportunity to amend the claims, drawing, or the remainder of the specification to limit the scope of the patent and steer clear of the prior art. *See, e.g.,* Judgment of May 6, 2010, Xa ZR 70/08 – *Maschinensatz*, (in German), discussed in Eike Shaper, *Restriction of Patent Claims in German Infringement Proceedings*, KLUWER PATENT BLOG (Dec. 30, 2010).

b. Reexamination

An issued patent can be challenged by third parties in a patent office reexamination proceeding in several countries including China, Australia, Canada, the United States and South Africa. In some countries, such as China, reexaminations resemble oppositions in that they can be based on virtually any patentability criteria, allow meaningful third-party participation and include oral hearings. However, unlike oppositions, initiation of a reexamination generally is available throughout the life of the patent.

Reexamination in the United States. is a more limited affair, particularly after passage of the AIA. The AIA eliminates inter-partes reexaminations, converting them to a new inter-partes review proceeding (discussed in Section 2.C *infra*), and thus has effectively returned the United

States to a purely ex parte reexamination regime. U.S. ex parte reexaminations can only be based on patents and printed publications that implicate novelty or non-obviousness concerns. *See* 35 U.S.C. §303. A reexamination can result in a patent being revoked in whole or in part, amended, or maintained as granted, and the files are open to the public throughout the proceedings.

c. Opposition and Post-Grant Review

In many countries, certain patent office challenges to a granted patent may only be initiated during a limited period of time after grant; for example, nine months in the EPO and six months in the JPO through an opposition proceeding. Post-grant opposition proceedings, such as those in the EPO, include the opportunity for oral hearings and significant participation by third parties. Moreover, the grounds for initiating an opposition generally include all patentability requirements such as subject matter, written description, lack of utility, and enablement. An opposition can result in a patent being revoked in whole or in part, amended, or maintained as granted.

The AIA has given the United States an opposition proceeding (effective September 16, 2012) called Post-Grant Review (PGR), which applies to patents obtained under the new first-inventor-to-file rules. PGR challenges must be initiated within the first nine months after a patent is granted, and can be based on most patentability criteria, unlike ex parte reexamination which is limited to issues of novelty and non-obviousness. The AIA also creates a new Inter Partes Review (IPR) proceeding (replacing Inter Partes Reexamination) which can be initiated after the nine month-from-grant window for PGR has closed but is limited to prior art issues based on patents and printed publications. Under both PGR and IPR, third parties can fully participate in proceedings, oral hearings are available, and discovery is available to both parties. In addition, the AIA creates a special PGR program (which will sunset in eight years) for review of covered business method patents that are not drawn to a technological invention and are asserted in pending litigation. Both oppositions and reexaminations have the potential to aid in the resolution of disputes that otherwise would need to be adjudicated in a court proceeding. For a detailed, insider's perspective on the new AIA PGR and IPR proceedings, *see* Joe Matal, A *Guide to the Legislative History of the America Invents Act: Part II of II*, 21 FED. CIR. B.J. 539, 598–613 (2012).

An added benefit of PGR may be the opportunity for the United States public to have greater participation in the patent system. In analyzing differences between challenges to Myriad Genetics' breast cancer gene patents (discussed briefly in Chapter 4), Professors Murray and Van Zimmeren note:

[A] comparative assessment reveals that interest groups in Europe effectively participated in challenging the Myriad patents far earlier than in the United States. In the United States the available formal methods for third-party participation are more limited than in Europe. Therefore, ongoing participation in patent decision-making is far less certain. In both jurisdictions, an interesting tension has emerged between the availability of third-party review at the internal administrative review stage and a subsequent invalidity review at the external review stage.
. . .

The internal opposition and appeal procedures of the EPC are structured so that "any" person may challenge the validity of a patent on broad terms. Thus, the internal administrative review of the EPC provides European "patent civil society" with the opportunity to participate in patent policy-making. . . . Achieving goals through external review of patents, though, has not been as simple in Europe. After the patent grant or the maintenance of the patent—potentially in amended form—the opportunity to challenge the patents in invalidity procedures before national courts remains open. However, the only opportunity to challenge a patent is to undertake external review of a patent in each individual member state of the European Patent Organization where the patent has been validated. This prompts a risk that different national courts will come to different conclusions as to the validity of each given patent. . . .

By contrast, when compared to Europe, the experience of patent civil society in the United States still remains underdeveloped. It was not until May 2009 that any significant challenge to the Myriad patents emerged. Members of the patent civil society were unable to utilize internal administrative avenues such as the current Patent Act to challenge the Myriad patents, because third parties are unable to oppose the grant of a patent under U.S. law (as was the case in Europe) . . . . The intense interest in Myriad demonstrates a desire to create a patent law amenable to the claims of interests beyond those of the patentee and its direct competitors.

Kali Murray & Esther van Zimmeren, *Dynamic Patent Governance in Europe and the United States: The Myriad Example*, 19 CARDOZO J. INT'L & COMP. L. 287, 321–325 (2011). We will further discuss the litigation challenges posed by the fragmented patent system in Europe in Chapter 10.

PART 3

MULTINATIONAL ENFORCEMENT

■ ■ ■

CHAPTER 10

COMPARATIVE APPROACHES TO PATENT INFRINGEMENT

■ ■ ■

A. DIRECT INFRINGEMENT

In all major patent systems, a patent gives its owner the right to exclude others from engaging in certain activities in relation to the claimed invention for a specified term. This right is expressed in TRIPS Article 28, which states that a patent confers on its owner the right "to prevent third parties not having the owner's consent from the acts of: making, using, offering for sale, selling, or importing . . . that product." Violation of this right is considered direct infringement. If the subject matter of the patent is a process, Article 28 further provides that the patent owner has the right "to prevent third parties . . . from using the process, and from the acts of using, offering for sale, selling, or importing . . . the product obtained directly by that process." These provisions appear straightforward; the difficulty arises in trying to determine when third-party activity actually infringes on the rights of the patent-holder. Such a determination requires interpretation of the patent claims at issue, approaches to which can vary significantly across jurisdictions.

1. CLAIM CONSTRUCTION

As noted in Chapter 1, patent rights are territorial and, other than the exceptions that will be discussed later in this Chapter, a patent owner generally must sue for infringement in each jurisdiction where infringement is allegedly taking place. This requires a firm understanding of the distinctive practices that surround claim interpretation in various jurisdictions. In the U.S., patent claims must be interpreted, or construed, to see what they cover, and whether their scope includes the third party's actions. After the patent claims are construed, they are "read on" to (i.e. compared with) the accused device to ascertain if each element of the claim is present, literally or equivalently, in the accused device. Furthermore, the claims are to be read in light of the remainder of the specification without reading limitations from the specification into the claims.

In the 1995 *Markman v. Westview Instruments, Inc.* decision, 52 F.3d 967 (Fed. Cir. 1995), aff'd, 517 U.S. 370 (1996), the Court of Appeals for the Federal Circuit (CAFC) held that claim construction is a question of law to be decided by judges, not juries. The court also identified the evidentiary sources appropriate for judicial consultation in the claim construction process; namely, *intrinsic* evidence consisting of the text of the claims, the remainder of the specification, and the prosecution history, if in evidence. Non-contradictory *extrinsic* evidence (i.e. everything else, including treatises, experts, and dictionaries) can also be consulted.

Following the *Markman* decision, judges routinely hold "Markman hearings" in the early stages of a trial, to determine the construction of the claims at issue. Because claim construction is generally determinative of infringement (i.e. whether the accused device comes within the claim terms) these proceedings often result in summary judgment decisions that send the question of the correctness of the judge's claim construction to the CAFC where, as a question of law, it is subject to non-deferential *de novo* review. Empirical studies have suggested that the three-judge CAFC panels reverse district court claim interpretations between 33 percent and 50 percent of the time, creating ill-will and dissatisfaction not only among judges, but also among litigants seeking certainty from the courts. Furthermore, in an attempt to create greater certainty and ostensibly to improve the notice function of patent claims, several CAFC judges began to use dictionaries as the definitive source for determining the meaning of (or "interpreting") a claim term despite the *Markman* intrinsic/extrinsic evidence distinction. The following *en banc* decision by the CAFC sought to bring clarity to the issue of claim construction.

EDWARD H. PHILLIPS V. AWH CORP.

United States Court of Appeals, Federal Circuit
415 F.3d 1303 (Fed. Cir. 2005)

■ BRYSON, Circuit Judge.

Edward H. Phillips invented modular, steel-shell panels that can be welded together to form vandalism-resistant walls. The panels are especially useful in building prisons because they are load-bearing and impact-resistant, while also insulating against fire and noise. Mr. Phillips obtained a patent on the invention, U.S. Patent No. 4,677,798 ("the '798 patent"), and he subsequently entered into an arrangement with AWH Corporation, Hopeman Brothers, Inc., and Lofton Corporation (collectively "AWH") to market and sell the panels. That arrangement ended in 1990. In 1991, however, Mr. Phillips received a sales brochure from AWH that suggested to him that AWH was continuing to use his trade secrets and patented technology without his consent. In February 1997, Mr. Phillips brought suit in the United States District Court for the District of Colorado charging AWH with infringement of claims 1, 21, 22, 24, 25, and 26 of the '798 patent.

[T]he district court focused on the language of claim 1, which recites "further means disposed inside the shell for increasing its load bearing capacity comprising internal steel baffles extending inwardly from the steel shell walls." Looking to the specification of the '798 patent, the court noted that "every textual reference in the Specification and its diagrams show baffle deployment at an angle other than 90 [degrees] to the wall faces" and that "placement of the baffles at such angles creates an intermediate interlocking, but not solid, internal barrier." The district court therefore ruled that, for purposes of the '798 patent, a baffle must "extend inward from the steel shell walls at an oblique or acute angle to the wall face" and must form part of an interlocking barrier in the interior of the wall module. Because Mr. Phillips could not prove infringement under that claim construction, the district court granted summary judgment of noninfringement.

Mr. Phillips appealed. A panel of this court affirmed. This court agreed to rehear the appeal en banc and vacated the judgment of the panel. We reverse.

I

Claim 1 of the '798 patent is representative of the asserted claims with respect to the use of the term "baffles." It recites:

Building modules adapted to fit together for construction of fire, sound and impact resistant security barriers and rooms for use in securing records and persons, comprising in combination, an outer shell . . . , sealant means . . . and further means disposed inside the shell for increasing its load bearing capacity comprising internal steel baffles extending inwardly from the steel shell walls.

. . . .

[W]e must determine the correct construction of the structural term "baffles," as used in the '798 patent.

II

. . . . It is a "bedrock principle" of patent law that "the claims of a patent define the invention to which the patentee is entitled the right to exclude." . . .

We have frequently stated that the words of a claim "are generally given their ordinary and customary meaning." *Vitronics,* 90 F.3d at 1582. We have made clear, moreover, that the ordinary and customary meaning of a claim term is the meaning that the term would have to a person of ordinary skill in the art in question at the time of the invention, i.e., as of the effective filing date of the patent application. . . .

Importantly, the person of ordinary skill in the art is deemed to read the claim term not only in the context of the particular claim in which the disputed term appears, but in the context of the entire patent, including the specification. . . .

Quite apart from the written description and the prosecution history, the claims themselves provide substantial guidance as to the meaning of particular claim terms. To begin with, the context in which a term is used in the asserted claim can be highly instructive. To take a simple example, the claim in this case refers to "steel baffles," which strongly implies that the term "baffles" does not inherently mean objects made of steel. . . Differences among claims can also be a useful guide in understanding the meaning of particular claim terms. For example, the presence of a dependent claim that adds a particular limitation gives rise to a presumption that the limitation in question is not present in the independent claim.

The claims, of course, do not stand alone. Rather, they are part of "a fully integrated written instrument," *Markman,* 52 F.3d at 978, consisting principally of a specification that concludes with the claims. For that reason, claims "must be read in view of the specification, of which they are a part." *Id.* at 979. As we stated in *Vitronics,* the specification "is always highly relevant to the claim construction analysis. Usually, it is dispositive; it is the single best guide to the meaning of a disputed term." 90 F.3d at 1582.

[O]ur cases recognize that the specification may reveal a special definition given to a claim term by the patentee that differs from the meaning it would otherwise possess. In such cases, the inventor's lexicography governs. In other cases, the specification may reveal an intentional disclaimer, or disavowal, of claim scope by the inventor. In that instance as well, the inventor has dictated the correct claim scope, and the inventor's intention, as expressed in the specification, is regarded as dispositive.

In addition to consulting the specification, we have held that a court "should also consider the patent's prosecution history, if it is in evidence." The prosecution history, which we have designated as part of the "intrinsic evidence," consists of the complete record of the proceedings before the PTO and includes the prior art cited during the examination of the patent. Like the specification, the prosecution history provides evidence of how the PTO and the inventor understood the patent. Yet because the prosecution history represents an ongoing negotiation between the PTO and the applicant, rather than the final product of that negotiation, it often lacks the clarity of the specification and thus is less useful for claim construction purposes. Nonetheless, the prosecution history can often inform the meaning of the claim language by demonstrating how the inventor understood the invention and whether the inventor limited the invention in the course of prosecution, making the claim scope narrower than it would otherwise be.

Although we have emphasized the importance of intrinsic evidence in claim construction, we have also authorized district courts to rely on extrinsic evidence, which "consists of all evidence external to the patent and prosecution history, including expert and inventor testimony, dictionaries, and learned treatises." *Markman,* 52 F.3d at 980. However, while extrinsic evidence "can shed useful light on the relevant art," we have explained that it is "less significant than the intrinsic record in determining 'the legally operative meaning of claim language.'"

We have viewed extrinsic evidence in general as less reliable than the patent and its prosecution history in determining how to read claim terms, for several reasons. First, extrinsic evidence by definition is not part of the patent and does not have the specification's virtue of being created at the time of patent prosecution for the purpose of explaining the patent's scope and meaning. Second, while claims are construed as they would be understood by a hypothetical person of skill in the art, extrinsic publications may not be written by or for skilled artisans and therefore may not reflect the understanding of a skilled artisan in the field of the patent. Third, extrinsic evidence consisting of expert reports and testimony is generated at the time of and for the purpose of litigation and thus can suffer from bias that is not present in intrinsic evidence. The effect of that bias can be exacerbated if the expert is not one of skill in the relevant art or if the expert's opinion is offered in a form that is not subject to cross-examination. Fourth, there is a virtually unbounded universe of potential extrinsic evidence of some marginal relevance that could be brought to bear on any claim construction question. In the course of litigation, each party will naturally choose the pieces of extrinsic evidence most favorable to its cause, leaving the court with the considerable task of filtering the useful extrinsic evidence from the fluff.

In sum, extrinsic evidence may be useful to the court, but it is unlikely to result in a reliable interpretation of patent claim scope unless considered in the context of the intrinsic evidence. Nonetheless, because extrinsic evidence can help educate the court regarding the field of the invention and can help the court determine what a person of ordinary skill in the art would understand claim terms to mean, it is permissible for the district court in its sound discretion to admit and use such evidence. . . .

III

Although the principles outlined above have been articulated on numerous occasions, some of this court's cases have suggested a somewhat different approach to claim construction, in which the court has given greater emphasis to dictionary definitions of claim terms and has assigned a less prominent role to the specification and the prosecution history. The leading case in this line is *Texas Digital Systems, Inc. v. Telegenix, Inc.,* 308 F.3d 1193 (Fed. Cir. 2002) . . . .

A

[*Texas Digital*] placed too much reliance on extrinsic sources such as dictionaries, treatises, and encyclopedias and too little on intrinsic sources, in particular the specification and prosecution history. While the court noted that the specification must be consulted in every case, it suggested a methodology for claim interpretation in which the specification should be consulted only after a determination is made, whether based on a dictionary, treatise, or other source, as to the ordinary meaning or meanings of the claim term in dispute. Even then, recourse to the specification is limited to determining whether the specification excludes one of the meanings derived from the dictionary, whether the presumption in favor of the dictionary definition of the claim term has been overcome by "an explicit definition of the term different from its ordinary meaning," or whether the inventor "has disavowed or disclaimed scope of coverage, by using words or expressions of manifest exclusion or restriction, representing a clear disavowal of claim scope." In effect, the *Texas Digital* approach limits the role of the specification in claim construction to serving as a check on the dictionary meaning of a claim term if the specification requires the court to conclude that fewer than all the dictionary definitions apply, or if the specification contains a sufficiently specific alternative definition or disavowal. That approach, in our view, improperly restricts the role of the specification in claim construction. . . .

The main problem with elevating the dictionary to such prominence is that it focuses the inquiry on the abstract meaning of words rather than on the meaning of claim terms within the context of the patent. Properly viewed, the "ordinary meaning" of a claim term is its meaning to the ordinary artisan after reading the entire patent. Yet heavy reliance on the dictionary divorced from the intrinsic evidence risks transforming the meaning of the claim term to the artisan into the meaning of the term in the abstract, out of its particular context, which is the specification. [T]here may be a disconnect between the patentee's responsibility to describe and claim his invention, and the dictionary editors' objective of aggregating all possible definitions for particular words.

[W]e do not intend to preclude the appropriate use of dictionaries. Dictionaries or comparable sources are often useful to assist in understanding the commonly understood meaning of words and have been used both by our court and the Supreme Court in claim interpretation. A dictionary definition has the value of being an unbiased source "accessible to the public in advance of litigation." . . .

We also acknowledge that the purpose underlying the *Texas Digital* line of cases—to avoid the danger of reading limitations from the specification into the claim—is sound. Moreover, we recognize that the distinction between using the specification to interpret the meaning of a claim and importing limitations from the specification into the claim can be a difficult one to apply in practice. However, the line between construing terms and importing limitations can be discerned with reasonable certainty and predictability if the court's focus remains on understanding how a person of ordinary skill in the art would understand the claim terms. . . .

In *Vitronics*, this court grappled with the same problem and set forth guidelines for reaching the correct claim construction and not imposing improper limitations on claims. In that process, we recognized that there is no magic formula or catechism for conducting claim construction. Nor is the court barred from considering any particular sources or required to analyze sources in any specific sequence, as long as those sources are not used to contradict claim meaning that is unambiguous in light of the intrinsic evidence. For example, a judge who encounters a claim term while reading a patent might consult a general purpose or specialized dictionary to begin to understand the meaning of the term, before reviewing the remainder of the patent to determine how the patentee has used the term. The sequence of steps used by the judge in consulting various sources is not important; what matters is for the court to attach the appropriate weight to be assigned to those sources in light of the statutes and policies that inform patent law. . . We now turn to the application of those principles to the case at bar.

IV

A

The critical language of claim 1 of the '798 patent—"further means disposed inside the shell for increasing its load bearing capacity comprising internal steel baffles extending inwardly from the steel shell walls"—imposes three clear requirements with respect to the baffles. First, the baffles must be made of steel. Second, they must be part of the load-bearing means for the wall section. Third, they must be pointed inward from the walls. Both parties, stipulating to a dictionary definition, also conceded that the term "baffles" refers to objects that check, impede, or obstruct the flow of something. The intrinsic evidence confirms that a person of skill in the art would understand that the term "baffles," as used in the '798 patent, would have that generic meaning.

The other claims of the '798 patent specify particular functions to be served by the baffles. For example, dependent claim 2 states that the baffles may be "oriented with the panel sections disposed at angles for deflecting projectiles such as bullets able to penetrate the steel plates." The inclusion of such a specific limitation on the term "baffles" in claim 2 makes it likely that the patentee did not contemplate that the term "baffles" already contained that limitation. Dependent claim 6 provides an additional requirement for the baffles, stating that "the internal baffles of both outer panel sections overlap and interlock at angles providing deflector panels extending from one end of the module to the other." If the baffles recited in claim 1 were inherently placed at specific angles, or interlocked to form an intermediate barrier, claim 6 would be redundant. . . .

Other uses for the baffles are listed in the specification as well. In Figure 7, the overlapping flanges "provide for overlapping and interlocking the baffles to produce substantially an intermediate barrier wall between the opposite [wall] faces":

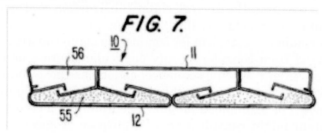

FIG. 7.

'798 patent, col. 5, ll. 26–29. Those baffles thus create small compartments that can be filled with either sound and thermal insulation or rock and gravel to stop projectiles.

The fact that the written description of the '798 patent sets forth multiple objectives to be served by the baffles recited in the claims confirms that the term "baffles" should not be read restrictively to require that the baffles in each case serve all of the recited functions. Although deflecting projectiles is one of the advantages of the baffles of the '798 patent, the patent does not require that the inward extending structures always be capable of performing that function. Accordingly, we conclude that a person of skill in the art would not interpret the disclosure and claims of the '798 patent to mean that a structure extending inward from one of the wall faces is a "baffle" if it is at an acute or obtuse angle, but is not a "baffle" if it is disposed at a right angle.

NOTES AND QUESTIONS

1. In *Phillips*, there really are two disputes to be resolved: (1) the meaning of the term "baffles" and (2) the appropriate methodology for construing claims. The court answered the first question clearly; the second less so. The court noted that "the specification is the single best guide" to the meaning of a claim term and criticized the *Texas Digital* panel's heavy reliance on dictionaries, but then stated that there is no "magic" formula, no particular order in which evidence is to be consulted. This failure to articulate a clear claim construction methodology has limited the benefit of the *Phillips* decision. Professors Wagner and Petherbridge have analyzed pre- and post- *Phillips* cases during the time period from May 15, 1996 to April 15, 2007. They identified a total of 712 total observable claim construction opinions and

found no meaningful change in court claim construction methodology. They conclude:

> Unfortunately, *Phillips* does not—at least to date—represent the Federal Circuit's finest hour. We find little here to suggest that the avowed goal of *Phillips*—to resolve the court's methodological disputes over claim construction—has been met in any measurable way. And we also find that the open-ended nature of the *Phillips* opinion, and its failure to resolve the longstanding split in claim construction jurisprudence, has undermined the Federal Circuit's efforts to develop a coherent and predictable jurisprudence.

R. Polk Wagner & Lee Petherbridge, *Did* Phillips *Change Anything? Empirical Analysis of the Federal Circuit's Claim Construction Doctrine*, in INTELLECTUAL PROPERTY AND THE COMMON LAW 33 (S. Balganesh ed., forthcoming Cambridge University Press, 2013).

What does this conclusion suggest for patent litigants? How should courts in the U.S. proceed with claim construction in light of the "guidance" provided in *Phillips*?

2. Prosecution history is considered part of the intrinsic evidence to be used in construing claims in the U.S.; however, in many countries, such as Germany, Canada, and the UK, its use is virtually non-existent. However, there are several countries where prosecution history is admissible, including the Netherlands, Italy, Switzerland, and China. For countries where prosecution history is admissible, should the claim interpretation of a court in one country influence a court in a different country? Are there any reasons countries should seek greater international consensus on the role of or appropriate approach to prosecution history in claim construction? For a cogent argument that prosecution history has no place in claim interpretation, *see* John R. Thomas, *On Preparatory Texts and Proprietary Technologies: The Place of Prosecution Histories in Patent Claim Interpretation*, 47 UCLA L. REV. 183, 188–89 (1999).

3. An important issue left unaddressed by the *Phillips* decision is whether the Federal Circuit should give any deference to the claim construction determination made by the trial court. In *Cybor Corp. v. FAS Technologies, Inc.*, 138 F.3d 1448 (1998), an *en banc* Federal Circuit ruled that claim construction was purely a question of law reviewed *de novo* with no deference to trial court determinations. Moreover, parties cannot obtain interlocutory review of a district court claim construction decision. In dissent, Judge Rader explained the fallacy of the majority's conclusion:

> Trial judges can spend hundreds of hours reading and rereading all kinds of source material, receiving tutorials on technology from leading scientists, formally questioning technical experts and testing their understanding against that of various experts, examining on site the operation of the principles of the claimed invention, and deliberating over the meaning of the claim language. If district judges are not satisfied with the proofs proffered by the parties,

they are not bound to a prepared record but may compel additional presentations or even employ their own court-appointed expert. An appellate court has none of these advantages.

Id. at 1477. What particular problems might *de novo* review of claim construction determinations create? What benefits might it provide?

––––––––––

In most countries, once a claim is construed, infringement can be determined by reading the claim onto the accused device to see if the device contains each element of the claim. If even one element of the construed claim is missing from the accused device, there is no infringement. However, if each element of the claim as construed is present in the accused device, literally or equivalently, the device infringes, even if it contains other elements (unless the claim contains language that limits its scope such as by a "consisting of" transition). This result is sometimes referred to as *absolute product protection*: If the claimed invention is present in an accused device, there is infringement, even if it is just one of many components making up a product.

The U.S. *Monsanto Co. v. McFarling* case, 488 F.3d 973 (Fed. Cir. 2007), provides an example of absolute product protection in action. The Monsanto Company owns numerous patents covering technology for genetically modifying plants to make them resistant to the herbicide glyphosate, sold under the trademark RoundUp®. Monsanto prohibits farmers planting the patented "RoundUp Ready®" seeds from saving any harvested seeds for replanting in a subsequent season. In *McFarling*, a farmer who saved and replanted seed in violation of Monsanto's stipulations was held to have infringed a patent claiming genetically modified plants, seeds, and the chimeric genes used in the modification. Although the seeds planted were new, and not the ones originally purchased from Monsanto, the court held that distinction to be irrelevant and that the patent claims infringed on an absolute product protection basis. It explained:

> Mr. McFarling asserts that the "unpatented germ plasm and second generation of genetically-altered soybeans is not a 'human-made' invention." But the fact that the germ plasm and the soybeans are not "human-made" is irrelevant to infringement. What is human-made are the chimeric genes claimed in the '605 patent, which are found in all of the infringing seeds at issue in this case. The principles of patent law do not cease to apply when patentable inventions are incorporated within living things, either genetically or mechanically."

> *Id.* at 978.

The following European Court of Justice (CJEU) decision, interpreting the EU Biotechnology Directive discussed in Chapter 4, also concerns Monsanto's patented RoundUp Ready® technology. However, the Court's construction of the scope of the claims imposes an interesting limit on absolute product protection for genetic information-based inventions.

MONSANTO TECH. LLC V. CEFETRA BV

Court of Justice of the European Union
Intervener in support of the defendant: Argentine State
Case C 428/08, (Grand Chamber), Eur. Ct. Justice (2010)

1. This reference for a preliminary ruling concerns the interpretation of Article 9 of Directive 98/44/EC of the European Parliament and of the Council of 6 July 1998 on the legal protection of biotechnological inventions (OJ 1998 L 213, p. 13) ('the Directive') . . .

Legal context

. . .

European Union law

5. Article 1 of the Directive provides that Member States are to protect biotechnological inventions under national patent law and that, if necessary, they are to adjust the latter to take account of the provisions of that Directive. It adds that the Directive is to be without prejudice to the obligations of the Member States pursuant, inter alia, to the TRIPs Agreement.

6. Article 2 of the Directive defines 'biological material' as any material containing genetic information and capable of reproducing itself or being reproduced in a biological system.

7. Article 3 provides that inventions which are new, which involve an inventive step and which are susceptible of industrial application are to be patentable even if they concern, in particular, a product consisting of or containing biological material. It further states that biological material which is isolated from its natural environment or produced by means of a technical process may be the subject of an invention even if it previously occurred in nature.

8. Recital 22 in the preamble to the Directive points out that the discussion on the patentability of sequences or partial sequences of genes is controversial. It states that the granting of a patent for inventions which concern such sequences or partial sequences should be subject to the same criteria of patentability as in all other areas of technology: novelty, inventive step and industrial application, and that the industrial application of a sequence or partial sequence must be disclosed in the patent application as filed.

9. Recital 23 in the preamble to the Directive states that a mere DNA sequence without indication of a function does not contain any technical information and is therefore not a patentable invention.

10. Recital 24 in the preamble to the Directive indicates that, in order to comply with the industrial application criterion it is necessary in cases where a sequence or partial sequence of a gene is used to produce a pro-

tein or part of a protein, to specify which protein or part of a protein is produced or what function it performs. . . .

12. Article 9, contained in Chapter II, entitled 'Scope of protection', provides:

> 'The protection conferred by a patent on a product containing or consisting of genetic information shall extend to all material . . . in which the product is incorporated and in which the genetic information is contained and performs its function.'

National law

13. Article 53 of the 1995 Netherlands Law on patents (Rijksoctrooiwet 1995) ('the 1995 Law') provides:

> '. . . A patent shall give the patent holder . . . the exclusive right:
>
> (a) to manufacture the patented product in or for its business, to use it, to bring it into circulation or to sell it on, to hire it out, to deliver it or otherwise trade in it, or to offer it, to import it or to have it in stock for any of those purposes;
>
> (b) to apply the patented process in or for its business, or to use, to bring into circulation or to sell on, to hire out or deliver the product derived directly from the application of that process, or otherwise to trade in that product, or to offer it, to import it or have it in stock for any of those purposes.'

14. Article 53a of that law reads as follows:

> '1. In respect of a patent on a biological material possessing specific characteristics as a result of the invention, the exclusive right shall extend to any biological material derived from that biological material through propagation or multiplication in an identical or divergent form and possessing those same characteristics.
>
> 2. In respect of a patent on a process that enables a biological material to be produced possessing specific characteristics as a result of the invention, the exclusive right shall extend to biological material directly obtained through that process and to any other biological material derived from the directly obtained biological material through propagation or multiplication in an identical or divergent form and possessing those same characteristics.
>
> 3. In respect of a patent on a product containing or consisting of genetic information, the exclusive right shall extend to all material in which the product is incorporated and in which the genetic information is contained and performs its function. . .'

The dispute in the main proceedings and the questions referred for a preliminary ruling

15. Monsanto is the holder of European patent EP 0 546 090 granted on 19 June 1996 relating to 'Glyphosate tolerant 5-enolpyruvylshikimate-3-phosphate synthases' ('the European patent'). The European patent is valid, inter alia, in the Netherlands.

16. Glyphosate is a non-selective herbicide. In a plant, it works by inhibiting the Class I enzyme 5-enol-pyruvylshikimate-3-phosphate synthase (also called 'EPSPS'), which plays an important role in the growth of the plant. The effect of glyphosate is that the plant dies.

17. The European patent describes a class of EPSPS enzymes which are not sensitive to glyphosate. Plants containing such enzymes survive the use of glyphosate, whilst weeds are destroyed. The genes encoding these Class II enzymes have been isolated from three different bacteria. Monsanto has inserted those genes into the DNA of a soy plant it has called RR (Roundup Ready) soybean plant. As a result, the RR soybean plant produces a Class II EPSPS enzyme called CP4-EPSPS, which is glyphosate-resistant. It thus becomes resistant to the herbicide 'Roundup'.

18. The RR soybean is cultivated on a large scale in Argentina, where there is no patent protection for the Monsanto invention.

19. Cefetra and Toepfer trade in soy meal. Three cargoes of soy meal from Argentina arrived in the port of Amsterdam on 16 June 2005, 21 March and 11 May 2006. Vopak made a customs declaration for one of the cargoes.

20. The three consignments were detained by the customs authorities pursuant to Council Regulation (EC) No 1383/2003 of 22 July 2003 concerning customs action against goods suspected of infringing certain intellectual property rights and the measures to be taken against goods found to have infringed such rights. They were released after Monsanto had taken samples. Monsanto tested the samples to determine whether they originated from RR soybeans.

21. Following the tests, which revealed the presence of CP4-EPSPS in the soy meal and the DNA sequence encoding it, Monsanto applied for injunctions against Cefetra, Vopak and Toepfler before the Rechtbank's-Gravenhage, on the basis of Article 16 of Regulation No 1383/2003, and for a prohibition of infringement of the European patent in all countries in which the patent is valid. The Argentine State intervened in support of the forms of order sought by Cefetra. . . .

23. Cefetra, supported by the Argentine State, and Toepfer, argue that Article 53a of the 1995 Law is exhaustive in character. It should be regarded as a lex specialis which derogates from the general protection

scheme established by Article 53 of the same law for a patented product. ~~If the DNA present in the soy meal can no longer perform its function in that substance, Monsanto cannot oppose the marketing of the soy meal solely on the ground that the DNA is present in it.~~ There is a connection between the limited patentability referred to in recitals 23 and 24 in the preamble to the Directive and the scope of the protection conferred by a patent.

24. Monsanto argues that the purpose of the Directive is not to limit the protection for biotechnological inventions that exists in Member States. The Directive does not affect the protection conferred by Article 53 of the 1995 Law, which is absolute. . .

32. In that context, the Rechtbank's-Gravenhage decided to stay the proceedings and to refer the following questions to the Court of Justice for a preliminary ruling:

'(1) Must Article 9 of Directive 98/44 . . . be interpreted as meaning that the protection provided under that provision can be invoked even in a situation such as that in the present proceedings, in which the product (the DNA sequence) forms part of a material imported into the European Union (soy meal) and does not perform its function at the time of the alleged infringement, but has indeed performed its function (in the soy plant) or would possibly again be able to perform its function after it has been isolated from that material and inserted into the cell of an organism?

(2) Proceeding on the basis that the DNA sequence described in claim 6 of patent No EP 0 546 090 is present in the soy meal imported into the Community by Cefetra and [Toepfer], and that the DNA is incorporated in the soy meal for the purposes of Article 9 of [the Directive] and that it does not perform its function therein:

does the protection of a patent on biological material as provided for under [the Directive], in particular under Article 9 thereof, preclude the national patent legislation from offering (in parallel) absolute protection to the product (the DNA) as such, regardless of whether that DNA performs its function, and must the protection as provided under Article 9 of [the Directive] therefore be deemed to be exhaustive in the situation referred to in that provision, in which the product consists in genetic information or contains such information, and the product is incorporated in material which contains the genetic information? . . .'

The questions referred for a preliminary ruling

The first question

33. By its first question, the national court asks, essentially, whether Article 9 of the Directive is to be interpreted as conferring patent right protection in circumstances such as those of the case in the main proceedings, in which the patented product is contained in the soy meal, where it does not perform the function for which it was patented, but did perform that function previously in the soy plant, of which the meal is a processed product, or would possibly again be able to perform its function after it has been extracted from the soy meal and inserted into the cell of a living organism.

34. In that regard, it must be noted that Article 9 of the Directive makes the protection for which it provides subject to the condition that the genetic information contained in the patented product or constituting that product 'performs' its function in the 'material . . . in which' that information is contained.

35. The usual meaning of the present tense used by the Community legislature and of the phrase 'material . . . in which' implies that the function is being performed at the present time and in the actual material in which the DNA sequence containing the genetic information is found.

36. In the case of genetic information such as that at issue in the main proceedings, the function of the invention is performed when the genetic information protects the biological material in which it is incorporated against the effect, or the foreseeable possibility of the effect, of a product which can cause that material to die.

37. The use of a herbicide on soy meal is not, however, foreseeable, or even normally conceivable. Moreover, even if it was used in that way, a patented product intended to protect the life of biological material containing it could not perform its function, since the genetic information can be found only in a residual state in the soy meal, which is a dead material obtained after the soy has undergone several treatment processes.

38. It follows from the foregoing that the protection provided for in Article 9 of the Directive is not available when the genetic information has ceased to perform the function it performed in the initial material from which the material in question is derived. . .

41. Monsanto argues, however, that its principal claim is for protection of its patented DNA sequence as such. It explains that the DNA sequence at issue in the case in the main proceedings is protected by the applicable national patent law, in accordance with Article 1(1) of the Directive. Article 9 of the Directive relates solely to an extension of such protection to other material in which the patented product is incorporated. In the case in the main proceedings, Monsanto is not, therefore,

seeking to obtain the protection provided for by Article 9 of the Directive for the soy meal in which the patented DNA sequence is incorporated. This case concerns the protection of the DNA sequence as such, which is not linked to the performance of a specific function. Such protection is indeed absolute under the applicable national law, to which Article 1(1) of the Directive refers.

42. Such an analysis cannot be accepted.

43. In that regard, it should be borne in mind that recital 23 in the preamble to the Directive states that 'a mere DNA sequence without indication of a function does not contain any technical information and is therefore not a patentable invention'.

44. Moreover, the import of recitals 23 and 24 in the preamble to, and Article 5(3) of the Directive is that a DNA sequence does not enjoy any protection under patent law when the function performed by that sequence is not specified.

45. Since the Directive thus makes the patentability of a DNA sequence subject to indication of the function it performs, it must be regarded as not according any protection to a patented DNA sequence which is not able to perform the specific function for which it was patented.

46. That interpretation is supported by the wording of Article 9 of the Directive, which makes the protection it provides for subject to the condition that the patented DNA sequence performs its function in the material in which it is incorporated.

47. An interpretation to the effect that, under the Directive, a patented DNA sequence could enjoy absolute protection as such, irrespective of whether or not the sequence was performing its function, would deprive that provision of its effectiveness. Protection accorded formally to the DNA sequence as such would necessarily in fact extend to the material of which it formed a part, as long as that situation continued. . .

50. Accordingly, the answer to the first question is that Article 9 of the Directive must be interpreted as not conferring patent right protection in circumstances such as those of the case in the main proceedings, in which the patented product is contained in the soy meal, where it does not perform the function for which it was patented, but did perform that function previously in the soy plant, of which the meal is a processed product, or would possibly again be able to perform that function after it had been extracted from the soy meal and inserted into the cell of a living organism.

The second question

51. By its second question, the national court asks, essentially, whether Article 9 of the Directive effects an exhaustive harmonisation of the protection it confers, with the result that it precludes national patent

legislation from offering absolute protection to the patented product as such, regardless of whether it performs its function in the material containing it.

52. That question is based on the premise, referred to in the order for reference, that a national provision such as Article 53 of the 1995 Law does in fact accord absolute protection to the patented product.

53. In order to answer the second question, it is appropriate to note that, in recitals 3 and 5 to 7 in the preamble to the Directive, the Community legislature states that:

— ffective and harmonised protection throughout the Member States is essential in order to maintain and encourage investment in the field of biotechnology;

— differences exist in the legal protection of biotechnological inventions offered by the laws and practices of the different Member States;

— such differences could create barriers to trade and hence impede the proper functioning of the internal market;

— such differences could well become greater as Member States adopt new and different legislation and administrative practices, or national case-law interpreting such legislation develops differently;

— uncoordinated development of national laws on the legal protection of biotechnological inventions in the Community could lead to further disincentives to trade, to the detriment of the industrial development of such inventions and of the smooth operation of the internal market. . .

55. It follows from those statements that the Community legislature intended to effect a harmonisation which was limited in its substantive scope, but suitable for remedying the existing differences and preventing future differences between Member States in the field of protection of biotechnological inventions.

56. The harmonisation decided upon is thus aimed at avoiding barriers to trade.

57. Moreover it represents a compromise between the interests of patent holders and the need for proper functioning of the internal market. . . .

60. It follows that the harmonisation effected by Article 9 of the Directive must be regarded as exhaustive.

. . . .

63. The answer to the second question is therefore that Article 9 of the Directive effects an exhaustive harmonisation of the protection it confers, with the result that it precludes the national patent legislation from offering absolute protection to the patented product as such, regardless of whether it performs its function in the material containing it. . .

NOTES AND QUESTIONS

1. As the CJEU's ruling in *Monsanto Tech. v. Cefetra* shows, how broadly or narrowly a claim is construed affects the patent owner's ability to enforce the patented claim against third parties. The ability to widely enforce biotech patents, such as those held by Monsanto, can be especially controversial and raise a host of broader policy issues, including issues related to international trade. As Dr. Heath of the EPO Board of Appeals notes:

> The freedom of international trade, one of the objectives of the WTO/TRIPS Agreement, may also be of concern when interpreting the Biotech Directive. If Monsanto's position were correct, similar cases could arise for the importation of cotton, the [RoundUp Ready®] variety of which Monsanto has started selling in India without corresponding patent protection. Any trace of the protected DNA in, say, imported jeans or t-shirts would allow the patentee to raid the premises of any manufacturer or shop commercially manufacturing or selling these goods—an interesting, but somewhat worrying scenario.

Christopher Heath, *The Scope of DNA Patents in Light of the Recent Monsanto Decisions*, 40 IIC 956 (2009). Should concerns about international trade, human rights, or regional harmonization be relevant to claim construction? How different is reliance on dictionary definitions of words used in a claim from reliance on the goals and objectives stated in international or regional patent agreements? What principles should guide claim construction when considerations related to patent harmonization are at issue?

2. *Monsanto Tech. v. Cefetra* generated immediate consternation and criticism for its perceived negative impact on the European biotechnology industry. According to some commentators:

> [T]here is a significant risk that countless biotechnology products are not protected by enforceable patent claims. An accused infringer, for example, could deny infringement by simply asserting that the patented polynucleotide or gene does not perform its function at the time of alleged infringement. Because many genes are only temporarily functional, or functional only in some tissues or organs, or have many functions, this defense may have merit. Furthermore, the opinion's impact may extend far beyond a narrow conception of the biotechnology industry. For example, the viability of patents claiming isolated DNA or RNA sequences used as reagents—

including reagents used in diagnostic methods such as gene tests and DNA chips—are now in jeopardy. . . . The ECJ decision is surprising because Article 9 of the Directive, which was an important basis for the ECJ's ruling, was intended to define what constitutes patentable subject matter when the claims in question cover living and replicating organisms. Article 9 was not intended to define the scope of enforceable rights in the context of alleged patent infringement.

Richard Peet et al., *The Future of Biotechnology Patents in the European Union: The Potential Impact of* Monsanto Technology LLC v. Cefetra et al. *on Patent Infringement*, INTELL. PROP. WATCH (Aug. 17, 2010, 6:43 PM), *available at* http://www.ip-watch.org/2010/08/17/the-future-of-biotechnology-patents-in-the-european-union. Read Article 9 of the Biotech Directive in conjunction with Recital 23. Are the authors correct that claim construction is an exercise entirely distinct from considerations of patent eligibility?

3. As the Court noted, Monsanto does not have a patent on Round-Up Ready® soybean seed in Argentina, where the soybean plants are grown. How relevant is that fact to this litigation?

4. According to Monsanto, the provisions of the Netherlands patent law arguably gave a stronger level of protection to biotechnology inventions than the EU Biotech Directive. Monsanto argued that Article 9 of the Directive should not be read to constrain a national law from giving a level of protection higher than prescribed by international or, in this case, regional law. By interpreting the provisions of the Directive as "exhaustive," the CJEU's decision effectively constrains the scope of rights EU member states can extend to biotechnology inventions. Is this prudent policy for the EU? What are the potential disadvantages of the CJEU's approach?

5. What are the benefits of the principle of exhaustive harmonization? Recall from Chapter 1, *supra,* that developing countries expressed significant concern over the impact of strong multilateral patent protection on their economic development goals. Given the stated objectives of the TRIPS Agreement, which include facilitating development goals, do you think courts in developing countries should adopt a principle of exhaustive harmonization in interpreting the scope of patent rights in national law?

---

2. DOCTRINE OF EQUIVALENTS

The Doctrine of Equivalents (DOE) is an equitable doctrine used in many countries to balance fairness to patentees with certainty regarding claim scope for third parties. Under the doctrine the patentee's right to exclude extends beyond the literal language of the claim to include substantially similar products. The origin of the doctrine can be traced at least to the 1853 *Winans v. Denmead* decision, 56 U.S. 330, 15 How. 330

(1853). Professors Meurer and Nard provide a useful description of events leading up to articulation of the DOE in the United States:

> The exact date of the creation of DOE is difficult to discern because the role of claims in patents has changed over time. The doctrine works to expand patent scope beyond the rights given by the claims, thus there could not be a DOE until rights were firmly associated with claims. Claims were not mentioned in the Patent Act of 1793; they first appear in the 1836 Act. Prior to the 1836 Act, however, patent attorneys as a norm began to include claim-type language in the patent specification.
>
> . . .To understand why this norm developed, one must appreciate that in the first half of the nineteenth century, courts helped inventors gain broad patent scope by setting generous standards for patent infringement—a precursor to the DOE. Early patent cases fleshed out the inchoate patent right by focusing on the "principle" of the invention. These decisions used such equitable language as "colorable differences," "copyist," and "pirated," and created linguistic tests such as "substantially the same" or "substantial identity" to gauge infringement. During litigation, the jury would peruse the written description to determine the principles underlying the inventive concept. The jury, however, had the difficult job of comparing the accused product with the patentee's disclosed invention because the jury was required to discern abstract principles of the invention from the patent document's textual description and schematic representations. As such, jurors may "find no infringement because they see so many superficial differences between the defendant's machine and the description of the patented invention." . . . .
>
> As the prominence of claims increased, the equitable standards for non-literal patent infringement coalesced into the doctrine of equivalents. Instead of searching for the principle of the invention, courts gradually shifted to a two-part analysis: first, interpret the claims and look for literal infringement; and second, expand patent rights as required by equitable considerations. The 1853 landmark decision *Winans v. Denmead* established the parameters of the DOE debate that remain applicable today. [In *Winans*,] the plaintiff requested the trial judge to instruct the jury that in determining infringement, similarity of form is less important than whether the "'defendants . . . constructed cars which, substantially, on the same principle and on the same mode of operation, accomplished the same result.'" The judge refused. . . . The Supreme Court, in a 5–4 decision, reversed and held that the jury instruction prayed for by *Winans* was appropriate. The majority accepted the notion that the claims play the

primary role in determining patent scope, but also insisted on a general role for equitable considerations that could expand patent scope.

Michael J. Meurer & Craig A. Nard, *Invention, Refinement and Patent Claim Scope: A New Perspective on the Doctrine of Equivalents,* 93 GEO. L. J. 1947, 1960–64 (2005). However, this equitable, fairness-based inquiry approved by the Court conflicts with the certainty and notice function that claims are expected to provide. The resulting tension has led courts to gradually constrict application of the DOE over time.

The Supreme Court revisited the DOE in *Warner Jenkinson Co. v. Hilton Davis Chemical Co.,* 520 U.S. 17 (1997), a case involving a claim to a dye purification process. During prosecution of the patent at issue, the patentee added a limitation that the purification process was performed at a pH from approx. 6.0 to 9.0 to overcome a prior art reference cited by the examiner showing a process operating above a pH of 9.0. However, the patentee gave no reason for including the 6.0 pH lower limit. After obtaining the patent, the patentee sued the defendant, whose process operated at a pH of 5.0. While conceding there was no literal infringement of the claim, the patentee argued that the claim was infringed under the DOE because 5.0 is equivalent to approx. 6.0. The Defendant countered that prosecution history estoppel barred application of the DOE as the patentee originally had sought a broad claim with no pH limitation but narrowed the claim by including the pH range in order to obtain the patent. The Supreme Court held that the DOE must be applied to each element of a claim (to avoid vitiating a claim element in its entirety) and that if an applicant made a narrowing amendment during prosecution without giving a reason (e.g., adding the lower limit of a pH of 6.0), this raised a rebuttable presumption that the amendment was made for a reason relating to patentability and prosecution history estoppel would apply.

While *Warner-Jenkinson* reaffirmed the viability of the DOE, the United States Court of Appeals for the Federal Circuit continued to whittle away at it until it ruled that a narrowing amendment made for *any* reason gave rise to prosecution history estoppel and completely precluded application of the DOE. The Supreme Court granted certiorari in the following decision, and breathed life back into the DOE. Nonetheless, the doctrine's condition remains precarious.

FESTO CORP. V. SHOKETSU KINZOKU KOGYO KABUSHIKI CO.

Supreme Court of the United States
535 U.S. 732 (2002)

■ Justice KENNEDY delivered the opinion of the Court.

This case requires us to address once again the relation between two patent law concepts, the doctrine of equivalents and the rule of prosecution history estoppel. . .

I

Petitioner Festo Corporation owns two patents for an improved magnetic rodless cylinder, a piston-driven device that relies on magnets to move objects in a conveying system. The device has many industrial uses and has been employed in machinery as diverse as sewing equipment and the Thunder Mountain ride at Disney World. Although the precise details of the cylinder's operation are not essential here, the prosecution history must be considered.

Petitioner's patent applications, as often occurs, were amended during the prosecution proceedings. The application for the first patent, the Stoll Patent (U.S. Patent No. 4,354,125), was amended after the patent examiner rejected the initial application because the exact method of operation was unclear and some claims were made in an impermissible way. The inventor, Dr. Stoll, submitted a new application designed to meet the examiner's objections and also added certain references to prior art. The second patent, the Carroll Patent (U.S. Patent No. 3,779,401), was also amended during a reexamination proceeding. The prior art references were added to this amended application as well. Both amended patents added a new limitation-that the inventions contain a pair of sealing rings, each having a lip on one side, which would prevent impurities from getting on the piston assembly. The amended Stoll Patent added the further limitation that the outer shell of the device, the sleeve, be made of a magnetizable material.

After Festo began selling its rodless cylinder, respondents (whom we refer to as SMC) entered the market with a device similar, but not identical, to the ones disclosed by Festo's patents. SMC's cylinder, rather than using two one-way sealing rings, employs a single sealing ring with a two-way lip. Furthermore, SMC's sleeve is made of a nonmagnetizable alloy. SMC's device does not fall within the literal claims of either patent, but petitioner contends that it is so similar that it infringes under the doctrine of equivalents.

SMC contends that Festo is estopped from making this argument because of the prosecution history of its patents. The sealing rings and the magnetized alloy in the Festo product were both disclosed for the first time in the amended applications. In SMC's view, these amendments narrowed the earlier applications, surrendering alternatives that are the very points of difference in the competing devices-the sealing rings and the type of alloy used to make the sleeve. As Festo narrowed its claims in these ways in order to obtain the patents, says SMC, Festo is now estopped from saying that these features are immaterial and that SMC's device is an equivalent of its own. . . .

II

The patent laws "promote the Progress of Science and useful Arts" by rewarding innovation with a temporary monopoly. U.S. Const., Art. I, § 8, cl. 8. The monopoly is a property right; and like any property right, its boundaries should be clear. This clarity is essential to promote progress, because it enables efficient investment in innovation. A patent holder should know what he owns, and the public should know what he does not. For this reason, the patent laws require inventors to describe their work in "full, clear, concise, and exact terms,"35 U.S.C. §112, as part of the delicate balance the law attempts to maintain between inventors, who rely on the promise of the law to bring the invention forth, and the public, which should be encouraged to pursue innovations, creations, and new ideas beyond the inventor's exclusive rights.

Unfortunately, the nature of language makes it impossible to capture the essence of a thing in a patent application. The inventor who chooses to patent an invention and disclose it to the public, rather than exploit it in secret, bears the risk that others will devote their efforts toward exploiting the limits of the patent's language. . . The language in the patent claims may not capture every nuance of the invention or describe with complete precision the range of its novelty. If patents were always interpreted by their literal terms, their value would be greatly diminished. Unimportant and insubstantial substitutes for certain elements could defeat the patent, and its value to inventors could be destroyed by simple acts of copying. For this reason, the clearest rule of patent interpretation, literalism, may conserve judicial resources but is not necessarily the most efficient rule. The scope of a patent is not limited to its literal terms but instead embraces all equivalents to the claims described.

It is true that the doctrine of equivalents renders the scope of patents less certain. It may be difficult to determine what is, or is not, an equivalent to a particular element of an invention. If competitors cannot be certain about a patent's extent, they may be deterred from engaging in legitimate manufactures outside its limits, or they may invest by mistake in competing products that the patent secures. In addition the uncertainty may lead to wasteful litigation between competitors, suits that a rule of literalism might avoid. These concerns with the doctrine of equivalents, however, are not new. Each time the Court has considered the doctrine, it has acknowledged this uncertainty as the price of ensuring the appropriate incentives for innovation, and it has affirmed the doctrine over dissents that urged a more certain rule. . . .

III

Prosecution history estoppel requires that the claims of a patent be interpreted in light of the proceedings in the PTO during the application process. Estoppel is a "rule of patent construction" that ensures that claims are interpreted by reference to those "that have been cancelled or rejected." The doctrine of equivalents allows the patentee to claim those insubstantial alterations that were not captured in drafting the original patent claim but which could be created through trivial changes. When, however, the patentee originally claimed the subject matter alleged to infringe but then narrowed the claim in response to a rejection, he may not argue that the surrendered territory comprised unforeseen subject matter that should be deemed equivalent to the literal claims of the issued patent. On the contrary, "[b]y the amendment [the patentee] recognized and emphasized the difference between the two phrases[,] . . . and [t]he difference which [the patentee] thus disclaimed must be regarded as material.". . .

A

The first question in this case concerns the kinds of amendments that may give rise to estoppel. ... We agree with the Court of Appeals that a narrowing amendment made to satisfy any requirement of the Patent Act may give rise to an estoppel. As that court explained, a number of statutory requirements must be satisfied before a patent can issue. The claimed subject matter must be useful, novel, and not obvious. ... In addition, the patent application must describe, enable, and set forth the best mode of carrying out the invention. §112 (1994 ed.) . . .

Petitioner contends that amendments made to comply with §112 concern the form of the application and not the subject matter of the invention. . . .

Estoppel arises when an amendment is made to secure the patent and the amendment narrows the patent's scope. If a §112 amendment is truly cosmetic, then it would not narrow the patent's scope or raise an estoppel. On the other hand, if a §112 amendment is necessary and narrows the patent's scope-even if only for the purpose of better description-estoppel may apply. . . .

B

Petitioner concedes that the limitations at issue-the sealing rings and the composition of the sleeve-were made for reasons related to §112, if not also to avoid the prior art. Our conclusion that prosecution history estoppel arises when a claim is narrowed to comply with §112 gives rise to the second question presented: Does the estoppel bar the inventor from asserting infringement against any equivalent to the narrowed element or might some equivalents still infringe? . . .

Though prosecution history estoppel can bar a patentee from challenging a wide range of alleged equivalents made or distributed by competitors, its reach requires an examination of the subject matter surrendered by the narrowing amendment. By amending the application, the inventor is deemed to concede that the patent does not extend as far as the original claim. It does not follow, however, that the amended claim becomes so perfect in its description that no one could devise an equivalent. After amendment, as before, language remains an imperfect fit for invention. The narrowing amendment may demonstrate what the claim is not; but it may still fail to capture precisely what the claim is. There is no reason why a narrowing amendment should be deemed to relinquish equivalents unforeseeable at the time of the amendment and beyond a fair interpretation of what was surrendered. Nor is there any call to foreclose claims of equivalence for aspects of the invention that have only a peripheral relation to the reason the amendment was submitted. . . .

This view of prosecution history estoppel is consistent with our precedents and respectful of the real practice before the PTO. . . .

When the patentee is unable to explain the reason for amendment, estoppel not only applies but also "bar[s] the application of the doctrine of equivalents as to that element." . . . These words do not mandate a complete bar; they are limited to the circumstance where "no explanation is established." . . .

[W]e hold here that the patentee should bear the burden of showing that the amendment does not surrender the particular equivalent in question. . . The patentee, as the author of the claim language, may be expected to draft claims encompassing readily known equivalents. A patentee's decision to narrow his claims through amendment may be presumed to be a general disclaimer of the territory between the original claim and the amended claim. There are some cases, however, where the amendment cannot reasonably be viewed as surrendering a particular equivalent. The equivalent may have been unforeseeable at the time of the application; the rationale underlying the amendment may bear no more than a tangential relation to the equivalent in question; or there may be some other reason suggesting that the patentee could not reasonably be expected to have described the insubstantial substitute in question. In those cases the patentee can overcome the presumption that prosecution history estoppel bars a finding of equivalence.

NOTES AND QUESTIONS

1. In *Festo*, the court justifies use of the DOE to expand a patentee's right to exclude beyond the literal scope of the claims based on the inherent limitations of language and the unforseeability of equivalents arising after the time of application. *Should* patentees be able to exclude others from using after-arising technology that they never contemplated? Consider the following critique:

> The DOE allows patent scope to grow over time as technology advances. In particular, patent owners exert control over products and processes that incorporate technology developed after the patent issues, and thus do not literally infringe. Expansion of scope is possible because equivalents are evaluated at the time of infringement, not the time of invention, filing, or issuance.

> The possibility that competitors could skirt literal claim language by making a minor modification based on later-developed technology generates ardent support for the DOE. . . .

> We believe . . . patent law's treatment of foreseeability is misguided. Courts mistakenly favor the patentee most strongly when the technology is least foreseeable. But unforeseeable technological developments do not justify application of the DOE, because the doctrine will not save refinement costs or significantly improve the incentive to invent in such cases. A patent applicant will not waste time refining claims to cover equivalents she cannot foresee. The DOE provides a social benefit when it diminishes the incentive for an inventor to invest in socially wasteful claim refinement. . . .

> Besides refinement cost savings, DOE policy must also be sensitive to inventor profit and the incentive to invent. No doubt, restricting the DOE will reduce incentives to some degree, but this hazard is probably overstated. First, notice that when an inventor foresees a high probability of a particular future substitute, the cost of claiming that substitute is probably low. Second, an inventor's incentive is not harmed much when, ex post, she is denied patent scope over technology that she did not foresee ex ante. The real incentive problem arises if an inventor believes there are many remote possible substitutes and the aggregate probability of some later developed substitute appearing is high. There is no statistical evidence suggesting this is a serious problem, and our impression from the case law and the history of technology is that few inventors have much to fear.

Michael J. Meurer & Craig A. Nard, *Invention, Refinement and Patent Claim Scope: A New Perspective on the Doctrine of Equivalents,* 93 GEO. L.J. 1947, 1996–1998 (2005). Do you agree with Professors Meurer and Nard?

2. The DOE survived *Festo* but in a more limited form than traditionally available because any narrowing amendment can trigger prosecution history

estoppel (PHE), leaving only three bases for rebutting the PHE presumption (unforeseeability of the equivalent, tangential relationship between amendment rationale and equivalent, or description limitations). However, in addition to PHE, a number of other doctrines limit application of the DOE, such as prior art (*see Wilson Sporting Goods Co. v. David Geoffrey & Assoc.*, 904 F.2d 677 (Fed. Cir. 1990)); disclosed but unclaimed embodiments (*see Johnson & Johnston Assoc. v. R.E. Serv. Co.*, 285 F.3d 1046 (Fed. Cir. 2002)); narrow claiming (*see Sage Prods., Inc. v. Devon Indus., Inc.*, 126 F.3d 1420 (Fed. Cir. 1997)); and the "all limitations" rule (*see Warner Jenkinson Co. v. Hilton Davis Chem. Co.*, 520 U.S. 17 (1997)). As a result, infringement actions are rarely won on the basis of the DOE. Professor Schwartz has posited another plausible theory for the decline of the DOE: a combination of doctrinal reallocation and doctrinal displacement. In *Explaining the Demise of the Doctrine of Equivalents*, 26 BERKELEY TECH. L.J. 1157 (2011), he argues:

> The theories of doctrinal reallocation and displacement explain the chain reaction resulting in the demise of the doctrine of equivalents. Initially, the Court of Appeals for the Federal Circuit reshaped patent litigation in *Markman*. There, it overruled previous precedent and held that claim construction was an issue of law that should be exclusively examined by a judge rather than a jury. Shortly thereafter, the Federal Circuit in *Cybor Corp. v. FAS Technologies* ruled that claim construction should be reviewed by the appellate court using the expansive de novo standard. These decisions triggered significant changes in patent litigation, not only in connection with claim construction, but also with respect to the doctrine of equivalents. Claim construction, which was significant but not critical before these decisions, rapidly became the centerpiece of patent litigation. Nearly contemporaneously, the doctrine of equivalents declined in importance. In effect, these doctrines switched places in terms of significance as a judicial tool. This switch occurred, in part, because both doctrines are essentially substitute ways for the court to evaluate the proper reach of an invention. When one means of evaluating scope—claim construction—became relatively easier for the court to apply, courts began to rely upon it more. As a result of this shift, patent litigation today is far different than litigation in the early 1990s.

Id. at 1160 (citations omitted).

Nevertheless, according to other scholars, the incidence of patentee wins under the DOE is not negligible. *See* Ted Sichelman & Stuart J.H. Graham, *Patenting by Entrepreneurs: An Empirical Study*, 17 MICH. TELECOMM. & TECH. L. REV. 111, 135 & n.133 (2010). For data on pre- and post-*Festo* patentee success rates on a DOE theory, *see* Lee Petherbridge, *On the Decline of the Doctrine of Equivalents*, 31 CARDOZO L. REV. 1371 (2010).

3. One of the questions created by the *Festo* decision concerns rebutting PHE when "the rationale underlying the amendment may bear no more than a tangential relation to the equivalent in question." The Federal Circuit has

upheld a finding of DOE infringement based on the "tangentially related" criterion rebuttal of PHE in at least two cases: *Insituform Tech., Inc. v. CAT Contracting, Inc.*, 385 F.3d 1360, 1368 (Fed. Cir. 2004), and *Primos, Inc. v. Hunter's Specialties, Inc.*, 451 F.3d 841, 849 (Fed. Cir. 2006). In *Insituform*, an amendment made to distinguish over the prior art based on *where* an element of the invention was located was considered only tangentially related to an equivalent directed to the *number* of such elements present. In *Primos*, an amendment related to element *spacing* was considered only tangentially related to element *shape*. Nevertheless, the "tangentially related" criterion is very narrow and "rebuttals under the tangential principle will be rare." *See Cross Medical Products, Inc. v. Medtronic Sofamor Danek, Inc.*, 480 F.3d 1335, 1346 (Rader, J., concurring).

Although the DOE originated in the U.S., a number of other jurisdictions have adopted the doctrine including Germany, France, and Japan. The following decision illustrates application of the DOE in another country, China, and for another kind of patent right: a utility model.

SHENZHEN TRIANGLE SCIENCE & TECHNOLOGY CO., LTD. V. COMPAQ

No. Gaozhichuzi 36/1998
Beijing High People's Court (2000)

■ Chief Judge ZHANG LUMIN

This Court accepted the case of patent infringement between the plaintiffs, Shengzhen Triangle Science & Technology Industrial Co., Ltd. (hereinafter referred to as Triangle Co., Ltd.), Ma Xiguang, and the defendant, Compaq Computer Corp. of the United States (hereinafter referred to as Compaq Corp.), on June 1, 1998. Compaq Corp. filed the request for invalidation with the Patent Reexamination Board of the Patent Office of the State Intellectual Property Office (hereinafter referred to as the Patent Reexamination Board) within the time limit for pleadings according to law, and this Court ruled suspension of the action on Aug. 18, 1998. The Patent Reexamination Board made the No. 2133 invalidation decision on April 27, 2000, which sustained the validity of the original right claim of that patent, and this Court resumed the trial on June 1, 2000 and organized a collegial panel according to law, which held an open trial of this case on Oct. 24, 2000.

The plaintiffs, Triangle Co., Ltd. and Ma Xiguang, jointly claimed that they were the co-owners of the No. 90204534 patent for utility model, which was a legal and valid patent in China. The notebook computers of model ARMADA 1 550T, etc. produced by the defendant, Compaq Corp., had fallen within the protection range of the foregoing patent for utility model. The notebook computers of the foregoing models produced by Compaq Corp. were sold in large numbers in China, and the Beijing Office of Compaq Corp. provided the after-sale service. The acts of Compaq Corp. had infringed upon their patent right and caused grave loss to them. Up to April 10, 1998, Compaq Corp. had gained 34,025,899.6 yuan directly from the sales. They, according to the law of China, asked the People's Court to order Compaq Corp. to stop its infringing acts and compensate for their economic loss of RMB 34,025,899.6 yuan, and bear the legal costs.

The defendant Compaq Corp. defended that neither literally nor under the doctrine of equivalents had the notebook computers of model ARMADA1 550T produced by it infringed upon the No. 90204534 patent for utility model, and asked the People's Court to reject the claims of Triangle Co., Ltd. and Ma Xiguang.

The authorized independent right claim [of the utility model patent] is "a kind of computer with seat grooves for replaceable battery and expansion board, including a computer main body, more than a group of battery packs and more than a group of expansion board packs, the characteristics are: there are two seat grooves set up at the rear of the computer main body, the size of which is suitable to accommodate the battery packs and the expansion board packs; there are contacts in those seat grooves and the positions of the contacts corresponded to those of the contacts of the battery packs for connection of circuit; and additionally there is fixed in the seat groove a circuit connection seat, which is interlinked with the main line, for butt joint with the connection part of the PC board of the specific lines extended from the expansion board packs." The China Patent Office altered the bibliographic items on July 22, 1997, the original "owner of the patent right, Ma Xiguang," was changed into the "owner of the patent right, Ma Xiguang, the co-owner of patent right, Shengzhen Triangle Science & Technology Industrial Co., Ltd."

Triangle Co., Ltd. purchased a Compaq notebook computer of model ARMADA 1 550T in the original packing from Beijing Founder Electronics Co., Ltd., and the seal of the Beijing Office of Compaq Corp. was put on the purchase registration card. There are a double bracket and a PC card seat groove on the left side of the computer body, the former may be used for installation of a floppy drive or another battery pack, and the latter may be used for installation of 32 bit or 16 bit PC card options of the size similar to that of a credit card; and there is a battery bracket on the right side of the computer body, which may be used for installation of rechargeable battery packs. On these grounds, Triangle Corp. and Ma Xiguang brought a charge of infringement upon their patent right against Compaq Corp. to this Court.

In the proceedings of the invalidation hearing [before the Patent Reexamination Board], the plaintiffs and defendant of this case had disputed over the understanding of the two terms "replaceable" and "additionally" in right claim 1, and the Patent Reexamination Board held that, according to the explanations of the patent specification and illustrations, the "replaceable" in right claim 1 shall be comprehended as "interchangeable;" and "additionally" shall be comprehended as "in addition." In the proceedings of invalidation hearing, the existing technologies quoted as evidence by Compaq Corp. and affirmed by the Patent Reexamination Office included: comparative document 1: page 176 of the magazine PC World released in 1989, involving a kind of GRIDCASE1 520 portable computer, which had a seat groove into which both battery packs and expansion board packs can be inserted and an external battery pack set up on the cover of the computer, but the battery packs cannot replace each other in the two seat grooves; comparative document 2: advertising model catalog . . . released in 1989, involving a kind of portable computer named as "The Book," which had a seat groove into which both battery packs and expansion board packs can be inserted and a seat groove, in which battery packs can be placed, set on the underside of the computer, but the battery packs cannot replace each other in the two seat grooves; comparative document 7: a patent of the United States, USP 4894792, released on Jan.16, 1990, involving a kind of portable computer, which had a seat groove at the rear of the computer and into which both battery packs and expansion board packs can be inserted, a seat groove set on the underside of the computer and into which rear additive expansion groupware can be inserted, and a seat groove on the side of the computer for storage inserted groupware. On these grounds, Triangle Co., Ltd. and Ma Xiguang argued that as this patent had two seat grooves with completely the same structure, and the sizes of the battery packs and the expansion board packs were completely the same, therefore the distinction between the foregoing existing technologies and the technical solution described in right claim 1 was that the seat grooves in the existing technologies were not interchangeable, while the seat grooves in the patent technical solution were interchangeable, moreover, it was this distinction that gave this patent the superior effect of free replacement and mutual substitution, and thus met the provisions of the Patent Law of China on creativeness. The Patent Reexamination Board agreed with the foregoing opinions of Triangle Co., Ltd. and Ma Xiguang, and held that right claim 1 was creative and thus sustained the validity of it based on those opinions.

This Court holds that Article 59 of the Patent Law of China provides that the protection range of patent right for utility model shall be based on its right claim, the specification and illustrations may be used to explain the right claim. . . . [W]hen the meaning of the terms in the right claim is unclear, the specification and illustrations shall be used to help understand the meaning of those terms; in the determination of the protection range of the patent right for utility model, due consideration shall be given to the statements made by the patent right owner on the restriction of the protection range of the right claim during the proceedings on validity of the patent right, and the patent owner shall be prohibited from going back on his word. The technical solution of right claim 1 of the No. 90204534 patent right for utility model in this case includes 7 technical characteristics: 1) having seat grooves for replaceable battery and expansion board; 2) a computer main body; 3) more than 1 group of battery packs; 4) more than 1 group of expansion board packs; 5) two seat grooves set up at the back edge of the main body and the size of which are suitable to accommodate the battery packs and expansion board packs; 6) all those seat grooves have contacts inside and the positions of the contacts correspond to those of the contacts of the battery packs to connect the circuit; 7) additionally there is fixed inside the seat groove a circuit connection seat linked with the main line for butt joint with the connection part of the PC board of the specific lines extended from the expansion board packs.

The two parties have different understandings of the meaning of "replaceable" in technical characteristic (1) and "additionally" in technical characteristic (7), and also disputed over whether the structures of the two seat grooves in technical characteristic (5) are the same. Since the Patent Reexamination Board has, on the basis of the specification and illustrations of the No. 90204534 patent, expressly explained in the No. 2133 invalidation decision that: "replaceable" in technical characteristic (1) shall be comprehended as "interchangeable," and "additionally" in technical characteristic (7) shall be comprehended as "in addition;" and since the owners of the patent right claimed in the statements of opinions submitted to the Patent Reexamination Board on Feb. 29, 2000 that the two seat grooves have the same structure and size and can be interchanged, these characteristics have made the patent right claim 1 of this case creative, and the Patent Reexamination Board has supported the foregoing arguments, the owners of patent right may not go back on their word on this point. [Thus], the protection range of right claim 1 shall be restricted jointly by the following technical characteristics: 1) having seat grooves for replaceable battery and expansion board; 2) a computer main body; 3) more than 1 group of battery packs; 4) more than 1 group of expansion board packs; 5) two seat grooves set up at the back edge of the main body and the size of which are suitable to accommodate the battery packs and expansion board packs; 6) all those seat grooves have contacts inside and the positions of the contacts correspond to those of the contacts of the battery packs to connect the circuit; 7) additionally there is fixed inside the seat groove a circuit connection seat linked with the main line for butt joint with the connection part of the PC board of the specific lines extended from the expansion board packs.

Since a floppy drive and another battery pack can be installed in the seat groove on the left side of the Compaq notebook computer ARMADA 1550 being charged with infringement, while battery packs and expansion board packs can be installed in the seat grooves described in right claim 1, Triangle Co., Ltd. and Ma Xiguang argued that the floppy drive shall fall within the category of expansion board, and the seat groove in the computer being charged with infringement is one with the same nature as that of the seat groove described in right claim 1. However, in the field of computer technology it is generally regarded that expansion refers to a method to increase the compatibility of computers, doing so by additive hardware is not the task of the basic system; an expansion board is a kind of circuit board inserted in the main line of the computer to increase additive functions or resources, and an expansion board in the notebook computer is a PC card of credit card size; a disc drive is one of the components of the basic system of a computer, an electronic mechanical equipment for reading and writing on the discs, therefore this Court holds that the disc drive is not a kind of expansion board, and the seat grooves in the computer being charged with infringement have different functions and qualities [to] those of the seat grooves described in right claim 1, so the arguments of Triangle Co., Ltd. and Ma Xiguang can't stand.

Compared with the 7 technical characteristics in right claim 1, the computer ARMADA 1 550T being charged with infringement has the technical characteristics (2), (3), (4), and (6), but doesn't have the technical characteristics (5) and (7), therefore the computer ARMADA 1 550T being charged with infringement is neither the same as nor equivalent with the technical solution of right claim 1, and doesn't fall within the protection range of right claim 1. Compaq Corp. hasn't infringed upon the patent right of Triangle Co., Ltd. and Ma Xiguang. In accordance with the provisions of the first paragraph of Article 59 of the Patent Law of the People's Republic of China of 1993, the following judgment is made:

The claims of the Shenzhen Triangle Science & Technology Industrial Co., Ltd. and Ma Xiguang are rejected. The acceptance fee of this case is 180,139 yuan, which shall be jointly borne by the Shenzhen Triangle Science & Technology Industrial Co., Ltd. and Ma Xiguang.

NOTES AND QUESTIONS

1. How did the plaintiffs' own arguments weaken the case? In analyzing infringement by equivalents, is the court using prosecution history estoppel, or something else? How does the Beijing High People's Court's analysis compare with that of the U.S. Supreme Court in *Festo*?

2. In 1998, the Supreme Court of Japan adopted the DOE in *Tsubakimoto Seiko v. THK K.K.*, 52 Minshū 113 (Sup. Ct., Feb. 2, 1998) and articulated a five-part test for equivalents:

> If there are elements that differ between the constitution described in a patented claim and [accused embodiment], the [accused embodiment] cannot be said to fall within the technical scope of the patented invention. On the other hand, even if there are elements [of

the claimed invention] that differ from the [accused embodiment], the [accused embodiment] may be equivalent to the constitution described in claim and may appropriately be said to fall within the technical scope of the patented invention if the following conditions are satisfied:

(1) the differing elements are not the essential elements in the patented invention;

(2) even if the differing elements are interchanged by elements of the [accused embodiment], the object of the patented invention can be achieved and the same effects can be obtained;

(3) by interchanging as above, a person of ordinary skill in the art to which the invention pertains [the "artisan"] could have easily achieved the [accused embodiment];

(4) the corresponding product and the like are not the same as the known art at the time of application for patent or could not have been easily conceived by an artisan at the time of application for patent; and

(5) there is not any special circumstances such that the [accused embodiment is] intentionally excluded from the scope of the claim during patent prosecution.

Chris T. Mizumoto & Yusuke Hiraki (trans.), http://www.softic.or.jp/en/cases/Tsubakimoto_v_THK.html (1998). How do these factors compare to the approach in the U.S. and China? Which approach seems easier to apply? Which seems more likely to result in a balance of fairness to the patentee and certainty for third parties trying to avoid infringing a patent?

3. For many years following the *Tsubakimoto* case, the DOE was largely rejected by courts in Japan. Former Tokyo High Court Judge Yukio Nagasawa blames this on the *Tsubakimoto* case requirement that a court find an "essential element", or part, of a claimed invention:

Between the Ball Spline [*Tsubakimoto*] decision and August 2002, there were 115 cases in which the doctrine of equivalent was invoked. Of these cases, the doctrine was applied and affirmed only in nine cases, which translates roughly to a mere 7.8% of the total cases where the doctrine was invoked. In other words, the court rejected the application of this doctrine in 92.2% of the cases. The main reason underlying the aversion of the Japanese lower courts towards applying the doctrine of equivalents is that the "essential part" requirement is unclear. Had the "essential part" requirement not existed, the doctrine of equivalents could have been applied to many more cases.

Nicholas Pumfrey et al., *The Doctrine of Equivalents in Various Regimes—Does Anybody Have It Right?*, 11 YALE J. L. & TECH. 261, 303–304 (2009). However, the doctrine is not dead in Japan. In 2009, the IP High Court found infringement under the DOE in the "Hollow Golf Club Head" case, *Yokohama Rubber Company v. Yonex*, 2077 Hanrei Jiho 123, (IP High Ct. June. 29, 2009). Arguing equivalents infringement thus remains a viable option for patentees litigating in Japan.

---

3. PURPOSIVE CONSTRUCTION

Recall that the EPO examines a single application that becomes a bundle of national patents in European Patent Convention (EPC) contracting states. Currently, there is no single court to adjudicate infringement of a European patent; a patentee generally must pursue actions in each jurisdiction in which infringement is occurring. Under the EPC, claim construction for infringement purposes is a national matter but is guided by EPC Article 69 and the Protocol on the Interpretation of Article 69. Article 69 of the EPC provides that "[t]he extent of the protection conferred by a European patent or a European patent application shall be determined by the terms of the claims. Nevertheless, the description and drawings shall be used to interpret the claims." The Protocol further states that:

> Article 69 should not be interpreted as meaning that the extent of the protection conferred by a European patent is to be understood as that defined by the strict, literal meaning of the wording used in the claims, the description and drawings being employed only for the purpose of resolving an ambiguity found in the claims. Nor should it be taken to mean that the claims serve only as a guideline and that the actual protection conferred may extend to what, from a consideration of the description and drawings by a person skilled in the art, the patent proprietor has contemplated. On the contrary, it is to be interpreted as defining a position between these extremes which combines *a fair protection for the patent proprietor with a reasonable degree of legal certainty for third parties*.

(Emphasis added).

A primary reason for the creation of the Protocol derived from the different approaches to infringement taken by the national courts at the time of the drafting of the EPC. In particular, the UK was perceived as taking a strict, literal approach to the construction of claims (which would tend to result in fewer findings of infringement), while Germany leaned toward the opposite extreme of using the claims as a guideline (tending to result in more findings of infringement).

Despite the admonition in the Protocol, European courts, particularly in the UK and Germany, continued to diverge in their approaches to claim construction, creating marked uncertainly for patentees since a patent might be found valid and infringed in one jurisdiction and valid and not infringed in another jurisdiction. Just such a situation occurred in the *Epilady/Improver* series of cases, where a UK court diverged from German and Dutch courts on the question of infringement. The UK and German decisions that follow illustrate some of the challenges faced by patentees suing for infringement of European patents with no centralized patent court system.

IMPROVER CORP. V. REMINGTON CONSUMER PRODS. LTD.

[1990] F.S.R. 181 (Pat. Ct.) (UK, 1989)

■ HOFFMANN J.:

This is an action for infringement of a European patent for an electrically powered cosmetic device for removing hair. The commercial embodiment of the plaintiff's invention is called "Epilady" and the defendant's device is called "Smooth & Silky." The defences are, first, that Smooth & Silky does not infringe the claims of the patent and secondly, that the patent is invalid for obviousness and insufficiency. In my judgment the patent in suit is valid but the defendant's device does not infringe. The action is therefore dismissed.

The Invention

Depilation means the removal of hair by the root, as opposed to shaving which leaves the root behind. The advantage of depilation is that the hair takes much longer to regenerate. Various methods have been used in the past for cosmetic depilation, but none was completely satisfactory. . . .

Epilady was invented by two Israelis in 1982. It consists of a small electric motor in a hand-held plastic housing to which is attached a helical steel spring held by its ends and stiffened by a guide wire to form a loop. The arcuate form of the spring causes the gaps between the windings to open on its convex side but to be pressed together on the concave side. When the spring is held close to the skin and rotated by the motor at about 6,000 revolutions per minute, hairs enter the gaps on its convex side and are gripped between the windings as the rotational movement brings them round to the concave side. The effect is to pluck them out of the skin.

Marketing of Epilady began in June 1986. It was an enormous commercial success. In the first two years over 5.8 million devices were made, generating a gross retail turnover in excess of US $340,000,000.

The Patent in Suit

The patent in suit is European Patent (UK) no. 0101656. . . .

The basic description of the patent in suit declares that—

"There is thus provided in accordance with an embodiment of the present invention an electrically powered depilatory device

including a hand held portable housing, motor apparatus disposed in the housing, and a helical spring composed of a plurality of adjacent windings arranged to be driven by the motor apparatus in rotational sliding motion relative to skin bearing hair to
be removed, the helical spring including an arcuate hair engaging portion arranged to define a convex side whereat the windings are spread apart, and a concave side corresponding thereto
whereat the windings are pressed together, the rotational motion
of the helical spring producing continuous motion of the windings from a spread apart orientation at the convex side to a
pressed together orientation at the concave side and for the engagement and plucking of hair from the skin, whereby the surface velocities of the windings relative to the skin greatly exceed
the surface velocity of the housing relative thereto." . . .

The description ends, however, with the following general statement,
which I shall later refer to as the "equivalents clause":

"It will be evident to those skilled in the art that the invention is not limited to the details of the foregoing illustrative embodiments, and that the present invention may be embodied in
other specific forms without departing from the essential attributes thereof, and it is therefore desired that the present embodiments be considered in all respects as illustrative and not restrictive, reference being made to the appended claims, rather
than to the foregoing description, *and all variations which come
within the meaning and range of equivalency of the claims are
therefore intended to be embraced therein*."

Claim 1 reads as follows:

an electrically powered depilatory device comprising:

a hand held portable housing (2);

motor means (4, 4') disposed in said housing; and

a helical spring (24) comprising a plurality of adjacent windings arranged to be driven by said motor means in rotational
sliding motion relative to skin bearing hair to be removed,
said helical spring (24) including an arcuate hair engaging
portion arranged to define a convex side whereat the windings are spread apart and a concave side corresponding
thereto whereat the windings are pressed together, the rotational motion of the helical spring (24) producing continuous
motion of the windings from a spread apart orientation at
the convex side to a pressed together orientation on the concave side and for the engagement and plucking of hair from
the skin of the subject, where by the surface velocities of the

windings relative to the skin greatly exceed the surface velocity of the housing relative thereto....

Smooth & Silky

Smooth & Silky also consists of a small electric motor in a hand held
housing but the element attached to the motor and used to extract the
hair is not a helical metal spring. Instead it is a cylindrical rod of elas-
tomerised synthetic rubber held by its ends to form an arc subtending
about 60°. I shall for convenience call it "the rubber rod." A number of
parallel radial slits have been cut into the rubber. The arcuate form of the
rod causes the slits to open on its convex side but to be pressed together
on the concave side. When the rod is held close to the skin and rapidly
rotated by the motor, hairs enter the gaps on its convex side and are
gripped between the walls of the slits as the rotational movement brings
them round to the concave side. The effect is to pluck them out of the
skin. . . .

Mr. Gross has been granted a patent [covering the Smooth & Silky
device] in the United States [U.S. 4,726,375] . . . .

Dr. Laming, a distinguished design engineer called as an expert witness by the defendants, said that Mr. Gross's specification contained
nothing which distinguished Smooth & Silky from Epilady by function.
The difference lay in their respective forms.

Infringement

The question of infringement turns upon a short but undoubtedly difficult point of construction, namely whether the rubber rod is a "helical
spring" as that expression is used in the claims of the patent in suit. The
proper approach to the interpretation of patents registered under the Patents Act 1949 was explained by Lord Diplock in *Catnic Components Ltd.
v. Hill & Smith Ltd.*[1982] R.P.C. 183, 242. The language should be given
a "purposive" and not necessarily a literal construction. If the issue was
whether a feature embodied in an alleged infringement which fell outside
the primary, literal or acontextual meaning of a descriptive word or
phrase in the claim ("a variant") was nevertheless within its language as
properly interpreted, the court should ask itself the following three questions:

(1) Does the variant have a material effect upon the way the invention works? If yes, the variant is outside the claim. If no—

(2) Would this (i.e. that the variant had no material effect) have been
obvious at the date of publication of the patent to a reader skilled in the
art. If no, the variant is outside the claim. If yes—

(3) Would the reader skilled in the art nevertheless have understood
from the language of the claim that the patentee intended that strict

compliance with the primary meaning was an essential requirement of the invention. If yes, the variant is outside the claim.

On the other hand, a negative answer to the last question would lead to the conclusion that the patentee was intending the word or phrase to have not a literal but a figurative meaning (the figure being a form of synecdoche or metonymy) denoting a class of things which included the variant and the literal meaning, the latter being perhaps the most perfect, best-known or striking example of the class. . . .

In the end, therefore, the question is always whether the alleged infringement is covered by the language of the claim. ... It is worth noticing that Lord Diplock's first two questions, although they cannot sensibly be answered without reference to the patent, do not primarily involve questions of construction: whether the variant would make a material difference to the way the invention worked and whether this would have been obvious to the skilled reader are questions of fact. The answers are used to provide the factual background against which the specification must be construed. It is the third question which raises the question of construction and Lord Diplock's formulation makes it clear that on this question the answers to the first two questions are not conclusive. Even a purposive construction of the language of the patent may lead to the conclusion that although the variant made no material difference and this would have been obvious at the time, the patentee for some reason was confining his claim to the primary meaning and excluding the variant. If this were not the case, there would be no point in asking the third question at all.

. . . Section 125 of the Patents Act 1977, which is declared by section 139(7) to be framed to have as nearly as practicable the same effect as Article 69 of the European Patent Convention, says that the invention shall be taken to be that specified in a claim, as interpreted by the description and drawings. Section 125(3) applies to English patents the Protocol on the Interpretation of Article 69 which, if I may paraphrase, says that Article 69 and section 125(1) mean what they say: the scope of the invention must be found in the language of the claims. Extrinsic material such as the description can be used to interpret those claims but cannot provide independent support for a cause of action which the language of the claim, literally or figuratively construed, simply cannot bear. On the other hand, the claims should not be interpreted literally but in a way which "combines a fair protection for the patentee with a reasonable degree of certainty for third parties."

Dillon L.J. said in his judgment at the interlocutory injunction stage of this action that Lord Diplock's speech in *Catnic* indicated the same approach to construction as that laid down by the Protocol. . . . I regard it as binding upon me. I must therefore ask Lord Diplock's three questions to ascertain whether "helical spring" should be interpreted to mean a class of bendy, slitty rods of which a close-coiled helical spring in its primary sense is a striking and elegant example but which includes the defendant's rubber rod.

(1) Does the variant have a material effect on the way the invention works?

The answer to this question depends upon the level of generality at which one describes the way the invention works. At one extreme, if one says that the invention works by gripping and pulling hair, there is obviously no difference; the same would be true of a pair of tweezers. At the other extreme, if one says that it works by gripping hairs between metal windings of circular cross-section wound in a continuous spiral around a hollow core, there obviously is a difference. . . . It seems to me that the right approach is to describe the working of the invention at the level of generality with which it is described in the claim of the patent. As I have said, Dr. Laming agreed that there was no difference between the descriptions in Mr. Gross's patent and the patent in suit of the way the inventions worked. The differences lay entirely in the descriptions of the hardware. In my judgment, at the appropriate level of description, the rubber rod works in the same way as the helical spring and the differences I have mentioned, so far as they exist, are not material.

(2) Would it have been obvious to a man skilled in the art that the variant would work in the same way?

. . . Dr. Laming and Dr. Sharp, the eminent engineer called as an expert by the plaintiff, agreed that it would have been obvious to the skilled man that the attributes which enabled the helical spring to function in the way described in the specification were that it was capable of rotating, capable of transmitting torque along its length to resist the forces involved in plucking hairs, *bendy* (to form an arc) and *slitty* (to entrap hairs by the opening and closing effect of rotation). They also agreed that it would have been obvious that any rod which had these qualities in sufficient degree and did not have other defects such as overheating or falling to bits would in principle work in the same way and that the rubber rod plainly belonged to that class. On this evidence the second question must in my judgment be answered yes.

. . .

(3) Would the skilled reader nevertheless have understood that the patentee intended to confine his claim to the primary meaning of a helical spring?

This brings one to the question of construction. Since the question is what the skilled reader would have understood, I set out the views of the rival experts.

Dr. Sharpe placed considerable emphasis on what I have called the equivalents clause. He said in his report:

> it would have been obvious to me that all the inventor want-
> ed a helical spring for was as a convenient rotating bent beam in
> which slits formed by the adjacent windings would open and
> close as it rotated. It would then have been equally obvious to me
> that he could not have intended to exclude equivalents like the
> [rubber] rod . . . in thinking of equivalents I fell driven by the
> last paragraph of the specification before the claims [the equiva-
> lents clause] to think that the inventor was trying to make me
> think of equivalents for the helical spring . . . some other element
> that would do the same job.

> . . .

Dr. Laming, on the other hand, said that a helical spring was a very specific engineering concept. It meant a bar or wire of uniform cross-section wound into a helix. This definition was also accepted by Dr. Sharpe, although he suggested that the rubber rod could also be regarded as a helical spring in a more literal sense because it was springy and had torque stresses running through it in a helical pattern. I do not think it would occur to the ordinary skilled man to think of the rubber rod as a helical spring. Dr. Laming thought that in the context of the specification the skilled man would also not understand a helical spring to mean a *genus* of bendy, slitty rods. The references to prior art did not suggest that the function of a helical spring was simply to be a bendy slitty rod. In the patents in which they had been used, they were plainly essential features. Dr. Laming said:

> My opinion is that there is no way of interpreting the
> [plaintiff's] specification such that anything other than a helical
> spring (as defined above) is intended. The simple reason for this
> is, in my view, that the inventor had in mind what he regarded
> as a novel use of a familiar and readily available engineering
> component and saw the nub and centre of the invention as that
> use.

> I have now read the European Patent several times and it is
> clear that nothing other than a helical spring is referred to. If
> there were alternatives to a helical spring which the inventor or
> draftsman of the patent had in mind he did not indicate any-
> where that such alternative might be used. This stands in con-
> trast to suggested alternatives with regard to e.g. alternative
> drive arrangements suggested in Column 6. . . .

> The flexibility conferred on the helical spring by its essential
> features is obtained for the elastomeric rod by quite other
> means—by its being made of a material of very low elastic modu-

lus, a material about 30,000 times more flexible than the steel of the spring. The difference of material is inherent in the difference between the two devices: the helical spring, if made of the elastomeric material, would be useless spaghetti; and the arcuate rod made of steel would be an undriveably rigid bar. . . .

If the [plaintiff's] specification contained anywhere such words as "or any other configuration of an elastic member or members whereby rotation of the member or members causes a spread apart orientation at one position and a pressed together orientation at another position or point in the cycle" then at least one might be led to think about alternatives to the helical spring. Whether I would have thought of an elastomeric rod in such a case is hard to say in hindsight but the likelihood is made less by consideration of the Figures 9–14 which show possible configurations which the patentee had in mind. Except possibly for the first (Fig. 9) these configurations could not be adopted by an elastomeric rod without some internal wire guide, and in that case, the friction developed between elastomer and guide would in my opinion be prohibitive.

On this last point Dr. Sharpe agreed.

Dealing with the equivalents clause, Dr. Laming said:

It is true that [in the equivalents clause] reference is made to embodiment 'in other specific forms' and it asks there for reference to be made 'to the appended claims rather than the foregoing description.' But what follows is a series of claims in which the variations are all on such matters as the angle subtended by the arcuate portion (claims 2, 3 and 18), the degree of opening of the windings (claims 5 to 8), various mechanical drive options (claims 13 and 14) and different surface speeds (claims 19 and 20). A constant feature of all the claims is the specification of a helical spring which itself is the only type of element mentioned in the text of the specification and shown in the figures.

In my judgment the difference between the experts depends upon how one construes the equivalents clause. The first part of the clause merely says that the description should not be used to restrict the meaning of the language used in the claims. That is not the question here. What matters is the final words: "*and all variations which come within the meaning and range of equivalency of the claims are therefore intended to be embraced therein.*" If this means: "whatever contrary impression the skilled man may be given by the language of the claims read in the context of the rest of the description, all references in the claims to hardware are deemed to include any other hardware which would in any circumstances function in the same way" then I think Dr. Sharpe must be right. In my judgment, however, the clause does not have so wide an effect. The words I have quoted say that the variation must still come within the *meaning* of the claims and the reference to "range of equivalency" means in my judgment no more than "don't forget that the claims must be interpreted in accordance with *Catnic* and the Protocol."

Thus interpreted, I do not think that "helical spring" can reasonably be given a wide generic construction and I accept Dr. Laming's reasons for thinking that a skilled man would not understand it in this sense. The rubber rod is not an approximation to a helical spring. It is a different thing which can in limited circumstances work in the same way. Nor can the spring be regarded as "inessential" or the change from metal spring to rubber rod as a minor variant. In Catnic Lord Diplock asked rhetorically whether there was any reason why the patentee should wish to restrict his invention to a support angled at precisely 90° C, thereby making avoidance easy. In this case I think that a similar question would receive a ready answer. It would be obvious that the rubber had problems of hysteresis which might be very difficult to overcome. The plaintiff's inventors had done no work on rubber rods. Certainly the rubber rod cannot be used in the loop configuration which is the plaintiff's preferred embodiment. On the other hand, drafting the claim in wide generic terms to cover alternatives like the rubber rod might be unacceptable to the patent office. I do not think that the hypothetical skilled man is also assumed to be skilled in patent law and he would in my judgment be entitled to think that patentee had good reasons for limiting himself, as he obviously appeared to have done, to a helical coil. To derive a different meaning solely from the equivalents clause would in my view be denying third parties that reasonable degree of certainty to which they are entitled under the Protocol.

The German decisions

The patent in suit is being litigated in a number of countries but the only one in which the action has come to trial is in Germany, where the *Landgericht* of Düsseldorf found in favour of the plaintiff. This naturally causes me concern because the *Landgericht* was interpreting the same patent according to the same Protocol and came to a different conclusion. It seems to me that the reason for the difference between me and my colleagues in Düsseldorf is that, having answered what I have labelled as Lord Diplock's first two questions in the same way as I have, they treated those answers as concluding the matter in favour of the plaintiff and did not find it necessary to ask the third question at all. The specification, they said, conveyed to the expert "the understanding that the configuration of the hair engaging portion as helical spring has to be understood functionally" and that the expert to whom the patent was directed would have "no difficulties in perceiving and understanding this meaning of the teaching of the invention." This does seem to me with respect to be an interpretation closer to treating the language of the claims as a "guideline" than the median course required by the Protocol. . . .

It may be said that the expert evidence before the *Landgericht* at the trial was different, but I doubt whether this could have been so. There was no real difference between the views of Dr. Sharpe and Dr. Laming on questions of engineering: the difference lay in the approach to construction, which is really a question of law.

NOTES AND QUESTIONS

1. In the *Improver* case, the court had to determine if a rubber rod-based depilatory device infringes a helical-spring-based depilatory device. Is the court assessing literal infringement, infringement under the doctrine of equivalents, or something else?

2. Despite concluding that use of the variant (rubber rod) instead of a helical spring would have no material effect on the way the invention worked (Protocol Question 1) and that this fact would have been obvious to a man skilled in the art (Protocol Question 2), the court still finds no infringement. Why? What evidence/argument do you think was most persuasive to the court? Do you agree with decision of non-infringement?

3. In *Phillips v. AWH*, the CAFC noted the danger of courts reading limitations from the specification into the claim instead of simply reading the claims in light of the specification. Did the UK court get this balance right or did it improperly limit the claims based on the specification? Can the line "between construing terms and importing limitations" really be "discerned with reasonable certainty and predictability" as stated in *Phillips*, p. 652 *supra*?

The following decision involves adjudication of infringement of the same European Epilady patent by the same device before a German appeals court.

GERMANY: EUROPEAN PATENT CONVENTION, ART.69 (1); PROTOCOL ON INTERPRETATION—"EPILADY GERMANY II"
24 IIC 838 (1993)

The plaintiffs accuse the defendant of infringement of European Patent 0101656. . . .

In June 1988, the defendant started distributing an electrically driven depilatory device, placing it into circulation in the Federal Republic of Germany under the designation, "Lady Remington Liberty". This device operates by means of an arcuate roll of rubber-like plastic, the smooth outer surface of which features a plurality of radial, spaced apart cuts which are distributed over the circumference of the roll and penetrate the plastic element partially only. By means of the motor, this roll is driven in a rotational motion about its longitudinal axis, so that the cuts open to form gaps at the convex side, and so that the side walls thereof are firmly pressed together when the cuts rotate to the concave side of the arcuate roll.

The plaintiffs asserted that the rubber roll provided with radial slits and used as hair-engaging element in the disputed depilatory device constitutes an equivalent to the helical spring provided by the invention. . . .

The defendant's admissible appeal is not successful on the merits. . . .

The starting point of the teaching of the patent in suit is the finding, which is known for instance from the state of the art mentioned in the patent specification, that a coil spring (helical spring) cannot only be used according to its actual purpose as a power unit, but, owing to its largely unlimited flexibility and to the gaps and clamping means resulting from the adjacent windings, is also suited to catch, clamp and pluck hairs out of the skin. This is rendered clear by the patent specification describing prior known hand-driven devices by correspondingly drawing attention to their mode of functioning. This, however, equally also applies to the subsequently described motor-driven depilatory device according to U.S. Patent 4,079,741, as the pertinent person skilled in the art easily recognizes even without express indication. According to the findings of the court's expert in the opinion of September 28, this person is an experienced college-educated engineer or a constructionally interested, academically trained engineer with a university degree. His knowledge must be of a certain scope, and he must be capable of fully recognizing and judging basic correlations. About the, as such atypical, use of a coil spring and the operation possible therewith, namely introduction of the hair into the gap, clamping of the hair by rotational or forward motion of movable windings and plucking of the hair, the teaching according to the patent in suit does not intend to change anything. This cannot be doubted in view of the description of U.S. Patent 4,079,741. Insofar, it is not the operation or the depilatory results achievable that are objected to, but solely the complex and expensive construction which makes the device unsuitable for home use. Only if said operation is too slow, as in the case of the known hand-operated or hand-driven devices, does it become inefficient and painful for the user. The court's expert did not express any doubts insofar, either; he also emphasizes that a coil spring in the described atypical use was already known as a suitable plucking means, and that the inventor was looking for a more efficient use of the known coil spring solution.

Accordingly, it is the object of the teaching of the patent in suit to suggest a motor-driven depilatory device with the described operation, so that efficient hair removal is ensured. In addition, however, the device according to its size, complexity, production costs and convenience of use should be suited for home use in such a way as is already the case for the electrical razor.

The solution according to the patent in suit (claim 1) makes use of the finding which is already revealed by Swiss Patent 268 696, i.e. that a coil spring is an elastic element which opens gaps on bending at the convex side and closes at the concave side, in a device which operates by motor-driven rotational motion of the windings of the spring, namely by a rotational motion which is quicker than the velocity at which the depilatory device is moved by the user's hand over the areas of the skin to be depilated. . . .

Patent claim 1 describes this solution of the problem of the patent by the following features:

The electrically powered depilatory device comprises

    1. a hand held portable housing,

    2. motor means positioned in said housing,

    3. a helical spring comprising a plurality of adjacent windings,

    4. the windings are arranged to be driven by said motor means in rotational sliding motion relative to skin bearing hair to be removed,

    5. said spring includes a hair engaging portion which

    a) is arcuate,

    b) defines a convex side whereat the windings are spread apart and

    c) defines a concave side corresponding to said convex side whereat the windings are pressed together,

    6. the rotational motion of the spring produces a continuous motion of the windings from a spread apart orientation at the convex side to a pressed together orientation at the concave side and for engagement with the hair and for plucking of hair from the skin of the subject,

    7. the surface velocity of the windings relative to the skin greatly exceeds the surface velocity of the housing relative thereto

The depilatory device, "Lady Remington Liberty", introduced in the German market by the defendant makes use of the teaching of the patent in suit as just explained.

The depilatory device distributed by the defendant fulfils features 1 and 2 literally. Features 3 to 7, however, are not given literally since the disputed embodiment uncontestedly does not feature a helical spring. The disputed embodiment instead has a massive roll-shaped body of a flexible and elastic rubber-like plastic material, featuring radial spaced apart cuts on its circumferential surface. This arcuate and motor-driven rubber roll is, however, a replacement means equivalent to the coil spring of the patent, so that features 3 to 7 of patent claim 1 are given in equivalent form.

First of all, the court . . . has no doubts that the disputed embodiment is identical in effect to a device making use of the wording of claim 1 of the patent in suit. The roll of the disputed embodiment unites a plurality of adjacent elements, namely the areas separated by the cuts (cf. feature 3); these areas are arranged to be driven by the motor means in rotational motion relative to skin-bearing hair to be removed (cf. feature 4). The roll comprises a hair-engaging portion which is arcuate, defines a convex side whereat the elements are spread apart and a concave side corresponding to the convex side whereat the elements are pressed together (cf. feature 5). The rotational motion of the roll produces a continuous motion of the elements from a spread apart orientation at the convex side to a pressed together orientation at the concave side for engagement with the hair and for plucking of hair from the skin of the subject (cf. feature 6). The surface velocity of the roll relative to the skin greatly exceeds the surface velocity of the housing relative to the skin (cf. feature 7). The disputed embodiment thus achieves that a hair that has reached the spaced apart areas of the roll is approached ever more closely by the walls of these areas as a consequence of the rotational movement, which walls then clamp the hair and pluck it out. With respect to the principle and success of the desired hair removal, which is efficient and suited for home use, the hair undergoes the same treatment as with a device using the wording of the patent in suit. In conjunction with this, reference can also be made to the description of the patent in suit, according to which wedge-shaped slits (gaps) are instrumental for the depilatory effect of the device. For, wedge-shaped gaps are also featured by the roll of the disputed embodiment. The fact that these—due to the different orientation and depth of their gaps in comparison with the inclined windings of a common coil spring—may move the hair differently before plucking it, namely bend it first, as to be seen from the private expert opinion, is therefore irrelevant for the question of identical effect. . . .

When evaluating the scope of protection of claim 1 of the patent in suit, however, the argument cannot be limited to the identity of effect only which, by the way, was also found, for example, by the British court (Justice Hoffmann) which had also dealt with the patent in suit and the disputed device. For the purpose of fairly delimiting the actual improvement of the field of technical knowledge achieved by an inventor on the basis of Art. 69(1) EPC and the Protocol on Interpretation, the protected invention will only be considered to be used if a person skilled in the art, on the basis of reflections progressing from the meaning of the patent claims, i.e. the invention described therein, could find out, with the help of his professional knowledge at the priority date, the modified means used with the disputed embodiment as a means being identical in effect for solving the problem underlying the invention; . . .

After the expert opinion, the court is convinced that a person skilled in the art—owing to the content of the claims of the patent in suit—was capable of arriving at the disputed embodiment in this sense.

The starting point for this conclusion is that a person skilled in the art will recognize by virtue of his professional knowledge that in the patent—in any case as far as the basic teaching of claim 1 is concerned—it is not a matter of the use of a "helical spring" as such. For, it is . . . used contrary to its common application or, as the expert also expressed, atypically. This fact was not sufficiently recognized in the court's judgment in the proceedings for issue of a preliminary injunction since it was only convincingly shown in the expert opinion; moreover, this fact was also given too little weight in the British court decision, which has already been mentioned, in this case probably mainly owing to the fact that the case was judged on the basis of the *Catnic* decision which was prior to Art. 69 EPC, and also owing to the additional fact that patent claim 1, which is of primary interest, was not placed in the foreground of consideration. The knowledge that, in the patent, the coil spring does not act as a power unit as usual, automatically results in the fact that those criteria of a helical spring are sought in order to determine why it is proposed in the patent. With this, however, a person skilled in the art in the field of interest here, and with the education mentioned by the expert and the skills resulting therefrom, will easily recognize that the coil spring is only proposed for the reason that it is an elastic cylindrical body which may be quickly rotated in the arcuate state and, above all, for the reason that it features—by virtue of its windings and their sides (walls) facing each other and separating the windings—means that stretch the surface of the body to form gaps at the convex side, while at the concave side they result in clamping areas with the help of which the hairs that entered the gaps may be clamped and plucked. In this way, to a person skilled in the art, the instruction of claim 1 of the patent in suit reads in a functional respect: Take a cylinder-shaped elastic element comprising separated walls of areas of material, to the effect that gaps will form on the convex side and clamping areas will form of the concave side if it is bent, and select—according to material and quality—an element that may be rotated at high speed when bent. If evaluated as a whole, the expert based his written opinion on this understanding. In view of the undisputed technical knowledge of the expert, both with respect to the technical field of interest here and with respect to his experience in patent litigation matters, the court does not see any reason not to follow the logic of the expert in that a person skilled in the art will actually understand the teaching of the patent in suit in this way. Moreover, the court's expert also confirmed this on inquiry of the defendant and the court. The basic thesis that a person skilled in the art will not interpret the coil spring as a spring, but as an elastic body with gaps is convincing, as it is obvious that the helical spring is not used as a spring per se, and as its use in accordance with the teaching of the patent in suit—and also, however, with the state of the art to be seen from the Swiss patent specification, for example—requires the abstraction by a person skilled in the art that this spring is an elastic element which opens at the convex side and closes at the concave side when bent, and which is furthermore so stable that it may be driven at relatively high speed. This abstraction therefore was professional knowledge in view of the state of the art, and it was rendered obvious by the claims of the patent in suit, respectively, if seen in the light of the description.

However, if the patent in suit conveyed this knowledge, it was also obvious to use a roll with cuts as in the accused embodiment as a hair-plucking element. . . . As opposed thereto, however, it is recognizably unimportant whether the body be completely hollow, feature a core or be massive, which is why a person skilled in the art could easily think of applying a massive roll with cuts. To produce the arcuate cut hair-plucking element of rubber or rubber-like plastic material could already be considered possible by a person skilled in the art for the reason that the wording of the patent in suit (claim 1) does not stipulate a certain material, but the question of the material is left open to the expert choice of a designing engineer proceeding on the basis of the patent in suit. Rubber-like plastic material is known to be a preferred material in conjunction with the use of an elastic, bendable element. . . .

The court also considers, as an indication of this finding, the history of the origin of the disputed embodiment as it is described in the British court decision which has been mentioned several times. The starting point was a device according to the patent with a metal coil spring. It was found that the use of this device was annoying because it plucked too many hairs at a time, but the principle of depilation according to the patent was not criticized. This points to the fact that the designing engineer of the disputed embodiment, having proceeded from the starting point assumed above, must have actually thought about what the "helical spring" really meant in the device presented to him. It further suggests that even though only metal coil springs had been used in the prior art, except for the so-called disk solutions, that fact did not actually represent an obstacle to a deviation therefrom.

Finally, it is also undisputed that it cannot be claimed that the disputed embodiment results in an obvious way from prior art (cf. in this respect Federal Supreme Court, 1986 GRUR 803, 806 – *Moulded Curbstone*). Insofar, it is sufficient to refer to the statements of the court's expert under No. 3 of his written expert opinion as the defendant had declared through its attorney during the oral proceedings that the so-called *Moulded Curbstone* objection was not raised.

NOTES AND QUESTIONS

1. In the UK *Improver* decision, the court concluded that the patent was valid, but was not infringed because the patentee intended to limit the scope of the invention to the use of a helical spring and did not contemplate any equivalent such as a rubber rod for hair removal. The German court, interpreting the same patent and the same EPC Article 69, reached the contrary conclusion that the defendant's rubber rod-based device did infringe claims in the patent. In a third decision, a court in the Hague also found infringement under a similar rationale as the German court. *See Improver Corp. v. Beska B.V. & Remington Products Inc.,* [Court of Appeals, the Hague], 20 Feb. 1992, 24 IIC 832 (1992) (Neth.). One possible reason for the different results can be traced to the language of EPC Article 69. The three official EPC languages are English, French, and German. The German word for "terms" in Article 69 is "Inhalt" which is perceived as having a broader meaning than the corresponding English and French words. Apparently the legislators were aware of the different meanings but were unable to agree on either narrowing the German or broadening the French and English. Because no one language dominates, all three versions are valid. For more on this topic *see* Christian von Drathen, *Patent Scope in English and German Law under the European Patent Convention 1973 and 2000*, 39 IIC 384 (2008); and Edward Armitage, *Interpretation of European Patents (Art. 69 and the Protocol on the Interpretation)*, 14 IIC 811 (1983).

2. Another difference between UK and German court proceedings concerns the use of experts. In the UK, each party can present expert witness testimony such as Lord Justice Hoffman considered in *Improver* (UK). However, in Germany, there generally is a single, court-appointed expert (parties are asked to propose a suitable expert) to assist the court as occurred in the German *Improver* case. Do you think the lack of a "battle of the experts" made any difference in the German *Improver* case outcome?

3. As noted in Chapter 2, EPC 2000 came into effect in May of 2008, and amended the Protocol on Article 69 to include a new Article 2, which states:

Equivalents

For the purpose of determining the extent of protection conferred by a European patent, due account shall be taken of any element which is equivalent to an element specified in the claims.

This new provision explicitly instructs courts to look beyond the literal claim language in determining infringement, allowing for a broadened scope of protection. While Germany has long accepted the DOE, the UK traditionally has been hostile to it. As further explained by Lord Hoffman:

There is often discussion about whether we have a European doctrine of equivalents and, if not, whether we should. It seems to me that both the doctrine of equivalents in the United States and the pith and marrow doctrine in the United Kingdom were born of despair. The courts felt unable to escape from interpretations which "unsparing logic" appeared to require and which prevented them from according the patentee the full extent of the monopoly which the person skilled in the art would reasonably have thought he was claiming. The background was the tendency to literalism which then characterised the approach of the courts to the interpretation of documents generally and the fact that patents are likely to attract the skills of lawyers seeking to exploit literalism to find loopholes in the monopoly they create. . . . If literalism stands in the way of construing patent claims so as to give fair protection to the patentee, there are two things that you can do. One is to adhere to literalism in construing the claims and evolve a doctrine which supplements the claims by extending protection to equivalents. That is what the Americans have done. The other is to abandon literalism. That is what the House of Lords did in the *Catnic* case . . . .

Since the *Catnic* case we have article 69 which, as it seems to me, firmly shuts the door on any doctrine which extends protection outside the claims. I cannot say that I am sorry because the *Festo* litigation suggests, with all respect to the courts of the United States, that American patent litigants pay dearly for results which are no more just or predictable than could be achieved by simply reading the claims. . . .

Although article 69 prevents equivalence from extending protection outside the claims, there is no reason why it cannot be an important part of the background of facts known to the skilled man which would affect what he understood the claims to mean. That is no more than common sense. It is also expressly provided by the new article 2 added to the Protocol by the Munich Act revising the EPC, dated 29 November 2000.

Kirin-Amgen Inc. v. Hoechst Marion Roussel Ltd., [2004] UKHL 46, [2005] 1 All E.R. 667 (Eng.), para. 41–42, 46, 49. Do you agree with Lord Hoffman's criticism of the DOE? Do you agree with his interpretation of Article 2 to the Protocol on Article 69?

NOTE ON POST-IMPROVER DEVELOPMENTS IN THE UK

The *Improver* questions can still inform the purposive construction of claims. However, in its 2003–2004 session, the House of Lords began to wean lower courts and litigants from their heavy reliance on the three Protocol/*Improver* questions in *Kirin-Amgen Inc. v. Hoechst Marion Roussel Ltd.*, [2004] UKHL 46. In so doing, it also provided a mini-treatise on patent claim construction. *Kirin-Amgen* involved the identification of the gene coding for human erythropoietin, one of the most important early biotech inventions. In the opinion, Lord Hoffmann explained:

> "[T]he Protocol questions" have been used by English courts for the past fifteen years as a framework for deciding whether equivalents fall within the scope of the claims. On the whole, the judges appear to have been comfortable with the results, although some of the cases have exposed the limitations of the method. When speaking of the "*Catnic* principle" it is important to distinguish between, on the one hand, the principle of purposive construction which I have said gives effect to the requirements of the Protocol, and on the other hand, the guidelines for applying that principle to equivalents, which are encapsulated in the Protocol questions. The former is the bedrock of patent construction, universally applicable. The latter are only guidelines, more useful in some cases than in others. I am bound to say that the cases show a tendency for counsel to treat the Protocol questions as legal rules rather than guides which will in appropriate cases help to decide what the skilled man would have understood the patentee to mean. . . .

> No doubt there will be patent lawyers who are dismayed at the notion that the Protocol questions do not provide an answer in every case. They may feel cast adrift on a sea of interpretative uncertainty. But that is the fate of all who have to understand what people mean by using language. The Protocol questions are useful in many cases, but they are not a substitute for trying to understand what the person skilled in the art would have understood the patentee to mean by the language of the claims.

Id. at para. 52 and 71.

Reinforcing the guidance from *Kirin-Amgen* that the Protocol/*Improver* questions are simply one means, but not the sole means, of engaging in a purposive claim construction, later courts also have relied on claim construction principles first articulated by Lord Justice Jacob in *Mayne Pharma Pty. Ltd. v. Pharmacia Italia* [2005] EWCA Civ 137:

> (a) The first, overarching principle, is that contained in Art 69 itself.

> (b) Art 69 says that the extent of protection is determined by the terms of the claims. It goes on to say that the description and drawings shall be used to interpret the claims. In short the claims are to be construed in context.

> (c) It follows that the claims are to be construed purposively-the inventor's purpose being ascertained from the description and drawings.

> (d) It further follows that the claims must not be construed as if they stood alone-the drawings and description only being used to resolve any ambiguity. Purpose is vital to the construction of claims.

(f) Nonetheless purpose is not the be-all and end-all. One is still at the end of the day concerned with the meaning of the language used. Hence the other extreme of the Protocol-a mere guideline-is also ruled out by Art 69 itself. It is the terms of the claims which delineate the patentee's territory.

(g) It follows that if the patentee has included what is obviously a deliberate limitation in his claims, it must have a meaning. One cannot disregard obviously intentional elements.

(h) It also follows that where a patentee has used a word or phrase which, acontextually, might have a particular meaning (narrow or wide) it does not necessarily have that meaning in context.

(i) It further follows that there is no general "doctrine of equivalents".

(j) On the other hand purposive construction can lead to the conclusion that a technically trivial or minor difference between an element of a claim and the corresponding element of the alleged infringement nonetheless falls within the meaning of the element when read purposively. This is not because there is a doctrine of equivalents: it is because that is the fair way to read the claim in context.

(k) Finally purposive construction leads one to eschew what Lord Diplock in *Catnic* called "the kind of meticulous verbal analysis which lawyers are too often tempted by their training to indulge."

Such guidance may not be as easy to apply as the brighter-line Protocol/*Improver* questions, but it represents the current approach to claim construction in the UK.

NOTES AND QUESTIONS

1. Do you consider the *Kirin-Amgen* and *Mayne Pharma* guidance on claim construction an improvement over the Protocol/*Improver* questions alone? Why or why not?

2. In an effort to bring Germany's approach to claim construction more in line with the UK, the German Supreme Court, or Bundesgerichtshof, in the *Schneidmesser I* (Cutting Blade I) decision, identified four questions to be considered in construing a claim. An article co-authored by German Supreme Court Judge Peter Meier-Beck describes the questions as follows:

> *Schneidmesser I* (Cutting Blade I), a fundamental German case on the doctrine of equivalents, divided the examination of the scope of protection into a series of questions, thereby referring back to the English model of purposive construction under *Catnic* and later elucidated by Justice (as he then was) Leonard Hoffmann in what came to be commonly called the *Improver* questions.

1. The first question is: Does the modified embodiment solve the problem underlying the invention by means which have objectively the same technical effect?

This question resembles the first *Improver* question, but it is not identical to it. Nor does it ask about how the invention "works" or the function-way-result test; rather, it only asks about the result of this effort. The identical result has to be achieved at least to a practically relevant degree. A merely similar effect is not sufficient. . .

If the answer to the first question is "no", the contested embodiment is outside the scope of the patent. If yes, we move on to the second question:

2. Was the person skilled in the art enabled by his expertise on the priority date to find the modified means as having the same effect?

This question is all about excluding those cases in which an inventive step was necessary to find the modified means as having the same effect. . . .

If either questions one or two are answered in the negative, there is no infringement by equivalents. However, if both are answered in the affirmative, we still have to ask a third question before finding for infringement. . . .

3. While answering question two, are the considerations that the person skilled in the art applies drawn from the technical teaching of the patent claim (so that the person skilled in the art took the modified embodiment into account as being an equivalent solution)?

Why is this third question necessary? Has everything necessary not been examined already, if the first two questions can be answered with a "yes"? That is not the case, for the following reasons: The first "*Schneidmesser*" question pertains only to an objectively identical "technical effect," i.e., a correspondence in the result that the invention aims at. But this correspondence and the fact that the person skilled in the art was able to recognize it without being inventive are not sufficient to bring the modified embodiment within the scope of protection. If this was only about including all variants that a person skilled in the art would have been able to do with the teaching of the patent, then the second question alone would be sufficient. But there is more at stake here: This is not only about what the person skilled in the art would have been able to do on the priority date knowing the patent, but about what he would have been able to do and would have done on the basis of the patent (of the patent claim). Again, one has to keep in mind that the exclusive patent right correlates to the invention's technical teaching made available by virtue of the patent being published. That is why the third question is about whether the considerations, which the person skilled in the art has to make, are sufficiently close to the technical meaning of the patent claim, i.e., whether they are drawn from the patent claim's teaching to the person skilled in the art. The technical teaching of the patent claim has to be the decisive basis for the consideration of the person skilled in the art, so that he recognizes the variant as an equivalent alternative to an embodiment which carries out the wording (in context) of the patent claim. . . .

4. Is the modified embodiment anticipated or made obvious by the state of the art?

This question, which is known as the *Formstein* objection [a.k.a. "*Moulded Curbstone*"] in German case law, is necessary to prevent a scope of protection (after the previous three questions have been answered in the affirmative) that is too broad in comparison to the state of the art, since it encompasses an embodiment, which— however rarely it may be the case—lacks novelty or at least was obvious to a person skilled in the art at the time of patenting. It is only the direct subject matter of the patent application that is examined for patentability during the grant procedure. The Patent Office does not determine what, having regard to the state of the art, the adequate scope of protection for the subject matter ought to be. Consequently, such a determination has to be made at the stage of infringement proceedings.

Nicholas Pumfreyet al., *The Doctrine of Equivalents in Various Regimes— Does Anybody Have It Right?*, 11 YALE J. L. & TECH. 261, 291–295 (2009).

What differences, if any, do you see between the UK and German approaches to claim construction? Are the approaches now consistent?

3. In the *AGA Medical Corporation v. Occlutech GmbH* litigation, an *Improver*-like situation arose—different infringement rulings in different European jurisdictions—but was averted by a 2011 decision of the German Supreme Court. The AGA Medical patent claimed a medical device and method for occluding blood vessels and claim 1 required the device to be "...characterized in that clamps are adapted to clamp the strands at the opposed ends of the device." Occlutech's accused device comprised a "sock" of braided material, having loose strands at one end only, which were held together by welding. The UK courts construed the claims as requiring "clamps" (plural) and "opposed ends" (plural) as essential elements thus the accused device did not infringe. The same result, on different reasoning, was obtained in the Netherlands, but lower and intermediate courts in Germany held the patent claims infringed. As explained by Lord Justice Patten in the UK decision, "they [the German courts] have decided that the language used has to be read as referring to the clamping of the opposed ends of the strands (rather than of the device) and that the use of two separate clamps in each device was not an essential feature or limitation on the scope of the claims." *Occlutech v. AGA Medical Corp.*, [2010] EWCA Civ 702, para. 31. Lord Patten also suggested that the different result on equivalents in Germany could be due to the absence of any inquiry corresponding to the third Protocol/*Improver* question. On appeal from the lower court decisions, the German

Supreme Court reversed and held the claims not infringed literally or equivalently. The Court also made specific reference to the correctness of the UK and Dutch decisions and took pains to correct the impression of a misalignment in the various approaches:

> Contrary to the interpretation of the English appeal court, which opined that the "cutting blade questions" contained nothing which corresponded to the third of the questions posed in *Improver v Remington* by J. Hoffmann as part of is account of Lord Diplock's interpretational approach in *Catnic*, the examination of the orientation to the claim therefore leads to the exclusion from the scope of protection of the patent of an embodiment which, although disclosed or which could be found in any case by the person skilled in the art, but for which the reader of the patent document must assume that—for whatever reason—it should not be placed under protection.

AGA Medical Corporation v. Occlutech GmbH, German Supreme Court, May 10, 2011, Case No. X ZR 16/09 para. 36. Later decisions by courts in Sweden and Italy also found no infringement, although those decisions are under appeal as of the time of this writing. European courts thus seem to be making a concerted effort to avoid the uncertainty occasioned by inconsistent rulings, a fact articulated by Lord Justice Hoffman when he stated:

> In my opinion there is no difference between Britain and Germany in what we understand the Protocol to Article 69 to mean and no difference in what we understand by fair protection for the patentee combined with reasonable certainty for third parties. That means that in practice we will decide infringement cases the same way or, if we decide them differently, the reason will be individual differences of opinion such as you can have between judges in the same jurisdiction.

Patent Construction, CIPA J., Nov. 2006, at 757. However, there can be numerous procedural differences in national courts that can substantively affect an infringement determination, such as the ability of each side to put forward expert witnesses, the availability of discovery, and more. Lord Hoffman appeared to give a nod to such distinctions in a later decision, *Conor Medsystems Inc v. Angiotech Pharmaceuticals Inc.* [2008] UKHL 49, para 3, noting:

> A European patent takes effect as a bundle of national patents over which the national courts have jurisdiction. It is therefore inevitable that they will occasionally give inconsistent decisions about the same patent. Sometimes this is because the evidence is different. In most continental jurisdictions, including the [EPO], cross-examination is limited or unknown. Sometimes one is dealing with questions of degree over which judges may legitimately differ. Obviousness is often in this category. But when the question is one of principle, it is desirable that so far as possible there should be uni-

formity in the way the national courts and the EPO interpret the [EPC].

Is uniformity in decisions always the preferred policy objective? When might it not be? Is it likely to be achievable on a consistent basis while there is no single European court system to adjudicate patent disputes? According to the EU Commission, the lack of uniformity in the European patent system is indeed problematic:

> The fragmented single market for patents has serious consequences for the competitiveness of Europe in relation to the challenges of the US, Japan and emerging economic powers such as China. The EU lags behind the US and Japan in terms of patent activity. Even in Europe, the US and Japan patent more than the EU: at the EPO 137 patents per million population are from the EU versus 143 patents from the US and 174 from Japan. The lack of critical patent mass at home translates in less patents that are filed in both the US, the EU and Japan, the so called triadic patents. Whereas Europe has 33 triadic patents per million population, the US has 48 and Japan has 102. Therefore, the US and Japan have respectively 45% and 209% more triadic patents than the EU.

Communication from the Commission to the European Parliament and the Council–Enhancing the Patent System in Europe, COM (2007) 165 final 2 (Apr. 3, 2007).

4. Signs abound that the 40-plus year effort to create a true EU patent and European patent court may be nearing completion. The European Commission, in conjunction with twenty-five EU member states, is moving forward with an enhanced cooperation initiative to create two EU regulations, one for a unitary EU patent that would be granted by the EPO, the other for a supporting translation regime. *See* Proposal for a Regulation of the European Parliament and of the Council Implementing Enhanced Cooperation in the Area of Creation of Unitary Patent Protection, COM (2011) 215 final (Apr. 4, 2011). Under the proposal, applicants could choose to pursue either the unitary EU patent instead of or in addition to the traditional European patent bundle granted by the EPO. Moreover, applicants could still choose to obtain individual patents from national offices. At the same time, an agreement to create a European patent court has also been pursued despite a variety of obstacles (*e.g.,* the role of national offices, fee splitting, location of the court) to implementation of both sets of initiatives. A March 2011 CJEU opinion on the incompatibility of a previously proposed EU and European patents court system with the EU treaties, inevitably constrains the framework for the proposed European patent court. Opinion 1/09 (Mar. 8, 2011). Moreover, on May 31, 2011, Spain and Italy, EU members that wanted a five-language unitary patent regime instead of the three-language regime of the current effort, filed a legal challenge against the unitary patent plan at the CJEU. While that challenge was rejected by the Court, Spain has recently launched a second legal challenge to the regime. EU bodies nevertheless are moving ahead with a plan designed to address the problems identified by the March

2011 CJEU decision. *See* Council of the European Union, Draft Agreement on a Unified Patent Court, Working Document No. 16741/11 (Nov. 11, 2011). And, on December 11, 2012, the European Parliament approved an EU patent package (comprising the unitary patent, language regime and court) for the twenty-five participating EU member states. While important details must still be resolved and ratifications remain, this is a large step forward for proponents of a unitary patent system in Europe.

B. INDIRECT INFRINGEMENT

When Party A makes, uses, sells, offers to sell, or imports a patented invention during the term of a patent (in the relevant territory), we normally say A has *directly* infringed the patent. Direct infringement is a strict liability offense with no knowledge requirement. But what if someone else, Party B, has facilitated A's infringement, by providing A with a component necessary to practice the invention or by otherwise inducing A to engage in infringing activities? B's behavior may qualify in some countries as *indirect* infringement. There are two primary kinds of indirect infringement: contributory infringement and active inducement of infringement. Standards for establishing liability can differ significantly from country to country, and in some cases such liability may be nonexistent.

1. UNITED STATES

Both contributory infringement and active inducement of infringement are provided for by statute in the U.S., and both have engendered confusion and contradictory decisions regarding the knowledge or mental culpability required for liability to accrue. 35 U.S.C. §271(b) and (c) provide:

> (b) Whoever actively induces infringement of a patent shall be liable as an infringer.

> (c) Whoever offers to sell or sells within the United States or imports into the United States a component of a patented machine, manufacture, combination, or composition, or a material or apparatus for use in practicing a patented process, constituting a material part of the invention, knowing the same to be especially made or especially adapted for use in an infringement of such patent, and not a staple article or commodity of commerce suitable for substantial noninfringing use, shall be liable as a contributory infringer.

In the following 2011 case, the U.S. Supreme Court articulated the relevant knowledge standard for both types of indirect infringement.

GLOBAL-TECH APPLIANCES, INC. V. SEB S.A.

Supreme Court of the United States
131 S. Ct. 2060 (2011)

■ Justice ALITO delivered the opinion of the Court.

We consider whether a party who "actively induces infringement of a patent" under 35 U.S.C. §271(b) must know that the induced acts constitute patent infringement.

I

This case concerns a patent for an innovative deep fryer designed by respondent SEB S.A., a French maker of home appliances. In the late 1980's, SEB invented a "cool-touch" deep fryer, that is, a deep fryer for home use with external surfaces that remain cool during the frying process. The cool-touch deep fryer consisted of a metal frying pot surrounded by a plastic outer housing. Attached to the housing was a ring that suspended the metal pot and insulated the housing from heat by separating it from the pot, creating air space between the two components. SEB obtained a U.S. patent for its design in 1991, and sometime later, SEB started manufacturing the cool-touch fryer and selling it in this country under its well-known "T–Fal" brand. Superior to other products in the American market at the time, SEB's fryer was a commercial success.

In 1997, Sunbeam Products, Inc., a U.S. competitor of SEB, asked petitioner Pentalpha Enterprises, Ltd., to supply it with deep fryers meeting certain specifications. Pentalpha is a Hong Kong maker of home appliances and a wholly owned subsidiary of petitioner Global–Tech Appliances, Inc.

In order to develop a deep fryer for Sunbeam, Pentalpha purchased an SEB fryer in Hong Kong and copied all but its cosmetic features. Because the SEB fryer bought in Hong Kong was made for sale in a foreign market, it bore no U.S. patent markings. After copying SEB's design, Pentalpha retained an attorney to conduct a right-to-use study, but Pentalpha refrained from telling the attorney that its design was copied directly from SEB's.

The attorney failed to locate SEB's patent, and in August 1997 he issued an opinion letter stating that Pentalpha's deep fryer did not infringe any of the patents that he had found. That same month, Pentalpha started selling its deep fryers to Sunbeam, which resold them in the United States under its trademarks. By obtaining its product from a manufacturer with lower production costs, Sunbeam was able to undercut SEB in the U.S. market.

After SEB's customers started defecting to Sunbeam, SEB sued Sunbeam in March 1998, alleging that Sunbeam's sales infringed SEB's patent. Sunbeam notified Pentalpha of the lawsuit the following month. Undeterred, Pentalpha went on to sell deep fryers to Fingerhut Corp. and

Montgomery Ward & Co., both of which resold them in the United States under their respective trademarks.

SEB settled the lawsuit with Sunbeam, and then sued Pentalpha. . . SEB claimed that Pentalpha had contravened §271(b) by actively inducing Sunbeam, Fingerhut, and Montgomery Ward to sell or to offer to sell Pentalpha's deep fryers in violation of SEB's patent rights.

Following a 5–day trial, the jury found for SEB . . . and also found that Pentalpha's infringement had been willful. Pentalpha filed post-trial motions seeking a new trial or judgment as a matter of law on several grounds. As relevant here, Pentalpha argued that there was insufficient evidence to support the jury's finding of induced infringement under §271(b) because Pentalpha did not actually know of SEB's patent until it received the notice of the Sunbeam lawsuit in April 1998.

The District Court rejected Pentalpha's argument, as did the Court of Appeals for the Federal Circuit, which affirmed the judgment . . . . Although the record contained no direct evidence that Pentalpha knew of SEB's patent before April 1998, the court found adequate evidence to support a finding that "Pentalpha deliberately disregarded a known risk that SEB had a protective patent." Such disregard, the court said, "is not different from actual knowledge, but is a form of actual knowledge."

We granted certiorari.

II

Pentalpha argues that active inducement liability under §271(b) requires more than deliberate indifference to a known risk that the induced acts may violate an existing patent. Instead, Pentalpha maintains, actual knowledge of the patent is needed.

A

In assessing Pentalpha's argument, we begin with the text of §271(b)—which is short, simple, and, with respect to the question presented in this case, inconclusive. Section 271(b) states: "Whoever actively induces infringement of a patent shall be liable as an infringer."

Although the text of §271(b) makes no mention of intent, we infer that at least some intent is required. The term "induce" means "[t]o lead on; to influence; to prevail on; to move by persuasion or influence." Webster's New International Dictionary 1269 (2d ed.1945). The addition of the adverb "actively" suggests that the inducement must involve the taking of affirmative steps to bring about the desired result.

When a person actively induces another to take some action, the inducer obviously knows the action that he or she wishes to bring about. If a used car salesman induces a customer to buy a car, the salesman knows that the desired result is the purchase of the car. But what if it is said that the salesman induced the customer to buy a damaged car? Does this mean merely that the salesman induced the customer to purchase a car that happened to be damaged, a fact of which the salesman may have been unaware? Or does this mean that the salesman knew that the car was damaged? The statement that the salesman induced the customer to buy a damaged car is ambiguous.

So is §271(b). In referring to a party that "induces infringement," this provision may require merely that the inducer lead another to engage in conduct that happens to amount to infringement, i.e., the making, using, offering to sell, selling, or importing of a patented invention. *See* §271(a). On the other hand, the reference to a party that "induces infringement" may also be read to mean that the inducer must persuade another to engage in conduct that the inducer knows is infringement. Both readings are possible.

B

Finding no definitive answer in the statutory text, we turn to the case law that predates the enactment of §271 as part the Patent Act of 1952. As we recognized in *Aro Mfg. Co. v. Convertible Top Replacement Co.*, 377 U.S. 476 (1964) (Aro II), "[t]he section was designed to 'codify in statutory form principles of contributory infringement' which had been 'part of our law for about 80 years.'" *Id.*, at 485–486, n. 6, (quoting H.R.Rep. No. 1923, 82d Cong., 2d Sess., 9 (1952)).

Unfortunately, the relevant pre–1952 cases are less clear than one might hope with respect to the question presented here. Before 1952, both the conduct now covered by §271(b) (induced infringement) and the conduct now addressed by §271(c) (sale of a component of a patented invention) were viewed as falling within the overarching concept of "contributory infringement."

. . . .

While both the language of §271(b) and the pre–1952 case law that this provision was meant to codify are susceptible to conflicting interpretations, our decision in *Aro II* resolves the question in this case. In *Aro II*, a majority held that a violator of §271(c) must know "that the combination for which his component was especially designed was both patented and infringing," and as we explain below, that conclusion compels this same knowledge for liability under §271(b).

C

As noted above, induced infringement was not considered a separate theory of indirect liability in the pre–1952 case law. Rather, it was treated as evidence of "contributory infringement," that is, the aiding and abetting of direct infringement by another party. *See* Mark Lemley, *Inducing Patent Infringement*, 39 U.C.D.L. REV. 225, 227 (2005). When Congress enacted §271, it separated what had previously been regarded as contributory infringement into two categories, one covered by §271(b) and the other covered by §271(c).

Aro II concerned §271(c), which states in relevant part:

"Whoever offers to sell or sells . . . a component of a patented [invention] . . ., constituting a material part of the invention, knowing the same to be especially made or especially adapted for use in an infringement of such patent, and not a staple article or commodity of commerce suitable for substantial noninfringing use, shall be liable as a contributory infringer." (Emphasis added.)

This language contains exactly the same ambiguity as §271(b). The phrase "knowing [a component] to be especially made or especially adapted for use in an infringement" may be read to mean that a violator must know that the component is "especially adapted for use" in a product that happens to infringe a patent. Or the phrase may be read to require, in addition, knowledge of the patent's existence.

This question closely divided the *Aro II* Court. In a badly fractured decision, a majority concluded that knowledge of the patent was needed. . . .

[T]he "holding in *Aro II* has become a fixture in the law of contributory infringement under [section] 271(c)," 5 R. Moy, Walker on Patents § 15:20, p. 15–131 (4th ed.2009)—so much so that SEB has not asked us to overrule it. Nor has Congress seen fit to alter §271(c)'s intent requirement in the nearly half a century since *Aro II* was decided. In light of the " 'special force' " of the doctrine of *stare decisis* with regard to questions of statutory interpretation, we proceed on the premise that §271(c) requires knowledge of the existence of the patent that is infringed.

Based on this premise, it follows that the same knowledge is needed for induced infringement under §271(b). As noted, the two provisions have a common origin in the pre–1952 understanding of contributory infringement, and the language of the two provisions creates the same difficult interpretive choice. It would thus be strange to hold that knowledge of the relevant patent is needed under §271(c) but not under §271(b).

Accordingly, we now hold that induced infringement under §271(b) requires knowledge that the induced acts constitute patent infringement.

III

Returning to Pentalpha's principal challenge, we agree that deliberate indifference to a known risk that a patent exists is not the appropriate standard under §271(b). We nevertheless affirm the judgment of the Court of Appeals because the evidence in this case was plainly sufficient to support a finding of Pentalpha's knowledge under the doctrine of willful blindness.

A

The doctrine of willful blindness is well established in criminal law. Many criminal statutes require proof that a defendant acted knowingly or willfully, and courts applying the doctrine of willful blindness hold that defendants cannot escape the reach of these statutes by deliberately shielding themselves from clear evidence of critical facts that are strongly suggested by the circumstances. The traditional rationale for this doctrine is that defendants who behave in this manner are just as culpable as those who have actual knowledge. . . .

This Court's opinion more than a century ago in *Spurr v. United States*, 174 U.S. 728 (1899), while not using the term "willful blindness," endorsed a similar concept. The case involved a criminal statute that prohibited a bank officer from "willfully" certifying a check drawn against insufficient funds. We said that a willful violation would occur "if the [bank] officer purposely keeps himself in ignorance of whether the drawer has money in the bank." Following our decision in *Spurr*, several federal prosecutions in the first half of the 20th century invoked the doctrine of willful blindness. . . . And every Court of Appeals—with the possible exception of the District of Columbia Circuit, has fully embraced willful blindness, applying the doctrine to a wide range of criminal statutes.

Given the long history of willful blindness and its wide acceptance in the Federal Judiciary, we can see no reason why the doctrine should not apply in civil lawsuits for induced patent infringement under 35 U.S.C. §271(b).

. . . .

B

While the Courts of Appeals articulate the doctrine of willful blindness in slightly different ways, all appear to agree on two basic requirements: (1) the defendant must subjectively believe that there is a high probability that a fact exists and (2) the defendant must take deliberate actions to avoid learning of that fact. We think these requirements give willful blindness an appropriately limited scope that surpasses recklessness and negligence. Under this formulation, a willfully blind defendant is one who takes deliberate actions to avoid confirming a high probability of wrongdoing and who can almost be said to have actually known the critical facts. . . . By contrast, a reckless defendant is one who merely knows of a substantial and unjustified risk of such wrongdoing, . . ., and a negligent defendant is one who should have known of a similar risk but, in fact, did not, *see* §2.02(2)(d).

The test applied by the Federal Circuit in this case departs from the proper willful blindness standard in two important respects. First, it permits a finding of knowledge when there is merely a "known risk" that the induced acts are infringing. Second, in demanding only "deliberate indifference" to that risk, the Federal Circuit's test does not require active efforts by an inducer to avoid knowing about the infringing nature of the activities.

In spite of these flaws, we believe that the evidence when viewed in the light most favorable to the verdict for SEB is sufficient under the correct standard. The jury could have easily found that before April 1998 Pentalpha willfully blinded itself to the infringing nature of the sales it encouraged Sunbeam to make.

SEB's cool-touch fryer was an innovation in the U.S. market when Pentalpha copied it. As one would expect with any superior product, sales of SEB's fryer had been growing for some time. Pentalpha knew all of this, for its CEO and president, John Sham, testified that, in developing a product for Sunbeam, Pentalpha performed "market research" and "gather[ed] information as much as possible." Pentalpha's belief that SEB's fryer embodied advanced technology that would be valuable in the U.S. market is evidenced by its decision to copy all but the cosmetic features of SEB's fryer.

Also revealing is Pentalpha's decision to copy an overseas model of SEB's fryer. Pentalpha knew that the product it was designing was for the U.S. market, and Sham—himself a named inventor on numerous U.S. patents,—was well aware that products made for overseas markets usually do not bear U.S. patent markings,. Even more telling is Sham's decision not to inform the attorney from whom Pentalpha sought a right-to-use opinion that the product to be evaluated was simply a knockoff of SEB's deep fryer. On the facts of this case, we cannot fathom what motive Sham could have had for withholding this information other than to manufacture a claim of plausible deniability in the event that his company was later accused of patent infringement. Nor does Sham's testimony on this subject provide any reason to doubt that inference. Asked whether the attorney would have fared better had he known of SEB's design, Sham was nonresponsive. All he could say was that a patent search is not an "easy job" and that is why he hired attorneys to perform them.

Taken together, this evidence was more than sufficient for a jury to find that Pentalpha subjectively believed there was a high probability that SEB's fryer was patented, that Pentalpha took deliberate steps to avoid knowing that fact, and that it therefore willfully blinded itself to the infringing nature of Sunbeam's sales.

The judgment of the United States Court of Appeals for the Federal Circuit is

Affirmed.

NOTES AND QUESTIONS

1. In his dissent, Justice Kennedy agreed with the majority that 35 U.S.C. §271(b) should be read in conjunction with §271(c) to include a knowledge requirement, but took issue with the standard of willful blindness:

> [H]aving interpreted the statute to require a showing of knowledge, the Court holds that willful blindness will suffice. This is a mistaken step. Willful blindness is not knowledge; and judges should not broaden a legislative proscription by analogy. . . . The Court invokes willful blindness to bring those who lack knowledge within §271(b)'s prohibition. . . . One can believe that there is a "high probability" that acts might infringe a patent but nonetheless conclude they do not infringe. . . . The alleged inducer who believes a device is non-infringing cannot be said to know otherwise. . . .

> [T]he Court appeals to moral theory by citing the "traditional rationale" that willfully blind defendants "are just as culpable as those who have actual knowledge." But the moral question is a difficult one. Is it true that the lawyer who knowingly suborns perjury is no more culpable than the lawyer who avoids learning that his client, a criminal defendant, lies when he testifies that he was not the shooter? The answer is not obvious. Perhaps the culpability of willful blindness depends on a person's reasons for remaining blind. Or perhaps only the person's justification for his conduct is relevant. This is a question of morality and of policy best left to the political branches. Even if one were to accept the substitution of equally blameworthy mental states in criminal cases in light of the retributive purposes of the criminal law, those purposes have no force in the domain of patent law that controls in this case. The Constitution confirms that the purpose of the patent law is a utilitarian one, to "promote the Progress of Science and useful Arts," Art. I, § 8, cl. 8.

Id. at 2072–73. Whose reasoning do you find most persuasive, that of the majority or of the dissent? Why?

2. Justice Kennedy further labeled the majority's new willful blindness standard as unnecessary. He argued:

> There is no need to invoke willful blindness for the first time in this case. Facts that support willful blindness are often probative of actual knowledge. Circumstantial facts like these tend to be the only available evidence in any event, for the jury lacks direct access to the defendant's mind. The jury must often infer knowledge from conduct, and attempts to eliminate evidence of knowledge may justify such inference, as where an accused inducer avoids further confirming what he already believes with good reason to be true. The majority's decision to expand the statute's scope appears to depend on the unstated premise that knowledge requires certainty, but the law often permits probabilistic judgments to count as knowledge.

The instant dispute provides a case in point. Pentalpha copied an innovative fryer. The model it copied bore no U.S. patent markings, but that could not have been a surprise, for Pentalpha knew that a fryer purchased in Hong Kong was unlikely to bear such markings. And Pentalpha failed to tell the lawyer who ran a patent search that it copied the SEB fryer. These facts may suggest knowledge that Pentalpha's fryers were infringing, and perhaps a jury could so find.

Id. at 2073. Does Justice Kennedy's argument suggest there is no meaningful difference between an actual knowledge and willful blindness standard?

3. Recall the *Contraceptive Method/British Technology Group* case (T 0074/93, 1995 Official J. Eur. Pat. Off. 712) from Chapter 5, in which the EPO denied patentability to a method of applying a contraceptive as not being industrially applicable. As it is unlikely that the patentee would have sought to sue individual women for direct infringement of such a patent claim, disallowing the claim prevented the patentee from suing other manufacturers of the contraceptive product for inducement of infringement by supplying the product with instructions for how it should be applied. Thus, enforcement of the statutory requirements of patentability during prosecution can affect not only *what* a patentee can sue on but also *who* it can sue for infringement.

---

2. EUROPE AND BEYOND

As with direct infringement, a diversity of approaches to indirect infringement result from the absence of a single European patent system and court. Nevertheless, efforts to harmonize national laws on the issue to comply with the Community Patent Convention have met with success in some European countries as discussed in the excerpt below.

PHILLIP JOHNSON, CONTRIBUTING TO THE WRONG: THE INDIRECT INFRINGEMENT OF PATENTS
5 J. Intell. Prop. L. & Practice 514 (2010)

The law of indirect infringement, or as it was still sometimes erroneously called contributory infringement, was introduced by section 60(2) of the Patents Act 1977 [UK], a provision which was intended to give effect to Article 30 of the original Community Patent Convention (renumbered Article 26 in the 1989 Luxembourg Agreement). . . :

Article 26

Prohibition of indirect use of the invention

1. A Community patent shall also confer on its proprietor the right to prevent all third parties not having his consent from supplying or offering to supply within the territories of the Contracting States a person, other than a party entitled to exploit the patented invention, with means, relating to an essential element of that invention, for putting it into effect therein, when the third party knows, or it is obvious in the circumstances, that these means are suitable and intended for putting that invention into effect.

2. Paragraph 1 shall not apply when the means are staple commercial products, except when the third party induces the person supplied to commit acts prohibited by Article 25.

. . . .

. . . The absence of a requirement that there be a direct infringer, as explained below, exemplifies the fact that indirect infringement should not be considered contributory infringement but rather as part of the patent monopoly. . . .

The early years of indirect infringement

The introduction of indirect infringement across the European Economic Community through the implementation of the Community Patent Convention during the late 1970s and early 1980s did not spur substantial litigation in the field. This meant that even after the law had been in place in the UK for over 15 years, any attempt at a detailed examination of indirect infringement has been frustrated. It has largely been based on textual analysis of the provisions, comparisons with jurisprudence under the unharmonized law and from the USA as well as mere hypothesis. A similar attempt at considering German law a little over 5 years later still had to rely largely on deduction rather than jurisprudence. The last decade has, however, seen an increasing reliance on indirect infringement, in particular, because of the rise of the internet. It is now possible to give some indication of the scope and effect of the provision on indirect infringement. . . .

The person supplies or offers to supply in the UK

The exclusive right extends to the supply of the 'means' and for this purpose, 'supply' would cover hire or lending. Indirect infringement does not include acts such as making or importing unless, and until, the means made or imported are supplied (or the offer made); and the German courts have held as such. Indeed, the terms 'supply' and 'offer to supply' are not used in relation to direct infringement, but it has yet to be argued whether 'supply' has a different meaning from 'disposal' as it has been interpreted in the context of 'putting on the market'. It may be that supply does not require physical possession although it was intended to have a narrower meaning based on commercial supply. . . .

Knowledge

The seller can only indirectly infringe a patent if he has actual or constructive knowledge of two things at the time of the sale. First, he must know that the 'means' supplied to put the invention into effect are suitable for putting the invention into effect and second, that those means are intended to put the invention into effect. Many cases will fail before they begin as there is insufficient knowledge. These knowledge requirements are cumulative and so a person who is aware the means supplied are suitable to put the invention into effect, but does not know (actually or constructively) that it is the purchaser's intention to do so, is not an indirect infringer. It is not necessary, however, for a person to know he is infringing a patent, only that the means may be used for putting the invention into effect. Accordingly, even if the supplier believed the supply was lawful and non-infringing, this is no defence. This means that it is unlikely that a person could have constructive knowledge of infringement where there are non-infringing uses (and increasingly less likely where those uses become more substantial). However, where the 'means' relate only to infringing uses, then any knowledge about the product's general purpose would probably be enough to impart the relevant knowledge.

Time knowledge must exist

The knowledge must exist at the time of the offer or the supply. As was made clear in *Qualcomm Inc v. Nokia*,[1] it is immaterial that it takes some time before the purchaser of those means puts the invention into effect or even if the purchaser changes his mind and does not actually use the items for that purpose. Conversely, if the seller believes that the purchaser intends to put the invention into effect, but in fact at the time of purchase that is not the case (although the purchaser subsequently changes his mind) there is still no infringement.

Comparison with the knowledge requirement to supply a process

The knowledge requirement for secondary infringement is therefore quite distinct from that for offering to supply a process for use. First, the seller does not need to have knowledge that a patent is in force; secondly, the seller does not need to have knowledge that the activity itself is infringing. Instead the seller's knowledge must relate to the invention itself, rather than the patent or the scope of the relevant monopoly.

---

[1] [2008] EWHC 329 (Pat), 243.

The intention

The intention to put the invention into effect is, according to *Cranway v. Playtech*,[2] a subjective intention. In other words, the person to whom the 'means' is supplied must actually intend to put the invention into effect. It is not enough that a reasonable person would infer such intent where it did not actually exist. If the seller did not know (actually or constructively) that such an intention existed, the person cannot be an indirect infringer. This approach can be contrasted with the German court's approach where it has been held that where the means are suitable for both infringing and non-infringing use then infringement requires a sufficient certainty that the intended use will infringe. Such a statement, however, only appears to relate to standards of evidential proof, rather than liability. . . .

Person entitled to work the invention

An infringing supply of the 'means' has to be to someone other than a licensee of the patent or a person entitled to work the invention. There are also some persons who are expressly stated to be entitled to work the invention such as Crown users, prior users, and those who began use when the patent was not in force (or patent application was terminated or with-drawn). The German courts have also held that a person is entitled to work the invention in relation to a particular article where the rights in that article have been exhausted and this will surely be the same under UK law.

Exceptions

A person wishing to rely on certain exceptions to infringement—namely acts which are done privately and for purposes which are not commercial; acts done for experimental purposes relating to the subject-matter of the invention; or acts which consist of the extemporaneous preparation in a pharmacy of a medicine for an individual in accordance with a prescription given by a registered medical or dental practitioner or consist of dealing with a medicine so prepared—are not entitled to work the invention for these purposes. The failure to include references to the other exceptions would suggest that a person relying on those exceptions is a person entitled for these purposes; although obiter comments were made to the contrary by Jacob J. in *Menashe Business Mercantile v William Hill*.[3]

Means relating to an essential element

The 'means' supplied by the defendant must be relating to an 'essential element' of the invention for there to be an indirect infringement. The German courts held in *Air Heater* that the means must be a 'physical ob-

---

[2] [2009] EWHC 1588 (Pat), [2010] FSR 3, 156.
[3] [2002] RPC 47, 23.

ject', but it is not clear that the same approach would be adopted in the UK as a CD-ROM (a mere carrier) of a computer program has been indicated to be such a 'means'. . . .

'Essential element'

There is very little case law on the meaning of an essential element under UK law. In *Anchor Building Products v Redland Road Tiles*,[4] a striking-out application, the Court of Appeal took the view that the means supplied (a type of sealing tape) were not an essential element as the claim required the use of a tape with an upwardly facing channel. In determining the essential element, the court adopted the approach of construing the scope of the relevant claim and seeing whether the use of the particular tape was an 'immaterial variation from that claimed. Further, in *Hazel Grove Limited v. Euro-League Leisure*,[5] it appears to be suggested that something which is not a subordinate part of the claim and is neither trivial nor low value might be an essential element; although it is far from clear or appropriate to use this as a basis of precedent.

German approach

A German court has held that the deciding factor in relation to the 'essential element' was whether the means was of essential or merely secondary importance to the patent. It further found that individual parts, already known in themselves but which are used in a patented combination, could be the subject of an indirect patent infringement. Another test used by the German courts in *Flow Meter*[6] was that the element has to functionally interact with the element realising the inventive concept, but this should be interpreted broadly so as to exclude only those things which do not contribute to the inventive concept. This has been interpreted broadly by the Bundesgerichtshof (Supreme Court) in *Pipette System*[7] so as to exclude only such means as do not contribute to realising the protected invention.

Dutch/Belgian approach

In *Sara Lee/Integro* (Coffee pods),[8] the Dutch Hoge Raad (Supreme Court) considered whether the supply of coffee pods (for a patented espresso machine using pods) amounted to indirect infringement. The court concluded that just because the pods were necessary to make the invention, work did not make them an essential element of the invention. Indeed, the court went further and suggested that the element is only essential where it distinguishes the teaching over the prior art. The same

---

[4] [1990]RPC 283.

[5] [1995] RPC 529, 5.1 (HHJ Ford).

[6] (2004) GRUR 758.

[7] (2007) GRUR 769.

[8] (2006) NJ 600.

case went before the Belgium court[9] where the court concluded that merely because a thing 'fitted' with an invention (such as the pod fitting with the machine) could not amount to an indirect infringement unless that thing also related to the patented invention (which it did not in that case).

To put the invention into effect

The essential element supplied must be used to put the invention into effect. In *Menashe Business Mercantile v. William Hill*, where the supply of the 'means' was a CD-ROM which enabled customers to use an online gaming system, it was held that putting the invention into effect must require:

. . . the means to be intended to put the apparatus claimed into effect: thereby requiring the claimed apparatus to become effective. Thus the means, the CDs, must be suitable for putting and be intended to put the claimed apparatus in a state of effectiveness, essentially to put into an infringing state in the United Kingdom.

This was clarified in *Cranway v. Playtech* to mean that it is an objective test that the invention can be put into effect. A similar approach was adopted by the German courts in the earlier *Air Heater* case. The means must also be designed in such a way to enable the purchaser to use them to put the invention directly into effect (i.e. without intermediary).

So it appears that the person supplying the means is an indirect infringer and the person who obtains that means must intend at least to be a direct infringer. There is some indication, however, that this may not always be required and that the issue will usually turn on whether a person has knowledge of the eventual use. Finally, it is essential that the invention is put into effect in the jurisdiction (e.g. the UK), rather than merely the effects of the invention are felt within that jurisdiction.

Non-infringing uses

The existence of non-infringing uses of the 'means' is usually not material to whether there is an infringement. This is because the person supplying the 'means' must know that they are going to be used to put the invention into effect. If there are non-infringing uses, of course, it will be more difficult to establish the requisite knowledge; and the greater the number of non-infringing uses, the more difficult it would be to establish knowledge.

No need for direct infringement

In Germany, it is not necessary to show that the patent supplied directly infringed the patent to obtain an injunction or information about supply chains, but it is necessary to show direct infringement to obtain compensatory damages. To the extent that direct infringement is not re-

---

[9] *See* De Visscher Comment [2004] EIPR N105.

quired must be right as it makes sense logically and contextually and it appears to have some support from Floyd J's judgment in *Qualcomm Inc. v Nokia* as well as before the French courts.

The spatial element

Indirect infringers need both to: (a) supply or offer to supply the means within the UK (or other relevant State); and (b) to know (actually or constructively) that the invention is going to be put into effect in that country. *Menashe Business Mercantile v William Hill* involved an interactive casino game which was hosted on a computer outside the jurisdiction, but required the players to install the program from a CD supplied by the defendant. It was agreed by the parties that the CD was a means relating to an essential element of the invention and that this had been supplied within the UK. The Court of Appeal found that the person in the UK who makes inputs to the host computer and receives outputs from it is using the invention and so putting it into effect in the jurisdiction, this case highlighting the need to properly identify what is being put into effect in the UK.

'Outsourcing'

In *Radio Clock II*,[10] the German Bundesgerichtshof decided that where the supply is from Germany to a foreign country and the product is due to return to Germany once completed (an act which, once committed, would be a direct infringement by importation) and the supplier was aware of the re-importation (rather than just infringement in another country), the double spatial requirement need not necessarily apply and the supplier may be an indirect infringer. It appears that the same conclusion was reached by the English courts in *University of Queensland v Siemens Magnet Technology Limited*.[11]

Staple commercial product

A person cannot be an indirect infringer if the supply or offer to supply is for a staple commercial product; unless the supply or the offer is made for the purpose of inducing the person supplied or to whom the offer is made to infringe the patent directly. It has been stated that the purpose of the staple commercial product proviso is to remove the need for traders to make enquiries of purchasers of products which are sold from their usual stock (as constructive knowledge may be sufficient). A seller who sells a staple commercial product is only liable for indirect infringement if he induced the purchaser to directly infringe the patent, in other words he is a joint tortfeasor in relation to the direct infringement.

---

[10] (2007) 38 IIC 607.
[11] [2007] EWHC 2258 (Pat), 59–61 (Pumfrey J.).

Custom-made products

A product which has been custom made cannot be a staple commercial product; even if it is of a general type of product which is widely sold. Indeed, during the negotiations leading to the original Community Patent Convention, it was stated that a staple commercial product does not include products specifically adapted for exploiting the patented invention. Instead, a staple commercial product is something which is of the kind 'needed every day and generally obtainable'. It is suggested that this does not exclude products which are available on a small scale, rather it is intended to protect sales 'off the shelf' or from pre-prepared catalogues in contrast to custom-made products.

Indications of inducement

The seller who sells a staple commercial product remains liable for indirect infringement if he induced the purchaser to directly infringe. For these purposes, it has also been suggested that the staple commercial product has to have been available at the time of publication of the patent specification, otherwise the product may have been a response to the availability of the invention to enable it to be used. The French courts have held that an indication in materials accompanying the sale of the means is good evidence of an inducement to use the staple commercial product for this end.

The future

The law of indirect infringement has developed rapidly over the last five years as courts across the European Union, particularly in Germany and in the UK, have started to grapple with the complexities of what started out as Article 26 of the Community Patent Convention. There is, however, a surprising conformity in the approaches adopted by the various European courts. Although there still remain distinctions in relation to what might be considered the central aspect of indirect infringement—the meaning of the essential element—it is hoped that a more or less uniform meaning will evolve over time through the cross-fertilization by national courts.

NOTES AND QUESTIONS

1. In the U.S., there can be no liability for indirect infringement (contributory or active inducement) without a direct infringer (or infringers, as discussed in note 4, *infra*). However, as the excerpt above notes, in Germany and certain other European countries, the presence of a direct infringer is not necessary for indirect infringement liability and injunctive relief. Thus, for example, a company may be found liable for indirect infringement in Germany if their customers intended to use their product (an essential element of a patented invention) in an infringement, even if the customers never actually

use it in that way. What are the advantages and disadvantages of the U.S. approach requiring direct infringement for indirect infringement liability? Which approach to indirect infringement is more consistent with the goals of patent law? Should there be a formal effort to develop a set of international guidelines on indirect infringement in light of increasing pressures to deepen levels of global patent harmonization?

2. Beyond Europe, approaches to liability for indirect infringement also can vary widely. Article 127 of South Korea's Industrial Property Law provides that the act of making an article exclusively used for an infringing product or process is considered to infringe the patent right. However, China's patent law does not yet provide liability for indirect infringement. Japan extends liability for indirect infringement as acts deemed to constitute infringement, but does not require proof of direct infringement. Japan Patent Act of 1959, as amended, art. 101. Thus in Japan, supplying an article exclusively used only to make or work a patented product or process, or essential to the patented product, is deemed to constitute infringement. However, infringement will not be found if the article may be used for other purposes (e.g., is a staple article of commerce). Additionally, Japan amended its patent law in 2002 such that even supplying an important element of the invention that is not an "exclusive use" article is considered indirect infringement if it is knowingly (i.e., in bad faith) provided for an infringing use. This created a third category of articles: staple, non-staple, and neutral-use. Thus, manufacture or supply of neutral-use articles may be infringement if there is sufficient bad faith on the part of the defendant. For a comparison of indirect infringement liability regimes in Japan, Germany, and the U.S., *see* Matthew T. Nesbitt, *Comment, From Oil Lamps to Cell Phones: What the Trilateral Offices Can Teach Us about Detangling the Metaphysics of Contributory Infringement,* 21 EMORY INT'L L. REV. 669, 692–700 (2007).

3. In *Nycomed Canada Inc. v. Teva Canada Ltd.*, 2012 FCA 195, the Canadian Federal Court of Appeals confirmed the absence of an action for contributory infringement in Canada affirming the trial court's decision and reasoning in striking out parts of pleadings that included such assertions. However, there is a well-established three-part test for active inducement of infringement. As articulated by the Federal Court of Appeals in *Weatherford Canada Ltd. v. Corlac Inc.,* 2011 FCA 228, para. 162 (Fed. C.A.):

> It is settled law that one who induces or procures another to infringe a patent is guilty of infringement of the patent. A determination of inducement requires the application of a three-prong test. First, the act of infringement must have been completed by the direct infringer. Second, the completion of the acts of infringement must be influenced by the acts of the alleged inducer to the point that, without the influence, direct infringement would not take place. Third, the influence must knowingly be exercised by the inducer, that is, the inducer knows that this influence will result in the completion of the act of infringement. The test is a difficult one to meet.

(citations omitted).

In the *Nycomed* case, the patentee had argued before the trial court that the Canadian Supreme Court in *Monsanto v. Schmeiser* (excerpted in Chapter 4, pp. 240–252, *supra*) had broadly interpreted the law to allow for contributory infringement liability. The trial judge (affirmed by the Federal Court of Appeals) disagreed:

> Nycomed relies heavily on the Supreme Court of Canada's decision in *Monsanto Canada Inc. v. Schmeiser*, 2004 SCC 34 (S.C.C.) and says . . . that, in *Monsanto*, the Supreme Court of Canada set out an "expansive and purposive interpretation of patent infringement and thus implicitly rejected discrete categories of infringement" . . . .
>
> To accept these submissions, I must be persuaded that the Supreme Court of Canada intended to move away from the Inducement Test when it made the statements on which Nycomed relies. . . The statements . . . are found in *Monsanto* at the paragraphs shown below. The emphasis is mine:
>
>> 34. The purpose of s. 42 [of the Patent Act] is to define the exclusive rights granted to the patent holder. These rights are the rights to full enjoyment of the monopoly granted by the patent. Therefore, what is prohibited is "any act that interferes with the full enjoyment of the monopoly granted to the patentee." . . . The guiding principle is that patent law ought to provide the inventor with "protection for that which he has actually in good faith invented." Applied to "use", the question becomes: did the defendant's activity deprive the inventor in whole or in part, directly or indirectly, of full enjoyment of the monopoly conferred by law?
>
> . . .
>
> [I]n my view, there are compelling reasons to conclude that the Supreme Court of Canada did not intend to signal such a fundamental departure from the well established Inducement Test. They include:
>
>> (i) The fact that *Monsanto* was a case of direct infringement;
>>
>> (ii) The Court's failure to mention contributory infringement;
>>
>> (iii) The fact that the language "even in part and even indirectly" can be read in a manner that is consistent with the Inducement Test in that "even in part" means "part of the patent" and "indirectly" refers to "inducement";
>>
>> (iv) The Supreme Court is careful to say in paragraph 32 that, in addition to being purposive and contextual, the inquiry into the meaning of use ". . . must be attentive to the wisdom of the case law". In its review of the relevant cases, the Court did not mention the established case law dealing with the Inducement Test.

For these reasons, I have concluded that *Monsanto* does not support the existence of a cause of action for contributory infringement.

Apotex Inc. v. Nycomed Canada Inc., 2011 FC 1441, at para. 22–28.

3. In *Akamai Technologies, Inc. v. Limelight Networks, Inc.,* and *McKesson Technologies, Inc. v. Epic Systems*, 692 F.3d 1301 (2012), the *en banc* Court of Appeals for the Federal Circuit eliminated the "single-entity direct infringement" prerequisite to a finding of active inducement of infringement (although it seemingly, and confusingly, retained the single entity requirement for direct infringement in the absence of an inducement allegation). As the court explained:

> When a single actor commits all the elements of infringement, that actor is liable for direct infringement under 35 U.S.C. §271(a). When a single actor induces another actor to commit all the elements of infringement, the first actor is liable for induced infringement under 35 U.S.C. §271(b). But when the acts necessary to give rise to liability for direct infringement are shared between two or more actors, doctrinal problems arise. In the two cases before us, we address the question whether a defendant may be held liable for induced infringement if the defendant has performed some of the steps of a claimed method and has induced other parties to commit the remaining steps (as in the *Akamai* case), or if the defendant has induced other parties to collectively perform all the steps of the claimed method, but no single party has performed all of the steps itself (as in the *McKesson* case).
>
> Requiring proof that there has been direct infringement as a predicate for induced infringement is not the same as requiring proof that a single party would be liable as a direct infringer. If a party has knowingly induced others to commit the acts necessary to infringe the plaintiff's patent and those others commit those acts, there is no reason to immunize the inducer from liability for indirect infringement simply because the parties have structured their conduct so that no single defendant has committed all the acts necessary to give rise to liability for direct infringement.
>
> A party who knowingly induces others to engage in acts that collectively practice the steps of the patented method—and those others perform those acts—has had precisely the same impact on the patentee as a party who induces the same infringement by a single direct infringer; there is no reason, either in the text of the statute or in the policy underlying it, to treat the two inducers differently. In particular, there is no reason to hold that the second inducer is liable for infringement but the first is not. . . . At the end of the day, we are persuaded that Congress did not intend to create a regime in which parties could knowingly sidestep infringement liability simply by arranging to divide the steps of a method claim between them.

Id. at 1306–1318.

By imposing liability for active inducement of infringement in the absence of a single direct infringer, the court resolved the issue of divided infringement liability, but may have created new uncertainties regarding the extraterritorial reach of the active inducement provision. According to Professor Holbrook:

> Before *Akamai*, direct infringement under 35 U.S.C. §271(a) was a prerequisite for active inducement under 35 U.S.C. §271(b). Section 271(a) contains territorial limits, and §271(b) does not. To infringe under §271(a), the activity must take place "within the United States." Because active inducement before *Akamai* required an act of direct infringement, induced infringement had territorial constraints.

> This state of affairs may change dramatically after *Akamai*. There, the Federal Circuit decoupled active inducement from §271(a), meaning that infringement under §271(b) is freestanding, and infringement is not defined by reference to other provisions of §271. The decoupling also means that, as a statutory matter, the court has removed the territorial constraints from active inducement.

Timothy R. Holbrook, *The Potential Extraterritorial Consequences of* Akamai, EMORY INT'L. L. REV. (forthcoming 2013).

Does the holding in *Akamai* bring the U.S. closer to other countries' formulations for indirect infringement or move it further away? Do you agree that expanded extraterritoriality is a cause for concern after *Akamai*? Why or why not?

CHAPTER 11

DEFENSES AND REMEDIES

■ ■ ■

A. DEFENSES AND EXCEPTIONS TO INFRINGEMENT

A variety of defenses are generally available to a party charged with patent infringement. The availability of a particular defense will vary by country, but common ones include non-infringement, patent invalidity, experimental/non-commercial use, prior use, exhaustion of rights, laches, estoppel, and inequitable conduct. Ignorance of the patent generally is not a defense to infringement. We begin with several of the most widely available defenses.

1. NON-INFRINGEMENT AND PATENT INVALIDITY

A party accused of patent infringement can always raise the defense of non-infringement: Her actions do not constitute an infringement of the patent right. Another common defense (often raised as a counterclaim) is patent invalidity, where the defendant argues that even if her actions constitute infringement, that is irrelevant because the patent claims are invalid and thus cannot be enforced against her.

Whether a challenge to the validity of a patent can be raised in a patent infringement action varies territorially. For example, while courts in the United States, the UK, France, the Netherlands, and Japan (only since 2000) can adjudicate both infringement and invalidity, in other countries, such as Germany and China, patent validity can only be challenged in a separate judicial tribunal or in a patent office nullity, opposition, or reexamination proceeding. In some countries, patents are presumed valid once granted, thus creating a higher evidentiary burden for challengers.

The following case involved a burden-of-proof challenge created by the presumption of patent validity in the U.S. patent statute.

MICROSOFT CORP. V. i4i LIMITED PARTNERSHIP
Supreme Court of the United States
131 S. Ct. 2238 (2011)

■ Justice SOTOMAYOR delivered the opinion of the Court.

Under § 282 of the Patent Act of 1952, "[a] patent shall be presumed valid" and "[t]he burden of establishing invalidity of a patent or any claim thereof shall rest on the party asserting such invalidity." 35 U.S.C. §282. We consider whether § 282 requires an invalidity defense to be proved by clear and convincing evidence. We hold that it does.

I

A

Pursuant to its authority under the Patent Clause, U.S. Const., Art. I, § 8, cl. 8, Congress has charged the United States Patent and Trademark Office (PTO) with the task of examining patent applications, 35 U.S.C. §2(a)(1), and issuing patents if "it appears that the applicant is entitled to a patent under the law," § 131. Congress has set forth the prerequisites for issuance of a patent, which the PTO must evaluate in the examination process. To receive patent protection a claimed invention must, among other things, fall within one of the express categories of patentable subject matter, § 101, and be novel, § 102, and nonobvious, § 103. Most relevant here, the on-sale bar of § 102(b) precludes patent protection for any "invention" that was "on sale in this country" more than one year prior to the filing of a patent application. . . .

Once issued, a patent grants certain exclusive rights to its holder, including the exclusive right to use the invention during the patent's duration. To enforce that right, a patentee can bring a civil action for infringement if another person "without authority makes, uses, offers to sell, or sells any patented invention, within the United States." § 271(a); *see also* § 281.

Among other defenses under § 282 of the Patent Act of 1952 (1952 Act), an alleged infringer may assert the invalidity of the patent—that is, he may attempt to prove that the patent never should have issued in the first place. *See* § 282(2), (3). A defendant may argue, for instance, that the claimed invention was obvious at the time and thus that one of the conditions of patentability was lacking. *See* § 282(2); *see also* § 103. "While the ultimate question of patent validity is one of law," . . . the same factual questions underlying the PTO's original examination of a patent application will also bear on an invalidity defense in an infringement action.

In asserting an invalidity defense, an alleged infringer must contend with the first paragraph of § 282, which provides that "[a] patent shall be presumed valid" and "[t]he burden of establishing invalidity . . . rest[s] on the party asserting such invalidity." Under the Federal Circuit's reading of § 282, a defendant seeking to overcome this presumption must persuade the factfinder of its invalidity defense by clear and convincing evidence. . . .

[In nearly 30 years] the Federal Circuit has never wavered in this interpretation of § 282.

B

Respondents i4i Limited Partnership and Infrastructures for Information Inc. (collectively, i4i) hold the patent at issue in this suit. The i4i patent claims an improved method for editing computer documents, which stores a document's content separately from the metacodes associated with the document's structure. In 2007, i4i sued petitioner Microsoft Corporation for willful infringement, claiming that Microsoft's manufacture and sale of certain Microsoft Word products infringed i4i's patent. In addition to denying infringement, Microsoft counterclaimed and sought a declaration that i4i's patent was invalid and unenforceable.

Specifically and as relevant here, Microsoft claimed that the on-sale bar of § 102(b) rendered the patent invalid, pointing to i4i's prior sale of a software program known as S4. The parties agreed that, more than one year prior to the filing of the i4i patent application, i4i had sold S4 in the United States. They presented opposing arguments to the jury, however, as to whether that software embodied the invention claimed in i4i's patent. Because the software's source code had been destroyed years before the commencement of this litigation, the factual dispute turned largely on trial testimony by S4's two inventors—also the named inventors on the i4i patent—both of whom testified that S4 did not practice the key invention disclosed in the patent.

Relying on the undisputed fact that the S4 software was never presented to the PTO examiner, Microsoft objected to i4i's proposed instruction that it was required to prove its invalidity defense by clear and convincing evidence. Instead, "if an instruction on the 'clear and convincing' burden were [to be] given," Microsoft requested the following:

> 'Microsoft's burden of proving invalidity and unenforceability is by clear and convincing evidence. However, Microsoft's burden of proof with regard to its defense of invalidity based on prior art that the examiner did not review during the prosecution of the patent-in-suit is by preponderance of the evidence.'

Rejecting the hybrid standard of proof that Microsoft advocated, the District Court instructed the jury that "Microsoft has the burden of proving invalidity by clear and convincing evidence." . . .

The jury found that Microsoft willfully infringed the i4i patent and that Microsoft failed to prove invalidity due to the on-sale bar or otherwise. . . . The Court of Appeals for the Federal Circuit affirmed. . . . We granted certiorari. . . .

II

According to Microsoft, a defendant in an infringement action need only persuade the jury of an invalidity defense by a preponderance of the evidence. In the alternative, Microsoft insists that a preponderance standard must apply at least when an invalidity defense rests on evidence that was never considered by the PTO in the examination process. We reject both contentions.

A

Where Congress has prescribed the governing standard of proof, its choice controls absent "countervailing constitutional constraints." . . . The question, then, is whether Congress has made such a choice here.

As stated, the first paragraph of § 282 provides that "[a] patent shall be presumed valid" and "[t]he burden of establishing invalidity of a patent or any claim thereof shall rest on the party asserting such invalidity." Thus, by its express terms, § 282 establishes a presumption of patent validity, and it provides that a challenger must overcome that presumption to prevail on an invalidity defense. But, while the statute explicitly specifies the burden of proof, it includes no express articulation of the standard of proof.

Our statutory inquiry, however, cannot simply end there. We begin, of course, with "the assumption that the ordinary meaning of the language" chosen by Congress "accurately expresses the legislative purpose." . . . But where Congress uses a common-law term in a statute, we assume the "term . . . comes with a common law meaning, absent anything pointing another way." . . . Here, by stating that a patent is "presumed valid," § 282, Congress used a term with a settled meaning in the common law.

Our decision in RCA, [*Radio Corp. of America v. Radio Engineering Laboratories, Inc.,* 293 U.S. 1, 9 (1934)], is authoritative. There, tracing nearly a century of case law from this Court and others, Justice Cardozo wrote for a unanimous Court that "there is a presumption of validity, a presumption not to be overthrown except by clear and cogent evidence." . . . Although the "force" of the presumption found "varying expression" in this Court and elsewhere, Justice Cardozo explained, one "common core of thought and truth" unified the decisions:

> [O]ne otherwise an infringer who assails the validity of a patent fair upon its face bears a heavy burden of persuasion, and fails unless his evidence has more than a dubious preponderance. If that is true where the assailant connects himself in some way with the title of the true inventor, it is so *a fortiori* where he is a stranger to the invention, without claim of title of his own. If it is true where the assailant launches his attack with evidence different, at least in form, from any theretofore produced in opposi-

tion to the patent, it is so a bit more clearly where the evidence is even verbally the same. . . .

The common-law presumption, in other words, reflected the universal understanding that a preponderance standard of proof was too "dubious" a basis to deem a patent invalid. . . .

Thus, by the time Congress enacted § 282 and declared that a patent is "presumed valid," the presumption of patent validity had long been a fixture of the common law. According to its settled meaning, a defendant raising an invalidity defense bore "a heavy burden of persuasion," requiring proof of the defense by clear and convincing evidence. . . . That is, the presumption encompassed not only an allocation of the burden of proof but also an imposition of a heightened standard of proof. Under the general rule that a common-law term comes with its common-law meaning, we cannot conclude that Congress intended to "drop" the heightened standard proof from the presumption simply because § 282 fails to reiterate it expressly. . . . On the contrary, we must *presume* that Congress intended to incorporate" the heightened standard of proof, "unless the statute otherwise dictates." . . .

We recognize that it may be unusual to treat a presumption as alone establishing the governing standard of proof. . . . But given how judges, including Justice Cardozo, repeatedly understood and explained the presumption of patent validity, we cannot accept Microsoft's argument that Congress used the words "presumed valid" to adopt only a procedural device for "shifting the burden of production," or for "shifting both the burden of production and the burden of persuasion." Whatever the significance of a presumption in the abstract, basic principles of statutory construction require us to assume that Congress meant to incorporate "the cluster of ideas" attached to the common-law term it adopted. . . .

B

Reprising the more limited argument that it pressed below, Microsoft argues in the alternative that a preponderance standard must at least apply where the evidence before the factfinder was not before the PTO during the examination process. In particular, it relies on *KSR Int'l Co. v. Teleflex Inc.,* 550 U.S. 398 (2007), where we observed that, in these circumstances, "the rationale underlying the presumption—that the PTO, in its expertise, has approved the claim—seems much diminished." . . .

That statement is true enough, although other rationales may animate the presumption in such circumstances. . . . The question remains, however, whether Congress has specified the applicable standard of proof. As established, Congress did just that by codifying the common-law presumption of patent validity and, implicitly, the heightened standard of proof attached to it.

Our pre–1952 cases never adopted or endorsed the kind of fluctuating standard of proof that Microsoft envisions. And they do not indicate, even in dicta, that anything less than a clear-and-convincing standard would ever apply to an invalidity defense raised in an infringement action. To the contrary, the Court spoke on this issue directly in RCA, stating that because the heightened standard of proof applied where the evidence before the court was "different" from that considered by the PTO, it applied even more clearly where the evidence was identical. . . . Likewise, the Court's statement that a "dubious preponderance" will never suffice to sustain an invalidity defense . . . admitted of no apparent exceptions. Finally, this Court often applied the heightened standard of proof without any mention of whether the relevant prior-art evidence had been before the PTO examiner, in circumstances strongly suggesting it had not. . . .

Nothing in § 282's text suggests that Congress meant to depart from that understanding to enact a standard of proof that would rise and fall with the facts of each case. Indeed, had Congress intended to drop the heightened standard of proof where the evidence before the jury varied from that before the PTO—and thus to take the unusual and impractical step of enacting a variable standard of proof that must itself be adjudicated in each case . . . —we assume it would have said so expressly.

To be sure, numerous courts of appeals in the years preceding the 1952 Act observed that the presumption of validity is "weakened" or "dissipated" in the circumstance that the evidence in an infringement action was never considered by the PTO. . . . But we cannot read these cases to hold or even to suggest that a preponderance standard would apply in such circumstances, and we decline to impute such a reading to Congress. Instead, we understand these cases to reflect the same commonsense principle that the Federal Circuit has recognized throughout its existence—namely, that new evidence supporting an invalidity defense may "carry more weight" in an infringement action than evidence previously considered by the PTO. . . . As Judge Rich explained:

> When new evidence touching validity of the patent not considered by the PTO is relied on, the tribunal considering it is not faced with having to disagree with the PTO or with deferring to its judgment or with taking its expertise into account. The evidence may, therefore, carry more weight and go further toward sustaining the attacker's unchanging burden. Ibid. (emphasis deleted) . . .

Simply put, if the PTO did not have all material facts before it, its considered judgment may lose significant force. . . . And, concomitantly, the challenger's burden to persuade the jury of its invalidity defense by clear and convincing evidence may be easier to sustain. In this respect, although we have no occasion to endorse any particular formulation, we note that a jury instruction on the effect of new evidence can, and when requested, most often should be given. When warranted, the jury may be instructed to consider that it has heard evidence that the PTO had no opportunity to evaluate before granting the patent. When it is disputed whether the evidence presented to the jury differs from that evaluated by the PTO, the jury may be instructed to consider that question. In either case, the jury may be instructed to evaluate whether the evidence before it is materially new, and if so, to consider that fact when determining whether an invalidity defense has been proved by clear and convincing evidence. . . . Although Microsoft emphasized in its argument to the jury that S4 was never considered by the PTO, it failed to request an instruction along these lines from the District Court. Now, in its reply brief in this Court, Microsoft insists that an instruction of this kind was warranted. That argument, however, comes far too late, and we therefore refuse to consider it. . . .

III

The parties and their *amici* have presented opposing views as to the wisdom of the clear-and-convincing-evidence standard that Congress adopted. Microsoft and its *amici* contend that the heightened standard of proof dampens innovation by unduly insulating "bad" patents from invalidity challenges. They point to the high invalidation rate as evidence that the PTO grants patent protection to too many undeserving "inventions." They claim that *inter partes* reexamination proceedings before the PTO cannot fix the problem, as some grounds for invalidation (like the on-sale bar at issue here) cannot be raised in such proceedings. They question the deference that the PTO's expert determinations warrant, in light of the agency's resources and procedures, which they deem inadequate. And, they insist that the heightened standard of proof essentially causes juries to abdicate their role in reviewing invalidity claims raised in infringement actions.

For their part, i4i and its *amici*, including the United States, contend that the heightened standard of proof properly limits the circumstances in which a lay jury overturns the considered judgment of an expert agency. They claim that the heightened standard of proof is an essential component of the patent "bargain," . . . and the incentives for inventors to disclose their innovations to the public in exchange for patent protection. They disagree with the notion that the patent issuance rate is above the optimal level. They explain that limits on the reexamination process reflect a judgment by Congress as to the appropriate degree of interference with patentees' reliance interests. Finally, they maintain that juries that are properly instructed as to the application of the clear-and-convincing-evidence standard can, and often do, find an invalidity defense established.

We find ourselves in no position to judge the comparative force of these policy arguments. For nearly 30 years, the Federal Circuit has interpreted § 282 as we do today. During this period, Congress has often amended § 282 . . . ; not once, so far as we (and Microsoft) are aware, has it even considered a proposal to lower the standard of proof, Moreover, Congress has amended the patent laws to account for concerns about "bad" patents, including by expanding the reexamination process to provide for *inter partes* proceedings. . . . Through it all, the evidentiary standard adopted in § 282 has gone untouched. Indeed, Congress has left the Federal Circuit's interpretation of § 282 in place despite ongoing criticism, both from within the Federal Government and without.

Congress specified the applicable standard of proof in 1952 when it codified the common-law presumption of patent validity. Since then, it has allowed the Federal Circuit's correct interpretation of § 282 to stand. Any re-calibration of the standard of proof remains in its hands.

For the reasons stated, the judgment of the Court of Appeals for the Federal Circuit is

Affirmed.

NOTES AND QUESTIONS

1. In *Microsoft Corp. v. i4i Limited Partnership et. al.*, the U.S. Supreme Court confirmed that the statutory presumption of validity codified in 35 U.S.C. §282 requires challengers to prove invalidity by clear and convincing evidence, even when the proffered evidence of invalidity was not considered by the patent office. This is not the only validity "presumption" embedded in the U.S. patent statute. Section 102 of the Patent Act states that "a person shall be entitled to a patent" unless the USPTO can establish that she is not so entitled. While there is not a clear and convincing evidence standard in the Office, Professor Seymore has argued that a strong presumption of validity during the prosecution stage is less than ideal for fostering innovation and encouraging high quality patents. He suggests replacing the presumption of validity during examination with one of unpatentability because:

> [T]he Patent Office must issue a patent unless it can affirmatively prove that the invention is unpatentable. The scales tip even further toward issuance if the examiner lacks the time, materials, or incentives to conduct a high-quality examination. And even though the applicant owes a duty of candor to the Patent Office, no one actually believes that everything that the applicant knows about the invention ends up before the examiner. Of course, this information deficit inevitably allows bad patents to slip through the cracks and further contributes to the patent quality problem. The bottom line is that anyone who files a patent application on anything starts off in a very good position.

Sean B. Seymore, *The Presumption of Patentability*, 97 MINN. L. REV. 990, 996 (2013).

What problems might such a change entail? What reasons justify a presumption of validity at the prosecution stage *and* during litigation? Is such a "double presumption" unduly favorable to patentees? Is it consistent with the policy goals of the patent system?

2. In a concurring opinion in *Microsoft*, Justice Breyer (joined by Justices Scalia and Alito) made the following distinction between applying the presumption to questions of law vs. fact:

> I write separately because, given the technical but important nature of the invalidity question, I believe it worth emphasizing that in this area of law as in others the evidentiary standard of proof applies to questions of fact and not to questions of law. . . . Thus a factfinder must use the "clear and convincing" standard where there are disputes about, say, when a product was first sold or whether a prior art reference had been published.

> Many claims of invalidity rest, however, not upon factual disputes, but upon how the law applies to facts as given. Do the given facts show that the product was previously "in public use"? 35 U.S.C. §102(b). Do they show that the invention was "nove[l]" and that it was "non-obvious"? §§ 102, 103. Do they show that the patent applicant described his claims properly? § 112. Where the ultimate question of patent validity turns on the correct answer to legal questions—what these subsidiary legal standards mean or how they apply to the facts as given—today's strict standard of proof has no application. . . .

> Courts can help to keep the application of today's "clear and convincing" standard within its proper legal bounds by separating factual and legal aspects of an invalidity claim, say, by using instructions based on case-specific circumstances that help the jury make the distinction or by using interrogatories and special verdicts to make clear which specific factual findings underlie the jury's conclusions. . . . By isolating the facts (determined with help of the "clear and convincing" standard), courts can thereby assure the proper interpretation or application of the correct legal standard (without use of the "clear and convincing" standard). By preventing the "clear and convincing" standard from roaming outside its fact-related reservation, courts can increase the likelihood that discoveries or inventions will not receive legal protection where none is due.

Microsoft, 131 S. Ct. at 2253.

Do you agree with reading this distinction into § 282? Is it consistent with the interpretation of § 282 by the majority?

3. Not all countries have as strong a presumption of entitlement to a patent as is present in § 102 of the U.S. patent statute. What factors could account for these differences in approach between the United States and these countries?

4. In some countries, particularly jurisdictions where patents are not examined substantively, no presumption during litigation attaches in practice although one may be provided for by statute. European patents generally are presumed valid (except during opposition proceedings) but what that means varies by country. For example, in Germany with its bifurcated system, patent invalidity cannot be asserted as a defense in an infringement action so the presumption of validity is strong in that sense. However, a court can choose to stay an infringement action until resolution of a pending nullity or opposition action it concludes is likely to succeed. *See* European Patent Office, *Patent Litigation in Europe: An Overview of the National Patent Litigation Systems in Europe* (2nd ed. 2010), *available at* http://www.epo.org/learning-events/materials/litigation.html, for detailed patent litigation information for thirty-seven countries.

5. The Indian Patent Act of 1970, as amended in 2005, explicitly denies a presumption of validity for issued patents even though they have undergone substantive examination. According to Article 13(4):

> The examination and investigations required under section 12 and this section shall not be deemed in any way to warrant the validity of any patent, and no liability shall be incurred by the Central Government or any officer thereof by reason of, or in connection with, any such examination or investigation or any report or other proceedings consequent thereon.

What are the ramifications of these different assessments of the validity of a patent for patent owners? For competitors?

2. EXPERIMENTAL USE

Most of the leading patent systems in the world provide that the unauthorized use of a patented invention for experimental or research purposes does not constitute an act of infringement. The United States, however, only recognizes an experimental use exception to claims of patent infringement in very narrow circumstances.

The purpose of the experimental use exception is to encourage scientific research and experimentation by freeing researchers from the chilling effects of potential patent infringement liability. Because the setting for much scientific research has traditionally been universities and other non-commercial sites, the act of using a patented invention for experimental purposes was not seen by countries that adopted an experimental use exception as depriving patentees of their exclusive rights, especially when those rights were balanced against the public interest of promoting science and technological innovation.

Today, the patent legislation of many countries expressly provides for experimental use exceptions that cover not only non-commercial experimentation, but also experimentation that may be commercially motivated. For example, § 11.2 of the German Patent Law provides that "[t]he effects of a patent shall not extend to . . . acts done for experimental purposes relating to the subject matter of the patented invention." Moreover, in keeping with the notion that non-commercial uses of a patented invention should also not constitute infringement, §11.1 of the German law extends the exception to "acts done privately and for non-commercial purposes."[1] Patentgesetz [Patent Act], Dec. 16, 1980, Bundesgesetzblatt [BHBl] at 501, (Ger.). Similarly, § 60(5) (a) and (b) of the UK Patent Act provides that an act does not constitute patent infringement if "it is done privately and for purposes which are not commercial" and if "it is done for experimental purposes relating to the subject-matter of the invention." *See* UK Patents Act 1977, c. 37, as amended, *available at* http://www.ipo.gov.uk/patentsact1977.pdf. The almost identical language of the two legislative texts stems from the fact that both echo the Community Patent Convention, a European treaty initially concluded in 1975 that never entered into force but has nevertheless had an important harmonizing effect on European patent legislation. Article 27 of the Community Patent Convention states that "the rights conferred by a Community patent shall not extend to (a) acts done privately and for non-commercial purposes; (b) acts done for experimental purposes relating to the subject-matter of the patented invention."

In *Monsanto Co. v. Stauffer Chemical Co.*, [1985] R.P.C. 515, a case from the UK Court of Appeal, Lord Justice Dillon had the opportunity to determine what kind of activities constitute "experimental purposes" and what kind fall outside its scope. His conclusion, which follows, has been generally accepted throughout Europe:

> Trials carried out in order to discover something unknown or to test a hypothesis or even in order to find out whether something which is known to work in specific conditions, e.g. of soil or weather, will work in different conditions can fairly, in my judgment, be regarded as experiments. But trials carried out in order to demonstrate to a third party that a product works or in order to amass information to satisfy a third party, whether a customer or a [regulatory] body . . . , that the product works as its maker claims are not, in my judgment, to be regarded as acts done' "for experimental purposes."

Id. at 542.

Recognition of a strong experimental use exception is not limited to Europe, however. Section 69(1) of the Japanese Patent Law, for example, provides that "[a] patent right shall not be effective against the working of the patented invention for experimental or research purposes." And in China, the right to engage in experimental use is provided not only in the Chinese Patent Law (Section 63), and explained in an advisory opinion of

---

[1] German Patent Law of December 16, 1980, as amended, available in English at http://www.wipo.int/wipolex/en/text.jsp?file_id=238776.

the Beijing Higher People's Court. Article 98 of the "Opinions of the Beijing High People's Court on Several Issues Relating to the Establishment of Patent Infringement (for Trial Implementation)" 2001 provides helpful guidelines on how the experimental use exception should be applied:

> Use for the purpose of scientific research and experimentation. Any act of using the patent concerned solely for the purpose of scientific research and experimentation is not deemed an infringement of the patent right. In this regard, a distinction should be made between the experimentation on the patented product and use of the patented product in experimentation.
>
> 1) The use of the patent concerned solely for the purpose of scientific research and experimentation should include the act of manufacturing the patented product solely for the purpose of scientific research and experimentation;
>
> 2) The use solely for the purpose of scientific research and experimentation is for the purpose of studying, testing or improving another person's patented technology and the result of this use is the making of a new technology achievement on the basis of the existing patented technology; and
>
> 3) The manufacture with or use of another person's patented technology in the course of scientific research and experimentation which is not for the purpose of research or improvement of another person's patented technology, with the result being not directly related to the patented technology, constitutes an infringement of the patent right.

HFG Law Firm and IP Agency in China, *Opinions of the Beijing Higher People's Court on Several Issues Relating to Patent Infringement Establishment (for Trial Implementation)*, in CHINA INTELLECTUAL PROPERTY LAW GUIDE ¶100-250 (2005).

Despite very early case law in the United States that sanctioned an experimental use exception, and an initial legislative effort to enact a broad exemption, only the most narrow experimental use exception exists in the United States today. Compared to most other nations, it can be said that U.S. case law gives patent owners the exclusive right to use their inventions virtually without qualification as to the purpose of the use or nature of the user. What remains from the common-law-based exception is an extremely limited rule that was reinforced by the Court of Appeals for the Federal Circuit in *Madey v. Duke University,* 307 F.3d 1351 (Fed. Cir. 2002). In *Madey,* scientists at Duke University used laboratory lasers to conduct basic research without a license from the owner of the laser equipment patent. Judge Gajarsa's summary of the rule stands out in strong contrast to the approach to experimental use adopted in much of the rest of the world:

> In short, regardless of whether a particular institution or entity is engaged in an endeavor for commercial gain, so long as the act is in furtherance of the alleged infringer's legitimate business and is not solely for amusement, to satisfy idle curiosity, or for strictly philosophical inquiry, the act does not qualify for the very narrow and strictly limited experimental use defense. Moreover, the profit or non-profit status of the user is not determinative.

Id. at 1362.

The only statutory recognition of an experimental use exception in the United States concerns the non-consensual use of a patented drug in the preparation of data to be submitted for approval to a governmental regulatory agency, such as the Food and Drug Administration (FDA). Section 271(e) (1) of the Patent Act was enacted in 1984 as part of the Patent Term Restoration Act, commonly known as the Hatch-Waxman Act (HWA). It provides as follows:

> It shall not be an act of infringement to make, use, offer to sell, or sell within the United States or import into the United States a patented invention (other than a new animal drug or veterinary biological product (as those terms are used in the Federal Food, Drug, and Cosmetic Act and the Act of March 4, 1913) which is primarily manufactured using recombinant DNA, recombinant RNA, hybridoma technology, or other processes involving site specific genetic manipulation techniques) solely for uses reasonably related to the development and submission of information under a Federal law which regulates the manufacture, use, or sale of drugs or veterinary biological products.

Section 271(e) is also called a "Bolar" exception to infringement because through it, Congress statutorily overruled the Federal Circuit decision in *Roche Products, Inc. v. Bolar Pharmaceutical Co.,* 733 F.2d 858 (Fed. Cir. 1984). In that case, before Roche's patent on its successful drug Dalmane® expired, Bolar obtained the active ingredient, florazepam, and conducted bioequivalence studies in order to seek FDA approval to market a generic version of Dalmane®. Roche sued Bolar for patent infringement and lost in the trial court where the judge ruled that Bolar's activities came within the common-law "experimental use" exception to patent infringement. On appeal, the U.S. Court of Appeals for the Federal Circuit reversed, narrowly construing the "experimental use" exception as not applying to tests having a commercial objective. According to the court:

It is well-established, in particular, that the *use* of a patented invention, without either manufacture or sale, is actionable. . . . Thus, the patentee does not need to have *any* evidence of damage or lost sales to bring an infringement action. . . . [W]e hold the experimental use exception to be truly narrow, and we will not expand it under the present circumstances. . . . Bolar's intended "experimental"' use is solely for business reasons and not for amusement, to satisfy idle curiosity, or for strictly philosophical inquiry.

Id. at 861–863.

Thus the *Bolar* decision created a de facto patent term extension for pharmaceuticals requiring FDA marketing approval, since generic competitors could not even begin the multi-year approval process until the patent expired.

The purpose of §271(e)(1) is to permit applicants seeking FDA approval for the manufacture and sale of generic versions of patented drugs previously approved by the FDA to use those patented drugs solely for purposes reasonably related to gathering data in support of their applications for approval. Such activity is therefore not considered to be patent infringement. In exchange for the experimental use exception, under the HWA up to five years of patent term can be restored to a pioneer drug firm for delays in obtaining FDA approval. For an overview of the HWA scheme and some of the challenges and opportunities it has created, *see* Michael A. Carrier, *Unsettling Drug Patent Settlements: A Framework for Presumptive Illegality*, 108 MICH. L. REV. 37 (2009).

Two Supreme Court cases have broadened somewhat the scope of §271(e) (1). In *Eli Lilly & Co. v. Medtronic, Inc.,* 496 U.S. 661 (1990), the Court held that §271(e) (1) covers not only data gathering on drugs, but also the testing of medical devices. And in the more recent case of *Merck KGAA v. Integra Lifesciences I, Ltd.,* 545 U.S. 193 (2005), the Court held that the provision also includes data gathering relating to clinical trials and pre-clinical testing of new drugs seeking FDA approval. It will be interesting to see whether the courts in the U.S. will continue to expand the scope of §271(e) (1) and, if so, what new uses will be permitted.

Many other countries have adopted *Bolar*-type regulatory review exemptions, often in addition to their more general experimental use provisions. For example, in the EU, Directive 2004/27/EC of the European Parliament and of the Council of 31 March 2004, amending Directive 2001/83/EC on the Community code relating to medicinal products for human use, provides in Article 10(6):

Conducting the necessary studies and trials with a view to the application of paragraphs 1, 2, 3 and 4 [applying for a marketing authorization for a generic medicine using the abbreviated procedure] and the consequential practical requirements shall not be regarded as contrary to patent rights or to supplementary protection certificates for medicinal products.

Member states were required to adopt legislation to implement the minimum requirements of the Directive, but, as with the EU Biotechnology Directive discussed in Chapter 4, members have significant discretion in implementation; thus conforming legislation varies by country with some having broad and some narrow interpretations of the *Bolar* exemption. Dr. Gwyn Cole provides a survey of the provisions in several member states. *See* Gwyn Cole, *Exemption from Infringement: The EU Bolar Directive*, IP Eur. Q. (2012), *available at* http://www.avidity-ip.com/assets/pdf/BolarJun12.pdf.

NOTES AND QUESTIONS

1. Which approach toward experimental use do you find more compelling—the United States or that of most other nations? Why do you think these similarly situated countries, at least economically and culturally, have such different approaches to experimental use? If you could reform United States policy toward experimental use, what changes would you make, if any? For varying views on whether the United States should codify an exception for experimenting "on" an invention, "with" an invention, or both, see, e.g., Janice M. Mueller, *The Evanescent Experimental Use Exemption from United States Patent Infringement Liability: Implications for University and Nonprofit Research and Development*, 56 BAYLOR L. REV. 917, 972 (2004); Katherine J. Strandburg, *What Does the Public Get? Experimental Use and the Patent Bargain*, 2004 WIS. L. REV. 81; and Rebecca S. Eisenberg, *Patents and the Progress of Science: Exclusive Rights and Experimental Use,* 56 U. CHI. L. REV. 1017 (1989).

2. Recent discussions have focused on the potential application of the experimental use exception to research tools, particularly within the context of genetic research. Those in favor of allowing nonconsensual use of research tools argue that the exception is necessary to diminish impediments to important areas of research. Those opposed argue that the exception would threaten the development of new means of diagnosis, as inventors would not be incentivized to create new patentable research tools that would be subject to the exception. For a thorough analysis of the issues involved, *see* Henrik Holzapfel and Joshua D. Sarnoff, *A Cross-Atlantic Dialog on Experimental Use and Research Tools*, 48 IDEA 123 (2008).

3. Should developing countries adopt a Bolar exception in their national patent laws? Is such an exception consistent with Article 30 of the TRIPS Agreement? With the considerations that animate international patent policy? *See* Carlos M. Correa, *The International Dimension of the Research Exception*, SIPPI Project, AAAS, Wash. D.C. (2005), *available at* http://sippi.aaas.org/Pubs/Correa_International%20Exception.pdf; Carlos M. Correa, *Multilateral Agreements and Policy Opportunities*, SIPPI Project, AAAS,

Wash. D.C. (2008), *available at* http://policydialogue.org/files/events/Correa_
Multilateral_Agreements_and_Policy_Opportunities.pdf. Recall that a Bolar-
type regulatory review exception was at issue in the *Canada—Patent Protection for Pharmaceutical Products* case in Chapter 3 (Report of the WTO Panel, Canada—Patent Protection for Pharmaceutical Products, WT/DS114/R,
(2000)). In paragraph 7.69 of the decision, the Panel noted that use for scientific experimentation is "one of the most widely accepted" exceptions in national patent laws.

3. EXHAUSTION OF PATENT RIGHTS/PARALLEL IMPORTATION

Under the First Sale Doctrine (FSD), the first sale of a patented item
in a territory releases that item from the purview of the patent-holder
and the buyer is free to do with the item as she wishes (except completely
reconstruct it) without being deemed an infringer. The FSD results in
what has been called the "exhaustion" of patent rights as to a particular
product. Thus exhaustion of patent rights is a defense to patent infringement. The critical question under the FSD is thus what is the relevant
"territory"? Is it a country, a region, or does a first sale of an item anywhere in the world exhaust a patentee's rights under all of its patents
covering that item in all jurisdictions? This is a subject on which countries have agreed not to agree. In fact, the lack of consensus is explicitly
stated in TRIPS Article 6:

> For the purposes of dispute settlement under this Agreement,
> . . . nothing in this Agreement shall be used to address the issue
> of the exhaustion of intellectual property rights.

The issue of exhaustion of patent rights often arises in the context of
"gray market goods"/parallel imports. These are genuine goods purchased
in a foreign market by independent third parties that are subsequently
resold into a domestic market to compete with goods of the authorized
distributor/patentee. Recently, the United States has sought to introduce
limits on some countries' ability to determine which exhaustion doctrine
they can adopt through regional and bilateral free trade agreements
(FTAs). For example, the leaked February 11, 2011 draft U.S. IP Chapter
of the Trans-Pacific Partnership Agreement (TPP), an FTA which involves nine countries in the Asia-Pacific region, includes a provision that
bans importation of certain genuine goods currently allowed under the
national laws of most countries pursuant to the exhaustion principle.
Although the draft provision applies only to copyrighted works, this effort
to narrow a flexibility provided in the TRIPS Agreement has attracted
much concern and criticism. Below, we look at the issue of exhaustion of
patent rights in the United States and other countries.

a. United States

The following case illustrates the U.S. approach to the territorial exhaustion of patent rights.

FUJI PHOTO FILM CO. V. JAZZ PHOTO CORP.

United States Court of Appeals, Federal Circuit
394 F.3d 1368 (Fed. Cir. 2005)

■ RADER, Circuit Judge.

On March 18, 2003, the United States District Court for the District of New Jersey entered final judgment against Jazz Photo Corp., Jazz Photo Ltd., and Jack Benun, a former Jazz director and consultant, (collectively Jazz) for infringement of Fuji Photo Film Co. Ltd.'s (Fuji's) patents. . . . Specifically, the district court found that Jazz's importation, sale, and use of over forty million refurbished disposable cameras directly infringed Fuji's family of U.S. patents directed to disposable cameras, also known as lens fitted film packages (LFFPs) . . . . Because the district court did not err in finding Jazz liable for direct and induced infringement, in awarding damages based upon the jury's reasonable royalty rate, in refusing to enhance those damages, or in denying Fuji a permanent injunction, this court affirms.

I.

Fuji and Jazz are no strangers to this court. Their dispute began in 1998, when Fuji commenced a proceeding before the International Trade Commission (ITC) against twenty-six respondents, including Jazz, under Section 337 of the Tariff Act of 1930, as amended, 19 U.S.C. § 1337. Through the ITC proceeding, Fuji sought to restrict the respondents' importation of refurbished LFFPs, alleging infringement of fourteen of its patents directed to LFFPs. LFFPs are simple, relatively inexpensive cameras that Fuji originally intended to be disposable after a single use. See, e.g., U.S. Patent No. 4,884,087 (issued Nov. 28, 1999), col. 6, ll. 14–18 (noting that "forming an opening in the film package makes it impossible to reuse the film package. Therefore it will be impossible to refill a new film into the used film package in order to reclaim a film package for reuse."). In response to public protest of the camera shell disposals, Fuji began a recycling program in 1991. Fuji subsequently learned that several companies, including Jazz, purchased used LFFP shells from foreign factories. These companies then refurbished the LFFPs by inserting new film through multiple steps. Then they resold the refurbished cameras. Upon learning of these resales, Fuji instituted the ITC proceeding.

The primary issue before the ITC was whether the respondents' refurbishment of Fuji's used LFFPs constituted permissible repair or impermissible reconstruction. Although the participating respondents did not disclose their respective refurbishment acts in their entirety, each acknowledged performance of at least eight common steps when refurbishing the Fuji LFFPs. [The eight refurbishment steps include: 1) removing the cardboard cover; 2) cutting open the cardboard case; 3) inserting new film and a new film receiving container; 4) replacing the winding wheel; 5) replacing the flash in relevant LFFPs; 6) resetting the counter; 7) resealing the outer case; and 8) adding a new cardboard cover.] The ITC administrative judge determined that those eight steps constituted impermissible reconstruction. . . . The ITC subsequently adopted the administrative judge's findings. . . . Accordingly, the ITC issued a general exclusion order and an order to cease and desist from further infringement of Fuji's patents. . . .

Before the ITC issued its final determination, Fuji filed suit against Jazz in the United States District Court for the District of New Jersey seeking damages and injunctive relief for direct and indirect infringement of its LFFP patents. Following the ITC's final determination, however, some of the ITC respondents filed an appeal with this court. The district court stayed its proceedings pending that appeal. In August 2001, this court reversed the ITC's final determination, finding instead that the eight-step refurbishment procedure constituted permissible repair. *Jazz Photo Corp. v. Int'l Trade Comm'n*, 264 F.3d 1094, 1110–11 (Fed.Cir. 2001) ["*Jazz*"]. Moreover, this court held that only LFFPs first sold in the United States qualified for the repair exclusion under the exhaustion doctrine. . . .

This court's holding in *Jazz*, however, was not entirely dispositive of the repair/reconstruction issue before the district court. In particular, Jazz acknowledged that its specific refurbishment procedures comprised a possible total of nineteen refurbishment steps, including the eight previously considered in *Jazz*. Accordingly, the district court lifted its stay and Fuji's lawsuit proceeded. . . .

Of relevance to this appeal, after a five week trial, the jury determined that: 1) Jazz infringed Fuji's patents by refurbishing 39,889,850 LFFPs; 2) Jazz willfully infringed by selling 1,209,760 newly-made LFFPs; and 3) Jazz owed a reasonable royalty of $ 0.56 per LFFP to compensate for infringement. . . . After the jury reached its verdict, the district court evaluated the repair/reconstruction issue as well as the underlying exhaustion issue.

In its analysis, the district court first determined that the nineteen steps were effectively sub-steps of the eight steps that this court previously deemed permissible repair. . . . As such, the district court then evaluated which of the eight Jazz Chinese factories performed these nineteen steps. Although Jazz had presented testimony regarding three Chinese factories, the district court rejected Jazz's proposed inference that its evidence represented the refurbishment activities at the remaining five Chinese factories. . . . Upon reviewing the record to adduce the number of refurbished LFFPs attributable to the three Chinese factories, the district court determined that the only evidence of record reflected 10%, or 4,009,937, of the LFFPs were permissibly repaired.

Recognizing that the repair affirmative defense is based upon the exhaustion doctrine, the district court next turned its analysis to the issue of foreign LFFP sales. . . . The district court interpreted this court's *Jazz* exhaustion precedent in holding that only first sales in the United States would serve as the appropriate basis for the repair affirmative defense. . . . Based on evidence presented by both parties, the jury determined that roughly 9.5%, or 3,809,442, of Jazz's refurbished LFFPs derived from United States first sales. . . . The district court then evaluated the nexus of refurbished LFFPs (1) that were first sold in the United States, and (2) which Jazz permissibly repaired. Recognizing the difficulty in requiring direct proof of the number of LFFPs fitting this description, the district court reasoned that it would be appropriate to infer that 9.5% of the 4,009,937 total potentially permissibly repaired cameras were attributable to United States first sales. Accordingly, the district court determined that Jazz's evidence supported a finding that 380,944 LFFPs fit these criteria. . . .

On appeal, Jazz challenges the district court's finding that it did not provide sufficient evidence that all eight of its Chinese supplier factories performed the nineteen repair steps. Jazz also disputes the district court's application of the exhaustion doctrine as enunciated in this court's holding in *Jazz*. . . . Fuji, in turn, cross appeals the district court's finding that Jazz sufficiently proved that 10% of its refurbished LFFPs fell within the repair safe harbor, as well as the district court's refusal to enhance damages and its denial of a permanent injunction. . . .

III.

. . . .

B. Exhaustion Doctrine

Jazz next argues that the district court misconstrued this court's holding regarding exhaustion in *Jazz*. In the alternative, even if the district court properly construed this court's exhaustion holding, Jazz contends that its effect should be purely prospective.

In *Jazz*, this court held that:

> To invoke the protection of the first sale doctrine, the authorized first sale must have occurred under the United States patent. . . . Our decision applies only to LFFPs for which the United States patent right has been exhausted by first sale in the United States. Imported LFFPs of solely foreign provenance are not immunized from infringement of United States patents by the nature of their refurbishment. *Id.* at 1105.

This court does not construe the "solely foreign provenance" language . . . to dictate a narrow application of the exhaustion principle. Specifically, this court does not read . . . the above language to limit the exhaustion principle to unauthorized sales. Jazz therefore does not escape application of the exhaustion principle because Fuji or its licensees authorized the international first sales of these LFFPs. The patentee's authorization of an international first sale does not affect exhaustion of that patentee's rights in the United States. Moreover, the "solely foreign provenance" language does not negate the exhaustion doctrine when either the patentee or its licensee sells the patented article abroad.

Read in full context, this court in *Jazz* stated that only LFFPs sold within the United States under a United States patent qualify for the repair defense under the exhaustion doctrine. . . . Moreover, Fuji's foreign sales can never occur under a United States patent because the United States patent system does not provide for extraterritorial effect. *Int'l Rectifier Corp. v. Samsung Elecs. Co.*, 361 F.3d 1355, 1360 (Fed. Cir. 2004) ("Further, it is well known that United States patent laws 'do not, and were not intended to, operate beyond the limits of the United States,'" quoting *Brown v. Duchesne*, 60 U.S. (19 How.) 183, 195 (1856)). In *Jazz*, therefore, this court expressly limited first sales under the exhaustion doctrine to those occurring within the United States. Accordingly, the district court correctly applied this court's exhaustion precedent.

NOTES AND QUESTIONS

1. The distinction between permissible repair (PR) and impermissible reconstruction (IR) can be difficult to define. In fact, it is rare to find cases where a party's actions are construed as IR as opposed to PR. Nevertheless, the refurbishment steps in *Fuji v. Jazz Photo* that were deemed PR for cameras first sold in the United States were considered to be infringement actions for cameras that had not been sold first in the United States. The court here is saying that the United States applies *domestic* exhaustion of patent rights: Once a patented product had been sold in the United States, it is free of the patent owner's claims and the product owner is free to use, sell, and offer to sell the product, as long as it does not *remake* (IR) the product. However, the owner of a U.S. patent can prevent gray market goods from being imported into the United States without permission, even though the goods were legitimately produced in their country of origin.

[handwritten margin note: clear holding]

2. In 2008, the United States Supreme Court decided *Quanta Computer, Inc. v. LG Electronics, Inc.*, 553 U.S. 617 (2008). There the Court held that the first sale of downstream goods "substantially embodying" a patented technology exhausted the patentee's rights in relation to those goods despite a license agreement between the patentee and the upstream provider of the goods, that explicitly did not extend to downstream third-party purchasers. Although *Quanta* did not deal directly with the issue of territorial exhaustion of patent rights, at least one lower court thought that it did, and that it in

essence overruled *Fuji v. Jazz Photo*, stating, "*Quanta's* holding—that exhaustion is triggered by the authorized sale of an article that substantially embodies a patent—applies to authorized foreign sales as well as sales in the United States." *LG Electronics v. Hitachi*, 655 F.Supp. 2d 1036, 1047 (N.D. Cal. 2009). The Federal Circuit disagreed, and noted (in a continuation of the Fuji/Jazz litigation):

> *Quanta Computer, Inc. v. LG Electronics, Inc.* did not eliminate the first sale rule's territoriality requirement. Three LG patents, relating to systems in which a micro-processor writes or reads memory unit data, were at issue in *Quanta*. LG licensed Intel to make, use, or sell combination products practicing these patents, but restricted Intel from passing a license on to Intel customers to make the patented combination by joining Intel's unpatented chips with components from a non-Intel source. . . . The license also stated that patent exhaustion applied when Intel sold its LG-licensed products. In a second agreement, Intel agreed to provide written notice to its customers that Intel's LG license did not extend to any subsequent purchaser's product made by combining an Intel product with any non-Intel product.

> Intel sold chips to Quanta without hardware to connect them in a working computer; it also provided Quanta with the required written notice. . . . LG's patents were not infringed until the chips were assembled with hardware, but the only reasonable and intended use for the chips was practicing LG's patents. . . . Quanta combined Intel's chips with non-Intel hardware so that LG's patents were practiced. . . . The Supreme Court resolved whether Intel selling chips to Quanta exhausted LG's patent rights in the chip-using system. . . . Holding the case governed by *United States v. Univis Lens Co.* . . . (exhaustion occurs when the only reasonable and intended use of the products sold is to complete the patented combination), the Court found that Intel's chips substantially embodied the patented invention and their unconditional, authorized sale by Intel thereby exhausted LG's patents. . . .

> Defendants assert that *Quanta* created a rule of "strict exhaustion," that the Court's failure to recite the territoriality requirement eliminated it. That case, however, did not involve foreign sales. Defendants rely on *Quanta's* footnote 6 because it contains the phrase "[w]hether outside the country." This phrase, however, emphasizes that *Univis* required the product's only use be for practicing–not infringing–the patent; and a practicing use may be "outside the country," while an infringing use must occur in the country where the patent is enforceable. Read properly, the phrase defendants rely on supports, rather than undermines, the exhaustion doctrine's territoriality requirement.

Fujifilm Corp. v. Benun, 605 F.3d 1366, 1371–72 (Fed. Cir. 2010) (citations omitted).

Thus, until such time as the Supreme Court chooses to directly address territorial exhaustion of patent rights, the U.S. remains a domestic exhaustion regime.

b. Europe

With its many, diverse member countries, the EU faces additional challenges on the issue of territorial exhaustion of patent rights as seen in the following case illustrating the EU approach to patent exhaustion.

MERCK & CO. v. PRIMECROWN LTD.

Court of Justice of the European Communities

Joined cases C-267 & C-268/95, 1996 E.C.R. I-6285, [1997] 1 C.M.L.R. 83

[Merck brought a patent infringement action in the UK Patents Court to prevent the parallel importation of pharmaceutical products from states where such products were not patentable—Spain and Portugal—into the UK. Spain and Portugal had joined the EEC but had not yet made patent protection available for such products. Transitional provisions gave Merck the right to prevent parallel imports until the end of the third year after which those countries made such products patentable.]

1. By two orders of 13 July 1995 . . . the High Court of Justice of England and Wales, Chancery Division, Patents Court, referred to the Court for a preliminary ruling under Article 177 of the EC Treaty questions concerning the interpretation of Article 47 and Article 209 of the Act concerning the Conditions of Accession of the Kingdom of Spain and the Portuguese Republic and the Adjustments to the Treaties (OJ 1985 L 302, p. 23, hereinafter "the Act of Accession") and of Articles 30 and 36 of the EC Treaty. . . .

3. Merck claims that Primecrown has infringed its United Kingdom patents for a hypertension drug marketed under the trade mark Innovace in the United Kingdom and under the trade mark Renitec elsewhere, for a drug prescribed in prostrate treatment, marketed under the trade mark Proscar, and for a glaucoma drug marketed under the trade mark Timoptol. It complains that Primecrown has carried out parallel imports of those products into the United Kingdom. Renitec and Proscar have been imported from Spain whilst Timoptol has been imported from Portugal.

4. Beecham has brought an action against Europharm for infringing its United Kingdom patents covering an antibiotic called Augmentin in the United Kingdom and Augmentine in Spain. Beecham complains that Europharm has imported this product from Spain into the United Kingdom with a view to applying to the competent authorities for an import licence which would allow it to import more of the product.

5. Merck and Beecham consider that they are entitled to oppose parallel imports of a drug for which they hold patents when, as in these cases, those imports come from a Member State where their products are marketed but were not patentable there.

6. Primecrown and Europharm refer, for their part, to the case-law of the Court on Articles 30 and 36 of the Treaty and in particular to the principle of the exhaustion of rights, as interpreted by the Court in its judgment in Case 187/80 *Merck v Stephar and Exler* ([1981] ECR 2063, hereinafter *"Merck v Stephar"* or *"Merck"*). They deduce from *Merck v Stephar* that, upon expiry of the transitional periods laid down in Articles 47 and 209 of the Act of Accession, they are entitled to import the products in question from Spain and Portugal where they have been marketed by, or with the consent of, the patent holders.

7. In *Merck v Stephar*, the Court referred to its case-law on Articles 30 and 36 of the Treaty according to which the proprietor of an industrial and commercial property right protected by the legislation of a Member State may not rely on that legislation to oppose the importation of a product which has been lawfully put on the market in another Member State by, or with the consent of, the proprietor of that right himself. The Court held that this case-law also applied where the product concerned was put on the market by, or with the consent of, the proprietor in a Member State where the product was not patentable. . . .

27. In substance, the High Court is seeking to ascertain whether it is necessary to reconsider the rule in *Merck v Stephar* or whether, having regard to the specific circumstances mentioned, its scope should be limited.

28. Merck and Beecham consider that there are weighty reasons for departing from the rule in *Merck v Stephar*. They point out first of all that an important change in the situation has occurred since *Merck*. At the time when the Court gave that judgment, it was the exception rather than the rule for pharmaceutical products to be patentable in Europe. Nowadays, such products are patentable in all the countries of the European Economic Area, with the exception of Iceland. Similarly, the Community institutions have emphasized the importance of patents in the pharmaceutical sector, in particular by the adoption of Council Regulation (EEC) No 1768/92 of 18 June 1992 concerning the creation of a supplementary protection certificate for medicinal products (OJ 1992 L 182, p. 1). Merck and Beecham then point to the increasingly serious financial consequences of maintaining the rule in *Merck* which, in their view, appreciably reduce the value of patents granted in the Community. Finally, they argue that the specific subject-matter of a patent can be exhausted only if the product in question is marketed with patent protection and that *Merck* is incompatible with the later case-law of the Court.

29. It is first necessary to recall the Court's reasoning in *Merck*.

30. In that judgment, the Court referred to its judgment in Case 15/74 *Centrafarm v. Sterling Drug* [1974] ECR 1147 in which it held, in paragraphs 8 and 9, that as an exception, on grounds of the protection of industrial and commercial property, to one of the fundamental principles of the common market, Article 36 of the Treaty admitted such derogation only in so far as it was justified for the purpose of safeguarding rights constituting the specific subject-matter of that property, which, as regards patents, is, in particular, in order to reward the creative effort of the inventor, to guarantee that the patentee has the exclusive right to use an invention with a view to manufacturing industrial products and putting them into circulation for the first time, either directly or by the grant of licences to third parties, as well as the right to oppose infringements.

31. In paragraphs 9 and 10 of *Merck*, the Court then stated that it followed from the definition of the specific purpose of a patent that the substance of a patent right lies essentially in according the inventor an exclusive right to put the product on the market for the first time, thereby allowing him a monopoly in exploiting his product and enabling him to obtain the reward for his creative effort without, however, guaranteeing such reward in all circumstances.

32. The Court held, finally, in paragraphs 11 and 13 of *Merck* that it was for the holder of the patent to decide, in the light of all the circumstances, under what conditions he would market his product, including the possibility of marketing it in a Member State where the law did not provide patent protection for the product in question. If he decides to do so, he must then accept the consequences of his choice as regards free movement of the product within the common market, this being a fundamental principle forming part of the legal and economic circumstances which the holder of the patent must take into account in determining how to exercise his exclusive right. Under those conditions, to permit an inventor to invoke a patent held by him in one Member State in order to prevent the importation of the product freely marketed by him in another Member State where that product was not patentable would cause a partitioning of national markets contrary to the aims of the Treaty.

33. For the reasons set out below, the arguments for reconsideration of the rule in Merck are not such as to call in question the reasoning on which the Court based that rule.

34. It is true, as Merck and Beecham point out, that it is now the norm for pharmaceutical products to be patentable. However, such a development does not mean that the reasoning underlying the rule in *Merck* is superseded.

35. The same is true in relation to the arguments based, first, on the efforts made by the Community institutions to give enhanced protection to holders of patents for pharmaceutical products and, second, on the con-

sequences of maintaining that rule for research and development by the pharmaceutical industry.

36. There can be no doubt now, any more than at the time when the judgment in *Merck* was given, that if a patentee could prohibit the importation of protected products marketed in another Member State by him or with his consent, he would be able to partition national markets and thereby restrict trade between the Member States. By the same token, if a patentee decides, in the light of all the circumstances, to put a product on the market in a Member State where it is not patentable, he must accept the consequences of his choice as regards the possibility of parallel imports.

37. The arguments put forward in the present cases have not shown that the Court was wrong in its assessment of the balance between the principle of free movement of goods in the Community and the principle of protection of patentees' rights, albeit that, as a result of striking that balance, the right to oppose importation of a product may be exhausted by its being marketed in a Member State where it is not patentable.

38. It is important to remember in this respect that the transitional measures provided for by Articles 47 and 209 of the Act of Accession were adopted in the light of the ruling in *Merck*. Although the Member States considered it necessary to postpone the effects of that ruling for a long period, they provided that, upon expiry of the transitional arrangements, Articles 30 and 36 of the Treaty, as interpreted in *Merck*, should apply in full to trade between Spain and Portugal, on the one hand, and the existing Member States, on the other.

39. Furthermore, the situations addressed by the ruling in *Merck* are set to disappear since pharmaceutical products are now patentable in all the Member States. If, upon accession of new States to the Community, such situations were to recur, the Member States could adopt the measures considered necessary, as was the case when the Kingdom of Spain and the Portuguese Republic acceded to the Community. . . .

44. The first question to be considered is whether the rule in *Merck* also applies where the patentee has a legal or ethical obligation to market or to continue to market his product in the exporting State. Here the national court is concerned to know what importance is to be attached to a requirement of that State's legislation or of Community legislation that, once the product has been put on the market in that State, the patentee must supply and continue to supply sufficient quantities to satisfy the needs of domestic patients.

45. The second question is whether the rule in *Merck* applies where the legislation of the exporting State not only grants to its authorities the right, which they exercise, to fix the sale price of the product but also prohibits the sale of the product at any other price. Here the national

court is concerned to know whether it is relevant that those authorities have fixed the price of the products at a level such that substantial exports of the product to the Member State of importation are foreseeable.

46. Merck and Beecham maintain in particular that, in the circumstances mentioned in the order for reference, their right to decide freely on the conditions in which they market their products is removed or considerably reduced. In their view, it follows from Pharmon that the rule in *Merck* does not apply in the present cases.

47. As to that, although the imposition of price controls is indeed a factor which may, in certain conditions, distort competition between Member States, that circumstance cannot justify a derogation from the principle of free movement of goods. It is well settled that distortions caused by different price legislation in a Member State must be remedied by measures taken by the Community authorities and not by the adoption by another Member State of measures incompatible with the rules on free movement of goods. . . .

48. The next question which must be examined is how far the rule in *Merck* applies where patentees are legally obliged to market their products in the exporting State.

49. In answering that question it is to be remembered, first, that in *Merck* the Court emphasized the importance of the fact that the patentee had taken his decision to market his product freely and in full knowledge of all relevant circumstances and, second, that it follows from Pharmon that a patentee who is not in a position to decide freely how he will market his products in the exporting State may oppose importation and marketing of those products in the State where the patent is in force.

50. It follows that, where a patentee is legally bound under either national law or Community law to market his products in a Member State, he cannot be deemed, within the meaning of the ruling in *Merck*, to have given his consent to the marketing of the products concerned. He is therefore entitled to oppose importation and marketing of those products in the State where they are protected.

51. It is for the patentee to prove, before the national court from which an order prohibiting imports is sought, that there is a legal obligation to market the product concerned in the exporting State. He must in particular show, for example by reference to decisions of the competent national authorities or courts or of the competent Community authorities, that there is a genuine, existing obligation.

52. According to the information given to the Court in these proceedings and as the Advocate General observes in points 152 and 153 of his Opinion, such obligations can hardly be said to exist in the case of the imports in question.

53. Finally, as regards the argument that ethical obligations may compel patentees to provide supplies of drugs to Member States where they are needed, even if they are not patentable there, such considerations are not, in the absence of any legal obligation, such as to make it possible properly to identify the situations in which the patentee is deprived of his power to decide freely how he will market his product. Such considerations are, at any rate in the present context, difficult to apprehend and distinguish from commercial considerations. Such ethical obligations cannot, therefore, be the basis for derogating from the rule on free movement of goods laid down in *Merck*.

54. In view of the foregoing, the answer to be given to the third question must be that Articles 30 and 36 of the Treaty preclude application of national legislation which grants the holder of a patent for a pharmaceutical product the right to oppose importation by a third party of that product from another Member State in circumstances where the holder first put the product on the market in that State after its accession to the European Community but before the product could be protected by a patent in that State, unless the holder of the patent can prove that he is under a genuine, existing legal obligation to market the product in that Member State.

. . . [I]n answer to the questions submitted to it by the High Court of Justice of England and Wales, Chancery Division, Patents Court, by orders of 13 July 1995, hereby rules:

Articles 30 and 36 of the EC Treaty preclude application of national legislation which grants the holder of a patent for a pharmaceutical product the right to oppose importation by a third party of that product from another Member State in circumstances where the holder first put the product on the market in that State after its accession to the European Community but before the product could be protected by a patent in that State, unless the holder of the patent can prove that he is under a genuine, existing legal obligation to market the product in that Member State.

NOTES AND QUESTIONS

1. In Joined Cases 267 & 268/95, *Merck & Co. v. Primecrown Ltd.*, 1996 E.C.R I-6285, [1997] 1 C.M.L.R. 83 (*Merck v. Primecrown* above), the European Court of Justice [ECJ] noted that the balance between the competing principles of free movement of goods in the common market and protection of patentee's rights swings in favor of free movement of goods in this case. Why is that? Applying the Court's reasoning, under what circumstances may a patentee block entry of parallel goods?

2. As the Court predicted, the accession of additional countries to the Community did result in new transitional measures being adopted to prevent, for a specified period of time, parallel importation of pharmaceutical

products from new member countries into old member countries. The Specific Mechanism in the EU Treaty Accession Act provides in part:

> With regard to the Czech Republic, Estonia, Latvia, Lithuania, Hungary, Poland, Slovenia or Slovakia, the holder or beneficiary, of a patent or supplementary protection certificate for a pharmaceutical product filed in a Member State at a time when such protection could not be obtained in one of the above-mentioned new Member states for that product, may rely on the rights granted by that patent or supplementary protection certificate in order to prevent the import and marketing of that product in the Member State or States where the product in question enjoys patent protection or supplementary protection, even if the product was put on the market in that new Member State for the first time by him or with his consent.

This mechanism, allowing patentees to stop parallel imports under the above-specified conditions, is operative until 2016 for the Czech Republic and Slovakia, 2017 for Slovenia, 2018 for Latvia and Poland, and 2019 for Hungary, Lithuania and Estonia.

3. The ECJ revisited the issue of pharmaceutical parallel imports in *Sot. Lélos kai Sia EE v. GlaxoSmithKline*, Joined Cases C-468/06 to C-478/06 (2008). There, GlaxoSmithKline (GSK) owned patents for its products Imigran (for migraines), Lamictal (for epilepsy) and Serevent (for asthma). GSK supplied products to the Greek market through wholesalers, who in turn, partly exported some of these products to other countries with higher price limits for the drugs. The wholesalers moved so much of the products, GSK had to temporarily stop supplying the wholesalers due to a shortage of the products. When GSK resumed supplying the wholesalers, it limited the amount supplied considerably, in an effort to stop the parallel importation of the products. The wholesalers sued GSK for abuse of a dominant position seeking damages for losses they had incurred and an order requiring GSK to resume supplying them with products at the original levels. The case eventually came before the ECJ on the question: Does the refusal to accept orders in order to limit parallel trade abuse the originator's (assumed) dominant position according Article 82 of the EC Treaty? Art. 82 EC provides in part:

> Any abuse by one or more undertakings of a dominant position within the common market or in a substantial part of it shall be prohibited as incompatible with the common market insofar as it may affect trade between Member States. Such abuse may, in particular, consist in . . . (b) limiting production, markets, or technical development to the prejudice of consumers . . .

In a decision with something for each party to like, the ECJ held that an undertaking occupying a dominant position and refusing to take ordinary orders from wholesalers in order to stop parallel imports by the wholesalers is abusing its dominant position. However, the court also held that it is for the national court to determine whether the orders are in fact ordinary in light of the size of the orders relative to the requirements of the national market and the previous business relations between the undertaking and the wholesalers. The court further noted that pharmaceutical companies are free to choose a vertically integrated distribution structure that would bypass the wholesaler problems completely. Who does this decision really favor, wholesalers or drug producers?

4. The primacy of the principle of free movement of goods in the Community has additional implications for patent owners when viewed in conjunction with the absence of an EU patent and EU patent court system. Recall the UK and German *Improver* decisions in Chapter 10. If, for example, a German court finds a European patent valid and infringed, and a UK court finds the same patent valid and not infringed, one would expect prices of the patented product to drop in the UK as it faces competitive pressure. *Merck v. Primecrown* suggests that third parties could then purchase genuine, patented products in the UK at a reduced price and re-sell them in Germany in competition with the patent owner. Such legal and economic uncertainty is likely to negatively impact the value ascribed to European patents and is further evidence of the need for a unified EU patent system.

c. Japan

As the following case illustrates, Japan has adopted an exhaustion regime that differs from both the United States and the EU in important ways.

Jinzo Fujino, Parallel Imports of Patented Goods: The Supreme Court Talks About Its Legality
22 AIPPI J. 163 (1997)

INTRODUCTION

On July 1, 1997, the Supreme Court of Japan handed down a long-awaited decision concerning parallel imports of patented goods ("BBS case"). . . The following is an English translation of the Supreme Court decision.

Petitioner: *BBS Kraftfahrzeug Technik AG*, Federal Republic of Germany; Intervenor: *Nippon BBS Kabushiki Kaisha*, Tokyo; Intervenor: *Washimeir Kabushiki Kaisha*, Fukui-shi, Japan; Respondent: *Kabushiki Kaisha Racimex Japan*, Tokyo; Respondent: *Kabushiki Kaisha Jap-Auto Products*, Tokyo

With respect to the case of injunction, etc. of patent infringement filed before the Tokyo High Court involving the above parties, the Tokyo High Court delivered its decision on March 23, 1995. Petitioner filed before this Court a petition to dismiss the High Court's decision in its entirety. This Court holds as follows. Petition to this Court is dismissed; and fees for the Petition should be borne by Petitioner.

GROUNDS

On "Reasons for Petition" by Sumio Takeuchi, Attorney to Petitioner and Intervenors:

I. This case was brought by Petitioner against Respondents who engaged in a so-called parallel importation by way of importing and reselling in Japan products manufactured and sold in the Federal Republic of Germany by Petitioner. In this case, Petitioner sought an injunction on importation and sale of products, and damages based on a patent right which Petitioner owns in Japan. The following facts were duly found final by the High Court.

(1) Petitioner owns, in Japan, a patent right entitled "Wheel for Automobile" (filed on October 29, 1983 claiming a priority based on a patent application filed before the European Patent Office on May 27, 1983), granted Patent 1629869 on December 20, 1991. (The patent is hereinafter referred to as the "subject patent" and the invention as the "subject patented invention.")

(2) Petitioner owns a patent right in Germany to cover an invention similar to the subject patented invention. (It was filed on May 27, 1983 before the European Patent Office with Germany and other countries as designated countries. It was granted a patent on April 22, 1987.) (This patent is hereinafter referred to as the "corresponding German patent.")

(3) Up until August 1992, Respondent, Jap-Auto Products imported aluminum wheels for automobiles, "BBS/RS,", and aluminum wheels for automobiles, "ROLINZER RSK," and sold them to another Respondent, *Racimex Japan. Racimex Japan* engaged in the sale of these aluminum wheels at least up until August 1992. It is likely that Respondents would continue their importation and sale. (Hereinafter, the aluminum wheels mentioned here are collectively referred to as the "subject goods" including both products already sold and those to be sold in the future.)

(4) The subject goods fall within the technical scope of the subject patented invention.

(5) The subject goods were manufactured as the product under the corresponding German patent, and sold by Petitioner in Germany after the German patent became effective.

II. In the petition to this Court, Respondents argue for what is called international exhaustion. Namely, the effect of the subject patent applicable to subject goods has exhausted because of legitimate distribution by Petitioner of the subject goods in Germany. Therefore, Respondents' importation and sale of the subject goods in Japan does not constitute infringement of the subject patent.

The High Court dismissed the claim filed by Petitioner against Respondents for injunction and damages under the subject patent. The High

Court reasoned that Petitioner manufactured and sold the subject goods as products under the corresponding patent in Germany. It was clear that Petitioner was provided an opportunity to secure remuneration for disclosing its invention. There were no admissible facts showing that such opportunity to secure remuneration was legally restricted when the subject goods were distributed. Legitimate distribution in Germany should be deemed to have caused the subject patent to be exhausted with respect to the subject goods.

III. The High Court decided that Petitioner's claims against Respondents for injunction and damages under the subject patent have no grounds. This Court is agreeable to the conclusion of the High Court decision. Reasons for this Court's agreement are as follows.

1. "The Paris Convention for the Protection of Industrial Property provides in Article 4*bis* that:

> (1) Patents applied for in the various countries of the Union by nationals of countries of the Union shall be independent of patents obtained for the same invention in other countries, whether members of the Union or not.

> (2) The foregoing provision is to be understood in an unrestricted sense, in particular, in the sense that patents applied for during the period of priority are independent, both as regards the grounds for nullity and forfeiture, and as regards their normal duration.

This provision denies the interdependence of patent rights and stipulates that a patent right of each country is independent from others with respect to its grant, changes and surrender. In other words, the existence of a patent right is not affected by the invalidation, forfeiture, expiration, etc. of a patent right in a different country. The question of whether a patentee is allowed to enforce its patent right under certain circumstances is not a matter stipulated in that provision.

Also, the principle of territoriality denotes, in the context of a patent right, that the grant, assignment, validity or the like of a patent right in each country is governed by the law of that country and that the patent right is effective only in the territory of that country.

When a patentee enforces its patent right in Japan, would such fact that a product subject to that patent right was already sold outside Japan by the patentee or the like, affect enforceability of the Japanese patent right? This question is a matter of interpretation of the Japanese Patent Law and is irrelevant to the Paris Convention and the principle of territoriality. It is clear from the foregoing that any interpretation in this respect, whatever interpretation it might be, is not in the breach of the provision of Article 4*bis* and the principle of territoriality.

2. A patentee has an exclusive right to commercially exploit its patented invention (*see*, Patent Law, Section 68). In the case of an invention of a product, acts of using, assigning or leasing constitute the exploitation of the invention. If so, acts of a commercial use or resale to a third party by the buyer who obtained products covered by the patent (hereinafter referred to as "Patented Product") from the patentee or its licensee, or acts of a commercial use or further sale or lease to others by the third party who obtained the patented products from the buyer would appear, on the surface, to constitute the exploitation of a patented invention to cause infringement of the relevant patent. However, in the case of the sale of patented products in Japan by the patentee or its licensee, a relevant patent in Japan should be deemed to have its right exhausted with respect to the product. In that case, the effect of the patent should no longer extend to the acts of use, assignment or lease of the patented product. This Court bases this interpretation on the following:

(i) The protection of an invention under the patent law has to be achieved in harmony with public interest;

(ii) In general, through the act of a sale, all rights adherent to the goods are transferred to the buyer. The buyer receives all rights which the seller has owned. When a patented product is placed on the market, the buyer enters into a deal with a prerequisite that he would obtain rights to freely use and resell the product as a business. If the sale of a patented product requires approval from the patentee for each transaction, the free flow of products on the market would be interrupted and the smooth distribution of patented products would be disturbed. This would result in adverse effects on the patentee's interests and would be contrary to the purpose of the patent law which aims at encouraging inventions by "promoting their protection and utilization so as to contribute to the development of industry." (*see*, Patent Law, Section 1);

(iii) On the other hand, a patentee receives proceeds including reward for disclosing its patented invention when the patentee sells its patented product. When it licenses the patent, it receives royalty payments. It can be said that an opportunity to secure a reward for disclosing its patented invention is guaranteed. Thus, once the patentee or its licensee sells Patented Products, there is no need to allow the patentee to obtain double profits through the process of distribution.

3. However, this rationale cannot be automatically applicable to the case where a patentee of a Japanese patent has sold its patented products outside Japan, because, in that case, the patentee may not have a patent for the same invention as covered by the Japanese patent (hereinafter referred to as the "counterpart patent"). Even if the patentee owns the

counterpart patent, it should be noted that its patent in Japan is separate from its counterpart patent in the country where the sale took place. In light of this fact, the patentee shall be free from any claim about double profits even if the patentee enforces its Japanese patent against the product which is a subject matter of the counterpart patent.

4. Now, the adjustment between the flow of products in international trade and the patentee's right is discussed below. In light of the fact that international trade is being conducted on a tremendously broad and sophisticated basis, it is necessary that freedom of trade including freedom to import should be paid utmost respect when a dealer in Japan imports a patented product marketed in a foreign country to put it in a distribution channel in Japan. Through economic transactions outside Japan, a seller transfers his rights to the product to a buyer. The buyer enters into a deal with the prerequisite recognition that he receives all rights which the seller has owned with respect to the product. In light of the status-quo of international trade in modern society, it is naturally anticipated that the buyer or a third party who purchased a patented product from the buyer can commercially import it into Japan, and commercially use it or resell it to others in Japan, even if the product is sold by the patentee outside Japan.

Thus, in the case where the owner of a patent in Japan or a person who can be recognized as an entity identical to the patent owner, sells its patented products outside Japan, a reasonable interpretation is that the patentee should not be allowed to enforce its patent in Japan against the buyer unless the buyer explicitly agrees to exclude Japan from the place of sale or use, and against a third party or subsequent buyers who purchased patented products from the buyer unless a notice of such agreement is clearly placed on the patented products. To be more specific:

(i) As was discussed earlier, it can be naturally anticipated that a patented product sold outside Japan might be imported into Japan. If the product was sold outside Japan without a reservation, it should be construed that the right to control the purchased product was implicitly given to the buyer and its subsequent purchasers without any restriction under the patent in Japan;

(ii) With respect to the right of the patentee, it is permissible for the patentee to reserve the right to enforce its patent in Japan when the patentee sells the product outside Japan. In the case where the buyer explicitly agrees with the patentee to an exclusion of Japan from the place of sale and use of the purchased product, and such exclusion is clearly indicated on the product, the subsequent purchasers will be in a position to learn the product is subject to certain restrictions irrespective of the involvement of other persons in the distribution process. They can fully decide whether or not to buy the patented product, taking into account the presence of such restriction; and

(iii) When the product is sold outside Japan by a subsidiary or an affiliated company which can be regarded as an entity identical to the patentee, such transactions should be deemed as the sale of the patented product by the patentee itself; or

(iv) The buyer of the patented product usually trusts in the free flow of the purchased product. That trust should be well protected. It should not matter whether or not the patentee has a counterpart patent in the country of first sale.

5. Now, the above will be applied to this case. According to the facts which the High Court found, both of the subject goods were sold in Germany by Petitioner who has the Japanese patent. Taking into account the fact that Petitioner did not argue and prove the existence of any agreement between Petitioner and Respondent for excluding Japan from the place of sale and use, and that of any clear notice of such exclusion on the subject goods, Petitioner is not allowed to claim for injunction and damages under the subject patent with respect to the subject goods.

The conclusion of the High Court is the same as that of this Court as discussed above. Therefore, this Court agrees to that decision.

NOTES & QUESTIONS

1. In *BBS Kraftfahrzeugtechnik AG v. Racimex Japan Corp.*, Case No. Heisei 7 (wo) 1988, 51 Minshu 2299 (July 1, 1997); *aff'g* Tokyo High Ct., AG No. 3272 of 1994 (Mar. 23, 1995) (the *BBS Wheels* case) the Japanese Supreme Court adopted international exhaustion: Sale of a patented product anywhere in the world exhausts the Japanese patent owner's rights and she cannot prevent such a product from entering Japan. The only exception noted by the court is where the buyer agrees that the product is not to be resold in Japan and the patent owner provides a notice on the product packaging that the good is not intended for sale in Japan. Thus, patent owners can contract around international exhaustion in Japan. An additional limitation on international exhaustion in Japan is where the patented product was first sold in a country where it was subject to price controls (e.g., a pharmaceutical product from Canada). In such a situation, the owner of the Japanese patent will be able to stop the product from being imported into Japan.

2. The case of *Canon v. Recycle Assist* (Japan Supreme Court, Case No. Heisei 18 (jyu) 826, 2007), added a gloss to Japan's international exhaustion regime in a *Fuji*-like context: refilled patented inkjet cartridges. The court reaffirmed the doctrine of international exhaustion but concluded that the actions amounted to impermissible reconstruction of the patented functionality (because an "essential element" of the patented invention had been modified) and thus constituted patent infringement, regardless of whether the cartridges were originally sold in Japan or in another country. After *Canon v.*

Recycle Assist, how would you describe the difference between the U.S. and Japanese approaches to exhaustion? For a recent review of the UK and German approaches to permissible repair and impermissible reconstruction, *see* Alistair Russell, *UK Court of Appeal Rejects German Approach and Confirms: You May Prolong the Life of a Patented Article but You Must Not Make a New One Under the Cover of Repair:* Schultz v. Werit, 34 EUR. INTELL. PROP. REV. 208 (2012).

B. REMEDIES

Although nations differ in the nature, breadth, and effectiveness of the enforcement remedies they employ to achieve the objectives of patent law, injunctive relief, compensatory damages, seizure of infringing goods, and even criminal penalties are part of the panoply of remedies on which nations rely in order to deter patent infringement and ensure the integrity of the patent system and the rights attendant thereto. Articles 43–48 of the TRIPS Agreement concern the remedies that authorities must have the power to order. These include injunctions (Article 44); damages, the awarding of expenses, including attorney's fees, and the recovery of profits and "pre-determined" damages (Article 45); and the destruction or disposal "outside the channels of commerce" of infringing goods and materials (Article 46). Countries also have the right to require infringers to provide information to patent-holders about the identity of third-party contributory infringers, "unless this would be out of proportion to the seriousness of the infringement" (Article 47), and in order to ensure balance and proportionality in enforcement, to order parties "wrongfully enjoined or restrained adequate compensation for the injury suffered because of such abuse" (Article 48).

Finally, Section 2 of the TRIPS Agreement recognizes that the imposition of civil remedies is the domain not only of judicial authorities, but frequently also of administrative authorities. This is the situation in China, for example, where victims of patent infringement are entitled to seek redress not only before the courts, but also before local administrative authorities, who are empowered to investigate and enjoin infringing behavior but may not award damages. Article 49 requires those authorities to comply with TRIPS obligations as follows:

> To the extent that any civil remedy can be ordered as a result of administrative procedures on the merits of a case, such procedures shall conform to principles equivalent in substance to those set forth in this Section.

As a patent is widely perceived as giving its owner the right to exclude others from practicing the claimed invention, injunctive relief is the remedy of choice in most infringement actions, judicial or administrative. Professors Merges, Menell, & Lemley note:

It is hard to put a precise dollar amount on a particular piece of patented technology, especially over a protracted period. This ... valuation problem is the key to understanding why the injunction, and not damages, is the standard remedy in a patent case ... [T]he various requirements of the "uniqueness" intellectual property law (e.g., novelty and non-obviousness in patent law) almost guarantee that its subject matter will not be amenable to treatment as a commodity.

Robert P. Merges, Peter S. Menell & Mark A. Lemley, Intellectual Property in the New Technological Age 378 (5th ed. 2010).

Such valuation problems are not geography-specific; injunctive relief is the preferred remedy around the world.

1. INJUNCTIVE RELIEF

In the majority of cases, the most important enforcement remedy a patent owner has is the right to permanent injunctive relief to stop present and future infringement of the owner's exclusive rights. The value of an injunction lies in the fact that without it:

[T]he right to exclude granted by the patent would be diminished.... The patent owner would lack much of the "leverage," afforded by the right to exclude, to enjoy the full value of his invention in the market place. Without the right to obtain an injunction, the right to exclude granted to the patentee would have only a fraction of the value it was intended to have, and would no longer be as great an incentive to engage in the toils of scientific and technological research.

Smith Int'l, Inc. v. Hughes Tool Co., 718 F.2d 1573, 1577–78 (Fed. Cir. 1983).

In the United States, the grant of an injunction is a federal judicial remedy. The Patent Act, 35 U.S.C. §283, provides that the "courts having jurisdiction of cases under this title may grant injunctions in accordance with the principles of equity to prevent the violation of any right secured by patent, on such terms as the court deems reasonable." In most countries, as in the United States, injunctive relief is a judicial remedy, although it is also available from the International Trade Commission, as discussed in Chapter 12, *infra*. In China, moreover, administrative authorities also have jurisdiction to enjoin infringing activity.

a. United States

Permanent injunctive relief has almost always been available in the United States following a final judgment of patent infringement. In *eBay Inc. v. MercExchange, L.L.C.,* 547 U.S. 388 (2006), the United States Supreme Court examined whether injunctive relief in patent cases should, absent exceptional circumstances, be awarded as a general rule.

eBay Inc. v. MercExchange, L.L.C.

Supreme Court of the United States
547 U.S. 388 (2006)

■ Justice THOMAS delivered the opinion of the Court.

. . .

I

Petitioner eBay operates a popular Internet Web site that allows private sellers to list goods they wish to sell, either through an auction or at a fixed price. Petitioner Half.com, now a wholly owned subsidiary of eBay, operates a similar Web site. Respondent MercExchange, L.L.C., holds a number of patents, including a business method patent for an electronic market designed to facilitate the sale of goods between private individuals by establishing a central authority to promote trust among participants. *See* U.S. Patent No. 5,845,265. MercExchange sought to license its patent to eBay and Half.com, as it had previously done with other companies, but the parties failed to reach an agreement. MercExchange subsequently filed a patent infringement suit against eBay and Half.com in the United States District Court for the Eastern District of Virginia. A jury found that MercExchange's patent was valid, that eBay and Half.com had infringed that patent, and that an award of damages was appropriate.

Following the jury verdict, the District Court denied MercExchange's motion for permanent injunctive relief. The Court of Appeals for the Federal Circuit reversed, applying its "general rule that courts will issue permanent injunctions against patent infringement absent exceptional circumstances." We granted certiorari to determine the appropriateness of this general rule.

II

According to well-established principles of equity, a plaintiff seeking a permanent injunction must satisfy a four-factor test before a court may grant such relief. A plaintiff must demonstrate: (1) that it has suffered an irreparable injury; (2) that remedies available at law, such as monetary damages, are inadequate to compensate for that injury; (3) that, considering the balance of hardships between the plaintiff and defendant, a remedy in equity is warranted; and (4) that the public interest would not be disserved by a permanent injunction. The decision to grant or deny permanent injunctive relief is an act of equitable discretion by the district court, reviewable on appeal for abuse of discretion.

These familiar principles apply with equal force to disputes arising under the Patent Act. As this Court has long recognized, "a major departure from the long tradition of equity practice should not be lightly implied." Nothing in the Patent Act indicates that Congress intended such a departure. To the contrary, the Patent Act expressly provides that injunctions "may" issue "in accordance with the principles of equity." 35 U.S.C. §283.

To be sure, the Patent Act also declares that "patents shall have the attributes of personal property,"§261, including "the right to exclude others from making, using, offering for sale, or selling the invention," §154(a)(1). According to the Court of Appeals, this statutory right to exclude alone justifies its general rule in favor of permanent injunctive relief. But the creation of a right is distinct from the provision of remedies for violations of that right. Indeed, the Patent Act itself indicates that patents shall have the attributes of personal property "[s]ubject to the provisions of this title," 35 U.S.C. §261, including, presumably, the provision that injunctive relief "may" issue only "in accordance with the principles of equity," § 283.

This approach is consistent with our treatment of injunctions under the Copyright Act. Like a patent owner, a copyright holder possesses "the right to exclude others from using his property." Like the Patent Act, the Copyright Act provides that courts "may" grant injunctive relief "on such terms as it may deem reasonable to prevent or restrain infringement of a copyright." 17 U.S.C. §502(a). And as in our decision today, this Court has consistently rejected invitations to replace traditional equitable considerations with a rule that an injunction automatically follows a determination that a copyright has been infringed.

Neither the District Court nor the Court of Appeals below fairly applied these traditional equitable principles in deciding respondent's motion for a permanent injunction. Although the District Court recited the traditional four-factor test, it appeared to adopt certain expansive principles suggesting that injunctive relief could not issue in a broad swath of cases. Most notably, it concluded that a "plaintiff's willingness to license its patents" and "its lack of commercial activity in practicing the patents" would be sufficient to establish that the patent holder would not suffer irreparable harm if an injunction did not issue. But traditional equitable principles do not permit such broad classifications. For example, some patent holders, such as university researchers or self-made inventors, might reasonably prefer to license their patents, rather than undertake efforts to secure the financing necessary to bring their works to market themselves. Such patent holders may be able to satisfy the traditional four-factor test, and we see no basis for categorically denying them the opportunity to do so. To the extent that the District Court adopted such a categorical rule, then, its analysis cannot be squared with the principles of equity adopted by Congress. . . .

In reversing the District Court, the Court of Appeals departed in the opposite direction from the four-factor test. The court articulated a "general rule," unique to patent disputes, "that a permanent injunction will issue once infringement and validity have been adjudged." The court further indicated that injunctions should be denied only in the "unusual" case, under "exceptional circumstances" and "'in rare instances . . . to protect the public interest.'" Just as the District Court erred in its categorical denial of injunctive relief, the Court of Appeals erred in its categorical grant of such relief.

Because we conclude that neither court below correctly applied the traditional four-factor framework that governs the award of injunctive relief, we vacate the judgment of the Court of Appeals, so that the District Court may apply that framework in the first instance. In doing so, we take no position on whether permanent injunctive relief should or should not issue in this particular case, or indeed in any number of other disputes arising under the Patent Act. We hold only that the decision whether to grant or deny injunctive relief rests within the equitable discretion of the district courts, and that such discretion must be exercised consistent with traditional principles of equity, in patent disputes no less than in other cases governed by such standards.

Accordingly, we vacate the judgment of the Court of Appeals, and remand for further proceedings consistent with this opinion.

It is so ordered.

Chief Justice ROBERTS, with whom Justice SCALIA and Justice GINS-BURG join, concurring.

I agree with the Court's holding that "the decision whether to grant or deny injunctive relief rests within the equitable discretion of the district courts, and that such discretion must be exercised consistent with traditional principles of equity, in patent disputes no less than in other cases governed by such standards," and I join the opinion of the Court. That opinion rightly rests on the proposition that "a major departure from the long tradition of equity practice should not be lightly implied."

From at least the early 19th century, courts have granted injunctive relief upon a finding of infringement in the vast majority of patent cases. This "long tradition of equity practice" is not surprising, given the difficulty of protecting a right to *exclude* through monetary remedies that allow an infringer to *use* an invention against the patentee's wishes—a difficulty that often implicates the first two factors of the traditional four-factor test. This historical practice, as the Court holds, does not *entitle* a patentee to a permanent injunction or justify a *general rule* that such injunctions should issue. . . At the same time, there is a difference between exercising equitable discretion pursuant to the established four-factor test and writing on an entirely clean slate. "Discretion is not whim, and limiting discretion according to legal standards helps promote the basic principle of justice that like cases should be decided alike." When it comes to discerning and applying those standards, in this area as others, "a page of history is worth a volume of logic."

Justice KENNEDY, with whom Justice STEVENS, Justice SOUTER, and Justice BREYER join, concurring.

The Court is correct, in my view, to hold that courts should apply the well-established, four-factor test—without resort to categorical rules—in deciding whether to grant injunctive relief in patent cases. The Chief Justice is also correct that history may be instructive in applying this test. The traditional practice of issuing injunctions against patent infringers, however, does not seem to rest on "the difficulty of protecting a right to *exclude* through monetary remedies that allow an infringer to *use* an invention against the patentee's wishes." Both the terms of the Patent Act and the traditional view of injunctive relief accept that the existence of a right to exclude does not dictate the remedy for a violation of that right. To the extent earlier cases establish a pattern of granting an injunction against patent infringers almost as a matter of course, this pattern simply illustrates the result of the four-factor test in the contexts then prevalent. The lesson of the historical practice, therefore, is most helpful and instructive when the circumstances of a case bear substantial parallels to litigation the courts have confronted before.

In cases now arising trial courts should bear in mind that in many instances the nature of the patent being enforced and the economic function of the patent holder present considerations quite unlike earlier cases. An industry has developed in which firms use patents not as a basis for producing and selling goods but, instead, primarily for obtaining licensing fees... For these firms, an injunction, and the potentially serious sanctions arising from its violation, can be employed as a bargaining tool to charge exorbitant fees to companies that seek to buy licenses to practice the patent. When the patented invention is but a small component of the product the companies seek to produce and the threat of an injunction is employed simply for undue leverage in negotiations, legal damages may well be sufficient to compensate for the infringement and an injunction may not serve the public interest. In addition injunctive relief may have different consequences for the burgeoning number of patents over business methods, which were not of much economic and legal significance in earlier times. The potential vagueness and suspect validity of some of these patents may affect the calculus under the four-factor test.

The equitable discretion over injunctions, granted by the Patent Act, is well suited to allow courts to adapt to the rapid technological and legal developments in the patent system. For these reasons it should be recognized that district courts must determine whether past practice fits the circumstances of the cases before them. With these observations, I join the opinion of the Court.

NOTES AND QUESTIONS

1. Of the three *eBay* opinions in this case, which do you find the most convincing? Why? How significant are the distinctions among the three opinions?

2. Justice Kennedy's concurrence refers to the fact that an "industry has developed in which firms use patents... primarily for obtaining licensing fees." Participants in that industry are sometimes pejoratively referred to as "patent trolls." Do you agree, as Justice Kennedy suggests, that patent trolls deserve less entitlement to an injunction than patent owners who choose to work their inventions? Why or why not? Should special rules be put in place to diminish the economic impact of patent trolls? According to some commentators, the "troll" hype may be greater than the reality:

> [W]e find little evidence that "trolls" are posing a serious problem. The number of patent licensing firms—the most obvious candidate for the role of troll—active in cases led in the study years was quite modest. Most of these licensing firms were small and they, for the most part, were equally likely to sue small, medium and large firms. However, there is some evidence that when a licensing firm sues a large firm they were less likely to pursue a judgment or a trial than were other small firms. Thus, our results suggest that patent litigation is not dominated by "trolls," but that the best candidates for the "troll" moniker do seem to behave differently when suing the largest firms than do other firms of similar size. Care needs to be used in interpreting this result, however, since the very fact that they were not present in large numbers may make it statistically difficult to analyze their behavior.

Gwendolyn P. Ball & Jay Kesan, *Transaction Costs and Trolls: Strategic Behavior by Individual Inventors, Small Firms and Entrepreneurs in Patent Litigation* 25 (Illinois Public Law and Legal Theory Papers Series No. 08–21, 2009), http://ssrn.com/abstract=1337166.

However, others see a more serious problem:

> Because of flaws in the patent system and government leaders' misunderstandings, there is an arms race of sorts happening in the tech industry that is sapping billions out of the economy and crushing technology startups. This system is enriching patent trolls—companies that buy patents in order to extort money from innovators. These trolls are like a modern day mafia. . . . The larger players can afford to buy patents to deter the trolls, but the smaller players—the innovative startups—can't.

> In a Sept. 2010 paper titled *Patent Quality and Settlement Among Repeat Patent Litigants*, [Mark] Lemley, John Allison of University of Texas, and Joshua Walker of Stanford Law School . . . found that repeat patent plaintiffs — "those who sue eight or more times on the same patents...are responsible for a sizeable fraction of all patent

lawsuits." Indeed, 106 out of roughly 1 million patents (or .0001 percent) in force were responsible for more than 10 percent of all patent assertions. This isn't based on the strengths of the patents; many of these are among the weakest and least defensible. When the most-litigated patents go to trial, slightly fewer than 11 percent of patent holders win their cases, compared with 47 percent of those that were litigated just once.

Vivek Wahdwa, *Where Are the Jobs? Ask the Patent Trolls*, Wash. Post, May 7, 2012, at 1, citing Mark A. Lemley et al., Patent Quality and Settlement among Repeat Patent Litigants, 99 GEO. L.J. 677 (2011). A recent study commissioned by the non-partisan Government Accountability Office found the following:

> [L]awsuits filed by monetizers [a.k.a trolls] increased from 22% of the cases filed five years ago to almost 40% of the cases filed in the most recent year. In addition . . . of the 5 parties in the sample who filed the greatest number of lawsuits during the period studied, 4 were monetizers. Only one was an operating company.

Sara Jeruss, Robin Feldman, & Joshua Walker, *The America Invents Act 500: Effects of Patent Monetization Entities on US Litigation*, 11 DUKE L. & TECH. REV. 357 (2012).

For further varying views on the innovation and patent litigation impact of trolls and other non-practicing entities, see, e.g., Colleen V. Chien, *Of Trolls, Davids, Goliaths, and Kings: Narratives and Evidence in the Litigation of High-Tech Patents*, 87 N.C. L. REV. 157 (2009); and John M. Golden, *"Patent Trolls" and Patent Remedies*," 85 TEX. L. REV. 2111 (2007)".

3. According to Professor Cotter, U.S. courts are much more careful in granting permanent injunctive relief post-*eBay*. He observes that injunctive awards have been made only three-quarters of the time to prevailing patentees, and that this remedy is far less likely to be available to non-practicing entities. *See* Thomas F. Cotter, *A Research Agenda for the Comparative Law and Economics of Patent Remedies*, in Patent Law in Global Perspective, *in* (PATENT LAW IN GLOBAL PERSPECTIVE, RUTH L. OKEDIJI & MARGO BAGLEY, EDS., Oxford University Press, forthcoming 2013). He further notes that the availability of injunctive relief is more common outside the United States despite the flexibility of the TRIPS Agreement on this issue, suggesting a possible trade-off between injunctive relief and the availability of other defenses:

> [T]he TRIPS Agreement appears to provide considerable leeway for nations to decide whether or under what conditions permanent injunctions should be awarded. The secondary literature nevertheless strongly suggests that permanent injunctions remain the norm in many countries. To the extent most other nations remain more firmly rooted than the United States post-*eBay* in the "property rule" camp, however, there could be a number of plausible explanations that merit further analysis. One that immediately leaps to mind is the somewhat greater receptivity of some patent systems to compul-

sory licensing. Even post-TRIPS, many industrialized nations have retained the option of compulsory licensing as a solution to the blocking patents phenomenon. Many of them also have in place more expansive exceptions for experimental use than is available in the United States. Conceivably, these exceptions could provide a needed safety valve in a substantial number of cases in which the public interest (in the language of *eBay*) would be "disserved" by injunctive relief, and in this manner relieve some of the pressure to deviate from the injunctive relief norm in cases in which do not fall within the scope of these exceptions; in other words, some cases may self-select out and wind up being negotiated rather than litigated. It also could be that the phenomenon of patent holdup is either not (yet?) perceived to be a problem in many countries other than the United States, in which case the need to confer discretion upon judges to deny requests for permanent injunctions may not appear pressing.

Id.

Which approach do you think is preferable? Having more defenses to infringement and administrative compulsory licenses but readily granting injunctive relief for proven infringement, or the U.S. approach with few defenses, and virtually no compulsory licenses (other than the *de facto* kind created when a judge denies a permanent injunction and allows for an "ongoing royalty")? For more on the patent holdup problem, *see* Mark A. Lemley & Carl Shapiro, *Patent Holdup and Royalty Stacking*, 85 TEX. LAW REV. 1991 (2007).

b. Europe: Cross-Border Injunctions

Just as patentees have sought to have foreign patent infringement adjudicated in U.S. and Japanese courts, they have sought similar relief in Europe. As noted in Chapter 1, the Brussels Regime (comprising the Brussels Convention (BC), Lugano Convention (LC), and the Brussels Regulation—which largely supplants the earlier two) provides EU-wide jurisdictional rules. It also allows courts to grant cross-border injunctions under certain circumstances. The basic premise of these provisions is that a defendant must be sued where she is domiciled, but there are several exceptions to this rule, such as in a tort action being sued where the tort occurred. Also, national courts have exclusive jurisdiction of issues of validity of IP rights. The following case is the latest in a series of decisions from the EU's highest court on the availability of cross-border injunctive relief.

SOLVAY SA v. HONEYWELL FLUORINE PRODUCTS EUROPE B.V.

Court of Justice of the European Union
Judgment of the Court (Third Chamber), 12 July 2012
Case C-616/10

1. This reference for a preliminary ruling concerns the interpretation of Articles 6(1), 22(4) and 31 of Council Regulation (EC) No 44/2001 of 22 December 2000 on jurisdiction and the recognition and enforcement of judgments in civil and commercial matters (OJ 2001 L 12, p. 1).

2. The reference was submitted in the course of proceedings between (i) Solvay SA, established in Belgium ("Solvay") and (ii) Honeywell Fluorine Products Europe BV, established in the Netherlands, and Honeywell Belgium NV and Honeywell Europe NV, both established in Belgium, (together "the Honeywell companies"), regarding the alleged infringement by various parties of a European patent.

LEGAL CONTEXT

. . . .

EUROPEAN UNION LAW

6. Recitals 11, [and] 15 . . . in the preamble to Regulation No 44/2001 [the Brussels Regulation] state:

'(11) The rules of jurisdiction must be highly predictable and founded on the principle that jurisdiction is generally based on the defendant's domicile and jurisdiction must always be available on this ground save in a few well-defined situations in which the subject-matter of the litigation or the autonomy of the parties warrants a different linking factor. . .

(15) In the interests of the harmonious administration of justice it is necessary to minimise the possibility of concurrent proceedings and to ensure that irreconcilable judgments will not be given in two Member States. . .

7. Under Article 2 of that regulation:

'1. Subject to this Regulation, persons domiciled in a Member State shall, whatever their nationality, be sued in the courts of that Member State.

2. Persons who are not nationals of the Member State in which they are domiciled shall be governed by the rules of jurisdiction applicable to nationals of that State.'

8. Article 6(1), which is part of Section 2 of Chapter II of that regulation, entitled 'Special jurisdiction', provides:

'A person domiciled in a Member State may also be sued:

(1) where he is one of a number of defendants, in the courts for the place where any one of them is domiciled, provided the claims are so closely connected that it is expedient to hear and determine them together to avoid the risk of irreconcilable judgments resulting from separate proceedings.'

9. According to Article 22(4) of that regulation:

'The following courts shall have exclusive jurisdiction, regardless of domicile:

. . .

(4) in proceedings concerned with the registration or validity of patents, trade marks, designs, or other similar rights required to be deposited or registered, the courts of the Member State in which the deposit or registration has been applied for, has taken place or is under the terms of a Community instrument or an international convention deemed to have taken place.

Without prejudice to the jurisdiction of the European Patent Office under the [Munich Convention], the courts of each Member State shall have exclusive jurisdiction, regardless of domicile, in proceedings concerned with the registration or validity of any European patent granted for that State.'

10. Article 25 of that regulation is worded as follows:

'Where a court of a Member State is seised of a claim which is principally concerned with a matter over which the courts of another Member State have exclusive jurisdiction by virtue of Article 22, it shall declare of its own motion that it has no jurisdiction.'

11. Pursuant to Article 31 of that regulation:

'Application may be made to the courts of a Member State for such provisional, including protective, measures as may be available under the law of that State, even if, under this Regulation, the courts of another Member State have jurisdiction as to the substance of the matter.'

The dispute in the main proceedings and the questions referred for a preliminary ruling

12. On 6 March 2009, Solvay, the proprietor of European patent EP 0 858 440, brought an action in the Rechtbank 's-Gravenhage for infringement of the national parts of that patent, as in force in Denmark, Ireland, Greece, Luxembourg, Austria, Portugal, Finland, Sweden, Liechtenstein and Switzerland, against the Honeywell companies for marketing a product HFC-245 fa, manufactured by Honeywell International Inc. and identical to the product covered by that patent.

13. Specifically, Solvay accuses Honeywell Flourine Products Europe BV and Honeywell Europe NV of performing the reserved actions in the whole of Europe and Honeywell Belgium NV of performing the reserved actions in Northern and Central Europe.

14. In the course of its action for infringement, on 9 December 2009 Solvay also lodged an interim claim against the Honeywell companies, seeking provisional relief in the form of a cross-border prohibition against infringement until a decision had been made in the main proceedings.

15. In the interim proceedings, the Honeywell companies raised the defence of invalidity of the national parts of the patent concerned without, however, having brought or even declared their intention of bringing proceedings for the annulment of the national parts of that patent, and without contesting the competence of the Dutch court to hear both the main proceedings and the interim proceedings.

16. In those circumstances, the Rechtbank's-Gravenhage decided to stay the proceedings and to refer the following questions to the Court of Justice for a preliminary ruling:

'Regarding Article 6(1) of [Regulation No 44/2001]:

> 1. In a situation where two or more companies from different Member States, in proceedings pending before a court of one of those Member States, are each separately accused of committing an infringement of the same national part of a European patent which is in force in yet another Member State by virtue of their performance of reserved actions with regard to the same product, does the possibility arise of "irreconcilable judgments" resulting from separate proceedings as referred to in Article 6(1) of [Regulation No 44/2001]?

Regarding Article 22(4) of [Regulation No 44/2001]:

> 2. Is Article 22(4) of [Regulation No 44/2001] applicable in proceedings seeking provisional relief on the basis of a foreign patent (such as a provisional cross-border prohibition against infringement), if the defendant argues by way of defence that the patent invoked is invalid, taking into account that the court in that case does not make a final decision on the validity of the patent invoked but makes an assessment as to how the court having jurisdiction under Article 22(4) of [that] Regulation would rule in that regard, and that the application for interim relief in the form of a prohibition against infringement shall be refused if, in the opinion of the court, a reasonable, non-negligible possibility exists that the patent invoked would be declared invalid by the competent court?

. . . .

ON THE QUESTIONS REFERRED

THE FIRST QUESTION

17. By its first question, the referring court asks, in essence, whether Article 6(1) of Regulation No 44/2001 must be interpreted as meaning that a situation where two or more companies established in different Member States, in proceedings pending before a court of one of those Member States, are each separately accused of committing an infringement of the same national part of a European patent which is in force in yet another Member State by virtue of their performance of reserved actions with regard to the same product, is capable of leading to 'irreconcilable judgments' resulting from separate proceedings as referred to in that provision.

18. First of all, it must be observed that Article 6(1) of Regulation No 44/2001 provides, in order to avoid irreconcilable judgments resulting from separate proceedings, that a defendant may be sued, where he is one of a number of defendants, in the courts for the place where any one of them is domiciled, provided the claims are so closely connected that it is expedient to hear and determine them together. . . .

20. Moreover, that special rule of jurisdiction must be interpreted in the light, first, of recital 11 in the preamble to Regulation No 44/2001, according to which the rules of jurisdiction must be highly predictable and founded on the principle that jurisdiction is generally based on the defendant's domicile and jurisdiction must always be available on this ground save in a few well-defined situations in which the subject-matter of the litigation or the autonomy of the parties warrants a different linking factor.

21. That special rule of jurisdiction, because it derogates from the principle stated in Article 2 of Regulation No 44/2001 that jurisdiction be based on the defendant's domicile, must be strictly interpreted and cannot be given an interpretation going beyond the cases expressly envisaged by that regulation.

22. In addition, that rule cannot be interpreted in such a way as to allow an applicant to make a claim against a number of defendants with the sole object of ousting the jurisdiction of the courts of the State where one of those defendants is domiciled. . . .

24. The Court has however stated in this connection that, in order for judgments to be regarded as at risk of being irreconcilable within the meaning of Article 6(1) of Regulation No 44/2001, it is not sufficient that there be a divergence in the outcome of the dispute, but that divergence must also arise in the same situation of fact and law (*see* Case C-539/03 Roche Nederland and Others [2006] ECR I-6535, paragraph 26; Freeport, paragraph 40; and Painer, paragraph 79).

25. As regards the assessment of the existence of the same situation, the Court has ruled, first, that the existence of the same situation of fact cannot be inferred where the defendants are different and the infringements they are accused of, committed in different Contracting States, are not the same. Secondly, it has held that the same situation of law cannot be inferred where infringement proceedings are brought before a number of courts in different Contracting States in respect of a European patent granted in each of those States and those actions are brought against defendants domiciled in those States in respect of acts allegedly committed in their territory (*see* Roche Nederland and Others, paragraphs 27 and 31).

26. A European patent continues to be governed . . . by the national law of each of the Contracting States for which it has been granted. By the same token, any action for infringement of a European patent must, as is apparent from Article 64(3) of that convention, be examined in the light of the relevant national law in force in each of the States for which it has been granted.

27. It follows from the specific features of a case such as that in the main proceedings that potential divergences in the outcome of the proceedings are likely to arise in the same situation of fact and law, so that it is possible that they will culminate in irreconcilable judgments resulting from separate proceedings.

28. As the Advocate General observed in point 25 of his Opinion, were Article 6(1) of Regulation No 44/2001 not applicable, two courts would each have to examine the alleged infringements in the light of the different national legislation governing the various national parts of the European patent alleged to have been infringed. They would, for instance, be called upon to assess according to the same Finnish law the infringement of the Finnish part of the European patent by the Honeywell companies as a result of the marketing of an identical infringing product in Finland.

29. In order to assess, in a situation such as that at issue in the main proceedings, whether there is a connection between the different claims brought before it and thus whether there is a risk of irreconcilable judgments if those claims were determined separately, it is for the national court to take into account, inter alia, the dual fact that, first, the defendants in the main proceeding are each separately accused of committing the same infringements with respect to the same products and, secondly, such infringements were committed in the same Member States, so that they adversely affect the same national parts of the European patent at issue.

30. In the light of the foregoing, the answer to the first question is that Article 6(1) of Regulation No 44/2001 must be interpreted as meaning that a situation where two or more companies from different Member

States, in proceedings pending before a court of one of those Member States, are each separately accused of committing an infringement of the same national part of a European patent which is in force in yet another Member State by virtue of their performance of reserved actions with regard to the same product, is capable of leading to 'irreconcilable judgments' resulting from separate proceedings as referred to in that provision. It is for the referring court to assess whether such a risk exists, taking into account all the relevant information in the file.

THE SECOND QUESTION

31. By its second question, the referring court asks whether Article 22(4) of Regulation No 44/2001 is applicable in proceedings seeking provisional relief on the basis of a foreign patent, such as a provisional cross-border prohibition against infringement, if the defendants in the main proceedings argue by way of defence that the patent invoked is invalid, taking into account that the court in that case does not make a final decision on the validity of the patent invoked but makes an assessment as to how the court having jurisdiction under Article 22(4) of that Regulation would rule in that regard, and that the application for interim relief in the form of a prohibition against infringement shall be refused if, in the opinion of the court, a reasonable, non-negligible possibility exists that the patent invoked would be declared invalid by the competent court.

32. It is apparent from the wording of the question referred for a preliminary ruling and the order for reference that the issue at the heart of the dispute in the main proceedings concerns a procedure for the adoption of an interim measure governed by the rule of jurisdiction set out in Article 31 of Regulation No 44/2001.

33. Consequently, the question asked must be construed as seeking to ascertain essentially whether Article 22(4) of Regulation No 44/2001 must be interpreted as precluding, in circumstances such as those at issue in the case in the main proceedings, the application of Article 31 of that regulation.

34. In this connection, it is apparent from Article 31 of Regulation No 44/2001 that the court of a Member State is authorised to rule on a claim for a provisional, including a protective, measure even if, under that regulation, the courts of another Member State have jurisdiction as to the substance of the matter.

35. Furthermore, as follows from Article 22(4) thereof, Regulation No 44/2001 lays down for a rule of exclusive jurisdiction according to which, in proceedings concerned with the registration or validity of patents, the courts of the Member State in which the deposit or registration has been applied for, has taken place or is under the terms of a Community instrument or an international convention deemed to have taken place, have exclusive jurisdiction.

36. Concerning, first of all, the wording of Articles 22(4) and 31 of Regulation No 44/2001, it should be noted that those provisions are intended to regulate different situations and each has a distinct field of application. Thus, whilst Article 22(4) concerns the attribution of jurisdiction to rule on the substance in proceedings relating to a clearly defined area, Article 31 is designed to apply regardless of any jurisdiction as to the substance.

37. Moreover, those two provisions do not refer to one another. . . .

40. It follows from this that Article 31 is independent in scope from Article 22(4) of that regulation. As noted in paragraph 34 above, Article 31 applies where a claim for provisional, including protective, measures is brought before a court other than the court which has jurisdiction as to the substance, so that Article 22(4), which concerns the jurisdiction as to substance, cannot, as a rule, be interpreted so as to derogate from Article 31 and, consequently, cause it to be disapplied. . . .

48. Accordingly, it must be established whether the specific scope of Article 22(4) of Regulation No 44/2001, as interpreted by the Court, affects the application of Article 31 of that regulation in a situation such as that at issue in the main proceedings, which concerns an action for infringement in which the invalidity of a European patent has been raised, at an interim stage, as a defence to the adoption of a provisional measure concerning cross-border prohibition against infringement.

49. According to the referring court, the court before which the interim proceedings have been brought does not make a final decision on the validity of the patent invoked but makes an assessment as to how the court having jurisdiction under Article 22(4) of the regulation would rule in that regard, and will refuse to adopt the provisional measure sought if it considers that there is a reasonable, non-negligible possibility that the patent invoked would be declared invalid by the competent court.

50. In those circumstances, it is apparent that there is no risk of conflicting decisions . . ., since the provisional decision taken by the court before which the interim proceedings have been brought will not in any way prejudice the decision to be taken on the substance by the court having jurisdiction under Article 22(4) of Regulation No 44/2001. Thus, the reasons which led the Court to interpret widely the jurisdiction provided for in Article 22(4) of Regulation No 44/2001 do not require that, in a case such as that in the main proceedings, Article 31 of that regulation should be disapplied.

51. In the light of all the foregoing considerations, the answer to the second question is that Article 22(4) of Regulation No 44/2001 must be interpreted as not precluding, in circumstances such as those at issue in the main proceedings, the application of Article 31 of that regulation. . . .

On those grounds, the Court (Third Chamber) hereby rules:

1. Article 6(1) of Council Regulation (EC) No 44/2001 of 22 December 2000 on jurisdiction and the recognition and enforcement of judgments in civil and commercial matters, must be interpreted as meaning that a situation where two or more companies established in different Member States, in proceedings pending before a court of one of those Member States, are each separately accused of committing an infringement of the same national part of a European patent which is in force in yet another Member State by virtue of their performance of reserved actions with regard to the same product, is capable of leading to 'irreconcilable judgments' resulting from separate proceedings as referred to in that provision. It is for the referring court to assess whether such a risk exists, taking into account all the relevant information in the file.

2. Article 22(4) of Regulation No 44/2001 must be interpreted as not precluding, in circumstances such as those at issue in the main proceedings, the application of Article 31 of that regulation.

NOTES AND QUESTIONS

1. In *Solvay*, the CJEU upheld the viability of cross-border injunctions in patent cases; however, the Court was not writing on a clean slate. In July 2006, the CJEU handed down two decisions on the same day that, at the time, seemed to spell the end of cross-border injunctions in patent cases: *Gesellschaft für Antriebstechnik mbH & Co. KG v. Lamellen und Kupplungsbau Beteiligungs KG*, 2006 E.C.R. I-6509, Case C-4/03 (*GAT v. LuK*), and *Roche Nederland BV v. Primus*, Case C-539/03, 2006 E.C.R. I-6535. In *GAT v. LuK*, LuK alleged that GAT was infringing two of its French patents. GAT then brought a declaratory judgment action in Germany asserting non-infringement and that the patents were invalid. The German Court, unsure of its jurisdiction, referred questions to the CJEU, which held that the exclusive jurisdiction rule of Article 16(4) of the Brussels Convention applied to all proceedings in which the issue of patent validity was raised, including declaratory judgment actions. In *Roche v. Primus*, U.S. patentees sued eight affiliated defendants in the Netherlands for patent infringement taking place in several EU countries, according to a common plan coordinated by the Netherlands-based affiliate (the "spider in the web" theory). The patentee based jurisdiction on the following Brussels Regulation provisions:

Brussels Regulation Art. 2

Subject to the provisions of this convention, persons domiciled in a Contracting State shall, whatever their nationality, be sued in the courts of that State.

Brussels Regulation Art. 6(1)

[A defendant domiciled in a Contracting State] may also be sued:

where he is **one of a number of defendants**, in the courts for the place **where any one of them is domiciled**. (Emphasis added).

However, the Regulation also requires that there "must exist, between the various actions brought by the same plaintiff against different defendants, a connection of such a kind that it is expedient to determine the actions together in order to avoid the risk of irreconcilable judgments resulting from separate proceedings." . . .

The patentee lost in the trial court but won on appeal and cross-border injunctions issued. The ECJ reversed, denying cross-border injunctive relief, holding that because patents are issued by different governments, there was no "connection of such a kind that it is expedient to determine the actions together in order to avoid the risk of irreconcilable judgments."

2. The CJEU decision in *Solvay* confines *Roche* to its specific facts by allowing a court, such as the Dutch court in this case, to assess whether there is a risk of irreconcilable judgments and to assume jurisdiction over the action if necessary. In other words, Article 6(1) does not apply when different companies, established in different Member States, all infringe different national parts of the same European patent, in their own country. In this case, Solvay had accused three related Honeywell companies (one Dutch, two Belgian) of infringing its European patent in several European countries and sought cross-border injunctions from the Dutch court. In framing questions for the CJEU, the Dutch court distinguished the facts from *Roche v. Primus* and *GAT v. LuK*, noting, among other things, that there was indeed the possibility of irreconcilable judgments. The court, under Article 2, had jurisdiction of the Dutch company and, since validity was not raised, it could issue cross-border injunctions for that company's activity in Belgium and elsewhere, yet a Belgian court would have jurisdiction over the same issues for the Belgian companies.

While *Solvay* was pending, Dutch courts continued to grant preliminary cross-border relief, such as in *Apple v. Samsung,* District Court of The Hague, 24 July 2011, where the court granted a preliminary injunction against three Dutch Samsung defendants. This practice has now been ratified by the CJEU, and we can expect to see more such injunctions issue in the future.

3. Patentees are not the only ones thinking strategically about patent infringement litigation. Savvy defendants have sought declaratory judgment actions of non-infringement in jurisdictions known to have very slow court proceedings such as Italy and Belgium. By bringing such an action before the patentee can sue for infringement elsewhere, the defendant potentially can drag out the litigation because, under the BC, another court would have to stay its action (Brussels Convention Article 21 requires all courts except the "first seized" to stay their proceedings). However, the usefulness of such "torpedo" actions has been limited by court decisions. For example, according to the Italian Supreme Court in *BL Macchine Automatiche Spa v. Windmoller & Holscher KG,* Cass., sez. un, 19 dicembre 2003, n. 19550, Giur. It. 2004, I, Il Corriere giuridico 2004 pp. 162–164 (It.), the court does not have jurisdiction if the patentee is not domiciled in Italy. Nevertheless, because it can take years for a slow court to even make the determination that it does not have jurisdiction, such torpedo actions remain a strategic option. *See* Isabella Bet-

ti, *Patents: The Italian Torpedo is Dead: Long Live the Italian Torpedo*, 3 J. INTELL. PROP. L. & PRAC. 6 (2008).

4. Consider the following hypothetical: You are a new associate in a law firm. One of the partners comes by and tells you that one of the firm's clients, ACME Products, has determined that a Belgian company is manufacturing and proceeding to sell a product very similar to ACME's best-selling widget, "The Widgerator®" in France, Italy, the Netherlands, and Germany. Your firm obtained patents on The Widgerator® in all of the countries in which the Belgian company is operating. The client wants to stop the perceived infringement, but wants to avoid protracted litigation in each country in which infringement is occurring. In fact, the client would like to sue for infringement of *all* of its patents on The Widgerator® in one court, one action, or at least in as few locales as possible. The partner asks you to investigate whether this is a viable option. Based on *Solvay v. Honeywell*, how would you respond?

2. DAMAGES

In addition to injunctive relief, monetary awards are a key remedy for patentees whose patents have been infringed. National approaches to damages vary significantly, as do the justifications that support particular categories of damage awards such as compensatory damages, enhanced damages, pre-judgment interest, and attorney's fees. Further, methods for calculating damages can vary from one jurisdiction to another. In the United States and other major economies, methods of computing patent damages for infringement typically fall into two main categories: the patentee's loss, measured by lost profits or a reasonable royalty, or disgorgement of the defendant's profits. For example, under UK law, a successful patent litigant is entitled to elect between damages (the patentee's loss) and an account of profits under Section 61 (1) (d) and 61 (2) of the 1977 Patents Act. Similar principles of election can be found in the patent statutes of other developed countries including Canada and Japan.

a. The Patentee's Loss

Courts in most countries exercise a significant amount of discretion in the methodology for computing damages. In the United States, according to the Federal Circuit Court of Appeals, the methodology for assessing and computing damages is within the "sound discretion" of the district courts. *See State Indus., Inc. v. Mor-Flo Indus., Inc.*, 883 F.2d 1573, 1576–1577 (Fed. Cir. 1989). However, disgorgement of a defendant's profits is only allowed in cases of design patent infringement (*see* 35 U.S.C. §289). Thus a patentee's loss is the only damages remedy available for utility patent infringement. Moreover, damages can be no less than a reasonable royalty by statute (35 U.S.C. §283). For a variety of reasons, a patentee may be unable or unwilling to establish her lost profits; thus calculation of a reasonable royalty rate—one the parties would have reached in a hypothetical pre-infringement negotiation—is the primary basis for U.S. patent infringement damages awards.

For many years, district courts in the United States used a 25 percent rule of thumb to assess a reasonable royalty. The 25 percent rule involved multiplying the number of infringing units sold by 25 percent of the value of the patented component, a number that may bear no relationship to the actual value of the patented contribution to the component and thus may result in a windfall for the patentee. The following case addressed the viability of this rule.

UNILOC USA, INC. V. MICROSOFT CORP.

United States Court of Appeals, Federal Circuit
632 F.3d 1292 (Fed. Cir. 2011)

■ LINN, Circuit Judge.

Uniloc USA, Inc. and Uniloc Singapore Private Limited (collectively, "Uniloc") appeal from the decision of the United States District Court for the District of Rhode Island granting Microsoft Corporation's ("Microsoft") motion for judgment as a matter of law ("JMOL") of non-infringement and no willful infringement of asserted claims of Uniloc's U.S. Patent No. 5,490,216 ("'216 patent"), and, in the alternative, granting a new trial on infringement and willfulness. Uniloc also appeals the district court's alternative grant of a new trial on damages. . . .

. . . Because the jury's damages award was fundamentally tainted by the use of a legally inadequate methodology, this court affirms the grant of a new trial on damages. . . .

I. BACKGROUND

Commercial software manufacturers like Microsoft lose significant sales as a result of the "casual copying" of software, where users install copies of a software program on multiple computers in violation of applicable software license conditions. Uniloc's '216 patent was an early attempt to combat such software piracy. . . .

Uniloc's '216 patent is directed to a software registration system to deter copying of software. The system allows the software to run without restrictions (in "use mode") only if the system determines that the software installation is legitimate. A representative embodiment functions as follows. First, a user intending to use the software in "use mode" enters certain user information when prompted, which may include a software serial number and/or name and address information. An algorithm on the user's computer (a "local licensee unique ID generating means") combines the inputted information into "a registration number unique to an intending licensee" (a "local licensee unique ID"). . . .

The accused product is Microsoft's Product Activation feature that acts as a gatekeeper to Microsoft's Word XP, Word 2003, and Windows XP software programs. Upon receipt of Microsoft's retail software program, the user must enter a 25–character alphanumeric product key contained within the packaging of Microsoft's retail products. If the Key is valid, the user is asked to agree to the End User License Agreement ("EULA"), by which the licensor-licensee relationship is initiated.

[The court affirmed the finding that Microsoft's product activation feature infringed the '216 patent.] . . .

A. NEW TRIAL ON DAMAGES

The jury here awarded Uniloc $388 million, based on the testimony of Uniloc's expert, Dr. Gemini. Dr. Gemini opined that damages should be $564,946,803. This was based on a hypothetical negotiation between Uniloc and Microsoft and the *Georgia–Pacific* factors. *See Georgia–Pacific Corp. v. U.S. Plywood Corp.*, 318 F. Supp. 1116 (S.D.N.Y.1970). Gemini began with an internal pre-litigation Microsoft document that stated:

> Product Keys are valuable for two major reasons. First, since Product Keys can be used to install a product and create a valid Product ID, you can associate a monetary value to them. An appraisal process found that a Product Key is worth anywhere between $10 and $10,000 depending on usage. Secondly, Product Keys contain short digital signature technology that Microsoft Research created. For these reasons, it is crucial that Product Keys are handled with maximum security.

Gemini took the lowest value, $10, and testified that this is "the isolated value of Product Activation." Gemini then applied the so-called "25 percent rule of thumb," hypothesizing that 25% of the value of the product would go to the patent owner and the other 75% would remain with Microsoft, resulting in a baseline royalty rate of $2.50 per license issued. Gemini justified the use of the rule of thumb because it has "been accepted by Courts as an appropriate methodology in determining damages, in [his] experience, in other cases." He then considered several of the Georgia–Pacific factors, with the idea being "to adjust this 25% up or down depending on how [the Georgia–Pacific factors] favor[ ] either party." At bottom, he concluded that the factors in favor of Uniloc and Microsoft generally balanced out and did not change the royalty rate. He then multiplied the $2.50 royalty rate by the number of new licenses to Office and Windows products, 225,978,721, to get a final reasonable royalty of $564,946,803. Gemini then "did kind of a check to determine whether that number was reasonable. It's obviously, you know, a significant amount of money. I wanted to check to make sure it was a reasonable number." The "check" was performed by "estimating the gross revenues for the accused products" by multiplying the 225,978,721 licenses by the average sales price per license of $85. The resulting gross revenue value was $19.28 billion. Gemini then calculated that his damages calculation resulted in a royalty rate over the gross revenue of Office and Windows of approximately 2.9%. Gemini presented this information in a demonstrative pie chart to accompany his testimony. . . . Gemini then opined that "in my experience, and data I've seen as far as industry royalty rates for software, which are generally above—on average, above 10% or 10, 11%, I felt that this royalty was reasonable and well within that range."

Microsoft had challenged the 25% rule in limine and attempted to exclude Mr. Gemini's testimony. The district court noted that "the concept of a 'rule of thumb' is perplexing in an area of the law where reliability and precision are deemed paramount," but rejected Microsoft's position because the rule has been widely accepted. The district court thus considered the use of the rule of thumb to be reasonable. Microsoft contested Gemini's use of the entire market value rule "check" because Product Activation was not the basis of the consumer demand for Microsoft's Office and Windows products. The district court agreed with Microsoft, and granted a new trial on damages, because the "$19 billion cat was never put back into the bag" and the jury may have "used the $19 billion figure to 'check' its significant award of $388,000,000." . . .

1. 25 PERCENT RULE

Section 284 of Title 35 of the United States Code provides that on finding infringement of a valid patent, damages shall "in no event [be] less than a reasonable royalty for the use made of the invention by the infringer, together with interest and costs as fixed by the court." In litigation, a reasonable royalty is often determined on the basis of a hypothetical negotiation, occurring between the parties at the time that infringement began. A reasonable royalty is the predominant measure of damages in patent infringement cases.

The 25 percent rule of thumb is a tool that has been used to approximate the reasonable royalty rate that the manufacturer of a patented product would be willing to offer to pay to the patentee during a hypothetical negotiation. Robert Goldscheider, John Jarosz and Carla Mulhern, *Use Of The 25 Per Cent Rule in Valuing IP*, 37 les Nouvelles 123, 123 (Dec. 2002) ("Valuing IP"). "The Rule suggests that the licensee pay a royalty rate equivalent to 25 per cent of its expected profits for the product that incorporates the IP at issue." *Id.* . . .

The underlying "assumption is that the licensee should retain a majority (i.e. 75 percent) of the profits, because it has undertaken substantial development, operational and commercialization risks, contributed other technology/IP and/or brought to bear its own development, operational and commercialization contributions." *Id.*

The rule was originally based on Goldscheider's observations of commercial licenses entered into by a "Swiss subsidiary of a large American company, with 18 licensees around the world, each having an exclusive territory." *Id.* The rights transferred were a portfolio of patents and other intellectual property apparently related to the patented products. *Id.* The term of each of these licenses was for three years, with the expectation that the licenses would be renewed. *Id.* at 123. The licensees "faced strong competition," and "were either first or second in sales volume, and probably profitability, in their respective market." *Id.*

According to its proponents, the veracity of the 25 percent rule has been "confirmed by a careful examination of years of licensing and profit data, across companies and industries." Goldscheider published a further empirical study in 2002, concluding that across all industries, the median royalty rate was 22.6 percent, and that the data supported the use of the 25 percent rule "as a tool of analysis.". . .

The 25 percent rule has, however, met its share of criticism that can be broadly separated into three categories. First, it fails to account for the unique relationship between the patent and the accused product. Second, it fails to account for the unique relationship between the parties. Finally, the rule is essentially arbitrary and does not fit within the model of the hypothetical negotiation within which it is based.

The admissibility of the bare 25 percent rule has never been squarely presented to this court. Nevertheless, this court has passively tolerated its use where its acceptability has not been the focus of the case, or where the parties disputed only the percentage to be applied (i.e. one-quarter to one-third), but agreed as to the rule's appropriateness. Lower courts have invariably admitted evidence based on the 25% rule, largely in reliance on its widespread acceptance or because its admissibility was uncontested. . . .

In *Daubert*, [*Daubert v. Merrell Dow Pharmaceuticals, Inc.*, 509 U.S. 579 (1993)], and *Kumho Tire*, [*Kumho Tire Co. v. Carmichael*, 526 U.S. 137 (1999)], the Supreme Court assigned to the district courts the responsibility of ensuring that all expert testimony must pertain to "scientific, technical, or other specialized knowledge" under Federal Rule of Evidence ("FRE") 702, which in turn required the judge to determine that the testimony was based on a firm scientific or technical grounding.

This court now holds as a matter of Federal Circuit law that the 25 percent rule of thumb is a fundamentally flawed tool for determining a baseline royalty rate in a hypothetical negotiation. Evidence relying on the 25 percent rule of thumb is thus inadmissible under *Daubert* and the Federal Rules of Evidence, because it fails to tie a reasonable royalty base to the facts of the case at issue.

The patentee bears the burden of proving damages. To properly carry this burden, the patentee must "sufficiently [tie the expert testimony on damages] to the facts of the case." If the patentee fails to tie the theory to the facts of the case, the testimony must be excluded. . . .

The bottom line . . . is that one major determinant of whether an expert should be excluded under *Daubert* is whether he has justified the application of a general theory to the facts of the case. Consistent with this conclusion, this court has held that "[a]ny evidence unrelated to the claimed invention does not support compensation for infringement but punishes beyond the reach of the statute." *ResQNet.com, Inc. v. Lansa, Inc.,* 594 F.3d 860, 869 (Fed.Cir.2010).

In *ResQNet, Lucent Technologies,* 580 F.3d 1301, and *Wordtech Systems, Inc. v. Integrated Networks Solutions, Inc.,* 609 F.3d 1308 (Fed.Cir.2010), this court determined that a patentee could not rely on license agreements that were "radically different from the hypothetical agreement under consideration" to determine a reasonable royalty. In Lucent Technologies, the patentee's expert relied in large part on "eight varied license agreements," four of which involved "PC-related patents," but either the specific subject matter of the patents was not explained to the jury or the license was "directed to a vastly different situation than the hypothetical licensing scenario of the present case," and four of which Lucent did not describe the relationship between the patented technology licensed therein and the licensee's products. This court noted that the "licenses relied on by the patentee in proving damages [must be] sufficiently comparable to the hypothetical license at issue in suit," and that the patentee's failure to do so "weighs strongly against the jury's award" relying on such non-comparable licenses. Similarly, in *ResQNet,* the patentee's expert "used licenses with no relationship to the claimed invention to drive the royalty rate up to unjustified double-digit levels," looking at licenses that did not mention the patents and had no "other discernible link to the claimed technology." This court rejected the expert's testimony, holding that the district court "must consider licenses that are commensurate with what the defendant has appropriated. If not, a prevailing plaintiff would be free to inflate the reasonable royalty analysis with conveniently selected licenses without an economic or other link to the technology in question." This court held that on remand, "the trial court should not rely on unrelated licenses to increase the reasonable royalty rate above rates more clearly linked to the economic demand for the claimed technology."

Similarly, in *Wordtech,* the patentee "introduced thirteen patent licenses that it previously granted to third parties for rights to some or all of the patents-in-suit" to argue to support the jury's damages determination. This court rejected eleven of the licenses because they were running royalty licenses (the patentee had only asked for a lump sum payment) and represented far lower rates than the jury returned. This court rejected the remaining two licenses (both for lump sum payments) because "[n]either license describe[d] how the parties calculated each lump sum, the licensees' intended products, or how many products each licensee expected to produce."

The meaning of these cases is clear: there must be a basis in fact to associate the royalty rates used in prior licenses to the particular hypothetical negotiation at issue in the case. The 25 percent rule of thumb as an abstract and largely theoretical construct fails to satisfy this fundamental requirement. The rule does not say anything about a particular hypothetical negotiation or reasonable royalty involving any particular technology, industry, or party. Relying on the 25 percent rule of thumb in a reasonable royalty calculation is far more unreliable and irrelevant than reliance on parties' unrelated licenses, which we rejected in *ResQNet and Lucent Technologies*. There, the prior licenses at least involved the same general industry and at least some of the same parties as the hypothetical negotiations at issue, and in *Wordtech* even involved licenses to the patents in suit entered into by the patentee-plaintiff. Lacking even these minimal connections, the 25 percent rule of thumb would predict that the same 25%/75% royalty split would begin royalty discussions between, for example, (a) TinyCo and IBM over a strong patent portfolio of twelve patents covering various aspects of a pioneering hard drive, and (b) Kodak and Fuji over a single patent to a tiny improvement in a specialty film emulsion.

It is of no moment that the 25 percent rule of thumb is offered merely as a starting point to which the *Georgia–Pacific* factors are then applied to bring the rate up or down. Beginning from a fundamentally flawed premise and adjusting it based on legitimate considerations specific to the facts of the case nevertheless results in a fundamentally flawed conclusion. This is reflected in *Lucent Technologies*, in which unrelated licenses were considered under *Georgia–Pacific* factor 1, but this court held that the entire royalty calculation was unsupported by substantial evidence.

. . . This court has sanctioned the use of the *Georgia–Pacific* factors to frame the reasonable royalty inquiry. Those factors properly tie the reasonable royalty calculation to the facts of the hypothetical negotiation at issue. This court's rejection of the 25 percent rule of thumb is not intended to limit the application of any of the *Georgia–Pacific* factors. In particular, factors 1 and 2—looking at royalties paid or received in licenses for the patent in suit or in comparable licenses—and factor 12—looking at the portion of profit that may be customarily allowed in the particular business for the use of the invention or similar inventions—remain valid and important factors in the determination of a reasonable royalty rate. However, evidence purporting to apply to these, and any other factors, must be tied to the relevant facts and circumstances of the particular case at issue and the hypothetical negotiations that would have taken place in light of those facts and circumstances at the relevant time.

In this case, it is clear that Gemini's testimony was based on the use of the 25% rule of thumb as an arbitrary, general rule, unrelated to the facts of this case. When asked the basis of his opinion that the rule of thumb would apply here, Gemini testified: "It's generally accepted. I've used it. I've seen others use it. It's a widely accepted rule." Upon further questioning, Dr. Gemini revealed that he had been involved in only four or five non-litigation related negotiations, and had recommended the 25% rule only once in a case involving a power tool. He did not testify that the parties here had a practice of beginning negotiations with a 25%/75% split, or that the contribution of Product Activation to Office and Word justified such a split. He did not base his 25 percent baseline on other licenses involving the patent at issue or comparable licenses. In short, Gemini's starting point of a 25 percent royalty had no relation to the facts of the case, and as such, was arbitrary, unreliable, and irrelevant. The use of such a rule fails to pass muster under *Daubert* and taints the jury's damages calculation.

This court thus holds that Microsoft is entitled to a new trial on damages.

2. ENTIRE MARKET VALUE RULE

As discussed above, Gemini performed "a check to determine whether" his $564,946,803 royalty figure was reasonable by comparing it to his calculation of Microsoft's approximate total revenue for Office and Windows of $19.28 billion. During trial, Gemini testified that his calculated royalty accounted for only 2.9% of Microsoft's revenue, and accented his point by reference to a prepared pie chart, showing Microsoft's $19.28 billion in revenue with a 2.9% sliver representing his calculated royalty rate. He concluded that 2.9% was a reasonable royalty based on his experience that royalty rates for software are "generally above—on average, above 10% or 10, 11%."

The entire market value rule allows a patentee to assess damages based on the entire market value of the accused product only where the patented feature creates the "basis for customer demand" or "substantially create[s] the value of the component parts." *Rite–Hite Corp. v. Kelley Co.,* 56 F.3d 1538, 1549–50 (Fed.Cir.1995). This rule is derived from Supreme Court precedent requiring that "the patentee . . . must in every case give evidence tending to separate or apportion the defendant's profits and the patentee's damages between the patented feature and the unpatented features, and such evidence must be reliable and tangible, and not conjectural or speculative," or show that "the entire value of the whole machine, as a marketable article, is properly and legally attributable to the patented feature."

Microsoft argues that Uniloc employed the entire market value of Office and Windows by virtue of Gemini's pie chart, his comparison of his calculated royalty to the total revenue Microsoft earns through the accused products, and Uniloc's attorneys' belittlement of Microsoft's expert's royalty figure as representing only .0003% of total revenue. Microsoft argues that Uniloc's use of the entire market value rule was not proper be-

cause it is undisputed that Product Activation did not create the basis for customer demand or substantially create the value of the component parts. Microsoft continues that Gemini's testimony tainted the jury's damages deliberations, regardless of its categorization as a "check."

Uniloc responds that: . . . (2) the entire market value of the product can be used if the royalty rate is low enough; and (3) the $19 billion figure was used only as a "check," and the jury was instructed not to base its damages determination on the entire market value, an instruction it should be presumed to have followed.

The district court agreed with Microsoft, and ordered a conditional new trial on damages. It noted that "Uniloc conceded customers do not buy Office or Windows because of [Product Activation] and said it would not base a royalty calculation on the entire market value of the products." As such, the use of the entire market value of Office and Windows in the form of the $19 billion figure was "irrelevant" and "taint[ed]" the jury's damages award. . . .

This court agrees with Microsoft and the district court that Uniloc's use of the $19 billion "check" was improper under the entire market value rule. . . .

. . . The Supreme Court and this court's precedents do not allow consideration of the entire market value of accused products for minor patent improvements simply by asserting a low enough royalty rate.

This case provides a good example of the danger of admitting consideration of the entire market value of the accused where the patented component does not create the basis for customer demand. As the district court aptly noted, "[t]he $19 billion cat was never put back into the bag even by Microsoft's cross-examination of Mr. Gemini and re-direct of Mr. Napper, and in spite of a final instruction that the jury may not award damages based on Microsoft's entire revenue from all the accused products in the case." This is unsurprising. The disclosure that a company has made $19 billion dollars in revenue from an infringing product cannot help but skew the damages horizon for the jury, regardless of the contribution of the patented component to this revenue. . . .

For the foregoing reasons, this court concludes that the district court did not abuse its discretion in granting a conditional new trial on damages for Uniloc's violation of the entire market value rule.

NOTES AND QUESTIONS

1. In *Uniloc USA, Inc. v. Microsoft Corp.*, 632 F. 3d 1292 (Fed. Cir. 2011), the Federal Circuit refers to, and reinforces the viability of, the *Georgia-Pacific* factors. These factors, compiled in the decision *Georgia–Pacific Corp. v. U.S. Plywood Corp.*, 318 F. Supp. 1116 (S.D.N.Y. 1970), are often consid-

ered by courts in reasonable royalty determinations. According to the *Georgia-Pacific* court:

A comprehensive list of evidentiary facts relevant, in general, to the determination of the amount of a reasonable royalty for a patent license may be drawn from a conspectus of the leading cases. The following are some of the factors mutatis mutandis seemingly more pertinent to the issue herein:

1. The royalties received by the patentee for the licensing of the patent in suit, proving or tending to prove an established royalty.

2. The rates paid by the licensee for the use of other patents comparable to the patent in suit.

3. The nature and scope of the license, as exclusive or non-exclusive; or as restricted or non-restricted in terms of territory or with respect to whom the manufactured product may be sold.

4. The licensor's established policy and marketing program to maintain his patent monopoly by not licensing others to use the invention or by granting licenses under special conditions designed to preserve that monopoly.

5. The commercial relationship between the licensor and licensee, such as, whether they are competitors in the same territory in the same line of business; or whether they are inventor and promoter.

6. The effect of selling the patented specialty in promoting sales of other products of the licensee; that existing value of the invention to the licensor as a generator of sales of his non-patented items; and the extent of such derivative or convoyed sales.

7. The duration of the patent and the term of the license.

8. The established profitability of the product made under the patent; its commercial success; and its current popularity.

9. The utility and advantages of the patent property over the old modes or devices, if any, that had been used for working out similar results.

10. The nature of the patented invention; the character of the commercial embodiment of it as owned and produced by the licensor; and the benefits to those who have used the invention.

11. The extent to which the infringer has made use of the invention; and any evidence probative of the value of that use.

12. The portion of the profit or of the selling price that may be customary in the particular business or in comparable businesses to allow for the use of the invention or analogous inventions.

13. The portion of the realizable profit that should be credited to the invention as distinguished from non-patented elements, the manufacturing process, business risks, or significant features or improvements added by the infringer.

14. The opinion testimony of qualified experts.

15. The amount that a licensor (such as the patentee) and a licensee (such as the infringer) would have agreed upon (at the time the infringement began) if both had been reasonably and voluntarily trying to reach an agreement; that is, the amount which a prudent licensee- who desired, as a business proposition, to obtain a license to manufacture and sell a particular article embodying the patented invention- would have been willing to pay as a royalty and yet be able to make a reasonable profit and which amount would have been acceptable by a prudent patentee who was willing to grant a license.

Id. at 1120.

Courts have broad discretion in selecting and evaluating these factors in any given case. And, as *Uniloc* illustrates, they are simply a starting point for the myriad factual assessments courts will need to make to reach a reasonable royalty determination.

2. Reasonable royalties are the most common remedy in many countries. *See, e.g., AlliedSignal Inc. v. DuPont Canada Inc.* (1998), 78 C.P.R. 3d 129, 176–181 (Can. Fed. Ct.) (listing, and approving, a set of thirteen factors the defendant's expert had used to calculate a royalty); *General Tire & Rubber Co. v. Firestone Tyre & Rubber Co.*, [1975] F.S.R. 273, 280–281 (UKHL) (appeal taken from Eng.) (opinion of Lord Wilberforce) (stating that judges should "take into account any licences actually granted and the rates of royalty fixed by them, to estimate their relevance and comparability, to apply them so far as he can to the bargain hypothetically to be made between the patentee and the infringer, and to the extent to which they do not provide a figure on which the damage can be measured, to consider any other evidence, according to its relevance and weight, upon which he can fix a rate of royalty which would have been agreed"); *id.* at 292–293 (opinion of Lord Salmon) (stating that, "when there is no established market rate, damages for infringement can be assessed only on the basis of what royalty a willing licensee would have been prepared to pay and a willing licensor to accept").

In the UK *Gerber Garment Technology v. Lectra Systems Ltd.*, [1997] R.P.C. 443 (A.C.) (Eng.) decision, the court stated:

> Infringement of a patent is a statutory tort; and in the ordinary way one would expect the damages recoverable to be governed by the same rules as with many or most other torts. We were referred to Halsbury's Laws of England (4th edn) vol.12 para 1128 and following, to establish the elementary rules (i) that the overriding principle is that the victim should be restored to the position he would have been in if no wrong had been done, and (2) that the victim can recover loss which was (i) foreseeable, (ii) caused by the wrong, and (iii) not excluded from recovery by public or social policy.

Id. at 452.

As a general matter, then, the patentee is entitled to recover any loss caused in fact by the infringement, as long as the loss is reasonably foreseeable in nature and public policy does not otherwise preclude recovery. Under *Gerber*, patentees in the UK have recovered lost profits on sales of convoyed goods where such losses are proximately attributable to the infringement, without the limitation imposed by U.S courts that the convoyed merchandise be functionally related to the patented products. *See, e.g., Rite-Hite Corp. v. Kelley Co.*, 56 F.3d 1538 (Fed. Cir. 1995).

Also in *Rite-Hite*, the Federal Circuit used a common, though not exclusive, four-factor test (called the "DAMP" test) to assess the patentee's entitlement to lost profits. Under the test, the patentee must show: (1) demand for the patentee's goods, (2) absence of acceptable non-infringing substitutes, (3) that the patentee had manufacturing and marketing capability to meet the demand, and (4) the profits the patentee would have made absent the infringement. Where a patentee is unable to meet the test (e.g., a non-practicing entity), a reasonable royalty award will be pursued.

3. In *Toei Tec K.K. v. Family K.K.*, Judgment of the Intellectual Property High Court, Case No. 2005(Ne) No. 10047 (September 25, 2006) (Japan), involving a patent for a massage chair, the court held that a patentee cannot combine damage calculations under Section 102(1) of the Patent Act, allowing damages incurred for goods that would have been sold but for the infringement, with Section 102(3) which allows damages measured by an ordinary licensing fee for infringing goods sold by the defendant beyond the patentee's marketing capacity. In interpreting Section 102 of the Japanese Patent Act, the court reasoned as follows:

> Article 102, para.1 provides for the method of calculating the amount of damages by applying the concept of lost profits which assumes how much profits the patentee may have earned if there were no act of working the invention that would constitute patent infringement, whereas Article 102, para.3 provides that the amount of royalties which the patentee would have been entitled to receive for the working of the patented invention that has actually been made by the infringer may be presumed to be the amount of damage sus-

tained by the patentee. Therefore, these provisions apply different approaches for calculating the amount of damage. Furthermore, if it were construed that royalties were also claimable for the quantity that the patentee would have been unable to sell, this would allow the patentee to be compensated for damage beyond the extent of lost profits which the patentee is rightfully entitled to claim for damages by reason of infringement. It is difficult to find a justifiable reason to allow such compensation of damage beyond lost profits."

Do you agree with the court's reasoning? Why or why not?

4. In a recent UK decision, *Fabio Perini SpA v. LPC Group Plc,* [2012] EWHC 911 (Ch.), Patents Court, England and Wales (Apr. 4, 2012), the court assessed damages for infringement of a process patent on a component of a machine based on loss of a contract to supply the entire machine. As two commentators explain:

> Perini, the patentee, had to demonstrate that the infringing act of PCMC/LPC had resulted in the loss of a contract to supply the relevant third party customers, namely LPC and Georgia Pacific (or the chance to supply) with its tailsealer product, which embodied the patented process. In assessing whether any such causal link had been established, the judge made the following observations:

>> -Where the infringing act relates to the use of a process, a patentee is not excluded, in principle, from claiming for loss of a contract to the extent that the infringing process is specifically written into the supply contract of the infringing apparatus, the premise being that such promotion of the infringing use could cause the patentee to lose a contract employing its patented method.

>> -No distinction in principle can be drawn between the infringement of a process patent as contrasted with a product patent. PCMC/LPC had argued that, where a customer is paying to achieve a result (i.e., a glued paper roll), he may not care how that result was achieved (in effect saying that there was no causal link), whereas with a product, this was different as the customer would have specifically wanted that product. The judge dismissed this argument on the basis that in either case the infringer would still be seeking a competitive advantage and so there was a causal link sufficient to ground the damages claim.

> *Total Damages*

> The amount of damages awarded to Perini was quite substantial given that (according to PCMC/LPC) the infringing tailsealer accounted for only six per cent of the total cost of the entire converting line. Based upon the evidence before the judge, Perini had successfully argued that it had lost the chance of a sale of the whole converting line (in which the tailsealer was one module) and not just the tailsealer itself.

Paul Joseph & Ben Mark, *Damages Inquiry: The Tail-End of a Long-Running Dispute*, 7 J. INTELL. PROP. L. & PRAC. 636 (2012).

Such damages determinations are quite fact-specific and the outcome can be quite difficult to predict. Thus, as noted by Messrs. Joseph and Mark "most assessments settle before reaching trial—if parties want certainty, settlement is the only option."

b. Defendant's Profits

The other primary measure of damages, disgorgement of a defendant's profits, is illustrated in the following seminal UK decision.

CELANESE INT'L CORP. V. BP CHEMICALS LTD.

[1999] R.P.C. 203 (Pat. Ct.) (Eng.)

■ LADDIE J:

. . .

1. By writ dated 19 June 1995, Hoechst Celanese Corporation [HC] commenced proceedings for patent infringement against BP Chemicals Ltd and Purolite International Limited in respect of patent EP (UK) 196,173 of which Hoechst Celanese was the registered proprietor. The matter came on before me for trial in January 1997. In a judgment dated 6 February 1997 I held the patent to be both valid and infringed. Following that, Hoechst Celanese took advantage of the procedure set out in Island Records Limited v. Tring International Plc [1995] FSR 560 and required BP to provide it with certain outline commercial information to allow it to make a more informed election before an inquiry as to damages and an account of profits. It chose an account. On 16 May, 1997 I made an order "[t]hat an account be taken of the profits derived by the Defendants and each of them from infringement of the Plaintiff's European Patent No. 0 196 173." . . .

TECHNICAL BACKGROUND

4. The invention in the patent in suit relates to a method for removing iodide compounds from acetic acid. Acetic acid is a chemical which is made on a large scale by a number of companies. It is used as a starting material in the manufacture of a number of different, more complex, chemical products. Some of its major uses include the manufacture of vinyl acetate monomer ("VAM"), acetic anhydride, and terephthalic acid. Each of the latter three chemicals in turn is used as a starting material for the manufacture of further, more complex, chemicals. VAM, which is of particular significance to the issues arising on this account, is used in the manufacture of a number of chemicals, the most important of which are polyvinyl acetate and polyvinyl alcohol. . . .

5. There are a number of processes used to manufacture acetic acid on a commercial scale. . . . BP, which is one of the largest producers of the

acid in the world, uses three different processes at its production facility at Hull. That facility comprises a number of production plants together with an extensive network of interconnecting pipework and storage tanks of differing sizes.

6. In the earlier part of this century one of the major routes used to produce the acid was based on the oxidation of readily available hydrocarbons such as butane, liquefied petroleum gas (LPG) and naphtha. There are a number of variants of this process. One is a naphtha oxidation process still used by BP at Hull in its DF2 and DF3 plants. In addition to acetic acid, a range of oxygenated products are synthesised in these plants including formic acid, propionic acid, ethyl acetate and methyl ethyl ketone. . . .

. . . During the 1980's, [BP] invested substantially in research and development to develop a new carbonylation process . . . to produce acetic acid and acetic anhydride at the same time from the same plant. They have to be separated from one another after synthesis. This modified . . . process was implemented in the A5 plant in June 1989. . . .

. . . .

IODIDE IMPURITIES

12. The basic . . . process as practised on A4 and the modified acetic acid/acetic anhydride process as practised on A5 both involve the carbonylation of methanol. This requires the use of a rhodium catalyst and methyl iodide as a promoter. The presence of the latter results in there being very small quantities of various iodides as impurities in the acetic acid produced on these plants. Since the chemical process in DF2 and DF3 does not use rhodium/methyl iodide, the same impurity problem does not exist in them. . . . The majority of customers do not consider the presence of these low levels of iodides a problem. However over the years it has been found that the iodide impurities in acetic acid can be a problem for VAM manufacturers. In their processes a palladium catalyst is employed [and] . . . [i]odides poison the catalyst irreversibly. . . . [M]ost VAM manufacturers demand that acid supplied to them does not have more than 10 ppb of iodides. It is not in dispute that distillation is one way of reducing the level of iodides in acetic acid. For example the A4 plant at Hull, prior to the period of infringement, achieved an acceptably low level of iodide in its acetic acid by means of distillation. At the same time the A5 plant was using a iodide-cleaning process based on silver nitrate, although with more variable results.

THE PATENT IN SUIT

13. HC's patent relates to a method for removing iodide compounds from acetic acid. The invention consists of contacting the iodide bearing acetic acid with a particular type of resin in a particular form loaded with silver (or mercury). All six of the claims in the patent are method claims

directed to the removal of iodide by the use of such a resin. If iodide-bearing acid is passed through a bed containing such a resin, it removes most of the iodides and can therefore be considered to guard the final product from excessive iodide content. Hence the piece of plant in which this process is operated is called a "guard bed."

14. In the early 1990s BP operated an infringing process in guard beds installed in their A4 and A5 plants. Since there is no iodide contamination on the DF plants, the process was not used there. In A4 and A5, a guard bed was installed between the existing purification stage and the storage tanks for the acid. The guard bed was therefore the last stage in the manufacture of the raw material which became the commercial product. A certain amount of blending and mixing also took place in some of the large storage tanks downstream of the guard beds at Hull so that the acid loaded, for example, into the hold of a ship for export to one of BP's customers would be the result of blending together acid either produced from only one plant (DF2, DF3, A4 or A5) or from more than one plant. Since the precise composition of the acid produced on a plant varies from time to time, for example, the precise iodide level fluctuates, and the composition of acids produced in one plant is likely to be different in some respects from that produced in another, the product shipped to the customer has an "averaged" composition. The result of the infringement was that low iodide acetic acid could be supplied to VAM manufacturers directly from A4 and A5. During the period of infringement a minor, though still substantial, part of the output of these two lines was supplied to such customers. BP says that it could always have met its VAM customer requirements (including BP's own VAM plant at Baglan Bay) either from its DF plants alone or by deliberately blending acid from DF (with no iodide) with acid from A4/A5 (with higher levels of iodide) even if the latter had not used the guard bed invention. It says that the existing pipework and storage tanks at Hull would have made this an easy thing to do and that blending was routine at Hull. Whether this would have been an easy thing to do and its relevance, if any, to this account will be considered below.

15. To appreciate the issues which arise on this account, it is useful to outline the parties' respective positions. Although these positions were refined during the course of the hearing, most of those refinements were in relation to numbers. By the end of the hearing, most of the figures had been agreed although there was still a large difference as to which of the figures were relevant to the account and . . . . where they had to be apportioned between infringing and non-infringing activities, the extent of that apportionment. The dispute as to the correct legal principles to apply to taking the account remained essentially intact to the end.

OUTLINE OF BP'S ARGUMENTS

16. BP argued that the order made after the trial, and indeed the only order which I could have made after HC had made its election, was to BP to account for profits "derived from infringement". This meant that it had to show how much it had profited or benefited by use of the invention and it had to pay the financial measure of that benefit over to HC. This was defined by BP as the additional profits arising as a result of its acid having been treated in infringement of the patent. BP said that the benefits, and therefore profits, derived from infringement can be assessed properly in one of two ways. The first is to calculate the difference between on the one hand the profits BP have received by the use of the guard bed and subsequent sale of the acid so treated and on the other hand the profits which would otherwise have been achieved but for its use. This gives rise to a figure which can be called a differential profit. This BP said was an example of the preferred incremental approach. The alternative is to determine what proportion of the total (i.e. gross) profits made from sale of the treated acid is attributable to the use of the guard bed. This is called an apportionment. It also said that the incremental approach is the best guide to apportionment. BP claimed that if the two approaches are adopted independently they ought to arrive at essentially the same figure but the incremental approach is more accurate and involves less guess work. BP's contention on this issue was expressed as follows . . .

> "The correct approach in assessing the profits derived from infringement is to assess the value of the benefits arising from using the guard bed, compared to the alternative which BP were most likely to have used otherwise, absent infringement."

Although BP did provide some material and put in a small amount of evidence relating to apportionment, it concentrated on supporting its incremental approach. . . .

23. BP said that this approach accords with the way management runs its business. When deciding whether to make an alteration to an existing process, management must try to balance the totality of expected benefits against the total expected costs of making the change and comparing that with the benefits/costs of either not changing at all or turning to another alternative. This is what happened here. BP management had to decide whether it would be advantageous to install guard beds on A4 and A5. Those deliberations resulted in two Capital Sanction Memoranda. For example the Memorandum relating to A4 expected BP to benefit from installing the guard bed. Briefly, the reasons for the change to A4 appear to have been as follows. BP wanted to use a new catalyst in the plant, the active ingredient in which was rhodium. Since rhodium was expensive and was gradually lost during the course of plant operation, BP considered ways of stabilising it so as to reduce those losses. A suitable

stabiliser was lithium iodide. However the introduction of that would, in turn, raise the iodide level of the final acetic acid. In order to reduce it again, the guard bed was introduced. Thus the guard beds were introduced so as to facilitate the introduction of the new catalyst. BP calculated the costs of the new catalyst and the guard bed and the savings to be made by it and, on the basis of their forecasts of how much rhodium they would save, they calculated that introduction of the lithium iodide/guard bed modification would save them a modest amount. The savings were dependent on the high cost of rhodium. The guard bed was introduced as a result. In fact the cost of rhodium fell precipitately. The expected savings never materialised. In fact BP was worse off.

24. Adopting this approach, Mr Boulton [BP's financial expert] concluded that BP saved nothing by incorporating the guard bed on A4 and only saved a comparatively small sum by doing so on A5. Mr Young Q.C., who argued the case on behalf of BP, said that this was not really forcing the court to hypothesise on what would have happened absent infringement. He pointed out that the Hull facility made sufficient low iodide acid to meet all its customer requirements both before and after infringement. That it would have been able to do so had it not infringed is not a matter of conjecture but a certainty. The only questions are how would it have done so and the size of the increased cost, if there was any, in doing so.
. . .

OUTLINE OF HC'S ARGUMENTS

25. HC said that the incremental approach favoured by BP is of no use in an account. The appropriate basis by which to assess the profits made from the process is by reference to the profits generated by the end product. The manufacture and sale of that product is the only purpose for operating the process in the first place. The product here is low-iodide acetic acid. Based on this it said that BP is liable for the whole of the profits made as a consequence of the disposal of that material. In other words BP should pay over the gross profits on the acetic acid made on the A4 and A5 plants during the period of infringement. In opening it accepted that apportionment was possible but not on the facts of this case. At that stage it sought some £180m, including interest.

26. In support of this basic proposition, HC argued as follows. The guard bed is effectively the last stage in the manufacture of acid on A4 and A5. The claims in the patent in suit are for a process for reducing the iodide content of that acid. However HC says that, in accordance with s.60 (1) (c) of the 1977 Act, when read in the context of Art. 64(2) of the European Patent Convention . . . . low-iodide acetic acid is a product obtained directly by means of the patented process. Therefore disposal of that acid is itself an infringement and low-iodide acetic acid can be regarded as "the product" of the invention. Whether that is true or not, that acid is what is aimed for by the patented process. Sale of the acid is a di-

rect exploitation of the invention. Prima facie, the defendant must account for all the profits made by the infringing business on the basis that it was being carried out on behalf of the patentee. . . .

27. HC went on to say that in relation to damages it is not permissible to say by way of defence that the defendant could have taken an alternative course which would also have inflicted the same or similar damage, and a number of cases confirm that the same principle applies in relation to accounts. Therefore the central plank of BP's case, namely the comparison of its financial position during infringement with its position if it had avoided infringement, is flawed. Nevertheless HC produced extensive evidence to show that BP could not or could not easily have avoided infringement because the non-infringing alternative routes either would not work or were not open to BP and that, in any event, it had understated how much those alternative routes would have cost, thereby understating the benefits which it had obtained by infringement. . . .

INCREMENTAL V. APPORTIONMENT APPROACHES

31. . . . I should start by explaining why I reject the suggestion that the incremental route is an alternative way of working out an apportionment. If these two routes arrive at similar figures it is a coincidence and no more. That this is so can be demonstrated as follows. If an infringer's process makes no profit overall, then whether infringement accounts for 10 per cent or 100 per cent of the profits, on an apportionment the plaintiff will recover nothing. A large percentage of zero is still zero. This was accepted as correct by Mr Watson. He said it was inherent in his case that if BP made no profits, HC would recover nothing. On the other hand an infringer may benefit very significantly from infringing even though the whole process makes no profit overall. For example if a process makes a loss of £1m p.a. with the infringing step but would have made a loss of £3m p.a. without it, the benefit to the infringer is £2m p.a. . . The two approaches are quite different and in most cases are likely to produce different figures. . . .

34. The reason for this difference is apparent. Apportionment looks at the profits actually made on the whole process or article and, where appropriate, splits them between those parts which infringe and those which do not. In the incremental approach it is neither necessary or relevant how many steps or integers there are in the process or article nor is it relevant what each one contributes, if anything, to overall profitability. Indeed whether the whole process or article is profitable or not is irrelevant. Under the incremental approach one is only looking at whether the infringing step is financially advantageous to the defendant when compared to the most likely alternative. As such it does give one indication of whether or not the defendant has benefited or enriched himself by use of the infringement. It also readily explains why it is a valuable analysis to the management of a company since it is one way of assessing which of a

number of alternatives is likely to be most cost effective or whether it is worthwhile making a change to an existing plant. If a plant is loss-making, modifications designed to reduce the loss will be attractive. . . .

GENERAL PRINCIPLES

35. A plaintiff who is successful in patent litigation has an entitlement to elect between damages and an account. The differences between them are considerable. Where the plaintiff seeks damages, the purpose of the inquiry is to determine what loss he has actually suffered. That loss may far exceed any gain made by the infringer through the infringing activity. Furthermore if the activity of the defendant infringes different rights held by different plaintiffs, he will have to compensate them all for the damage they have suffered. In this respect there is no upper limit on the compensation he may have to pay. The more damage he inflicts, the greater the financial burden imposed on him. In working out quantum the court has to determine what acts of infringement have been committed (an issue which may have been resolved on the trial as to liability) and what damage has been caused, in the legal sense, by them. In doing this the court is not allowed to speculate on whether the defendant could have avoided infringement and, if so, what damage would have been inflicted on the plaintiff by such alternative legitimate activities. It may be that a non-infringing activity would have inflicted the same or more financial damage on the plaintiff. If so it could be said that the plaintiff is no worse off as a result of the infringement than he would have been if a non-infringing course of action had been adopted by the defendant. But this is irrelevant to an inquiry as to damages. . . . The fact that the plaintiff could have been damaged by actions of the defendant for which it had no legal redress does not detract from the fact that the damage was inflicted by activities for which it is entitled to redress.

36. An account of profits is very different. Instead of looking to the harm inflicted on the plaintiff it considers the profit made by the infringer. The defendant is treated as if he conducted his business and made profits on behalf of the plaintiff. A number of consequences flow from this. One of them is that the maximum payment which can be ordered is the total profit made by the defendant. It may be that that figure far exceeds the damage suffered by the plaintiff. . . . The hope of obtaining more is the normal reason why plaintiffs elect an account in those comparatively rare cases in which they do so. Furthermore there is only one profits "pot". If different plaintiffs seek accounts in respect of different infringing activities of a defendant within a single business, the totality of the profits ordered to be paid should not exceed the total profits made by the defendant in that business. . . .

37. Although an account may give rise to a very different figure to that on an inquiry as to damages, they both proceed on a common principle of legal causation. On an inquiry the court is trying to determine what

damage has been caused, in a legal sense, by the defendant's wrongful acts. It has to decide whether the breach was the cause of the loss or merely the occasion of it. . . . In an account the court is trying to determine what profits have been caused, in a legal sense, by those acts. . .

38. One consequence of this is that where the defendant carries on multiple businesses or sells different products and only one infringes, he only has to compensate the plaintiff for the damage inflicted by the infringements or he only has to account for the profits made by the infringements. For example in this case no question of BP having to account in respect of acetic acid from the DF plants arises. Similarly, save in respect of the period of the stay early this year where special circumstances are said to exist, it is not suggested that BP must account for the acetic anhydride made on the A5 plant. As Lord Watson said in United Horse Shoe and Nail v. Stewart (1888) 5 R.P.C. 260, it would be unreasonable to give the patentee profits which were not earned by use of his invention.

39. A further consequence of these common principles is that it should be no answer to an account that the defendant could have made the same profits by following an alternative, non-infringing course. The question to be answered is "what profits were in fact made by the defendant by the wrongful activity?". It should not matter that similar profits could have been made in another, non-infringing way. . . .

41. . . . Imagine a case where the plaintiff invents and patents an entirely new process for making an entirely new product. The defendant infringes the patent by using the process to make the products which he sells at a profit. There is little doubt that he would have to account to the patentee for the profits so made. Now imagine that, quite independently and at the same time, some other inventor invents another new process for making the same product but does not patent it so that the infringer could have made the same product in a non-infringing way. The fact is that he did not do so. The profits he made were made by use of the patented invention and he should account for them. The existence of alternatives may push down the market price for the products and thereby depress the profits actually made, but that is another matter.

42. If this is right, it cuts both ways. Just as the defendant cannot reduce the profits by saying that he could have made all or most of them if he had taken a non-infringing course, so also the plaintiff must take the defendant as he finds him. He cannot increase the profits by saying that the defendant could and should have generated higher profits. . . .

43. Although the infringer cannot avoid paying over profits by relying on possible non-infringing alternatives, the patentee, as noted above, cannot recover profits which were not earned by use of his invention. I have already referred to a case where the defendant has two businesses, one infringing and the other not. But the same approach should apply where only part of a product or process infringes. Profits attributable to

the non-infringing parts were not caused by or attributable to the use of the invention even if the use of the invention was the occasion for the generation of those profits. . . .

47. Sometimes the court may come to the conclusion that all the profits are attributable to the act of infringement. . . . Similarly, the court may come to the conclusion, as a matter of fact, that the invention was the essential ingredient in the creation of the defendant's whole product or process. If so, it may be appropriate not to apportion. . . .

48. However, once it is conceded or proved that an apportionment is appropriate, the court must do its best to split the profits between infringing and non-infringing parts.

[The court then engaged in a detailed assessment of BP profits and losses and apportionment of profits between infringing and non-infringing parts.]

127. The figures calculated in accordance with the above principles are set out in the confidential annex to this judgment. The result is that I have come to the conclusion that BP made a gross profit of £94.64M on A4 and a loss of £89.1M on A5 acid. It follows that nothing is payable to HC in respect of A5 acid. As far as A4 is concerned, 0.6% of the gross profit is to be taken as the part attributable to the use of HC's process. This gives a base allocated profit of £567,840 before tax. . . .

144. For the reasons set out above, I will order BP to pay to HC, £567,840 less an appropriate deduction for corporation tax. I realise that in so doing, I have arrived at a figure which is smaller than that arrived at by BP. I did at one stage consider using the latter as a lower limit below which I could not go. However I do not think that would be right. For the reasons given above, the basis on which BP arrived at its figure is flawed. Although it would have resulted in the payment of a larger sum to HC, that was entirely attributable to notional incremental profits made on the loss-making A5 acid production.

NOTES AND QUESTIONS

1. After apportioning the value of the invention to the value of the end product, the court in *Celanese Int'l Corp. v. BP Chemicals Ltd.*, [1999] R.P.C. 203 (Pat. Ct.) (Eng.) awarded a mere 0.3 percent of what the plaintiff sought. Do you think this percentage is consistent with the goal of patent damages?

2. Which do you think is better: to allow a patentee to disgorge an infringer of profits made due to the infringement, to require the patentee to establish the profits she would have made, or to settle for a reasonable royalty? What benefits and drawbacks do you see to each approach?

Some commentators have identified an unexpected negative side effect of the patent-holder's ability to pick the type of damage calculation and the variable nature of court calculations. They may be facilitating "trolling" behavior:

> Surprisingly from an economic standpoint, damages awards may not only be calculated following different rationales within one jurisdiction, but it lies (to the largest extent) within the discretion of the patent holder (and not the court!) to pick the type of remedy he/she prefers (namely, "lost profits, "infringers profits," (unjust enrichment) and "reasonable royalty rates"). The real problem occurs, however as the courts' interpretation of these damages awards regulations in some cases renders "being infringed" a more profitable option than legitimate negotiation between the patent holder and the potential infringer in the first place—eventually opening the floodgates for the "troll business."

Markus G. Reitzig, Joachim Henkel & Christopher Heath, *On Sharks, Trolls, and Other Patent Animals—Being Infringed as a Normatively Induced Innovation Exploitation Strategy* (2006), http://ssrn.com/abstract=885914.

Should the court, not the patent-holder, pick the type of remedy for infringement? Why or why not?

3. In *Monsanto Canada Inc. v. Schmeiser*, [2004] 1 S.C.R. 902, the Supreme Court of Canada adopted the principle of considering the availability of non-infringing substitutes to reverse an award of the defendant's profits on the ground that the defendant would have earned the same profit had he planted non-infringing canola: "A comparison is to be made between the defendant's profit attributable to the invention and his profit had he used the best non-infringing option." *Id.* at 938–939. As stated by the Court, "it is settled law that the inventor is only entitled to that portion of the infringer's profit which is causally attributable to the invention. ... The preferred means of calculating an accounting of profits is . . . the value-based or "differential profit" approach, where profits are allocated according to the value contributed to the defendant's wares by the patent. . . . A comparison is to be made between the defendant's profit attributable to the invention and his profit had he used the best non-infringing option . . ." *Id.* at para. 101–102.

This differential approach was rejected by the court in *Celanese* where it held "[a] further consequence of these common principles is that it should be no answer to an account that the defendant could have made the same profits by following an alternative, non-infringing course. The question to be answered is "what profits were in fact made by the defendant by the wrongful activity?" It should not matter that similar profits could have been made in another, non-infringing way." *Id.* at para. 39. In your opinion, which court has the better argument?

4. In BGH 1.Zivilsenat, 02.11.2000–*Gemeinkostenanteil* (Germany), the BGH held that for purposes of determining a defendant's profits, the defendant may not deduct overhead costs that would have been incurred even absent the infringement. Instead, defendants may deduct "merely the variable costs . . . for the production and distribution of the infringing objects but not

the fixed costs." The latter, the court stated, presumably would have been incurred in any event, though "[i]f and to the extent that fixed costs and variable overheads can in exceptional cases be directly ascribed to the infringing objects, these are . . . to be deducted from the proceeds when calculating the profit from the infringement. . . ." On remand the defendant could attempt to prove "the extent to which overheads incurred can be ascribed directly to the production of the infringing jewelry." It is viewed as a significant case in that it would seem to permit much higher awards of defendant's profits than were available in Germany in the past.

————————

U.S. patent owners frequently criticize other countries for the inadequacy of their patent infringement damage awards. China has particularly been singled out for criticism. As the following article indicates, however, damage awards in China can be significant:

TIM MALLOY & YUFENG (ETHAN) MA, *IP ENFORCEMENT IN CHINA:* CHINT V. SCHNEIDER ELECTRIC
Portfolio Media, New York (Oct. 10, 2007)
IP Law 360

Saturday, Sept. 29, 2007, marked dual milestones in IP enforcement in China. First, a record breaking damage award of $45 million was rendered for patent infringement. Second, it was rendered for a "small invention" patent. These are formally called "utility model" patents in China, and can be rapidly obtained simply through registration without elaborate examination.

French electrical company Schneider Electric was ordered to pay its Chinese rival Chint Group 333 million yuan (about $45 million U.S.) in damages for infringement of a Chinese utility model patent. Since 1999, the two companies have battled each other through 25 patent lawsuits, including seven in China and the remainder in other countries. This latest award is record-breaking in light of the enormous amount.

Not long ago, a U.S. trade official noted that awards in the vast majority of Chinese IP infringement suits were less than $100,000 and many people had expressed the view that Chinese patents were useless because they were rarely and anemically enforced. Yet one cannot ignore this record breaking damage award even despite the fact that it favored a Chinese company over a "foreign" entity.

What is even more interesting about this case, however, is that this huge award is based on a utility model patent, i.e., a "small invention" patent, and not a regular Chinese "invention patent" that corresponds— albeit confusingly—with so-called utility patents in the United States. The utility model patent involved in the *Chint v. Schneider* case is ZL97248279.5.

Chint applied for this patent on Nov. 11, 1997. Not long after filing, it was registered, and it enjoys a 10-year term from the application date until Nov. 11, 2007. The patent deals with high cut-off, small circuit-breakers, which sell for less than $1.50 per unit.

NOTES AND QUESTIONS

1. On April 15, 2009, Chint and Schneider agreed to an unprecedented settlement of $23 million (RMB 157 million) in the above-mentioned case. The settlement amounted to approximately half the damages awarded in the previous two years by the Wenzhou Intermediate People's Court. While the number of judicial infringement proceedings is increasing markedly in China, the question remains whether the damage award in *Chint v. Schneider Electric* is simply an outlier or whether it signals the start of a trend.

2. As you look at the range of remedies provided, what common threads do you identify? What are the major differences? Is patent enforcement an area that is ripe for harmonization? Why or why not?

3. As the importance of patents in China increases, we may see more of a different type of remedy: apology. As Professor Nguyen explains:

> Both injunctions and damages are available and routinely obtained by the prevailing Chinese intellectual property owners.11 In addition to these remedies, the prevailing owners frequently avail themselves of the statutorily available apology remedy as well. . . .

> [However the remedy of apology] is not always afforded in patent infringement cases. . . [T]he Supreme People's Court [has] held that "[m]aking an apology is mainly a way of bearing the liability for damaging the aggrieved party's personal interests or commercial credit standing. While patent right is mainly a kind of property interest, hence this method generally does not apply to cases on dispute over patent infringement." . . .

Apology was ordered, however, as a remedy in a case where the court found the defendant guilty of patent infringement. In Institute of Organic Chemistry of Chengdu Under the Chinese Academy of Sciences v. Chengdu Zhengda Electric Apparatus Factory, the patentee brought a patent infringement action against the defendant, Zhengda, for manufacturing and selling air re-purifiers in violation of plaintiff's three patents: the "purifier of duplication machine ozone," the "purifier of room air," and "a kind of low-noise impeller of the centrifugal blower fan." The Higher People's Court of Sichuan Province affirmed the lower court's infringement finding only with respect to "a kind of low-noise impeller of the centrifugal blower fan" patent . . . [In addition to a damages award] The Court accepted the infringement finding, and the finding that the defendant knew the impellers used in the metal blower fans in the Zhengda re-purifiers were the same as those contained in the plaintiff's relevant patent. The defendant nevertheless manufactured and sold the infringing product for several years. The Court upheld the lower court's order with respect to making an apology. Specifically, the defendant, Zhengda Factory, was instructed to make public apologies to the plaintiff in three publications: China Patent, Sichuan Daily, and Chengdu Evening Paper, for the purpose of "clearing up ill effects." Xuan-Thao Nguyen, *Apologies as Intellectual Property Remedies: Lessons from China*, 44 CONN. L. REV. 883, 886, 918–919 (2012) (citations omitted). Should other countries make the remedy of apology available in patent cases?

4. In *Samsung Electronic (UK) Ltd. v. Apple Inc.*, [2012] EWCA Civ 1339, the design infringement case excerpted in Chapter 8, the UK Court of Appeals upheld an order requiring Apple to publicize the fact that Samsung tablets had been found non-infringing. As Sir Robin Jacob explained:

> I should first consider whether or not there is power to grant a publicity order of this short- publicity by an intellectual property claimant that has failed in his action for infringement. Publicity orders in intellectual property cases are quite a new thing at least in this jurisdiction. Prior to the Enforcement Directive 2004/48/EC they were, so far as I am aware, unknown here. . . . The Enforcement Directive changed that, providing expressly for publicity orders where the IP right holder has been successful. The purpose (Recital 27) was to act as a "supplementary deterrent to future infringers and to contribute to the awareness of the public at large." The Directive does not provide for publicity orders the other way round—where a party has successfully defended an unjustified claim of infringement or has obtained a declaration of non-infringement. . .

> I have come to the firm conclusion that such an order is necessary now. The decision of the Oberlandesgericht received much publicity. What was the ordinary consumer, or the marketing department of a potential Samsung customer to make of it? On the one hand the media said Samsung had won, on the other the media were saying that Apple had a German Europe-wide injunction. Real commercial uncertainty was thereby created. A consumer might well think "I had better not buy a Samsung—maybe it's illegal and if I buy one it may not be supported". A customer (and I include its legal department) might well wonder whether, if it bought Sansung's 7.7 it might be in trouble before the German Courts. Safest thing to do either way is not to buy.

> Of course our decision fully understood actually lifts the fog that the cloud of litigation concerning the alleged infringement of the Apple registered design by the Samsung Galaxy 10.1, 8.9 and 7.7 tablets must have created. And doubtless the decision will be widely publicized. But media reports now, given the uncertainty created by the conflicting reports of the past, are not enough. Another lot of media reports, reporting more or less accurately that Samsung have not only finally won but been vindicated on appeal may not be enough to disperse all the fog. It is now necessary to make assurance doubly so. Apple itself must (having created the confusion) make the posi-

tion clear: that it acknowledges that the court has decided that these Samsung products do not infringe its registered design.

The acknowledgement must come from the horse's mouth. Nothing short of that will be sure to do the job completely.

Id. at paras. 70, 71, 83, 84.

In addition to the newspaper notice, the Court required the following notice to be posted on Apple's website for one month:

On 9th July 2012 the High Court of Justice of England and Wales ruled that Samsung Electronic (UK) Limited's Galaxy Tablet Computers, namely the Galaxy Tab 10.1, Tab 8.9 and Tab 7.7 do not infringe Apple's registered design No. 0000181607-0001. A copy of the full judgment of the High Court is available on the following link [link given]. That Judgment has effect throughout the European Union and was upheld by the Court of Appeal on ..... A copy of the Court of Appeal's judgment is available on the following link [...]. There is no injunction in respect of the registered design in force anywhere in Europe.

Id. at para. 87.

Should more jurisdictions adopt the remedies of apology and/or corrective publicity? Under what circumstances should such relief be available?

3. CRIMINAL PENALTIES

The United States does not provide criminal penalties for patent infringement, but a large number of countries do, particularly when the infringement is committed willfully and on a commercial scale. Countries that impose criminal penalties tend to view willful infringement not just as a private wrong, but also as an offense against the state because the infringement breaches the state's exclusive grant to the patent owner and undermines the state's right to control that grant. As the list below indicates, most countries that criminalize patent infringement are those with civil law rather than common law legal systems, perhaps reflecting differences in the two systems' conceptions of what constitutes a crime.

Criminal penalties, which generally consist of fines, prison sentences, or both, are useful when a country's enforcement system offers inadequate injunctive relief or the likelihood of receiving adequate damages is slim. A suit alleging criminal infringement must usually be initiated by the patent owner, but the proceedings are generally controlled by a public prosecutor. The quality of the enforcement consequently depends heavily on the quality of the prosecution.

The following countries all provide criminal penalties for patent infringement: Algeria, Angola, Argentina, Austria, Bahrain, Barbados, Bolivia, Brazil, Burundi, Canada, Chile, China, Columbia, Costa Rica, Cuba, Denmark, Dominican Republic, Ecuador, Egypt, Finland, Germany, Ghana, Guatemala, Haiti, Iceland, Indonesia, Iran, Iraq, Italy, Japan, Kenya, Korea, Kuwait, Lebanon, Lesotho, Libya, Macedonia, Madagascar, Malta, Mexico, Mongolia, Nepal, Netherlands, Nicaragua, Norway, Panama, Paraguay, Peru, Philippines, Poland, Portugal, Romania, Russia, Sri Lanka, Sudan, Suriname, Sweden, Switzerland, Syria, Tanzania, Thailand, Turkey, Uruguay, Venezuela, Yugoslavia, Zaire, Zambia, and Zimbabwe. *See* 2A J.W. Baxter et al., WORLD PATENT LAW AND PRACTICE App. 2A.00 (2008).

NOTES AND QUESTIONS

1. What justifications support criminal enforcement of patents? Should there be any limits on the nature and scope of criminal penalties for infringement? If so, what norms should inform such limits? If you were asked to design an enforcement regime for a country desirous of modernizing its patent system, what elements would you include, what would you exclude, and why?

2. The U.S. remedy of enhanced damages, in theory, takes the place of criminal penalties. Which remedy do you think has the greatest potential to deter patent infringement? Should deterrence be the primary goal of criminal penalties?

CHAPTER 12

MULTINATIONAL ENFORCEMENT OF PATENT RIGHTS

■ ■ ■

A. OVERVIEW OF INTERNATIONAL OBLIGATIONS

Recall from Chapter 1 that concern over the lack of protection, and thus inability to enforce patent rights in global markets, was a primary motivation for the establishment of an international patent system. Beginning with the Paris Convention, multilateral patent agreements—both substantive and procedural—have been aimed at ensuring that patent owners can secure and enjoy the benefits of patent protection across different jurisdictions. Efforts by patent owners to enforce their rights begin at the national level, and providing a means of patent enforcement is the duty of individual nations. Without the ability to enforce the exclusive rights accorded by a patent, protection is meaningless.

You have learned in earlier Chapters of this casebook that prior to the TRIPS Agreement, countries had varying levels of patent protection including, in some cases, the exclusion of entire subjects such as pharmaceutical inventions, from domestic patent laws. In addition, many developing and least-developed countries did not have effective legal processes through which patent owners could enforce even those rights that were provided for in their domestic patent legislation. Strong dissatisfaction with this state of affairs led to efforts on the part of the United States, Japan and the EU to extend the TRIPS negotiations beyond basic prohibitions on infringement, like predecessor treaties had done, to establish minimum global standards for the enforcement of intellectual property rights. The unprecedented success of the TRIPS negotiations with regard to the enforcement agenda is reflected in the Preamble to the TRIPS Agreement, which states that WTO members recognize the need for "new rules and disciplines concerning the provision of effective and appropriate means for the enforcement of trade-related intellectual property rights, taking into account differences in national legal systems."

Effective national laws are a prerequisite to securing the benefits of the patent system, particularly by ensuring that private entities have legal recourse to enforce their patent rights. The TRIPS Agreement is the first international agreement to set minimum standards to govern private enforcement of patent rights. It makes national compliance with those standards subject to the WTO dispute settlement procedures. The TRIPS enforcement standards, which all WTO members must incorporate in their domestic laws, are thus an important aspect of the global enforcement architecture designed to facilitate these ends.

1. THE TRIPS ENFORCEMENT STANDARDS

The leading developed countries tend to share common objectives for patent enforcement; namely, discouraging infringement, penalizing infringers, and preserving the rights of patent-holders. Part III of the TRIPS Agreement, which sets forth the minimum enforcement standards, can best be described as a collection of good enforcement practices that most of these countries had already implemented before the TRIPS Agreement was adopted. Nevertheless, many developed countries had to modify some practices in order to achieve full conformity with the Agreement.

Section 1, Article 41 of Part III sets out the general obligations and standards that countries have to meet to achieve TRIPS compliance. It provides in part as follows:

> 1. Members shall ensure that enforcement procedures as specified in this Part are available under their law so as to permit effective action against any act of infringement of intellectual property rights covered by this Agreement, including expeditious remedies to prevent infringements and remedies which constitute a deterrent to further infringements. These procedures shall be applied in such a manner as to avoid the creation of barriers to legitimate trade and to provide for safeguards against their abuse.

> 2. Procedures concerning the enforcement of intellectual property rights shall be fair and equitable. They shall not be unnecessarily complicated or costly, or entail unreasonable time-limits or unwarranted delays.

Section 2 of Part III sets parameters for the civil and administrative provisions and remedies that countries must put into place, and in so doing it adds some essential detail to the general obligations and standards set forth in Section 1. For example, concerning the fair and equitable procedures required by Article 41.2 quoted above, Article 42 provides that defendants must receive timely and sufficient written notice of claims, and that all parties must have a right to representation, to present and respond to evidence, and to preserve confidential information. Article 43 further provides that judicial authorities must have the capacity to order the production of evidence and, in cases where a party fails to produce the evidence requested, countries may allow authorities to make rulings on the basis of the available evidence.

Next, Section 3 of Part III requires WTO member countries to ensure that the judicial bodies "have the authority to order prompt and effective provisional measures . . . to prevent an infringement of any intellectual property right from occurring, and . . . to preserve relevant evidence in regard to the alleged infringement" (Article 50.1). Where appropriate, particularly where there is a likelihood of irreparable harm or the destruction of evidence, judicial authorities must be able to order provisional remedies on an ex parte basis without notice to the alleged infringer. The provisional measures are to be accompanied by safeguards, however, such as requiring the patent-holder to provide security and for revocation of the measures where the patent-holder does not promptly initiate proceedings for a decision on the merits (Article 50.3–50.8).

NOTES AND QUESTIONS

1. Part III of the TRIPS Agreement, as summarized in the section above, essentially prescribes rules of judicial and administrative conduct for all WTO member states. The detail and specificity of some of the provisions are more similar to what one might expect in a domestic statute and quite unprecedented for an international treaty. Why do you think countries like the United States and Japan were willing to agree to such nationally intrusive provisions? What normative or policy concerns do you think influenced the design of these enforcement provisions in TRIPS? If you represented a developing or least-developed country during negotiations over Part III of the TRIPS Agreement, what objections would you have raised, if any?

2. Review from Chapter 1, the Federal Circuit's reasoning in *Voda v. Cordis Corp.*, *supra,* p. 45, about the role of international treaties in judicial enforcement of patents. Do you agree that the concerns and goals of international agreements such as TRIPS should have no place in a court's analysis in an infringement case, even when the treaty provisions incorporate explicit directions regarding what judicial authorities must have the power to do?

3. The enforcement provisions of the TRIPS Agreement were widely considered by scholars and commentators as the most significant aspect of the Uruguay Round of multilateral trade negotiations. *See, e.g.,* Andreas F. Lowenfeld & Rochelle Cooper Dreyfuss, *Two Achievements of the Uruguay Round: Putting TRIPS and Dispute Settlement Together*, 37 VA. J. INT'L L. 276 (1997). In this important article, Professors Lowenfeld and Dreyfuss cautioned that WTO enforcement of TRIPS obligations, including the enforcement provisions, must reflect an understanding that countries at different stages of development can and must strike a balance between incentives to create and access to knowledge goods. They observed:

> [T]he cost to member states of enforcing intellectual property rights is formidable. Monitoring is expensive, the obligation to destroy infringing materials entails high social costs, and countries with weak civil justice systems must spend the money to create them. . . . Even after these costs are borne, the TRIPS Agreement may present a

significant problem to developing countries. . . . [I]t can be argued that a technologically undeveloped country that agrees to the TRIPS Agreement is handicapping itself. Instead of following the strategy (which many developed countries once pursued) of absorbing the world's knowledge base and coming up to technological speed before protecting foreign intellectual property, a country that enters into the TRIPS Agreement . . . before it has a creative community in place, may well raise the costs of acquiring the knowledge it needs. The TRIPS Agreement might, therefore, improve the *incentives* for a developing country's citizens to become innovative, but put the *cost* of becoming innovative out of reach.

Id. at 302–303.

Do you agree? Reflect on the justifications for the international patent system which you studied in Chapter 1. What counterarguments about the effect of the TRIPS Agreement on innovation incentives could you make? Professors Lowenfeld and Dreyfuss suggest that the argument that prevailed in the Uruguay Round was that "by providing secure protection for intellectual property, a member state can remain in the mainstream of technological progress, while denying protection might leave it on the sidelines of innovation." *Id.* at 303. Recall from Chapter 1 that similar arguments were made to encourage developing countries to accede to the international patent treaties once they became independent sovereign nations. Given the concerns expressed to the United Nations in the 1970s by countries such as Brazil about the negative effects of the international patent system on national development goals, why do you think the developed countries made this same argument three decades later? Is a globally harmonized approach to patent enforcement a necessary prerequisite for encouraging domestic innovation?

4. As noted earlier, the TRIPS Agreement is the first intellectual property treaty to provide for enforcement measures as part of the substantive obligations imposed on WTO member states. Note that Article 41 states that countries only have to make sure that the standards set forth in Part III are "available"—there is no requirement that countries must actually secure the range of procedural options enumerated. Why do you think the TRIPS Agreement is framed in this way? If you were representing a patent owner, how much solace would you take in these provisions? If you were negotiating on behalf of the United States what provisions would you have wanted to change? If you were negotiating on behalf of developing and least-developed countries what provisions would you have wanted to include?

5.   Article 41.5 of the TRIPS Agreement states:

It is understood that this Part does not create any obligation to put in place a judicial system for the enforcement of intellectual property rights distinct from that for the enforcement of law in general, nor does it affect the capacity of Members to enforce their law in general. Nothing in this Part creates any obligation with respect to the distribution of resources as between enforcement of intellectual property rights and the enforcement of law in general.

Paragraph 5 was inserted at the urging of developing countries which were concerned that they would be required to devote a disproportionate amount of their scarce resources to establishing a distinct judicial system for adjudication of intellectual property rights. This provision makes clear that countries may use the existing legal infrastructure to address intellectual property enforcement. However, Article 41.1 arguably still requires countries with weak civil justice systems to expend resources to ensure that intellectual property owners can take "effective" action against acts of infringement. So, in one way or another, developing countries are obligated to strengthen their institutional capacity to enforce patent rights or face the prospect of trade sanctions.

2. IMPLEMENTING THE ENFORCEMENT PROVISIONS OF THE TRIPS AGREEMENT

Like most treaties, the TRIPS Agreement is addressed to national governments. In most countries, private parties cannot rely on its enforcement provisions to pursue an infringement action in court but instead must petition their governments to take action on their behalf before the WTO. WTO member countries may bring a complaint against another member country whose laws arguably do not comply with the enforcement standards. Two early complaints by the United States alleged that inadequate measures by Denmark and Sweden affected the enforcement of intellectual property rights in violation of TRIPS Article 50, which deals with provisional measures. Article 50 requires that judicial authorities in member states "shall have the authority to order prompt and effective provisional measures." On May 14, 1997, in *Denmark—Measures Affecting the Enforcement of Intellectual Property Rights* (DS 83), the United States requested dispute settlement consultations with Denmark on the grounds that Denmark failed to provide TRIPS-conforming ex parte provisional measures as required by Art. 50.5. Two weeks later, on May 28, 1997, the United States requested consultations with Sweden on the same grounds in *Sweden—Measures Affecting the Enforcement of Intellectual Property Rights*. In December 1998, Denmark, Sweden, and the United States notified the WTO that all parties had reached mutually agreed solutions following the enactment of amending legislation in Denmark and Sweden. The following Notification of Mutually-Agreed Solution concerns the resolution of the complaint filed against Sweden:

SWEDEN—MEASURES AFFECTING THE ENFORCEMENT OF INTELLECTUAL PROPERTY RIGHTS

WT/DS86/2
IP/D/10/Add.1
11 December 1998
World Trade Organization

NOTIFICATION OF MUTUALLY-AGREED SOLUTION

The following communication, dated 2 December 1998, from the Permanent Mission of the United States, the Permanent Delegation of the European Commission and the Permanent Mission of Sweden to the Chairman of the Dispute Settlement Body, is circulated pursuant to Article 3.6 of the DSU.

The United States of America and the European Communities— Sweden wish to notify the Dispute Settlement Body that they have reached a mutually satisfactory solution to the matter raised by the Government of the United States in WT/DS86/1, dated 2 June 1997, concerning the obligations of the European Communities and the Government of Sweden under the Agreement on Trade-Related Aspects of Intellectual Property Rights (TRIPS) to make available prompt and effective provisional measures *inaudita altera parte* in civil proceedings involving intellectual property rights.

To fulfill this obligation, inter alia, the Parliament of Sweden passed legislation on 25 November 1998 amending Sweden's Copyright Act, Trademarks Act, Patents Act, Design Protection Act, Trade Names Act, Act on Protection of Semiconductor Products, and Plant Breeders Protection Act. This legislation grants judicial authorities in Sweden the authority to order provisional measures in the context of civil proceedings involving intellectual property rights. Specifically, the legislation provides that if there is reason to believe that a person has taken or is about to take action to infringe intellectual property rights, the court may order a search for infringing materials, documents or other relevant evidence. The search may be ordered *inaudita altera parte* if there is a risk that materials or documents could be removed, destroyed or altered. The legislation will come into effect on 1 January, 1999.

Based on these developments, the European Communities—Sweden and the United States have agreed to terminate consultations on this matter and the United States wishes formally to withdraw this matter from further attention under the provisions of the Dispute Settlement Understanding. This agreement is without prejudice to the rights or obligations of either Member under the Agreement Establishing the World Trade Organization.

NOTES AND QUESTIONS

1. Review the chart in Chapter 3, p. 156, illustrating the dispute resolution process of the WTO. What are the advantages or disadvantages of the consultations phase of the process? Why do you think countries accused of TRIPS violations are willing to allow their accusers to trigger the dispute settlement process rather than comply ex ante with the provisions of TRIPS Part III? Below, Professor Okediji examines the way countries may strategically choose to engage the WTO dispute process:

> With its mandatory system of adjudication, and the availability of sanctions, it would seem that the trade regime does not suffer from the weakness of other public international law arrangements; an effective system of enforcement presumably obviates the need for alternative justifications for state compliance with TRIPS obligations. However, the importance of steady, cooperative relations in the international sphere still imposes voluntary compliance as the model for enforcing legal obligations among sovereign states... [D]espite the import of the new dispute settlement system, the provisions of the DSU reinforce the primacy of cooperative dispute resolution as the optimal strategy for promoting stable international relations and strong global markets. Article 3 of the DSU cautions members to "exercise. . . . judgment as to whether action under these procedures would be fruitful. . . . A solution mutually acceptable to the parties to a dispute and consistent with the covered agreements is *clearly to be preferred*."

> It is useful to think of the DSU process as a kind of market where information about an actor's grievance is bought and sold. Disputing Members also bargain over the terms and conditions of informal dispute settlement opportunities. . . . In such a market, the various stages of DSU adjudication serve as "signals" from the complaining party, who invokes the formal process. . . .

> Under the DSU, parties may choose to opt out of the formal process, and settle the dispute informally. It is conceivable that the possibility of opting out dilutes the strength of each signal, thus making the actions of the parties harder to predict or assess. However, the fact that opting out of the formal process is subject to *mutual agreement* alleviates this problem, because neither party can be sure what conditions will induce the other to agree to opt out. Consequently, the signals triggered by each stage of the formal process will be the most accurate source of information regarding what the other party believes about the alleged violation. The parties can then evaluate the information against the risk of sanctions and/or the costs of involuntary compliance.

> An important point is that the closer the relationship between the disputing parties, that is, the more they share political or economic interests, the more likely that there will be bargaining chips to facil-

itate an agreement to opt out of the DSU system. This is particularly true where the disputing parties are developed countries that both feel strongly about their individual positions [as suggested in the U.S.—Sweden, U.S.—Denmark cases]. Rather than risk undermining the integrity and credibility of the DSU system by refusing to implement Pane/Appellate Body decisions, the disputing developed countries may choose instead to settle their dispute through alternative means. . . The lesser the degree of interdependence between parties (and in the absence of convergent interests/shared alliances), the more difficult agreeing to opt out may be for parties, because they have no long-term interest at stake. The political economy of international society suggests that countries with "thin" relationships should be encouraged to invest in voluntary compliance, because they have no direct or immediate incentive to pay attention to the signals sent by the other country in the dispute. The lack of incentive to acquire information, and the resulting asymmetries may mean that disputes that can and should be easily resolved will instead go through the entire DSU process. Thus, interdependence facilitates the optimal condition of voluntary compliance.

Ruth L. Okediji, *Rules of Power in an Age of Law: Process Opportunism and TRIPS Dispute Settlement, in* HANDBOOK OF INTERNATIONAL TRADE, VOLUME II: ECONOMIC AND LEGAL ANALYSES OF TRADE POLICY AND INSTITUTIONS 42–72 (E. KWAN CHOI & JAMES C. HARTIGAN EDS., 2005).

Are there any disadvantages in allowing countries to opt out of the formal DSU process as Professor Okediji describes above? Do you think developing and least-developed countries can effectively exercise the signaling functions of the DSU process? Why or why not? What factors may strengthen the possibility of voluntary *cooperation* in intellectual property matters between developed and developing/least-developed countries?

2. Pursuant to TRIPS Article 63.2, once a country has amended its laws pursuant to the TRIPS Agreement, or made any other legislative changes bearing upon its obligations under TRIPS, it must publish such laws and notify them to the TRIPS Council, the body charged with oversight of TRIPS compliance. TRIPS Article 68 provides as follows:

The Council for TRIPS shall monitor the operation of this Agreement and, in particular, Members' compliance with their obligations hereunder, and shall afford Members the opportunity of consulting on matters relating to the trade-related aspects of intellectual property rights. It shall carry out such other responsibilities as assigned to it by the Members, and it shall, in particular, provide any assistance requested by them in the context of dispute settlement procedures. In carrying out its functions, the Council for TRIPS may consult with and seek information from any source it deems appropriate.

What are the advantages and disadvantages of requiring countries to notify the Council for TRIPS of changes in their intellectual property laws? What should be the consequences of a country's failure to notify? Could Article 68 above be interpreted to empower the Council for TRIPS to inform WTO members when another member country's laws are inconsistent with TRIPS?

3. The enforcement provisions of the TRIPS Agreement represent a material departure from the compliance model adopted by the Paris Convention and other international intellectual property treaties. As Professor Reichman notes:

> Under these "Great Conventions" . . . state practice treated the adoption in domestic law of a statute that more or less embodied an international minimum standard as sufficient to discharge a given state's international responsibility, even if the domestic law in question were laxly or loosely enforced. . . . What mattered was that member states strictly observed national treatment in the application of such laws, and not that the laws themselves, as implemented, fulfilled the spirit of the Conventions. Under the TRIPS Agreement, in contrast, adopting legislation that complies with international minimum standards becomes only the starting point. States must further apply these laws in ways that will stand up to external scrutiny . . . then they must adequately enforce them in compliance with detailed criteria concerning procedural and administrative matters, including remedies. Rights holders who cannot translate substantive victories into effective remedial action at the local level may eventually trigger the WTO's dispute-settlement machinery if their own states choose to question the good faith of the accused state's judicial and administrative organs.

Jerome H. Reichman, *Enforcing the Enforcement Procedures of the TRIPS Agreement*, 37 VA. J. INT'L L. 335, 338–39 (1997). What justifies this change in enforcement models in international intellectual property agreements?

3. WILLFUL INFRINGEMENT ON A COMMERCIAL SCALE: U.S. V. CHINA AND IMPLICATIONS FOR PATENT ENFORCEMENT

Section 5 of Part III, Article 61 of TRIPS states that "Members *may* provide for criminal procedures and penalties to be applied in . . . cases of infringement of [patent] rights, in particular where they are committed willfully and on a commercial scale." The same provision requires the application of criminal penalties and procedures in cases of willful, commercial-scale trademark counterfeiting or copyright piracy. Where countries adopt criminal penalties for patent infringement, the available remedies include imprisonment, fines, and the seizure, forfeiture, and destruction of infringing goods, materials, and the implements used in their manufacture. As discussed in Chapter 11, *supra*, many countries provide criminal penalties for patent infringement.

On April 10, 2007, the United States filed a complaint against China in the WTO requesting consultations concerning the protection and enforcement of intellectual property rights in China. While the U.S. complaint focused on alleged violations by China of copyright and trademark obligations under the TRIPS Agreement, the case offers an interpretation of, inter alia, Article 61 and thus has important implications for the enforcement of patent rights.

CHINA—MEASURES AFFECTING THE PROTECTION AND ENFORCEMENT OF INTELLECTUAL PROPERTY RIGHTS

WT/DS362/1
IP/D/26
G/L/819
16 April 2007

REQUEST FOR CONSULTATIONS BY THE UNITED STATES

The following communication, dated 10 April 2007, from the delegation of the United States to the delegation of China and to the Chairman of the Dispute Settlement Body, is circulated in accordance with Article 4.4 of the DSU.

My authorities have instructed me to request consultations with the Government of the People's Republic of China ("China") pursuant to Articles 1 and 4 of the *Understanding on Rules and Procedures Governing the Settlement of Disputes* ("DSU") and Article 64 of the *Agreement on Trade-Related Aspects of Intellectual Property Rights* ("TRIPS Agreement") (to the extent that Article 64 corresponds to Article XXII of the *General Agreement on Tariffs and Trade 1994*) with respect to certain measures pertaining to the protection and enforcement of intellectual property rights in China.

I. THRESHOLDS FOR CRIMINAL PROCEDURES AND PENALTIES

The first matter on which the United States requests consultations concerns the thresholds that must be met in order for certain acts . . . to be subject to criminal procedures and penalties. . . In this regard, the measures at issue include:

(1) the Criminal Law of the People's Republic of China (adopted at the Second Session of the Fifth National People's Congress on 1 July 1979 and revised at the Fifth Session of the Eighth National People's Congress on 14 March 1997) ("Criminal Law"), in particular Articles 213, 214, 215, 217, 218, and 220. . . .

Articles 213, 214, and 215 of the Criminal Law describe certain acts of trademark counterfeiting that may be subject to criminal procedures and penalties. However, under Article 213, criminal procedures and penalties are available only "if the circumstances are serious" or "if the circumstances are especially serious". Under Article 214, criminal procedures and penalties are available only "if the amount of sales [of commodities bearing counterfeit registered trademarks] is relatively large" or "if the amount of sales is huge". Under Article 215, criminal procedures and penalties are available only "if the circumstances are serious" or "if the circumstances are especially serious".

Articles 217 and 218 of the Criminal Law describe certain acts of copyright piracy that may be subject to criminal procedures and penalties. However, under Article 217, criminal procedures and penalties are available only "if the amount of illegal gains is relatively large, or if there are other serious circumstances" or "if the amount of illegal gains is huge or if there are other especially serious circumstances". Under Article 218, criminal procedures and penalties are available only "if the amount of illegal gains is huge". . . .

The Criminal Law itself does not define the terms "serious", "especially serious", "relatively large", and "huge" as used in the above-referenced articles. Instead, these terms are defined in the December 2004 Judicial Interpretation and the April 2007 Judicial Interpretation by reference to "illegal business volume" (stated in terms of the value of products produced, stored, transported and sold), "illegal gains" (stated in terms of profit), or number of "illegal copies".

Additionally, where the thresholds are defined in terms of "illegal business volume", Article 12 of the December 2004 Judicial Interpretation provides that value ordinarily is calculated according to "the prices at which such products are actually sold" or "the labeled prices or the actual prices found to be sold at after investigation". In other words, it is the price of the infringing goods as opposed to the price of the corresponding legitimate goods that determines "illegal business volume". The lower the actual or labeled prices of infringing goods, the more of them an infringer can sell or offer for sale without reaching the thresholds in the Criminal Law that are defined by reference to "illegal business volume".

The United States understands that acts of trademark counterfeiting and copyright piracy occurring on a commercial scale in China that fail to meet the thresholds are not subject to criminal procedures and penalties in China. The lack of criminal procedures and penalties for commercial scale counterfeiting and piracy in China as a result of the thresholds appears to be inconsistent with China's obligations under Articles 41.1 and 61 of the TRIPS Agreement.

II. DISPOSAL OF GOODS CONFISCATED BY CUSTOMS AUTHORITIES THAT INFRINGE INTELLECTUAL PROPERTY RIGHTS

The second matter on which the United States requests consultations concerns goods that infringe intellectual property rights that are confiscated by Chinese customs authorities, in particular the disposal of such goods following removal of their infringing features. . . .

Specifically, the United States understands that Article 27 of the Customs IPR Regulations and Article 30 of the Customs IPR Implementing Measures set forth a hierarchy of requirements for the disposal of goods that infringe intellectual property rights and that are confiscated by Chinese customs authorities. Under that hierarchy, the customs authorities often appear to be required to give priority to disposal options that would allow such goods to enter the channels of commerce (for instance, through auctioning the goods after removing their infringing features). Only if the infringing features cannot be removed must the goods be destroyed. The requirement that infringing goods be released into the channels of commerce under the circumstances set forth in the measures at issue appears to be inconsistent with China's obligations under Articles 46 and 59 of the TRIPS Agreement. . . .

IV. UNAVAILABILITY OF CRIMINAL PROCEDURES AND PENALTIES FOR A PERSON WHO ENGAGES IN EITHER UNAUTHORIZED REPRODUCTION OR UNAUTHORIZED DISTRIBUTION OF COPYRIGHTED WORKS

The fourth matter on which the United States requests consultations concerns the scope of coverage of criminal procedures and penalties for unauthorized reproduction or unauthorized distribution of copyrighted works. In particular, it appears that unauthorized reproduction of copyrighted works by itself—that is, unauthorized reproduction that is not accompanied by unauthorized distribution—may not be subject to criminal procedures and penalties. Likewise, it appears that unauthorized distribution of copyrighted works by itself—that is, unauthorized distribution that is not accompanied by unauthorized reproduction—may not be not subject to criminal procedures and penalties.

In this regard, the measures at issue include the Criminal Law, in particular Article 217, as well as any amendments, related measures, or implementing measures.

Article 217 establishes the availability of criminal procedures and penalties for certain acts of copyright piracy, including "reproducing and distributing [*fuzhifaxing*] a written work, musical work, motion picture, television programme or other visual works, computer software or other works without permission of the copyright owner" and "reproducing and distributing an audio or video recording produced by another person without permission of the producer".

To the extent that wilful copyright piracy on a commercial scale that consists of unauthorized reproduction—but not unauthorized distribution—of copyrighted works, and *vice versa*, may not be subject to criminal procedures and penalties under the law of China, this would appear to be inconsistent with China's obligations under Articles 41.1 and 61 of the TRIPS Agreement.

The United States notes that Article 2 of the April 2007 Judicial Interpretation addresses the phrase "reproducing and distributing" [*fuzhifaxing*], and we look forward to discussing this matter with China during our consultations.

Following failed consultations with China, the United States requested the establishment of a Panel pursuant to the DSU. On December 13, 2007, the director-general composed the Panel. On January 26, 2009, the Panel released its report in the case (*see* WTO, *China—Measures Affecting the Protection and Enforcement of Intellectual Property Rights*, WT/DS362/R), and on March 20, 2009, the WTO Dispute Settlement Body adopted the Report. Both China and the U.S. accepted the report's findings. The following comment attempts to shed insight on the report's lengthy, thorough, and complex analysis:

JAMES MENDENHALL, WTO REPORT ON CONSISTENCY OF CHINESE INTELLECTUAL PROPERTY STANDARDS
ASIL Insight, Apr. 3, 2009

On March 20, 2009, the World Trade Organization (WTO) Dispute Settlement Body adopted the report of the dispute settlement panel in *China—Measures Affecting the Protection and Enforcement of Intellectual Property Rights (China—IPR)*. The report addressed three claims brought by the United States alleging that certain Chinese measures are inconsistent with the WTO Agreement on Trade-Related Aspects of Intellectual Property Rights (TRIPS). The panel upheld, at least in part, two of the three U.S. claims, but found that the United States did not present sufficient evidence to support its most important allegation, *i.e.*, that certain volume and value thresholds established for defining criminal counterfeiting and piracy are inconsistent with TRIPS.

Previous dispute settlement decisions had touched on the general enforcement obligations in TRIPS, but only in a superficial way. The panel in the *China-IPR* dispute was thus faced with a series of novel questions, and, as would be expected, the standards adopted by the panel merit further refinement. For example, while the report draws a roadmap for framing future claims regarding criminal thresholds, it is less clear how a government could apply some of the standards before bringing a claim. Still, the report may provide a basis for further engagement with China on the issue of IPR enforcement and may, therefore, ultimately lead to stronger IPR protection.

CRIMINAL THRESHOLDS

Under Chinese law, acts of counterfeiting and piracy are criminal only if the amount of infringing material exceeds certain quantity or value thresholds, *e.g.*, 500 copies of a DVD or approximately $7,000 worth of counterfeit goods. The United States alleged that the thresholds create a safe harbor for businesses engaged in commercial activities such as distribution of infringing products and are inconsistent with Article 61 of the TRIPS Agreement, which requires the criminalization of "wilful trademark counterfeiting or copyright piracy on a commercial scale." In support of this claim, the United States provided, along with the measures themselves, industry reports detailing the volume of infringing material seized during police raids (which in many cases fell below the thresholds) and other anecdotal data.

The critical issue with respect to this claim was the meaning of the phrase "commercial scale," a term never before interpreted by a WTO panel or the Appellate Body. The panel concluded that "commercial scale" activity means something different than "commercial" activity. Specifically, the term "commercial scale" implies a certain size threshold and not a qualitative assessment of the purpose of the activity. Furthermore, according to the panel, the threshold cannot be interpreted in the abstract but varies with respect to individual products and markets. According to the panel, "counterfeiting or piracy 'on a commercial scale' refers to counterfeiting or piracy carried on at the magnitude or extent of typical or usual commercial activity with respect to a given product in a given market." In any given case, commercial scale "may be large or small. The magnitude or extent of typical or usual commercial activity relates, in the longer term, to profitability."

Despite the panel's reference to profitability, there is no indication that the panel believed that profitability is the critical defining characteristic for "commercial scale" activity. In fact, the panel appeared to conclude that the profitability or purpose of an individual operation is irrelevant. Under the standard enunciated by the panel, the critical question is whether the infringing activity is equal to or larger than the usual size of a business operation with respect to a given product or market. While the panel recognized that the Chinese measures "exclude certain commercial activity from criminal procedures and penalties," it found that this was insufficient to prove that the measures are inconsistent with TRIPS.

The panel emphasized the importance of evidence to establish a claim that quantitative thresholds are inconsistent with Article 61. It found that "the United States did not provide data regarding products and markets or other factors that would demonstrate what constituted 'a commercial' scale in the specific situation in China's marketplace." According to the panel, the press articles that the United States provided were merely anecdotal, while the raid data did not provide enough context to assess how the seized quantities related to typical or usual commercial activity with respect to the market and product at issue.

. . . .

RELEASE OF SEIZED COUNTERFEIT GOODS INTO THE STREAM OF COMMERCE

China's customs regulations give customs authorities the following options for disposing of IPR-infringing goods seized at the border: (i) Customs may hand the goods over to public welfare bodies for public welfare undertakings; (ii) if the holder of the intellectual property wishes to buy the goods, Customs may sell them; (iii) if the first two options are not possible, and if Customs can "eradicat[e] the infringing features," then the goods may be auctioned; or (iv) when eradication is impossible, Customs may destroy the goods.

The United States argued that the customs regulations are inconsistent with Article 59 of the TRIPS Agreement, which requires that competent authorities have the authority to order destruction or disposal of infringing goods. The United States asserted that the Chinese regulations created a "compulsory scheme" that precluded destruction or proper disposal of infringing goods if one of the first two options listed above were possible. The panel rejected China's claim that customs authorities were not authorized to destroy or properly dispose of infringing goods in large part based on China's clarification of the powers granted to its authority.

The panel accepted the U.S. claim that the third option in the Chinese regulations is inconsistent with TRIPS Article 46, (as referenced in TRIPS Article 59), stating that "the simple removal of the trademark unlawfully affixed shall not be sufficient, other than in exceptional circumstances, to permit release of the goods into the channels of commerce."

One point in the panel's reasoning is of particular interest. TRIPS Article 59 requires that competent authorities "shall have the authority to order the destruction or disposal of infringing goods in accordance with the principles set out in article 46." The panel report made it clear that "[t]he obligation is to 'have' authority not an obligation to 'exercise' authority." According to the panel, "the obligation that competent authorities 'shall have the authority' to make certain orders is not an obligation that competent authorities shall exercise that authority in a particular way, unless otherwise specified." The United States had not challenged the manner in which China applied its customs regulations, but only the regulations as such. Thus, this statement does not preclude a future WTO claim, based on appropriate factual evidence, that the authority granted to an enforcement authority is never used and is effectively a nullity. Such a claim might be based not only on Article 59 but also Article 41 of the TRIPS Agreement, which requires that enforcement procedures be "available . . . so as to permit effective action against any act of infringement. . . ." Assembling the necessary evidence could be challenging, however.

CONCLUSION

China will now have a reasonable period of time to implement the panel's recommendations. . . . The . . . claims that the United States won are relatively discrete, and China can comply with the related rulings through surgical amendments to its regulations. Whether the panel's finding on the thresholds claim will have a significant impact on China's IPR enforcement regime remains to be seen. Significantly, the panel did not find that China's criminal enforcement scheme was consistent with TRIPS Article 61, but only that United States had failed to prove its claims. Consequently, the panel report gives a roadmap for future challenges that should be of interest to private parties adversely affected by China's current thresholds or any other thresholds of a similar nature. At the very least, the report may provide a basis for further constructive dialogue with China.

NOTES AND QUESTIONS

1. In commenting on the China panel report, Professor Yu sees benefits for both the United States and China:

[T]hrough the present dispute, the United States sent a strong signal to China about its willingness to use the WTO process to resolve disputes. This signal, in turn, may lead to further negotiations both within and without the intellectual property arena. . . .

Second, through the WTO process, the United States has learned a great deal about China's legal reasoning and WTO strategies. The panel report also reveals how the WTO panels will evaluate China's unique legal structure and measures (such as those judicial interpretations that have normative effects). This information is useful not only for the U.S. administration, but also for American rights holders. . . .

Third, through the various submissions and oral statements, the United States and its rights holders successfully obtained on record detailed information about how censorship regulations, customs procedures, and criminal thresholds operate in China. . . . In the future, all of this information will be very useful to protect the interests of rights holders. The United States will also be able to use this information as well as claims China made before the WTO panel to induce China not to change its position. The collected information therefore will create an estoppel effect, providing certainty, clarity, and predictability in the area. . . .

The panel report enables China to understand better its TRIPS obligations through the eyes of a neutral third party. It provides both certainty and clarity to the country's TRIPS-related obligations. More importantly, the report provides the reformist factions within the Chinese leadership with an important push for stronger reforms within the country. In China, the reformists are constantly challenged by their more conservative counterparts, who are uncomfortable with the country's rapid socio-economic changes and the resulting social ills. By providing the much-needed external push that helps reduce resistance from conservative leaders, the panel report has helped accelerate reforms in the area of intellectual property protection and enforcement.

In addition, China's participation in the WTO process has helped the country raise what I have called the "WTO game." In addition to human resources, litigation capital, and legal capacities, a successful player will need more finely-honed skills and a deeper knowledge of the different facets of this game. The more a country plays the WTO game, the more familiar and better it will become. . . . Any experience China earns in the intellectual property area can also spill over into other areas covered by the various WTO agreements. . . . Finally, the gains in the panel report will put China in a better bargaining position in its ongoing intellectual property-related negotiations with the United States.

Peter K. Yu, *The TRIPS Enforcement Dispute*, 89 Neb. L. Rev. 1046, 1103–1108 (2011). Do you agree with Professor Yu?

2. Like all litigation, complaining parties must assess the risk of loss and weigh the consequences of such loss for future interactions with other market actors. While the United States did not "lose" as such in the China case, the panel's ruling and interpretation of the TRIPS provisions at issue were not as favorable for U.S. economic interests as had been expected. In particular, the perceived value of having successfully limited an expansive interpretation of the TRIPS enforcement provisions may have weakened the ability of the United States to threaten other countries with what may be one-sided views of what the TRIPS standards require. In your view, is this a positive or negative consequence of the China dispute?

3. Despite the well-recognized importance of the WTO dispute settlement system to intellectual property enforcement, TRIPS disputes have been far less numerous and significant than was imagined at the conclusion of the Uruguay Round. Further, while many scholars and commentators anticipated—consistent with the geopolitical conditions that dominated the Round—that TRIPS adjudication would be a primary mechanism to discipline free-riding by developing and least-developed countries, indeed most TRIPS disputes have been between the *developed* countries. Professor Okediji suggests that this surprising development may be attributable to the incomplete nature of the TRIPS Agreement, and the relative power parity between the developed countries during negotiations. She argues that the alliances that made the TRIPS Agreement possible required developed countries to largely ignore normative differences in their own laws in favor of an agreement that would bring developing countries into a stronger international intellectual property system. As a result, if diplomacy fails and interests do not converge, WTO dispute settlement becomes the only avenue for redress in intellectual

property disputes between powerful countries. *See* Ruth L. Okediji, *Public Welfare and the Role of the WTO: Reconsidering the TRIPS Agreement*, 17 EMORY INT'L L. REV. 819, 842–854 (2003). For a recent analysis focusing on TRIPS dispute settlement compared to other trade areas, *see* Joost Pauwelyn, *The Dog that Barked But Didn't Bite: 15 Years of Intellectual Property Disputes at the WTO*, 1 J. INT'L DISP. SETTLEMENT 389 (2010). To date, only twenty-eight intellectual property disputes have been adjudicated within the WTO system. Of these, only three were patent cases.

B. REGIONAL ENFORCEMENT INITIATIVES

1. THE EUROPEAN DIRECTIVE ON THE ENFORCEMENT OF INTELLECTUAL PROPERTY RIGHTS

In 2004, the European Union adopted Directive 2004/48/EC on the Enforcement of Intellectual Property Rights. The Directive, which builds on the enforcement provisions of the TRIPS Agreement and applies to patents and all other intellectual property rights, is illustrative of a growing trend within the EU to "regionalize" intellectual property standard-setting; in other words, to set regional standards for intellectual property protection to which all EU member countries must adhere.

Article 3 requires EU Member States to provide enforcement measures, procedures, and remedies that are "fair and equitable" and not "unnecessarily complicated or costly or entail unreasonable time-limits or unwarranted delays." The provision goes on to state:

> Those measures, procedures and remedies shall also be effective, proportionate and dissuasive and shall be applied in such a manner as to avoid the creation of barriers to legitimate trade and to provide for safeguards against their abuse.

Among the Directive's provisions are those relating to evidence, provisional and precautionary measures, corrective measures, and damages, and a principal target of the Directive seems to be commercial-scale infringement. For example, the Directive requires EU member states to provide not only for the presentation of evidence regarding the alleged infringement, but also "in the case of an infringement committed on a commercial scale" to order up the alleged infringer's "banking, financial or commercial documents" when requested by the patent-holder (Article 6.2).

The Directive's required enforcement measures give judges an extensive array of remedies. Judges must be authorized to issue preliminary injunctions in order to prevent imminent infringement, including ex parte orders, as well as permanent injunctions. They must also be authorized to order the removal of infringing goods or provide for their destruction, require the losing party to bear the legal costs, compel the infringer to disseminate information about the infringement, and order the payment of damages. Although the level of damages for patent infringement in Europe is generally lower than in the United States, judges who set damages are required to take into account the following factors in accordance with Article 13.1:

(a) [T]hey shall take into account all appropriate aspects, such as the negative economic consequences, including lost profits, which the injured party has suffered, any unfair profits made by the infringer and, in appropriate cases, elements other than economic factors, such as the moral prejudice caused to the right holder by the infringement;

or

(b) as an alternative to (a), they may, in appropriate cases, set the damages as a lump sum on the basis of elements such as at least the amount of royalties or fees which would have been due if the infringer had requested authorisation to use the intellectual property right in question.

Article 9.2 of the Directive provides for the remedy of a precautionary seizure (roughly the equivalent of an attachment) of an alleged infringer's property, including bank accounts and other assets. The provision states:

In the case of an infringement committed on a commercial scale, the Member States shall ensure that, if the injured party demonstrates circumstances likely to endanger the recovery of damages, the judicial authorities may order the precautionary seizure of the movable and immovable property of the alleged infringer, including the blocking of his/her bank accounts and other assets. To that end, the competent authorities may order the communication of bank, financial or commercial documents, or appropriate access to the relevant information.

The excerpt below comments on a 2007 case from the Court of Genoa, Italy, in which the patent owner, the Dutch company Philips, sought a precautionary seizure of the assets of Princo Corporation, the alleged infringer, in order to ensure the recovery of damages at the conclusion of the infringement proceedings.

LAURA ORLANDO, "PIRACY" PROVISIONS UNDER THE ENFORCEMENT DIRECTIVE AND PATENT INFRINGEMENT
2 J. INTELL. PROP. L. & PRAC. 642 (2007)

Princo Corporation, Ltd v. Koninklijke Philips Electronics, Docket no. 3213/07, Court of Genoa, 18 April 2007.

The Court of Genoa has issued its first decision on the application to patent infringement of the remedies introduced by Directive 2004/48 on the Enforcement of Intellectual Property Rights, dismissing the appeal filed by Princo against a precautionary seizure order over its movable and immovable property issued by a judge of the Genoa IP Chamber on the grounds that the patent infringement was committed intentionally and on a commercial scale.

LEGAL CONTEXT

The ruling was issued on the grounds of Article 9 of Directive 2004/48. This Article establishes that in the case of an infringement committed on a commercial scale, the Member States should ensure that, if the injured party demonstrates circumstances likely to endanger the recovery of damages, the judicial authority may order the precautionary seizure of all the defendant's assets, including bank accounts. Such provision was implemented in Article 144bis of the Italian IP Code. For the purposes of the application of this, Article 144 of the Italian IP Code also specified that the infringement of IP rights carried out intentionally and on a commercial scale falls within the definition of acts of piracy.

FACTS

Philips sued Princo before the Court of Genoa for the infringement of its patent rights following the importation into Italy of a batch of unlicensed CD-Rs manufactured by Princo and seized by the Italian customs authorities. After the preliminary seizure of the single batch and injunction order, proceedings on the merits were instigated. In these proceedings, the appointed Court expert witness quantified damages owed to Philips based not only on the single batch of products seized but rather on the overall number of unlicensed importations of Princo CD-Rs carried out in the relevant period.

Upon the findings of the Court expert witness, Philips requested and obtained an order of precautionary seizure over all Princo's movable and immovable property, including its bank accounts, with a view to ensuring the recovery of damages to be awarded at the end of the liability proceedings.

Princo appealed against the precautionary seizure order before the Panel of the Court, which dismissed the appeal and confirmed the seizure order on the grounds that the activity of manufacture and destination for the Italian and European market of unlicensed CD-Rs, being both wilful and systematic, met the requirements provided by Italian law for "piracy on a commercial scale."

ANALYSIS

The precautionary order was issued pursuant to Art. 144bis of the Intellectual Property Code. This Article (recently introduced in Italy through the implementation of the Enforcement Directive) establishes that the seizure of the infringer's assets can be requested whenever the damaged party claims the existence of circumstances that may jeopardize monetary compensation.

The defendant claimed that the seizure order obtained by Philips in the preliminary proceedings should be revoked, by arguing, inter alia, that (i) no infringement of Philips' patents had occurred, as Princo would not have participated in any act of importation in Italy of the contested discs, and (ii) no damages should be awarded to Philips, as all the contested goods had been held by the customs authorities and seized before being put on the market; (iii) consequently, the seizure order of all the defendant's assets provided for by the IP Code in order to guarantee the payment of damages lacked sufficient grounds.

The Court dismissed all these arguments.

I.   INFRINGEMENT

As to the first argument, the Court found that Princo (directly or through other entities) had for years been trying to introduce into the European and US markets unlicensed goods in competition with those covered by Philips' patents and sought to challenge Philips' relevant patents in many jurisdictions, without success. According to the Court, in the present case Princo was continuing to challenge Philips' patents throughout "circumventive operations," i.e. both using triangular schemes of importation of goods through countries where the customs controls are less efficient and using a chain of exporters/retailers aimed at reducing the risks of being charged with being the direct promoter of the importations.

II.   DAMAGES

The second argument was dismissed on the ground that the applicable set of rules for the protection of IP rights allows rights holders to claim damages also in view of imminent violations, without the need that the goods actually reached the market. The Court also concluded that, at the moment when the border detention takes place, the sale of the infringing goods to the Italian importer has already taken place and the exporter of counterfeit goods has already gained a profit. Accordingly, the actual damage to the right holder, being deprived of the due profits due to the failure by the importer to purchase the goods through licensed channels, has already occurred.

III.   GROUNDS FOR SEIZURE

As to the grounds for the measure, the Court held that the requirements provided for by the relevant provision—i.e. the existence of circumstances that may jeopardize monetary compensation or lead the Court to believe that the losing party may fail to comply with the order of compensation—could be considered *ipso facto* in this specific case without the need to produce further evidence. Indeed, according to the Court, the acts carried out by the defendant met the specific requirements of "piracy," i.e.

the wilful and systematic usurpation of IP rights. Accordingly, a precautionary seizure order as introduced by the Enforcement Directive could be granted automatically. In calculating the capped amount for the precautionary seizure, the Court took into account the standard royalty applicable in the field for the licence of the technology at issue and, after having multiplied that royalty by the number of unlicensed discs involved, doubled the resulting amount for punitive purposes.

NOTES AND QUESTIONS

1. In July 2005, the EU proposed a Directive on Criminal Measures Aimed at Ensuring the Enforcement of Intellectual Property Rights, COM (2005) 276 final, to supplement the Directive on the Enforcement of Intellectual Property Rights, Directive 2004/48/EC, which is limited to civil enforcement. The draft directive provides that "Member States shall ensure that all intentional infringements of an intellectual property right on a commercial scale, and attempting, aiding or abetting and inciting such infringements, are treated as criminal offences" (Article 3). The draft directive came under considerable criticism and ultimately was withdrawn. Do you think requiring criminal liability for patent infringement is a wise policy?

2. In December 2000, the European Union adopted Council Regulation No. 44/2001 on Jurisdiction and the Recognition and Enforcement of Judgments in Civil and Commercial Matters, 2001 O.J. (L 12) 1. Article 22(4) of the Regulation expressly establishes exclusive jurisdiction over intellectual property rights as follows:

The following courts shall have exclusive jurisdiction, regardless of domicile:

4. in proceedings concerned with the registration or validity of patents, trademarks, designs, or other similar rights required to be deposited or registered, the courts of the Member State in which the deposit or registration has been applied for, has taken place or is under the terms of a Community instrument or an international convention deemed to have taken place.

Without prejudice to the jurisdiction of the European Patent Office under the Convention on the Grant of European Patents, signed at Munich on 5 October 1973, the courts of each Member State shall have exclusive jurisdiction, regardless of domicile, in proceedings concerned with the registration or validity of any European patent granted for that State. . . .

The Regulation thus makes clear that even in respect of European patents that may be valid in several European countries, enforcement of patent rights in each designated country is governed by the law and courts of that country, just as you learned in Chapter 10.

2. FREE TRADE AGREEMENTS

As discussed in Chapter 3, following the conclusion of the Uruguay Round, the United States and other developed countries embarked on a series of negotiations for free trade agreements (FTAs) with many developing countries and regions. Many of the agreements include a Chapter on intellectual property protection that, in many cases, extends intellectual property obligations beyond the minimum standards required by the TRIPS Agreement. In general, the heightened patent obligations in the FTAs cover things such as widened scope of protectable subject matter, constraints on limitations and exceptions recognized under TRIPS or other intellectual property treaties, and proposing stronger enforcement obligations. These so-called "TRIPS-plus" agreements have been heavily criticized for upsetting the balance between incentives for innovation and ensuring the dissemination and accessibility of public knowledge goods. Particularly as relates to pharmaceutical patents, TRIPS-plus provisions in certain FTAs facially constrain the ability of developing-country partners to exercise the limitations related to ensuring an optimal supply of essential medicines as recognized in the 2001 Doha Declaration on TRIPS and Public Health. For example, FTAs between the United States and Peru, the United States and Columbia, and the United States and Panama all contain provisions requiring data exclusivity of clinical test data for at least a five-year period. *See* Bryan Mercurio, *TRIPS-Plus Provisions in FTAs: Recent Trends*, in *Regional Trade Agreements and the WTO Legal System* 215, 227–228 (Lorand Bartels & Frederico Ortino eds., 2006); and, e.g., United States—Peru Trade Promotion Agreement, Apr. 12, 2006, http://www.ustr.gov/trade-agreements/free-trade-agreements/peru-tpa/final-text. This is neither required by TRIPS, nor reflective of U.S. law which, while protecting data exclusivity, has always done so with strict caps on the periods. *See, e.g.,* 21 U.S.C. §355(c)(3)(E), 21 U.S.C. §355(j)(5)(F).

The expansion of substantive and procedural rights for patent-holders contained in many FTAs is reinforced by an explicit delimiting of flexibilities that historically have served to provide residual space for the exercise of sovereign autonomy over innovation policy, and in the design of intellectual property laws to serve identified public welfare goals that are meaningfully related to domestic local conditions. Combined with stronger enforcement obligations, FTAs are viewed by some commentators as particularly pernicious to developing countries, even when they are consistent with the substantive principles of the TRIPS Agreement. *See, e.g.,* Reto H. Hilty & Thomas T. Jaeger, *Legal Effects and Policy Considerations for Free Trade Agreements: What's Wrong with FTAs?* (Max Planck Institute for Intellectual Property, Competition & Tax Law Research Paper No. 10–02, 2010); Anselm Kamperman Sanders, *Intellectual Property, Free Trade Agreements and Economic Development,* 23 GA. ST. U. L. REV. 893 (2007).

While FTAs do not usually incorporate institutional dispute settlement characteristics such as the WTO dispute resolution system, greater commitments to enforce the TRIPS-plus provisions are regarded as more likely to generate compliance by developing countries precisely because violations of these provisions are subject to bilateral (and often closed) discussions without the benefit or obligation to reflect the general objectives of the TRIPS Agreement as set out in the Preamble, or in Articles 7 and 8. Further, enforcement of patent rights pursuant to the provisions of an FTA does not require a lengthy adjudicative process in which arguments can be coordinated to weave a common theme regarding the overarching policies of the treaty as is usually evident in the WTO TRIPS dispute settlement process. Rather, FTAs, which are more like privately negotiated contracts than publicly designed statutes, are more likely to be interpreted—and enforcement obligations of member states more seriously monitored—and enforced in the manner most satisfying to the immediate goals of the parties which, in many cases, is reflective of the short-term demands of powerful domestic interest groups. Nevertheless, FTAs could be strategically important for patent owners to the extent they delineate geographical spaces in which enforcement of rights could be far more accessible in regions with economic significance. In other words, FTAs offer a more cohesive set of geographical, legal and economic boundaries for enforcement of patents than does the TRIPS Agreement. For a list of U.S. FTAs in force, *see* Office of the U.S. Trade Representative, *Trade Agreements*, http://www.ustr.gov/trade-agreements.

C. ADMINISTRATIVE AND BORDER ENFORCEMENT

In several countries, courts are not the only forum available for patent enforcement. Customs officials and other agencies have the authority to make initial determinations of infringement (often based on evidence submitted by a patentee or exclusive licensee) and enjoin importation of infringing goods. Further, in major patent-granting countries such as the United States and China, administrative agencies serve to supplement court systems as part of a coordinated approach to enforcement. In the United States, the International Trade Commission (ITC) is a quasi-judicial federal agency authorized through § 337 of the Tariff Act of 1930 (19 U.S.C. § 1337) to, among other things, adjudicate cases that concern imports of allegedly infringing products. Foreign and domestic patent owners often initiate an ITC proceeding over litigation (or in addition to it) because of the ITC's power to grant exclusion orders that ban all imports of the alleged infringing product. Since amendments in 1988 made it easier for patentees to use the ITC process, it has become a powerful forum for patent enforcement. By 2007, 94 percent of all § 337 investigations by the ITC involved patent infringement allegations. In 2010, all but four of the active § 337 investigations at the ITC involved allegations of patent infringement. *See* U.S. Int'l Trade Comm'n, *Year in Review, Fiscal Year 2010*, 14 http://www.usitc.gov/publications/year_in_review/pub 4212.pdf (2010). The ITC reportedly conducts more patent adjudications than any district court in the United States. *See*, Taras M. Czebiniak, Note, *When Congress Gives Two Hats, Which Do You Wear? Choosing Between Domestic Industry Protection and IP Enforcement in § 337 Investigations*, 26 BERKELEY TECH. L.J. 93, 103–104 (2011).

In China, patent rights can be enforced through a regional administrative system as well as through the courts. As the following excerpt explains, there are certain advantages to adopting an administrative route for patent enforcement.

JEFFERY M. DUNCAN, MICHELLE A. SHERWOOD & YUANLIN SHEN, A COMPARISON BETWEEN THE JUDICIAL AND ADMINISTRATIVE ROUTES TO ENFORCE INTELLECTUAL PROPERTY RIGHTS IN CHINA

7 J. MARSHALL REV. INTELL. PROP. L. 529 (2008)

China offers two distinct routes for enforcing IP rights. The route most familiar to U.S. companies is the judicial route, namely the bringing of an infringement action in the courts. The other route is to bring an administrative action. The use of a government agency to enforce intellectual property rights is a somewhat "foreign" concept to most U.S. companies. Nevertheless, as explained below and depending on the circumstances, this may be the best route. . . .

[W]hen utilizing administrative proceedings, a patent holder requests administrative action in front of an IPO [local intellectual property office]. Established in the designated cities, independent regions, and the provinces, the local IPO's are overseen by SIPO [the State Intellectual Property Office of China]. This marks a difference between the United States Patent and Trademark Office ("USPTO") and SIPO. Whereas SIPO supervises the local IPO's which have authority to enforce IP rights throughout the country, the USPTO only has authority to examine and issue patents. *[handwritten: difference b/w USPTO v. SIPO]*

Bestowing on an administrative agency, such as the local IPO's, quasi-judicial authorities, which would be highly unusual in the United States, is reportedly very common in China. One theory posited is that China has traditionally not embraced the concept of "separation of power," which is a fundamental concept in the U.S. system. In any case, although granted the authority to judge patent disputes, the local IPO's often take a mediation approach, rather than adjudication. This appears to be consistent with the theory that the Chinese traditionally prefer to resolve disputes privately. As such, a neutral and detached government agency like a local IPO can be involved as a mediator to thereby facilitate opposing parties in making concessions and compromises towards a settlement.

The local IPO's do not have an established appeal procedure. Thus, if one of the parties is dissatisfied with the decision of the local IPO, that party would have to bring an infringement action in the People's Courts to change the result.

ADMINISTRATIVE PROCEDURE

The Measures for Administrative Enforcement of Patent, promulgated by SIPO in 2001, govern the procedure for a patent enforcement action before a local IPO. In order to initiate such a proceeding, a patent holder must file a written request to the administrative authorities for patent affairs to handle an infringement dispute. The patent holder must clearly identify the respondent and the matter at issue and certify that it has not instituted court proceedings in the People's Court in respect to the specific infringement dispute. The patent holder may request the relevant administrative authorities at county-level and above at the place of the infringer's domicile or location of the infringing act to handle the case. The patent holder should also submit proof of his right and evidence of the infringing act. If an agent is appointed to submit the request, an authorization letter should also be furnished.

The administrative authorities responsible for handling IP disputes will make a decision whether a complaint will be processed within a fixed time upon receipt of the request and inform the applicant of its decision. The time is seven days for patent actions and fifteen days for copyright actions. A written explanation will be given to the applicant if the decision is negative.

Upon receipt, the IPO will forward the request to the respondent, i.e. the accused infringer, within fourteen days from receipt of the request. The respondent then has only fifteen days to submit a written defense. If the respondent fails to answer within the given time, the action will proceed without its participation. The IPO generally issues a decision within a few months. If the agency decides that infringement has been proven, the IPO may issue an order to cease manufacturing and selling the infringing products, and to destroy all existing infringing products. The IPO may also confiscate illegal earnings based on the illicit income earned by the infringing party. However, the IPO is not to award money damages to the plaintiff. Upon the request of the interested party, however, the IPO may mediate resolution of claims for compensation.

If the respondent is not satisfied with the IPO's decision, the law permits him to institute legal proceedings in the court in accordance with the Administrative Procedure Law of China within fifteen days from the date of receipt of the decision. However, the decision of the IPO regarding patent infringement and the punishment rendered will continue to be enforced during the court proceedings. Where an interested party is dissatisfied with the administrative punishment decision made by the administrative authorities, he may, within three months from receipt of the notification of the decision, institute administrative proceedings with the People's Court in the place where the administrative authorities are located. If no proceedings are instituted and the decision is not performed at the expiration of the specified period, the administrative authorities may request the People's Court for compulsory execution thereof.

Thus, for example, in a patent infringement case, where the parties are not willing to consult with each other or the consultation fails, the patentee or any interested party may institute a legal proceeding with a competent People's Court, as discussed above, or request the relevant administrative authority for patent affairs to handle the matter. If the case is referred to an administrative authority and such authority establishes infringement, it has the power to order the infringing party to stop the infringing act immediately. If, within the time limit, the order is not complied with, the administrative authority for patent affairs may approach the People's Court for enforcement of the administrative order. If any party is not satisfied with the administrative order, it may, within fifteen days as of receipt of the administrative order, institute a legal proceeding with a competent People's Court.

In a case of passing off and false marking, the administrative authority has the right to order the person or entity to stop and to rectify the act. Further, the administrative authority may confiscate illegal income and impose a fine of no more than three times the value of illegal income or, if there is no income, a fine of no more than RMB 50,000. In a case of attempting to pass off a non-patented product as a patented one, for example, by false marking with a fictitious patent number, the administrative authorities may order the person or entity to stop, announce a public criticism and/or impose a fine of up to RMB 50,000.

To curb patent infringement and especially patent counterfeiting, the agency has recently been given additional power to examine the alleged infringing party, and other relevant parties, to inspect the premises of the alleged infringing act, to inspect or copy relevant documents, and, if reasonable evidence of the illegal activities is provided, the power to seize or confiscate relevant products or equipment. . . .

ADVANTAGES AND DISADVANTAGES OF THE ADMINISTRATIVE ROUTE

The administrative route can provide a quick, efficient and low-cost remedy, specifically when the case of infringement is clear, when there are minimal damages, and when it is not likely that the infringer will contest the infringement allegations. If, however, the accused infringer is likely to strongly dispute the allegations and challenge any administrative decision in court, it is more efficient to forgo the administrative approach and directly seek a remedy in court. Another disadvantage of the administrative route is that the local IPO may be influenced by local government officials keen to protecting their local industries. Because the local IPO does not have authority to award damages to the plaintiff, the only way the plaintiff can walk away with money is through a mediation conducted by the IPO. If the mediation fails, the parties may institute a legal proceeding.

While administrative proceedings with the appropriate IPO are effective to end infringing activity in a relatively short time, they are ineffective in imposing punishment or damages. First, it is difficult to calculate the amount of the offender's illegal earnings. Second, the maximum fine seems low compared with the potential profit of an infringer. Further, the amount of compensation for patent infringement is calculated based on the infringer's profits earned during the infringement period or the amount lost by the patent holder during the same period. In many cases, however, the infringing party's loss is much greater than the infringer's illegal earnings. Such compensation appears to be an insufficient deterrent against patent infringement. . . .

The administrative route is faster and less expensive, often resulting in an administrative injunction being issued against the infringer. However, where a patent owner is [not] satisfied with enjoining the infringer's activity alone and wishes to recover damages, it is advisable to take the judicial route instead. In either route, court or IPO facilitated mediation has been quite successful in resolving IP infringement disputes.

Section 4 of Part III of TRIPS, entitled Special Requirements Related to Border Measures, obliges WTO member countries to adopt measures that permit right holders who have valid grounds for suspecting the importation of infringing goods into the country, to seek the assistance of customs authorities in blocking the importation of those goods. The section was adopted primarily to prevent the importation of counterfeit trademark or pirated copyright goods. It does not oblige member countries to apply the border measures to patented goods, but Article 51 *permits* countries to do so, provided the countries respect the same safeguards that apply to trademark and copyright measures. Typical safeguards include requiring the applicant to provide security or an equivalent assurance sufficient to protect the defendant and the competent authorities from potential abuse.

The ability to stop infringing goods from crossing the borders of a particular territory can be a powerful enforcement tool for patent-holders. As the following excerpt and notes discuss, the United States, EU, and Japan all have effective border enforcement regimes in place for intellectual property infringement. While the systems differ in form and procedure, they all have the same goal: allowing the entry of non-infringing goods with minimal harm to the importer, and the detention of infringing goods that would injure the rights of intellectual property owners, a balance that can be difficult to achieve.

Tyson Winarski & Adam Hess, INTERNATIONAL TECHNOLOGY TRADE WARS: DEFENDING PATENTED ELECTRICAL TECHNOLOGY AT THE INTERNATIONAL TRADE COMMISSION

INTELL. PROP. TODAY, Nov. 2008
(http://www.iptoday.com/articles/2008-11-winarski.asp)

Patents are the primary means by which companies establish legal rights to a technology (essentially granting the owner a limited monopoly). When competitors infringe those patents, patent owners have conventionally gone to Federal District Court to seek out damages and injunctive relief for patent infringement. However, when foreign imports are the source of patent infringement, patent owners can and should look outside the box and seek to enforce their patent rights in front of the International Trade Commission ("ITC"). Pursuant to Section 337 of the Tariff Act of 1930 (19 U.S.C. §1337), the ITC has the authority to redress unfair trade practices caused by imports into the United States, such as those caused by patent, copyright, and trademark infringement. . . .

Over the past decade, the ITC has received 195 complaints requesting the institution of investigations pursuant to Section 337 alleging patent infringement as the underlying unfair act. Of these 195 complaints, 89 alleged infringement of electrical and electronics-based patents. Indeed, over 46 percent of all complaints received by the ITC over the past decade for patent infringement concern electrical technologies. The remaining 54 percent involved pharmaceutical, mechanical, and chemical technologies. . . . The accused products in these complaints largely involve imports from Asia. Over the past 10 years, 79 percent of the accused products originated in Asia. Of the remaining 21 percent, 10 percent were exports from Europe and 8 percent were exported either from Canada or Mexico.

[T]he ITC is a U.S. government body that has jurisdiction over, among other things, determining whether foreign imports violate U.S. patent rights. Other governments, such as the European Union and Japan, have analogous customs systems that have jurisdiction over the importation of goods that are accused [of infringing] patent rights held in those countries.

Seeking relief from the ITC for patent infringement has many unique advantages. In addition to a jurisdictional reach that far exceeds the scope of the Federal District Courts making it a useful forum for dealing with foreign entities, the expedited nature of a Section 337 patent infringement proceeding before the ITC provides swift and cost effective relief. Section 337 proceedings before the ITC proceed on a fast track. The statute requires that the ITC conduct and conclude its investigation "at the earliest practicable time." To fulfill this requirement, the ITC generally concludes its investigation and issues an order within 12 to 15 months. This forum's speed often results in another benefit: lower legal costs. Further, the expedited nature and fixed schedule of 337 proceedings before the ITC provide a level of certainty with respect to the financial outlay involved, much more so than its Federal District Court counterpart.

A patent owner's successful enforcement of its patent rights before the ITC earns it an exclusion order against continued importation of the accused articles and/or a cease-and-desist order barring the sale of the subject articles held in inventory by the infringers in the United States. Exclusion orders are enforced by the U.S. Bureau of Customs and Border Protection, and the Commission itself enforces cease-and-desist orders. Parties who wish to settle their claims with the ITC before imposition of an exclusion order or cease-and-desist order may agree to a consent order. Under a consent order, the Commission is permitted to maintain jurisdiction over the matter to monitor the compliance of the settling party. Consent orders represent a cost effective method for parties who are infringing a patent to extricate themselves from an ITC proceeding. These remedies are very distinct as ITC Section 337 investigations are *in rem* and are directed toward the infringing products rather than the foreign parties. . . .

[T]he *in rem* nature of the proceedings and remedies available at the ITC, particularly the extraordinary remedy of a general exclusion order, also allows domestic patent holders to obtain substantial prospective relief without filing a series of actions against numerous foreign infringers (*i.e.,* a general exclusion order stops the subject articles at the U.S. border, notwithstanding the exporters/importer's identity). To avail itself of this remedy, a patent owner must establish a "widespread pattern of unauthorized use" of the proprietary product and difficulty distinguishing the source.

A further advantage afforded to patent owners is the dual track proceeding. While patent owners seek an exclusion order against foreign importation against the ITC, patent owners can and often do simultaneously pursue a patent action in Federal District Court for monetary damages (a remedy that is not available to a patent owner before the ITC due to the *in rem* nature of that proceeding). This "one-two punch" of pursuing both an ITC and Federal District Court action for patent infringement can prove extremely effective for patent owners seeking to protect their domestic patent rights in gross.

The ability to pursue parallel actions before both the ITC and Federal District Court and the fast-track investigation of the ITC are fueling an expansion of patent litigation at the ITC under Section 337. For much of the 20th century, patent owners relied little upon the ITC for substantive relief. Rather, patent owners have looked almost exclusively to the Federal District Courts to enforce patent rights. During much of the 1990s, patent-related 337 complaints hovered relatively constant between a mere 6 to 11 complaints per year. However, with the recovery in the tech sector and economy in 2004 and continued expansion of high-tech foreign imports due to inexpensive overseas labor, the ITC received an unprecedented 31 Section 337 patent complaints in 2004. In each of the three subsequent years, the ITC broke its own record for number of complaints filed. 2007 proved to be the ITC's most active year on record with over 40 complaints filed. For 2008, the ITC has so far received 26 filed complaints, putting it on track to receive approximately the same number of complaints as it did in 2007. . . .

With the increasingly international scope of business and technology today, more and more patent owners can expect that infringing goods will come from outside the United States. When such goods cross the U.S. border, patent owners should not forget the ITC as a preeminent forum to redress patent infringement. The ITC can provide patent owners with fast and decisive relief against infringement and reach infringing goods that would traditionally be outside the jurisdiction of Federal District Courts.

NOTES AND QUESTIONS

1. If a country were considering adopting a new administrative patent enforcement regime, would you recommend the Chinese system, the ITC approach, or something else entirely? Why or why not? In both Chinese administrative action and the ITC action, injunctive relief is available but not damages. Does that meaningfully lessen the attractiveness of these actions?

2. The above excerpt discusses the strengths and benefits of the ITC. However, there are also significant concerns about the role of the ITC process in enforcement of patent rights. In the wake of the *eBay v. MercExchange* decision discussed in Chapter 11, courts no longer routinely grant injunctions upon a finding of infringement. This has made the ITC an even more attractive venue for patentees seeking injunctive relief. As Professors Chien and Lemley explain:

> In the wake of the Supreme Court's 2006 *eBay Inc. v. MercExchange, L.L.C.* decision, district courts rarely grant injunctions in patent infringement cases to patent-assertion entities (PAEs, also known as "patent trolls"). PAEs assert patents as a business model, traditionally using the threat of an injunction to reach a favorable settlement with the defendant. That threat often results in patent holdup. As Justice Anthony Kennedy articulated in his eBay concurrence, a holdup problem results when "an injunction . . . can be employed as a bargaining tool to charge exorbitant fees." By requir-

ing federal courts to consider the equities of a particular case before granting an injunction, eBay solved much of the patent system's holdup problem. But the Court's ruling didn't eliminate injunction-based holdup because another jurisdiction routinely grants injunctions in patent cases: the International Trade Commission (ITC). In the past five years, both PAEs and product-producing companies have flocked to this once-obscure trade agency in search of injunctions or the credible threat of injunctions.

As the Commission itself explained: "[S]ince the U.S. Supreme Court's 2006 eBay decision, which has made it more difficult for patent-holders that do not themselves practice a patent to obtain injunctions in district courts, exclusion orders have increasingly been sought by non-practicing entities that hold U.S. patents." The result is that the ITC is busier with patent cases than it has ever been before.

The double standard in patent law about when an injunction is available has drawn the scrutiny and, in some cases, the fury of the mainstream media, commentators, practitioners, Congress, and the Federal Trade Commission. In effect, the ITC's practices have undone many of the desirable consequences of eBay. The ITC issues exclusion orders that prevent the importation of a product. Exclusion orders can have a dramatic impact because, to comply with them, a company must pull its products from the market and redesign them. Many household devices, including computers, flat-screen televisions, GPS devices, and printers, have been the subjects of ITC section 337 investigations. In 2011, every major smartphone maker was embroiled in an ITC dispute. As the impact of this trade agency has grown, mainstream commentators have warned that the ITC "could do great economic harm to . . . U.S. industries that [are] growing rapidly." Calls for legislative reform of the ITC have also intensified based on the perception that the ITC's exclusion orders are "economically destructive and inflexible." The difficulty is that the ITC can't award damages; it can only exclude products in what might seem to be an all-or-nothing affair.

Colleen V. Chien & Mark A. Lemley, *Patent Holdup, the ITC, and the Public Interest*, 98 CORNELL L. REV. 1, 2–5, (2012). Professors Chien and Lemley suggest the ITC should use its discretionary powers to deny exclusion orders in appropriate cases, or to flexibly tailor the scope, timing, and bonding requirements of such orders.

3. Some scholars are also concerned about the ITC awarding exclusion orders in cases involving standards-essential patents (SEPs) that are subject to reasonable and non-discriminatory (RAND) licensing conditions:

ITC exclusion orders generally should not be granted under § 1337(d)(1) on the basis of patents subject to obligations to license on "reasonable and non-discriminatory" (RAND) terms. Doing so would undermine the significant pro-competitive and pro-consumer benefits that RAND promises produce and the investments they enable. . . . Holders of SEPs put aside their rights to exclude when they agree to make their technology available on terms that are reasonable and non-discriminatory and imply that legal remedies (i.e. monetary damages) are adequate. Through their promises, patent holders have traded the right to exclude for the privilege of being declared essential to the standard. . . .

Patent owners may legitimately worry that without the threat of an injunction, infringers will turn down reasonable offers. We are sympathetic to these concerns. However, district courts are in a better position to deal with them by imposing attorneys' fee sanctions for bad behavior or enhanced damages in certain situations. District courts also can issue injunctions, even for SEPs subject to RAND commitments, if the equities favor doing so. . . .

As one of us has written elsewhere: "There is at least one situation where an ITC action and exclusion order on the basis of a RAND patent may be appropriate, however. [] In the cases when the district court lacks jurisdiction over a defendant but the in rem jurisdiction of the ITC is available, the ITC provides the patentee with its only recourse." In such cases, ITC review and relief may be appropriate, provided that the other prerequisites to relief have been met.

Colleen V. Chien et al., *RAND Patents and Exclusion Orders: Submission of 19 Economics and Law Professors to the International Trade Commission*, 2, 8 (2012) *available at* http://ssrn.com/abstract=2102865.

How the ITC responds to these concerns could have a significant impact on U.S. patent litigation, competitive conditions, and consumer access to a variety of products.

4. In 2003, Japan instituted a new customs enforcement procedure for IP rights. So far, this option largely has been used by trademark owners, but it is garnering increasing interest as a potential tool for patent-holders as well.

In revising the Customs Tariff Law (CTL) which governs Customs service actions, Japanese lawmakers closely studied U.S. International Trade Commission (ITC) proceedings and modeled several aspects of their system on ITC actions. For example, the CTA allows a patentee to stop the importation of infringing goods without court action and possibly without knowing the identity of the importer. Under the CTL, a patentee may submit a written request to the Director-General of Customs (D-GC) requesting import suspension of accused goods and providing supporting documents (e.g., a copy of the patent, photos and descriptions of infringing devices, and instructions on how to identify them).

If the D-GC decides to initiate the proceeding to determine if infringement exists and imports should be suspended, he will inform both parties and they will have ten working days to submit evidence (e.g., expert opinions) regarding the allegedly infringing goods. The D-GC is aided in making his determination by the presence of IP experts in each regional customs office and also by the availability of recourse to the JPO for opinion assistance. Importation of the goods will be suspended during the proceeding; however, the D-GC may require the patentee to post a bond to cover damages to the importer if infringement ultimately is not found. The D-GC will examine all of the submitted evidence and arguments and make a decision within a month (extendable) as to whether the accused goods infringe and the goods should be seized and destroyed. If the D-GC finds for the patentee, the import suspension can last for up to two years (renewable). There is a danger, however, that if the patent is later found to be invalid either in a court proceeding or at the JPO, the patentee could be liable for damages for the suspended importation. The following flowchart illustrates the main features of the proceeding.

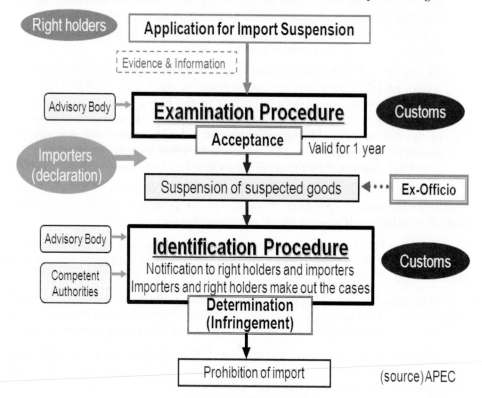

Source: World Customs Organization.

This proceeding is most useful where infringement is easy to ascertain, where there is no significant question regarding the validity of the patent (an issue that the D-GC can take into consideration), and where the patentee is making a product that embodies the patent that can be used in a direct comparison with the allegedly infringing product. *See* Teruo Doi, *Japan, in* 5 INTERNATIONAL ENCYCLOPEDIA OF LAWS: INTELLECTUAL PROPERTY 248 (Hendrik Vanhees ed., 2007).

5. Unlike the Japanese procedure, under EU Regulation 1383/2003, 2003 O.J. (L 196) 7, which came into effect July 1, 2004, EU customs officials do not assess infringement themselves; that decision is the province of national courts. The regulation allows IP owners to request that Customs detain infringing goods at an EU border for up to twenty days while the IP owners initiate an action in a national court for a determination of infringement; there is not a specialized forum for like issues such as the ITC. Thus the determination of infringement can take years, literally, while the products remain in detention. The procedure is somewhat complicated by the national character of patent rights and the system of goods movement in the EU. As explained by two commentators:

> The EU operates as a Customs Union, so that goods are free to move across national borders once they have been cleared by Customs. Also, goods can move from one country to another and can be stored in the EU without being Customs cleared, under so-called transit regimes. However, to be traded they must be Customs cleared at a certain point of entry. The Regulation provides for detention of products, which are not (yet) Customs cleared.

> Each country has its own national Customs authorities, to whom detention requests must be addressed . . . the transit-regimes can cause the physical point of entry to differ from the point of entry for Customs purposes (point of Customs clearance). The point of Customs clearance is the last point in the supply chain for Customs detention.

> [Thus] an applicant must have patent protection in either the country of the physical point of entry into the EU or the Customs point of entry, but preferably both. It is also necessary to identify the infringing products, where they come from, when and where the goods are likely to arrive in the EU, and their further distribution. The applicant must further provide proof of patent ownership. . . . Normally, the national Customs authorities will grant the request within a few weeks and issue a detention order for the specified products.

Jasper Helder & Francis van Velsen, *Why Customs Can Help Patent Owners*, MANAGING INTELL. PROP. (March 30, 2005) *available at* http://www.managing ip.com/Article.aspx?ArticleID=1321510.

The IP owner must accept liability for any wrongful detention of goods in its request to Customs and must pay to keep goods in detention and to pay for any damage Customs or third parties incur. Also, if the IP owner fails to initiate legal action in a national court within twenty working days of the start of detention, or if the goods are ultimately determined not to infringe, the IP owner is liable for damages. However, there is still the possibility for abuse, as competitors can be blocked from entering markets with goods that are later determined clearly to not infringe. Owners of the goods may obtain their release from detention by paying a security/bond fee, as long as a national court has not ordered pre-judgment seizure or other precautionary relief during the twenty-day period. Not surprisingly, parties often find it more satisfactory to settle the detention issue out of court than to wait for a judicial resolution.

The TRIPS-consistency of EU Regulation 1383/2003 recently came under question in response to the seizure of generic drugs en route to Nigeria from India. In February 2009, customs officials in the Netherlands seized a consignment of abacabir sulphate tablets under claims that the consignment contained counterfeit goods. Manufacture of the tablets had been funded by the United Nations agency, UNITAID, as part of a program by the Clinton Foundation. According to some reports, seventeen other such incidents had occurred in 2008 and in May 2009, a shipment of the widely used antibiotic, amoxicillin, destined for Vanuatu from India was seized in Frankfurt. *See e.g.*, Melissa O. Nonaka, *Enough Is Enough: India's Fight Against Seizures of Lawful Generic Medicines,* 16 Mich. St. U. J. MED. & L. 37, 38 (2011); Health Action Int'l, Press Release, *Another Seizure of Generic Medicines Destined for a Developing Country, This Time in Frankfurt,* IP-WATCH (Jun. 5, 2009), http://www.ip-watch.org/weblog/wp-content/uploads/2009/06/june-5-press-release-frankfurt-seizure.pdf.

GlaxoSmithKline, which owns the patent for amoxicillin, subsequently reported that the shipment did not infringe its trademarks. None of these incidents revealed any violations of patents or trademark rights. Following the 2009 seizures, India initiated a request for consultations with the EU pursuant to the WTO dispute settlement process.

EUROPEAN UNION AND A MEMBER STATE—SEIZURE OF GENERIC DRUGS IN TRANSIT

WT/DS408/1
19 May, 2010

REQUEST FOR CONSULTATIONS BY INDIA

The following communication, dated 11 May 2010, from the delegation of India to the delegations of the European Union and the Netherlands, and to the Chairman of the Dispute Settlement Body, is circulated in accordance with Article 4.4 of the DSU.

My authorities have instructed me to request consultations with the European Union (the "EU") and the Kingdom of the Netherlands (the "Netherlands") pursuant to Article 4 of the Understanding on Rules and Procedures Governing the Settlement of Disputes, Article XXII:1 of the General Agreement on Tariffs and Trade 1994 (the "GATT 1994") and Article 64.1 of the Agreement on Trade-Related Aspects of Intellectual Property Rights (the "TRIPS Agreement"), regarding the repeated seizures of consignments of generic drugs originating in India at ports and airports in the Netherlands on the ground of alleged infringement of patents subsisting in the Netherlands while these consignments were in transit to third country destinations (the "measures at issue").

Based on complaints of alleged infringement by alleged owners of patents over the last two years, customs authorities in the Netherlands have seized a substantial number of consignments of generic drugs from India in transit through the Netherlands. India understands that these seizures were made by applying the so-called "manufacturing fiction" under which generic drugs actually manufactured in India and in transit to third countries were treated as if they had been manufactured in the Netherlands. These consignments were initially detained and later, either destroyed or returned to India. In a few cases, the consignments were permitted to proceed to the destination country after considerable delay. Available evidence confirms that the customs authorities seized at least 19 consignments of generic drugs in 2008 and 2009 while in transit through the Netherlands, 16 of which originated in India. An illustrative list setting forth relevant details of some of these seizures is provided in the Annex to this request.

The measures at issue also include the reiterated conduct and practice of seizing generic drugs in transit on the ground of alleged patent infringement and the following, among other, laws, rules, regulations, guidelines and administrative practices of the EU and of the Netherlands but only to the extent that they authorise or require the seizure or destruction of drugs in transit on the ground of alleged patent infringement:

(a) Council Regulation (EC) No. 1383/2003 of 22 July 2003;

(b) Commission Regulation (EC) No. 1891/2004 of 21 October 2004;

(c) Council Regulation (EEC) No 2913/92 of 12 October 1992;

(d) Directive 2004/48/EC of the European Parliament and of the Council of 29 April 2004;

(e) Regulation (EC) No 816/2006 of the European Parliament and of the Council of 17 May 2006;

(f) Relevant provisions of the Patents Act of the Kingdom of the Netherlands, 1995 (*Rijksoctrooiwet 1995*) (the "Patents Act"), as amended, including, without limitation, the provisions of Chapter IV thereof, especially Articles 53 and 79, and relevant rules, regulations, guidelines and administrative practices;

(g) Relevant provisions of the General Customs Act of the Netherlands (*de Algemene douanewet (Adw)*) (the "Customs Act"), as amended, including, without limitation, Articles 5 and 11 and relevant rules, regulations, guidelines and administrative practices;

(h) Customs Manual VGEM (30.05.00 Intellectual Property Rights, Version 3.1) (*Douane Handboek VGEM, 30.05.00 Intellec-*

tuele eigendomsrechten, 6 April 2009, Versie 3.1) including, without limitation, the provisions of Chapter 6 and of other relevant Chapters;

(i) The Public Prosecutor's Office Guide to Intellectual Property Fraud 20005A022 of 1 February 2006 (*Aanwijzing intellectueleeignendomsfraude 2005A022*) and the Public Prosecutor's Office Directive (2005R013);

(j) Relevant provisions of the Criminal Code of the Netherlands (*Het Nederlandse Wetboek van Strafrecht*) including, without limitation, the provisions of Article 337, and relevant rules, regulations, guidelines and administrative practices; and

(k) Relevant provisions of the Criminal Procedure Code of the Netherlands and relevant rules, regulations, guidelines and administrative practices.

This request also covers any amendments, replacements, extensions, implementing measures and any other related measures with respect to the laws, rules, regulations, guidelines and administrative practices of the EU and of the Netherlands set forth above.

India considers that the measures at issue are, in several respects, inconsistent as such and as applied, with the obligations of the EU and the Netherlands under the following provisions of the GATT 1994 and of the TRIPS Agreement:

1. Paragraphs 2, 3, 4, 5 and 7 of Article V of the GATT 1994 because the measures at issue, *inter alia*, are unreasonable, discriminatory and interfere with, and impose unnecessary delays and restrictions on, the freedom of transit of generic drugs lawfully manufactured within, and exported from, India by the routes most convenient for international transit;

2. Article X of the GATT 1994, including, without limitation, Article X:3, because the measures at issue, *inter alia*, are not administered in a uniform, impartial and reasonable manner;

3. Article 28 read together with Article 2 of the TRIPS Agreement, Article 4*bis* of the Paris Convention, 1967 and the last sentence of paragraph 6(i) of the Decision of the General Council of August 30, 2003 on the Implementation of Paragraph 6 of the Doha Declaration on the TRIPS Agreement and Public Health (the "August 30, 2003 Decision") because a cumulative reading of these provisions confirms, *inter alia*, that the rights conferred on the owner of a patent cannot be extended to interfere with the freedom of transit of generic drugs lawfully manufactured within, and exported from, India;

4. Articles 41 and 42 of the TRIPS Agreement because the measures at issue, *inter alia*, create barriers to legitimate trade,

permit abuse of the rights conferred on the owner of a patent, are unfair and inequitable, unnecessarily burdensome and complicated and create unwarranted delays; and

5. Article 31 of the TRIPS Agreement read together with the provisions of the August 30, 2003 Decision because the measures at issue, *inter alia*, authorise interference with the freedom of transit of drugs that may be produced in, and exported from, India to Members of the World Trade Organization with insufficient or no capacity in the pharmaceutical sector that seek to obtain supplies of such products needed to address their public health problems by making effective use of compulsory licensing.

India considers further that the measures at issue also have a serious adverse impact on the ability of developing and least-developed country members of the World Trade Organization to protect public health and to provide access to medicines for all. Accordingly, the provisions of the TRIPS Agreement referred to above must be interpreted and implemented in light of the objectives and principles set forth in Articles 7 and 8 of the TRIPS Agreement, the Doha Ministerial Declaration on the TRIPS Agreement and Public Health adopted on 14 November 2001 and in the light of Article 12(1) of the International Covenant on Economic, Social and Cultural Rights, which recognizes the right of all persons to the enjoyment of the highest attainable standard of physical and mental health.

We reserve the right to raise additional claims and legal matters regarding the measures at issue during the course of the consultations.

We look forward to receiving your reply to this request to set a mutually convenient date for these consultations.

India's request for consultations was joined by Brazil after drugs being shipped from India to Brazil were seized in the Netherlands. The dispute was resolved during the consultations phase when the EU reportedly indicated its willingness to deal with the dispute without resort to the establishment of a WTO panel. The EU and India entered into a formal Understanding of principles to guide EU border enforcement procedures. Reports also indicate that the principles in the Understanding will be reflected in a proposal to replace Regulation 1383/2003. However, consistent with the resolution of trade disputes generally, the case will not be finally resolved until compliant regulation is enacted in the EU. *See* WGM Editorial: *India and the EU Reach Understanding on Seizure of Indian Generic Drugs*, World Generic Markets, Sept. 9, 2011, 2011 WLNR 17882218; *see also India, EU Reach "Interim Settlement" over Generic Drugs Row*, BUS. STANDARD, July 29, 2011, at 5.

D. MULTINATIONAL PATENT LITIGATION

1. SPECIALIZED COURTS

As you learned in Chapter 11, a typical defense in a patent infringement suit is that the patent in question is invalid. In most countries, the court hearing the infringement action also has jurisdiction to rule on the invalidity defense. In Germany, however, those procedures take place in separate courts. Specialized courts within the German district court system have exclusive jurisdiction in patent infringement suits, and it is in those courts that owners of German patents seek injunctive relief and money damages against alleged infringers. The specialized courts do not have jurisdiction to hear questions of patent validity, however. They are required to assume that the patents before them are valid and they are bound by the patents' wording. Questions of patent validity are heard by the German Federal Patent Court (*Bundespatentgericht*), a centralized court established in 1961 made up of both legally and technically qualified judges. If an alleged infringer wishes to argue that the asserted patent is invalid, the infringer must file a separate invalidity action before the German Federal Patent Court.

When an invalidity action is brought before the Federal Patent Court at the same time as an infringement action is pending before a specialized court, the specialized court usually suspends the infringement action until the Federal Patent Court has issued its decision. This is especially so if the specialized court considers that the invalidity action has a likelihood of success. The specialized court has no obligation to suspend its proceedings, however, if it concludes that the defendant has instituted the invalidity action merely to cause delay. Decisions issued by the Federal Patent Court issues bind the specialized courts; therefore, if the Federal Patent Court declares the patent invalid, the specialized court must dismiss the infringement action. The decisions of both courts are subject to appeal to the Federal Court of Justice, which has ultimate jurisdiction over both the Federal Patent Court and the specialized courts.

Other countries also use a bifurcated system in patent litigation. In Japan, for example, the Japanese district courts hear infringement proceedings and the JPO handles hearings on validity. Starting in 2005, Japan established an Intellectual Property (IP) High Court as a special branch of the Tokyo High Court. The IP High Court hears appeals from district courts and the JPO. Since invalidity is an affirmative defense to an infringement claim, a court in Japan may issue an independent determination about validity in the context of a patent infringement case despite the bifurcated system. An alleged infringer may still pursue invalidation of a patent through the JPO using parallel revocation proceedings. The infringement litigation may be suspended until the JPO invalidation hearing has been concluded. The evidence used in court during the infringement proceeding is available to the JPO to use during its consideration of the patent's validity.

Common law countries such as the United States and United Kingdom do not have a system of specialized courts for patent litigation. However, in the UK, most cases are heard in the Patents Court in the Chancery Division of the High Court. Since 1990, a Patents County Court (PCC) also exists in the UK as an alternative to the Patents Court and High Court. The PCC offers less expensive and simplified procedures than the High Court, although the same streamlined procedures are now available in all courts following reforms made in 1998. Cases in the PCC can be argued by solicitors or patent agents. As of June 14, 2011, the PCC can only hear cases with a maximum value of £500,000 (excluding interest and costs). *See* Patents County Court (Designation and Jurisdiction) Order 1994 SI No. 1609, amended by High Court and County Courts Jurisdiction (Amendment) Order 2005 SI No. 587; Patents County Court (Financial Limits) Order 2011 (SI 2011/1402).

In the United States, patent cases are heard by federal district courts with appeals going to a specialized appellate court—the Court of Appeals for the Federal Circuit. Flowing from these different court structures, countries adopt specific procedural rules, case management procedures and other litigation processes which, often, impose significant burdens on patent owners.

2. ISSUE PRECLUSION

It may be quite difficult for a patent owner to consolidate multinational infringement actions in one jurisdiction, one lawsuit. However, there are still ways that a patent owner may be able to reduce the time and costs associated with bringing multiple lawsuits. One promising tool is issue preclusion. In the U.S., for example, courts are constitutionally required to give full faith and credit to the rulings of other states, but not to the rulings of courts in other countries. Foreign judgments are recognized, if at all, on the basis of comity. As discussed in *Voda v. Cordis, supra* Chapter 1, p. 45, there has to have been: 1) the opportunity for full and fair trial, 2) conducted following regular proceedings, 3) before a court of competent jurisdiction, 4) after due citation or voluntary appearance of defendant, 5) under a system of justice likely to render fair judgment between citizens of its own country and citizens of another. If these requirements are met, then "the merits of the case should not, in an action brought in this country upon the judgment, be tried afresh." *See Hilton v. Guyot,* 159 U.S. 113 (1895).

Recognized judgments may have preclusive effect. While claim preclusion is generally not going to be available (different patents are involved so the legal issues are not identical), issue preclusion, also known as collateral estoppel, may be used so that once a fact is decided between two parties in litigation, that factual finding is binding against them in future litigation. For issue preclusion, the cause of action need not be identical; rather, the following elements must be satisfied: 1) each of the two lawsuits involved the issue that is now under consideration as potentially precluded from re-litigation, 2) that issue was actually litigated in the earlier (foreign) lawsuit, 3) determination of that issue was necessary to a final decision there, and 4) the losing party had an opportunity to litigate that issue fully and fairly. The following case illustrates the successful use of issue preclusion in U.S. patent litigation.

NORTHLAKE MARKETING & SUPPLY, INC., v. GLAVERBEL, S.A.

958 F. Supp. 373 (N.D. Ill. 1997)

MEMORANDUM OPINION AND ORDER

■ SHADUR, Senior District Judge.

This distressingly protracted litigation is at long last approaching the day of reckoning (that is, trial) on the patent issues that divide the litigants. But after the parties' counsel had at long last submitted and this Court had entered the final pretrial order that states the game plan and places the case in readiness for trial, defendants Glaverbel, S.A. ("Glaverbel") and Fosbel, Inc. ("Fosbel")-collectively "Glaverbel-Fosbel"-have filed a combined Fed.R.Civ.P. ("Rule") 56 and Rule 16 motion in an effort to streamline what remains in the case. Although this Court often rejects such late-in-the-day submissions in favor of sorting everything out at trial, in this instance the Glaverbel-Fosbel motion serves a constructive purpose in narrowing the boundaries for the required evidentiary presentation. . . .

Northlake's Count II

Unlike their position on the other claims, Glaverbel-Fosbel do not launch a global attack on Northlake's Count II claim of the invalidity of the patents in suit. Instead Glaverbel-Fosbel try to narrow the issues on that claim in two respects:

1. They seek to bar Northlake's contention that a British document entitled "Carbonization Section Report, CN 385, Design and Development of a Silica Welding Apparatus," constitutes a prior "publication" in Great Britain and is hence to be considered as prior art.

2. They contend that Northlake has identified no evidence to justify the factfinders' consideration of any asserted violation of the "on sale" or "public use" restrictions of 35 U.S.C. § 102(b).

As to the first of those matters, Glaverbel-Fosbel point to the Belgian litigation in which Glaverbel prevailed against Northlake in an infringement action involving three Glaverbel-owned Belgian patents. That prior litigation is not asserted by way of claim preclusion but rather as issue-preclusive: There the Belgian court determined that the document at issue was found "in a private library" and that it could not qualify as having been printed or published because under Belgian law those terms refer to documents "available to the public."[1]

To begin with, it is of course true that as between a Belgian court and this District Court the same full faith and credit that is applicable to the rulings of other courts in this country under the Constitution and 28 U.S.C. § 1738 does not apply. But the case law from our own Court of Appeals teaches that the same result is still called for here, because proceedings in a Belgian tribunal are considered "fundamentally fair" (*Ingersoll Milling Mach. Co. v. Granger,* 833 F.2d 680, 686–88 (7th Cir.1987)), and Northlake has posed no quarrel in that respect. And although the standard of *law* applied by the Belgian tribunal is not the same as ours, the just-recited *factual* findings of the Belgian court, which Northlake is not entitled to relitigate or dispute in this action, conclusively demonstrate that the document is not a "printed *publication*" under the United States patent laws (35 U.S.C. § 102(b)) either.

[The Court then analyzed and ruled favorably on the second portion of the Glaverbel-Fosbel motion]

Thus Glaverbel-Fosbel have also succeeded on both facets of their issue-narrowing motion as to Count II. This action has been substantially contracted in both that and the other respects dealt with in this opinion.

CONCLUSION

Glaverbel-Fosbel have succeeded in their current effort to . . . narrow the issues in Complaint Count II for purposes of trial.

NOTES AND QUESTIONS

1. What benefits of issue preclusion does the *Northlake Marketing* case illustrate? How can issue preclusion be used strategically by litigants facing patent suits in multiple jurisdictions? Are there disadvantages to employing issue preclusion as a litigation strategy?

---

[1] Rule 44.1 deals with the determination of foreign law, such as that of Belgium in this case. Glaverbel-Fosbel has properly established what the Belgian court *did*. As for the legal significance of that ruling in terms of issue preclusion (the legal concept as framed in American law), neither side has offered anything for this Court's consideration. This opinion has accordingly adopted the same approach that is applicable in diversity cases where parties have not spoken to a choice-of-law question: It has looked instead to the law of the forum . . . . And that approach is consistent with what 9 Charles Wright & Arthur Miller, *Federal Practice and Procedure: Civil* 2d § 2447, at 659–60 (2d ed.1995) consider the preferable view . . . . In this instance that seems particularly appropriate, given the universality of American law in barring a litigant from relitigating an issue that has once been resolved in a full-blown litigated dispute between the same parties.

2. In a different *Northlake Marketing v. Glaverbel* opinion dealing with different factual findings to which issue preclusion applied, the district court was careful to note:

> [I]n this Court's view, the Opinion left no room for any belief that this Court's ruling included any element of attributing preclusive effect to the Belgian court's determinations of substantive patent *law* (which would necessarily pose questions of Belgian rather than United States law), as contrasted with that court's determinations of *fact* (as to which this Court determined the question of preclusiveness as a matter of United States law).

986 F. Supp. 471, 478–79.

The U.S. Court of Appeals for the Federal Circuit has been open to recognizing foreign factual findings of the type at issue in *Northlake Marketing v. Glaverbel;* however, it has refused to recognize foreign legal rulings. For example, in *Medtronic, Inc. v. Daig Corp.,* 789 F.2d 903 (Fed. Cir. 1986), the court refused to adopt a German court ruling on the obviousness of a U.S. patent corresponding to a litigated German patent. Moreover, not all courts are even willing to adopt foreign factual findings. For example, in *Cuno Inc. v. Pall Corp.,* 729 F. Supp. 234 (E.D.N.Y. 1989), the district court refused to adopt factual findings made by a British court, noting that time would not necessarily be shortened and citing the Federal Circuit's aversion to preclusion where questions of law and fact were mixed. *Id.* at 239.

3. Issue preclusion can be a useful litigation tool, but its adoption by U.S. courts is far from guaranteed. In *Quad/Tech, Inc. v. Q.I. Press Controls B.V.,* 413 Fed. Appx. 278 (Fed. Cir. 2011), the Federal Circuit affirmed a district court's refusal to consider a patent infringement judgment from Germany in ruling on a preliminary injunction request. Quad/Tech asserted that Q.I. had lost (and then failed to appeal) a patent infringement suit in Germany and asked the district court to "adopt Q.I.'s acceptance of the judgment in Germany as an admission of infringement of a virtually identical claim." The district court refused, noting that Quad/Tech had failed to provide sufficient evidence of the German judgment (it relied solely on an affidavit from a corporate VP describing the judgment), and that "foreign patent determinations are not binding in litigation concerning United States patents and patent law." *Quad/Tech, Inc. v. Q.I. Press Controls B.V.,* 701 F.Supp.2d 644, 655 (E.D. Pa. 2010). Thus, the adoption of issue preclusion remains discretionary with the court.

4. U.S. law provides a potentially useful tool for multinational patent litigation in 28 U.S.C. § 1782 entitled "Assistance to foreign and international tribunals and to litigants before such tribunals." This provision allows documents and testimony to be procured in the U.S. for use in foreign litigation. It provides in part:

> a. The district court of the district in which a person resides or is found may order him to give his testimony or statement or to produce a document or other thing for use in a proceeding in a foreign

or international tribunal, including criminal investigations conducted before formal accusation. The order may be made pursuant to a
letter rogatory issued, or request made, by a foreign or international
tribunal or upon the application of any interested person and may
direct that the testimony or statement be given, or the document or
other thing be produced, before a person appointed by the court. By
virtue of his appointment, the person appointed has power to administer any necessary oath and take the testimony or statement.
The order may prescribe the practice and procedure, which may be
in whole or part the practice and procedure of the foreign country or
the international tribunal, for taking the testimony or statement or
producing the document or other thing . . .

Id.

Such a tool can be a boon to litigants where significant information is only available in the U.S. or where discovery may be limited in the litigation
forum.

3. EXTRATERRITORIAL APPROACHES

The territoriality of patent law generally means that patent owners
who have obtained patents in multiple jurisdictions must enforce those
patents in those separate jurisdictions inefficiently and often at considerable monetary and temporal expense. Not surprisingly, patent owners
have sought creative ways to minimize such litigation. One approach of
having a single court adjudicate infringement of foreign patents was discussed in Chapter 1 in the *Voda v. Cordis* and *KK Coral* cases, and in
Chapter 11 in the *Solvay v. Honeywell* cross-border injunction case. A second approach is to extend the reach of a domestic patent to cover activity
taking place in another country. Efforts to extend the territorial reach of
patents have had a fair amount of success in the U.S. where Congress has
statutorily expanded the reach of U.S. patents. The following two cases
illustrate the somewhat surprising ability of U.S. patents to encompass
activity occurring beyond U.S. borders.

TRANSOCEAN OFFSHORE DEEPWATER DRILLING, INC. V. MAERSK CONTRACTORS USA, INC.

United States Court of Appeals, Federal Circuit
617 F.3d 1296 (Fed. Cir. 2010)

■ MOORE, Circuit Judge.

Transocean Offshore Deepwater Drilling, Inc. (Transocean) appeals
from a final judgment of the U.S. District Court for the Southern District
of Texas. The district court, on summary judgment, held that the asserted
claims of the patents-in-suit are invalid, not infringed, and that defendant Maersk Contractors USA, Inc. (Maersk USA) did not act willfully. For

the reasons set forth below, we reverse-in-part, vacate-in-part, affirm-in-part, and remand.

BACKGROUND

Transocean asserted claims 10–13 and 30 of U.S. Patent No. 6,047,781 ('781 patent), claim 17 of U.S. Patent No. 6,068,069 ('069 patent), and claim 10 of U.S. Patent No. 6,085,851 ('851 patent) against Maersk USA. The patents-in-suit share a common specification. The patents relate to an improved apparatus for conducting offshore drilling. In order to exploit oil and other resources below the sea floor, the disclosed rig must lower several components to the seabed including the drill bit, casings (metal tubes that create the wall of the borehole), and a blow-out preventer (BOP) that sits atop the well to prevent rupture during extended drilling. The structure for lowering these elements and rotating the drill is called the derrick. The derrick includes a top drive to rotate the drill and drawworks to move components (such as the drill, casing, and BOP) to and from the sea floor. . . .

A conventional rig utilized a derrick with a single top drive and drawworks. Because it could only lower one element at a time, the rig performed the many steps involved in drilling a well in series. Transocean attempted to improve the efficiency of this time-consuming process with the system described in the patents-in-suit. The patents describe a derrick that includes two stations-a main advancing station and an auxiliary advancing station-that can each assemble drill strings and lower components to the seabed. . . . This "dual-activity" rig can significantly decrease the time required to complete a borehole. . . .

DISCUSSION

. . . .

II. INFRINGEMENT

The infringement issues in this case are unusual and require a discussion of the factual background. Transocean accused Maersk USA's DSS-21 rig of infringement. Maersk USA's Danish parent company, Maersk A/S, contracted with Keppel FELS Ltd. in 2005 to build the accused rig in Singapore. Later, Maersk A/S negotiated with Statoil ASA (a Norwegian company) for Statoil's use of the accused rig. The companies came to an agreement for use of the rig and Maersk USA and Statoil Gulf of Mexico LLC (Statoil), a Texas Corporation, signed a contract in Norway. The contract specified that the "Operating Area" for the rig was the U.S. Gulf of Mexico but that Statoil had the right to use the rig outside the Operating Area with certain limitations. . . .

The contract also included mention of Transocean's U.S. patents. Maersk USA specifically retained the right to make "alterations" to the accused rig "in view of court or administrative determinations throughout the world." One of these "determinations" came when Transocean assert-ed the same patent claims in this case against another competitor, Glob-alSantaFe Corp. (GSF). Transocean prevailed in that case and the court issued an injunction requiring GSF to install a "casing sleeve" on one of its two advancing stations. . . . This casing sleeve prevents the auxiliary advancing station from lowering a drill string into the water. . . . The dis-trict court in GSF held that this avoids infringement because the cased advancing station can no longer advance tubes to the seabed as the inde-pendent claims require. Before delivering the rig to the U.S., Maersk USA learned of the injunction against GSF and modified the accused rig with the same casing sleeve to prevent one of the stations from advancing pipes to the seabed.

The district court granted summary judgment of noninfringement af-ter determining that there was no sale or offer to sell under 35 U.S.C. § 271(a). The court relied on the undisputed facts that the negotiation and signing of the contract took place outside the U.S. and that the contract gave Maersk the option to alter the rig to avoid infringement. *Id.* The dis-trict court also held that Transocean was collaterally estopped from argu-ing that the modified rig that Maersk USA delivered to Statoil (that in-cluded the casing sleeve to prevent advancing tubular members to the seabed) infringed the patent claims because this design was adjudicated as noninfringing in the GSF litigation. . . .

A. OFFER TO SELL

Section 271(a) defines infringing conduct: "whoever without authority makes, uses, offers to sell, or sells any patented invention, within the United States . . . infringes the patent." 35 U.S.C. § 271(a). An offer to sell is a distinct act of infringement separate from an actual sale. An offer to sell differs from a sale in that an offer to sell need not be accepted to con-stitute an act of infringement. . . . We analyze an offer to sell under § 271(a) using traditional contract principles. . . . There is no dispute that there was an offer to sell in this case, but Maersk USA argues that the offer was made in Norway, not the United States, thereby absolving it of § 271(a) liability.

Maersk A/S (a Danish company) and Statoil ASA (a Norwegian com-pany) negotiated the contract that is the subject of this alleged offer to sell. Their U.S. affiliates, Maersk USA and Statoil executed the contract in Norway. The contract included an "Operating Area" of the U.S. Gulf of Mexico. The district court held that because the negotiations and execu-tion took place outside the U.S., this could not be an offer to sell within the United States under § 271(a).

Transocean argues that to hold that this contract between two U.S. companies for performance in the U.S. is not an offer to sell within the U.S. simply because the contract was negotiated and executed abroad would be inconsistent with *Litecubes, LLC v. Northern Light Products,*

Inc., 523 F.3d 1353 (Fed. Cir. 2008) (holding that a foreign company cannot avoid liability for a sale by delivering the product outside the U.S. to a U.S. customer for importation). Transocean argues that a contract between two U.S. companies for delivery or performance in the U.S. must be an offer to sell within the United States under § 271(a).

Maersk USA argues that . . . for there to be an offer to sell within the U.S., the offer activities must occur within the U.S. It argues that the negotiations and execution outside the U.S. preclude offer to sell liability in this case.

This case presents the question whether an offer which is made in Norway by a U.S. company to a U.S. company to sell a product within the U.S., for delivery and use within the U.S. constitutes an offer to sell within the U.S. under § 271(a). We conclude that it does. Section 271(a) states that "whoever . . . offers to sell . . . within the United States any patented invention . . . infringes." In order for an offer to sell to constitute infringement, the offer must be to sell a patented invention within the United States. The focus should not be on the location of the offer, but rather the location of the future sale that would occur pursuant to the offer.

The offer to sell liability was added to the patent statute to conform to the April 1994 Uruguay Round's Trade-Related Aspects of Intellectual Property Agreement (TRIPS). The underlying purpose of holding someone who offers to sell liable for infringement is to prevent "generating interest in a potential infringing product to the commercial detriment of the rightful patentee." . . . The offer must be for a potentially infringing article. We are mindful of the presumption against extraterritoriality. *Microsoft Corp. v. AT&T Corp.,* 550 U.S. 437, 441 (2007). "It is the general rule under United States patent law that no infringement occurs when a patented product is made and sold in another country." *Id.* This presumption has guided other courts to conclude that the contemplated sale would occur within the United States in order for an offer to sell to constitute infringement. . . . We agree that the location of the contemplated sale controls whether there is an offer to sell within the United States.

The statute precludes "offers to sell . . . within the United States." To adopt Maersk USA's position would have us read the statute as "offers made within the United States to sell" or "offers made within the United States to sell within the United States." First, this is not the statutory language. Second, this interpretation would exalt form over substance by allowing a U.S. company to travel abroad to make offers to sell back into the U.S. without any liability for infringement. This company would generate interest in its product in the U.S. to the detriment of the U.S. patent owner, the type of harm that offer to sell within the U.S. liability is meant to remedy. *Id.* These acts create a real harm in the U.S. to a U.S. patentee. . . .

We hold that the district court erred because a contract between two U.S. companies for performance in the U.S. may constitute an offer to sell within the U.S. under § 271(a). The fact that the offer was negotiated or a contract signed while the two U.S. companies were abroad does not remove this case from statutory liability. We therefore vacate the district court's summary judgment of noninfringement.

B. SALE

The parties begin with the same territoriality argument presented in the context of an offer to sell. Transocean argues that a contract between two U.S. companies for performance in the U.S. constitutes a sale under § 271(a). Maersk USA responds that this cannot be a sale within the U.S. because all negotiations and execution of the contract took place in Norway and the contract did not provide for performance only in the U.S.

The parties further dispute whether the device that was sold was "the patented invention." Transocean argues that we should analyze infringement based on the schematics that accompanied the contract. Maersk USA argues that this was not an infringing sale because it reserved the right to alter the rig to avoid infringement. Finally, Maersk USA argues this cannot be a sale under § 271(a) because the rig was not complete at the time of contracting. It argues that "in order for there to have been a sale within the meaning of 35 U.S.C. § 271(a), the entire apparatus must have been constructed and ready for use," citing *Ecodyne Corp. v. Croll-Reynolds Engineering,* 491 F. Supp. 194, 197 (D.Conn.1979).

As with the offer to sell, we hold that a contract between two U.S. companies for the sale of the patented invention with delivery and performance in the U.S. constitutes a sale under § 271(a) as a matter of law. Maersk USA's first argument, that the location of negotiation and contracting should control is contrary to our precedent in *Litecubes.* There, we held that a sale does not only occur at a "single point where some legally operative act took place." . . . We may also consider other factors such as the place of performance. Maersk USA's argument that Statoil could use the rig outside the U.S. ignores the plain language of the contract, which includes an "Operating Area" of the U.S. Gulf of Mexico. It also ignores the fact that Maersk did in fact deliver the rig to U.S. waters. Maersk USA's remaining arguments regarding the right to alter the final design and the fact that the rig was not complete at the time of contracting do not change the result. Maersk USA and Statoil signed a contract and the schematics that accompanied that contract could support a finding that the sale was of an infringing article under § 271(a). The fact that Maersk USA, after the execution of the contract, altered the rig in response to the GSF injunction is irrelevant to this infringement analysis. The potentially infringing article is the rig sold in the contract, not the altered rig that Maersk USA delivered to the U.S.

Finally, we reject Maersk USA's claim that the entire apparatus must have been constructed and ready for use in order to have been sold. Our precedent establishes that a contract can constitute a sale to trigger infringement liability. *See NTP, Inc. v. Research in Motion, Ltd.,* 418 F.3d 1282, 1319 (Fed.Cir. 2005). A "sale" is not limited to the transfer of tangible property; a sale may also be the agreement by which such a transfer takes place. *Id.* In this case, there was a contract to sell a rig that included schematics. On summary judgment, we must draw all justifiable inferences in favor of the nonmovant, Transocean. Transocean argues that these schematics show sale of the patented invention. This is a genuine issue of material fact sufficient to withstand summary judgment.

We conclude that the district court erred in granting summary judgment that there was no sale within the U.S. in this case. As with the offer to sell, there remains a dispute over whether the unmodified rig that was sold was the patented invention, a question not reached by the district court thus far.

NOTES AND QUESTIONS

1. In *Transocean Offshore Deepwater Drilling, Inc. v. Maersk Contractors USA, Inc.,* Maersk was held liable for patent infringement based on a contract negotiated in Norway for a product that never even entered the U.S., since the product actually sold was modified prior to delivery to avoid infringement. Should U.S. patentees be able to reach such wholly foreign activity? What problems might this decision create and for whom?

2. The court's broad holding in *Transocean* could also create liability in an even stranger set of circumstances. As hypothesized by Professor Holbrook:

> Suppose that the party making the offer to sell the invention actually owns the patent in the jurisdiction in which the negotiations take place. The negotiations, and offer to sell, include sales to the United States. In a global marketplace, such an offer could be made in the context of negotiations dealing with product or products in multiple countries. Under the broad reading of *Transocean's* holding, an offer in this context would infringe a U.S. patent, even though the offeror is negotiating in a country where he owns the patent. Indeed, the offeror would be exposed to liability in the US even if the sale is never completed and even though the offeror owns the patent in the given country. Infringement of a patent is strict liability, so there would be infringement even if the offeror were unaware of the U.S. patent. It is in this way that the potential broader holding of *Transocean* has considerable extraterritorial impact and risks creating conflicts with foreign jurisdictions.

Timothy R. Holbrook, Essay, *Territoriality and Tangibility after* Transocean, 61 EMORY L. J. 1087, 1120 (2012).

Is the broad holding of *Transocean* necessary to adequately protect and incentivize patentees or has the court gone too far? Does the TRIPS Agreement provide any remedies for this extraterritorial reach by U.S. courts? Does global harmonization offer a compelling reason to empower national courts to reach activities beyond its territorial borders?

In the following case, the U.S. Court of Appeals for the Federal Circuit (CAFC) addressed a type of geographically "divided" infringement, in which all steps of a method claim were not performed in the United States.

NTP, INC. V. RESEARCH IN MOTION, LTD.

United States Court of Appeals, Federal Circuit
418 F.3d 1282 (Fed. Cir. 2005)

■ LINN, Circuit Judge.

Research In Motion, Ltd. ("RIM") appeals from a judgment of the U.S. District Court for the Eastern District of Virginia ("district court") entered in favor of NTP, Inc. ("NTP") following a jury verdict that RIM's BlackBerry TM system infringed NTP's U.S. Patents Nos. 5,436,960 ("the '960 patent"); 5,625,670 ("the '670 patent"); 5,819,172 ("the '172 patent"); 6,067,451 ("the '451 patent"); and 6,317,592 ("the '592 patent") (collectively, "the patents-in-suit") and awarding damages to NTP in the amount of $53,704,322.69. The court, in a final order also appealed by RIM, permanently enjoined any further infringement by RIM, but stayed the injunction pending this appeal. . . .

I. BACKGROUND

The technology at issue relates to systems for integrating existing electronic mail systems ("wireline" systems) with radio frequency ("RF") wireless communication networks, to enable a mobile user to receive email over a wireless network.

A. OVERVIEW OF ELECTRONIC MAIL TECHNOLOGY

Traditional email systems operate in the following manner: To send an email, a user begins by composing a message in his or her email client. . . When the message is sent, it is transferred first from the sender's machine to his or her ISP. The sender's host then uses a domain name server to identify the recipient's ISP mail server and its associated internet protocol ("IP") address. A connection is then established by the sender's host with the recipient's ISP mail server, facilitating transfer of the message. The message is next sorted by the recipient's ISP mail server into the recipient's particular "mailbox," where it is stored until the recipient initiates a connection with the server and downloads the message off the server onto his or her personal machine. This configuration is commonly referred to as a "pull" system because emails cannot be distributed to the user's machine without a connection being initiated by the user to "pull" the messages from the mail server.

B. PROBLEMS WITH THE PRIOR ART SYSTEMS

As societal dependence on email and computers increased throughout the 1990s, so did the demand for mobile internet access. . . . Available methods of remote internet access were cumbersome and inefficient for the traveling businessperson, however. . . .

C. THE PATENTS-IN-SUIT

Inventors Thomas J. Campana, Jr.; Michael P. Ponschke; and Gary F. Thelen (collectively "Campana") developed an electronic mail system that was claimed in the '960, '670, '172, '451, and '592 patents. . . . NTP now owns these five patents-in-suit.

Campana's particular innovation was to integrate existing electronic mail systems with RF wireless communications networks. In simplified terms, the Campana invention operates in the following manner: A message originating in an electronic mail system may be transmitted not only by wireline but also via RF, in which case it is received by the user and stored on his or her mobile RF receiver. The user can view the message on the RF receiver and, at some later point, connect the RF receiver to a fixed destination processor, i.e., his or her personal desktop computer, and transfer the stored message. . . . Intermediate transmission to the RF receiver is advantageous because it "eliminat[es] the requirement that the destination processor [be] turned on and carried with the user" to receive messages. . . .

D. THE ACCUSED SYSTEM

RIM is a Canadian corporation. . . . RIM sells the accused BlackBerry system, which allows out-of-office users to continue to receive and send electronic mail, or "email" communications, using a small wireless device. The system utilizes the following components: (1) the BlackBerry handheld unit (also referred to as the "BlackBerry Pager"); (2) email redirector software . . . and (3) access to a nationwide wireless network. . . .

The BlackBerry system uses "push" email technology to route messages to the user's handheld device without a user-initiated connection. There are multiple BlackBerry email "solutions" that interface with different levels of the user's email system. In the Desktop solution, the BlackBerry email redirector software, the Desktop Redirector, is installed on the user's personal computer. . . . Also at issue in this case is RIM's Internet solution of the BlackBerry system. . . . In either version, the BlackBerry email redirector software merges seamlessly with the user's existing email system. . . . When new mail is detected in the Desktop solution, the Desktop Redirector is notified and retrieves the message from the mail server. It then copies, encrypts, and routes the message to the

BlackBerry "Relay" component of RIM's wireless network, which is located in Canada. . . . [T]he message travels through the BlackBerry Relay, where it is translated and routed from the processors in the user's email system to a partner wireless network. That partner network delivers the message to the user's BlackBerry handheld, and the user is "notified virtually instantly" of new email messages. This process, accomplished without any command from the BlackBerry user, is an example of "push" email architecture. . . . There are significant advantages to "push" email architecture. Most importantly, the user is no longer required to initiate a connection with the mail server to determine if he or she has new email.

. . .

B. INFRINGEMENT

. . . RIM contends that because the BlackBerry Relay is located in Canada, as a matter of law RIM cannot be held liable for infringement under 35 U.S.C. § 271. . . .

1. CLAIM CONSTRUCTION

A determination of infringement is a two-step process. The court must first correctly construe the asserted claims, and then compare the properly construed claims to the allegedly infringing devices, systems, or methods. . . .

2. SECTION 271(A)

Section 271(a) of title 35 sets forth the requirements for a claim of direct infringement of a patent. It provides:

> Except as otherwise provided in this title, whoever without authority makes, uses, offers to sell, or sells any patented invention, within the United States or imports into the United States any patented invention during the term of the patent therefor, infringes the patent.

35 U.S.C. § 271(a) (2000).

The territorial reach of section 271 is limited. Section 271(a) is only actionable against patent infringement that occurs within the United States.

Ordinarily, whether an infringing activity under section 271(a) occurs within the United States can be determined without difficulty. This case presents an added degree of complexity, however, in that: (1) the "patented invention" is not one single device, but rather a system comprising multiple distinct components or a method with multiple distinct steps; and (2) the nature of those components or steps permits their function and use to be separated from their physical location.

In its complaint, NTP alleged that RIM had infringed its patents by "making, using, selling, offering to sell and importing into the United

States products and services, including the Defendant's BlackBerry TM products and their related software. . . ." NTP's theory of infringement tracks the language of section 271(a). In the district court, RIM moved for summary judgment of non-infringement, arguing that it could not be held liable as a direct infringer under section 271(a). According to RIM, the statutory requirement that the allegedly infringing activity occur "within the United States" was not satisfied because the BlackBerry Relay component of the accused system is located in Canada. The Relay component is alleged to meet the "interface" or the "interface switch" limitation in the '960, '670, '172, and '451 patents. . . .

. . . In the district court, the jury found direct, induced, and contributory infringement by RIM on all asserted claims. The asserted claims included both systems and methods for transmitting an email message between an originating processor and a destination processor. By holding RIM liable for contributory infringement and inducing infringement, the jury necessarily found that its customers are direct infringers of the claimed systems and methods.

On appeal, RIM argues that the district court erred in its interpretation of the infringement statute. RIM does not appeal the jury's finding that its customers use, i.e., put into service, its systems and methods for transmitting email messages. RIM has, however, appealed whether any direct infringement, by it or its customers, can be considered "within the United States" for purposes of section 271(a) . . . . For section 271(a) to apply, RIM asserts that the entire accused system and method must be contained or conducted within the territorial bounds of the United States. RIM thus contends that there can be no direct infringement as a matter of law because the location of RIM's Relay outside the United States precludes a finding of an infringing act occurring within the United States. . . .

The question before us is whether the using, offering to sell, or selling of a patented invention is an infringement under section 271(a) if a component or step of the patented invention is located or performed abroad. . . . Pursuant to section 271(a), whoever without authority "uses, offers to sell, or sells any patented invention, within the United States . . . during the term of the patent therefor, infringes the patent." 35 U.S.C. § 271(a). The grammatical structure of the statute indicates that "within the United States" is a separate requirement from the infringing acts clause. Thus, it is unclear from the statutory language how the territoriality requirement limits direct infringement where the location of at least a part of the "patented invention" is not the same as the location of the infringing act.

RIM argues that *Deepsouth* [406 U.S. 518 (1972)] answers this question. However, *Deepsouth* did not address this issue. . . . In that case, however, both the act of making and the resulting patented invention were wholly outside the United States. By contrast, this case involves a system that is partly within and partly outside the United States and relates to acts that may be occurring within or outside the United States.

Although *Deepsouth* does not resolve these issues, our predecessor court's decision in *Decca Ltd. v. United States,* 210 Ct.Cl. 546, 544 F.2d 1070 (1976), is instructive. In *Decca*, the plaintiff sued the United States for use and manufacture of its patented invention under 28 U.S.C. § 1498. The claimed invention was a radio navigation system requiring stations transmitting signals that are received by a receiver, which then calculates position by the time difference in the signals. At the time of the suit, the United States was operating three such transmitting stations, one of which was located in Norway and thus was outside the territorial limits of the United States. Only asserted claim 11 required three transmitting stations. Thus, in considering infringement of claim 11, the court considered the extraterritorial reach of the patent laws as applied to a system in which a component was located outside the United States. . . . In analyzing whether such a system was "made" in the United States, however, the court focused on the "operable assembly of the whole" language from *Deepsouth* and concluded that "[t]he plain fact is that one of the claimed elements is outside of the United States so that the combination, as an operable assembly, simply is not to be found solely within the territorial limits of this country." The court recognized that what was located within the United States was as much of the system as was possible, but the court reached no clear resolution of whether the accused system was "made" within the United States. Nevertheless, the court said, "Analyzed from the standpoint of a use instead of a making by the United States, a somewhat clearer picture emerges." The court concluded that "it is obvious that, although the Norwegian station is located on Norwegian soil, a navigator employing signals from that station is, in fact, 'using' that station and such use occurs wherever the signals are received and used in the manner claimed." In reaching its decision, the court found particularly significant "the ownership of the equipment by the United States, the control of the equipment from the United States and . . . the actual beneficial use of the system within the United States." . . .

Decca provides a legal framework for analyzing this case. As our predecessor court concluded, infringement under section 271(a) is not necessarily precluded even though a component of a patented system is located outside the United States. However, as is also evident from *Decca*, the effect of the extraterritorial component may be different for different infringing acts. In *Decca*, the court found it difficult to conclude that the system had been made within the United States but concluded that the system had been used in the United States even though one of the claim limitations was only met by including a component located in Norway. Not only will the analysis differ for different types of infringing acts, it will also differ as the result of differences between different types of claims. Because the analytical frameworks differ, we will separately analyze the alleged infringing acts, considering first the system claims and then the claimed methods.

a. "USES . . . WITHIN THE UNITED STATES"

The situs of the infringement "is wherever an offending act [of infringement] is committed." The situs of the infringing act is a "purely physical occurrence[ ]." In terms of the infringing act of "use," courts have interpreted the term "use" broadly. . . . The ordinary meaning of "use" is to "put into action or service." Webster's Third New International Dictionary 2523 (1993). The few court decisions that address the meaning of "use" have consistently followed the Supreme Court's lead in giving the term a broad interpretation.

The use of a claimed system under section 271(a) is the place at which the system as a whole is put into service, i.e., the place where control of the system is exercised and beneficial use of the system obtained. Based on this interpretation of section 271(a), it was proper for the jury to have found that use of NTP's asserted system claims occurred within the United States. RIM's customers located within the United States controlled the transmission of the originated information and also benefited from such an exchange of information. Thus, the location of the Relay in Canada did not, as a matter of law, preclude infringement of the asserted system claims in this case.

RIM argues that the BlackBerry system is distinguishable from the system in *Decca* because the RIM Relay, which controls the accused systems and is necessary for the other components of the system to function properly, is not located within the United States. While this distinction recognizes technical differences between the two systems, it fails to appreciate the way in which the claimed NTP system is actually used by RIM's customers. When RIM's United States customers send and receive messages by manipulating the handheld devices in their possession in the United States, the location of the use of the communication system as a whole occurs in the United States. This satisfactorily establishes that the situs of the "use" of RIM's system by RIM's United States customers for purposes of section 271(a) is the United States. . . .

We reach a different conclusion as to NTP's asserted method claims. Under section 271(a), the concept of "use" of a patented method or process is fundamentally different from the use of a patented system or device. Although the Supreme Court focused on the whole operable assembly of a system claim for infringement in *Deepsouth*, there is no corresponding whole operable assembly of a process claim. A method or process consists of one or more operative steps, and, accordingly, "[i]t is well established that a patent for a method or process is not infringed unless all steps or stages of the claimed process are utilized."

Because a process is nothing more than the sequence of actions of which it is comprised, the use of a process necessarily involves doing or performing each of the steps recited. This is unlike use of a system as a whole, in which the components are used collectively, not individually. We therefore hold that a process cannot be used "within" the United States as required by section 271(a) unless each of the steps is performed within this country. In the present case, each of the asserted method claims of the '960, '172, and '451 patents recites a step that utilizes an "interface" or "interface switch," which is only satisfied by the use of RIM's Relay located in Canada. Therefore, as a matter of law, these claimed methods could not be infringed by use of RIM's system.

Thus, we agree with RIM that a finding of direct infringement by RIM's customers under section 271(a) of the method claims reciting an "interface switch" or an "interface" is precluded by the location of RIM's Relay in Canada. As a consequence, RIM cannot be liable for induced or contributory infringement of the asserted method claims, as a matter of law.

b. "OFFERS TO SELL, OR SELLS"

. . . [W]e [now] must consider whether RIM could have directly infringed the method claims under the "sell" or "offer to sell" prongs of section 271(a) . . . .

Because the relevant precedent does not address the issue of whether a sale of a claimed method can occur in the United States, even though the contemplated performance of that method would not be wholly within the United States, the issue is one of first impression. We begin with the language of the statute. Section 271(a) does not define "sells" or "offers to sell," nor does the statute specify which infringing acts apply to which types of claims. . . . [T]he precise contours of infringement of a method claim have not been clearly established.

. . . The definition of "sale" is: "1. The transfer of property or title for a price. 2. The agreement by which such a transfer takes place. The four elements are (1) parties competent to contract, (2) mutual assent, (3) a thing capable of being transferred, and (4) a price in money paid or promised." Black's Law Dictionary 1337 (7th ed.1999). Thus, the ordinary meaning of a sale includes the concept of a transfer of title or property. The definition also requires as the third element "a thing capable of being transferred." . . . It is difficult to envision what property is transferred merely by one party performing the steps of a method claim in exchange for payment by another party. . . .

Congress has consistently expressed the view that it understands infringement of method claims under section 271(a) to be limited to use. The committee reports surrounding the passage of the Process Patents Amendments Act of 1987 indicate that Congress did not understand all of the infringing acts in section 271(a) to apply to method claims. The Senate Report explains, "Under our current patent laws, a patent on a process gives the patentholder the right to exclude others from using that process in the United States without authorization from the patentholder. The other two standard aspects of the patent right—the exclusive right to make or sell the invention—are not directly applicable to a patented process." S.Rep. No. 100–83, at 30 (1987) . . . .

In 1994, Congress passed legislation to implement the Uruguay Round of the General Agreement on Tariffs and Trade. Uruguay Round Agreements Act, Pub.L. No. 103–465, 108 Stat. 4809 (1994). That legislation modified section 271(a) to include the infringing acts of offering to sell and importing into the United States. The portion of the Uruguay Round being implemented in the modification of section 271(a) was the Agreement on Trade-Related Aspects of Intellectual Property Rights. That agreement clearly spells out the rights to be protected. It states:

1. A patent shall confer on its owner the following exclusive rights:

(a) where the subject matter of a patent is a product, to prevent third parties not having the owner's consent from the acts of: making, using, offering for sale, selling or importing for these purposes that product;

(b) where the subject matter of a patent is a process, to prevent third parties not having the owner's consent from the act of using the process, and from the acts of: using, offering for sale, selling, or importing for these purposes at least the product obtained directly by that process.

The agreement makes clear that claimed processes are to be directly protected only from "the act of using the process." . . .

In this case, we conclude that the jury could not have found that RIM infringed the asserted method claims under the "sells" or "offers to sell" prongs of section 271(a). We need not and do not hold that method claims may not be infringed under the "sells" and "offers to sell" prongs of section 271(a). Rather, we conclude only that RIM's performance of at least some of the recited steps of the asserted method claims as a service for its customers cannot be considered to be selling or offering to sell the invention covered by the asserted method claims. The sale or offer to sell handheld devices is not, in and of itself, enough. Thus, we conclude as a matter of law that RIM did not sell or offer to sell the invention covered by NTP's method claims within the United States.

c. "IMPORTS INTO THE UNITED STATES"

. . . [W]e must consider next whether the jury could have found that RIM imported any of the processes covered by the asserted method claims in violation of section 271(a) . . . . We hold . . . that for the same reasons that the jury could not have found that RIM infringed the method claims under the sale or offer for sale prongs, it could not have found infringement by importation under the facts of this case.

3. SECTION 271(F)

. . . Because we have determined that the system claims are infringed under section 271(a), we need not consider infringement of the system claims under section 271(f) and will limit our infringement analysis under section 271(f) to the method claims at issue.

The statute provides:

> (1) Whoever without authority supplies or causes to be supplied in or from the United States all or a substantial portion of the components of a patented invention, where such components are uncombined in whole or in part, in such manner as to actively induce the combination of such components outside of the United States in a manner that would infringe the patent if such combination occurred within the United States, shall be liable as an infringer.

> (2) Whoever without authority supplies or causes to be supplied in or from the United States any component of a patented invention that is especially made or especially adapted for use in the invention and not a staple article or commodity of commerce suitable for substantial non-infringing use, where such component is uncombined in whole or in part, knowing that such component is so made or adapted and intending that such component will be combined outside of the United States in a manner that would infringe the patent if such combination occurred within the United States, shall be liable as an infringer.

35 U.S.C. § 271(f) (2000) (emphases added).

While it is difficult to conceive of how one might supply or cause to be supplied all or a substantial portion of the steps of a patented method in the sense contemplated by the phrase "components of a patented invention" in section 271(f), it is clear that RIM's supply of the BlackBerry handheld devices and Redirector products to its customers in the United States is not the statutory "supply" of any "component" steps for combination into NTP's patented methods. By merely supplying products to its customers in the United States, RIM is not supplying or causing to be supplied in this country any steps of a patented process invention for combination outside the United States and cannot infringe NTP's asserted method claims under section 271(f) as a matter of law.

4. SECTION 271(G)

The next question is whether RIM can be said to "import[ ] into . . . or offer[ ] to sell, sell[ ], or use[ ] within the United States a product which is made by a process patented in the United States" and thus infringe under 35 U.S.C. § 271(g). . . .

RIM argues that the product created by the NTP process is data or information, and that *Bayer AG v. Housey Pharmaceuticals, Inc.,* 340 F.3d 1367 (Fed.Cir.2003), held that section 271(g) does not cover the production of intangible items. NTP counters that *Bayer* held only that a "product" cannot be "information in the abstract." . . .

In *Bayer,* we considered whether research data from the performance of a method to identify substances, which inhibit or activate a protein affecting characteristics of the cell, was "a product which is made by a process." We held that "the production of information is not covered" by section 271(g), explaining that the process must be for the "manufacturing" of "a physical article." In this case, the relevant claims are directed to methods for the transmission of information in the form of email messages. Because the "transmission of information," like the "production of information," does not entail the manufacturing of a physical product, section 271(g) does not apply to the asserted method claims in this case any more than it did in *Bayer.*

NOTES AND QUESTIONS

1. As *Transocean v. Maersk* and *NTP v. RIM* both illustrate, the territorial reach of 35 U.S.C. §271(a) is greater than one might reasonably expect. Further, U.S. patent law also has explicitly extraterritorial provisions in Sections 271(f) and (g). Thus there is the potential for significant extraterritorial patent infringement liability, which can be problematic in an integrated global economy. As one commentator explains:

> The problem with applying U.S. patent law extraterritorially is that it extends U.S. law to activities occurring in foreign nations that should be governed by the foreign sovereigns' laws. On many occasions, another country's law on validity, infringement, or priority may be different from U.S. law, and outcome determinative with respect to the rights of the parties. For example, this situation could occur in countries that require absolute novelty for patentability, or countries that define patent law subject matter differently than the U.S.

Dariush Keyhani, *Patent Law in the Global Economy: A Modest Proposal for U.S. Patent Law and Infringement without Borders*, 54 VILLANOVA L. REV. 291, 291–292 (2009).

However, others question whether the law even reaches far enough to provide sufficient protection for patentees. For example, while the CAFC upheld the finding of infringement of certain system and apparatus claims in *NTP*, it vacated the infringement findings for the method claims. According to Professor Wasserman:

> [T]he territorial nature of patent law creates an opportunity for divided infringement. Even if the inventor owns patents in each relevant country, no country's patent law may cover the infringer's activity. The result is a legal no-man's-land: A patented invention is being infringed, but no country's law provides protection for the patentholder. Potential infringers who take advantage of this legal gap are able to circumvent patent law. . . . Divided infringement undercuts the incentive to innovate, the primary purpose of the patent system. The extraterritorial reach of patent law should be expanded to prevent divided infringement.

Melissa Feeney Wasserman, Note, *"Divided Infringement: Expanding the Extraterritorial Scope of Patent Law,"* 82 N.Y.U. L. REV. 281, 282 (2007). Does the holding in the CAFC Akamai Technologies, Inc. v. Limelight Networks, Inc. case discussed in Chapter 10, *supra* (that inducement of infringement can be found even if no single entity engages in direct infringement), alleviate Professor Wasserman's concern?

Professor Wasserman proposes allowing U.S. courts to extend the extraterritorial reach of U.S. patents using a "substantial effects test" limited by comity concerns to account for the impact on other sovereign nations. Do you agree that the reach of U.S. patents should be further extended? Should foreign courts adopt a similar approach with respect to their national patents?

2. Which strategy is most consistent with international patent policy: domestic adjudication of foreign patents (as in the *K.K. Coral v. Marine Bio* and *Solvay v. Honeywell* cases), or extending the territorial reach of domestic patents to cover foreign activity? What are the potential benefits and harms of each approach?

As discussed in the following excerpt, unlike the CAFC, the Supreme Court, in *Microsoft Corp. v. AT&T Corp.,* 550 U.S. 437 (2007), has chosen to strictly construe the territorial limits of U.S. patents.

KENDRA ROBINS, NOTE, EXTRATERRITORIAL PATENT ENFORCEMENT AND MULTINATIONAL PATENT LITIGATION: PROPOSED GUIDELINES FOR U.S. COURTS
93 VA. L. REV. 1259 (2007)

Patent law is traditionally territorial in scope. Territoriality in patent law generally means that a patent owner can exclude others from making, using, offering to sell, or selling his or her patented invention in the jurisdiction that granted the patent and nowhere else. The primary statute in the Patent Act that governs patent infringement—35 U.S.C. § 271(a)—also illustrates the territoriality of patent infringement, providing that a person who "without authority makes, uses, offers to sell, or sells any patented invention, within the United States or imports into the

United States any patented invention during the term of the patent therefor, infringes the patent." Congress, however, has expanded the effective territorial scope of U.S. patents by adding Sections 271(f) and (g) to the Patent Act. . . .

In *Deepsouth Packing Co. v. Laitram Corp.*, the Supreme Court . . . expressly declined to extend the extraterritorial reach of U.S. patent law. Deepsouth Packing Company made all of the components of a shrimp deveining machine within the United States and then shipped the components to foreign customers for assembly and use abroad. In a 5–4 decision, the Court held that Deepsouth's practice of shipping the unassembled machine abroad did not constitute infringement because there was no "making" in the United States within the meaning of 271(a). The Court noted that an inventor who needs protection in foreign markets can seek foreign patent protection. The Court also remarked that Congress is free at any time to redefine the scope of patent protection.

In 1984, twelve years after *Deepsouth*, Congress enacted Section 271(f) in order to overrule the Supreme Court's holding in *Deepsouth* and "to close a loophole in patent law." Section 271(f)'s legislative history also explains that the amendments sought to make the patent system more "responsive to the challenges of a changing world" and to "avoid encouraging manufacturing outside the United States." Congress divided Section 271(f) into two Subsections: 271(f)(1) and 271(f)(2). Section 271(f)(1) imposes liability on exporters of unassembled components of what would be an infringing device if it were built in the United States when the exporter actively induces the assembly of the device outside of the United States. In contrast, Section 271(f)(2) imposes liability on anyone who exports a patented device's component that is either not a staple article of commerce or that has no substantial noninfringing use if the exporter knows that the component's only use is in the patented device and also knows that it will be combined into the completed device outside of the United States.

Four years later, Congress enacted the Process Patent Amendments Act ("The Process Act"), another amendment concerning the territorial scope of U.S. patents, which added Section 271(g). Prior to the enactment of Section 271(g), a manufacturer could perform a patented process abroad and import the products of this process into the United States without any fear of liability. The addition of Section 271(g) attempted to close this additional loophole in patent law by imposing liability for anyone who imports into, sells in, or uses in the United States an unpatented component "made by" a process covered by a U.S. patent. Although the U.S. Court of Appeals for the Federal Circuit has not hesitated to extend "component" software patents extraterritorially under Section 271(f), the Federal Circuit has refused to apply Section 271(g) to the importation of "intangible information" into the United States.

Understanding Sections 271(f) and (g) and courts' interpretations of these statutes is critical for appreciating their effects on the extraterritorial application of domestic patent law and the willingness of courts to extend domestic patent law abroad. Although the text of Sections 271(f) and (g) seemingly limits these statutes' extraterritorial reach by requiring some nexus between the foreign conduct and the conduct occurring within the United States, recent cases illustrate that the Federal Circuit has been willing to stretch the text of these statutes in order to find such a connection. This extension, however, raises several important policy concerns, and the Supreme Court reversed the Federal Circuit's expansive decision in *AT&T Corp. v. Microsoft Corp.*, narrowly interpreting Section 271(f) as applied to foreign duplication of software.

[In *AT&T v. Microsoft*] AT&T sued Microsoft for the infringement of a patent covering certain speech codecs that are included in Windows. Microsoft generated its source code in the United States and then shipped it abroad to foreign OEMs who, pursuant to their license agreement with Microsoft, generated copies of the software that were then installed on computers that were sold abroad. Microsoft argued that software could not be a "component" under 271(f) and that the copies were manufactured abroad rather than "supplied" from the United States. The Federal Circuit [found] that

> [g]iven the nature of the technology, the "supplying" of software commonly involves generating a copy. . . . Accordingly, for software "components," the act of copying is subsumed in the act of "supplying," such that sending a single copy abroad with the intent that it be replicated invokes § 271(f) liability for those foreign-made copies.

Judge Rader, dissenting in *AT&T*, criticized the majority's provision of "extraterritorial expansion to U.S. law by punishing under U.S. law 'copying' that occurs abroad." Instead, he argued that "[t]his court should accord proper respect to the clear language of the statute and to foreign patent regimes by limiting the application of § 271(f) to components literally 'shipped from the United States.'"

On April 30, 2007, the U.S. Supreme Court reversed the Federal Circuit 7–1, concluding that Microsoft was not liable for the alleged infringing acts occurring outside the United States. The Court focused on two questions related to Section 271(f): (1) whether software can be considered a "component" under Section 271(f); and (2) whether the foreign-made software copy was "supplied" by Microsoft "from the United States."

[T]he Court held that only software in a tangible medium could qualify as a "component" amenable to "combination" under Section 271(f). Consequently, the master copy of the computer code (not the computer code itself) qualifies as a "component.". . . In light of the Court's answer to the first question, the Court treated the master copy of the computer code as the only item supplied by Microsoft from the United States. The Court, agreeing with Judge Rader's dissent, found that nothing in the text of Section 271(f) addresses copying. The Court concluded that "[t]he absence of anything addressing copying in the statutory text weighs against a judicial determination that replication abroad of a master dispatched from the United States 'supplies' the foreign-made copies from the United States within the intendment of § 271(f).". . .

While at first glance the extraterritorial application of U.S. patent laws may seem to reflect a general domestic economic interest— discouraging foreign manufacturing of goods—extending U.S. patent laws abroad raises [several] policy concerns. . . .

First, with regard to economic policy, Section 271(f) in general and the recent extraterritorial patent law decisions [discussed above] set up a complicated incentive structure for companies. Commentators have suggested that Section 271(f) is bad economic policy because it punishes companies who produce components domestically and export them, while rewarding those who move all production offshore.

Second, the extraterritorial application of U.S. patent law intrudes on the sovereignty of foreign states. The fact that the Canadian government filed an amicus brief supporting the petition for rehearing [*NTP v. RIM*] *en banc* highlights this sovereignty concern. The Canadian government asserted that the Federal Circuit's decision "raises the risk that Section 271(a) may be accorded inappropriate extraterritorial application, contrary to basic principles of comity affecting Canada and the United States." Similarly, the Federal Circuit's willingness to extend U.S. patent law to activities occurring in Europe intrudes on the sovereignty of the European countries involved. In *AT&T*, the Supreme Court reiterated the general principle that "courts should 'assume that legislators take account of the legitimate sovereign interests of other nations when they write American laws'" and therefore applied a narrow construction of Section 271(f) to the facts of the case. In the wake of *AT&T*, courts should rethink their willingness to extend U.S. patent law. Because of the Paris Convention, the Patent Cooperation Treaty ("PCT"), and other agreements, access to patent protection throughout the world is now more readily available to inventors such that they can file for patent protection internationally, rather than arguing for the extension of their U.S. patents. Multinational patent litigation therefore can provide a means for parties to litigate related foreign patents efficiently.

NOTES AND QUESTIONS

1. The above excerpt identifies two policy concerns militating against extraterritorial application of U.S. patent laws: economic concerns and sovereignty concerns. However, a recent article makes the case that such extrater-

ritorial action, and the resulting concerns, should be viewed as beneficial, in that it may facilitate negotiation of a global patent enforcement treaty:

> One of the primary reasons development of a global patent enforcement system has stalled is that territoriality creates advantages for states. Chief among these is keeping foreign plaintiffs from litigating patent infringement claims against domestic defendants. By erecting high barriers to suing domestic defendants, each nation reaps a net benefit, while a net harm—unchecked global infringement—is felt throughout the rest of the world (at least where the potential plaintiff holds a patent). Thus, each nation has incentives to maintain the territorial system, even though it may not produce the most efficient outcomes. The collective action problem can best be conceived in terms of a repeated prisoner's dilemma. Countries have two options available to solve the problem of global infringement—enter into a treaty to provide a multinational enforcement mechanism, or maintain the strict territorial system of patent rights that requires enforcement in each individual country. With the strict territorial approach, the costs for a domestic business to remedy global infringement are astronomical. Under a global enforcement treaty, however, the costs are drastically reduced. Domestic plaintiffs would only need to litigate their infringement claims once, and they would receive a judgment that could be enforced in all states that were party to the treaty. Thus, all countries are better off under a treaty system than a strict territorial regime. . . .
>
> Extraterritorial enforcement of U.S. patent law is more likely to place pressure on the political branches to negotiate and reach an international agreement for global patent enforcement. First, and most significantly, statutory interpretations that construe U.S. patent law extraterritorially apply to all parties—not simply the parties in the litigation. For example, if U.S. courts move toward the adjudication of foreign patent claims, foreign defendants will only be subject to U.S. jurisdiction in limited circumstances. They must be infringing a U.S. patent within the United States as well as a foreign patent in a foreign jurisdiction, and they must be infringing patents that are substantially similar. On the other hand, anyone may potentially infringe a U.S. patent that is applied extraterritorially. As long as the U.S. court has personal jurisdiction (and traditional jurisdictional exceptions, such as *forum non convenient* do not apply), there is at least some risk that any foreign conduct is infringing a U.S. patent. Unlike the possibility of multinational litigation, extraterritorial application of U.S. patent law will force foreign parties to consider U.S. law in all cases, not just those in which they have made an affirmative decision to enter the U.S. market. The potential for extraterritorial application of U.S. law has already provoked responses from foreign governments, thus demonstrating its potential for creating international discord.

Timothy A. Cook, Note, *Courts as Diplomats: Encouraging an International Patent Enforcement Treaty Through Extraterritorial Constructions of the Patent Act*, 97 VA. L. REV. 1181, 1210, 1217–18 (2011).

Which argument do you find most compelling? Is extraterritorial application of U.S. patent laws beneficial or harmful in the global patent arena?

2. In arguing that U.S. courts should explicitly consider foreign law when determining *whether* to apply a U.S. patent to activities outside of the United States, Professor Holbrook identifies some concerns with the current approach:

> The apparently simplest approach to dealing with territoriality issues is to strictly limit patent infringement to acts entirely within the United States, much like the Supreme Court has done in *Deepsouth* and *Microsoft*. . . . A strict adherence to the territoriality principle would make it much easier to predict whether there should be infringement. Congress could then address any concerns legislatively, as it did in adopting §§ 271(f) and (g). This approach would be consistent with the Supreme Court's insistence on clear signals from Congress that it intends to extend the reach of American law outside the territorial U.S. . . .

> This colloquy between the courts and Congress does have significant downsides however. Congress must react to the courts' overtures, which can take time. For instance, *Deepsouth* was decided in 1972, and Congress did not overrule it with § 271(f) until 1984. Such delays could be costly to the affected patent holders, particularly for those whose patent terms expire during the period of delay. Moreover, congressional action will always be piecemeal and reactive; it is unlikely that Congress would be able to anticipate various ways that companies would arbitrage the system to take advantage of the rules of territoriality. Instead, a problem would develop and Congress would respond. In contrast, the courts will be the first to confront these scenarios and would be better situated to address them up-front.

> The position of the courts on the "front lines" of these issues highlights another problem with adhering to territoriality. Faced with these scenarios where a seeming injustice is being perpetrated against a patent holder, a court may engage in arguably tortured statutory constructions to combat the situation. Instead of waiting for Congress, the courts may try to address the problem, resulting in odd and disingenuous statutory interpretations like those of *Eolas* and *AT&T*. It was precisely this concern that motivated the Federal Circuit to afford § 271(f) such broad protection in the *Microsoft* case:

> Were we to hold that Microsoft's supply by exportation of the master versions of the Windows software-specifically for the purpose of foreign replication-avoids infringement, we would be subverting the

remedial nature of § 271(f), permitting a technical avoidance of the statute by ignoring the advances in a field of technology-and its associated industry practices-that developed after the enactment of § 271(f). It would be unsound to construe a statutory provision that was originally enacted to encourage advances in technology by closing a loophole, in a manner that allows the very advances in technology thus encouraged to subvert that intent. Section 271(f), if it is to remain effective, must therefore be interpreted in a manner that is appropriate to the nature of the technology at issue.

Such a strained interpretation undermines the territorial approach, subverts Congress's role in the process, and only serves to create uncertainty. It also shows that courts may feel compelled to act unilaterally to remedy perceived unfairness that may arise due to changes in technology, short-circuiting the Supreme Court's preferred deference to Congress.

Timothy R. Holbrook, *Extraterritoriality in U.S. Patent Law*, 49 WM. & MARY L. REV. 2119, 2142–43 (2008).

How valid are these concerns? How *should* the territorial reach of a patent be determined?

3. Some commentators are less optimistic about the prospects of wholesale reform efforts to address the problems associated with having to litigate patent infringement claims in multiple jurisdictions. They note that the creation of an international court would still likely led to follow-up proceedings in domestic courts; negotiating a treaty could be a lengthy and unpredictable process; and exercising jurisdiction over foreign patents generates political ire over perceived loss of national sovereignty. *See* James Pooley & Vicki Huang, *Multinational Patent Litigation: Management of Discovery and Settlement Issues and the Role of the Judiciary,* 22 FORDHAM. INTELL. PROP. MEDIA AND ENT. L. J. 46 (2011). In their article, Pooley and Huang identify divergences in national procedural laws as a significant challenge to harmonizing multinational patent enforcement. They offer three proposals for judges to enhance the efficiency and efficacy of global patent litigation with regard to the existence and scope of discovery and the ability to settle the case: 1) order parties to undergo global mediation; 2) order a global case-management conference; and 3) promote networks of judges involved in the dispute in various jurisdictions. *See id.*, at 64–66. What do you think of these proposals? Are they consistent with the TRIPS Agreement? Do they need to be?

INDEX

References are to Pages

ABANDONMENT OF APPLICATION
Prior art, abandoned application as, 112

ABANDONMENT OF INVENTION
Generally, 415

ABANDONMENT OF PATENT
Paris Convention, 86
Strategic considerations, 112

ABBOTT, FREDERICK
Pharmaceutical patents, TRIPS waivers,
190

ABBOTT LABORATORIES
Compulsory license request after
infringement finding, 192

ABSOLUTE NOVELTY
China, 579

ABSTRACT IDEAS
Patentability, 298, 310, 332

ABSTRACTS
Applications for patents, 591

ABUSES OF PATENT RIGHTS
Paris Convention, 88
TRIPS, 153

ACTA
See Anti-Counterfeiting Trade Agreement,
this index

**ACTIVE INDUCEMENT OF
INFRINGEMENT**
See Infringement of Patents, this index

**ADMINISTRATIVE ENFORCEMENT
OF PATENT RIGHTS**
China, 827
Injunctive relief for patent law violations,
831
International Trade Commission, this
index
Multinational regulatory enforcement, 826
et seq.
Patent and Trademark Office, this index
Post-Grant Proceedings, this index
TRIPS, 757

**ADMINISTRATIVE PROCEDURE ACT
(APA)**
Patent and Trademark Office procedure
challenges, 108

ADMINISTRATIVE PROCEDURE LAW
China, 828

AESTHETIC CREATIONS
Domestic law restrictions on patentability,
225
European Patent Convention, 285

AFRICA
History of patent law, 12

**AFRICAN REGIONAL INDUSTRIAL
PROPERTY ORGANIZATION
(ARIPO)**
Generally, 132

**AGREEMENT ON TRADE-RELATED
ASPECTS OF INTELLECTUAL
PROPERTY RIGHTS**
See TRIPS Agreement, this index

AGROCHEMICAL PATENTS
Data exclusivity provisions in free trade
agreements, 219
Exclusive marketing rights, 157
Genes, pesticide resistant, patentability
Generally, 241
Moral utility issue, 389
TRIPS, 151
US, 164

ALGERIA
Criminal penalties for infringement, 801

ALGORITHMS
Patentability, 304

ALITO, SAMUEL
Indirect infringement, 707

AMERICA INVENTS ACT (AIA)
Business methods patents, 311
Enactment, 73
First to file versus first to invent, 73
Global vs domestic novelty, 422
Grace periods, prior art, 428
Harmonization, 416
Idiosyncrasies, 415, 417
Inequitable conduct, 620
Inter Partes Review, this index
Interference proceedings effects, 76
Inventive step requirement, 439
Inventors' rights, 87
Novelty requirement, 416
On-sale bar, 84
Patent Law Treaty implementation, 630

Post-grant review, 643
Printed publication bar, 73, 424
Prior art
    Generally, 75
    Grace periods, 428
    Priority rights principle, 73
    Public disclosure as prior art, 416
    Public-use bar, 74
    Reexamination, 643
    Translations, 75
TRIPS compliance, 150

**AMERICAN INVENTOR'S
    PROTECTION ACT OF 1999 (US)**
First to file versus first to invent, 419, 619

**AMERICAN SOCIETY FOR THE
    PREVENTION OF CRUELTY TO
    ANIMALS**
Higher life forms patentability, 232

AMIN, TAHIR
Data exclusivity provisions in free trade
    agreements, 219

AMOXICILLIN
Confiscations of pharmaceutical shipments,
    838

ANDEAN COMMUNITY OF NATIONS
    Generally, 545
Disclosure of origin requirement, 545
Genetic resources, 542, 543

ANGOLA
Criminal penalties for infringement, 801

ANIMAL LEGAL DEFENSE FUND
Higher life forms patentability, 232

ANTICIPATION
Generally, 108, 396
See also Novelty Requirement, this index
Enablement, anticipatory, 410
Inherency and, 414

**ANTI-COUNTERFEITING ACT OF
    2008 (KENYA)**
Generally, 214

ANTI-COUNTERFEITING CODE
US support for, 138

**ANTI-COUNTERFEITING TRADE
    AGREEMENT (ACTA)**
Bilateralism, post TRIPS, 217
Non-governmental organizations
    opposition, 217

ANTI-PATENT MOVEMENT
History of patent law, 5, 7

APA
See Administrative Procedure Act, this
    index

APOTEX, INC.
AZT patentability, 374
Indirect infringement, 721

APPLICATIONS FOR PATENTS
Generally, 589 et seq.
See also Prosecution, this index
Abandonment of application
    Priority implications, 73
    Revival, 110
Abstracts, 591
Candor duty of inventors, 730
Central claiming, 604, 608
China
    Generally, 60
    Internationalized applications, 601
Claims, this index
Combination inventions, functional claims,
    606
Complex technologies impacting
    administrative procedures, 41
Construction of claims, 608
Continuation applications
    Generally, 46, 149
    US, 612
    Continuing and regular applications,
        612
Costs and fees
    Generally, 590
    Patent Cooperation Treaty, 112
Developing countries, internationalized
    applications issues, 604
Disclosures in
    Generally, 509 et seq., 591
    See also Disclosure Requirements,
        this index
Divisional applications, 612
Drafting claims, 606
EU
    Generally, 45
    Multiple inventions, 611
European Patent Office
    Claims, 604
    Swiss-type claims, 607
Filing formalities
    Generally, 589
    Patent Cooperation Treaty unified
        filing system, 93
First to file versus first to invent priority
    rights, 73
Foreign filings
    Government permission
        requirements, 589, 604
    Licenses, 602
Foreign/domestic application conflicts,
    priority rights principle, 73
Formal requirements, Patent Cooperation
    Treaty, 116
Gaming of the patent system through
    claims drafting, 608
Harmonization, 601
Independent and dependent claims, 603
Internationalized applications
    Generally, 79, 590 et seq.
    China, 600
    Developing country issues, 601
    Foreign filing licenses, 602
    Pharmaceutical patents, 600
    Preliminary examinations, 105

Risks, 602
Translation requirements, 598
US, 602
Utility models, 602
WTO requirements, 590
Inventors' identification rights, 630
IP5 applications, 590
Japan, multiple inventions, 611
Means plus function claims, 606
Multinational filing, Patent Law Treaty,
115, 630
Multiple inventions, 611
Novelty requirement, applications filed
earlier but published after, 405
Omnibus claims, 604, 606
Paris Convention, 602
Patent Cooperation Treaty
Generally, 602
Formal requirements, 116
Procedure, 79
Stages of patent application, 100, 106
Unified filing system, 93
Patent Law Treaty
Generally, 602
Multinational filing, 115, 630
Patent Prosecution Highways, 117
Pendency delays, 41
Peripheral claiming, 605
Pharmaceutical patents, internationalized
applications, 600
Preliminary examinations, international,
105
Priority rights principle, foreign/domestic
application conflicts, 73
Provisional applications
Generally, 609
TRIPS, 149
Publication of applications and search
reports
Generally, 105
Patent Cooperation Treaty, 94
Regular and continuing applications, 612
Restriction practice, 113, 612
Revival of abandoned applications, 110
Risks, internationalized applications, 602
Searches of Prior Art, this index
Secrecy orders, 603
South Korea, 60
Specification disclosures, 509, 589
Stages of patent application, Patent
Cooperation Treaty, 100, 106
Strategic considerations, 112
Swiss-type claims, 607
Technology transfer, patent applications as
catalysts for, 105
Translation of Patents, this index
Triadic patents, 590
Trilateral cooperation, 119
Trilateral Cooperation Offices, 590
TRIPS
Generally, 602
Provisional applications, 149
Types of applications, 609
Unified filing system, Patent Cooperation
Treaty, 93

Unity of invention objections, 612
US
Internationalized applications, 602
Multiple inventions, 611
Utility models, internationalized
applications, 602
Written descriptions
Generally, 521
See also Disclosure Requirements,
this index
WTO requirements, internationalized
applications, 590

ARGENTINA
Criminal penalties for infringement, 801
Technology transfer proposal, 57
WIPO development proposal, 57
Working requirements proposal, 57

ARIPO
See African Regional Industrial Property
Organization, this index

ARISTOTLE
History of patent law, 3

ASIA
History of patent law, 12

ASSOCIATION OF SOUTHEAST
ASIAN NATIONS (ASEAN)
Generally, 141
Patent examination cooperation, 121

ATOMIC WEAPONS
Patentability, 226

AT&T CORP.
Microsoft litigation, territorial limits of
patents, 863

ATTORNEY'S FEES AWARDS
Generally, 775
English rule, 621
TRIPS, 757

AUSTRALIA
Business methods and software
patentability, 311
Diagnostic methods patentability issues,
331
Gene patents, 331
Innovation patents, 554
Inventors' rights, 638
Patents of addition, 622
Transpacific Partnership Agreement, 217
Utility requirement, 345
Vancouver Group worksharing group, 121

AUSTRIA
Criminal penalties for infringement, 801
Inventors' rights, 632

AUSTRIA-HUNGARY
History of patent law, 5

AZT (DRUG)
Limitations on patent rights, 200
Patentability, 374

BACTERIA
Life forms patentability, 227

BAGLEY, MARGO A.
Biotechnology patentability, 278
Geographical limitations on prior art, 423
Knowledge transfer, 421, 423
Limitations on patentability, 276, 282, 390, 545

BAHRAIN
Criminal penalties for infringement, 801

BALL, GWENDOLYN P.
Transaction costs and patent trolls, 763

BARBADOS
Criminal penalties for infringement, 801

BASHEER, SHAMNAD
India's pharmaceutical industry, 163
TRIPS compliance pressures, 216

BAYER CROPSCIENCE
Seed patents, genetic resource challenges, 552

BAYER HEALTHCARE AG
Compulsory licensing of pharmaceuticals, 192

BAYH-DOLE ACT OF 1980 (US)
Government-funded inventions, manufacturing restrictions, 185
Inventors' rights, 637
Technology transfer policy, 457

BEIER, DAVID
TRIPS origin, 140

BELGIUM
Compulsory licensing, 92, 194
Disclosure of origin requirement, 545
International Depository Authority, 531
Paris Convention, 69
Substantive patent examination, 588, 615

BELLO, JUDITH HIPPLER
WTO dispute settlement authority questions, 162

BENEFICIAL OR MORAL UTILITY
Generally, 382
See also Moral Utility Doctrine, this index

BERNE CONVENTION
Generally, 139, 178
Human rights, 32

BERNE DECLARATION (NGO)
Seed patents, genetic resource challenges, 552

BEST MODE
See Disclosure Requirements, this index

BETTI, ISABELLA
Torpedo, Italian, 774

BILATERALISM, POST-TRIPS
See also Free Trade Agreements, this index

Anti-Counterfeiting Trade Agreement enactment, 217
Central America-Dominican Republic Free Trade Agreement, 218
Data exclusivity provisions in free trade agreements, 219
Regional free trade agreements, 216
Scope of patent protection matters, 217
Transpacific Partnership Agreement, 217
TRIPs-Plus agreements, 216

BIODIVERSITY ACT
India, 544

BIOINDUSTRY ASSOCIATION (BIA)
Generally, 371

BIOLOGICAL DIVERSITY ACT
India, 552

BIOLOGICAL RESOURCES
Convention on Biological Diversity, 541

BIOPHARMACEUTICAL INDUSTRY
US economy importance, 22

BIOTECH DIRECTIVE
Generally, 664

BIOTECHNOLOGY
Disclosure of origin requirement, 539
EU
    Generally, 665
    Biotechnology Directive, 355
Genetic Resources, this index
Patentability
    Generally, 226 et seq.
    See also Life Forms, Patentability of, this index
    US, 278
Piracy, disclosure of origin requirement to combat, 540
Traditional Knowledge, this index
Utility requirement, 345

BIOTECHNOLOGY DIRECTIVE (EU)
Generally, 355

BIPARTISAN TRADE PROMOTION AUTHORITY ACT OF 2002 (US)
Generally, 215

BOLAR EXCEPTION
Infringement, 735

BOLIVIA
Criminal penalties for infringement, 801
WIPO Development Agenda, 57

BONADIO, ENRICO
Human embryo research, 277

BORDER ENFORCEMENT OF PATENT RIGHTS
Generally, 826 et seq.
See also International Trade, this index
Commercialization vs production level patent enforcement, 60

Confiscations of Infringing Goods, this
    index
Customs enforcement, 830
Customs Tariff Law, Japan, 835
Destruction of infringing goods, TRIPS, 757
EU, 841
Exclusion orders, International Trade
    Commission, 831
Multinational enforcement of patent rights,
    830

BRAGA, CARLOS ALBERTO
GATT and TRIPS, 136

BRAZIL
Compulsory licenses, 185, 194
Criminal penalties for infringement, 801
Design protection, 559
Development status changes, 60
Examination for patents, 615
Genetic resources, 544
International patent system and
    developing countries, 56
Patent Cooperation Treaty, membership
    considerations, 97
Pharmaceutical patents, 185
Technology transfer proposal, 56
Utility requirement, 345
WIPO development proposal, 57
Working requirements
    Compulsory licenses to enforce, 185
    WIPO proposal, 57

**BRAZILIAN ASSOCIATION OF
    INTELLECTUAL PROPERTY**
Utility requirement, 345

BREWSTER, RACHEL
Domestic origins of international
    agreements, 37

BREYER, STEPHEN
Business method patents, 297

BRUNEI DARUSSALAM
Transpacific Partnership Agreement, 217

BRUSSELS CONVENTION
Jurisdictional expansion, 45
Territoriality restrictions, elimination, 45

BRUSSELS REGULATION
Cross-border injunctive relief, 765, 773
Territoriality restrictions, elimination, 45

BUDAPEST TREATY
Deposits of microorganism samples, 530
Disclosure requirement, samples, 530

BURDEN OF PROOF
Claim construction questions, 653
Examinations for patents, 621
Invalidity defense to infringement, 727
Patent and Trademark Office, 621
Prosecution, 621
TRIPS, infringement issues, 154

BURK, DAN L.
Chemical patents, utility requirement, 345

BURUNDI
Criminal penalties for infringement, 801

**BUSINESS METHODS AND
    SOFTWARE, PATENTABILITY
    OF**
Generally, 284
See also Software, this index
Algorithms, patentability, 304
America Invents Act, 311
Australia, 311
Breadth of business methods, 308
China, 311
Diagnostic methods patentability
    compared, 328
Disclosure aspects of business method
    operational details, 308
Domestic law restrictions on patentability,
    225
EU, 284
European Patent Office, 293
First Inventors Defense Act of 1999, 306
Infringement issues, 284
Injunctive relief to enforce, 759
Japan, 284, 311
New Zealand, 312
Post-Grant Review, 643 et seq.
Prior user rights, 420
TRIPS, 312
UK, 284
US, 296
Vagueness of business methods, 309

CAFTA-DR
See Central America-Dominican Republic
    Free Trade Agreement, this index

CALVERT, JANE
Utility standards, 372

CAMBODIA
ASEAN Patent Examination Cooperation
    Program, 121
Patent Cooperation Treaty, membership
    considerations, 98

CANADA
Criminal penalties for infringement, 801
Damages, this index
Design protection, 560
Grace periods, prior art, 430
Indirect infringement, 722
Inventive Step Requirement, this index
Life forms patentability, 233, 241
New uses of known substances,
    patentability, 320
Patent Protection of Pharmaceutical
    Products case, Bole exception, 742
Pharmaceutical Patents, this index
Plant protection, 584
Prior art, grace periods, 430
Prosecution history use in construction of
    claims, 655
US pharmaceuticals purchases, 218
Utility requirement, 345, 374
Vancouver Group worksharing group, 121

CANCER RESEARCH
Harvard Oncomouse, this index
Life forms patentability incentives, 233

CANDOR, DUTY OF
Generally, 730
Comparative law, 600
US, 620

**CAPABLE OF INDUSTRIAL
  APPLICATION**
Useful and, synonymous use of terms, 435

CATERPILLAR (COMPANY)
US role in global economy, 20

CBD
See Convention on Biological Diversity,
  this index

**CENTRAL AMERICA-DOMINICAN
  REPUBLIC FREE TRADE
  AGREEMENT (CAFTA-DR)**
Bilateralism, post TRIPS, 218

**CENTRALIZED ACCESS TO SEARCH
  AND EXAMINATION (CASE)**
Vancouver Group, 121

CETUS (COMPANY)
Assignments of rights by inventors, 637

CHEMICAL PATENTS
Agrochemical Patents, this index
Inventive step requirement, chemical arts
  EU, 486
  US, 458
Patentability, 314
Utility requirement, 342, 345

CHEVRON OIL
US role in global economy, 20

CHIEN, COLLEEN V.
Exclusion orders, 834

CHILE
Criminal penalties for infringement, 801
Transpacific Partnership Agreement, 217

CHINA
Absolute novelty, 578
Administrative Procedure Law, 282
Applications for patents, 60
Business methods and software
  patentability, 311
Consistency of Chinese remedies for
  infringement, 817
Criminal penalties for infringement, 801
Damages, 801
Design patents, 579
Development status changes, 60
Disclosure of origin requirement, 544
Examinations for Patents, this index
Experimental use defense, 733
Generic drug production, 192
Global patent application filings, 40
Injunctive remedies, 799
Internationalized applications, 602

Invalidity defense to infringement, 723
Inventive Step Requirement, this index
Inventors' rights, 631
IP5 initiative, 120
Life forms patentability, 276
Multinational enforcement of patent rights,
  811 et seq.
Novelty Requirement, this index
Patent Law, 497
Pharmaceutical patents, inventive step
  requirement, 502
Prior art
  Generally, 398
  Global vs domestic, 427
Prosecution history use in construction of
  claims, 655
Reexamination, this index
Regulatory enforcement, 827
Remedies for infringement
  Generally, 798
  Apology remedy, 799
  Consistency of Chinese standards,
    818
US compared, inventive step requirement,
  500
Utility models, 553
WIPO membership, 616
WTO membership, importance of Chinese
  participation, 819

CHISUM, DONALD S.
Novelty requirement, 413

CHOICE OF LAW ISSUES
Extraterritorial approaches to enforcement
  of patent rights, 847

CHUN, DONGWOOK
Harmonization of patent laws, 122

CLAIMS
Generally, 603
Burden of proof, claim construction
  questions, 652
Central claiming, 604, 606
Combination inventions, functional claims,
  606
Comparative claim construction, 649
Construction of claims in infringement
  actions
  Generally, 649 et seq.
  Infringement of Patents, this index
  Prosecution History Estoppel, this
    index
  Purposive Construction, this index
Costs of excessive claims, 606
Design patents, omnibus claims, 605
Dictionary use in construction, 651, 654
Disclosure requirement, enablement, 509
Drafting claims
  Generally, 603
  Gaming the patent system, 608
Election demands, 611
Enablement, disclosure requirement, 509
European Patent Office
  Generally, 604

Swiss-type claims, 607
Excessive claims, costs, 606
Extrinsic evidence use in construction, 652, 655
Functional claims, 606
Gaming of the patent system through claims drafting, 608
Germany, construction, 700
Independent and dependent claims, 603
Law, construction questions as matters of, 649, 655 673
Limiting number of, 608
Means plus function claims, 606
Omnibus claims, 604, 606
Ordinary and customary meaning, 652
Patented invention and claimed invention, terms distinguished, 608
Peripheral claiming, 605
Person of ordinary skill in the art standard, construction by, 653
Prosecution history use in construction of claims
    Generally, 649
    See also Prosecution History
        Estoppel, this index
    Comparative practice, 655
PTO regulations, 609
Purposive Construction, this index
Reading on claims, 650, 656
Restriction practice, 611
Specifications confusing claims construction, 693
Standard of appellate review of construction questions, 656, 673
Swiss-type claims, 607

CLIMATE CHANGE
Globalization of patent law and, 18, 91, 165

CLINTON, BILL
Uruguay Round Agreements Act, 148

CLINTON FOUNDATION
United Nations generic drugs programs, 838

CLONING
Embryonic stem cells, 279
Gene Patents, this index
Human beings, 263, 272
Life Forms, Patentability of, this index

COLLABORATIVE RESEARCH AND TECHNOLOGY ENHANCEMENT ACT (CREATE)
Inventive step requirement, 456

COLLECTIVE ACTION PROBLEMS
Institutional theory of treaty formation, 38

COLOMBIA
Criminal penalties for infringement, 801
Free trade agreement, 217

COLONIAL ERA
History of patent law, 12

COMBINATION INVENTIONS
Functional claims, 606

COMMISSION ON INTELLECTUAL PROPERTY RIGHTS, INNOVATION, AND PUBLIC HEALTH
Intellectual property rights and public health, 165

COMMUNITY PATENT CONVENTION (CPC)
Creation, 125

COMPARATIVE EXAMINATIONS
See Examinations for Patents, this index

COMPARATIVE PATENTABILITY REQUIREMENTS
Generally, 223 et seq.
Business Methods and Software, Patentability of, this index
Examinations, quality improvements, 42
Life Forms, Patentability of, this index
Procurement, 509 et seq.
Subject matter of patents, 225 et seq.

COMPARATIVE PROCUREMENT REQUIREMENTS
Generally, 509 et seq.
Applications for Patents, this index
Design Patents, this index
Disclosure Requirements, this index
Examinations for Patents, this index
Plant Protection, this index
Prosecution, this index
Utility Models, this index

COMPULSORY LICENSING
Brazil, 185
Developed vs developing countries use, 92
Domestic law requirements, 89
Guinea, 194
History of patent law, 70
India, 192
Jordan, 194
National emergencies, 186
Noncommunicable diseases treatment pharmaceuticals, 191
Paris Convention, 70, 87
Pharmaceuticals, noncommunicable diseases treatments, 191
Public health policy, 194
Singapore, 197, 198
Thailand, 192
TRIPS requirements
    Generally, 153
    US compliance, 93
Working requirements enforcement
    Generally, 89
    Brazil, 185

COMPUTERS
See also Business Methods and Software, Patentability of, this index
Design patents, 561, 572

CONFIDENTIALITY
Data Exclusivity Provisions, this index
Disclosure Requirements, this index

**CONFISCATIONS OF INFRINGING
GOODS**
EU, 824, 841
India, 841
Multinational enforcement of patent rights,
817
Pharmaceuticals, 841
TRIPS, 757

CONSOLIDATION OF LAWSUITS
Multinational enforcement of patent rights,
846

CONSTITUTION (US)
History of patent law, 4

CONSTRUCTION OF CLAIMS
Generally, 647 et seq.
Infringement of Patents, this index
Prosecution History Estoppel, this index
Purposive Construction, this index

CONTINUATION APPLICATIONS
See Applications for Patents, this index

**CONTINUATION-IN-PART
APPLICATIONS**
See Applications for Patents, this index

CONTRIBUTORY INFRINGEMENT
See Infringement of Patents, this index

**CONVENTION ON BIOLOGICAL
DIVERSITY (CBD)**
Human rights issues, 40
Membership, 540
National control of biological resources, 541
Sovereignty over genetic resources, 547
Traditional knowledge study, 548

**CONVENTION ON JURISDICTION
AND THE ENFORCEMENT OF
JUDGMENTS IN CIVIL AND
COMMERCIAL MATTERS**
Generally, 45

**CONVENTION ON THE GRANT OF
EUROPEAN PATENTS**
See European Patent Convention, this
index

COOK, TIMOTHY A.
International patent enforcement, 868

COSTA RICA
Criminal penalties for infringement, 801
Genetic resources, 542

COSTS AND FEES
See Maintenance Fees, this index
Applications for patents
Generally, 590
Excessive claims, 611
Grants of patents, 639

Patent Cooperation Treaty application
costs, 112
Searches of prior art, 103
Substantive examinations, 617
TRIPS expenses, 757

COTTER, THOMAS F.
Permanent injunctions, 764

COUNTERFEIT PRODUCTS
See also Piracy, this index
Border Enforcement of Patent Rights, this
index
Human rights challenges to TRIPS
compliant laws, 199
Multinational Enforcement of Patent
Rights, this index
Parallel Imports, this index
TRIPS compliant laws, human rights
challenges, 199

CPC
See Community Patent Convention, this
index

CREATE
See Collaborative Research and Technology
Enhancement Act, this index

**CRIMINAL PENALTIES FOR
INFRINGEMENT**
Generally, 801
Enhanced damages, 802
EU, 824
Multinational enforcement of patent rights,
criminal procedures issues, 815
Policy considerations, 802
Purposes, 803
US, 801

CROUCH, DENNIS
Novelty requirement, 334

CUBA
Criminal penalties for infringement, 801
WIPO Development Agenda, 57

CULTURAL PROTECTIONS
Generally, 26
Genetic Resources, this index
International Covenant on Economic,
Social, and Cultural Rights, this
index
Traditional Knowledge, this index
United Nations Educational, Scientific and
Cultural Organization, 139

CUSTOMS LAWS
Border Enforcement of Patent Rights, this
index
Confiscations of Infringing Goods, this
index

CUSTOMS TARIFF LAW
Japan, 835

CZECH REPUBLIC
Parallel imports, 750

DAMAGES
Generally, 775 et seq.
Attorney's fees awards, 775
Canada
    Generally, 775
    Defendant's profits as measure, 797
China, 798
Criminal penalties for infringement,
    enhanced damages in lieu of, 801
Defendant's profits as measure
    Generally, 775 et seq.
    Canada, 797
    China, 801
    Disgorgement, 788
    Germany, 801
    UK, 787
Disgorgement, 788
Elections by patent holder, 796
Enhanced damages in lieu of criminal
    penalties for infringement, 802
Four-factor or DAMP test, 786
Georgia-Pacific factors, 787
Germany, defendant's profits as measure,
    797
Lost chance damages, 787
Lost profits damages, 786
Market value measure of damages, 782
Patentee's loss as measure, 775 et seq.
Pre-judgment interest, 775
Process patent infringement, 787
Reasonable royalty as measure, 775, 785
Technology patents, injunction vs damages
    protection, 758
TRIPS, 757
UK
    Generally, 786
    Defendant's profits as measure, 788
US, 775 et seq.
Valuation problems, 758

DAMP TEST
Lost profits damages, 786

DATA EXCLUSIVITY PROVISIONS
Agrochemical patents, 218
Free trade agreements containing, 218, 641
Pharmaceutical patents, 218, 229, 641

DATE OF INVENTION
See also Priority, Right of, this index
TRIPS, 149

**DECLARATION OF THE RIGHTS OF
    MAN (FRANCE)**
History of patent law, 5

DEEPSOUTH PACKING CO.
Litigation addressing extraterritoriality of
    US patent laws, 864

**DEFENSES AND EXCEPTIONS TO
    INFRINGEMENT**
Generally, 723 et seq.
Bolar exception, 735
Experimental Use Defense, this index
First sale doctrine

    Exhaustion of Patent Rights, this
        index
    Parallel Imports, this index
Inequitable Conduct Defense, this index
Invalidity defense
    Generally, 726 et seq.
    See also Validity of Patent, this index
Non-infringement defense, 723
Parallel Imports, this index

DENMARK
Comparative examination, 631
Criminal penalties for infringement, 801

DEPENDENT CLAIMS
Independent claims distinguished, 603

DERENYI, EUGENE F.
Business method patents, 312

DESCRIPTIONS
See Disclosure Requirements, this index

DESIGN PATENTS
Generally, 559
China, 578
Computers, 560, 572
Constrained design aspects and design
    freedom aspects, 569
EU, 575
Functional design features, 573
Informed user test, 561, 572, 576
Novelty requirement
    Generally, 560, 573
    China, 578
    US, 575
Omnibus claims, 605
Ordinary observer test, 572, 573
Patent Law Treaties Implementation Act,
    580
Point of novelty test, 573, 625
Priority rights, 572
Registered Community Designs, 559
UK, 561
US
    Generally, 559
    Novelty requirement, 575
    Patent Law Treaties Implementation
        Act, 580

**DESTRUCTION OF INFRINGING
    GOODS**
See also Confiscations of Infringing Goods,
    this index
TRIPS, 757

DEVELOPING COUNTRIES
See also Least Developed Countries, this
    index
Alternative forms of intellectual property
    protection proposals, 66
Balancing incentives to create and
    resulting opportunities for free
    competition, 182
Brazil, development status changes, 60
China, development status changes, 60

Compulsory licensing, developed vs
    developing countries use, 92
Cultural differences as to property rights,
    62
Development status changes, 60
Dispute Settlement Understanding
    involvement, 819
Experimental use defense, 738
Flexible TRIPS provisions
    Generally, 184
    Public health policy, 164
Foreign patent ownership in third world,
    58
Free trade agreements, proposed benefits,
    219
Genetic resources advocacy, 185, 546
Harmonization concerns, 43
History of patent law, 12
India, development status changes, 60
Intellectual property policies, 142
Internationalized patent applications
    issues, 602
Inventive step requirement, 444
Multinational enforcement of patent rights,
    807
Patent Cooperation Treaty, membership
    considerations, 98
Piracy concerns of developed countries, 21
Post-TRIPS tug-of-war between developed
    and developing countries, 185
Property rights, cultural differences as to,
    62
Quest for a global patent
    Framework, 56
    Rich/poor divide concerns, 41
South Africa, development status changes,
    60
South Korea, development status changes,
    60
Traditional knowledge protection advocacy,
    185
TRIPS
    Acceptance, 180
    Alternative forms of protection
        proposals, 66
    Enforcement impacts, 807
    Flexibilities
        Generally, 184
        Public health policy, 164
        Resistance, 142
Utility standards, policy considerations,
    354
WIPO voting blocs, 15
WIPO Development Agenda, 57
WTO memberships, 17

DEVELOPMENT ROUND
TRIPS, 215

DIAGNOSTIC METHOD PATENTS
Australia, 332
Business method patentability parallels,
    327
Exclusions, 225
Machine or transformation test, 330
Patentability issues, 321, 381

Pharmaceutical patent combinations, 321
TRIPS, 152
US, 322

DIRECT INFRINGEMENT
See Infringement of Patents, this index

DISCLOSURE OF ORIGIN (DOO)
    REQUIREMENT
Generally, 539 et seq.
Andean Community of Nations, 545
Biotechnology inventions, 539
China, 544
Country source disclosures, 550
EU, 545
European Union Commission study, 548
Genetic resource protections, 539, 541
Source disclosures, 541
Traditional knowledge protections, 540
TRIPS recognition, 543, 550
US opposition, 540
WIPO recognition, 543
WTO recognition, 543, 550

DISCLOSURE REQUIREMENTS
Generally, 509 et seq.
See also Data Exclusivity Provisions, this
    index
Applications for patents, disclosures in
    Generally, 509, 589
    Secrecy orders, 603
Best mode, 538
Biological materials, written description,
    530
Business method operational details, 307
China, disclosure of origin requirement,
    544
Claims enablement, 518
Completeness, 509
Drawings, 530
Eight factors relevant to enablement, 514
Elements disclosure, 514
Enablement
    Generally, 509 et seq.
    See also Enablement Requirement,
        this index
European Patent Office
    Enablement, 509
    Written description, 529, 532
Exclusivity, disclosure in exchange for, 344
Genetic resources disclosure proposals, 115
Innovation protection, 509
Origin of invention. See Disclosure of
    Origin Requirement, this index
Person having ordinary skill in the art
    standard, 509
Pharmaceuticals enablement, 515
Priority implications, 522
Quid pro quo of patent exclusivity, 344, 537
Samples, 531
Source of invention. See Disclosure of
    Origin Requirement, this index
South Korea, written description, 521
Specifications, disclosures in, 509, 589
Sufficiency, 509
Trade secrets protection compared, 419

Traditional knowledge disclosure
    proposals, 115
UK
    Written description, 531
US
    Disclosure of origin requirement
        opposition, 540
    Enablement, 514
    Written description, 522, 537
    Working examples, enablement, 519
Written descriptions
    Generally, 521
    Biological materials, 530
    Drawings, 530
    Enablement requirement
        distinguished, 523, 538
    European Patent Office, 529, 531
    Patent and Trademark Office report,
        531
    Samples, 531
    South Korea, 521
    UK, 531
    US, 522, 537

DISCOVERIES
Patentability, 225

DISCOVERY
TRIPS, discovery in aid of infringement
    actions, 757

DISCRIMINATION
Chinese infringement remedies,
    consistency of standards, 817
Foreign applications
Generally, 107, 618
National Treatment, this index
Reasonable and non-discriminatory
    licensing conditions, 835

DISGORGEMENT OF PROFITS
Remedies for infringement, 788

DISPUTE SETTLEMENT BODY (DSB)
Human rights considerations, 28
Transparency criticisms, 28

**DISPUTE SETTLEMENT
    UNDERSTANDING (DSU)**
Generally, 154 et seq.
Canada vs EU patent protection of
    pharmaceutical products, 167
Complaints
    Generally, 155
    Non-violation complaints, 166
Consultations to resolve disputes, 812, 813,
    815
Creation, 16
Developing and least-developed countries
    involvement, 819
Enforcement of reports, 154
EU vs Canada, patent protection of
    pharmaceutical products, 167
India vs US, protection for pharmaceutical
    and agricultural chemical products,
    158
Initiation of DSU measures, 155

Judicial review of proceedings, 154
Market analysis of dispute resolution
    processes, 809
Mechanisms of settlement, 155
Non-violation complaints, 166
Panels, 155
Patent case resolutions, 157
Remedies, 166
Sanctions, 16
Suspension of trade concession remedies,
    166
TRIPS flexibilities, justification for, 184
WTO authority questions, 162

DIVISIONAL APPLICATIONS
See Applications for Patents, this index

DNA
Generally, 347
See also Gene Patents, this index
Patentability, 331

DOCTRINE OF EQUIVALENTS (DOE)
Generally, 665 et seq.
After-arising technology, 672
Comparative practice, 674
Expert testimony, 689
France, 674
Germany, 674, 700
History of doctrine, 665
Japan, 674
Non-literal infringement, 666
Policy considerations, 672
Prosecution history estoppel and, 668, 673
Purposive construction distinguished, 680,
    697, 698
Standard of appellate review, 673
US, 674

**DOHA DECLARATION ON THE TRIPS
    AGREEMENT AND PUBLIC
    HEALTH**
Generally, 148, 186
TRIPS adoption, 189

DOHA ROUND
Exclusive marketing rights, transition
    periods, 157
HIV/AIDS declaration, 186
Public health policy declaration, 186
TRIPS flexibilities, 187

**DOMESTIC ORIGINS OF
    INTERNATIONAL
    AGREEMENTS**
Generally, 38

DOMINICAN REPUBLIC
Criminal penalties for infringement, 801
WIPO Development Agenda, 57

DOO
See Disclosure of Origin Requirement, this
    index

DOUBLE PATENTING
Generally, 405, 639

DOW JONES INDEX
Generally, 19

DRAHOS, PETER
Patent Cooperation Treaty membership,
    developing country considerations, 98
Patent office operations, 608

DREYFUSS, ROCHELLE COOPER
Substantive Patent Law Treaty
    negotiations, 42

DRUGS
See Pharmaceutical Patents, this index

DSB
See Dispute Settlement Body, this index

DSU
See Dispute Settlement Understanding,
    this index

DUFFY, JOHN F.
Non-obviousness requirement, 436

DUNCAN, JEFFREY M.
Judicial and administrative enforcement of
    international property rights in
    china, 827

DUNN, KYLA
Cloning embryonic stem cells, 278

DUTFIELD, GRAHAM
Pharmaceuticals, patentability, 313

DYESTUFFS
Patentability, 314

EAPO
See Eurasian Patent Organization, this
    index

EARLY HARMONIZATION EFFORTS
Generally, 6

ECJ
See European Court of Justice, this index

ECUADOR
Compulsory licenses, 194
Criminal penalties for infringement, 801
WIPO Development Agenda, 57

EGYPT
Criminal penalties for infringement, 801
Searches of prior art, Patent Cooperation
    Treaty guidelines, 113

ELECTRICAL TECHNOLOGY
Multinational enforcement of patent rights,
    831

ELIGIBLE SUBJECT MATTER
See Subject Matter of Patents, this index

EL-SAID, HAMED
Access to pharmaceuticals in developing
    countries, 219

EL-SAID, MOHAMMED
Access to pharmaceuticals in developing
    countries, 219

EMBRYONIC STEM CELLS
Cloning technology, 279
Patentability, 263

EMERGING TECHNOLOGIES
Utility requirement problems, 345

EMORY UNIVERSITY
Inventors' rights, 636

EMPLOYEE INVENTORS
Generally, 631
See also Inventors, this index
Japan, 636
Nigeria, 638
Transfers of rights, 631

**EMPLOYEES' INVENTION ACT
    (DENMARK)**
Generally, 632

**EMPLOYEES' INVENTION ACT
    (SWEDEN)**
Generally, 631

**EMPLOYEES' INVENTIONS ACT
    (GERMANY)**
Generally, 631

EMR
See Exclusive Marketing Rights, this index

ENABLEMENT REQUIREMENT
Generally, 509 et seq.
Anticipatory enablement, 405
Claims, enablement of, 518
Eight relevant factors, 514
European Patent Office, 509
Inventive step distinguished, 509
Novelty distinguished, 509
Pharmaceuticals, 515
Presumptive enablement, 516
Specification disclosing, 509
Specification enabling the invention, 110
US, 514
Working examples, 519
Written description distinguished, 523, 538

**ENFORCEMENT OF INTELLECTUAL
    PROPERTY RIGHTS DIRECTIVE
    (EU)**
Generally, 824

ENFORCEMENT OF PATENT RIGHTS
Administrative Enforcement of Patent
    Rights, this index
Border Enforcement of Patent Rights, this
    index
Commercialization vs production level
    enforcement, 59
Confiscations of Infringing Goods, this
    index
Dispute Settlement Understanding, this
    index

Extraterritorial Approaches to
    Multinational Litigation, this index
Jurisdiction, this index
Multinational Enforcement of Patent
    Rights, this index
Regional Patent Enforcement Initiatives,
    this index
Remedies for Infringement, this index

ENGLAND
See United Kingdom, this index

ENGLISH RULE
Attorney fee awards, 621

ENHANCED DAMAGES
Criminal penalties for infringement,
    enhanced damages in lieu of, 802

ENVIRONMENTAL PROTECTION
Patentability exclusions, 225

EPC
See European Patent Convention, this
    index

EPO
See European Patent Office, this index

EQUAL TREATMENT
See National Treatment, this index

EQUIVALENTS
See Doctrine of Equivalents, this index

ERSTLING, JAY A.
Comparative patent examination practices,
    623

EST
See Expressed Sequence Tags, this index

ESTONIA
Parallel imports, 750

ETHICS
See also Moral Duties, this index
Patentability implications of ethical
    violations involved in making
    invention, 277

**EURASIAN PATENT ORGANIZATION
    (EAPO)**
Generally, 133

**EUROPEAN COURT OF JUSTICE
    (ECJ)**
Cross-border injunctive relief, 768, 774
Parallel imports, 750

EUROPEAN FREE TRADE AREA
Patent protection levels, 215

**EUROPEAN GENERIC MEDICINES
    ASSOCIATION**
Generally, 319

**EUROPEAN PATENT CONVENTION
    (EPC)**
Generally, 124
Article 69, 680, 693

London Agreement, 125
Oppositions, 126
Post-Grant Review, 644
Purposive Construction, this index
Translation issues, 125
Utility requirement, 354 et seq.

EUROPEAN PATENT COURT
Proposals, 702

EUROPEAN PATENT OFFICE (EPO)
Business methods and software
    patentability, 293
Claims in patent applications, 607
Climate change and patent protection, 165
Disclosure Requirements, this index
Discrimination against foreign applicants,
    618
EU harmonization, 485
European Patent Convention, this index
Inventive step requirement
    Generally, 467
        Japanese Patent Office compared,
            487
IP5 initiative, 120
Life forms patentability, 256
New uses of known substances,
    patentability, 319
Novelty requirement, 392, 418
Patent Law Treaty adherence, 115
Priority rights principle, 86
Purposive Construction, this index
Searches of prior art, 102
Software patentability, 294
Swiss-type claims, 607
Translations, 628
Trilateral cooperation, 119

**EUROPEAN PATENT
    ORGANIZATION**
Generally, 644

EUROPEAN UNION
Applications for patents
    Generally, 45
    Multiple inventions, 611
Bilateralism, post TRIPS, 215
BioTech Directive, 665
Biotechnology Directive, 355
Biotechnology patents, 665
Business methods and software
    patentability, 285
Canada pharmaceutical products patent
    protection, EU dispute, 167
Confiscations of infringing goods, 824, 841
Convention on Jurisdiction and the
    Enforcement of Judgments in Civil
    and Commercial Matters, 45
Criminal penalties for infringement, 801
Cross-border injunctions, 765
Customs enforcement of patents, 841
Customs officials enforcement of patent
    rights, 841
Design patents, 575
Design protection, 559

Directive on the Enforcement of Intellectual Property Rights, 824
Disclosure of origin requirement, 550
Enforcement of Intellectual Property Rights Directive (EU), 824
Exhaustion of patent rights, 744 et seq.
Experimental use defense, 733, 736
Extensions of patent terms, 641
Extraterritorial approaches to enforcement of patent rights, 770
Grace periods, prior art, 432
Harmonization, 485
Infringement of Patents, this index
Injunctive relief, 765
Inventive step requirement, 454, 466 et seq.
Jurisdiction
    Generally, 45
    Infringement, 680, 701
    Injunctive relief, 769
    Recognition and enforcement of judgments, 826
Life forms patentability, 257
Multinational enforcement of patent rights
    Generally, 824
    Customs officials, 837
Multiple invention applications, 611
Parallel imports, 747 et seq.
Parallel proceedings, strategic considerations, 774
Patent court proposals, 702
Patent term extensions, 641
Piracy, 823
Plant protection, 582
Prior art, grace periods, 432
ProTon Europe, 420
Purposive Construction, this index
Recognition and enforcement of judgments, 826
Regional enforcement initiatives, 820
Registered Community Designs, 560
Strasbourg Convention, 443
Term extensions, 641
Territoriality restrictions, elimination, 44
TRIPS, bilateralism following, 215
University patent filing activities, US vs Europe, 420
Utility models study, 558
Utility Requirement, this index

EUROPEAN UNION COMMISSION

Disclosure of origin requirement study, 545

EVERGREENING

Generally, 319, 496
See also Term of Patent, this index
Inherency doctrine and, 414

EXAMINATIONS FOR PATENTS

Generally, 615 et seq.
See also Prosecution, this index
Administrative Procedure Act challenges to prosecution decisions, 111
America Invents Act, substantive examinations, 620
Belgium, 615

Brazil, 615
Burden of proof, 619
Candor, Duty of, this index
China, 615
Claims, election demands, 611
Comparative examinations
    Generally, 623 et seq.
    Denmark, 631
    EU, 623
    Japan, 631
    Quality improvements, 42
    Translations, 628
    USPTO, 629
Comparative law, substantive examinations, 589, 615
Costs of substantive examination, 615
Denmark, comparative examination, 631
Discrimination against foreign applicants, 111, 619
EU
    Comparative examination, 623
    US practices compared, 623
India
    Generally, 615
    Foreign applicants, 621
International preliminary examinations, 105
Japan, comparative examination, 631
Nigeria, 615
Organisation Africaine de la Propriete Intellectuelle, 615
Preliminary examinations, international, 105
Presumptive validity based on substantive examination, 616
Prima facie case, 442
Project Exchange Program to expedite and improve patent examination and reduce backlogs, 629
Quality of patent examinations, improving, 42
Reexamination, this index
Registration system alternatives to substantive examinations, 615
Russia, 615
Singapore, 615
Soft-look systems, 614
South Africa, 615
Substantive examinations
    Generally, 615 et seq.
    America Invents Act, 620
    Comparative law, 591, 615
    Costs, 615
    Litigation challenges as alternative, 614
    Presumptive validity based on, 616
    Registration system alternatives, 615
    US, 621
Uganda, 615
US
    Comparative examinations, 630
    Duty of candor, 620
    EU practices compared, 623
    Substantive examinations, 619

Utility models, examination requirements, 558

EXCEPTIONS TO INFRINGEMENT
See Defenses and Exceptions to Infringement, this index

EXCLUSION ORDERS
International Trade Commission, 826

EXCLUSIVE MARKETING RIGHTS (EMR)
Agrochemical patents, 157
Least developed countries, 157
Pharmaceutical patents, 157
Transition periods, 157

EXCLUSIVE RIGHTS IN TRIPS AGREEMENT
Generally, 152

EXCLUSIVE RIGHTS OF PATENT OWNERS
Disclosure in exchange for as quid pro quo of patent system, 344
Infringement protection
Generally, 651
See also Infringement of Patents, this index
Injunctive enforcement, 761
Innovation tensions, balancing, 521
International Union for the Protection of New Varieties of Plants, 586
Parallel Imports, this index
Post-TRIPS era limitations, 195
Process patents, TRIPS, 153

EXHAUSTION OF PATENT RIGHTS
Generally, 738 et seq.
See also Parallel Imports, this index
EU, 747 et seq.
First sale doctrine, 738
Foreign vs domestic first sales, 741
Free trade agreements limiting, 738
Gray market goods, 738
Japan, 754 et seq.
Permissible repair vs impermissible reconstruction, 742
Refurbishment of secondhand goods, 739
Territorial limits, 738, 743
Trans-Pacific Partnership Agreement, 738
TRIPS, 738
US, 739

EXPENSES
See Costs and Fees, this index

EXPERIMENTAL USE
Prior art determinations, experimental vs public uses, 423

EXPERIMENTAL USE DEFENSE
Generally, 732 et seq.
Bolar exception to infringement, 735
China, 733
Developing countries, 737
EU, 733, 736

Food, Drug, and Cosmetic Act compliance, 735
Genetic research, 737
Germany, 732
Hatch-Waxman Act, 735
Japan, 733
Pharmaceutical patents, 735
Regulatory authority, activities necessary to meet requirements of, 735
TRIPS, 737
UK, 733
US, 732, 734

EXPERT TESTIMONY
Doctrine of equivalents, 689
Infringement, 699
US, 783

EXPLOITATION OF PATENT
See Working Requirements, this index

EXPORT OF INTELLECTUAL PROPERTY
Generally, 140

EXPRESSED SEQUENCE TAGS (EST)
Research functions, 352
Utility requirement, 347

EXTENSION OF TERM OF PATENT
See Term of Patent, this index

EXTRATERRITORIAL APPROACHES TO MULTINATIONAL LITIGATION
Generally, 847 et seq.
See also Multinational Enforcement of Patent Rights, this index; Parallel Proceedings, this index
Choice of law issues, 869
Convention on Jurisdiction and the Enforcement of Judgments in Civil and Commercial Matters, 45
EU, 770
Geographically divided infringement, 857
Japanese view, 51
Process patents, 864
Software, 856
Treaties, 45
US laws
Generally, 45, 851
Policy considerations, 866
Process patents, 864

FAO
See United Nations Food and Agriculture Organization, this index

FAST TRACK AUTHORITY
Bipartisan Trade Promotion Authority Act of 2002, 215
Patent Prosecution Highways, 117

FDI
See Foreign Direct Investment, this index

FEES
See Costs and Fees, this index

FERTILIZERS
See Agrochemical Patents, this index

FILING
See Applications for Patents, this index

FINLAND
Criminal penalties for infringement, 801

FIRST INVENTORS DEFENSE ACT OF 1999
Business methods and software patentability, 306

FIRST SALE DOCTRINE (FSD)
Generally, 738 et seq.
Exhaustion of Patent Rights, this index
Foreign vs domestic first sales, 741
Parallel Imports, this index
Territorial limitations on exhaustion of patent rights, 738, 743

FIRST TO FILE VERSUS FIRST TO INVENT
Generally, 414
America Invents Act, 73
American Inventor's Protection Act of 1999, 419, 619
Priority, Right of, this index
University patent filings, 421

FOLKLORE
See Traditional Knowledge, this index

FOOD, DRUG, AND COSMETIC ACT
Compliance, experimental use defense, 735

FOREIGN DIRECT INVESTMENT (FDI)
Intellectual property protection and, 61

FOUR-FACTOR TEST
Lost profits damages, 786
Permanent injunctions, 759

FRANCE
Doctrine of equivalents, 674
Gene patents, 262
Invalidity defense to infringement, 723
Inventive step requirement, 437
Inventors' rights, 632

FREE RIDERS
Least developed countries, 137
TRIPS, 180

FREE TRADE AGREEMENTS (FTA)
Generally, 215
Bilateralism, post TRIPS, 216
Central America-Dominican Republic Free Trade Agreement, 218
Data exclusivity provisions, 218, 641
Developing countries, proposed benefits, 219
European Union, this index
Exhaustion of patent rights limitations, 742
Jordan, 219

Multinational enforcement of patent rights, 826
North American Free Trade Agreement, this index
Regional agreements, 216
Regional enforcement initiatives, 826
TRIPS enforcement mechanisms compared, 830

FSD
See First Sale Doctrine, this index

FUJINO, JINZO
Parallel imports, 751

FUKUNAGA, YOSHIFUMI
WIPO minimum standards agreements, 14

FUNCTIONAL CLAIMS
Generally, 606

GADBAW, R. MICHAEL
TRIPS development, trade leverage as instrument of, 144

GANA, RUTH L.
See also Okediji, Ruth L., this index
Creativity impacts of globalization on third world, 62

GATS
See General Agreement on Trade in Services, this index

GATT
See General Agreement on Tariffs and Trade, this index

GCC
See Gulf Cooperation Council, this index

GENERAL AGREEMENT ON TARIFFS AND TRADE (GATT)
Geographic indications, 137
Historical context for global patent cooperation, 16
Intellectual property issues, 137
Marks of origin, 137
Special and differential treatment approach, 136
Trade names, 137
TRIPS relationship, 136
US domestic law conformance, 22

GENERAL AGREEMENT ON TRADE IN SERVICES (GATS)
Creation, 16
US compliance, 167

GENERAL ELECTRIC CO.
US role in global economy, 20

GENE-RELATED PATENTS
Generally, 241
See also Life Forms, Patentability of, this index
Australia, 331
France, 262
Germany, 262

Seeds, 242
Utility requirement, 346

GENERIC DRUGS
See also Pharmaceutical Patents, this
   index
Biosimilars, 192
China production, 192
European Generic Medicines Association,
   319
India production, 152, 192
Multinational enforcement of patent rights,
   841
United Nations generic drugs programs,
   838

GENETIC RESEARCH
Experimental use defense, 737
Importance of, 240
Life forms patentability incentives, 240
Netherlands, 587
Public policy considerations, 240
Risks, 230

GENETIC RESOURCES
Andean Community of Nations, 545
Brazil, 545
Convention on Biological Diversity, 540,
   548
Costa Rica, 542
Developing countries, 547
Disclosure of origin requirement protecting,
   539, 541
India, 545
Nagoya Protocol, 552
Patent Cooperation Treaty disclosure
   requirement proposals, 115
Seeds, patentability, 552
Sovereignty over, 546
Sovereignty proposals, 547
WIPO study, 552

**GENETIC USE RESTRICTION
   TECHNOLOGIES (GURT)**
Plant protection, 586

GENEWATCH (NGO)
Plant protection, 552

GEOGRAPHIC INDICATIONS
GATT protections, 136
Paris Convention, 69

GEOGRAPHIC LIMITATIONS
Exhaustion of patent rights, 738, 743
Extraterritorial Approaches to
   Multinational Litigation, this index
Novelty requirement, 421
Prior art, 421
Searches of prior art, 103

GEOGRAPHIC REGIONS
See Regional Patent Regimes, this index

GERMANY
Claim construction, 698
Criminal penalties for infringement, 801

Damages, defendant's profits as measure,
   798
Doctrine of equivalents, 674, 700
Employees' Inventions Act, 631
Experimental use defense, 732
Gene patents, 262
History of patent law, 5
Infringement of Patents, this index
Invalidity defense to infringement, 723
Inventive step requirement, 437, 485
Inventors' rights, 631
Life forms patentability, 265
Pharmaceutical patents, 164
Plant protection, 582
Presumption of validity of patents, 732
Prosecution history use in construction of
   claims, 655
Purposive construction, 680, 697, 698
Utility models, 554, 558
Validity of patents, presumption of validity,
   732

GHANA
Compulsory licenses, 194
Criminal penalties for infringement, 801

GIRTZ, CHRISTIAN J.
Comparative patent examination practices,
   623

GLAXOSMITHKLINE
Parallel imports litigation, 750

GLOBALIZATION OF PATENT LAW
See also Harmonization of patent laws, this
   index
Alternative forms of intellectual property
   protection proposals in developing
   countries, 66
Creativity impacts of globalization on third
   world, 62
Historical Context for Global Patent
   Cooperation, this index
Justifications for a Global Patent
   Framework, this index
Minimum standards agreements, 14
Multinational Enforcement of Patent
   Rights, this index
Patent application filings, global, 41
Patent Cooperation Treaty, this index
Procedural Patent Agreements, this index
Quest for a global patent framework, 41 et
   seq.
Resolution 2000/7, 36
Statistics of Worldwide Patent Activity,
   this index
Substantive Patent Agreements, this index
WTO role, 18

GOODYEAR CO.
US role in global economy, 20

GRACE PERIODS
America Invents Act, 428
European Patent Convention, 86
Harmonization of grace periods, 433
Patent Cooperation Treaty, 114

Prior art, 428
Substantive Patent Law Treaty, 123

GRANTS OF PATENTS
Generally, 639 et seq.
See also Prosecution, this index
Corrections, post-grant, 642
Fees, 639
Inter Partes Review, this index
Interference Proceedings, this index
Nullity proceedings, 642
Oppositions, this index
Post-Grant Proceedings, this index
Standing to challenge granted patents, 643
Statistics of Worldwide Patent Activity,
    this index
Trigger of patent term, 640

GRAY MARKET GOODS
Generally, 738
See also Parallel Imports, this index

GREAT BRITAIN
See United Kingdom, this index

GREECE
Inventors' rights, 631

GREENE, BOB
US role in global economy, 19

GREENPEACE (NGO)
Plant protection, 552

GUATEMALA
Criminal penalties for infringement, 802

GUINEA
Compulsory licenses, 194

**GULF COOPERATION COUNCIL
    (GCC)**
Generally, 133

GURT
See Genetic Use Restriction Technologies,
    this index

**HAGUE AGREEMENT CONCERNING
    THE INTERNATIONAL DEPOSIT
    OF INDUSTRIAL DESIGNS**
Generally, 580

HAITI
Criminal penalties for infringement, 802

HARHOFF, DIETMAN
German Employees' Inventions Act, 631

HARMONIZATION OF PATENT LAWS
America Invents Act, 415
Applications for patents, 601
Developing countries, harmonization
    concerns, 43
EU and European Patent Office, 485
Grace periods, prior art, 433
Historical harmonization efforts, 6
Independence principle conflicts, 123
International Congress on Industrial
    Property, 6

Paris Convention measures, incorporation
    in TRIPS, 147
Patent Cooperation Treaty achievements,
    113
Prior art grace periods, 433
Remedies for infringement, 799
Substantive Patent Law Treaty
    negotiations, 42
Substantive Patent Law Treaty proposal,
    122
TRIPS, Paris Convention measures
    incorporation, 147
Utility requirement, 370
Vienna Congress for Patent Reform, 6
WIPO goals, 42

HARVARD ONCOMOUSE
Generally, 233
European Patent Office, 255

HATCH-WAXMAN ACT OF 1984 (US)
Experimental use defense, 735
Patent term extensions, 641

HCHR
See United Nations High Commissioner for
    Human Rights, this index

HEATH, CHRISTOPHER
BioTech Directive, 664, 797

HELDER, JASPER
Customs enforcement of patents, 837

HELFER, LAURENCE R.
Human rights framework for intellectual
    property, 31

HENKEL, JOACHIM
Patent trolls, 797

HERBICIDES
See Agrochemical Patents, this index

HESS, ADAM
Electrical technology protection, 831

HIGHER LIFE FORMS
See Life Forms, Patentability of, this index

HIPPODAMUS OF MILETUS
History of patent law, 3

HIRAKI, YUSUKE
Doctrine of equivalents, 679

**HISTORICAL CONTEXT FOR
    GLOBAL PATENT
    COOPERATION**
Generally, 3 et seq.
Anti-Patent Movement, this index
Developing country roles, 12
General Agreement on Tariffs and Trade,
    16
Harmonization efforts, 6
International Congress on Industrial
    Property, 6
Mercantilist trade policies, 6

Paris Convention for the Protection of Industrial Property, 6
Territoriality problems, 6

HISTORY OF PATENT LAW
Generally, 3 et seq.
Africa, 12
American view of monopolistic patent laws, 10
Anti-patent movement, 5, 7
Asia, 12
Colonial era, 12
Compulsory licensing, 70
Constitution (US), 4
Developing countries, 12
Doctrine of equivalents, 665
Harmonization efforts, 6
Industrial revolution pressures, 43
National treatment principle, 13
Novelty requirement, 10
Paris Convention for the Protection of Industrial Property, 5
Property rights view of patents, 11
TRIPS, 135
Utility requirement, 5

HIV/AIDS
Doha Declaration, 186
Global access to medicines campaign, 193
Human rights impacts of patent protections, 36
TRIPS compliant counterfeiting laws, human rights challenges, 199

HOISL, KAREN
German Employees' Inventions Act, 633

HOLBROOK, TIMOTHY R.
Active inducement of infringement, 722
Extraterritorial approaches to enforcement of patent rights, 869

HOLLAND
See also Netherlands, this index
Anti-patent movement, 5, 7
History of patent law, 5

HUMAN CLONING
Generally, 261, 272

HUMAN EMBRYONIC STEM CELLS
Patentability, 263

HUMAN EMBRYOS
Patentability, 259

HUMAN RIGHTS
Achieving human rights ends through intellectual property means, 35
Balancing developing country needs against intellectual property rights, 27
Berne Convention, 32
Controversial nature of, 33
Convention on Biological Diversity mandates, 40
Counterfeiting laws, TRIPS compliant, human rights challenges, 201

Domestic limits on intellectual property imposed by, 34
Expanding intellectual property through, 33
Expansion of international human rights regime, 33
External limits on intellectual property imposed by, 34
HIV-Aids pandemic, human rights impacts of patent protections, 36
International Covenant on Economic, Social, and Cultural Rights, this index
Justifications for a global patent framework, 25
Limits on intellectual property imposed by, 34
Negative impact of globalization, 29
Non-governmental organization roles, 35
Paris Convention, 32
Patent rights, human rights-based limitations, 198
Property rights in patents, tensions created, 25
Protection of intellectual property
    Human rights approach, 25
    Human rights ends achieved through, 34
    Human rights framework for, 31
Resolution 2000/7, this index
Rome Conventions, 32
TRIPS
    Generally, 32
    Compliant counterfeiting laws challenges, 201
    Criticisms by High Commissioner for Human Rights, 30, 35
United Nations Food and Agriculture Organization, 40
United Nations Sub-Commission on the Promotion and Protection of Human Rights, this index
Universal Declaration of Human Rights, 31
WIPO tensions, 36
WTO dispute resolution system, 29

HUMANE FARMING ASSOCIATION
Higher life forms patentability, 232

HUNGARY
Parallel imports, 750

HYBRID SEEDS PROTECTION
Generally, 586

ICELAND
Criminal penalties for infringement, 802

ICESCR
See International Covenant on Economic, Social, and Cultural Rights, this index

IDA
See International Depository Authority, this index

IIPA
See International Intellectual Property
    Alliance, this index

IMPERMISSIBLE RECONSTRUCTION
See Exhaustion of Patent Rights, this index

**IMPLEMENTING REGULATIONS OF
    THE PATENT LAW (CHINA)**
Priority rights, 402

IMPORTATION RIGHTS
Paris Convention, 87

IMPORTS
Border Enforcement of Patent Rights, this
    index
Confiscations of Infringing Goods, this
    index
Parallel Imports, this index

INDEPENDENCE PRINCIPLE
Harmonization conflicts, 123
Paris Convention, 86
Territoriality tensions, 44

INDEPENDENT CLAIMS
Dependent claims distinguished, 603

INDIA
Biodiversity Act, 545
Biological Diversity Act, 553
Compulsory licenses, 192, 194
Confiscations of infringing
    pharmaceuticals, 841
Development status changes, 61
Examination for patents
        Generally, 615
        Foreign applicants, 621
Generic drug production, 152, 192
Genetic resources, 544
Inventive step requirement, new uses of
    known substances, 496
Patent Act
        Generally, 161
        TRIPS compliance, 319
Patentability, ordre public standards, 552
Patents of addition, 622
Pharmaceutical industry
        Generally, 315
        Confiscations of infringing goods, 841
        Development, 196
        Disputes with US, 158
        TRIPS compliance, 163
Plant protection, 584
Presumption of patent validity, 732
Protection for pharmaceutical and
    agricultural chemical products, 158
Protection of Plant Varieties and Farmer's
    Rights Act, 584
US vs India dispute settlement, protection
    for pharmaceutical and agricultural
    chemical products, 158
Validity of patents presumption, 732

**INDIA PROTECTION FOR
    PHARMACEUTICAL AND
    AGRICULTURAL CHEMICAL
    PRODUCTS CASE**
Generally, 164

INDIGENOUS SOCIETIES
See also Least Developed Countries, this
    index
Innovation rights protections, 541

INDIRECT INFRINGEMENT
See Infringement of Patents, this index

INDONESIA
ASEAN Patent Examination Cooperation
    Program, 121
Compulsory licenses, 194
Criminal penalties for infringement, 802

INDUCEMENT OF INFRINGEMENT
See Infringement of Patents, this index

**INDUSTRIAL APPLICATION
    STANDARD**
Generally, 373, 375
See also Utility Requirement, this index
Usefulness requirement compared, 435

INDUSTRIAL DESIGNS
See also Design Patents, this index
Hague Agreement, 580
Paris Convention, 69

**INDUSTRIAL PROPERTY LAW
    (BRAZIL)**
Generally, 345

INDUSTRIAL REVOLUTION
History of patent law, 43

INEQUITABLE CONDUCT DEFENSE
Generally, 390, 723
See also National Treatment, this index
America Invents Act, 620
Comparative prosecution requirements,
    622

INFORMED USER TEST
Design patents, 561, 571, 576

INFRINGEMENT OF PATENTS
Generally, 647 et seq.
Absolute product protection, direct
    infringement, 656
Active inducement of infringement as
    indirect infringement, 703, 718
After-arising technology, 672
Bolar exception to infringement, 735
Border Enforcement of Patent Rights, this
    index
Brussels Convention expansion of
    jurisdictional limits, 45
Burden of proof
        Claim construction questions, 649
        Invalidity defense to infringement,
            723
        TRIPS, 154

Business methods patents, infringement
issues, 284
Canada
    Indirect infringement, 721
    Prosecution history use in
        construction of claims, 655
China, prosecution history use in
    construction of claims, 655
Claim construction questions
    Generally, 647 et seq.
    Burden of proof, 649
    Comparative construction, 647
    Dictionary use, 651 654
    Extrinsic evidence, 652, 655
    Federal Circuit, 655
    Law, questions as matters of, 649,
        655, 673
    Literal and purposive construction
        distinguished, 680
    Markman hearings, 648
    Ordinary and customary meaning,
        649
    Person of ordinary skill in the art
        standard, 649
    Prosecution History Estoppel, this
        index
    Purposive Construction, this index
    Specifications confusing claims
        construction, 693
    Standard of appellate review, 656,
        673
    US methodology, 649, 655
Commercialization vs production level
    enforcement, 59
Comparative claim construction, 647
Confiscations of Infringing Goods, this
    index
Contributory infringement, 703
Criminal Penalties for Infringement, this
    index
Damages, this index
Declarations of non-infringement, litigation
    seeking, 571
Defenses and Exceptions to Infringement,
    this index
Deliberate indifference, indirect
    infringement, 708
Dictionary use in construction of claims,
    651, 654
Direct infringement
    Generally, 647 et seq.
    Absolute product protection, 656
    After-arising technology, 672
    Claim construction questions, above
    Definition, 647
    Doctrine of Equivalents, this index
    Essential elements, 679
    Indirect and direct infringers, 722
    Indirect infringement distinguished,
        703
    Literal infringement, 666
    Non-literal infringement, 666
    Purposive Construction, this index
Discovery in aid of infringement litigation,
    761

Doctrine of Equivalents, this index
Essential element, indirect infringement,
    714, 718
Essential elements, direct infringement,
    679
EU
    Absolute product protection, 656
    Indirect infringement, 715
    Jurisdiction, 680, 701
Exclusive rights exercise, 647
Exhaustion of Patent Rights, this index
Experimental Use Defense, this index
Expert witnesses, 695
Extraterritorial Approaches to
    Multinational Litigation, this index
Extrinsic evidence in construction of
    claims, 648, 651
First sale doctrine
    Exhaustion of Patent Rights, this
        index
    Parallel Imports, this index
Geographically divided infringement,
    extraterritorial approaches to
    enforcement of patent rights, 857
Germany
    Indirect infringement, 718
    Prosecution history use in
        construction of claims, 655
    Purposive construction, 680, 697, 698
Indirect infringement
    Generally, 703 et seq.
    Active inducement of infringement,
        703, 718
    Canada, 719
    Contributory infringement, 703
    Deliberate indifference, 708
    Direct and indirect infringers, 722
    Direct infringement distinguished,
        703
    Discovery rights, 760
    Essential element, 714, 718
    EU, 715
    Germany, 718
    Intent, 705
    Knowledge standard, 703
    Single actor direct infringement, 721
    South Korea, 719
    US, 703 et seq.
    Willful blindness doctrine, 708, 710
    Willfulness, 708
Inducement of infringement as indirect
    infringement, 703, 718
Intent, indirect infringement, 705
Invalidity defense
    Generally, 723 et seq.
    See also Validity of Patent, this index
Italy, 655
Jurisdiction
    Generally, 647
    EU, 680, 701
Knowledge standard, indirect
    infringement, 703
Law, claim construction questions as
    matters of, 649, 655, 673
Literal infringement, 666

Markman hearings, claim construction questions, 648

Netherlands, prosecution history use in construction of claims, 655

Non-infringement defense, 723

Non-literal infringement, 666

Ordinary and customary meaning employment in claim construction, 649

Parallel Imports, this index

Patent markings, 709

Presumptions, 54, 59, 247

Product patents and process patents distinguished, 787

Production level vs commercialization enforcement, 59

Prosecution History Estoppel, this index

Publicity orders, 800

Purposive Construction, this index

Reading on claims, 647, 656

Remedies For Infringement, this index

Right-to-use studies, 704

Scope changes, TRIPS compliance, 149

Single actor direct infringement, 721

South Korea, indirect infringement, 719

Standard of appellate review, 656, 673

Summary judgment practice, 649

Switzerland, prosecution history use in construction of claims, 655

Territorial nature of patent rights, 647

TRIPS
     Administrative enforcement, 757
     Burden of proof, 154

UK
     Absolute product protection, 656
     Prosecution history use in construction of claims, 655

US
     Absolute product protection, 656
     Claim construction questions, 649, 655
     Indirect infringement, 703 et seq.
     Infringement scope changes, 149
     TRIPS compliance, 147

Utility models, 558

Validity questions implied, 45

Willful blindness doctrine, indirect infringement, 708, 710

Willfulness, indirect infringement, 708

INHERENCY
Generally, 406
See also Novelty Requirement, this index
Anticipation by, 414
Prior art, inherency in, 406 et seq.
UK, 412
US, 409

INJUNCTIVE RELIEF
Generally, 758 et seq.
Brussels Regulation, 765, 773
Business method patents, 759
China, 801
EU
     Cross-border injunctions, 765
     Jurisdiction, 765

Exclusion orders, 835

Exclusive rights principle, 758

Four-factor test, permanent injunctions, 760

International Trade Commission, 833

Jurisdiction
     EU, 765
         Strategic considerations, 774
         Lugano Convention, 765

Parallel proceedings, strategic considerations, 774

Patent trolls, injunction rights considerations, 763, 833

Permanent injunctions, four-factor test, 760

Strategic considerations, 774

Technology patents, injunction vs damages protection, 758

TRIPS, 757, 765

US
     Generally, 758 et seq.
     Restrictions on injunctions, 93

INNOVATION
See also Research and Development, this index
Australia, innovation patents, 553
Democratizing innovation, 24
Disclosure requirement to protect, 509
Distributed innovation, 24
Exclusive rights tensions, balancing, 521
Experimental Use Defense, this index
Indigenous and local communities, protection of rights of, 541
TRIPS objective to promote, 147
User-centered processes vs manufacturer-centric development systems, 24

INNOVATION PATENTS
Generally, 553

INSTITUTIONAL THEORY
Treaty formation, 38

INSTITUTIONALISM
Generally, 38

INTELLECTUAL PROPERTY CLAUSE (US)
History of patent law, 4

INTELLECTUAL PROPERTY COMMITTEE (IPC)
Uruguay Round activities, 142

INTELLECTUAL PROPERTY RIGHTS
See Property Rights in Patents, this index

INTER PARTES REVIEW (IPR)
America Invents Act, 643
Prior art issues, 643
Procedure, 643

INTERFERENCE PROCEEDINGS
Generally, 415, 429
America Invents Act affects, 76
Priority issues, 522

INTERNATIONAL BUSINESS
MACHINES
Business method patents, 296

INTERNATIONAL CONGRESS ON
INDUSTRIAL PROPERTY
Harmonization, 6

INTERNATIONAL COURTS
European Court of Justice, this index
European patent court proposals, 702
International Court of Justice, 15
Proposals, 873

INTERNATIONAL COVENANT ON
ECONOMIC, SOCIAL, AND
CULTURAL RIGHTS (ICESCR)
Controversial nature of human rights, 31
Intellectual property protection, human
rights approach, 26
Moral and material interests of authors
and inventors, 25

INTERNATIONAL DEPOSITORY
AUTHORITY (IDA)
Disclosure requirement, samples, 531

INTERNATIONAL ENFORCEMENT
Enforcement of Patent Rights, this index
Extraterritorial Approaches to
Multinational Litigation, this index

INTERNATIONAL INTELLECTUAL
PROPERTY ALLIANCE (IIPA)
US economy, effect of copyright protection,
23

INTERNATIONAL PATENT LAW
DEVELOPMENT
See Globalization of Patent Law, this index

INTERNATIONAL TRADE
Border Enforcement of Patent Rights, this
index
Commercialization vs production level
enforcement of patent rights, 59
Confiscations of Infringing Goods, this
index
Free Trade Agreements, this index
Intellectual property laws importance to,
140
Justifications for a global patent
framework, 19
Parallel Imports, this index
Paris Convention development
considerations, 66
Trade leverage as instrument of TRIPS
development, 145
TRIPS development, trade leverage as
instrument of, 145
United States Trade Representative use of
trade leverage policies, 145
Unusual intellectual property laws as
barriers, 22, 23

INTERNATIONAL TRADE
COMMISSION (ITC)
Exclusion orders, 826

Injunctive relief for patent law violations,
833
Multinational enforcement of patent rights,
831, 835

INTERNATIONAL UNION FOR THE
PROTECTION OF NEW
VARIETIES OF PLANTS (UPOV)
Generally, 583
Exclusive rights, 585
Farmers' rights, 585
Research and development impacts, 586

INTERNATIONALIZING OF PATENT
APPLICATIONS
Generally, 590 et seq.
See also Applications for Patents, this
index

INTERNET PROCESSES
Patentability, 332

INVALIDITY OF PATENT
See Validity of Patent, this index

INVENTION
Claimed invention and patented invention,
terms distinguished, 608
Multiple inventions, patent applications
for, 611
Origin of invention. See Disclosure of
Origin Requirement, this index
Patented invention and claimed invention,
terms distinguished, 608
Unity of Invention, this index

INVENTION PRIORITY
Generally, 414 et seq.
See also Novelty Requirement, this index

INVENTIVE STEP REQUIREMENT
Generally, 435 et seq.
See also Prior Art, this index
Advance over prior art principle
Distinguished, 435
Japan, 437
Advantageous effects, Japan, 495
America Invents Act, 439
Analogous art doctrine, 455
Arbitrary nature of obviousness decisions,
485
Canada, new uses of known substances,
496
Causation effect of prior art, Japan, 492
Challenge of the requirement, 438
Chemical arts
EU, 486
US, 458
China
Generally, 497
US approach compared, 500
Collaborative Research and Technology
Enhancement Act, 456
Commercial success standard, 442
Developing country standards, 444
Doctrine of inventive step, 435 et seq.
Enablement distinguished, 509

EU
    Generally, 454, 466 et seq.
    Japanese approach compared, 496
    New uses of known substances, 496
European Patent Office
    Generally, 466
    Japanese Patent Office compared,
       487
Evidence, 504
Failure of others standard, 442
Flash of creative genius, 436
France, 437
Germany, 437, 485
Hindsight bias, Japan, 487
Hindsight dangers, 453
India, new uses of known substances, 496
Japan
    Generally, 487 et seq.
    Advance over prior art, 437
    Advantageous effects, 495
    EU approach compared, 496
    European Patent Office compared,
       487
    Patent Act, 487
Licensability as measure, 443
Long felt but unsolved need standard, 441
Motivation effect of prior art, Japan, 492
New uses of known substances, 496
Non-obviousness, 435
Novelty distinguished, 396, 435
Objective approach, 454
Obvious, use of term, 437
Origins of inventive step, 435
Paris Convention, 443
Patent Cooperation Treaty, 505
Person having ordinary skill in the art
    standard
    Generally, 438
    Japan, 495
Pharmaceuticals
    China, 502
    New uses of known substances, 496
Presumptions, Japan, 492
Problem solution approach
    Generally, 454, 467
    EU, 466
    UK, 467, 475
PTO Guidelines, 455, 457
Secondary considerations, 444
Subjective nature of obviousness decisions,
    485
Teaching, suggestion, or motivation
    approach, 444
Treatment method, Japan, 490
TRIPS, 496
UK
    Generally, 437, 443
    Problem-solution approach, 475
Unexpected effects
    Japan, 495
Unexpected results
    China, 501
US
    Generally, 439 et seq.
    Chinese approach compared, 500

    New uses of known substances, 496
    Patent Act of 1952, 436
Utility models and patents distinguished,
    553, 558

INVENTORS
Candor, Duty of, this index
Employee Inventors, this index
Prosecution roles
    Generally, 630 et seq.
    See also Prosecution, this index
Rights of inventors
       See also Employee Inventors,
          this index
    Assignments by inventors, 636
    Australia, 636
    Bayh-Dole Act, 631
    Paris Convention
       Generally, 87
       Identification rights, 630
       US, 631, 635

**IP5 (PATENT WORKSHARING
    INITIATIVE)**
Applications for patents, 590
Member states, 590
Patent prosecution, 120

IPC
See Intellectual Property Committee, this
    index

IPR
See Inter Partes Review, this index

IRAN
Criminal penalties for infringement, 802
WIPO Development Agenda, 57

IRAQ
Criminal penalties for infringement, 802

ISRAEL
Inventors' rights, 631

**ISSUE PRECLUSION,
    MULTINATIONAL
    ENFORCEMENT**
Generally, 843
Recognition and enforcement of judgments
    in Europe, 824
US, 846

ITALY
Criminal penalties for infringement, 802
History of patent law, 5
Inventors' rights, 631
Pharmaceutical patents, 164
Prosecution history use in construction of
    claims, 655
Torpedo, Italian, 775

ITC
See International Trade Commission, this
    index

JACKSON, JOHN H.
WTO dispute settlement authority
    questions, 162

JAMES I (ENGLAND)
History of patent law, 4

JANIS, MARK D.
Written description requirements in UK and European Patent Office, 531

JAPAN
Applications for patents for multiple inventions, 611
Business methods and software patentability, 284, 311
Comparative examination, 631
Criminal penalties for infringement, 802
Customs Tariff Law, 835
Design protection, 559
Discrimination against foreign patent applicants, 618
Doctrine of equivalents, 679
Employee inventors, 631
Exhaustion of patent rights, 754 et seq.
Experimental use defense, 733
Extraterritorial approaches to multinational litigation, 51
Grace periods, prior art, 430
Invalidity defense to infringement, 723
Inventive Step Requirement, this index
Inventors' rights, 631, 632
Life forms patentability, 264
Moral utility doctrine, 382
Multiple invention applications, 611
Novelty requirement, 396
Parallel imports, 751
Patent Prosecution Highways, 117
Person having ordinary skill in the art standard, 495
Pharmaceutical patents, 164
Prior art
    Global vs domestic, 427
    Grace periods, 430

JAPANESE PATENT OFFICE (JPO)
IP5 initiative, 120
Trilateral cooperation, 119

JAY, JOHN
Property rights of patent holders, 9

JOHNSON, PHILLIP
Indirect infringement, 711

JORDAN
Compulsory licenses, 194
Free trade agreements, 219

JUDICIAL REVIEW
Dispute Settlement Understanding proceedings, 154

JURISDICTION
Brussels Convention expansion of jurisdictional limits, 45
EU
    Generally, 45
    Convention on Jurisdiction and the Enforcement of Judgments in Civil and Commercial Matters, 45

Injunctive relief, 765
Recognition and enforcement of judgments, 820
Extraterritorial Approaches to Multinational Litigation, this index
Infringement suits
    Generally, 647
    EU, 680, 701
Injunctive relief
    EU, 765
    Strategic considerations, 774
Multinational Enforcement of Patent Rights, this index
Parallel Imports, this index
Recognition and enforcement of judgments in Europe, 820
Territoriality, this index

JURISDICTIONAL STRIPPING
Generally, 51

JUSTIFICATIONS FOR A GLOBAL PATENT FRAMEWORK
Generally, 18
Human rights justification, 25
International institutional justification, 37
International trade, 19
Piracy concerns, 21
User-centered innovation process, 24

KASTENMEIER, ROBERT W.
TRIPS origin, 140

KENNEDY, ANTHONY
Indirect infringement, 710
Permanent injunctions, 762

KENYA
Criminal penalties for infringement, 802
Parallel imports, 206
WIPO Development Agenda, 57

KESAN, JAY
Transaction costs and patent trolls, 763

KEYHANI, DARIUSH
Extraterritoriality of patent laws, 862

KIEFF, F. SCOTT
Registration systems vs substantive patent examinations, 613

KNOWLEDGE
Indirect infringement, knowledge standard, 703
Patentability of knowledge, 547
Public knowledge goods, 825
Traditional Knowledge, this index

KOREA
See South Korea, this index

KRONSTEIN, HEINRICH
Paris Convention for the Protection of Industrial Property, 6

KUWAIT
Criminal penalties for infringement, 802

LAO PDR
ASEAN Patent Examination Cooperation
Program, 121

LATVIA
Parallel imports, 750

LAWS OF NATURE
Moral duties to disclose, 334
Novelty inquiries, 333
Patentability, 229, 299, 328

LC
See Lugano Convention, this index

LEAD COMPOUND APPROACH
Inventive step, 486

**LEAHY-SMITH AMERICA INVENTS
ACT OF 2011 (US)**
See America Invents Act, this index

**LEAST DEVELOPED COUNTRIES
(LDC)**
See also Developing Countries, this index
Compulsory licensing, developed vs
developing countries use, 92
Development status changes, 61
Dispute Settlement Understanding
involvement, 819
Exclusive marketing rights, transition
periods, 157
Foreign patent ownership in third world,
59
Genetic Resources, this index
Historical context for global patent
cooperation, 13
Intellectual property policies, 142
Inventive step requirement, 443
Multinational enforcement of patent rights,
803
Traditional Knowledge, this index
TRIPS enforcement impacts on developing
countries, 804
TRIPS pharmaceutical patent
requirements, 152
Utility standards, policy considerations,
354

LEBANON
Criminal penalties for infringement, 802

LEDER, PHILIP
Harvard oncomouse, 233

LEFSTIN, JEFFREY A.
Enablement requirement, 538

LEGALITY
Patentability implications of moral
violations involved in making an
invention, 276

LEMLEY, MARK A.
Abstract ideas limitation on patentability,
311
Chemical patents, utility requirement, 345
Examination for patents, soft-look systems,
614

Exclusion orders, 834

LERNER, JOSH
Patent examination discrimination against
foreign applicants, 111

LESOTHO
Criminal penalties for infringement, 802

LEX SPECIALIS
Treaty interpretation rules, 28

LIBYA
Criminal penalties for infringement, 802

LICENSING
Compulsory Licensing, this index
Inventive step requirement, licensability as
measure, 442
On-sale bar implications, 84
Patent trolls, injunction rights
considerations, 763, 833
Prior user rights, 419
Reasonable and Non-Discriminatory
Licensing Conditions, this index
Technology use licenses, 242

LIEGSALZ, JOHANNES
Patent examinations in China, 615

LIFE CYCLE MANAGEMENT
Pharmaceutical patent terms, extension
strategies, 319

LIFE FORMS, PATENTABILITY OF
Generally, 226 et seq.
Bacteria, 227
Canada, 233, 241
China, 276
Cloning human beings, 261, 272
Comparative approaches, 257 et seq.
EU, 257
European Patent Office, 255
Genetic research risks, 230
Genetic research uses, 240
Germany, 265
Harvard oncomouse
Generally, 233
European Patent Office, 255
Higher life forms, 232
Human embryonic stem cells, 264
Japan, 264
Lower life forms, 226
Moral utility doctrine, 382
Risks of genetic research, 230
Stem cells, 265
US
Generally, 226, 278
Weldon Amendment, 283

LIFE PROTECTION
Patentability exclusions, 225

LISBON AGREEMENT
Deceptive indications of source of goods,
139

LITHUANIA
Parallel imports, 750

LONDON AGREEMENT
European Patent Convention, 125

LOON, NG-LOY WEE
Singapore law on compulsory licensing, 198

LOUWAARS, NIELS
Plant protection, 587

LOVE, JAMIE
Drug costs policy, 193

LOWENFELD, ANDREAS F.
TRIPS enforcement impacts on developing
    countries, 805

LUGANO CONVENTION (LC)
Injunctive relief, 765
Territoriality restrictions, elimination, 45

MA, YUFENG
Damage awards in China, 798

MACEDONIA
Criminal penalties for infringement, 802

**MACHINE OR TRANSFORMATION
    (MOT) TEST**
Generally, 305, 309, 323
Business method patents, 296
Process patents, 298

MADAGASCAR
Criminal penalties for infringement, 802

MADRID AGREEMENT
Deceptive indications of source of goods,
    139

MAILBOX APPLICATIONS
Pharmaceutical patents, 164

MAILBOX SYSTEM
TRIPS, 157

MAINTENANCE FEES
Paris Convention, 89

MALAYSIA
ASEAN Patent Examination Cooperation
    Program, 121
Compulsory licenses, 194
Transpacific Partnership Agreement, 217

MALLOY, TIM
Damage awards in China, 798

MALTA
Criminal penalties for infringement, 802

**MARKETING EXCLUSIVITY
    PROTECTION**
Pharmaceutical patents, 641

MARKMAN HEARINGS
Infringement, claim construction, 648

MARKS OF ORIGIN
GATT, 137

MATHEMATICAL METHODS
Domestic law restrictions on patentability,
    225

**MAX PLANCK INSTITUTE FOR
    INTELLECTUAL PROPERTY,
    COMPETITION AND TAX LAW**
TRIPS exceptions, three-step test, 179

MCCARTHY, J. THOMAS
Justifications for a global patent
    framework, 19

MEDICINES
See Pharmaceutical Patents, this index

MEIER-BECK, PETER
Germany's approach to claim construction,
    699

MENDENHALL, JAMES
Consistency of chinese intellectual property
    standards, 815

MENELL, PETER S.
Valuing technology for damages purposes,
    757

MERCANTILIST TRADE POLICIES
Historical context for global patent
    cooperation, 6

MERGES, ROBERT P.
Novelty requirement, 334

MEURER, MICHAEL J.
Doctrine of equivalents, 666

MEXICO
Criminal penalties for infringement, 802
Inventors' rights, 631

MFN
See Most-Favored-Nation Treatment, this
    index

MIAO, EMILY
Pharmaceuticals, internationalized patent
    applications, 598

**MICROBIOLOGICAL PROCESS
    PATENTS**
TRIPS, 152

MICROSOFT CORP.
AT&T litigation, territoriality limits of
    patents, 863

MINISTERIAL CONFERENCE
World Trade Organization, 17

MIZUMOTO, CHRIS T.
Doctrine of equivalents, 679

MONGOLIA
Criminal penalties for infringement, 802

MONSANTO CO.
Gene patent litigation, 240

MORAL DUTIES
Generally, 225
Inventive activities, immoral or illegal, 276
Laws of nature, moral duties to disclose, 334
Life creation, moral issues, 226
Pharmaceutical patents, morality objections, 314

MORAL UTILITY DOCTRINE
Generally, 276, 382 et seq
Life forms patentability, 384
Obnoxious or mischievous inventions, 383
US, 280, 388

MOST-FAVORED-NATION (MFN) TREATMENT
TRIPS, 147

MOT
See Machine or Transformation Test, this index

MOZAMBIQUE
Compulsory licenses, 194

MUELLER, JANICE M.
Novelty requirement, 413

MULTINATIONAL ENFORCEMENT OF PATENT RIGHTS
Generally, 645 et seq.
See also Extraterritorial Approaches to Multinational Litigation, this index
Administrative and border enforcement, 826 et seq.
Border Enforcement of Patent Rights, this index
China, US vs, 811
Commercial scale willful infringement, 811 et seq.
Confiscations of infringing goods, 813
Consolidation of lawsuits, 843
Consultations to resolve disputes, 807, 808, 812
Criminal procedures issues, 812
Customs laws. See Border Enforcement of Patent Rights, this index
Defenses and Exceptions to Infringement, this index
Denmark, US vs, 807
Developing countries, 803
Domestic enforcement of treaty mandates, 805
Electrical technology, 831
EU customs officials, 837
European Directive on the Enforcement of Intellectual Property Rights, 820
Free trade agreements, 825
Generic drugs, 839
Implementation of TRIPS enforcement mechanisms, 807 et seq.
Infringement of Patents, this index
International Trade Commission, 826, 831
Issue preclusion
    Generally, 843
    US, 845
Jurisdictional stripping

Generally, 51
    See also Jurisdiction, this index
Least developed countries, 803
Minimum standards agreements, 14
Overview of international obligations, 803 et seq.
Paris Convention TRIPS provisions compared, 811
Procedural Patent Agreements, this index
Recognition and enforcement of judgments in Europe, 824
Regional Enforcement Initiatives, 820
Remedies for Infringement, this index
Specialized courts, 842
Substantive Patent Agreements, this index
Sweden, US vs, 808
TRIPS
    Compliance standards, 804 et seq.
    Costs of compliance, 805
    Domestic enforcement of treaty mandates, 804
    Implementation of enforcement mechanisms, 807 et seq.
    Nationality intrusive measures, 805
    Paris Convention provisions compared, 811
    Preamble, 803
Unfair trade practices claims, 831
US
    China dispute, 811
    Denmark dispute, 807
    Issue preclusion, 845
    Sweden dispute, 808
    Willful infringement on a commercial scale, 811 et seq.

MURRAY, KALI
Myriad patent challenges, 643

NAFTA
See North American Free Trade Agreement, this index

NAGOYA PROTOCOL
Genetic resources, 551

NAKIMURA, SHUJI
Employee inventors, 636

NARD, CRAIG A.
Doctrine of equivalents, 666

NATCO PHARMA (COMPANY)
Compulsory licenses, 192

NATIONAL EMERGENCIES
Compulsory licenses, 186

NATIONAL TREATMENT
Generally, 70
History of patent law, 13
Paris Convention, 70
Paris Convention for the Protection of Industrial Property, 70
Patent prosecution, discrimination against foreign applicants, 111, 618
TRIPS, 147
WIPO, 15

NATURAL PROCESSES
Practical utility, natural processes aiding,
248

NATURE
See Laws of Nature, this index

**NATURE OF INTERNATIONAL
PATENT LAW**
Generally, 3 et seq.

NCD
See Noncommunicable Diseases, this index

NEPAL
Criminal penalties for infringement, 802

NETHERLANDS
See also Holland, this index
Criminal penalties for infringement, 802
Genetic research, 585
Invalidity defense to infringement, 723
Prosecution history use in construction of
claims, 655

NEW ROUTE
Patent prosecution worksharing proposal,
121

NEW USES OF KNOWN SUBSTANCES
Patentability, 319

NEW YORK UNIVERSITY
Invention licensing revenue, 636

NEW ZEALAND
Patents of addition, 622
Software patentability, 312
Transpacific Partnership Agreement, 217

**NEW ZEALAND INFORMATION AND
COMMUNICATIONS
TECHNOLOGY GROUP**
Software patentability, 312

NEWMAN, STUART
Moral utility doctrine, 383

NEWNESS
See Novelty Requirement, this index

NGUYEN, XUAN-THAO
China, apology remedy for patent
infringement, 799

NICARAGUA
CAFTA-DR, 218
Criminal penalties for infringement, 801

NIGERIA
Examination for patents, 615
Inventor's rights, 638

NO PATENTS ON LIFE (NGO)
Seed patents, genetic resource challenges,
552

**NONCOMMUNICABLE DISEASES
(NCD)**
Compulsory licenses for treatment
pharmaceuticals, 191

WHO report, 191

**NON-GOVERNMENTAL
ORGANIZATIONS (NGO)**
Anti-Counterfeiting Trade Agreement
opposition, 217
Human rights activities, 33
Transpacific Partnership Agreement
opposition, 217
WIPO and WTO activities, 32

NON-INFRINGEMENT
Defenses and Exceptions to Infringement,
this index
Validity of Patent, this index

NON-OBVIOUSNESS
Generally, 435 et seq.
See also Inventive Step Requirement, this
index

NORDIC PATENT INSTITUTE
Search services, 105

**NORTH AMERICAN FREE TRADE
AGREEMENT (NAFTA)**
US domestic law conformance, 22

NORTHWESTERN UNIVERSITY
Invention licensing revenue, 636

NORWAY
Criminal penalties for infringement, 802

NOVARTIS (COMPANY)
Pharmaceutical patents, mailbox
applications, 164

NOVELTY REQUIREMENT
Generally, 391 et seq.
Absolute novelty, China, 579
Anticipation, 108, 396
Anticipatory enablement, 405
Anticipatory references, 410
Applications filed earlier but published
after, 405
China
Generally, 398, 418
Absolute novelty, 578
Design patents, 578
Comparative approaches, 396
Defining novelty, 391 et seq.
Design Patents, this index
Domestic vs absolute novelty, 391, 421 et
seq.
Enablement distinguished, 509
European Patent Office, 392, 418
Evergreening, inherency doctrine and, 414
Experimental vs public uses, 423
First to file versus first to invent, 415
Geographical boundaries, 421
Global vs domestic novelty, 391, 421
Grace periods, prior art, 428
History of patent law, 6
Inherency, this index
Invention priority, 414 et seq.

Inventive step distinguished, 396, 435
Japan, 397
Laws of nature, novelty inquiries, 334
On-sale bar, 416
Person having ordinary skill in the art
    standard, 391
Pharmaceuticals, inherency, 412
Photographic novelty, 405
Printed publication bar, 415
Prior art, definition of term
    Generally, 391
    Prior Art, this index
    Searches of Prior Art, this index
Prior User Rights, this index
Public use bar, 416
Searches of Prior Art, this index
Secret prior art applications, 405
Secret prior user, 419
Sine qua non of patentability, 391
Statute of Monopolies, 391, 421
Statutory bars, US, 415
Temporal limitations on prior art, 428
Territorial limitations on prior art for
    novelty determinations, 391, 421 et
    seq.
UK
    Inherency, 412
US
    Generally, 396
    America Invents Act, this index
    Design patents, 575
    First to file versus first to invent, 415
    Global vs domestic novelty, 421
    406
    Statutory bars, 415
Utility models, 553
Utility patents, 560
Venetian Patent Act of 1474, 391

NUCLEAR WEAPONS
Patentability, 226

NULLITY PROCEEDINGS
Post-grant, 641

NUNHEMS (COMPANY)
Seed patents, genetic resource challenges,
    552

NUTRITION POLICIES
TRIPS balancing of intellectual property
    rights and obligations, 148, 151

OAPI
See Organisation Africaine de la Propriete
    Intellectuelle, this index

OBAMA, BARACK
Patent Law Treaties Implementation Act
    signing, 580

OBJECTIVES OF PROTECTION
Scope of protection relationship, 12

**OBNOXIOUS OR MISCHIEVOUS
    INVENTIONS**
Moral utility doctrine, 383

OBVIOUSNESS
See also Inventive Step Requirement, this
    index
Non-obviousness, 435 et seq.

**OFFICE FOR HARMONIZATION IN
    THE INTERNAL MARKET
    (OHIM)**
Registered Community Designs, 559

OKEDIJI, RUTH L.
Global intellectual property norms, 92
History of patent law, 12, 99
Patent law in developing countries, 12, 99
TRIPS dispute resolution mechanisms, 809
WIPO, 92
WIPO dispute settlement, 819

OMNIBUS CLAIMS
Generally, 606

ON-SALE BAR
America Invents Act, 73
Licensing, 84
Novelty requirement, 416
Priority rights principle, 84

OPPOSITION
Generally, 642
See also Post-Grant Review, this index
European Patent Convention, 126
UK, 127

ORDINARY OBSERVER TEST
Design patents, 572, 573

ORDRE PUBLIC PROTECTIONS
Generally, 255
India patentability limitations, 552
Patentability exclusions, 225, 277

**ORGANISATION AFRICAINE DE LA
    PROPRIETE INTELLECTUELLE
    (OAPI)**
Generally, 132
Examination for patents, 615
TRIPS-plus provision adoptions, 215

ORIGIN OF INVENTION
See Disclosure of Origin Requirement, this
    index

ORLANDO, LAURA
EU piracy suppression, 821

ORNAMENTAL DESIGN
See Design Patents, this index

ORPHAN DRUGS
Special protections, 641

OXFAM
Anti-Counterfeiting Trade Agreement, 217

PANAMA
Criminal penalties for infringement, 802
Free trade agreement, 217

PARAGUAY
Criminal penalties for infringement, 802

PARALLEL IMPORTS
Generally, 738 et seq.
See also Exhaustion of Patent Rights, this
    index
Czech Republic, 750
Defenses to infringement, 738 et seq.
Estonia, 750
EU, 744 et seq.
European Court of Justice, 750
Exhaustion of patent rights doctrine,
    territorial limits, 738, 744
First sale doctrine, 738
Gray market goods, 738
Hungary, 750
Japan, 751
Kenya, 206
Latvia, 750
Lithuania, 750
Pharmaceuticals, 744, 750
Poland, 750
Portugal, 744
Slovakia, 750
Slovenia, 750
Spain, 744
Territorial limitations on exhaustion of
    patent rights, 738, 744
TRIPS, 216
UK, 744

PARALLEL PROCEEDINGS
Injunctive relief, strategic considerations,
    774
Italian Torpedo, 775
Jurisdictional stripping, 51

**PARIS CONVENTION FOR THE
    PROTECTION OF INDUSTRIAL
    PROPERTY (PC)**
Generally, 14
Abandonment of patent, 87
Abuse of patent rights, 88
Applications for patents, 602
Compulsory licensing, 69, 87
Copyrights, 69
Design patents, priority rights, 572
Fees, 89
Geographic indications, 69
Grace periods, prior art, 430
Historical context for global patent
    cooperation, 6
History of patent law, 5
Human rights, 32
Importation rights, 88
Independence of patents principle, 86
International trade considerations during
    development, 67
Inventive step requirement, 443
Inventors' rights, 87, 630
Maintenance fees, 89
Multinational enforcement, TRIPS
    provisions compared, 811
National treatment principle, 70
Patent Cooperation Treaty interaction, 79
Prior art grace periods, 430
Priority rights, 71, 572
Procedural nature, 70

Procedural Patent Agreements, this index
Revisions, 14
Signatories, 69
Special agreements between members, 90
Trademarks and trade names, 69
TRIPS Agreement incorporation, 16
TRIPS harmonizations, 147
Unfair competition measures, 69
Union for the Protection of Industrial
    Property, 90
WIPO formation, 14
Working requirements, 87

PATENT ACT (JAPAN)
Inventive step requirement, 487

PATENT ACT OF 1791 (FRANCE)
History of patent law, 5

PATENT ACT OF 1970 (INDIA)
Generally, 163, 621

PATENT ACT OF 2005 (INDIA)
Generally, 163

PATENT ACT OF 1790 (US)
History of patent law, 5

PATENT ACT OF 1836 (US)
History of patent law, 229

PATENT ACT OF 1870 (US)
History of patent law, 229

PATENT ACT OF 1952 (US)
Generally, 73, 229
Inventive step requirement, 436

PATENT ACT (SOUTH KOREA)
Generally, 521

**PATENT AND TRADEMARK OFFICE
    (PTO)**
Administrative Procedure Act challenges to
    prosecution decisions, 111
Backlog reform measures, 629
Burden of proof, 619
Claims regulations, 609
Comparative examination, 629
Design patent applications, 580
Green Technology Pilot Program, 629
Guidelines
    Inventive step, 455, 457
    Utility, 346, 352, 374
IP5 initiative, 120
Prior user rights report, 420
Project Exchange Program to expedite and
    improve patent examination and
    reduce backlogs, 629
Rule-making authority, 609
Trilateral cooperation, 119
Written description report, 531

**PATENT COOPERATION TREATY
    (PCT)**
Generally, 93 et seq.
Applications
    Generally, 79, 601
    Formal requirements, 116

International stages, 100
National stages, 106
Unified filing system, 93
Costs of PCT applications, 112
Designated offices, 97
Developing countries, membership
    considerations, 98
Enabling provisions, US interpretation,
    107
Examinations, 105
Framework, 95
Genetic resources disclosure requirement
    proposals, 115
Global patenting activity, 94
Growth in filings, 94
Harmonization achievements, 113
Impact on international filings, 113
International preliminary examinations,
    105
International searches, 102
International searching authorities, 96
International stage of patent applications,
    100
Inventive step requirement, 505
Membership considerations, developing
    countries, 98
National searches, utilization of PCT
    guidelines, 113
National stage of patent application, 106
Opt out provisions in revised rules, 114
Origins, 94
Paris Convention interaction, 79
Person having ordinary skill in the art
    standard, 505
Preliminary examinations, international,
    105
Prior art searches, 94
Priority claims, 96
Priority disputes, 79
Procedural irregularities
    PCT reforms, 114
    Validity effects, 111
Publication of applications, 94, 105
Publication of search reports, 105
Receiving Office Guidelines, 95
Reformation of PCT Regulations, 113
Regional networks of patent offices, 98
Reports of prior art searches, 103
Searches
    International, 102
    National, 113
Signatories, 94
Stages of patent application
    International stage, 100
    National stage, 106
Supplementary searches of prior art, 104
Traditional knowledge disclosure
    requirement proposals, 115
Translation functions, 98
Unified filing system, 93
Unity of invention requirement, 103, 113
US, enabling provisions interpretation, 107
WIPO, International Bureau role, 97

PATENT DIVIDE
Generally, 56

**PATENT EXAMINATION
    COOPERATION (ASPEC)
    PROGRAM**
Generally, 121

PATENT LAW (CHINA)
Generally, 497, 616

PATENT LAW (FRANCE)
Generally, 632

**PATENT LAW TREATIES
    IMPLEMENTATION ACT OF 2012
    (US)**
Generally, 630
Design patents, 580

PATENT LAW TREATY (PLT)
Generally, 115
American Invents Act implementation, 630
Applications for patents
    Generally, 602
    Multinational filing, 115, 630
Regional patent offices, 115
US ratification, 115, 630

PATENT PROPERTY RIGHTS
See Property Rights in Patents, this index

PATENT PROSECUTION
See Prosecution, this index

**PATENT PROSECUTION HIGHWAYS
    (PPH)**
Generally, 117, 121
Japan, 117

PATENT TERM
See Term of Patent, this index

PATENT TERRITORIALITY
See Territoriality, this index

PATENT TROLLS
See Trolling, this index

PATENT VALIDITY
See Validity of Patent, this index

**PATENT WORKSHARING
    INITIATIVES**
See Worksharing, this index

PATENTABILITY
See Scope of Patent Protection, this index

PATENTS ACT (UK)
Paris Convention interaction, 79

**PATENTS AND DESIGN ACT OF 1932
    (UK)**
Generally, 437

PATENTS OF ADDITION
Australia, 622
India, 622
New Zealand, 622

PC
See Paris Convention, this index

PCT
See Patent Cooperation Treaty, this index

PEET, RICHARD
EU biotechnology patents, 665

PEOPLE'S REPUBLIC OF CHINA
See China, this index

PERMISSIBLE REPAIR
See Exhaustion of Patent Rights, this index

PERSONS HAVING ORDINARY SKILL IN THE ART (PHOSITA)
Ascertaining the level of ordinary skill in the pertinent art, 444
Claim construction questions, 653
Disclosure standard, 509
Groups of inventors as a PHOSITA, 495
Infringement, claim construction questions, 653
Inventive step standard
    Generally, 438
    Japan, 495
Novelty standard, 391
Patent Cooperation Treaty, 506
Specifications standard, 362, 509
Utility determinations, 346

PERU
Criminal penalties for infringement, 802
Transpacific Partnership Agreement, 217
WIPO Development Agenda, 57

PESTICIDES
See Agrochemical Patents, this index

PETHERBRIDGE, LEE
Claim construction methodology, 655

PETTY PATENTS
Generally, 553
See also Utility Models, this index

PGR
See Post-Grant Review, this index

PHARMACEUTICAL PATENTS
See also Public Health Policy, this index
Biopharmaceutical industry, importance to US economy, 23
Brazil, 185
Canada
    Generally, 164
    EU dispute, 167
    US pharmaceuticals sales, 218
China, inventive step requirement, 502
Compulsory licenses for noncommunicable diseases treatment pharmaceuticals, 191
Confiscations of infringing goods, 838
Data exclusivity provisions in free trade agreements, 219, 641
Diagnostic method patent combinations, 321
Disclosure requirement, enablement, 514

EU vs Canada dispute, 167
Evergreening strategy to extend patent term, 320, 496
Exclusive marketing rights, 157
Experimental use defense, regulatory compliance, 736
Extensions of patent terms, 641
Generic Drugs, this index
Germany, 164
Global access to medicines campaign, 193
Incentivizing research, 194
India, this index
Internationalized patent applications, 598
Inventive step requirement
    China, 502
    New uses of known substances, 496
Italy, 164
Japan, 164
Life cycle management of patent terms, 319
Mailbox applications, 164
Marketing exclusivity protection, 641
Methods patents, 314
Morality objections, 314
Noncommunicable diseases, compulsory licenses for treatment pharmaceuticals, 191
Novelty requirement, inherency, 412
Orphan drugs, special protections, 641
Parallel imports disputes, 744, 750
Patent term extensions, 640
Patentability issues
    Generally, 313
    India, 315
    Methods patents, 314
    Morality objections, 314
    New uses of known substances, 319
    TRIPS, 314
Public interest requirements for protection, Brazil, 185
Regulatory compliance, experimental use defense, 735
Research and development costs, 193
Switzerland, 164
Term extensions
    Generally, 643
    See also Evergreening, this index
TRIPS
    Generally, 152, 315
    Waivers, 190
US
    Generally, 164
    Canadian pharmaceuticals sales, 218
Utility requirement, 345
WIPO research initiative database, 194

PHILIPPINES
ASEAN Patent Examination Cooperation Program, 121
Criminal penalties for infringement, 802

PHOSITA
See Persons Having Ordinary Skill in the Art, this index

PHOTOGRAPHIC NOVELTY
Generally, 405

PIRACY
See also Counterfeiting, this index
Biopiracy, 539
Biotechnology inventions, 539
Developing countries/developed country
    tensions, 21
Disclosure of origin requirement for
    biotechnology patents to combat, 539
EU piracy suppression, 820
Multinational Enforcement of Patent
    Rights, this index
Software, 21
TRIPS, piracy concerns motivating
    development, 136, 140
United States Trade Representative report,
    22

PIRES DE CARVALHO, NUNO
Genetic resources, disclosure of origin
    requirement protecting, 541

PLANT PATENT ACT (PPA)
Generally, 581

PLANT PROTECTION
Generally, 581 et seq.
Breeder's rights and patent rights conflicts,
    586
Canada, 583
Distinctness, utility distinguished, 582
Enforcement, 584
EU, 582
Exclusive rights, 585
Genetic use restriction technologies, 586
Germany, 582
Greenpeace views, 552
Hybrid seeds, 586
India, 584
International Union for the Protection of
    New Varieties of Plants, this index
Patents
        Omnibus claims, 606
        TRIPS, 152
Post-TRIPS concerns, 584
Seeds, utility patent protection, 581
Sexually and asexually produced varieties,
    581
South Korea, 581, 586
Technological control mechanisms, 586
Terminator and traitor seeds, 586
TRIPS
        Generally, 580, 583
        Post-TRIPS concerns, 584
        TRIPs-plus agreements, 583
US
        Generally, 581
        Utility patents, 583

**PLANT VARIETY PROTECTION ACT
    (PPVA)**
Generally, 581

PLT
See Patent Law Treaty, this index

POINT OF NOVELTY TEST
Design patents, 573, 625

POLAND
Criminal penalties for infringement, 802
Parallel imports, 750

POMPIDOU, ALAIN
Generally, 294

PORTUGAL
Criminal penalties for infringement, 802
History of patent law, 5
Parallel imports, 744

POST-GRANT PROCEEDINGS
Generally, 641
Corrections, 642
Inter Partes Review, this index
Interference Proceedings, this index
Nullity proceedings, 642
Opposition, this index
Post-Grant Review, this index
Reexamination, this index

POST-GRANT REVIEW (PGR)
Generally, 643 et seq.
America Invents Act, 643
Business method patents, 643
European Patent Convention, 644
Opposition, 643
Priority challenges, 643
Procedures, 644
Standing to challenge granted patents, 643

PPA
See Plant Patent Act, this index

PPH
See Patent Prosecution Highways, this
    index

PPVA
See Plant Variety Protection Act, this index

PRACTICAL UTILITY
Natural processes aiding, 248

PRINTED PUBLICATION BAR
America Invents Act, 74, 426
Date determinations, 393
Expansive definition, 425
Novelty requirement, 405
US, 423

PRIOR ART
Abandoned application as, 112
Advances over prior art, inventive step
    requirement distinguished, 435
America Invents Act, public disclosure as
    prior art, 416
Anticipatory enablement, 405
Anticipatory references, 410
Applications filed earlier but published
    after, 405
Canada, grace periods, 429
China
        Generally, 397
        Global vs domestic prior art, 428
EU, grace periods, 431
Experimental vs public uses, 423

Geographical limitations, 421
Grace periods
    Generally, 428
    Canada, 429
    Harmonization of grace periods, 433
Inherency in prior art, 406 et seq.
Inter Partes Review, prior art issues, 643
Inventive step analysis
    Generally, 444
    See also Inventive Step Requirement,
        this index
    Advance over prior art distinguished,
        435
    Analogous art doctrine, 454
    Causation effect of prior art, 492
    Prior art measurement, 444
    Prior art motivating, 492
Japan
    Global vs domestic prior art, 427
    Grace periods, 429
Paris Convention, grace periods, 432
Patent Cooperation Treaty searches, 94
Priority rights, prior art determinations
    for, 75
Public disclosure as prior art, America
    Invents Act, 416
Relevant prior art, 102
Searches of Prior Art, this index
Secret prior art, 405, 444
Secret prior users, 418
Temporal limitations, 428
Territorial limitations on prior art for
    novelty determinations, 391, 421 et
    seq.
Thailand, grace periods, 429
TRIPS, grace periods, 432
Written vs oral disclosures, 103

PRIOR USER RIGHTS
Generally, 418
Business method patents, 419
PTO report, 420
Secret prior users, 418

PRIORITY, RIGHT OF
Abandoned applications, 75
Design patents, 572
Disclosure requirement, priority
    implications, 522
European Patent Office, 86
First to File Versus First to Invent, this
    index
Foreign/domestic application conflicts, 73
Leahy-Smith America Invents Act, 73
On-sale bar, 84
Paris Convention for the Protection of
    Industrial Property, 71
Patent Cooperation Treaty
    Priority claims, 96
    Resolution of disputes, 79
Post-grant review, 643
Prior art determinations for, 75
Provisional applications to secure, 609
TRIPS, 149
US and US approaches compared, 76
US policy controversy, 85

PROBLEM-SOLUTION APPROACH
See Inventive Step Requirement, this index

**PROCEDURAL PATENT
    AGREEMENTS**
Generally, 69 et seq.
See Regional Patent Regimes, this index
Objectives, 69
Patent Cooperation Treaty, this index
Patent Law Treaty, this index
Patent Prosecution Highways, this index
Patent worksharing initiatives, 117
Substantive patent agreements
    distinguished, 69, 135

**PROCESS PATENT AMENDMENTS
    ACT OF 1988 (US)**
Generally, 864
Software, PPAA applicability, 864

PROCESS PATENTS
Chemicals, utility requirement, 341
Exclusive rights of patent owners, TRIPS,
    153
Machine or transformation test, 297
Microbiological processes, TRIPS, 152
Product patents distinguished
    Generally, 153
    Infringement, 787
Remedies for infringement, 787
Territorial scope, 864
TRIPS, exclusive rights of patent owners,
    153
US
    Generally, 860
    Territorial scope, 864

PROCUREMENT
See Comparative Procurement
    Requirements, this index

PRODUCT PATENTS
Exclusive marketing rights, 157
Exclusive rights of patent owners, 153
Process patents distinguished
Generally, 153
Infringement, 787
TRIPS
    Exclusive rights of patent owners,
        153
    Negotiations, 152

**PROFITS OF DEFENDANT AS
    DAMAGES**
Generally, 788 et seq.

PROJECT EXCHANGE
PTO program to expedite and improve
    patent examination and reduce
    backlogs, 629

PROPERTY RIGHTS IN PATENTS
Balancing developing country needs
    against, 27
Climate change and patent protection, 165
Cultural differences as to, 63
Developed vs developing countries debates,
    142

Foreign patent ownership in third world, 59
Genetic Resources, this index
History of patent law, 11
Human rights tensions, 25
Third world, foreign patent ownership in, 59
Traditional Knowledge, this index

PROSECUTION
Generally, 589 et seq.
Abuse of rights, Paris Convention, 88
America Invents Act, inequitable conduct claims, 620
Applications for Patents, this index
ASEAN Patent Examination Cooperation Program, 121
Burden of proof, 619
Comparative law
    Filing, 589
    Substantive examinations, 589, 613
Costs and fees, 589
Definition, 589, 613
Discrimination against foreign applicants, 111, 618
Examinations for Patents, this index
Filing formalities, 589
Foreign applicants
    Discrimination against, 111, 618
    Government permission requirements, 589, 602
Global patent application filings, 41
Grants of Patents, this index
Inequitable Conduct Defense, this index
Inventors, identification, 630
Inventors' roles
    Generally, 630 et seq.
    Employee Inventors, this index
    Professional assistance, 630
IP5 initiative, 120
New Route worksharing proposal, 121
Patent Cooperation Treaty, this index
Patent Law Treaty, multinational filing, 115, 630
Patent Prosecution Highways, this index
Patentability requirements
    Generally, 613 et seq.
    See also Examinations for Patents, this index
Registration systems vs substantive examinations, 613
Post-Grant Proceedings, this index
Presumptive validity based on substantive examination, 613
Procedural irregularities
    PCT reforms, 114
    Validity effects, 111
Professional assistance for inventors, 630
Registration system alternatives to substantive examinations, 613
Searches of Prior Art, this index
Soft-look systems, 614
Strategic considerations, 112
Trilateral cooperation, 119
Triway initiative, 120

Vancouver Group worksharing group, 121

PROSECUTION HISTORY
Generally, 54, 652

PROSECUTION HISTORY ESTOPPEL
Generally, 599, 670
Comparative law, 627
Doctrine of equivalents and, 667, 673

PROTECTION OF PLANT VARIETIES AND FARMER'S RIGHTS ACT (INDIA)
Generally, 584

PROTON EUROPE (NETWORK)
Generally, 420

PROVISIONAL APPLICATIONS
See Applications For Patents, this index

PTO
See Patent and Trademark Office, this index

PUBLIC HEALTH POLICY
Commission on Intellectual Property Rights, Innovation, and Public Health creation, 165
Commission on Intellectual Property Rights, Innovation, and Public Health report, 165
Compulsory licenses, 194
Doha Declaration, 186
Infectious diseases, human rights impacts of patent protections, 37
Pharmaceutical Patents, this index
Quest for a global patent, public health policy concerns, 42
TRIPS balancing of intellectual property rights and obligations, 148, 151
TRIPS flexibilities, 164

PUBLIC ORDER AND MORALITY
See also Moral Utility Doctrine, this index
Patents endangering, 152, 255, 276

PUBLIC PATENT FOUNDATION
DNA patentability, 331
Plant protection, 253

PUBLIC USE BAR
America Invents Act, 74
Novelty requirement, 404

PUBLICITY ORDERS
Remedies for infringement, 800

PUMFREY, NICHOLAS
Doctrine of equivalents, 679

PUNTA DEL ESTE DECLARATION
Uruguay Round negotiations, 135

PURPOSIVE CONSTRUCTION
Generally, 680 et seq.
Doctrine of equivalents distinguished, 686, 689, 696
European Patent Convention Article 69, 680, 693

European patent court proposals, 702
German infringement adjudications, 681, 689, 689
Literal construction distinguished, 683
Specifications confusing claims construction, 689
UK infringement adjudications
Generally, 681
Improver litigation, developments after, 696

PYRAMID OF KNOWLEDGE
Patentability, pyramid-of-knowledge analysis, 308

QUEEN MARY INSTITUTE
Disclosure of origin regimes study, 545

QUEST FOR A GLOBAL PATENT FRAMEWORK
Generally, 41 et seq.
Applications for patents, central filing, 46
Creativity impacts of globalization on third world, 62
Developing countries, 56
International patent system and developing countries, 56
Public health policy concerns, 42
Quality of patent examinations, improving, 42
Rich/poor divide concerns, 41
Substantive Patent Law Treaty negotiations, 42
Territoriality principle tensions, 45
United Nations Conference on Trade and Development report, 58

RAND
See Reasonable and Non-Discriminatory Licensing Conditions, this index

RAUSTIALA, KAL
Human rights implications of intellectual property protection, 37

RCD
See Registered Community Designs, this index

REAGAN, RONALD
Intellectual property laws, importance to international trade, 140

REASONABLE AND NON-DISCRIMINATORY (RAND) LICENSING CONDITIONS
Standards-essential patents, 834

REEXAMINATION
Generally, 642
China, 398, 558, 674
Third-party participation, 642
US, 642, 729

REGIONAL PATENT ENFORCEMENT INITIATIVES
European Directive on the Enforcement of Intellectual Property Rights, 820

Free trade agreements, 825
Multinational enforcement of patent rights, 820
Recognition and enforcement of judgments in Europe, 824

REGIONAL PATENT OFFICES
Patent Law Treaty, 115

REGIONAL PATENT REGIMES
Generally, 124 et seq.
European Patent Convention, this index
Patent Cooperation Treaty, regional networks of patent offices, 98

REGIONAL PATENT SYSTEMS
African Regional Industrial Property Organization, 132
Eurasian Patent Organization, 133
Gulf Cooperation Council, 133
Organisation Africaine de la Propriete Intellectuelle (OAPI), 132
Procurement, 133

REGISTERED COMMUNITY DESIGNS (RCD)
EU design patents, 559

REICHMAN, JEROME H.
Multinational dispute resolution, 811
Substantive Patent Law Treaty negotiations, 42
TRIPS, developing countries acceptance, 180

REITZIG, MARKUS G.
Patent trolls, 797

REMEDIES FOR INFRINGEMENT
Generally, 757 et seq.
Apology remedy, China, 799
Attorney's Fees Awards, this index
China
Generally, 798
Apology remedy, 799
Consistency of Chinese standards, 815
Confiscations of Infringing Goods, this index
Criminal Penalties for Infringement, this index
Damages, this index
Discovery in aid of infringement actions, 757
Disgorgement, 788
Harmonization, 799
Indirect infringement, willfulness, 705
Injunctive Relief, this index
Jurisdiction restraints on injunctive relief, strategic considerations, 774
Pre-judgment interest, 775
Process patents, 787
Publicity orders, 800
TRIPS
Generally, 757
Confiscations of infringing goods, 757
Valuation problems, 758

Willfulness, indirect infringement, 705

REPUBLIC OF KOREA
See South Korea, this index

RESEARCH AND DEVELOPMENT
See also Innovation, this index
Collaborative Research and Technology
        Enhancement Act, 456
Experimental Use Defense, this index
Incentivizing pharmaceutical research, 194
International Union for the Protection of
        New Varieties of Plants impacts, 583
Pharmaceutical patent costs, 193
User-centered innovation process, 24
Utility requirement, research impacts, 346
WIPO research initiative database, 194

**RESEAU SEMENCES PAYSANNES
        (NGO)**
Plant protection, 552

**RESOLUTION 2000/7 (HUMAN
        RIGHTS)**
Generally, 26
Developed country responses, 30
Global patent law rules effects, 37
Intellectual property protection, human
        rights approach, 26

RESTRICTION PRACTICE
Applications for inventions, 113

REVIEW
Inter Partes Review, this index
Post-Grant Proceedings, this index
Post-Grant Review, this index

RIFKIN, JEREMY
Moral utility doctrine, 383

RIGHT OF PRIORITY
See Priority, Right of, this index

RISCH, MICHAEL
Abstract ideas limitation on patentability,
        310

ROBERTS, GWILYM V.
Comparative patent examination practices,
        623

ROBERTS, JOHN
Permanent injunctions, 761

ROBINS, KENDRA
Extraterritorial patent enforcement, 863

ROMANIA
Criminal penalties for infringement, 802

ROME CONVENTIONS
Human rights, 32

ROUND-UP READY SEEDS
Patent infringement litigation, 241, 389,
        656

ROYALTIES
Damages, reasonable royalty as measure,
        775, 784

RUSSIA
Criminal penalties for infringement, 802
Examination for patents, 615

RWANDA
Compulsory licenses, 194

SAFRIN, SABRINA
Disclosure of origin requirement, 546

SALES
See On-Sale Bar, this index

SANCTIONS
Dispute Settlement Understanding, 16

SARNOFF, JOSHUA D.
Theological influences on patentability, 334

SCHERER, ISABELLE
Canada pharmaceuticals sales to US
        consumers, 218

SCHOFF, KELL
Intellectual property protection, human
        rights approach, 26

SCHWARTZ, DAVID L.
Doctrine of equivalents, 673

SCIENTIFIC THEORIES
Domestic law restrictions on patentability,
        225

SCOPE OF PATENT PROTECTION
See Validity of Patents, this index
Abstract ideas, 298, 309, 332
Aesthetic creations, domestic law
        restrictions on patentability, 225
Algorithms, 304
Atomic weapons, 226
Bilateralism, post TRIPS, 217
Biotechnology
        Generally, 226 et seq.
        See also Life Forms, Patentability of,
                this index
Business methods, domestic law
        restrictions, 225
Chemicals, 314
Claims drafting, gaming of the patent
        system through, 608
Cloning human beings, 261, 272
Comparative patentability requirements,
        225 et seq.
Comparative procurement requirements,
        509 et seq.
Diagnostic methods patents, 381
Discoveries, domestic law restrictions on
        patentability, 225
DNA, 331
Domestic law restrictions on patentability
        Generally, 225
        TRIPS, 152
Dyestuffs, 314
Environmental protection exclusions, 225

Ethical violations involved in making an invention, patentability implications, 276

Examination requirements
    Generally, 613 et seq.
    See also Examinations for Patents, this index
    Registration systems vs substantive examinations, 613

Exclusions, 225

Gaming of the patent system through claims drafting, 608

Genetic resources challenges, 551

Harmonization efforts, 225

Human embryos, patentability limitations, 259

India, ordre public standards, 551

Internet processes, 332

Knowledge, 547

Laws of nature, 229, 299, 328

Legal violations involved in making an invention, patentability implications, 276

Life Forms, Patentability of, this index

Life protection exclusions, 225

Machine or transformation test, 305, 310

Mathematical methods, domestic law restrictions on patentability, 225

Moral considerations, US, 278, 388

Moral violations involved in making an invention, patentability implications, 276

New uses of known substances, 319

New Zealand, software, 312

Non-obviousness
    Generally, 435 et seq.
    See also Inventive Step Requirement, this index

Novelty Requirement, this index

Nuclear weapons, 226

Nullity proceedings, post-grant, 641

Objectives of protection relationship, 12

Opposition. See Post-Grant Review, this index

Ordre public and morality protection exclusions, 225, 276

Ordre public protection exclusions, India, 551

Pharmaceutical Patents, this index

Post-Grant Review, this index

Presumptive validity based on substantive examination, 613

Pyramid-of-knowledge analysis, 308

Scientific theories, domestic law restrictions on patentability, 225

Seed patents, genetic resources challenges, 552

Sine qua non of patentability, 391

Software
    Domestic law restrictions on patentability, 225
    New Zealand, 312
    US, 226

Standing to challenge granted patents, 641

Statutory bars, US, 226

Surgical methods, 225, 381

Theological influences on patentability, 334

Therapeutic methods, 225, 381

TRIPS
    Generally, 151
    Domestic limits, 152

US
    Moral considerations, 388
    Morality consideration exclusions, 278
    Software, 226
    Standing to challenge granted patents, 641
    Statutory bars, 226

Utility Requirement, this index

SEARCHES OF PRIOR ART

See also Prosecution, this index

European Patent Office, 102

Fees, 103

Geographic restrictions, 103

International searches, Patent Cooperation Treaty, 102

International searching authorities, Patent Cooperation Treaty, 96

National searches, Patent Cooperation Treaty guidelines, 113

Publication of applications and search reports, 105

Reports of searches, 103

Searching authorities, 102

Supplementary searches, 104

United States Patent and Trademark Office (USPTO), 102

Written vs oral disclosures, 103

SECONDHAND GOODS

Exhaustion of Patent Rights, this index

Parallel Imports, this index

SECRECY

Applications subject to secrecy orders, 603

Data Exclusivity Provisions, this index

Disclosure Requirements, this index

Patents and trade secrets compared, 419

Prior art, secret, 405, 444

Trade protection agreements secretly negotiated, 217

SECRETAN, JACQUES,

Unions for the Protection of Intellectual Property, 36

SEEDS

Gene patents, 242

Hybrid seeds protection, 586

Patents, genetic resources based patentability challenges, 552

Terminator and traitor seeds, 586

Utility patent protection, 581

SEP

See Standards-Essential Patents, this index

SEYMORE, SEAN B.

Anticipatory enablement, 405

Presumptive validity, 730

SHEN, YUANLIN
Judicial and administrative enforcement of
    international property rights in
    china, 827

SHERWOOD, MICHELLE A.
Judicial and administrative enforcement of
    international property rights in
    china, 827

SICHELMAN, TED
Abstract ideas limitation on patentability,
    310

SIERRA LEONE
WIPO Development Agenda, 57

SINGAPORE
ASEAN Patent Examination Cooperation
    Program, 121
Compulsory licenses, 197
Examination for patents, 615
Transpacific Partnership Agreement, 217

SINGLE REFERENCE RULE
Novelty requirement, 396, 405, 506

SLOVAKIA
Parallel imports, 750

SLOVENIA
Parallel imports, 750

SOCIAL RIGHTS
See International Covenant on Economic,
    Social, and Cultural Rights, this
    index

SOFT-LOOK SYSTEMS
Examination for patents, 614

SOFTWARE
See also Business Methods and Software,
    Patentability of, this index
Domestic law restrictions on patentability,
    225
Extraterritorial approaches to enforcement
    of patent rights, 852
Patentability
    European Patent Office, 293
    New Zealand, 312
    US, 226, 864
Piracy, 21
Process Patent Amendments Act
    applicability, 864

SOTOMAYOR, SONIA
Invalidity defense to infringement, 724

SOUND PREDICTIONS DOCTRINE
Utility requirement, 374

**SOURCES OF INTERNATIONAL
    PATENT LAW**
Generally, 3 et seq.

SOUTER, DAVID
Business method patents, 296

SOUTH AFRICA
Design protection, 559
Development status changes, 61
Examination for patents, 615
WIPO Development Agenda, 57

SOUTH KOREA
Applications for patents, 61
Criminal penalties for infringement, 802
Design protection, 559
Development status changes, 61
Free trade agreement, 217
Indirect infringement, 719
Inventors' rights, 631
IP5 initiative, 120
Plant protection, 581, 583
Written description, 521

SOVEREIGNTY
Genetic resources
    Sovereignty over, 547
    Sovereignty proposals, 546
TRIPS, national sovereignty tensions, 164

SPAIN
History of patent law, 5
Parallel imports, 744

SPECIAL AGREEMENTS
National treatment principle exceptions, 71
Paris Convention, 90

**SPECIAL AND DIFFERENTIAL
    TREATMENT APPROACH**
GATT, 136

SPECIALIZED COURTS
Multinational enforcement of patent rights,
    842
Multinational patent litigation, 842

SPECIFICATIONS
Generally, 82, 125
Applications for patents, 509, 589
Claim construction questions,
    specifications confusing, 689
Construction of claims based on, 250
Enablement of invention by, 110
Enablement requirement, specification
    disclosing, 509
Person having ordinary skill in the art
    standard, 362, 509

SPECULATIVE INVENTIONS
Potential vs immediate benefits, 339

SPLT
See Substantive Patent Law Treaty, this
    index

SRI LANKA
Criminal penalties for infringement, 802

**STANDARDS-ESSENTIAL PATENTS
    (SEP)**
Reasonable and non-discriminatory
    licensing conditions, 834

STANDING
Granted patents, standing to challenge, 641

STANFORD UNIVERSITY
Assignments of rights by inventors, 637

STATISTICS OF WORLDWIDE PATENT ACTIVITY
Generally, 41
China and South Korea, 120
Examinations volume, 615
Newly developed economies, 61, 100
Patent Cooperation Treaty, 94, 100

STATUTE OF MONOPOLIES OF 1623 (ENGLAND)
History of patent law, 4, 10
Novelty requirement, 391, 421

STATUTORY BARS
Patentability, US, 226, 415

STEM CELLS
Embryonic stem cells
Cloning technology, 278
Patentability, 263
Life forms patentability, 265

STEVENS, JOHN PAUL
Business method patents, 296

STEWART, TIMOTHY
Harvard oncomouse, 233

STILLING, WILLIAM J.
Hatch-Waxman Act, patent term extensions, 640

STOKLEY, LINDA
TRIPS, US patent law changes to implement, 148

STORY, JOSEPH
Moral utility doctrine, 383
Useful invention, 339

STRASBOURG CONVENTION
Generally, 443

STRONG VS WEAK PATENT REGIMES
Technology transfer implications, 62

SUB-COMMISSION
Resolution 2000/7, this index
United Nations Sub-Commission on the Promotion and Protection of Human Rights, this index

SUBJECT MATTER OF PATENTS
See Scope of Patent Protection, this index

SUBSTANTIVE EXAMINATIONS
See Examinations for Patents, this index

SUBSTANTIVE PATENT AGREEMENTS
Generally, 135 et seq.
Objectives, 69

Procedural patent agreements distinguished, 69, 135
TRIPS Agreement, this index

SUBSTANTIVE PATENT LAW TREATY (SPLT)
Negotiations, 42
Proposal generally, 122

SUDAN
Criminal penalties for infringement, 802

SUMMARY JUDGMENT PRACTICE
Infringement, 648

SUPPLEMENTARY PROTECTION CERTIFICATES
Generally, 641
Medicinal products, 737
Term of patent, 641

SURGICAL METHODS PATENTS
Patentability, 225, 381
TRIPS, 152

SURINAME
Criminal penalties for infringement, 802

SUSPENSION OF TRADE CONCESSIONS
WTO remedy, 166

SWAZILAND
Compulsory licenses, 194

SWEDEN
Criminal penalties for infringement, 802
Inventors' rights, 631

SWISSAID
Plant protection, 552
SWISS-TYPE CLAIMS
Applications for patents, 607

SWITZERLAND
Anti-patent movement, 7
Criminal penalties for infringement, 802
Patent applications, Swiss-type claims, 607
Pharmaceutical patents, 164
Prosecution history use in construction of claims, 655

SYRIA
Criminal penalties for infringement, 802

TAIWAN
Compulsory licenses, 194

TAKENAKA, TOSHIKO
Japan, novelty/priority relationships, 430

TANZANIA
Criminal penalties for infringement, 802
WIPO Development Agenda, 57

TARIFF ACT OF 1930 (US)
Generally, 831

TARIFFS
Customs Tariff Law, Japan, 835

General Agreement on Tariffs and Trade, this index

TAX REDUCTION STRATEGIES
Patentability, 311

TECHNOLOGY TRANSFER
Argentine proposal, 57
Bayh-Dole Act, 457
Brazilian proposal, 57
Patent applications as catalysts for, 105
Strong vs weak patent regimes, 62
TRIPS objective to promote, 147
Utility requirement, technology transfer considerations, 351

TEMPORAL LIMITATIONS ON PRIOR ART
Generally, 428

TERM OF PATENT
EU extensions, 641
Evergreening, this index
Extensions, 640
Hatch-Waxman Act extensions, 640
Life cycle management pharmaceutical patent terms, extension strategies, 319
Orphan drugs, special protections, 641
Pharmaceutical patents extensions, 641
Supplementary protection certificates, 641
Trigger of patent term, 639
TRIPS
          Generally, 149
          Extensions, 640
          US, extensions, 640

TERMINATOR SEEDS
Generally, 584, 586

TERRITORIAL EXHAUSTION OF PATENT RIGHTS
See Exhaustion of Patent Rights, this index

TERRITORIAL LIMITATIONS ON PRIOR ART
Generally, 391, 421 et seq.

TERRITORIALITY
See also Extraterritorial Approaches to Multinational Litigation, this index; Jurisdiction, this index
EU, 45
Historical context for global patent cooperation, 6
Independence tensions, 44
Infringement of patents, 647
Quest for a global patent, territoriality principle tensions, 45
US laws, extraterritoriality, 46

THACHER, J.M.
Vienna conference participation, 8

THAILAND
ASEAN Patent Examination Cooperation Program, 121
Compulsory licenses, 192, 194

Criminal penalties for infringement, 802
Prior art, grace periods, 429

THERAPEUTIC METHODS PATENTS
Patentability, 225, 381
TRIPS, 152

THIRD WORLD
See Developing Countries and Least Developed Countries, this index

THIRTEENTH AMENDMENT (US)
Inventions comprising humans, 280

THOMAS, CLARENCE
Permanent injunctions, 759

THROW AWAY UTILITIES
Generally, 353

TILL, IRENE
Paris Convention for the Protection of Industrial Property, 7

TK
See Traditional Knowledge, this index

TOKYO ROUND
Generally, 136, 138

TPP
See Transpacific Partnership Agreement, this index

TRADE LEVERAGE
TRIPS development, trade leverage as instrument of, 144

TRADE NAMES
GATT, 137

TRADE PROTECTION AGREEMENTS
Secret negotiation, 217

TRADE REGULATION
Paris Convention, 88

TRADE SECRETS
Patent protection compared, 419

TRADEMARKS AND TRADE NAMES
Paris Convention for the Protection of Industrial Property, 69

TRADE-RELATED ASPECTS OF INTELLECTUAL PROPERTY RIGHTS
See TRIPS Agreement, this index

TRADITIONAL KNOWLEDGE (TK)
Generally, 539
Convention on Biological Diversity, 540
Convention on Biological Diversity study, 548
Disclosure of origin requirement protecting, 539
Patent Cooperation Treaty disclosure requirement proposals, 115
Property rights, 540
WIPO folklore study, 552

TRAITOR SEEDS
Plant protection, 586

TRANSFORMATION
See Machine or Transformation Test, this index

TRANSLATION OF PATENTS
European Patent Convention, 125
European Patent Office, 627
Internationalized applications, 599
Internationalized patent applications, 599
Patent Cooperation Treaty functions, 98

TRANSPACIFIC PARTNERSHIP AGREEMENT (TPP)
Bilateralism, post TRIPS, 217
Exhaustion of patent rights, 738
Non-governmental organizations in opposition to, 217

TRANSPARENCY
Dispute Settlement Body transparency criticisms, 29

TREATIES
Collective action problems inhibiting, 40
Dispute Settlement Understanding, this index
Domestic enforcement of treaty mandates, 805
Domestic origins of international agreements, 38
Extraterritorial approaches to enforcement of patent rights, 46
Free Trade Agreements, 215
Institutional theory of treaty formation, 38
Interpretation rules
    Generally, 28, 169
    Lex specialis, 28
Patent Cooperation Treaty, this index
Patent Law Treaty, this index
Procedural Patent Agreements, this index
Substantive Patent Agreements, this index
Vienna Convention on the Law of Treaties, interpretation rules, 28, 169
WTO obligations conflicts, 28

TREATMENT METHOD
Inventive step requirement, Japan, 487

TRIADIC PATENTS
Generally, 590

TRILATERAL COOPERATION
Applications for patents, 119

TRILATERAL COOPERATION OFFICES
Applications for patents, 590

TRIPP, KAREN
TRIPS, US patent law changes to implement, 148

TRIPS AGREEMENT
Generally, 135 et seq.
Abuses of patent rights, 153
Administrative enforcement, 757

Agrochemical patents, 152
Alternative forms of protection proposals, 66
America Invents Act changes in US patent law, 150
Applications for patents
    Generally, 602
    Provisional applications, 149
Attorney fee awards, 757
Balancing of intellectual property rights and obligations, 148
Bilateralism, Post-TRIPS, this index
Burden of proof of infringement, 154
Business methods and software patentability, 312
Capable of industrial application and useful, synonymous use of terms, 435
Compulsory licensing
    Generally, 153
    US compliance, 93
Confiscations of infringing goods, 757
Consensus problems, 144
Costs of compliance, multinational enforcement of patent rights, 805
Council functions, 17
Counterfeiting laws, TRIPS compliant, human rights challenges, 199
Creation, 16
Damages, 757
Date of invention determinations, 149
Destruction of infringing goods, 757
Developing Countries, this index
Development Round, 215
Diagnostic methods patents, 152
Disclosure of origin requirement, 539, 547
Discovery in aid of infringement actions, 757
Discrimination against foreign patent applicants, 618
Dispute Settlement Understanding creation, 16
Doha Declaration, incorporation in TRIPS, 189
Doha Round, this index
Domestic law mandates, 148
Domestic limits on patentability, 152
Domestic patent laws tensions, 18
Domestic priority systems, 149
Economic context of development, 135
Efficient breach of treaty provisions, 162
Enforcement
    Generally, 154 et seq., 757
    See also Dispute Settlement Understanding, this index
EU bilateralism, post TRIPS, 215
Exceptions to rights conferred, 167
Exclusive rights
    Generally, 153
    Post-TRIPS era limitations, 195
Exhaustion of patent rights, 738
Expenses, 757
Experimental use defense, 737
Extensions of patent terms, 640
Flexibilities
    Generally, 184

Doha Declaration, 187
Public health policy, 164
Free riders, 180
Free trade agreements enforcement
mechanisms compared, 825
GATT relationship, 136
Grace periods, prior art, 432
High Commissioner for Human Rights
criticisms, 30, 35
History of patent law, 135
Human rights, 32
Human rights concerns, Resolution 2000/7
expression, 27
Human rights-based limitations on patent
rights, 198
Implementation of enforcement
mechanisms, 807 et seq.
Indian Patent Act compliance, 318
Infringement
Burden of proof, 154
Scope changes, 149
Injunctive relief, 757, 764
Innovation promotion, 147
Intellectual property issues treated in
GATT, 137
Interpretation rules, 28, 169
Inventive step requirement, 496
Mailbox system, 157
Microbiological process patents, 152
Minimum standards of protection
mandates, 143
Ministerial declaration, 136
Most-favored-nation treatment principle,
147
Multinational enforcement of patent rights
Compliance standards, 804 et seq.
Costs of compliance, 805
Implementation of enforcement
mechanisms, 807 et seq.
Nationality intrusive measures, 805
Paris Convention provisions
compared, 811
TRIPS Preamble, 803
National sovereignty tensions, 164
National treatment principle, 147
Nationality intrusive measures, 805
Nutrition policies, balancing of intellectual
property rights and obligations, 148,
151
Overview, 143
Parallel imports, 216
Paris Convention harmonization, 147
Paris Convention provisions incorporated,
16
Patent term requirements
Generally, 149
Extensions, 640
Patentable subject matter standards, 151
Pharmaceutical patents, 152, 314
Piracy concerns motivating TRIPS
development, 136, 140
Plant protection
Generally, 581, 583
Patents, 152
Post-TRIPS concerns, 584

Political context of development, 135
Post-TRIPS era
Generally, 186 et seq.
Bilateralism, post-TRIPS, this index
Counterfeiting laws, TRIPS
compliant, human rights
challenges, 199
Development Round, 215
Doha Round, this index
Exclusive rights limitations, 195
Human rights-based limitations on
patent rights, 198
Plant protection concerns, 584
Tug-of-war between developed and
developing countries, 185, 186
Preamble
Generally, 151
Multinational enforcement, 803
Principles and objectives, 147
Prior art grace periods, 432
Priority rights principle, 149
Process patents, exclusive rights of patent
owners, 153
Pro-competitive strategy for implementing,
181
Product patents, exclusive rights of patent
owners, 153
Product patents negotiations, 152
Provisional applications, 149
Public health policies
Balancing of intellectual property
rights and obligations, 148, 151
Doha Declaration, 186
Flexibilities, 164
Public order or morality, patents
endangering, 152
Remedies
Generally, 154 et seq., 757
See also Dispute Settlement
Understanding, this index
Resolution 2000/7 expression of human
rights concerns, 27
Scope of patent protection
Generally, 151
Domestic limits, 152
Standards of protection, 148
Structure of agreement, 146
Surgical methods patents, 152
Technology transfer promotion, 147
Term extensions, 640
Therapeutic methods patents, 152
Trade leverage as instrument of TRIPS
development, 144
Uruguay Round creation, 135
US
Bilateralism, post TRIPS, 215
Compulsory licensing requirements,
93
Patent law changes to implement,
148
Useful and capable of industrial
application, synonymous use of
terms, 435
Utility requirement, 345, 374
Waivers, pharmaceutical patents, 190

WTO dispute settlement authority
    questions, 162

TRIPS-PLUS AGREEMENTS
Generally, 215 et seq.
Bilateralism, Post-TRIPS, this index
Data Exclusivity Provisions, this index
Organisation Africaine de la Propriete
    Intellectuelle adoption, 215
Plant protection, 583
Public knowledge goods, 825
US impacts, 218

**TRIWAY (PATENT WORKSHARING
    INITIATIVE)**
Patent prosecution, 120

TROLLING
Injunction remedies, 763, 833

TURKEY
Criminal penalties for infringement, 802

UDHR
See Universal Declaration of Human
    Rights, this index

UGANDA
Examination for patents, 615

UNCTAD
See United Nations Conference on Trade
    and Development, this index

**UNDERSTANDING ON THE RULES
    AND PROCEDURES
    GOVERNING THE SETTLEMENT
    OF DISPUTES**
See Dispute Settlement Understanding,
    this index

UNESCO
See United Nations Educational, Scientific
    and Cultural Organization, this index

UNFAIR COMPETITION
Paris Convention for the Protection of
    Industrial Property measures, 69

UNFAIR TRADE PRACTICES
Multinational enforcement of patent rights,
    831

UNHCHR
See United Nations High Commissioner for
    Human Rights, this index

UNION CARBIDE
US role in global economy, 20

**UNION FOR THE PROTECTION OF
    INDUSTRIAL PROPERTY**
See Paris Convention, this index

UNITED KINGDOM
Business methods and software
    patentability, 284
Damages
    Generally, 775
    Defendant's profits as measure, 788

Design patents, 560
Disclosure requirement, 531
Experimental use defense, 733
Infringement of Patents, this index
Inherency, novelty requirement, 412
Invalidity defense to infringement, 724
Inventive step requirement
    Generally, 437, 443
    Problem solution approach, 467, 475
London Agreement, 125
Novelty requirement, inherency, 412
Oppositions, 126
Parallel imports, 744
Priority rights principle, US approach
    compared, 76
Problem-solution approach to obviousness
    determinations, 467
Prosecution history use in construction of
    claims, 655
Purposive construction, infringement
    adjudications
    Generally, 681
    Post-Improver developments, 696
US patent law development based on UK
    laws, 22
Utility requirement, 356
Vancouver Group, 121

**UNITED NATIONS CONFERENCE ON
    TRADE AND DEVELOPMENT
    (UNCTAD)**
International patent development concerns,
    58

**UNITED NATIONS EDUCATIONAL,
    SCIENTIFIC AND CULTURAL
    ORGANIZATION (UNESCO)**
Intellectual property discussions, 139

**UNITED NATIONS FOOD AND
    AGRICULTURE ORGANIZATION**
Human rights issues, 41

**UNITED NATIONS HIGH
    COMMISSIONER FOR HUMAN
    RIGHTS (HCHR)**
TRIPS criticisms, 30, 35

**UNITED NATIONS SUB-COMMISSION
    ON THE PROMOTION AND
    PROTECTION OF HUMAN
    RIGHTS (UNSCPPHR)**
Generally, 26
Patent rights, human rights-based
    limitations, 198
Resolution 2000/7, this index

UNITED STATES
Agrochemical patents, 164
America Invents Act, this index
Applications for Patents, this index
Bilateralism, post TRIPS, 215
Biopharmaceutical industry importance, 23
Biotechnology patentability, 278
Business methods and software
    patentability, 296

Canadian pharmaceuticals purchases, state laws, 218
Chemical compounds, utility requirement, 339
Compulsory licensing, TRIPS requirements compliance, 93
Convention on Biological Diversity membership, 540
Copyright protection, importance to US economy, 23
Criminal penalties for infringement, 801
Damages, 775
Date of invention determinations, 149
Design Patents, this index
Diagnostic method patents, 321
Disclosure of origin requirement opposition, 540
Disclosure Requirements, this index
Discrimination against foreign patent applicants, 618
Doctrine of equivalents, 678
Domestic priority systems, TRIPS compliance, 149
Examinations for Patents, this index
Exhaustion of Patent Rights, this index
Experimental use defense, 732, 733
Expert testimony standard, 779
Export of intellectual property, 140
Extensions of patent terms, 640
Extraterritorial application of US laws
    Generally, 46
    Policy considerations, 866
Extraterritorial approaches to enforcement of patent rights, 847
Foreign vs domestic intellectual property inconsistencies, 218
Free trade agreements, Jordan, 219
GATT conformance, 22
General Agreement on Trade in Services compliance, 167
Global economy, US role, 19
Global patent application filings, 41
History of patent law, 10
India vs US dispute settlement, protection for pharmaceutical and agricultural chemical products, 158
Infringement of Patents, this index
Injunctive relief
    Generally, 758 et seq.
    Restrictions, 93
Invalidity defense to infringement, 724
Inventive Step Requirement, this index
Inventors' rights, 637, 636
Issue preclusion, multinational enforcement of patent rights, 845
Jordan free trade agreement, 219
Life forms patentability
Generally, 227, 278
Weldon Amendment, 283
Monopolistic patent laws, American view, 10
Morality protections, patentability exclusions, 278
Multinational Enforcement of Patent Rights, this index

NAFTA conformance, 22
New uses of known substances, patentability, 319
Non-obviousness
Generally, 435 et seq.
See also Inventive Step Requirement, this index
Novelty Requirement, this index
Patent Cooperation Treaty, enabling provisions interpretation, 107
Patent law changes to implement TRIPS, 148
Patent Law Treaties Implementation Act of 2012, this index
Patent Law Treaty ratification, 115, 630
Patent Prosecution Highways, 117
Patent term extensions, 640
Patent territoriality view, 46
Patentability
    Morality protections, 278
    Software, 226
Pharmaceutical patents
    Generally, 164
    Disputes with India, 163
Piracy concerns motivating TRIPS development, 140
Plant Patent Act, 581
Priority rights principle, UK approach compared, 76
Priority rules controversy, 85
Process patents
    Generally, 860
    Territorial scope, 864
Public interest view of patents, 10
Reexamination, this index
Software patentability, 226
Standing to challenge granted patents, 641
Statutory bars to patentability, 226, 415
Term of patent protection
    Extensions, 640
    TRIPS requirements, 149
Transpacific Partnership Agreement, 217
TRIPS
    Bilateralism, post TRIPS, 215
    Compulsory licensing requirements compliance, 93
    Patent law changes to implement, 148
    Piracy concerns motivating development, 140
United Kingdom patent laws adoptions, 22
University patent filing activities, US vs Europe, 421
Uruguay Round Agreements Act, 148
Utility models, 558
Utility Requirement, this index
Weldon Amendment, 283
Working requirement, 88

UNITED STATES TRADE REPRESENTATIVE (USTR)
Free trade agreements benefits to developing countries, 219
Piracy report, 22
Trade leverage policies, 145

UNITY OF INVENTION
Generally, 611
Patent Cooperation Treaty, 103, 113

UNIVERSAL COPYRIGHT CONVENTION
Generally, 139

UNIVERSAL DECLARATION OF HUMAN RIGHTS (UDHR)
Generally, 31

UNIVERSITIES
Bayh-Dole Act, technology transfer policy, 457
Inventors' rights, Bayh-Dole Act, 637
Patent filing activities, US vs Europe, 421

UNIVERSITY OF MINNESOTA
Technology licensing revenue, 637

UNSCPPHR
See United Nations Sub-Commission on the Promotion and Protection of Human Rights, this index

UPOV
See International Union for the Protection of New Varieties of Plants, this index

URUGUAY
Criminal penalties for infringement, 802

URUGUAY ROUND
Agenda, 138
TRIPS creation, 135
WTO creation, 16

URUGUAY ROUND AGREEMENTS ACT
Enactment, 148

USED PRODUCTS
Exhaustion of Patent Rights, this index
Parallel Imports, this index

USEFUL
Capable of industrial application and, synonymous use of terms, 435

USPTO
See Patent and Trademark Office, this index

USTR
See United States Trade Representative, this index

UTILITY MODELS
Generally, 553 et seq.
Applications, internationalized, 602
China, 553
EU study, 558
Examination requirements, 558
Germany, 553, 558
Infringement, 558
Innovation patents, 553
Innovative vs inventive step, 554, 558
Internationalized applications, 602
Novelty requirement, 553

Patents distinguished, 554, 558
Petty patents, 554
Procurement of protection, 553
US, 558
WIPO, 553

UTILITY PATENTS
Novelty requirement, 560
Plants, utility patent protection, 581
US, plant protection, 583

UTILITY REQUIREMENT
Generally, 337 et seq.
Australia, 345
Beneficial or moral utility, 382, 382 et seq.
Beneficial societal use, 389
Beneficial utility, 339
Biotechnology inventions, 345
Brazil, 345
Canada, 345, 374
Capable of industrial application, 345
Capable of industrial application and useful, synonymous use of terms, 435
Chemical compounds, 339
Chemical inventions, 345
Chemical patents, 342
De-minimis-test approach, 351
Developing country standards, policy considerations, 354
Distinctness requirement for plant patents, utility distinguished, 581
Downstream development facilitation through, 373
Emerging technologies, 346
EU, 354 et seq.
Expressed Sequence Tags, 347
Gene-related patent inventions, 346
Harmonization, 370
History of patent law, 5
Industrial application doctrine, 375
Moral Utility Doctrine, this index
Natural processes aiding practical utility, 248
Personal or private use, 375
Persons having ordinary skill in the art determinations of utility, 347
Pharmaceuticals, 346
Plant patent distinctness, utility distinguished, 581
Policy aspects, US, 344
Practical exploitations, 345
Practical utility
Generally, 339 et seq.
Natural processes aiding, 248
Research impacts, 346
Sound predictions doctrine, 374
Specific utility, 352
Speculative inventions having potential vs immediate benefits, 339
Technology transfer considerations, 351
Threshold of utility, 337
Throw away utilities, 353
TRIPS, 345, 374
UK, 356
Upstream research, 339 et seq.
US

Generally, 339 et seq.
Chemical compounds, 339
European and Japanese standards
    compared, 353
Moral utility doctrine, 383
New-and-useful statutory provision,
    370
Policy aspects, 344
PTO Utility Guidelines, 346, 352, 374
Usefulness and utility, 339
Usefulness
    Capable of industrial application and,
        synonymous use of terms, 435
    US, 339
Venetian Patent Law of 1474, 337

VAITSOS, CONSTANTINE V.
Quest for a global patent framework, 58

VALIDITY OF PATENTS
See also Subject Matter of Patents, this
    index
Burden of proof, invalidity defense to
    infringement, 724
Germany, presumption of validity, 732
India, presumption of validity, 732
Invalidity defense to infringement
Generally, 724 et seq.
Burden of proof, 724
Nullity proceedings, post-grant, 641
Patent prosecution procedural
    irregularities
    Generally, 111
    PCT reforms, 114
Presumptive validity, 724, 732
Standing to challenge granted patents, 641

VALUE
Market value measure of damages, 782

VAN VELSEN, FRANCIS
Customs enforcement of patent rights, 837

VAN ZIMMEREN, ESTHER
Myriad patent challenges, 643

VANCOUVER GROUP
Patent prosecution worksharing group, 121

VAVER, DAVID
TRIPS compliance pressures, 216

VENETIAN PATENT ACT OF 1474
Novelty requirement, 391

VENETIAN PATENT LAW OF 1474
History of patent law, 3
Utility, 337

VENEZUELA
Criminal penalties for infringement, 802
WIPO Development Agenda, 57

**VIENNA CONGRESS FOR PATENT
    REFORM**
Harmonization, 6

**VIENNA CONVENTION ON THE LAW
    OF TREATIES**
Interpretation rules, 28, 169

VIETNAM
ASEAN Patent Examination Cooperation
    Program, 121
Patent Cooperation Treaty, membership
    considerations, 98
Transpacific Partnership Agreement, 217

**VOLUME OF GLOBAL PATENT
    FILINGS**
See Statistics of Worldwide Patent Activity,
    this index

VON HIPPEL, ERIC.
Democratizing innovation, 25

VOTING RIGHTS
WIPO, 15
WTO, 17

WAGNER, R. POLK
Abstract ideas limitation on patentability,
    310
Claim construction methodology, 655

WAGNER, STEFAN
Patent examinations in China, 615

WAHDWA, VIVEK
Patent trolls, 764

WALT DISNEY COMPANY
US role in global economy, 19

WASSERMAN, MELISSA FEENEY
Territoriality and divided infringement,
    863

WEAK PATENT REGIMES
See Strong vs Weak Patent Regimes, this
    index

WEISSBRODT, DAVID
Intellectual property protection, human
    rights approach, 26

WELLCOME FOUNDATION LTD.
AZT patentability, 374

WHO
See World Health Organization, this index

**WILLFUL INFRINGEMENT ON
    COMMERCIAL SCALE**
Generally, 811 et seq.

WINARSKI, TYSON
Electrical technology protection, 831

WIPO
See World Intellectual Property
    Organization, this index

**WISCONSIN ALUMNI RESEARCH
    FOUNDATION**
Embryonic stem cells, patentability, 263

WORKING REQUIREMENTS
Argentine proposal, 57
Brazil
       Compulsory licenses to enforce, 185
       Proposal, 57
Compulsory licenses to enforce, 89, 185
Manufacturing and policy-oriented
       perspectives, 338
Paris Convention, 87
US, 88

WORKSHARING
Generally, 117, 122
IP5, 120, 590
New Route worksharing proposal, 121
Triway initiative, 120
Vancouver Group, 121

**WORLD HEALTH ORGANIZATION
       (WHO)**
Commission on Intellectual Property
       Rights, Innovation, and Public
       Health creation, 165
Commission on Intellectual Property
       Rights,Innovation, and Public
       Health, 165
Noncommunicable diseases report, 191

**WORLD INTELLECTUAL PROPERTY
       ORGANIZATION (WIPO)**
China, 615
Development Agenda, 57
Disclosure of origin requirement, 539
Dispute resolution procedures, 15
Enforcement mechanisms, 14
Folklore study, 552
Formation, 14
Genetic resources study, 552
Global patent application filings, 41
Harmonization goals, 43
Human rights tensions, 36
International Bureau, Patent Cooperation
       Treaty role, 97
International patent system and
       developing countries, 57
Minimum standards agreements, 14
National treatment principles, 15
Non-governmental organization activities,
       33
Patent Cooperation Treaty, International
       Bureau role, 97
Research initiative database, 194
Substantive Patent Law Treaty, 42, 122
Utility models, 553
Voting blocs, 15

**WORLD TRADE ORGANIZATION
       (WTO)**
Chinese membership, importance, 819
Creation, 16
Developing country memberships, 18
Disclosure of origin requirement, 539, 547
Dispute settlement authority questions,
       162
Enforcement of treaties
       Generally, 154 et seq.

See also Dispute Settlement
           Understanding, this index
Establishment, 16
General Agreement on Tariffs and Trade,
       16
Governance structure, 17
Internationalized patent applications, 590
Ministerial Conference, 17
Non-governmental organization activities,
       33
Patent applications, internationalizing, 590
Secretariat, 17
Suspension of trade concessions, 166
Treaties conflicting with WTO obligations,
       28
Voting rights, 17

WTO
See World Trade Organization, this index

WRITTEN DESCRIPTIONS
See Disclosure Requirements, this index

YING, DONALD J.
Employee inventions, 639

YU, PETER K.
Importance of Chinese participation in
       WTO process, 819
TRIPS objectives and principles, 195

YUAN, ARTHUR TAN CHI
Novelty and prior art in China, 398

YUGOSLAVIA
Criminal penalties for infringement, 802

ZAIRE
Criminal penalties for infringement, 802

ZAMBIA
Compulsory licenses, 194
Criminal penalties for infringement, 802

ZIMBABWE
Compulsory licenses, 194
Criminal penalties for infringement, 802